CLINICAL PSYCHIATRY

W. Mayer-Gross (1889–1961)

MAYER-GROSS SLATER AND ROTH

CLINICAL PSYCHIATRY

THIRD EDITION BY

Eliot Slater

M.A., M.D. (Camb.), F.R.C.P. (Lond.), D.P.M.

Honorary Physician, Royal Bethlem and Maudsley Hospitals
Director, M.R.C. Psychiatric Genetics Research Unit
Institute of Psychiatry, London

AND

Martin Roth

M.D. (Lond.), F.R.C.P. (Lond.), D.P.M.

Professor of Psychological Medicine, Royal Victoria Infirmary
and University of Newcastle upon Tyne
Director of Department of Psychological Medicine, Newcastle General Hospitals
Honorary Director, M.R.C. Group on the Relation of Functional
and Organic Illness

BAILLIÈRE, TINDALL & CASSELL
LONDON

Baillière, Tindall and Cassell Limited
7 & 8 Henrietta Street, London WC 2

First edition 1954
Reprinted 1955
Second edition 1960
Reprinted 1961
Third edition 1969
Reprinted 1970
Reprinted 1972

ISBN 0 7020 0001 9

Published in the United States by
The Williams and Wilkins Company, Baltimore

Printed in Great Britain by
Lowe & Brydone (Printers) Ltd, London
Bound by The Newdigate Press Ltd, Dorking

CONTENTS

CONTENTS

CHAPTER V SCHIZOPHRENIA

CHAPTER VI EXOGENOUS REACTIONS AND SYMPTOMATIC PSYCHOSES

CHAPTER VII ALCOHOLISM, DRUG ADDICTION AND OTHER INTOXI-CATIONS

CHAPTER VIII THE EPILEPSIES

LIST OF PLATES

PREFACE TO THE THIRD EDITION

We have to record with deep regret the loss of our senior colleague, Willy Mayer-Gross, who died at the age of 72 on the 14th February, 1961. Mayer-Gross was educated in the German school of psychiatry, and was a pioneer contributor, with such other great men as Beringer, Gruhle and Jaspers, to the remarkable flowering of clinical psychiatry in the development of 'phenomenology', i.e. the exact study and precise description of psychic events, which are a primary requisite for their understanding. Mayer-Gross came to Britain in 1933, and from that time the effect of his presence, and that of his close colleague and friend Erich Guttmann, was shown, perhaps more than in anything else, in a far-reaching educative process. This process, which extended through the length and breadth of British psychiatry, succeeded in rejuvenating the ingrown habits of thought of the British approach, till then bogged down in the unproductive generalities of Meyerian psychobiology. The sceptical and empirical spirit so imparted was enough to hold in check a tendency towards undisciplined theorizing, to which our younger psychiatrists might otherwise have become addicted; and instead of that we have seen the building up of a tradition of thinking for oneself without undue deference to authority, and concerning oneself with clinical research and with practical issues, above all the problems of treatment.

Since our last edition in 1960, and the death of Mayer-Gross in 1961, the changes that have overtaken psychiatry in this as in other lands have been both extensive and profound. Perhaps the most important of these is the increasing involvement in the study of epidemiology of mental disorder, its social causes, its consequences and the problems of rehabilitation. Much of the work undertaken in this field has been marked by the precise definition of variables and the use of valid and reliable measures even in relation to phenomena such as intra-family attitudes, which up to quite recently have been thought insusceptible of measurement. Perhaps partly because the use of the classical variables of sociology (social class, economic status, isolation, urbanization, mobility) has failed outside the fields of delinquency and mental subnormality to reveal any significant factors in causation, attention is now being diverted towards the social microcosm of the family and its influence on the development of instability and of mental disorder. In the next decade the familial tendency to schizophrenia as to neurosis will probably be studied to an increasing extent with the aid of sociological and psychological as well as clinical and genetical tools. Such multidisciplinary endeavours are in a modern spirit of enquiries in human biology and should help to provide psychiatry with that complementarity of vision that is so badly needed at the present stage of its scientific development. However, we must remember that even if specific social influences can be clearly established as contributors to the processes which culminate in neurotic, psychopathic, drug-addicted or sexually deviant personalities (to take some of the likely candidates) the problem of alleviating these disorders by social measures or by any measures which the social sciences suggest would remain to be solved. We know a very great deal about the major contributors to death and disability in early and late life which our passionate addictions to smoking, drinking and driving motor-cars burden us with. But even when shown the way, civilized communities evince an absolute unwillingness to tackle these social disorders in any radical way.

Of little less importance is the progress which has been made in physical methods of treatment, with which have gone advances in defining the physiological and biochemical bases of mental disorder. In retrospect, it can be seen that at the time of our first edition we already stood on the brink of a psychopharmacological era. A wide range of substances has been developed for the treatment of schizophrenia, paranoid, depressive and anxiety states. In many instances their efficacy has been established with repeated controlled trials. In addition to transforming therapeutics in psychiatry, and bringing an increasing range of psychiatric disorders under observation, the study of the new psychotropic drugs has stimulated the development of heuristically valuable hypotheses about the biochemical mechanisms underlying mental disorder. This has not been without setbacks. Until a few years ago it looked possible that the biochemical basis of schizophrenia would be clarified in the foreseeable future. These hopes have faded. However, in the last decade, a far more promising prospect has opened up in the depressive disorders; the evidence that the metabolism of catechol- and indol-amines is in some manner associated with depressive symptoms comes from a number of independent sources. It would be surprising if important further advances were not made in this field within the next decade; and if they came they would have far-reaching effects on our thinking about the commonest forms of psychiatric illness.

Another new arrival is the methodological advance by which it is becoming possible to use for scientific purposes the great mass of information which is assembled by the psychiatrist about the individual patient. We are now in a position to apply advanced techniques such as multivariate and principal component analysis to large bodies of case material. The impact of these developments has so far been most marked in the fields of classification and diagnosis; but we are at the brink of a revolution that is likely to transform psychiatric research as a whole.

What then, one might ask, is the future of clinical psychiatry with all these vigorous newcomers in the field? The most significant result of all the self-criticism to which psychiatry has subjected itself, the scepticism of the value of the clinical interview, of psychiatric history-taking, of the validity and function of diagnosis and the clinical criteria on which diagnostic judgements are based, all these and the vast amount of scrupulously conscientious work which has been invested in them, have led to the validation of the basic clinical methods and clinical concepts. Effective support has not been found for the idea that mental illness is a myth, and the literature of clinical psychiatry a mythology. Attempts to find substitutes for diagnostic classifications in cluster analysis of psychometric ratings have led back once again to the Kraepelinian groupings. On our last edition, one of our reviewers wrote: 'Those who believe that all human behaviour, whether normal or abnormal, is both meaningful and purposive, will have little sympathy with the authors' views'. We are content that this should be so, since the number of those who share that belief must be diminishing day by day.

It has been the task of the two revising authors to try to do justice to all the great changes to which we have referred, and to integrate them into a living framework. Perhaps psychiatry has now already progressed beyond the stage in which textbooks by only a few authors can be justified. However, the sciences do not advance solely by the accumulation of ever more facts; it is also necessary to arrive at statements of an increasing generality, to provide modes of interpretation, i.e. hypotheses, of an increasingly extensive explanatory and predictive power. A major task to be met in a textbook is the placing of facts and observations in perspective and to see them in relation to one another. The author who takes it upon himself to review a much wider field than that in which his own best work has been done, or that with which he is most familiar, will surely disclose to the informed reader errors of fact and emphasis and the biases which his own restricted experience necessarily involves. But what he should be able to give to the reader in compensation for these deficiencies is a picture of the entire scene as it is visualized by a single observer placed at an elevation over one part of the whole map. While the multi-author textbook will remain indispensable for many purposes, above all for detailed study of any part of the whole terrain, the general reader needs in addition the synoptic study in which parts are brought into relation with the whole.

In this edition the least changes have been made in Chapter I Introduction, and Chapter II Examination of the Psychiatric Patient. The amount of new matter required to bring Chapter VIII The Epilepsies and Chapter XII Mental Subnormality up to date, though substantial, has not been very large. It has been necessary to alter thoroughly the Chapters III Personality Deviations and Neurotic Reactions, IV Affective Disorders, V Schizophrenia, VII Alcoholism and Drug Addiction, and X Ageing and the Mental Diseases of the Aged. Chapter XIII on Administrative and Legal Psychiatry has been thoroughly revised and in fact re-written. And there is a new Chapter on Social Psychiatry.

ACKNOWLEDGEMENTS

THE authors of this text feel indebted to a great number of people, much greater than can be enumerated and named here. They are the many medical colleagues, collaborators and students who were given the opportunity of reading parts of the book or of listening to lectures and discussions at which some of the content was presented. They willingly pointed out omissions or inadequacies, gave advice and suggested improvements as well as criticized the views expressed by the authors. To all those unnamed helpers we extend our first thanks; they have given the encouragement and the interim satisfaction without which it it so difficult to sustain progress in work of this kind.

In the preparation of this third edition we have been particularly helped by Dr. A. J. Coppen and Dr. J. L. Gibbons who gave valuable advice about Chapter IV, and by Dr. I. Kolvin and Dr. D. W. K. Kay whose useful criticisms and suggestions are incorporated into the chapters on Child Psychiatry and Ageing and Mental Diseases of the Aged respectively. We are also indebted to Dr. J. Tanner who provided the photographs of somatotypes and to Mr. Hubert D'Havrincourt who gave us permission to use the photographs of Pavlov and Freud which had originally appeared in *World Health*, a W.H.O. publication. We are grateful also to Dr. G. L. Gryspeerdt who went to great trouble in the preparation of the photographs of air encephalograms. We also owe a debt of gratitude to Professor B. Cronholm of the Karolinska Institute, Stockholm, who supplied photographs of drawings by Carl Frederick Hill and Ernst Josephson. For the photographs of karyotypes of four subjects with chromosomal abnormalities, our thanks are due to Dr. J. Kahn. We are indebted to Sir Charles Symonds for valuable and detailed criticism of the chapter on the Epilepsies.

The chapter on Administrative and Legal Psychiatry could not have been completed without the willing support of colleagues in this country and abroad. The data it contains have been furnished and literature has been provided by the following: for Switzerland by Professor M. Bleuler; for Spain by Professor J. J. Lopez Ibor; for Portugal by Professor H. J. de B. Fernandes; for Belgium by Dr. Jacques de Busscher; for Holland by Dr. P. van der Esch; for Norway by Professor Ødegaard; for Denmark by Professor Erik Strömgren; for Sweden by Professor Ottosson; for Greece by Dr. G. Lyberi; for Italy by Dr. G.

Bonfiglio and Dr. G. Pampiglione; for France by Dr. Henri Duchenne and Dr. P. Pichot; for Eire by Dr. J. N. P. Moore; for Scotland by Dr. H. B. Craigie; for Northern Ireland by Dr. W. McCartan. Dr. M. Guttmacher suggested sources of information on Legal Psychiatry in the U.S.A.

We would also like to express our indebtedness to the numerous authors of books and other publications on which a text of this kind must be based. As explained before, it is written with a view to display and to preserve the clinical knowledge accumulated during the last century and built on the achievements of the last three generations of psychiatrists. In spite of our effort to provide a full list of references, there must be many details in a volume of this kind for which the original or another important source is not quoted. We ask the authors to accept our apologies for these omissions and our assurance that we are very much aware of the short-comings of our selection of literary references.

We should like especially to thank the following: Springer Verlag, Heidelberg, for permission to make use of the *Handbook of Mental Diseases*, edited by Bumke, in its various parts; Butterworth & Co. (Publishers) Ltd., London, for the use of material from the article on Affective Psychosis in the *British Encyclopaedia of Medical Practice*, vol. 10; to the editor and publishers of the *Journal of Mental Science* for the Schema for the Examination of Organic Cases (reproduced with slight alterations); Professor A. J. Lewis for the Scheme for Case-Taking used in the Institute of Psychiatry, Maudsley Hospital, London, and Dr. R. S. Illingworth for the Table of Normal Developmental Data in Chapter XII. We also thank Dr. McMenemey for permission to reproduce plates XIII and XV.

We should also like to express our gratitude to Miss Susan Allison for the thoughtful, efficient and dedicated effort she has devoted to the production of this volume. She did a great deal to stimulate, sustain and collate the work of the authors and without her indefatigable contribution the preparation of this third edition would not have been possible.

CHAPTER I

INTRODUCTION

THE FOUNDATIONS OF PSYCHIATRY

THIS book is based on the conviction of the authors that the foundations of psychiatry have to be laid *on the ground of the natural sciences*. In it the attempt is made to apply the methods and the resources of a scientific approach to the problems of clinical psychiatry. It is obvious that in the present stage of development of our specialty such a plan can only be carried out in a partial way, and that much of our clinical knowledge today belongs more to medical art than to science. Nevertheless we have kept to this aim because we believe that it is only from an organic connexion between the natural sciences, biology, medicine and psychiatry, and from the arduous but reliable scientific methods of investigation and discussion that lasting advances can be made.

It seems necessary to make such a statement at the outset, because now, as so frequently during the hundred years of its existence, psychiatry is in danger of losing its connexion with the body of medicine. These recurrent crises can be traced to two main causes: to the influence of psychiatric practice on the knowledge and the attitude of psychiatrists, and to the peculiar position of psychiatry between medicine and neurology on the one side and philosophy and psychology on the other.

The primary concern of *the practising psychiatrist*, within the walls of an institution or at large, is to treat and to help his patients. He must try to do this even where knowledge is inadequate and the results of past research provide him with no or an insecure foundation. He will then turn to any tool to hand. When, for instance, the discoveries in cerebral anatomy and pathology of the eighties and nineties of the last century proved of little help in the understanding of mental patients, and when at the same time Kraepelin's nosological classification was of little use when it came to their treatment, it was natural for psychiatrists to be allured by the psychopathological theories of Freud, which promised an explanation of the whole before the details had been elaborated. Similar manifestations of impatience, attempted short cuts and deviations from the slow advance of science, have happened before and happen now. Whenever a new branch of scientific activity appears with some relevance to human behaviour, or whenever a new philosophical movement meets a popular response, psychiatrists seize upon it and try out its implications in their own field. This also is a way of breaking new ground, which must, however, if it is to bear fruit, be worked over by the methods of science.

This instability in the attitude of psychiatrists is made all the easier by the subjectivity and the *lack of precision of psychological data*. Mental events can only be described in words which are themselves often open to varied interpretations. Many terms used in psychiatry are taken from everyday language and are not clearly defined. Special terms, on the other hand, have been taken over from psychiatry into ordinary speech, so that their meaning has been watered down and become ambiguous. Much of the psychiatric literature of today owes its existence to the possibility of playing with words and concepts; and the scientific worker in psychiatry must constantly bear in mind the risks of vagueness and verbosity.

The harm that these tendencies have done and may yet do to the psychiatrist and to his reputation is not to be minimized; strict attention to scientific standards in clinical work is needed now more than ever. It is well to remember that as recently as 150 years ago the treatment of mental aberrations, excepting the care of the dangerous psychotic, was regarded as the province of the philosopher and the theologian. In this country before the First World War, whoever took up psychiatry was considered a failure, a man unable to make his way in medicine or surgery. Psychotherapy was regarded as identical with charlatanry, and the institutional psychiatrist as only fitted to act as society's custodian of its degenerate or dangerous members.

That this has now changed, and that the psychiatrist is recognized as a physician of standing as well as a counsellor in social problems of general interest, is due to the cautious industry of responsible research workers and to the impartial collection of careful clinical observations. With this in mind the following critical review of present-day tendencies in psychiatry should be read.

Although practising psychiatrists of all schools share much in common, there is rather too much dissension for the present state of psychiatry to be regarded as entirely healthy. Wide differences about fundamental issues exist between what is thought and taught in different centres. These differences inspire attitudes of dogmatism, and there is not the open-mindedness there should be. Rapid advances are being made, but are judged or even ignored on the basis of preconceptions. The solid acquisitions of knowledge from the past, where they conflict with current modes of thought, are not being reformulated where necessary, but are being neglected and even forgotten. Psychiatry is not only being split into a number of schools, but is also, which is more regrettable, being *divorced from the parent science of medicine*. There are indeed psychiatrists who, so far from regretting the split, clear-sightedly do what they can to widen it. Growth in every field, in the number of practising psychiatrists, in the amount of time given to psychiatric teaching of under-graduate and postgraduate students, in the claims made by psychiatrists to be heard in their own and in related fields, in public esteem and support, has led to a corresponding decrease of self-criticism. The normal progress of scientific advance, by which facts are first accumulated and confirmed, and then have fitted to them a theory whose critical implications are subjected to test, has been interrupted by a flight into the air. Theoretical exposition follows theoretical exposition in ever-growing complexity, and the need constantly to check theory by seeking at every point for new facts is forgotten.

Some of the correctives to these tendencies suggested in the previous edition of this textbook may have reflected a too narrow conception of the scope of psychiatry as a discipline. It is desirable that psychiatrists should attempt to define the social and environmental conditions under which the individual thrives or breaks down. It is also to the good that they should round off their knowledge and understanding of disease by studying patients who manage to survive in the community at large, as also those suffering from mild and sub-clinical forms of psychiatric disorder. Estimates of incidence and prevalence of the main forms of psychiatric disorder have to be made if the mental health services are to be well-planned, and observations on the social setting of health and disease might ultimately enable the psychiatrist to make some contribution towards preventive programmes. The psychiatrist cannot, therefore, ignore the social sciences and must play his part in defining those 'environmental, domestic, occupational, economic, habitual and nutritional factors without which the intimate (or specific) causal factors cannot find their opportunity' (Ryle, 1948). But he must retain a sense of proportion and, in practical work as in research, direct his main energies to those tasks in the field where needs are most pressing, development most promising, and where his special skills and experience are most likely to make him effective. His special gifts and insights are derived from intimate familiarity with the phenomena of mental disorder and, while he will not wish to define these too rigidly, they should, if he is wise, provide for him the focus of interest. For if he should disperse his activities over too wide a field, he will inevitably fall a victim to superficiality and error.

It therefore seems to us far-fetched to claim that sociology or cultural anthropology occupy as basic a position in relation to psychiatry as do the mental and biological sciences. Within their respective fields the quantitative relation between the known and the unknown is entirely different. Our knowledge of medicine and physiology is detailed, relatively precise and capable of clear definition. Our knowledge of sociology is scanty, imprecise and not easily capable of confirmation or refutation. Our knowledge of medicine gives us information about individuals; sociological knowledge gives us information only about groups, from which deductions about the individual are notoriously subject to error. Medicine teaches us much about the causes of ill-health, the mode of operation of those causes, and the reasons why they show their effects in particular symptoms. Sociology is largely a study of normal people, and has made so far little contribution to our knowledge of the causes of illness. There is no culture or society on record in which the major psychoses have been found to be absent. Nor are any free from neurotic disorders, which are generally regarded as having a much closer association with social and environmental factors.

The argument in favour of an intimate relationship between psychiatry and medicine might still be regarded as trifling if, in fact, the *applicability of neurological and medical concepts in psychiatry* were very restricted. This is far from being the case. The organic psychoses, the psychiatric sequelae of cerebral trauma, the epilepsies, encephalitis, alcoholism and the intoxications, occupy a considerable part of the territory which it is the duty of psychiatry to cover. Furthermore, this field is constantly being enlarged. Entirely unsuspected relations, some of them of great theoretical importance, between physical and mental changes are constantly being discovered. The addition of cerebral surgery to the psychiatrist's weapons has opened a new path to the solution of problems as well as to treatment. Recent work with the electroencephalograph provides an instance of the transformation of ideas which may result from the application of neurophysiological concepts and methods to psychiatric problems. The organic connexion between psychiatry on the one side and medicine and physiology on the other is itself a region of rapid further growth.

Another *objection to the divorce of psychiatry from medicine* is that when it is so deprived of its natural foundations it can be swayed by every wind that blows. New doctrines arise and are propagated, and find in many minds a ready application. There is no longer a standard of reference by which they may be criticized. The newer schools which would elevate psychiatry to a loftier position make little or no use of experiment, clinical observation, painstaking follow-up study, even statistical analysis and argument. The psychiatrist is content if he can interpret his findings in terms which happen to be fashionable. Diagnosis becomes unpopular, and is allowed only secondary importance; what is exalted in its place is interpretation and understanding.

The emphasis on the contribution of sociology and anthropology derives from the view that, since man is a social animal in intimate association with his cultural environment, the level of organization which should be studied to provide an appropriate framework for psychiatry is that at which individual human beings are integrated with communities. There would be something to be said for this view if psychiatry could be justifiably described as the 'science of behaviour' (Masserman). It would then have to aim at giving a complete account, not only of the clinical disorders that provide the daily work of most psychiatrists, but also of human motivation and behaviour as manifested in social and political life, in art and religion. But this would involve a grandiose and *unwarranted expansion of the scope of psychiatry*. A complete account of human behaviour in this sense would demand contributions not only from psychiatry, sociology, psychology and anthropology, but also from economics, history, literature and all the sciences—in fact, from all branches of human knowledge.

Much contemporary work in the field of psychopathology reflects a shift of interest from the characteristics of groups, such as 'schizophrenics', to actual persons, the differences between them, and their relations with one another. An *excessive preoccupation with individuals* is heuristically sterile. Physics would not have advanced very far if every natural phenomenon had been regarded as unique rather than as a member of a class of similar phenomena. Progress depends on recognizing similarities in phenomena which may, superficially, differ very greatly, for from these similarities we may deduce general causes.

We may take as an analogy the logic employed in a *statistically planned experiment*, such as is conducted by the experimental biologist. In interpreting his findings he will attempt first of all to separate out the effects of general causes—the difference between two breeds, or the presence or absence of a soil fertilizer. These are the 'main effects'. If there are more than one of them, he will also be able to measure the effect of 'interactions' between them. Finally he will come down to individual variation, which will be classifiable, statistically, as 'error'. If he were to start at the opposite end, and try to cover as much as possible of the total differences observed by individual variation, he would never discover anything else at all.

So it is in psychiatry. Individual schizophrenics differ from one another almost as much as normal individuals, but they do have similarities, and aspects in which they differ from normals as a class. Their risks of suicide, of tuberculosis and of early death are increased; their chances of successful social adjustment are diminished; their ways of thinking and of feeling show consistent and characteristic differences from those of normal people. Within the schizophrenic group further *classification is useful*; there are sex differences, age differences, differences in clinical type of illness, which are significant for prognosis and treatment. If these classifications are never made, the information they provide naturally never accrues, and it is gratuitous to assert that they are 'little guide'. Furthermore, if we are going to allow ourselves only one method of treatment, e.g. psychotherapy, and apply it in every case, no information of a general kind can possibly be relevant to treatment; but such an approach takes us back to the days of universal purging and bleeding.

If we forgo the *making of a diagnosis*, we also forgo all application of the extensive knowledge which has been accumulated in the past. This would be sheer folly; we cannot wilfully ignore what is known, and if we wish to do so we are under the psychological necessity of proving (or believing) that the knowledge is false knowledge, or that it is irrelevant. If we refrain from diagnosis we shall be left in the individual case without the help of general concepts. The wise physician never neglects the individual peculiarities of his patient; but he will first see how far he can be fitted into general patterns, and he will not mistake a quality which is characteristic of the group, such as thought disorder or auditory hallucination, as either without significance or as something to be interpreted by the life-history of that one patient alone.

All-embracing explanations and concepts such as those often advanced by psychoanalysts are of dubious value in the light of recent advances in the philosophy of science. It has been argued by Popper (1963) that the greater the explanatory power of a hypothesis, the less is its scientific usefulness. No testable predictions can be based on theories which explain everything and are not capable of refutation. The most useful hypothesis is the one which has the greatest *a priori* improbability; and no sooner is it formulated than one should make the most strenuous efforts to refute it. Our confidence in it will increase with every well-designed effort at refutation which it survives. As has been emphasized by Perley and Guze (1962), an important function of a diagnosis is that of a prediction which can be confirmed or refuted. What are predicted are such significant features as the range of causes which may be shown to be responsible for the condition when further investigated, its course and outcome, etc.

Diagnosis is not a matter of merely naming and labelling. Ideally it implies judgment of causation; and even if this is possible in only the most tentative way, it always includes a plan of action, e.g. of treatment. In medicine we have to deal with causes of all kinds, and not only those that are both necessary and sufficient. In searching for a cause of some phenomenon, we are really *searching for a quantitative relationship*. If A is the necessary and sufficient cause of B, then there is a one-to-one relationship between A and B. If A is a necessary but not sufficient cause, then there is no B without A, but A may be combined with X or Y instead of with B. If the variety of these Xs and Ys is very great, the causal relationship, though it still exists, is thereby weakened. If A is neither necessary nor sufficient, then there are As without Bs and Bs without As, and the strength of the causation will depend on the proportionate relationship between AB to A on the one hand and B on the other. From this one may deduce the reason why the remoter antecedents of an illness are of little consequence. We can, if we like, lose our way in a causal network; but we need not do so if we take into account the quantitative aspect of causation. It is at this point that so much psychiatric thought loses cogency and direction. Quantitatively important causes are tangled in a knot of others whose quantitative relation with the effect we are interested in is slight or entirely unknown. It is, for instance, maintained by some psychoanalysts that during the birth-pangs of the mother the infant suffers 'anxiety', and that this is the cause of anxiety symptoms in later life. This doctrine appears to be meaningless, for an experience which is shared by all human beings cannot be the cause of a difference between some human beings and others.

In analysing the causes of a given state we are led to postulate factors which hold in this case and do not hold in others. We deal, in fact, in terms of *differences*. In considering the causes of an abnormal mental state it is relevant to inquire whether there is a family history of mental illness, for if that is the case the patient is differentiated from others. Recent studies have also adduced evidence that psychiatric patients differ from normal subjects in respect of the circumstances of their early childhood and upbringing. In a wide range of disorders, including psychoneuroses (Barry and Lindemann, 1960), depressive states (Brown, 1961), delinquency (Glueck and Glueck, 1950), the affective disorders of the aged (Kay, Beamish and Roth, 1964b) and psychiatric patients in general (Gregory, 1958), the frequency with which one or other parent had been lost in childhood has proved greater than in the general population. The specificity of the psychological effects of such deprivations is considered to be greater by some authors (Bowlby, 1960) than others (Lewis, 1954). The important thing is that a start has been made in putting to some sort of objective test hypotheses about the early origins of psychiatric disorder which owe something to psychoanalytic thinking. But that this constitutes no more than a beginning is illustrated by Wootton's review of twenty-one systematic studies of delinquents (Wootton, 1959); the evidence about the aetiological role of such factors as poverty, lower social status, poor employment record, broken home, mother's employment outside the home and low educational attainment proved to be uncertain and imprecise. There is as yet only an insecure foundation of hard fact about the early origins of psychiatric disorder. Few psychiatrists would doubt that deprivation and vicissitude in childhood contribute something to emotional instability and neurotic breakdown. But the precise extent and significance of this contribution remains uncertain.

The need in psychiatry for a scientific approach is overwhelming; by neglecting it we introduce every year a greater degree of confusion. Its requirements are simple. Where a particular quality is attributed to a sample of the population, e.g. those suffering from mental illness, it must be shown, unless it is self-evident, that the same quality is found in other samples to a lesser degree or in lower frequency. *Control studies*, gathered either by the investigator's own hand, or by other means, must be available. The formulation of hypotheses in a precise form should follow and be based on the facts. The major logical consequences of the hypotheses should then be drawn, and those selected for further investigation which might produce critical results, i.e. ones which could prove fatal to the hypothesis.

THE FIELD OF PSYCHIATRY

Psychiatry has been defined by Curran and Guttmann (1949) as that branch of medicine whose special province is the study, prevention and treatment of all types and degrees of mental ill-health, however caused. We might, perhaps, go a little further and say that *psychiatry is that branch of medicine in which psychological phenomena are important as causes, signs and symptoms, or as curative agents.* In either case we shall regard our subject-matter and our approach to it as essentially medical and our final concern as being with the health of individuals. Such definitions are now no longer fashionable, and many modern authors would prefer to define psychiatry as the study of human behaviour, or as the study of interpersonal relationships.

The first of these modern re-definitions represents an undue expansion, the other an undue restriction of our field, and each of them has its dangers. If the psychiatrist claims, because he can understand certain human problems, that his concepts can be expanded and applied to *human behaviour* as a whole, he will misjudge the range of his hypotheses and land in superficiality and error. His inordinate ambition will drive him by facile psychologizing to obscure rather than to illuminate aspects of life with which he has no special acquaintance. His day-to-day work is with persons behaving in an abnormal or at least unusual way, and this gives him a bias in perspective. Making use of the notions with which he is familiar, he will tend to regard quite normal phenomena as pathological. Even within the field of psychiatry it is easy to misapply concepts in this way, and much of what has been written on the subject of neurosis is vitiated because the underlying mechanisms were regarded as pathological. If any phenomenon, such as the occurrence of anxiety, is almost universal in the human race, then it is not to be wholly explained by morbid mechanisms.

Still more, then, is it likely that concepts taken from mental pathology and applied in such fields as anthropology and sociology, will shed a delusive light. We should, rather, proceed in the opposite direction, and try to map the range of normal variation before we feel sure of what is abnormal. Unfortunately, for obvious reasons, little has been done in this way.

The contrary tendency, to confine psychiatry to such an aspect of behaviour as *interpersonal relations*, is nearly as dangerous. Anatomical, physiological, biochemical, neurological and other modes of investigation are thereby excluded or regarded as of secondary importance, when they can contribute much to our understanding. The definition of psychiatry so framed is really a cloak for a hypothesis of the causation of mental abnormality, namely that it is due to disturbances of emotional relationships between individuals.

If, however, the definition we gave is accepted, we still have to delimit the concerns of psychiatry from those of psychology, the social sciences, general medicine and neurology. In every case there is a large border territory which is equally and desirably of interest to workers on both sides of the line.

Psychiatry and Medicine

The general physician and the neurologist regard physical manifestations as a prime focus of interest, and it is really only in this rather unimportant feature that they distinguish themselves from the psychiatrist. It has of late been increasingly recognized that psychological factors, especially the bodily manifestations of emotional changes, play a perceptible part in illness over the whole field of medicine. The physician employs such physical methods of investigation as examination of the urine, of the blood, of his patient's reflexes. This does not mean that he has to ignore higher and more complex phenomena, nor that he can afford to be indifferent to his patient as a personality with a life-history of his own. But it is, and should remain, a primary purpose to discover whether or not there is some malfunction at the lower level. If the physician can exclude bodily disease, or define the limits within which its effects are to be traced, and then continue to treat the patient and his symptoms as a whole, as he may properly do, then he is to some extent taking on a psychiatric function. The fact that the psychiatric aspect of medical illness can never be ignored, is not an argument for referring every patient to a psychiatrist, but for equipping with a psychiatric grounding every medical man who has to handle patients.

Psychiatry and Sociology

The close relation of psychiatry to social conditions is recognized in Anglo-Saxon countries by the employment, as a most valuable aid, of the services of the *psychiatric social worker*. The training of these workers was inaugurated by Adolf Meyer in 1918, and it includes a one- to two-year course in psychiatry after taking a social science degree.

The *importance of social factors* in psychiatric illness and of psychiatric factors in social problems had been recognized long before. Since the beginning of this century generations of psychiatrists have given attention to such subjects as the influence of social and economic factors on the suicide rate, the fertility of the dull and backward, the influence of social insecurity upon the rate of admission of old patients to mental hospitals, the contribution which is made to juvenile delinquency by the psychopathic ringleader, or the proportion of crimes of violence which is attributable to the early schizophrenic. The effect of psychiatric factors on employment and working capacity, on family life, social and political life, and on crime, have also been studied for decades.

The findings of psychiatry have also made their contribution to a number of important *social developments* that have occurred during the past half-century—to the evolution of new methods of education which lay emphasis upon a freer expression of the child's personality, the liberalization of the methods of children's upbringing in general, the emergence of a franker and more open attitude towards the problems of sex, and the development of a more humane and rational attitude towards the treatment of criminal offenders.

In recent years the increasing rate of discharge of psychiatric patients into the community and the facilities for supervision and aftercare that have had to be created to render them viable there have led to a growing interest in the social aspects of psychiatry. Attempts have been made to determine the prevalence and incidence of different forms of psychiatric disorder in the community and, as comparison of the findings in different areas was clearly desirable, this has in turn directed attention to the need for more precision and uniformity in the definition of psychiatric disorders. Once differences in prevalence have been established, which are independent of variations in the use of terms and examination procedures, the possibility arises of seeking for environmental factors that may have caused or contributed to these differences. Attempts have also been made to investigate the influence of variables such as social isolation and mobility, emigration and economic and urban-rural differences upon the rate of occurrence of mental disorder. Epidemiological and social studies of this nature have exerted a beneficent effect by encouraging psychiatrists to apply themselves to the problems of sampling, controlled comparison and statistical analysis, in short to the utilization of scientific techniques as good as the situation would permit. They have stimulated interest in studies of the patient's relations in the home, at work and in the wider community, and have fostered a more realistic appreciation of the size of the problem of mental ill-health and of the social and medical services required to meet the enormity of the challenge they offer. Potentially such studies carry the hope of discovering fresh causes of mental disorder, or at any rate of narrowing down the area to be scanned in the search for such causes. However, it has to be admitted that so far no mental disturbances specific for certain cultural or social settings have been identified. All the known forms of psychiatric disorder occur in every culture that has been thoroughly investigated and, although their prevalence and detailed symptomatology may vary from one setting to another, the form of schizophrenia, obsessional states and depression is essentially the same in Newcastle and New York as it is in Hong Kong and Calcutta. In short, epidemiological research is more likely to reveal social variables correlated with differences in prevalence and outcome than to define specific causes of mental disorder.

Social psychiatry has, then, exerted a valuable influence in broadening clinical perspectives and in fostering a scientific approach towards certain problems of mental disorder. Attempts should be made to investigate with the aid of objective techniques the contribution made to the causation of mental disease by disturbances in interaction between the individual on the one hand and the family and wider community on the other. But to encourage the hope at the present time that enquiries along these lines will ultimately help us to explain and control mental disorder is to travel along the same road as the enthusiasts of the mental hygiene movement of half a century ago who saw themselves as the midwives of the 'Sane Society'.

Psychiatry and Psychology

The relations between psychiatry and psychology are much closer than between psychiatry and sociology. Some of the concepts which have been evolved by psychologists, some of their techniques, and many of their observations are of fundamental importance in psychiatry. Nevertheless it would be absurd to maintain that psychology can be to psychiatry what physiology has been to medicine, not only because the claim would be exaggerated, but also because it implies that psychiatry and medicine are mere cousin-sciences. The reason why psychology has not been able to provide even more of the basic knowledge and the basic ideas of psychiatry lies in their separate histories.

At the end of the last century and at the beginning of the present one, psychology was concerned with elementary phenomena, such as sensory perception, reaction time, intelligence, memory, learning and other functions which are not usually affected in the commonest psychiatric illnesses. If psychologists studied the more complex phenomena, such as personality, character, instincts and emotions, they did so under the shadow of philosophical theories which often had little or no basis in factual observation. During the last forty years the development of the two young sciences has not brought them closer together, as might have been expected; apart from *some points of contact* they have tended to diverge. The contacts were made by a few rare personalities: Wundt, Kraepelin; Binet, Ribot, Janet; Henry Head; McDougall, William Brown, Fluegel; Koehler, Goldstein. In general there has been rather little transference of ideas from one field to the other; and scientists on one side have taken little interest in the problems and difficulties of their colleagues on the other. As a result both have suffered.

Because of the inadequacies of academic psychology, psychiatrists had to provide their own psychology. The result has not always been what one would have wished. Psychoanalysis is a striking example of what a neurologist could do in evolving a theory of normal psychology, a mechanistic mythology which is far behind what contemporary psychology has to offer. To this day analytic theorists in the field of child psychiatry almost totally ignore all the achievements of the Buehler school, of Piaget, Gesell, Katz and many others.

Psychiatrists, however, have not lacked some justification. They came across observations which threw new light on normal mental life, for instance the peculiar loss of reality feeling in depersonalization and derealization, the loss of the self in passivity phenomena, the disturbance of the body schema seen in some localized neurological lesions, disturbances of the sense of familiarity in the *déjà vu* phenomenon. For such things as these psychology could offer little in terminology, or standards of comparison, or theory, which would be useful in the description or elucidation of pathological changes.

Of recent years, however, there has been a considerable degree of *rapprochement between psychology and psychiatry*. Psychologists, such as Page (1947), and Landis and Bolles (1950), have produced interesting text-books of abnormal psychology. Gardner Murphy has based his psychology of personality (1947) on biological concepts. Eysenck (1952) has used psychometric techniques and the statistical device of factor analysis to isolate constitutional modes of variation on the affective side. He has particularly developed the concept of dimensions of personality, reaching the position of regarding 'psychoticism' and 'neuroticism' as primary modes of quantitative variation. He and his colleagues (Eysenck, 1960c) have attempted to apply psychometric techniques and concepts over a large part of the psychiatric field.

Psychometric techniques, especially in the cognitive field, have proved of invaluable assistance in dealing with the problems of mental deficiency and backwardness, and in the organic psychoses. A limited number of psychologists have turned their attention to the specific psychological defects associated with localized lesions of the brain, and the border territory between psychology and neurology is being explored. Although here the ground is much less secure, advances have been made in the analysis and measurement of temperamental traits of personality. Psychologists have proved their value as members of the psychiatric team both in child-guidance clinics and in clinics and hospitals for adults. One method of closing the gap between psychology and psychiatry is, however, to be regarded with some reserve, namely the tendency shown for the psychologist, for example in the application of learning theory in therapy, to take over the functions of a doctor and to engage in individual treatment. Some psychologists have shown unusual ability in this field, and it would be a pity if they were discouraged. However the selection of cases for such treatment should always be made by the doctor and psychiatrist.

However far the *rapprochement* goes, we still cannot expect that psychiatry will ever be able to base itself on psychology alone. The psychiatrist can never lose his interest in what is happening in the bodily field, or cease to seek, wherever he can, the most direct contacts with physiology and medicine. Furthermore the primary concern of the psychiatrist is with the morbid mental states; and however much is known about the psychology of the normal individual, in the pathological field some new laws will be found to operate.

CONTEMPORARY SCHOOLS OF PSYCHIATRY

Kraepelin's System and its Influence

It says much for the fluidity of present-day psychiatry that there are a number of contemporary schools, some of which do not accept the most basic tenets of the others. Modern psychiatry begins with Kraepelin, before whose attempts to bring system and order conceptions were even more chaotic than they are today. *Kraepelin's approach was nosological.* By following up groups of patients over many years he attempted to discover common features in the conditions from which they suffered which would be of value in assessing prognosis. He was led to the description of diseases of which the two most important are manic-depressive insanity and dementia praecox. It is on the basis of his work that we are now able to classify mental disorders into three main classes, the organic psychoses, the endogenous psychoses without known structural pathology, and the deviations of personality and reactive states. Kraepelin's ideas proved practical and fertile, although they required and received considerable subsequent modification. Kraepelin himself recognized this, and was always ready to change his theoretical point of view. The nosological conception which he took from medicine has proved too valuable to be entirely discarded, even by the most fanatically 'psychodynamic' schools. Even now, such conditions as Pick's disease, general paresis and cerebral arteriosclerosis are allowed to retain their dignity as disease entities, though the similar standing of manic-depressive psychoses and schizophrenia may be disputed.

What do we mean by *disease*? In special contexts the word may convey different meanings; but by it we generally mean a condition in which there is some physical change in the body which will not be completely reversible if it goes too far. In the latter case a structural alteration will usually be found, but in any case there will be functional changes, whose nature will be determined by their physical basis. The body will react to these changes by compensatory ones of a kind to halt and repair the original process and restore normal function. Mentally there will be a similar readjustment for the same purpose. All these processes and counter-processes together produce a *total alteration of the individual* which will be recognizable as to a certain extent specific and unique among similar pictures; and it is this to which we give the name of disease. There is in fact a large element of constancy in these syndromes, whatever the constitution and personality of the individual patient who is affected. Argyll-Robertson pupils, a characteristic Lange gold curve and increase of the cells in the cerebrospinal fluid may be shown by prince or pauper, and in either case are diagnostic of cerebral syphilis.

The *deficiencies of Kraepelin's system*, which led later to much modification, was his treatment of neurotic and psychopathic states. He saw no fundamental difference between these conditions and the psychoses, and did not realize the desirability of such a concept as psychogenic reaction. The popularization of this new idea was largely the work of Adolf Meyer. It proved a fruitful concept within the field of personality deviations and the neuroses, but it has added little to our understanding of the psychoses. In that field Meyer's approach led to a better appreciation of the patient's personal peculiarities and needs, of the individual features in the clinical picture, of the secondary reactions of the personality to the primary process, but not of the central psychotic symptoms themselves.

There is no reason why there should be differences of principle between the nosology of psychiatry and that of other branches of medicine. The ultimate aim of clinical medicine is to discover the causes of disease, to classify diseases by their causes, and to base prevention and treatment on this aetiological knowledge. Even general medicine has achieved so much in only a minority of instances, and it is hardly surprising that psychiatry lags behind. But it would be *absurd to accept intermediate solutions as final*, and to give up the struggle for an aetiological classification because, in the single century since psychiatry became a branch of scientific medicine, progress on the absolute scale has not been more striking. Knowledge accrues, like more material goods, not only by capital gains, but also as interest on capital in hand—and in psychiatry we started from nothing, at a later date, and in a more difficult field of endeavour, than workers in general medicine.

Such *aetiological knowledge* as we have, has to be applied. Intermediate solutions are useful as well as necessary. As in other branches of medicine, the physician has to treat his patients more or less rationally; and he cannot postpone diagnosis and therapy until the causes of the illness are fully known.

Diagnosis needs a classification which is based on a definite *system;* and it is here that special difficulties arise. In any text-book of medicine, after the illnesses known to be due to micro-organisms and poisons, diseases of unknown aetiology are discussed in chapters headed 'Illnesses of the Heart', '. . . of the Lungs', '. . . of Metabolism', etc. In psychiatry such a classification is obviously impossible, because the brain is in any case the final common pathway of all symptoms. The pathology of the brain, as it stands today, is of little help in differentiating diagnostic groups. But it is often forgotten that, from a functional point of view, the anatomy of the brain is almost entirely unexplored. The brain, with its 10^{10} cells of unequalled variety arranged with an unequalled complexity, is more like a complex of different organs than one single one. We already know of the existence of important local chemical and enzyme differences from region to region, but it seems that our knowledge in this field is only now beginning to grow and that we shall find certain functional disturbances of a psychiatric kind associated with lesions of different functional systems. The temperamental disturbances of the psychopath resemble those of the epileptic, which are themselves associated with disturbances of function of central structures, perhaps the hypothalamus. The oculogyric crises of the post-encephalitic are often accompanied by obsessional symptoms, and again a hypothalamic dysfunction is beginning to appear probable. All the specific cognitive and intellectual disturbances, the dysphasias, disturbances of spatial orientation, acalculias, etc., are associated with localized lesions of the temporal and parietal lobes. With lesions of the temporal lobe, moreover, the peculiar experience of *déjà vu* is connected. Lesions of the posterior part of the hypothalamus are liable to cause disturbance of normal sleeping-waking mechanisms. It was possible to construct a symptom complex of 'diencephalosis' (Staehelin, 1944) and even to base a number of psychiatric symptoms on primary disturbances in the diencephalon (Guiraud). The temperamental changes caused by lesions of the frontal lobes are now beginning to be well known. Recent advances in anatomy and physiology look likely to transform the aetiological basis of psychiatry within our life-times.

Much of this was not known in Kraepelin's earlier days, when diagnosis had to be based almost solely on clinical symptoms, a very unsatisfactory state of affairs against which he pitted his endeavours the whole of his life. When he found that neither cerebral anatomy nor biochemistry fulfilled his expectations, he put his hopes on the *course of the illness* and its final outcome. He collected *life histories*, which he extended into the patient's family, hoping that heredity might provide the key for a 'natural' grouping and for diagnosis. This was really the method of descriptive analysis of symptoms extended in time and expanded to cover groups rather than individuals. Many aetiological unknowns remained.

There were limitations and inadequacies in Kraepelin's views. One was his belief in a 'natural system' of diseases, like Linnaeus's system of classification of plants, which only needed to be discovered. It was also mistaken to use general paresis as the standard pattern for psychiatric disease entities, as it set too high a standard. Like his contemporaries in other branches of medicine, he based diagnosis on Virchow's anatomic-pathological concepts. Since then we have developed a much more *functional view of aetiology*, as of pathology, and recognize both primary and secondary factors as converging in the causation of disease. It is no paradox for us that heredity and constitution have been found to play their part in tuberculosis. We, unlike Kraepelin, recognize the mutual interdependence of the different organs of the body, such as appears, for instance, in the pathogenesis of anaemia. We appreciate the significance of diathesis, of temporary predispositions, and of subclinical states of ill-health which have abolished the sharp dividing line between health and disease.

The spread of these newer ideas in psychiatry was facilitated by the intensive *study of symptomatology* which was stimulated by Kraepelin's views and the controversy they engendered. Kraepelin's 'chase after the phantom of nosological entities', as it was stigmatized by one of his earliest and most ardent opponents, has not been in vain. And the diagnostic groupings which Kraepelin himself never regarded as final, still retain their pragmatic validity and have even been accepted by such workers as Adolf Meyer, who have renounced the principle of aetiological diagnosis.

Two new developments have created fresh possibilities of great importance for carrying forward the scientific work of classification and objective diagnosis begun by Kraepelin. The first is the development of a number of effective remedies for psychiatric disorders. These have provided a new and important external criterion for testing the validity of classifications established primarily on symptomological grounds. Differences in response to treatment can help to define lines of demarcation between clinical entities, although classification cannot be decided by responses to treatment alone as the relatively nonspecific effects of penicillin and cortisone exemplify. The second is the development of modern statistical techniques such as factorial analysis and discriminant function analysis. With the aid of the former, relatively precise tests can be applied to the clinical data systematically recorded in large numbers of patients so as to ascertain whether co-varying clusters of features are present. With the aid of the latter, the discriminating value in diagnosis of each of the clinical features of a disorder can be determined so that this need not be decided by subjective impression, tradition or authority. A good example of the employment of both therapeutic response and modern statistical techniques to advance knowledge of classification was the study of depressive disorders by Kiloh and Garside (1963).

Wernicke and the Cerebral Localizers

Although Freud's world-wide recognition and influence have set him on a higher pedestal than Wernicke's, Wernicke was at least the equal of Freud and of Kraepelin in power of penetration in observation and thought. Freud and Wernicke were contemporaries and were both pupils of Meynert in Vienna; but Wernicke died untimely and by accident in 1905. Wernicke and Kraepelin were having a revolutionary effect on psychiatric teaching at a time when Freud's doctrines were still restricted to small conventicles and were banned from official cognizance.

Wernicke's ideas are based, like those of Hughlings Jackson, on observation in the *borderland between psychiatry and neurology*. His discovery of 'sensory aphasia' suggested to him that all psychic functions might have their representation in the brain. He regarded the cerebral cortex as constituting, in its anatomical arrangement of fibres and cells, the organ of association. 'The first principle of classification must be that of the anatomical order, in other words that of the natural grouping and succession of psychological changes.'

The *reflex arc* was his functional unit, and the principles it involved could be extended to the highest mental activities. Its three functional aspects, sensitivity, interneural association and motor output, could be separately disturbed, by increase, decrease or malfunction. Wernicke thought it was justifiable to apply this principle even in the case of psychological disturbances for which no localized cerebral representation had, so far, been discovered.

The theory was a mechanistic one and, because of its mechanical and strictly anatomical ideas, inferior to Hughlings Jackson's similar though more functional principles. The latter's concept of stratification of mental function, of integration on different levels of the C.N.S. and of release of lower-level function after disturbance on the higher level, have only lately influenced psychiatric theory. Henri Ey (1963) was able to trace Jacksonian ideas in Bleuler's system and has himself orientated his general psychiatry on these ideas.

Both theories, Wernicke's and Jackson's, are, because of their generality, very adaptable. Within its framework Wernicke and his pupils tried to arrange the whole of psychiatric experience. This has led, in the case of Kleist and his school, to a pigeon-holed localization of functions and personality traits which reminds one at times of the phrenology of Gall and Spurzheim. Wernicke, on the other hand, made a number of important *psychological discoveries* which have become permanent additions to psychiatry. He was the first to speak of 'autochthonous ideas', as a passivity symptom in schizophrenia; he distinguished delusions of explanation from primary delusions, and failure of retention from disturbances of memory in general; he clarified the difference between over-valued ideas and delusions proper.

His universal concept of '*sejunction*', used as we use dissociation to describe and explain certain psychopathological phenomena, was the forerunner of Bleuler's theory of splitting. Wernicke was the first, preceding Bleuler, to discriminate between the primary symptoms, directly produced by the disease process itself, and the secondary symptoms which are the reactions of the personality to the primary disturbances.

Psychiatry is in debt not only to Wernicke but also to his pupils Liepmann, Bonhoeffer, Kleist and others, for much original work. The analysis which Freud attempted from inside, by psychological understanding and self-analysis, Wernicke approached from outside, behaviouristically. On one occasion he insisted that all psychiatric symptoms, including the spoken word, had to be investigated as *disturbances of motor behaviour*.

Psychobiology

The psychobiological school, founded by Meyer, derived its strength from the emphasis it placed on understanding the patient as a man. This essential aspect of clinical psychiatry had been largely ignored by Kraepelin and his closer followers, although it was later emphasized by Kretschmer among others. For the psychobiologist *the individual patient is unique*, a unity which cannot be broken down into separate aspects, nor classified in a category of simple disease entities. Meyer required of his students that they should make the most detailed studies of the personalities and the past histories of their patients, and try to interpret the illness itself as a psychobiological reaction, involving both physical and mental aspects, to immediate stresses and past habits of adjustment. He largely ignored the effect of genetical causes in influencing the make-up of the personality, and concentrated his attention on social, psychological and other environmental causes. The schizoid personality, therefore, had meaning for him as a faulty development, which had been progressively determined by a series of inadequate reactions to real life. Schizophrenia was a withdrawal into illness from a reality which had taken on an intolerable quality for the enfeebled personality. The cardinal principles of his philosophy were the unity of body and mind, the necessary combination of psychological and biological aspects in all causes of mental illness, and the uniqueness of the individual patient. From a purely philosophical point of view this was an improvement on the dualistic philosophical basis of Germanic psychiatry.

The weakness of Meyer's system was that it went too far in the opposite direction. Concentration on individual aspects of mental illness leads to the jettisoning of the knowledge which has been accumulated in studies of series of individuals; and it makes any decision, as to what is relevant among the vast mass of data accumulated about each patient, to a large extent arbitrary. Moreover, the arrangement of the causal factors in their order of importance in a given case was naturally considered misleading in the Meyerian scheme. For causation was regarded as a process, and to select any one link in the continuous causal chain for special emphasis was to distort its true character.

Graduates of the psychobiological school were confined to treating every patient as a problem of a unique kind, and were therefore not encouraged to use methods of treatment which were applicable to classes of patients. Such methods of treatment as convulsive therapy, insulin coma, etc., found no logical place in the schema, and were in practice largely neglected. Meyer was a great teacher, and his pupils were filled with an entirely wholesome respect for and devotion to the individual personality of the patient. But the only treatment which developed naturally from the primary assumptions was a form of psychotherapy, sometimes called 'personality analysis', which though useful has not proved outstandingly successful in practice.

It is also difficult to overlook the weakness of a system that ranges all types of reaction, neurotic, psychotic and organic, side by side, as if there were little to choose between them in depth of abnormality or in the causative factors involved. Meyer's enthusiasm in the fight against Kraepelinian classification led him to throw out the baby with the bathwater. Perhaps the greatest weakness in the Meyerian approach was that it encouraged no precise general formulations. Theoretical expressions emanating from this school are almost uniformly vague. Heuristically the Meyerian approach was almost entirely sterile.

Psychoanalysis

An attempt of a very different kind to escape from the difficulties of fitting psychiatry into medicine was made by Sigmund Freud (1856–1939). Freud was a neurologist, and his theory takes a *mechanistic* form such as one might expect from a neurologist of the nineteenth century; and it was based on the *dualistic* approach to body and mind which was universal in Continental psychiatry in his time. This dualism remains unresolved today, and is even now the greatest source of weakness in Freudian theory.

The *original observation* from which Freud started his life-long research is reported in a monograph with Breuer in 1895. This describes the treatment of a hysterical patient by means of hypnosis. During a hypnotic session the patient re-lived an incident in her remote past, till then forgotten; in the re-living she showed the most lively emotions, and after it experienced substantial relief from her symptoms. His reflexions on this observation led Freud directly to his conception of the unconscious, to the concept of repression, and to the view that emotion attached to repressed memories could affect the individual's responses to events of the present. All these ideas were revolutionary for their time, and represented a great advance; in one or another form they are generally accepted today. Nevertheless, he was not the originator of the idea that important mental processes went on in 'the unconscious', which had, in fact, been debated for centuries (Whyte, 1962).

While other schools of psychiatry directed their main interest to the natural history of mental disorders, their constitutional basis, their causative and releasing factors, Freud and his followers turned their attention to psychological influences and the 'dynamics' of the interaction of personality and environment. The change of emphasis was an important one, and itself constituted a significant advance. The first person whom Freud took as a subject for intensive observation was himself; and ever since then, the utterances of persons undergoing analysis have made up a large part of the body of data on which psychoanalytic theory has been based. Furthermore, the patients who have contributed their own part have been, in almost overwhelming majority, persons suffering from reactive (neurotic) rather than endogenous disorders. From this it has followed that the most valuable additions to understanding, which have stemmed from the psychoanalytic school, have been in the field of normal psychology. Freud and his successors have done relatively little practical work with psychotic patients; Freud's acquaintance with the psychology of paranoia, for instance, was gained from a book written by Schreber, and from no personal knowledge of the patient. It is not surprising, therefore, that the field of pathological psychology, as shown in psychotic states, has been left almost entirely unilluminated by psychoanalytic theory—so much so that many analysts find it difficult to understand that there are differences between the normal and the diseased, between the neurotic and the psychotic, or between reactive and endogenous disorders.

However, in the field of normal psychology, which is certainly of great significance and relevance to any study of the abnormal, psychoanalysis has provided important new insights. Outside psychiatry, moreover, it has had a profound influence on contemporary thought in wide and diverse fields. Psychoanalytic theory is concrete, complex, coherent and highly integrated. Some of its most important tenets may be briefly summarized and discussed.

THE UNCONSCIOUS. Freud's teaching on the unconscious mind is fundamental to the entire theory. There are many observations which support the occurrence of mental processes apart from the awareness of the subject, and they may be of a high order of integration. Thus the actions which may be carried out in sleep-walking may be of any order of complexity. The phenomena of post-hypnotic suggestion are instructive, in that what emerges into consciousness is a goal-directed idea, a tendency to perform some specific action apparently of the subject's own free will, while the essential motivation, the suggestion imparted by the hypnotist, is not remembered. Freud took the view that a very large part of the mental life of the normal individual went on below the level of awareness, and that a great part of his everyday behaviour was determined in the same kind of way as the phenomena of post-hypnotic suggestion; such actions, and such things as the symptoms of the hysteric, are due to unconscious ideas which control behaviour without the subject being aware even of their presence.

Freud distinguished between the conscious, the preconscious and the unconscious. What was preconscious could be brought into consciousness by the mere direction of attention. On the other hand, attempts to bring unconscious material into consciousness met, he thought, with resistance. This was attributed to an active force repressing such unconscious ideas, which was named the Censor. The Censor could, however, be overwhelmed by ideas of great power rising up from the unconscious, as occurred in psychoses; or it could be evaded by these ideas taking on some disguise, and more easily so when the individual was asleep. Thus repressed ideas could appear in a disguised form in dreams, and the study of dreams was thought to be a valuable source of information about unconscious processes.

INSTINCT. In Freudian theory it is a fundamental function of the central nervous system to attempt to annul or neutralize nervous stimulation. This hypothesis is taken as axiomatic; and it is interesting that it has also recently provided the basic assumption of certain schemes produced by physiologists and mathematicians, which attempt to explain the properties of the reflex arc on purely physical principles. It may then be seen that the stimulation which arises from the environment alone can only provide reactions of a very simple kind. However, Freud held, stimulation also arises from within, for the annulment of which very complex behaviour may be required. The animal engaged in hunting down its quarry, for instance, may be compelled to behave in a complex and intelligent way for many hours on end before hunger can be stilled. This stimulation from within is the source of instinct.

Freud made consistent efforts to simplify the *conception of instinct*. For a time he thought that the postulation of one instinct would be sufficient, but in the end had to content himself with two. These are the love instinct and the death instinct. The first is held to inspire all forms of behaviour which serve preservation of the self and the species. The second is a contrarily oriented drive towards destruction, even destruction of the self. It is often in

PLATE I

Ivan P. Pavlov (1849–1936)

Sigmund Freud (1856–1939)

conflict with the first, but at times may unite with it to stimulate a form of behaviour satisfying to both, as in eating.

A large part of Freudian theory is concerned with the development of the *sexual instinct* from earliest infancy to adult life, and with the perversions, diversions and frustrations it may undergo. Freud maintained that the first manifestations of sexuality occurred soon after birth, and were then not primarily concerned with genital function. The function of sexuality was to obtain pleasure from certain zones of the body, the 'erogenous zones'. At different stages in development, different zones took on a special importance, so that the infant and child passed through oral, anal and phallic phases. After this, development in the two sexes diverged, and there was a period of latency, precipitated in the male by the threat of castration. Much of the aetiology of neurosis in the adult is attributed to fixation of the libido, or sexual energy, on to infantile erogenous zones; and in the psychotic patient there might be a regression to an earlier level of fixation.

THE OEDIPUS COMPLEX. The first object of infantile desire is the mother's breast, and from this the child's love becomes attached to the mother herself. She maintains her place in the child's affections by being a provider of satisfactions of many kinds. If her love fails, it is believed, the development of personality will be perverted from the beginning.

The role of the father, in Freudian theory, is more remote. For the boy, especially, he appears late on the scene and then in the guise of a rival for the mother's love. The pattern of affective relationships within the family determines trends and attitudes which persist throughout life; and in them is to be sought the source of the loves, jealousies, rivalries and hatreds which in adult life affect personal relations between men and between man and society. To a faulty development of the Oedipus complex is also attributed the causation of numerous neuroses.

THE STRUCTURE OF THE PSYCHE. As has been said, Freud divided the mind into conscious and unconscious parts, between which stands the censorship. In the deepest layers of the unconscious lies the 'id', a well of energy supplying the motive force of conduct. In the conscious there is the 'ego', but the ego too has its roots in the unconscious. The function of the ego is to direct conduct so as to supply the satisfactions demanded by the id, but in a socially acceptable form. In the unconscious part of the ego, extending into the conscious part, is the 'superego', the Freudian equivalent of conscience. Its function is to warn the ego against infractions of its code, and to punish such infractions as they occur. It is invariably much stricter in its standards and harsher in its punishments than rational considerations alone would justify. This is so because it is itself non-rational, largely submerged in the unconscious from which it derives its energy, and represents the preventive and punitive aspects of the parents. Applied to psychopathology, the id–ego system is used to explain neurosis as the result of a conflict between ego and id, and psychosis as the submerging of ego in id, which has assumed control.

GENERAL CRITICISM. This short exposition, which will contain nothing new for the majority of readers, is sufficient to show how Freud was able to bring a high level of order and systematization into a great range of rather chaotic material. It is not surprising that, impinging on the rational psychology prevalent at the beginning of the century, the impact that his theory had was a tremendous one which has indeed not yet lost its impetus. It will also be apparent how ill it fits, in important ways, with any modern neurophysiology. We may briefly comment on these.

The Freudian unconscious is conceived of as space, when what corresponds to it from the neurophysiological point of view must be thought of as an integrated complexity of adaptive functions of the nervous system, proceeding below the level of awareness. From this point of view, activity at the spinal, medullary and higher levels up to the thalamus may rightly be thought of as unconscious. Neuronic pathways exist of course between these centres and the cortex; and there is no *a priori* impossibility in the psychoanalytic claim that, by appropriate training, more direct channels of communication between cortical and sub-cortical activities can be established, by which 'repressed' memories, emotions and tendencies can be subjected to conscious awareness. Conscious and unconscious mental processes would appear to shade into one another, and to be merely at the opposite fringes of a continuous spectrum. What has been conscious sinks, as a memory, at first into a preconscious level at which it is still readily available, and then into deeper levels from which its recall is progressively more difficult. Association with powerful affects may ensure its integrity against the processes of re-organization, generalization and dissolution to which it is otherwise subject; and in that case it will be capable of re-emerging, naked or disguised, on the occurrence of an appropriate stimulus.

Re-stated in some such way as this, Freudian teaching on the unconscious would be reconcilable with our knowledge from other sources about the working of the nervous system, and would become a working hypothesis of heuristic value. In some respects the views he propounded are generally accepted. The reality of unconscious mental life, its predominantly emotional and non-rational nature, and its significance in motivation, are concepts which represented a revolutionary advance. It is as a result of Freud's work that no psychiatrist now could content himself with superficial and rational-sounding explanations of conduct. Men are indeed moved by drives and motives of whose nature they have little awareness and understanding, by which they may be pressed towards a goal which means the destruction of all they would claim they valued. Conduct is surely a better guide to a man's personality than his preferred estimate of himself. It must, however, be noted that the Freudian picture is a very incomplete one. In the unconscious there is room also for the occurrence of rational and non-affective processes. These may be seen, for instance, in so-called conditioning processes, and in the development of skills and habits. Gestalt phenomena, such as those in which an intuitive solution of a long considered problem is reached, or in which the chess-player suddenly becomes aware of the existence of a subtle combination, also depend on unconscious mechanisms.

On the subject of instinct, a concept which has been practically abandoned in modern biology, it is to be noted how far into the metaphysical we are taken by the Freudian formulation. The postulation of antithetical causes, such as mutually opposed forces, will enable one to explain in a facile way phenomena of almost any kind. The love instinct and the death instinct are scarcely more than the ancient forces of good and evil dressed up in new costume. The whole formulation, especially the concept of a death instinct, now dropped by many of Freud's successors, is essentially unbiological. There is no reason to think that innate tendencies of adaptive value, i.e. the behavioural manifestations of what we call instinct, should have any single or simple primary basis. While all innate modes of reaction tend to serve a biological function, and so can be regarded as manifestations of a primary instinct of self- and race-preservation, it is unhelpful to be content with such a general idea. If we think of 'instinctual' behaviour as lying somewhere in complexity and modifiability between the simple reflex arc and behaviour directed by consciousness, we have a truer model. We may then find it no matter for surprise that such behaviour, though in general tending to fulfil a biological requirement, may also be shown in circumstances in which its effects are no longer advantageous; and we may think it more useful to imagine an infinity of 'instincts' than one.

The great service provided by Freud's work on sexual development was to draw attention to a whole range of behaviour, especially in the child, from which both medical men and psychiatrists had in Freud's day rather shied away. However the extreme emphasis which he placed on sexual motivations has proved a source of confusion. The assumption, for instance, that the pleasure which the infant can be supposed to derive from certain stimulations, e.g. of the lips, is 'sexual', is unnecessary. For Freudian theory there are no pleasures other than sexual ones, a hypothesis which flies in the face of observation and self-observation. Considering the significance of eating for maintaining life in the body, there is no need to suppose that the pleasure derived from it and from the satisfaction of hunger is not an adaptive mechanism which exists in its own right. In the same way it is forced and unconvincing to attribute to sexuality the satisfaction derived from the relief of tension in bowel or bladder, from cutaneous stimulation and muscular activity, from play in children, sport in adults, and the exercise of intellectual and artistic appreciations or creative powers.

The importance which Freud placed on the mother's love for the welfare of the child has recently been the focus of much interest and some experimental study, and has raised echoes far outside the field of medicine. There is an increasing amount of evidence, e.g. from experiments on nurturing young animals, that the young and growing creature prospers if, in addition to the satisfaction of all known biological needs, it receives love and tenderness from those that care for it. However, we do not know in what way development is thwarted if this affective atmosphere is lacking, nor what, if any, are the defects of personality likely to be shown by the deprived individual on reaching adult life. The subject should not be regarded as adequately clarified. One of the faults of an all too naïve interpretation of Freudian ideas has been the popular misconception that the child must not only be loved, but loved for every instant of the day, never be punished, never be restricted, never suffer even for a few moments from any feeling of withdrawal of love. Freud's account of the relationship of the child to his father is now quite out of date. The repressive father, whom Freud took as a standard, is now a much less formidable figure. The belief that the affections of the child are early set in a rigid pattern, not subsequently to be altered, needs extensive modification. The neurophysiology and the psychology of the infant and of the adult are so different that it is misleading to try, as Freud did, to equate one with the other, or even to suppose that processes of the same kind are at work.

That part of Freudian theory which anatomizes the psyche into ego, superego and id will have to be entirely reformulated before it can be fitted into any general scheme of understanding of mental processes. We have already pointed out the unacceptability of any system by which processes are reified into things. Thus the functions of the superego may be seen, in a Pavlovian terminology, as a series of conditioned reflexes, imprinted on the genetically prepared individual by affectively toned experience, of which those which have been instilled most firmly and from the earliest times will be those most deeply placed in the 'unconscious'. Society being as complex as it is, it need not surprise us that conflict arises, both between these conditioned reflexes and primary urges, and between them and the reasonable requirements of the situation.

Then again Freud used too narrow a framework to describe the influence of social environment. The family is the purveyor of a social and cultural tradition, and the relationships within it reflect the operation of fundamental social and economic forces extending far beyond its limits. Freud's blind spot for the significance of the *extra-familial environment* has, however, been largely corrected by the interest taken by many of his followers of the present day in interpersonal relations and social psychiatry.

Finally the theory is inadequate in that it leaves all too little place for the influence of *reason and insight* on human behaviour. Freudian doctrine, if pressed too far, would lead to a cult of unreason. If we are unaware of the reasons for some of our activities, we do not have to remain so, for we have the means of exploring them. If from non-rational urges our activity takes a particular slant, it is constantly being modified by the dictates of reason and by our appreciation of objective reality. And if once we gain an increased insight into our motivations, a new factor enters to make differences of a lasting kind.

The modern adherent of the Freudian psychoanalytic school does not accept the whole of Freud's teachings as unalterable dogma. As psychoanalytic theory changes and evolves, it may well be that a rapprochement between this and the other schools will become possible. Freud has done more than any other thinker to teach psychiatrists to look at the development of personality historically. To this extent psychoanalytic teaching has come to stay; it has been partly integrated into psychiatric practice and has formed the starting point of a certain amount of research. However, if the remaining distance is to be narrowed, some further change in attitudes will be essential. It must be realized that, despite its claim of comprehensiveness, the whole of the existing body of doctrine is inadequate to cover all forms of human behaviour; that psychological processes are manifestations of physiological ones in another dimension; that any kind of pathology, or disease process, introduces new factors of which not even the rudiments may be seen in the normal. On the methodological side, room must be made for scepticism, for the experimental test, and for the abandonment of what has proved fallacious. It is time that the subject should be taught as any other subject, to be accepted or doubted by the student in the light of his reason. It would be best to abandon altogether that process of indoctrination which is called a teaching analysis. There is but one truth; and in our asymptotic approach towards it the worker in the field of human psychology has to submit himself to the same disciplines as obtain in every other science.

Pavlovian Psychiatry

Almost contemporaneously with Freud, towards the end of the last century, I. P. Pavlov (1849–1936) was making a contribution to psychology and psychiatry of a very different kind and of probably more lasting importance. Pavlov was a *physiologist* who came to interest himself in the way and the extent to which physiological processes might be influenced by psychic stimuli occurring in the form of signals. As he had been engaged on a study of digestion, he investigated the effect of such stimuli on the process of salivation. The presentation of food to a dog causes the secretion of saliva, an unconditioned or primary reflex; but Pavlov showed that on this simple basis a complicated psychic structure might subsequently be raised. If together with the presentation of the food, the dog were presented with a sensory cue, such as the ringing of a bell, and this were repeated every time the dog was fed (re-inforcement), in time the dog would respond by salivation to the ringing of the bell alone. The bell becomes a conditioned stimulus, and the secretion of saliva in response to it a conditioned reflex. The exploitation of this simple observation in a brilliant series of experiments has added a new dimension of understanding and of investigation in psychology and psychiatry.

The potentiality, exhibited in the auditory-salivary conditioned reflex, is an entirely general one. Any unconditioned reflex may form the basis, and the sensory stimulus to be associated with it may be of any kind. In human experimentation, for instance, a reflex which is conveniently made use of is the eye-blink to a puff of air; and this may be readily conditioned to other cues. The generality of the process has made the theory of conditioning of great importance to the psychology of learning, especially as non-reflex, habitual and voluntary behaviour can be linked to cue stimuli in a similar way. Responses, moreover, do not have to be shown in a form involving nervous excitation, but can equally well be inhibitory. Pavlov and his associates worked out the laws describing conditioning processes in a systematic way, finally applying them to the theory of experimental neuroses. Their experimental methods have been very widely copied, especially in the United States; but their theoretical formulation has been less generally accepted, perhaps because the relevant literature has not been accessible in a simplified and pre-digested form. The best statement of this kind known to us is that by H. K. Wells (1956), which is the source of much of what now follows.

Pavlov maintained that all animal behaviour can be accounted for in terms of reflex and response, leaving no residue to be explained by 'instincts'. Through reinforcement or the lack of reinforcement, conditioning processes are going on throughout life, new conditioned reflexes (CRs) being formed and old ones being extinguished. The process is an adaptive one, enabling the animal to respond in a biologically adequate way to regularities in the environment; and as the environment is constantly changing, so CRs must constantly be learned and un-learned. The establishment of a CR opens up a nervous pathway, which must be through the medium of the cortex, since decortication abolishes all CRs, though the unconditioned reflexes are retained. As has been said, inhibitory reflexes are built up, as well as excitatory ones: and it has been shown that the inhibited state is not simply a lack of susceptibility to excitation, but rather the formation of a resistance to it. When first formed, the CR is in a very generalized form, and not only the specific cue stimulus, but also others resembling it, are effective. However, life furnishes the circumstances necessary for concentration or specialization of the response, as re-inforcement with the specific stimulus is persisted with, and inhibitory responses are attached to similar but different stimuli.

Many of the *inhibitory responses* are seen as having a protective function. They will not only ensue on prolonged action of a CR without re-inforcement, but also after ultra-maximal stimulation. Over the normal physiological range, increase in intensity of the conditioned stimulus leads to an increase in the response, but only up to a limit; beyond this limit a paradoxical phase is seen, in which increasing strength of stimulus is matched with decreasing intensity of response. Localized areas of inhibition in the functional systems of the cortex may develop in this and other ways; generalized protective cortical inhibition is seen in sleep, and local inhibition can be thought of as local sleep. The entire behaviour of the animal is determined by the balancing of excitatory and inhibitory processes, and the adaptation of these to the external world. It is believed that the process begins with the earliest days of life, so that a totally unmodified unconditioned reflex can only be seen in the newly born. After that, the primary reflexes become the foci of a nexus of CRs, with indirect as well as direct attachments; for one CR may be the cue to a second CR, causing the latter to mediate the response.

The sensory cues of CRs are considered together as constituting a *signalling system*. Man is distinguished from other animals by having a *second signalling system, in speech*. A verbal stimulus may play its part by acting as the cue for a sensory cue, as when a CR which has been developed to the ringing of a bell is brought into action by hearing the statement 'I am going to ring the bell'. Cues based on the first and second signalling systems attach themselves to the unconditioned reflexes from a very early time in development; and the response of one CR may be the cue for a second CR. Accordingly every unconditioned reflex is thought of as becoming 'covered' with CRs of various complexity knitting together with them to form fused reflexes, or complex acts. The second signalling system involves the whole mental life of man. No thinking is possible, it is maintained, in other than verbal or comparable symbolic form. Consciousness, and not the Unconscious, plays the dominant role in man's psychic life; and the determining elements of human mental activity are not in the lowest level, the instinctual level as maintained by Freud, but rather in the highest, in the speech system.

Psychic properties are thought of, not only as being formed in the course of the life experience of an individual, but also as consisting of stages and links of stages of formation. These links and stages must progress from the simplest and most elementary mechanisms to more and more complex ones. If earlier links are missing or badly formed, then some deficiency appears in later ones. Such a deficiency may, however, be eliminated by building up the missing link through a conditioning process. This principle has been used, it is claimed successfully, in education, e.g. in teaching tone-deaf children to sing.

Pavlov recognized the existence of constitutional differences between individuals, which occurred as a result of differences in the accumulation of acquired characteristics. He thought of variation in the *force* of nervous processes of excitation and inhibition, the *equilibrium* of these processes, and their *mobility*. The four main types of temperament are the weak inhibitory, the quiet equilibrated, the lively equilibrated, and the strong excitable; variations and sub-types could be added. Both of the extreme types, the weak inhibitory and the strong excitable, are more liable than the others to one or another form of nervous breakdown. Thus the weak inhibitory type has a lower functional limit of working capacity of the cortical cells, and under stimulation rapidly develops protective or transmarginal inhibition, which readily irradiates.

Experimental neuroses in dogs were first produced by calling for the development of a feeding response to a painful stimulus, with inhibition of the unconditioned response of withdrawal. Different forms of neurosis, inhibitory and excitatory, were produced, depending on the personality of the dog. Transmarginal stimulation alone, e.g. in the combination of a variety of extremely strong stimuli such as an explosion together with the swinging of the platform on which the dog stood, could also produce such a neurosis. Other methods were the development of extremely delicate differentiations, the requirement of a conditioned response to every fourth stimulus, the quick and direct transition from inhibitory to excitatory stimuli, and the re-shaping of a dynamic stereotype. All these forms of stress could be classified as overstrain of excitatory capacity, of inhibitory capacity or of mobility. Even the dogs of equilibrated temperament could be caused to develop experimental neuroses, if overloaded sufficiently.

The symptoms shown by the *experimental animals* when reduced to a neurotic state were all regarded as 'hypnotic phases', in which excitatory and inhibitory elements were present. In the equalization stage, all stimuli, weak or strong, produce the same effect; in the paradoxical phase strong stimuli produce no effect, and only weak ones work; in the ultraparadoxical stage inhibitory stimuli have a positive effect. If mobility is overstrained, 'isolated pathological points' appear in certain parts of the cortex, which are conceived of not as literally spatial designations, such as localized groups of cortical cells, but rather as functional dynamic structures, such as the various analysers, auditory, visual, motor, etc. The result is a pathological inertness or a pathological lability. In the one the CR is fixed, frozen, and cannot be changed or extinguished, so leading to a mechanical repetition of the response; in the other no CR can be fixed but at the best remains highly unstable, leading to chaotic behaviour. In all such neuroses numerous psychosomatic effects are observed, and there is disturbance of bodily functions as a whole.

The brain is also open to disturbance from internal causes, such as chemical, metabolic and endocrine changes, intoxications, castration, a period of heat, pregnancy. When so disturbed, the animal is less easily conditioned, and there is decline and instability of existing CRs.

Pavlov's conception of neurosis is therefore a chronic disturbance of higher nervous processes, a deviation from the normal working of the hemispheres, but a functional and not a structural change. Thus hysteria is a psychic disorder resulting from exhaustion of the brain: the first signalling system is imperfectly controlled by the second signalling system; the patient is chronically 'hypnotized' to some degree. Even in the case of schizophrenia, all the symptoms are in one or other of the various phases of hypnosis, apathy, dullness, immobility or playfulness, and are the expression of a chronic 'hypnotic' state. The Pavlovian treatment of such states relies in the main on rest, with medication and the management of abundant sleep, and on training.

Pavlov's view of the *development of personality* is that it depends on early training. People are taught to develop such character traits as perseverance and strength of will; and training also is responsible for the qualities of equilibrium and mobility. In man, with his second signalling system, a further dimension of variation is introduced over and above those available to other animals. Thus, in the 'artist' type the first signalling system is dominant over the second, and imagination and emotion are partially divorced from the regulating influence of ideas or verbal abstractions. In the 'thinker' type, the second signalling system achieves an excessive domination, and we have a dogmatist, an intellectual, living in a world of abstract ideas. These are extremes, between which most of the genuine artists and thinkers are to be found, i.e. in a state in which both first and second signalling systems are to some extent equilibrated.

The *principal neuroses* Pavlov classified as neurasthenia, psychasthenia and hysteria. Neurasthenia is the disorder of the middle human type. There are first periods of weakness and fatigue, due to the fact that there has been an excess of excitation and activity. There follows a weakening of inhibitory processes, lack of restraint, irritability, decline in self-control. Then excitatory processes begin to weaken, reacting quickly but soon lapsing into exhaustion. Finally there is irradiating transmarginal inhibition, and drastic lowering of all activity. Psychasthenia is the disorder of the thinker type, and shows itself in an abundance of socially unnecessary inhibitions, feeble emotions, painful doubts, incapacity to react to new situations, and the substitution of profitless reasoning for effective action. Hysteria occurs mainly in the artist type, with highly emotional and imaginative thinking, a tendency to substitute fantasy for reality, and rash impulsiveness. There is predominance of the first over the second signalling system, of subcortical activity over cortical. As regulation by the first signalling system weakens, activity becomes chaotic, irradiating transmarginal inhibition and a variety of hypnotic phases develop. The essential causes for all such disorders are to be sought in strains, shocks and conflicts.

The above provides a brief outline of work that has been in progress over a number of decades and is embodied in a vast literature. The Pavlovian classification of personality, for example, was based upon the features of *balance* of excitation against inhibition and the *strength* and *mobility* of conditioning processes. In man the presence of the second signal system provides a further dimension. Recent Soviet work has included studies of interoceptive conditioning in which conditioned and unconditioned stimuli or both are delivered to the mucosal lining of a viscus. The responses so generated have been shown to obey the laws of conditioning although they were largely unconscious in character (Bykov, 1959; Razran, 1961). As the functioning of the kidneys, the endocrine and nervous systems have been claimed, in these studies, to undergo sustained changes, they would appear to be of some importance for the field of psychosomatic medicine. Soviet workers have also carried out extensive enquiries into schizophrenia and have claimed, among other things, that conditioned reflexes are difficult to establish in schizophrenics and that they also show, in common with brain-damaged subjects, defective 'orienting' reflexes which are considered to be regulated by the reticular arousal system (Lynn, 1963).

The Pavlovian scheme has become the main foundation of Soviet psychiatry, and is readily reconciled with their other prevailing ideas along economic and social lines. *Treatment* in psychiatry, on this approach, eschews such methods as pre-frontal leucotomy, and becomes essentially psychotherapeutic and re-educative. In Anglo-American psychiatry, Pavlovian ideas began to cause extensive echoes during the Second World War, the development of such ideas in a setting of war psychiatry being especially associated with William Sargant. Indeed, the particular form of war neuroses, with anxiety states or hysterical dissociative symptoms being released under stress ('transmarginal stimulation'), was such as to make them readily understandable along Pavlovian lines. This approach led to the use of 'abreactive' methods of treatment. To take an example, the soldier who had become paralysed in one arm after being involved in a grenade explosion, could be looked on as having developed a locus of transmarginal inhibition. To cure it, the forces isolating this 'pathological point' must be broken through. An effective way of doing this was to put the patient into a hypnotic state with drugs, and then to get him to return in memory to the traumatic incident and to live it through. This would be likely to be accompanied by an extreme state of excitement and fear, followed by collapse into a momentary state of total higher nervous inhibition. After this, in a satisfying proportion of cases, nervous re-integration, with relief of the paralysis, would be found to have occurred.

In recent years the concepts of Pavlov, Watson, Hull and Skinner have been applied in the treatment of neurotic disorders. Behaviour therapy has made use of techniques such as reciprocal inhibition in the extinction of neurotic symptoms; and Wolpe (1958), who has written an influential book on the theoretical basis and practical aspects of the treatment, as also a number of his followers (Eysenck (ed), 1960b) have claimed favourable and lasting results with it. It has exerted a beneficent effect in stimulating a fresh interest in the establishment of a rationally-based and systematic treatment of neurotic disabilities and in the objective evaluation of the results achieved. However, the precise value of these and related forms of treatment remains, at the present time, uncertain.

The attempt to analyse the pathogenesis of neurotic symptoms as manifestations of normal and abnormal conditioning has hardly made more than a start in Western psychiatry, and we are all too ignorant of what the progress has been in the USSR. The approach is, at least, a most interesting and promising one. It is doubtful whether so much can be said of the possibilities of Pavlovian interpretations of the pathogenesis of schizophrenia and other psychotic states. But even if, once again, the advance made is more in the field of normal than pathological psychology, it yet may well prove of great importance for future developments.

Existential Analysis and Related Theories

Under this heading we may describe a variety of attempts to solve the problems of psychopathology by the use of philosophical short-cuts, instead of the relatively slow method of investigation with the disciplines of natural science. From its nature, existential analysis appeals to those of a philosophical or metaphysical cast of mind, especially those who find scientific methodology too materialistic or technological. The school of thought associated with the name of existentialism has become particularly prominent in certain countries of Western Europe, and has its adherents in philosophy and literature as well as in psychiatry. It represents a revival of similar movements in the history of thought which have sprung up in past eras, especially that which occurred in the first half of the nineteenth century, when romantic writers and philosophers such as Carus, Schelling and Schlegel, tried to keep pace with the new discoveries of natural science by using the method of philosophical discussion to reach conclusions on the 'nature' of animals, of organs of the body and their functions, or of the universe itself.

One of the first steps of the modern romantics was to free psychology from what was regarded as the Cartesian prejudice, i.e. the requirement that subject and object should be separated as a start to scientific thinking, especially in psychology. The existentialist, abandoning this division, wishes to start by using as a basic unitary concept for the understanding of all human life the awareness of the individual of himself in his world, 'Being-in-the-World'; from this are to be derived the concept of 'ontology', the doctrine of being, and the basis of all philosophy. In the formulation of the German philosopher Heidegger, the primary Being-in-the-World is a state of solitude and anxiety, with the awareness of approaching death as the only certain knowledge. This pessimistic outlook had a natural appeal to the younger generation of postwar Europe, especially when it was spiced, as in the case of some French existentialists, by an element of irresponsible hedonism.

It would however be wrong to link this particular mode of popularization with the work of such serious and humane psychiatrists as L. Binswanger, V. von Gebsattel and E. W. Straus, who for a number of years had advocated a more direct, more total and less piecemeal approach to psychiatric patients and their symptoms. By putting subjective experience into the centre of psychology, and linking it with the phenomenology of Jaspers, they aimed at what, for lack of a better description, one may call the opposite of behaviourism; this brackets together all objective phenomena, while the existential school is only interested in the interpretation of the subjective.

Giving their modes of approach such various names as 'constructive-genetic anthropology', 'existential analysis' and 'existential anthropology', these workers use empathy to 'understand' the 'world' of the depressive, the obsessional, the manic or the patient with ideas of reference. Putting themselves into the patient's situation, they use the totality of this understanding to interpret individual symptoms. Sometimes the interpretations are plausible, or even obvious; sometimes they are defined in a new and more precise terminology; or they may be capable of illustration from novels or poetry. Other interpretations represent attempts to abstract a general principle of explanation for the patient's experience. Thus certain syndromes are derived from non-psychological principles such as 'time' or 'vital energy'. The experiences of depression are due to a standstill of subjective time, while the manic with flight of ideas is living in a momentary present in a festive enjoyment of his existence; paranoid experiences are related to a special abnormal way of looking at the world, and so forth.

It is obvious that the words of everyday language and their meaning must play an important part in this psychopathology. The meanings of the words we use to describe the emotional aspects of experience are often far from definite; and it is by using this halo of vagueness of meaning as a starting point for its hypotheses that existentialism can make a direct appeal to the feelings, at least of those who find a purely scientific approach unsatisfying. There are fundamental differences between this school and that other school, Freudian psychoanalysis, which also puts the patient's subjective experiences and the words in which they are described in the centre of the picture. While Freudian interpretations are based on the hidden sexual symbolism of certain words, existentialism makes much of the supposed hidden psychological insight inherent in certain metaphorically used phrases, such as 'encounter' ('Begegnung'), 'course of life' ('Lebensweg'), etc. Furthermore, in contrast to psychoanalysis, existentialism is concerned with the ego only, with higher human motifs, and neglects early childhood experiences, instinctual drives and all that we share with the animals, to such an extent that it becomes at times totally unrealistic. 'Being-in-the-World' then becomes synonymous with 'Being-in-the-Academic-World-of-Europe'.

The great differences in level of originality and critical judgment between the representatives of the existentialist school have to be emphasized, as well as the variety of their basic views. It is hardly more than a few negative characteristics that they all have in common, and which allocate them their special position in psychiatric theory. Although they frequently refer to phenomenology, what they practise is not strictly to be so named. Phenomenology is a factual approach, based on the work of Jaspers, and differs from existentialism by seeking no aid from philosophical short-cuts. Existentialists and cognate theorists either deny that psychology can be a part of natural science, or else consider that any part of psychology which can be scientific is irrelevant for the understanding and treatment of psychiatric patients. For the existentialist, even the patient's body is only of importance as far as the patient is aware of it and experiences it as part of himself and the world. Binswanger, who ranks as their philosophical spokesman, has said: 'the ground and soil, in which psychiatry can take root as a science in its own right, is neither cerebral anatomy or physiology, nor biology, neither psychology, characterology and typology, nor the science of the person, but man ('der Mensch')'. Thereby psychiatry for the existentialist becomes entirely isolated from all other modes of study of the mentality of man, and would seem to be deprived of all possibility of fertilizing them in turn.

The Multidimensional Approach

The observations for which we have to account in psychiatry are of a very complex and varied kind. Any single and simple hypothesis can be regarded with suspicion from the start, as it will almost certainly prove inadequate to cover the whole range of observation. This does not mean that such a theory should be rejected out of hand. It should, rather, be carefully tested and its implications explored; for it may provide a useful framework for a limited range of data, suggest fruitful subjects for research and, if it is substantiated, eventually prove capable of organization into a larger scheme. In order that science should progress, the mind needs *working hypotheses* in order to grasp and dissect its experiences; and no harm is done if these hypotheses are only partial, or even faulty, provided they are invariably regarded with scepticism. As Popper (1963) has shown, we need hypotheses in order to refute them. We shall need hypotheses of somewhat different kinds to account for the occurrence of confusional states in vitamin deprivation and for the delinquencies of a badly brought up boy. The psychiatrist, however, needs also at least the adumbration of a *general theoretical scheme* in which partial hypotheses may find their place.

An inkling of the breadth that such a scheme must assume is given by a preliminary glance at the *variety and the paradoxical qualities of our material.* We know, for instance, that physical changes in the body, especially in the blood and in the brain, tend to be followed by changes in the mental state; but also that changes in the mental state may have bodily changes as a consequence. In some respects the pattern of development of the personality is determined by genetical factors; but man is also flexible and adaptable, and his character is influenced by the world in which he grows up and lives. Mental health is affected, often in a far-reaching way, by changes in the physical environment; but man lives also in a world of ideas, by which his behaviour is largely governed. As medical men we are primarily concerned with the individual; but man is a social animal, his behaviour is moulded by the society in which he lives, and his health is affected by his relations with other individuals and with the community as a whole. Some mental illnesses have an easily recognizable anatomical pathology; but other abnormal states, so far from having an identifiable physical basis, are of such a nature that they can only depend on changes of a functional, probably chemical, and rapidly reversible kind. There are syndromes which have constant features, irrespective of the qualities of the individuals who are affected by them; but the individual, whatever the change he undergoes, brings into it features which are constant to himself.

If we are to order such a variety of experience in any comprehensible way, we must have something in the nature of *dimensions*, or *ordinates*, by which phenomena may be arranged and compared. A change which a man undergoes may be of greater or less degree, and it may occur before or after another change. These are *scales of reference* which everyone uses; the psychiatrist has to envisage many others. Among these is the *functional–organic scale*. We recognize that there can be no structural change without a change in function, and that any functional change presupposes some kind of structural modification; yet in some cases the structural change is the primary one, or of massive effect, and in other cases it can be for all practical purposes neglected. It is important to realize how far along this scale any particular change is to have its estimated place. With a similar proviso, we must employ a *physiogenic–psychogenic scale*, and try to order the factors which affect human behaviour towards the pole of a physical mode of operation or towards the pole of operation as ideas. We must think also in terms of simplicity or complexity, of changes which affect primary and basic activities or those of the highest order, or having effects which are extended or limited and localized. If we attempt to think in this way we shall find that our many dimensions of reference will be meaningfully related to one another, that even complex data can be lucidly approached, and that we shall not be tempted to extend the application of partial hypotheses outside their appropriate fields.

If we follow a human being through the whole of his life-span, we see that he begins as a lowly and undifferentiated organism, almost indistinguishable from other organisms in a comparable state of development, even those belonging to other genera. As development proceeds there is an increasing degree of *differentiation*. At the time the infant is born, he is, from a neurological point of view, a mid-brain preparation, without co-ordinated cortical activity, and without consciousness in any adult sense. Nevertheless individual peculiarities are already beginning to appear, and the infant is distinguishable from others, not only by such physical characteristics as the blood agglutinogens, but also by such temperamental qualities as placidity or restlessness. The new-born infant, in fact, already has to some extent a personality. We do not know as yet the extent to which infantile traits of temperament are correlated with the adult traits he will show later on.

It is difficult to imagine causes other than *genetical* for personality differences shown so early, and sufficiently marked for nurses and for mothers to recognize one baby from another. Yet *environmental factors* may have already exercised an important, even a critical influence, on the individual. An attack of rubella which affected the mother during pregnancy may have caused a structural defect in the child; so may a birth injury, or an incompatibility between the foetal and the maternal blood. Such grossly pathological factors are likely to cause not only general and undifferentiated effects, such as an eventual mental deficiency, but also specific ones, such as a congenital heart lesion, a porencephaly or kernicterus. If such a structural change does occur, the constitution of the individual is permanently altered, and will show the effects throughout life.

As development proceeds, the infant is subjected to influences coming both from within and from without, that are both of a genetical and an environmental kind and we shall envisage *genetical and environmental factors* in mutual interaction. As the individual gets older, genes hitherto latent in their effects will begin to influence the course of development, themselves being called into activity by an environmental change. In the normal child, the genes involved will be the multitudinous genes of minor effect, producing changes which are all within physiological limits. It may occur, however, in the unusual case, that the child carries a *major mutant gene*, whose effect is large and harmful and quite specific. For instance the child may have inherited from father and from mother a gene which causes an incapacity to metabolize phenylalanine along normal pathways. In that case, whatever his other genetical and environmental advantages, he will need a special diet to develop intellectually beyond the defective level. However, we can place *no time-limit* on the period of latency of a mutant gene. In the case of Huntington's chorea or Pick's disease, it may be fifty years or more before it begins to show its eventually disastrous effects.

Even in the case of the mutant genes responsible for grossly pathological changes, there are few that are entirely sure of their effects. In most cases they have a *variability* which allows both the environment and the rest of the genetical constitution to exercise some influence. The presence of a mutant gene may be necessary for, say, the predisposition to schizophrenia; but having the predisposition one may yet well escape having the disease. Constitutional or environmental advantages may prevent one Huntington gene-carrier from developing the disease until advanced old age, while another develops it in the early thirties.

In the case of individuals, and they compose the majority, who have no mutant gene likely to cause mental abnormality before the senium, the *genetical make-up* will still influence development. We can see this especially with qualities of a *quantitative* kind in which there is a good deal of *individual variation*. A well-studied example is that of stature, of which the hereditary basis is polygenic, but which is known to be markedly influenced by environmental factors, e.g. of a nutritional kind. It is almost certainly true that differences in *intelligence*, and probably true that differences in *temperament*, are also, like adult stature, the product of an interaction between heredity and environmental causes.

Just as genetical causes influencing development may be single and gross or multi-tudinous and slight, so also may *environmental causes*. An encephalitis or a severe head injury may permanently alter the personality and give a particular slant to further develop-ment; a toxaemia or an infection may cause a very severe but entirely reversible change. These factors will be relatively rare, although of the greatest importance in psychiatry, which is more concerned with the sick than the healthy. As a rule the environ-ment will be compatible with health, but still exercise a persistent guiding influence. The *environment in its psychological aspects*, inspiring habit patterns based on confidence or fear, trust or suspicion, aggressiveness or submission, independence or conformity, will deter-mine the way in which the potentialities of the individual, not otherwise entirely unbounded, will be realized. The successes and failures, the interests which are encouraged and those which are frustrated, the unfolding of intellectual powers and special gifts and handicaps, though it might seem primarily in the intellectual field, will have their influence on the temperament. Paths of development once entered on will tend to continue in a benign or vicious spiral, as if development had its own momentum.

The importance of learning and habit-formation in both normal and abnormal develop-ments of personality, and the significance of learning theory for psychiatry have only recently received adequate recognition. Evidence has been adduced, for example, that pro-longed separation of a child from its mother is liable to produce serious and lasting distortion of personality development, many such children subsequently becoming affectionless and delinquent individuals (Bowlby, 1953). A more recent reappraisal of the evidence (*Depriva-tion of Maternal Care*, W.H.O., 1962) has thrown doubt on some of the claims originally made. The effects appear neither as specific, invariable, lasting nor as irreversible as had been originally claimed, although it is generally agreed that adverse effects are produced in some children. There is also fairly strong evidence that insufficient maternal warmth and stimulation are liable to give rise in certain infants to a picture resembling mental retardation (Clarke and Clarke, 1958) unassociated with brain damage or any other causal agent. The phenomenon can be reversed by the provision of a satisfactory mother substitute and may therefore have considerable practical importance in view of the marked social gradient in the incidence of the commonest forms of mental subnormality.

At any particular instant of time the individual himself, and not only the environment in which he is placed, is in a *state of flux*. The environment provides stimuli, biochemical, sensory, ideational, etc., which necessitate some reaction; and the mode of reaction will be determined by the totality of predispositions which have been developed through past interactions between the constitution and the environment. The genetical equipment will have contributed to this, but also learned patterns of response which have now become habitual, physical changes which have resulted from earlier accidents or diseases, and other effects of past environments. As a result of the *momentary interaction*, some form of behaviour will be shown, which itself has consequences for the environment and the individual. It is possible to look on the interaction as *fully determined* within a range of probabilities; and this mode of approach is the only one which is heuristically justified for scientific purposes.

As the individual develops, so his constitution constantly changes. Although the genetic equipment is always the same, at different times of his life a different constellation of genes is playing the critical role. The constitution is very different at the age of seven from what it is at seventeen, at forty-seven or seventy-seven. At these ages, also, the type of environmental factor which is important for further development will change. At any particular time, the reactions of an individual are the *compound result of a complexity of forces*. How shall we go about the analysis of this complexity?

The problem is slightly different if we are attempting to draw some general conclusion, or if we are trying to sort out the causes which have conspired to bring on some illness in a single individual. In the former case we shall have to work with *grouped data*. There are very few conclusions which can be reliably based on a single observation. If we wish, for instance, to discover whether alcoholism can precipitate schizophrenia, we might begin by collecting a number of patients suffering from the so-called chronic alcoholic hallucinosis, and studying the resemblances and differences between them and a group of schizophrenics comparable in family background, past personality, clinical picture and prognosis. In any such study purely individual features shown by particular cases are necessarily submerged. But we shall learn nothing about the aetiological connexion between alcohol and schizophrenia by the study of a single case showing both conditions.

When, on the other hand, we are faced by a *single patient* and required to come to conclusions about the causes of his illness, we shall have to proceed on the basis of the knowledge we have already accumulated by investigations of series. We shall try to see how far his case falls in line with others, showing some similarity in one or other aspect of personality or clinical state. Classifications of many kinds will be indispensable tools; and before we can put our fingers on what is individual to his case, we shall have to delimit the aspects which can be assigned as the effect of more general causes.

The total observational material can be broken down in this way into parts which can be assigned wholly to some specific factor, and others which have to be attributed to a combination of factors. This is to employ the *multidimensional diagnosis*, whose value was so strongly emphasized by Kretschmer and Birnbaum. The operative causes are arrayed in a hierarchy, some of them being more fundamental than others. The individual features of the case were recognized for what they were by first sorting out the features accounted for by more general attributes.

One might ask why a greater importance should be assigned in interpretation to qualities in which a man resembles other men than to those in which he is peculiar to himself. Does not this minimize the value and importance of personality? The answer lies in our conception of individuality. The individuality of a man lies in the respects and the degrees in which he differs from other people, so that even to discover what they are, we must first exclude those respects in which he is like others. Furthermore, the *individual in himself is unknowable*, and we can only begin to understand him by using the method of comparison. Finally, the investigation of the causes of illness can only proceed by abstraction, by getting away from singularities to generalities, and in this it resembles all other sciences. We must find room in our general scheme for all kinds of causes.

Experienced clinicians of all ages have practised the same principles in other branches of medicine and surgery where, however, for reasons explained earlier, the disentanglement of the essential from the accidental is easier. When all the symptoms are psychological, much careful scrutiny and patient observation, based on a wide clinical experience, is needed. From the cross-section before the physician at the moment of his examination, he has to decide what is '*pathogenetic*' and how far '*pathoplastic*' elements contribute to the picture.

If for instance it was correct, as Bostroem suggested some time ago, that the morbid cheerfulness and hilarity of the early general paretic is only found in patients of cyclothymic constitution, some with pyknic physique, while other constitutional types react with another clinical picture to the same infection—this would prove that the clinical picture and the causation of illness belong to *different dimensions*: the euphoria being a pathoplastic contribution of the patient's constitution while the disturbance as a whole was due to the action of the micro-organism on the brain.

On the same principle more intricate pictures in which genetical or early acquired constitutional factors combine with factors of the outer or inner environment, can be analysed and the contribution of each to the appearance of the disease estimated, before arriving at a final diagnosis suited to direct our action.

Symptoms of different dimensions may follow one another in time in the same patient and wrongly be considered equivalent: a beginning schizophrenic illness, for instance, may be disguised as one of the neurotic reactions: what first appears are features at the disposal of every average individual in a situation of stress. Whatever neurotic symptoms prevail in the picture, may be decided by the patient's special life situation: anxiety symptoms in an immature adolescent, uncertain of himself; hysterical symptoms in an unhappily married young woman, or in a prisoner who shows pseudo-dementia and a paranoid reaction, and so on. Behind these symptoms—in fact less definite and more vague neurotic pictures are the more common precursors of schizophrenia—the illness proper with its characteristic and specific symptoms will one day make its appearance. If similarly vague neurotic reactions are due to a slowly growing cerebral neoplasm, the appearance of papilloedema or other neurological signs will clear the situation. As soon as, in the case of schizophrenia, thought disorder, emotional blunting, auditory hallucinations, etc., are suspected, become probable or recognizable, the secondary nature of what may have appeared a pure neurotic reaction, is established.

For multidimensional diagnosis in psychiatry it is not only essential to have the knowledge of symptoms and signs and an idea of their common occurrence and combinations in clinical pictures, but also to be able to range their specificity, their significance and their relation to situations in the various phases of human life.

Depression, probably the most common presenting symptom of psychiatric patients today, may serve as an example of the *varying diagnostic validity* of such a symptom according to the dimension in which it appears. It may be the only and overriding feature of a depressive neurotic reaction, motivated by the patient's life situation and well understood if one knows his history. In another case, it may be less easily comprehended from the circumstances, but here the depressive picture occurs in a constitutionally predisposed individual of the cyclothymic type. Depression, especially of the recurrent type, is, of course, the most common symptom of affective disorder. As such it is not only deeper and of longer duration than in the first-mentioned case, but ranges in a different dimension. In another dimension again depression is the sequela of an attack of influenza or of infective hepatitis; it may also be the leading symptom of a cerebral arteriosclerosis in a middle-aged patient. Mental recovery paralleling physical convalescence in the first case and an organic deterioration appearing after some time in the arteriosclerotic discloses the diagnostic value of the depressive symptom in these patients. In view of the varying significance of the symptom—the foregoing examples do not exhaust all possibilities—it seems equally one-sided to classify every psychosis with some depressive admixture among the affective group as to disregard depressive elements in a clinical picture because depression can have so many different meanings in the totality of the syndrome.

In conclusion it should be remembered that the multidimensional approach cannot be expected to allocate every unusual feature to some primary or secondary cause or to solve every diagnostic problem. Its dimensions are not necessarily limited to what is known of mental mechanisms and their physical concomitants today—other points of view will arise in the psychiatry of the future and there is *room for new observations*. For example, the dividing line between pathoplastic and pathogenic and between functional and organic has recently been found to be nothing like as sharp and immutable as one might have supposed. Thus it has been found that disorders closely simulating schizophrenia may arise in association with long-standing epilepsy or as the result of addiction to the amphetamine group of drugs. Organic features may be minimal or absent in the psychiatric picture and the schizophrenia-like illness does not appear to be a pathoplastic effect arising from innate disposition. These and other examples of an overlap between the functional and organic territories have important implications for classification, diagnosis and clinical research in psychiatry. In the light of this, it should be clear that, although some theoretical framework is necessary to give cohesion and direction to psychiatric practice and scientific enquiry, it should always be regarded as tentative and applied with flexibility so that fresh knowledge and insight can be rapidly accommodated. But for the reader of this text, if the intentions of the authors have been realized, it should be impossible to accept as general, a partial and narrow theory.

CHAPTER II

EXAMINATION OF THE PSYCHIATRIC PATIENT

ADOLF MEYER and his students, who have formed the psychobiological school which has had such a large influence on Anglo-American psychiatry, drew attention to the great importance of the psychiatric interview with its various aspects of history-taking and examination. They pointed out also the *therapeutic significance* of this preliminary study. From their viewpoint, nearly everything of clinical importance would be derived from the study of the patient as an individual, and precise and detailed knowledge was therefore required of the way in which the patient's personality differed from that of other men, how it had grown, and how it had been influenced by all the events of his life. A whole philosophy and a theory of the causation of mental illness were implied in the method of examination (Muncie, 1948).

Psychiatrists of other schools have learned much from psychobiological teaching. But, in the opinion of the authors, it has led to a lack of sense of proportion, to a forgetfulness of pathological factors, and an immersion in detail which have not in the long run been profitable. They favour, therefore, a somewhat more robust method. If treatment is to be begun when it has the best chances of success, a *provisional diagnosis* at least should be reached within the first week after the patient's admission. In difficult cases, that diagnosis may be incomplete. It may, for instance, be decided that there are indications of pituitary disorder, in the elucidation of which a long series of physical tests may be necessary; or the diagnosis may simply consist of a provisional exclusion of organic illness or endogenous psychosis, an acceptance of the symptoms as most probably a neurotic reaction, which therefore calls for more detailed study of the personality. In order that one may get so far in the time allowed, the method of examination should be such as to focus attention on crucial points, while subtleties may be left to emerge more gradually as the time for a personal acquaintance with the patient extends.

If a man has a physical illness, he comes to his doctor with a *complaint*. The complaint points to the direction in which its cause is to be sought, and narrows the field of enquiry. The careful physician makes a full examination of all systems, but with a mind that is sensitized to a limited range of possibilities; his taking of the history will also be governed by the same principle. Let us suppose that his enquiries come to nothing. Less likely possibilities then arise for consideration, and further questions about the past history and further tests and examinations will then be made. We will suppose that all fail, and the patient still persists with his complaint. It is now attributed to 'imagination', 'nerves', 'lack of will power', or is labelled as 'functional' or 'psychological'. If the physician has the courage of his conviction he will now refer the patient to a psychiatrist.

The psychiatrist proceeds in exactly the same way, but in a field which has been left almost untouched by the physician. He will pay attention to matters which the latter has dismissed as personal or accidental. His mind will be alert to the possibility of diseases

C

which do not show themselves in abnormalities of structure or of the simpler functions of the body, but in complexities of behaviour or such even less tangible matters as deviations of mood. These must be judged against the personal environment, and he will necessarily be interested in the circumstances of his patient's life, his hopes, fears, conflicts and disappointments. Nevertheless he will be driven to make use of just such an *orderly system of investigation* as is employed by the physician. The general and comprehensive survey will not be neglected, but detailed investigation will be confined to the fields in which it is most hopeful, in which the major possibilities arise.

The physician examines his patient system by system; similarly the psychiatrist must make his examination methodically and attempt to describe his findings under headings, such as those of affect and intellect.

Physical complaints often disguise mental abnormality. On the other hand, psychiatric patients often have no complaint to make, and *lacking insight* into their condition, come to the psychiatrist only on the advice of relatives or friends. Whereas a man may be able to regard and to describe a disturbance of stomach or bladder function with a measure of detachment, and be the best available informant about his trouble, a different state of affairs is the rule in psychiatry. If there is mental disorder, the whole of the functions of the mind are distorted in some way, and the information that the patient provides suffers the same distortion. Where there is no gross mental disorder, and interest centres on the patient's personality, he is likely, as an observer, to be if anything in even worse case. No man is able to appraise his own personality in any adequate way, being held within its own bounds—just as our astronomers are unable to see the shape of the galaxy in which the solar system revolves.

For all these reasons the information which can be provided by *the independent observer* is of more crucial significance in psychiatry than in any other branch of medicine. Even from a relative or friend, however, wholly impartial information should not be expected. They too are to some extent within the patient's circle, motivated by sympathies and antipathies, and with their own axes to grind. The psychiatrist, while attempting to get all available information, should avoid making any formulation of the case which he has yet to see, not even to himself and least of all to the relative. He will not be surprised if any preliminary construction he makes fails to correspond with what he finds in the patient himself.

In history-taking and the examination of the patient himself two methods may be followed. They are not alternatives, and it is best if they are combined, for each has its own deficiencies. The *free interview* may deteriorate into a conversation on the social level, and may provide hints and indications rather than solid facts; all too easily important themes may be forgotten and left untouched. The method of *questionnaire* has other defects. It is uncomfortable for the patient, who may feel like a pupil in the presence of his schoolmaster; and the information that is obtained may consist in a mass of detail, without highlight or relief, which it is very difficult to organize into a coherent picture. The best plan is therefore to have the framework of a questionnaire in mind, but to allow the patient to tell his own story. As the story unfolds, it is fitted into the framework, so that any gaps that are still left are apparent. Further questioning will then fill up the gaps and will clarify points of salient importance.

As information comes in, a general outline of the case will be forming in the mind of the psychiatrist. This will itself lead to modifications of the plan of examination. The psychiatrist, however, must avoid any disclosure of this plan, and above all avoid giving the patient any feeling that he is being treated as a 'case' only. It is as easy to err on one side as on the other. If a background of experience in the wards of a mental hospital leads too easily to a dehumanized attitude, a predominant interest in individual psychotherapy may concentrate attention all too much on peculiarities of the patient's situation and on his understandable difficulties and preoccupations, while fundamental ways in which he differs from normal men are obscured. The psychiatrist must be both *neutral and sympathetic*. He must give the patient rein and allow him to advance his own interpretations without correction. As far as possible he must keep an open mind and guard himself against preconceived ideas. In no case, at this early stage, should he be tempted into pushing his own point of view. It is easy to play the prophet and saviour; and it is a standing danger of psychiatric practice that the psychiatrist may become inflated with ideas of his own superiority, and regard himself as gifted with supernormal and all-embracing powers of insight. In trying to avoid this danger, a psychiatrist may fall into another—that of subordinating himself to the patient and allowing himself to be influenced, against his clinical judgement, by the patient's desires and whims.

Psychiatric examination proceeds by, as it were, taking a longitudinal and a cross-section of the patient's life. It is simplest to begin with the longitudinal section, by taking the patient's *biography*. Without it, the cross-section, the comprehensive view of the patient's state at the time of examination, will appear unclear, confused and difficult to understand. Time relations are lost, and what is fleeting and insignificant may be taken to be permanent and important. If the history is taken first, the findings on examination are brought into a natural relation to one another; and further enquiry will be needed to trace back into the past the roots of only those findings whose appearance in the present state is unexpected and difficult to interpret.

If they are accessible at all, psychiatric patients are, even more than others, interested in their own lives and like to talk about themselves. While the patient describes his life, he gives us an opportunity to see how he speaks, thinks, judges, feels; how he has reacted to events in the past, how he deals with the objective world and with people around him, and what are his ideas on moral, religious, political and sexual questions. Observations will be made which properly belong to the account of the present state, and though to be embodied in it, must be recorded at the time they are made. It is useful to note down the actual words the patient uses to describe his most important symptoms, and indeed to record any very individual and characteristic phraseology on a subject of interest.

It is well-tried psychiatric practice to record findings *in writing*, nor has the advent of new technologies replaced the need. A sound-recording of what the patient says does indeed provide in permanent form and for ready reference very much more than the psychiatrist can capture in his notes. It is, however, entirely unselective. For the young specialist it is of the utmost importance to keep his ideas clear by formulating in writing what he has found. Only so can he learn from case to case, and get his clinical knowledge in proper perspective. If sound-recordings are available, they should be played over so that a written presentation, from which all inessentials are omitted, can be prepared. When the records are complete, they should be rounded off by a *formulation*. This is in essence a detailed statement of the diagnosis in multidimensional terms. It will contain a classification of the disorder and a specification of the factors, physical, constitutional and psychogenic, which have contributed to its appearance. It will also contain a short plan for further investigation and for treatment. This formulation is a much more difficult matter than the description of past and present in extended form, and will test all the psychiatrist's powers of judgement and wealth of experience. Even for the student, however, it is a necessary exercise. *Well-kept case records* are the basis of all progress in clinical medicine, and are indispensable for research.

Only in the course of time can the psychiatrist develop the art of eliciting by tactful questioning all he has to know. Long training is needed to learn how to overcome the patient's resistance, to be aware of where his tale is biased, where information has been withheld and where it has been coloured by an emotional attitude. The beginner is inclined to take every statement the patient makes at its face value. In this he has been encouraged by psychoanalytic teaching that fabrications and even deliberate falsifications have their value as symptoms. He must, however, beware of an *uncritical credulity*. It is the objective world in which we live and to which the subjective world must pay deference. It is even more important to know what the facts are than to know what the patient makes of them.

One final warning seems apposite. Not only beginners but experienced psychiatrists are liable to make an excessive use of *technical terms*, and especially ones with an implied interpretation. It is useless to record that the patient has feelings of passivity, unless his actual experience is also recorded in simple everyday language, and preferably the words he has used himself. Such slovenly habits lead to the production of records on which no later observer can place any reliance. Throughout the record, language should be as precise and simple as possible. Psychiatric histories are often held up to ridicule for their length and literary flourish. Length is often unavoidable; great experience is required to write a short history which is also complete. While any good novelist can give points and a beating to most psychiatrists in the description of human personality, the psychiatrist should avoid taking even great writers as a model. To adopt another metaphor, it is his job to produce a scientific photograph and not a portrait in oils. His own personality should not be allowed to intrude.

Recently, there has been a growing tendency, particularly in the course of clinical research, to supplement the clinical examination with standard rating scales so as to provide more detailed and quantifiable information on some aspects of the clinical picture. Measures for anxiety (Taylor, 1953), depression (Hamilton, 1960; Zung, 1965; Lubin, 1965; Beck, 1961), ward behaviour (Lucero and Meyer, 1951) and, in the case of organic disorders, for memory (Cronholm and Ottosson, 1963a) and brain damage (Walton and Black, 1957) have been among the scales widely used as adjuncts to psychiatric examination, and comprehensive psychiatric rating scales such as those of Wittenborn (1955) and the multidimensional scale for psychiatric patients (Lorr, 1953) have been applied in the course of experimental and other enquiries. Such scales can, in special circumstances, provide a valuable adjunct to the clinical examination but are no substitute for it (Roth, 1967).

As we have said, the taking of the history and the description of the mental state should follow a *general scheme*. The one added to this chapter is used at the Institute of Psychiatry, Maudsley Hospital, London, and has been designed on the basis of a scheme first published by Kirby (1921). The beginner will find it useful in many ways. It will stop him forgetting one or another of the many aspects and fields of examination. It will also provide him with a vocabulary of special terms, and of words taken from common speech especially useful in the description of psychiatric conditions. Most modern languages are rich in words descriptive of inner experiences, emotional states and their expressions, as also of features of personality and temperament. These words do not as a rule come easily to a medical man, and it is therefore useful to obtain a familiarity with them.

The most important caution in the use of the scheme is not to be too rigidly bound by it. A slavish adherence may stand in the way of putting the patient at ease, and, when time is limited, may cause it to be spent unprofitably. The scheme properly demands that negative as well as positive findings should be recorded. Some *negative findings* may be of the greatest importance; but the unimaginative recording of all of them will lead to an account of the patient which is devoid of all life or descriptive value. Only experience can teach what ways, in which the patient does *not* depart from normality, are worth special mention. It is better for the beginner to be too circumstantial than too selective.

In working with the scheme it is important to keep the *separate sources of information* distinct. What is said about the patient by himself, and by his wife, and by his other relatives or friends, should not be confused. The place in which they may be welded into a single structure is in the final formulation. Furthermore the several main subdivisions are often best begun on separate pages. During the taking of the history, notes can be made about the patient's behaviour during interview, and characteristic passages recorded in the Mental State under 'sample of talk'. The following paragraphs may be regarded as more detailed comments on the use of the scheme.

History

Although it would be more orderly, it is not advisable to begin with the family history; results may be later written up in this order. The relative, and still more the patient himself, is usually full of the events of his recent life, and wants to discuss his latest problems. He will give more reliable information about the remoter past when relieved of this pressure. When he is describing psychotic experiences, it is important to pick up all threads leading backwards into the historical development and to follow them later on.

The *family history* should not be confined to manifest cases of psychosis, epilepsy, addiction, etc.; short personality studies of parents and siblings should be obtained, if the informant is sufficiently educated and intelligent. These sketches should be life-like and free from clichés. There is often great reluctance to disclose a family history of mental disorder or psychopathy, and this is a section where both patient and relatives are most unreliable. Where they do not actually suppress information, they will often make use of euphemisms designed to mislead themselves and others. On the other hand, this information is important, because where the case is difficult diagnostically, a knowledge of the nature of psychotic illnesses in other members of the family is very helpful. Because of the value of twin studies for genetics, it is always worth noting if the patient is a twin.

The significance of *the first five years of life* is not likely to be underestimated. Relatives provide the principal source of information; on the other hand, the patient's own account of his emotional relations with other members of the family is more pertinent than that of others. This is also true of his *school life*. It may, however, be possible to get an objective report about his educational success or failure; and in the case of adolescents the views of a schoolmaster who knows the boy well are very valuable. An indication of low intelligence from the school record is of great importance for diagnosis and prognosis in any psychiatric illness.

The period which centres around *puberty* is specially important for the many mental abnormalities which show themselves for the first time at this age. The psychiatrist must, however, make a large allowance for individual variation in the age of onset of sexual maturation, its speed and duration, and the mental reaction to which it gives rise. It may establish itself as a natural growth without any great psychological upset or other complications. On the other hand primary restlessness before puberty, masturbation and emotional pre-occupations centring on it, transient homosexuality, hero-worship, crushes, and the whole turmoil caused by sexual excitation may be seen in young people who later develop along entirely normal lines. It is important, but to a degree which can be over-estimated, to have an account of how the patient experienced this critical phase in his life; for instance, with the elderly melancholic it is absurd to delve for material in this field. The introspective adolescent, for whom the importance of these enquiries is obvious, is usually only waiting for a chance to unburden himself. In *adolescence* the first signs of asocial or antisocial inclinations often become evident, so also do other neurotic features and indications of personality disorder such as anxiety reactions, phobias, abnormal dependence on parents or other relatives. Finally habits are formed, such as indulgence in alcohol, sexual perversions, etc.

The *work record* is also of importance. One wants to know how and why the patient chose his occupation, whether he felt a vocation from the start, and followed a straight line, or whether he came to it by trial and error. *Military service* as a conscript is often a test of mental stability. In the case of older subjects, the record of degree of occupational success, in the level attained, the frequency of change, the frequency and duration of spells of un-employment, furnishes the most objective and reliable evidence of the man's capacity for social adaptation, of his temperamental stability and of his abilities.

In the *marital history*, the doctor should interest himself not only in the purely sexual side, but also in the patient's solution of the familial and inter-personal problems of married life. A childless marriage presents a special problem. The attitude of the patient to his children throws light on his emotional life in its more general aspects. It is worth noting how women have reacted to pregnancy and childbirth; and it may be remembered that the advent of the first child is often a time of considerable emotional strain, even for the father.

In taking the *medical history*, attention should be paid not only to the more severe physical illnesses, but also to periods of ill-health, malaise and semi-invalidism, and of more minor ailments such as chronic chest complaints, digestive upsets, headaches, periods of exhaustion and inertia. Psychiatric illness is often disguised by indefinite physical complaints.

The delineation of the *pre-morbid personality* is probably the most difficult task that the case record demands, but is one of great importance. The aim in view is to provide a comprehensible portrait, but this does not mean that contradictory features and inconsistencies of character should be slurred over. From this section, much that is of great practical importance will eventually be derived, and it should provide the basic information from which one can decide which of the patient's symptoms represent an exaggeration of pre-existing traits, and which are specific features of the illness. To some extent, therefore, the psychiatrist will be led by clues from the history of the illness itself; if he is told that the patient has become irritable and aggressive, he will want to know, and will specially enquire, whether he was at all an irritable or aggressive man before ever the illness began. But all the outstanding qualities of the personality are of interest, and not merely those on which a pathological process or neurotic development has thrown the spotlight. Lists of adjectives are sterile and uninformative reading and should be avoided. Illustration by a recounting of incidents in which the patient has behaved in a way typical for him is, on the other hand, very helpful.

When the patient is asked about his *present illness*, he will not infrequently say that he does not consider himself ill at all. Even when he has consented to see a specialist, he may try to minimize his abnormalities, and explain everything as the natural outcome of circumstances. Some psychiatric patients ask the doctor to treat their wife or husband, as the case may be, insisting that it is the latter who is abnormal. This situation is most likely to arise when one of the parties has delusional ideas; but may occur in other cases when there is a good deal of marital disharmony. In a surprisingly large minority of these cases both parties will be found to be abnormal; and it is sometimes found that the second of a married pair, who has remained in the background, is the more seriously abnormal, when the first has already been treated for a relatively minor condition for weeks or months.

Every attempt should be made to get the history in *precise and meaningful terms*. Although vague expressions, such as nervousness, shock, worry, etc., are very useful in phrasing non-committal leading questions, they should lead to answers of a more precise type. Such indefinite descriptions should be eschewed in the written record. *Leading questions* cannot usually be avoided. They have played their part if they lead to an answer which is clearly spontaneous and made with inner conviction. When however the informant merely accepts in a passive way the suggestions offered by the doctor, the response should be regarded with suspicion. It will then be found useful, in order to clarify the real state of affairs, to lead first in one and then in a diametrically opposed direction. Direct questions are likely to be needed to elicit an account of delusions, hallucinations, aggressive tendencies and any suicidal inclination; on all these points the account given by friends and relatives is of special value. The doctor should never forget to enquire about *suicidal tendencies*, at least when there is any suggestion of depression or of behaviour of an unpredictable type.

We have already emphasized the great value of *information from friends and relatives*. One should never be satisfied, no matter what the nature of the case, with the patient's story alone. An objective history should be obtained as early as possible. If the relatives do not accompany the patient to hospital, and cannot be brought to attend at an early date, a psychiatric social worker should visit the home and obtain the necessary information. Valuable as this aid is, the doctor should try to make his own contact with the relatives. Other *objective sources of information* may be tapped—the school-teacher, the employer, the family doctor, and other hospitals where the patient has been treated. One should never rely on second-hand accounts of a previous illness when a direct report can be obtained. Other documentary evidence may also be obtained, such as the patient's letters, diaries, drawings, etc.

In many acute psychoses the patient does not co-operate. *Unconscious patients* are usually admitted to a general hospital, although they are not infrequently psychiatric cases. Among the many physical causes of unconsciousness, one should not forget that some are the results of suicidal attempts, such as trauma sustained in a street 'accident' and carbon-monoxide poisoning. In most cases the circumstances under which an unconscious patient has been found and the physical signs will disclose the nature of the condition. In some, however, more than one cause is involved, or there are other sources of difficulty. Cerebral injury in an accident which has been caused by alcoholic intoxication, a suicidal attempt with barbiturates made by a severely undernourished depressive patient, coma caused by an overdose of an anticonvulsant drug taken by an epileptic in a depressive mood swing, are some examples of the difficult diagnostic problems encountered in cases of unconsciousness.

More frequently than unconsciousness, a degree of *clouding of consciousness*, of stupor or excitement, may interfere with history-taking and a full examination; or the patient may merely be too restless or distracted. In all such states a full description should be recorded at the time, as the state may be a transient one. The findings made on a full and immediate *physical examination* must also be noted. While the examination of unconscious psychiatric patients is largely identical with that of similar cases in general medicine, *stuporose patients* offer special difficulties. A scheme of examination of these cases, designed by Kirby, is included in this chapter (p. 46).

Mental State

The description of general behaviour should include all the outward signs which are noted in passing—the expression of the face and especially of the eyes, posture, general character of movements and gestures, dress, tidiness or otherwise of clothes, hair, nails. Included under the same head should be a judgement of the patient's sensorium, that is his state of consciousness, awareness of the surroundings and of his own relation to them.

Orientation is dealt with in a more detailed way under a separate heading. Almost every patient, if he can give an answer at all, is oriented about his own person. Only in the severest cases of organic dementia and the lowest degrees of idiocy can personal orientation, that is awareness of the identity, name and personal status, be lost. If a patient assumes a delusional identity, e.g. that she is the Mother of Christ, this does not mean a disturbance of personal orientation. Orientation in place is best observed from the patient's behaviour and by means of asking him about his whereabouts. Understandable ignorance, e.g. of the name of the hospital to which he has just been admitted, is not evidence of disorientation; but it is clear that there is some spatial disorientation if, as in some cases of occupational delirium, the patient can give the name of the hospital but behaves as if he were in a public bar or in a tailor's shop. In some focal cerebral lesions there may be a disturbance of the power to appreciate spatial relationships which does not amount to a gross disorientation. This may be tested by asking the patient to draw a plan of the position of his bed in the ward, or the layout of the rooms in his own home. Such patients show their disturbance by losing their way in the ward, as for instance when going to the lavatory. Orientation in time may be disturbed when spatial orientation is still preserved. Minor degrees are important. The patient may be able to state the year and month, and yet be unable to give the day of the week, or the time of day, or to say how long he has been in hospital.

In observing *the patient's talk*, outward signs are of interest. Does he speak with a stammer or lisp? Is the inflexion, or dialect, in accordance with his education, and appropriate to the situation? Does he search for words, or use odd expressions? Does he repeat himself? Do speech and gestures match? Does a pressure of talk go with poverty of words, or other sign of dysphasia? A special scheme for the examination of organic states, including their focal signs, will be found in the present chapter (p. 48).

In describing the *mood*, it should be related to the topics discussed. The influence of mood on thinking and behaviour may be tested by discussing matters of emotional significance to the patient. This, however, must be done with tact; only harm is done by stirring up an excessive emotional reaction which may alienate the patient from his doctor for good. Shallowness, superficiality or absence of mood are, of course, as important an indicator of abnormality as a mood which is excessive or unduly sustained.

Tests of *memory*, *general information*, *judgement* and *insight* are most difficult to evaluate, especially if the patient is in an acutely psychotic state. Results may mislead, because the patient is preoccupied with morbid ideas and does not really co-operate. In all these cases it is much more important to observe *how* the patient deals with the problems set him, than to register final success or failure. If he is unlikely to co-operate, it is not worth while persisting with these tests, which may then be postponed to a later date. One should, however, record the refusal to co-operate, and its probable reasons.

In all cases where there are doubts about the *intellectual endowment*, and the patient is not too emotionally disturbed or otherwise incapacitated from applying himself, a systematic intelligence test should be given. If a psychologist is available, the choice of test and its application should be left to him, and the result judged in consultation. In children, the Terman and Merrill revision of the Stanford-Binet test is widely used. For adults the Bellevue-Wechsler test is useful, and is well standardized for patients in the U.S.A. Among non-verbal tests, Raven's Matrices test is standardized for the British population of all ages, and can be applied to children and adults of any nationality, whatever their native tongue. It can be conveniently combined with Raven's Mill Hill Vocabulary Test; from the two together, an assessment can be made of native intelligence and of knowledge acquired by education and of intellectual deterioration.

If possible, a full *physical examination* should precede rather than follow the mental examination. Observation of the patient's conduct at this time is often most revealing; clues will be obtained about his attitude towards his own body, his special sensitivities or hypochondriacal preoccupations. Entirely new aspects of the case may come to light, not only through the physical findings but also through what one sees of his psychological reaction to the situation.

In summing up the history and mental and physical state, the psychiatrist should try to reach, even after the first examination, a *preliminary diagnosis*. The reasons for it should be given, an estimate made of its reliability, and the differential diagnosis should be discussed. This should be followed by a view of the prognosis and an outline of proposals for further investigation and treatment.

SCHEME FOR CASE-TAKING
History

Name   Age

(If taken from relatives or friends, state the *Informant*, his name, relation to the patient, intimacy and length of acquaintance, impression of informant, reliability, etc. Do not collate into one the accounts from several informants until the summary is reached. Information obtained from the patient must be explicitly marked as such. If information is obtained from several sources put the additional information on supplementary sheets.)

COMPLAINTS (or REASON FOR ADMISSION) and their duration.

FAMILY HISTORY

Father. Occupation. Health, age, or age at time of death, and cause of death. Personality.
Mother. Health, age, or age at time of death, and cause of death. Personality. Are the parents related by blood?

Siblings. Enumerated by year of birth with Christian names, ages, marital condition personality, occupation, health or illness. Stillbirths to be included.

Social position and general efficiency of family. Any familial diseases, alcoholism, abnormal personalities, mental disorder, epilepsy (state whether unknown or none).

Home atmosphere and influence. Any salient happenings among parents and collaterals during patient's early years. Emotional relationship to parents, siblings, nurse, etc. Note particulars which might be required for further enquiries, e.g. names of hospitals where relatives have been treated.

PERSONAL HISTORY: Date of birth and place. Mother's condition during pregnancy. Full-term birth? Normal delivery? Breast or bottle fed?

Early development. Delicate or healthy baby. Precocious or retarded. Time of teething, talking, walking, cleanliness as to excreta.

Neurotic symptoms in childhood. Night-terrors, walking in sleep, tantrums, wetting the bed, thumb-sucking, nail-biting, faddiness about food, stammering, mannerisms, fear-states, model child. (Particularize these.)

Health during childhood. Infections, chorea, infantile convulsions. Any effect of illness on development. Play. Spontaneous games in childhood. Make-believe. Organized games, especially during adolescence.

School. Age of beginning and finishing. Standard reached. Evidence of ability or backwardness. Special abilities or disabilities. Hobbies and interests. Relationship to schoolmates. (Nicknames, bully or butt.)

Occupations (in some detail). Age of starting work. Jobs held in chronological order, with wages, dates, reasons for change. Satisfaction in work. Present economic circumstances. Ambition. Satisfaction or reasons for dissatisfaction.

Menstrual history. Age at first period. How regarded. Regularity, duration and amount. Pain. Psychic changes, especially in premenstruum. Date of last period. Climacteric symptoms.

Sexual inclinations and practice. Sexual information, how acquired, of what kind, how received. Masturbation; sexual fantasies; prudery; homosexuality; heterosexual experiences, apart from marriage.

Marital history. Duration of acquaintance before marriage and of engagement. Husband's age, occupation, personality. Compatibility. Mode and frequency of sexual intercourse. Sexual satisfaction or frigidity. Contraceptive measures.

Children. Chronological list of children and miscarriages, giving years of birth, names, personality, etc., of former.

Medical history. Illnesses, operations, and accidents. Chronologically and in detail.

Previous mental illness (detailed account). Dates, duration, symptoms of attacks; in what hospital or out-patient department.

PERSONALITY BEFORE ILLNESS. In this description of the personality *prior to the beginning of the mental illness*, do not be satisfied with a series of adjectives and epithets, but give illustrative anecdotes and detailed statements. Aim at a picture of an individual, not a type. The following is merely a collection of hints, not a scheme. It will not be possible to cover all the items listed in the course of the first interview, but an attempt should be made, particularly in cases of neurosis or affective disorder, to elicit evidence about all aspects of pre-morbid personality in the course of explorations extending over a period.

1. Social relations: to family (attachment, dependence); to friends, groups, societies, clubs; to work and workmates (leader or follower, organizer, aggressive, submissive, ambitious, adjustable, independent).

2. Intellectual activities, hobbies and interests: books, plays, pictures preferred; memory, observation, judgement, critical faculty.

3. Mood: bright and cheerful or despondent; worrying or placid; strung-up or calm and relaxed; optimistic or pessimistic; self-depreciative or satisfied; mood stable or unstable (with or without any occasion).

4. Character.

 (a) Attitude to work and responsibility; welcomes or is worried by responsibility; makes decisions easily or with difficulty; haphazard and slapdash or methodical and meticulous; rigid or flexible; cautious, foresightful and given to checking or impulsive and slipshod; persevering and determined or easily bored and discouraged.

 (b) Interpersonal relationships; self-confident or shy and timid; insensitive or touchy and sensitive to criticism; trusting or suspicious and jealous; emotionally-controlled or quick-tempered and irritable; tactful or outspoken; enjoys or shuns self-display; quiet and restrained or expressive and demonstrative in speech and gesture; interests and enthusiasms sustained or evanescent; tolerant or intolerant of others; adaptable or unadaptable.

 (c) Standards in moral, religious, social and health matters: level of aspiration high or low; perfectionistic and self-critical or complacent and self-approving in relation to own behaviour and achievement; steadfast in face of difficulties or intolerant of frustration; selfish and egotistical or unselfish and altruistic; given to much or little concern about own health.

 (d) Energy, initiative: energetic or sluggish; output sustained or fitful. Fatiguability: any regular or irregular fluctuations in energy or output.

5. Fantasy life: frequency and content of daydreaming.

6. Habits: eating (fads); alcohol consumption; self-medication with drugs or other medicines. Specify amounts taken recently and earlier. Tobacco consumption; sleeping; excretory functions.

PRESENT ILLNESS

Detailed coherent account, in chronological order, of the illness from the earliest time at which a change was noticed until admission to hospital. Give data which will permit the sequence of various symptoms to be dated approximately.

SUMMARY OF HISTORY

Under the headings:

1. Complaint.
2. Family history.
3. Personal history.
4. Personality.
5. Present illness.

Mental State

General behaviour. Description as complete, accurate, and life-like as possible, of what doctors and nurses observe in the patient's behaviour, especially anything abnormal. (The following points may be considered, though not exclusively.)

Does the patient look ill? Is he in touch with his surroundings in general and in particular? Relationship to other patients, to the nurses, to the doctor who examines and treats him. How does he respond to various requirements and situations? What gestures, grimaces or other motor expressions? Tics, mannerisms. Much or little activity? Is it constant or abrupt or fitful? Spontaneous or how provoked? Free or constrained? Slow, stereotyped, hesitant, or fidgety? Tenseness, scratching or rubbing. Do movements and attitudes have an evident purpose or meaning? Do real or hallucinatory perceptions seem to modify behaviour? Does the patient, if inactive, resist passive movements, or maintain an attitude, or obey commands, or indicate awareness at all? Eating; sleep; cleanliness in general, and as to excreta. Way of spending the day.

If the patient does not speak, the description of his mental state may be limited to a careful report of his behaviour (see p. 46).

Talk. The form of the patient's utterances rather than their content is here considered. Does he say much or little, talk spontaneously, or only in answer, slow or fast, hesitantly or promptly, to the point or wide of it, coherently, discursively, loosely, with interruptions, sudden silences, changes of topic, comments on happenings and things at hand, appropriately, using strange words or syntax, rhymes, puns? How does the form of his talk vary with its subject?

Sample of talk. Conversation should be recorded with physician's remarks on left side of page, and patient's on right. It should be representative of the form of his talk, his response to questioning and his main preoccupations. Its length will depend on its individual significance. In later sections of the mental state, it will be desirable to record the patient's reported experiences (e.g. hallucinations, delusions, attitude to illness) in his own words, but the sample required at this point need not aim at being comprehensive.

Mood. The patient's appearance may be described, so far as it is indicative of his mood. His answers to 'How do you feel in yourself', 'What is your mood', 'How about your spirits', or some similar enquiry should be recorded. Many varieties of mood may be present—not merely happiness or sadness, but such states as irritability, suspicion, fear, unreality, worry, restlessness, bewilderment, and many more which it is convenient to include under this heading. Observe the constancy of the mood, the influences which change it; the appropriateness of the patient's apparent emotional state to what he says.

Delusion and misinterpretation. What is the patient's attitude to the various people and things in his environment? Does he misinterpret what happens, give it special or false meaning, or is he doubtful about it? Does he think anyone pays special attention to him, treats him in a special way, persecutes or influences him bodily, or mentally, in ordinary or scientific or preternatural ways? Laughs at him? Shuns him? Admires him? Tries to kill, harm, annoy him? Does he depreciate himself in any regard, his morals, possessions, health? Has he grandiose beliefs?

These matters may be complicated or concealed and may need much enquiry. If a whole conversation dealing with them is reported here, resume the main points at the end.

Hallucinations and other disorders of perception. Auditory, visual, olfactory, gustatory, tactile, visceral. The source, vividness, reality, manner of reception, content, and all other circumstances of the experience are important; its content, especially if auditory or visual, must be reported. When do these experiences occur, at night, when falling asleep, when alone? Any peculiar bodily sensations; feeling of deadness? Unreality?

Compulsive phenomena. Obsessional thoughts, impulses, or acts. Are they felt to be from without, or part of the patient's own mind? Does their insistence distress him? Does he recognize their inappropriateness? Relation to his emotional state? Does he repeat actions, such as washing, unnecessarily, to reassure himself?

Orientation. Record the patient's answers to questions about his own name and identity, the place where he is, the time of day, and the date. Is there anything unusual to him in the way in which time seems to pass?

Memory. This may be tested by comparing the patient's account of his life with that given by others, or examining his account for intrinsic evidence of gaps or inconsistencies. Information which he gives about his previous life, his personality, sexual experiences, etc., should not be inserted here but included as a supplementary part of the history, and its source indicated. There should be special enquiry for recent events such as those of his admission to hospital and happenings in the ward since. Where there is selective impairment of memory for special incidents, periods, recent or remote happenings, this should be recorded in detail, and the patient's attitude towards his forgetfulness and the things forgotten specially investigated.

Record the patient's success or failure in grasping, retaining, and being able to recall spontaneously or on demand three or five minutes later a number, a name and address, or other data. Give the patient the 'Cowboy' or 'Donkey and Salt' story to read and ask him to repeat it in his own words; record his repetition of the story verbatim if possible, and say whether he sees the point of it. See how many items of the Logical Memory Test he can repeat immediately, and how many after an interval of five minutes. Give him digits to repeat forwards, and then others to repeat backwards, and record how many he can repeat immediately. In administering this test the digits should be given with equal intervals and not grouped.

(In describing the state of the patient's memory, do not merely record the conclusions reached but give the evidence first, and describe such facts of behaviour as seem to indicate whether he was attending, trying his hardest, being distracted by other stimuli, etc.)

Attention and concentration. Is his attention easily aroused and sustained? Does he concentrate? Is he easily distracted? Preoccupied? To test his concentration ask him to tell the days or months in reverse order, or to do simple arithmetical problems requiring 'carrying over' (112 − 25), subtraction of serial sevens from 100 (give answers and time taken).

General information. Tests for general information and grasp should be varied according to the patient's educational level and his experiences and interests, but the answers to the following should be recorded in all cases:

Name of the Queen and her immediate predecessors.

The Prime Minister.

Capitals of France, Germany, Italy, Spain, Scotland.

Date of beginning and end of the Second World War.

Six large cities in England.

Intelligence. Assess the patient's intelligence. Use his history, his general knowledge, problems of reasoning. You may employ standardized tests. Observe discrepancies in the results of various methods, and try to interpret them.

Insight and judgement. What is the patient's attitude to his present state? Does he regard it as an illness, as 'mental' or 'nervous', as needing treatment? Is he aware of mistakes made spontaneously or in response to tests? How does he regard them and other details of his condition? How does he regard previous experiences, mental illnesses, etc.?

What is his attitude towards social, financial, domestic, ethical problems? Is his judgement good? What does he propose to do when he has left the hospital?

SUMMARY OF MENTAL STATE

Under the headings:

1. Behaviour and talk.
2. Mood.
3. Preoccupations, morbid beliefs, disorders of perception.
4. Sensorium.
5. Attitude to illness.

Cowboy Story

A cowboy went to San Francisco with his dog which he left at a friend's while he went to buy a new suit of clothes. Dressed in his grand new suit, he came back to the dog, whistled to it, called it by name, and patted it. But the dog would have nothing to do with him in his new hat and coat, and gave a mournful howl. Coaxing was of no avail, so the cowboy went away and put on his old suit, and then the dog immediately showed its wild joy on seeing its master as it thought he ought to be.

Logical Memory Test

Jimmy Stevens/used to play football/for a local team/and became well-known/as a Forward./ Ten years ago/ he went/to Arsenal/ and became/one of their/leading players./ He is now/a sergeant-major/in the army./ Yesterday/he returned/to his home town /and scored/all five goals/against Swansea.

Examination of Non-co-operative or Stuporose Patients

(*Kirby*, 1921)

The difficulty of getting information from non-co-operative patients should not discourage the physician from making and recording certain observations. These may be of great importance in the study of various types of cases and give valuable data for the interpretation of different clinical reactions. It is hardly necessary to say that the time to study negativistic reactions is during the period of negativism, the time to study a stupor is during the stuporose phase. To wait for the clinical picture to change or for the patient to become more accessible is often to miss an opportunity and leave a serious gap in the clinical observation. Obviously it is necessary in the examination of such cases to adopt some other plan than that used in making the usual 'mental status'. The following guide was devised to cover in a systematic way the most important points for purposes of clinical differentiation.

I. GENERAL REACTION AND POSTURE

(*a*) Attitude voluntary or passive.
(*b*) Voluntary postures comfortable, natural, constrained or awkward.
(*c*) What does the patient do if placed in awkward or uncomfortable positions.

(d) Behaviour toward physicians and nurses: resistive, evasive, irritable, apathetic, compliant.

(e) Spontaneous acts: any occasional show of playfulness, mischievousness or assaultiveness. Defence movements when interfered with or when pricked with pin. Eating and dressing. Attention to bowels and bladder. Do the movements show only initial retardation or are they consistent throughout?

(f) To what extent does the attitude change? Is the behaviour constant or variable from day to day? Do any special occurrences influence the condition?

II. FACIAL EXPRESSION. Alert, attentive, placid, vacant, stolid, sulky, scowling, averse, perplexed, distressed, etc. Any play of facial expression or signs of emotion: tears, smiles, flushing, perspiration. On what occasions?

III. EYES. Open or closed. If closed, resist having lid raised. Movement of eyes: absent or obtained on request; give attention and follow the examiner or moving objects; or show only fixed gazing, furtive glances or evasion.
Rolling of eyeballs upward. Blinking, flickering, or tremor of lid. Reaction to sudden approach of threat to stick pin in eye. Sensory reaction of pupils (dilation from painful stimuli or irritation to skin of neck).

IV. REACTION TO WHAT IS SAID OR DONE. Commands: show tongue, move limbs, grasp with hand (clinging, clutching, etc.).
Motions slow or sudden. Reaction to pin-pricks. Automatic obedience: tell patient to protrude the tongue to have pin stuck into it.
Echopraxia: imitation of actions of others.

V. MUSCULAR REACTIONS. Test for rigidity: muscles relaxed or tense when limbs or body is moved.
Catalepsy, waxy flexibility. Negativism shown by movements in opposite direction or springy or cog-wheel resistance.
Test head and neck by movements forward and backward and to side.
Test also the jaw, shoulders, elbows, fingers and the lower extremities.
Does distraction or command influence the reactions?
Closing of mouth, protrusion of lips ('Schnauzkrampf').
Holding of saliva, drooling.

VI. EMOTIONAL RESPONSIVENESS. Is feeling shown when talked to of family or children?
Or when sensitive points in history are mentioned or when visitors come?
Note whether or not acceleration of respiration or pulse occurs; also look for flushing, perspiration, tears in eyes, etc. Do jokes elicit any response?
Effect of unexpected stimuli (clap hands, flash of electric light).

VII. SPEECH. Any apparent effort to talk, lip-movements, whispers, movements of head.
Note exact utterances with accompanying emotional reaction (may indicate hallucinations).

VIII. WRITING. Offer paper and pencil. Irresponsive or partially stuporose patients will often write when they fail to talk.

SCHEMA FOR THE EXAMINATION OF ORGANIC CASES, ESPECIALLY WITH FOCAL LESIONS

(Mayer-Gross and Guttmann, 1937)

The following tests have been selected to supplement a routine neurological and psychiatric examination. They are less suitable for finding out if there is an organic illness. Their application is intended to reveal the *special incapacity* caused by brain damage which has already been diagnosed. For more detailed examination and the problems of localization of function we refer to Klein and Mayer-Gross (1957), McFie (1960) and Piercy (1964).

It is best not to offer the tests in a set order, but to find out by taking a few sample tests which the patient does best, and then gradually work up to the more difficult ones (otherwise the patient may get upset and it will be impossible to assess his abilities).

It must be remembered that some organic patients are easily tired and that others do not show any fatigue at all. Both kinds of behaviour have to be noticed.

It is not sufficient to state only whether the patient succeeded or failed in the test, but his actual performance and his answers should be recorded, whenever possible, in his own words. The patient's subjective experiences and his attitude towards them are of as much value in organic cases as in so-called psychological conditions. Hallucinations and illusions in all sensory fields have to be noted.

(1) MOOD. Is the mood labile? Is there preservation of emotional expression? Is the emotional reaction exaggerated, perverted, lacking; is there a preference for one kind of emotion? Is the habitual mood in keeping with the pre-morbid personality? Do not overlook changes of personality caused by organic diseases like encephalitis lethargica.

A conversation on topics of emotional importance for the patient will give more information here than special tests. Shades of euphoria ('*Witzelsucht*', jocularity, lack of seriousness, etc.) are diagnostically more important than depressions, which are more frequently of secondary character. Various euphoric states have been put forward as localizing signs of lesions of the frontal lobe, the orbital region, the di- and mesencephalon. Lack of appreciation of the person's own symptoms, combined with euphoria, is an important symptom of damage of the orbital cortex. Moral deterioration may result from irreparable lesions of the same region; also foci in the periventricular grey matter produce changes of personality. Irritability and apathy may be signs of general organic deterioration.

(2) ORIENTATION. Record even slight impairment. Distinguish the patient's orientation from his capacity to orientate himself in new surroundings. What aid does he use for it? Is there a common factor among the ways in which his disorientation shows itself?

Episodic loss of visual orientation has been described as a sign of fits originating in the occipital lobe. When disturbances of subjective time experience are present, a special examination of the capacity for estimating and reproducing time intervals may be indicated. Route-finding and topographic difficulties are associated with parietal lesions.

(3) ATTENTION AND ADAPTABILITY. Is the patient's attention easy to attract? Can he concentrate his attention on his task for some period? Can he be distracted easily, and by what, or is he imperturbable to any stimulus? (Bourdon's test.)

The ease with which the patient's attention may be obtained varies according to the sensory field in which the stimulus is applied. There may even be differences between the various parts of the visual field (see p. 51). Remember that attention and concentration are influenced by fluctuations of consciousness. Distractibility of attention may be a symptom of organic impairment. ('Unselected responsiveness to stimuli', 'hypermetamorphosis'.)

How far is the patient able to change from one topic or test to another? How far does this ability depend on his being interested and how far on the actual situation, especially the way in which the test is presented to him?

Perseveration, an extremely common symptom of organic disease, is often an obstacle to testing these cases. It can be present in various degrees, and may extend to words, phrases, actions or to the total behaviour. It is more likely to occur where the patient meets a difficulty, and can serve as an indicator of his shortcomings. Furthermore, an extreme 'selectiveness to stimuli' may interfere with the patient's adaptability. The patient fails in everything that does not fit into the situation. He appears therefore quite undistractible (can be tested by Heilbronner's pictures, where the perseverating patient sticks to his first interpretation throughout the whole scale of the pictures). Some performances can be carried out when approached one way, but are impossible when attacked in another way ('focusing disturbance', *Einstellstörung*').

(4) MEMORY. Disturbances of remembering are always the most easily recognizable signs of an organic illness.

Besides the tests usually applied, detailed regard should be paid, if there is amnesia, to the dates of its beginning and its end. Was it complete while it lasted? Are there fragments or islands of memory?

It is important to observe the memory without the patient being aware of the purpose of the examination. Recollection of facts is often better when it is incidental than when it is deliberate. How much does the amnesia cover the time before and after the lesion which caused it? Did the amnesic period coincide with a disturbance of consciousness (retrograde and anterograde amnesia)? Are there special memory defects, e.g. for dates, numbers, visual or verbalized impressions?

Non-language tests of memory are of special importance in all cases where there is the slightest suspicion of a dysphasic disorder (see below).

Does the patient fabricate, does he do so spontaneously or in response to suggestion only? Memory disturbances of a specific kind are associated with lesions of the hippocampus and bilateral temporal lesions.

(5) USE OF NUMBERS. Can the patient read and write figures and numbers of two or more digits? Has he a general concept of numbers and measures? (inhabitants of London, are there thousands or millions? Height of a man, of a horse, a dog, inches or feet? Weight of a man, 5 stone or 50?).

Can the patient add, subtract, divide or multiply? Let him do it on paper as well as in his head, with plain numbers as well as in concrete problems. Can he count objects, recognize dots on dominoes and similar groupings? Can he guess without counting how many matches are lying in front of him? Can he divide them into two or three equal groups? Let him compare a few big objects with many small ones of the same kind (buttons). Can he count money?

While disturbances in writing single figures generally belong to the field of agraphia, mistakes in the sequence of figures and loss of the position value are a characteristic arithmetical disturbance *sui generis*.

Multiplication tables being most automatized are of little use for testing arithmetical ability. Counting of objects one by one is entirely different from recognizing dots arranged in a group at one glance. This again is different from estimating the size of an unorganized multitude. Disturbance of all these performances may be observed with lesions of the occipito-parietal convexity.

(6) SPEECH. What is the patient's *spontaneous speech* like? Does he articulate correctly? Does he hesitate or stammer (which can be a sign of aphasia)? Notice his modulation and the inflexion of voice. Is his voice monotonous or does it fade away? Can he repeat words or sentences? (words he understands and unknown words like Artaxerxes, Lysistrata). Can he recite automatic word series? (days of the week, months of the year, a prayer or poem).

Notice the *grammar* in his spontaneous speech; if necessary ask him to tell a story. Test his capacity to conjugate or parse. Ask him to build up a sentence using three given words: hunter, fox, field; child, scissors, hurt; gun, soldier, battle.

Does he produce any paraphasic utterances?

Does the patient *understand* single words? (e.g. objects: Give me the pencil! Where is the door?). Does he understand simple or more complicated sentences? (orders: Open the window. Take the chair and put it in the corner. Open your mouth, shut it again and point to your right eye). [Memory disturbance and apraxia may interfere with this.] Can he distinguish words which sound alike and can he use them correctly? (father, farther; breeze, breathe; boat, bought; task, tusk).

Does he notice and can he correct mispronounced words? Can he find the right words? Names of objects and pictures, abstract nouns, proper names? (Colour-names: see p. 51.)

In cases of severe disturbance: how far are *emotional utterances* preserved? (swearing, interjections). Can he indicate the number of syllables in words which he cannot utter? (Lichtheim's test of inner language). Is any former command of *foreign languages* impaired? Is his *vocabulary* poor? (Tell me the names of flowers, pieces of furniture, etc. Find opposites to given words such as good, outside, quick, empty, many, friend, etc. Find rhymes to words like fair, round, patch, etc.)

Since all the tests mentioned earlier require for their performance full command of speech, it is advantageous wherever there is any suspicion of dysphasia to examine for it before doing other tests. Dysphasia is often overlooked, or is mistakenly regarded as due to confusion, dementia or hysteria. By means of the above scheme only a coarse outline of the patient's speech impairment can be arrived at. For detailed analysis, systematic examination must be carried out as proposed by Weissenburg (1935) and Muncie (1948).

This scheme has been made as elastic as possible, since this is more necessary in the field of aphasia than anywhere else. The variability of the findings and the adaptability of the patient can yield more information than an artificial constancy in the result.

A series of tests such as employed by Head (1926) has not been recommended here; with them it would be difficult to allow for individual differences in linguistic gift and education, and to take into account the extent to which the patient's ability to learn is preserved. Moreover the tests do not cover the whole wide field of the use of language.

It is generally agreed that the brain lesions which produce aphasia are located in the left hemisphere when the patient is right-handed and vice versa. Furthermore foci producing expressive (motor) dysphasia are to be found in the anterior parts of the brain, those producing the receptive (sensory) forms further back. The finer localization of other subdivisions of dysphasia is still very much under debate. Just as in assessing the results of verbal tests the patient's previous level of intelligence must be taken into account, so in using intellectual tests due regard must be paid to the speech disturbance, since this might notably interfere with the intellectual process—much more so, indeed, than any other focal lesion would.

When speech is disturbed the following *non-language tests* may be employed as substitutes for the methods suggested before: Pintner-Paterson substitution test; Knox's cube test; Porteus mazes; sorting of objects or of small pictures of objects; form-colour test (sorting cardboard pieces of various shapes, sizes, and colours); portrait test (show the patient a portrait and then ask him to find it when it is mixed with eight others).

The interpretation of the results of these non-language tests is only possible after carrying out the tests for agnosia and apraxia.

(7) VISUAL AND RELATED FUNCTIONS. Measure first the visual acuity and record the field of vision either by rough testing or on the perimeter with different colours. Scotomata? blinking reflex? optokinetic nystagmus? reaction to strong stimuli, e.g. bright light?

Are there any visual hallucinations? illusions? (note alterations of size, shape and colour). How are moving objects perceived? (too slow, too fast, stationary). If necessary, test with stroboscope or cinema. Is there a consistent distortion of visual space? Is there evidence of visual disorientation?

VISUAL ATTENTION. Ask him to name or to find various letters or numbers of objects drawn all over the surface of a blackboard. Does he neglect those in any particular region?

VISUAL MEMORY OR IMAGERY. Get him to show the size of a well-known object with his hands (a cat, a horse, etc.). Does he remember the colour of objects mentioned to him? Get him to describe his house or the situation of his bed in the ward. Wertheimer's test (two isosceles right-angled triangles of the same size, cut out from paper, are shown to the patient, who has to indicate what figure would be formed by putting these two triangles together, side by side, in various ways. The answer can be a square, a diamond, or a larger triangle).

Can he recognize, when he sees them, objects, gestures and simple happenings? Can he name them? Can he recognize pictures of single objects and scenes? Is he able on request to pick one out of a large number of pictures (or letters) spread on the table?

Can he recognize and name simple geometric patterns? (triangle, square, circle). Can he disentangle them in Abelson's test?

Can he connect two given dots by a straight line? Can he find the middle of a straight line or of a circle?

Ishihara's test for colour-blindness.

Perception of *colours*? Can he name them? Can he sort out colours on request (Holmgren's wools)?

Can he tell the time from the *clock*? Can he set the hands of a clock to a given time?

Can he use a *map*? Can he find the points of the compass? Can he point to visible objects in different parts of the room? Can he demonstrate and name *directions*—above, below, horizontal, perpendicular, etc.?

Can he guess distances? Can he see perspective correctly?

Methods of examination which usually are regarded as neurological have been put at the top of this list, since their results are often modified by central visual disturbances, in which case the responses obtained are much less constant than they are after lesions of the more peripheral part of the visual apparatus. Disturbances of specific, i.e. here visual, attention (such as '*Seelenlähmung des Schauens*', Balint) and also specific fatigue can produce phenomena which may be mistaken for hysterical ones, because of their lack of constancy. One-sided absence of the blinking reflex or optokinetic nystagmus may be due to hemianopia or to partial disturbance of attention. Inadequate response to optic stimuli (even to sudden and strong ones) can be an initial or residual symptom of visual agnosia.

In spite of constitutional differences with regard to the faculty of visualization, a certain amount of visual imagery can be expected from everyone. The distinctness and range of images can be interfered with by cerebral lesions; in particular, the ease with which they are recalled can be diminished. Purely subjective anomalies of vision such as micropsia, macropsia and other distortions cannot be described by the patient except by comparison with such visual memory as he has preserved.

By testing with pictures minor disturbances of visual perception may be revealed in patients who are able to recognize objects. Others do well with pictures of single objects, but fail in understanding a scene if this requires them to bring the parts of the pictures into proper relation ('comprehension-disturbance', Pick). Children's toy books can be used for examinations of this kind.

Some of these tests could have been given under other headings as well, but are mentioned here for the sake of convenience. For instance, impairment of colour-names really belongs to aphasia, but may occur independently. Inability in setting a clock may be a sign of apraxia, or agnosia, or secondary to disturbances in the use of numbers. Failures in spatial tests can be of various origin: recognition of the points of the compass depends on the distinction of left and right (see below). Pointing may be disturbed by apraxia. Immediate orientation in space is dependent on the 'body-image'. This central representation of one's own body can be disturbed by a lesion of the parietal lobe as well as by damage to the vestibulo-cerebellar system (see below).

Roughly speaking, disturbances of visual perception and related functions such as those mentioned are to be found after lesions of the occipital lobes. Perceptual anomalies of a lower level occur after lesions of the calcarine area whereas more complex disturbances appear when wider areas of the occipital lobe, including its convexity, are involved.

Can he *read* letters, words, sentences—aloud and silently? Is there a difference between writing and print? Does he keep to the line? Does he understand written sentences, e.g. requests? Does he notice mistakes in spelling? Can he read words in which single letters are struck out?

All tests of visual perception may be increased in difficulty by shortening the time of exposure (tachistoscope).

Alexia may occur with, and be dependent on, aphasic disorders of all kinds. Aphasics who cannot read aloud can still often understand what they read silently to themselves.

Of special interest is the interdependence of alexia and agraphia, though both can occur separately. Patients may be unable to recognize single letters, or they may be able to do so, but unable to read words as a whole.

Mild alectic disturbances are discovered only when the test is made harder, e.g. by giving words in which single letters have been struck out. This can be an insuperable obstacle for an alectic patient, although a normal person hardly notices the difference. Lesions in cases of alexia may be found either in the parietal or in the occipital lobe.

(8) AUDITORY PERCEPTION. Does he recognize *noises*? (whistling, rattling, banging, barking, mewing, etc.). Does he recognize objects from sounds? (match-box, coins, brush). Reaction to strong auditory stimuli? (slammed door). Can he point towards noises coming from different directions? ('acoustic localization').

Understanding of spoken *language:* see under (6).

Music. Is he able to recognize tunes, to repeat them, to sing spontaneously? Use of musical instruments if possible. Can he repeat a *rhythm*, knocked out to him on the table? Can he roughly estimate intervals of time?

An exact examination of the peripheral hearing is of the same importance as the examination of visual acuity and visual field. The interaction of peripheral and central disturbances in the province of hearing are closer than in seeing, but much less known, since the methods of distinguishing them are still somewhat defective.

Central disturbances of auditory perception are to be observed after lesions of the temporal lobes, the gyri Heschl (gyrus temporalis transversus ant.) specially. Double-sided lesions are probably necessary to produce defects.

(9) TACTILE PERCEPTION AND 'BODY IMAGE'. Does the patient recognize materials and objects by feeling? Does he recognize numbers written on his skin? Can he describe the direction of a line drawn on his skin? Can he imitate postures of his limbs from one side to the other and imitate the examiner's postures? Can he point to parts of his own body or other people's? (Head's finger-nose-ear test).

Does he recognize and name and demonstrate *single fingers*? Can he distinguish between *right and left*? Can he do this on a person sitting opposite to him?

Is there any anomaly of the awareness of his own body or parts of it?

The routine examination of superficial and deep sensation must precede the application of these tests. In all doubtful cases standardized stimuli should be used, such as von Frey's set of hairs, or dividers. Not only quantitative anomalies, but also qualitative variations of sensation have to be recorded, such as are to be observed especially after thalamic lesions. The recognition of surface of material, e.g. silk, velvet, paper, wood, can be disturbed without impairment of the common skin sensation. The same is true with regard to the recognition of shapes and objects. Numbers written on the skin are generally recognized independently of their orientation in space. These functions are found disturbed after lesions of the post-central gyrus and the adjacent parts of the parietal lobe.

When using the finger-nose-ear test, one has to bear in mind that the results depend to some extent on the patient's memory and speech. Sometimes the disturbances appear only when the patient has to cross the mid-line of his body with the hand to carry out the test. *Finger agnosia* may be found as a relatively isolated disturbance, often together with difficulties in distinguishing right and left (asomatognosia). Both are due to lesions in the lower parietal lobe, generally of the left side. Disturbances of the body image have been observed as loss of orientation in respect to parts of the body (autotopagnosia), wrong localization of it, symmetrical displacement (alloaesthesia), loss of self-perception of pareses and other disturbances of function (anosognosia). Bilateral disturbances of these kinds are particularly associated with lesions of the left hemisphere.

(10) MOTILITY. Does the patient's motor behaviour as a whole show anything exceptional with regard to amount, tempo, co-ordination and harmony of movements?

Observe the patient's behaviour, especially when he carries out movements requiring some skill, such as throwing and catching a ball, jumping over an obstacle, carrying a tray with several objects.

Is there any anomaly in spontaneous *facial expression*? Can he produce facial expressions on request—smile, look astonished, etc.? Can he nod 'yes' and 'no', whistle, click his tongue, pout, lick his upper lip, close one eye? Can he make *gestures* correctly? (beckoning, military salute, threatening, waving good-bye. To be tested with each hand separately).

Single movements of joints and limbs might be disturbed without paralysis: moving of single fingers, of the toes, opening and closing the hands, doing 'physical jerks' with arms or legs. Notice especially synkineses of the other side.

Can he *imitate* all the movements and postures demonstrated to him? Can he perform activities on his own body correctly? (scratching, twisting moustache).

How does he perform *purposive activities* with objects? (using scissors, a key, threading a needle, putting a letter into an envelope and posting it, combing his hair while holding the glass, etc.).

Try activities with particular difficulties in space: putting on spectacles, forming a string into a bow, folding a napkin.

Purposive make-believe activities (knocking at a door, using a hammer and nail, using a typewriter, playing the violin).

Poverty as well as abundance of spontaneous movements can be a symptom of organic disease. The disturbances may be noticeable in the whole body or be limited to parts of it. They may be caused by lesions in various areas of the brain. Slowness and rapidity of movements, well known after lesions of the extra-pyramidal system, may be produced by lesions at a higher level as well. The same holds true for tic-like, choreiform and similar hyperkineses. Their diagnostic value can be assessed only within their particular setting. They can be of organic origin, even if they appear only under the influence of emotions.

There is a form of apraxia limited to the face. It is characterized by the inability to carry out expressive movements deliberately, while the automatic expressive movements are preserved.

Mild cases of apraxia may appear just 'clumsy', severe ones confused. Apraxia may be confined to one limb or one side of the body. Purposive make-believe activities reveal the disturbance more easily than ordinary activities with objects do. Lesions in cases of apraxia are to be found in the corpus callosum, the parietal lobe and, possibly, in the frontal lobe; and bilateral apraxia always involves the dominant hemisphere.

CONSTRUCTIONAL ACTIVITIES. Can the patient imitate patterns of matches, blocks or mosaics? Free construction without pattern? Does he recognize his mistakes? Constructional apraxia is associated with lesions of the non-dominant hemisphere.

DRAWING. Can he draw on request a cross, triangle, house, man or elephant? Can he copy simple drawings? Can he trace? Defects in this field are also related to the right hemisphere more than to the left.

WRITING. Can the patient write down letters, words, sentences dictated to him? Can he write his signature? In cursive and block letters? Can he answer a question in writing? Can he copy from print? Guide his finger so that he writes letters and ask him to read them. Can he put together single wooden letters to form a word?

Constructional disability is relatively independent of other apractic disturbances. As a rule, disturbances in drawing and in constructing occur together. The inability is generally so striking in cases of this kind that the usual standardized performance tests are of no use; they are much too difficult. Only such gross inability is of diagnostic value, since the average person's performances in these tests, especially in drawing, are poor. The tests are especially useful, since they are independent of vocabulary and memory. The lesions in cases of constructional disturbances are to be found in the lower parietal lobe, near to the occipital lobe.

Disturbances of writing are most commonly combined with disturbances of language and secondary to them. All types of dysphasic disorders are reflected in the patient's writing; but there are also isolated agraphias. Agraphia may interfere with the writing of the single letter, construction of words or the arrangement of the lines. The signature being a fixed stamped pattern is often the *ultimum moriens*. Figure-writing, too, plays a particular part (see above). Some patients, though unable to write, preserve the ability to draw letters. Disturbances of writing can be observed independently of reading disturbances.

The Reliability of the Psychiatric Interview

A number of enquiries have been undertaken in recent years to determine the reliability of methods of examination of the psychiatric patient which are modelled on the psychiatric interview (Spitzer *et al.*, 1964; Wing *et al.*, 1967). The most comprehensive investigations have been those undertaken by Wing and his colleagues. Their technique preserves the essentially clinical character of the interview although this is converted into a highly systematized and structured procedure. The five trained interviewers who took part in this investigation achieved a satisfactory degree of reliability in the provisional diagnosis and also in the clinical scores recorded. In the psychotic section, the correlation between two observers for judgements as to the presence of 'auditory hallucinations' reached 0·919; for 'delusional experiences and disordered thoughts', 0·945 and for 'blunting of affect', 0·862. In non-psychotic features correlation for anxiety in the last group of interviews was 0·939; for depression, 0·883. In assigning patients to diagnostic categories, complete agreement between pairs of clinicians was achieved in 84 per cent. and partial agreement in 7 per cent.

CHAPTER III

PERSONALITY DEVIATIONS AND NEUROTIC REACTIONS

HISTORICAL DEVELOPMENT OF THE CONCEPT OF PSYCHOPATHY

PSYCHIATRIC interest in the individual who, though neither insane nor intellectually defective, behaves socially in an abnormal way, begins in 1835 with Prichard who coined the term 'moral insanity'. Among criminals Prichard observed those who showed loss of feeling, loss of control and loss of all ethical sense, and he thought that the abnormality shown by these men was on a par with mental disease, although shown at a different level. A further step was taken by Koch (1891) in his book *Die psychopathischen Minderwertig-keiten.* We owe to him the terms 'psychopathic', 'psychopathic inferior' and 'constitutional inferior' all of which are in current use. Moebius in 1900 brought in the idea of 'degeneration' from French psychiatry, to help to explain clinical findings; but he was ahead of his time in thinking also of normal variation, and in writing 'the psychopath is a morbid variety of the normal' ('*eine krankhafte Spielart der Norm*'). All these views, relating psychopathy with insanity, with some form of organic deterioration, and with normal variation, have found their followers, so that even to recent times there has been great confusion as to what was to be meant by the term 'psychopathic personality'.

This confusion has also been in part due to doubt about what aspects of the mind should be included in the personality. At one time authors, such as Wilmanns and Gruhle, wished to include intellectual functions within the concept of the personality; mental defect would then be one form of psychopathy. On the whole, however, authors both in Europe and America have agreed that intellectual functions were best excluded from consideration, and the concept of the personality restricted to *the affective and conative aspects of the individual* as a whole. This development was a necessary one for any clarity. While it remained true that in the handling of the individual patient it was necessary to take not only neurotic and psychopathic aspects of the case into account but also intelligence and mental abilities, as much might also be said of social and cultural aspects. Clinical experience showed that psychopathic character traits, neurotic symptoms and emotional disturbances took very much the same form in the man of high as of low intellectual ability: that, in the language of statistics, the two variables (temperament and intellect) were largely independent of one another, and that quite distinct vocabularies were required for an adequate description of events in the affective and the intellectual field.

The isolation of the two fields, necessary as it was, had, however, some undesirable consequences. Apart from the clinical description of certain pathological forms of imbecility, human variation in mental ability became the province of *non-medical psychologists.*

Ignoring pathological causes, they concerned themselves with developing testing techniques for mapping the range of the normal. The affective aspects of the personality were left to the *medical psychologists*, by whom description in terms of pathology was favoured, leading to a radically different approach. The similarities between the two aspects of the individual were thereby obscured and came to be largely forgotten.

The next source of confusion, which has not been so easily resolved, is the difficulty, primarily clinical and secondarily theoretical, of distinguishing abnormalities of personality from psychosis on the one hand and neurosis on the other, and of marking the boundary between all three and the realm of the normal. The difficulty has been met in some quarters, notably in the *school of Adolf Meyer*, by denying the validity of the distinction between any two of these three abnormal manifestations. For Meyer and his followers the individual was a psychobiological unity. Any unusual or morbid manifestation was a mode of reaction to particular features in the environment; and psychosis, psychopathic personality and neurosis were different parts of a psychiatric spectrum showing a gradation by infinitesimal degrees from one extreme to the other. The development of the personality was itself regarded as the result of a series of reactions to environmental forces; and endogenous and hereditary determinants were allowed but little importance and received scant attention.

For this school the complex case in which a deviation of the personality and neurotic and psychotic symptoms were all to be seen in the clinical picture represented no particular puzzle, at least theoretically. No attempt was made to order clinical features in a *hierarchy of relative significance*, or to attain any clarity in either diagnosis or prognosis. On the one hand the formulation of reaction types, lined up in single file, was so flexible that almost any combination of clinical findings could be easily explained; on the other hand it was so lacking in precision that its predictive and heuristic value was small and it proved sterile as a ground for the growth of new theories and new ideas.

The contribution to the discussion made by disciples of the *school of Freud* has not been a very helpful one for psychiatrists who do not belong to that school. For the psychoanalyst the basic disturbance in psychopathic personality, psychosis and neurosis alike, is a deviation from the normal line of psychological development which has taken place in early childhood. This deviation is conceived in terms of a fixation of the libido in the anal or the early or late oral stages. What is postulated, in fact, is an abnormality of constitution, but due to environmental causes. In the case of the 'psychopathic personality' it is visible on the surface, in the 'psychotic' and the 'neurotic' not openly manifested until the outbreak of symptoms. In addition, the psychotic shows in the course of his illness the phenomenon of regression to an infantile level of libido-fixation. Although Freud himself left room in the formulation for the effects of an inherited and inborn constitution in modifying subsequent events, he and his followers have given this little attention; and in general both the initial disturbance in development and the later neurotic or psychotic state are thought of as occurring in response to environmental psychological factors. Freud's conception allows a fairly clear distinction to be drawn between 'neurotic' and 'psychotic' illnesses, according to the point at which, in infantile development, libido has become fixed and whether or not regression is taking place. 'Psychopathic personality', on the other hand, becomes a concept of little practical value, a congeries of different states, individual members of which may be more nearly related to the neurotic or the psychotic types of constitution. In general, in psychoanalysis the use of such terms as psychopathic, neurotic and psychotic has come to have less and less significance, and a fundamentally different formulation is used for diagnostic, therapeutic and prognostic purposes.

In the *German school of psychiatry*, much attention and dispute have been attracted to the problem of the aetiological relationship between deviations of personality and psychosis. For Kraepelin, 'psychopathic personalities' were *formes frustes* of psychoses, or personalities who had deviated from a normal line of development as a result of hereditary or organic environmental factors. Kahn distinguished 'episodic', 'periodic' and 'lasting' psychopathic personalities and psychopathic developments, which might occur as the result of a disease process or of the normal reaction between individual and environment. Jaspers was the first to formulate the sharp distinction between *development of personality* and *disease process*, giving rise to much controversy and theoretical progress. The development of the personality, whether or not along psychopathic lines, was for Jaspers, apart from the effects of age, an understandable sequence of changes. It was understandable because it was closely related to normal reactions, and there was a continuous scale of transitions between normality on one side and psychopathy on the other. On the other hand alterations in the personality due to a disease process (psychosis) showed something new and strange, not deducible from what was known of the personality, age, and circumstances of life.

Kretschmer took an opposite view, and saw for instance every possible transitional stage between the schizothyme, the schizoid and the schizophrenic. The ordinary events of life involved the individual in changes which were not to be sharply distinguished qualitatively from those caused by disease, and development might occur not only in a smooth curve but also in sudden jumps, as for instance at puberty. The main stream of German psychiatric teaching, however, did not follow this course; and the concepts of development and of process came to assume a central importance. The clinical distinction between what was to be regarded as deriving from one or the other was to be made by the criterion of 'understanding' the symptoms, or by what was called '*empathy*'. It was recognized that psychopathic and neurotic behaviour has its roots in normal behaviour, differs from it only in degree, and can be thought of as a distortion of normal psychology. No sharp lines of distinction can be drawn, either between the normal and the psychopathic, or between the different forms of psychopathic and neurotic reaction. When the opponents of this view pointed out that even in a psychosis the content of the delusions could always be related to previous circumstances in an understandable way, the answer was that the vital point was not content but the form of the symptoms. Even the form of the symptoms is understandable in a neurotic state, but is not so in some aspects of psychotic conditions. Thus one may understand that certain experiences may readily cause a response in the development of anxiety or of an over-valued idea, but not in the appearance of hallucinations or delusions.

From the clinical point of view, distinctions drawn along these lines proved extremely useful. By their use it became possible to distinguish between schizophrenic illness and the reactive disturbances of paranoid, sensitive or autistic personalities, with advantages in the treatment of states of both kinds. The nuclear symptoms of schizophrenia were delineated, and it became for the first time possible to recognize with fair certainty post-schizophrenic defect states.

The symptoms and sequelae of organic disorders of known pathology were also clarified and patients in whom symptoms of this kind were intermingled with neurotic reactions could be appraised and assessed clinically with greater sureness. It was possible to *order the symptoms* in a given case *in a hierarchy*, denoting those which indicated structural changes and those which represented a reaction of the personality to the changed internal and external environment. Work in which these levels of action and reaction were incorporated, such as the structural analysis of Birnbaum and Kretschmer's multidimensional diagnosis, became possible. Beyond the field of the schizophrenic and organic psychoses, the method was pressed into the analysis of the affective psychoses. A considerable degree of success was attained here in differentiating the primary from the secondary mood changes, a vital from a reactive depression (K. Schneider), manic-depressive and involutional psychoses from a variety of neurotic states. But in this field the instruments of analysis, the nuclear symptoms of the endogenous change, were both less numerous and less characteristic, and in the individual instance a satisfactory distinction was often impossible. The method of distinguishing between one symptom and another by the readiness with which it may be understood from the known personality and circumstances leads to distinctions which are relative and often very subjective; and with certain symptoms, such as ideas of reference, in many cases it proves indecisive.

In *British and American psychiatry* the concept of 'psychopathic personality', as a class of phenomena at the same generalized level as 'psychosis', never emerged. The more basic concepts of development and process, familiar to psychiatry on the European continent, were largely unknown. Instead, efforts were made along purely clinical lines to describe a syndrome, to delineate a being who could be classified as a 'psychopath'. These efforts could only lead to confusion, as each author moulded his definition of psychopathy on his own experience and predilections; and there came to be as many definitions as authors. Thus for Henderson the psychopath is both antisocial or asocial and incorrigible, for Cheney he is emotionally immature, for Levine he is lacking in foresight, for North non-constructive, for Bullard an egoist and a social misfit. Although Henderson for one recognizes the 'creative' psychopath, for most authors strong antisocial tendencies are requisite. All agree in regarding the aetiology as entirely obscure but unrelated with that of psychosis and neurosis.

In their review of the subject in 1944 Curran and Mallinson drew attention to this unsatisfactory confusion of ideas. However, they adhered to the view, shared by many psychiatrists, that the concept of psychopathic personality must be limited clinically, and that to make it coextensive with abnormal personality would lead only to further confusion. They recognized three classes of psychopathic personality: vulnerable personalities, i.e. those who 'when pinched by circumstances, are liable to develop neurotic and psychotic as well as psychopathic reactions'; unusual or abnormal personalities or characters, i.e. those who deviate markedly from the common run, but are not necessarily unstable or socially undesirable; and 'sociopathic' personalities, whose cardinal feature is asocial or antisocial behaviour. These three classes fade into one another, into the neurotic and into the psychotic. The concept remains a clinical one, without aetiological implications.

The attempt to delimit psychopathy as a clinical syndrome has now become fossilized in the Mental Health Act (1959). Section 4 (4) reads:

'In this Act "psychopathic disorder" means a persistent disorder or disability of the mind (whether or not including subnormality of intelligence) which results in abnormally aggressive or seriously irresponsible conduct on the part of the patient, and requires or is susceptible to medical treatment.'

In effect this clause equates 'psychopathic disorder' with antisocial conduct. Persons coming within the definition make up a group with no common clinical or aetiological feature; and the definition excludes personality deviants which clinically and aetiologically are closely related, e.g. so-called inadequate psychopaths. Furthermore, aggressive or irresponsible conduct is likely to be the only evidence which can be offered that there is disorder or disability of the mind. It is unfortunate that a modern statute, of prime significance to psychiatry in this country, should be conceptually so ill-founded.

MODERN DEVELOPMENT OF THE CONCEPT OF PSYCHOPATHY

In German psychiatry the importance given to the ideas of process and development led to a sharp distinction being drawn between psychosis on the one side and *psychopathic personality and neurosis* on the other. Between the last two, however, the distinction was much more fluid. There was, in fact, a strong tendency to link up psychopathic personality with psychoneurosis in calling the latter 'psychopathic reaction', 'psychogenic reaction' or 'abnormal psychological reaction' (Lange). It had long been recognized that neuroses frequently occurred in personalities which could be classified as psychopathic, and that the mode of reaction corresponded with the most outstanding traits of the personality in which it occurred, e.g. hysterical conversion symptoms in a hysterical personality. Some peculiar personalities were most easily understood if they were regarded as suffering from the result of a psychotic process in the past; but in this case the assumption could frequently be confirmed by a diligent search of the past history and the discovery that a mild psychotic episode had actually occurred. Such cases were, however, relatively rare; and the majority of psychopathic personalities must be interpreted along other lines. It was at this point that Kurt Schneider made an important contribution to the subject.

Schneider pointed out that *the term 'abnormal'* was used in two different ways, the *statistical* and the *ideal*, and that it is only in its former sense that it can usefully be applied scientifically. If, for instance, we attempt to use 'abnormal' in the sense of failing to conduce to satisfactory function, a subjective element is introduced into the definition, for what is satisfactory to one observer in one environment will be unsatisfactory to another in a different environment. In the statistical sense, 'abnormal' merely means 'deviating from the average', and the average can be found by a process of objective enquiry. Schneider recognizes that any deviation from the average must always be a matter of degree, and that there are many varieties of abnormal or deviant personality that suffer from no disabilities and are the cause of no trouble. He defines psychopathic personalities as those *abnormal personalities who suffer from their abnormality or cause society to suffer.* These two classes clearly correspond with the neurotic and the psychopath of British and American psychiatry; but in Schneider's formulation the distinction is purely one of convenience, and without aetiological, symptomatic, diagnostic, prognostic, or other significance.

This conception supplies an approach to the problems of psychopathy which is comprehensive and rational. We are taken away from philosophical conceptions back to observations of fact. We are not put in the painful position of distinguishing on theoretical grounds between the psychopath and the eccentric, between the paranoid litigant and the fanatical social reformer. Fundamentally similar types of personality are not put on opposite sides of a supposedly aetiologically significant dividing line, because from society one attracts approval and the other condemnation. The difference between the neurotic, who suffers himself, and the psychopath who causes society to suffer, is no longer the difference between someone who is ill, and the proper recipient of medical aid, and someone who is not, and is an enemy of society. It is no longer a source of puzzlement, that an abnormal personality can at one time be calling for the aid of his doctors, at another bringing misery and disgrace on his relatives, and finally be applauded in history for positive achievements beyond the reach of the average.

Another advantage is that Schneider's formulation can be *translated into biometrical terms*. The concepts which he left somewhat vague and indeterminate then take on a mathematical precision. The qualities of temperament and personality can be regarded as varying from individual to individual in much the same way as stature, body-weight, quantitatively variable psychological attributes in general, or, in the field of psychiatry, intelligence. These are graded characters, and have to be measured quantitatively. When measurements of things like these are made on a large number of persons chosen at random from the population, and the measurements are plotted along a scale divided into equal intervals against the frequencies with which they are represented, a 'normal' curve is observed. In such a curve the measurements which are most commonly represented in the population are concentrated at or near the average value; and the frequencies of more extreme values to either side fall off at a regular and increasing rate. At any point on the scale it is possible to say just how frequently that, or an even more extreme, degree of variation from the average will be found.

A very similar view was taken by the Swedish psychiatrist, Sjöbring (1963), who considered that temperamental traits could be considered as distributed in a normal curve, and even when shown in an extreme degree could be distinguished from the results of pathological change, such as are shown by the post-schizophrenic. He described four dimensions of variation, one of them being 'capacity' (intelligence), and the three others 'stability', 'solidity' and 'validity'. At the negative extreme of the first are the sub-stable, the warm, interested in others, extensively active personalities; the super-stable are cold, interested in ideas, intensively active. The sub-solid are quickly reactive, flexible, subjective; the super-solid are slow, objective, self-possessed. The sub-valid are retiring, tense and anxious; the super-valid expressive, venturesome, self-confident. All shades of difference in all of these four dimensions are shown by normal people and even very unusual normal personalities can be described in terms of deviation along one or more of these dimensions. However, Sjöbring retained the concept of psychopathic personality as a qualitatively abnormal phenomenon, to be accounted for as the result of a pathological process. Sjöbring's pupils have found his scheme very helpful clinically, particularly, for instance, in leading to the detection of a change of personality which, being of a nature foreign to the personality itself, suggests a pathological process. Sjöbring's formulation is in some ways superior to that of Schneider, who, in the clinical part of his work, reverted to the use of types of personality and departed from his own concept of modes of variation.

Both Schneider and Sjöbring, therefore, believed that men varied in their temperamental traits in many ways, by infinitesimal degrees and between wide extremes, and that we should look for the *cause of psychopathy in this normal variation*. Strong support for this view was provided by clinical experience during the Second World War. During the First World War of 1914–18, psychiatric attention was concentrated on the clinical manifestations of neurosis ('shell shock') and on its psychological causes. During the second war, attention was also given to the constitutional background. It was found that the liability to neurotic breakdown varied with the degree of stress imposed, but also with the degree of constitutional instability. This constitutional factor could be detected and to some extent measured by such psychiatric findings as a family history of nervous illness, a past history of nervous breakdown or an irregular work record, etc. The detection of the constitutionally unstable became supremely important in all questions of selection of personnel, especially the choosing of officers, air-crew, etc. The relation between liability to neurotic breakdown and abnormalities of personality became obvious, and led to the formulation of the 'neurotic constitution' (Slater, 1943; Slater and Slater, 1944).

According to these authors, the *constitutional liability to neurosis* varied quantitatively, but was not of a unitary kind. Some men were highly susceptible to stress of one kind, others to another. The very mode of breakdown and the type of symptoms exhibited varied from patient to patient, necessitating different diagnostic labels, different prognoses, different methods of treatment. Although it was possible to diagnose one neurotic patient as suffering from an anxiety state and another from hysteria, in the majority of patients symptoms of both kinds could be found. The diagnostic groups faded into one another. The nature of the symptoms, however, was found to have close associations with the basic personality of the patient, and somewhat less close ones with the type of stress to which he had been subjected. Certain types of environment had a preferential effect in producing anxiety symptoms, others minor states of depression, others again a hypochondriacal preoccupation, e.g. syphilophobia. In general, however, *formes frustes* of the eventually incapacitating neurotic symptoms could be found in the patient's past life, and were associated with the make-up of his personality.

It was pointed out that if we regard the disposition to neurosis as *due to a number of distinct qualities*, each of them subject to normal variation, clinical observations could be accounted for. In any one quality the man who would be liable to a neurosis would be likely to show a constitutional deviation from the average value to one extreme. In this respect he would be more susceptible to certain specific stresses, and if the stress passed a certain level of intensity, to breakdown. Once having broken down, he would be likely to show symptoms of a specific and related kind. But the majority of men who were likely to break down under stress would be those, as the laws of chance would compel one to postulate, who showed *minor deficiencies along a number of different lines* rather than those who showed an extreme deficiency along one line only. Under ordinary circumstances one would therefore expect to find in one's clinical material a mixture of different types of stress, breakdown occurring among men of constitutional susceptibility of a mixture of kinds, and clinical syndromes in which patients with symptoms of a pure type would be in a minority. One would, moreover, expect to find *genetical factors of a multifactorial kind* playing a part in the predisposition to nervous breakdown.

From the point of view of a discussion of the problems of psychopathic personality, this theory has three advantages. It accounts for the *incidence of neurotic symptoms* and their relation to qualities of personality in an orderly and comprehensive way. It provides an account of the *genetical basis of the neurotic disposition*. And finally it brings the neurotic personality into a comprehensible *relation with the psychopathic personality*, neurotic symptoms into relation with psychopathic behaviour. The first of these three aspects has already been adequately dealt with, and the second will be treated in a separate section (p. 63). It remains to consider the third.

It is clear that this theory is applicable not only to the development of symptoms of illness in the individual under stress, but to *human behaviour in general* in any given set of environmental circumstances. Tachycardia, sweating, feelings of fear, insomnia, depression, faints, fugues and all the other phenomena which we call neurotic symptoms, are easily thought of as manifestations of a given personality and constitution in circumstances favourable to their development. We could also consider tendencies to seek relief in alcohol, outbursts of temper, wandering, dereliction of duty, lying and thieving, and acts of ruthless cruelty in the same light. There can be no fundamental distinction between them; and such distinction as there is depends on their social effects and their liability to be dealt with by doctors or by other agents of society. We must indeed expect to find 'psychopathic' traits in the man, who, in his medical contacts, is generally classified as 'neurotic', and 'neurotic' traits in the 'psychopath'. Admittedly, certain types of susceptibility are particularly likely to lead their possessor into circumstances in which he himself suffers the main consequences. An unusually marked tendency to anxiety reactions is one such. But elsewhere consequences will be more evenly divided between the individual and society, as is the case with those tendencies, sometimes called 'hysterical', which will at one time show themselves as headaches or loss of memory, at another as social parasitism, pseudologia, or persistent shoplifting. In still other cases, such as men with a grossly hypertrophied egoism, symptoms of illness are little likely to appear and the whole effects of the abnormality of personality will be seen in personal relationships and career.

We see, then, that the *classification of human beings into types* represents an oversimplification, however useful it may be practically. If we had no means of measuring the body, we should have to classify people into tall and short, and fat and thin. For medical purposes, we replace such crude categories by actual measurements. When we can make an adequate number of reliable psychological measurements, we shall be able to abandon the use of such terms as 'obsessional personality' and 'hysterical psychopath', for measurements or indices which will be more informative. We have not as yet reached this point, but we are progressing in that direction. Psychologists are elaborating such tests, and the work of Eysenck and his collaborators (1960c) has shown how they may be used to discriminate between neurotics and normals. Sheldon and his collaborators (Sheldon, Stevens and Tucker, 1940; Sheldon and Stevens, 1942) have found continuous variation in both the physical and the temperamental field and high correlations between measurements along the two kinds of scales. Their findings provide support for the view that the physiological and psychological attributes of the individual are but aspects of an underlying unity, and therefore aspects of one another. However, their observations have since been questioned on statistical and other grounds (see pages 70 and 193).

In this book we shall attempt to deal as far as we can in terms of *modes of variation* and *modes of reaction*, and to eschew the classification of either individuals or their non-pathological reactions into watertight compartments. For purposes of clinical description, however, it will be necessary to describe types in which some feature is given a central position and other variables are ignored. This is justifiable in so far as it conduces to clarity and brings into relief all the ways in which some single quality may manifest itself.

AETIOLOGICAL ASPECTS OF CONSTITUTION

Heredity

In the previous section we have seen how, in a number of qualities of personality of immediate psychiatric interest, human beings vary in a way that conforms to the normal curve. This suggests that in each case variation is controlled by a great number of single determining factors, whose effects may be additive to one another. These determining factors might be either genetical or environmental in nature.

In the general field of animal and plant genetics the concept of harmonious interaction between a *multiplicity of genes*, in determining characters which have to be considered quantitatively, has now an established place. Even those genes which produce single, specific and large effects are found to be subject, in the extent and the degree and the time of their manifestation, to the qualifying influence of the rest of the genetic constitution, usually referred to as modifying genes. It is indeed generally believed that evolutionary advance and the formation of species has very largely occurred by the accumulation of modifying genes producing effects of different kinds, those which are favourable being accumulated through natural selection. As no single gene possessed by the individual can be thought of as being quite without effect on any part of the body or on any vital function, it follows that these modifying genes involve the totality of the genetic constitution.

The type of variation in any quantitative character produced in this way will necessarily tend to follow the normal curve. And the concept of genetical determination of attributes of personality accordingly fits very well with our observed findings in respect of any one character. But it also fits very well with numbers of characters taken together. As many of the genes which have a considerable effect in determining the degree of one quality will be identical with those which have a main share in determining a second quality, we must expect, on genetical grounds, to find some *correlation between different qualities* taken two at a time, a correlation which will be much greater in the case of some pairs of qualities than in the case of other pairs. This also is observed in psychometric psychology. The genetical theory leads us also to expect some correlation between psychological qualities and somatic ones, such as had indeed been found and is the basis of the work on physical constitution in psychiatry by Kretschmer and his followers.

This genetical theory is adequate to explain the observed facts of variation, and it is supported by independent evidence that genetic factors do indeed play a large part in the formation of personality and in determining various psychological tendencies. This evidence is derived from work on twins and from family investigations.

The *literature on this subject* is very large indeed, and there is no need to examine it in detail. It suffers from various defects, principally from the fact that clinical psychiatrists have not been able to examine their subjects by scales of measurement, but only by clinical impressions which have often amounted to no more than a finding that a certain quality was or was not present in fairly marked degree.

EVIDENCE FROM TWINS. A fair amount of work has been done by psychologists on normal twins, enough to show that there are extensive resemblances in temperament and character between monozygotic (MZ) twins, greater than those which obtain between dizygotic (DZ) twins or ordinary sibs. A striking piece of work in this field is the report by Newman, Freeman and Holzinger (1937) on nineteen pairs of MZ twins reared apart from early years. Despite very different environments there were marked resemblances between the twins both in the clinical impression they gave and their reactions to psychological tests of temperament; but the resemblance was less close than in the field of intelligence.

Shields (1962) has reviewed the work done on separated MZ twins since that of Newman, and has provided an extended report on 44 such pairs which he had investigated himself, together with 44 control pairs of MZ twins, not separated. Most of the twins of the S series had been separated by the age of three months, but some much later. The separated pairs were no less alike than the control pairs in physique, intelligence or temperament tests; the correlation in 'neuroticism', for instance, was $+0.53$ in the S series and $+0.38$ in the C series. The author's own personality ratings were more successful than the M.P.I. test in detecting the differences produced within pairs by environmental separation.

Monozygotic twins in both series were found to resemble one another in a variety of ways, in mannerisms, voice, tastes, and sexual behaviour. Deviations in the disposition to quick temper, anxiety, emotional lability, rigidity, and cyclothymic traits were often concordant in both S and C series. Some but not all childhood neurotic traits, e.g. enuresis, but not sleep-walking, tended to be concordant. The differences found between members of the separated pairs seemed to be just as frequent in pairs separated after the age of four as in those separated soon after birth.

Most of the work that has been done on normal twins, however, has little reference to clinical psychiatry. In the field of psychopathology the best body of knowledge has been accumulated by twin studies of crime. The first in this field was Johannes Lange. The result of his work was to show that in ten out of thirteen cases the uniovular twin of a criminal was himself criminal, one of the exceptions being provided by a pair in which one had become criminal after a head injury. Not only was there concordance between the twins in respect of criminality, but also in the actual type of crime, the favoured criminal technique, the age of manifestation, etc. Thus one pair were both repeatedly guilty of robbery with violence, and in another pair both brothers engaged in a long series of frauds on some of the wealthiest men in Germany, using their gains to travel about the country with cars and secretaries as if they were princes. There was, in fact, very close similarity between the brothers in the personality make-up, out of which criminal activities had grown. In the seventeen same-sexed binovular pairs, on the other hand, there were only two cases in which both of the pair were criminal, and there was little similarity in character. The effect of Lange's work, which attracted very great attention at the time, was to suggest that, apart from such accidents as organic cerebral disease, the make-up of the personality was determined almost exclusively by hereditary factors; and that social behaviour was itself the almost inevitable product of the personality.

To some extent Lange's work was confirmed by Rosanoff in U.S.A. (1934). Rosanoff collected 340 pairs of twins, divided approximately equally into three groups of adult criminals, juvenile delinquents and children with behaviour problems. In all three groups there was a very striking conformity between the uniovular pairs, which was not matched by the binovular ones. Rosanoff's work is not adorned with the detailed and fascinating character studies which make up such a large part and much of the value of the work of Lange; but he shows that in the discordant uniovular pairs the criminality of the one twin is as often as not of a rather accidental nature. Such factors as this, as well as inadequacy of information, may account for the fact that only two-thirds out of all the uniovular adult pairs were concordant. Rosanoff distinguishes between criminality, the objectively observed criminal behaviour, and criminalism, the 'strong and persistent constitutional tendency which manifests itself under various conditions of no special difficulty or strain'. This work has been reported in greater detail later (Rosanoff, Handy and Plessett, 1941).

A necessary correction to the work of Lange was provided by that of Kranz (1936) and of Stumpfl (1936). Both of these workers made *systematic studies in the criminal population* of North and South Germany respectively, with every effort to get an inclusive and unbiased collection, in which binovular pairs would be as well investigated as the uniovular ones. Their results went to show that Lange was in every way right in his view that the make-up of the personality was determined, at least to a preponderant extent, by hereditary factors; but that Rosanoff had been equally right in thinking that accidental and environmental factors played a large part in determining whether or not that personality actually descended into a life of crime. Family tradition was important, as was shown by the fact that among

D

male binovular pairs there was a considerable measure of concordance. Two brothers, of dissimilar character, might both be led into crime, though of a dissimilar kind, by the effect of bad example and other psychological and environmental influences.

The possible contribution of genetical factors to the causation of homosexuality will be discussed later (p. 169). Apart from this, most of the systematic twin work in the field of neurotic and personality disorders has been carried out in the Genetics Unit at the Maudsley Hospital. Thus Slater (1953) in a series of about 300 twin pairs found 8 MZ and 43 DZ pairs with concordant diagnoses in the co-twins in only 2 of the former and 8 of the latter. Work by Shields (1954) on schoolchildren showed that MZ twins resembled one another closely in the type of neurotic reaction shown, but much less markedly in the degree. The main factors determining whether a child became neurotic seemed, in fact, to be environmental, though the mode in which a neurotic reaction was shown was influenced more by hereditary factors.

A study of 12 MZ and 12 DZ pairs, in which the index twin was diagnosed as suffering from 'hysteria' was reported by Slater (1961). The remarkable observation was made that there was no indication whatever that genetical factors made any contribution to the specifically hysterical nature of the symptomatology. Not one of the 24 co-twins received a formal diagnosis of hysteria; 3 MZ and 2 DZ pairs were concordant in receiving a diagnosis of neurosis in a wider sense; and, using the widest form of classification, 5 MZ and 4 DZ pairs were concordant in which both members of the pair had received treatment from psychiatrist or general practitioner for neurotic symptoms. The fact that, however we look at it, no difference is to be found between the MZ and the DZ pairs, cannot be reconciled with a major contribution to the aetiology from the genetical side. The implications of this work are further discussed on page 104.

Parker (1964 b, c) investigated 21 pairs of twins, in which the index case had received a diagnosis of neurosis or personality deviation at the Bethlem Maudsley or Belmont Hospitals during 1959–61. He considers that twin work has very limited usefulness in unravelling the interaction of heredity and environment in the causation of mental illness; and he is strongly critical of the use of diagnostic classification in the field of neurosis and personality deviation, and in the application of the concept of concordance to clinical data so classified. However, his observations led him to cast doubt on the theory that the high concordance rate for psychiatric disorder in MZ twins could be attributed to mutual identification (1964b); and the tabulated data he shows (1964c) reveal remarkable similarities in diagnostic classification of index twins and co-twin.

All the twins admitted to the Bethlem Maudsley Hospitals during 1948–1958, with a diagnosis by the hospital psychiatrist in the index case of neurosis or personality deviation, are now being reviewed. Follow-up information has been obtained about 384 individuals. Case summaries were prepared (by J. Shields) on all individuals in whom there was any psychiatric symptomatology, and 'blind' diagnoses were then made on these summaries (by E. Slater). In this material there were 80 MZ and 112 DZ pairs; and the diagnostic classifications made on the MZ pairs grouped under the categories of the International Classification of Diseases, 1947, are shown in the table below. It should be noted that, with the benefit of follow-up data, some of the Maudsley diagnoses of neurotic and psychopathic states had to be altered to psychotic ones or to epilepsy. Nevertheless, with all the admitted weaknesses of psychiatric diagnosis and despite the grave defects of the I.C.D. 1947 schema, there is a remarkable degree of similarity in the diagnoses made on twins and co-twins. Omitting those co-twins who were regarded as 'within normal limits', we have 40 pairs in which both twins received a psychiatric diagnosis; in 25 pairs the diagnosis in twin and co-twin fall into the same group, as against an expectation of 11·4.

Index Twin	Monozygotic Co-Twin						
	Psychoses 300 301 353			Neuroses 310 311–8		Personality disorders 320–4	Normal	Total
Psychoses								
300 Schizophrenic	2	—	—	—	1	1	2	6
301 Manic-depressive	—	3	—	3	1	—	4	11
353 Epilepsy	—	—	—	—	—	—	1	1
Psychoneurotic Disorders								
310 Anxiety reaction	—	—	—	7	—	1	9	17
311–8 other neuroses	—	—	—	—	—	3	9	12
Disorders of Character, etc.								
320–4 Pathological personality etc.	2	—	2	1	—	13	15	33
Totals	4	3	2	11	2	18	40	80

The finding that genetical factors probably play a major part in some neurotic states and some personality deviations, and a minor one in others, has received support from the work of Gottesman (1962, 1963). This worker investigated normal schoolchildren aged 14 to 18, 24 MZ and 24 DZ pairs. The findings obtained with the Minnesota Multiphasic Personality Inventory (M.M.P.I.) are of considerable interest. The values of H ('heritability index') for the ten scales of the M.M.P.I. are, in order of ascending value:

	Scale	H
3 Hy	hysteria	0·00
6 Pa	paranoia	0·05
5 Mf	pathological sexuality	0·15
1 Hs	hypochondriasis	0·16
9 Ma	hypomania	0·24
7 Pt	psychasthenia	0·37
8 Sc	schizophrenia	0·42
2 D	depression	0·45
4 Pd	psychopathic deviation	0·50
0 Si	social introversion	0·71

Commenting on his work Gottesman remarks, 'It would appear that neuroses with hypochondriacal and hysterical elements have no or low genetic component, while those with elements of anxiety, depression, obsession and schizoid withdrawal have a substantial genetic component under the environmental conditions obtaining for this particular adolescent sample.'

The evidence from the study of twins, therefore, leads us to the view that hereditary factors play an important role in the development of personality. The influence of the environment has been demonstrated most clearly in the small proportions of individuals affected by organic disease and injury. One must suppose also that the influences of early home life, affection or rejection, upbringing, training and education have a powerful effect in moulding the development of the personality.

EVIDENCE FROM FAMILY INVESTIGATIONS. While the study of twins leads us to the view that hereditary factors play an important role in the development of personality, we are left in the dark about the nature of these factors and their specificity. For information on this aspect we have to turn to investigations of families.

Of all neurotic syndromes, the evidence relating to genetical predisposition is best with the obsessional neuroses. Luxenburger (1930) examined the parents and sibs of 71 obsessionals, and found anankastic qualities in 15 per cent. of fathers, 6 per cent. of mothers and 14 per cent. of sibs. Lewis (1935a) found even higher proportions—37 per cent. of parents and 21 per cent. of sibs showed mild or severe obsessional traits. Both Lewis and Luxenburger favour the view that the anankastic or obsessional predisposition is a specific one. An opposite view was taken by Brown (1942); but in his material the obsessional, anxious and hysterical relatives are found clustering in the families of, respectively, the obsessional, anxious and hysterical probands. The most recent report is that of Rüdin (1953). She found that 5 per cent. of the parents and 2 per cent. of the sibs of her obsessional patients had had an obsessional illness, and, in addition, 5 per cent. of the parents and 3 per cent. of the sibs had obsessional personalities.

The data relating to anxiety states are less in amount. McInnes (1937), examining the relatives of 50 anxiety neurotics, found that 15 per cent. of the parents and 15 per cent. of the sibs had had anxiety neuroses also; among the relatives of psychiatrically normal controls the corresponding figures for parents and sibs were 4 per cent. and 5 per cent. Brown found 21 per cent. of parents and 12 per cent. of sibs of anxiety neurotics had had anxiety neuroses, i.e. conditions producing some temporary social incapacity; but such conditions were found with about half those frequencies in the relatives of obsessionals and hysterics. Cohen (1951) investigated the families of army recruits suffering from 'neurocirculatory asthenia' (N.C.A.). Among the relatives of the acute cases the frequency of N.C.A. was hardly higher than in the relatives of a control group; but it was very high in the relatives of chronic cases—18 per cent. in fathers, 55 per cent. in mothers, 13 per cent. in brothers and 12 per cent. in sisters. Among the children of these patients N.C.A. was common, but there was no evidence of hysteria, depressions or obsessional neurosis.

When we turn to hysteria, the evidence is conflicting; it will be discussed in the section on Hysterical Reactions on page 103.

An important recent advance, the discovery of the XYY syndrome, has had to find place in a postscript on p. 691.

Somatic Factors

The association between temperamental traits and bodily build has been observed from the earliest times; Hippocrates described *homo apoplecticus* and *homo phthisicus* in the fifth century B.C. A valuable review of the field has been provided by Linford Rees (1960). The modern approach has differed from that of earlier observers in that we now think of quantitative variation along a number of dimensions where they used to think in terms of bodily types. Some of the more commonly used and better founded typologies are shown in the table below, which is an extract from a much larger table given by Rees.

	1	2	3
1908 Sigaud	digestive	muscular	respiratory-cerebral
1919 Viola	megalosplanchnic	normosplanchnic	microsplanchnic
1921 Kretschmer	pyknic	athletic	leptosomatic
1940 Sheldon	endomorph	mesomorph	ectomorph
1945 Rees and Eysenck	eurymorph	mesomorph	leptomorph
1953 Lindegård	fat factor high	muscle factor high	length factor high.

In dimensional terms, it seems that there are three modes of measurement which are likely to be fairly independent: (1) body size, (2) relation between height on one side and breadth and depth on the other, and (3) the relation between the shoulder girdle and the pelvic measurements.

BODY SIZE. The relation between body size and psychological and psychiatric manifestations has not proved very important. Stature, as a principal component of body size more stable than weight or volume, proves to be a characteristic which is sensitive to environmental differences, especially in the quality of nutrition enjoyed in childhood and adolescence; and it is, accordingly, more closely related to the social history and background of the individual than to his mental make-up. Furthermore, in so far as it is found to be associated with differences in attitudes, it may have caused them along psychogenic rather than biological pathways. It is probably for the social reasons mentioned that microsomatic men have been found to have, compared with the meso- and macro-somatic, on average a lower intellectual capacity, lower educational records, a higher proportion of the unskilled, and a poorer work record. In personality, those on the macrosomatic side tend towards rebelliousness and aggressiveness, those of the microsomatic side towards weak, dependent, anxious and hypochondriacal traits. Persons deviating towards either extreme have expectations of nervous breakdown which are larger than those pertaining to the mesosomatic. They have higher incidences of childhood symptoms, and a higher proportion are prone to be of unstable personality.

BODILY PROPORTIONS. Variation in the proportionate development of the adult body, either linearly towards relatively greater height, or circumferentially towards greater breadth and depth in trunk measurements, has attracted much attention; and investigations of this aspect of the bodily constitution have been fertile in ideas. Kretschmer (1936) was particularly successful in starting psychiatrists to think along these lines. He considered that pyknic individuals tended to be cyclothymic, and were more than normally liable to manic-depressive psychoses; schizothymic individuals and still more schizophrenics tended to be leptosomatic. The physical and the psychiatric modes attained popular usage, and became combined with the psychological typology of C. G. Jung by which people were classified into extroverts and introverts.

An advance was made by Sheldon and his collaborators, who employed large scale photography and measurements of normal individuals. Instead of the individual being classified as falling into one type or another, he was graded by being given 0 to 5 points along a three-dimensional scale. By associated psychological testing the three physical dimensions of endomorphy, mesomorphy and ectomorphy were correlated with three temperamental dimensions of viscerotonia, somatotonia and cerebrotonia. Viscerotonia

shows itself in relaxation, love of comfort, sociability; somatotonia in vigour and assertive-
ness; cerebrotonia in restraint and inhibition. Sheldon found correlation coefficients of
the order of +0·8 between variations along the physical and psychological dimensions;
but subsequent workers have been unable to confirm these very high values.

In the investigations by means of direct measurements of the living body carried out
by Rees and Eysenck (1945), Eysenck (1947) and Rees (1950 a, b, c), hysterical personality
traits, hysterical symptoms and hysterical diagnoses were found to be associated with
deviation towards the eurymorphic (pyknic) pole in both sexes. Depressive characteristics
in both sexes, and to a lesser extent both anxious and obsessional characteristics, were
associated with deviation towards the leptomorphic pole. Work based on Sheldon's formulation has also associated anxiety and obsessionality with ectomorphy; and ectomorphs have
been found to be more liable to neuroses than persons of other types. Delinquents both
male and female have been found to be more mesomorphic than control samples (Glueck
and Glueck, 1950; Gibbens, 1957).

The Sheldon terminology tends to become complicated, with the use of three dimensions which are supposed to be independent, since workers can and do classify not only
by an excess of development along one dimension but also by a deficiency. Thus one can
find ectopenic, mesopenic and endopenic individuals; and according to Sheldon hysteria
is associated with ectopenia, neurasthenia with mesopenia, and psychasthenia with endo-
penia. Sheldon's work has been criticized on the grounds that the evidence provided does
not support the postulation of more than two independent types of temperament. His
schema is three times as complex as that of a simple linear mode of distribution between
two poles (e.g. the formulation of Rees and Eysenck) and there is no evidence that it is
any more efficient.

ANDROGYNY. From developmental studies of the normal population Tanner (1951)
proposed the use of an index whose numerical value in centimetres is given by 3 × bi-
acromial diameter − bi-iliac diameter. This index has been found to be normally distributed
in each sex with a mean of 90·1 ± 4·7 for men and 78·9 ± 4·6 for women; the misclassification between the sexes is of the order of 12 per cent. (see also pp. 192–3 and Plates I–V).

This index has been applied to psychiatric patients suffering from effort syndrome,
neurosis, homosexuality (male), depression and schizophrenia. Rey and Coppen (1959)
found that patients of both sexes had a significantly lower (more feminine) androgyny
score and a narrower bi-acromial diameter than their control groups. Proceeding from the
masculine to the feminine poles, the order in which the means were distributed was (1)
controls, (2) homosexuals, (3) neurotics, (4) depressives, and (5) schizophrenics. The
findings relating to schizophrenics were later confirmed by Cowie, Coppen and Norman
(1960).

It seems that this interesting anthropometric feature, which is likely to have correlations
with traits of temperament, has received insufficient attention.

BRAIN-WAVE PATTERNS. A certain amount of progress has been made in defining
the association between variation in personality and the electro-physiology of the brain
both in normal subjects and in psychiatric patients. The electroencephalogram has proved
to be nothing like as sensitive an instrument in the study of the human personality and its
variations as had been hoped in the early days after Berger's discovery. However, certain
findings now rest on a firm basis. Electrophysiologists are agreed that, when they are taken
under standard conditions, the pattern of the brain-waves is very constant to the individual.

Lennox, Gibbs, and Gibbs (1945) have also shown that uniovular twins resemble each other so closely in this respect, that it is possible to diagnose uniovularity from the E.E.G. alone with only a small margin of error. The genetical basis for the individual pattern is thereby established. Lennox and other workers have also found that a tendency to 'dysrhythmia', which is very common in epilepsy, is also shown in excess by the parents and other relatives of epileptics.

The pattern of the brain-waves is different in childhood from what it becomes in adult life, and what is normal for the child is abnormal for the adult. This observation has led to the concept of *maturation*, and it seems probable that electroencephalographic maturation proceeds step by step with psychological maturation. Much of the psychiatric abnormality shown in the behaviour disorders of early adult life can be related to *emotional immaturity*, and tends to disappear as the individual passes into the thirties and forties; and it is among persons of this type that E.E.G. abnormality is particularly common. In this context it is of interest that behaviour disturbances are more frequent in boys than in girls and that maturation of the E.E.G. tends to proceed at a slower rate in the former (Rey, Pond and Evans, 1949). There is evidence also that the immaturity of personality found in the psychopath is associated with corresponding anomalies in the electrophysiology of the brain. In an enquiry into 104 non-epileptic psychopaths by Hill (1952) three types of abnormality were defined, all of them reflecting defective maturation of the cerebrum. In Hill's as in other studies (Cohn and Nardini, 1958–9) the E.E.G. abnormalities have been most marked and consistent in psychopathic individuals manifesting aggressive behaviour. The commonest abnormality found by Hill was excess of bilateral rhythmic theta activity with an amplitude greater than or equal to the alpha rhythm; this occurred in 22 per cent. of subjects. It was seen at highest amplitude in the temporal and central regions, failed to respond to visual attention and was accentuated by hyperventilation. In 3·2 per cent. of subjects variants of the alpha rhythm were present. Perhaps the most specific and important abnormality was the occurrence in 14 per cent. of cases of foci of 3 to 5 cycles per second activity in the posterior temporal regions, this anomaly being found in only 2 per cent. of controls. The focal slow activity was often greater in amplitude than that of the alpha rhythm and in a proportion of cases it was unilateral, right-sided foci being commoner than left. It is probably relevant that epileptic patients with temporal lobe foci often show inter-seizure anomalies of behaviour reminiscent of those found in aggressive psychopaths.

The pattern of the brain-waves is also related to the physiological state of the body, and tends to become abnormal if the individual is subjected to such physiological stresses as over-breathing, lowering of the blood sugar, over-hydration by drinking large quantities of fluid, etc. It is under these circumstances, also, that abnormal behaviour is most likely to appear; and it seems that those individuals who are most inclined to impulsive and aggressive acts are also those who show a *constitutional instability of nervous control*.

However, little success has attended the attempts made to correlate the E.E.G. with finer variations in personality structure. A few studies are perhaps worthy of mention. In a recent study by Savage (1964a) high scores for extraversion were found to be significantly related to high alpha amplitude. Shagass and Jones (1958) found that the sedation threshold (estimated by measurements made on the E.E.G. after administration of 0·5 mg./kg. body weight of amylobarbitone sodium injected intravenously by means of a special technique) was significantly different in individuals manifesting different types of neurotic disturbance; thus the threshold was 2·79 mg./kg. in conversion hysteria, 4·78 mg./kg. in neurotic depression, and 5·27 mg./kg. in anxiety states, as compared with 3·09 mg./kg. in non-patient controls. The results have been confirmed by some authors and called into question by others. The important lesson taught by recent investigations, however, is that careful quantification of both psychological variables and E.E.G. phenomena in the course of enquiries in this field tends on the whole to yield more informative and meaningful findings than those recorded in the earliest E.E.G. studies in psychiatry. One of the most striking facts is that abnormalities in the E.E.G. tend to become commoner as the section of the population brought under investigation becomes more abnormal, particularly if the abnormality includes propensities for aggressive and explosive behaviour. Thus the frequency of E.E.G. abnormalities is at a minimum (5 per cent.) in individuals highly selected for emotional stability such as flying personnel (Williams, 1941). It is greater (15 per cent.) in the general population (Hill and Watterson, 1942), still greater (26 per cent.) in a neurotic population (Williams, 1941c), and higher still (65 per cent.) among aggressive psychopaths (Hill and Watterson, 1942). In an enquiry in a group of subjects who had committed murder without motive and little or no provocation, 73 per cent. were found to have an abnormal E.E.G., while among those obviously insane when their crimes were committed the incidence was 86 per cent. (Stafford-Clark and Taylor, 1949). The E.E.G. is of course important in the diagnosis of epilepsy and in the localization of focal lesions in the brain; but it is also of some relevance for the study of the psychophysical constitution.

Psychological Factors

As the whole of any Western Society is based on the possibility of influencing the development of character by education, tradition and other psychological forces, it would seem superfluous to demand any proof of the role that psychological factors play. It is still, however, far from settled just how far personality is amenable to moulding in this way. The work of anthropologists, such as Margaret Mead, has shown that in different cultures human personality can develop along widely divergent lines, even in such apparently fundamental aspects as the relationship between parent and child, male and female dominance, and pacifism or belligerence. It can fairly be objected that the societies studied differ, not only in their cultural tradition, but also in their genetic make-up; but even with this proviso we must allow *wide latitude for human plasticity*, particularly in the years of infancy and childhood, and for the play of environmental psychological forces in shaping personality.

The mode in which psychological determinants act is almost as much disputed as their total effect. A reasonable theory is provided by the experiments and the theories of Pavlov, which would in fact describe the learning of socially acceptable modes of behaviour, the control of emotional expression, etc., *in terms of conditioning* (see Chapter I, p. 20). As the infant grows into a child, and the child into an adult, the nervous system is growing organically; neural pathways are being successively myelinated and brought under more precise central control, by which more and more refined modes of response to the environment become available. Together with organic growth, the child develops habitual responses to constantly recurring stimuli or complexes of stimuli. Individual stimuli which regularly recur together become organized into 'Gestalten', which can then act as a single stimulus. The phenomena of affection for the mother, which are shown early in infancy, can in this way be accounted for as correlates for her significance to the child as a provider of food, warmth and physical comfort. A very deeply ingrained conditioned response of this kind will have its effect throughout the whole of later life, and we find no difficulty in understanding how different cultures may differ by the effect of their various traditions of upbringing and education of the child.

What is true of societies will also be true of individuals. If in one family there is no curb placed on egoism and displays of temper, or no encouragement given to the overcoming of natural childish timidities, we may expect that its members will in later life differ from those brought up under better-regulated conditions. A violent and brutal father might inspire in his children a habitual tendency to anxiety reactions, or a mother's over-solicitude might lead to an attitude of rebelliousness. There is no difficulty in imagining such relations, or in discovering them when they are present, as they often are. But in the observation of clinical cases one sees also very frequently character developments which are only explained along such lines in a forced and unreal way; and unless we are biased we may see that other factors than those mentioned can play a part. When, for instance, one only out of a large family of siblings, brought up in a sensible and affectionate home, grows up into an unreliable, boastful, hysterical trickster, processes of psychological conditioning are unlikely to be the whole explanation. Such phenomena become readily explicable if we are prepared to consider genetic causes, but if we are not, we are compelled to adopt some more abstruse and complex theory.

The *Freudian approach* to this sort of problem is to try to relate character development to psychological stresses in very early life, and to the prevailing state of emotional integration at the time of their occurrence. Thus the occurrence of anxiety symptoms in adult life is thought to be but a reflexion of the earliest anxieties experienced by the infant at the withdrawal of the maternal breast, and even of the primary 'anxiety' experience at the time of birth itself. The difficulties raised by such a hypothesis are as great as those that are solved. The theory, of course, offers no explanation at all of the fact that the emotion of anxiety takes the exact form, physiologically, that it does. But it is an even more important defect of the theory that other emotions, such as anger, are given the same explanation. We are still left in doubt why it is that one individual develops one pattern of response, and someone else another.

The *form of later symptoms* is, however, hypothetically also determined by the libidinal stage reached by the individual at the time of critical psychological experiences. Some forms of aggressiveness are associated with the fixation of some part of the libido in the oral stage; and tendencies to obsessionality, hypochondriasis and depression with libidinal fixation in the anal sadistic stage. The schizoid personality derives its roots from an earlier stage of infantile narcissism, and schizophrenia itself involves a regression to this level. The most important role in character formation is, however, assigned to the superego, which is itself formed from the child's experience of his parents' attitudes, encouraging or discouraging, towards his own behaviour. A part of the superego is made up by the ego-ideal, the perfected figment of the self towards which the individual is driven to strive. Actual behaviour is determined by a balancing between the influences on the ego of libidinal drives on one side and superego prohibitions on the other, under the constant check of the reality principle. There is room in the theory for constitutional variations, e.g. in the primary strength of the libido, but these are not felt to be worth serious research.

The evidence which is used to support these theories is derived solely from analytic interviews, which provide an essentially non-communicable experience. It is to psychoanalysis that we owe, however, the modern emphasis on the historical dimension in personality development and in the genesis of psychiatric disorder. Psychiatry cannot dispense with this dimension, least of all in the neuroses and personality disorders. As far as one can see ahead, the longitudinal or historical aspects of causation will be relevant in the investigation of neuroses as well as the cross-sectional ones. The difficulty at the present time is that the reconstruction of the past has been undertaken with insufficient rigour to promote the growth of a body of scientific knowledge. A valuable review of the role of 'Childhood upbringing and other environmental factors' in personality development and psychiatric disorder (O'Connor and Franks, 1960) has shown how little consistent and reliable information has accumulated in relation to such questions as the precise effects of parental attitudes, maternal deprivation and other aspects of early childhood experience on later development. There is, however, no reason to suppose that more stringent, carefully-planned enquiries could not yield more useful information. In the meantime, the hypothesis that neuroses and their associated personality patterns have to some extent been learned in the course of development and can in part be explained by vicissitudes and advantages in the formative years of personality growth, accords so well with clinical experience that it would be unreasonable to ignore it.

Pathological Factors

STRUCTURAL AND ORGANIC. The outbreak of epidemic encephalitis lethargica at the end of the First World War, with its sequelae of post-encephalitic personality changes and disorders of behaviour, turned the minds of many psychiatrists to a consideration of the relationship of deviations of personality to the *structural integrity of the brain.* Thought was stimulated along two lines. On the one hand it was held possible that all deviations of personality of an extreme degree might, by dint of much further research, prove to have a basis in pathological change. On the other hand, the problems of relationship between psychiatric symptoms and cerebral localization were thrown widely open. An outstanding exponent of this school of thought was Kleist. He anatomized the psyche into the three aspects of somatopsyche, with its seat in the grey matter of the third ventricle, the thymopsyche and the autopsyche, both of them localized in the thalamus and the pallido-striate region. He distinguished correspondingly between the somatopsychically abnormal, such as hysterics and sex perverts, those with thymopsychic deficiencies, such as the emotionally unstable, the anxious and the cold and unfeeling, and psychopaths with autopsyche abnormalities, such as the egoistic, the paranoid and the obsessional. It was to some extent a matter of indifference whether the actual deviations of personality observed were regarded as due to hereditary factors which had caused some abnormality of development of the hypothetically affected part of the brain, or whether this part had suffered change from some structural organic process.

It is now generally accepted that much of the emotional activity of the individual, with which qualities of personality are intimately bound up, proceeds *along paths radiating from thalamic and hypothalamic centres.* This has been shown, not only by the changes that occur in previously habitual patterns after epidemic encephalitis, but also after brain trauma or with cerebral neoplasms in these parts. But there is much to show that the focus of attention should not be on this part of the brain alone, but rather that other parts of the brain may be the ones more directly involved, although probably those parts which have some fairly direct connexion with the thalamus and hypothalamus. Thus it is generally accepted that character changes of a rather subtle kind are fairly constantly to be observed after the operation of prefrontal leucotomy, in which the frontothalamic radiation is principally affected.

If the conception that much of the individual qualities of a man's personality are in some way connected with the structural make-up of some particular part of his brain is not one that calls for much in the way of criticism, neither is it one that leads us very far. *The personality changes* that have been found to be *associated with gross damage to the hypothalamus* are of a rather limited kind, and are very far from covering the whole range of psychopathic personality as clinically observed. It was the much more speculative opinion, usually adopted by those psychiatrists who concerned themselves with the cerebral localization of personality, that morbid changes in the brain are to be called into account for all cases of psychopathy which called for criticism, and has in fact been severely criticized by Schneider. Schneider considers that the term psychopathy should be used to describe either the extreme variant, or that which from a teleological point of view lies under some sort of disadvantage. Patients whose personalities have suffered disadvantageous change after encephalitis, or after head injury, should not be ranked as psychopaths, however close clinical resemblances may be between them and well-known types of constitutional psychopaths. For him the class of psychopaths is to be rigidly restricted to individuals whose abnormality is inborn, even though not necessarily due exclusively to hereditary factors.

This view seems to us unduly restrictive and one that leads to artificial distinctions. The moment of birth seems an arbitrary point at which to distinguish between different kinds of determinants, and an absolute distinction between the effects of heredity and environment is equally impossible. We must suppose that the personality of a man has been affected by the experiences through which he has passed, as well as by his original hereditary make-up and such gross noxae as brain diseases and traumata which he may have suffered. We are led to a *conception of constitution*, as the momentary product of original endowment and of all the physical and psychological processes of the past, and one which therefore is constantly changing as the individual passes through life. The man who has suffered a brain trauma or an attack of encephalitis has a constitution which has been altered by their effects, and if in consequence he shows traits of personality which lead to illness or social consequences, there is no reason why he should not be classified as psychopathic. This provides a self-consistent conception of psychopathy as a clinical variant, which may then be investigated aetiologically without preconceptions.

Examining then the whole range of psychopaths who are met with clinically, we find that many of their number, although probably still considerably the smaller part, are so because of the fact that they have suffered *some destructive lesion* in the past. It is probable that the nature of many of these lesions is unknown; those we are aware of are numerous in their variety, and they have made their effects felt at almost any point in life, before and after birth.

Prenatal processes and injury at birth producing such conditions as Little's disease, and the other pathological causes of imbecility and idiocy, do not impair the intellect alone, but also leave their marks on the personality. In any hospital for the care of the mentally deficient, there is a high proportion of patients who show psychopathic features, or periodic or lasting emotional disturbances. A significant development in recent years has been the increasing attention paid to the possible importance of minimal degrees of cerebral damage incurred during pregnancy or childbirth upon psychiatric disability during childhood and adult life. Evidence has accumulated that limited damage which does not result in overt neurological signs or symptoms may contribute to causation of disabilities which have not previously been regarded as organic in character. Pasamanick and his colleagues have conducted retrospective enquiries into the birth history of patients suffering from cerebral palsy, behaviour disorder and speech difficulties. They found that abnormalities during the prenatal and perinatal periods were significantly greater among their cases than among controls (Rogers, Pasamanick and Lilienfeld, 1955). The views of this group were well summarized in a paper by Knobloch and Pasamanick (1959): 'Some time ago we constructed a hypothesis of a "continuum of reproductive causality". According to this hypothesis there is a lethal component of cerebral damage which results in foetal and neonatal deaths, and a sub-lethal component which gives rise to a series of clinical and neuro-psychiatric syndromes depending on the degree and location of the damage'. They go on to state that, in addition to well-known sequelae such as epilepsy and mental sub-normality, minimal brain damage may give rise to tics, behaviour disorders and learning difficulties. The conclusions drawn by these authors have often been criticized on various grounds such as, for example, their failure adequately to control social class which could have contributed to the disabilities under consideration (Pond, 1961). They have, however, performed a valuable service in drawing attention to an important field of enquiry that has received inadequate attention. Observations along similar lines have been published by Stott (1957). Prechtl (1960) has, on the basis of prospective studies, described a choreiform syndrome in children who had suffered from perinatal hypoxia and also a hypokinetic syndrome associated with hypotonia, drowsiness and apathy alternating with irritability which he also attributes to minimal brain damage. The findings in this area must be weighed with caution and criticism but the concepts of 'minimal brain damage' and 'the invisible lesion' are of some importance in psychiatry. It has become clear in a number of fields that clinically evident neurological damage and cognitive defect do not occur until the extent of brain damage exceeds a certain threshold. The view that some disorders of emotional life and personality may be associated with lesions that have not reached this threshold is supported by indirect evidence and is therefore a plausible one. It certainly merits careful investigation.

In the same way *postnatal injuries and diseases*, such as birth injury, cerebrospinal meningitis, congenital lues, etc., also leave marks on the personality of the same non-specific kinds. Chorea, occurring rather later in childhood, also commonly leaves some mental sequelae, of which the most common are a tendency to jerkiness and lack of smoothness in motor co-ordination, lack of emotional control, obscene utterances, and tendencies to anxious and hysterical reactions (see p. 381).

In adult life a psychopathic development may occur after lesions of the brain, especially of the frontal cortex and, as has already been said, in the neighbourhood of the hypothalamus and mid-brain. Perhaps the commonest of these syndromes is seen in the subject of cerebral contusion. If this is at all extensive, it is likely to leave behind a change in the personality, by which neurasthenic, hysterical and paranoid reactions are favoured, and one is likely to see inadequate control of mood variations, both endogenous and psychogenically precipitated, tendencies towards hypochondriasis, irritability and aggressiveness, and a general lack of initiative and energy.

The character changes which are brought about by prefrontal leucotomy vary much from case to case; but among their common features is a tendency to the short-circuiting of emotional reactions, to a greater immediacy of response with a diminished power of procrastination and reflection, reduced insight, forethought and consideration for others, and, what is often the purpose of the operation, a lesser tendency to worry.

In summary, we may say that structural damage to the brain is likely to leave some effects on the personality; but that the change produced will depend on the original constitutional make-up as well as on the site and extent of the lesion. We are yet far from a cerebral localization of the psychopathic symptoms most commonly seen, but there are reasons to hope that further knowledge in this field will accrue with time.

SPECIAL FORMS OF REACTION AND OF PERSONALITY

The Depressive Reaction

OCCURRENCE IN THE NORMAL. Fluctuations in the mood state, either in the direction of excitement, elation and euphoria, or contrariwise in the direction of depression, unhappiness and malaise, are of daily occurrence to any normal man. The extent, the duration, and the direction of the change depend both on the circumstances which have called it forth, and on the constitution of the individual. Normal changes in the upwards direction, however, are exceedingly seldom of such a degree that the attentions of the doctor are required, and they are of little medical importance. It is sufficient to remember that they occur, and that their significance in the past history of the individual patient may be considerable.

The fluctuations in the depressive direction, on the contrary, may easily reach such a pitch that the subject is incapacitated, and has to call for the help of a doctor. As a *suicidal depth* is not infrequently reached, there may be need for specialized psychiatric treatment, sometimes in a mental hospital.

A depressive mood change as severe as this may be produced, either by *exceptional circumstances* in an individual of fairly average constitution, or by events of a more ordinary kind in those who are naturally liable to *instability of mood*. It is, perhaps, rather surprising that many normal people can go through events of the most tragic kind, and yet never reach such a depressed state that they are incapacitated or take their own lives. Nevertheless, personal tragedy is a commonplace in this world, and severe reactive depressions are seen from time to time by the psychiatrist, where the whole of the effective causes can be regarded as environmental in nature. As a rule such states are produced by a sudden critical change, the death of a wife, the loss of a job, the threat of scandal or imprisonment, the breaking of a love-affair, and are much less frequently precipitated by a more gradual accumulation of miseries. Many Jews committed suicide in Vienna when that city was occupied by Hitler's troops; but there were very few suicides in the concentration camps.

PHYSIOLOGICAL BASIS. The physiological basis of depressive states is still largely unknown. Certain poisons have an almost universal effect in causing depression, the toxin of influenza, for instance, reserpine and the sulphonamide drugs. Physical illness is commonly associated with the depressions of later life and the illness is often reactive in type (see Chapter X, p. 569). In the depressed state, the biochemical regulation of the body is altered. There is usually some rise of blood-pressure, but the action of the heart is commonly slowed. All gastric and intestinal movements are also slowed down, and there is, subjectively, loss of appetite and constipation. A marked degree of psychomotor retardation is uncommon, and is usually regarded as a sign of a depression of the endogenous type; nevertheless a minor degree is usual in reactive states, if the depression be only severe enough. The skin loses its healthy flush, and the circulation in the extremities may be somewhat reduced.

The sections on the biochemical, physiological and cerebral aspects of manic-depressive psychosis (see pp. 198–204) should be read in conjunction with this section. In many physiopathological and aetiological enquiries no sharp distinction between the varieties of depression is attempted. There is, moreover, probably some overlap in the clinical picture and aetiological basis of neurotic and endogenous forms of depressive illness, although the extent of this is in dispute.

ASSOCIATIONS. Reactive states, in which a melancholy mood is the only psychological feature of any importance, are rather commoner than pure anxiety states, but still unusual. As a rule there are other neurotic features, among the most frequent of which are symptoms of a neurasthenic kind (q.v.). Anxiety and hypochondriasis are also often seen, and at times hysterical features or irritability may colour the picture.

Organic states are very commonly the prime cause of a depression. Depression is sometimes the presenting symptom of general paralysis, and not uncommonly of arteriosclerotic dementia. Acute physical illness, or convalescence therefrom, may precipitate an attack; and depressive features are frequent in the symptomatic psychoses. There is hardly a single organic syndrome which has not at some time or another been found to be associated with depression.

Among the endogenous psychoses, schizophrenia is important as a frequent cause of depressive reactions; and the severe depressive state in the young patient has to be regarded with some suspicion on this account.

PREDISPOSITION. The predisposition to depressive reactions is difficult to distinguish from the cyclothymic constitution; the two must be regarded as distinct, but they are probably related. Depressive reactions are of more than normal frequency in those who also suffer unmistakably endogenous variations in mood, and the patient with a good capacity for self-observation will at times describe the entirely *different subjective experience* of the two types of illness. One of our patients, for instance, suffered from more than one endogenous depression, but was also depressed for three years after the death in battle of her fiancé; this latter depression was for her an experience of a different nature, as though she was consistently low-spirited she had none of the psychomotor retardation and sensation of almost physical illness and ineptitude which she had learned to know in her endogenous phases. Manic-depressive psychoses are comparatively rare, whereas depressive reactions are fairly common.

In the majority of patients who suffer from a reactive depression the constitutional make-up plays a significant role. Genetical factors, doubtless of a multifactorial kind, enter the picture; and it is common to hear of other relatives being unstable in mood, or having suffered from a similar illness. The past personality of the patient shows a *greater lability* than usual. He is elated by pleasant occurrences, cast down by disappointments, more than most of his circle. Alternatively, he may be described as being placid enough, but likely to brood upon unpleasant events, to be unable to throw things off easily, and even, constantly of a *mildly pessimistic nature*. The relation between personalities of this type and those that belong to the manic-depressive group is clinically a close one; but the outstanding feature of the cyclothymic disposition, the tendency to moods that come 'out of the blue', that have their own recurrent rhythm, is lacking. The man who is predisposed to a reactive depression may have had more than his fair share of mood swings, but they have been precipitated by circumstances of an appropriate kind. All his depressions are 'understandable', though they may have reached a degree and duration beyond the commonly accepted limits of the 'normal'.

Women are rather more liable to this sort of instability than men, though the difference is not a very marked one. In the experience of most psychiatrists, reactive depressions are rather more evenly distributed between the sexes than are the endogenous ones. *Age* also plays a part. Children, though profoundly depressed by trivialities, are almost immune to lasting changes of mood. The capacity for prolonged mood changes appears at puberty, and in adolescence may reach a considerable degree, even sufficient to allow of suicide, a catastrophe which may be precipitated by an unhappy love-affair, or by a failure at an examination. Nevertheless, failing an untimely termination of this kind, youthful resilience usually allows rapid recovery. In middle life the tendency is to a longer duration, and depressive illnesses become more frequent. The tendency increases with age up to the senium. In the later age groups, organic deterioration plays some part in increasing the tendency towards depression.

Psychological factors cannot play any notable part in creating the predisposition to depression, although they enter largely into precipitation.

PRECIPITATION. The common immediate cause of a depressive reaction is an incident, a grief, a loss or a disappointment, which would produce some lowering of spirits even in the most normal. To result in psychological illness, either the incident has been of an uncommonly grave nature, or the individual to whom it has occurred is unduly susceptible, or his susceptibility has been increased by such a thing as recent physical illness. Not uncommonly the final straw is illness itself, particularly septic illnesses and toxaemias; influenza very commonly causes in convalescence a very severe depressive state. In other cases, the precipitating incident has come at the end of a long series of disappointments and frustrations.

CLINICAL FEATURES. Reactive depressions show, as a rule, only a graver degree of the changes observable in the normal man when temporarily cast down. The marks of a gross physiological change, retardation and inhibition, agitation, delusional ideas, depersonalization, are nearly always lacking. Even self-reproachfulness is only slight, though self-evaluation is disturbed. *Good contact with reality* is maintained. The most notable feature is the mood change itself. The patient feels unhappy, unfit to cope with day-to-day affairs or to face the future, which seems a gloomy one. Lack of energy, difficulties in concentration, early and excessive fatigue and other neurasthenic symptoms are frequent. An endless circle of unpleasant thoughts goes round in his head, and he finds it difficult unaided to throw himself out of his preoccupations. Although his judgement of the future and of his own affairs is impaired by his consistent gloom, there is no tendency towards the formation of outspoken delusions. Once he can temporarily cease to contemplate his melancholy state, and apply his mind to realities, there is an immediate upsurge in the direction of greater normality. It is a feature of these conditions, which carries great diagnostic weight, that the patients can be distracted from their woes, and in cheerful company, or at some place of entertainment, return for the time being to their usual selves.

Sleep is commonly disturbed, and may be interrupted by unpleasant dreams. But a particular tendency to waking in the early morning is unusual, and there is *no diurnal rhythm* in the depth of depression such as is seen in the endogenous depressions. If there is a change during the day, it is usually towards a worsening of the depression when the patient is tired in the evening. The patient retains his responsiveness, and by turning his mind, even for a few minutes, onto a cheerful topic, his mood can be lightened. In interview, for instance, he can be brought to smile at some absurdity or a play of humour.

His depression is connected in the closest and most logical way with its psychogenic causes; and he can tell his questioner exactly what it is that is making him unhappy and why. Somatic manifestations are not prominent, although there may be some tendency towards constipation, and a hypochondriacal attitude towards the illness.

DIFFERENTIAL DIAGNOSIS. The most important differential problem is to distinguish between these reactive states and endogenous depressions (see Chapter IV, p. 219). Important data can be derived from the family history, from the account received of the past personality and of previous psychiatric illness. The man who is susceptible to reactive depressions will often describe previous attacks of depression, but they will be seen to be themselves reactive to a psychogenic precipitant and to have persisted only as long as the unfavourable circumstances themselves lasted. There will be no history of depressions coming 'out of the blue'. The personality will not be that of the cyclothymic, but rather of the over-labile asthenic, perhaps, with some obsessional traits. The present illness will be traceable to a definite point in time at which events took an unfavourable turn. The clinical state will show in its lability and responsiveness to circumstances that it has no deeper biological basis. Retardation and severer degrees of inhibition will not be seen in any but the gravest reactive states, and are then not very pronounced.

The next important point that should attract enquiry is the existence or not of any basis in physical illness, and especially so where psychogenesis seems inadequate and the past record not that of an excessively unstable man. In older patients, vascular disease is very commonly accompanied by a mild degree of depression, not distinguishable clinically from psychogenic states.

Finally the question must be asked whether depression is an entirely *secondary symptom*, and whether there are indications of other types of psychiatric illness, of schizophrenia for instance. Such conditions will hardly be missed when a full examination of the mental status is made. The depression which is not uncommonly the first symptom of an oncoming schizophrenia does not usually give the impression of being a psychogenic reaction.

COURSE, PROGNOSIS AND OUTCOME. These reactions almost invariably remit in due course, as the patient recovers from physical ill-health, or his circumstances take a turn for the better, or the passage of time allows him to forget a loss or a disappointment. He will then return to his normal frame of mind, which may, of course, be of a naturally gloomy turn. The risk of suicide, however, is not inconsiderable, especially as psychomotor inhibition and indecisiveness are not present to prevent its being attempted; but the danger is seldom so great as to call for certification. At the height of his illness the patient may feel suicidal, but once he can be brought beyond this point the danger diminishes rapidly. Those depressive states which cause over many months an unceasing danger of suicide, with repeated attempts necessitating the closest possible watch, are not the reactive depressions. The danger of chronicity is negligible, unless the personality itself is of the unremittingly depressive and pessimistic type. As a rule, these illnesses are not of long duration, and *two to four months* see the patient through the worst of his trouble. They are, however, highly dependent on the circumstances that have called them forth, and if these are of a permanently unfavourable kind, disability may be prolonged. The man who has, at a relatively advanced age, lost a position of a type that he can hardly expect to get again, and the man whose domestic circumstances are of a permanently worrying and frustrating kind, will not find it easy in any circumstances to regain a cheerful level of spirits.

TREATMENT. The treatment of these states is in the first place of a simply psychotherapeutic kind, guided by common sense. If the circumstances which have precipitated illness can be repaired, or the patient can be shown how they may be surmounted, the outlook for early recovery is good. That type of *psychotherapy* which devotes attention to establishing self-knowledge and understanding is very appropriate. Lengthy psychoanalysis is hardly ever called for. It is very often desirable to secure some *change of milieu*, and a temporary release from an environment that constantly reminds the patient of his troubles; and it is well if the new environment is of a gently stimulating kind, and not unprovided with distractions. For this reason, admission to hospital is not always the best thing, although if the hospital be of the type of a rehabilitation centre, and well supplied with opportunities for social engagement and occupation it can hardly be bettered.

The advent of anti-depressive drugs has transformed the treatment of this group of disorders. Recent enquiries have placed the differential diagnosis between endogenous and reactive depression on a more precise and quantitative basis (see Chapter IV, p. 222). Where systematic clinical appraisal shows the patient to be suffering from an unequivocally neurotic form of depression the drug of choice is probably a monoamine oxidase inhibitor such as phenelzine which can be given in initial doses of 15 mg. three times a day or isocarboxazid, 10 mg. t.d.s. This can be combined with tranquillizing agents such as chlordiazepoxide in doses of 10 mg t.d.s. As the patient shows signs of improvement in 10 to 14 days the dosage of these drugs can be reduced. However, medication with a mono-amine oxidase inhibitor has frequently to be maintained for a period of 8 to 12 weeks to achieve a stable remission and some patients require treatment for longer periods. Cheese, broad beans, Marmite and similar yeast extracts must be excluded from the diet. Where the diagnosis is more doubtful owing to the presence of one or two endogenous features such as early morning awakening or consistent retardation, tryptizol in doses of 25 mg. daily, rising to a total of 150 to 200 mg. daily should be tried. If a monoamine oxidase inhibitor has been the first drug administered, a period of three weeks should be allowed to elapse before any drug of the imipramine group is given. If drug treatment fails to elicit a response or if the patient is persistently suicidal or if a swift response to treatment is for some reason imperative, electroconvulsive treatment may have to be used. It is rarely indicated nowadays and, if it is used, the number of treatments should be kept to a minimum. In patients with prominent anxiety or with hysterical features in their personality the results have to be carefully watched as unpleasant side-effects or an exacerbation of symptoms are common. Nevertheless, E.C.T. sometimes plays a useful part in helping the patient to throw off inertia and depression which persist, as if of their own momentum, after the patient has in his mind dealt with and disposed of the main psychological sources of his current attack of illness. If E.C.T. is used without dealing adequately with the patient's reasons for feeling depressed, the response, if any, is likely to be short-lived and amnesia, hysterical manifestations and exacerbated anxiety will be common complications.

The Neurasthenic Reaction

DEFINITION, OCCURRENCE IN THE NORMAL. The symptoms that are commonly called neurasthenic involve as their central feature a reduction in the capacity for the output of energy.

The term 'neurasthenia' was coined by G. M. Beard who, in his book on *American Nervousness* (1880), took up the time-honoured idea of a varying tonus of the nervous system which might be sthenic or asthenic. The term was generally accepted, and neurasthenia became a fashionable diagnosis for all kinds of neurotic conditions, which were supposed to originate from mental weakness and nervous over-sensitivity. The concept of over-sensitivity was added to that of asthenia, probably because of the everyday observation that those who are fatigued or weak after illness are particularly sensitive to pains, discomforts, anxieties and irritations. Pierre Janet (1908) emphasized the sensitiveness of certain neurotics, and described as 'psychasthenics' a group of patients closely related to the obsessional. Since Janet's time controversy has been endless, and many of the unjustifiable generalizations of later authors have themselves in turn been discarded. What remains as valid is that certain symptoms and a certain type of personality can best be described by comparison with the normal state of subjective fatigue.

Fatigue is shown in the physical field as a reduction in the amount of spontaneous movement, lassitude, bodily relaxation and some loss of tone, lack of power and of certainty and precision in movements, and possibly some retardation. In the mental field, similarly, there is a reduced capacity for mental effort and lack of initiative and willingness to undertake new activities. Thought may tend to wander and is less successfully directed toward a specific goal.

These symptoms, not in themselves unpleasant if they can be indulged, are a normal experience towards the end of a day's activities. They are frequently not total in their incidence, i.e. they relate to a continuation of the activities which have been persisted in for many hours, but may not be associated with other activities which would be a change from the first. Nevertheless in the fatigued state, even a fresh activity produces more rapid tiring than it would in the same person after rest.

PHYSIOLOGICAL BASIS. The occurrence of *mental fatigue*, as a physiological phenomenon, has often been doubted. Some authorities incline to the view that its basis is purely emotional. Nevertheless physiological work does suggest that fatigue occurs at the synapse, and a reflex arc becomes fatigued more rapidly than a neuromuscular preparation. One might assume that the larger the number of synapses involved, as in more complicated forms of behaviour, the earlier would fatigue ensue.

Emotional factors certainly enter the picture. One tires more rapidly with an unpleasant than with a pleasant activity. Where activity is of a stereotyped kind, and involves the endless repetition of essentially the same process, the subject rapidly becomes 'bored', which is not the same as tired. The emotion of ennui is relieved at once by a change of occupation and leaves no sequela, but it is otherwise with fatigue. The individual becomes tired, rather than bored, if the occupation is so stereotyped as to be uninteresting, but at the same time demands unremitting attention, as for instance when decisions are called for from time to time. Even interesting work can be very fatiguing; fatigue will then creep up on the subject without his being aware of it, but make its presence overwhelmingly felt if there is an interruption or interest flags.

Activities which produce mental and physical tension, such as those which are accompanied by anxiety, are usually rapidly tiring. Fatigue, in this case, appears to involve the autonomic system, so that after a prolonged period of over-activity there is a drop in autonomic tonus. A fall in blood pressure is as a rule accompanied by the experience of lassitude and anergia; and those whose blood pressure is consistently low tire rapidly, and tend to show a lower energy output than those with a higher level.

The role of sleep, and the sleep mechanism by which fatigue is normally overcome, must be mentioned in this connexion. People vary much in their ability to derive benefit from quite short periods of sleep; very energetic men seem to have more than their share of this capacity. Neurasthenics, on the other hand, tend to suffer from *insomnia* although on going to bed they feel both tired and sleepy. In the normal, an emotional conflict or preoccupation with an insoluble personal problem may prevent quiet refreshing sleep, and a state of over-wakefulness and restlessness ensues which shows all the characteristics of a neurasthenic reaction.

PREDISPOSITION. There is much individual variation in the susceptibility to fatigue and in the level of energy output normally engaged in; and this is probably connected with autonomic tonus and endocrine balance. The subthyroid patient and the patient with a consistently low blood pressure tend to be found at one end of the scale, their opposites at the other.

Bauer (1921) drew attention to the *physique of the neurasthenic*—his narrow build, thin bones, flaccid muscles, small heart, general infantile appearance, and lack of 'turgor'. He also described excitability of the autonomic centres shown in vasomotor lability, blushing, cold and blue extremities, and red nose; and he noted the mental content of phobias and the relation to obsessional reactions. Weakness of the instincts, 'psychosexual infantilism', frigidity and fear of pregnancy in the female, and failure in marriage, have been associated with neurasthenia by Mathes (1924). Slater (1945) found that in a group of neurotic soldiers those whose sexual lives were conducted at a low level of activity and interest distinguished themselves from the remainder by being even more often of asthenic physique and having less constitutional resistance to neurotic breakdown.

Apart from these bodily and endocrine relations, the neurasthenic is *allied to the anxious* constitution. The man who is over-liable to anxiety is also likely to get tired easily. There are many people who go through life, without evidence of marked variation from the normal in endocrine or autonomic functions, who yet are consistently anergic, easily dismayed and discouraged, and who have less than average powers of persistence. Men of this type were common among the neurotic casualties in the armed forces during the last war. Maxwell Jones (1946) showed that patients suffering from anxiety states, 'effort syndrome' and related conditions, when tested with the ergograph, felt exhausted at a time when estimations of the blood lactic acid and other physiological tests showed that they had as yet suffered little ill effect from the physical effort they had expended. In some it was likely that the state of fatigue was a hysterical conversion symptom determined by the special situation and the wish to escape from further service; but in others there appeared to be a more lasting feebleness of conative powers, of will and purpose.

Any debilitating physical illness may cause or contribute to a neurasthenic tendency, and 'organic neurasthenia' is generally accepted by physicians. Organic diseases such as syphilis, intoxications, arteriosclerosis, encephalitis and trauma, frequently present neurasthenic symptoms in their early stages or in their milder forms.

A similar state of temporary duration may also be seen in the man of psychiatrically fairly normal disposition who, as a result of severe environmental stress, has gone through a severe and prolonged anxiety reaction. Although a very minor degree of depression is clinically very difficult to distinguish from organic neurasthenia, depressive reactions are less likely to leave the neurasthenic aftermath which one sees after recovery from severe anxiety states.

Age is an important predisposing factor. Neurasthenic states are practically never seen in children, except as the actual concomitants of physical illness. Although children tire very rapidly, they also show great resilience, and their ready distractibility protects them from fatigue states of any duration. In youth, also, the tendency is small, although it is at this time that one first sees the chronic neurasthenic personality showing itself in its true colours. In middle life the instinctual drive supplied by the endocrine system begins to give out, and neurasthenic states begin to become common. The tendency is further increased when degenerative changes in the brain begin to make their effects felt.

CLINICAL FEATURES AND ASSOCIATIONS. States in which neurasthenic symptoms are accompanied by no others are rare in psychiatric experience; but the symptoms themselves are common, especially in depressive illnesses, anxiety states and organic deteriorations. Neurasthenic symptoms may be the first ones to be seen in arteriosclerotic, senile or syphilitic dementia. Depressive illnesses, both endogenous and reactive, almost always involve some degree of lassitude, inertia, fatigue and loss of initiative. A neurasthenic picture is not infrequently seen in the course of schizophrenic illnesses; and the hebetude which accompanies schizophrenic impairment of personality bears a resemblance to organic neurasthenia. The circulatory disturbances seen so commonly in the chronic schizophrenic may be partly responsible.

In the way of clinical description, there is not much to add to what has already been said. Symptoms of *lassitude and lack of conative drive* are usually accompanied by some loss of spirits and of cheerfulness. On clinical examination there is a reduction of activity, and in the field of mental testing there is commonly some slight retardation and an impairment of concentration. Where, as is often the case, the picture has arisen in a patient who is constitutionally liable to such a reaction, evidence will be obtained from the previous history of the occurrence of similar reactions, and of a deficiency of drive which will have had effects on the conduct of a career, on the choice of a marriage partner, and elsewhere.

While the picture of pure neurasthenia as described by the psychiatrists of fifty years ago seems to have become rather a rarity, patients are still seen whose sole complaint is weakness and hypochondriacal concern with their lack of mental energy. They are often at the same time restless in an aimless fidgety manner, over-sensitive to noise and light, and easily irritated by the presence of others. They avoid company, live a solitary carefully regulated life, and are incapable of following any regular occupation.

DIFFERENTIAL DIAGNOSIS, COURSE, OUTCOME AND TREATMENT. A neurasthenic reaction must always be investigated from the aetiological point of view, as it seldom arises—apart from the constitutionally asthenic personality—as a primary state. The exclusion of an organic basis is especially important. If an underlying factor is found, the course, outcome and treatment will depend entirely on this finding.

The differential diagnosis from a state of depression will often be difficult, but must be attempted because of the possibility of treatment, in the case of a primarily affective disorder, by convulsion therapy. It must not be forgotten that a constitutional asthenic may suffer from an endogenous depression; and the constitutional depressive who belongs to the cyclothymic group of personalities, and is liable to occasional exacerbations of depression and anergia, is often mis-diagnosed as a chronic neurasthenic. Sometimes it is only the result of convulsive treatment, entered into empirically, which will disclose the affective nature of an apparently neurasthenic state.

In the *'chronic neurasthenic'*, the future depends on the estimate which is made of the underlying personality, the extent to which environmental stresses have contributed to the existing incapacity, and the extent to which these stresses can be avoided in future. Because of their poverty of symptoms, cases of long standing are rarely accessible to psychotherapy, persuasive, suggestive or analytical. They frequent the surgeries of general practitioners and are as a rule satisfied with the prescription of a tonic medicine or some other placebo. These patients are frequently helped by monoamine oxidase inhibiting drugs, which may be given for some weeks at a time with intermissions. Some patients feel nearly normal on a dose of dexamphetamine; but great care must be used with this drug which is markedly prone to produce habituation.

The Anxiety Reaction

OCCURRENCE IN THE NORMAL. Anxiety reactions are a fundamental mode of response in the normal adaptation to environmental circumstances of particular kinds. They carry an unpleasant emotional tone, which may, perhaps, have survival value in predisposing the individual to avoid circumstances which evoke the reaction. Such circumstances are those which impose an expectation of danger or distress, or the need for a special effort, the time for which is not yet. The state is only likely to arise when effective action, whether avoidance or attack, cannot yet be taken. In its extremer degrees anxiety becomes fear; but common to all its degrees is the subjective experience of tension and of unpleasant anticipation. This is even true when the danger, for instance, is past before the reaction becomes manifest. This may easily occur when the speed of events outstrips that of the body's physiological change. The sudden apprehension of a motor accident, for example, followed by its immediate passing, may be succeeded after the event by the almost contemporaneous experience of anxiety and of relief.

All normal persons are prone to such reactions, before examinations, before a critical interview or during it, before making a public address or appearing on the stage, and so forth. *Fear-evoking situations* were exceedingly common for all classes of the population in belligerent countries during the war, and the sound of the air-raid siren, or the whistle of an approaching bomb, were almost universally effective stimuli.

In ordinary life circumstances of these kinds are mostly of a non-recurrent nature. When they are recurrent, *habituation* can occur in either of two directions. Where a succession of such experiences provides an increasing confidence that they will be surmounted successfully, the stimulus gradually loses its effect. Where no such confidence can be gained, or where experience gives an increasing background of failure or humiliation, *sensitivity* increases too.

PHYSIOLOGICAL BASIS. The physiological basis lies in an overall increased nervous activity mainly of the autonomic nervous system, both sympathetic and parasympathetic (Gellhorn, 1943). In general there is a rise in the concentration of adrenalin in the blood, itself causing a mobilization of sugar reserves from the liver, a rise in blood pressure and increased frequency of the heart, sometimes exophthalmos. The skin goes pale and sweats, the mouth goes dry. Respirations become deeper and more frequent. The muscles lose tone or become tremulous. Parasympathetic phenomena may be seen in frequency or urgency of micturition, increased peristalsis and diarrhoea, even an uncontrolled voiding of the bladder or rectum, and raising of the hair. If the emotional state is more prolonged there may be increased muscular tone, accompanied by a feeling of tension, restlessness and the recurrence of fidgety agitated movements, often of a stereotyped form. Digestive functions, appetite and sleep are often affected, and cause in their turn a physical deterioration.

Many of these physiological changes occur in other mood states such as those of anger or sexual excitement. For this reason it is not surprising that one sees from time to time emotional states in which two or more of these qualitative tones are present at once, or in which one tone is succeeded and supplanted by another.

Recent enquiries have demonstrated that anxiety is associated with increased activity of the pituitary-adrenocortical system. In elegant experiments, Mason and his co-workers (Mason, 1959) have shown in monkeys that anxiety-provoking circumstances, such as first transfer from home cage to experimental cage or restraining chair, are associated with a marked rise in the level of 17-hydroxycorticosteroid in plasma and urine. During the week-ends when animals were left undisturbed, 17-OHCS levels showed a consistent fall. Similar observations have been made in anxious human subjects (Persky, 1957; Glocking et al., 1961). In an investigation in which careful quantified assessments of behaviour were made by two independent psychiatrists, a significant and linear relationship was found between degree of anger and anxiety and change in 17-OHCS level (Persky et al., 1958). Admission to hospital, surgical procedures and competitive sports are associated with similar changes. There is also some evidence to suggest that these changes may be under cerebral control. Thus stimulation of certain parts of the amygdaloid nucleus produces an increase of alertness in monkeys and cats and more intense stimulation provokes changes suggestive of fear or anger (Kaada, 1959). In conscious monkeys stimulation of the amygdaloid complex produces a marked rise in plasma 17-OHCS levels. Anxiety is a very common component of attacks of temporal lobe epilepsy and a short-lived, sharply defined attack of anxiety ('ictal' anxiety) is a well-known phenomenon in this condition. That the limbic system plays a role of profound importance in the regulation of emotional life has been known since the classical work of Klüver and Bucy (1939) on the effects of bilateral temporal lobectomy in primates.

Some anxiety-provoking stimuli have been shown to produce an increase in forearm blood-flow (Harper et al., 1965; Kelly, 1966) and this increased diversion of blood to the musculature may be related to the tendency of anxious subjects to suffer attacks of fainting.

ASSOCIATIONS. Anxiety neurosis is the commonest form of neurotic illness seen in clinical practice in highly-developed countries. It is commonly associated as a secondary effect, with some degree of depression; not infrequently anxiety develops in what was originally an essentially depressive disorder of the neurotic or reactive kind. The distinction between anxiety neurosis and neurotic depression is nevertheless a valid one although the disorders overlap in their clinical features. An association of particular importance is that with the phobic anxiety states. Subjects who are predisposed to the development of anxiety reactions frequently suffer from isolated phobias of thunder and lightning, certain animals, lifts, heights or water. Such circumscribed phobias commonly begin in childhood and are frequently lifelong but are not often seen in the psychiatric clinic as they cause little incapacity. On the other hand phobias of the kind originally described by Westphal (1871) under the heading of 'agoraphobia', which make the patient incapable of venturing unaccompanied into the street and may render him housebound, are seen frequently because of the severe disability they cause. Phobic states have been classified by some workers with obsessional states and by others with hysterical reactions. There is a good deal to suggest that their affinities are with the anxiety neuroses. Thus phobias will frequently develop following stress in an individual already suffering from a simple anxiety neurosis. Where an anxiety state continues for some time, the physiological upset caused often leads to hypochondriacal bodily preoccupations and to fears of organic illness. Cardiac neuroses and emotional reactions dominated by venerophobia and cancerophobia mainly belong with the anxiety states, although the physical accompaniments of emotion may be elaborated in a bizarre manner. The tension, and incapacity to turn attention away from unpleasant ideas, may set up a neurasthenic state in which there is a deficiency of energy and initiative, a decrease in powers of concentration and enhanced susceptibility to fatigue. In those who are susceptible to such reactions or in circumstances that favour an escape into invalidism, tendencies to hysteria are often brought into the open; and in military practice in war-time *combinations of anxiety and hysterical symptoms* were seen much more frequently than either in pure culture. Severe depersonalization and derealization are most often seen in clinical practice in the setting of anxiety states commonly of the 'agoraphobic' kind. The anxiety in most subjects so affected is acute in onset and intense. These and other observations suggest affinities between depersonalization and dissociative states.

Anxiety reactions can be engendered by primarily organic conditions, the most direct connexion being seen in thyrotoxicosis where the severe anxiety is frequently terminated by correction of the metabolic disturbance. In rare cases of tumour of the adrenal medulla or phaeochromocytoma, paroxysmal attacks of anxiety and fear of impending death with raised arterial tension occur; they are terminated by removal of the growth. The early symptoms of essential hypertension are frequently those of an anxiety neurosis precipitated by communication of the diagnosis to the patient or an unfavourable verdict at an examination for life insurance. Symptoms of anxiety are prominent in the post-concussional syndrome. The post-choreic seems to be more than normally susceptible to anxiety states; and tendencies towards worry, fidgetiness and agitation are almost the invariable concomitants of oncoming senility. Cerebral arteriosclerosis and Parkinsonism are also often accompanied by manifestations of anxiety.

Among the endogenous psychoses, *involutional melancholia* is most frequently accompanied by anxiety, fear, tension and agitation. But depressive psychoses of the manic-depressive type in younger patients may also elicit these symptoms, most often where there is the constitutional background of an anxious personality. Anxiety is not a very common symptom of schizophrenic psychoses, but in individual cases it may be prominent. Panic states may occur, usually under the pressure of terrifying delusions and hallucinations.

However, although anxiety may arise in a great diversity of psychiatric conditions, it is most commonly seen in the somewhat over-susceptible but otherwise normal man, as a reaction to strains and stresses of a type which most people have to go through at some time or another. Anxiety neurosis in this sense is one of the commonest conditions in psychiatric practice and occupies a central position within the psychoneuroses.

PREDISPOSITION AND ITS COMMENCEMENT. Genetical factors probably play a considerable role in determining the degree of constitutional predisposition (see p. 62). Inheritance is almost certainly of the multifactorial type. Sex is not of very great importance, although the incidence of anxiety symptoms is rather greater in the female than the male. It is common to find a phobic anxiety of the 'agoraphobic' kind in more than one member of the family, often in more than one generation. The disorder is commoner in women and the illnesses of mother and daughter may show a striking similarity. The extent to which this familial trend can be attributed to heredity or to learning remains to be determined.

In general anxiety is associated with *immaturity* on the one hand, with *advanced age* on the other. Anxiety symptoms, fear of the dark, of strangers, of larger beings such as big dogs or elder children, of being left alone, nightmares and night-terrors, some forms of travel-sickness, etc., are almost universal in children, but are usually so well understood that they only cause difficulty in management when they reach an extreme degree. These anxious tendencies usually pass off satisfactorily as the child grows older, but may return at adolescence. At this time of life there is usually an increase in anxiety, but the symptoms tend to take a rather different form from that seen in childhood. The adolescent is likely to feel insecure above all in certain kinds of social environment, e.g. when meeting members of the opposite sex, or in connexion with the manifestations of developing sexual functions. So it is that we see at this time the first appearance of a stammer, hypochondriacal worries about masturbation, nocturnal emissions, or imagined abnormalities of the sexual organs, and socially, shyness, exaggerated reserve, awkwardnesses and gaucheries, even behaviour of a superficially aggressive and boorish type.

As the individual passes into adult life these tendencies to generalized anxiety tend to subside. However, specific phobias of thunder, lightning or animals, which are prominent in childhood frequently remain unaltered throughout life, although most individuals have contrived to minimize the disability they suffer by the time they reach adult life. A relatively high proportion of acute phobic anxieties commence more or less abruptly in the middle or late twenties although much less disabling and more variable symptoms of tension in shops, vehicles and churches may have appeared previously in adolescence. Middle life is of all times that which is most free from anxiety symptoms. With the climacteric in women and the involutional period in men, the tendency to anxiety is likely to increase again, and with advancing age shows no tendency to diminution. Agitation, tension and anxiety are common in senescence.

Organic factors may play a part in bringing about an enhanced tendency to anxiety. The readjustment of biochemical equilibrium which women go through at the time of the menopause very commonly has this effect, and the premenstrual tension state is a well recognized syndrome (see Chapter VI, p. 371). Any circumstance which has depressed physical health below its usual level may also do so, as for instance debilitating disease, or prolonged strain with loss of weight and inadequate sleep. Over-activity of the thyroid may be the cause, as well as the result of increased anxiety, and most subjects of Graves's disease show some psychological as well as physical manifestations of it. Head trauma, acute infections such as influenza, cerebral arteriosclerosis and many lesions of the central nervous system may also have this effect. Situational anxiety is a relatively common interictal disability of temporal lobe epileptics (Harper and Roth, 1962) and anxiety may be prominent during the epileptic attack.

Psychological factors are commonly assigned great significance in determining the anxious predisposition. Particular experiences in childhood, which have been highly charged with emotion, but which have been later repressed, may be the cause of specific phobias. These causes seem to operate principally along the line of pre-conditioning. The mechanism was seen in a simple form in the neurotic casualties of war; a soldier, for instance, who had been subjected to circumstances of great strain and fear, might thereafter for a number of years be startled or even terrified whenever he heard sounds which recalled those of a falling bomb, or the passage of a shell, or even that of an aeroplane overhead. If the growing child is subjected to feelings of fear in a great number and variety of circumstances, as for instance when he is brought up by a stern and rigid parent, he may come to have a very generalized susceptibility to anxiety, and to that extent to suffer a real alteration of his personality. However, in many subjects, particularly those suffering from phobic anxiety states, the opposite of this situation appears to have obtained during childhood. The patient has been markedly over-protected in early life and a relationship of unusual closeness and intensity appears to have been formed, most often with the patient's mother. This may have fostered anxiety-proneness by denying the patient adequate experience in handling independently the normal stresses and buffetings of life. To some extent the neuroses that subsequently develop may be regarded as the result of learning. However, specific traumatic experiences in childhood forming the starting point of the later anxiety neurosis can be traced only in a minority of cases.

Traits of immaturity and marked dependence are relatively common among patients with severe phobic anxiety and phobic anxiety-depersonalization states, particularly where these have begun in early life. In addition to emotional immaturity, it is common to find sexual frigidity among the women (who constitute some two-thirds of the cases) and a deficient capacity for adult tenderness and affection. Their dependent and other traits complicate their interpersonal relationships and render them particularly susceptible to any threat to their sense of security. However, such features are not specific and among those with anxiety states of late onset there are personalities whose previous adjustment has been relatively effective and successful. Nor is this group of neuroses confined, as has been claimed, to one type of personality constitution. Anxiety neuroses occur both in those with predominantly hysterical and those with mainly obsessional personalities, and can thus be regarded as normal responses, in exaggerated form, to stresses that provoke fear or insecurity.

PRECIPITATION. Before the anxious man presents himself to a doctor as a patient, he has nearly always reached a breaking-point. It is therefore usually the case that some straw has broken the camel's back—some single incident has pushed him beyond the last limit of adaptation. This precipitating factor, which has played the critical role in bringing on illness and incapacity, is nearly always of a psychological kind. As a general rule, however, it will be the last in a chain of such events, some of them psychological, some physical. An evaluation of the man's state demands an appreciation of all the factors which have exhausted his reserves, without excessive emphasis being laid on the last of them. Every man has a limit to what he can go through, and some can tolerate less than others. In the appreciation of the individual case, some effort should be made to decide how far the circumstances have been unusual, how much of the causation is to be sought in inadequate powers of adaptation. The precipitating cause of illness is usually one of the misfortunes to which all are liable, the death of a wife, the loss of a job, an attack of influenza.

To a limited extent these views require qualification in the light of recent observations. Psychological stresses of a calamitous nature are more prone to be followed by anxiety states than other forms of neurosis and this holds also for physical illness. The neuroses that begin shortly after an operation or dental treatment that required an anaesthetic often take the form of a simple or phobic anxiety state and the same appears to hold for neuroses beginning acutely in the puerperium. The explanation resides partly in the fearful ordeal these situations present to subjects so predisposed.

CLINICAL FEATURES. The anxiety state is likely to arise in the person who is habitually subject to responses of this kind. He is therefore likely to show some features of personality which adumbrate his potentialities—to be insecure, to complain that he has 'an inferiority complex', to be *doubtful of his powers of achievement*, to blame himself to excess for his failures, to be subject to tensions, worries, to magnifying his difficulties, to anticipating the worst. In the physical field, he will report his susceptibility tc the bodily manifestations of anxiety shortly to be discussed, and, very often, to occupy his mind with these feelings and to be exaggeratedly conscious of his visceral functions. His basic mood is likely to be apprehensive, and even to tend towards the side of depression, although many anxious people exhibit a considerable degree of drive and productivity. In males physical illness appears a particularly important precipitant (see p. 143).

Comparative enquiries (Gurney, Roth and Garside, 1970) have shown that patients with anxiety states tend to be more dependent and immature in their pre-morbid personality than subjects with depressive reactions. They also appear to be a more unstable group as judged by a wide range of indices. They are more in need of advice and support in everyday life as well as in critical situations. They are on the whole less capable of assuming responsibility without help and support and are dependent for their feeling of security on the nearness of certain key figures, usually mother or husband or both. Immaturity of appearance is common, sexual coolness or frigidity is found in a high proportion of instances and the capacity for giving free expression to adult tenderness and affection is often ill-developed. Despite this psychosexual immaturity it has been found that the rate of marriage among female phobic patients is significantly higher than in the general population of comparable age (Roth, 1959a), a finding that possibly reflects the more urgent quest for security and support. However, such features are not invariable. Among those who develop phobic or anxiety states in middle age or later there are many with well-adjusted and normal personalities and, in some of these, illness appears unaccountably to follow relatively trivial stresses where much more onerous ones have been previously handled in a courageous and effective manner. This feature, as also the abrupt step-like onset and failure of so many cases to respond to favourable change in their familial or social environment or to systematic psychotherapy over long periods, suggests that perpetuation of these disorders is perhaps under the control of relatively autonomous physiological mechanisms. It is facts such as these that have led some workers to talk in terms of 'endogenous' or 'vital' anxiety states (Lopez Ibor, 1950, 1966). There is no distinct group of endogenous disturbances, but lasting anxiety states with an onset that is defined with some sharpness, in the setting of a stable personality, cannot be regarded as simple reactions differing from the passing tensions of everyday life only in a quantitative manner. That a predisposition to this form of breakdown has been fashioned in some degree by the vicissitudes of the patient's upbringing and development there can be no doubt. But there are reasons for regarding the neurotic disturbance as an illness under the control of mechanisms not operative during ordinary personality functioning. These arguments are particularly applicable to the chronic disturbances of the 'agoraphobic' group which are most difficult of all to explain as exaggerations of the reversible anxiety reactions that are in some measure suffered by everyone in critical situations.

Although there are subjects in whom the time of onset of symptoms of anxiety is difficult to determine, the illness usually has a clearly-defined onset and follows one or a succession of traumatic experiences. These are very rarely sufficient causes of illness, but the pendulum in recent years has probably swung too far towards negating the importance of precipitating factors. Many patients break down following severe stresses while in other cases these are often of the overwhelming kind that could be expected to tax even relatively normal personalities to breaking point.

The mood is one of fearful anticipation, perhaps exacerbated at times to reach a panicky degree. There is a strong *sense of tension*, of being 'strung-up', which shows itself objectively in an increase of muscular tonus, perhaps some tremor of the hands, and the strained face and furrowed brow. Inwardly there is a sense of restlessness and incapacity for relaxation, shown to the observer in small fidgety movements of the hands, clenching of the hands, picking at the fingers, an unquiet pacing up and down, and often in repetitive movements of a stereotyped kind, such as a facial tic or grimace. The affective state is experienced as highly unpleasant, and often shows a fair degree of genuine depression; it is at least never euphoric. Sleep is almost always disturbed to some degree. As a rule there is a difficulty in getting off to sleep; but sleep when it occurs may be felt as restless and unsatisfying, broken perhaps in the early hours, commonly interrupted by dreams, which may themselves take on a frightening or nightmare quality. Ordinary mental functions are interfered with. The patient finds difficulty in applying himself to his usual occupations, complains of *difficulty in concentration*, perhaps even difficulties in memory and recall, loss of interest and lack of pleasure in favourite hobbies. He usually becomes irritable, short-tempered and impatient, and tolerance for frustration is lowered.

The features described so far are common to all forms of anxiety neurosis. The more specific features may be described under the heading of the two main sub-divisions of this group of disorders; (1) simple anxiety states, (2) phobic anxiety states. Although there is some degree of overlap between these two groups of phenomena, they differ in prognosis and in the form of treatment they require.

Simple Anxiety States. The patient suffers from almost continual free-floating anxiety and somatic symptoms dominate the clinical picture. The *cardiovascular system* shows a heightened and unstable tone, with rapid action of the heart, subjective experience of palpitations, throbbing of the vessels, fainting feelings. There is a sense of pressure on the chest, and (especially in circumstances which are likely to promote such feelings, such as the underground railway) a sense of choking or suffocation. The *alimentary functions* are disturbed. Lack of appetite and of all pleasure in food is common. The mouth may be dry, and it may be almost impossible to swallow. Dyspepsia is very common, and may be felt in sinking sensations in the abdomen, a sense of fullness in the stomach, pain before or after meals (often increased by excessive smoking), burning sensations, waterbrash, nausea and even vomiting. It is probably true that, in the chronically anxious individual, the persistence of gastric dysfunction with locally excessive secretion and hyperaemia, may lead to the development of peptic ulcer. The bowels are often disturbed in action, with a tendency to constipation or looseness. Frequency of micturition is common, especially as a manifestation in the acute anxiety attack, but less common in the chronic state. Sexual functions are interfered with. In women there may be *amenorrhoea* or, sometimes, periods excessive in frequency or degree; in men *impotence*, either as an ejaculatio praecox or as the failure to maintain erection. Further symptoms of involvement of the nervous system are flushing, pallor and a tendency to sweat; there are also subjective experiences of giddiness, distinct from the dizziness of the threatened faint, and the well-known 'tension headache'.

Anxiety may be increased at times under certain circumstances such as crowded shops or vehicles or social gatherings from which it is difficult to depart in an inconspicuous manner. This situational exacerbation is neither consistent nor prominent and the patient is rarely sufficiently disabled to need the support of a companion in everyday activities. However, in their very severe form, simple somatic anxiety states merge with the 'agoraphobic' anxiety states to be described in the next section.

No patient shows all these symptoms at once, and for each patient there is an individual *locus minoris resistentiae*, with a special liability to somatic manifestations of one particular kind. If this specific form of symptom is of a relatively unusual type, unaccompanied by gross and more obvious manifestations of anxiety, the anxious basis may be missed. Clinical investigation may then be pursued along purely somatic lines, with ineffective results. It is this type of patient who provides the bulk of the cases who have received so much attention of late and have led to a better appreciation of *psychosomatic interrelations*.

Phobic Anxiety States. These conditions were hitherto described with the aid of a long list of Greek and Latin names depicting morbid fears of animals, feathers, pointed objects, the dark, water, heights, thunder and lightning, blood, dentists and hospitals. These terms provide little help in classifying patients seen at the clinic. The great majority of these specific phobias are of little clinical importance in that they are readily circumvented and rarely sufficiently disabling or disturbing to lead the patient to seek psychiatric help. However, phobias centering on different themes tend to cluster into certain broad groups and the lines of demarcation which appear to be taking shape at the present time can perhaps be regarded as a further development of a distinction originally suggested by Freud in 1895 which differentiated the phobias of those objects and situations which everyone fears to some extent, such as death, illness and snakes, from phobias of circumstances which inspire no fear in the normal individual, e.g. 'agoraphobia'.

Recent observations (Gelder and Marks, 1966) call for a classification reminiscent in certain ways of that suggested by Freud but differing from it in important respects. The most significant distinction is not between objects or situations which everyone does or does not fear to some extent but between monosymptomatic phobias (which include themes that are the object of universal dread together with others that do not normally inspire fear) and phobic anxieties of a more intricate nature with a complex clinical picture. The former usually commence in childhood (Marks and Gelder, 1966a) and are usually well encapsulated and non-disabling (Roth, 1960). The agoraphobic and allied states on the other hand generally commence fairly suddenly in adult life often during the decade 25 to 35 years. There are certain other differences between the groups to which reference will be made later.

The term agoraphobia was first used by Westphal (1871) to describe three male patients with fear of wide streets and open spaces who were sometimes compelled to seek the aid of passers-by. The term is a misnomer for the condition to which it is commonly applied at present in that it is not so much open spaces the patients fear, as being at a distance from familiar surroundings without some supporting figure to whom they can turn in case of need (Roth, 1959a, 1960). All three of Westphal's patients were men whereas the majority of patients in clinical practice are female and it is in women that the condition is seen in its most typical form. The original description emphasized that fainting never occurred but recent observations indicate that many patients come close to syncope; approximately 15 per cent. of patients report one or more syncopal attacks by the time they come under observation.

The illness begins abruptly in the majority of cases, often after some severe stress such as a bereavement, separation or serious physical illness which brings about a sudden change for the worse in the patient's circumstances. Traits of dependence on other individuals are conspicuous and the stresses which precede the onset of symptoms often appear to threaten some individual in the patient's personal environment with whom his sense of security is closely bound up. It is of interest that the majority of patients are young married women. This may partly reflect the higher frequency of marriage among these patients (Roth, 1959a), but is probably related also to the fact that many of these subjects have been moved by marriage from a wide family circle to the relative isolation in which the young housewife often lives most of the day. That this situation exposes these subjects to stress is already evident in the lengths to which they have often gone, even before breakdown, to ensure that someone from the immediate family circle is at home with them during the day. Some patients travel long distances to spend a large part of the day with a mother or a close relation. This conspicuous dependence on some member of the family tends to be transferred to the husband in varying degrees after marriage. He may be compelled to change his shift to avoid night work or to travel 20 to 25 miles to take lunch at home. It is when this dependence transferred onto the marriage partner fails or is threatened or undermined by death or illness that some of the patients begin to manifest phobic symptoms.

In a substantial proportion of cases a mild or moderate anxiety state exists for months or a longer period before the relatively abrupt development of the phobic anxiety state. In fact 'agoraphobic' or phobic anxiety-depersonalization states may be regarded as simple anxiety states on which certain specific symptoms are superimposed, those in particular that tend in their extreme form to give rise to the completely housebound housewife.

The anxiety is at its most intense in enclosed spaces such as shops, vehicles, cinemas, theatres or churches, particularly when the patient finds himself surrounded by a crowd of people. He then begins to feel hot, flustered, tremulous, foolish and panic-stricken. Waiting in such a crowd or a tube tends to cause mounting anxiety which leads the patient to take flight in fear and embarrassment. When questioned about these experiences some patients describe fear of developing a panic-attack or exhibiting anxiety in the presence of others, of fainting or being *seen* in a helpless or uncontrolled state which they regard as humiliating and embarrassing in the extreme.

Once a syncopal attack has occurred the phobias are almost invariably intensified and some patients are wholly incapacitated from shopping or even walking alone in the streets thereafter. Tetany induced by hyperventilation sometimes occurs and has a similar effect in intensifying the phobic symptoms. Although anxiety is at its most intense if the patient is in a crowded enclosed space, some degree of tension persists during the whole of the time and the physiological concomitants described in relation to simple anxiety are frequently present in severe form. Broken sleep interrupted by terrifying dreams is a common feature particularly in the acute stage, and after a period of months, anorexia, loss of weight and general exhaustion may cause the patient's appearance to become pallid, haggard and drawn. Severely affected patients are not only unable to leave their homes but also to remain in them alone. However, the presence of a spouse, a parent or a close friend relieves anxiety to a sufficient extent for the patient to travel, go shopping or visit a cinema where she will tend to choose a seat near the exit. Some patients can manage outings if they are wheeling their baby in a pram, others will venture out at night or when wearing dark glasses though rarely without a good deal of apprehension.

A variable colouring of depression is present as is often the case with all forms of anxiety neurosis and is particularly marked in older patients. Although the depressive affect is rarely of the persistent unresponsive kind, suicidal ideas are reported by more than a third of the cases and suicidal acts by one in ten patients.

More than two-thirds of the patients describe associated symptoms of depersonalization or derealization (Roth, 1969; Roth and Gurney, 1971) and recent enquiries (Roth, 1968; Roth and Gurney, 1969) have shown that within the affective disorders it is with anxiety states and phobic disorders in particular that these symptoms are associated rather than with the depressions. Only in a minority of patients is the depersonalization continuous and unrelenting; most subjects reporting intermittent or episodic unreality feelings of varying intensity particularly in the chronic stage of disorder (see also p. 119).

The unreality feelings described by the patient include complaints of feeling like an automaton or being outside himself, the passive spectator of the activities in which he is engaged. Movement may feel clumsy, contrived and unnatural. Although observation may reveal little beyond slowness and deliberation in action, the patient complains that he cannot do anything properly. There is frequently derealization; the world becomes unfamiliar, still, remote and strange. Nothing appears to excite sensation and there is a feeling of deadness within; trees, flowers or the countryside no longer excite pleasure or any other emotion. The patient is distressed by the failure of those closest to him to arouse feelings of affection. Closely associated with the unreality feelings are other features reminiscent of a disturbance of temporal lobe function although these are prominent only in a minority. There may be *déjà vu* or *jamais vu* experiences, distortion of visual perception and fleeting hallucinations mainly of a hypnagogic character.

As he is falling asleep the patient may hear a voice calling his name or see an apparition of a dead relative at the foot of the bed. Some patients describe olfactory hallucinations of a 'burning' or 'peardrops' smell, or an odour linked with some emotionally disturbing experience which is recollected with hallucinatory vividness. The sudden surges of dread of their surroundings described by some very disturbed patients or the fear of looking at faces on the cinema or television screen or at their own reflexion in the mirror are probably related to depersonalization and derealization. These latter phenomena are probably more closely related to the anxiety than to other features of the disorder.

It was perhaps experience with this group of disorders that led Nils Antoni (1946) to state that there were psychiatric conditions which bore a resemblance to the dreamy state and the psychic equivalents of epilepsy. Migraine is significantly more common in these cases than in the general run of neuroses. It seems particularly to be associated with cases showing prominent depersonalization, although headaches are often in abeyance while the unreality feelings are present in a severe form. Some patients discover to their surprise that they are capable of taking prompt and appropriate action in harrowing circumstances while experiencing depersonalization. There is some evidence for the view that depersonalization reflects the working of a preformed cerebral mechanism that tends to confine anxiety within tolerable limits (Roth and Harper, 1962). However, a substantial proportion of patients simultaneously experience anxiety and depersonalization so that the effectiveness of any such mechanism can only be incomplete and the precise nature of the relationship between the phenomena remains uncertain (see p. 121).

A wide range of other clinical features may be present, usually in a variable form. Hypochondriacal preoccupations or self-scrutiny are marked in about half the cases and isolated obsessional symptoms of a ruminative nature or hysterical features are manifested in about the same proportion. The incidence of these features depends to a considerable extent on the personality background which varies between fairly wide limits. Although shy, introverted subjects are common within the group and scores for introversion prove to be significantly higher than in other forms of affective disorder (Gurney, Roth and Garside, 1970), such traits are by no means confined to them. A proportion of subjects have prominent hysterical personality traits and exhibit histrionic importunate behaviour, and somatic conversion symptoms may be prominent in association with the phobic anxiety in these cases. It is of interest that hysterical traits are significantly correlated with depersonalization phenomena. There may be a variable depressive colouring that persists over months. The resistant core of the illness consists, however, of the situational phobias, combined in about 40 per cent. of cases with severe depersonalization.

The aetiological basis of the disorder remains for the present obscure. A family history of neurosis has been elicited in about a fifth of the parents and 10 per cent. of the sibs of these patients and a hereditary factor probably contributes in causation. However, many of the clinical observations suggest that psychological factors play an important part in the genesis of the disorder. As the origin of isolated animal phobias or fear of water can sometimes be traced to traumatic experiences in early life and can also be generated experimentally (as in the well-known example of the baby rendered fearful of a furry toy animal by the use of a loud noise while he handled it) attempts have been made to explain 'agoraphobic' states in terms of modern learning theory. It has been found (Roth, 1969) that subjects with this form of disorder report phobic symptoms in childhood significantly more often than patients with other forms of affective disturbance. Although these phobias tend to fade after the first decade, phobic anxiety in adult life could conceivably arise from generalization of a morbid fear learned in early childhood. However, the evidence for this view is on the whole unconvincing. It is difficult to explain an illness with a symptomatology as wide ranging as that found in agoraphobic states in terms of learning alone. Monosymptomatic phobias lend themselves more readily to explanations along these lines, and recent investigations have shown that they can be readily reversed by behaviour therapy (Marks and Gelder, 1965). However, the response of severe phobic anxiety-depersonalization states to behaviour therapy is in most cases transient and unsatisfactory (Gelder and Marks, 1966).

Varieties of Phobic Anxiety. The following classification of illnesses with phobias as the dominant feature is mainly based on the observations of Marks and Gelder and a recent report (Marks, 1967) in which psycho-physiological findings by Lader, Martin and Kelly are included.

1. Specific animal phobias. The symptoms are confined to animals such as birds or dogs or cats or to feathers or insects. The phobias tend to be the sole complaint although it may be a superimposed general anxiety state which brings the patient under observation. The condition generally begins in childhood when fears tend to be limited to single animals with little generalization to other objects or situations. Symptoms tend to persist into adult life but respond well to treatment. Patients show a low neuroticism score, normal habituation of the galvanic skin response to repetitive stimulation and normal forearm blood-flow.

2. Specific situational phobias. These individuals have phobias of particular situations such as heights or thunderstorms or darkness. In these, too, the phobias are restricted to a specific theme and there is no generalized anxiety. Onset may be at any time from childhood into old age. Some patients may be incapacitated through compulsion to listen to weather reports and spending long periods in fearful anticipation. The symptoms persist over many years but respond quite well to behaviour therapy. The physiological responses tend to be similar to those in animal phobias.

3. Social anxieties. These individuals complain of fear of eating meals in the presence of others, of blushing or of trembling and making themselves conspicuous in other ways in public. There is said to be little generalized anxiety but on the present evidence there is no

very clear line of demarcation from the next group although there is a higher proportion of men among these cases than in other forms of phobic anxiety.

4. Agoraphobic or phobic anxiety-depersonalization states. About three-quarters of the patients are women and onset is generally in the third or late part of the second decade. There is a wide range of situational anxieties as already described and much general anxiety. Patients show high Cornell neuroticism scores and tend to be introverted; the galvanic skin response shows many spontaneous fluctuations and habituation following repetitive stimulation, is slow. Kelly and Walter (1968) reported that phobic patients did not differ from normals in respect of resting blood-flow, but recent observations suggest that, in relaxation, forearm blood-flow is increased and habituation following repetitive auditory stimuli is significantly slower than in normal subjects (Brierley, 1968). Response to treatment tends to be poor or ill-sustained.

Lasting disability results in a large number of instances. Fear of leaving the house unaccompanied remains as the main feature of the illness. Many patients become totally housebound and others are reduced to a very circumscribed existence. Depersonalization tends to subside in the course of time in most cases but may remain severe. Some degree of disablement from situational phobias is, in addition, usual even in these cases. Many patients achieve a *modus vivendi* but at the cost of considerable restriction (see also p. 133, phobias in obsessional states).

DIFFERENTIAL DIAGNOSIS. For the patient with pronounced physical manifestations of anxiety, differentiation from the corresponding organic syndrome is important although sometimes very difficult. In a case of dyspepsia, for example, it is important to decide how far psychological mechanisms are playing a part, and whether any structural lesion actually exists. The 'effort syndrome' so common in soldiers during the war needed to be differentiated from the incapacity for effort caused by organic disease of the heart. Once the physician is alive to the possibilities of mistake, it is usually not difficult to avoid error; it is to the naive of either school that disagreeable experiences, through forgetting either the organic or the psychological side, will occur.

The differential diagnosis from thyrotoxicosis is a matter of great practical as well as theoretical importance particularly since it is demonstrated (Wayne, 1960) that traditional physical signs are not as consistent in patients with hyperthyroidism as had been previously supposed. In thyrotoxic patients there are usually such features as loss of weight in the presence of ravenous appetite, extreme intolerance of heat, an enlarged vascular thyroid sometimes with a bruit, and ocular signs including exophthalmos; the latter is, however, neither invariable nor peculiar to hyperthyroidism. Moreover, as far as psychiatric features are concerned, the symptoms of anxiety appear out of a relatively clear sky, often after a trivial or no precipitant; the patients on the whole tend to be more stable than those with ordinary anxiety neuroses, a history of previous breakdown being less frequent and the general overall effectiveness and achievement of the personality being better. The age of onset of hyperthyroidism is generally later than that of anxiety neuroses. In a recent computer analysis of the clinical features of 45 hyperthyroid and 90 euthyroid patients with emotional disturbance, the features that differentiated to a significant degree between the two groups included neuroticism (as measured by the M.P.I. scale), presence of a psychological precipitant for the illness, depersonalization, age of onset, panic attacks, hysterical symptoms and clinical assessment of the personality as neurotic, in addition to physical signs such as exophthalmos, changed appetite pattern, tachycardia, and bruit etc.

(Gurney, Roth and Harper, 1966). However some anxiety states commence in middle or late life and can be identified as such on clinical grounds in the majority of cases; only in a minority is the diagnosis so uncertain even after full physical and psychological evaluation that laboratory tests have to be employed to exclude hyperthyroidism. Reference has already been made to the anxiety states associated with essential hypertension, the post-concussional syndrome and tumours of the adrenal medulla (p. 87).

Differentiation from other psychiatric syndromes is often more difficult. It is far from uncommon for an endogenous depressive illness to begin with symptoms chiefly shown as some form of anxiety, and the same may be true of cerebral arteriosclerosis or schizophrenia. If it is remembered that the diagnosis of an 'anxiety state' carries with it very little in the way of aetiological implications, and is in fact much more of a label than a diagnosis in the true sense, there is some safeguard against regarding a provisional conclusion as a final one, and treating the patient along the wrong lines. Careful enquiry into the past history will usually disclose, in such conditions as manic-depressive, schizophrenic or organic states, that the anxiety symptoms now being shown are not habitual modes of reaction, that they are not to be accounted for by a change in the external circumstances, and that some primary cause must be sought for.

It is important to attempt differentiation of different forms of anxiety neurosis from depressive disorders. Difficulties are created by the frequency with which the depressive colouring is present particularly in the severe forms of anxiety state and by the commonness of symptoms of tension, anxiety and agitation in depressive illness. The view has been expressed by a number of authors that the various forms of anxiety state and depressive illness merge insensibly with one another. Yet clinical observation suggests that the response of these two broad groups to treatment differs. The symptoms of patients with anxiety neurosis are frequently exacerbated by tricyclic compounds and even more so when electroconvulsive therapy is administered. The latter treatment can give rise to serious complications and we have seen patients with anxiety neurosis in whom a long course of E.C.T. had given rise to persistent and severe depersonalization. In a recent enquiry (Roth, 1969) an attempt has been made to sharpen the lines of demarcation between these two groups of disorders by carrying out a systematic comparison of 145 subjects tentatively allocated either to one of the forms of anxiety neurosis or to one of the depressive disorders. Patients with anxiety neurosis proved on the whole to be more unstable than the depressives in respect of a range of biographical and personality indices, which differentiated to a statistically significant degree between the groups. They more often had a family history of neurosis or personality disorder, a poor relationship with one parent, and neurotic traits and phobias in childhood. They fared worse at school, achieved a poorer social adjustment, showed more personality traits of anxiety, immaturity, dependence and hysterical tendencies and more often manifested anergic symptoms. The breakdown had been more often preceded by psychological or physical stresses and the onset of illness was more abrupt and tended to occur at an earlier age. The illness itself was more often characterized by tension and anxiety symptoms, panic attacks, situational phobias, depersonalization and related symptoms, attacks of unconsciousness and a colouring both of hysterical and obsessional features. The anxiety states had also shown higher scores for neuroticism both on clinical and psychometric measures and lower scores for extraversion. To determine the best means of separating the two groups, a multiple regression analysis was carried out making use of 58 composite items. Fifteen cases in which the diagnosis was considered to be in doubt were omitted from the analysis. The diagnostic index was constructed from the weighting coefficients of the 13 items which proved to have the highest discriminating value and these are shown together with their scores in the table. The distribution of diagnostic scores for all patients is shown in Fig. 1 and it is a clearly bimodal one. Anxiety states and depressive disorders occupy different parts of the distribution with a small amount of overlap and it will also be seen that most of the doubtful cases are now allocated either to the depressive or to the anxiety half of the distribution. Patients with phobic anxiety are to be found at the left hand extreme and endogenous depressions at the opposite extreme of the distribution

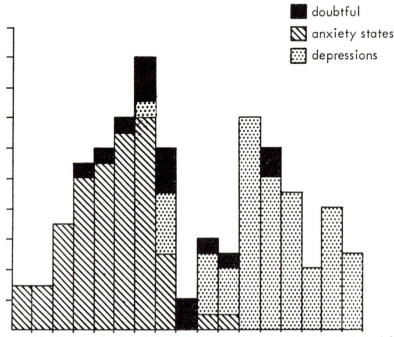

■ doubtful

▨ anxiety states

▦ depressions

FIG. 1. Distribution of patients' diagnostic scores using a 13-item scale derived from multiple regression analysis of 58 clinical items in 130 patients with anxiety neurosis or depressive states. The distribution of 15 cases where diagnosis was doubtful is also shown. For the sake of clarity only the main groups are indicated by different shading. The absolute scores range from +91 to −40 (see facing page).

with the simple anxiety states and neurotic depressions in between. A fairly clear differentiation between the two groups of disorders can therefore be achieved but this requires taking account of a wide range of clinical and biographical features in addition to the affective disturbance judged to be predominant. The distribution shown is clinically meaningful in a number of ways. At the extreme ends are the two groups of disorders most difficult to explain in terms of reactive or learned emotional responses alone. Clinical and psychological measures have shown the 'agoraphobic' states at one extreme to have the most unstable, and the endogenous depressions at the other, the most stable personalities. The anxiety-agitation and depressive-retardation clusters of features have emerged as relatively distinct from a number of recent factor-analytic and other studies (Hamilton and White, 1959; Hordern, et al., 1965).

The differential diagnosis of phobic anxiety states from temporal lobe epilepsy and other disorders with temporal lobe lesions has been discussed elsewhere (p. 460). Here it need only be said that attacks of anxiety of very sharp onset and determination, lasting no

DIAGNOSTIC INDEX

The scores (derived from regression coefficients) are those of the 13 best clinical discriminators between anxiety states and depressions. (Scores from +91 to +26 place patients in the 'anxiety' section, from +25 to +12 in the 'doubtful' section, and from +11 to −40 in the the 'depressive' section.)

Neurotic traits in childhood	many	+	10
	few	+	5
	none		0
Dependent traits in personality	present	+	6
	absent		0
Physical illness associated with onset	severe	+	16
	moderate/mild	+	8
	none		0
Panic attacks	more than 3/week	+	20
	less ,, ,, ,,	+	10
	none		0
Situational phobias	marked	+	6
	moderate	+	3
	none		0
Derealization	marked	+	2
	moderate	+	1
	none		0
Anxiety features	many	+	12
	few	+	6
	none		0
Depressed mood	severe	−	18
	moderate	−	9
	none		0
Early wakening	present	−	4
	absent		0
Suicidal tendencies	acts	−	12
	ideas	−	6
	none		0
Retardation	present	−	6
	absent		0
Obsessional features in illness	marked	+	4
	moderate	+	2
	none		0
Neuroticism (M.P.I.)	41 – 48	+	15
	33 – 40	+	12
	25 – 32	+	9
	17 – 24	+	6
	9 – 16	+	3
	0 – 8		0

more than seconds, are always suspect as organic in origin. Further, the orderliness of the march of events in epileptic attacks contrasts with the marked variability in which the symptoms succeed one another in anxiety states lacking an organic basis.

COURSE, PROGNOSIS AND OUTCOME. Anxiety reactions may run almost any course from the single severe attack occurring as the result of exceptional strain in the constitutionally fairly stable individual, and passing off without serious sequela in a fairly short space of time, to a state so severe, chronic and intractable that the patient is permanently, partially or even completely, disabled. Between these two extremes are seen the patients who have periodic recurrences of acute attacks, exacerbations of a personal predisposition which otherwise is of only minor significance in their lives. Prognosis in the individual case depends very much on these individual factors, on the assessment that is made of the constitutional aspect on the one side, the weight that must be assigned to environmental precipitation on the other.

Those in whom attacks of anxiety prove short-lived and reversible when external stresses are removed are only infrequently seen in the clinic. It is probably true to say that the distinction between the neurotically-ill subject and the individual with normal anxieties is that the former fails to recover emotional equilibrium; an emotional reaction tends to evolve into a 'process'. We have, moreover, been made aware recently of the difficulties in predicting the outcome of neurotic illnesses. The formerly accepted criteria of stability, assets and achievements, in the pre-morbid personality, the presence of under-standable and severe precipitating factors, the possibility of modifying environmental and social circumstances so as to ease pressures on the patient, which were regarded as indicative of a good prognosis and their opposite as portending poor outcome, provide a basis only for imprecise predictions. An unstable individual lacking in persistence and with hysterical traits will sometimes appear to surmount an anxiety reaction within a short time whereas a stable, effective individual with many personality assets developing his first illness in the mid-forties may unaccountably progress to a chronic, crippling, phobic anxiety neurosis. The generally accepted criteria already quoted influence the progress of the disorder and are of value in prediction, but there are also unknown factors that will require more research to define. Many patients present for treatment after their illness has been in progress for months or years. It is possible that this long period of untreated illness serves to render the symptoms more firmly ingrained. There is much to be said for early treatment particularly where specific neurotic habits or aversions have to be unlearned. Specific object phobias generally commence early in life, cause a circumscribed disability and carry a relatively benign prognosis; they respond favourably to behaviour therapy.

TREATMENT. In the acute stage of an anxiety neurosis immediately following upon the impact of some severe stress or environmental pressure the simplest and most effective method of treatment is to remove the patient from these disturbing factors, sedate him with the aid of *drugs* such as chlordiazepoxide in doses of 40–50 mg. daily, together with doses of barbiturate adequate to secure sleep at night. Psychological help at this stage should be confined to support, reassurance and simple explanation. A period of almost complete rest is desirable in the acute phase and, if the manifestations of anxiety can be temporarily damped down, conditioning effects can sometimes be avoided. However the majority of cases seen by the psychiatrist present months or longer following the appearance of symptoms when the patient is already suffering from a number of well-established and more or less severely disabling symptoms. For these patients aims of treatment are twofold. In the first place the most severe manifestations of anxiety, and the associated depression, phobic symptoms, unreality feelings and panic attacks need to be brought under control by measures aimed directly at the disabling symptoms.

Secondly, some attempt has to be made, when the acute phase has passed, to help the patient acquire some understanding of the vulnerable facets in his personality that have contributed to his breakdown and as far as possible the manner in which they have arisen. Although no specifically effective treatments exist there are a number of measures that will bring symptomatic relief. For patients with simple anxiety neuroses and minimal phobic symptoms the combination of a monoamine oxidase inhibitor with a tranquillizing drug is frequently very helpful. Phenelzine in doses of 15 mg. thrice daily combined with chlordiazepoxide 10 mg. thrice daily often brings about a marked reduction of tension and depression, restores sleep, enables the patient to resume some of his daily activities and raises morale. The change may be evident within seven to ten days but two or three weeks may elapse before improvement sets in.

In patients with severe phobic symptoms and unreality feelings, the associated anxiety and depressive symptoms will frequently show improvement on these measures but the phobic aversions, unreality feelings, panics and other disabling symptoms are rarely alleviated to a significant extent. In patients whose phobic symptoms are of less than two to three years' duration and in whom there was a sharply defined onset for the illness, a course of thiopentone injections will often bring relief, and sometimes patients with symptoms of longer duration or with severe exacerbations of the illness are helped. In patients with extreme tension and recurrent attacks of panic, few other measures confer the same degree of short-term relief. Twenty millilitres of 2·5 solution of thiopentone are used and the treatment begins with the rapid injection of 3 ml. This causes a mild alteration of consciousness in most cases. Thereafter 1 ml is injected at one minute intervals, each injection being given as rapidly as possible. It helps to prevent blocking of the needle if a slight positive pressure is maintained on the plunger so as to keep the needle full of thiopentone. With this technique, the majority of patients go into a light sleep in which their cough and lash reflexes are maintained. This stage is achieved after about 15 ml. in most cases, but there is a considerable variation from case to case in the amount required to reach this stage. If the patient has a very low sedation threshold and falls asleep within two or three minutes, further thiopentone is withheld until he awakes and then a slow injection rate is proceeded with. The majority of patients awake spontaneously five to ten minutes after sleep has been induced by this technique. The same procedure is then adopted at subsequent injections. The treatment should not be administered to patients with cardiac, respiratory or other serious systemic disease and, although difficulties rarely arise with the techniques described, means for dealing with respiratory arrest should always be close at hand as a precaution. The spacing is two to three injections per week and improvement generally begins after three to four treatments. Some subjects become very drowsy and lethargic after two or three injections and it is then advisable to allow longer intervals of time to elapse between injections.

No deliberate encouragement is given to the patient to abreact, but where he spontaneously initiates discussion after awakening, he is permitted to ventilate emotionally-laden topics. In some subjects a succession of traumatic experiences preceding the illness that had not emerged in the course of ordinary interviews may be described. However, the occurrence of abreaction appears to have little bearing upon the result of treatment. The majority of patients show some relief from symptoms of anxiety and, after three to five injections, situational anxiety with its associated symptoms is usually alleviated, sometimes to a marked degree. The opportunity created by such relief should be seized for pressing ahead with treatment along other lines. Deconditioning and desensitization procedures can with advantage be initiated at this stage.

However, although the majority of patients show initial improvement on treatment with thiopentone and patients with symptoms of 6–12 months' duration may achieve a complete remission, subjects with several years of continuous disability relapse in a high proportion of instances. Exaggerated hopes should not therefore be encouraged in the chronic case even if a remission has been induced, for this is all too likely to prove fleeting (King and Little, 1959).

Psychotherapy. In most patients with symptoms of a lasting nature, some form of psychological help should be given. All patients require a good deal of support, reassurance and simple explanation about the nature of the illness. In the acute stage of the disorder psychological measures should go no further than this. After the acute symptoms have died down, the psychotherapy provided in a hospital setting will take one of many forms, from discussions in a group of similarly affected patients designed to develop better understanding of the symptoms and some reduction of health consciousness to treatment of a more formal and carefully-planned kind. In the majority of patients who present with free-floating anxiety, pharmacological treatment combined with psychological help of a simple, superficial kind will suffice. The majority of such patients make a good recovery in a matter of months.

More intensive psychotherapeutic measures should be reserved for patients with anxieties of a situational or 'agoraphobic' kind and those in whom persistent, groundless fears of cardiac, venereal or other disease figure prominently in the picture; in these a chronic and severely disabling illness threatens unless symptoms can be relieved at a relatively early stage. Psychotherapy offers the advantage of giving the patient a chance to unburden himself of all his worries in turn, and to discharge his tension in talking to a sympathetic listener. In going over the same ground again and again, it is quite likely that environmental causes of anxiety or frustration will appear, of which the patient himself is hardly aware; he may then be given the courage to put them right. Furthermore, the penetration of the investigation into early years will help the patient to understand his own personality and to realize his weaknesses.

Many patients acquire some understanding of the extreme dependence they have carried over from an earlier stage of development; this can then be used to promote some change in their attitude to relationships with others. The patients' role in interpersonal relationships, including that with their spouses, is prone to be passive, clinging and demanding. Such immaturity in emotional development cannot be overcome by psychotherapy alone but a beginning can be made. Attitudes of inflexibility and unadaptability also frequently come to light, and here again the patient can be aided to begin the task of easing the grip of the habitual, unsatisfying routine which has often for long restricted and circumscribed his life. Approximately 60 per cent. of patients with situational phobias or phobias of disease can be enabled, with the aid of combined pharmacological and psychological measures, to return to work or household duty although some measure of restriction in movements or activities remains in many of these patients. The remaining 40 per cent. are left with a more severe disability. It is possible that, if treatment could be more often instituted at an earlier stage, better results would be obtained.

Behaviour therapy, which is described later (see p. 184), is specially applicable to cases in which anxiety is directed towards some specific situation or object. The technique generally recommended is that of desensitization by reciprocal inhibition of the phobia with deep mental and physical relaxation for which hypnosis may be required. Not all patients with situational anxiety are capable of co-operating and this method of treatment and the technique of graded exposure to the feared situations, at first in the company of some supporting figure who then gradually retires from the scene, may have to be employed. Behaviour therapy achieves good results with monosymptomatic phobias but success with agoraphobic cases is more limited. It is not yet certain that the 50 per cent. of patients who gain substantial relief represents a higher degree of success than that achieved by simple psychotherapy and other measures (Marks and Gelder, 1965). Behaviour therapy is not wholly distinct from psychotherapy in that the two types of procedure have certain features in common and may be combined in the management of individual cases.

Psychoanalysis is far too time-consuming and expensive a treatment to be called for in the majority of cases, and is best reserved for those cases who are grave and chronic enough to merit this method of attack, who have a personality sufficiently endowed with intelligence and staying power to be likely to profit from it. One need not be an adherent of psychoanalysis to believe that *prolonged individual therapy* can be helpful.

For the majority of patients, some individual but more superficial method along the lines described above will be found to be adequate. This may also be conveniently combined with treatment along medical lines. A maintenance dose of phenelzine 15–30 mg. and chlordiazepoxide 10–20 mg. over a period of weeks or a few months helps many patients. Severe panic attacks should be combated with Amytal 50–100 mg. At the times when the patient comes to report progress, opportunity is taken to discuss his difficulties with him, to encourage him to face and deal with them, and to salve with reassurance his feelings of insecurity and insufficiency.

Measures of this kind will be found inadequate to deal with the very severe and chronic case; and for patients of this kind, in whom all else has failed, the operation of leucotomy, in one or another of its forms, may come in question. Where it has been thought necessary, and has been tried, results have proved very encouraging.

Hysterical Reactions

THE UNITY OF THE SYNDROME. The concept of 'hysteria' has recently come under strong attack, from a number of authors and from a number of sides. It seems very doubtful whether its status as a syndrome can still be maintained. The evidence will be summarized under the headings of genetical basis, personality background and follow-up studies.

Genetical Basis. The earlier evidence is conflicting, while more recent evidence suggests that the genetical contribution is far from strong. Kraulis (1931) took a group of hospitalized patients who were psychopathic in a general sense as well as being subject to hysterical symptoms; 9 per cent. of the parents and 15 per cent. of the children had hysterical reactions, and there was a raised prevalence of abnormalities of personality among the sibs. Much lower figures were given by McInnes (1937) for the families of 30 hysterical patients. Of the 60 parents two suffered from anxiety states and two from hysteria; of the 117 sibs two suffered from anxiety states and none from hysteria. Brown (1942) found high rates: 19 per cent. of the parents and 6 per cent. of the sibs of his hysterics had hysterical symptoms causing social incapacity, paralyses, amnesic fugues, hysterical fits, etc. An investigation of psychopathic swindlers and liars by von Baeyer (1935) showed that, genetically, they constituted a heterogeneous group; among the relatives hysterical and cyclothymic traits of personality separated, like strands that had been accidentally woven together in the persons of the probands.

In more recent years we have the important study of Ljungberg (1957). Unfortunately no statement is made of the criteria on which a diagnosis of hysteria in the relatives is made, a deficiency which is the more to be regretted as no estimate is made of the incidence of other types of neurosis than hysteria among the relatives. The incidence of 'hysteria' in the fathers, brothers and sons of hysterical probands was respectively 2, 3 and 5 per cent., and in their mothers, sisters and daughters 7, 6 and 7 per cent. respectively, as against an estimated 0·5 per cent. for the general population. Fremming's figure (1951) for the expectation of psychoneurosis in the general population is 1·79 per cent. for men and 2·65 per cent. for women, figures which those of Ljungberg do not greatly exceed. Among the parents and sibs of the twin pairs reported by Slater (1961) there was no single individual who had been diagnosed as suffering from a hysterical illness, and the incidence of abnormal personalities did not seem to be high. There was, however, an unexpectedly high number (7 per cent.) of individuals suffering from endogenous affective psychoses.

The evidence from the twin series (Slater, 1961) was even more striking. Among the 12 MZ and the 12 DZ partners of the 24 hysterical propositi there was no single individual who had been given a diagnosis of 'hysteria'. However 3 of the MZ and 2 of the DZ partners had at some time been diagnosed as neurotic; and in all there were 5 MZ and 4 DZ partners who had had neurotic symptomatology in some form. Both the low concordance rates, and the equality of the concordance rates in MZ and DZ pairs, speak against setting a high value on the significance of a specific genetic contribution to the aetiology.

Personality Background. Most recent studies of the genetical background on which a hysterical neurosis develops have failed to show that it is of a specifically hysterical type. Ljungberg, indeed, found that in 21 per cent. of his probands the pre-morbid personality had been of the hysterical type, essentially in respect of suggestibility. But there were other common modes of deviation, e.g. the psycho-infantile 10 per cent., and the psychasthenic 8 per cent. More than half, 55 per cent., of the probands were of 'non-deviating' personality. Slater found, by comparing proband with co-twin, that the hysterical patient differed from his twin most often by being more anxious (9:0), more timid and shy (11:1), and endowed with less energy and initiative (11:4). The preponderance in respect of hysterical traits such as excitability, suggestibility, shallow affects, selfishness, histrionic traits, was less, and shown in a quarter of the cases, 3 MZ and 3 DZ pairs. A psychometric study by Ingham and Robinson (1964) also showed that hysterics could not be grouped into a single category.

Chodoff and Lyons (1958) studied a carefully sifted group of patients with conversion reactions from which all neurological disorders had been excluded. The personalities of these patients were of all kinds: passive-aggressive, emotionally unstable, inadequate, schizoid, paranoid, etc.; but there was only one example of the hysterical personality. Ziegler, Imboden and Meyer (1960) also found that only a minority of patients with conversion reactions showed 'hysterical' personalities. On the other hand they noticed a striking association with depression; 30 per cent. of their patients had depressive symptoms, and when they examined a sample of 100 depressives, they found conversion symptoms in 28. Stephens and Kamp (1962) also found no predominance of hysterical personalities in patients diagnosed as suffering from hysterical and dissociative syndromes; they thought the commonest personality deviation was of the passive-dependent type.

FOLLOW-UP STUDIES. Follow-up studies have shown that, unless the operational definition of 'hysteria' is drawn in a question-begging way, any group of hysterics fragments over the course of time into a variety of syndromes. Thus in the study by Ljungberg, there was a heavy incidence of psychosis in the probands over a follow-up which extended in some cases as long as 15 years: 3 per cent. became schizophrenic, 2 per cent. manic-depressive, 3 per cent. had epilepsy and 4 per cent. had other psychoses. The twin probands studied by Slater, who were followed up for an average period of 75 months, had to be rediagnosed in nearly all cases; temporal lobe epilepsy, other forms of epilepsy, schizophrenia, manic-depressive illness, anxiety-tension states and organic illness proved to be the primary condition in the bulk of cases.

Ziegler and Paul (1954) took all the women who had been diagnosed as suffering from 'psychoneurosis hysteria' at the Boston Psychopathic Hospital from 1927 to 1932. There were 66 of these women, and 22 had been re-hospitalized later with a psychotic diagnosis, including 12 diagnoses of dementia praecox, 9 of manic-depressive psychosis and 2 of organic psychosis. The authors concluded: 'These cases were thought to have a kind of uniformity twenty-five years ago; now the extreme diversity in mental status raises the question whether the given criteria are not so imprecise as to be non-functional; whether they do not create the illusion of defining an entity where there is none.'

If hysterics are selected by the presence of conversion symptoms in an uncomplicated setting, favourable recovery rates and some evidence of uniformity may be found. Out of the 90 patients with recent onset whom Carter (1949) succeeded in contacting after a lapse of 4 to 6 years, 70 per cent. were well; however two patients had become schizophrenic. However, in a follow-up of 3 to 10 years made by Gatfield and Guze (1962), 4 out of 24 patients with conversion symptoms developed clear signs of neurological disease (tabes, motor paresis, basal ganglia disease, cerebral tumour), with a further case in which the fits proved to be focal. The authors conclude that conversion symptoms arise with a variety of psychiatric and neurological conditions as cause; and that the prognosis is not good, many patients becoming chronic.

Observational support for the existence of 'hysteria' as a unitary syndrome has been claimed by Purtell, Robins and Cohen (1951). The patients were diagnosed by the authors, and were compared with a control series. There were significant differences between the two groups of patients, hysterics and non-hysterics, in the frequencies of a number of findings, e.g. the number of past hospitalizations, the variety of symptoms, the degree of social adjustment, etc. However, there is no evidence that the differences found were not the consequence of the criteria of selection; and no evidence that the hysterics constituted a homogeneous group.

Guze and Perley (1963) avoid the difficulties by an operational definition which itself determines the expected course of the illness. For them 'hysteria' is an illness which starts early in life, which occurs mainly in the female, and which is shown by recurrent symptoms in many different organ systems. Conversion symptoms are included, but there are many others: pains of all kinds, menstrual disorders, anxiety symptoms, an excess of hospitalizations and of operations, attention-getting and manipulative behaviour. So defined, this syndrome is a stable one (Perley and Guze, 1962) and in 11 out of 17 patients the diagnosis was confirmed on follow-up. In this sense, then, hysteria is a serious illness which runs a chronic course, lasting many years without remission. It is also a very rare one. According to Guze and Perley, the main value of such a formulation is to enable one to reject the diagnosis in a case in which conversion symptoms are prominent, but which lacks the required characteristics.

In a follow-up study of patients given a diagnosis of hysteria in a neurological hospital, Slater (1965) found that after a lapse of time which averaged 9 years, out of 85 patients 12 had died, 14 had become totally disabled, 16 partially disabled, and 43 (50 per cent.) were independent, though of these only 19 were symptom-free. The frequency of mis-diagnosis was very high. In cases where the diagnosis of hysteria had been coupled with an organic diagnosis, the subsequent course of the illness was that of the underlying disease process and the hysterical manifestations were of very temporary duration. In 28 out of the 85 patients no organic diagnosis was made at the time of hospital admission, but an organic basis for the condition was subsequently demonstrated. Among the non-organic patients there were two schizophrenics and 7 patients with recurrent endogenous depressions. The diagnosis of 'hysteria' could only be sustained in 21 patients (25 per cent.) and even in them two very different types of condition were found. There were seven patients, mostly very young, who had acute and temporary psychogenic reactions in the form of a conversion syndrome (like the patients investigated by Carter); and 14 suffering from a lasting personality disorder (resembling the patients accepted as hysterical by Guze and Perley).

Analysing the criteria which appeared to be in use by clinicians for diagnosing hysteria, Slater considered that the following emerged in order of frequency of application: (1) absence of relevant physical findings, (2) multitudinous symptoms, (3) evidence of psycho-genesis, (4) presence of a suspect symptom such as aphonia or amnesia, (5) behaviour on the part of the patient which is undesired by the physician, such as attention-seeking, playing-up, self-pity and self-concern, histrionic behaviour, and either emotional over-reaction or *belle indifférence*.

It seems, then, that wherever we touch the syndrome of hysteria, whether the probe we use is a genetic one, or a follow-up study, whether we concern ourselves with pathology or personality or symptom-clusters, the syndrome fragments. If we are to introduce system and order, we shall have to do so at more than one level. We may do so with the following postulates.

The mental mechanisms of response to suggestion, self-suggestion and dissociation are within the repertoire of all mankind. When a dissociative process, or the response to suggestion, takes the form of a symptom we may justly speak of the symptom being hysterical. This, however, does not justify us in saying that the patient is suffering from 'hysteria'. The commonest cause of hysterical symptoms in clinical practice is an acute anxiety state. Having diagnosed the nature of one or more of the symptoms shown by the patient, we are still left with the problem whether all the symptoms are of this kind or whether some are psychopathologically different; and we are still left with the need to formulate a diagnosis of the underlying state.

The great majority of patients exhibiting hysterical symptoms are of normal, and not even particularly 'hysterical', personality. In the young, one commonly sees as the personality basis some degree of emotional immaturity. Hysterical symptoms appearing for the first time after the age of forty are very commonly associated with an unidentified organic disorder or an endogenous psychosis, particularly a depression. Cyclothymic personality make-up seems to aid the manifestation of temporary hysterical mechanisms.

The hysterical personality, so called, is a well-known but not very common polar extreme of one mode of normal variation. It will be described in following pages. But the manifestations to which such personalities are predisposed, include a wide range of deviant modes of behaviour, in which quite other mechanisms than those of suggestion and dissociation are involved.

The final position to which we are led is that it will be safe to use the term 'hysterical' in its adjectival applications, e.g. to a symptom or constellation of symptoms. 'Hysteria' as the name of a specific syndrome or disorder of the mind is a term we shall avoid as the malady so signified lacks definition, pathology, pathogenesis, unitary symptom structure, unitary course or outcome.

DEFINITION OF THE TERM 'HYSTERICAL'. In British psychiatry it is usual to call those states hysterical in which some motivation for the symptoms can be discovered. The criterion breaks down in practice for two reasons. Many patients are seen with symptoms which all would call hysterical, in whom no motivation for the symptom can be discovered despite intensive enquiry. Furthermore, intensive enquiry will frequently persuade the psychodynamically minded clinician that there is motivation for symptoms which few psychiatrists would accept as hysterical. 'Motivation' is not an observational datum but a judgement of a very high degree of subjectivity. Many hysterical symptoms are psychogenic, i.e. precipitated by a psychological rather than a physical cause, brought on by an idea which has assumed importance in the patient's mind. Nevertheless, no one would call hysterical the reactive anxieties and depressions, the insomnia or dyspepsia that goes with mental tension, and such normal phenomena as fainting at the sight of blood.

When one reviews the enormous range of what one has to call hysterical, the quality that emerges as the most plausible single feature constant to all cases is the tendency to dissociation, to a breakdown in central nervous integration (Janet, 1893–4, 1907, 1910). This can be seen in unmistakable form in hysterical paralyses, anaesthesias, twilight states, losses of memory; but it is also visible in the *'belle indifférence'*, which permits the hysterical patient to suffer distressing complaints without their normal emotional consequences. The quality of lack of genuineness, of dramatization and exaggeration, which attaches to so many hysterical complaints, even those such as headaches or disorders of visceral function which are not hysterical on the face, depends on the ability of the patient to dissociate himself from his symptoms, to regard them as being hardly a part of himself. So it is that a patient can confront his doctor with his symptoms, and put on him the whole onus of their cure.

OCCURRENCE IN THE NORMAL. Hysterical symptoms are commonest at the two ends of life, before the organization of the central nervous system has yet achieved maturity, and after it has entered on its decline. The thwarted child, who flies into a tantrum, is behaving normally for his age; but exactly similar behaviour in the adult is regarded as hysterical. The same can be said of childish terrors, sleep-walking, day-dreaming and the telling of romances in which the teller himself comes to believe. Most of the 'behaviour disorders' of children depend on inadequacy, owing to immaturity, of mechanisms of central control, on emotional over-reaction, and the greater liability to breakdown of central integration (see Chapter XI, p. 634). In age, we have to do with the release of hysterical tendencies by an organic impairment of these same functions. It is therefore only likely to occur when structural deterioration is affecting those parts of the brain chiefly concerned with emotional and vegetative control, especially the frontal areas. So it is that some people fail to show hysterical traits even though some degree of senile dementia can be demonstrated clinically; in others the appearance of a hysterical symptom is the first sign of the advances made by an unsuspected organic process.

In adult life, the tendency to grossly hysterical manifestations is sufficiently small for most individuals to be safeguarded against any ordinary strain. The tendency to react to stresses with hysteria in some form is however a quality in which there is much *individual variation* of a quantitative kind. If it could be measured, there is no reason to think it would not show a normal spread of variation from individual to individual. The occurrence of a hysterical syndrome will then, if the stress situation is not unusually severe, be found to be associated with an abnormal degree of constitutional instability, or if the constitution is of average stability arise only under circumstances of exceptional stress.

There is no reason to think that men are any less liable than women to dissociative symptoms; nevertheless the diagnosis of 'hysteria' is more commonly made in women than in men. Chodoff and Lyons (1958) have made the penetrating and witty comment that the traditional description of the hysterical personality is a description of women in the words of men. A patient will often be diagnosed as suffering from 'hysteria' if the symptoms, of whatever kind, are coloured by hysterical traits of personality, or bear some suggestion of undue liveliness or exaggeration, not to speak of the histrionic. A male clinician will regard a woman who breaks into tears, on what he thinks is insufficient cause, as hysterical; while he will accept without mental criticism the behaviour of the man who puts on the show of a stiff upper lip.

PHYSIOLOGICAL BASIS. *Experimental hysteria in animals* has been chiefly studied by physiologists of the school of Pavlov. It occurs, for instance, if an animal is trained to react in one way to a stimulus of one kind, in another way to a stimulus which differs from the first only in degree, e.g. to bells of different tones. When these two stimuli in successive experiments are approximated, the point is reached when the animal is stimulated in two different directions at once. What appears then is excited or disorderly ('hysterical') behaviour and a state in which not only pre-existing conditioned reflexes are abolished, but new ones cannot be learned. Such neurotic states might persist for some time, though they might also be successfully treated, for instance, by the administration of bromides. The liability of the experimental animals to such disturbances, the severity and duration of the neurosis, were found to differ very much from animal to animal, and Pavlov was impelled to postulate constitutional differences between his dogs. Pavlov's interpretation of his findings suggests that localized areas of stimulation or inhibition are set up in certain parts of the cortex, which then maintain their activity in isolation from the rest of the nervous system; various types of stereotyped activity, such as tremors, panicky reactions, or an uncontrolled excitement at the exhibition of any sort of stimulus, would then persist, despite their inappropriateness to the immediate circumstances.

Many of the hysterical phenomena which occur in human subjects may be interpreted along the same lines. The acute hysterical reactions of soldiers shocked in battle in war-time, and reacting with functional paralyses, tremors, or losses of memory, followed on a single but very severe stimulus, such as the near explosion of a bomb, mine or shell. This stimulus could be regarded as a form of ultra-maximal stimulation in the Pavlovian terminology. Alternatively those hysterical reactions which have been the favoured subjects of psychoanalytic investigation and interpretation can be regarded as the result of incompatibility between the reaction appropriate to the circumstances of the present and responses conditioned by experiences of the remote past. The man with a phobia of crossing a bridge shows a specificity of response such as we have learned to associate with *conditioned reflexes*, and the psychoanalytic exploration of such a case nearly always shows some traumatic incident in past history which has determined the choice of this particular stimulus. Focal hysterical symptoms like this often respond to treatment by psychoanalytic means, treatment which is designed to bring repressed memories into consciousness, or, looked at in the Pavlovian way, to re-establish functional integration in the nervous system.

Just as in experimental physiology, an ultra-maximal stimulus may initiate a neurotic response, so it may also abolish an old and well-established stereotypy. The acute hysteria of soldiers often responded to stimulation of the nervous system by the inhalation of small quantities of ether, by inducing the patient to relate the events of the past in a dramatic way, to re-live the past, and by psychological means to induce a state of excitement, in short by '*abreaction*'. This corresponds to the old observation of the paralysed hysterical patient who springs from her bed at the cry of 'Fire!'. The abreaction of emotion was a feature of Freud's first successfully treated patient, and abreaction in a less dramatic form plays a part in psychoanalytic treatment even today.

ASSOCIATIONS. Any illness or neurotic state which arises in a person of hysterical temperament is likely to take on a hysterical colouring, i.e. symptoms, themselves of another kind, may be exaggerated or dramatized, or may be accepted by the patient in an attitude of complacency. This effect is one which is independent of the nature of the primary disorder.

Organic illnesses are very commonly a basis on which hysterical symptoms may flourish, and this may occur in either of two ways. *Organic damage to the brain*, especially in the frontal lobes, may create or greatly increase a natural disposition to hysterical manifestations. Hysterical symptoms occur (though not very commonly, according to Pratt, 1951) in advanced cases of disseminated sclerosis, when plaques have formed in the brain as well as in the spinal cord, and in cerebral arteriosclerosis; they may occur also with cerebral tumour, general paresis, meningovascular syphilis, and as transient features in the acute encephalopathies. They are not infrequent in early idiopathic epilepsy. They are, on the other hand, rare in chronic encephalitis, and in lesions confined to the parieto-temporal or occipital lobes, or to the hypothalamus or other parts of the brain. Hysterical symptoms are frequent in some types of *mental defect*; and persons of dull and backward intelligence seem to be more liable to dissociative symptoms than are the superior or average. The appearance of hysterical manifestations secondary to an organic lesion is of great clinical importance when the underlying lesion cannot itself be clearly demonstrated. This is frequently the case after cerebral traumata. The occurrence of hysterical symptoms in an unhysterical personality during convalescence from *severe concussion* may at times be a reliable sign that some material degree of damage has been done to the brain.

The second way in which organic lesions may predispose to hysteria is by providing a focus for the development of a constellation of ideas. A partial organic paresis of a limb may, for instance, come to be exaggerated by a disability of a hysterical nature. This mechanism is of very frequent occurrence in cases coming under the Workmen's Compensation Acts, and among pension neurotics in general.

The endogenous psychoses may also provide a basis for the release of hysterical phenomena. This is seen not infrequently in involutional melancholias and at times also in schizophrenia and the manic and depressive states of cyclothymia. The hysterical symptoms are as a rule transitory and readily distinguishable from those of the more primary condition.

Hysterical symptoms are very frequent in neurotic reactions to which one would be tempted to give a different name; above all anxiety symptoms are often accompanied by hysterical ones. There is to some extent a reciprocal relation between these two. The case which begins in an acute form as a nervous breakdown under stress, and in which anxiety symptoms take up the whole of the foreground, may in course of time take on a more and more hysterical appearance, while the manifest anxiety recedes; and the patient whose conversion symptom is abolished by suggestive therapy may relapse into a state of anxiety such as he had not previously shown. In the acute neurotic reactions produced by *battle experience during the war*, symptoms of both kinds were more often seen combined than in pure culture. As the advantage to be gained by illness became more and more important to the patient, the syndrome usually drifted, failing recovery, more and more to the hysterical side. In the psychogenic or reactive depressions, also, some hysterical symptoms are quite often seen. Of all forms of neurosis the obsessional neurosis alone seems to show little tendency to complicate itself with hysterical symptoms; and though occasional patients are seen in whom both obsessional and hysterical phenomena appear, they are uncommon.

PREDISPOSITION: THE 'HYSTERICAL' PERSONALITY. We have already discussed (p. 103) the genetical contribution to predisposition, and the actual evidence relating to the personality traits associated with hysterical illnesses. As has been seen, there is no great specificity in either. Nevertheless, there is a mode of variation in personality, which brings persons at one of the extremes (corresponding fairly closely to the 'sub-solid' extreme in Sjöbring's nomenclature) into a class which is of great social and clinical interest, and one which in British psychiatry is designated as 'hysterical'. People of this kind are probably more than normally liable to dissociative symptoms, and are therefore predisposed to hysterical manifestations in our sense; but they are prone to a great variety of other modes of behaviour which cause them to be a nuisance rather than cause them to be ill.

The traits of personality we have in mind are in large part covered by the ideas of affective immaturity and affective instability. It is what has the appearance of childish behaviour in the adult which tempts one to call him hysterical. In the child, as in the patient, we see reactions which are brisk and appropriate to emotional stimuli, but superficial and with little staying power. Quick but evanescent enthusiasms, infatuations, easy laughter and tears, moods like April showers show the rapidity of response, and, underlying it, the lack of depth of emotion. Like the child, the patient tends to be egocentric. The whole external world is seen only in the light of his own interests. In affection he tends to be possessive; a clear grasp is maintained of his rights and of the duties of others.

A personality of this type is largely immune from any serious disturbance, and feels at home in the stormiest situations. The passionate scenes, the accusations, tears, protestations and reconciliations which exhaust his partner, are for him a welcome stimulation. In a few minutes they are forgotten, and he then cannot understand how the other should be so slow to forgive and forget. The seriously histrionic personality will exaggerate such scenes to their fullest extent, so that a stagey dramatic quality emerges, which only their author himself finds completely convincing. Everything is valued in superlatives. Describing his own illness, a characteristic phraseology is used: his headaches are 'terrible', his nerves are 'shattered', his relatives have behaved 'abominably' or 'like angels'.

In the shallower personalities of this type there is an incapacity for insight which plays havoc with social relations and with possibilities of therapy or education. Attempts at psychotherapy which depend on developing insight are met with either active resistance or by psychological blindness. The capacity for self-deception is often shown in a readiness for outright lying. One may never be able to say how much of the symptoms have been deliberately assumed and how much the patient has hoodwinked himself into them. The opportunities for error on the part of the clinician are multiplied; even genuine organic symptoms may be lent an unreal stamp.

The potentialities for conflict with society are also enhanced. Von Baeyer (1935) and Cleckley (1941) have made valuable studies of antisocial people of this stamp. Cleckley, indeed, was so impressed by the abnormality of the mental state of these patients that he postulated a malignant psychological process and called it 'semantic dementia'. There seems, however to be no need to explain the downward path taken by these individuals as due to an inherent change, when it can so easily be seen as a psychological chain-reaction, each stage facilitating a descent into the next. The pseudologic swindler is well known to the criminologist. He is characterized by his lively imagination, the plausibility of his conceits, adorned by a wealth of circumstantial detail, the capacity for adaptability to circumstances which will often bring him through scrape after scrape, and the capacity for auto-suggestion which permits him to gain a belief in his own lies, and to live completely in the situation he has created for himself.

The temperamental quality which, run to an extreme, brings its holder into such trouble, in a milder form adds to the richness of human variety and human intercourse. Able men and women may show such traits, and derive much advantage from them. One finds them in the occupations where the talents of a showman are employed, in the demagogues, the revivalist preachers, players on stage or screen, popular lecturers, dance-band leaders, high powered salesmen; and people of the right quality are attracted to these occupations by the glare of publicity in which they are conducted. It is, however, difficult for such a personality to be contented for long, whatever his success. No life situation can meet all the demands he makes, least of all his own. Whatever his attainments, he is persuaded they are still greater than appears. Sometimes he is unable to persuade himself that his exploits have obtained the recognition they deserve. The fault then must lie in the blindness, stupidity or ill-will of others. From this springs the paranoid quality which we may find combined with the many other colourful strands which go to the make-up of these complex personalities.

PRECIPITATION. There is little that is specific about the precipitating causes of hysterical illness. The sudden breakdown of the previously normal personality may occur under almost any sort of sharply imposed emotional strain—an accident, a disappointment, an overwhelming stimulus such as the explosion of a bomb, the excitement and fear produced by the experiences of the first night of marriage in the emotionally immature bride. As a general rule, even these acute episodes will have been heralded by a previous period of *mounting emotional tension*. In the majority of patients, this prodromal phase can be clearly shown, and it often passes by infinitesimal stages into the full-blown hysterical state.

A workman falls from a scaffold, and is almost unhurt but frightened. His cautious foreman has him taken to hospital. There he has to wait, for examination, for an X-ray, before he is allowed to go home. His doctor thinks it best he should take a few days off. His original feelings of being shaken and dazed gradually develop through symptoms of persistent headache, fear of returning to work, under the eventual spur of possibilities of compensation, into hysterical tremors, multiple pains, and a disabling conversion hysteria. Motivation for illness, which was of no effect originally, becomes the factor which prevents normal processes of recovery. Prolonged and repeated examinations, an excess of medical attention, doubts about the diagnosis, every factor which helps to concentrate his attention on his symptoms, aids in the progress of the illness.

The only type of stimulus which seems to be rather particularly associated with later hysterical manifestations is that which involves some *disturbance of consciousness*. Thus it was found in the last war that hysterical fugues were rather commonly precipitated by an initial very mild concussion or dazing from an otherwise insignificant head trauma. Where consciousness is already impaired, as for instance in toxic confusional and amnesic states, hysterical symptoms are facilitated; even a very partial and temporary disturbance of consciousness might be sufficient to start a hysterical dissociation, which thereafter might become self-maintaining.

In the onset of many hysterical states *suggestion* has played an important role. This may have been either direct or indirect. As an example of the less direct type of suggestion, the accident neurosis may be quoted. The hypothetical workman who fell off a scaffold, cited above, will have derived from his foreman's concern the idea that he might have done himself serious damage, an idea which is reinforced by his doctor's telling him to take a few days off work, and by the extent of the examinations made in hospital. Some of the questions he has been asked by the doctors he has seen will have suggested the likelihood of such symptoms as headaches. On the other hand, the appearance of a tremor of the hands may have occurred in the first instance without suggestion, being an anxiety symptom, but be perpetuated by hysterical mechanisms (Kretschmer, 1948). Direct suggestion is often employed diagnostically, and the classical stigmata of hysteria, anaesthesia of the palate and cornea, narrowing of the visual fields, glove and stocking anaesthesia, are only seen in hysterics when the doctor who is examining them has himself implanted the idea (Babinski, 1901).

A hysterical dissociation of consciousness, and the appearance of hysterical amnesias, anaesthesias, etc., can be brought about in suitable subjects, not all of them of a constitutionally highly hysterical type of personality, by *hypnosis*, which depends for its initiation on direct suggestion. Professional hypnotists sometimes give public exhibitions of their powers as a means of livelihood. A subject, self-selected from the audience, is by direct suggestion, put into a trance in which he is oblivious to the rest of the environment but attendant only on the commands of the hypnotist. Anaesthesias, super-normal rigidity or flaccidity of the muscles, feats of balancing, etc., can then be demonstrated, and commands given which would be carried out later at a signal after the hypnotic state had been ended— the so-called *post-hypnotic automatism*. It seems to be established that hypnotism can produce in the suitable subject a physiological state which is not otherwise obtainable. Thus a sufficient anaesthesia has been obtained to allow a painless childbirth, or the performance of a surgical operation. Changes of temperature by hyperaemia of one of a pair of extremities have been produced; and on occasion a hysterical twilight state has been so deepened that the subject was no longer responsive to the hypnotist, and has 'slept' for two or three days on end, so that tube-feeding had to be used. These phenomena all signify a splitting of consciousness, which may go down to a considerable depth, when visceral control is affected.

Hypnotism is used, not very frequently or very successfully, for the treatment of hysterical states. It is of considerable interest psychologically, and might repay more intensive study than it has received.

One of the reasons why hypnotism is not frequently used in treatment is that doctors vary very much in their powers as hypnotists. It is essential that the hypnotist believes implicitly in his own powers, as if he does not he is not likely to be convincing to others.

It seems to be true that the most successful hypnotists are themselves of a somewhat hysterical type of personality. Those who have reason to doubt their hypnotic powers may employ aids of a chemical kind in introducing the hypnotic state, particularly such general sedatives, hypnotics and anaesthetics as ether, nitrous oxide, and the rapidly acting barbiturates such as Amytal and Pentothal. A prolonged period of *over-breathing*, causing alkalinity of the blood, also produces that slight impairment of consciousness which favours dissociation. Hysterical patients may bring this about in themselves, and hysterical fits most commonly begin with a stage of over-breathing.

CLINICAL FEATURES. It would not be profitable to detail here all the symptoms which may result from dissociative processes. Some of the most common are disturbances of sensation, anaesthesiae and paraesthesiae, disturbances of motility, ataxias, spastic and flaccid paralyses, choreiform and athetoid movements, tremors. It is a common tendency to regard all such symptoms as hysterical, once investigation has failed to show any organic basis. This is quite often an error. Torticollis, facial tics, stammers, are very seldom hysterical; and such things as Parkinsonism are not infrequently mis-diagnosed as hysterical in their early stages.

More interesting than these bodily manifestations are the mental ones. These involve, in some form or another, a disturbance of consciousness, which may be at different levels. The most superficial form, and one which has attracted much attention from the dramatic form the symptoms take, is seen in the *double and multiple personalities*, which have been described by Morton Prince, McDougall and others. The patient describes herself at different times as being one or another of several different personalities. These different personalities may be endowed with superficially different character traits, and may or may not be aware of each other's existence. Thus a girl who is by turns 'Mary' and 'Margaret', may be quiet, studious and obedient as Mary, and unaware of Margaret's existence. When she becomes Margaret, however, she may be gay, headstrong and wilful, and refer to Mary in contemptuous terms. It seems that these multiple personalities are always artificial productions, the product of the medical attention[1] that they arouse.

Spontaneous hysterical splitting of the personality is more common, but probably not more genuine. From time to time in the newspapers is recorded the story of a man who has disappeared from his usual haunts, and is discovered months or years later, living in a different town, under a different name, following a different occupation. When he is discovered, he claims a *complete loss of memory* for his previous existence, and cannot be proved a liar. As a general rule, it may be assumed that in some way his earlier life was intolerable (very often his marital situation), and that he ran away from it to start again.

Such incidents have begun with a hysterical fugue, and hysterical fugues are so common that there are few psychiatrists who have not met many examples. In war they were frequently precipitated by emotional experiences of a highly traumatic kind, severe shelling and bombing, after psychological powers of resistance had been reduced by physical exhaustion, loss of confidence and by surrounding chaos and disintegration; under these circumstances they often occurred in fairly well-integrated personalities. They were also, however, common, and then in personalities of a more hysterical stamp, while the soldier was on leave but on his way back to the front, or in similar circumstances when motivations of a quite obvious kind were playing a role. In peace-time, fugues are nearly always an *escape from a disagreeable situation*, which has quite often only arisen because of some petty crime by the patient. More often than not they arouse the suspicion of the psychiatrist

[1] And also literary interest.   There are many novels on this theme.

that not all the memory-loss is genuine. In the fugue state the patient may wander from his usual environment, travel to strange towns, spend the night in doss-houses or under bridges, and finally, when the money in his pocket has all been spent, be brought to the doctor in a dirty, unshaven, physically exhausted state. Nevertheless, if he has been observed during his dissociated state, his behaviour has shown signs of being fairly well integrated; while he has money in his pocket, for instance, the subject of the hysterical fugue will not go for long without food and drink. In this way these states can be distinguished from the fugue states occasionally seen in epileptic, schizophrenic and depressed patients.

In the neurotic casualties of war, fugue states were often observed in association with *amnesic gaps* in the recollection of the past, although these were also observed independently. Soldiers arriving in hospital after breaking down in battle, were often unable to remember the events of several days together, those days in which their nervous breakdown had occurred. These memories could be recalled under hypnosis, or barbiturate narcosis and suggestion, and were then found to be always of a painful kind, and often of a nature to *undermine* the patient's feelings of *self-respect*. It is a hysterical trait to think better of oneself than a true insight would allow, so that the hysterically disposed are particularly susceptible to emotional traumata of that kind, as well as particularly likely to react to them (as to anything unpleasant) by a process of forgetting.

The hysterical fugue bears resemblances to *somnambulism*, which is however to be regarded as a normal phenomenon, at least in childhood. Certain theories of hysteria (Sollier) are based on the similarity of hysterical states to sleep and dream. Sleep-walking, as its name implies, is a state of dissociated consciousness, in which phenomena of the sleeping and the waking states are combined. The degree of complexity of behaviour, as Pai (1946) has shown, may vary very widely. Muttering, calling out or even talking, fragmentary or almost coherent, may take place in sleep; and in isolated instances the somnambulist may be brought to carry on a rational conversation. As in the hypnotic state, some of the highest cortical centres must then be active, while others, notably those involved in self-awareness and self-criticism, are isolated. Motor activity, getting out of bed and back again at the simplest level, up to going for a long walk, or even taking up some occupation at the highest level, also occurs. These phenomena are not to be clearly distinguished from the necessary activity of a simple kind that takes place at all times in sleep. In normal sleep there is a good deal of bodily movement, stimulated by feelings of bodily discomfort and of a kind to remedy them. Many people, moreover, disturbed by a full bladder at night, are able to cope with the situation without properly waking up at all.

Hysterical amnesia is sometimes seen as a part of a more widespread disturbance of intellectual functions, *hysterical pseudodementia*. Here the patient will claim a loss of memory for large sections of his past life, refuse to recognize relatives, deny all knowledge of, say, arithmetical methods. Nearly always there is much that is not genuine in the symptoms, which are used in the most consistent way to defeat investigation; as with the hysterical fugue, there is very often a discreditable incident to be concealed. Sometimes the defence is very successful, and we have known an embezzler avoid a severe prison sentence by its means.

Hysterical pseudodementia is an ill-defined syndrome most typically represented by the Ganser state (1898); many clinicians regard the two as coterminous and identical. However, typical Ganser states are rare (Goldin and Macdonald, 1955). These authors quote Wertham's definition, 'a "Ganser reaction" is a hysterical pseudostupidity which occurs almost exclusively in gaols and in old-fashioned German psychiatric textbooks'. It is rare in gaols too;

and the experienced prison psychologists consulted by Goldin and Macdonald could muster between them only a single dubious case. Ganser's criteria included the giving of approximate answers ('How many legs has a horse?' 'Three') and apparently foolish answers which yet show that the patient has understood the question ('Where are you?' 'Berlin, in Russia'). Ganser insisted that these responses were not simulated, and that the patients were genuinely ill and were not trying to deceive him; frank malingering accordingly should not be classified as a Ganser state. He said they tried to find an answer, but had difficulty in focusing attention. Other symptoms were auditory and visual hallucinations, disorientation, a twilight state of fluid character and short duration, and amnesia for the whole episode after reversion to normal. Ganser thought the condition was hysterical, with or without added psychosis.

This is now the general view. States of hysterical pseudodementia, loosely defined, are not very uncommon; they are nearly always an ephemeral episode in the course of a psychosis (epilepsy, schizophrenia, organic cerebral disease). Organic symptoms that take on hysterical colouring under the influence of emotional stress are, of course, seen in many circumstances. In shipwreck survivors during the war, Anderson (1942b) reported the occurrence of massive hallucinations, such as of a shore in sight, which were experienced in common by several men; the phenomenon was hysterical, but predisposed to by the effects of exposure, starvation and thirst in causing some impairment of normal consciousness.

Hysterical trances occur spontaneously, but bear every resemblance to the similar trances brought about by hypnotism. Emotional experiences of a highly complex kind may occur, e.g. of a religious kind, including massive and complicated visual and auditory hallucinations, internally coherent, and the receipt of 'messages' supposedly from God or His angels. Like all hysterical phenomena, these show the common feature of being the type of manifestation which one associates with a high level of consciousness. The messages which have been received, by accepted saints among others, usually after periods of fasting and vigil, are not chaotic or disorganized, but bear the stamp of the personality of the recipient, and may contain elements of genuine and exalted mysticism. *Vegetative phenomena*, occurring by mechanisms which we are not yet in a position to understand, may also occur. The evidence which relates to the production of the stigmata of Christ by ardent though simple-minded believers, to the ability to live for days without nourishment but also without gross metabolic disturbance, the ability of students of Yoga to reduce animation to a remarkably low level, or to handle fire, is not of a kind to satisfy, as yet, the scientific enquirer; but there is certainly a case for enquiry. Little would be gained by calling these phenomena hysterical, because neither the psychological mechanism nor its physiological correlates are really understood at present. But they are no doubt *closely related to the dissociative symptoms of the hysterical patient*.

The phenomenon of chronic addiction to invalidism and to medical or surgical disorders which are deliberately simulated by the patient, has received a good deal of attention in recent years and is well known to doctors who work in general hospitals. It is almost invariably found in individuals with many grossly hysterical traits of personality whose special craving is for the sympathy and concern and the sense of participation in high drama that treatment in hospital provides. The syndrome has become known by the unfortunate eponym of Munchausen syndrome (Asher, 1951; Hawkings, Sim and Tibbets, 1956; Roth, 1962). The commonest of the simulated illnesses are pyrexias of unknown origin, haemorrhages which may bring haemoglobin down to dangerous levels, acute abdominal emergencies, cutaneous artifacts or deeper wounds which become infected and necessitate amputation of a limb, multiple abscesses from which *Escherichia coli* is usually cultured, and more rarely, neurological disorders. The blend of conscious and unconscious mechanisms in the psychogenesis of hysterical symptoms is particularly well illustrated by this phenomenon. The physical symptoms and signs are consciously feigned but the reasons which impel the patients to seek these morbid satisfactions are concealed from them. In one of our patients, a middle-aged nun, a succession of physical illnesses was successfully simulated over a period of more than 25 years. The conditions for which she received investigation and treatment included multiple haemorrhages, acute abdominal emergencies, pyrexias of unknown origin, suspected hyperthyroidism, multiple abscesses and septic arthritis of several joints from each of which a pure culture of *E. coli* was obtained and which subsequently led to the amputation of a thumb. In the course of her last admission to hospital there were found in her locker, syringes, needles, catheters, textbooks of medicine and hundreds of tablets of various kinds, including thyroid extract. She was the child of cold and remote medical parents, largely absorbed in their work. Her case-history was in fact reminiscent of the account of two psychoanalysts, man and wife, busily engaged the whole day long in their work; when their only child was asked one day what he would like to be when he grew up he instantly replied, 'A patient'.

This account will have given some impression of the immense variety of hysterical manifestations. It is a point of some interest how much the favoured type of manifestation has varied during the course of human history from age to age, from the hysterical fits and casting-out of devils of the pre-scientific era, the pilgrimages of the flagellants of the Middle Ages, and such other communal psychoses affecting primitive communities as were seen in the witch-hunts of the seventeenth century (e.g. the Salem witches), down to the days of neurasthenia and railway-spine at the time of Beard. The prevalence of a disposition to hysteria probably remains unaltered through the centuries, but its manifestation is *responsive to the 'Zeitgeist'*, and above all to the preoccupations, interests and theories of the medical men of the time. Under the influence of Charcot and his school were seen the 'attitudes passionelles', now never observed, 'traumatic neurosis' after Oppenheim and other neurologists, in the 1914–18 war ataxias, paralyses, astasia-abasia; and in the last war 'effort syndrome'.

DIFFERENTIAL DIAGNOSIS. In accordance with the principles with which we concluded the introductory part of this section, we may say that the clinician who makes a diagnosis of 'hysteria' will always be in error. All that he is entitled to say, even after the most complete examination of past history and present status is that certain named phenomena, e.g. particular symptoms, are hysterical and that hysterical mechanisms are in evidence. Even then, all that is said thereby is that the phenomena named are to be explained by normal psychopathological mechanisms and do not presuppose a basis in pathology. The demonstration that one or several symptoms are due to dissociation does not enable one to conclude that all the rest must be so too. When a conclusion has been drawn that some or all of the presenting symptoms are dissociative, it is still necessary to make up one's mind about the aetiology and the basic state. This may at times be found to rest on a markedly deviant personality; but very much more often the personality will be found to be normal, and the state on which a hysterical superstructure has been reared will prove to be an anxiety state, a depression, or an organic change.

Often it is not easy to establish that the symptoms are hysterical, and a full examination of the past history and the present clinical state will be required. Clues will be obtained during history-taking in indications of a hysterical type of personality and behaviour patterns in the past which indicate a tendency to hysterical reactions. A carefully taken account of the present illness will show that *pathogenesis has proceeded via the intermediation of consciousness*. Finally the symptom itself may be found clearly to have a strong personal significance to the patient, to be perhaps an effective defence against some environmental threat, or to have a symbolic meaning connected with events in the past history. In clinical examination the findings will be such as could not be simply explained by an organic lesion. A paralysed arm, for instance, may be paralysed only for deliberate and voluntary movements, but still react normally in automatic movements initiated by a voluntary movement of the opposed arm. A hysterical anaesthesia will not correspond to the distribution of an anaesthesia caused by interference in any anatomical pathway. Hysterical fugues, amnesias, twilight states will show a disturbance of consciousness which is self-contradictory, i.e. leaving some functions, in which the highest levels of consciousness are involved, unaffected.

Despite indications of these kinds differential diagnosis may be made difficult by the simultaneous occurrence of symptoms directly referable to an organic lesion. As has been said, organic symptoms are often *overlaid by hysterical elaborations* and exaggerations, and it may then be very difficult to say where the organic disability ends and the functional one begins. This is especially true in diseases of the digestive system (nervous dyspepsia, achalasia, ulcerative colitis), of the cardiovascular and respiratory systems (cardiac neuroses, angioneurotic oedema, hay fever, asthma), and the skin ('dermatitis', hyperhidrosis). As an example of the interlocking of psychological and physical mechanisms, anorexia nervosa is discussed in an appendix to this section. Furthermore, organic brain disease may itself predispose to hysterical reactions. Mistakes of both kinds are common, both the wasteful expenditure of time and trouble on the investigation of hysterical conditions along standard medical lines, and the recognition of a hysterical overlay while its underlying organic cause is missed.

COURSE, PROGNOSIS AND OUTCOME. The majority of hysterical symptoms clear up spontaneously soon after their first occurrence, as the situation which had produced them alters. Nevertheless, many hysterical illnesses continue for years. Ljungberg found that, though 62 per cent. of patients had recovered in the first year, 20 per cent. were still ill fifteen years later. In the series reported by Slater (1961) the outcome tended to be even worse.

Reasons for the continuance of symptoms may be many, and lie either within the patient or in his environmental circumstances. Gross and long-persisting hysterical symptoms are nearly always found in association with personalities of a markedly hysterical structure; but the commonest finding then is that one symptom has passed off only to be replaced by another. The type of circumstance which is most likely to lead to long duration is one which provides the patient with *significant gain from his illness*. This gain need not be commensurate with the suffering which the illness itself involves. Among the long-standing pension neurotics left behind by the 1914–18 war there were many who drew a few shillings a week on account of their disability, but were effectively prevented by it from maintaining themselves at a very much higher standard of living. The long persistence of a hysterical symptom itself aids its further continuation. A conditioned state of the central nervous system has been set up which can only be abolished by energetic and appropriate interference. An important factor leading to chronicity is the existence of a partner, consort, sib or parent, who believes in the patient's illness and constantly supports it.

Nevertheless hysterical conditions are such that, notwithstanding their duration or the unfavourable qualities of the personality in which they have arisen, the *possibility of cure* is never entirely abolished. Kraepelin and others have pointed out the relative youthfulness of hysterical patients, and have concluded that the tendency to hysteria diminishes with increasing age. Kraepelin's figures refer to admissions to a psychiatric hospital; but the majority of milder hysterics are never hospitalized; indeed only a minority are ever seen by a psychiatrist. It seems, however, to be true that a full social adaptation after a stormy hysterical phase not infrequently occurs after the age of thirty, even in patients of markedly hysterical personality.

TREATMENT. The treatment of hysterical illnesses will depend on a thorough understanding of the personality of the patient and of the circumstances which have conspired to produce illness. As a rule, therefore, it will not be begun until after a *careful history* has provided the physician with an idea of the patient's strengths and weaknesses of personality, the extent to which certain modes of reaction are ingrained or subject to variation, the present sources of emotional stress, etc. There are certain exceptions to this general rule. It is not possible to get into sufficient contact with a patient who appears to be mute or amnesic, unless the mutism or amnesia can first be disposed of. In such patients, a few sessions of treatment by hypnosis or by suggestion under narcosis may well precede psychiatric exploration, and the obtaining of the history will very likely be best continued while the patient is under control of this kind.

When the history is complete, and the available facts have been analysed, the physician will be able to assess the nature and extent of the therapeutic problem. In rare cases it may then be seen that hysterical patterns of behaviour have been so lifelong, the patient's capacity for social adaptation so defective, that treatment is practically hopeless. As a rule, however, it will be found that the main part of the disability is due to certain symptoms, and other symptoms are of less practical importance. These most important symptoms, moreover, will probably not be ones which are entirely habitual, but to a certain extent facultative, and due to a particular constellation of emotional factors. *Alternative satisfactions for the patient's psychological needs* will be available, and an alternative mode of reaction can be suggested to him which, while still fitting his personality, will be less disturbing socially or less disabling. In treatment it is important to keep one's aim within what is practically attainable and not to attempt to educate the patient into a way of life which is entirely foreign to him. For this reason the belief of some psychotherapists, that they should be content with nothing less than the remodelling of the patient's personality and the abolition of all hysterical tendencies, seems to us the equivalent of throwing away the substance for the shadow.

In the course of the therapeutic analysis, an understanding will be obtained of the environmental factors which have aided in the causation of the illness. Very frequently these or some of them, will be of a remediable nature. The attitude taken towards the patient's symptoms by his immediate friends and relatives will often fall into this category; and a considerable amount of explanation and persuasion may have to be given to a husband or wife, parent or child. At other times, contact may have to be made with teachers or employers, a change of work may have to be arranged; and in general there is considerable scope for treatment along social lines. Manipulation of the environment so as to exclude its more traumatic features is needed more often than not.

In the course of study of the patient's case, the physician will gain a great measure of insight into the factors that determine his usual modes of reaction. If a certain amount of this insight can be passed on to the patient, so that he too may know where his weaknesses lie and thereby be guarded against them, it is all to the good. In general, however, treatment in this way comes up against the barrier of an *incapacity for insight*, often showing itself in an apparent unwillingness to accept the most obvious explanation, which is a constitutional trait of an intractable kind. It will be found necessary to wrap up the insights which the patient must have in a sugar-coating of some sort in order to make them acceptable.

Treatment of the disabling symptoms themselves will nearly always be by one or another means of suggestion. With insufficient previous preparation, suggestion will often bring about a cure, followed by immediate relapse. It is therefore desirable, before even any specifically directed suggestion is begun, to have a course mapped out for the patient during convalescence and after recovery and return to normal life, which he understands and has accepted. He must in fact be willing to get well before he is asked to give up his symptom. This will often involve negotiations, which may even take on a bargaining character, especially if concessions are going to be demanded of the patient's relatives.

The longer the disabling hysterical symptoms have lasted, the more carefully planned the *scheme of treatment* will have to be. In acute hysterical reactions, such as were seen in great abundance during the war, quite simple suggestive, or merely restorative, measures often brought about a permanent cure. Thus a man who was brought into a field aid-post with a gross tremor, or an amnesic state, after being dazed and then terrified by mortar fire, very frequently made a complete recovery with a heavy dose of sedative and twelve to sixteen hours' sleep. Only when a motivation for illness became established, after being sent down the line, did treatment begin to become difficult.

Suggestion, which plays such a central part in the treatment, may be given in many ways, over a long time and in small doses in the course of conversations in which explanation and persuasion are also playing a role, or in single intensive sessions. If the latter method is used, then every effort is made to increase the patient's momentary suggestibility up to a maximum. This may be done by hypnosis, by a very light narcosis under ether inhalation or intravenous barbiturate, or by the building up of a situation of emotional tension which is brought to a dramatic climax (as in some religious meetings). Any symptomatic improvement obtained must be grasped firmly, and the patient cannot be allowed to slip back. If, for instance, he has been paralysed and can be brought to walk, he should do so publicly, so that he is committed to his improvement. Where the hysterical syndrome is attributable to a single traumatic incident in the past, *abreactive procedures* will often be effective; under suggestion the patient is brought to relive this buried incident and to bring out all the emotion it caused at the time. This by itself is often enough, but it may also be necessary for him to look at this emotion in the cold light of day, as it were, and be able to discuss it in reassuring circumstances. Treatment by methods of psychological exploration, such as psychoanalysis, depends for its success as much on the discovery of such incidents in a forgotten past as on the elucidation of the factors in the present situation which aid the continuation of the illness.

Depersonalization

There are many vivid and arresting descriptions of the experience of depersonalization in the writings of mystics and saints and such an experience was probably the starting-point of Wordsworth's 'Ode on the Intimations of Immortality from Recollections of Early Childhood'. The phenomenon began to attract the interest of non-medical psychologists towards the end of the last century and the earliest theories are to be found in the writings of Krishaber (1872), Ribot (1882) and Taine (1870) who attributed the phenomenon to a disturbance of sense perception. Janet (1908), whose book *Obsessions and Psychasthenia* contains some excellent accounts of the phenomenon, considered that hyperactivity of memory in a setting of narrowed consciousness was the essential factor in causation. The experience, in his view, arose from the contrast between recollection of the former healthy personality and the present state. Theories along psychological, psychodynamic and organic lines have continued to proliferate throughout the past seven decades.

A turning-point of psychiatric interest in the phenomenon was marked by the publication of a classical monograph by Schilder in 1914 and a later work in 1935. He described depersonalization as 'a state in which the individual feels himself changed throughout in comparison with his former state. This change extends both to the self and the outer world, and leads to the individual not acknowledging himself as a personality. His actions seem to him automatic. He observes his own actions like a spectator'.

In another work (Schilder, 1928) this description was expanded. 'To the depersonalized individual the world appears strange, peculiar, foreign, dream-like. Objects appear at times strangely diminished in size, at times flat. Sounds appear to come from a distance. The tactile characteristics of objects likewise seem strangely altered, but the patients complain not only of the changes in their perceptivity but their imagery appears to be altered. Patients characterize their imagery as pale, colourless and some complain that they have altogether lost the power of imagination. The emotions likewise undergo marked alteration. Patients complain that they are capable of experiencing neither pain nor pleasure; love and hate have perished with them. They experience a fundamental change in their personality, and the climax is reached with their complaints that they have become strangers to themselves. It is as though they were dead, lifeless, mere automatons. The objective examination of such patients reveals not only an intact sensory apparatus, but also an intact emotional apparatus. All these patients exhibit natural affective reactions in their facial expressions, attitudes, etc., so that it is impossible to assume that they are incapable of emotional response'.

A number of distinct components of the phenomenon may be defined, in this as in other descriptions. For the alienation of the outer world the term '*derealization*' was coined by Mapother. There appears to be a subjective distortion of perception, for not only may the size of objects appear to be altered but their shapes may be twisted, colours dimmed and faces changed, unfamiliar and frightening. Some patients complain of an unearthly stillness in the world. One of Mayer-Gross's (1935) patients once said 'The world looks perfectly still, like a post-card. It is standing still; there is no point in it. A bus moves along without purpose. It does not feel real. Everything in vision is dead; branches of trees are swaying without purpose'.

Many patients complain of a subjective experience of *bodily change*. The head may feel large or numb, or the body below the neck feel dead and lifeless. Some patients use bizarre terms to describe their experience. They refer to their heads 'filled with cotton-wool' or their bodies 'made of marble'. A quasi-delusional form of expression may be employed to convey the experiences but, unless a transition to schizophrenic illness is taking place, further enquiry reveals that these descriptions carry an implicit 'as if' qualification. The arms may feel heavy, swollen, or the hands held up before the patient arouse a sense of unfamiliarity or dread.

In the '*automaton*' experience the patient feels as if he were a passive and indifferent spectator of his own activities. Movements appear forced, affected, puppet-like, and require a special act of will. His voice sounds unfamiliar, and he is bereft of spontaneity in thought, speech and action. Closely associated with these features is a compulsive *self-scrutiny* which appears from descriptions given by the patients to aggravate the situation in a vicious circle. Schilder was inclined to attach special importance to this self-scrutinizing tendency which he considered to be fundamental to the whole disturbance. Bizarre *hypochondriacal ideas* are quite often expressed by patients whose attention appears set in a state of self-observation. Despite the complaints of robot-like behaviour devoid of all feelings of fulfilment or satisfaction, objectively patients appear to carry out tasks in a normally prompt and efficient manner. The loss of the specific feelings that accompany action ('*aktionsgefühle*') has been held by Loewy (1908) to be the central feature of depersonalization phenomena.

The patients' *inability to feel emotion* even towards those dear and close to them is a distressing component of the syndrome but, as it is quite often found independently of the other features, it is probably less specific than '*aktionsgefühle*' for depersonalization.

The patient finds the experiences *difficult to render into words*. There is a continual feeling that the personality is not involved in events and a quality of estrangement from and unfamiliarity with the self that makes the individual fearful or uncomfortable when left alone. He has feelings of doubt about his own identity. His reflexion in the mirror appears unfamiliar and feelings of unreality may be heightened when he hears his own name spoken. He fears a sudden failure of memory, a lapse into blankness and total loss of identity. The physical experiences include feelings of floating in space and of blunted sensation all over the body which leads some patients to touch, punch or prick themselves repeatedly in an attempt to provoke a sense of reality. The experience is like a dream from which some vivid, dramatic event might at any moment bring awakening.

Most of the patients presenting in clinical practice with depersonalization symptoms of the kind described will be found to be suffering from an *anxiety neurosis* very often with prominent *phobic features*. The feelings of anxiety rarely become manifest in objective disturbances of conduct, but there is a fear of some sudden violent explosion of conduct with loss of control and lapse into madness. These feelings, as also the sense of unreality and detachment, are aggravated in unfamiliar surroundings and by being away from the protection and security conferred by close friends and relatives. Patients are therefore disinclined to leave the home and family circle and attacks of panic may break through if excursions far from home are attempted. These patients with situational anxiety belong to the group of *phobic anxiety-depersonalization* cases (see p. 94), although intense and persistent unreality feelings are found in only a minority.

Another group in which depersonalization may dominate the clinical picture is made up of immature, markedly obsessional, introspective young people in whom depersonalization often begins abruptly. These cases are relatively rare and their representation in the literature of depersonalization is out of proportion to their numerical importance. This is probably because of their psychopathological interest, the vivid and differentiated descriptions of their experiences many of these patients provide, and the long duration of the symptoms. The term '*primary depersonalization syndrome*' can perhaps be applied to this group, for the depersonalization does not appear to be secondary to some other psychiatric disorder, although difficulty in establishing personal relationships and in negotiating adolescence in general, and an abnormal degree of self-absorption, withdrawal into phantasy or rumination about fate, time and death are common features. There may have been fleeting attacks of unreality feelings previously, but the illness is generally of abrupt onset. The adolescent cases described by Meyer (1959, 1961) probably belonged to this group, as also a number of those studied by Shorvon *et al.* (1946), who considered that depersonalization occurred in the form of an independent syndrome.

Many of the cases of 'primary depersonalization syndrome' and the far more common cases of depersonalization in the setting of an anxiety neurosis, have, in recent years, been classified under the heading of 'pseudo-neurotic schizophrenia', particularly by North American authors. The ineffability of the patients' experience, the difficulty of arriving at satisfactory explanations in terms of psychopathology alone, and the long drawn out nature of the illness have all contributed to the adoption of this nomenclature. There is, however, no evidence that depersonalization sustained for months or years without complicating psychotic features bears any relationship to schizophrenic illness.

When depersonalization does occur during the evolution of unquestionable schizophrenic psychosis it is fleeting in character, the clinical events march swiftly and delusional and hallucinatory experiences are never very far off. Moreover, even prior to the stage of actual delusion, careful examination reveals perplexity, affective incongruity and a tendency to make near-delusional misinterpretations of events in the patient's environment as well as of his subjective experiences. It is of interest, moreover, that in a recent phenomenological enquiry into schizophrenia and related illnesses (McClelland et al., 1968), depersonalization was found to be associated with the non-nuclear rather than the nuclear cases. The main constituents of the former were cases with cerebral lesions and schizophreniform illnesses following some severe stress in which a strong colouring of anxiety or depression were usual.

Depersonalization is often held to have affinities with obsessive-compulsive states but the relationship, if any, is a complex one requiring further elucidation. Unreality feelings are found in only a minority of true obsessive neuroses and are rarely more than a transient experience that comes on at the peak of bouts of intense rumination or ritualistic behaviour. They may occur in any kind of personality setting although the long-sustained depersonalization syndromes of near-adolescence appear to develop mainly in individuals with conspicuous obsessional personality traits. In hysterical subjects depersonalization presents in a particularly florid and differentiated manner and the experiences described are of great psychopathological interest. However, the term 'hysterical depersonalization syndrome' is a misnomer in that it confuses a description of personality with the diagnosis of a syndrome or illness. These patients are usually subjects with prominent hysterical personality traits who have developed an anxiety neurosis (often with marked phobic features) following a severe and clearly defined stress.

Depersonalization occurs in only a small minority (10 to 12 per cent.) of the patients with depressive illness and is generally confined to the complaint of blunting or deadness of feeling which is the least specific part of the depersonalization syndrome. When depersonalization is prominent and presents in its complete form, the diagnosis of depression requires careful reconsideration. Attention has already been drawn to the evidence (p. 94) that it is with the affect of anxiety and not with depression that depersonalization is most closely associated.

Relatively little is known about depersonalization as it occurs in the course of *everyday experience* or in situations not easily accessible to clinical observers. The menacing and intolerable circumstances in which those arriving in Nazi concentration camps found themselves evoked feelings of depersonalization in the majority of inmates and these persisted for some weeks after their arrival (Kral, 1951). Similar experiences have been reported by survivors of shipwreck, those rescued from drowning or those who have narrowly escaped death in other circumstances. The following account of an experience in a situation of danger given to us by a psychiatrist exemplifies in a particularly clear manner *the relationship between fear, anxiety and depersonalization*. The man in question was driving at some speed on a wet road surface and as he cornered fast the car skidded. He immediately experienced a dream-like detachment and found himself steering mechanically and aware of his actions as if he were contemplating some unfortunate victim from a distance. After spinning round several times and narrowly avoiding oncoming traffic the car finally came to a halt facing in the opposite direction. The driver felt quite calm but when bystanders spoke to him their voices seemed muffled and the surrounding countryside appeared still, remote and unreal. His own voice sounded unfamiliar. He drove on feeling quite calm, arrived at his clinic and rang for his first patient. As the patient entered the psychiatrist's depersonalization suddenly lifted and he became aware that he was perspiring and trembling severely and his heart was pounding at a rapid rate.

Transient unreality feelings are also experienced quite often by the bereaved and by persons given to rumination about abstract problems of life and death. Only a small number of such subjects develop an actual illness which brings them under psychiatric observation. In all these situations there is a strong undercurrent of anxiety and this is also true of the depersonalization that develops in association with the perceptual distortions, hallucinations and heightened arousal promoted by hallucinogenic drugs.

Some transient experiences of depersonalization in normal subjects begin in states of fatigue or during a period of relaxation after intense emotional experience (Roberts, 1960; Sedman, 1966). Little is known about the psychopathology of this phenomenon.

There have been numerous attempts at a unifying explanation of depersonalization phenomena. Among the views expressed by psychoanalysts have been a flight from the fear of psychic castration, erotization of thinking with a consequent clash of homosexual and heterosexual tendencies and a narcissistic self-scrutiny that seeks to compensate for deficient affection and admiration in childhood. None of those views is very fruitful for clinical understanding or investigation. The view that depersonalization is an abortive form of schizophrenia (Galdston, 1947; Nolan Lewis, 1949) implies that a wide range of neurotic disturbances have affinities with schizophrenia and is also unacceptable because this psychosis so rarely develops in depersonalized patients. Ackner's view (1954) that depersonalization reflects 'relative failure of integration of experience into the total organization of psychic functioning' is difficult to follow in view of the rarity of this complication in most forms of psychiatric disorder. Many workers have referred in some perplexity to the widely different psychiatric disorders in which depersonalization occurs (Oberndorf, 1950). However, recent observations indicate that illnesses are not equal in this respect; depersonalization is common in some, very rare in others. The view that depersonalization is a specific form of constriction of consciousness (or 'arousal') that is closely related to anxiety and has the effect of attenuating its influence upon behaviour has a little in common with the view of Oberndorf (1950) that it is a defence against anxiety arising from threats to the ego (from the id or super-ego) and also with Mayer-Gross's concept (1935) of a 'preformed functional response of the brain'. According to this view the factor held in common by most of the clinical settings of depersonalization is severe anxiety. It would therefore be expected to be commonest in disorders in which anxiety frequently mounted to the level of panic. If a close functional relationship between anxiety and depersonalization exists, it would be reasonable to expect that there would be a correspondingly close relationship between them in a neurological sense. Anxiety is in fact prominent in depersonalization associated with organic disease, as in temporal lobe epilepsy, as well as with the functional variants and it seems likely that the two types of phenomenon utilize a common final pathway. These recent hypotheses about depersonalization have some heuristic value and are open to further critical evaluation.

The treatment of depersonalization syndromes is that of the underlying psychiatric disorder and has therefore been mainly dealt with in the section on anxiety neuroses. In the rare cases of 'primary depersonalization syndrome' treatment is difficult. Davison's (1964) demonstration that temporary relief could be conferred by intravenous injections of Methedrine and that this was accompanied by a slight increase in frequency of the alpha rhythm in the E.E.G., is of considerable interest. It does not, however, provide, for the present, a practicable form of therapy and carries a risk of addiction. In cases with prominent anxiety a course of thiopentone injections may prove beneficial (see p. 94).

Anorexia Nervosa

This is a condition almost confined to women in the years of adolescence and early adult life, although it also occurs rarely in young men; it may occur as early as fourteen and is seldom seen after the age of thirty. In its most typical form it begins as an *attempt at dieting* for the sake of slimness by a healthy well-nourished girl, and in its earliest stages would probably be fairly easily reversed. The psychiatrist does not see the patient until she has lost some fifteen kilograms, and by her refusal to take any more than a few bites of food a day is causing her relatives the greatest anxiety. Both mental and physical changes are then in the foreground, and prolonged treatment will be called for before recovery.

The *constitutional factors* in aetiology are important. The patient will have shown signs in earlier years of hysterical tendencies, often also of obsessional traits, and there may be a family history of psychopathy or neurosis. There are, however, constitutional factors of a physical type, which have remained latent until the anorexia is well advanced, but then disclose themselves. These are shown in a pattern of somatic reaction which is almost unique, and which may one day be found to have some physiological basis. Organic hypothalamic lesions will, in rare instances, produce severe anorexia (White and Hain, 1959) while injury to the ventro-medial nuclei tends to produce over-eating and obesity. It is possible, therefore, that anorexia nervosa arises from a functional disturbance of the balance of activity of the two main centres concerned with the control of appetite.

Psychogenic factors also play an important part. The dynamic situation within the family is nearly always found to be out of the ordinary, most typically with an over-protective dominant and obsessionally rigid mother, who is being driven into extremes of anxiety by her daughter's behaviour. Minor psychological abnormalities are relatively common round about puberty; some patients being conspicuously tomboyish, others showing prudishness or disgust with matters relating to sex including the development of their secondary sexual characteristics. A proportion of the patients are obese in the pre-anorexic period and many have a strong interest in food. A history of feeding difficulties in childhood is relatively common (Kay and Leigh, 1954). The illness nearly always arises out of some *conflict situation*, e.g. an engagement to marry which the patient secretly does not feel willing to carry out, impaired relations with the parents, a disappointment over a job, or some similar situation which it will often need painstaking investigation to disclose. These patients put up considerable resistance to psychotherapeutic exploration and, by diverting the physician's attention onto their prominent physical symptoms, for a long while successfully prevent it.

Physically the patient is invariably thin and sometimes has lost so much weight that the skin seems to be lying loosely over bones only just beneath the surface. Loss of weight down to five stone or even less is common. The skin itself is dry and papery, without normal suppleness and elasticity, and it may show a prominent growth of downy hair on the extremities and trunk. The basal metabolic rate is greatly reduced, blood pressure is low, and the circulation in the extremities is poor; hands and feet are cold and may be blue. There is amenorrhoea, which has usually lasted from very early in the illness, and is sometimes reported to have antedated the most obvious signs of loss of appetite. There is an obstinate constipation, probably attributable to the small intake of food and fluid.

The anorexia is profound. The patient has *no desire for food* of any kind, and most foods, especially the more nutritious, are regarded with repulsion. The strongest resistance is made to taking an adequate diet, even to taking food at all. The doctor will often obtain promises from the patient to take a sufficient meal; but, though she says she tries, she really makes no effort to eat. All her efforts are in the opposite direction. Much cunning will be shown in disposing of food by other ways than eating it. Hiding-places will be found where it can be concealed until it can be disposed of down the lavatory. Many patients can make themselves vomit at will, and so get rid of even such food as they have eaten. If anything is taken voluntarily, it will be something without nutritive value, such as sips of water and fruit or salads. Milk and fats are especially abhorrent.

Despite her physically reduced state, the patient nearly always shows a remarkable degree of *energy, alertness and initiative*. Up to the time of admission to hospital, she will frequently have been engaging in usual social activities, even dancing, swimming and playing tennis. In many cases she does not herself feel ill, and her anorexia is hardly so much a symptom to her as a guiding principle of her life; in others there are complaints of symptoms of a non-specifically neurotic kind.

The *differential diagnosis* is from the secondary anorexias. There is no depression, nor any symptom of a schizophrenic kind; and it is hardly possible to mistake the condition for a psychotic state. The exclusion of organic disease, such as carcinoma of the stomach, or tuberculosis, is also easy, as no signs will be found of these diseases, and the characteristic well-being combined with anorexia and amenorrhoea are rarely seen in organic disease. In hypopituitarism there is very rarely gross loss of weight nor anorexia, and the signs of endocrine dyscrasia are more prominent; there is nearly always atrophy of pubic and axillary hair, and often also of the breasts. Furthermore, the condition will have most frequently come on slowly in childhood, or abruptly after the puerperium. In the anorexias secondary to other psychiatric disorders the complete syndrome described above is rarely seen. A further feature is that onset of such secondary anorexias is usually long after or before puberty (King, 1963).

For effective *treatment* to be undertaken, it is essential that the patient be admitted to hospital and placed under the closest nursing supervision. It is much better if a nurse can personally assist at every meal and by persuasion and persistence see that an adequate amount of it is taken. The first meals will be the most difficult, and once the patient's routine refusal can be overcome the battle is half over. Failure with such simple measures is nearly always attributable to insufficient or insufficiently-skilled *nursing*. At the same time *psychological exploration* is called for, and when the facts have been elicited, an attempt must be made to get the patient to see her illness in a less peculiar light and to solve the problems which have caused breakdown. Adjuvant measures, the giving of a liquid diet which can more easily be measured and controlled, the giving of insulin, or of a course of modified insulin treatment, even at times tube-feeding, should not often be called for.

A considerable advance in treatment in recent years has been through the use of phenothiazines. Chlorpromazine in effective doses (300–1,000 mg. daily) produces a tranquil state in the patient, in which she will accept adequate nourishment. High calorie diets combined with strict nursing supervision (Russell and Mezey, 1962) can, however, yield rapid results without the marked lethargy high dosage phenothiazines cause in some patients. Sustaining long term improvement is the main problem.

Failing effective treatment, the *outcome* in anorexia nervosa is surrounded by dangers. Patients not infrequently die of inanition or intercurrent disease such as tuberculosis; and of those whose lives are saved but who have still resisted therapy, some pass into a chronic state in which a partial anorexia is maintained. In a recent follow-up study, Kay and Schapira (1965) found evidence to suggest that the prognosis for survival in this disorder may have improved in recent years. Thus, whereas there were 6 deaths among 38 cases followed up in 1954, only 1 of 27 recent cases died. Nevertheless, some degree of chronic disability remained, in many cases, years after discharge from hospital. A good initial response to treatment in hospital was a favourable sign, but relapse had occurred in some instances even after a satisfactory initial gain in weight. In 60 per cent. of patients some disturbance of appetite continued, while more than half either remained underweight or showed a marked fluctuation in weight. The menses were irregular or completely absent in nearly 60 per cent. of the female patients traced three or more years after admission. In some patients amenorrhoea appears to persist despite satisfactory gain in weight. However, normal menstruation with pregnancy and lactation was found to occur in some instances after many years of amenorrhoea suggesting that permanent endocrine damage is rare. Approximately a third of the patients had achieved a good recovery with a few residual symptoms, though sexual frigidity and difficulties in social adjustment were common. A further third were underweight and showed more or less severe neurotic symptoms; menses were irregular in a few cases. In just under a third of the cases the patients were markedly underweight, amenorrhoeic and still largely preoccupied with food and often with the functioning of the bowels. As some degree of chronic disability is so common and the disorder, even with modern treatment, occasionally proves fatal, leucotomy may have to be considered in a few of the most difficult and resistant cases. However, if effective treatment can be begun early, a satisfactory degree of improvement may be anticipated in a high proportion of cases.

Obsessional States

DEFINITION. The essential nature of the obsessional or compulsive symptom lies in its appearance as a mental content, an idea, image, affect, impulse or movement, with a *subjective sense of compulsion overriding an internal resistance*. This resistance from the healthy part of the personality, in which the symptom is recognized as strange or morbid, is the essential characteristic by which truly compulsive phenomena can be distinguished from other phenomena of a related or similar kind. If the personality as a whole identifies itself with the idea, e.g. the idea of contamination, we have to deal with a delusional idea rather than with a compulsive one. *Over-valued ideas fall* somewhat between these two forms of symptom; they are accepted without struggle by the patient, but not without intermittent doubts.

Compulsive symptoms tend to take on a *precisely determined form*, and to be *repetitive*, especially if they consist in a movement or have a motor component, as with a gesture. Thus there is a resemblance to other phenomena showing some but not all of these qualities. We may compare the compulsion with motor tics, which occur without the mediation of consciousness, but often arouse an internal sense of compulsion and futile resistance. It may also be compared with formalized repetitive experiences without this subjective reaction, such as mannerisms of various kinds, the 'doodling' of the absentminded man, and rituals. In the individual patient these phenomena, of a related but not strictly compulsive kind, may be combined with typical compulsive symptoms.

If we consider obsessional illnesses from a purely symptomatological point of view, we have to take into account the fact that *compulsive symptoms* can be found in normal people, in persons suffering from functional and organic psychoses and from neurotic reactions. When we consider matters from an aetiological viewpoint, we note that there is a group of *persons, commonly called obsessional,* showing a constitutional syndrome, a well-marked constellation of character traits, who tend to suffer from a variety of illnesses, in which compulsive symptoms are usually prominent. It is necessary to keep these two aspects distinct, and in the section below we shall confine our use of the word 'obsessional' to the constitutional syndrome in rather the same way as Kahn used the word 'anankastic', and our use of the word 'compulsive' to the symptom.

OCCURRENCE IN THE NORMAL. Phenomena of a kind related to the compulsive are frequently observed in children in pre-pubescent years. Much of the *play of children* takes on a formalized and repetitive quality. Children will walk along the street making a hop at every fourth step, or treading on the paving-stones and not on the cracks between, or tapping with a stick in a rhythmic way on the palings they pass. Coming to their own home, they may have a particular ritual for entering, by taking two steps up and one down in climbing the steps to the front door. These modes of behaviour become associated with fantasy and ideas of good and evil. The cracks between the paving-stones represent deep gulfs into the earth; to step on one of them would be to fall. To enter the home without the climbing ritual would somehow be bad or unlucky. The child may be perfectly prepared to admit that these ideas are nonsensical, but they still have some sort of validity. After a time the force of habit may assert itself, and the compulsion to continue in a set ritual may become so strong that it is imperative even against the strongly expressed demands of the parents and the wishes of the child to regain his liberty of action. This is a common mode of onset of the obsessional neuroses of children. As a rule these childish habits are outgrown, and have little significance in the later development of personality.

Very similar to the compulsive symptoms of the normal child are the *superstitions of the adult.* Some harmless and meaningless act, such as the spilling of salt at table, comes to take on in popular tradition a symbolic meaning for good or ill. The irrationality of the idea will be admitted, but a sense of discomfort accompanies an infraction of the requirements of the superstition (e.g. that a pinch of the spilt salt should be thrown over one's left shoulder), and the superstition-ridden will affirm that, really, it is better to be 'safe'. Such a superstition is genuinely compulsive in nature, but it has arisen from mental mechanisms common to all normal people, the association of a symbolic value and an affective tone to an idea or an act by a process of conditioning, and without rational justification.

Childish rituals and superstitious acts resemble in many ways the rituals of animistically religious *primitive peoples.* They also live in fear and try to govern their threatening world by strict rules, which will prevent chance events from disturbing the regularity of their narrowly ordered environment. Superstitions are relics of the magical beliefs of our ancestors, and under some circumstances civilized man will revert to the mental attitude on which they are based. Goldstein has shown that brain-injured patients with personality defects also have an extreme *'organic orderliness'* which borders on compulsive behaviour. This can be interpreted as a defensive mechanism, allowing them to master their restricted environment in spite of their defect.

Another symptom experienced at some time by most normal adults, which bears a close resemblance to the compulsive, or is perhaps genuinely compulsive in nature, is the simple *persistence of some content of the mind* when it has ceased to serve any adaptive purpose. One of the commonest forms this takes is the way a tune will run in the head, although the subject does his best to turn his mind to other things. Tunes or snatches of rhyme are particularly prone to have this effect, no doubt owing to their rhythmic quality. This quality is one that is met widely in compulsive symptoms. However, it need not always be present. Most brain-workers are familiar with nights when they have difficulty in getting off to sleep, owing to a compulsive turning over in their minds of recollections of the day past, or plans for the morrow; any event or prospect which has an affect of frustration, irritation or tension bound up with it is particularly likely to act as a focus for rumination.[1]

PHYSIOLOGICAL BASIS. It is worth bringing these three aspects of compulsive symptoms in the normal, i.e. the frequency of occurrence in children, their rhythmic or repetitive nature, their increased incidence in states of fatigue and hypnagogic states, into relation with *neurological findings*. Thus compulsive symptoms, often in association with oculogyric crises, occur in association with epidemic encephalitis, while Hillbom (1960) has described the occurrence of severe obsessive-compulsive neurosis in patients suffering from brain injuries with epilepsy following gunshot wounds of the head. Some workers have also described a higher incidence of E.E.G. abnormalities in severely obsessive patients but the anomalies reported are of a subtle and borderline kind and further evidence relating to this problem is needed. There is therefore evidence to suggest that, underlying the three aspects of compulsive symptoms described above, there is likely to be a unitary disturbance of cerebral function.

ASSOCIATIONS. Compulsive symptoms are occasionally seen in organic states, but probably with a greater than chance frequency only in the late stages of encephalitis lethargica. This disease has the capacity to release such symptoms even in those not predisposed. There can be no doubt that the relation is a causal one. In cases that have come under our observation the compulsive symptoms, which were of the form of ruminations ('Why am I?', 'Why are men men?'), occurred only during the actual occurrence of oculogyric crises. They have, however, also been observed in the post-encephalitic apart from the crises. It has been suggested that they are due to an *abnormal state of wakefulness*; the peculiar division of personality, one part initiating the compulsion, the other resisting it and trying to free itself, is facilitated by an uneven spread of wakefulness in the central nervous system, as one also sees in the hypnagogic state.

Better known than in the organic states, are the compulsive symptoms seen in the endogenous psychoses. In involutional melancholia they are frequent, but usually anchored in the basis of an obsessional personality. In *schizophrenia* compulsive symptoms arise not uncommonly without such a basis, apparently owing to the localized effect of the process on one aspect of mental function. It has often been debated whether these symptoms are related to the similar ones seen in true obsessional states, and it is generally suspected that their pathogenesis is different. The schizophrenic may feel himself compelled to carry out certain rituals under the influence of an extraneous power; in these cases the formal disorder of thought distinguishes itself from that seen in the similar obsessional symptom,

---

[1] Described in French psychiatry as '*mentisme*' (Dumont de Monteux, 1867). See G. Heuyer and A. Lamache (1929).

in that the subject has *no insight* into the irrationality of his act. The delusional nature of the phenomenon can usually be elicited. Again, the catatonic patient may engage in a series of mannerisms so complicated and formalized that it closely resembles an obsessional pattern; but he will often be able to report that it is carried through without any sense of internal resistance.

Much has been written about the theoretical possibility that delusional ideas in paranoid schizophrenia may be first present as compulsive ideas and later become delusions, through loss of insight and the *abandoning of resistance* to their overwhelming power. In fact, in the life-history of individual patients, this development happens very rarely if it happens at all. Stengel (1945) thinks that the desires and fears which the obsessional idea served to suppress and control may appear in the form of delusions. The compulsion itself is not projected, but something that was represented by the compulsion in a distorted and unrecognizable form (see also Chapter V, p. 283).

Compulsive symptoms are quite common in *manic-depressive psychoses*, especially in depressions. They are then often monosymptomatic. A depressed woman, for instance, may complain that she feels the impulse, whenever she sees the carving-knife, to pick it up and cut her infant's throat. The idea is inexpressibly horrible, and arouses acute feelings of anxiety. Patients with this sort of symptom often show the extraverted, cycloid type of personality usual in manic-depressive disorders, without notable obsessional traits. As the severity of the illness lessens, the compulsive symptom lessens too, and no permanent habit-pattern is set up. These symptoms bear a resemblance to feelings not uncommon in normal people, which are sometimes called 'contrast ideas', e.g. the impulse to shout a blasphemy in church, the feeling, when standing at the edge of a cliff, that against one's will one might throw oneself over.

From time to time one sees the rare cases of *recurrent endogenous obsessional neuroses*. These are people who, in time of health, show no noteworthy obsessional traits, but who have phases in which compulsive symptoms appear out of the blue and rapidly mount up to complete incapacitation. Any depression seen may appear to be entirely secondary, and the whole of the foreground of the picture may be filled by the compulsions. Nevertheless these illnesses remit and relapse in very much the same way as cyclothymic illnesses, may show just as much regularity of timing, and are probably to be included, from the aetiological point of view, in the manic-depressive disorders (see Chapter IV).

Compulsive symptoms are frequent in certain of the neurotic reactions, such as neurasthenic and anxiety states; rare in others, such as hysterical reactions. Causally, however, the relationship is to be seen the other way round. Persons of obsessional temperament are liable to certain neuroses, and comparatively immune to others; and when one of the favoured neurotic reactions occurs, it is likely to be coloured by patterns of behaviour which are *constitutionally determined*. An obsessional temperament is likely to suffer from an anxiety neurosis, in which compulsive symptoms may then appear; but there is no tendency for anxiety to release compulsive symptoms in those who are not so predisposed.

PREDISPOSITION. The role of genetical factors in predisposing to obsessional states was discussed on page 64. The suggestion is at the least a plausible one that the prevalence of obsessional personalities in the parents of obsessional patients is due to the fact that such parents cause their children to become obsessional by the way they bring them up. We must suppose that such forces play a part; but the fact that within a sibship one finds only

F

a minority of obsessional individuals, even when both parents are themselves obsessional, suggests that upbringing alone can hardly be the whole of the story. Compulsive symptoms are likely to flourish in persons of a particular sort of personality, and the more marked the personality deviation, the more likely is it that symptoms will occur. The qualities of this personality are in themselves normal, and are shown to some extent by the majority of healthy individuals, but in the obsessional neurotic they usually reach a rather extreme degree. These qualities are very distinctive and tend to be associated together, so that a recognizable *personality syndrome* is formed. There is a specificity about the obsessional personality which is lacking from the merely anxious or neurasthenic. An excellent description has been given by Pierre Janet (1908).

The outstanding features of this type of personality are its rigidity, inflexibility and lack of adaptability; its conscientiousness and love of order and discipline; and its persistence and endurance even in the face of obstacles. A high ethical value must indeed be set on many of the *character-traits of the obsessional*—his dependability and reliability, his punctuality, precision, scrupulousness in matters of morals, his capacity for self-effacement and even self-immolation on the altar of a principle. If we are to try to cover all the traits he shows with one term, one might say that the obsessional shows an unusual degree of mental 'inertia' (but not inertness), taking the word from physics for a metaphorical use. That is to say, he is difficult to move, but set moving in a given direction, persists in it and is difficult to stop or to deflect.

The rapid and easy but superficial adaptability of the hysteric is not for him; and in fact we find that persons of obsessional temperament very rarely show hysterical symptoms. Swift variations of mood and energy are also foreign, and the path of the obsessional, lacking brilliance, is dull but dogged. Minor obsessional traits add a *quality of worth and stability* to a personality, and proved valuable assets to men of outstanding achievement (e.g. Dr Johnson). If, however, they are present in marked degree, they are usually so hampering as to prevent any remarkable feat of originality. Such a man finds himself most at home in a world in which all is ordered, and little left to personal initiative. The obsessional, *par excellence*, is found in the ranks of the Civil Service, though, admittedly, usually in its lower ranks. He tends to find for himself a religion which is cut and dried, and is more frequently found, for instance, among Plymouth Brethren and Scottish Presbyterians than among Catholics, and in the Catholics more frequently among Jesuit priests than those governing themselves with a less rigid discipline. *Adherence to rules and regulations* provides an internal security which is otherwise difficult to attain; and this may show itself in a petty sabbatarianism. The love of order and discipline is extended to others; and obsessional people tend to be strict parents and domineering masters.

Coupled with this rigidity there is often an internal insecurity. *High standards* are set for personal performance, and much anxiety is felt if these standards cannot be maintained, or are maintained with difficulty. Many obsessionals have their first nervous breakdown when given added responsibility or authority; or when they are given work of an unfamiliar kind. A common manifestation of an obsessional state is as a 'promotion neurosis'. An obsessional librarian, for instance, who was called up into the Royal Air Force, proved brilliant in theory, passed all the examinations, was absolutely reliable in the upkeep of the machines, but broke down when he had to fly alone and to make quick decisions in a fight with the enemy.

Persons of obsessional disposition are more than normally liable to several distinct clinical syndromes. They are, first, liable to frank obsessional states, which will be more fully described in the clinical section below. They are also subject to *involutional depressive states*, and to clinically closely similar states which occur in earlier years. They are very liable to *anxiety neuroses*, usually with anxiety symptoms clustering about the focus of some compulsive idea such as a groundless fear of disease; and they are liable to vaguer neurotic conditions in which symptoms of neurasthenia or *hypochondriasis* predominate. The occurrence of *depersonalization* is often stated in literature to be associated with the obsessional personality (Shorvon, 1946). In fact depersonalization may occur in any kind of personality setting, but there is evidence to suggest that it has some correlation with hysterical traits (Roth *et al.*, 1965) and it usually forms one component of an anxiety neurosis. However, the 'intellectual obsessive' type of depersonalization probably identical with the 'primary depersonalization syndrome' of other writers (Skoog, 1965) is prone to occur in young men with pronounced obsessional traits in their pre-morbid personality. This condition may, with its ruminative, self-scrutinizing features prove disabling over a period of years. It has figured prominently in the literature of depersonalization (see p. 119).

PRECIPITATION. These less specific neurotic reactions which occur in obsessional personalities are subject to the general laws which seem to hold good for neurotic reactions; i.e. they occur under psychological and physiological stress of an exceptional kind, and once the stress is removed, they show a spontaneous tendency towards remission. The stresses are most usually of a kind to provoke anxiety, but may take a specific form, as the subject may be immune to some situations likely to produce anxiety in the average man, but liable to feel anxiety in situations which would cause most people little distress of mind. As has been said, these stresses may be of the kind to demand adaptation to a change of circumstances, a relaxation of established habits, an increase in responsibility, or a situation which puts a demand on flexibility of attitude or confident self-reliance.

True obsessional states are much less frequently traceable to environmental factors of these kinds, and are but rarely of rapid onset at a given point in time. For the most part they develop insidiously as the *result of a vicious circle*. The patient has, for instance, the compulsive thought that after touching any foreign object the hands are dirtied. This is countered by washing. After a single washing of the hands the thought recurs, and has to be countered by more washing. At every recurrence of the thought, there are symptoms of anxiety. As the number of washings increases, to the immediate anxiety associated with the compulsive thought is added the normal anxiety caused by the failure of the countermeasures to abate distress and that caused by being caught in a net of such irrational behaviour. Further measures are invented to deal with these aspects; a resolution is made that three washings on any single occasion must be enough. These defences too break down. The magic power of the number three may be insufficient, and three times three washings be called for; or a phobia of a miscount may arise; or a doubt that the towel on which the hands were wiped was itself unclean. Very gradually over the course of years, or in minor or major exacerbations and remissions, matters may go from bad to worse, so that at last all normal activity is hampered and frustrated, normal life can no longer be coped with, and admission to hospital has to be arranged.

The course of the illness is, therefore, largely determined by *endogenous factors* and their immediate repercussions. Nevertheless, one also sees patients in whom remissions and relapses are attributable to environmental circumstances. Mild obsessional symptoms may only become troublesome after, say, the death of a relative, with the feelings of guilt that insufficient care and affection had been shown, or with some other similar stress. The passing of the situation of stress may then not bring relief, because the new and graver pattern of behaviour has become ingrained.

CLINICAL FEATURES. By the time the patient comes for treatment, he is probably in middle life, but the *history* is elicited that he has suffered since early years from minor forms of the symptoms of which he now complains. Intelligence is, more often than not, better than average, and the patient is unlikely to be of the poorest economic class. His occupation will most likely be one to some extent attuned to the obsessional disposition, such as clerk, librarian or skilled craftsman, but is rarely of a kind to demand brisk executive action. The family history will show an incidence of obsessional personality, and perhaps of frank compulsive symptoms, far in excess of normal expectations. More often than not, one or other, or perhaps both, of the parents will have been of rigid and inflexible type, and the early environment one of strict puritanical discipline 'with much insistence on rectitude, obedience and cleanliness' (Kringlen, 1965). Neurotic symptoms have often been prominent in childhood and, in some instances, these symptoms have been compulsive in character from the beginning. There may be a history of actual nervous breakdown, an anxiety state, a mild depression or an obsessional state, earlier in life. Apart from this there may be a history of psychosomatic complaints, constipation, dyspepsia and even peptic ulcer.

The presenting symptoms may not be of a compulsive type, but rather those of depression, anxiety, asthenia, which are indeed seldom absent. Only on enquiry may their connexion with phobias, ruminations, compulsive rituals, etc., appear. The patient is probably of *asthenic physique*, with a narrow, lined, intense face, his whole manner speaking tension and even agitation. The central symptoms will be a selection from a wide range, of which only the most common forms can be mentioned. For the best clinical description yet written the reader should consult Janet's work of 1908.

Compulsive rituals are perhaps the most frequent, and of these, those of washing one of the most typical. The patient is compelled to wash, usually the hands only but sometimes as much as the whole body, after contacts of certain kinds, e.g. with strangers, or with objects that might have been in contact with strangers, or with a chair on which a fleck of dust has been seen, or after the performance of any excretory function, or after the occurrence to the mind of some compulsive thought, e.g. of a sexual kind. Clothes, and articles of furniture, or of the meal-table, may also be involved. The washings themselves will probably be governed by a ritual consisting in several formal stages, each of which has to be performed with meticulous accuracy. Similar to the washing rituals are those of arranging. Clothes when removed have to be carefully folded, put away in assigned places, and when resumed have to go on in a certain order. Books and papers, pictures and articles of furniture have to keep to a special position, generally of a geometrical regularity or symmetry; one patient flew into rages with his children if they moved the table or chairs in their living-room, another became acutely distressed in the doctor's consulting-room if the pens, pen-tray and ink-pot were not symmetrically disposed in relation to one another. Other rituals concern touching: before the spoon can be lifted it must be tapped four times on the table, before retiring for the night the light must be switched on and off three times. Yet others concern defences against phobic dangers: a round of the apartment has to be made to ensure all doors and windows are locked against intruders, or the fire has to be raked out to the last particle to ensure against fire in the night.

Where there are rituals there is usually also *folie de doute*, i.e. the doubt that the ritual has not been carried through according to prescription. *Folie de doute* may also exist apart from this, and takes the form of *endless recheckings*. The book-keeper has to check and recheck the addition of columns of figures, the clerk to reassure himself again and again that the letters for posting have gone into the right envelopes, the postman to sweep out with his fingers the floor of the post-box to make sure that no letter has been left, even reopening the locked box to do so. One of our patients had the need to assure himself that he had observed every slightest sensation and movement that occurred in the process of masturbation. No other fantasy accompanied this act than this necessity for the intensest observation. If, as was nearly always the case, he felt he had failed in this, he had to wait in the greatest anxiety until the next day when his sexual powers should have recuperated sufficiently for another attempt.

Then there are the *phobias*, usually associated with bizarre and imaginary dangers. One patient cannot see or handle any piece of string, however short or unsuitable for the purpose, because he might strangle himself with it. A girl is unable to travel in any public conveyance because she might look at the trousers of male travellers and see the shape of the concealed genitals. A young man was unable to tolerate company of any kind, even that of his work-mates, or to go into a restaurant or train, because his nose might go red; when friends arrived to share an evening meal, he went out into the garden and was found there stripped to the waist rubbing his nose with snow to prevent it from getting congested. Such phobias may take paradoxical forms. One of our patients feared that if he were required to lose a tooth he would be unable to stand the operation. This led him to dentist after dentist to put himself to the test, until he at last succeeded in getting his entire set of healthy teeth extracted. All these phobias have to be distinguished from simple anxiety symptoms which may show a superficial similarity, but differ by lacking a compulsive quality combined with insight and the subjective experience of an internal resistance. Thus the claustrophobic patient who is unable to travel in trains because of mounting somatic symptoms such as tachycardia and shortness of breath, more often than not shows no compulsive basis; the anxiety is spontaneous, not dependent on a primary compulsive idea, and is immediately felt in the somatic field. A further feature that differentiates the patient with an obsessional neurosis is that he generally suffers from a multitude of phobias and his preoccupations shift freely and frequently among the themes of disease, contamination, sex, violence, and death (see pp. 95–6, phobias in anxiety states).

Obsessional *ruminations* also occur, and seem, of all obsessional symptoms, those most frequently combined with *depersonalization and derealization*. They may develop out of the contrast ideas already mentioned as experienced occasionally by normal persons. When called on to get down to urgent business affairs the patient is hamstrung by a repetitive and endless turning over of thoughts of an irrelevant kind, which lead nowhere. If he is a religious man, he may be unable to concentrate his mind on his devotions, because of the intrusion of sexual thoughts and imagery. Sleep may be prevented by a compulsive enumeration of the doings of the day. Hypochondriacal preoccupations, and a compulsive pondering of somatic feelings and of bodily functions, are also common. These often develop in association with a compulsive self-scrutiny which is particularly prone to interfere with physiological activities such as breathing, swallowing and falling asleep, that demand a smooth coordination of voluntary and automatic, conscious and unconscious, functions (Skoog, 1965). Such disturbances are therefore specially frequent in patients who lose their sense of spontaneity and in whom self-scrutiny and unreality feelings then appear to aggravate one another in a vicious circle. Not infrequently rumination may take a pseudophilosophical form, as when the recurring thoughts are of the nature of questions such as 'Why did God make the world?', 'Who created God?', 'Why are there so many different forms of substance?'. But these questions may as easily be of an openly nonsensical type, which cannot imaginably have any answer. A common form of obsessional preoccupation is with *numbers*. As we have seen, number often enters into obsessional ritual. Some patients are compelled to note and record in their minds the licence numbers of cars passing in the street, or the numbers on bus and train tickets, and to perform arithmetical operations on them. Yet another common preoccupation is with the *idea of death*. The patient is oppressed by the sense of its inevitability, and by the resistless passage of time which brings it ever nearer. Every tick of the clock marks another step on the road. As a rule, it is neither the state of being dead, nor even the process of dying, which is contemplated with horror, but merely that for the individual personality it is the end of all. Many famous men have been affected in this way: Edgar Allan Poe, for one, was morbidly fascinated by death in all its aspects.

Disciples of Freud have rightly pointed out the *symbolic meaning* of many obsessional symptoms. Some of these meanings have some general validity and are exemplified in many patients. An important part of psychoanalytic doctrine is derived from the symbolizations studied in obsessional patients, and those symbols most regularly employed in applications of the theory have found their origin in compulsive symptoms. Other symbolizations are valid only for the individual patient, and their intimate relationship to his past history has in many reported cases been uncovered by psychoanalytic exploration.

Other, non-Freudian, psychiatrists and philosophers have paid great attention to obsessional symbolism. E. W. Straus and E. von Gebsattel, for instance, have analysed in the most detailed way the distorted world of the obsessional and his attitude to such concepts as time, space, death and existence. Straus (1948) makes *disgust* the central theme of the psychology of the obsessional.

DIFFERENTIAL DIAGNOSIS. Where compulsive symptoms are shown, the first step in diagnosis is to decide whether these arise on the basis of an obsessional personality, or whether they represent something new. In the latter case a primary cause is to be sought for, in a possible organic lesion, or, more likely, in the upsurge of a manic-depressive or schizophrenic psychosis. Where the symptoms can be demonstrated as mere *exacerbations of pre-existing personality traits*, diagnosis does not often give rise to much difficulty. It must be remembered, however, that obsessional personalities are peculiarly subject to involutional depression and to depersonalization symptoms; and in a particular case careful analysis may be required to estimate the relative importance to be attributed to symptoms of anxiety, depression, and at times depersonalization, as well as to the more obtrusive compulsive phenomena. Both prognosis and treatment will often depend on this analysis.

COURSE, PROGNOSIS AND OUTCOME. When one is concerned with a compulsive colouring to a melancholic or schizophrenic state, course, prognosis and treatment will be those of the more fundamental condition, and the compulsive symptoms in themselves will affect the outcome but little. Stengel (1945) has, however, published a number of cases in which compulsive symptoms appeared *in the course of a schizophrenic psychosis*, and found that the illness tended to run a benign course to a good remission. The change from obsessive neurosis to schizophrenic illness has been reported in a number of follow-up studies. Müller (1957) reported this change in 7 of 57 obsessionals, while Kringlen found that 6 out of 91 patients with an obsessional illness were suffering at follow-up from a psychosis or borderline psychosis. However, the symptomatology in these cases appears often to carry a strong stamp of the initial obsessional illness with the qualities of insight and resistance removed. They appear to have, therefore, some affinity with the many cases of indubitably obsessional illness in which insight fluctuates and in which a change (often reversible with the aid of physical treatments) from obsessions to delusions may be observed. The status of these cases deserves further study. Some such patients may suffer from 'obsessional psychoses' with a relatively benign prognosis rather than illnesses of a schizophrenic kind. The prognosis is that of the supervening state, when an involutional depression or a depersonalization syndrome arises in an obsessional personality. The obsessional is also liable to an *anxiety state* which appears without any notable increase in compulsive symptoms. This condition, as has been remarked above, usually occurs in response to some situation of stress; but it may persist when the situation has changed favourably. As a general rule the patient will then settle down very slowly into that degree of placidity which is normal to him; but the process may take a long time and involve a length of social incapacitation which may do permanent damage to his career. Contrary to what is usually said about obsessional disorders, these states are very susceptible to handling on a superficial level. *Psychotherapy*, of no very intensive kind, principally devoted to an explanation and evaluation of symptoms, reassurance, and education in methods of meeting them, has often a valuable therapeutic effect, provided the therapist's aim is not set too high. Social and environmental adjustments, especially if the situation of stress has not been abolished, may also be called for. Medical treatment of a sedative type will also aid in restitution. The prognosis, in fact, is good if effective treatment is adopted, though less favourable if nothing is done. In the latter case chronicity of an originally acute syndrome may supervene.

The outlook in the true obsessional state is less favourable. In this the compulsive symptoms occupy the centre of the picture, and the whole of the anxiety and depression are secondary to them. The history will probably be found to extend back for years before the time when the patient is first seen, and will show a gradual ingravescence, the progressive elaboration of rituals, an *increasing incapacity* to break away from abnormal patterns of behaviour and to maintain some social adjustment. These patients can be aided by sedative drugs for the countering of secondary anxiety, and are often suitable subjects for leucotomy. But social and environmental factors have rarely played an important part in causation, and so are not susceptible to therapeutic attack. The value of psychotherapy is almost solely in keeping up such useful activity as remains possible. Future expectations must be judged on the basis of the past. The outlook is not unfavourable if the symptoms have been mild, and especially if there has been some fluctuation in their gravity with periods of comparative health. But in those patients whose illness has run an undeviating course, the outlook is at best maintenance *in statu quo*, more usually imperceptible decline downhill.

From these chronic states must be distinguished the *cyclic obsessional conditions*, distinguished by rapid onset, in a personality of comparatively non-obsessional but rather cycloid type, and often by a history of earlier breakdown from which recovery after weeks or months was made. When patients of this relatively rare type are seen, a confident prognosis of spontaneous recovery may be made.

A study by Pollitt (1957) provides a warning against taking too gloomy a view of the prognosis in obsessional states, and suggests that an episodic course is more common than is generally supposed. In an investigation of 150 obsessional patients followed up for a mean period of three and a half years, 100 had had previous attacks which had cleared up before the onset of the present illness; and 21 out of 30 (non-leucotomized) patients followed for four or more years had become socially adapted. The outlook for recovery was, of course, much better in patients with a short duration of illness than in others. In a recent follow-up study of 91 patients with phobic and/or obsessional illness 13 to 20 years after admission, Kringlen (1965) found a less favourable outcome. In three-quarters of the cases the disability could be largely regarded as unchanged; this group included 27 patients who were slightly improved and six who were not. Only one quarter of the patients were described as much improved. There had been few remissions. An obsessive pre-morbid personality and a severely disturbed clinical picture at first admission to hospital were both of poor prognostic omen and so were marked nervousness in childhood and unmarried status.

TREATMENT. Treatment has already been touched on; and it will indeed often be found that much can be done along the lines suggested, i.e. superficial psychotherapy, environmental readjustment and perhaps some sedation, especially in obsessional states in which anxiety is prominent. With one exception, these measures should always be tried before more drastic treatments, until the patient's capacity for response, or his lack of it, has been evaluated. The exception arises when symptoms of depression are very marked. Depressive symptoms in the obsessional personality, even when superficially they appear to be reactive in nature, nearly always respond to treatment by *convulsive therapy*; and this should not be withheld unduly long. Convulsive therapy will also be found of value in other syndromes to which the obsessional personality is liable, such as states in which there is some depression, but whose hypochondriacal or neurasthenic aspects are more prominent.

In a proportion of typical obsessional patients, drugs of the imipramine group may help to abate the symptoms, sometimes to a marked degree, even where evidence of an underlying depressive illness is lacking. Some 15 to 20 per cent. of patients will be found to respond in this way. Full doses of imipramine or one of its analogues (200–250 mg.) will be needed initially and, after a period of 4–5 weeks, dosage can usually be reduced to a maintenance dose of 100–150 mg. daily. This may have to be continued for a period of months or years. In the presence of an exacerbation of symptoms the drug may have to be re-established in full doses for a period. A number of our patients have maintained a satisfactory adjustment on medication along these lines over a period of years.

Obsessional patients are rarely benefited by conventional psychoanalysis, as Sigmund Freud himself pointed out. However, as already indicated, psychotherapy along simple supportive and explanatory lines is found helpful by patients and regular interviews should form part of the management of the illness in every case. Evidence from a number of surveys suggests that a relatively short history of symptoms is of good prognostic omen. The significance of this finding is uncertain. But in the present state of knowledge it should be taken to imply that intensive treatment ought to be given at the earliest possible stage in the development of the illness. It is to be hoped that the growing knowledge and experience of psychiatric disorder among family doctors will decrease the proportion of cases that are now presenting for treatment after the illness has been established for 5 or 10 years or more.

When other methods of treatment have failed, the physician will have to consider *prefrontal leucotomy*. The modern very modified operation in which only the frontothalamic radiation in the inferomedial quadrant of the frontal lobe is interfered with, produces little adverse personality change (Sykes and Tredgold, 1964). In properly chosen patients, the benefits of this treatment are considerable. The symptoms of tension and anxiety can above all be expected to improve, and with them will go tendencies to painful and useless rumination. Compulsive rituals which have been built up over the course of years cannot be expected to lose their grip immediately. The patient will usually report that these modes of behaviour do not seem to have their old compelling power, but he may still persist in them to some extent. In very few of our patients have we seen these symptoms abolished immediately; they have, rather, diminished in the course of months after the operation, as careful re-education and discipline implanted new patterns of behaviour. This post-operative re-educative therapy is generally vital for success.

The judgement as to when to intervene with surgery presents many difficulties. On the one hand there is the possibility that, in course of time, the patient's symptoms will abate to a sufficient degree to enable him to achieve some social adjustment; as Kringlen points out, ageing in some cases appears to exert an effect much like leucotomy though less striking. On the other hand, psychiatrists have to take account of the fact that, on available evidence, the chances of a successful result following surgery are to some extent adversely affected by long duration of symptoms. As further observations are made, it may prove possible in course of time to resolve this dilemma with the aid of factual evidence. For the present there would appear to be a strong case for operating relatively early (i.e. within 5–7 years of commencement of symptoms) in patients whose symptoms are severe and disabling from the start, who fail to show improvement with all available therapies of a conservative nature, and in whom there were severe obsessional traits in the pre-morbid personality though not without compensatory assets and achievements. The operation should not be carried out in patients who are without substantial personality assets and who have never enjoyed a period of relatively stable and effective adjustment, nor is it justifiable in patients with brain damage or defective intelligence.

Irritability

OCCURRENCE IN THE NORMAL. In this account we are not concerned with the quality, sometimes called 'irritability', of excessive sensitivity to external stimuli, but with *tendencies to anger* in its milder or severer forms. Such emotions are commonplaces of everyday life and are familiar to all of us. They are a mode of response to psychological stimuli of a particular kind, such as those in which the individual is threatened in some way, or is frustrated in a purposive course of action. They may then have the effect of stimulating aggressive action against the threat, or of overriding the impediment to action. Some people 'work themselves up' into anger when faced by frustration, knowing that such a state of mind gives them an energy, fearlessness, aggressiveness or determination they would otherwise be incapable of. The capacity for such emotions is therefore an aid to successful adaptation. Very commonly, however, as they disturb equanimity, they lead to impulsive and ill-considered behaviour, which defeats its own ends. An important cause of irritation are distractions which interfere with orderly thinking, and are particularly felt when an effort is being made at mental concentration, or relaxation. Simple examples are the flashing on and off of lights when one is trying to sleep, or the banging of a door when one is trying to write a letter. Stimuli which recur in a variable and unpredictable way are particularly effective.

Irritation and anger involve a state of *tension*, and this mounts to a certain pitch before it results in a discharge. A *latent period* during which tension mounts, is always found in the normal, even in the baby who starts to cry after the withdrawal of the nipple or in the man who kicks the chair, over which he has just stumbled. In pathological mental states, however, we may see explosive aggressive action follow almost instantaneously on its causative stimulus, or occur out of a blue sky without any detectable precipitation at all.

PHYSIOLOGICAL BASIS. Cannon (1928) has emphasized the reflex character of the outburst of anger. All the bodily adjustments of an enraged animal are such as to render the organism more efficient in a struggle: the more rapid heart-beat, the redistribution of the blood, the increase of red corpuscles in the blood, the dilatation of the bronchioles, the liberation of sugar from the liver and the secretion of adrenalin. Some of the adjustments are the same as those in anxiety. They are all made through the *mediation of the autonomic system,* and effective stimuli can be of quite a simple physiological form, such as asphyxia or very vigorous muscular exercise. Cannon also showed that a phylogenetically ancient part of the brain near the thalamic region is indispensable for getting the full rage response in cats. Under cortical control this centre is damped down and the time during which it will maintain a discharge is abbreviated. Masserman (1943) was able to produce rage in cats by electrical stimulation of the hypothalamic region, this response being reduced by hypnotic drugs and greatly increased even by very small doses of metrazol or picrotoxin.

The experimental evidence that the centres in the neighbourhood of the thalamus which are responsible for the rage reaction are normally *inhibited by higher centres* accords well with psychiatric observations. Irritability is most likely to appear when the function of these higher centres is impaired in some way, by structural damage, by toxins, or by physiological changes such as hypoglycaemia. The tired man and the sleepy man are especially liable to irritability; and irritability is a common feature of the early stages of alcoholic intoxication. A slight degree of cerebral anoxaemia tends also in this direction, and people who live in high altitudes are said to be more irritable than where the air is less thin. Calcium metabolism or the parathyroid glands may also be involved, as subjects of·tetany sometimes suffer from irritability at the time of their attacks, and even between them.

Some further elucidation of the physiological basis of irritability has been brought by the *electroencephalograph.* The fully-conscious but resting brain shows an alpha rhythm which varies from individual to individual, but is commonly at from 8–12 cycles per second. Its source is in the occipital cortex. As sleep comes on, and in certain other states, a theta rhythm at a much slower rate becomes more and more prominent. It arises from a different part of the brain, probably from hypothalamic centres. The same phenomenon occurs when the physiological state is altered in other ways, e.g. by hypoglycaemia, hydraemia or alkalosis. If the electrical changes are of a sufficient degree, they are likely to be accompanied by minimal changes of consciousness or alterations of the mood state. Persons who are of irritable and aggressive disposition are more likely than the average to show a demonstrable theta rhythm even in the resting state, and are more susceptible than others to such physiological stresses.

Irritability accompanying fatigue and sleepiness has already been mentioned. Most normal people are more *irritable* than is their habit *in the mornings.* This may be because a slight degree of sleepiness persists for some time after waking, or because of a lowered blood-sugar. The taking of breakfast may by itself be enough to annul it. Irritability returns at the end of the day with associated feelings of fatigue; it tends to be more marked in brain workers than in those whose day is spent in physical exertion, perhaps because of the added influence of emotional stresses. Some people convert emotional tensions arising from worry or anxiety or any other cause into irritability. Many women, also, are more than usually irritable at one stage of the menstrual cycle, the particular stage being different in different individuals.

ASSOCIATIONS. Both organic lesions and functional upsets may cause an increase of irritability. *Brain trauma* is clinically a very common antecedent to a change of personality towards increased irritability. The irritability appears early after the injury, and tends very slowly to pass off in the course of time, although after a serious head injury the personality is permanently affected to some degree. Irritability has also been noted as an undesirable sequela of prefrontal leucotomy, but is by no means always observed.

The organic changes brought by *advancing age* are an important cause; but it may well be that the irritability of the elderly is as much determined by their emotional situation as by physical regressive changes, and is in the nature of a personality reaction. They frequently find themselves having to cope with loneliness, discontent, isolation, lack of appreciation and awareness of failing powers, while the personality which has to surmount these handicaps is becoming rigid and failing in adaptability. The 'catastrophic reaction', noted by Goldstein as a response to failure in a psychological test, may take the form of an outburst of irritation as easily as one of tears or a refusal to try further. Irritability is noted in all the organic psychoses, cerebral arteriosclerosis, general paresis and the presenile dementias. It is often prominent in Huntington's chorea and may lead to antisocial acts and the need for hospitalization.

Irritability is prominently associated with *epilepsy*, in which very violent outbursts of rage with or without gross disturbance of consciousness occur (see p. 467). A psycho-motor equivalent of a fit may show itself only in this form. Patients will be seen who are liable to periods of hours or days at a time in which irritability is greatly increased, and an outburst of rage is triggered off by comparatively trivial stimuli. Careful electroencephalographic study of these patients often proves illuminating, and there can be no doubt that some of them are masked epileptics. Even though the patient himself may never have had a fit, it will often be found that a near relative was epileptic.

Hill and Watterson (1942) have drawn attention to a group of psychopaths whose disorder they called '*dysrhythmic aggressive behaviour disorder*', owing to the frequency with which abnormalities of the electroencephalographic record could be demonstrated. Clinical experience confirms the existence of such a personality syndrome. The subjects are nearly always men in early adult life. There may be a family history of epilepsy or the patients themselves may have had convulsions in infancy or an isolated fit at puberty. In physical build they tend to be of the muscular athletic type, and physically energetic. Temperamentally they are emotionally unstable, and particularly liable to anger and aggression and to an impulsiveness of behaviour. Clinically they correspond with Schneider's '*explosive psychopaths*'. They frequently come in conflict with society, and may find themselves in prison for crimes of violence; they also attempt and carry out suicide. The dominant mood is variable, and periods of sulkiness or depression, as also of irritability, follow an irregularly phasic form. They tend to be heavy sleepers, and there may be a history of enuresis in childhood. Libido is generally strong and can be very excessive, and sexual activity may take an aggressive form. Though very difficult to control by social means, they often respond well to anti-epileptic drugs, or to amphetamine of which they tolerate large doses.

Among the other endogenous states, irritability is particularly associated with *manic-depressive syndromes* (Mayer-Gross, 1937). It is even more frequently shown in manic and hypomanic states than in depression, and in the latter may more often take the form of a querulous resentfulness than any tendency to outright anger. The depressive state, with its tendencies towards inhibition, is likely to damp the effects of the more positive manifestations of irritability. Irritability is not in any way characteristic of schizophrenia, although a cold surliness or sudden outbursts of aggression may imitate it.

Irritability is a prominent feature of certain neurotic reactions. It is the more likely to arise if sleep is being interfered with. It is a well-known aspect of the chronic *compensation neurosis*, and is no doubt then induced by the emotional situation. These patients lead a restless life of medical examinations, court sessions and investigations in hospital. Their mind is filled with ill-digested medical facts and the half-understood and apparently conflicting opinions of experts. Emotional frustration, increasing discontent after repeated disappointments and lack of useful occupation provide the necessary setting for irritability to become constant. Lewis (1935*b*) found that irritability was a common complaint among chronic neurotics with a long record of unemployment.

PREDISPOSITION. There seems to be no need to postulate an especial association between irritability and any other feature of the personality. Individual susceptibility to reactions of anger is probably a character trait like any other, and liable to the same amount of *quantitative variation*. Men seem to be on the whole more irritable than women, but this may be no more than a liability on their side to express irritation in an open and aggressive way. Irritability varies with age. The control of anger is least in infancy and gradually grows with increasing maturity until the involutional period sets in, when it lessens once more with regressive changes in the brain. Although the environment plays a prominent and important part in releasing anger, and in causing temporary phases of irritability, it is doubtful whether by itself it can do much in altering the predisposition otherwise than by a direct effect on the structure of the brain. A life which is in some mild degree unhealthy, such as life in the tropics for white men, may have such an effect; the peppery colonel, retired, of the Indian Army, was at one time a stock figure for the novelist. Irritability has also been reported by explorers living a life of great hardship in the Arctic and Antarctic. Early upbringing with excessive indulgence and a permitted display of temper without fear of rebuke, no doubt facilitates a behaviour pattern which resembles constitutional irritability. Such persons, however, are well able to maintain control when they know that it is important for them to do so. Emotional frustration, constant and continuing over many years, also predisposes to irritability. The Civil servant, who is kept in rigid control at his work, may give vent to daily irritations once he gets home in the evening.

PRECIPITATION, CLINICAL FEATURES. Much need not be said on the subject of precipitation. There is a good deal of individual variation, both in the normal and in the pathological subject, in the *susceptibility* to particular irritants. Some are particularly susceptible to slights to their vanity, others are intolerant of any thwarting of their desires. Among emotionally indifferent stimuli, *noise* seems to be particularly likely to produce irritation. This is so much so, that it has been made the guiding principle of various tests of neuroticism. Alcohol may serve to release irritable or violent and destructive behaviour in individuals of aggressive or psychopathic make-up.

The clinical features are interesting but insufficiently studied. There is a sense of tension which is likely to culminate by a trigger reaction in an explosion. If the discharge is on a grand scale, the affective state may be cleared up completely; but it is also possible for small, partially controlled outbursts to go on sputtering, as it were, keeping tension within bounds but not completely disposing of it. A *major discharge* lasts only a short time, rarely more than minutes, during which there is a considerable interference with normal consciousness and a great increase in automaticity of reactions. These are themselves motor, shown in words or deeds, and aggressive in quality. Consciousness is narrowed, so that certain objects only are attended to. Even severely painful stimuli may not be subjectively experienced at all. Apart from the *narrowing of the field of attention*, there is often also some degree of dazing. Actions may be bizarrely inappropriate to any rational consideration of the circumstances, and a few instants later be profoundly regretted. Subsequent to the attack there may be a feeling of euphoria, or one of lassitude and depression.

DIAGNOSIS, PROGNOSIS, TREATMENT. A complaint of irritability provokes enquiry along many lines, and little can be said about differential diagnosis other than that organic and epileptic causation should not be forgotten. The prognosis will entirely depend on what diagnosis is eventually made. Treatment will also primarily depend on this, but specific treatment for the symptom itself is often important. The symptom is relieved by drugs which have their main effect on consciousness, i.e. sedatives such as phenobarbitone and stimulants such as amphetamine. The second of these is more generally useful than the first, but individual susceptibility varies, and they can often be advantageously combined. If it is found that outbursts of irritation are occurring regularly in association with some form of physiological stress, e.g. when insufficient meals are taken over a part of the day, an appropriate regulation of personal habits will often secure improvement. Attention to sleep for the same reason will often prove beneficial. Equally, if it can be found that there is some psychological cause of frustration, an appropriate social or emotional readjustment may be possible.

Hypochondriasis

OCCURRENCE IN THE NORMAL. The normal individual, as he himself may discover by *introspection*, is subject at all times to somatic sensations slightly below the level required to claim the attention of consciousness—feelings of tingling, hotness or coldness in the limbs, even slight pains of a dull or sharp quality, feelings of fullness in the stomach, of distension in bladder or rectum, headaches or sensations of tightness or pressure on the head, etc. These sensations, as a rule, pass unheeded and do not form the subject of complaint.

The *constant stream of sensation* reaching the central nervous system forms the background from which special perceptions stand out and receive their location as if from a grid; this is probably the physiological basis of the body scheme or body image.

In hypochondriacal states these sensations secure conscious appreciation and are felt to be the cause of *discomfort or malaise*, and may even interfere with normal activity and so become the symptoms of illness. There is the usual amount of normal variation in the liability to hypochondriasis, and some people are much more susceptible than others. Nevertheless the tendency is sufficiently universal to provoke commercial exploitation by the manufacturers of laxatives, backache pills, patent medicines, and remedies which may be sold across the counter without a doctor's prescription. This *commercial exploitation* itself increases the diffusion of the tendency through the population, and has, for instance, been sufficient to produce what almost amounts to a national hypochondriacal neurosis centred on constipation. Dyspepsia, headaches and gynaecological complaints are also very frequent manifestations. Among the chronic attenders at any hospital out-patient department or in any doctor's surgery will be found a high proportion of people who have nothing worse the matter with them than hypochondriacal preoccupations.

PHYSIOLOGICAL BASIS. From the physiological point of view we may think of a hypochondriacal preoccupation with a particular organ or function as a *disturbance of the body
image*. The image is distorted, and that part which is the source of disagreeable images
occupies an increasing and disproportionate place in consciousness. There are resemblances
between a hypochondriacal dyspepsia, for instance, and a causalgia.

Developments in information theory (Wiener, 1961) may provide us with the means of
understanding how morbid sensory phenomena could be produced by a breakdown in the
systems of communication in the brain, even without any structural lesion. At the present
time work in this field appears to be largely speculative and concerned with simplified
models rather than with living organisms.

PREDISPOSITION AND PRECIPITATION. There is a constitutional basis for hypochondriasis;
it is associated with certain traits of personality, and one not infrequently finds families
with many hypochondriacal members, and all of the latter showing the same *personality
pattern*. Nevertheless environmental causes predominate. Among physical predisposing
factors is age. The elderly tend to become hypochondriacal, perhaps in part because of
their increasing self-centredness. Physical disease, which concentrates attention on one
part of the body, will lead to the appearance of imagined discomforts in that part. Concentration may be directed to the body generally. The hypochondriasis of athletes and
medical students is well known. For some individuals it may be enough to pick up a
medical book in a second-hand book store and to read in it for a little, for all sorts of
hypochondriacal anxieties to appear. A large popular literature, in both books and 'Health'
magazines, is devoted to the stimulation and the satisfaction of this appetite. Much of the
widespread mild hypochondriasis is *iatrogenic*; doctors, by satisfying a complaint with
medical remedies, aid its perpetuation. Any condition which causes intermittent pain or
discomfort, or remains undiagnosed for a long period, or is repeatedly subjected to medical
examination, does not permit the patient to forget its existence, and so leads to unjustified
preoccupation. This is probably a main reason why hypochondriasis is so often a prominent
aspect of compensation neurosis.

Every psychiatrist has met patients in whom hypochondriacal symptoms filled the
whole foreground of the picture, and in whom there was little else to observe. These
patients are probably in a minority and more commonly hypochondriasis is accompanied
by symptoms of other kinds. These are most usually of a depressive, anxious or hysterical
nature in that order of frequency. Nevertheless, when hypochondriacal symptoms loom
large in the clinical picture, the outcome tends to prove more unfavourable than in patients
with simple depressive and anxiety states (Kreitman *et al.*, 1965). There appears, moreover,
to be an inverse relationship between the prominence of hypochondriacal features and the
degree of emotional disturbance manifested by the patient.

In considering the phenomenology of hypochondriacal states there is an interesting and
important sex difference to be borne in mind. The majority of persistently hypochondriacal
men present initially with an anxiety neurosis in the setting of a more or less markedly
obsessional personality. In women, on the other hand, chronic hypochondriacal symptoms
are often associated with a relatively bland or complacent affect and the personality background reveals more hysterical traits although motives for escaping into illness may be
difficult to define. The clinical picture shows some overlap in the two sexes, but the difference between the syndromes is unlikely to be a purely pathoplastic one, since the mode
of onset and course of the disorders also differ in important respects. Thus a high proportion

of male cases present in middle age. There is commonly a history of marked but not disabling health consciousness and athleticism and some cases will be found to have devoted many years' effort to the cultivation of bodily prowess (Little, 1966). The precipitating stress frequently creates or is imagined to present a threat to physical well-being and the hypochondriacal complaints are initially manifest in a setting of severe anxiety. The symptoms are frequently focused on the heart, but may be concerned with abdominal or genital discomfort, muscular pain and weakness, strange feelings in the head or in the spine for which erroneous or bizarre explanations are advanced. These anxiety symptoms are somatic in nature, and when they occur have an adequate physiological causation. But by the frequency of their recurrence they promote a sense of *uneasy awareness of bodily function* and an anticipation that, at any moment, things are likely to go wrong. So it is that a patient with 'effort syndrome' may be always conscious of the action of his heart, may abandon a physical task at the slightest feeling of discomfort, and conclude that his inadequate performance is attributable to organic disease.

The obsessional drive of many of these patients has come to be directed in a perfectionistic way towards the achievement of bodily fitness. Their tendency to rumination and incapacity to throw off dominating ideas forms favourable ground for the development of hypochondriasis. Owing to the inflexibility of their mental processes these patients are not easily relieved by assurances that there is nothing organically wrong. Such assurances are countered by doubts which are themselves often of a compulsive character. Exaggerated concern with bodily fitness can frequently be explained to some extent historically. But in most respects these patients may be effective personalities and, until their special Achilles' heel has been defined by careful enquiry, their illness may be difficult to understand. Yet the hypochondriacal tendencies of athletes have become well known. It has been said that on the long marches across Europe prisoners of war in German hands were forced to undertake, some physical-training instructors were brought at an unexpectedly early stage to the point of exhaustion or collapse. Ardent devotion to athletic pursuits continued well beyond youth may be an over-compensation for real or imagined physical inferiorities; hence the disproportionate effect of stresses that threaten physical integrity.

In the hysterical type of hypochondriasis the patient is frequently female and the disorder usually fulfils a role for which some emotional justification can be discovered although rarely does it provide a wholly satisfactory explanation for the illness. The symptoms are very often those which arose originally from a directly pathological cause, but have been perpetuated by a mental dissociation which has its justification in the advantages attained by remaining unwell. The symptoms represent the *figment of an illness* with which the patient has already been made familiar. Monosymptomatic hypochondriases are usually of this kind, and, from the ease with which they may be maintained, despite evidence of the unreality of any organic basis, may be exceedingly difficult to treat. Alternatively, hysterical hypochondriases may be picked up by a process of imitation, from association with other patients with adequate physical grounds for the symptoms of which they complain. The psychological character of the disability is often overlooked and many patients have undergone a succession of laparotomies, gynaecological and orthopaedic operations before their referral for psychiatric advice. Many of these patients seek to secure vicariously through illness and invalidism, the sympathy, affection and concern of which they feel deprived in their personal relationships. The deprivation arises in part from their own emotional shallowness and excessive demands. A proportion of these patients advance elaborate and bizarre physiological explanations for their symptoms to which they adhere with a near-delusional tenacity. They may come for consultation armed with specimens of pus, blood or some mysterious fluid which they claim had discharged from one or other orifice. Some authors are inclined to regard these patients as schizophrenics but the evidence for this is unconvincing. The clinical picture may remain unaltered over many years and the personality shows no sign of deterioration.

In depressive reactions attention is likely to become fixed on bodily disturbances, largely because these disturbances are actually occurring. There is a *real lowering of physiological performance*, which is appreciated as such, and becomes the centre of attention because it provides the fuel for gloomy rumination. However, the diagnosis of depressive disorder in the presence of prominent hypochondriacal symptoms should always be tentative until there has been an opportunity for observing the course of the illness over a period. It should be regarded as proven only in those cases in which both the hypochondriacal and the depressive symptoms are eliminated or markedly improved by anti-depressive remedies.

OCCURRENCE IN PSYCHOTIC STATES. In the organic psychoses, the opposite of hypochondriasis is likely to occur. Owing to defective insight, the patient is likely to make light of his difficulties, real though they may be. Nevertheless hypochondriasis is also seen, particularly in those with a constitutional tendency in that direction which has been exaggerated by the process. This occurs perhaps most frequently in early senile and arteriosclerotic states.

In manic-depressive psychoses hypochondriasis is not as a rule common, though it may be seen, and then more often in the depressive than in the manic state. A symptom of the 'vital depression' which has been emphasized by Kurt Schneider as an almost pathognomonic feature is the sense of a *physical localization of the 'depression'*, e.g. as a sense of pressure on or in the chest. In the involutional depressions hypochondriasis is frequently in the foreground, and may take an extreme and even a *delusional form*. The patients complain of constipation, and the complaint becomes exaggerated into the delusion that the bowels are entirely blocked—a belief that is not shaken by the daily passage of a stool. Dyspepsia and lack of appetite and a sense of fullness in the stomach after meals becomes the focus of beliefs that food is rotting in the stomach and is not digested. And so with other disordered appreciations of bodily functions.

These symptoms are very similar to corresponding ones in schizophrenia, in which hypochondriacal delusions, first appearing as paraesthesiae or complaints of physical discomfort, are very frequent. In *schizophrenia simplex* hypochondriasis may be the only positive symptom while the emotional flattening is not easily recognized and often overlooked. As the disease progresses the existence of a delusional or hallucinatory basis for the hypochondriasis may become more apparent. But in the early stages its nature is often obscure, and it may lead to repeated physical investigations without the discovery of any abnormal finding.

DIFFERENTIAL DIAGNOSIS, COURSE, OUTCOME AND TREATMENT. The prognosis and the treatment of hypochondriacal states depend on making an adequate *aetiological diagnosis*. This has very frequently to be by a process of exclusion. Physical investigation is generally necessary to exclude a local organic basis for the symptom complained of, although the terms in which the complaint is made will often indicate that the condition is more likely to be psychological than physical. Thereafter a full psychiatric case-history and examination will probably be needed, as the symptoms which will be critical diagnostically may be submerged by the dominant bodily preoccupations and not easy to elicit. By this means, the great majority of patients will be found to fall into the three main categories: the anxiety states, hysterical disorders and depressive illnesses, as already described. With certain reservations already made the prognostic and therapeutic implications are those of the principal illness of which the hypochondriasis forms a part. A small residuum will, however, be found in which no other really significant features can be discovered. These will be mainly patients with *constitutional hypochondriacal tendencies*, and very often with an otherwise *rigid and obsessional personality*. In this small group of patients, treatment is exceedingly difficult and often unrewarding. Very commonly they resist all efforts to modify their symptoms by environmental readjustment, psychotherapy, and such other measures as come for consideration in the individual case. There is some evidence to suggest that thoughtless or inept communications by doctors about the symptoms or illnesses of patients may help to initiate or reinforce hypochondriacal symptoms. In a study by Ruesch (1951) it was estimated that doctors had, in this way, contributed to the causation of hypochondriasis in 13 per cent. of cases. A prophylactic approach to the problem must, therefore, include better education of doctors about the nature and causes of hypochondriacal symptoms. Very commonly, also, patients' notions have been fixed by prolonged periods of physical investigation or unguarded statements about its interpretation, which have left a belief, never to be completely shaken, that even though no physical abnormality has yet been discovered, one day it will be. These patients drift from doctor to doctor, the addicts of every new method of treatment that becomes fashionable, the predestined victims of the quack.

It has to be borne in mind, however, that the drugs introduced in recent years for the treatment of psychiatric illness, particularly those of the antidepressive group, have not yet been given adequate trial in these difficult cases. Careful review of the history and clinical picture of the illness should always be undertaken and the associated affective symptoms which may have been more prominent at an earlier stage defined. A full course of treatment with antidepressive drugs should be given in all cases with some depressive symptoms, and this is well worth while even in patients when the hypochondriasis appears to be primary. In patients with features of anxiety and tension, attempts should be made to bring this under control with the aid of sedative and tranquillizing drugs; chlordiazepoxide (Librium) or Valium in doses of 10 mg. thrice daily may be found helpful. Where all such methods fail and symptoms of long duration appear to have become firmly ingrained, the only chance of producing recovery rests with one of the modern forms of prefrontal leucotomy. Success will often be incomplete in illnesses of long duration but patients' preoccupation with and distress over somatic symptoms will usually fade in the weeks or months following operation. Whether or not leucotomy can be considered, will depend on the psychiatrist's judgement of many other important aspects of the case, such as the underlying personality, the degree of disability, and the possibility of rehabilitation.

The Paranoid Reaction

OCCURRENCE IN THE NORMAL. Paranoid reactions are based on the mechanism of *projection* and this appears to be a universal mode of thinking. Primitive man was accustomed to think of natural forces as conscious entities, capable of feeling good or ill will towards him. The tendency to projection as between men, i.e. the belief that others are experiencing the same feelings as oneself, and the tendency to self-reference, i.e. the assumption that outside events are directed towards oneself in a meaningful way, have probably been an aid to human survival, inspiring a sensitivity to the environment which otherwise might not have been given.

Some paranoid reactions are almost universal, e.g. the idea, on entering a crowded restaurant, that all eyes are directed towards one; the idea, when a roomful of friends stop talking at one's entry, that they have been talking about oneself. Such ideas are evanescent, and insight into their probable unreality is either present from the beginning or returns after a few moments of doubt. They *carry no conviction* and do not lead to action. Their nature and content are easily explained by the situation in which they are experienced, and a knowledge of the state of mind of the subject; it may be that he is wearing a new suit; or he may be feeling secretly guilty because of some real offence; or he may simply be a shy and reticent recluse, who has lacked self-confidence all his life. It is only when the tendency to projection persists, becomes habitual and gains influence on the life and behaviour of the subject, that the reaction can be called morbid and made the object of medical attention.

The resemblance of the paranoid reaction to such normal 'beliefs' has always attracted psychiatric attention. In fact, there is no way of discriminating between the two in a purely descriptive way, except by emphasizing the *egocentric nature* of the paranoid reaction. Even this, however, may not always be obvious.

The distinctive features of the paranoid reaction are its *inner coherence and logic*, and its systematic development along paths every step of which can be understood from the viewpoint of normal psychology. Given the special situation—e.g. that of a prisoner who believes he has been wrongly judged, or a refugee in a strange country whose language he cannot understand—we can easily conceive how the mechanism of projection leads to the development of his ideas from stage to stage. However, one must be careful not to force *psychological interpretation*. If that is done one will overlook more alien symptoms such as the primary delusions which are specific to schizophrenia. Much of the age-old controversy on 'paranoia' has arisen from the difficulty of distinguishing between paranoid reactions and paranoid schizophrenia (see Chapter V, p. 288). To avoid confusion it is helpful to adhere to the rule that the paranoid reaction is a mental development which can be understood from a full knowledge of the situation and the personality of the patient, and that if features are present which cannot be so understood, the diagnosis is in doubt.

Little is known of the *physiological basis* of paranoid reactions. Chronic abuse of certain intoxicants, such as cocaine and alcohol, can cause habitual paranoid reactions; and excessive physical exhaustion, such as has been experienced by explorers in arctic regions, seems to have a similar effect. But the contribution of constitutional and psychological influences to these observations cannot be clearly distinguished from possible physiological factors. It does appear, however, that mild impairment of consciousness does tend to enhance the tendency to paranoid misinterpretations. The elderly person who, following some surgical procedure, exhibits paranoid symptoms in the setting of a clear or almost clear sensorium is not uncommon in clinical practice. The E.E.G. shows some abnormality in a proportion of such cases.

ASSOCIATIONS. Paranoid reactions are common wherever a personality, even a normal one, is affected by an *acute impairment of function*, as in the organic and symptomatic psychoses and in intoxications. The paranoid ideas which occur in these conditions can often be understood as the patient's attempts to interpret his hallucinations, or to find some cause in the environment to account for his incapacities. They are, however, not universal in these conditions and rarely form an essential part of the clinical picture.

Many paranoid symptoms in schizophrenia are of a similar kind; they are attempts to preserve order and system in a world shaken to its foundations by primary disturbances of thinking, emotions, volition and the self. But beyond this, the schizophrenic experiences primary delusions, sudden unmotivated convictions or apprehensions of meaning, apparently unconnected with the past or present situation, unexpected, bewildering, but nevertheless firmly believed and of decisive influence and great importance for the patient. *Primary delusions* may attach themselves to trivial events, but also to hallucinations and similar phenomena. When they are found, we are not dealing with a paranoid reaction, but with a schizophrenic illness. On the other hand, in the simple, hebephrenic and catatonic type of schizophrenia primary delusions may be absent and the reactive paranoid ideas, if they occur at all, can be of a transient and fleeting character.

Paranoid ideas in the affective disorders are again of a different nature because they arise directly *out of the prevalent affect*. In involutional melancholia ideas of self-reference and persecution express the feeling of unworthiness and of guilt: the patient, magnifying the sins and errors of the past and accounting himself a criminal, thinks he is despised; he interprets distant noises as the cries of his tortured children, punished for his misdeeds; he believes the world is coming to an end because of his intolerable crimes. Although paranoid symptoms in these cases are sometimes absurd and far-fetched, especially if they refer to bodily complaints, their origin can still be traced to the primary affective change (see Chapter IV, p. 209).

Paranoid symptoms in the *affective disorders* of younger patients are much less frequent, but follow the same pattern. In depressive phases they are easily derived from the feeling of inadequacy, unworthiness and hopelessness. Delusional ideas of a grandiose kind may occur in manic phases. Whereas ideas of reference usually have a persecutory tone, in the manic state they may take on an opposite quality, and the patient feels that other people are doing all they can to help him to a great position. Manic hyperactivity can also lead to the idea of hostility of the environment. The patient does not realize that he is ill, and understandably takes amiss the rebuffs and the restraint for which his disturbed conduct calls. *Paranoid fanaticism and litigiousness* also derive some of their drive and persistence from a hypomanic excess of energy. Patients of this kind have been found to be constitutionally hyperthymic, as well as being paranoid psychopaths.

Paranoid symptoms of a mild type are not infrequent in the neuroses where other symptoms take the foreground; they are distinctly commoner in association with hysterical symptoms than with anxiety, and they are shown also by irritable and aggressive psychopaths.

PREDISPOSITION. Genetical factors probably play a part in the predisposition to paranoid reactions. Even in symptomatic and organic psychoses and in alcoholism one can often find evidence that the prepsychotic personality was to some degree of a paranoid type; and a *tendency to touchiness and sensitivity* runs in families. As tendencies of this kind are so much a matter of quantitative variation, we must expect the genetical basis to be multifactorial. There is, on the other hand, some evidence that paranoid reactions and developments are not infrequently found among the blood relatives of schizophrenics. Over-sensitiveness, egocentricity and rigidity of attitude, the principal features predisposing to paranoid reactions, are found in certain *schizoid personalities*. A single genetical factor may be responsible in these cases.

There seems to be no general difference between *the sexes* in liability to paranoid reactions, although some observations suggest predilections of one sex for certain forms. Querulous and litigant psychopaths seem always to be men; this is at least true of the famous examples published in the literature. 'Involutional paranoia' as described by Kleist, in our view a form of late paranoid schizophrenia, is mainly an illness of middle-aged women.

It is well known that schizophrenia coming on in the later ages is particularly likely to take a paranoid form, but the same is true of all psychoses, including endogenous depression. Paranoid symptomatology is frequent in the organic dementias, senile and arteriosclerotic, which have a late age of onset. Apart from the psychoses, however, and in the undamaged personality, it is during adolescence that paranoid reactions are most likely to occur. Gaucherie and social uncertainty are, of course, the rule at this time of life; and the shyness, sensitivity and liability to think oneself belittled which afflict young people can be accounted for by their awareness of these handicaps.

It is a clinical commonplace that *chronic deafness* predisposes to the development of a paranoid attitude. The cause must lie in the sense deprivation, but it is noteworthy that the blind do not seem to be particularly liable to become paranoid even when, as is sometimes the case, they suffer from visual hallucinations. It may be that deafness has a so much more disturbing effect because it is a greater barrier between man and man; blindness chiefly intervenes between man and the inanimate world.

Deafness is not alone among physical disabilities as a predisposing cause. Any *physical defect* which puts the patient at a disadvantage aids the development of paranoid traits, especially such things as a disfiguring naevus, a hare-lip, a withered arm, or a limp which cannot be concealed.

Psychological factors sometimes play a role. The man who has risen in the world, but cannot rid himself of an uneducated accent, or who finds himself in the company of intellectual superiors, or in any unfamiliar social milieu, is liable to the increased sensitivity and tendency to self-reference which a *doubt of inferiority* may bring. Attempts have been made to implicate psychological predisposing factors in a more recondite way; and it has been suggested that early upbringing, infantile experiences and disturbances of emotional relationships within the family may lead to paranoid traits in the adult personality. Knowledge about the precise character of such influences is lacking but one would anticipate that anything fostering a sense of inferiority in the child might in later life contribute in some degree to a tendency to paranoid behaviour.

PRECIPITATION. While a paranoid personality usually develops by infinitesimal degrees over the course of years, often without any indication of environmental precipitation, the appearance of a florid paranoid syndrome is more often precipitated by some sudden stress. This may take the form of a *physical illness* of almost any kind. In the wards of a general hospital it is common to see acute but usually mild and short-lived paranoid reactions after comparatively mild disturbances, even for instance an aseptic operation on the knee-joint. Illnesses involving some degree of toxaemia or exhaustion are particularly liable to produce such a reaction. Where toxaemia is not important, it may be possible that depletion of vitamin reserves may be the operative factor.

Psychogenic precipitants are also important, and these are most often of the type that provides an *assault on the patient's self-esteem*. Promotion is delayed, or given to another; a marriage engagement is broken; a case at law fails; reproof or punishment is received in what seems an unjust way. But almost any difficulty may play this role. If there is little pre-disposition large noxae are required; if there is much, then circumstances can scarcely be conceived in which the patient does not find material for distrust.

The isolation in *prison* and especially in solitary confinement is a most fertile soil for paranoid reactions. Birnbaum (1908) has made a study of such cases. Some prisoners devel-oped fantastic delusions of being pardoned or acquitted and indemnified, which disappeared when they were allowed to mix with others or when the sentence had been concluded. Para-noid reactions in prisoners of war, isolated by language from their environment, have also been observed (Allers, 1920; Eitinger, 1960).

Much has been made in earlier literature of the '*key event*' ('*Schlüsselerlebnis*') from which a paranoid reaction makes its start: a small injustice from which a long sequence of lawsuits originated, a small sign of affection which is supposed to have kindled the delusional love. Such key events are no more than the spark in the powder barrel, and have obviously more literary than psychological interest.

While they are conceived in isolation, paranoid reactions show a particular tendency to spread by psychological contagion. In the narrow circle of the family this tendency may be the cause of *folie à deux*, as when a husband takes on and believes the delusions of his para-noid wife. In such circumstances one usually finds that one member of the pair or more of affected persons is suffering from an organic or endogenous illness, while the others are ill only in a social sense. These healthier members of the affected group distinguish themselves clinically by the more reasonable expression of their false beliefs and their greater accessi-bility to rational argument. The *spread by contagion* of delusional ideas may, however, take place on a much larger scale. In primitive communities whole villages have come to be dominated by, for instance, a belief that they were subject to the machinations of witches. Here the psychopathology of the paranoid reaction touches the problems of suggestion and mass psychology.

CLINICAL FEATURES. Acute paranoid reactions are most likely to arise in persons of emotion-ally labile disposition, sensitive and touchy, and with a contradictory pride and lack of self-confidence; they are often emotionally immature, and not infrequently are *adolescent or in early adult life*. The train is often laid by a habit or some circumstance which is associated with feelings of shame and which the patient would wish to keep concealed—such as the habit of masturbation or of some sexual perversion, an irregular love-affair, an illegitimate birth, secret drinking. The match is set by an actual or imagined discovery. At once the guilty secret is known; it is whispered on all sides; acquaintances look at him queerly, avoid him, conspire against him. The patient becomes filled with anxiety. His sensitiveness increases a hundredfold, and nothing occurs in his environment which is not attentively examined for its possible relation to his delusions. This secondary emotional reaction may at times take an extreme degree, so as to lead to severely depressed states, attempts at suicide, or even an emotionally determined disturbance of consciousness with confusion and hallucinatory phenomena, whose illusional basis can, however, still be seen. Provided this extreme disturbance does not occur, the patient retains his capacity for coherent thought and emotional *rapport* with those other parties who are not, for the moment, involved in his delusions. The physician, for instance, can usually reassure him to some extent, and will find him, unlike the schizophrenic, not entirely inaccessible to rational argument. The psychogenic nature of the syndrome is shown in its *modifiability by environmental changes*, and by the favourable prognosis. After some weeks or months the disturbance will often pass off and leave an intact personality behind; and this will occur all the earlier if the patient can be taken away from the environment which is involved in his ideas. However, a proportion of acute and sub-acute paranoid reactions continue for long periods and may become chronic.

The personality also remains intact in the *subacute paranoid development*, unless there is an underlying organic illness of progressive nature causing deterioration. The paranoia of the deaf, for instance, comes on, not in the earliest stages when hearing is still good, but only when it is so bad that much of what passes is still heard but not sufficiently clearly to be understood. This state is one in which illusions are particularly likely to occur. It may be compared with the special liability of both normal persons and the subjects of confusional psychoses to suffer from visual illusions in dim and uncertain lights. Just as the tendency disappears when light dims to absolute darkness, so the deaf and paranoid patient sometimes recovers from delusional symptoms when a total deafness supervenes. For a time the illness gets worse and then it improves again. At its height half-heard remarks are interpreted falsely, as referring to the patient and implying some criticism or threat. Fragmentary experiences may be built into a delusional system, usually of a coherent and quite plausible kind, such as that the family are finding the patient an incubus, and are plotting to have her sent away. There may be depression and irritability; but a normal affect is also shown at times, and intellectual powers and the main features of the personality are preserved unimpaired.

Chronic paranoid developments are infrequent and often too involved for a short description. Arising out of the effect of unfavourable circumstances on a predisposed personality, they are commonly slowly progressive. The paranoid reaction itself causes ill-advised or inappropriate behaviour, which brings further difficulties for the patient, and increases his paranoid tendencies. Nevertheless if the vicious circle can be broken, if the patient can be removed into an entirely different environment, recovery, or at least improvement, may still occur. We have seen an officer of a municipal service, who was intensely paranoid against his superior officer and the service as a whole after years of submission in a posting from which he could get no promotion, make a satisfactory recovery, when it proved possible to secure, not promotion, but transfer to a different and more favourable situation.

Many psychiatrists have thought that among the causes of a paranoid reaction was a conflict between a man's own opinion of himself and the esteem in which he was held by others. Intelligent schoolmasters, condemned to live among bucolic oafs who regarded their culture as so much ridiculous eccentricity, have suffered in this way; so have artists and writers whose reception by the critics and their colleagues has been consistently unfavourable and who have not found a public. Cranks and eccentrics trying to convert society to their peculiar beliefs may respond to the hostility they often arouse with paranoid ideas; but also serious pioneers and *reformers*, who find great difficulty in convincing others, may develop a paranoid attitude, which can be of service in providing them with the fanaticism and driving power to secure interest for their new ideas and eventual success.

An important part in paranoid developments is played by the *over-valued idea*. This may take on any quality from that of the loftiest altruism to a narrow egoism. With the fanatical reformer, it may appear as an abstract ideal of justice, perhaps for some limited section of the community with which the subject has identified himself. The paranoid *litigant*, who drags his case from court to court, and even turns on his legal advisers, may feel that he is fighting not for himself alone but for a wider principle. In either case the patient may secure a considerable following from his stubbornness and courage in the extremes of adversity, and from the apparent rationality of his claims and the fire with which they are presented. Other paranoid individuals take a less active line, and beyond boring their acquaintances with the tale of their wrongs, take no positive step to put things right.

These cases may show very little in the way of psychologically abnormal findings. Careful history-taking will usually serve to define some Achilles' heel in the personality that has been struck by recent stress or adversity. There may have been long-standing feelings of inferiority about some physical defect or deformity, illegitimacy or other disadvantage that has exerted a profound effect in the shaping of the personality. A severe physical illness or a decline in potency may serve in a previously jealous or insecure person, to initiate a syndrome of delusional jealousy. Though on superficial examination the psychiatric disorder may present as a 'kink' in development, more careful enquiry will often reveal the strands of continuity with long-standing oddities of personality. As far as the presenting clinical picture is concerned, there is likely to be a complete humourlessness, and a lack of all sense of proportion. The patient has but a *single scale of reference*, by which all the conduct of others is judged and misjudged. His preoccupations have but one restricted theme, which is the hub around which the whole of his life is made to turn. His attitude to others, and his approach to reality, are distorted by many misinterpretations, which are themselves logically interlocked. The affective state is normal, or would be normal if the facts were what the patient believed; and there is no formal thought disorder. Any inappropriateness of affect or disorder of thought would suggest, not a chronic paranoid reaction, but an underlying schizophrenic psychosis.

The paranoid syndromes that arise as the result of physical illness are dealt with under the Symptomatic Psychoses. At this place it is only worth noting that in very mild conditions of this kind the paranoid symptoms may be the *only sign of a disturbance of cerebral metabolism*. A patient who is being treated in hospital for some minor condition, particularly one which involves some surgical interference or other injury, or who has gone through an uncomplicated childbirth, or who is attending an out-patient clinic where bromides have been administered, begins to complain of paranoid symptoms. The neighbours, or the patients in nearby beds, are whispering about her; it is generally bruited about that she has had an illegitimate child, or has been treated for V.D.; people keep out of her way as much as possible. These symptoms slowly subside as physical recovery proceeds (or as measures are taken to secure the elimination of the bromide), but may last for some weeks after the bodily state has apparently returned to normal. Even at their height it may be impossible to demonstrate any disturbance of consciousness, of orientation, of memory or intellectual functions, although behaviour is likely to be upset by the emotional reactions to the paranoid ideas.

DIFFERENTIAL DIAGNOSIS. The differential diagnosis of paranoid reactions is a matter of crucial importance, and often one of great temporary difficulty. The possible aetiological factors require close investigation, and this will generally be first along the organic line. If an appropriate *organic cause* can be found, the case will need to be considered in that light, and further treatment and prognosis determined thereby. It is worth remembering that mental changes in old age sometimes take on the form of paranoid symptoms before the signs of deterioration make their appearance.

If no organic cause can be discovered, it will then be necessary to exclude the possibility of a paranoid psychosis, especially of the schizophrenic kind. This will be supported by the discovery of primary delusional experiences, of hallucinations, thought disorder, abnormality or flattening of the affective state, or a change in personality of a destructive kind. As will be described in the chapter on schizophrenia (p. 288), these symptoms are sometimes not easily elicited and if the observer prides himself in following the threads of psychological development backwards into the patient's past, he may easily be led by the nose and overlook primary schizophrenic symptoms. There is no paranoid idea so bizarre that it cannot be 'understood' by a strong effort of will, especially if recourse is had to the flexible concepts of psychoanalysis. It is a useful practical rule to remember that paranoid reactions and developments are rare, while paranoid schizophrenia is a rather common psychiatric illness.

Before the possibility of schizophrenia can be eliminated, the case will have to be considered as a whole from both the constitutional and the psychopathological sides. Evidence will be taken about the family history and family background, the nature and the development of the personality, and the psychogenic factors which have played their part in precipitation. And the issue will often be settled by a careful and unbiased examination of the mental state.

Whereas the differential diagnosis between a paranoid reaction and paranoid schizophrenia does not often present great difficulty, the situation is not quite so clear when it comes to differentiating between paranoid reactions and paranoid psychoses that are not unequivocally of a schizophrenic kind. In the light of the experience of the last 50 years the distinction within the paranoid disorders between personality 'developments' and 'processes' is less clear than it was when Jaspers first made it. To qualify as an example of personality development a paranoid reaction should be initiated by stresses and events adequate to explain the disorder of conduct that follows, the clinical picture should be 'comprehensible' in that it should show the patient to be responding to and elaborating experiences in a manner characteristic for him. Cases that fail to satisfy these criteria should fall naturally into the class of disease 'process' in that they should reflect the entry of entirely new psychological phenomena into the life history, in the absence of experiences or adversities sufficient to explain the onset of symptoms; the form and character of these should be incomprehensible. In the 'process' there is a kink in development at one particular point in the patient's life, whereas 'the development is merely one variant of normal psychological life which continues in a straight line, as it were'.

However, delusional states of jealousy whether arising understandably from stressful experiences or out of a clear sky tend to pursue a chronic and intractable course uninfluenced by environmental events. The symptomatology may be bizarre with an elaborate delusional system, falsification or fabrication of evidence against the spouse, pseudo-hallucinatory experiences and aggressive behaviour which may culminate in murder. Clear strands of continuity with pre-morbid personality are frequently present and the illness may, in this way, be partly understandable. However, the evolution of paranoid jealousy syndromes in individuals with lifelong tendencies to jealousy does not always follow a straight line; the commencement of the paranoid illness may prove difficult to explain even when all the circumstances are known. Not only are these 'psychoses' and 'reactions' not sharply distinct from each other but neither can be very clearly demarcated from those cases where alcoholism or other organic factors contribute in causation (Johanson, 1964). The paranoid disorders of subjects whose symptoms centre in delusions that some smell emanates from them or that their physical appearance draws adverse comment and requires surgical modification, may also start in a step-like and unaccountable manner. Clear starting points for such disorders may be found in the mode of onset and pre-morbid personality but to 'understand' them requires too much subjective interpolation.

Some workers regard all such disorders as schizophrenic. This is unsatisfactory for although many of these cases, as also morbid jealousy 'reactions', tend to pursue a chronic course, personality deterioration does not occur and the psychiatric disturbance remains well encapsulated. The failure of these disorders to respond to an appreciable degree to electroconvulsive treatment or phenothiazines also throws doubt upon their schizophrenic basis. Nor is it satisfactory to resuscitate the Kraepelinian concept of paranoia to accommodate such patients. Some starting point in personality can often be defined in some cases, while hallucinations occur in others. At the present time these problems of classification cannot be resolved with the aid of general directives or principles. Only systematic clinical enquiries into paranoid disorders along a broad front, aided by statistical techniques, would be likely to give us a classification which provides a sound basis for prediction of course and outcome of treatment. The subject of the differential diagnosis of paranoid disorders has also been discussed in Chapter V, page 293.

COURSE, PROGNOSIS AND OUTCOME. The prognosis is usually excellent in those cases where the syndrome has arisen almost entirely from psychological isolation or from psychological contagion with a closely associated primary source, as in *folie à deux*—that is if the isolation can be broken and the primary source removed. The outlook is also good in the acute paranoid reactions, as there is a natural tendency to recovery once the psychological forces which are causing an extreme sensitivity can be dealt with. In chronic paranoid developments, more often than not, all attempts to modify the situation fail, and the patient continues in his vicious circle of ill-advised aggressiveness, self-protection, misinterpretation, spread of the delusional ideas, and increased watchfulness. In those few patients for whom it is possible to make an effective break in this chain, the outlook is still dubious. We have, however, seen a case of litigiousness that persisted over years and impoverished a reputable tradesman and his family, coming to a sudden stop with the emigration of the whole family overseas. The one-time patient seemed to have left his past behind, and rebuilding his business from the scrap-heap, lived a contented life.

More often a change of environment does not cure the rigidity of attitude and stubbornness of opinion, nor remove the natural sensitivity and tendency to suspicion, the main components of the paranoid personality. Incorrect ideas of the past will often be maintained for years, though they now have a less direct effect on conduct; and the new life situation may be as productive of new difficulties as the old.

TREATMENT. As will have been gathered from the last paragraphs, treatment is often difficult. Psychotherapy of a superficial kind and attempts at *correcting environmental stresses* are called for, and will be of great aid in acute psychogenic paranoid reactions. Efforts of the same kind should be made also in the chronic states, but with due caution. A woman who is having difficulties with one set of neighbours owing to her paranoid tendencies, may not profit for more than a month or two by a removal to a new district, arranged, perhaps, at the cost of great financial sacrifice by her family. As a rule there is little of a radical kind that can be done in this way. A continued superficial psychotherapy, directed towards reassurance, the provision of sensible practical advice, and encouragement to keep manifestations of delusional ideas within social bounds, will often help the patient to maintain a social front for many years. In patients who show agitation or restlessness or who are distressed in other ways, a full course of phenothiazines should always be tried; some mitigation of symptoms is usual though the results are variable. In severely disturbed and agitated patients, those in whom an acute illness shows no signs of waning following a removal from the stressful environment and administration of tranquillizing drugs, a course of electroconvulsive treatment should be attempted. Where measures of this kind fail, and the chronically paranoid patient is becoming too difficult to manage outside or inside a hospital, the question of *prefrontal leucotomy* may be worth considering, especially as paranoid schizophrenics with a well-preserved personality have given favourable results with this treatment—after less drastic procedures had failed. Though the paranoid ideas may not be cured, the affect underlying them is diverted, and socially passable behaviour may be maintained.

The Unstable Drifter

Some abnormalities of temperament only become manifest as transient reactions, e.g. under stress; others appear as *permanent features of the personality*. Among the latter are those which represent a minus variation, i.e. a lack or deficiency; and one of the most common of them is a form of mental instability, covered by the German term '*Haltlosigkeit*' for which there is no equivalent English noun, which is shown in a drifting, irresponsible aimless life.

What such a person lacks is persistence and strength in will-power, mental concentration and interests. None of his affects has a lasting quality. One can say of him that *he lives in the present only*. His immediate wishes, affections or disgruntlements rule him completely, and he is indifferent about the future and never considers the past. This gives a shifting, kaleidoscopic quality to the personality, at the same time robbing it of solidity and depth.

Moods are superficial, interests those that exercise a shallow attraction. Lasting aims are replaced by whims and insubstantial ambitions; enthusiasms are quickly aroused, and as quickly dropped. The calls of duty and honour, because of their lack of immediate personal application, are hardly felt. Even considerations of the most selfish interest may be disregarded, if they are of a long-term nature and do not apply to the circumstances of the moment. It is not any lack of wit which brings the subjects of this deviation of personality into trouble. They have the intelligence to see that a present course of action will land them in disaster after a few months or weeks. But they cannot identify their present selves with the future to come; the machinery for forethought is available, but they seem unable to act according to their insight. Such insights as they do gain are superficial and never penetrate an inner core of complacency; and they are clever at concealing, both from themselves and others, this lack of real understanding by an exercise of verbal agility. From the cognitive point of view their most characteristic defect is the *inability to learn from experience* or to profit from their failures and disappointments.

As with other normal traits of personality, a pathological process can in special circumstances lead to much the same development. It seems likely that the *frontal lobes* and the thalamo-frontal radiation provide part of the mechanism by which, in the normal individual, affects are given persistence, and behaviour is directed along self-consistent lines. A change in personality towards instability is by no means infrequent after cerebral contusion, is sometimes seen in the earliest stages of organic psychoses, and may become a feature of the personality after prefrontal leucotomy. Chronic alcoholics and drug addicts quite often are unstable psychopaths; but this is more likely to be because the trait led to the addiction, than because the chronic intoxication has caused destructive changes in the brain which are responsible for a change of personality.

The habitual behaviour of the unstable drifter shows some similarity to a very mild hypomania. In fact, many drifters are sanguine and always optimistic about their future; they are pleasant company and likeable clubmen and political yes-men. Both the hypomanic and the psychopath show, in different ways, a quality of distractibility. But here all resemblance ends. Of all psychiatric syndromes, the *hysterical personality* provides the nearest analogy to the unstable psychopath. The two are often seen combined, and in the irresponsible psychopath there is an emotional immaturity very like that of the hysteric. Kraulis (1931) found a rather high proportion of unstable drifters among the relatives of hysterics; and this suggests a genetical relationship.

The traits of instability of purpose, lack of forethought, suggestibility, egoism and superficiality of affect, which contribute to the make-up of the unstable psychopath, are to some extent normal in childhood. Young persons are frequently brought to the psychiatrist because, through such traits, they have got into trouble; and a favourable prognosis may yet be given if the traits of personality are not too marked, or the circumstances which produced the misbehaviour are of an exceptional kind. Much will depend on whether the psychiatrist can feel that the patient himself has learnt a lesson. Even at this stage the true psychopath will distinguish himself by the glibness and insincerity of his protestations. Dispassionate enquiry, from which ethical expressions are excluded, will show that he blames himself not at all, and only hopes to be extracted from his difficulties in order to continue as before on much the same path. However superficial their affects, personalities of this type often show an apparent warmth; not infrequently they have qualities of charm; and they are always ready to accept help and to depend on others. These features often permit them to impose on their friends and relatives to an almost unbelievable extent. Mothers, in particular, will often go on protecting an errant son from the worst effects of his failures, even though the financial drain is severe and other relationships in the family are strained. In such cases it is often found that the *foolish indulgence of the mother* has contributed to the unfavourable character-development of her son.

Because of his lack of responsibility and steadiness the drifter is entirely *at the mercy of his environment*. He appears highly adaptable, kneadable like wax in the hands of the circle of persons surrounding him. He takes on the views and advice of his more or less benevolent friends. He is easily persuaded to give up a suitable post when tempted by vague and flattering promises, and to drift into debts and transient unemployment. After several changes of this kind his family may send him overseas where, after a promising start, once again he proves a failure and if not financially supported may finish up as a vagabond or in trouble with the law.

If born into circumstances where family support cannot be given for long or to any great extent, the unstable drifter is likely to find himself in adult life among the hangers-on of semi-illicit undertakings or among the ranks of the state-supported *chronically unemployed*. By taking on a general hypochondriasis he may even come to be regarded as disabled. However poor his circumstances, some help is usually not lacking. He is the perfect object of philanthropy, and sometimes finds a not unsatisfactory refuge in some philanthropically supported colony. There his story of conversion and reform may form the text for pamphlets and appeals. He is, in fact, the prototype and pattern for 'proofs' of every doctrine of extreme environmentalism, just as the callous emotionally cool psychopath is the prototype of the 'born criminal' of Lombroso.

The scrapes into which the unstable psychopath may be led are legion. An excellent clinical description of the life-histories of patients of this kind has been given by Cleckley (1941). Although the patient himself may show no sign of wickedness or ill-will towards society, he easily falls into the *company of criminals*. Left to himself, his criminal acts are likely to take such forms as obtaining money on false pretences, petty theft, the giving of valueless cheques, forgery and embezzlement. It is temperamentally impossible for him to save, or to maintain any secure financial position, or to keep steady employment. He squanders his money, or risks and loses it in gambling or wild speculations to which he is easily persuaded. *He never learns*, and his losses and failures teach him nothing. He is always on the brink of a disaster which, however much it worries his relatives, causes him no sleepless nights. Very often he brings further deterioration on himself by *alcoholism*.

The treatment of such a personality is almost hopeless, under the present ordering of society. Any treatment would demand time and presents difficulties—and the surmounting of difficulties and perseverance over any prolonged time are both beyond the powers of these patients. It sometimes happens that the psychopath who has been convicted of an offence is put on probation on the condition that he gives responsible relatives control over his affairs and puts himself in the hands of a psychiatrist. The prospects of psychotherapy are forlorn; and the best that can be obtained will be reached through *social control* and, perhaps, some *attempt at training*. The settlement of such personalities in colonies and hostels is successful only if psychopaths of a more active type are excluded and the moral atmosphere is kept favourable by well-chosen *leadership and supervision*. Under the Criminal Justice Act, psychopaths with such propensities have in recent years been referred by the courts for treatment in psychiatric hospitals but this has proved unsatisfactory. Psychiatric hospitals in general do not dispose of the very special facilities that are required to handle such patients, nor are they able to provide the planned retraining and the kind of constructive group activity which these patients require.

The prognosis is not entirely hopeless, at least in the youthful psychopath, as an emotional immaturity is often involved and the patient may with time grow out of the worst of his weaknesses.

Probably the most important function of the psychiatrist when dealing with these patients is to protect their relatives and friends from ruining themselves in hopeless attempts at reclamation. With most of these patients a time comes when the relatives will be best advised to hold their hands, to try no longer to hush up the scandal, and to allow the patient to go to prison, or otherwise suffer unsheltered the consequences of his deeds.

The Cold and the Emotionally Callous

In previous sections we have treated tendencies to anxiety, to depressive reactions, to irritability, etc., as dimensions of the personality along which normal variation may occur. It is justifiable to take the warmth or coldness of the personality, i.e. the *presence or absence of feelings of sympathy*, as another dimension. In this respect people vary between wide limits, and at one pole the extreme variants are likely to show abnormalities of behaviour which are of grave psychiatric import. In contrast to the anxious personalities, there are the phlegmatic; in contrast to the irritable, there are the placid; and in contrast to those who are liable to reactive depressions, there are those who maintain stability of mood under even severe strain. But the phlegmatic, the placid and the stable, even when they show these qualities in rather extreme form, are seldom likely to suffer thereby. So it is also in respect of warmth of sympathy. We all know persons of very warm and sympathetic temperament, who suffer acutely in the misfortunes of others, people to whom all and sundry run at the first sign of trouble, and who themselves become the victims of any trickster with a hard-luck story. But it is rarely indeed that this engaging trait of character leads to a need for psychiatric advice. It is those at the opposite pole, *the cold, the callous and the unfeeling*, who at times cause dangerous repercussions, and about whose state and disposal the psychiatrist is called to advise.

This deviation of personality development has been a focus of psychiatric and medico-legal interest and debate for many years. There seems to be no purpose in discussing at this point all the theories which have been raised to account for the clinical findings which have been made. These theories have already been outlined in the general section on the aetiology of psychopathy. There is no more evidence here, than in other types of psychopathy, for postulating either psychosis or organic structural change as a necessary basis for even an extreme deviation of personality. It is principally the *incomprehensibility*, the 'un-understandability', of some of the almost inhuman behaviour to which this deviation may lead which has provided an intuitive justification for the assumption of some form of pathology. As Schneider (p. 60) has pointed out, we can see all gradations from the compassionate to the cool personalities, and from the cool to the cold and callous; and in the majority of cases the aetiological basis is to be sought in normal variation. Nevertheless there are some cases in which a pathological process has played a part.

Organic psychoses, notably general paresis, can lead to a preferential reduction of the power to react to human situations in an emotionally adequate way, and may therefore cause a coldness and insensitivity which grossly impairs social adjustment. This is likely only in an early stage, and before long more widespread changes will be visible. Old age and senile changes in the brain can produce a similar effect. A more important cause is *schizophrenia*. In some cases the schizophrenic process may cause a destruction of some affective qualities of the personality, while leaving others almost unimpaired; and among emotionally callous psychopaths there are a small number who appear, after careful enquiry, to have had in earlier life a mild and usually clinically unclear mental illness, from which the unfavourable turn in character development can be traced. There is also probably an excess of persons of this type among the close *relatives of schizophrenics*, in which the genetical relationship is clear although the affected person never had any mental illness. Other types of pathological process, such as those accompanying epilepsy and encephalitis, though they may cause a character change which leads to antisocial acts, do not seem to bear any special relationship to the phenomenon we are describing. Furthermore, there is no reliable evidence that this quality of personality is to be accounted for as a kind of *mental deficiency*. The high-grade mental defective can be guilty of acts of unfeeling cruelty; but when he is, it will usually be found that he is not unfeeling in his personal relations generally, and that the act is explained by his simply having no clear understanding of what he was doing, e.g. that pain and bodily harm could result.

The social and legal importance of the emotionally callous psychopath is considerable. Although extreme variants are rare, yet in greater or lesser degree, this quality of personality contributes to the make-up of society's most ruthless, *dangerous and incorrigible criminals*. However, it must not be assumed that the emotionally callous are invariably criminal; psychiatric experience is biased, as it is only when these people are also criminal that they are likely to come under observation. There are many 'normal' men who, cold and unfeeling though they may be, are also cautious, conventional and socially correct, and never offend against the law. They are kept on permissible paths by prudence and considerations of expediency; and it is their subordinates, business associates, consorts and children who suffer, perhaps not through any act of spite, but through their incapacity for warmth and sympathy. Their *lack of capacity for human feeling*, and their lack of need for the affection, the friendship and the understanding of others, is like a blind spot in the personality. Whole aspects of life mean very little to them; but that which remains may yet provide an adequate and unexceptionable field for self-expression. Some of these abnormal personalities may through sternness, asceticism and sincere ideals, win respect and regard; and they have probably played a conspicuous part in the annals of religious persecution.

A relative incapacity for warm emotional responses is a character trait more likely to be found among men than women, although in the latter it is not unknown. The female constitution, naturally endowed with maternal feelings, which in any case tend to be stronger than their paternal equivalent, is better protected against such a development. The genetical constitution is probably one important cause, and the trait tends to be shown early in life. This is also helped by the *emotional immaturity of the child*, which forms a favourable background for its manifestation. Some children, who in later life turn out to be quite normal individuals, torture small animals rather out of an innocent curiosity than any spirit of genuine cruelty. Children, too, will persecute each other, or band together to make the life of an adult miserable, with a lack of comprehension of what they are doing which is reminiscent of the mental defective. These normal children, however, will not show any generalized lack of feeling.

The child who is to grow up into a callous psychopath will have a record of another kind also. He will have been found generally unresponsive, incapable of friendship, or even of a natural affection to his parents. For reasons, into which genetical and environmental causes may both enter, his parents have frequently shown some of the same traits too, so that *home life* has been lacking in warmth, and the child's chances of making satisfactory adjustments have been reduced. It is remarkable how emotional callousness or coolness in one or a few members of a household leads to an atmosphere of estrangement, bitterness and resentment which may spread over the life of all members of the family, destroying all warm human relations. The psychiatrist meets such families among the relations of schizophrenic patients. The atmosphere is presented with great realism in some of the novels and plays of Strindberg.

One of our patients was subjected in childhood to systematic mental torture by his father. The father would keep him at home till he was certain to be late for school, or prevent him from doing his home-work, or send him out on errands so that he might be in trouble for truanting, all in order that he should be punished by the schoolmaster. The father himself took a particular pleasure in beating the boy for things he knew he had not done, in extorting a confession, and then beating him again for lying. This lad grew up into an unstable and psychopathic man, but not of the emotionally callous type. It is by no means shown that coldness and cruelty towards the child tend to make him grow the same way; in our experience they are more likely to produce insecurity and anxiety tendencies.

Recent experience before and during the last war has demonstrated in the clearest way that it is possible to *train normal individuals into an emotional callousness* which permits them to carry out the cruellest acts. This is confirmed by such psychiatric evidence as is available about the personalities of guards in Nazi concentration camps, the personnel of the secret and political police, the officials entrusted with the mass extermination of Jews, and even the German medical men who under the Nazi political system undertook brutal and often meaningless experiments on living human subjects. Little has been written about the personalities of these individuals. But from the communications of psychiatrists who have examined them, it seems clear that they were originally men and women of a fairly average type, if somewhat egoistic and with a limited horizon, who were brought to do these acts by training and indoctrination, and permitted their original repugnance to be overcome by considerations of personal security and of their future careers (L. Alexander, 1948). What was true in such marked degree of some, has held also to a lesser extent with all of us. When human suffering is widespread and any personal effort to mitigate it seems unavailing, the sense of pity becomes fatigued, and it is possible that over a long time it may atrophy. Those, such as doctors and nurses, who spend their days surrounded by people in discomfort, pain and unhappiness, though they may retain their kindliness, become more and more impersonal in their attitude. If, as in wards for the incurable and in the asylums of the past, little can be done to give compassion effective expression, the personality suffers and tends to become increasingly calloused.

Such circumstances are, however, of an unusual kind; and in ordinary life, the cold and unfeeling are mostly those who are so by nature. They seldom seek psychiatric advice of their own volition. Friendless though he may be, the emotionally cold psychopath is protected against an unhappy loneliness by his own lack of feeling. He will find an adequate outlet in the pursuit of his career, or such relatively crude, impersonal or intellectual satisfactions as his temperament makes available. Though he may, in moments of sincerity, express himself as a cynic, yet out of enlightened self-interest he may play up to what is expected of him. The trait of coldness is *not necessarily combined with aggressiveness*, sadism or lust for power; but when it is, the danger to society at once becomes very great. The criminal acts of the callous and the calculating by no means always take the form of offences against the person; they may as easily be shady financial dealings. The criminal of this type, when he comes to be examined by the psychiatrist, has usually been betrayed by other and additional deficiencies of personality, particularly by any element of impulsiveness or lack of forethought.

The Sexually Perverse

It is the usual practice in psychiatric text-books to include sexual perversion either under the general heading of neurosis or, more commonly, of psychopathic personality. If from this it were assumed that every sexually perverse individual was either neurotic or psychopathic, one would fall into error. *What is regarded as a perversion* in one society in one part of the world, or at one epoch, may be not only acceptable but even normal behaviour in another society at another time or place. Even the word 'perversion' is open to objection; according to Freud and his followers, every infant is 'polymorphously perverse'. Kinsey remarks (1948): 'It is not possible to insist that any departure from the sexual mores, or any participation in socially taboo activities, always, or even usually, involves a neurosis or psychosis, for the case-histories abundantly demonstrate that most individuals who engage in taboo activities make satisfactory social adjustments.' This view agrees with psychiatric experience. If masturbation were counted among the perversions, and there is no good reason why it should not be, the great majority of normal people would have to be regarded as perverts at some time in their lives. It is not only true that most persons, who choose for preference a deviant sexual activity, are free from other important psychiatric symptoms and are no source of difficulty to society or themselves; but equally true that most people, whose sexual lives fairly closely fit accepted patterns, have minor predilections of a fetishistic or sado-masochistic kind or socially inhibited homosexual tendencies, which differ only in degree from an outspoken perversion.

This is not to deny that there are relationships of a causal kind between *sexual perversion and neurosis or psychopathy*. If the personality is in other ways abnormal, sexual behaviour is likely to be affected as well as other functions; the aggressive and the cruel, for instance, are likely to be sadistic in their love relationships. Furthermore, perverse ideas, bringing with them a consciousness of social and religious disapproval, may prove the starting-point of an anxious, depressive or obsessional neurotic state. Many people do, in fact, consult a psychiatrist with sexual difficulties as the presenting symptom. They may need medical help, either because their sexual abnormalities are part and parcel of other disturbances of a neurotic or psychopathic kind; or because they think, rightly or wrongly, that their sex behaviour is having a bad influence on their physical or mental well-being; or because their sexual habits are interfering with their social relations in family and community life.

A sexual activity is usually regarded as perverse if it has no immediate *connexion with reproduction*, and still more so if it tends to replace sexual activity which could lead to reproduction. For this reason, even coitus if conducted with contraceptive precautions would by some churchmen be regarded as a perversion. On the other hand, activities, such as kissing, which are a normal part of foreplay before sexual intercourse, are accepted even by the strictest as in themselves normal. If, however, the sexual urge is satisfied at such a half-way stage, as in the exhibitionists, the frotteurs, etc., and the intermediate activity becomes an end in itself, once more we may speak of a perversion. Inevitably, when we are forced to define and re-define in this way, an element of hair-splitting cannot be avoided.

The phenomena of sexual perversion are best understood if they are traced to their origin in the *physiological development of the reproductive instinct* in man. There is no doubt that Freud was right in pointing out that this instinct did not appear fully fledged after puberty, but had been developing during the long years of human childhood. In these earlier years it was physiologically incapable of expressing itself in the adult form, but was confined to partial activities and associated with different levels of behaviour, different regions and organs of sensation and expression. Many of these childish activities irresistibly remind one of corresponding aspects of adult sexuality, and are therefore found reprehensible by adults, suppressed, and made taboo.

The activities themselves are of many kinds, varying from emotions of personal affection and their expression, to such localized mechanisms as penile erection and the genital play of infants. They also include behaviour of a psychologically preparatory nature, imitations of grown-up activities, playing with dolls, playing 'mother and father', curiosity about the details of reproduction, etc. These modes of development do not as a rule progress step by step. Times of relative standstill alternate with others in which there is rapid progress in emotional life, and in a focusing of interest on the opposite sex, on persons with whom a sexual relation would be possible, and, among all organs, on the genitals. There is in fact a convergence towards adult sexuality. Much of this development follows the *principle of trial and error*, and there are great individual variations. It is difficult to say how much social customs, especially the peculiar taboos which surround sex in Western civilization, contribute to the great variation in prepubertal maturation. Perhaps it is only after puberty that these extrinsic factors play their main role. At puberty itself, there is a further process of integration, and a greater co-ordination between the higher and lower centres in the nervous system. Even then, however, in our Western culture, although physiologically and anatomically normal sexual function is possible, it is further delayed by psychological barriers and social sanctions.

The whole process can be interpreted as one of *progressive specialization*, whose final aim is the preservation of the species. If the sexual instinct is given the central place in human life, and sexual pleasure is regarded as the prime origin of all human values, as is the case for the psychoanalyst, then one will naturally be inclined to interpret the whole of childish development by the aid of the sexual principle. In this view, sucking, feeding, weaning, excretory functions, training, movement, emotional expression, aggression, submission, speech, curiosity, play, and indeed whatever happens in the child's life, are manifestations of the flux and the development of the libido. All the complicated and sometimes clumsy adaptive efforts made in the course of sexual development come to be held responsible, not only for maladjustment in childhood, but also for later neurotic and psychotic illness—although the same history of developmental difficulties and vagaries can be found in normal and well-adjusted people.

The extreme *sexualization of the child's life* is a singular weakness of Freud's teaching. It is combined with a remarkable 'adultomorphism', that is the application to childish behaviour of concepts and terms taken from the psychology of the sexually mature. Indifference and carelessness towards small animals, which children torture and destroy like lifeless objects, are called sadism; their experimental play with sensitive parts of their bodies is called narcissism; their pride and curiosity in their physique, exhibitionism. This misuse of words exemplifies the superficiality of psychoanalytic psychology. It would be wrong to overlook Freud's insight and courage, when he tore the veil which in the late Victorian age covered the quasi-sexual behaviour of the 'innocent' child. But he cloaked his theory, for the sake of simplicity, in an out-dated psychology; and he made no attempt to understand the child as a being living in its own world, conceiving it only as an adult reduced in size.

The studies of Havelock Ellis and of Freud have shown that sexual behaviour is capable of very *wide variation*, and of *easy deviation* from normal paths by psychological factors operating in early years. Sexual inclination has a generalized aspect which is retained to some extent throughout life, and never becomes completely focused on one sex or one person. It can indeed reach its goal, as in masturbation, without the co-operation of another individual of any kind. The variation in the time-curve of sexual and psychosexual maturation is equally great, and so are the quantitative differences in individual intensity of sex drive, which, according to Kinsey, are correlated with the time of maturation. It is in this biological variation, and in the variety of psychological experience in prepubertal and early adolescent life, and in the conditioning processes which these latter initiate, that we can seek for the causes of the sexual perversions.

IMPOTENCE AND FRIGIDITY. Although they are not strictly speaking perversions, impotence and frigidity may be discussed here. Many perversions, but especially homosexuality, may lead to impotence in attempts at normal sexual intercourse. Both impotence and frigidity are normal at a fairly advanced age; but in this respect there is an enormous range of individual variation. In Kinsey's material, a 50 per cent. incidence of impotence in the male was only reached after the age of seventy-five. Frigidity in women is commoner than impotence in men; and there is evidence that it comes on at an earlier age as a physiological change. Lifelong and complete impotence, that is incapacity for an erection, does exist, but is very rare, and is generally associated with some endocrine abnormality such as pituitary dwarfism.

G

By far the greater number of patients who complain of impotence are impotent only on occasion—even if those occasions are the most critical ones for them. Apart from absolute impotence, there are great *individual variations in the strength of the libido*, which are to some extent correlated with other features of the personality. Men of very weak libido tend to be of pyknic or asthenic rather than athletic build, and to have temperaments of an un-aggressive and anergic type. They appear also to be more subject than others to neurotic illness. In women, frigidity is associated with tendencies to hysterical manifestations.

Among the patients who complain of impotence, the majority are found to suffer from an anxiety syndrome. Successful coitus demands the co-operation of lower and higher regulatory centres, which are themselves under the influence of emotion. Excessive mental excitement, or an anticipatory anxiety, feelings of excessive respect, or disgust, for the partner, inhibitions due to prejudice or reticence, may lead to *failure at the first attempt* at coitus, followed by a vicious circle of further anxiety and further failure. If the physical urge is very strong, these psychological obstacles will at some time be overwhelmed; the vicious circle will then be interrupted, and normal sexual habits will be developed. If, however, it is very temperate, at least for the particular partner concerned, the barrier may grow, and become almost insurmountable. Fears of venereal disease, of pregnancy, or of impotence itself, perhaps attributed to past masturbatory habits, may play their part in preventing erection or causing premature ejaculation. Anticipatory anxiety is the usual cause of impotence or frigidity during the honeymoon, and in the male is likely to take the form of ejaculatio praecox. Many men are in any case subject to a quick orgasm; according to Kinsey, three-quarters of the average male population reach an orgasm within two minutes. No equivalent of ejaculatio praecox is known in the female, in whom the orgasm is almost always by male standards greatly delayed.

Ignorance and erroneous ideas about sexual matters play an important part in these disturbances; and therapy is often only a matter of enlightenment and instruction. It is best if treatment of this kind can be given to both partners. It is much easier if one can ensure the co-operation of the wife, and her readiness to accept failures in the hope of better things to come, when one is asked for help by a man whose anxieties have conditioned him into a faulty response. It is often the conscientious, slightly obsessional subject of high ethical standards who is afflicted in this way; and much tact and patience is required before the doctor can be fully informed, and be in a position to give acceptable counsel. Impotence and frigidity which are based on weak libido are much more difficult to treat.

Impotence and frigidity may be the early *signs of a serious mental illness*, such as general paresis or other organic psychoses. They are regularly found in morphinism and severe alcoholism, although in the latter impotence is sometimes associated with increased sexual appetite. In endogenous depressions libido and potency are reduced or abolished, and this may also occur in schizophrenia. In the schizophrenic youth, before it eventually subsides, sexual activity may for a short time be increased, even to the point of what are sometimes called satyriasis and nymphomania. Hypomanics and manics often have for a time an increased sexual drive, which may be a subject of complaint if it conflicts with their moral standards; in severer manic states, however, the libido is soon lost.

MASTURBATION. Masturbation is the typical example of an activity which, strictly, may be regarded as a perversion, and which is yet essentially a *preparatory practice* both before and after puberty. It is seen in many of the higher animals; and in man is a commonly used substitute for intercourse, especially in social strata where premarital intercourse is taboo.

As it is so easily performed, and an effort is needed to overcome the habit and to adapt to a partner, it may persist to a late age in sensitive, reticent, shy and weak-willed persons. Young men may have years of their lives made unhappy by a continuous struggle against something they consider morally sinful or physically harmful. Their concern over frequent defeats may lead to neurasthenic reactions with hypochondriacal fears; and it may delay maturation and prevent the development of an assured and self-reliant personality. Old women's tales of the damaging effect of masturbation on bodily and mental powers are still widespread, and are sometimes supported by a religious condemnation which stems from the Old Testament. In the predisposed person, such a conflict may lead to a transient paranoid reaction. Fears of these kinds may be redressed by giving the patient *a clear insight into the biological facts*; and such a process of re-education is an important part of the treatment of the neurotic reactions, which may, however, also need other measures.

In men, masturbation may persist after heterosexual intercourse has begun, and even during marriage, if the sexual drive is strong and it is needed as an additional outlet. This is of no medical significance, and may even be advantageous if the married partner has less sexual desire.

Masturbation is usually carried out with the aid of an *erotic fantasy*; however, in those of dull imagination it may be an almost purely physical act, and we have observed its occurrence as an obsessional compulsion with a negligible erotic content. The fantasies are as a rule of a normal heterosexual kind, but of a type determined by previous experience and instruction. In the constitutional homosexual, the fantasies also will be homosexual. As the main incidence of masturbation is at an age when young males are thrown much in their own company, and have a very limited access to the female, it has been thought that the practice can lead to a conditioned homosexuality. This has never been proved. It is, however, likely that a similar *mechanism of conditioning* plays a part *in the rarer sex perversions*, such as fetishism, exhibitionism, sadism and masochism; those circumstances which attended the first sexual experience come to carry a sexual tone, however accidental the original connexion might have been. It is certainly true, though the cause may be quite different, that all these deviations, including homosexuality, are found in persons whose usual sexual outlet is masturbation with the aid of a specific fantasy. In exhibitionists and fetishists, masturbation may be the only sex activity.

FETISHISM. It is very usual, even among quite normal people, to place a particular value on some feature or physical quality in persons of the opposite sex, or of the same sex in the case of homosexuals, and to feel a sexual attraction to this single trait. One man may pay special attention to a woman's eyes, and another to the shape of her legs. Although this aspect of normal psychology may provide part of the basis from which a fetishism may grow, we cannot speak of fetishism being present until this *partial feature takes a central importance* and comes by itself to provide an adequate cause for sexual excitation. In common parlance, fetishism is restricted to a sexual preoccupation with entirely inessential and accidental features, such as articles of clothing. Tactile and odorous qualities seem to play a special role in determining these fetishisms; and so it happens that among the commonest objects involved are female underclothing, especially of silk, leather articles, especially shoes, fabrics like velvet and furs, etc.

In taking the case-history from a fetishist, one will often find that the *first sexual experiences* were associated with sensory impressions of these kinds, and the development of the fetishism can be accounted for along lines of conditioning. There will usually, however, also be a *constitutional factor* in the form of temperamental difficulties in making normal social and sexual contacts, or in a generally inadequate libido. In many cases, however, these first sexual experiences remain buried and inaccessible, until they can be revealed by a very prolonged process of enquiry. Psychoanalysts have proved very successful in ferreting out these remote psychological precipitants; but even if such an end can be attained, the problems of further treatment may remain as difficult as ever.

Fetishists may be caused a good deal of unhappiness by their abnormality, especially through feeling themselves isolated from the rest of society. Psychotherapeutic help is then best given by *explanation and reassurance*, and if the subject is still young, by pointing out the ways in which he might advance towards more normal sexual and emotional relations, giving up his fetishism only by easy stages. If he can find a helpful and sympathetic partner, she can play the major role in this treatment. These patients are rather seldom of an anti-social, uncooperative or grossly psychopathic type; but of course, the more abnormal the basic personality is, the more difficult treatment will be. The psychiatrist will in any case have to cope with secondary neurotic symptoms of the anxious or depressive type.

Perhaps the principal psychiatric significance of the fetishisms is in the *medico-legal field*. Fetishists may have to steal in order to obtain their object, and the stealing itself may become part of the sexual ritual. When apprehended, they may seek to raise the defence of irresistible impulse. This can seldom be supported psychiatrically; but if the offence is a first one, a claim can legitimately be made that psychiatric treatment be tried before any severe punishment is inflicted. As fetishism is a very limited form of sexual deviation and acquired by conditioning, it is not surprising that successful treatment with behaviour therapy has been reported (Clark, 1963a; Raymond, 1956). Help along these lines and general psychological support should enable the therapist to educate the patient into keeping his impulses within socially innocuous limits.

TRANS-SEXUALISM AND TRANSVESTISM. Transvestism is a deviation of personality in which gratification is afforded by wearing the garb of the opposite sex. The term covers a wide range of different phenomena which have been classified in papers by Ellis (1928) and Hamburger (1953). The following classification is based on the descriptions provided in these studies and upon an enquiry into 36 cases of male and female persons with transvestite tendencies (Ball, 1965; Roth and Ball, 1963). Three main varieties may be recognized.

1. *Symptomatic Transvestism.* The cross-dressing in this form is a symptom of some other sexual deviation, most commonly homosexuality or fetishism, and is employed as a means to sexual excitement and gratification. This is the most widely recognized form of trans-vestism and is probably responsible for the commonly held and erroneous view that it is always a manifestation of homosexuality.

2. *Simple Transvestism.* In this variety the subject confines himself to cross-dressing which, in itself, brings gratification without genital excitation or interest in homosexual behaviour. As these subjects rarely seek advice, the incidence of this condition is unknown but it is probably relatively high and sometimes comes to light in persons seeking medical advice for other reasons. The subject lives as an ordinary male and cross-dresses in secret or wears feminine undergarments regularly under his male clothing (Lukianowicz, 1959; Wyrsch, 1944).

3. *Trans-sexualism.* In this deviation cross-dressing is part of a more profound and generalized sexual and personal maladjustment. The individuals affected have a conviction

that borders at times on the delusional that they are members of the opposite sex (that is females, since the phenomenon is far commoner in the male sex). There is no sexual excitement from dressing up but a firm belief that the chosen clothing, though opposed to the individual's morphological sex, is more appropriate to his personality; a feeling of happiness and contentment is conferred by wearing feminine dress, whereas male clothes render the individual self-conscious and ill at ease. Although romantic infatuation with members of the same sex is common and there may be fantasies of pregnancy and motherhood, desire for homosexual intercourse is confined to a small proportion of subjects, and where physical gratification has been experienced this has been more often than not heterosexual. Although libidinal drive is usually weak some of the subjects marry and beget children. These individuals present in the psychiatrist's clinic on account of their intense and unrelenting ambition to achieve a change of sex, or at any rate some anatomical alteration that will bring them closer in appearance to the opposite sex. In rare instances self-castration has been attempted following prolonged frustration of this aim.

There is some degree of overlap between simple transvestism and trans-sexualism, in that a substantial proportion of cases of the former appear to harbour beliefs about their intrinsic femininity which are more or less clearly defined, without feeling compelled to embark upon a quest to achieve change of sex by surgical means. Moreover, the majority of cases of trans-sexualism pass through a stage in which the desire for change of sex is not yet firmly crystallized.

The situation is different as far as transvestism and trans-sexualism in women is concerned. Both transvestite and trans-sexualist women are almost invariably active and dominant partners in a homosexual relationship. This was the situation in every one of the ten patients studied in the department of one of the authors during 5 years. Complete cross-dressing as an isolated phenomenon is rare and trans-sexualist women commonly seek plastic surgery to 'change sex' or bring about an alteration in appearance that will make them more closely resemble men. A severe degree of abnormality of personality is the almost invariable setting for this phenomenon.

The causation of trans-sexualism is obscure; nuclear sex is generally male (Barr and Hobbs, 1954) but a mosaic Klinefelter (XY/XXY) with trans-sexualism has been described (Dowling and Knox, 1963) and both trans-sexualism (Money, 1963) and transvestism (Overzier, 1958) have been described in typical Klinefelter cases. There is some evidence also that a genetic factor may contribute to causation (Ball, 1965).

In the enquiry by Roth and Ball (1963) it was found that, in a high proportion of male cases (94 per cent.), there had been extreme dependence on, and a strong preference for, the mother of the family. It was of interest that the father of the majority had either been absent for long periods during the formative years (59 per cent.) or insignificant in the family setting or had had a personality marked by coldness, hostility or psychopathic traits (77 per cent.). The child had thus been driven into an exclusive relationship with the mother, even when she had herself possessed some abnormal traits. The hazards connected with this kind of family setting might, as in the case of homosexuality, be more widely disseminated with *prophylactic* intention, so that the environment to which the developing child is exposed may be modified by all available means. It has to be remembered, however, that the family setting in question is not a specific one, having been described also in relation to other psychiatric disorders and not to sexual deviations alone. Even if prophylactic measures were practicable their effect would very likely prove limited.

The phenomenon is readily recognizable *in childhood* as affected individuals show, from a very early age, a consistent preference for girls as playmates and for girlish games. Cross-dressing usually begins between the ages of 5 and 8 years and is at first carried out in secret or during the parents' absence. If opportunities for therapeutic intervention during the childhood or adolescent transvestite state could be more frequently found, there might be a chance of more effective psychotherapy and social reorientation.

During *adolescence* transvestite boys and girls will frequently co-operate in treatment as their propensities often cause conflict, anxiety, shame and increasing isolation from others. It may be possible to help the intelligent and co-operative patient to view compulsive cross-dressing objectively as a disability to be surmounted.

At a later stage in the development of trans-sexualism the patient treats his anomaly as a treasured possession and he is rarely prepared to relinquish it. Co-operation in any treatment aimed at transforming his sexual orientation is withheld or is incomplete. In strongly motivated patients, temporary successes may be achieved, but cure is infrequent, as the trans-sexualist patient looks to the doctor to confirm his anomaly, not to eradicate it. There have been a number of reports of transvestites successfully treated with aversion therapy (Barker *et al.*, 1961; Glynn and Harper, 1961, Blakemore *et al.*, 1963 *a, b*; Marks and Gelder, 1967). Only a small minority will co-operate in such forms of treatment and, for such a generalized disorder of personality, the rationale seems crude. But further exploration, particularly in young patients, is called for.

Some patients whose social adjustment has wholly broken down may be enabled to start a new life once permission has been obtained to re-register them as women for employment purposes. Dressed as women, they achieve a new sense of ease and contentment and are partly freed from the trapped and hunted feeling they experience while posing as women at their work without official sanction. However, before helping the patient to take the crucial step of assuming feminine attire and employment, the physician must take care to define to the patient his attitude to the further demands that will almost invariably follow this concession. Once permitted to dress and work as a woman, the patient will usually plead sooner or later that the situation places him in a painful predicament. Removal of the hated male genitalia would, it is claimed, enable the patient to live without the dread of being found out in deceitful and possibly illegal, conduct. If operation is refused, self-castration may be attempted by a determined patient. If it is carried out, it will almost certainly be followed by yet further demands for plastic surgery, e.g. plastic operations for creation of a vagina and enlargement of the breasts.

The problem of operative treatment in trans-sexualist patients raises many social and ethical, as well as psychological problems. A number of cases have gone on record in which operation has been followed by an improved social adjustment and a release of latent abilities and talents (Bättig, 1952; Boss, 1952, Hamburger *et al.*, 1953). The patients are often gifted, and the possibility of improvement of this sort cannot be lightly set aside.

A number of workers have expressed themselves in favour of the operation (Hamburger, 1953; Hamburger *et al.*, 1953). Others such as Dukor (1951) have conceded that, in cases associated with a great deal of suffering, operation may be justified; but the outcome may be unfortunate and even disastrous, as indicated by a few reports of patients who have bitterly regretted the operation and pleaded for a reversal of the change. A good many operations have now been carried out and a systematic, detailed, long-term evaluation would appear to be desirable. Until reliable information has been assembled, pleas for operation must be regarded as a hazard in all cases, particularly where the personality is unstable or psychopathic. In such subjects narcissism is conspicuous, and dress and demeanour provocative. Some work as female impersonators in night-clubs and others practise as homosexual prostitutes. There will usually be other indices of instability and social maladjustment. They are probably homosexuals with chameleon-like propensities rather than trans-sexualists, and it is difficult to justify the operations that have been undertaken in this group. In the general run of trans-sexualists oestrogens will often bring some relief, but only in rare exceptional instances is there any indication for the operations for which they plead.

EXHIBITIONISM. The exhibitionist is a common class of offender, but his perversion consists in elevating to a central position a normal aspect of sexual relations, the display of the naked body or of the genitals alone. The *tendency towards self-display* is itself normal, and is made use of in socially accepted form both in the way that men and women dress, and in the amount of undressing which is allowed, e.g. on a bathing beach or in evening dress. The earliest manifestations of this natural tendency are seen in some of the sexually-toned play activities of young children. The mutual inspection of the genitals which is often indulged at this early age may be the point from which the conditioning begins.

The adult exhibitionist, who is almost invariably a man, is a public nuisance. He may haunt dark streets, parks or field paths, and on encountering a woman or girl, throw open his overcoat to expose his erect penis, perhaps throwing the light of a torch on it, or perhaps masturbating. The motivation is often obscure; he may feel that this display excites the woman, or he may derive satisfaction from her dismay and even terror. The women and girls of a neighbourhood may be set in fear by knowing that such a man is lurking about. The exhibitionist is usually, but not always, of an inadequate and *ill-adjusted personality*, and his libido feeble. He is, extremely commonly, a recidivist; and this perversion is very difficult to treat. Psychotherapy is usually almost useless, and punishment also is often quite ineffective; some of these offenders have had as many as thirty or more periods of imprisonment and still continue undeterred. Many of these patients are helped to curb their tendencies by long-term psychiatric support and supervision. Counselling of the spouse is important in married cases since exhibitionist acts are often triggered off by outbursts of domestic strife.

SADISM AND MASOCHISM. The meaning of these terms has been so extended by psycho-analysis, that they are now only used with peril by the psychiatrist. For the psychoanalyst, sadism has come to mean any attitude or activity with an element of aggression, masochism any tendency towards submission or the voluntary acceptance of an experience with a quality of 'un-pleasure'. It is only because of the baseless Freudian doctrine that the springs of all activity are to be found in sexuality, that these words could be so misused. The *aggressiveness of the male* and the greater *dependence of the female* are more likely to have their origin in the necessary conditions for the organization of mammalian family life and in evolutionary processes which have brought us through tribal societies to the structure of society of today, than, as is commonly supposed, in the mere position and mutual relation of the male and the female in the act of coitus.

Aggressiveness and submissiveness enter into all human relations, and it is therefore only to be expected that they should colour courtship and mating. There is *much individual variation* in qualities of temperament which affect the liability to these opposed mental attitudes, and processes of training and habituation also have their effect. So it is that

Mead has been able to report isolated primitive societies in which other than our accepted social and sexual relations are the standard, and that there is in these respects a good deal of difference between North American, European, Latin, Semitic and Oriental cultures.

From the psychiatric point of view sadism and masochism are best considered in their narrower *sexual connotation*. The sadist derives sexual pleasure from the inflicting of pain, humiliation or violence on his partner, the masochist from submitting to such things. Although, as any other person with deviant sexual tendencies, the masochist may at times need help and guidance, it is the sadist who is responsible for social and legal problems. Even so, as East (1938) points out, sadists who derive pleasure from whipping their partner may find willing victims, and so not become offenders. Nevertheless parents, and occasionally teachers, who 'punish' and ill-use children in their care, may go to serious lengths. Even if there may not be cause for legal action in the criminal courts, there still may be adequate reason for removing the victimized children from their charge. Sexually motivated acts of violence against the person are a *substantial proportion of all serious crimes*, and may take the gravest of all possible forms in murder. Such cases may become notorious, as for instance the infamous Peter Kürten, the Düsseldorf murderer, who was tried on nine counts of murder and confessed to others. His father was grossly psychopathic, and Kürten himself tortured animals while he was still of tender years, and may be said to have committed his first murder at the age of nine, when another boy fell off the raft from which they were bathing and Kürten prevented him from climbing back. Kürten proceeded from less to more extreme acts as he failed to reach orgasm with acts of lesser violence. (Critchley, personal communication.)

Although sadism may inspire rape, not every rapist is a sadist; many are merely men of brutal habits who take the directest path towards their goal of normal sexual intercourse, callously brushing aside any obstacle. Sadism may well take forms which are *not immediately identifiable as sexual*. No doubt there were sadists, in the strict sense, among the Nazi war criminals who tortured and killed their victims and derived sensual satisfactions therefrom, though without making any specifically sexual assault. Nevertheless, the majority of these men were probably moved more by hatred and by a training in ruthlessness and violence than by specifically sexual feelings. To call them sadistic would, perhaps, be generally accepted, but might still be a straining of the concept. Freudian explanations of such behaviour seem unduly facile, and further investigation, for which there was adequate opportunity, might well have been made. Psychoanalysis associates sadism with anal-erotism and with homosexuality. This association has never been clinically established.

BESTIALITY. The obtaining of sexual satisfaction by this method is, according to Kinsey (1948), not infrequent among farmers' boys in certain rural districts of the U.S.A. As a rule it is a transient deviation and a substitute for normal sex relations, being replaced by the latter when the opportunity arises. In the experience of European psychiatrists, it may lead to torturing the animal. The psychiatrist is usually consulted when the perversion becomes notorious and the subject of legal procedure. The offender in such cases is usually found to be a *mental defective* of the lower high-grade or lower grade, who because of his dullness has been unable to find a human partner. Recent reports by Shenken (1960, 1964) suggest that, occurring in persons of better social background, bestiality is likely to be the product of severe neurotic or psychotic illness.

HOMOSEXUALITY

GENETICAL BASIS. In 1940 the interesting hypothesis was proposed by Lang that homosexuals of either sex were representatives of genetical intersexes. Intersexes were known in other species and had, in fact, been elaborately studied. Evidential support for this hypothesis was provided by the demonstration that the sex ratio shown by the sibs of male homosexuals showed a marked preponderance of males, a finding which could be accounted for if it were supposed that the male homosexual was a genetic female. This view in its original simple form can no longer be supported. Genetic sex is determined by the presence of a Y chromosome. The normal male is of XY constitution, the normal female XX. However Klinefelter cases, with genetic constitution XXY or XXXY are males; and deletion of the Y chromosome, leaving the constitution XO, causes the production of a female with Turner's syndrome. Examination of cells from the buccal mucosa of 50 male homosexuals (Pare, 1956) showed absence of the chromatin body, i.e. the existence of only one X chromosome corresponding to the XY constitution.

However, the possibility of some chromosomal anomaly is not to be entirely dismissed. Slater (1962) showed that the birth order and maternal age of male homosexuals was shifted to the right, with late appearance in birth order, and late maternal age. The shift was in the same direction, but only about half as marked, as in the case of mongolism. These findings are susceptible of the alternative hypothesis that it is the elderly mother who is most likely to produce around her son the psychological influences which might drive him in the direction of homosexuality (Davis, 1962).

Psychological tests, e.g. those of Terman and Miles, have been developed which differentiate one sex from the other. They show, however, such a wide individual variation that there is some overlapping, some males for instance giving a score which would more commonly be given by a female. Male homosexuals subjected to this test gave scores which were about half-way between the male and female means (Terman and Miles, 1936). An analogous result on a differential vocabulary test was obtained by Slater and Slater (1947). A group of 15 male trans-sexualists gave scores on the Terman and Miles test which were in every instance well within the female range (Ball, 1966). These findings indicate that as far as mental constitution is involved *the two sexes are not sharply differentiated* from one another; in respect of a differential mental trait the curve of distribution is U-shaped, with a certain amount of overlapping. Homosexuals tend to fall into this intermediate position between the two sexes in mental habits, interests and avocations and in their knowledge and use of words. One may therefore say that, irrespective of whether or not genetical intersexes exist, in mental make-up there are persons who tend to take an intermediate position between the sexes and to be characteristic of neither.

The most impressive evidence in favour of a genetic basis for homosexuality has been presented by Kallmann (1952) who investigated eighty-five pairs of twins, forty of them monozygotic and forty-five dizygotic. Most of his subjects were more or less exclusively homosexual. He was able to trace thirty-seven of the twin partners of the uni-ovular propositi and found that all were homosexually inclined, twenty-eight of them exclusively so. He was able to trace twenty-six of the non-identical twins and of these only three had homosexual trends of any description, an incidence which did not depart from that to be expected in the population at large. A further finding of considerable importance was that emulation or seduction can have played little or no part in deciding the concordance of the identical pairs; the twin partners claimed that they had veered towards a homosexual pattern of life independently of one another.

That heredity plays some part in the causation of a proportion of cases of homosexual behaviour may be regarded as established. But the nature and importance of this hereditary influence cannot be reliably assessed at the present time. In Kallmann's material, which was obtained to some extent with the co-operation of the New York State Department of Correction, criminal and abnormal personalities were over-represented; one subject was schizophrenic and twenty-two others schizoid, severely unstable or alcoholic. The material therefore could not have been representative of homosexuals in general. Moreover, it is hazardous to draw conclusions about the relative importance of environment and heredity from twin studies alone. Parker (1964a) has criticized the literature that deals with the genetics of homosexuality, and has described two MZ and one DZ pair who were discordant. Other reports have appeared of identical twins discordant for homosexuality (Rainer et al., 1960; Klintworth, 1962).

A specific genetic or constitutional basis for homosexuality would lead one to expect biochemical or endocrine differences from normal subjects. A number of investigators have reported differences of this nature. Thus Myerson and Neustadt (1942) have found a lowering of the androgen/oestrogen ratio in homosexuals. They suggested that the vigour of sexual drive was related to androgen level and its direction to the relative amount of oestrogens. There has been no confirmation for these findings and it seems highly improbable, if several per cent. of the population are indeed exclusively homosexual, that they can be sharply differentiated from the remainder of the general population by means of simple biochemical tests of this nature. It would seem more likely that we are dealing with a variant of the norm whose causes will probably prove to be multifactorial. Coppen's (1959) finding that the androgyny score of *male* homosexuals was shifted towards the feminine side, more so than in a control neurotic group, is of some interest for the problem of the homosexual constitution.

OCCURRENCE IN THE NORMAL. The *frequency of homosexual behaviour* varies very greatly from time to time and from place to place. In the golden age of Greece, homosexuality was not thought of as being in any way discreditable, but rather the reverse; homosexual relations between the males of the free citizenhood, especially between an older and a younger man, were thought to be valuable to both and must have been engaged in by a high proportion of the population.

Estimates as to the frequency of homosexuality at the present time vary widely. Hirschfeld was the first worker to conduct a large scale survey (Hirschfeld, 1944). From an enquiry into the sexual life of almost 9,000 German subjects, he concluded that 2 per cent. of men were wholly, and 3·4 per cent. partly, homosexual in inclination. However, only 50 per cent. of the subjects replied to his questionnaire. G. V. Hamilton (1929) carried out a survey of the sexual life of 100 married men and 100 married women. Forty-six men and twenty-three women admitted to relationships with their own sex that had involved some stimulation of sexual organs. Only forty-four of 100 married women denied all memory of homosexual play in early life, while in seventeen of the men homosexual experiences were reported to have taken place after the age of 18.

According to the Kinsey Report (Kinsey et al., 1948) at least 30 per cent. have had homosexual experience to the point of orgasm between the beginning of adolescence and old age. Ten per cent. of the population were more or less exclusively homosexual for at least 3 years between the ages of 16 and 55; 4 per cent. were judged to be exclusively homosexual throughout their lives. The second Kinsey Report (Kinsey et al., 1953) revealed the smaller incidence of 13 per cent. of homosexuality among 6,000 white women, much of this having occurred in the form of short-lived experiences. Persistent homosexuality was unusual; among single women 4 per cent. remained more or less exclusively homosexual between the ages of 20 and 55 years, as compared with approximately 12 per cent. among men. No study comparable in scale and thoroughness with the Kinsey enquiries has been carried out in Europe. But even so, the discrepancy between the figures recorded in his surveys and the far smaller incidence registered in more limited European studies is difficult to explain. Thus homosexuals made up only 1 per cent. of all male Service patients admitted to one psychiatric unit during the Second World War. In a survey of unselected material of male private psychiatric patients, Curran and Parr (1957) found that 5 per cent. of the cases had been homosexuals. Homosexuals would tend to be over-represented in a group such as this, but the fact that the incidence was between 2 and 5 per cent. in all diagnostic groups is noteworthy. Taking all the evidence into consideration, it would seem likely that the hard core of exclusively homosexual male individuals makes up between 2 and 5 per cent. of the general population. If this is accepted, homosexuality can hardly be regarded as a pathological variant in the ordinary sense.

From an enquiry carried out by Ford and Beach (1951) into 76 primitive societies, two important points emerged. In the first place some form of homosexuality was considered to be quite normal in the majority of societies: the second finding was the relative rarity of female homosexuality which was observed in only 17 of the cultures studied. This preponderance of homosexuality in the male in a wide range of cultures makes it unlikely that the male preponderance in highly-developed societies is wholly the product of social and legal prejudice as some workers have suggested. The differential sex incidence is more likely to have some biological explanation.

FACTORS IN THE GENESIS OF HOMOSEXUALITY. On balance, it does not seem likely that heredity alone will ever provide more than part of the explanation for the majority of cases with exclusively homosexual tendencies.

Much emphasis has been placed in the past upon the contribution made by experiences in the course of personality development. The effect of homosexual seduction and the pattern of sexual arousal in early adolescence have been among the more obvious factors considered. Recent enquiries have provided little support for such views. During investigation of 100 Borstal lads aged 16–21 years, Gibbens (1957) found that 30 per cent. of those with known homosexual tendencies had had advances made to them, whereas 33 per cent. of those without such tendencies had had identical experiences. In an enquiry by Parr (1957) no significant difference was found in the psychosexual experience of day school and boarding school boys during early and later life. Parr concluded that the role of boarding schools and sexual segregation had probably been exaggerated. In a detailed analysis of 200 cases, he found no evidence to suggest that early seduction had played a significant part in causing homosexuality.

The theory advanced by some psychoanalysts that the sources of male homosexuality are to be sought in unconscious castration fear or survival of infantile anal eroticism rests on little evidence. However, the view that an especially intimate and intense emotional bond with the mother, together with a weak, unsympathetic, unattractive or brutal father, play some part in moulding the personality of the homosexual, is supported by a number of psychological investigations and by autobiographical descriptions recorded by homosexuals. Some thirty years ago Terman and Miles (1936) investigated 77 passive male homosexuals between 17 and 44 years of age and arrived at the following conclusions. 'If the case history data supplied by these individuals can be accepted as anywhere near the truth, the psychosocial formula for developing homosexuality in boys would seem to run somewhat as follows: too demonstrative affection from an excessively emotional mother—a father who is unsympathetic, autocratic, brutal, much away from home or deceased; treatment of the child as a girl, coupled with lack of encouragement or opportunity to associate with boys—over emphasis of neatness, niceness and spirituality, lack of vigilance against the danger of seduction by older homosexual males . . . .' The life histories of Marcel Proust and André Gide conform in many particulars with the first part of this description. A study by West (1959, 1960) has shown that the combination of an abnormally intense relationship with the mother and an unsatisfactory relationship with the father was far commoner among homosexuals than among control subjects. Roth and Ball (1963) found a statistically significant difference in this respect between a group of 27 homosexuals and 94 neurotic controls, though comparison with trans-sexualists (see p. 165) showed that this family pattern was not specific for homosexuals.

Other factors must almost invariably be concerned in causation. In the life-histories of many homosexuals a strong puritanical component which involves suppression of all matters concerned with sex appears also to be involved. Sexual relationships are in consequence hedged round with feelings of guilt. General inadequacies of personality which inhibit the transition from the all-male society of many boys during puberty and adolescence to the heterosexual groupings of adult life probably make a further contribution.

PSYCHOLOGICAL AND PSYCHIATRIC ASPECTS. Male homosexuals are frequently classified into the active and the passive type; female homosexuals into the masculine and feminine. The active male homosexual is defined as one who in sexual relationships with another male takes the active role making his partner adopt the female position in intercourse, or to submit to, rather than to perform, sodomy, etc. The active physical role is usually accompanied by the active, seeking, courting and dominating role mentally. If the two are of disparate ages, the older man is more likely to be the active one. On the other hand the effeminate type of male homosexual will prefer the more passive role throughout his life. *Mutatis mutandis* the same may be said for female homosexuals. The active male and the passive female are frequently of fairly normal psychosomatic constitution; adopt their homosexual behaviour as a *pis aller*, or, as frequently occurs, out of an abundance of sexual urge and interest and as part of a polymorphous perversity. The passive male and the active female homosexual are much more likely to show contrasexual traits of physique and mind, and to be irreversibly and solely homosexually inclined.

There is, however, *no sharp distinction between activity and passivity*, as a lasting trait, and most homosexuals are to be found somewhere away from the extremes on a scale of infinite gradation between the two. Furthermore the mental and physical aspects of activity or passivity may not go together. Variation in course of time, or with change of partner, may occur, and out of a desire to explore every sort of physical gratification, reversal of roles may occur between the same partners on different occasions. Even with these reservations, however, it is broadly true that homosexuals tend to fall into one or other of these two classes and not to be unclassifiably midway between.

The Danish poet Herman Bang, himself an avowed homosexual, described the two types as follows: 'In inborn homosexuality there are a great number of shades and grades. One class of man is male in every other respect and even more male than most men; only in their sex life they are separated from the rest of men. They love definitely male men, just as a heterosexual man loves a woman. If we put this class at the right wing, the left wing is formed by the pronounced women among the homosexuals, that is by men who are only men by name; the body's form is pronouncedly female and the so-called soul is almost entirely female. This is expressed in everything, behaviour, walking and talking, especially in the movements of the hands. These men sew and embroider, they take on occupations such as cooks, waiters, ladies' tailors, milliners; I have never met a homosexual men's tailor, if he was a tailor, the homosexual always made ladies' dresses. Between the two extremes there is a host of transitional cases in which at times the male is preponderant in appearance and emotional life and at other times, the female is more pronounced.' The idea that in love-making the homosexual is either only man or only woman, is mistaken according to Bang (quoted from Kahn, 1928).

Among recent classifications that of Scott (1957) based on a study of sixty-three males and nine females is useful, although it has the disadvantage of being based on a number of different principles, including criteria such as pattern of social adjustment, clinical features, response to treatment and age.

His first group of *adolescents and mentally immature adults* consists of a group of young people in whom the final pattern of sexual adjustment is not yet decided and in whom homosexual conduct may prove to be merely one stage in development. Of his second group of *severely damaged personalities*, one type is inadequate and downtrodden and another deeply resentful and antisocially inclined. Of these, the latter are socially dangerous—both to other homosexuals, whom they victimize, and to society. The other variety in this sub-group appears to be rare and one wonders from the description given whether they are not really trans-sexualists, lacking desire for physical contact, who exploit their propensities in flirtation or actual prostitution. The third main group consists of *relatively intact personalities* who lead an active homosexual life but manage to combine this with a reasonable social adjustment. The fourth group are *latent and well-compensated homosexuals* with strong traits of character, rarely seen in the clinic until perhaps late in life. The last group includes individuals with *serious mental disablement*, including those with psychoses, organic brain damage and extreme personality defects. They are apt to injure their victims, are socially dangerous and should be segregated 'till rendered harmless by ageing or specific treatment'.

There is a general impression among psychiatrists that homosexuals tend to be of more than average intelligence and in surveys (Scott, 1957; Parr, 1957) the lower classes tend to be under-represented, although as Parr points out, this may be due to the fact that offenders from these sections of the community are more commonly seen in law courts and prisons. There is a high level of artistic sensibility, and interests in painting and music, as also a fastidious taste in dress and furniture, are common. Many homosexuals have achieved distinction in art, the theatre and cinema, whereas the active or aggressive type of Lesbian may strive to succeed in the professions, such as law or medicine.

According to the psychoanalytic theory, homosexuality reflects a warping of personality development, the anomalous choice of love object having been determined by castration fear; it may be regarded therefore as a form of neurotic disturbance. Unfortunately opportunities for a systematic psychiatric enquiry into the personality of homosexuals drawn at random from the general population rarely present themselves. Neurotic disturbance, psychopathy, alcoholism and other anomalies of personality are certainly common among homosexuals studied by psychiatrists even when referral has not been decided by medical causes. On the other hand there is a substantial proportion of relatively normal personalities even within this population. Thus 68 of 150 out-patients studied by Parr were found to be free from any gross personality disorder, neurosis or psychosis during their adult lives. Moreover, no definite pattern of personality associated with homosexuality has been described, although some psychiatrists of experience have described indecision, procrastination and uncertainty about his role as relatively common features (Scott, 1957).

Homosexuals tend to be more promiscuous in their relationship with each other than heterosexual individuals and this tendency is not confined to those with associated psychiatric disorder. The lack of stability of homosexual relationships, the difficulty in establishing fresh contacts with advancing age and the denial of the roles of parent and grandparent, which may continue to provide fulfilments for the normal individual after the waning of sexual passion, makes the plight of the ageing homosexual a difficult and pathetic one. Some of the psychiatric disturbances, particularly the alcoholism, depression and suicide (O'Connor, 1948) which are common in homosexuals, may be related to such factors. Instability, over-compensation and paranoid tendencies are relatively frequent psychiatric complications in homosexuals as with other isolated and spurned minority groups; they are more likely to be due to social than to psychodynamic factors.

LEGAL ASPECTS AND TREATMENT. Constitutional homosexuals of both sexes are acutely aware of their position in society, suffer from it, and frequently regard it as unjust. Although female homosexuals are immune to criminal prosecution for their activities, the position of the male is very exposed. He has to fear, not only a prison sentence but more frequently social disgrace, and sometimes blackmail.

The possibilities of a *prophylactic approach* to the problem of homosexuality have hardly been explored, for there are few well-established facts, and cause, effect and the play of chance are difficult to disentangle from one another. It seems, nevertheless, logical to attempt to apply such few facts as have accumulated. Boys born relatively late and reared in families marked by a strong predominance of feminine influence, with an intense exclusive relationship between mother and son would appear to be specifically vulnerable to homosexuality. It is quite possible that only a proportion of children brought up in such a setting becomes sexually deviant and we cannot be certain that such anomalies in parent–child relationships do not merely reflect a constitutional anomaly in the child to which the mother responds. But the special hazards of this pattern of family relationships ought to be more widely known not only among psychiatrists but among physicians, social workers, school-teachers and the general population.

In *adolescence* homosexual behaviour may be a transitional stage in development and the possibility of ultimately achieving an adult heterosexual pattern of life always exists. It is unwise to assume that exclusively homosexual behaviour is established until the age of 25 has been passed. The anxiety and sense of isolation that accompany homosexual practices may lead the adolescent to attach himself to a coterie who have banded together to insulate themselves from the hostility and ridicule which society accords to them. Loyalty to such a group may serve to prolong immature sexual conduct and the remorse and fear generated by adolescent homosexual experiment may prevent heterosexual friendships being made. Hence persistent homosexual behaviour, even in adolescence, calls for expert help. The aim of the therapist is to mitigate guilt and anxiety and to help the patient to develop heterosexual contacts. A good deal can be done with these early cases by helping them through simple psychotherapy to gain insight into some of the factors behind their deviant behaviour.

In *older patients* with long-established and exclusively homosexual behaviour unassociated with heterosexual desire, attempts at a complete sexual reorientation are futile. Treatment has to aim at the more limited objectives of improved social adjustment, reduction of anxiety and an attempt to impart a more sensible and realistic perspective about the relative importance of sexual activities in the patient's total life pattern; these frequently loom disproportionately large. A dispassionate and understanding approach to the patient helps him to bridge the gulf between that side of his life in which the sexual and passionate part of his nature finds expression and the workaday world in which he is compelled to conceal his secret.

It must be remembered that in embarking upon a course of treatment aimed at correcting his deviation, the homosexual is preparing to abandon not only a form of sexual deviation but a whole way of life that can offer variety and excitement, and a select society in which aesthetic and emotional sensibility is at a premium; the new way of life he strives to adopt may appear mundane.

Psychotherapy has a better chance of success in subjects in whom some degree of sexual ambivalence exists or those in whom heterosexual life has been inhibited by lack of opportunity or failure. A talented, earnest person, who dislikes his perversion and has a desire for change, is a favourable subject in whom a more stable compromise may be achieved in the course of systematic and sustained psychological help.

Precise knowledge about the results of psychotherapy in various forms of homosexuality is lacking but there is no evidence to suggest that orthodox psychoanalysis yields results that are superior to those gained by less time-consuming forms of psychological help. Penological methods are probably harmful but, in the case of seriously damaged, aggressive, unscrupulous personalities or those who seduce young boys, imprisonment sometimes provides the only means of protecting society. Probation provides help in a proportion of cases. Stilboestrol is useful in a small minority of patients desirous of curbing sexual drive but hormonal treatments are otherwise worthless. In recent years successes have been claimed for deconditioning processes. These methods appear crude and banal in relation to a long-established deviation of a fundamental drive but the successes reported deserve further evaluation (see p. 185). Drugs may be useful in the control of anxiety.

Homosexual activities enter at times into matrimonial cases and into prosecutions for blackmail. In British law the homosexuality of either partner may be cited as evidence of cruelty in an action for divorce. The male homosexual may be involved in legal proceedings in a criminal prosecution with heavy penalties and the opinion of a psychiatrist is not infrequently sought in such cases. This might well be done more often than is at present the case.

PSYCHOLOGICAL TREATMENT OF NEUROSIS AND PSYCHOPATHY

Psychotherapy refers to systematic treatments employing psychological means aimed at relieving the patient of his symptoms and helping him to understand and modify his conduct so as to enable him to live a happier and better-adjusted life. It is a special kind of learning experience and there is, therefore, no very sharp distinction between this form of treatment and the more recently introduced 'behaviour therapies' which derive their inspiration directly from learning theory. However, whereas in behaviour therapy symptoms are regarded as bad habits which have to be unlearned, most forms of long-term psychotherapy are directed towards remoulding the deficiencies of personality from which the symptoms have sprung. Failure to attend to such Achilles' heels in a patient's personality is held to make recurrence of neurotic symptoms inevitable, while attempts to reshape them are thought to reduce the chances of relapse into neurotic disability. These views at present are not supported by an adequate amount of evidence.

As far as qualifications for the psychotherapist are concerned we can do no better than quote some comments of Jaspers (1913a).

'Certainly a psychotherapist should have a training in somatic medicine and in psychopathology, both of which have to be scientifically based. If he has no such training he would only be a charlatan, yet with this training alone he is still not a psychotherapist. Science is only a part of his necessary equipment. Much more has to be added. Among the *personal prerequisites*, the width of his own horizon plays a part, so does the ability to be detached at times from any value-judgement, to be accepting and totally free of prejudice (an ability only found in those who generally possess very well defined values and have a personality that is mature). Finally, there is the necessity for fundamental warmth and a natural kindness. It is therefore clear that a good psychotherapist can only be a rare phenomenon and even then he is usually only good for *a certain circle of people* for whom he is well suited. A psychotherapist for everyone is an impossibility. However, force of circumstances makes it the psychotherapist's usual duty to treat everyone who may ask his help. That fact should help him to keep his claims to modest proportions.'

In ordinary psychiatric practice psychotherapy is generally combined with other procedures such as drug therapy, abreactive treatment, and attempts made in collaboration with a psychiatric social worker to modify the patient's social and familial environment in order to reduce the amount of stress to which he is exposed.

During the past thirty to forty years patients with neurotic disorders have been turning to an increasing extent to the psychiatrist for help in combating their disability. Yet psychotherapy, despite the passing of several decades in which it has been practised on an extensive scale, remains to a large extent an *empirical procedure*. There are two main lines of approach to the treatment of the neurotic patient. Although their indications differ they are not mutually exclusive. The first is that applicable to the mild or moderate disability of short duration occurring in a relatively stable personality. *Reassurance and simple explanation* as to the nature of the disability, advice about the management of current problems and constructive help in the organization of the patient's life to enable him to make the best possible use of his personality assets and minimize his deficiencies, are the main ingredients of therapy. With the help of a psychiatric social worker the patient's family and employer can be brought into collaboration with the psychiatric team in planning the patient's future. In this form of *supportive psychotherapy* advice and supervision are usually maintained over a period of weeks or months. In the severely disabled patient, treatment is directed towards a more radical *alteration of the patient's attitude* to life and his reactions to his environment. Complete recovery is rarely achieved by means of psychotherapy in a case of long-standing or severe neurosis; but, if the patient is willing and capable of making an intelligent and determined effort to surmount his difficulties, the attempt to help him by psychotherapy should be made.

Some degree of success in such cases is assured to any psychiatrist who has training and experience in the treatment of neurotic patients, the gift of empathy and a willingness to devote regular sessions to psychotherapeutic work. Most patients are grateful for any form of psychotherapeutic help and support, provided no extravagant hopes have been encouraged and the treatment has not involved a heavy financial sacrifice in the ill-founded expectation of a cure. Rümke (1963) stresses that before deciding on psychotherapeutic treatment the doctor should form an idea of the patient's personality to discover what may be considered changeable, because deviations of personality rooted in the constitution are not likely to be altered by deeper therapy. To ignore the limitations of this treatment and so raise expectation of change will lead to harmful disappointment and loss of confidence in both doctor and patient.

The essential condition for some degree of success in psychological treatment is *a relationship with the patient* that is based on a respect for his personality, a tolerance for his deficiencies and sympathy and understanding for his predicament. The establishment of such a relationship with the neurotic patient requires humanity, wisdom, maturity and empathy as well as psychiatric experience. As the neurotic patient gradually learns that someone he regards with respect and invests with authority does not respond with criticism and moral condemnation (as may even those closest to him) to an account of his innermost thoughts, guilt-laden memories and urges, he is able, perhaps for the first time in his life, to talk with a freedom that has a cathartic effect. Therefore, if the psychiatrist feels in doubt about his ability to tolerate and respect a neurotic patient, he should not undertake to treat him. Disapproval of a patient's conduct is sometimes necessary but criticizing him as a person, and treatment by moral exhortation are futile and can be disastrous.

It has long been known and has been rightly emphasized by psychoanalysts that, although the most important conflicts troubling the patient and the experiences that have warped his relationships with others may become apparent to the psychiatrist after a few sessions, *a direct exposition of these facts is rarely helpful* either in the relief of symptoms or the cultivation of insight. For the neurotic patient, as the normal individual, disguises from himself the real and often non-conscious character of his motives by rationalizations that present his personality in a favourable light. He prefers an interpretation of his experience which buffers him against the unpleasant knowledge of failure, exonerates him from blame and protects him from guilt. A direct presentation of his problems 'in a nutshell' is too damaging to his self-esteem. It is only when he has come to feel complete confidence in the therapist's acceptance of him, that he can begin to face an objective evaluation of himself. Only by slow degrees and over a long period can he assimilate the self-knowledge with which the treatment equips him.

As the history of the patient's early life and upbringing and early adjustment unfolds, it emerges to what extent and in what manner his attitudes to others, of the same and the opposite sex, in authority or subordinate position to him, have been moulded by his *relationship with his parents and other individuals* in his environment. He may also reveal opposing tendencies in his make-up that he has been striving to reconcile. His ethical or religious beliefs may be in conflict with biological urges or worldly demands that violate them, a desire for self-assertion and success may conflict with his need for the love and respect of those with whom he lives and works. Many neurotic patients have to learn that they give little, but expect a great deal out of life. Often the patient's difficulties issue from an attempt to tackle his problems by a pattern of behaviour that has repeatedly failed in the past. Yet he may be as unaware of the consistent and pre-determined character of this response as of the reasons why it takes this peculiar form.

The therapist attempts to impart what the patient has to learn by laying emphasis on certain topics, as distinct from others, by asking for elaboration when events are touched upon that teach important lessons. He will ask questions that the patient has avoided and request him to draw conclusions that he has shirked in the past. When certain events, individuals, objects or symbols seem to have a special and yet obscure significance for the patient, his associations around these themes may throw light on their meaning in his life.

In many cases it is valuable to ask the patient to explain and justify his views on such matters as religion, sexual behaviour, politics, racial discrimination, his attitude to work, success, the bringing up of children and to illness and death. In these ways *the patient is gradually brought face to face with himself*. In the later stages of treatment intervention may take a more direct form in explanations and suggestions for re-orientation. But decisions and plans for future action are left, as far as possible, to the *initiative of the patient*.

Ziskind (1957) has pointed out that the process of 'insight' psychotherapy usually involves inculcating the patient with the therapist's clinical point of view even though the therapist's 'non-directive' approach is calculated to avoid inculcation. The specific conflict of which the patient is made aware will vary with the orientation of the therapist, whether it be to Freud, Adler, Jung or to any other system. Despite his desire to give no direction, the therapist inevitably seizes upon disclosures on the patient's part which conform with his theories and ignores those which do not. In this way his own orientation is emphasized and imprinted upon the treatment he gives. As a method of eliminating this indirect indoctrination, Ziskind advocates that the clinician should directly explain the nature and purpose of psychotherapy and share openly with the patient a well-defined series of goals towards which treatment is to be directed. These he suggests, should be:

1. That the patient be brought to accept that his symptoms are psychogenic in origin.

2. That the current stresses from which the patient suffers be uncovered and worked through.

3. That what is morbid (i.e. neurotic) in the patient's reaction to these stresses be revealed and worked through.

4. That any specific traumatic experiences occurring in the patient's childhood be brought to light and their significance explained.

There is much to commend this directness of approach. The aims will of course vary in detail from case to case.

This outline of the strategy in psychotherapeutic procedure is specially applicable to the patient who is intelligent enough to understand the therapist's intentions, and young and adaptable enough to accept counsel and to act on it. The approach to treatment has to be modified to meet conditions that in the majority of patients are far from these ideals. Before embarking upon psychotherapy, the positive role of certain neurotic reactions and habits has to be taken into account. The probable benefits of treatment need to be weighed against the repercussions in the patient's professional or family life if he is to be freed in large measure from his symptoms. There seems little doubt that the creative abilities of men such as Darwin or Dickens were partly associated with neurotic or psychopathic trends in their personality.

The *frequency* with which *interviews* have to be given varies from case to case, but a 40–60 minute session once or twice weekly is quite adequate in most cases. Some patients feel more comfortable 'particularly in the initial stages of treatment' if they are allowed to talk without having to face the psychiatrist. *Reclining on a couch* while the psychiatrist sits to one side of the patient may bring freedom from constraint and lead to a more spontaneous production of information. In the course of a prolonged period of treatment the patient will often come to feel an exaggerated *attachment* for the person to whom he has unburdened himself. This may change, particularly when things are going badly, to an exaggerated *hostility*. Such exaggerated emotions are understandable when an anxious and insecure person has become dependent for his hopes of recovery upon a person invested in the patient's mind with authority and prestige. But there is no good reason for supposing that they involve in every case a revival of conflicting feelings identical with those experienced towards one or other parent in childhood, as suggested in the analytical concept of 'transference'. Nor is there impressive evidence that the success of treatment depends wholly on the extent to which the nature of such a relationship can be laid bare and the emotions linked with it given free expression.

After 3–6 months of such simple psychotherapy many neurotic patients show *considerable improvement*. They report that they feel more calm and secure, more confident that in future they will be less at the mercy of their neurotic difficulties. Where there have been phobias, compulsions or attacks of anxiety, they may occur with diminished frequency and be experienced with less apprehension. Having been encouraged to look upon his life as a continuous whole and helped to understand something about the forces that have made him what he is, the patient may adopt a more dispassionate and tolerant view of himself and others. An intelligent man may in this way learn to direct his energies in a more purposeful manner, to adopt a more philosophical attitude towards life and to sift the trivial from that which is of more lasting value in his activities and aspirations.

The psychiatrist should, however, not deceive himself by attributing the improvement to the therapeutic procedure alone; the acute exacerbations that occur in the course of neuroses have a *natural tendency to improvement*. In most cases one has merely helped this process of recovery on its way. The patient is also more able to cope with the residual disability or with any recurrence of symptoms, and there is consequently less disorganization of his life. But specific disabilities such as phobias, compulsions, depersonalization, sexual deviation, and hysterical conversion symptoms resist complete eradication, even when psychological factors in causation have been laid bare, and traumatic experiences have been relived and abreacted. Psychoanalysts would hold that the patients cling to their defences. But it would seem more likely that constitutional factors play some part and the mechanisms underlying neurotic symptoms also have their own impetus and can be influenced only within certain limits by psychological measures.

With simpler psychotherapy as with *psychoanalysis* many neurotic patients improve, but cures are rare. There appears to be no evidence to suggest that the patient with a severe neurosis has been helped more and his improvement lasts longer following three years of analysis than if he had been under the less disturbing and exacting attentions of a wise and sympathetic psychiatrist of any other school. After making allowances for the tendency to spontaneous improvement or recovery in the neuroses, any success achieved in the course of psychotherapy is probably due as much to the personality of the therapist as to the theories of psychopathology he holds.

The outlook of some intellectuals of our time is often so coloured by cynicism, ennui and a preoccupation with the destructive and sordid in human nature that their adjustment to life tends to be a precarious one. Not infrequently they turn to the psychoanalyst to explain and alleviate their unhappiness. Jung is probably right in holding that some neurotic subjects seeking help are really groping for *some system of religious belief* which will provide them with a source of strength and render their lives meaningful. These probably include the individuals whose problems were in former times dealt with by the priest, the confessor or the head of the family; the hesitant, the guilt-ridden, the excessively timid, those lacking clear convictions with which to face life. Psychoanalysis, in explaining religion, art, politics, social phenomena, literature, sport, as well as mental illness, as forms of sublimation of the conflicts generated during the period of infantile attachment to the parents, does, in fact, seem to provide an all-embracing explanation for human aspirations and activities. It may achieve for some of these patients what religious conversion will do for others.

We must give what help we can to the patient with a neurosis; this will, in the present state of our knowledge, often take the form of psychotherapy aided by treatment with drugs and, in patients with circumscribed phobias or deviant sexual tendencies, behaviour therapy. As Marks and Gelder (1966b) have pointed out, there is a good deal of common ground between these two forms of treatment and in practice they may complement each other. Abreactive techniques have a valuable role in treating certain types of neurotic patient (see p. 181). The aid of relatives and friends in the rehabilitation of a patient and the reordering of his life should always, where possible, be enlisted. But it cannot be claimed that we know how to cure neurotics; no specific treatment is known and certainly no psychological treatment that can claim successes as striking as those achieved in depressive illness with the aid of anti-depressive drugs or electroconvulsive treatment.

SPECIAL TECHNIQUES IN PSYCHOLOGICAL TREATMENT

Hypnosis

Suggestion plays some part in many forms of medical treatment and the 'placebo responses' of which so much has been written in recent years are attributed to its potency. In the formal technique of hypnosis the efficacy of suggestion is exploited for the relief of symptoms. The popularity of hypnosis has been subject to marked fluctuations but it has finally settled into a modest position in the armamentarium of psychiatric therapies. Hypnosis is useful only as an adjunct to other forms of treatment and should never be undertaken without careful preliminary psychiatric exploration. It is wholly contraindicated in psychotic patients and in most subjects with prominent hysterical traits in their personality. It has, however, a limited value in eliminating hysterical symptoms that have survived long after the traumatic experiences and conflicts that initiated them have passed. Among the most favourable cases are those in whom conversion symptoms such as aphonia, paralysis or amnesia arising in a state of severe anxiety (the hysterical symptoms of the so-called 'fright neurosis') continue unchanged when the emotional disturbance has died down. Hypnosis may also prove effective in patients with monosymptomatic phobias or isolated hypochondriacal symptoms, and particularly those that initially arose in a setting of acute anxiety. In more generalized phobic anxieties the benefits of hypnosis are prone to prove evanescent. In some stages of the management of chronic psychosomatic disorders such as asthma, migraine and spastic colon, hypnosis may prove of value but clinical judgement of a high order is needed and, in the presence of disabling physical illness, collaboration with a general physician is desirable.

Treatment should begin by giving the patient a simple, matter-of-fact explanation of the objectives of hypnotic treatment and the procedures that will be followed. The approach should be friendly and sympathetic and aimed at securing his co-operation. It is unnecessary and undesirable to introduce a note of mystery or drama into the proceedings and the psychiatrist should take care to avoid suggestions that he is in a position of authority or dominance over the patient. In the induction of hypnosis a variety of procedures is followed but they are all based on the same principle. The patient reclines in a comfortable position on a couch in a quiet room in which the lights have been dimmed. He is asked to place himself in a position of comfort and relaxation. When he appears quiet and composed, he is invited to fix his gaze on the tip of a pencil or on a coin held just above the eyes while the physician tells him in a quiet, steady tone of voice that his limbs are relaxing more and more, his eyelids are feeling heavier and closing slowly and that he is growing more and more fatigued and drowsy. The suggestions are repeated until voluntary movement gradually wanes, the eyelids droop, the patient adopts a relaxed and immobile posture and breathing becomes deep and regular. At this point he is told that he will be asleep before the physician has counted up to ten and the counting then begins. Throughout the procedure, the precise suggestions made to the patient are varied according to the reactions towards relaxation and drowsiness observed by the physician. When the hypnotic state is established, suggestions can be made to eliminate hysterical or phobic symptoms. Feelings of tightness in the chest or the head may be countered by suggestions that breathing is proceeding with greater ease or comfort and that tension in the head has subsided. When the physician wishes to terminate a hypnotic session he gives warning that he will count backwards from ten to one and that at the end of the count, the patient will feel fully awake, alert and well. The count-down is then proceeded with.

At a later stage, when the procedure for inducing the hypnotic state is well established suggestions can be made that the symptoms will be relieved and appear with less frequency between sessions of treatment. Although the physician must avoid extravagant or histrionic display and maintain a composed and serene demeanour he should have complete confidence in his ability to induce a hypnotic state. However, even the most experienced practitioners may require a number of sessions to induce a satisfactory degree of hypnosis in some patients.

Abreaction

The hypnotic session can be utilized to revive and bring into consciousness forgotten and other traumatic experiences, a process that is often associated with the discharge of pent-up emotion. The catharsis thus induced may result in emotional relief after the end of the abreactive session, although only in cases in which the trauma has been a relatively recent, specific one is the benefit likely to be of a lasting nature. Abreaction promoted under hypnosis was utilized by Breuer and Freud in the early days of psychoanalysis and was at first regarded as the specific curative mechanism in the treatment of hysteria. It was later abandoned but rediscovered during the Second World War (Sargant and Slater, 1940; Grinker and Spiegel, 1945; Sargant and Shorvon, 1945). The most commonly used abreactive agent is a $2\frac{1}{2}$ per cent. solution of sodium thiopentone which is injected slowly at the rate of about 1 ml. per minute. When deep and regular respiration is established and before consciousness is lost, the patient is encouraged to recall and re-enact the experiences that were associated with the onset of symptoms. When traumatic experiences are recounted it is desirable that the therapist should encourage a free expression of emotion, and some workers claim that this emotional catharsis is essential for the success of the treatment. However, patients with anxiety states of recent onset given a course of thiopentone injections often abreact little or not at all, yet derive benefit.

In patients who are markedly inhibited, obsessional and tongue-tied and in whom there is reason to believe that some recent traumatic experience has been 'lost' or 'buried', it has been found useful (Sargant and Slater, 1963) to combine a $2\frac{1}{2}$ per cent. solution of sodium thiopentone with Methedrine in a dose of 10 mg. which can subsequently be increased to 40 mg. to 50 mg. if required. The injection is given at the same rate as intravenous barbiturate. Most patients are thus induced to talk in a fluent, rapid manner. Recent traumatic experiences are often vividly re-enacted to the accompaniment of intense emotion and excitement. Selection for this form of abreaction should be undertaken with great care; there is considerable hazard of addiction in highly unstable and psychopathic subjects.

Ether administered through an open mask has been used with soldiers to induce an excitatory abreaction. The expression of emotion is generally of a more violent nature, the patient becomes intensely excited, reaching a climax of terror in which he may scream, shout and become angry or aggressive. The climax of excitement is followed by sudden quiescence and cessation of effort in which the patient is unresponsive. This crescendo of excitement followed by collapse is considered to have therapeutic value and some workers regard the content of the memories abreacted as being of no material importance. Accordingly the therapist attempts to stimulate the patient's excited and aggressive behaviour and recordings of the noise of battle may be utilized to lend a quality of verisimilitude to the patient's recovered memories. The procedure may be repeated on a number of occasions until a feeling of relaxation and well-being has been induced. It is not without risk and should not be employed on other than young subjects of robust physique in whom evidence of physical disability or disease has been rigorously excluded. Ether abreaction proved a useful first aid measure in cases fresh from the battlefield but there is little evidence that it has a place of value in peace-time psychiatric practice.

Group Therapy

During recent years, this form of treatment has attracted growing attention, because of the possibilities it offers for providing some help to a relatively *large number of patients*. It is often useful in some cases inaccessible to individual psychotherapy, and its possibilities in the treatment of individuals whose disability is predominantly a failure of social adjustment have been explored in units devoted to the treatment of severely handicapped psychopathic and neurotic patients. The best known of these units was run by Maxwell Jones (Jones, 1952) on 'therapeutic community' lines for patients who had severe difficulties in their interpersonal relationships and had in a majority of cases had a highly disturbed background and a long history of social maladjustment. Treatment at this unit was conducted exclusively in groups on the assumption that through the social pressures applied by the patients on each other in a democratic and permissive community, their behaviour could become gradually more adapted to reality. The same techniques have been applied in the programmes of treatment organized for criminal psychopaths in some countries (Stürup, 1952) and in some residential establishments for young delinquents. Some workers have also reported encouraging results with group treatment in chronic alcoholic subjects (Walton, 1961). Others have applied the technique to groups of patients with some other disability in common such as chronic schizophrenia, anxiety neurosis, drug addiction or to the families of patients with psychiatric disorder. A monograph has been devoted to the theory and practice of group therapy by Foulkes and Anthony (1957) whose orientation is psychoanalytical.

The simplest type of treatment takes the form of *explanatory lectures* in which the aetiology and mechanism of symptoms is described. This helps to banish the morbid and erroneous ideas which neurotics often accumulate about their illness, and to instil some degree of insight. Moreover, to the socially isolated and friendless individual, preoccupied with his complaints, it is instructive to compare his own predicament with that of other individuals afflicted in a similar manner whether they are more or less successful in grappling with their disability. By means of these and other interactions he is encouraged to draw upon the experience and example of a group as well as to contribute to it.

Some group treatments aim at a more *systematic approach* to the problems of the individual members. Members of the group are carefully selected and comprise from eight to ten patients meeting for a session of half an hour to one-and-a-half hours each week. The choice of topic is left to the patients, and discussion of private and emotionally significant subjects is encouraged. The therapist remains as far as possible in the background intervening only to guide and interpret the discussion at suitable points. His role is always important because it is his conduct of the meetings that determines whether the pattern of interaction between the members and their influence upon each other will prove enlightening and constructive or otherwise. The technique of group treatment has been considerably influenced by the views of Slavson (1950), who originally introduced group therapy for problem children. He stressed the importance of a permissive atmosphere, in which the child's aggressiveness and anti-social behaviour is tolerated. Through the affection and acceptance of the therapist, the child can be gradually guided to a less egocentric and more socially acceptable pattern of conduct.

In *psycho-drama*, the patient presents dramatized episodes from his life, with the aid of a cast which he selects from among the other patients and nurses. In attempting to bring his characters to life, he has in some measure to identify himself with them. As a result he may begin to see them and himself in a more objective and tolerant light. His insight may be further deepened in the discussion which follows the play, and in which the patients take part freely. At the end, the doctor sums up and emphasizes the points that are of crucial importance in relation to the patient's own problem, as well as those that are of general significance for the group that forms the audience (Jones, 1952).

A combination of group and individual forms of treatment is used at the *Institution for Criminal Psychopaths*, at Herstedvester in Denmark, where under the directorship of Stürup an attempt is being made to re-socialize criminal offenders. Under Section XVII of the Danish Criminal Law, patients suffering from mental disorder other than insanity or mental defect, may be sent to the Psychopathic Prison on an *indeterminate sentence*. Release can be sanctioned only by the court which convicted the prisoner, and this is usually done on the recommendation of the medical superintendent (Taylor, 1949). Some of the patients suffer from life-long anomalies of behaviour that have brought them into conflict with society since adolescence or childhood; they are, in other words, *severely disturbed psychopaths*. Among them are sex perverts, drifters, 'epileptoids', but also epileptics with psychopathic trends and cases of psychopathy following cerebral injury and other organic diseases of the brain.

The institution resembles a hospital rather than a prison in its structure and has ample *facilities for occupation* directed towards social resettlement of the inmates. While no one is compelled to work, luxuries such as cigarettes and newspapers can be purchased only with money earned by voluntary labour. There is a *lively social life*, with facilities for sports, games and entertainments, but also opportunities for further education. The ability to make a suitable adjustment to work and social life in the institution is one of the criteria determining fitness for discharge.

When first admitted, the patient is over-optimistic, but, when, after a few months, he comes to realize that he is separated from society for an indefinite period, he gives way to despair. This stage is used to help and encourage him to overcome his problems. The doctor in charge of the patient now spends long sessions with him, attempting to deepen his insight and put him on the road to a new adjustment. In favourable cases, there follows a *maturing period*, in which the patient shows evidence that he is capable of a cooperative and constructive life in the society that had judged him unfit for liberty. All the individuals around him—orderlies, his family, fellow-detainees, as well as the physician—collaborate in remoulding the patient's attitude. Treatment by the doctor alone is, according to Stürup, futile. The regulations of the Institution are based on the assumption that the patient is to a large extent *responsible for his behaviour*. Only great emotional stress is accepted as an extenuating factor diminishing responsibility for anti-social conduct. The patient is helped to adjust to laws which, while resembling in most respects those operating in the outside world are, in some ways, more logical and just.

Stürup (1952) has pointed out that difficult problems arise in the doctor–patient relationship because this is over-shadowed to a much greater extent than usual by the *responsibility of the physician to society*. Yet some 50 per cent. of the patients admitted have been successfully rehabilitated. Patients are discharged on parole and carefully followed up by welfare workers, who make every attempt to help them to hold down a job at which they can earn their own living. The Herstedvester experiment will doubtless be given detailed study in coming years. The experience gained there has paved the way for the establishment of similar institutions such as Grendon Underwood in England.

Behaviour Therapy

The past decade has seen the development of a variety of treatments derived from learning theory. The various methods have been subsumed under the heading of '*behaviour therapy*' which owes its inspiration to workers such as Pavlov, Hull, Skinner and Mowrer who have applied theories of learning to abnormal human behaviour. An early application of learning theory to psychotherapy was undertaken by Jones (1924) who treated a child with a severe phobic aversion to animals, fur objects and similar articles. The child was deconditioned by feeding him in the presence of a rabbit in a cage which was initially placed at some distance from the child and then gradually brought nearer. The explicit application of learning theory to the treatment of neurotic subjects on a large scale was first undertaken by Wolpe (1954, 1958). He has given a full account of his techniques of treatment in a number of papers. Eysenck and his co-workers (Eysenck, 1960b; Eysenck and Rachman, 1965a) have developed a general theory of neurosis in terms of theories of learning and have related the concepts of neuroticism and extraversion/introversion to these theories.

The exponents of behaviour therapy postulate that, although the neurotic patient may be genetically predisposed to develop a neurotic illness, his neurotic symptoms are learnt; 'neurotic symptoms are learned patterns of behaviour which for some reason or another are unadaptive' (Eysenck, 1960a). Anxiety is 'usually the central constituent of this behaviour, being invariably present in the causal situation' (Wolpe, 1961). Phobias may, for example, be regarded as conditioned fear reactions. It will follow that the laws of learning can be applied to such behaviour. Learning theory not only explains how new patterns of behaviour are acquired but also how they may be unlearned or eliminated by a process of extinction or by inhibition. Accordingly, neurotic behaviour may be unlearnt by using methods embodying these processes.

Once having developed an anxious or neurotic response to a particular situation the affected individual tends to avoid exposure to this situation. This serves to perpetuate the neurotic disability. For conditioned anxiety reactions can only be extinguished by repeated failure to reinforce them so that extinction cannot occur so long as the patient avoids the noxious circumstances. Moreover, as the patient responds to the anxiety-provoking situation by withdrawing from it, avoidance behaviour tends to become reinforced since this leads to a reduction in anxiety (Rachman and Costello, 1961). This is what Eysenck (1960b) refers to as 'the vicious circle which protects the conditioned fear response from extinction'. However, neurotic behaviour may, under some circumstances, result 'not only from the learning of an unadaptive response, but from the failure to learn an adaptive response' (Eysenck 1960a). Enuresis is an example of this.

The treatment that occupies a central place in Wolpe's techniques is 'reciprocal inhibition' which has been described by him in the following terms: 'If a response antagonistic to anxiety can be made to occur in the presence of anxiety-provoking stimuli so that it is accompanied by a complete or partial suppression of the anxiety responses, the bond between these stimuli and the anxiety responses will be weakened' (Wolpe, 1958). To inhibit and extinguish anxiety Wolpe makes use of three types of response which are antagonistic to it. These are assertive or approach responses, relaxation responses, sexual responses and other 'pleasant' responses in the life situation.

In the 'reciprocal inhibition' technique employed by Wolpe the first step is to construct an anxiety hierarchy derived from the clinical history, information obtained at interview and psychological test responses. The hierarchy consists of a list of stimuli ranked in order of their potency in provoking anxiety in the patient; these can subsequently be confronted in imagination by the patient as graded stimuli. The patient is given training in deep muscle relaxation often using hypnosis (Jacobson, 1938), and treatment commences by his being asked to imagine a situation which ranks at the bottom of the anxiety hierarchy while he is completely relaxed. If relaxation is undisturbed this is followed by imagining the next item on the list and so on. Treatment proceeds until the first situation in the hierarchy can be presented without disturbing the relaxed state.

The advantages claimed for this technique are that the prime aim of the treatment can be clearly stated in every case, it can be carried out before an unconcealed audience, it does not entail collecting a large number of anxiety-producing objects, the therapists can be interchanged if desired, the method is relatively brief, demanding an average of thirty sessions, and lastly it is more efficacious than other methods of psychotherapy. Wolpe (1961) has claimed that in a series of 210 patients treated, 89 per cent. showed marked improvement. Unfortunately, these were a selected group; some being rejected from the series even after treatment had been started, and controls were not used.

Other techniques that have been used by behaviour therapists have included aversive conditioning using chemical or electrical methods (Blakemore et al., 1963a), extinction based on negative practice (Jones, 1960) and avoidance learning (Lovibond, 1963).

Reciprocal inhibition has been mainly employed for the treatment of anxiety-driven avoidance responses such as phobic states or obsessional disorders. In the case of maladaptive approach responses, such as alcoholic addiction or deviant sexual behaviour, an *aversive deconditioning* technique has usually been employed, consisting of repeated association of the habit or substance in question with some unpleasant stimulus. The usual technique in alcoholics on whom it has been used for some three decades, has been to give a succession of 9–12 treatments in which the sight, smell and taste of alcohol has been associated with the onset of nausea induced by drugs such as apomorphine or emetine (see p. 409). This form of treatment has fallen out of favour for a variety of reasons. It was unpleasant and arduous and the results obtained were equivocal. In addition, the technique employed by some clinicians has been criticized on theoretical grounds by some workers (Eysenck and Rachman, 1965a). More recently aversive techniques have been applied to the treatment of sexual disorders, and electrical stimuli are increasingly replacing drugs. However, Raymond (1956) successfully treated a man with a fetish for handbags and perambulators whose condition had resisted psychoanalytic therapy. The treatment consisted of exhibiting to the patient a collection of handbags and perambulators immediately before the onset of nausea provoked by apomorphine. The programme of deconditioning was arduous, consisting of 2 hourly sessions day and night for a week followed by further sessions 8 days and 6 months later. This patient is said to have shown marked improvement in his social and occupational adjustment in addition to elimination of the fetish.

The efficacy of 'massed practice' is attributed to the fact that the evocation of any response tends to generate reactive inhibition which dissipates with time. If, however, the patient is encouraged voluntarily to perform the behaviour pattern in question in rapid succession for a period of time, reactive inhibition builds up and extinction of the undesired behaviour is promoted. Applying these principles in the treatment of tics, Yates (1958) showed that the optimal technique was massed practice of the tics followed by prolonged rest to permit the dissipation of reactive inhibition. The results were in accord with experimental findings and theoretical expectations.

The introduction of behaviour therapy has been valuable in certain ways. It has a rationale that is firmly based on the results of experimental psychology and it leads to deductions that may be tested by experimental methods. It has, therefore, stimulated a renewed interest in psychological methods of treatment and assessment of results by objective and controlled investigations.

However, the value of the treatment and the validity of the theory of neurosis from which it derives must be judged by the successes achieved. If the symptoms reflect faulty learning and constitute the whole of the neurosis, it should be possible to achieve lasting cures by unlearning the symptoms; that is by extinguishing maladaptive conditioned reflexes. In seeking answers to these questions one meets the difficulty that many of the enquiries reported by behaviour therapists have been uncontrolled and are therefore of little scientific value. The results of some more objective recent enquiries (Meyer and Gelder, 1963; Marks and Gelder, 1965) suggest that in isolated animal and other object phobias treatment is often successful although relapses occur in some cases within a relatively short time. In the milder forms of agoraphobia treated in out-patients, behaviour therapy induced more symptomatic improvement than individual or group psychotherapy given to matched controls (Gelder, Marks, Sakinofsky, and Wolff, 1964). Ashem (1963) and Clark (1963b) also describe the successful treatment of monosymptomatic phobias, which Freeman and Kendrick (1960) had previously shown to be particularly suitable for reciprocal inhibition treatment. The results recorded in isolated cases of patients with circumscribed disabilities of a fetishistic or fetishist-transvestite kind combined are likewise promising. However, the value of behaviour therapy in patients suffering from more widespread and pervasive neurotic disorders is far from being established.

Despite long and arduous treatment averaging 4–5 months Marks and Gelder (1965) found that patients with the severe and extensive situational anxieties found in phobic anxiety-depersonalization or agoraphobic cases showed an improvement rate of 55–60 per cent.

at the end of treatment. This was better than the result in controls but the difference was related to more frequent and longer treatment. At the end of the year patients on behaviour therapy were not significantly better than controls, and the majority of patients showed considerable residual disability. In a prospective controlled trial of behaviour therapy in 20 patients with severe agoraphobia (Gelder and Marks, 1966), the results were found to differ little from those achieved with brief re-educative psychotherapy. Seven out of ten patients had improved symptomatically in each group at the end of treatment. Although phobic patients had shown more improvement in their ability to work at the termination of treatment, this advantage was lost at follow-up. As Cooper (1963) points out, in addition to the behaviour therapy other factors, including the emotional inter-relationship between therapist and patient, probably influence the results. Other therapists (Meyer and Gelder, 1963) have also commented on the marked dependence on therapists that is prone to develop in the course of treatment.

Further, in addition to the phobic symptoms, patients of the agoraphobic kind commonly have a rich symptomatology which often includes derealization, panic attacks, syncope, temporal lobe features, depressive and hypochondriacal symptoms, and the development of all these features, following stresses, which are in some instances trivial, is difficult to explain in terms of learning theory alone. Although the value of behaviour therapy seems fairly well established in patients with neurotic and other disabilities of a very circumscribed nature, when it comes to the more diffuse disabilities that are far more common in everyday psychiatric practice the verdict of 'not proven' returned by Cooper (1963) appears justified. However, behaviour therapy and learning theory have not only fostered more rigorous methodology in the treatment of neuroses and deviations and in the assessment of results of such treatment but have shed valuable light on psychopathological problems. There is a certain parallelism in the results achieved in relation to phobic symptoms on the one hand and sexual deviations on the other. Behaviour therapy succeeds in monosymptomatic phobias and cases of fetishism or fetishistic transvestism. This appears somewhat paradoxical in that symptoms generally arise early in life in the former whereas in the latter disordered behaviour does not appear until adolescence or much later in adult life. It is not the duration of symptoms but the extent to which personality functioning as a whole is affected that may decide the outcome. Although the effects of behaviour therapy show a remarkable specificity both in relation to phobic states and sexual deviations (impotence for example rarely complicates aversion treatment), symptomatic improvement is often followed by general improvement in social adaptation. In a recent study of faradic aversion treatment in five fetishistic and transvestite subjects with well-adjusted personalities, sexually deviant desires and practices were extinguished in all cases. On careful evaluation of the patients' attitudes and measurements the penis transducer provided objective confirmation that the changes in attitude and behaviour were real. A surprising finding was the disappearance of associated masochistic behaviour in one subject and of tendencies towards trans-sexualism in another, as the fetishist symptoms were extinguished. These observations suggest that fetishist and transvestite deviations may be the primary components of some more complex forms of sexual maladjustment and that the treatment of the cross-dressing child or adolescent may prove the most useful approach towards the intractable problem of trans-sexualism. However, such hopes probably go beyond the promise of existing observations. The most encouraging results have been achieved with disorders that can be regarded as relatively simple learned responses, and even in these the results of long-term follow up studies are awaited.

CHAPTER IV

AFFECTIVE DISORDERS

(Manic-depressive Psychoses and Constitution, Involutional Melancholia)

DEFINITION

THE term 'affective disorders' is used for a group of mental diseases with a primary disturbance of affect from which all the other symptoms seem more or less directly derived. The affect is of a special kind, varying between the poles of *cheerfulness and sadness*. This is clearly expressed in Kraepelin's term 'manic-depressive insanity'. Affective disturbances can be found in nearly all psychoses, but mainly as secondary alterations; and these disorders are not thereby qualified for inclusion in the affective group of mental diseases. Anxiety and irritability may, however, play an important part in some cases of affective disorder. The illness has a second characteristic: periodicity. In typical cases elevation or depression of mood alternate with free intervals in which there is a complete return to the normal. In fact, the capacity for recovery from the single attack without impairment of mental integrity is the third characteristic of the illness.

Around the nucleus of the periodic manic-depressive illness, first described by Falret (1854, 1864) and Baillarger (1853/4) under the name of '*folie circulaire*', other French psychiatrists grouped many variants of periodic disorders containing depressive or manic phases only, with longer or shorter lucid intervals, and gave each variant its special name. It was Kraepelin who saw that the different forms belong to one nosological entity; he included isolated attacks of mania and depression, and, after some hesitation, also the depressions of later life (involutional melancholia) into his manic-depressive insanity. After the concept was established, *borderline states* were described with mild or attenuated forms of the principal symptoms: the depressive, hypomanic and cyclothymic constitutions, lately summed up under the term *cycloid* or *cyclothymic temperaments*. Although they may exist independently, they often constitute soil on which the severer disorders grow.

Far commoner than the attenuated forms of manic-depressive psychosis are the neurotic depressions which figure so prominently in contemporary clinical practice. The immediate response these conditions make to modern antidepressive remedies is similar to that seen in endogenous depression. This may suggest that they have some inherent metabolic or endogenous basis and lead to classification of such conditions with the manic-depressive psychoses. Yet their long-term response to treatment differs markedly from that of endogenous depressions proper and so does their clinical profile. It is probable that the concept of manic-depressive psychosis has become unnecessarily blurred in recent years in clinical practice and the time has come to redefine it with the aid of systematic clinical and modern statistical techniques. Clinical, genetic and prognostic criteria ought to be applied afresh to psychiatric disorders in which depressive symptoms figure prominently. Recent studies suggest (Kiloh and Garside, 1963; Carney *et al.*, 1965; Angst and Perris, 1967) that there may be qualitative as well as quantitative distinctions to be made among the depressive disorders. The next few years should see more studies along such lines. These should ultimately enable us to define the lines of demarcation between conditions such as manic-depressive psychosis, involutional melancholia and neurotic and reactive depressions with greater precision.

INCIDENCE

Estimations of the incidence of mental illnesses have been made from samples of the general population in Germany, Switzerland and, very extensively, in Scandinavia. The prevalence of affective disorders is not a very meaningful concept since only a small proportion of persons, who at some time in their lives have an affective illness, will be found suffering from it at the time of investigation. It is accordingly customary to consider the expectation of illness, which is equivalent to the risk of having such an illness at some time in one's life, given survival to an advanced age. The following estimates may be quoted:

Expectation of manic-depressive illness			as percentage in	
Date	Region	Author	Males	Females
1938	(pooled)	Slater	0·36	0·4
1946	Norway	Ødegaard	0·6	0·8
1951	Denmark	Fremming	1·02	2·2
1954	Sweden	Larsson and Sjögren	0·9	1·2
1959	U.K.	Norris	0·8	1·4
1964	Iceland	Helgason	1·8	2·5

The amount of variation from country to country is not very great, and is probably not significant. Nevertheless, it is probable that there are differences between populations which may depend on differences in physical environment, culture, race, etc., i.e. may be due to environmental or genetic factors. In his study of an isolated Swedish population living north of the Arctic Circle, Böök (1953a) found a virtual absence of affective disorder, though schizophrenia was about three times as common as in other places; there is some evidence that affective illness is commoner in people of Jewish stock than in Gentile families living alongside them (Weinberg and Lobstein, 1936); and in their study of an American religious endogamous sect, the Hutterites, Eaton and Weil (1955) found schizophrenic illness rare, depressive illnesses common. There is also some evidence that affective disorder is more frequent in the upper social strata than in the general population. In a recent enquiry into the epidemiology of mental disorders in Iceland (Helgason, 1964) the highest morbid risk for manic-depressive psychosis was found in the first of the three social classes into which the population was subdivided. The discrepancy was greatest in men ($3 \cdot 36 \pm 0 \cdot 85$ in Class I, as against $1 \cdot 99 \pm 0 \cdot 53$ in Class III).

A suggestive feature of the figures given in the table is the tendency to find larger estimates in recent years. This is perhaps most plausibly explained as evidence of greater willingness on the part of the patient to seek admission to hospital for a depressive illness, and, perhaps, a greater hope of receiving benefit from doing so. Furthermore, with the increasing readiness of hospitals to admit patients with neurotic syndromes, the possibility arises that neurotic depressive reactions may come to be included under manic-depressive states. This may help to explain the fact that, from the figures provided by the Registrar General for the year 1960, such high values are derived: an expectation for males of 2.4 per cent., and for females of 3·9 per cent. of admission to hospital for a manic-depressive reaction during a life-span of 75 years.

The greater frequency of admission affects not only manic-depressive but all forms of mental disorder. In the Registrar General's tabulation for the years 1952 to 1960 the following percentage increases are found:

Per cent. increase from 1952–1960 in rate of first admissions	Males	Females
Manic-depressive reaction	79	98
Schizophrenia	9	23
Senile and presenile psychoses	12	34
Psychoneuroses	50	54
Disorders of character, behaviour and intelligence	111	80

The distribution of onset of manic-depressive reaction by age is a matter of considerable interest, and is shown in the following table and in Fig. 2. In both sexes the peak is found in the 55–65 age group; but age of onset tends to be lower in the female and the means of the two distributions are for males 53·2 and for females 50·6 years. The table also shows the shift in sex ratio which occurs with age. In earlier ages the risk is almost twice as great in females as in males, but parity is achieved by old age.

FIRST ADMISSION RATES FOR MANIC-DEPRESSIVE REACTION FOR 1960

Age from	First admissions rates per million		M/F ratio*	Per cent. of risk to 75 survived	
	Males	Females		Males	Females
10–	3	3			
15–	71	138	0·55	0	0
20–	177	350	0·58	2	2
25–	273	593	0·53	5	6
35–	399	741	0·57	16	21
45–	456	771	0·66	33	40
55–	646	825	0·82	52	60
65–	529	756	0·76	78	81
75+	268	299	0·92	100	100

* based on average of years 1952–1960.

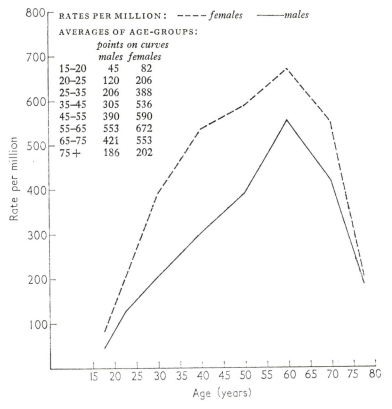

RATES PER MILLION: ---- *females* ——— *males*

AVERAGES OF AGE-GROUPS:

	points on curves	
	males	*females*
15–20	45	82
20–25	120	206
25–35	206	388
35–45	305	536
45–55	390	590
55–65	553	672
65–75	421	553
75+	186	202

FIG. 2. First admissions for manic-depressive reaction, 1952–1960.

BASIC PERSONALITY

Something is known about conditions which may be contributory aetiological factors. First among these are particular mental and physical features present before the illness and in the free intervals. In a carefully studied group of 100 manic-depressives Lange (1928) found that more than three-quarters had previously shown a *cycloid type of temperament*. Although this type of personality is not a *sine qua non* for the development of the psychosis the affinity between affective psychosis and cycloid temperament is aetiologically important, especially since Kretschmer (1936) related both to a particular type of bodily constitution.

Kretschmer gave a list of qualities of personality, which he subdivided into three groups: (i) the sociable, good-hearted, kind, and easy-going; (ii) the elated, humorous, lively, and hot-tempered; and (iii) the quiet, calm, serious, and gentle. The first group of qualities is characteristic of all cyclothymics, and the second and third of hyper- and hypothymic types of cycloid personality respectively. Kretschmer found such types of personality not only among his patients before the onset of any illness but also among their relations, even those who never became psychotic.

If Kraepelin's original conception of the manic-depressive constitution is adopted, four types may be distinguished (see the accompanying table). They have been considered the *'basic states'* from which the psychoses rise like mountain peaks from a structurally similar level plain. The table shows the proportions in which types of constitution are severally liable to different types of psychosis.

RELATIONSHIP BETWEEN PERSONALITY AND PSYCHOSIS
(*from Kraepelin*)

Personality	Psychosis		
	Depressive %	Manic %	Manic-depressive %
Depressive	64	8	27
Hypomanic	35	23	41
Irritable	45	24	30
Cyclothymic	35	11	53

The table shows that the depressive psychosis is commoner than the manic in all types of constitution, even in the hypomanic type.

PHYSICAL CONSTITUTION

The pyknic bodily build, described by Kretschmer and associated with the cycloid temperament and with affective psychoses, is seen in its most characteristic form in middle-aged men. Large visceral cavities (thoracic, abdominal, and cranial), a tendency to fat on the trunk, especially in its lower part, slightly built shoulder-girdle, and slender extremities tapering to small hands and feet are the main characteristics. A stocky build, a broad face the features of which are not sharp or prominent but rounded like the face, a short and massive neck, and a fat and rotund abdomen complete a characteristic picture. Many other more detailed characters may be used for the diagnosis of the pyknic type in young people and in females, who are less characteristic. Anthropological measurements and indices have been used but have proved to be of comparatively little additional value, because a carefully chosen index of measurements, as applied by Linford Rees and Eysenck (1945), correlates highly, as the authors have shown, with the clinical diagnosis of the bodily constitution. The percentage of pyknics found by Kretschmer among manic-depressive patients has also been reached by some of his followers; others have reported much less striking figures. The large amount of work done on this subject in many countries has confirmed that the pyknic habitus is more frequent in patients suffering from affective disorders than in the average population.

The pyknic habitus corresponds to Sigaud's typus digestivus and to the arthritic habitus of French medicine. Arthritics are predisposed to gout, diabetes mellitus, rheumatism, and arteriosclerosis, but seem to be less liable to tuberculosis than the average. A positive correlation between gout and affective psychoses has been established, and a large percentage of mentally healthy patients with diabetes mellitus have been found to be of pyknic constitution (Lange, 1928).

Sheldon has developed the idea of correlating physique and mental features on a wider scale, using more exact methods of measurements and up-to-date statistical methods as described in the preceding chapter. His aim was not to construct a pure or ideal type, but to develop a scheme of dimensions in which every person could be placed along each of

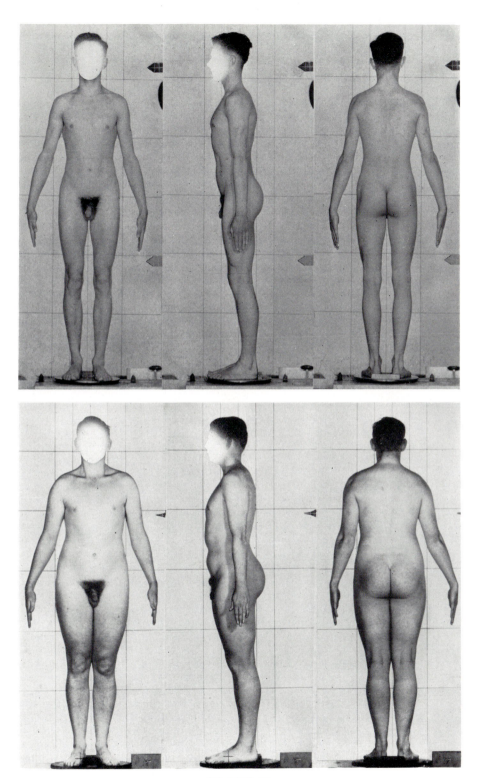

PLATE II

Above: average physique (344), age 19   Below: extreme in endomorphy (632), age 21

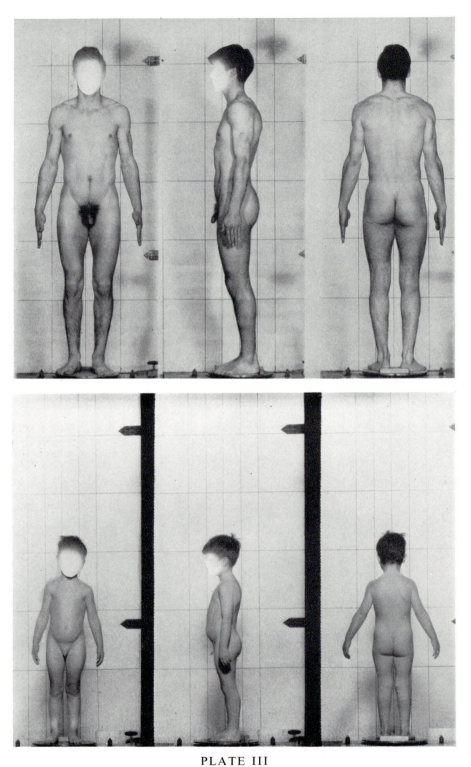

PLATE III

Extreme in mesomorphy (2½62), age 20, and the same individual aged 5 years

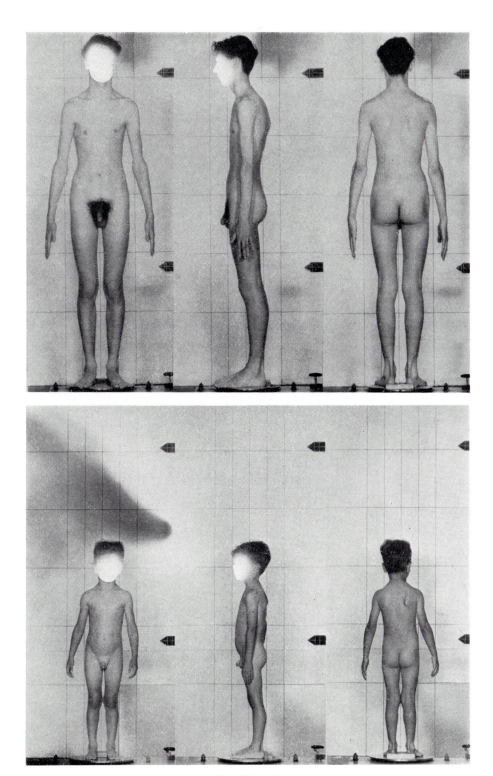

PLATE IV
Extreme in ectomorphy ($1\frac{1}{2}26\frac{1}{2}$), age 17, and the same individual aged 5 years

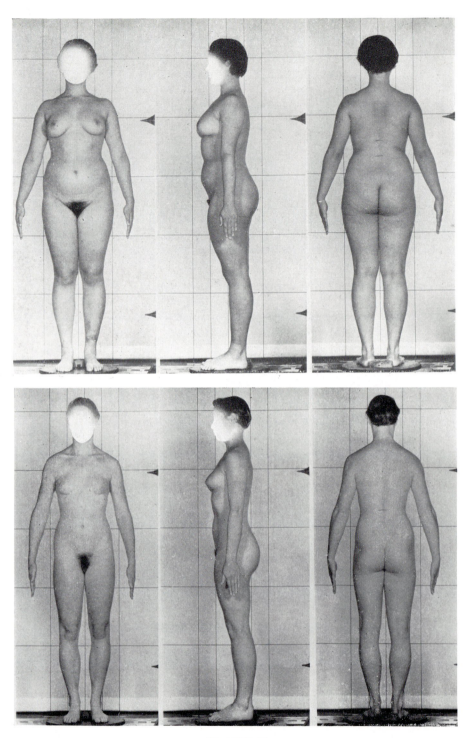

PLATE V

Above: extreme in endomorphy ($6\frac{1}{2}31\frac{1}{2}$), age 19   Below: extreme in mesomorphy ($452\frac{1}{2}$), age 19

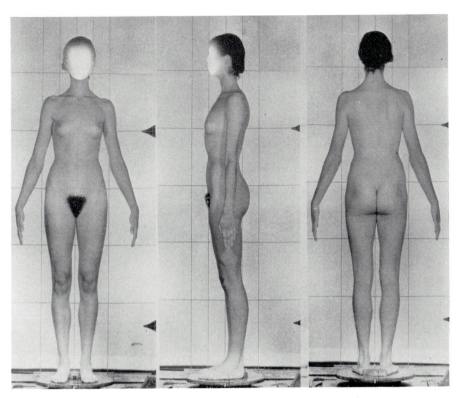

PLATE VI

Extreme in ectomorphy ($32\frac{1}{2}5\frac{1}{2}$), age 18

The photographs for Plates II–VI were kindly supplied by
Professor J. M. Tanner, Institute of Child Health, London.

the three accepted axes. A formula of three numerals could be found to express the strength of the primary components of physique. Sheldon's 'somato-types': endomorphy ('massive digestive viscera'), mesomorphy ('bone, muscle and connective tissue predominating') and ectomorphy ('fragility, linearity and delicacy throughout the body') have obvious relations to Kretschmer's pyknic, athletic and leptosomatic types, but he also describes the average individual as showing almost an even balance among the three primary components. In his work on temperament he proceeds on similar lines, again starting from normal male material. Kretschmer's manic-depressive pyknics are, according to Sheldon, fat mesomorphs or a mixture of endomorphy and mesomorphy, the latter predominant. The cyclic temperament is supposed to be a similar mixture with a considerable contribution from Sheldon's third temperamental component. The validity of Sheldon's hypothesis that the three components of physique are derived from the three primary germinal layers and are the origin of three independent types of physique has been called in question by recent investigators. A factorial analysis by Howells (1952) suggests that ectomorphy and endomorphy are not independent factors but opposite poles of a single continuum. A similar conclusion was reached by Ekman (1951) who suggests that two rather than three components are required to account for Sheldon's data. Sheldon's conclusions have also been called into question on statistical grounds (Lubin, 1950). Further work on somatotyping continues, however, and Tanner see Plates II–VI) has produced interesting data including long-term studies showing development from 5 to 20 years of age.

The *endocrine system*, with its evident influence on bodily habits and its subjection to a biological periodicity, has been held responsible by some for the fluctuations of mood in affective psychoses. On the other hand, the relevant evidence is complex and difficult to interpret. A high proportion of women are subject to menstrual and premenstrual depression, but recent enquiries have shown these mood changes to be neurotic rather than endogenous in character and highly correlated with neuroticism (Kessel and Coppen, 1963). Their relevance for the aetiology of manic-depressive psychosis is therefore doubtful. Again, the menstrual periods may cease during a severe affective psychosis but this change is more common in schizophrenia and probably no more common in affective psychosis than in severe neurotic disturbances. Attacks of mania do occur in association with Graves's disease but are so rare that they are unimportant. As far as myxoedema is concerned, the clinical picture tends to be varied and in cases free from clouding of consciousness, a predominantly paranoid illness is more common than a depressive one. It is possibly of some interest for the aetiology of endogenous depressive psychoses that a dysphoric type of depression is so commonly seen in association with a wide range of endocrine disorders (Michael and Gibbons, 1963). The administration of ACTH or cortisone, particularly in high dosage, is generally associated with mood changes mainly in the direction of euphoria, though in a proportion depressive symptoms predominate. The more severe psychotic reactions that occur in about 5 per cent. of cases have been regarded as depressive by some workers although they appear, in most instances, to combine paranoid, schizophrenic, depressive and organic features in varying proportions.

One of the observations suggesting an endocrine effect is the different *frequency* of affective illnesses *in the two sexes*. The admissions to psychiatric clinics and hospitals show that women outnumber men in a proportion of about 3 to 2. It has been pointed out that women are more ready than men to accept treatment, especially institutional treatment; that in men the diagnosis is often more difficult, and the illness is more likely to take an aberrant form, e.g. recurrent alcoholism; and that suicide is commoner in men

H

and may forestall the diagnosis; however, it seems doubtful whether all these factors can account for the whole of the difference between the sexes.

Manic-depressive illnesses show an especially *high incidence in late spring* and early summer, a phenomenon which is true of mental illnesses in general; and individual manic-depressives have their own season of the year in which they are especially likely to fall ill (Slater, 1938). Lange (1928) compared the periodicity of manic-depressive illness with the periodicity of biological functions shown by animals in *hibernation*, which shows an even closer relationship with seasonal changes.

PSYCHOPATHOLOGY

The psychopathology of the affective disorders can most easily be described by reference to the *similarity of the abnormal affect with normal emotions* of the same kind.

Sad people usually tend to be more silent than their wont and to find difficulty in concentrating on indifferent matters. The patient's sadness deepens to a morbid depression, and the difficulty in concentration becomes retardation of all thought and action. Normal cheerfulness usually brings with it greater freedom and ease of speech and movement and a stimulation of all psychological activity; and the manic state shows corresponding symptoms: lack of inhibition, apparent quickness of psychological reaction, distractibility, and flight of ideas. Elation of mood is accompanied by a feeling of *general well-being*, which in the manic state is manifested as lack of insight; a gloomy mood disposes to preoccupation with gloomy thoughts, and in the depressive are found a *hypochondriacal attitude and exaggerated complaints* of bodily ill-being. Powerful emotions of any kind militate against normal sleep, and in both types of affective psychosis insomnia is prominent. The total affective state colours not only the individual outlook but also the impression gained of the environment. An affect of this kind can be seen in the preconceptions and the misinterpretations of manics and depressives and even supply a partial interpretation of their delusional ideas.

The parallelism between abnormal and normal emotional reactions can be overemphasized; and the attempt to derive the symptoms of manic and depressive states along the line of 'understanding' (i.e. seeing in the abnormal only what is normal but in an extreme form) can easily be overdone in this as in many other fields of psychopathology.

There are, in fact, many exceptions to the general scheme. Depressives are often not noticeably inhibited but are restless and talkative without any sign of retardation. On closer examination the over-activity of manic patients is often found to be repetitive and non-productive. Depressive patients may show a complete failure of all insight, deny that they are ill, and hold steadfastly to their *ideas of guilt and punishment*. Manic patients may feel unwell and complain of their nervousness and excitability. Anxiety in depressives and irritability in both types of patient further complicate the picture; most clinicians agree that pure and uncomplicated manic and depressive states are rare. Kraepelin found it necessary to introduce a third classification of *'mixed forms'*, in which manic and depressive symptoms are inextricably intertwined. Such mixed forms are not infrequent, especially at the onset of a manic or depressive phase and at approaching recovery. Practically, however, the use of the term should be somewhat restricted and it should not be used to cover every slight deviation from the classical type.

Psychological phenomena in the cyclothymic constitutions have only a limited relevance to those of the graver affective psychoses. Schneider (1920) considers that the reactive and psychogenic depressions can be distinguished from endogenous depressions by the symptoms alone, the depressive affect in endogenous depressions having a quality of its own—'*vital depression*'. By this term attention is drawn to the deeper stratum of the personality involved in endogenous depression, a stratum closely connected with the somatic concomitants of the affect. The idea may be of help in differential diagnosis in some cases, but it is too indefinite to be a generally useful criterion. Subtle analyses of various forms of depressive illness have been made by Weitbrecht (1952), who tries to single out one group with marked somatic complaints and hypochondriacal sulkiness under the term 'endoreactive dysthymia'. The group of patients so covered seem to be, partly at least, the same as those classified by Schneider as suffering from vital depression.

One group of workers on the Continent, influenced by philosophers such as Scheler and Heidegger, have applied their method of 'existential analysis' ('*Daseinsanalyse*') to the affective psychoses; a well-known article by L. Binswanger has analysed the flight of ideas in a manic patient. The results of this and similar analyses by v. Gebsattel, E. Straus and others may give the possibility of a more refined communication with the patient, clarify details in his behaviour, and provide a fuller clinical picture and a better understanding in the single case. But it is not very generally applicable, and provides no answer to the more troublesome clinical problems. No psychopathology wearing the mantle of philosophy can tell us, for instance, why this or that symptom has appeared in this particular case while others have failed to appear. Attention to the patient as a whole, which this school emphasizes so much, may be taken too far, and is of little aid in elucidating details.

In psychoanalytic thinking (Abraham, 1911; Freud, 1927) melancholia is conceived as the individual's reaction to the loss of a love-object. As the love-object has been partially assimilated or introjected into the patient's own personality, the sadistic tendencies inherent in the ambivalent relationship with the love-object are turned inwards. This is the explanation given by psychoanalysis for the combination, in severe depressive illnesses, of some features of mourning with tendencies to self-destruction. Abraham also lays emphasis on the tendency to oral eroticism; owing to the fixation of libido at the oral level, the disappointments in love relationships experienced in early life recur in adulthood. The comparison with mourning first made by Abraham has entered into much subsequent psychoanalytic thinking. As Freud pointed out, in mourning as in melancholia there is the same psychic pain, the same temporary inability to acquire a new love-object due in each to a withdrawal of libido. Manic and hypomanic symptoms are regarded by psychoanalysts as a form of defence against feelings of depression and disappointment. The gulf between ego and superego is bridged and the patient is thus enabled to project himself without reserve or inhibition into the outer world and thus to shut out the disturbed and conflict-ridden inner one. An interesting psychodynamic study of elation has been published by Lewin (1950).

Dynamic psychologists have doubtless made a start in seeking for the explanations of certain puzzling features of the peculiarly human phenomenon of intense depression or melancholia. The combination of egotism and aggressiveness with extreme self-reproach, self-depreciation and attempted suicide requires fuller explanation than can be provided by investigations of the cross-sectional clinical picture. The psychoanalytic ideas for all their diversity and contradiction have therefore added something to our understanding of the content of the symptoms of depressive psychosis. It is doubtful, however, whether they have helped in any way to define its causes.

Lewis (1934) considered depressive states as a paradigm of *adaptive reaction of the organism* to an intolerable situation. This interpretation seems well suited to explain certain reactive depressive states and can, perhaps, be applied to depressions following severe infections and other exhaustive conditions ('organic neurasthenia', see Chapter III, p. 83). Endogenous depression leading so frequently to self-destruction can only by a 'tour de force' be ranged as an adaptive reaction to life.

AETIOLOGY, PHYSIOPATHOLOGY and BIOCHEMISTRY

Heredity

Genetical aspects of the predisposition to affective psychoses have been investigated in recent years by a number of workers. The results of earlier work, as described in the last edition of this book, were to suggest that the factor responsible was a single autosomal dominant gene of reduced penetrance and somewhat variable expressivity. Later work has tended to confirm this view, which was supported by the large-scale investigations of Stenstedt (1952, 1959). In his work on manic-depressive psychosis, Stenstedt found that approximately 12 per cent. of the first degree relatives of his probands, i.e. their parents, sibs and children, suffered from a manic-depressive psychosis; and that there was no excess of mental disorders of other kinds. In his study of involutional melancholia the corresponding figure was only 6 per cent., and Stenstedt concludes that this form of disorder is genetically heterogeneous, with a considerable admixture of exogenous states. Similar findings were made by Hopkinson (1964); morbidity risks were approximately twice as great in the first degree relatives of patients with onset before 50, as in the relatives of late onset cases. The risk figures observed correspond fairly well with those of Stenstedt and earlier workers. A well-documented twin study has been contributed by da Fonseca (1959); he found rather higher incidences in the parents, sibs and children of his probands, 23, 19 and 22 per cent. respectively. Concordance rates in the twins were 75 per cent. in MZ and 38 per cent. in DZ twins. The results are comparable with those of Kallmann (1950).

Alternative hypotheses have not been lacking. Thus, on the basis of a review of the literature, Ordonez Sierra (1962) proposes a two-gene theory: gene A the phasic gene, and gene B inhibiting its manifestation, both dominant and with respective frequencies of 0.013 and 0.36. The cycloid temperament is regarded as distinct from predisposition to psychosis and a graded character. Leonhard, Korff and Schulz (1962) offer a similar model, on the basis of family studies in 104 cases, i.e. a specific factor for manic-depressive illness, which can show itself in cyclothymia, but for the appearance of illness needing an independent affective temperament of non-specific determination. This idea is based on the results obtained by classifying affective psychoses into bipolar manic-depressive ones on one side and monopolar ones on the other. Finally, there is a theory of a radically different kind, offered by a statistical expert (Burch, 1964 a,b,c,) namely, that in all three major syndromes, manic-depressive, schizophrenic and involutional psychoses, we have to do with an autoimmune reaction. In manic-depressive psychoses two genes are hypothesized, both dominant, one X-linked and one autosomal; and the manifestation of the illness is brought about by three specific random events, leading, most probably, to a somatic mutation, with the appearance of a 'forbidden clone' of cells. This theory looks a great deal too complex to be justified by the rather rough and ready estimates we have of the basic data, especially bearing in mind the uncertainties of diagnosis.

A much more attractive hypothesis arises from the work of Edwards (1960) on quasi-continuous variations. He shows that continuous variation, e.g. in the predisposition to disease, may simulate mendelism if the disease is relatively common, say with a frequency greater than one in 1,000 and there is a threshold effect, by which a degree of variation beyond a limit manifests as an all or none reaction. Mechanisms of this kind are in fact common in medicine. On this model Edwards shows that the expected incidence of manifest disorder in the first degree relatives of sufferers should approximate to $\sqrt{p}$ where p is the frequency of the disorder in the general population. We are now faced with the difficulty of knowing what is the frequency of manic-depressive illness in the general population. If it is as low as 0.4 per cent. then we should expect only 6.3 per cent. of parents, sibs and children to be similarly affected; if it is as high as 3 per cent. then the incidence in first degree relatives should be 17 per cent. Our observational data would fit the second but not the first.

On any hypothesis the relatively greater incidence of affective psychoses in the female than in the male requires explanation. The suggestion by Burch, that an X-linked dominant gene is involved, was previously made by Rosanoff, Handy and Plesset (1935). This would be incompatible with the finding that there is no tendency on the part of affected males to pass on the predisposition exclusively to their daughters. Most workers have not been impressed by any great difference in the sex distribution of the affected children of manic-depressive fathers and manic-depressive mothers. However, this may not apply to all the clinical sub-groups of the affective psychoses. Winokur (1967) found one affected father to 8 affected mothers among the parents of male manics, but an equal distribution of 8 affected fathers to 8 affected mothers in the parents of female manics. An equivalent finding does not seem to have been made by Perris in his investigation of the families of bipolar manic-depressives.

It would be reasonable to suppose that the sex difference in liability to recurrent affective illness could be put down to a more general cause. The imposition of phasic variation is likely to produce more exaggerated peaks and troughs in a spontaneously rhythmic than in a stable constitution. This idea is supported by the fact that the sex ratio tends towards parity after the years of female reproductivity. It is, accordingly, highly interesting that both Angst (1966) and Perris (1966), while finding the usual female preponderance in manic-depressive illnesses in general, and in unipolar recurrent depressive psychoses, have found approximately equal representation of the sexes among the affected relatives of bipolar patients (i.e. those who have had both manic and depressive phases). This aspect of the problem therefore remains open.

Heterogeneity in the causation of the affective psychoses is not to be disregarded. Some psychiatrists regard endogenous and reactive depressions as polar extremes of a quantitatively variable phenomenon. There is, however, strong evidence that a qualitative distinction is to be drawn between the two types of illness; and the majority of clinicians find the distinction useful in practice, especially so in treatment. The difference between patients who respond to amine-oxidase inhibitors and those who respond to the imipramine group of antidepressants may, indeed, be based on genetical factors (Pare, Rees and Sainsbury, 1962). Further evidence comes from the study of atypical psychoses, in which affective and schizophrenic features are found combined. Leonhard (1934) has demonstrated families with affected members in which such psychoses ran true; the appearances were such as to be attributable to a dominant gene. Furthermore, atypical psychoses were only found in a high proportion of cases in atypical x atypical crossings, in which the children of doubly psychotic parents were studied (Elsässer, 1952). Kurosawa (1962), Mitsuda (1962) and Angst (1966) also observed this tendency for the clinical type of atypical psychoses to run true. The evidence suggests that specific genes may be responsible for these rare, atypical syndromes.

Remarkable findings, of a convergent kind, which suggest genetic heterogeneity in the affective psychoses have recently been reported by Angst (1966), Perris (1966) and Winokur and Clayton (1967). Angst and Perris (1967) have also collaborated in a joint comparison and analysis of their individual findings. In essence what emerges is that there may be a rather specifically genetically determined syndrome which most typically manifests as a recurrent cyclic psychosis with both manic and depressive phases, but may exhibit only the depressive half of the picture. Angst thinks that manifestation as depression is about three times as common as in a manic state. Distinct from this syndrome is another, which shows only as a depression, which may also run a phasic course. There is accordingly a good deal of clinical overlap, since the two varieties of depressive state are not easily distinguished clinically. However, among affected relatives of bipolar patients there is a higher incidence of affective illness and a more equal sex representation. Moreover bipolar psychoses are found almost exclusively among the relatives of bipolar probands. The following table from Perris illustrates the relationships:

Affective illness shown as	Numbers of relatives of 138 bipolar and 139 unipolar probands	
	Bipolar	Unipolar
Bipolar psychosis	58	2
Unipolar psychosis	3	44
Not classifiable	14	16
Suicide	32	24

Involutional melancholias, whose position in the affective series has long been disputed, would be assigned by Angst to the unipolar syndrome, and indeed regarded as not differing from other such illnesses except in the age of onset. Nearly all the schizoaffective and mixed psychoses which Angst found were among the relatives of his schizoaffective probands; among the relatives in this group were also typical affective psychoses and typical schizophrenias which however tended to be of a relatively benign kind.

Evidence for the existence of two types of affective disorder has also been reported by Winokur and Clayton (1967). One of these types might be attributable to a dominant gene: it was the families with affected persons in both parental and filial generations, i.e. with the 'dominant' type of family history, who included nearly all the manic patients. It may be said accordingly that the line of thought suggested by Leonhard and his co-workers in Germany in 1962—that at least two distinct genotypes are involved in the manic-depressive syndrome —has now been supported by evidence gathered in Sweden, Switzerland and the U.S.A., support so wide and so strong that this viewpoint must be taken very seriously. In further clinical investigations it will be incumbent on the research worker to distinguish between the unipolar and the bipolar modes of reaction.

Neurological Basis of Depression

An increasing amount of research has been directed in recent years to physiological and biochemical aspects of affective disorder. Although no relevant pathological changes of a gross kind have ever been found at post mortem in the brain of patients who had suffered from affective disorder, there has been a good deal of suggestive evidence implicating the brain as the final pathway to the causation of this group of psychiatric disturbances. Numerous diseases of the central nervous system, including general paralysis and cerebral arteriosclerosis, are commonly accompanied by affective symptoms, especially of a depressive kind. In arteriosclerotic psychosis, a depressive colouring of the organic syndrome was found in more than a quarter of the cases. The features of the manic syndrome, such as overactivity, hilariousness and an excessive feeling of well-being, have long been known to follow lesions in the orbital parts of the frontal lobes. Manic states occasionally alternating with depression have also been observed in patients with diencephalic lesions. A small number of convulsions will occasionally turn a depressive patient into a hypomanic and similar changes have recently been found during treatment of patients suffering from endogenous depression with imipramine and allied substances (Barker *et al.*, 1960). Such facts point to a central mechanism for the regulation of affective life, possibly under the control of specific biochemical processes (see next section). Further evidence about the cerebral activities possibly concerned with affective disorders may come from investigations of the mode of action of convulsive treatment and prefrontal leucotomy. Convulsive treatment leads to the development of rhythmic bilaterally synchronous bursts of slow waves which are seen at high voltage, particularly in the prefrontal areas. The changes can be potentiated by intravenous thiopentone (Roth, 1951). The frequency of relapse in an endogenous depressive illness following E.C.T. has been shown to be related to the amount of measured slow activity in the E.E.G. (Roth *et al.*, 1957) and there is evidence to link the E.E.G. changes with increased activity in a diencephalic pacemaker. The operation of prefrontal leucotomy involves severing of the fibres linking the prefrontal cortex with the dorsomedial and anterior nuclei of the thalamus which are themselves relay stations for cortical projection from the posterior hypothalamus. Here also, a quantitative principle appears to operate; the number of fibres divided and, to a lesser extent, the site of the lesion affect the outcome of the operation (Meyer and Beck, 1954) inadequate lesions being associated with an unsatisfactory result. Changes in sleep rhythm, appetite, body weight, the menstrual cycle and libido after electroconvulsive treatment and leucotomy probably reflect changes in the activity of the corresponding diencephalic regulating centres, and possibly there are physiological mechanisms common to the two treatments (Roth and Garside, 1962).

Brain Monoamines and Depression

Recent biochemical research has not only advanced our knowledge of the mode of action of antidepressive drugs but also added to our understanding of the physiopathology of affective disorders. It has been shown, for example, that most of the 5-hydroxytryptamine 5-HT) and noradrenaline (NA) in the brain is concentrated in subcortical areas in the neighbourhood of upper mid-brain, hypothalamus and third ventricle (Vogt, 1954). Whereas in most parts of the brain catecholamines and 5-HT are found together, the limbic system contains a high concentration of 5-HT and little NA, while the corpus striatum contains the greater part of all the dopamine to be found in the brain (Brodie and Costa, 1962). Drugs such as the monoamine-oxidase inhibitors, reserpine (Serpasil) and, to some extent, imipramine, which exert a striking effect upon emotional life, have been shown to give rise to specific biochemical changes in diencephalic centres.

An impressive body of evidence has accumulated to support the view that monoamine-oxidase inhibitors achieve their effects by releasing NA in the brain. The authors have made extensive use here of an important review article by Brodie and Costa (1962). Species differences in the excitatory effects of monoamine-oxidase inhibitors appear to be closely related to variations in the rate at which they cause NA levels to rise in the brains of different experimental animals. Monoamine-oxidase inhibitors give rise to an increase in excitation in animals such as the mouse, but not in dogs or cats. The difference appears to be related to the rapid rise in NA levels in the brain of the former but not of the latter group in whom 5-HT is released but not NA. The administration to mice of the NA-inhibitor MO-9-11 followed twelve hours later by the compound alpha-methyl-M-tyrosine, which releases brain NA without affecting 5-HT, elicits intense motor excitation for a period of two hours or more. The animals dart at great speed from one side of the cage to the other and also show extreme exophthalmos, hyperthermia and exquisite sensitivity to noise or touch. These effects appear to be due to the high level of free NA available at receptor sites, which may facilitate activity in neuronal pathways associated with central adrenergic mechanisms. It is, therefore, tempting to suppose that the antidepressant action of monoamine-oxidase inhibitors in man is due to an increase in brain NA, especially since iproniazid administration approximately doubles the concentration of both 5-HT and NA in the human brain stem (Ganrot et al., 1962).

It is well known that patients who have received reserpine whether for a psychiatric illness or in the course of treatment for hypertension are prone to present with a severe depressive syndrome that often has endogenous features. It is of considerable interest, therefore, that administration of reserpine appears to be associated with equally specific biochemical effects. These consist of blockage of the storage of 5-HT which depletes the stores of the amine but gives rise to an increased concentration of 5-HT at the reactive sites. It has been contended by Costa et al. (1962) that it is not the depletion of NA that causes the 'sedation' in animals and possibly depressive effect in man, as was originally claimed. Thus agents which deplete NA but not 5-HT do not give rise to sedative effects.

Attempts have been made to potentiate the antidepressive effects of MAO inhibitors by the simultaneous administration of tryptophan and tranylcypromine (Coppen et al., 1963). It was found that the effect of tranylcypromine was accelerated. The effect was a relatively specific one in that, in further studies, no potentiation of the action of imipramine could be produced with added tryptophan (Pare, 1963). The interpretation of these results is difficult, in that tryptophan could be expected to give rise to the production of both 5-HT and tryptamine at the catecholamine reactive sites. There is some evidence, however, to suggest that in man, as in the cat, a great increase in 5-HT at the reactive sites (as produced for example by the administration of nialamide) may have excitatory or antisedative rather than soporific effects (Resnick et al., 1963).

These important enquiries have now been carried further at the Karolinska Institute (Hillarp et al., 1966). Using a fluorescent histochemical technique it has been shown that, in the rat brain, there are monoaminergic neurones of three types with 5-HT and NA and DOPA as their mediators. Thus 5-HT accumulates almost exclusively within nerve terminals of the specific 5-HT neurones. A marked increase at the terminals of 5-HT neurones alone and also in their axons and cell bodies was produced by MAO inhibitors. As expected, tetrabenazine caused complete disappearance of 5-HT and NA from the appropriate neurones while imipramine had no detectable effects. These observations suggest that the monoamine-oxidase inhibitor group of antidepressive drugs exert their effects by influencing the concentration in the diencephalon of a number of transmitter substances each with its own specific effect upon certain groups of neurones. The possibility that affective psychoses are associated with changes in the activity or balance of activity in such neurones will doubtless receive increasing attention in the near future.

The effects exerted by imipramine, one of the most effective antidepressive agents, differs, as might have been expected, from those of MAO inhibitors. But much evidence has accumulated to suggest that imipramine may exert its effects by potentiation of endogenous catecholamines at the reactive sites in the brain (Scheckel and Boff, 1964). Thus both imipramine and desmethylimipramine augment the stimulating effect of DOPA and amphetamine. Sedative doses of tetrabenazine depress conditioned avoidance behaviour and this depression is reversed by MAO inhibitors. Imipramine however stimulates such behaviour when given with a non-depressant dose of tetrabenazine, a dose which selectively frees NA leaving DOPA and 5-HT levels unchanged (Scheckel and Boff, 1964). A technique that has been developed for measuring NA uptake by the intact rat brain after intraventricular injection of tritiated NA has shed further light on the situation. Uptake is markedly reduced by imipramine, desmethylimipramine and amitriptyline but not by chlorpromazine nor by a chemical relative of imipramine without clinical antidepressant action (Glowinski and Axelrod, 1964). Tricyclic compounds also reverse the reserpine syndrome probably by blocking the reuptake of NA through the synaptic membrane thus giving rise to an accumulation of NA at postsynaptic sites (Sulser et al., 1964), an effect these compounds have also been shown to produce in central neurones (Carlsson et al., 1966). All these findings have strengthened the view that the antidepressive effects of tricyclic compounds are due to enhancement of NA at receptor sites.

In attempting to account for the experimental and other observations Brodie and Costa have made use of the concepts formulated by Hess (1954) in relation to the integration of autonomic function in the diencephalon. In Hess's scheme, one component of the system, the ergotrophic component, promotes expenditure of energy by integrating behaviour patterns that prepare the body for positive action. In contrast, the other or trophotropic system, promotes recuperative patterns of behaviour. Its activation elicits drowsiness, increased central parasympathetic output, decreased motor activity and diminished responsiveness to external stimuli. It was suggested that this system is predominant in sleep, hibernation and states of apathy, whereas the ergotrophic system, which is balanced in a state of reciprocal opposition to the trophotropic one, is predominant in states of excitement or mania. Drugs producing antidepressive or sedative effects may affect the balance of one opposing component against the other. This schema will doubtless prove to be an over-simplification but it does provide tentative explanations for a diversity of facts within a simple conceptual framework, is supported by experimental observations and is broadly in accord with many of the known effects of drugs that produce affective changes in man.

It will be clear from the foregoing that there is a good deal of evidence that antidepressive drugs may exert their effects by increasing the concentration of monoamines in the diencephalon. However, it does not necessarily follow that depressive illness is caused by a corresponding deficiency of monoamines. It has to be remembered also that much of the experimental work has been done on animals and that no satisfactory animal models of depression or mania exist. Notwithstanding these reservations, the monoamine theory probably represents a significant step forward in knowledge of the underlying basis of affective disorders.

Monoamine oxidase Inhibitors and Diet

In recent years monoamine oxidase inhibitors have been found to produce a serious side-effect which has some clinical resemblance to the hypertensive crisis associated with phaeochromocytoma. Tranylcypromine (Parnate) a non-hydrazine MAO inhibitor has been found most commonly responsible, but phenelzine (Nardil) which is a hydrazine drug, has been found to produce similar effects, though less commonly. The usual syndrome consists of severe headache, commonly occipital in distribution, associated with nausea, vomiting and palpitations, together with a rise in systolic and diastolic blood-pressure. In some cases, however, there is also nuchal rigidity, photophobia and loss of consciousness. Neurological complications may in fact develop, subarachnoid and intracranial haemorrhage have been described in a number of subjects (Dorrell, 1963a, b; Blackwell, 1963a; Blackwell and Marley, 1964) and there have been some fatalities. The association between these symptoms and the ingestion of cheese is now well established (Thomas, 1963; Blackwell, 1963b). In some of the patients pre-existing arterial disease has been present, cerebral atheroma having been described by Mason (1962) and an aneurysm of the posterior communicating artery by McClure (1962). It is clear that in all such patients, as also in hypertensives, the use of these drugs is contra-indicated. The crises appear to be determined by the absorption of pressor amines of the phenyl-ethylamine group (which includes tyramine) in unmodified form. From the intestine they pass into the liver and then probably into the systemic circulation to act on peripheral adrenergic receptors. In addition to cheese, yeast extracts such as Marmite, broad beans and matured wine have been the cause of the crises, the mechanism being similar to that in relation to cheese. The monoamine-oxidase inhibitors probably interfere with the normal oxidation of the toxic substances in the gut and liver. Some aspects of the mechanism remain obscure in that not all patients who take both cheese and monoamine-oxidase inhibitors develop side-effects, nor is it clear why tranylcypromine, rather than other substances has been so often reported as the cause of a crisis. The subject of interactions of monoamine-oxidase inhibitors with other drugs and certain components of diet has been discussed in a comprehensive review article by Sjöqvist (1965).

Hypertensive crises and loss of consciousness may also follow from the potentiation of the effects of tricyclic compounds (imipramine and amitriptyline) and prolonged coma, together with hypothermia, may follow from their interaction with morphine or pethidine (Laurence, 1963). The number of these toxic effects now reported is large, some workers claim that 20 per cent. of cases treated with tranylcypromine are affected (Cooper et al., 1964). The fact that a group of antidepressive drugs can exert such striking effects on arterial tension has considerable theoretical interest and may be of some relevance for the patho-physiology of depressive disorders. The production of serious depressive symptoms by a number of hypotensive drugs is likely to be an opposite effect exerted on the same system. The latest drug incriminated in this way is methyldopa. In a series of 63 cases studied by Raftos et al. (1964) severe depression was reported in 7, occurring in each case within a few days of commencing treatment and disappearing within 2–7 days of discontinuing the methyldopa. A recent report (Haskovec and Rysánek, 1967) suggesting that reserpine may markedly augment the antidepressive effect of imipramine by liberating monoamines on to cerebral receptor sites requires further evaluation.

Electrolyte Distribution and Endocrine and Metabolic Change in Affective Disorder

The application of modern scientific techniques has brought to light subtle changes in electrolyte distribution and of endocrine function in the course of affective disorders. The precise significance of the changes remains to be determined. Crammer (1959) studied two patients, one of them a man aged 49 who had bouts of stupor lasting 2 days followed by a manic disturbance during the following 4 days. On a strictly controlled food and fluid intake, he retained about 220 m/Eq. sodium and gained 0.75 kg. in weight during the depressed phase. However, the weight gain varied with the amount of sodium in the diet and the mood changes were uninfluenced when weight change was abolished by dietary control. Gibbons (1960) studied 24 adult patients with endogenous depression. The levels of exchangeable sodium and potassium were within normal limits but re-examination after a period of some weeks revealed a highly significant decrease of exchangeable sodium in the recovered group (200 m/Eq.) while the control cases showed an insignificant increase of 30 m/Eq. The changes were identical with those in 10 of the patients who had received a constant diet throughout the period of investigation. The possibility that the electrolyte changes give rise to the mood disturbances has been discussed by Gibbons (1963). In view of the lack of specificity in the association between mood change and electrolytes and the ease with which their relationship can be altered by dietary changes without corresponding mood alteration, he concludes that changes in water and electrolyte metabolism are more likely to be effects than causes of the mood change. Russell (1960) using the metabolic balance technique found only insignificant losses of sodium during the recovery period. However, Coppen and his co-workers (Coppen and Shaw, 1963; Coppen 1965b) have reported electrolyte changes of a different character. In an investigation of the distribution of water and electrolytes in a group of 23 patients suffering from severe depression the authors employed a multiple isotope technique and total body counting. Each patient was studied initially during the depressed phase and, later, after recovery had been observed. They were unable to confirm changes in total exchangeable sodium nor was there any significant change in extra-cellular sodium. However, residual sodium (which includes intra-cellular and bone sodium) was very significantly increased during depression, and diminished in both male and female patients after recovery. Total body water, extra-cellular fluid and extra-cellular chloride were all greater after recovery. There was no variation in other indices of mineral metabolism. However, a somewhat unexpected finding was the increased ratio of exchangeable sodium to total body potassium both during and after illness, suggesting that there may be some subtle constitutional difference between depressed and normal subjects. Similar but quantitatively more marked changes in residual sodium than those found in depressive illness have been recorded by these workers during attacks of mania (Coppen, Malleson and Shaw, 1965). These interesting findings await confirmation.

The electrolyte changes may be connected with the increase in adrenocortical activity that has now been demonstrated in severe depressive illness by a number of workers. Board, Wadeson and Persky (1957) found significantly higher mean values of plasma 17-hydroxycorticoids in depressed patients than in normal controls. The levels tended to fall with clinical improvement. The most consistent correlations with depressive affect have been observed by Gibbons and McHugh (1962) who studied 17 depressed patients during 18 periods of stay in hospital. Plasma cortisol was measured at weekly intervals through periods of eight to twelve weeks. The mean level before treatment was 22 mg. falling to 10 mg. with clinical recovery induced either by E.C.T. or imipramine. Spontaneous recovery produced a similar decline. In general, the more severe the depression the higher was the cortisol level. Some link with the electrolyte changes may exist in that Woodbury et al. (1957) have shown that cortisol lowers the electro-shock threshold. The change is associated with an increase in intra-cellular sodium. It is of interest also that depression is a characteristic mood disturbance of Cushing's disease although simple euphoria is a commoner correlate of corticoid treatment. However, the increased secretion of cortisol is not invariable even in severe depressions and is of a far smaller order than that associated with established cases of Cushing's disease.

Anderson and Dawson (1962) having previously noted that the blood level of acetyl-methylcarbinol (AMC), a breakdown product of pyruvic acid, was raised before and during the onset of the depressive phase of manic-depressive illness, found that in 98 cases of depressive illness there was a significant positive correlation between a high fasting level of blood AMC and such clinical features as verbal retardation, preoccupation with ideas of guilt and self-blame. There appeared to be a relationship between the high AMC level and sodium retention (Anderson and Dawson, 1963). The clinical features of cases with low AMC levels corresponded to the picture of neurotic depression.

Neurophysiological Changes in Depression

Another group of findings that may have some relationship with the reported electrolyte and endocrine changes is the change in cortical reactivity in 'psychotic depression' reported by Shagass and Schwartz (1963). They measured the cycle of cortical reactivity by comparing the amplitudes of responses to paired stimuli separated by varying intervals. The cortical potentials were recorded from scalp leads using averaging techniques. They found that in normal individuals there was initial recovery of full responsiveness during the first 20 m.sec. This was followed by diminished responsiveness with a second peak of recovery at about 120 m.sec. However, in 21 psychotic depressives, the mean recovery was less than 50 per cent. at any time within the first 20 m.sec. The administration of E.C.T. with or without imipramine was associated with a recovery of normal responsiveness particularly in the first 20 m.sec. E.C.T. may therefore owe its effectiveness to normalization of cortical reactivity. The changes in cortical reactivity are regarded by the authors as secondary to unidentified neurophysiological changes which may underlie the experience of depression. It is noteworthy that in these studies neurotic patients, including those suffering from depression, showed no difference from normal ones.

In earlier studies, Shagass and Jones (1958), using an electro encephalographic technique of measuring the sedation threshold with a barbiturate, showed that cases of endogenous depression (even in the presence of severe agitation) had a significantly lower sedation threshold that those with neurotic depression. Nymgaard (1959) using a modified technique reached similar conclusions but Ackner and Pampiglione (1959) were unable to confirm the findings of Shagass and his co-workers.

Investigations with methylamphetamine (Roberts, 1959b) have both physiological and diagnostic interest. The threshold for the production of stimulation (15 per cent. increase in systolic blood pressure; 25 per cent. increase in pulse rate and behavioural changes) with slow intravenous injection of Methedrine was markedly lower in neurotic depression than in psychotic depression. Moreover, whereas in the former the result was a 'normalization of symptoms', in the latter symptoms were intensified.

The earlier observations of Strongin and Hinsie (1939), suggesting that the parotid secretion rate was reduced in endogenous depression, have been confirmed recently by Busfield et al. (1961). It is of interest that, although mild and severe depressions did not differ, endogenous depression had a significantly lower parotid secretion rate than exogenous cases.

PRECIPITATION

What is needed to provoke a phase of manic or depressive illness in these temperamentally allied personalities is entirely unknown. In many cases the stimuli of everyday life seem sufficient to start an attack; in a few, physical illness, childbirth or the menopause, or possibly the metabolic changes associated with them, can be held responsible. Thus Dalton (1959) found that in 46 per cent. of cases in which onset of psychiatric illness was so acute that immediate admission to hospital was required, the women were admitted in the premenstrual or menstrual phase. Psychological traumata of an emotional kind are frequently cited, but their influence is always difficult to assess. Many of the *'causes' of breakdown* given by the relatives of patients are symptoms of the oncoming illness; but depressive illnesses follow emotional shocks with a more than random frequency. Illnesses of this kind at first appear as an understandable and adequate emotional reaction to the blow of fate which has produced them and from that develop into a picture abnormal both in the intensity and the duration of the affective change. The interpretation of the first attack is difficult; not infrequently the subject of such a 'reactive' illness develops on a later occasion a similar psychosis without any preceding emotional shock; and a depressing experience may be followed by a hypomanic illness. Much of what has been written on the subject of psychogenesis has been from the view point of those who believe that the distinction between 'endogenous' and 'reactive' depressions is a quantitative one. The evidence is now growing strong that this is not so, and that we have to do with a qualitative difference. In their study of depressive states along factor-analytic lines, Kiloh and Garside (1963) found that the syndromes of neurotic and endogenous depression were likely to be independent. The occurrence of 'psychological disturbances clearly related to the onset of the illness, and which appeared to the observer to play an important role in its genesis' was found to be a distinctive feature of neurotic depression, correlating with this diagnosis highly significantly ($r = 0.65$).

Although differentiation between an *endogenous and reactive depression* may be difficult, sometimes extremely so in the single case, it should be attempted and can succeed in the majority of patients (see Diagnosis, page 219). It should be remembered that affective psychoses can occur in persons without a noticeably cycloid temperament; and although some of these illnesses show unusual features derived from the patient's personality, which make diagnosis difficult, others represent typical attacks of depression or mania.

CLINICAL PICTURE

Affective Constitutions

THE CONSTITUTIONAL DEPRESSIVE. This temperament frequently passes unrecognized because the constitutional depressive is quiet and reserved, and likes to remain in the background. He takes everything as a heavy burden and is always inclined to see the sad side of any event. He is pessimistic, easily moved to tears or to prolonged brooding and lacks self-confidence. He is, as Kretschmer pointed out, not always sad, but he responds more easily to depressing events. Some people of this type are deeply religious, with a piety purely emotional, without bigotry or fanaticism.

While most of these persons *lack somewhat in energy and drive*, yet they are efficient within restricted fields, e.g. as civil servants. They live a quiet and secluded existence with a few friends but are not unsociable. Indeed their gentle melancholy, their *pessimism often enlivened by a quietly ironic humour*, may not be without charm. They may be considered by themselves or their relatives as 'nervous', but they rarely come to the psychiatrist for treatment. They may develop minor obsessional traits or hypochondriacal preoccupations. This tendency, or more severe fluctuations of mood, may bring them to consult a practitioner; but they readily relinquish his assistance and drift back to their home-made remedies and self-devised routine. The type is common but is not easily described, for it is as varied as the normal human personality.

THE CONSTITUTIONAL HYPOMANIC. This temperament is the counterpart of the depressive and equally frequently goes undiagnosed. An abundant flow of energy, liveliness, sociability, enthusiasm and resistance to fatigue are the main characteristics. Hypomanics are realistic, quick to grasp opportunities, versatile and often rather superficial. They are full of ideas, have a natural skill in dealing with people and in mastering situations. Having little tenacity, they are taken in by the impression of the moment and easily diverted from their aim by something new. They have many friends, *see the best in everybody and everything* and are never discouraged by failures. Such types are common and are often found in positions of importance, where their abundant energy has brought them. But they may have got into difficulties from their unbalanced optimism, made themselves enemies through a streak of ruthlessness, or failed at critical moments through a sudden relapse into a mood of depression and defeatism.

Hypomanics are found among company directors, politicians, journalists, commercial travellers, etc. There are many variants, some of which are well described in picturesque language by Kretschmer. If handicapped by some physical ailment, the hypomanic may develop a most tiresome form of hypochondriasis which takes him from one consulting-room to another. If opposed by bureaucracy or wronged by some small injustice, some hypomanics develop into querulous litigants and, because of their enormous energy, are most difficult to influence.

On the whole, however, constitutional hypomanics and depressives rarely show asocial or antisocial tendencies and are *well adapted* and valuable members of human society.

THE CONSTITUTIONAL CYCLOTHYMIC. Alternations of mood from the depressive to the hypomanic, each lasting a period of months or longer, neither producing an excessive change, is the picture of the cyclothymic constitution. It is perhaps less frequent than the other two 'basic states', but its existence in artists and writers has attracted some attention, especially as novelists like Björnsen and H. Hesse have given characteristic descriptions of the condition. Besides those whose swings of mood never intermit, there are others with more or less prolonged *intervals of normality*. In the hypomanic state the patient feels well, but the existence of such states accentuates his feeling of insufficiency and even illness in the depressive phases. At such times he will often seek the advice of his practitioner, complaining of such vague symptoms as headache, insomnia, lassitude, and indigestion. The removal of septic foci in appendix, teeth, tonsils, or sinuses, a cure at a spa, a course of Weir Mitchell treatment, a sea-cruise, hydrotherapy, massage, light and electrical treatment, or psychotherapy will produce a rapid cure, provided that the change to normality or to a hypomanic state is already fated to take place. In typical cases such alternative cycles will last a lifetime. In cyclothymic artists, musicians, and other creative workers the rhythm of the cycles can be read from the dates of the beginning and cessation of productive work.

Some cyclothymics have a *seasonal rhythm* and have learned to adapt their lives and occupations so well to it that they do not need medical attention.

Affective Psychoses

DEPRESSION. From the general appearance alone the beginning of a depression is not difficult to recognize. The patient looks tired and self-concerned. Often the sadness of mood is reflected as much in posture and movement as in facial expression. With the appearance of retardation the normal wealth and freedom of expression and gesture diminish. An expression of indifference may disguise the real mood. An 'omega figure' between the eyebrows and Veraguth's folds of the upper lids have been considered characteristic, but 'analysis feature by feature is less informative than a single glance' (Mapother and Lewis, 1937).

The history of *change in the patient's behaviour* is characteristic and important; he retires from usual social activities, avoids his friends in the street, and, if forced into company, seems bored and inattentive and takes little interest in topics that usually elicit an active response. Productivity in all spheres diminishes: the sermons of the priest become dull and lifeless; students find themselves bored and disappointed by their teacher; the letters of the business man remain unanswered, even unopened. Work takes longer than formerly and is carried out with greater difficulty. The housewife is never finished in time with her household duties, leaves important things undone, and becomes increasingly negligent of her personal appearance. An atmosphere of listlessness and indolence pervades the whole life of the patient. Conscious of the change in himself, he may strive to hide it from those about him, perhaps with some temporary success. With immense effort he carries out his ordinary duties, but avoids anything new or out of his ordinary routine, and seeks to protect himself from demands that he knows he will not be able to meet. An observant friend or relative may notice the change but mistake it for fatigue or bodily illness. The practitioner may be consulted, who, deceived in his turn, may advise a change of environment, a visit to a spa, a sea-cruise, or a life of gaiety and increased social activity, which only accentuate the patient's *feeling of insufficiency*. Or some bodily symptom, which has been the centre of the patient's increased tendency to self-observation, is made the focus of medical or even surgical attack.

Suicide, or the attempt at it, is often the first alarming symptom of a depressive illness; it is the first and last symptom of many depressive illnesses, occurring when retardation is not evident and the patient's relatives have not noticed that he is ill. In most cases these attempts are desperately earnest, and suicide is by far the greatest danger threatening the patient. Suicide is often carefully planned, and the means chosen are often selected regardless of the amount of bodily pain and suffering they may cause. The gas-oven, drowning, strangulation, shooting, and poisoning are the commonest methods. It is not rare for depressives to *kill their relatives*, especially their young children, before taking their own lives, to save them, as they believe, from a life of misery and despair.

The patient may come to the physician with any of many *complaints*, the number of which correspond to the manifold ways in which the illness is experienced subjectively. The complaint may be one of sudden and complete loss of interest and enjoyment in usual pursuits; of an uncomfortable realization of diminishing quickness of thought and action; of difficulty with customarily easy mental activities; of inability to reach any decision, even in trifling matters; of 'loss of will power'; or of a feeling of incapacity, only abolished by taking increasing quantities of alcohol or coffee. Bodily symptoms may be to the fore; e.g. a general feeling of fatigue, of pressure in the head or chest, of heaviness of all limbs, of sleeplessness, loss of appetite, and constipation. On the basis of these and other unpleasant physical sensations an exaggerated hypochondriasis may develop, the patient remaining querulously convinced of his constipation or insomnia even after it has been adequately treated, or making some other physical symptom the subject of fresh complaint. This hypochondriasis may be shown also in psychological symptoms, such as exaggerated fears and anxieties, especially the fear of going mad; such symptoms, and also self-reproach and delusional ideas of guilt, may constitute the only complaint made by the patient.

An initial mood of indifference in depressive states may last for a considerable time but sooner or later is replaced by one of *sadness*, which may be of any degree from comparatively slight to a hopeless despair overwhelming the whole of the mental life. With this there is a diminished capacity for normal affective response to sad as well as happy events, a phenomenon which is merely one aspect of a *generalized insufficiency of all mental activities*. This insufficiency has been much emphasized by French authors, who have considered it (under the name of '*asthénie*') to be the central symptom of the psychosis. Whatever is experienced seems to be painful. Even enjoyable experiences have this effect, partly by making the patient more acutely aware of his incapacity for normal appreciation, partly because he is at once sensible of any unfortunate aspect they may have; he may in fact show considerable ingenuity in seeing the bad side of everything. Past, present, and future are alike seen through the same dark and gloomy veil; the whole of life seems miserable and agonizing. The depth of the affect cannot easily be measured from its *outward expression*. The silent shedding of tears may be seen in an otherwise expressionless face; another patient will mock at himself and at his complaints with a grim and sardonic but surprising humour or call himself a fraud or a fool; in another a sudden smile or expression of gaiety will deceive the physician about the severity of the underlying emotion.

Anxiety in some form or other is very often part of the mood, oftener indeed than one would gather from the spontaneous utterances of the patients. Direct questioning will reveal it often enough, and it is partly responsible for the delusional ideas. It may be manifested principally in the form of anxiety attacks, occurring most often at night or in the early morning; they may last for hours, during which the patient clings in panic terror to those around him; or there may be a milder but a lasting state of fear, which occupies so much of the affective picture that the presence of an underlying depression is almost a matter of speculation.

Retardation, as may clearly be discerned from the descriptions of intelligent patients, is not the same as the absorption of energy and interest by grief. Although some patients, devoid of other spontaneous activity, talk freely about their personal preoccupations, in others the whole mental life shows a uniform retardation, and they may mistakenly be regarded as slothful, stupid or demented, until with approaching recovery retardation recedes and mental activity is regained. Especially in the higher functions of will, purpose and decision is the retardation experienced as an almost intolerable burden. The patient feels incapable of initiating or following any complex sequence of thought; the power of imagination fails; ideas and images lose their vividness; memory does not respond promptly to attempts at recollection; the capacity for self-expression diminishes, and speech is an effort.

This subjective retardation does not always correspond to that observed objectively and is accentuated for the patient by his general gloomy outlook; he feels his mental faculties are worse than they are and is afraid of progressive deterioration. The observed retardation of movement and speech is often combined with a sense of inner restlessness, of unquiet brooding on perpetually recurring topics of hopelessness and gloom, 'a ceaseless roundabout of painful thought' (Mapother and Lewis). As retardation increases, even comparatively simple actions take unduly long and are performed as though against resistance. Finally, a state of *stupor* or semi-stupor may be reached, in which all activities, even the simplest, both spontaneous and reactive, show the same phenomenon. Stupor is seldom complete in depressions. The ocular movements usually escape an otherwise universal motor inhibition, and the patients continue to keep themselves clean in defaecation and micturition.

It is, perhaps, the subjective awareness of general retardation present even in milder cases which leads to the characteristic feeling of inability to feel. More probably an additional factor of obscure origin is needed to produce this symptom which is really a form of *depersonalization*. In depressions depersonalization is usually restricted to the change in emotional response. The patient complains of and seems to be deeply upset by an awareness that he cannot feel pleasure or pain, that he has lost his ability to love his dear ones, his affection for his wife and children, that everything that aroused his emotion before leaves him indifferent and cold. Depersonalization extends in some cases to his will and actions, which appear forced or mechanical, to his own body which is felt as dead or strange. It may also include the outer world (derealization), which is then described as unreal, unnatural or as seen through a mist. The full picture of depersonalization and derealization is, however, rare in true depressive illness (see p. 119).

Delusional ideas, though not infrequently present, are not essential to a depressive illness. Only a very few patients take an objective attitude to their symptoms, as does the normal man to symptoms of physical illness; almost all have some feelings of guilt, which may be the source of *self-reproach* taking many forms; the patient will attribute his failure to insufficient effort, culpable neglect, misuse of former abilities, extravagant living, or masturbation or other sexual practices. The illness is regarded as a punishment for these and many other sins. The whole of the past life is gone over with such misdeeds in view, and a formidable catalogue is compiled and repeated in and out of season as a justification of present misery.

Everything that occurs to the patient is interpreted in the light of the overmastering delusion. He feels himself universally despised and avoided; his sins are bruited abroad and are the subject of the contemptuous conversations of others; doctors and nurses draw aside their clothing to avoid infection as they pass his bed. Delusional fears spring from the breeding-ground of a *dominant anxiety*; permanent breakdown of health, incapacity ever to work again, exclusion from all decent society, cancer, tuberculosis, death, damnation and hell stand like spectres round the bed. It is hopeless to argue with the patients about these ideas; they cannot be convinced nor more than momentarily comforted, though sometimes they apparently *welcome an opposition* that permits an endless repetition of their ideas. Ideas of persecution are not based on the primary idea of a hostile environment but are rather secondary to self-humiliation. The patient is watched by detectives, that he may not escape his deserved punishment; the poison in his food is to save him from a public execution; others avoid him to escape infection from his moral decay.

Hallucinations are rare in typical depressive states. Misinterpretations and illusions in conformity with the psychotic content are common. The distinction, however, is sometimes difficult to draw. It is often not easy to discover what, if any, is the perceptual basis for some of the statements made by patients, for example, that derisive remarks are made about them by people around, and that their own bodies give off a foul smell. Many of the illusory experiences occur in the hypnagogic state and at night. The patients say that they see grimacing faces at night, or horrible scenes are enacted before their eyes; they hear the rattling of chains or the screams of tortured relations. It is possible that the hypochondriacal complaints have at times an illusional or hallucinatory basis, when, for instance, the complaint is made that inside the body there is but an emptiness, the food is stagnating in the belly, the intestines are rotting, and the bowels are blocked. These symptoms are also related to depersonalization.

Intelligence and memory are unimpaired in depressive states, as far as they are accessible to testing. Severe retardation may simulate stupidity or even dementia; but the moment the patient becomes accessible his faculties are found to be intact. Consciousness remains lucid, even in states of stupor and overmastering retardation. This may be discovered by investigation after recovery from such states; and care should be taken not to make tactless or hurtful remarks in front of an apparently completely self-absorbed and inattentive patient.

Depressive illness in aged subjects is particularly prone to be mistaken for a dementing process owing to the frequent occurrence of marked apathy and retardation and the transient clouding of consciousness that may be present in the early and acute phases of a severe illness. The presence of physical disability and mild memory defect, both common in ordinary old people, may heighten the impression of organic psychiatric disturbance. There is also a small group of functional psychoses in early and middle life in which some confusion or apparent intellectual deterioration, confirmed by psychometric investigation, may be present. Clinical studies have shown that many such patients suffer from atypical depressive illness (Kiloh, 1961). The diagnosis is suggested by the relatively short history and rapid onset of the illness, the patient's intermittent lucidity, a history of previous attacks of a similar nature and the presence of a depressive or manic-depressive hereditary trend in the family. The E.E.G. is usually normal and there is a prompt and dramatic response to antidepressive drugs or electroconvulsive treatment in most cases.

Disturbance of sleep is the most important of the bodily symptoms. Insomnia sometimes precedes all other psychological symptoms, and restoration of sleep may be the first sign of approaching recovery. The patients may have difficulty in getting to sleep, but most typically wake early in the morning and are unable to fall asleep again. Sleep is unrefreshing and not infrequently disturbed by horrible dreams. In the course of investigations in 27 patients with endogenous, and 7 with reactive, depression Hinton (1963) could not demonstrate any difference in the duration of sleep or its distribution throughout the night between the two groups nor could he discover any difference in their degree of restlessness. Costello *et al.* (1965) also failed to demonstrate any characteristic pattern of wakefulness in 6 patients with endogenous depression. Nevertheless the subjective experience of early-morning awakening is consistently reported in clinical enquiries (Foulds, 1962; Kiloh and Garside, 1963; Carney *et al.*, 1965) and probably has diagnostic value.

Anorexia is but one aspect of the inertia of the whole digestive and metabolic system. Food may be resolutely refused for this reason; but other motives, such as desire for death and belief in an utter unworthiness, even of being fed and supported by others, not infrequently play a part. Occasionally increased appetite is found (Post, 1956). Constipation is very common, sometimes fairly severe, and is of great moment to the patients, so much so that slight constitutional depressives are sometimes treated for years for '*nervous dyspepsia*'. Loss of weight may occur very early and may be out of proportion to the diminished intake of food. Increase of body-weight is a common herald of recovery and has been shown to result from increased caloric intake (Russell, 1960). Menstruation may diminish, and not infrequently ceases during a depressive phase, and sexual desire and potency are reduced. The general bodily appearance indicates a lowering of all bodily activities. The skin is dry, the vasomotor responses are sluggish, and the patient looks years older than he does when in health.

An important and significant symptom of endogenous depression—but also of mania —is the *daily fluctuation* of mood and of the total state. Improvement of all symptoms usually occurs towards evening, the retardation and depressive mood particularly showing a change for the better. In the morning, however, the patient wakes direct from sleep into his characteristic sombre mood or is normal for a few minutes, before, as he says, the depression comes down 'like a cloud'.

Recent studies of metabolism in depressive states have already been described (pp. 202 –204). All the indications are that there will be further progress in this field in the near future. For the present none of the metabolic changes demonstrated appears likely to emerge as a primary cause of the affective change. But follow-up of the available clues may well lead to the definition of primary metabolic changes of this nature. An old observation is the impairment of glucose tolerance in endogenous depression. Re-investigating older observations, Pryce (1958, 1964) was unable to confirm any close parallelism between impairment of glucose tolerance and emotional state.

MANIA. Manic psychoses are rarer than depressions, even when allowance is made for the fact that mild manic or hypomanic states are more likely than a mild depression to escape notice. The manic patient neither feels nor looks ill and on examination commonly presents a *picture of perfect physical health.* The manic attack not infrequently begins with a slight mood of depression, lasting a few days only, and gradually changing to a mood of increasing elation, accompanied by increased activity and restlessness.

After a short sleep the patient rises early to a day of continuous and joyous activity. The housewife has most of her ordinary work done before breakfast and spends the rest of her day in an unnecessary spring-cleaning or in dressing herself up in bright colours, with a plentiful but often inartistic use of cosmetics, and in running round to visit all her friends, regardless of whether they are likely to want to see her or not. The business man shows un- usual enterprise, is full of plans, which, inspired or not, he regards with uncritical optimism, and takes considerable and unjustifiable risks in carrying out his ideas. The patient is self- assertive, boastful, and easily irritated when others fail to conform with his plans. Nothing is done quickly enough for him; no one can compare with him in efficiency and success. The past and present he regards with self-satisfaction, the future with radiant self-confidence. He is in an excellent humour with all the world, and indifferent trifles may tickle him to a loud hilarity. Sexual desire and enterprise are increased and in women may be the source of serious trouble and the main reason for seeking the doctor's advice.

The *hyperactivity* in manic states is rarely fruitful, but in a favourable combination of circumstances it may lead to real, occasionally to brilliant, success. The chances of success are usually impaired by lack of sense of proportion and by inability to keep to any fixed purpose. A history of fussy and ill co-ordinated activity, of writing innumerable letters to distant acquaintances or strangers, particularly those in higher walks of life, and of the initiation of proposals of improvement in matters outside the patient's province, are typical manifestations of manic behaviour.

Thanks to the feeling of general well-being there are usually no *complaints*. The patient, however, may often be persuaded to consult a practitioner by increasing sleeplessness and a not infrequent feeling of 'nervousness'. In a more severe state, the irritability and distractibility are felt by the patient as unusual, even abnormal, and may lead to a sense of helplessness, of which advantage should be taken to secure medical advice. But all mild manics and hypomanics fail to show the slightest insight during the episode and even very little afterwards. They find life supremely enjoyable, are convinced of their increased powers and efficiency, never feel tired, are scornful of the very idea of taking medical advice and utterly opposed to accepting it.

The *mood* shows all degrees between an infectious jollity, a sparkling and cloudless hilarity, and wild excitement. Even in the slighter changes the patient, though for a time he may be amusing, even exhilarating, company, is likely to become boring and overbearing. He can respond in a qualitatively adequate manner to events not fitting into his prevailing mood, and shed tears over the loss of a near relative; but in an instant the cheerful elation returns. The tendency to domineer and to order others about leads to conflicts with the environment. These are not all taken in good part by the patient, who on such occasions easily flies into a rage. Attacks of temper are usually soon over and very seldom leave any ill-feeling with the patient, who after them is his usual sunny self; but this volatility and irritability are prominent symptoms of the psychosis and are not infrequently combined with mischievousness and even aggressiveness. Such symptoms may make treatment in hospital difficult and demand the greatest tact and firmness. The patient takes violent likes and dislikes, passes judgement on others without the least tact, and makes jokes and witticisms which though without ill-will are likely to wound. He is as devoid of insight into the minds of others as into his own and at all times expresses his feelings with a childish lack of control. Manics change their medical attendants as quickly as their topics of interest. Generally speaking, the fundamental characteristics of the personality are expressed much more clearly in the manic state than in the depressive, and the clinical state therefore varies much more from case to case. The classical type, with a purely hilarious affect, is rather seldom seen.

The *stream of thought* is more rapid than normal or is at least so experienced by the patient. The output of talk is incessant and shows the characteristic 'flight of ideas', i.e. talk and thought are controlled less by sequence of meaning than by casual associations: similarity of sounds and words, rhyming, punning, and all sorts of word-play, as well as by associations from every sort of object in the environment, which readily engage the patient's distractible attention. The superficial impression of a great range of ideas is fallacious; their range is really very limited. Beneath the apparently illogical flow may be discovered an underlying trend of ideas, influencing the associations, as long as the manic excitement is not too severe. At the height of a severe manic attack, the flow of speech breaks down into a scattered sequence of single words, perhaps merely an enumeration of the perceptions of the moment. This is due to the disturbance of attention, which is also shown in the flight of ideas of less severe states.

The *attention* of the manic patient is intense but fleeting; it is occupied completely at any one moment by an object or idea, which, however, it is unable to retain for any space of time. In a few moments he is completely absorbed by something else. This means a very high distractibility. The patient is unable to keep to any topic, to finish any task, even, in the more severe states, to finish a sentence; every object in the environment is no sooner perceived than it exerts, as it were, a forced response, which drives the patient on his headlong path. It is therefore impossible from the usual tests to form any judgement of the preservation of intelligence or memory, which, however, remains intact as can be shown in less distractible cases.

There is no sharp boundary between the natural conceit of the manic and grandiose ideas which may become *delusional*; but fixed delusions are very uncommon, and what is seen is, instead, a playful fabrication, readiness to accept any grandiose suggestion offered, or gasconades of self-conceit or ideas of persecution developed from the restraints imposed by the environment. The last is also responsible for some querulousness, which is almost the rule. Transient hypochondriacal complaints also occur with some frequency.

Manic excitement in its most severe form leads to *confusion*, in which the typical symptoms of mania are obscured. Consciousness, which is clear in the less severe states, becomes clouded, illusions and hallucinations may be observed, and the condition may resemble a delirium. These states are seriously debilitating and may endanger life. *Sleep* is severely disturbed in these graver psychoses, but it is also shortened in the milder forms. Another bodily symptom is the exhaustion which supervenes on months of hyperactivity and reduced sleep. The intake of food may be seriously interfered with, for the manic may never take an uninterrupted meal, being constantly diverted to something else. *Body-weight*, which increases in the milder stages, rapidly drops, and very careful nursing is required. Daily fluctuations in mood similar to those occurring in depressive states are seen in manic psychoses.

The possibility that the atypical features in manic confusion or delirium are due to nutritional deficiencies of the same kind as those sometimes causing delirium in infective illness, cannot be excluded. Similar delirious states can occur in depressive illness and here again a specific deficiency caused by insufficient food intake should always be suspected. It must, however, be remembered that as mild manic attacks are so much coloured by the underlying personality of the patient, they frequently have atypical features. The excessive emotional expression sometimes brings out hysterical features; and the motor excitement is not infrequently reminiscent of catatonia. (See Differential Diagnosis, p. 219.)

INVOLUTIONAL MELANCHOLIA. With increasing age the comparative frequency of mania drops, whereas that of depression rises. In later life emotional reactions tend to take a depressive form. This is true not only for normal people: where an emotional colouring is added to the picture of psychoses of known aetiology, such as general paresis, arterio-sclerosis and senility, it is usually depressive. Even cases of typical recurrent manic-depressive psychosis tend to depression during the involutional period; and at this time of life a depressive illness attacks many who have never suffered in any similar way before. Such an attack may be the only one, or it may be the first of a series of recurrent depressions or the first attack of a relapsing manic-depressive illness. That organic and functional changes associated with the climacteric or involution should precipitate such breakdowns can be readily understood, but exactly what endocrine or metabolic alterations are responsible is still unknown. With the increasing longevity of the general population, the depressions of later life become more frequent, and constitute perhaps one-half or one-third of the total of affective psychoses.

If we leave out of account the first depressions, in middle age, of persons of cyclothymic temperament, the *personalities* who are especially liable to involutional depression have called for other descriptions—as rigid, obsessional, conscientious characters, but also as over-anxious, timid and sensitive types (Anderson, 1936). A part of the affective psychoses of the involution are undoubtedly manic-depressive in nature. But that they are not all of this kind is shown by different hereditary relationships, a different personality background, a different prognosis and different response to treatment. There are symptomatic differences which are only in part attributable to the influence of age on the clinical picture. The paranoid element is often noticeable; and family studies often show the coincidence of involutional depressions and schizophrenias in the same family. However Stenstedt (1959) was unable to confirm any genetical relationship to schizophrenia. He found that the incidence of endogenous affective illnesses in the parents and sibs of involutional depressives, once exogenous cases had been excluded, did not differ materially from the corresponding figures for manic-depressives. In an investigation (Tait *et al.*, 1957) of 54 female patients first admitted between the ages of 40 and 55 years, only a minority of cases were found to manifest bizarre hypochondriasis, nihilistic delusions and great agitation and the incidence of such features was no greater in the endogenous cases than in the control subjects. Affective involutional psychoses are, therefore, a somewhat *heterogeneous group*; but their several kinds are not easily distinguished clinically.

Psychogenic causes have been searched for and found: disappointments, unfulfilled ambitions, the recognition of missed opportunities, threats to security, increased responsibility after a promotion for which the patient had been waiting for years, etc.—factors of stress, real or supposed, which, at this phase of life, can probably be detected in most middle-aged people. Because they frequently form the content of the patient's complaints and of his delusional ideas, they have too willingly been accepted as effective causes. Their validity is difficult to assess, especially as their presence or absence does not seem to influence the prognosis (Anderson); and the removal of the 'cause' has little influence on the course of the attack.

The *symptoms of involutional melancholia* differ to some extent from those of depressions occurring in youth and in the prime of life: (i) besides the profound depression, anxiety is a conspicuous element of the affective state; (ii) retardation is usually not prominent, and the anxiety is expressed by severe restlessness and agitation; (iii) there is often a rich development of delusions centring in the patient's feeling of guilt, frequently hypochondriacal and grossly bizarre. It must be stressed however that such features are not specific for the depressions of the involutional period. Moreover, with the growing influx of milder cases of affective disorder into the psychiatric clinic in recent years the relative frequency of such features has declined. In Stenstedt's study the Cotard symptom of bizarre hypochondriacal, negativistic delusions was present in only 10 per cent. of cases and was found to be without special aetiological significance.

The *onset* is usually *insidious*, with a progressive irritability and peevishness, increasing worry about health, business affairs, or financial circumstances, an increasing restlessness, and apprehensiveness. The expression becomes one of extreme misery; the patient wrings his hands, weeps and moans constantly, and repeats over and over in a monotonous and stereotyped way a phrase or phrases expressive of his misery, abasement or self-reproach. In bed his attitude is bowed and often somewhat rigid, but there may be free use of gesture or restless, fumbling, picking movements of the fingers. He is not lost to his environment but notices it only to interpret it in the light of his preoccupations or depressive ideas. The cries or screams of other patients signify that they are being subjected to torture, for which he is somehow responsible; if another looks at him, it is a look of contempt or pity; the vaguely heard conversation of others is on the subject of his misdeeds. His delusional ideas are legion and tend in their *depressive setting* to have a *touch of the grandiose*.

His sins are so horrid that he has destroyed the happiness of the whole world; catastrophes and misfortunes that he reads of in the paper and the illnesses of the patients round him are all to be traced to him; to provide him with food they are being starved; nothing will go aright until he is destroyed; a horrible fate awaits him; he is to be tortured, and his body will be torn to pieces, but he will never die. Equally manifold are the hypochondriacal ideas: his bowels are blocked; he has not been able to defaecate for years; his intestines are full of filth, are rotting, have rotted away; he is empty inside, has no body at all, and everything he eats falls into empty space. This description, accurate for the days when no effective treatment was available, now rarely applies in all its severity.

In spite of these absurd ideas, consciousness is clear, and there is no formal disorder of thought or intellectual defect in cases uncomplicated by organic changes. Nevertheless the *refusal of food* and the *exhaustion* due to the continual agitation may reduce the patient to a pitiful state. Fortunately, convulsion treatment is very effective and relieves much mental and physical suffering. Even so, constant and devoted nursing is required, not least because of the serious danger of suicide.

In fact, many of the depressive ideas in later life are *centred around death* which is at the same time dreaded and desired. Often the demanding and *egotistic demonstrativeness* of the patient, exacting for relatives and nurses, is reminiscent of hysteria and may be misjudged as such by laymen and doctors. If hysterical behaviour appears for the first time in life in a middle-aged or elderly patient, one should always think of a beginning melancholia, or of the appearance of an organic cerebral condition.

MIXED AND ATYPICAL FORMS. It is possible to regard the typical case of involutional melancholia as a *mixed psychosis* with depressive affect and manic hypermotility. Somewhat similar pictures with a mixture of manic and depressive elements may be seen at other times, especially in transitional periods, when a manic phase is followed by a depression, or vice versa. The clinical picture may offer great diagnostic difficulties and is often mistaken for schizophrenia. These mixed forms, however, are comparatively rare. One of the least uncommon is *manic stupor*, in which the patient lies quiet, speechless, and inaccessible, but the facial expression is one of elation. Later, after recovery, the patient can report that his mind was filled with a constant turmoil of streaming ideas, which so occupied and filled his consciousness that he was unable to react to anything else.

In a broad grouping of affective disorders based mainly on symptomatology as used here, there is always a temptation and indeed a possibility of including atypical pictures of a periodic course leading to recovery. As mentioned before, mild cases of depression and mania may derive most of their positive and obtrusive symptoms from the original personality which may reveal itself in the psychotic state. *Periodic obsessional states* are a typical example and workers who find cases of obsessional illness of good prognosis or responding to psychological treatment should suspect it to be basically an affective disorder. There are also the not infrequent 'exogenous' admixtures arising from a nutritional or toxic condition due to the patient's inadequate care of himself and the malnutrition which results from the mental state. Periodic hallucinosis, stupor, excitement and paranoid phases have been described by Kleist (1921) and Schroeder (1926) and these authors have suggested separating them as '*degeneration psychosis*' from the main part of manic-depressive illness. The idea of 'degeneration' originates in this context from the marked hereditary taint found in families in which these atypical psychoses occur. Familiar types of atypical affective psychoses have been observed in several members of the same family ('oneiroid type', Mayer-Gross, 1924).

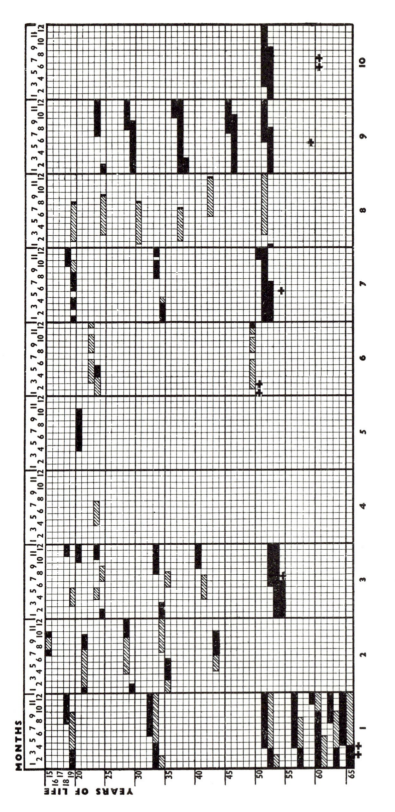

FIG. 3. Diagram of the observed courses of affective psychosis in ten patients. 1, 2, 3. Cyclic course. 4. Single mania. 5. Single depression. 6. Two manic phases, followed by short depressions. 7. Three depressive phases. 8. Periodic mania. 9. Periodic depression. 10. Involutional melancholia.

    + Death from physical causes.
    ++ Suicide.
    Black—Depression.
    Shaded—Mania.

(from Gruhle)

The genetical interpretation of these findings has been discussed at the beginning of this section. Some of these atypical psychoses may arise through the co-existence in one individual of more than one morbid predisposition.

COURSE AND PROGNOSIS

Although periodicity is an important character of the affective psychoses, rather less than one-quarter of a large series of patients had only one attack in their lives (Rennie, 1942). In such cases the illness is nearly always depressive, often severe and of prolonged duration, and often determined by physical illness, e.g. the puerperium, or by overpowering psychological difficulties. Other persons escape with two illnesses, which are then usually in adolescence or youth and middle age. Many patients have repeated illnesses at intervals of four to ten years. In this series *every sort of combination* can be found: depressive illnesses only; severe depressive illnesses followed by slight hypomanic phases, the existence of which can only be ascertained by specific questioning; alternating severe depressive and manic phases with or without periods of normality; recurrent mania with or without depressive phases; 'mixed forms' alternating with either mania or depression; a single manic or depressive illness in a series of psychoses of complementary colouring; and, rarest of all, true cyclothymia alternating continuously from mania to depression. Twenty-one of the last were found in 347 depressive patients observed by Kirchhof (1942). The first attack is depressive in 70 to 80 per cent. of all cases. The average *duration of a single attack* of mania or depression is about six months, the duration usually becoming longer with advancing age. However, many patients give a history of previous attacks of short duration, not severe enough to need hospital treatment; and rare cases are observed which fluctuate every few days or even day by day. Generally speaking, cases with a single severe attack or attacks followed by long intervals of normality have a better outlook than those in which the symptoms are milder but the intervals shorter or in which mild symptoms persist even in the times of comparative normality. In Rennie's material (1942) of 208 cases of pure affective disorder followed up for over thirty years, only 21 per cent. had a single attack in life; 79 per cent. had second, 63 per cent. third attacks, and 45 per cent. had fourth attacks. On the whole, Rennie's observations confirm the findings of earlier work on prognosis, although it would seem doubtful from his reference to the clinical picture of his cases, whether his material contained affective disorders alone.

The more purely affective the symptoms the better is the *prognosis of the single attack.* The presence of *atypical features*, e.g. depersonalization, severe hypochondriasis, and paranoid symptoms, augur a more prolonged course but do not indicate that complete recovery will not occur. However, in a proportion of the patients in whom such features are very prominent, the illness pursues a chronic course. Patients with a continuous alternation of hypomanic and depressive phases may require hospital treatment only during their depressions, but many of them end their lives in mental hospitals, requiring continuous treatment in advanced age. Manic phases are considered by some an indication of a less hopeful prognosis for the life as a whole. Relapsing manics frequently require certification, whereas periodic depressives may be treated as 'informal' patients or out of mental hospitals altogether. *Chronic mania* also occurs, this state supervening at the end of a series of illnesses from which there has been recovery and providing a lasting and terminal picture of shallow and monotonous hilarity, querulousness and irritability.

It is of some interest that there is evidence for some correlation between body build and the outcome of treatment in affective psychosis. Earlier studies by Rees (1944) demonstrated differences in body build between patients manifesting symptoms of anxiety, obsession and neurotic depression who had ectomorphic physique as distinct from manic-depressive subjects who were found to have eurymorphic physique. More recently Hamilton and White (1960) found a correlation of +0.29 between pyknic build and successful outcome: the material consisted of 20 endogenous and 29 reactive depressives.

The relation between the *manic-depressive and the arteriopathic diathesis* is of prognostic importance. If definite signs of cerebrovascular disease are present, which is sometimes the case, the prognosis is thereby made worse. Early focal neurological symptoms such as dysphasia, slight pyramidal signs, emotional incontinence or mild epileptiform attacks, the occurrence of brief bouts of clouded consciousness or an unusually fluctuating course, may be found if looked for, and provide the hint of an underlying cerebral arteriosclerosis. In these cases progressive intellectual deterioration may be expected. The organic mental and physical changes are of course irrecoverable, but the affective symptoms will often subside temporarily, or a remission may be induced for a period by antidepressive drugs or convulsant therapy. However, treatment by physical methods in these cases should be decided on only after careful thought.

Progressive mental deterioration does not result from manic-depressive psychosis. Though hospital treatment over years may lead to a narrowing of interests, social isolation, and extreme dependence on hospital care, secondary dementia from manic-depressive psychosis does not exist. If dementia occurs, it is due to the same causes (e.g. arterial disease and senility) as in persons of normal constitution and differs in no way from the changes seen in them, except that *hypomania in senility* may disguise an early deterioration by youthful freshness of physical appearance and mental versatility. Similarly *senile depressives* often appear much more demented through anxiety, restlessness and retardation than they are on the basis of their organic defect. Hence the often surprising improvement of all mental abilities after convulsion treatment. It is a common error in mental hospitals to mis-diagnose as senile dementia the case of the elderly patient who has had a first attack after the age of sixty-five.

The prognosis of atypical cases and especially of affective psychoses with schizophrenic admixture is good for the single attack. In some the periodicity with regular full remissions remains preserved throughout life. In others the schizophrenic component seems to gain the upper hand, so to speak, and a chronic schizophrenic picture, often of a paranoid kind, develops in later life and with it a progressive deterioration. Even so, *fluctuations of mood may persist* and a certain warmth of personality allowing good rapport with their environment can be detected in these patients in spite of their delusionally distorted view of the world.

Patients with affective psychoses die from suicide, from cerebrovascular catastrophe, or from intercurrent disease. The risks of the last, however, are increased in severe depressions and manias. Starvation and hypermotility may reduce the patient to such a cachectic· state that the expert attention of physician and nurses may with difficulty save him from untimely death. The death rate in depressive psychoses has been greatly diminished by convulsive therapy. At the Royal Edinburgh Hospital the death rate in depressive patients was 16 per cent. in males and 14 per cent. in females during the years 1900–39, before E.C.T. was available. In the years 1940–48, while it still remained as high in untreated patients, in the patients treated by E.C.T., who were probably a prognostically less favourable group, it fell to 2 per cent. or less (Karagulla, 1950; Slater, 1951).

The course of the affective psychoses has been modified by physical treatment methods, especially convulsion treatment (see pp. 228, 232) in so far as the single attack of depression and mania can be considerably shortened. It is, however, doubtful whether this treatment has any influence on the frequency of attacks. Prefrontal leucotomy, on the other hand, has a definite *effect on periodicity* (Jones and McCowan, 1949) and seems sometimes to abolish relapses altogether. Sykes and Tredgold (1964) found that only three out of 29 recurrent depressives had any relapse over a follow-up period of three to five years after orbital undercutting.

DIAGNOSIS AND DIFFERENTIAL DIAGNOSIS

Affective disorder may be the initial sign of a schizophrenic or an organic psychosis, e.g. general paralysis, arteriosclerosis, and cerebral tumour. In the majority of cases some evidence of organic involvement, in the form of memory impairment, brief bouts of clouding or of loss of consciousness, or early personality change, will be present in addition, or will be elicited on careful history-taking. But occasionally the picture will be that of a purely depressive or less often manic psychosis. A careful physical examination must therefore be carried out in every case, and should be repeated in the event of any unusual development. If physical findings are negative, the diagnosis may be facilitated by a *history of similar illnesses*. If both manic and depressive illnesses have occurred, the diagnosis of affective psychosis may be regarded as established. Further help may be obtained from a family history of similar psychoses in the nearer relations and from the patient's psychological and somatic constitution. Nevertheless a constitutional cyclothymic may have an affective psychosis precipitated by the organic process involved in general paralysis or oncoming senility.

Though the symptoms of an affective psychosis are easy to recognize after they have fully developed, at the time of their first appearance they may be diffuse and vague. They may take the form of physical symptoms; and clinical acumen in the differential diagnosis between a depressive and some form of physical illness may be necessary. Ziegler (1939) collected 111 cases of depression 'who first came to a surgeon's or internist's office for the relief of bodily ailments' and gave a brief report of how they were grossly and universally misunderstood. The exclusion of physical illness must rest entirely on negative findings in the physical examination. Unfortunately general medicine is not always able to provide such a clear negative answer in cases of dyspepsia, cardiovascular disturbances, or similar *'functional' complaints* of a mild type. If they occur periodically and have an effect on the patient's well-being exceeding by far the objective findings, affective disorder should be suspected as the underlying cause of the physical disability and psychiatric treatment instituted.

Many depressions are mistaken for neurasthenic or anxiety reactions or some other form of *psychoneurosis*. If one holds the view, as many psychiatrists do, that there is no difference in kind, but only one of degree between neurotic reactions, including reactive depression, and affective disorders, one will not be in the least surprised when a case labelled neurasthenia develops into an agitated involutional melancholia. If, however, as the authors believe, a real distinction exists demanding different practical measures in each of the two alternatives, the differential diagnosis must be made with great care. It is a common mistake to regard the cyclothymic with mild fluctuations of mood as a neurotic. Even experienced psychiatrists regularly blunder in this way, with unfortunate results for the patient who is then subjected to time-wasting and unprofitable psychotherapy. On the other hand the growing influx of milder forms of affective disturbance into the psychiatric clinic in recent years creates the opposite danger. It is becoming increasingly recognized that a substantial minority of patients whose illness first appears in middle life or old age suffer from neurotic disturbances rather than endogenous affective psychosis.

In milder cases features of the original personality and the psychic content supplied by recent or remote emotional experiences make up so much of the clinical picture that the primary lowering of mood may be missed until prolonged observation has made it unmistakable. Care must be taken not to accept unreservedly the patient's explanations, that, for instance, his 'nervous breakdown' is due to his failure in business or to a disappointment in love, when the sequence of events was really the reverse. There can be no direct measure of the relative part played by *external and constitutional factors* in the development of a state of depression or excitement; nevertheless it is important both from the prognostic and the therapeutic point of view to diagnose between, for example, a constitutional recurrent depressive, a hysterical type of personality suffering from a largely psychogenic depression, and a comparatively normal type of personality in a state of depression reactive to particular external circumstances.

Differentiation of *cyclothymic and reactive depression*, the subject of lively argument between psychotherapists and psychiatrists of thirty years ago (Curran, 1937) is again topical because reactive depressions have of late become more frequent in the psychiatrist's consulting-room, since their psychological nature is recognized at an earlier stage and they are sent to the specialist before more severe neurotic symptoms have appeared. The evidence of repeated attacks of depression may be misleading because the personality predisposed to this type of psychoneurotic reaction may show it whenever he is in difficulties. If family history, constitutional make-up, and the objective data of the patient's life are fully known and collated with the clinical picture, a decision can be reached in most cases, provided these factors are not merely enumerated but weighed with judgement and insight, and the observer does not lose his way in a thicket of unimportant details. The life-history of the reactive depressive shows that all his depressions have been in response to the stress of circumstance, and that a purely endogenous mood change is unknown to him. The cyclothymic person on the other hand will know at once what is meant when enquiry is made about endogenous mood changes; and the daily fluctuation in mood will also be familiar to him. The depressive mood of the reactive patient is much more responsive to the immediate environment than an endogenous depression, and will generally be alleviated for a few hours by such distractions as the society of cheerful friends. Any degree of retardation is most unusual in reactive states; and insomnia, when it occurs, is a difficulty in dropping off to sleep and not, as is generally the case in endogenous depressions, a tendency to wake in the early hours.

Severe alcoholic intoxication is sometimes mistaken for a manic state. Since the manic at the beginning of his psychosis is often given to alcoholic over-indulgence, the distinction may be impossible before the patient has returned to sobriety. Hyperkinesis in children suffering from encephalitis epidemica may be mistaken for manic excitement. Specific neurological signs may be absent, but the history usually discloses the real nature of the illness. States of excitement in patients with toxic goitre may show every psychological characteristic of mania or at times closely resemble an agitated depression. Some authors assume an intrinsic connexion between thyrotoxic and affective disorders; but, besides the obvious physical signs, the subjects of thyrotoxic psychoses usually show some dimming of consciousness or at least a fluctuation in its clearness.

Only when manic excitement is severe are *clouding of consciousness and confusion* observed. Generally speaking, depression and mania occur in a setting of clear consciousness. This serves to differentiate affective disorders from similar psychoses accompanying fever or other physical illness, from post-traumatic confusion, and from epileptic twilight states, in which mood changes may be prominent.

Epileptic mood swings occurring as equivalents can have all the characteristics of an endogenous depression including suicidal tendency; the history of seizures and the E.E.G. will clear up the diagnosis. The differential diagnosis of manic-depressive from post-infectious depression ('organic neurasthenia') may also be difficult, although retardation is often absent in the latter, irritability may be marked and even the leading symptom. Severe depressive reactions not infrequently follow the administration of sulphonamides and vanish with their discontinuation.

The *differential diagnosis* between an affective psychosis and schizophrenia is important and often difficult. The differentiation is simple in all cases in which schizophrenic thought-disorder, incongruity of affect, and a bizarre quality of the behaviour are easily recognized, however prominent the mood change may appear. The schizophrenic symptoms, however, may be much more vague. The schizophrenic may complain of increasing shallowness of affect, of a feeling of loss of sympathy, and of depression of spirits, using very similar words and phrases to the depressive; but the setting is different. The schizophrenic lacks the warmth and natural expression of the depressive. The same similarity of symptoms and difference of setting are seen in the schizophrenic complaint of loss of energy and will-power, which may closely resemble the subjective experience of retardation. The distinction here may be impossible, until a short and unexpected outburst of bizarre hyperactivity incompatible with retardation indicates schizophrenia.

In general it may be said that the schizophrenic, in contrast to the depressive, shows a withdrawal from reality and a remote absorption in psychotic fantasy, a stiffness of movement, a lack of consistency in expression and emotional attitude, and the primary development of delusions unrelated to the affective background. On the other hand the occurrence of a single apparently schizophrenic symptom in an affective setting is not of great diagnostic significance, especially in young people. Lange (1922) collected catatonic symptoms in manic-depressives and found them fairly common about the age of twenty years. Cases of mania are seen with catatonic features, in which the outcome is no worse than in the classical types. Very similar hallucinations may be found in depressives and in schizophrenics. *The single symptom is less important than the total picture* provided by history, constitution, personality, and interaction of personality and symptoms. Schizophrenic disorders are commoner than affective psychoses when the latter are strictly defined. Many practitioners mistakenly believe that schizophrenic psychoses are largely irrecoverable, and are thereby led by an optimism out of touch with reality to regard any case as affective so long as affective symptoms occur. A schizophrenic psychosis, particularly in late life, may commence in the setting of a profound depression. The undue prominence of paranoid and schizophrenic symptoms, which also tend to grow more pronounced with each successive relapse following treatment, should give the clue to the diagnosis. The differential diagnosis between a schizophrenic and an affective disorder, though often very difficult, is extremely important not merely from the scientific but also from the severely practical viewpoints of therapy and prognosis. When differential diagnosis seems impossible, it may be remembered that combinations of the two psychoses, though uncommon, do occur. Such a diagnosis should be made only when there is strong positive evidence on both sides. It is as a rule better to postpone judgement than to make an arbitrary diagnosis without sufficient justification.

Recent Statistical Enquiries into Diagnosis and Prediction of Outcome

The classification of depression has recently been investigated with the aid of objective methods of examination, and the statistical techniques of principal component and discriminant function analysis. Many of these studies have been conducted in the course of pharmacological and other treatments. It has been found that following treatment with E.C.T. (Roberts, 1959a; Hamilton and White, 1959; Rose, 1963; Carney, Roth and Garside, 1965; Mendels, 1965a) and imipramine (Kiloh and Ball, 1961), significantly better results are achieved in endogenous than reactive cases with each form of treatment. As far as pre-frontal leucotomy is concerned most workers agree that there is a differential effect in the two main groups of depression. Most of the workers who have studied large series have reported better results in 'reactive' than in endogenous depression (Partridge, 1949; Pippard, 1955; Elithorn, 1959). But Sykes and Tredgold (1964) recently reported excellent results in 'recurrent depressive illness'. In the studies carried out by Kiloh and his colleagues a discriminant function analysis of the data from 97 patients all treated with imipramine showed that one cluster of symptoms was correlated positively and a second cluster of symptoms correlated negatively with a good response to imipramine. The first cluster corresponded to the clinical picture of endogenous depression while the second included features often regarded as characteristic of neurotic depression. In a further enquiry a factorial analysis was carried out on an enlarged material of 143 patients (Kiloh et al., 1962, 1963). Two factors were extracted. The first was a general factor for which the majority of the depressive features studied had positive loadings. It was shown statistically, however, that the data were not consistent with the presence of a single depressive syndrome. A second bipolar factor extracted differentiated between neurotic and endogenous depression. The clinical features significantly correlated with a diagnosis of endogenous depression were early-morning wakening, depression worse in the morning, qualitative change in affect, retardation, duration of symptoms of one year or less, age 40 years or above, depression regarded as being of considerable depth, failure of concentration, weight loss of 7 lbs. or more and a history of previous attacks. The items have been cited in order of the magnitude of their correlation with the diagnosis. On the other hand, the following features correlated significantly with a diagnosis of neurotic depression; responsiveness of depression (to environmental change), presence of a precipitant, self-pity, variability of illness, hysterical features, inadequacy, initial insomnia, depression worse in the evening, sudden onset, irritability, hypochondriasis and obsessionality. These authors also summarized a considerable body of observations from literature concerned with hereditary factors, physiological and biochemical changes, prognosis and differential responses to treatment, providing confirmation for the independence of reactive and endogenous depression. Lopez Ibor (1962) made similar observations to those of Kiloh and his colleagues, eliciting a better response with imipramine in patients manifesting 'vital sadness' than the treated depressive group as a whole. However Fleminger and Groden (1962) could find no relationship between response to treatment with imipramine and the presence or absence of agitation, anorexia, anxiety, apathy, early awakening, hypochondriasis, self-reproach, and suicidal ideas among other features.

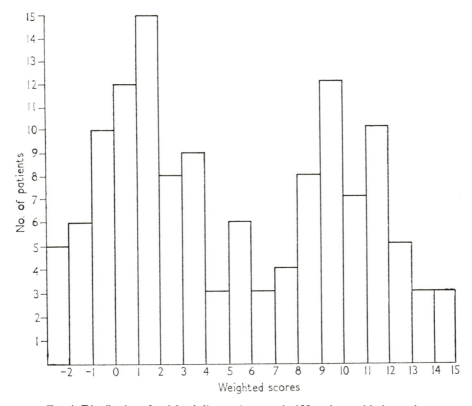

FIG. 4. Distribution of weighted diagnostic scores in 129 patients with depression.

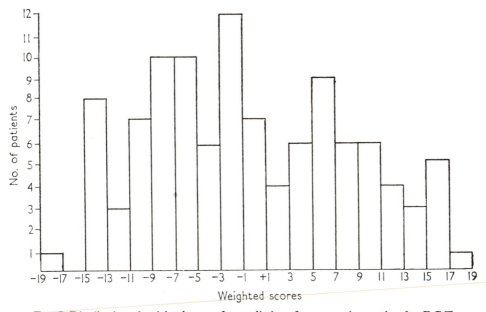

FIG. 5. Distribution of weighted scores for prediction of outcome six months after E.C.T.

Carney, Roth and Garside (1965) investigated 129 in-patients suffering from depressive illness and treated with E.C.T. An analysis yielded three significant factors. The first of these was a bipolar factor closely similar to that extracted by Kiloh and Garside. In this enquiry the outcome of the illness was investigated at 3 months and again at 6 months after the completion of treatment. There was a clear difference in outcome between the endogenous and neurotic groups of depression. On the basis of a multiple regression analysis (from which 13 'doubtful' cases were excluded) the 18 best predictive features were chosen and three series of weighted coefficients were calculated for differential diagnosis between the two varieties of depression and for the prediction of E.C.T. response at 3 and 6 months respectively. The distribution of the weighted diagnostic item scores is shown in histogram form in Fig. 4. There is a clearly bimodal distribution corresponding with the distinction between endogenous and neurotic depression. The result is similar to that earlier recorded by Hamilton and White (1959). Their material comprised only 67 patients, however, and the distribution of factor scores did not depart from the norm to a significant degree. Distribution of the weighted scores for the prediction of the results of E.C.T. at 6 months after treatment is shown in Fig. 5; the bimodality of this distribution is not quite as clear cut as that for the diagnostic weights. It was found that the outcome of E.C.T. could be better predicted by the direct use of the weights for E.C.T. response than from the diagnostic weights alone. From the original 18 diagnostic and predictive weights simplified weights have been derived both for diagnostic purposes and for prediction of outcome. The table shows the ten features of greatest discriminating and predictive value. The original weights have been converted to whole numbers for the sake of simplicity.

WEIGHTS FOR DERIVING DIAGNOSTIC AND E.C.T. PREDICTION INDICES

Feature	Diagnostic Indices	E.C.T. Indices Outcome at 6 months
3. Adequate personality	+1	
4. No adequate psychogenesis	+2	
7. Distinct quality..	+1	
8. Weight loss	+2	+3
10. Pyknic		+3
11. Previous episode	+1	
12. Early wakening		+2
15. Depressive psychomotor activity ..	+2	
16. Anxiety	−1	−2
18. Nihilistic delusions	+2	
19. Somatic delusions		+2
20. Paranoid delusions		+1
25. Worse p.m.		−3
26. Blame others	−1	
27. Self-pity		−1
29. Hypochondriasis		−3
33. Hysterical features		−3
35. Guilt	+1	

To use this table the presence of any relevant feature is scored as indicated by the weights given in the table. If a feature is absent it is ignored. For example, if a patient has adequate personality, weight loss, early wakening, blames others and has guilt feelings and/or delusions of guilt, his diagnostic index score is $+1 \ +2 \ -1 + 1 = +3$, and his E.C.T. index score is $+3 \ +2 = +5$. Reference to the distribution of diagnostic and predictive scores (Figs. 4 and 5) will show that anyone with a diagnostic score of 6 or more is likely to be endogenous, and with a score of 5 or less neurotic. The E.C.T. scores are not so clear cut, but a score of 1 or more suggests a good result after 6 months, whereas a score of 0 or less will tend to be associated with a relatively poor result. In an enquiry conducted by Nyström (1964) into 188 personally studied patients and 254 others treated at another clinic, the results obtained were similar in certain respects to those reported by Carney et al. He also found that the outcome of treatment with E.C.T. could be better predicted from the clinical features present than from classification into 'endogenous' or 'reactive' groups. Among features significantly associated with a favourable outcome were early awakening, moderate and severe retardation of speech and motor activity, profound depression of mood, short duration of illness, previous E.C.T. with good effect and pyknic build. Seclusiveness, ideas of reference, depersonalization, obsessive-compulsive symptoms, demonstrative behaviour, duration of illness over one year, age below 35 years, and tendencies towards irritability, tension and a 'hysteroid' attitude in the pre-morbid personality were associated with a poor outcome. Mendels (1965, a,b,c) found considerable overlap in the symptoms of endogenous and reactive forms of depression, most patients conforming to the picture of endoreactive dysthymia (Weitbrecht, 1953), but the two syndromes differed markedly in their response to E.C.T. In this study also weighted scores allocated to clinical features proved better predictors of outcome than diagnosis. Among factors associated with a good response to E.C.T. 3 months after treatment, were family history of depression, early morning awakening, delusions and psychomotor retardation. Neurotic traits in child or adult life, inadequate pre-morbid personality, precipitating factors and emotional lability were associated with a poor prognosis.

In some recent enquiries findings discrepant in certain respects with those of Kiloh et al. (1962) and Carney et al. (1965) have been recorded. McConaghy et al. (1967) found that neither component extracted from an analysis of 40 features in 100 patients differentiated the groups generally associated with endogenous and neurotic depression and Rosenthal and Gudeman (1967 a,b) found normal rather than bimodal distribution of patients' scores on an endogenous depressive factor. It is of interest, however, that patients differing in their mean scores on this factor differed significantly in respect of independently derived ratings of premorbid personality, personal history and the presence of a precipitant for the illness. Differences in the patient population studied may be responsible for some of these discrepancies.

Further observations are needed but other lines of evidence have also to be taken into account. If neurotic and endogenous depressions are the milder and more severe forms of the same illness, the more favourable response of the latter to all forms of antidepressive treatment is difficult to explain. Lewis (1950), a champion of the unitary view, pointed out that milder forms of illness tended to pursue a chronic course. If endogenous depressions are qualitatively distinct these paradoxes are resolved. That there is some degree of continuity in clinical features over the whole territory of depressive illness is not in question, but that there is discontinuity and qualitative variation also is suggested by much of the evidence including the findings of Perris and Angst in relation to unipolar and bipolar

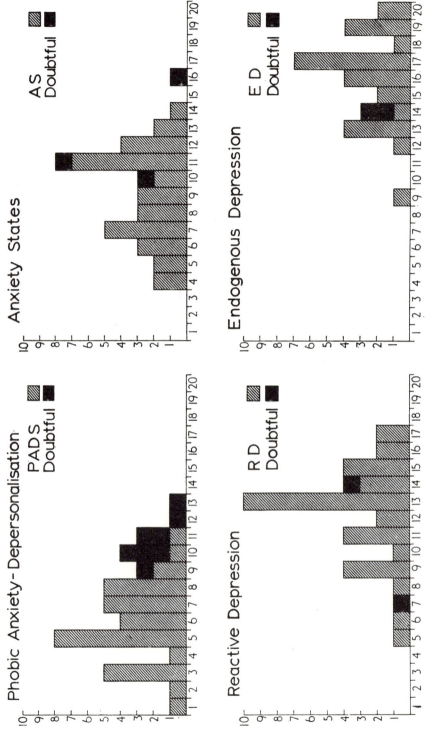

Fig. 6. Factor scores on component 1 of 145 cases (15 in whom diagnosis was doubtful) using 58 items listed in accompanying table.

depressions (p. 198). It is difficult to regard the man who responds to bereavement with mania and to inheriting a fortune with depression as a variant of the norm.

The differentiation of anxiety states from depressive disorders has already been discussed (p. 97). There is some measure of overlap between the two broad groups but with the aid of modern statistical methods a satisfactory degree of separation between them, as also between their main subdivisions, can be achieved. In a principal component analysis of the clinical features of the 145 patients with anxiety states and depressive disorders already discussed, three significant components were isolated, all of which appeared to be clinically meaningful (Roth, 1969). Figure 6 shows the distribution of patients' factor scores on the first component. It will be seen that the four groups into which the patients were tentatively allocated (phobic anxiety-depersonalization states, simple anxiety states, neurotic depressions and endogenous depressions) occupy different parts of the distribution. The 58 clinical items used in the analysis and their loadings on this first component are shown in the table. With the aid of the two other components the overlap between the groups could be reduced to a considerable extent (see p. 98). When the distribution of patents' scores and the loadings of clinical features with respect to the three main components was examined, the separate clustering of the endogenous depressive and

ITEM WEIGHTS ON FIRST COMPONENT

145 patients: 58 items. The number of grades used in scoring each item is indicated in parentheses

Family history (2)	+0·2861	Situational phobias (3)	+0·5959
Poor relationship with parents (2)	+0·3364	Other phobias (3)	+0·4032
Parental deprivation (2)	+0·1281	Depersonalization (3)	+0·4611
Over-protection (2)	+0·2916	Derealization (3)	+0·5178
Neurotic traits: childhood (3)	+0·5204	Anxiety symptoms (4)	+0·4131
Phobias: childhood (3)	+0·4724	'Dizzy' attacks (2)	+0·4602
Poor school adjustment (2)	+0·3405	Temporal lobe features (3)	+0·6436
Unstable work record (2)	+0·0726	Attacks of unconsciousness (3)	+0·4018
Marital disharmony (2)	+0·3379	Depressed mood; severity (3)	−0·1839
Other domestic difficulties (2)	−0·0720	Persistent depression (2)	−0·4926
Poor social adjustment (2)	+0·2624	Reactivity of depression (2)	+0·3963
Sensitive: paranoid (2)	+0·3491	Depression: worse a.m. (2)	−0·4070
Anxiety traits (3)	+0·5512	Loss of interest and energy (2)	−0·2068
Irritability of mood (2)	+0·4400	Affective loss (2)	+0·0642
Immaturity (2)	+0·5490	Early awakening (2)	−0·5363
Dependence (2)	+0·5166	Suicidal tendencies (3)	−0·1105
Obsessional traits (3)	+0·1154	Hypochondriacal ideas (3)	+0·1629
Psychopathic traits (3)	+0·1692	Agitation (2)	−0·0923
Hysterical traits (3)	+0·4675	Retardation (2)	−0·4947
Anergic traits (2)	+0·3460	Delusions (2)	−0·1886
Personality disorder (3)	+0·6303	Episodes of hypomania (2)	−0·1362
Previous breakdown (3)	+0·1793	Hysterical symptoms (3)	+0·4241
Sudden onset (2)	+0·1322	Obsessional symptoms (3)	+0·4640
Age of onset young (5)	+0·6610	Aggressive outbursts (3)	+0·2702
Duration (4)	−0·4565	Alcoholism (2)	+0·0211
Psychological stress (3)	+0·2829	Current physical illness (3)	−0·1987
Physical stress (3)	−0·0278	Male sex (2)	−0·3896
Tension (3)	+0·1553	Neuroticism (M.P.I.) 6	+0·4110
Panic attacks (3)	+0·5962	Introversion (M.P.I.) 6	+0·3474

phobic anxiety groups proved to derive partly from the appearance of novel features with the onset of illness—retardation, delusions and early awakening in the former; situational phobias, panic attacks, depersonalization and attacks of unconsciousness in the latter. This clearly demarcated 'process'-like character of the phobic cases together with the common depressive colouring explain the frequency with which a diagnosis of endogenous depression is made in this disorder.

TREATMENT

ENDOGENOUS DEPRESSION. The use of *convulsion therapy* in the affective disorders requires a section to itself; but the possibility of treatment by this method should not blind the clinician to the more *general aspects of treatment*. This should, where possible, be of a conservative kind. Given time, in nearly every case one can expect a spontaneous remission, so that drastic, and above all destructive, methods of treatment should be applied with the greatest caution. The first duties of the physician are to guard his patients against the dangers of the illness, and to provide them with relief from the worst symptoms.

By far the most serious danger is, in states of depression, that of *suicide*. Since the risk is greatest at the beginning of the illness, before retardation has paralysed the patient's activity and capacity for taking decisions, the responsibility rests largely with the practitioner who sees him first. He must not only deal with the fixed ideas of biased relations but also with deception on the part of the patient, who will dissimulate his weariness of life. If he speaks of it openly, this is often mistakenly taken as a sign that the danger is not real—which is far from true. Even a slight suspicion of suicidal inclination should ensure the patient's removal to a place where he can be kept under observation night and day. Unless there are facilities for this at home, he should be removed to a *psychiatric hospital*. Nowadays there are departments of psychological medicine in general and teaching hospitals, where the facilities will exist for adequate observation, and security will be sufficient for even a seriously suicidal patient. Where such units are not available, the admission ward of a mental hospital, where the patient can go as an informal patient, is preferable by far to makeshift arrangements in a general hospital or nursing home. There is no generally applicable rule for judging the danger of suicide in an individual case, and even competent experts are liable to make occasional mistakes. An unsuccessful attempt at suicide at the beginning of the illness, on the other hand, facilitates the subsequent management.

It is a common mistake to try to cheer up a depressive by sending him on a cruise, making him travel or go on a holiday, and forcing social activities on him. The same mistake is made with the hypomanic, to provide him with an outlet for his increased flow of energy. Both states, however, should be treated in a quiet environment with as little distraction as possible, unless of a specifically prescribed kind. If the state is at all a severe one, therefore, the most suitable place is a special hospital. The early depressive is often easily persuaded to *enter the hospital as an informal patient* and usually adapts himself well to hospital life. At many centres day hospitals are available, and may provide all that is needed. Many mild recurrent depressives, on the other hand, may suffer a social disadvantage by too early an admission to hospital, particularly if their jobs are endangered by too high a share of sick leave in the past. With such patients, while some working routine can be maintained, and there is no risk of suicide, admission to hospital can be postponed for a time; and in the case of a mild and short-lived mood state it may be possible to avoid sick leave altogether. The patients may then be helped over the worst of their symptoms by such simple measures as the securing of adequate sleep, and the administration of antidepressive drugs along the lines described below. If convulsive therapy is required, it is often available at a neighbouring out-patient clinic. The dangers which have to be avoided in the hypomanic patient are of another nature, and unless his state is very mild indeed admission to hospital is likely to be imperative. The risk he runs is that he will perform some ill-considered, tactless or unwise action which will prejudice his future. This is so difficult to predict or to guard against that it is by far the best thing if the patient can be persuaded to protect himself by going into hospital.

In hospital the severely depressed patient, retarded or agitated, should be first treated in bed. This is also desirable for the manic patient, but much more difficult to carry out. Each should be nursed in a quiet room with as little outside stimulation as possible. Relatives should only be admitted if they have understanding of the case and co-operate with the medical staff.

In true endogenous depression any attempt at systematic psychotherapy is contra-indicated as it often leads to a deepening of the patient's sense of worthlessness. But it is essential to penetrate the barrier created by the patient's self-torment and despair and to establish a warm rapport with him—a difficult task which requires much patience and skill. Explanations about the benign and recoverable character of the illness, the manner in which it generates the morbid ideas expressed by the patient and reassuring objections against his self-accusations may appear to make no impression, but are frequently recalled with gratitude by the patient after recovery. Even the speechless patient expects words of comfort and encouragement and resents if it he is overlooked. Though apparently completely self-absorbed, he is sensitive to tactless handling and will only be driven into deeper depression if he feels he is not under sympathetic care. Adequate time spent in making contact with, and gaining the confidence of, the patient usually reaps rewards when it comes to persuading him to accept medication or other physical treatment.

It is not uncommon for resentment or animosity towards some close relation or a marriage partner to surge up during a depressive attack and to give rise to strained relations and even to precipitate actions which may prejudice the chances of a reconciliation. Such antipathy has frequently died down after recovery from the illness and a seemingly ill-matched couple may, after successful treatment of the sick partner, resume a long-established *modus vivendi*. It is well to remember, therefore, that intense feelings of hostility and anger may be, to some extent, conditioned by the psychotic illness and, although rarely without some real foundation, they may be exaggerated out of all proportion to the true state of affairs. The patient, as also his relations, may need to be carefully advised and guided to prevent them from taking precipitate actions, the effects of which may prove to be irrevocable.

The bodily constitution of both depressive and hypomanic patients needs careful watching, when agitation or excitement and insufficient feeding have brought it to a low level. Depressive patients (especially the elderly) are frequently admitted in a state of emaciation and exhaustion and it is advisable in such cases to administer a high-potency vitamin preparation intramuscularly for a period as an adjunct to other physical treatments. It is essential to promote sleep from the beginning by adequate dosage of hypnotics such as sodium amylobarbitone (200–400 mg.) or butobarbitone (100–200 mg.). Where the patient continues to waken early in the morning despite adequate doses of normal hypnotics, a long-acting preparation, such as sodium quinalbarbitone in doses of 100 mg., may be added. Under no circumstances should the patient be entrusted with quantities of these substances adequate for a suicidal attempt and, in profoundly depressed and determined suicidal patients, special care must be taken to ensure that hypnotics administered are, in fact, being taken and not saved up for an attempt.

It is important for the patient to be kept occupied but care must be taken not to overtax his powers, and coercion in any form or degree is wholly unjustified. To obtain the best results with *occupational therapy* it should be given with a due appreciation of the psychiatric state and of the patient's talents, failings, likes and dislikes and given by someone skilled in its management. Loss of spontaneity and difficulty in concentration convert even simple tasks into an ordeal, and in the most severe cases all activity may reinforce the sense of failure and inadequacy.

As far as specific treatment for endogenous depression is concerned, where a swift effect is needed in a profoundly depressed and suicidal patient, electroplexy probably remains the treatment of choice. But where there is no urgency or where the patient is frail, exhausted or physically ill, a trial of one of the antidepressant drugs is greatly to be preferred. Many cases of endogenous depression can with advantage be treated at home provided satisfactory arrangements for careful and regular out-patient supervision can be made. Many drugs are recommended for use and a number of these have had their efficacy established with the aid of controlled therapeutic trials. Among these, perhaps the best tried preparation is imipramine (Tofranil) which is administered in initial doses of 25 mg. four times daily increasing within 7–10 days to a maximum total dosage of 150–250 mg. daily. Only in rare instances need the maximum dosage taken be above 200 mg. daily. The dosage should be maintained at this level for a period of three to four weeks, and then reduced over 10–14 days to a maintenance dosage of 75–100 mg. daily. The precise period for which treatment with this and other antidepressant drugs is required remains to be determined. There appears to be some individual variation in the needs of different patients, but, as a general rule, maintenance dosage for a period of four to six months is required and in many cases relapse follows discontinuation of treatment even after this period. The side-effects of dryness in the mouth, difficulty in initiating micturition and constipation give rise to little difficulty in cases of endogenous depression. It is surprising how little patients with this disorder complain of such symptoms, despite the fact that careful enquiry will often show them to be present. Hypotension is also common and the blood pressure should be checked regularly, particularly in elderly patients.

Among alternatives for imipramine is amitriptyline hydrochloride which has been shown in some controlled trials (Burt *et al.*, 1962; Hordern *et al.*, 1963; Garry and Leonard, 1963) to be at least the equal of imipramine in the treatment of endogenous depression. It is given in doses of 50 mg. three times daily reduced on maintenance to 25 mg. three to four times daily. It is less prone to produce tension, perspiration and tremor than imipramine and frequently exerts something of a soporific effect which is useful in some cases but a disadvantage in others. Among new tricyclic compounds the secondary amines, desipramine, nortryptiline and protryptiline are possibly more stimulating in very retarded patients but tend to exacerbate anxiety. There is no convincing evidence that these or tertiary amines such as trimipramine are superior to amitryptiline or imipramine.

For the present, there would appear to be little to indicate that *any one type of endogenous depression*, being specially susceptible, is particularly worthy of a preliminary trial on pharmacological treatment. On the whole the more closely the picture approximates to that of classical endogenous depression the more likely a favourable response to imipramine (Kiloh *et al.*, 1962). But stuporous and persistently deluded or hallucinated patients often fail to respond in the authors' experience and require E.C.T. Further clinical experience may serve to define groups in terms of clinical picture, age of onset, duration and sex, which respond specifically to pharmacological or to electroconvulsive treatment. If there is no response, it is unjustified to prolong treatment with drugs for longer than three or four weeks and, in the more severe cases, it may have to be abandoned earlier and electroplexy begun.

With beginning convalescence, the risk of suicide once more becomes serious as retardation fades. The patient should not be discharged from hospital until there are grounds for regarding the recovery as stable. Useful assistance in deciding this point and in helping the patient to adapt himself to outside life is provided by short excursions and week-ends at home. Relatives often press for early discharge, even when in early convalescence the *risk of suicide* is still appreciable; and the hospital psychiatrist may need the assistance of the family practitioner to induce them to take a sensible view.

Environmental stresses play a very limited part in causing endogenous depression and are rarely more than precipitating factors. Resolving the difficulties in which the patient may have become enmeshed before his illness will not, therefore, cure him but will often help him once recovery begins. Moreover, a minority of patients with endogenous depression have lifelong emotional and personality problems similar to those in patients with neurotic affective disturbances. Some patients harbour ambitions that are beyond their capacity to fulfil, others are seeking unawares 'to have their cake and eat it'. Some patients are prevented from making an adequate adaptation to their difficulties by refusal to face them squarely; they may be able to do so with help. Other unstable persons continue to respond to difficulties in interpersonal relationships in a way that previous experience should have taught them was bound to fail. Psychotherapy aimed at deepening the patient's insight into such problems and into the way in which he may unwittingly expose himself to undue stress or conflict, may help to reduce the chances of further breakdown.

MANIA. Cases of mania or severe forms of hypomanic illness require admission to hospital as the patient's lack of restraint and impaired judgement may jeopardize his career or social position. The milder attacks of hypomanic illness can be treated at home under the supervision of the general practitioner, but only if it is possible to ensure a wise and flexible supervision of the patient's activities. An intelligent and responsible relative who is prepared to remain at home with the patient may meet the needs of the situation. But only a very small proportion of hypomanic cases can be managed in this manner.

Most of the milder cases of mania respond fairly rapidly to phenothiazines and an initial intramuscular dose of 50 mg. repeated within four to six hours, and followed thereafter by 50–100 mg. doses orally at 6-hourly intervals, brings the excitement, overactivity and insomnia under a reasonable degree of control. In cases with an extreme degree of psychomotor overactivity other measures will be necessary. The drug haloperidol (which is related in structure to gamma-amino-butyric acid) given in an intravenous injection of 3–5 mg., often reduces manic excitement in a dramatic manner. The dose should be repeated at 6-hourly intervals until the patient's condition is sufficiently subdued. Maintenance dosage consists of 1 or 2 mg. thrice daily, taken by mouth. Extra-pyramidal side-effects are common and severe and may have to be counteracted with orphenadrine hydrochloride (Disipal), 50 mg. thrice daily. Treatment with haloperidol should be undertaken only in hospital, but maintenance treatment for a period is often necessary when the patient returns home.

Drug treatment may fail to bring the excitement under sufficiently rapid control and, as an emergency measure, a short course of E.C.T. administered at intervals of one to two days, according to progress, may be required. The minimum number of treatments necessary to render the condition manageable should be given.

In some patients manic excitement and irritability become chronic or relapse rapidly follows a seemingly complete recovery. Lithium carbonate, originally introduced by Cade (1949), plays a valuable part in the management of such chronic or relapsing cases. The drug is provided in 250 mg. tablets and an initial dosage of 750–1000 mg., in four divided doses, is required for the control of symptoms. After a week or so, dosage may be changed to a maintenance dose of two to three tablets daily which should be adjusted later in accordance with the clinical improvement and side effects. This treatment should not be administered unless regular estimations of plasma lithium can be arranged. In some cases a therapeutic effect is not achieved unless a minimum plasma level of 1 m/Eq. per litre can be maintained. The dosage may have to be raised to $1\frac{1}{2}$–2 gm. daily in the initial stages to bring plasma lithium to this level and subsequent dosage needs to be adjusted to maintain it at this level. Toxic effects appear when the plasma lithium concentration rises above 2 ml. Eq. per litre. The patient complains of some of the following symptoms: dizziness, headache, blurring of vision, weakness and tremor, diarrhoea and anorexia. In the presence of any such complications the drug should be discontinued immediately. After a few days, dosage can often be resumed at a lower level. Toxic effects rarely arise on maintenance therapy. The drug is wholly contra-indicated in patients with renal or cardiac disease.

Hypomanics and manics without the slightest insight into their condition are not accessible to psychological treatment; but the transition from hospital to normal life may be considerably eased by the skill of a sympathetic and understanding doctor. Convalescence is often difficult, and return to outside life with its distractions and irritations may precipitate a recurrence of the symptoms.

Mixed states in which depression and manic features occur simultaneously or in which manic and depressive attacks follow one another without normal intervals present problems of the greatest difficulty for therapy. It is probably best in these cases to avoid convulsive treatment as far as this is possible. It has been suggested (Schou, 1963) that imipramine and its analogues as well as lithium salts act as stabilizers of mood disturbance, whether manic or depressive, but the evidence for this is, at present, unconvincing. A certain proportion of mixed cases respond to imipramine alone. In others careful and systematic trial of a combination of imipramine with haloperidol or with lithium carbonate has to be undertaken. Most cases are eventually brought under control but months or years may elapse before a satisfactory stabilization is achieved.

Convulsive Therapy

Convulsive therapy finds by far its most important application in the treatment of affective disorders and, wisely used, may transform the outlook at least for the attack. The mistake that is most frequently made nowadays is its excessive or too indiscriminate use. The authors have seen no good results from battering the patient with more than one fit a day for days in succession, but they have seen the most serious and lasting losses of memory and amnesic patches extending over months or even years as a result of this treatment, which then themselves form the germ of new complaints in a cyclothymic or neurotic patient.

Of all the affective syndromes *involutional depression* is most susceptible to benefit from convulsive treatment. Once the diagnosis can be confidently made, the treatment should be begun—that is to say, provided there are no overriding contra-indications. It is probably best to give the treatment twice a week for the first three or four treatments, after which the frequency might drop to once weekly. Others prefer to give three treatments weekly for two weeks and wait for the result of this course. In general the length of treatment should be judged by the results obtained. If no sign whatever of improvement has been obtained with the first six treatments it is best to revert to more conservative measures for one or two months, after which a second attempt can be made.

Treatment should not necessarily be continued until the last traces of depression have disappeared. Once he is well on the way to recovery, the depressive will often go the rest of the way himself. The spacing of the convulsions should be adapted to the individual patient. Although the convulsion is an all-or-nothing reaction, one fit exactly like the other, clinical discrimination should be applied to its *proper timing and spacing*. The amount of slow activity generated in the E.E.G. by a given course of E.C.T. varies markedly in different individuals (Roth *et al.*, 1957) with an identical illness, and courses of treatment which do not vary in spacing or number are therefore probably unphysiological. However it is well known that, if a course of E.C.T. is brought to an end as soon as the main symptoms have been relieved, relapse commonly follows. It is therefore necessary to prolong the course beyond this point; the final number of treatments administered being based on careful clinical appraisal. Thus, when the first series of six fits has initiated recovery, one to three carefully spaced treatments may be needed to remove the last traces of the illness, such as slight inertia in the morning. In the case of psychosis the number of E.C.T. given should very rarely be less than three or more than ten. The appearance of mild hypomania following a short course of treatment in a depressive patient should be taken as a signal to stop the treatment. It usually disappears after a few days or a week; but if it is followed by a relapse into depression, some more spaced-out treatments may help the patient to gain his equilibrium.

It should not be forgotten that a succession of fits, even as infrequently as once a week causes *some impairment of memory*, and therefore an attempt should be made to keep the number given as low as possible. In the great majority of cases the damage is transient and memory and retention if disturbed at all return to normal after about a month. The patients themselves consider the complaint negligible when compared with their sufferings during the depressive illness. However, unexpected and severe memory loss may occur and we have seen at least one severe dysmnesic syndrome lasting two months in a patient of thirty after a few convulsions given for a reactive depression. Sustained impairment of intellectual function is much more likely in the presence of cerebrovascular or other cerebral disease, but there is very little evidence that the changes produced are irreversible or that the administration of E.C.T. in such cases carries an appreciable risk of producing cerebral infarction or damage. In other cases one has to balance the hazard of producing some quite sustained intellectual impairment, possibly an attack of confusion, against the benefits derived from bringing relief for the depression, which in these cases carries an appreciable risk of suicide (see Chapter X, p. 559). Throughout the course of the convulsive treatment an eye should be kept open for signs of a confusion which lasts for more than the few hours immediately succeeding the fit, and for disturbances of memory and impairment of grasp and concentration.

Recurrent affective disorders of a more typically manic-depressive type do not respond so regularly to convulsive therapy as do the involutional melancholias; but the treatment is still far superior to anything known before its introduction and may considerably shorten the single attack of depression or mania, reduce the time in hospital and mitigate suffering and distress. It is always worth trying, although not infrequently treatment fails to have an effect, or produces only a temporary improvement. This is particularly likely to happen if treatment is given early in the affective swing, while it is gathering momentum or is still at its height. Success, however, is very probable if the biological change has passed its zenith, and yet the patient remains stuck fast in a depression. Often the past history will give one some idea of how long, in the individual patient, the normal length of the illness should be. We have seen patients who have been allowed to go on untreated for two years, after an early failure with electrical treatment, but have then recovered after two or three treatments. One patient, who had recovered once after treatment given at the end of one phase, failed to respond when it was given early in the next one, and was so discouraged that he took his life. This is a typical incident illustrating the danger of treating an endogenous depression without adequate supervision, and also of the *risk of suicide during and immediately after convulsive therapy*. Convulsions may remove the motor inhibition without clearing up entirely the background of unhappiness or despair—factors which are not entirely interdependent as we know from the occurrence of mixed states. On the other hand the number of suicidal attempts which will be encountered in patients who have once come under observation and control will be lessened considerably by energetic treatment.

Electrical convulsive therapy is less effective for manic and hypomanic states than for depressions. Good results are obtained from time to time; a *greater number of more closely spaced convulsions* is needed for a satisfactory result. On the whole, the treatment should be used according to the same principles as in the manic-depressive depressions, that is to say with caution, and with an effort to choose the most propitious time.

The *setting in which the treatment is given* is of some importance. Each patient should be treated singly in a room by himself and not behind a screen in the ward where other patients anxiously observe the noises (epileptic cry and stertorous breathing) while they are waiting for their turn. Privacy in treatment is no less necessary with the greatly improved modern method of administering an intravenous anaesthetic (thiopentone sodium) and a muscular relaxant (suxamethonium) before giving the electrical treatment.

The method of choice for convulsive treatment at present is the application of an alternating electric current of 70 to 120 volts for 0·4–0·6 of a second. The technical details are laid down in handbooks of physical therapy (Sargant and Slater, 1963; Kalinowsky and Hoch, 1961). Convulsive therapy is now almost always modified by giving first an intravenous injection of barbiturate and then a muscular relaxant. The anaesthetic most commonly used is thiopentone sodium which is given in doses 0.2–0.25 gm. in 4–5 ml. water. This is injected over a period of 30–35 seconds and is followed immediately by an injection of 30 mg. of scoline given through the same needle. It is essential to ensure that the patient is adequately oxygenated before electric current is passed to initiate convulsion. Apart from the general desirability of this, there is some reason to suppose that anoxia plays a part in deciding the degree of memory impairment. The occurrence of a fit is sometimes difficult to judge but a slight rhythmic twitching of the facial muscles and toes normally provides a reliable indication that the fit is in progress. It is important to administer the intravenous barbiturate first as the experience of progressive paralysis in the conscious state is terrifying. Immediately the fit is over, oxygenation should be begun again with the aid of a pressure-bag and maintained until a satisfactory red colour is achieved and spontaneous respiration is established. Speaking generally, the more simple apparatus with reliable timing is to be preferred to complicated machines which because of their refined build are sometimes apt to break down. The same holds true of the type of electrodes used; reliable contact can be achieved by cleansing the skin with a salt solution or a contact jelly, and that is all that is needed. As the current within the range of strength and time mentioned above is free from danger, it seems unnecessary to start with the lowest possible dose in each case because 'subconvulsive shocks' are often very unpleasant for the patient and apt to increase his apprehension. They should be avoided as far as possible. If the patient has taken phenobarbitone before the beginning of the convulsive therapy, the first treatments may need a relatively high voltage because of the anti-epileptic effect of these drugs. Much detailed study has been given to modifications of the electrical impulses: wave form, pulse strength and duration, intervals between pulses, polarity, have all been varied; and apparatus has been recommended to produce some special variation, the claim being made that it reduces the post-convulsive confusion and the disturbance of memory. Frequent claims have, for example, been made for the therapeutic advantages of types of apparatus that deliver unidirectional pulses which are considered to yield superior results and to cause less marked memory impairment. Careful enquiries (Cronholm and Ottosson, 1963 b) have failed to confirm these claims. In a group of important studies Ottosson (1960 a,b,c) has shown that the depression-relieving effects of E.C.T. are due to the generation of 'seizure activity' and not (or only to a minor extent) to other effects exerted by the current. The therapeutic effect of grand mal seizures is similar whether the electrical stimulus was liminal or supraliminal although improvement tended to be somewhat more rapid when a supraliminal stimulus was used. Seizures modified by lidocaine were slightly less effective than unmodified seizures. Of particular importance was the finding that the mechanism whereby therapeutic results and memory defects were produced were independent of each other; the latter consisted of an impairment of retention and was related to the electrical energy administered. There would therefore appear to be some advantages, as far as memory impairment is concerned, in techniques that involve the passage of the smallest quantity of electrical energy required to generate a fit.

If there is no adverse outside influence, depressive patients accept convulsion treatment *without dread or anxiety*. Many consent willingly to further applications when they feel its effect on their condition, in spite of some vague, half-conscious memory of the procedure. We have seen many recurrent depressives return and ask for the treatment when they felt their oncoming attack. Conversely, gossip about it in hospital wards or out-patient clinics and ill-informed and exaggerated literary and journalistic descriptions can easily produce an atmosphere of fear infecting all patients.

The effect produced is illustrated by a *patient's spontaneous description*, written three years after her discharge from hospital:

'. . . after the second treatment I could taste my food for the first time and felt I had an appetite. I had been so fond of sweets and after I got depressed I could not look at sweets, but just after the second treatment one of the ladies gave me a bit of chocolate. It tasted so good and I just wanted more, and I got better every day after that.

'I could not bear to hear a bird singing or hear the sound of a motor horn when I went in at first, but after the electrical treatment everything was different, and I certainly have felt no bad effects and I can concentrate on reading, sewing, wireless or listening even to a quarrel with my two girls and I never bother at all.'

Since the induction of *convulsions by electricity* (Cerletti and Bini, 1938) has become the standard method, analeptic drugs have gone out of use for this purpose. However, some clinicians still insist that fits produced by *leptazol*, the drug applied by Meduna when he first established the treatment, have an effect in certain patients refractory to electrical convulsive therapy, especially in cases of agitated melancholia. A possible explanation could be that the initial feeling of dread, after the injection of the drug before the convulsion, has some additional influence on the patient. This initial dread is absent when electricity is used. The general theory, however, that fear is the curative factor in convulsion treatment has no foundation in fact.

The part that *leucotomy or similar operative procedures* may play in the treatment of the affective psychoses is not yet fully explored. There can be no doubt that it will often bring about the rapid cessation of a depressive illness. As the cerebral effects of electrical treatment are reversible, leucotomy should only be employed when convulsive therapy has failed and the outlook appears hopeless without it. Caution is especially required in the cyclical affective psychoses, and every case should be judged on its merits. The personality changes seen after leucotomy often destroy those delicate emotional features which are the greatest asset of the cyclothymic. In involutional melancholias, which have failed to respond to convulsive therapy, leucotomy has given satisfactory results, and most observers have found a recovery rate between 60 and 80 per cent. Here again we know at least of one patient who changed into a picture of persisting hypomania with reckless aggressiveness, in its social effects much worse than the pre-operative hypochondriacal depression. A few cases have also been observed in which there has been a subsequent relapse, a phenomenon which it is not very easy to understand.

CHAPTER V

SCHIZOPHRENIA

DEFINITION

THE term schizophrenia is used here for a group of mental illnesses characterized by *specific psychological symptoms* and leading, in the majority of cases, to a disorganization of the personality of the patient. The symptoms interfere with the patient's thinking, emotions, conation and motor behaviour, and with each in a characteristic way. The disorganization of personality often results in chronic invalidism and life-long hospitalization in spite of the absence of gross physical signs or symptoms.

Unfavourable outcome and onset in youth or early manhood provided the guiding principle for Kraepelin in unifying varied clinical pictures under the name of 'dementia praecox' in 1896. The term had been first used by Morel (1860) to designate a smaller group of similar kind. These were cases of what till then had been regarded as not one but many different diseases, and Kraepelin's new concept was opposed by most contemporary psychiatrists. 'By a stroke of genius' (Adolf Meyer) Kraepelin assembled into the newly established *disease entity* the masses of what were then, and still are, chronic inmates of mental hospitals. His classical description of the illness has not been surpassed and has stood the test of time. The concept slowly gained recognition. It was confirmed and consolidated by Bleuler who in his monograph *The Schizophrenias* (1911), by an intimate study of a broad clinical material, made an important attempt at establishing a primary disturbance common to all cases of the group. From the nature of this fundamental disturbance he coined the term 'schizophrenia' using the plural because of uncertainty of the aetiological unity of the group. This uncertainty still persists. Bleuler's schizophrenia included a somewhat wider range of patients than Kraepelin's dementia praecox, and embodies the milder cases without a clearly defined psychotic attack which Kretschmer later described under the name of schizoids.

Numerous attempts have been made to subdivide the large group without success. In later editions of his text-book Kraepelin himself singled out 'presenile paranoia', '*Spaetkatatonie*' (late catatonia) and 'paraphrenia' as sub-groups, placing them either inside, or bordering on the 'dementia praecox–circle'. These subdivisions have not found as general an acceptance as his main grouping, although the problems of classification of some of these groups are far from settled (see p. 294). Conversely, diseases which he and others had considered separate entities, such as involutional and alcoholic paranoia, have proved to be closely related to the large schizophrenic aggregate. This has resisted dissolution so far and has been taken over in the psychobiological system of Adolf Meyer as the '*parergasic reaction type*'. The effort by Kleist and his pupils to split it up again into numerous small entities, with different syndromes and outcome, must appear, in the absence of any established pathology, as a retrograde step towards the pre-Kraepelinian confusion of the nineteenth century.

INCIDENCE

With so much controversy about the boundaries, one would hardly expect to get reliable data on the prevalence of schizophrenia in the general population. Such estimates are, in fact, affected by errors from a wide variety of sources. Fashions in diagnosis change from time to time; in the U.S.A., for instance, there has been a greater readiness to make a diagnosis of schizophrenia in recent years. The breadth or narrowness of concept involved in a diagnostic classification also varies from country to country, and in this respect the general practice differs a good deal between North America and Europe. There are marked differences in diagnostic practice between private and public mental hospitals; and in the former there is a widespread tendency to avoid the diagnosis of a psychosis, and particularly the diagnosis of schizophrenia. There are differences between university clinics, out-patient clinics, and regional hospitals; and, even within the group of regional hospitals, the diagnostic practice of one hospital may differ from that of its neighbours. Certain clinical syndromes such as states of depersonalization, 'schizo-affective' disorders and 'psychogenic psychoses', tend in particular to be classified in one way by some hospitals and in another way by others. Nevertheless, in the case of schizophrenia, most hospitals in Europe tend to be guided by Kraepelinian concepts, so that they show a gratifying degree of consistency in clinical approach. On this basis, the bulk of 'schizophrenic' patients would be acceptable as such to the great majority of clinicians. Prevalence rates and expectancies calculated from clinical observations classified by this generally agreed system of diagnosis show themselves to be comparable from country to country, and from one decade to the next.

Variations in the incidence of schizophrenia along ethnic, cultural and social lines have attracted a great deal of attention. A number of reports (e.g. Faris and Dunham, 1939) showed that schizophrenics tend to come from the most depressed social classes and from the slum areas of great cities. The same trend has been found in national figures, as for instance, in Britain. However, recent work (e.g. Clausen and Kohn, 1959; Goldberg and Morrison, 1963) suggests that these findings are to be interpreted in the opposite sense from the one which first seemed plausible. The parents of schizophrenics, and the circumstances into which they are born, show the same social distribution as that of the general population; what has happened is that the schizophrenic has himself drifted down the social scale, often as the result of a slow process which may have antedated the onset of manifest psychosis. However, a limited contribution by adverse environmental and exogenous factors to the causation of schizophrenia is not excluded by the available facts (Kay and Roth, 1961). The steep social class gradient in the prevalence of schizophrenic illness therefore deserves further enquiry both from the genetical and the sociological point of view.

There is nothing to support the view that large ethnic groups differ markedly in their liability to schizophrenic illness. The notion that primitives, untouched by civilization, are even relatively immune has never found evidential support. As Hoch has noted (1961), there is a wonderful change in the underprivileged country once psychiatric facilities are made available: 'Whereas they formerly claimed that they had no psychotic patients, their culture being such that it didn't produce schizophrenia, as soon as a hospital is built it is filled, and immediately they are made to build another hospital.' On the other hand, small, inbreeding, partially isolated subcultures may be found to have raised or lowered expectancies of one or another psychosis. Thus the North American religious sect of Hutterites have been found to have very little schizophrenia but rather more than their share of manic-depressive illness; while the North Swedish, geographically isolated, population investigated by Böök had practically no manic-depressives, but nearly three times the usual incidence of schizophrenia.

The more important estimates of the expectancy of schizophrenia for members of the general population in several countries, and the data provided by the Registrar General for England and Wales in 1960 (together with some further estimates calculated from them) are shown in the accompanying tables. On the basis of the Registrar General's figures one may calculate the expectancy of schizophrenia for males as 1.13 per cent. by the age of 55, 1.23 per cent. by the age of 75; for females the corresponding figures are 1.08 per cent. and 1.30 per cent. These estimates, based on hospital returns for the country as a whole, are in good agreement, not only with Norris's estimates using national data for 1953, but also with most of the estimates made for samples of out-bred populations. Arctic Sweden and the populations of Geneva and of Iceland differ rather sharply from the general mean.

EXPECTANCY OF SCHIZOPHRENIA IN THE GENERAL POPULATION

Date Author	Region	Expectancy (per cent.)		
		Males	Females	Both
1946 Ødegaard	Norway	1·92	1·79	
1948 Sjögren	Sweden	—	—	0·83
1950 Strömgren	18 investigations in Central and Northern Europe	—	—	0·72
1951 Fremming	Denmark	0·75	1·02	0·88
1953 Böök	Arctic Sweden	2·59	2·75	2·66
1954 Larsson and Sjögren	Sweden (Rural)	1·6	1·6	1·6
1956 Essen-Möller	Sweden (Rural)	—	—	1·1
1959 Norris	U.K. (National data)	1·07	0·93	
Norris	U.K. (area of 3 mental hospitals)	0·93	1·16	
1962 Garrone	Switzerland	1·9	2·9	2·4
1964 Helgason	Iceland	0·57	0·9	

ADMISSION RATE FOR SCHIZOPHRENIA IN ENGLAND AND WALES IN 1960

Age Group	Annual admission rate per million		Sex ratio M/F	Proportion (per cent.) of total risk survived	
	M	F	M/F	M	F
10 to	11	13	0·87	0	0
15 to	247	224	1·18	0	0
20 to	458	283	1·46	10	9
25 to	403	350	1·15	29	20
35 to	254	275	0·95	62	47
45 to	119	195	0·58	82	68
55 to	70	139	0·48	92	83
65 to	30	84	0·42	98	94
75 plus	23	68	0·38	100	100

There is little difference in the risk of schizophrenia for males and for females except that, in England and Wales at least, the age of onset in women tends to fall rather later than in men. This results in a striking change in the sex ratio of new admissions at various ages, with a marked preponderance of males at earlier ages especially between 25 and 35, and an increasingly greater preponderance of females at ages after 45. It seems probable that this is a characteristic of the illness which is to be found in Western countries generally; but whether its causes are to be sought for in biological or social factors is an open question.

AETIOLOGY AND PATHOLOGY

(1) Heredity

The genetical contribution to the aetiology of schizophrenia, though resting on a mass of well-observed and analysed data, is constantly called in question, especially by writers who believe that psychodynamic factors are prepotent. An example of recent criticism from this point of view has been provided by Jackson (1960). It seems desirable, therefore, to review the evidence with special reference to recent work.

WORK ON TWINS. The biological difference between monozygotic (MZ) and dizygotic (DZ) pairs of twins provides the means of making the most sensitive single test of the significance of hereditary factors. A balanced review of the logic of this approach, and of the results that have been obtained in psychiatry, has been provided by Essen-Möller (1963). If there are genetical factors involved in causation, then we must expect a much greater degree of similarity between members of MZ pairs than between members of (same-sexed) DZ pairs, since the former are genotypic replicas of one another and the latter share only half of their genetical equipment in common. This somewhat simplified statement stands despite the qualifications which the theorist feels called on to make, for example, regarding the effect of cytoplasmic inheritance, of somatic mutations, transfer of genetic material from one twin to another. All such phenomena are, as far as is known, sufficiently infrequent or of such limited extent in their effect on the total genotype, that when one is working with a series of patients and using statistical methods their effect can be ignored. Their significance, however, has to be borne in mind in a number of rare and interesting individual cases.

The principal caution, which is advanced in the way of interpreting the results of twin investigations along genetical lines, is that the environment of MZ pairs is much more alike for the two members of the pair than it is for the two members of DZ pairs. There is certainly some truth in this contention, mainly because individuals of different genetical make-up and different predispositions will seek out different environments for themselves, while MZ pairs of twins not infrequently cling together to share a life lived much in common. This objection however, remains of an entirely theoretical kind. It has never been shown that the environments of members of MZ pairs are more alike than the environments of DZ pairs in respect of any single feature which is known to have any connexion with mental illness. Until we know what to look for, we have no means of measuring the allowance we should make for such hypothetical environmental differences between MZ and DZ pairs. If we were to be ruled by this consideration we should have to abandon twin observations of all kinds as having no relevance to the problem of distinguishing between genetical and environmental contributions to aetiology.

The other main line of objection amounts, in effect, to the proposition that twins, especially MZ twins, suffer under a variety of disabilities in the development of 'ego identity'. According to Jackson (1960) 'the identity problem of the schizophrenic . . . could find no better nidus than in the intertwining of twin identities, in the ego fusion that in one sense doubles the ego (since the other is felt as part of the self) and in another halves it (since the self is felt as part of the other)'. As has been pointed out by Rosenthal (1960, 1963) who is himself a keen but discriminating critic of twin methodology, all such theories lead to an expectation that mental illness (e.g. schizophrenia) will be more frequent in twins than in singletons, more frequent in members of same-sexed (SS) than of opposite-sexed (OS) pairs, and more frequent in SS MZ than in SS DZ pairs. None of these expectations is borne out: the incidence of schizophrenia in the twin-born is the same as in non-twins.

Interest has recently been aroused by reports showing a much lower degree of concordance between members of MZ pairs in respect of schizophrenia than that found by earlier workers. Essen-Möller (1963) reviewed the major contributions made up to that time, including only SS paris, and showed a crude concordance, uncorrected for age, of 69 per cent. in the MZ pairs as against 13 per cent. in the DZ pairs. The Japanese workers Inouye and Kurihara (Inouye, 1961) found much the same picture, 60 per cent. concordance in the MZ pairs and 18 per cent. in the DZ pairs. Preconceptions were accordingly violently jarred when Tienari (1963) reported a large unselected series of twins from Finland, male pairs only, in which there was zero concordance in the 16 MZ schizophrenic pairs. This was indeed difficult to understand, though the work of Kringlen (1966) and of Gottesman and Shields (1966) helps us to resolve this apparent contradiction. The data provided by all these workers are shown in the table below.

	Concordance in absolute numbers			
	SS DZ	MZ pairs		
		Male	Female	Total
Essen-Möller (results of 5 series summed)	59/448			194/280
Inouye, Kurihara	2/11	12/21	21/34	33/55
Tienari	1/19	0/12		0/12
Kringlen	13/94	12/27	7/23	19/50
Gottesman and Shields	3/33	5/13	5/11	10/24

The older material has been repeatedly criticized for being clinically unrepresentative, since in most series not only fresh admissions but also a standing hospital population were used, in which therefore severe psychoses leading to chronic illness would find more than their fair place. For Tienari's material it is claimed that the selection is based on a sounder principle, the starting material having been all same-sexed twins born in Finland from 1920–1929. However, even here selective factors may have influenced the results since female pairs were not investigated, and only living twins were taken, by which the ascertainment of those who became schizophrenic may well have been incomplete.

It is a remarkable feature of the survey that Tienari found no single case of affective psychosis. Of the 17 psychotic patients 14 are diagnosed as suffering from schizophrenia, and one each from schizo-affective psychosis, 'border-line' schizophrenia, and reactive psychosis. However, three of the schizophrenics (608, 32, 462) had gross brain lesions and most psychiatrists would unhesitatingly have diagnosed them as suffering from organic psychoses; in a fourth pair (74) both twins had thyrotoxicosis, and in addition the co-twin had a hyperpietic brain syndrome. To make the case material comparable with other studies it seems best to omit the more obviously organic states and, as is recorded in the table above, to allow zero concordance in a total of 12 pairs.

Fortunately Tienari provides adequate case summaries, from which it appears that his clinical material does not differ so much from that of other workers as one might have thought from his figures alone. There are close resemblances between the members of a number of his MZ pairs, and in one case (989) most judges would consider that both brothers were schizophrenic. Nevertheless, one must agree that concordance within MZ pairs is surprisingly low in this series. Shields (1965) has pointed out that concordance rates tend to be low in all the Scandinavian series, including those of Essen-Möller in Sweden and Kringlen in Norway; and these studies as a group differ from those conducted in America, Britain, Denmark, Germany and Japan. It is possible that concordance rates might be lower in Norway, Sweden and Finland than elsewhere in the world; it might be that the population in these lands is genetically more homogeneous than in other countries, so that genetical differences between individuals lose in significance to the environmental ones.

However the main cause for the lowering of the estimates of concordance which recent studies have brought is probably due to the fact that recent workers have been careful to guard against the effects of selection in favour of severe psychoses. Gottesman and Shields have confirmed the suggestion made by Rosenthal that the more severe the illness the more likely is it to prove concordant within MZ twin pairs. In their material there was 17 per cent. concordance in the 12 MZ pairs in which the proband's illness was a mild one, 75 per cent. in the 16 pairs where it was severe. The corresponding figures in the DZ pairs was 0 per cent. and 22 per cent. The method of selection employed by Gottesman and Shields was the follow-up of an uninterrupted series of hospital in-patient and out-patient admissions, in which twinship was ascertained at the time of admission. An equally satisfactory or even better method of selection was used by Kringlen, by means of a cross check between all twin births recorded at a national central office and all persons registered in the National Register of Psychosis. The twins taken were those born 1901 to 1930, and who were therefore in the 35 to 64 age group on investigation. The results are much the same in both these modern studies. Concordance in MZ pairs, estimated as 38 to 42 per cent., is markedly and significantly greater than in SS DZ pairs, 9 to 14 per cent. The twin evidence for the existence of a genetical contribution to a large part at least of the illnesses we call schizophrenic remains very strong.

Noteworthy contributions to twin theory have been made by Rosenthal in a series of papers (1959, 1960, 1961, 1962 a,b), especially in criticizing processes of case-selection, and in rebutting the idea that the special environment in which twins live may be an aetiological factor. He has also pointed out that in one twin series (Slater, 1953) there were several observations which suggested schizophrenia might be broken down into genetically and non-genetically determined syndromes. However, apart from the findings that severer ill-nesses go with higher concordance rates, similar observations have not been made in the later series of Kringlen and of Gottesman and Shields.

Rosenthal has also reported the very striking case of the Genain quadruplets (1963). These were four monozygous girls, all of whom became schizophrenic, though with psycho-ses of widely different severity; obviously in this case the genetical predisposition must have been identical in all four girls. Rosenthal discusses at length the possible aetiological models for schizophrenia, and classifies them into monogenic-biochemical, diathesis-stress, and life-experience theories; his own preferences tend towards the second of these.

GENETIC HETEROGENEITY. The work of Rosenthal, and the interesting suggestion that within the group of schizophrenias forms may be distinguished which are respectively genetically and non-genetically caused, has already been referred to. In the chapter on the symptomatic schizophrenias, forms of schizophrenic illness are discussed, which at some stage in their life history are clinically indistinguishable from the nuclear group of schizo-phrenias, but which appear to have no specific genetical basis. The general thesis that schizo-phrenia covers a variety of different conditions may therefore be accepted; but from this it does not follow that the great bulk of cases, especially those in which the illness begins in early adult life without obvious precipitant, are not to be regarded as belonging to a uniform group. It may well be that the fringe psychoses represent only a small minority of all cases diagnosed schizophrenic, since those that have been identified are all relatively infrequent.

A more difficult problem arises when we come to consider whether the nuclear group of schizophrenics is itself heterogeneous. This is constantly suggested anew, but usually with very little supporting evidence. However, there are observations bearing on this point. One of the earliest suggestions made by clinicians was that there was a special form of schizophrenia associated with mental subnormality—'Pfropfschizophrenie'. Repeated inves-tigations of this possibility, from the earliest by Brugger in 1928 to the most recent by Hallgren and Sjögren (1959), conclusively negative this. The latter workers, for instance, found that cases in which schizophrenia was combined with low-grade defect were present in the population they investigated in statistical excess; but the incidence of schizophrenia in the sibs of defectives, and the incidence of mental defect in the sibs of schizophrenics, were not raised. There was in fact no suggestion of any biological link between the two conditions.

An interesting attempt to break down schizophrenia into clinical-genetical subgroups was made by Schulz and Leonhard (1940). Leonhard classified the case records of schizo-phrenic probands into those who were, by his criteria, 'typical' (i.e. patients with progressively deteriorating disorders) and those who were 'atypical' (e.g. suffering from recurrent phasic disturbances, etc.); this was done without any knowledge of the family histories, data which had already been collected by Schulz. It was found that the incidence of schizophrenia in the 300 sibs and the 200 parents of the probands was higher in the families of 'atypical' than in the families of the 'typical' probands. The difference was not so great in the sibs (7.8 per cent. to 5.5 per cent.) as in the parents (5.6 per cent. to 0.9 per cent.). The suggestion arises that this method of clinical analysis might be separating disorders caused by a domin-ant gene from those caused by a recessive one. It would be quite in accordance with our understanding of genetics for the severe disorder to be associated with recessive inheritance, the milder one with dominant inheritance.

The view that all the endogenous psychoses are genetically related to one another has been systematically advanced by Mitsuda (1957, 1962). Thus, in his view, there are independent schizophrenic, manic-depressive, epileptic and 'degeneration' psychoses, each overlapping with the others to some extent; and within each major psychosis there are partially independent sub-illnesses, which also overlap. Atypical schizophrenic psychoses would have some kinship with atypical manic-depressive psychoses; and within the large group of atypical psychoses families with dominant and with recessive inheritance are to be found.

However, there seems to be no sound evidence for genetical kinship between manic-depressive illness and schizophrenia. The lack of connexion is not quite so sure in the case of involutional melancholia, since it seems that late schizophrenic illnesses may take a depressive form, and are not infrequently diagnosed as cases of affective psychosis.

The independence of schizophrenic and manic-depressive illnesses is supported by observations from many fields. Follow-up studies have shown that in the majority of cases, 'schizo-affective' disorders and illnesses of a clinically intermediate type become in the course of time more and more clearly schizophrenic in nature. On the genetical side, three groups of findings support the distinction:

1. In the many studies which have been made of the near relatives of probands with endogenous psychoses, the risk of manic-depressive illness in the relatives of schizophrenics, and the risk of schizophrenia in the relatives of manic-depressives, have not been found to be significantly greater than in the general population.

2. In all the large numbers of twin pairs that have now been reported, there has been no MZ pair in which one member showed a schizophrenic and the other a manic-depressive illness.

3. The endogenous psychoses which are found in the children of parents, both of whom have suffered from either a manic-depressive or a schizophrenic illness, conform to one or the other of these types, depending on the mating from which the children descend. There is no tendency for the merging of one stereotype with

Parental mating	Children over 16	Normal	Minor Abnormalities	Psychotic	Schiz.	Man.-dep.	Atypical	Other
N. Type								
34 S×S	96	38	30	28	$20\frac{3}{8}$	—	—	—
20 M×M	47	28	5	14	1	$9\frac{1}{2}$	2	1
19 S×M	68	35	14	19	$6\frac{2}{3}$	$6\frac{2}{3}$	1	2
23 A×S	91	53	23	15	8	$1\frac{1}{2}$	3	$\frac{2}{3}$
21 A×M	55	32	12	11	—	$4\frac{2}{3}$	$4\frac{1}{2}$	—
17 A×A	67	27	16	24	5	$5\frac{1}{2}$	$10\frac{1}{2}$	$\frac{2}{3}$
134 all	424	213	100	111	(88 certain + 23 doubtful)			

the other. The results which we owe to Elsässer (1952) are shown in the table above. It will be seen that matings between a manic-depressive and a schizophrenic produce manic-depressives and schizophrenics; and that matings between parents both of whom have had 'atypical' endogenous psychoses show a marked tendency for the manic-depressive and schizophrenic predispositions to 'mendelize' out in the next generation.

EMPIRICAL RISKS IN THE FAMILIES OF SCHIZOPHRENICS. Kallmann, collating his own observations with those of others, has provided the figures for the table below. The striking feature of this table is the sharp and steady rise in the risk of schizophrenia as the subjects investigated approach more closely in genetical relationship to the index case, e.g. from step-sibs 2 per cent., to half sibs 7 per cent., full sibs 14 per cent., and MZ twins 86 per cent. Environmental effects are possibly shown in the greater risk to consorts and step-sibs of schizophrenics than that of the general population, and the greater risk in MZ pairs for co-twins who had lived with the index case than for those who had been separated for the past five years or more.

Expectation of schizophrenia (as percentage)	
General population	0·9
Relatives of schizophrenic probands	
a. *Not related by blood*	
Step-sibs	1·8
Spouses	2·1
b. *Related by blood*	
First cousins	2·6
Nephews and nieces	3·9
Grandchildren	4·3
Half-sibs	7·1
Parents	9·2
Full sibs	14·2
Dizygotic co-twins	14·5
Dizygotic co-twins of same sex	17·6
Children	16·4
Children of two schizophrenic parents (Elsässer)	39·2
Monozygotic co-twins living apart	77·6
Monozygotic co-twins living together	91·5

(Data mainly from Kallmann)

Other observers have found risks comparable with those reported by Kallman, if somewhat lower. The risk for sibs has been estimated by Johanson (1958) as from 3·8 to 7·6 per cent., Slater (1953) 5·4 per cent., Hallgren and Sjögren (1959) 5·7 per cent., Alanen (1963) 7·3 per cent., Bleuler (1941) 10·0 per cent., Kallmann (1938) 11·5 per cent. and Garrone (1962) 14·6 per cent. Attention has been drawn to the fact that these estimates are lower than those associated with DZ twins. However, the nature of genetical field studies is such that one obtains much better and more reliable information about twins than about sibs. The investigator makes a strong effort to see all co-twins; but, when investigating a sibship, he usually has to be content with seeing one only of several sibs, so that the bulk of his information is hearsay. It is, therefore, very doubtful whether the DZ twins of schizophrenics have any greater risk of schizophrenia than the sibs. If it could be shown that they did, the finding could be plausibly related with the greater homogeneity of the environment of a pair of twins than a pair of sibs.

A feature of the familial data which has confused many authors is that, when the parents of schizophrenics are investigated, larger numbers of schizophrenic mothers than of schizophrenic fathers have usually been found. Both Alanen and Bleuler and, following them, Jackson, have interpreted this finding in support of the view that it is psychogenic rather than genetical factors which play the predominant role in the causation of schizophrenia. 'The very facts, which used to be taken as a "proof" of the genetical causation of schizophrenia, are today accepted by many researchers as demonstrating the familial tensions to which schizophrenics have been exposed, and thereby the probability of psychic causation' (Bleuler, 1963).

However, it was always difficult to reconcile with this interpretation the co-existent fact that all investigations have shown that the sex of a schizophrenic parent is not relevant to the fate of his children. Male schizophrenics have just as high a proportion of schizophrenic children as female schizophrenics do. Essen-Möller (1963) has shown convincingly that the reason for the difference in the findings when one proceeds from the index case to the parents, and from the index case to the children is due to a difference in the selective factors involved. Parents are selected for health, and to have had a schizophrenic child, must have reached the age attained at the time of his birth, not only without dying but also most probably without having suffered from a schizophrenic breakdown. Men marry later than women and have their schizophrenic illnesses earlier in life. So it is that, at the time of the birth of the individual who eventually becomes a schizophrenic index case, the father has survived a larger part of his schizophrenic risk period than the mother has. Reliable estimates of the respective proportionate risks can be made; and if they are taken into account, the observed proportions of schizophrenic fathers to schizophrenic mothers fit the expected proportions very well.

An interesting development in the clinical and psychodynamic approach to the causation of schizophrenia has risen from the psychometric study of parents (McConaghy, 1959). The work of Lidz and his co-workers (Lidz et al., 1957 a,b; 1958 a,b; Fleck et al., 1957) may be instanced. Forms of thought disorder, which are regarded as of the schizophrenic kind, are found in a high proportion of the parents. In this sense therefore, a high proportion of the parents of schizophrenics are found to be schizophrenic. Their children, the probands, have themselves become schizophrenic, not via genetical transmission it is thought, but by psychic contagion. Both the reliability of these findings and their interpretations must await independent confirmation (see also p. 317).

MODEL GENETICAL HYPOTHESES. Reviewing the facts discussed in the preceding pages, we may conclude that the evidence is very strong that the genetical constitution of an individual contributes a large part of his total potentiality of becoming schizophrenic. Furthermore, the schizophrenic disposition appears to be fairly specific and does not involve predisposition to other mental or bodily disorders. There are two main working hypotheses which may be used to explain the known facts and supply a foundation for further research: these are respectively of a polygenic and of a monogenic kind. The hypothesis advanced by Burch (1964*b*) (i.e. that schizophrenia is an auto-immune disorder resulting on the appearance of a forbidden clone of cells caused by two successive somatic mutations, in individuals predisposed by homozygosity for two recessive genes at two independent loci) will only have to be seriously considered if *ad hoc* research shows that auto-immunization is taking place in schizophrenics.

The polygenic hypothesis in schizophrenia is based on considerations advanced by Edwards (1960, 1963). These considerations can be put briefly as follows. No single-gene hypothesis, dominant, recessive or intermediate, can account for the observational data without the supplementary hypothesis of a reduced manifestation rate. Furthermore the factors which determine whether, in the predisposed individual, manifestation of the psychosis does or does not occur, are generally supposed to be polygenic. It would therefore be a step in the direction of simplicity if one postulated polygenic factors only and left out the hypothetical single gene. It can be shown that polygenic factors are responsible in a number of all-or-none reactions, a typical example being the harelip–cleft palate syndrome. Union of the embryonic layers involved can be pushed forwards or back in time, in a quantitatively variable way, as the result of quantitatively variable genetic constitution; but if union of these layers is delayed beyond a certain point in embryonic development, then it never occurs. In other cases quantitative variation may be transformed into qualitative differences by the passing of a threshold; biochemical thresholds, hormonal switch-mechanisms, mechanical events such as the bursting of an artery, may be the means by which a 'normal' individual is transformed into a case of disease. Edwards advances theoretical reasons for expecting that in diseases which are common in the community, genetical predisposition is likely to make its effects felt along such pathways as these, rather than through the agency of specific genes.

The hypothesis is a useful one, because precise predictions can be based upon it. Edwards shows that the incidence of a common disorder (a disorder is 'common' if more than one person in a thousand is subject to it) will be found in the first degree relatives of index cases in a proportion represented by $\sqrt{s}$ where s is the frequency of the condition in the general population. If the older figures for the incidence of schizophrenia in the population are taken as about 0·8 per cent., then about 9 per cent. of the sibs and of the children of schizophrenics should become schizophrenic in turn; if 1·2 per cent. is taken as the expectation in the general population, then the incidence in the first-degree relatives of schizophrenics should be 11 per cent. These figures are quite close to those actually reported. Other lines of evidence lending support to the view advanced by Edwards can be cited. The monogenic theory, particularly when dominant or intermediate inheritance is postulated, always requires some qualification in that marked variations in such characteristics as age of onset, degree of affective colouring, type of disease, its course, and other features, have to be explained by the action of polygenes. The existence of symptomatic schizophrenias often found in association with little or very low incidence of schizophrenic illness in the first-degree relatives is more difficult to accommodate within a monogenic than a polygenic theory. Edwards (1963) has pointed out that when concordance within MZ pairs is high, say 80 per cent., and at least twice as great as concordance in DZ pairs, the presence of genes of high specificity may reasonably be assumed in the majority of cases. The observed differences between the concordances in schizophrenia are of this order; 69 per cent. in MZ and 14 per cent. in DZ pairs. But the interpretation of such data presents some difficulties in the case of common disorders. It is often held that a polygenic hypothesis is

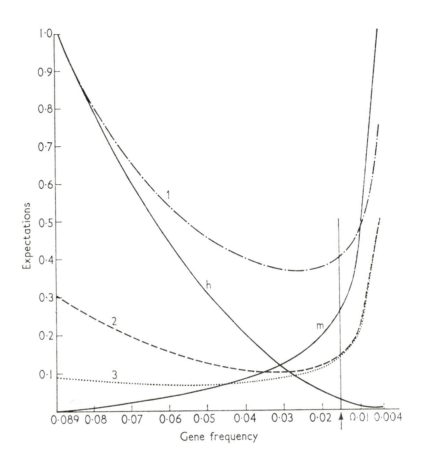

Fig. 7. Theoretical expectations of incidence of schizophrenia in relatives of schizophrenics (broken lines) with varying gene frequency and varying penetrance. 1=children of two schizophrenics; 2=sibs of schizophrenics; 3=children of one schizophrenic; h=proportion of all schizophrenics who are homozygous; m=manifestation rate of gene in heterozygote. (After Slater, 1958.)

inconsistent with the presence of specific biochemical, physiological changes between schizophrenic and normal subjects. This is not necessarily the case. Idiopathic epilepsy is almost certainly determined by multi-factorial inheritance. Yet in a high proportion of cases electroencephalographic changes of a highly specific kind, such as the spike and wave complex, are to be found. This suggests that when quantitative variation has been pushed beyond a certain threshold, qualitatively distinct physiological and biochemical changes may become manifest.

The polygenic hypothesis has been adopted by Gottesman and Shields (1967) and by Kringlen (1967) but needs more evidence. Moreover, a polygenic basis for some forms of schizophrenia, as for example those associated with exogenous causes, is not necessarily incompatible with a specific genetic basis for most of the cases encountered in clinical practice. Not only is the weight of evidence in favour of a specific, genetic basis too weighty to be discounted on the basis of theoretical considerations, but the monogenic theory is heuristically more productive; specific biochemical, physiological and psychological differences between schizophrenic and normal subjects are more likely if a specific hypothesis is accepted.

As our knowledge of the biochemical basis of human variation increases, so our theories of genetical causation are likely to pass from unifactorial to multifactorial form and back again. Under the all-or-none classification, diabetic or normal quantitative variation in the efficiency of sugar metabolism was found, which suggested polygenic inheritance. This was a step forward from a primitive one-gene hypothesis. Now it has been found that, under the quantitative variation, there are qualitative differences between individuals in respect of a circulating anti-insulin. Adult diabetics are likely to come from the heterozygotes, and infantile and childhood diabetics from the homozygotes who carry this body in their serum. On such general considerations as these, it seems desirable to fit a single gene hypothesis to the genetics of schizophrenia if one can; and then see what there is left that cannot be so accounted for.

This is no place to discuss the earlier two-gene theories, and the single-gene theories involving simple dominance or recessivity. The only single-gene theory deserving consideration is that of an intermediate gene, such as was first postulated by Böök (1953 a,b) to account for the findings in the north Swedish isolate he investigated. This theory (Slater, 1958) is that all the homozygotes, carrying the hypothetical specific schizophrenic gene, become schizophrenic, while only a proportion m of the heterozygotes do; m is, in fact, the manifestation rate in the heterozygote. If we write s for the frequency of schizophrenia in the general population, and p for the frequency in the population of the schizophrenia gene, then the relation holds: $s = 2mp + p^2$. For s we can enter the best estimate we have of the incidence of schizophrenia in the general population, and we can then calculate what values p must take with every value of m from 1, i.e. complete dominance, to 0, i.e. complete recessivity. Furthermore, if we know the values of m and p, we can calculate the expected incidence of schizophrenia in the relatives of schizophrenics. The interrelation of these expectations to the gene frequency, on the assumption that s, the incidence of schizophrenia in the general population, is 0.8 per cent. is shown in Fig. 7. At the point marked by the arrow and line we have something near the best fit we can get between observation, in the three key classes of relatives named, and expectation on the intermediate gene hypothesis. If we take a higher estimate of the incidence of schizophrenia in the general population, we can still get a tolerable fit between observation and expectation, as may be seen in the table on p. 250.

We may briefly note the consequences of this theory. If 0·8 per cent. is the best estimate of the incidence of schizophrenia in the general population, then at a gene frequency of 0·015 we have a situation not far removed from dominance. Less than 3 per cent. of all schizophrenics are homozygotes, and about 97 per cent. of the population are homozygous normals and without genetical predisposition to schizophrenia. Of the heterozygotes only 26 per cent. actually become schizophrenic, so that a large part of the causative factors would have to be looked for elsewhere, for example in environmental precipitants.

One suggestion arising from Fig. 7 is worth brief mention. It will be seen that the line drawn at points of closest correspondence between observation and expectation lies near to the lowest points in the curves of incidence in first degree relatives. Such a coincidence might arise as the result of the operation of natural selective forces on an evolutionary time scale. The effect is one of balancing gene frequency against manifestation rate to produce

s	p	m	h	2. Sibs	3. Ch. of 1	1. Ch. of 2
0·008	0·015	0·263	0·028	0·144	0·143	0·396
0·012	0·030	0·191	0·075	0·125	0·118	0·384
0·012	0·025	0·233	0·052	0·133	0·130	0·393

(The frequencies per cent. may be derived from this table by multiplying each figure by 100.)

Expected incidence of schizophrenia in relatives of schizophrenics, at stated incidence of schizophrenia in the general population, and stated gene frequency. Incidences in the sibs of schizophrenics, in the children of one schizophrenic parent, and the children of two parents, both schizophrenic, are shown.

s = incidence in general population; m = frequency of manifestation in the heterozygote; h = proportion of all schizophrenics who will be homozygotes; p = gene frequency.

the lowest incidences in the relatives of schizophrenics for a given incidence of schizophrenia.

The genetical model offered by this hypothesis can be fitted into the balanced polymorphisms, which have recently received wide attention. It is, in fact, generally supposed that where we find genes of common occurrence, dividing the population into genetically distinct strains, each of the allelomorphic forms of the gene will be associated with some biological advantage and disadvantage. One form of such a balanced polymorphism arises where the heterozygote has an advantage over both types of homozygote; and it is this balanced state, or 'morphism' in the terminology of Julian Huxley, which could account for the genetics and the epidemiology of schizophrenia. Huxley, Mayr, Osmond and Hoffer (1964) suggest that the Sc gene is too common to be in balance with its obvious disadvantages (such as the reduction of fertility of schizophrenics by 30 per cent.) without selective advantages. Such advantages, however, can actually be found in the high resistance of schizophrenics to surgical and wound shock, to dangerous concentrations of insulin, and to other stresses. It would seem, they conclude, that the Sc gene causes an error of metabolism and one which may result in a substance interfering with the normal integration of perception. This hypothesis is one which is fertile in ideas for further research along many lines. However, future progress in the genetics of schizophrenia will probably have to wait for advances in other fields, such as the biochemical, which may provide us with the means of recognizing the gene-carrier.

(2) The Schizoid Constitution

Observant clinicians early realized that many schizophrenics had shown *mental peculiarities before the illness* proper began. Similar features were also found in the blood relatives of the patients. It was difficult to say precisely what these peculiarities were. Berze (1910) mentioned certain characteristics in the patient's parents: lack of insight into the illness of their children, shyness and eccentricity. Bleuler was inclined to see in these eccentrics 'latent schizophrenics'. He insisted that the psychosis had often only quantitatively increased features of character present in relatives or in the pre-psychotic personality of the patient himself.

It was Kretschmer (1936) who took up these observations and constructed a comprehensive *theory of the schizophrenic constitution.* He coined the term schizoid and built a symmetrical system parallel to the system of relations between basic affective constitutions and affective psychoses. In his opinion, the psychology of the pre-psychotic, the psychotic and the post-psychotic (remitted) schizophrenic is identical with that of the schizoid, the non-psychotic blood relative of the patient. 'Only if one considers all these as one and the same, can one arrive at a correct picture.'

Kretschmer's theory of the psychoses and their constitutional background, of which the schizoid personality and the associated bodily constitution is one part, appears at first acquaintance complete in itself. Its weaknesses are especially apparent in the field of schizophrenia. He and his pupils have made every attempt to replace the original intuitively conceived concepts by more exact, experimental and quantitative methods. From the first he neglected to provide figures of the distribution in the general population, both for his psychological and physical types. Even if this were corrected and allowance made for other difficulties and discrepancies of method, strong objections to some of his fundamental ideas would remain. The validity of identifying the symptoms of a psychosis leading to personality deterioration with certain superficially similar features in the patient before the illness or in his relatives has not been accepted outside Kretschmer's own school.

On the other hand the existence of the *schizoid constitution* itself has been generally recognized. One of the more cautious followers of Kretschmer, Manfred Bleuler, includes the following types among the more severe schizoids: the suspicious-oversensitive, the pedant, the reckless and callous, the paranoid, the shy and delicate, the fanatic, the bigotedly pious and the eccentric. Among 351 schizophrenics in hospital, Bleuler found 34 per cent. belonging to one of these types prior to their psychosis, but a further 29 per cent. with less marked, single schizoid features. Judged on pre-psychotic history, schizophrenics were twice as often schizoid as the (non-schizophrenic) parents of the patients, three times more frequently so than their siblings and over fifty times more than the average population. Rather similar findings were made by Slater (1953) in the families of twin propositi suffering from schizophrenia. The deviations of personality which were typical of schizophrenic families, rather than the families of cases of affective, psychopathic or organic disorder, could be grouped into four sets of traits: paranoid traits showing themselves in suspiciousness, sensitivity, resentful, jealous and critical attitudes; eccentricities, such as pedantic, humourless, cranky and bigoted ways; lack of feeling, seen in impassive, cool, calculating, unsympathetic, unkind and selfish personalities with little capacity for warmth and often naturally reserved; and finally a tendency to anergia. Psychopathic personalities of other types were found to be no more frequent among pre-psychotic schizophrenics and among their relatives than in the general population (M. Bleuler, 1941a). Other observers, using different criteria, have estimated the figure of pre-psychotic schizoid persons in schizophrenia at about 50 per cent.

Results somewhat at variance with those of Bleuler are described in a preliminary report of a study designed to investigate the relative importance of environmental and hereditary aspects of schizophrenia. Atkinson *et al.* (1968) found a higher incidence of psychiatric disorder and abnormal personalities within families of schizophrenic patients that within control families of neurotic or acute surgical patients. The excess of total abnormality—comprising psychosis, neurosis and personality disorder—reached statistically significant levels both in parents and among siblings. In addition, non-psychotic first degree relatives of schizophrenics were found to achieve mean scores on tests of thought disorder which lay between the means for schizophrenic patients and control groups (Romney, 1967). (See also p. 317.) There was no evidence of bimodality in the distribution of psychological test scores, nor did the distributions of abnormality in the families of 73 schizophrenic patients correspond to simple Mendelian ratios. The relatively high incidence of abnormal personalities in the first degree relatives, over and above the small group who had an indubitably schizophrenic illness, is of particular interest. It conforms to findings in other studies and was reported, for example, by Heston (1966) among the adopted children of schizophrenic mothers. Whether these abnormal personalities have any affinity constitutionally with the proven cases of schizophrenia or reflect the operation of generally adverse environmental factors within the family, or whether perhaps both these influences are at work, deserves careful investigation. If they are indeed formes frustes they are preferable to the psychosis.

While the relation of schizoid personality and schizophrenia has been established, one still has to remember that 30 to 50 per cent. of cases show *no mental abnormality before the outbreak* of the schizophrenic disease. The relation of schizophrenia to one or more types of bodily build is still under debate except for a general agreement that it is unusual in persons of the typical pyknic physique. If it occurs, careful reconsideration of the diagnosis seems advisable (see Differential Diagnosis, p. 320).

(3) Endocrines

The rarity of schizophrenia in children before puberty, its frequent commencement in adolescence, the similarity of the clinical picture to mental immaturity ('hebephrenia'), the release of schizophrenia by the puerperium and a second wave of higher incidence at the time of the menopause—all pointed to the endocrine system as a possible factor in aetiology. The dysplastic physique observed by Kretschmer in schizophrenic subjects, although found in a small proportion of cases only, also suggests possible endocrine anomaly as does the frequent delay of sexual maturity in schizophrenics with poor development of secondary sex characteristics. The earlier work in this field was reviewed by Müller (1944). In more recent years modern techniques of endocrine investigation have been applied to the problem. In the 1950s attention was mainly directed to the pattern of excretion of 17-ketosteroids and indirect indices of adrenocortical activity shown by blood eosinophil and lymphocyte counts, investigations of urinary uric acid, phosphates and electrolytes. As these measures are poorly correlated with adrenocortical activity, it is not surprising that some workers (Pincus and Hoagland, 1950) observed diminished and others increased adrenocortical activity. Utilizing the more precise measure of plasma level of hydroxycorticosteroids, Bliss *et al.* (1955) demonstrated an interesting difference between acute and chronic cases of schizophrenia. In 27 cases of schizophrenia of recent onset, 19 were judged to be emotionally disturbed and they had a mean plasma 17-hydroxicorticosteroid level of 22 μg/100 ml. In contrast, in 8 emotionally undisturbed patients, the mean level was 13 μg. In chronic cases the observed plasma levels of 14 μg/100 ml. did not differ from the level in normal subjects and the response to the administration of ACTH in schizophrenics was normal. Treatment with E.C.T. led in acute cases to a transient rise of 17-hydroxycorticosteroid levels which reached a maximum within an hour; they returned to the previous level within four hours. The degree of change showed no correlation with the therapeutic effect of E.C.T. As Michael and Gibbons point out (1963), correlations of increased adrenocortical activity appear, as in the case of states of depression and anxiety, to be with the disturbance of affect rather than the schizophrenic illness as such.

Recent enquiries into thyroid function in schizophrenia have yielded uncertain results.

Lingjaerde *et al.* (1960) reported a mean uptake of 39 per cent. in 27 schizophrenics; this was not significantly different from the results in other diagnostic groups. On the other hand, Stevens and Dunn (1958) reported low normal radio-iodine uptake in 28 cases. Utilizing a more elegant index of thyroid function, the It value, which is based on the initial rate of uptake of radio-iodine by the thyroid and the actual uptake at 24 hours, Reiss and his colleagues (Batt *et al.*, 1957) found that, in two-thirds of the patients with schizophrenia, the results were within normal limits. However, among schizophrenic men 19 per cent. had decreased and 15 per cent. increased thyroid activity; in women the figures were 14 and 21 per cent. respectively. Stoll and Brack (1957) obtained similar results in chronic schizophrenics, but found neither a relationship between clinical improvement and change in thyroid activity nor any impressive changes in clinical state when attempts were made to rectify thyroid activity with the aid of thyroid hormone or antithyroid medication. We see, therefore, that there is very little evidence that endocrine disturbance plays any significant part in the aetiology of schizophrenic illness. The fact that sufferers from myxoedema, hyper- or hypothyroidism, Addison's and Cushing's disease and acromegaly bear no resemblance to schizophrenics—although combinations of these with schizophrenia have been observed in rare cases—also speaks against an endocrine aetiology. Marked tolerance for thyroid extract has been reported in the past among long-standing schizophrenics as compared with normal subjects, but these observations need to be repeated with the aid of more modern and better-controlled techniques. Therapeutic administration of a wide range of endocrine preparations has been tried in schizophrenics without success.

Investigations on a large scale have been carried out by Manfred Bleuler and his collaborators (1954), with the aim of elucidating the pathology of schizophrenia by studying the endocrine anomalies sometimes found in combination with it. A number of families showing such combinations were collected and their hereditary relations were analysed. Valuable documentary material was thus accumulated, but almost no light was thrown on the central problem. In most cases the endocrinological abnormality seems to have been a mere coincidence, although it might have had some effect on the clinical course of the psychosis. Women, for instance, with signs of virilism or an endocrine obesity tended to have a poor outlook, schizophrenia in their cases leading to severe deterioration. The failure of this large-scale research project to yield the expected result is not to be laid entirely at the door of psychiatry. Techniques of endocrinological investigation are not sufficiently advanced to measure and interpret the minor abnormalities with which the psychiatrist is so often faced.

(4) **Biochemical and Physiological Aspects**

1. EARLIER STUDIES. Clinicians and research workers vary in their views of the essential nature of the schizophrenic process and of the breadth of variability to be allowed to its clinical manifestations. To this may be attributed the varying results of investigations into its metabolism. In one of the earlier editions of his book, Kraepelin classified dementia praecox as a metabolic disease; and many clinicians have pointed to the pale, unhealthy appearance, the cyanosed extremities, lack of appetite and loss of weight of the patients, who in fact *rarely show robust physical health*. In an illness that may last a life-time or whose acute attacks last for at least several months, the patient's inactivity or hyper-activity may influence his metabolism and any variation may well be the result of the illness and not its cause. If, as many believe, schizophrenia is an aggregate comprising different diseases showing identical psychological symptoms, discrepant findings are what one would expect.

Persistent investigations by the Worcester group of workers under Hoskins resulted in a large number of single findings, but none with aetiological significance: the schizophrenic is less than normally responsive not only to thyroid and oxidative stimulants, but also to insulin and adrenaline, to moist heat, to cold, and to strong emotions. He has a low blood pressure, his heart rate and circulation time are slow. His circulation adapts poorly to physical effort. In the same way vestibular function, as measured by the number of nystagmus beats after caloric or rotatory stimulation, are below par in adaptation; and his postural steadiness is impaired if assessed in sway experiments. The same workers found an inability to maintain differential levels under stress as shown in the difference between oral and rectal temperatures or between systolic and diastolic blood pressures. Hoskins (1946) who at one time suggested that these findings might be explained as signs of *physiological 'withdrawal'* from the ordinary environment corresponding to the mental withdrawal of the schizophrenic, later speaks in more general terms of 'numerous *defects of adaptive efficiency*'.

The methods used in these and many similar studies of schizophrenic metabolism seem unsatisfactory because the single data have been collected from a large number of patients exhibiting all the variegated clinical states occurring in schizophrenia. Even the most careful statistical analysis cannot overcome the probable lack of homogeneity of the basic clinical material. Gjessing (1947) avoided this difficulty by his method of serial studies continued for years on a few patients who, because of the periodicity of their illness, could serve as their own controls. He chose *periodic catatonia*, a comparatively rare form, accounting for only 2 per cent. of all cases of schizophrenia, and recorded carefully over years the physiological and psychological changes. By registering intake and output, movements, circulation, blood picture and all autonomic signs in the psychotic phase as well as in the free interval, he found *phasic variations in the total nitrogen balance* associated with the periodic mental changes. Catatonic stupor as well as catatonic excitement were accompanied by nitrogen retention, or compensatory excretion of nitrogen after retention in the free interval. Simultaneous changes in autonomic function he referred to an abnormal storage of nitrogen and its supposed toxic effect. This hypothesis was supported by the effect of thyroxin in his cases. Combined with a low-protein diet, it apparently catabolized the excessive nitrogen thus abolishing the periodic psychosis (see section on therapy). In more recent work undertaken in collaboration with his son, L. Gjessing (1961), the length of the interval between attacks was manipulated by varying intake of protein and by controlling BMR by the administration of thyroxine. The reduced protein intake tended to prolong intervals between the attacks. He also suggested that the autonomic changes associated with catatonic states have a diencephalic origin.

In studies by Crammer (1957, 1959) on periodic psychoses both schizophrenic and affective, the focus of interest was on changes in body-weight, which were found to depend on water metabolism. However it was not possible to form a hypothesis to explain the periodicity.

Gjessing's work has been confirmed by workers in Britain, Scandinavia and Germany, e.g. by Greving (1941). The latter also described together with Jahn (1936) certain changes in the formation of red blood cells which they referred to a hypothetical, histamine-like substance, to which the somatic symptoms of schizophrenia could be attributed.

2. RECENT BIOCHEMICAL THEORIES. THE TOXIC METABOLITE THEORY. The view that substances such as mescaline and bulbocapnine bear a chemical resemblance to the toxin responsible for schizophrenia is not altogether new, but was revived by Hoffer *et al.*

(1954) who suggested that this substance might be an indole compound derived from adrenaline and similar in structure to mescaline, lysergic acid diethylamide 25, harmine and other hallucinogens. Mescaline and adrenaline are similar in chemical structure and adrenochrome, the first oxidation product of the latter, has an indole nucleus. Early claims that adrenochrome was psychotomimetic proved to have little foundation. Adrenolutin, another derivative of adrenaline, has been claimed to produce thought disorder resembling that found in schizophrenic subjects (Hoffer, 1957). However, serious doubt has been cast on the adrenochrome and adrenolutin theories by the studies of Axelrod which have defined the main pathways for the metabolism of epinephrine and norepinephrine. These involve O-methylation to metanephrine or normetanephrine. The findings have been confirmed in man (La Bross, Axelrod and Kety, 1958) and the enzyme concerned with the O-methylation of catecholamines, catechol-O-methyl transferase, has also been identified. Ninety per cent. of the end-products of these processes have been indentified in human urine, 53 per cent. as metanephrine and its conjugates (La Brosse, Axelrod and Kety, 1958) and 30 per cent. as vanilmandelic acid (Kirshner, Goodall and Rosen, 1958).

The substances adrenochrome and adrenolutin were not found as break-down products in these enquiries. It is possible that breakdown of adrenaline in schizophrenics proceeds along different paths, but this has been rendered improbable by studies (Pollin, Cardon and Kety, 1961) in which 12 schizophrenic and 12 control subjects were given intravenous adrenaline and their responses compared. Although there were some minor differences in behaviour in the two groups, assay of the tritium labelled metabolites in the urine showed that practically none of the adrenaline administered could have been metabolized via adrenochrome or its derivatives in either schizophrenics or normals.

More recently Hoffer and Osmond (1962) have described an unidentified substance in the urine of schizophrenics which takes on a mauve colour on the plate paper chromatogram. The phenomenon is not, however, confined to schizophrenics, having also been observed by these workers in children with mental retardation. The authors have named this condition 'malvaria'.

Observations in this field took a dramatic turn with a publication by Heath and his colleagues (1957, 1958) of their observations that the injection of the serum of schizophrenic patients produced catatonic and other schizophrenic symptoms in monkeys and man. They identified the active substance as an enzyme similar to a copper-containing enzyme, ceruloplasmin, and claimed that it can be fractionated from the serum of the schizophrenic but not of normal individuals. Heath has named this substance 'taraxein' and believes that it is responsible for the more rapid oxidation of adrenaline by schizophrenic than by normal serum. However attempts to reproduce this work have led to contradictory results and the claims made by the Tulane workers cannot be regarded as confirmed (Bond, 1958; Kety 1958; Robins 1957; Siegal et al., 1959).

Although there is a little evidence to suggest a specific schizophrenic toxin, observations continue to be reported to suggest that the body fluids of the schizophrenic contain a substance, as yet unidentified, which exerts toxic or lethal effects when injected into animals. Thus Sjövall (1947) has repeated some earlier experiments by Weichbrodt on the toxic effects of schizophrenic serum in a series of carefully controlled experiments which show that schizophrenic serum is more often and more rapidly lethal than that of normals. In studies carried out by Wada and Gibson (1959) on extracts prepared by McGeer, Brown and McGeer (1957) of the aromatic constituents of normal and schizophrenic urine, behavioural changes were confined to animals injected intra-cisternally or intra-ventricularly with extracts obtained from schizophrenics; they included behavioural changes such as intense rage and automatism in cats and cataleptiform episodes in monkeys. Plasma from schizophrenics has also been shown to produce impairment of new learning capacity in the rat and abnormalities in the web-spinning behaviour of spiders.

A study by Smith and Sines (1960) claims to have demonstrated an odour peculiar to the sweat of a proportion of schizophrenic patients. These workers collected specimens of sweat from schizophrenics and from control subjects with organic psychoses under treatment in the same ward who did not have the odour. It was claimed that rats could be trained to differentiate to a significant degree between the sweat collected from the two groups. That some of these toxic effects are likely to be non-specific and secondary is suggested by the studies of Rodnight and Aves (1958) who investigated a number of previous reports that the urine of psychotic patients often contained abnormal indoles. They showed that the level of such substances in depressives bore no relation to their clinical state and could be reduced by administration of antibiotics. They concluded that the indoles were probably of intestinal origin, the sluggish peristalsis of these patients being responsible. In subsequent studies they suggested explanations along similar lines for the occasional finding of excessive indoleacetic acid or 5HIAA in the urine of psychotic subjects.

The recent discovery by Friedhoff and van Winkle (1962) of a substance they identified as 3,4-dimethoxyphenyl-ethylamine (DMPE) in the urine of 15 out of 19 schizophrenic patients has revived interest in the hypothesis originally advanced by Osmond and Smythies and Harley-Mason (1952) that abnormal methylation of catecholamines might be of aetiological importance for schizophrenic illness. The results obtained by other workers have been variable. Takesada et al. (1963) found DMPE in 70 out of 78 schizophrenic patients but the same result was obtained in 50 per cent. of neurotic subjects and normal controls. The most striking results have been recorded by Bourdillon et al. (1965) who found a substance which yielded a pink colour on chromatographic analysis in the urine of 46 out of 73 schizophrenic patients but none in 16 non-schizophrenic subjects. Moreover, in subjects who manifested Kurt Schneider's first-rank symptoms and were regarded as free from paranoid delusions, 80 per cent. excreted a substance which yielded a 'pink spot' in contrast to patients who were Schneider-negative and showed paranoid features of whom only 15 per cent. excreted the substance. The biochemical and clinical enquiries were conducted independently. The authors used the term 'pink spot' as they felt that further enquiry would be needed to establish the precise identity of the biochemical substance concerned. There are numerous sources of artifact in biochemical investigations of schizophrenics as Kety (1959) has pointed out. Recent observations (Keuhl et al., 1966) have shown that schizophrenics are unlikely to have any special tendency to excrete DMPE, and that large doses of this substance are without significant effects in humans (Hollister and Friedhoff, 1966).

THE NEURO-HUMOURAL DISEQUILIBRIUM THEORY. A suggestion was independently made by Woolley and Shaw (1954a) and Gaddum (1953) that schizophrenia might result from 'a disorder of serotonin metabolism. This hypothesis was prompted by the fact that LSD 25, which has marked hallucinogenic effects, also possesses strong antiserotonin properties. It was suggested that these might give rise to a replacement of serotonin in the appropriate receptors by LSD (in virtue of the similarity of the two substances) thus giving rise to serotonin deficiency or competition between LSD and serotonin for the enzyme monoamine-oxidase which could lead to an accumulation of serotonin in the brain. By analogy, the unknown biochemical cause of schizophrenia might act in a similar way as an antagonist of serotonin. However, schizophrenics have not been found to have any anomaly of serotonin metabolism (Kopin, 1959) nor do all serotonin antagonists appear to have hallucinogenic properties.

Although the enquiries of the past ten to fifteen years began with high hopes, they have failed to identify the biochemical causes or correlates of schizophrenia in a convincing manner and Kety (1959) in a critical review of the biochemical aspects of schizophrenia, has cautioned against optimism that specific biochemical defects are likely to be identified in the near future. Yet these enquiries have made important contributions to basic knowledge in neurochemistry and neuropharmacology and these may ultimately aid the search for the causes of schizophrenic illnesses.

(5) Central Nervous System

Many workers in search of a somatic causation of schizophrenia end up with the diencephalon, the regulating centre of both metabolism and endocrines. There are, in fact, some physical symptoms which can be related to the *autonomic nervous system*, such as an increased tolerance to insulin, deviations in shape and size of cutaneous capillaries, vago-insulin predominance as described by Gellhorn (1943). This writer speaks of a slackness of central autonomic function in schizophrenia and explains the results of physical therapies such as convulsion and insulin treatment by their stimulating effect on the hypothalamus. Sleep disturbances in schizophrenics have been related to the diencephalic sleep centre, and Gjessing refers to the *diencephalic region* from which the periodic mental and physical changes in his patients are regulated.

Encephalitis lethargica produces hyperkinetic and akinetic signs sometimes reminiscent of catatonic motor behaviour. During the epidemics after the First World War the similarity was frequently commented on and in a few cases the development of a schizophreniform psychosis has been seen after encephalitis lethargica. But in the very large number of cases the mental state of the sufferer remained entirely unaffected or showed mild organic disturbances with no relation to schizophrenia. In post-mortem examination of catatonic patients, on the other hand, no lesions could be discovered in the areas mainly affected in encephalitis.

The search for *cortical changes in schizophrenia* has never ceased since modern histopathological methods were introduced in cerebral pathology. Many abnormalities, both of the cortical cells, of the glia and the capillaries, have been described and various authors have pointed to this or that finding as characteristic of schizophrenia. There is no doubt that histopathological examination reveals certain changes in the brain of schizophrenics, but they are so uncharacteristic and in many cases so minute that their interpretation is very difficult. Some, like the swelling of oligodendroglia, are found in many other forms of mental illness. Others may be due to terminal disease or to post-mortem changes. They certainly cannot be clearly distinguished from the latter. Findings in biopsy material, recovered during leucotomy operations, are regarded by critical observers as artifacts due to the process of fixation (Wolf and Cowen, 1952).

Recent years have seen a new wave of interest in the neuropathology of schizophrenia. At a discussion on the histopathology of schizophrenia at the International Congress of Neuropathology in 1952, the Vogts (1952) reaffirmed their belief in the occurrence of fatty degeneration of nerve cells and *Schwunderkrankung* in the brain of schizophrenics. Control material was used in these enquiries although the observations were not fully reported.

K

It was claimed that certain areas including the prefrontal, anterior cingula and the third convolution of the temporal lobes, as also the corpus striatum and the anterior and medial nuclei of the thalamus, were consistently involved while the hypothalamus was free of definite change. A number of workers reported gross pathological changes in subjects who had in life shown schizophrenic symptoms. Bruetsch (1952) described gross damage due to rheumatic occlusive endarteritis (frequently with rheumatic heart disease) in 9 of 100 'schizophrenic' subjects. Considered in isolation these and other observations reported at the Congress appeared to have little significance: when they are related to recent work on the symptomatic schizophrenias undertaken in a more modern spirit, a clearer perspective emerges. There can be no doubt, as will be further indicated in the section on symptomatic schizophrenia (p. 299), that cerebral lesions are associated under certain conditions, with psychiatric disorders difficult to differentiate from schizophrenic illness. In the schizophrenia-like psychoses of chronic epileptics, a focal lesion is found in one or both temporal lobes in a high proportion of instances (Slater et al., 1963). The findings could not be explained in terms of fortuitous association of cerebral disease with a latent predisposition to schizophrenia. Of particular interest was the long interval, 14 years, in the case of epilepsy, that separated the commencement of cerebral disease from the onset of a psychosis. Davison (1966) has shown that schizophrenia and cerebral disease are associated more often than can be explained by chance and that the diencephalon and brain stem are the commonest sites of the lesion.

NEUROPHYSIOLOGY. A number of anomalies have been described in the E.E.G. of schizophrenics but hardly any of those reported on the strength of qualitative observations have stood the test of time. More recently Heath, making use of in-dwelling electrodes, has reported differences between schizophrenics and non-schizophrenic subjects (Heath, 1962a and b). He describes spiking and slow-wave activity from the hippocampus confined to psychotic episodes and subsiding during periods of remission. In schizophrenics the abnormal discharges are more marked in the septal region than in the hippocampus or the amygdala, whereas in patients with epilepsy the converse is true. These findings await independent confirmation; artifacts are difficult to exclude with the techniques employed. Quantitative analysis of the E.E.G. of chronic schizophrenics has recently suggested that it may be characterized by a lower mean energy content and less variability than that of normal controls, in that drug-induced changes in the clinical status of these patients may be accompanied by corresponding E.E.G. changes (Goldstein et al., 1963; Sugerman et al., 1964). Investigating the palmar skin potential Venables and Wing (1962) found no differences between schizophrenics and controls, but withdrawn schizophrenics were less responsive than either 'active' cases or controls and bi-phasic responses were significantly more common in normal than in schizophrenic subjects. It is claimed by Lovett-Doust (1962) that the capillary morphology of schizophrenic subjects shows an anatomical immaturity in common with other forms of mental disease but that in schizophrenics there is, in addition, a far longer cycle for spontaneous oscillation of the capillary circulation than either in normal subjects or in those with other forms of functional or organic mental disorder. He relates these findings to the lower responsiveness to environmental stimulation shown by schizophrenics. The techniques of examination are not free from the risk of subjective error but, with further development, they may prove one of the useful tools for the investigation of the schizophrenic constitution.

(6) **Precipitation**

(*a*) BODILY ILLNESS. With the prevailing uncertainty about the causation of schizo-phrenia, the possibility of a *physical precipitation* has attracted attention. There has been more theorizing and speculation than is warranted by the actual frequency of coincidence of bodily and mental illness. Three observations are of interest: (1) a schizophrenic illness may break out during or immediately after an infective disease or childbirth, and, conversely, an intercurrent infection may have an effect on a chronic schizophrenia; (2) schizophrenia starting during the course of a bodily illness may take an atypical form; (3) schizophrenic symptoms may be seen in organic cerebral disease.

In view of these observations Bumke at one time proposed to range schizophrenia among the *symptomatic psychoses*. Because of the similarity of some schizophrenic symptoms to those of delirium and subacute delirious states, he suggested 'that schizophrenic symptoms are nothing but a certain type of exogenous reaction (in Bonhoeffer's sense) for which a disposition exists in the brains of some persons and which may be released by various kinds of noxae'. If the noxa is acute and massive, delirium or another symptomatic psychosis may result; if it acts insidiously, it may lead to an ordinary schizophrenic illness.

This attempt to link up schizophrenia with the so-called exogenous reaction type, i.e. with mental symptoms in infectious and toxic disease, has not proved very fruitful. Some facts are against the hypothesis: symptomatic psychoses are infrequent, much rarer than schizophrenia; infections and childbirth are frequent. *Puerperal psychosis*, for instance, has been estimated to occur in only 0·14 per cent. of women in childbirth while the expecta-tion for a schizophrenic attack between twenty and forty is roughly 0·5 per cent. at least. If the schizophrenic predisposition were akin to that for symptomatic psychosis, many more schizophrenic attacks would be expected to start in childbirth than actually do. According to Runge (1911) only about 37 per cent. of all puerperal psychoses are or become schizophrenic. Seelert (1929) calculated the probability of schizophrenic illness coinciding with pregnancy, puerperium and lactation in young women and doubts whether the con-clusion of a causal connexion can be drawn; the concurrence of the two events may be entirely coincidental. Moreover, infective illnesses are so frequent and universal that the manifestation of schizophrenia at the same time may also be the result of chance.

Clinical authorities have also maintained the precipitating action of infections and the puerperium. The frequency of outbreak of schizophrenia in the latter has been contrasted with its relative rarity during pregnancy. There is no conclusive evidence that patients who became schizophrenic at childbirth, would not otherwise have fallen ill; such data as are available from the study of monozygotic twins are inconclusive. Cases in which there has been *relapse into a second attack* of schizophrenia after the delivery of a second child are known, but also others with one or more uneventful births both before and after a single puerperal schizophrenia. Schizophrenia may appear for the first time after the second or the third delivery. These statements hold equally true *mutatis mutandis* for schizophrenia starting in connexion with infective disease. Nevertheless, the occurrence of a puerperal schizophrenia is sufficient, in the view of many clinicians, to justify the termination of a later pregnancy.

The influence of acute *febrile infections on chronic schizophrenics* has for a long time attracted the attention of psychiatrists. During such an illness all the more prominent symptoms, such as stupor, mannerisms, hallucinations, delusional ideas, may disappear and the patient who was hitherto regarded as severely deteriorated and withdrawn may become accessible, show adequate emotions naturally expressed and take an interest in his surroundings. This improvement may be transient and with the return of physical health the psychosis may return. In some cases the remission may be lasting and lead to discharge from hospital. On the other hand, in the majority of instances chronic schizophrenics affected by infectious diseases show not the slightest alteration of their psychotic behaviour. They remain negativistic and deluded and are, therefore, very difficult to treat or to nurse.

The mechanism of the improvement when it occurs is not well understood. There may be some direct influence on the unknown physical disorder underlying the disease. In view of the known tendency to *'habit formation'* in schizophrenia, the curative effect may be purely psychological. The apparently deteriorated patient may remain inaccessible although the schizophrenic process has come to a standstill. If the bodily disease occurs at this moment, the change of surroundings, the personal attention and the physical suffering may free him from symptoms which he carries on by habit—just as a change of ward or hospital or an accident, such as an outbreak of fire or bombing by enemy action, can lead to unexpected improvement.

The observation that schizophrenia starting during an infection or at childbirth often shows *symptoms appertaining to symptomatic psychoses* (see Chapter VI, p. 374) is of clinical and diagnostic importance. This is what one would expect from the modifiability of the picture in early schizophrenia. We shall find the same influence of the psychological situation, personality and milieu on the clinical picture when discussing the precipitation by psychological factors. This is only an instance of the general rule in psychiatry that positive symptoms are much more easily observed than negative ones, and hence factors which produce positive features will tend to be given undue prominence in an appraisal of the clinical picture. Negative symptoms or deficiencies, are submerged until they become manifest at a later stage. It is an ill-founded conclusion that the observation of symptoms of, say, delirium in the initial stages of a schizophrenic illness proves that the latter has been precipitated by the bodily illness responsible for the delirium.

However, recent observations suggest that the association of physical illness and schizophrenia may not be wholly fortuitous. McClelland, Roth *et al.* (1968) examined this association in a sample of 168 patients, compared with a control group admitted with affective illness to a psychiatric hospital over the same period. 34.5 per cent. of the schizophrenic cases were found to have physical illness. In the age group 41–60 there was significantly more physical illness in schizophrenics than in the affective controls and in the 18–40 group the trend was in the same direction but the difference was not significant either in this group or in those aged 60 and over.

Impaired hearing and vision and physical deformities were significantly in excess within the schizophrenic group as a whole, while cardiovascular and lung disease were significantly more common in the control group. Lesions of the CNS were commoner in the schizophrenics but the difference just failed to reach significance.

(*b*) PSYCHOLOGICAL PRECIPITATION. The schizophrenia-like psychogenic psychoses with their abrupt onset and short duration are discussed on page 302. Here we are concerned with the broader problem of psychogenic precipitation of schizophrenic psychoses typical both in form and in evolution. It seems improbable that a severe mental illness leading to deterioration and destruction of the personality could be psychogenically determined, even if a strong genetic predisposition is assumed. One should, therefore, approach with sceptical reserve the rare cases in which a schizophrenic illness seems to be *precipitated by emotional upset,* mental conflict or other psychological or social difficulties. On closer enquiry in many of these cases the situations or emotional conflicts to which a precipitating force is assigned prove to be but the earliest social effects of the beginning of the illness itself. It would, however, be far-fetched to deny a psychological precipitation in some of the cases reported on, in which the outbreak of the psychosis has been associated with the loss of close friends and relatives, professional failure, extreme mental and physical exhaustion, a threat to life, the break-up of the family circle, or the strain of facing grave decisions on marriage or occupation. In almost every instance one will find serious predisposing factors on which the psychological event acts as a trigger. Even if the patient's mind is full of ideas concerned with the events which are presumed to have caused the attack and the sequence of experiences seems to fit these events and is easy to understand, one should still be reluctant to trust to appearances. Only by a *tour de force* can the primary symptoms on which the diagnosis of schizophrenia is based, be understood as the outcome of an emotional conflict. If these primary symptoms are present, then they are features which refute any purely psychogenic theory; if they are absent, then the diagnosis of schizophrenia should be reconsidered.

However, if the predisposition is present, the response of the predisposed person to a situation of stress may take the form of a schizophrenic illness—at least one is tempted to think so. The remarkable fact is the *scarcity of cases* in which such a precipitation is plausible. Neither the First nor the Second World War increased the incidence of schizophrenia in any of the belligerent countries. No greater incidence has been observed among prisoners of war and in concentration camps or among victims of mass catastrophes such as earthquakes, accidents in mines, etc.

An astonishing improvement is sometimes seen in chronic schizophrenics after a change of ward, discharge home, or some emotional stimulation. If these events take place at the right moment in a patient whose illness is at an inactive stage, they may have an unexpectedly favourable effect. In many other patients not at such a susceptible stage, they are without effect. In fact, these miracles of mental healing are a *contrast-effect in neglected chronic wards*: because they happen among the most deteriorated patients, they are so memorable. It is one of the tasks of the psychiatrist treating hospitalized chronic patients to pay attention to the tendency of schizophrenics to get bogged down in stereotypies of thinking and behaving. He has to combat this morbid mechanism and the formation of habits. If that is done according to the principles first developed by Bleuler and his school, miraculous psychological cures will disappear, every patient will be kept at his best possible level and the general behaviour will maintain a higher standard (see section on Treatment, p. 327).

A fact which has been used to support the view that the psychological situation plays an important role, is that schizophrenia is relatively frequent among criminals serving *long-term sentences of imprisonment.* Among a number of men serving life sentences Rüdin (1909) found forty-seven who showed signs of abnormality and twenty-one who suffered from schizophrenia. Similar findings have been repeatedly made since; West (1963), for instance, found seven psychotics in 50 men made subject to preventive detention, five at least being schizophrenic. The most probable explanation of the accumulation of the illness among incorrigibly anti-social men is that of Wilmanns (1940). He related the criminal career to a schizoid make-up or an insidious schizophrenic personality change. These men became criminals because of their schizophrenic constitution, and under the conditions of long-term detention in solitary confinement their psychosis became manifest.

In short, *psychological factors*, in spite of a widespread belief in their influence, do not frequently precipitate a schizophrenic illness or attack. The psychological situation has, however, considerable effect on the established schizophrenic illness. The term 'schizophrenic reaction' introduced to suggest a transient psychogenic schizophrenic illness has little foundation in fact and should, in the view of the authors, be avoided.

The neurotic reactions which may be symptoms of an early schizophrenia, and their relation to the psychological situation, are described and discussed under 'Clinical Picture' (p. 277).

PSYCHOGENESIS

In recent years undaunted efforts have been made to elucidate the problems of psychogenesis in schizophrenia. The subject has been reviewed by Kind (1966). Some of the evidence that psychotic states, clinically typically schizophrenic in form, may arise under severe psychogenic stresses, is discussed in the section on symptomatic schizophrenia (p. 299). However, more far-reaching claims are made than that psychological stresses may precipitate a schizophreniform psychosis. It is believed that apparently irreversible schizophrenic processes may be caused by disturbance of the child's emotional relationships with other members of the family, especially the mother; and that such processes may be reversed by psychotherapy. Thus Sechehaye (1954) reported the striking case of a girl suffering from severe deteriorative hebephrenic psychosis, who seemed to respond to psychotherapy and who made a remarkable recovery. Such work has been taken up systematically by the Zurich school under the inspiration by Manfred Bleuler, as has been reported by Benedetti (1964) who has been very active in this field. However inspiring for the psychotherapist, this work is of limited evidential value for the problems of aetiology. Kind comments that the rather scanty successes of psychotherapy cannot be taken as proof of psychogenesis; statistically they have no weight, and it is not possible to dismiss the objection that they are the results of spontaneous remission.

A second line of study has been the intensive investigation of family relationships such as has been conducted by Lidz, Fleck and their co-workers, and reported in a number of papers over the last sixteen years (Fleck, 1963). Only some 15 to 17 young patients were investigated, but very intensively, hundreds of hours being spent in interviews with all available members of the family, and even teachers and nannies. In every one of these families a very abnormal state of affairs was discovered, but one that varied widely from family to family. A majority of the patients had at least one parent who was either actually schizophrenic or definitely paranoid; and schizophrenic thought disorder could be demonstrated by psychometric methods. The relationship of the child to the parent was likely to be distorted by the 'double bind' (i.e. the conflict caused by the demands of each parent on the child being mutually incompatible or antagonistic). One of the weaknesses of this study is that it is by no means clear that any one, either of the parents or of the probands themselves, would be diagnosed as schizophrenic by any European psychiatrist. Not only is the American concept of schizophrenia much wider than the concepts applied in all countries of Europe, but Lidz himself has denied the usefulness of attempting to fit psychiatric disorder into a diagnostic classification. Nothing has been reported about these families which could not readily be accounted for if the probands were a group of children with severe behaviour disorders, but not actually schizophrenic.

This objection cannot be raised to the work of Alanen (1958), which was not only very thorough, but was also based on Langfeldt's concept of schizophrenic and schizophreniform psychoses. He examined personally 100 mothers of young patients in the University Clinic at Helsinki, and took as controls the mothers of 20 neurotics from a medical ward and 20 healthy students. While 84 of the mothers of schizophrenics were at least severely neurotic, with salient symptoms of anxiety and aggressiveness, there were only three abnormal mothers in the control series. Fear and aggression characterized the early relationships between mother and child; and most of the mothers had been particularly disturbed emotionally at the time of the birth of the schizophrenic patient and during his infancy. All these abnormalities were more marked in the mothers of the schizophrenics than in the mothers of the schizophreniform patients.

The difficulties which lie in the way of coming to reliable judgements in this field are illustrated by the work of Ernst (1956) at Zurich. Out of 50 female schizophrenics under his care in Burghölzli, 7 came from abroad; in 35 out of the 43 remaining cases routine investigation had already shown that family relationships were very disturbed. Ernst now investigated the 8 cases in which family circumstances seemed to be fairly normal. In all but one of them exhaustive research finally showed that the patient had been subjected to severe stresses from within the family, and in only one was the family regarded as an integrated one. It is very difficult to know what weight to give to such findings. It is not the usual clinical experience to find that all but a very small minority of schizophrenic patients have been subjected to emotional stresses much more severe than most children and young people cope with; the suggestion arises from the work of Ernst that this is only because practically all psychiatrists up till now have not looked at the childhood of their patients sufficiently carefully. This is certainly a possibility; but other possibilities have to be taken into account. Ernst went into his intensive investigations determined to discover anything and everything that was discoverable, and the halo effect of such an emotional attitude on the part of the investigator can be very great.

This consideration applies also to a large part of the other work in this field which offers us for consideration as objective matter results based on highly subjective impressions. It is claimed that the cool and impartial observer will never discover for himself all that his patients have to reveal; only if the psychotherapist puts himself into close emotional rapport with his patient, and participates in his feelings, can he understand him and come to appreciate what a terrible time he has gone through. Insights of such a kind may well be of inestimable value for the treatment of the individual patient; but they are very unreliable as basic data for aetiological research. Practically all this work is retrospective. The investigator relies on what his patients and their relatives can tell him, not so much about the events of one, two or three decades ago, as about their emotional inter-relationships of that far-off time. No allowance is made for the falsifications of memory that must occur, and it is difficult to see how an allowance could be made. With the observer and interpreter himself pre-committed to a particular aetiological theory, it becomes impossible for the outsider to know what solid ground there is.

One must also note that this work is not capable of being repeated and confirmed by others. All the objective data, which would appear to be relevant to theories of psychogenesis in schizophrenia, such as the incidence of broken homes, duration of breast-feeding, time at which toilet training was established, occurrence and duration of separation between parent and child, all these have been found to show no significant differences between schizophrenic and control groups. It is, in fact, only the subjective data which do show such a difference; and they vary a great deal from one investigator to the next, so that it is hardly possible to speak of the work of one confirming the work of another.

When one examines the conclusions that are drawn, one finds that the parents have been subjected to a moral judgement, one might even say a harsh one, and have been found wanting. Terms of moral condemnation are in fact employed: it is said that the parents have 'failed' their children and have failed them 'lamentably'. It is above all the mothers who are condemned. They have shown either excessive strictness, or excessive indulgence. They have been indecisive and ambivalent, or have shown a covert harshness and moral inflexibility. They have been rejecting or covertly rejecting or over-protective. They have shown either a cool detachment or an excessive devotion. One investigator, according to Kind, found that a special type of gentle yet restrictive control and domination under the guise of self-sacrificing mother love had a particularly devastating effect. Where parent and child are both normal, the relationship between them is found to have been pathological. It is difficult to resist the conclusion that we are being offered an account of mothers who by and large are within the normal range of human variation, but who are very much mothers. It seems to have been their maternity even more than their humanity which has aroused so much indignation.

It is to be regretted that it has been predominantly the psychotherapist, pre-committed to a theory and emotionally involved with his patients, who has penetrated into this field. If his discoveries had proved to be to some degree correlated with data which could be confirmed by the independent observer, we should have been able to advance much farther. We must suppose that the totality of environmental factors plays a large part in the aetiology of schizophrenia, and it seems likely that the experiences of the child may affect his development in such a way as to make him more or less susceptible to schizophrenic illness. At present, however, we are still very much in the dark about what the nature of these experiences may be, and what kind of twist may be given to the processes of development to increase the risk of schizophrenia.

PSYCHOPATHOLOGY

As long as no known physical pathology of schizophrenia exists, the psychology of the disease must be of primary importance even to those who, like the authors, believe that it has a physical cause. Psychological symptoms are at present the *basis of our diagnosis and therapeutic action* and any theory of the illness has to be founded on its psychopathology. In fact, much of the psychopathology of psychoses, and of neuroses as well, has been developed on schizophrenic material and in connexion with the phenomena observed in schizophrenia.

Before Eugen Bleuler's work appeared, and in some respect anticipating his concept of 'splitting', Stransky (1914), using a metaphor from neurology, proposed 'intrapsychic ataxia' as the basic symptom of dementia praecox. He described a lack of co-ordination between emotions ('thymo-psyche') and thinking ('noö-psyche'), which is now generally accepted and referred to as incongruity of affect. Bleuler found the splitting within the thinking itself, and being an adherent of Wundt's association psychology, thought the *loosening in the association of ideas* was the primary and fundamental disturbance. Through the loosened links in the chain of associations instinctual desires and unconscious wishes can intrude into the consciousness of the patient; his repressed complexes gain the upper hand and can entirely rule his life and behaviour. The result is the disruption or distortion of his personality. He is at the mercy of his emotions and withdraws from reality whenever it is opposed to the whim of his complexes.

The introduction of Freudian theory into Bleuler's psychology of schizophrenia had been prepared by Jung (1907) who was working with Bleuler at that time. However, while Jung, using his diagnostic association studies, thought that the psychology of schizophrenia was identical with that of dreams, hysteria and other neurotic conditions, Bleuler maintained the view that the *dissociation of thinking* was of a primary kind, and independent of influences arising from the unconscious. Other symptoms, although not of the same order as the disturbance of thinking, and thought by Bleuler to be primary, are: weakening of will-power, emotional stiffness and flattening, and ambivalence. Delusions, hallucinations and catatonic symptoms are regarded as secondary or accessory. Autism (withdrawal) is placed somewhere between these two groups in Bleuler's system, and freely used to explain other symptoms.

Bleuler was on the *search for a fundamental disturbance*, hoping that the symptoms could then be explained as the reaction to it of the patient's mind. This idea was taken up in a systematic way by Berze (1914). He thought that 'insufficiency and lowering of psychic activity', based on organic damage of unknown nature, is the primary symptom of schizophrenia. Patients often describe lack of will-power and lack of control and spontaneity; and Berze gives a striking collection of such descriptions. The lowered mental activity may prevent the making of a clear distinction between what is real and what is imaginary, so that the schizophrenic indulges in delusional ways of thinking and behaving. Other authors have used as a comparison the half-waking state of the normal person going to sleep. A person in this state may have similar difficulties in thinking clearly and in distinguishing between reality and imagination. To explain the over-activity and increased productivity in certain schizophrenic states, Berze resorts to the idea that in them there has been a removal of inhibitions which are part of normal activity: schizophrenic excitement is, according to this theory, really unproductive and on a lower level of psychological performance. It is therefore not incompatible with the reduction of energy required by the theory of insufficiency of mental activity. Another important distinction which Berze drew between symptoms of the acute illness, and symptoms of defect and adaptation after the acute disease process has come to a standstill, has been widely recognized and has proved most fruitful. Some of the most striking symptoms of chronic schizophrenics, grotesque stereotypies of speech and behaviour, negativisms and many difficulties in institutional life have almost disappeared, since the tendency to *'habit formation'* (Adolf Meyer) has been acknowledged as a typical defect of the patient of this type, and has been given appropriate treatment.

The earlier psychopathological theories of schizophrenia are numerous and complex. For a lucid description and critique the work by Fish (1962) should be consulted. Nearly all theories show their inadequacy by 'explaining' only part of the symptomatology—the negative symptoms but not the positive ones—or are so vague as to have no heuristic value, as is the case with existentialist theories.

During the past decade hypotheses about the nature of the fundamental psychological disturbance underlying schizophrenic symptoms have been put to the test by investigations of schizophrenic subjects and controls with the aid of carefully designed tests. Some of these enquiries have brought together the approaches of experimental psychology, psychodynamics and genetics. The results derived from this integrated approach have been fruitful and promising. One of the starting points was Norman Cameron's (Cameron, 1939) concept of over-inclusiveness in thinking as the essential defect; this was defined as an inability to preserve conceptual boundaries, resulting in incorporation of irrelevant ideas leading to vagueness and confusion of thought. Payne (1962) has suggested that over-inclusiveness may arise from 'breakdown in a hypothetical filter mechanism which normally screens out those stimuli, both internal and external, which are irrelevant to a task in hand, to allow the most efficient processing of incoming information'. Over-inclusive thinking is said to be confined to schizophrenic patients but occurs in only about half the cases studied, these being very largely acute schizophrenics (Payne, 1962). It appears to be a relatively specific disorder largely independent of general intelligence and of the general retardation seen in many psychotic patients. However, it influences performance of a variety of tests and emerges as a clearly defined factor when test inter-correlations are factor analysed. Payne has suggested that over-inclusive thinking may be related to the presence of delusions but this is as yet unsupported by satisfactory evidence.

Tests of the object-classification and sorting kind have also been used by Lovibond (1954) and McConaghy (1959). The latter showed that one or both parents of schizophrenic patients show a disorder of conceptual thinking on the Lovibond test. This result was strikingly at variance with that obtained in control subjects. As such techniques provide a possible means of identifying schizoid personalities, the implications for enquiries along both genetical and psychopathological lines are of importance. Lidz *et al.* (1958*b*) have drawn attention to the distortions of communication which frequently result in families of schizophrenic patients owing to the schizoid or paranoid personalities of one or both parents; these may undermine the patient's ability to test reality and to assess and respond appropriately to the emotional responses of other members of the family. However, such 'transmission of irrationality' may merely render manifest an inborn predisposition to schizophrenic illness. Indeed McGhie (1961), who found the mothers of schizophrenics to differ from those of neurotics in characteristic ways, points out that explanations of schizophrenia in terms of warped mother–child relationships have also to account for the fact that most siblings of schizophrenics survive their early rearing in such a way as to achieve a satisfactory adjustment in adult life. He concludes that both genetic predisposition towards 'inadequate ego development' and family influences which may help to loosen the patient's hold on reality have to be invoked to account for schizophrenia. As these new techniques of investigation may serve to identify both possible carriers of abnormal genes and sources of abnormal psychological influence within the family, they may also help to define the relative importance of these two factors. It is, perhaps, expecting too much to hope to define a fundamental psychological disturbance underlying all schizophrenic symptoms, especially as there is doubt whether the present concept of schizophrenia is uniform *from the aetiological point of view*. In the present state of our knowledge all that can be done is to group the *essential psychological abnormalities* as they affect the different mental functions and to build up from these abnormalities the most typical syndromes.

(1) Disturbance of Thinking

When we refer to schizophrenic thought disorder, we mean an *abnormality of the thought process*, and not any abnormality of the ideas which it may express. One aspect is shown in the splitting and loosening of associations, which Bleuler regarded as the fundamental symptom of schizophrenia, and which is in fact a most characteristic and important one. But the disturbance has other aspects than a simple disconnexion of thought, or the putting together of overtly disconnected ideas.

In early cases it often appears as a 'woolly' vagueness, or as an inconsequential following of side-issues which lead away from the main topic of conversation. The effect is very puzzling, if a suspicion of schizophrenia is not already in mind; and the clinician may only become aware that there is something amiss when ten minutes of earnest enquiry have led nowhere. The patient's thought is directed by alliterations, analogies, clang associations, associations with the accidents of his environment, symbolic meanings, and the condensations into one of several, perhaps mutually contradictory, ideas. The effect is sometimes rather like that of wit, and indeed may be on occasion genuinely witty; and the patient may therefore appear facetious or jocular when speaking about serious subjects. Words are used out of context, as it were, a concrete meaning being employed when the abstract one would be appropriate, and vice versa. The schizophrenic clings to unimportant detail, in this resembling the epileptic, permits the aim of his thinking to slip out of sight, and lacks discrimination in his thinking processes. (See also Plates VII and VIII.)

A young patient said: 'I feel that everything is sort of related to everybody and that some people are far more susceptible to this theory of relativity than others because of either having previous ancestors connected in some way or other with places or things, or because of believing, or by leaving a trail behind when you walk through a room you know. Some people might leave a different trail and all sorts of things go like that.' This patient claimed that this statement was a clear one, and showed signs of anger when asked to elucidate it.

The following example is from a letter: 'I have just looked up "simplicity" and the dictionary says "sim = one, plicare = to fold, one fold". I told Dr H—— that I dreamed he returned to me the story I sent him which he had folded six times when I had folded it once making it double. Jesus said that the sheep he called would make one fold. I thought at the time that the Latin for six is sex, and that the number of the Beast is 666. Is sex then beastly? I think I will leave you to puzzle out the difference between 6 and 666 and 6 fold in substitution of one fold; for the number of the Beast is a mystery.'

It is necessary to give such illustrations here—others will be given when the symptoms are discussed—because even the lengthiest description cannot convey the impression of schizophrenic thought disorder with the immediacy of an example. The art productions of schizophrenics often represent their thought and feeling in a particularly clear manner (Plate X). On the other hand, it must be remembered that the *negative symptoms*, the gaps, the poverty, the indefiniteness and vagueness are not fully represented in such examples. Furthermore, what they show is necessarily formulated in spoken or written language, and may correspond to what, in the thinking process, may be a more severe or a qualitatively different disturbance; for of course the patient tries to overcome his difficulties, and in his expressions the primary disturbance and the secondary adjustments it requires are not easily separated.

Some patients have no insight into the disorder, and consider that their vagueness is profundity and their deviant associations originality; in this way their interest may be turned to *philosophical and mystical subjects*, and, if they are active and productive, may impel them to write books, join societies and address meetings. Generally, however, and especially in early cases, some insight is retained, and the patients complain of perplexity and bewilderment, of difficulties in concentration, or of a feeling of emptiness. Other and more characteristic things may be complained of. It is impossible to provide any adequate illustration of *'thought-blocking'*, in which the patient is aware of a sudden pause in the flow of thought, and may show it in his behaviour, or of *'pressure of thoughts'*, in which he feels that a multitude of ideas are racing through his mind. Both symptoms are diagnostic of schizophrenia. The following self-description is, however, pertinent, and provides a good idea of the subjective experience of thought under duress, which is seen in the schizophrenic complaint of *'thought-withdrawal'*, *of thoughts spoken aloud or echo de pensée and of thoughts being put into his mind:*

'All sorts of "thoughts" seem to come to me, as if someone is "speaking" them inside my head. When in any company it appears to be worse (probably some form of self-consciousness). I don't want the "thoughts" to come but I keep on "hearing" them (as it were) and it requires lots of will power sometimes to stop myself from "thinking" (in the form of "words") the most absurd and embarrassing things. These "thoughts" do not mean anything to me, and cause "lack of concentration" in whatever I am doing at work, etc. When listening to music I find that the words of the song come to me involuntarily, or if I don't know the particular song that is being played, I seem to "make up words" to the song against my will. Another thing similar to the above is the fact that if there is any banging or such-like noise going on, I do the same thing, which is to "think up" words to "rhyme"—as you might say—with whatever noise I can hear.'

The psychometric testing for thought disorder is discussed on p. 316. Thought disorder is often *difficult to detect* and may be entirely absent while the patient is questioned by the psychiatrist at an interview holding his full attention. Yet when he is led to express himself freely, for instance by explaining a proverb or repeating a short fable, such as 'The Cowboy Story' or 'The Donkey and the Salt', it may be easily demonstrated. Other patients only exhibit the impairment of thinking under a certain emotional stress, for instance when speaking in a larger company or under the influence of alcohol.

Laconic answers, such as 'Maybe', 'Perhaps', 'I don't know', are often given from embarrassment due to disordered thought of which the patient is more or less aware. Similarly the monotonous repetition of phrases like 'I want to go home', 'I want to see my mother', without any affect or attempt to put these aims into effect, is often nothing but a sign of *emptiness and vagueness of ideas*. The patient tries to hold on, so to speak, to something concrete while everything else in his mind is diffused, hazy and insipid.

Many authors have made the theory of schizophrenic thought disorder a subject of special studies. Bleuler (1921) himself followed up the part played by 'autistic' or 'dereistic' (not adapted to reality) thinking within the psychology of the normal. In this study he took more account of the content than of the functional disturbance of thinking. More attention is paid to the *functional side of the disorder* in N. Cameron's (1938) subdivision of three types of disorganization of thought in schizophrenia; 'asyndesis', a paucity of functional connecting links; 'metonymy', a poor approximation instead of the correct word, totally inadequate verbal productions which seem however to satisfy the patient; and finally 'interpenetration' where ideas related to reality and to fantasy are mixed inseparably. Cameron's types suffer from an attempt to combine too many aspects—logic, semantics, relation to reality, and social relations—for their formation.

Paul Schilder's (1920) theory of schizophrenic thought is not, like Bleuler's, based on the outmoded views of association of ideas in a continuous chain. Conscious thinking is, in his view, guided by a *determinative idea*. It has a goal towards which clear and relevant thoughts progress, surrounded by a fringe of less important, less precise ideas and recollections which accompanies the main train of thoughts all the time. The schizophrenic is, according to Schilder, unable to keep to the determinative idea and to focus his attention on the centre. Associated ideas from the fringe constantly interfere with the clearness of his thinking; hence the peculiar character of schizophrenic thought which is beside the point, disjointed, but often not entirely meaningless. This formulation clearly has affinities with the modern concept of 'over-inclusion' that was discussed above.

(2) Disturbance of Emotions

The schizophrenic's emotions are not the mere accompaniment of his mental life, inclusive of his symptoms. They can be primarily disturbed in their character, their intensity and in their relation to other psychic experiences.

Emotional blunting in the established schizophrenic was regarded by Kraepelin as characteristic of the personality change in chronic cases. He spoke of 'affective dementia' in contrast to the 'intellectual dementia' seen in patients with demonstrable brain damage.

The loss of capacity for experiencing certain emotions may be an early symptom and, in some cases, for a long time the only sign of the disease. The flattening of emotional reaction progresses from the more refined and tender *feelings of sympathy* and regard for family and friends, to primitive emotions of fear, rage, hilarity and eroticism. The latter often persist when differentiated responses have long been blunted. The theory of a primary withdrawal can explain the schizophrenic's loss of interest in his appearance and his lack of regard for the feeling of others. It cannot, however, account for the *rapid fluctuations of emotion* observed in many schizophrenics, nor for the incongruity between affect and thought and action. Transient states of elation, ecstasy, desolation, dread or panic, bewildering the patient, are frequent in early schizophrenia. They may occur in sudden bursts side by side with emotional blunting and the absence of warm human feelings. They may be the basis of delusional ideas or combine with primary delusions in an acute schizophrenic attack.

An intelligent young man gave the following description:

'During the day I feel emotions of a sentimental nature (I think) which seem to be entirely on their own inside me without any particular accompanying processes of thought. But sometimes I may eventually build thoughts or imagined scenes on these feelings. But when these emotions slide away I realize that without them I would have to force myself to believe I was concerned and keen about something.'

Incongruity of affect and accompanying thought can be considered as a further example of splitting of personality. It sometimes appears as if only the patient's *expression of emotions* is not in step with his flow of ideas or of talk. But from many descriptions the dissociation between feeling and thinking is beyond doubt. The appropriate emotion is in other cases only delayed in time so that the patient speaks of a bereavement with carelessness followed by a flood of tears some time later when an indifferent subject is being discussed. A trifling affair may arouse wild fury and an incident pregnant with pathos may be treated with levity.

Blunting of emotion and the other primary emotional disturbances are partly or wholly responsible for callous and apparently motiveless *crimes of violence* which sometimes are the first sign of a beginning schizophrenia (Wilmanns, 1922). They include homicide, suicide, sexual attacks or self-mutilation. The lack of feeling removes civilized restraint; but a delusional misinterpretation or a hallucinatory command may also contribute to the antisocial act. On the other hand, the weakness of will and indecision of the schizophrenic prevents the execution of such deeds in most cases where otherwise the risk might arise. The actual number of crimes committed by established schizophrenics is, in fact, relatively small.

The incapacity of the schizophrenic for emotional contact with other human beings is probably also at the root of the physician's impression of chill and distance when confronted with the patient. This lack of 'rapport', the 'pane of glass' preventing the doctor from establishing ordinary human relations, in spite of all effort to do so, is of great diagnostic value because it is a 'physiognomic' perception of the *disturbed feelings of sympathy* in the patient. It may enable an outsider to detect the illness at a time when the relatives often schizoid themselves, have failed to observe anything abnormal (see Diagnosis, p. 314).

(3) Disturbances of Volition

Here again the most common disturbance is a blunting of will power, Berze's basic insufficiency of activity. Complaints of patients about the *weakening of their will*, their inability to make decisions or to act, are not rare; but many do not seem to realize their reduced activity and efficiency. They have ready, though often vague or empty, excuses if asked why they are inactive, spend their days in bed, and do not progress in their work; or they regard these matters as requiring no explanation. A young student finds it natural to waste many months staring into space preparing to write the outlines of a new philosophy or religion, which will never be written. Such behaviour is closely related to autistic day-dreaming and to catatonic stupor; in fact many abnormalities of volition become manifest in catatonic signs.

Besides indecision from weakness of will, there is often at the same time *stubbornness and persistence* in a negative attitude to all requests: *negativism*. The peculiar gesture of half proffering and half withdrawing his hand in a handshake has long been recognized as a physiognomic sign of schizophrenia. Bleuler introduced the term 'ambivalence', applying it to the whole field of motivations in schizophrenia. Psychoanalysis has extended its use, finding similar contrasting motivations in many instances of normal emotional life. In schizophrenics ambivalence is mainly due to weakness of volition.

The latter can be theoretically attributed to *disturbance of the self*. In fact, some workers have made the weakness or loss of the self the central symptom of schizophrenia. The *passivity phenomena* in which this loss is best seen are indeed very characteristic of schizophrenia. The patient tells us that his thoughts, feelings, speech and action are not his own. His thoughts are put into his head by an outside influence; his emotions are artificially made; he is made to laugh, to cry, to remain mute, to utter nonsensical words or obscene phrases, to perform bizarre movements, or to act against his will. Catatonic hyperkinesis and akinesis are often experienced in this way, but not always. There are all transitions from full self-identification with the abnormal behaviour to complete passivity with full insight into the strange and alien nature of the experiences and the behaviour arising out of them. The patient may interpret the experience of passivity in a delusional manner by maintaining that he is influenced by hypnosis, guided by God, wireless waves, telepathy, or manipulated by certain persons or agencies (Plate XI). There are obvious relations between passivity and hallucinations and both phenomena may be based on the same mechanisms—but in fact they occur independently.

Closely related to the ecstatic states in acute schizophrenia, a loosening or *blurring of the boundaries of the self* is often experienced: the patient feels that he is part of the plants, animals, clouds, or of the whole world, and that they are part of himself. His empathy and feeling of unity may extend to all mankind—or he may complain that will power and energy are sapped from him by a hostile outer world which has reduced him to a robot without a self. French workers have comprehended disturbances of volition and self under the concept of '*automatisme*' (Baillarger). Lévy-Valensi (1925) distinguishes '*automatisme sensitive—sensoriel*' (= hallucinations), '*automatisme moteur*' (= catatonia) and '*automatisme supérieur*' (= loss or disturbance of self). They give very illustrative descriptions of the phenomena; '*prise de la pensée*', '*pensée divulguée*'; '*ma pensée est mise dans la rue*'; '*c'est comme si mes projets étaient sur un écran*'.

Disturbance of volition and of the self, loss of self-control, negativism and ambivalence can be accompanied by doubt, perplexity, uncertainty and distress, especially in early stages of the illness. One patient said 'It's peculiar; it's just as if I were being steered around, by whom or what I don't know.' Habit-formation and flattening of affect later lead to uncomplaining acceptance of the symptoms or to more or less consequential *delusional explanations* of what is experienced.

(4) Catatonic Symptoms

Although they can be regarded as purely physical and are to be explained in neurological terms, catatonic symptoms have their psychopathology. Hence they have been termed '*psychomotor*' *symptoms*. More detailed description will be given in the section on clinical picture. Many catatonic signs are only the outward expression of the disorders of volition already described. Milder signs of catatonia such as awkwardness, immobility, stilted and ungraceful movements seem simply to express the mental attitude of the patient: he shows his peculiarity of feeling in the way he walks or dances or behaves in company. Stupor, catalepsy, mannerisms, stereotypies may also be understood as purely neurological signs, being observed in organic brain diseases such as encephalitis lethargica, cerebral tumours, epilepsy, etc. In schizophrenia they are, however, often meaningful; and the most absurd utterances and actions can represent ideas and complexes. The longer they persist the more abbreviated and distorted they become. Kläsi (1922) has analysed a number of such inveterate stereotypies and revealed their original meaning and derivation. However, it would be erroneous to conclude from his interesting analyses of relatively complicated symptoms that, because these activities have a meaning, their causation is psychological.

Stupor, for instance, the most common catatonic symptom, does not in all patients, nor even in the majority of cases, signify a withdrawal into a world of delusional fantasies. Many *stuporose patients* experience nothing in this state. Careful and thorough examination afterwards reveals no content whatsoever, although the patient was at the time fully aware of his surroundings and is now willing to furnish all possible information. In other cases, the patient seems to have been in a dozing, semi-conscious state, and has no recollection of what was going on around him during his stupor. Finally, some patients seem to be entirely unaware of their motionless, passive condition in stupor, and deny that they behaved abnormally. One patient who had been stuporose for weeks, had had to be spoon-fed and taken to the toilet with resistance and great difficulty, spoke for the first time when her relatives visited her, and complained that she was bored and had nothing to do in the hospital.

The abnormal motor behaviour in catatonia takes place, neurologically speaking, on such a *high level of integration* that it is easily influenced and coloured by psychological factors. It can be both caused and abolished by mental and environmental influences; and it may mirror the mental attitude of the patient and his other schizophrenic symptoms—dissociation of thinking, affective and volitional disturbances. This also explains why gross catatonic features have become rather rare recently, since treatment in modern hospitals directs the patient's activities into less asocial and more useful channels.

(5) Primary Delusions

Delusional interpretations of symptoms, such as passivity or emotional outbursts, are of a secondary nature. They merely show that the patient's powers of reasoning and judgement are well preserved, and that he tries to keep order and system in the world of his experience. The primary (or autochthonous) delusion, on the other hand, is a *disturbance of function* at a much more fundamental level, as was first pointed out by Gruhle (1915). Gruhle made it clear that it is not a disturbance of sensory perception: the patient does not feel there is any alteration of the colour or shape of things. Nor is it a disturbance of apperception: the patient is aware that the object at which he is looking is, say, a table. And finally it is not a disturbance of intelligent grasp: the patient can say that it is a rococo table. The disturbance is one of symbolic meaning, and the table signifies that the world is twisted like its legs. The experience is an immediate one, appears out of the blue and without precursor or explanation. While it puzzles the patient, it carries with it its own *sense of conviction*. Interpretative delusions occur in most psychoses, primary delusions are almost pathognomonic for schizophrenia. In their purest form they appear suddenly, fully developed, and are immediately and firmly believed by the patient.

A young wife, herself a doctor, travelled with her children to visit her husband who had been called up for war service, at a nearby aerodrome. While the train stopped at a station, she suddenly realized that all the passengers in her carriage were hostile towards her and her family, that they were disguised Roman Catholic priests and wanted to kill her. She left the train immediately and with her children returned home, where she fell into an acute catatonic psychosis the following night. In another case, a young woman was listening to the B.B.C. news bulletin when she suddenly realized that the announcer was talking about her (Gillies, 1949).

After having made a good recovery, an intelligent working-class girl wrote this description of the start of her illness. 'We got off the bus and entered the cinema. I don't quite know how to say this but it seemed like a place for prostitutes. Inside were people and as they went through the doors I knew they were there to judge me and would give their verdict. At first I enjoyed the film then it became disjointed and I realized that the actors were not who they were supposed to be and that it was all to fool me in some way. We went into the café afterwards and a switch like an electric switch seemed to be moved across my mind and suddenly I was laughing and everything was fine, then I heard someone say, "She knows", and I suddenly understood they were all there to have a look at me and I thought "Perhaps I'll only get a light sentence". Once more it was like being judged. Then my cousin said, "Oh, you've woken up, have you?", with a double meaning it seemed, as if I had suddenly woken up to the meaning of life.'

The peculiar *disturbance of symbolization* producing the experience of primary delusion is most obvious and most easily demonstrated in early cases. The rapid growth of secondary interpretations naturally obscures their origin when the illness has progressed. It was Gruhle who, on the basis of Neisser's observations, first pointed out the primary nature and the importance of this symptom in schizophrenia. Many critics, however, still maintained its secondary nature, and held that its occurrence could be explained by the delusional idea which it embodies. Projection of guilt feelings, they said, would produce the idea of persecution, compensation for feelings of inferiority, the idea of a messianic mission and of universal recognition, etc.

However, in many cases any clear ideational content is missing from the experience of primary delusions: the patient knows that some trivial observation, such as a few chairs in a row, or the reflections of the sunlight in the street, has *some important significance* for him, but he does not know what it means. He is stirred to the depths by some lines in the newspaper; he knows that they are of great significance for the state of the world and for humanity, but is unable to say what they indicate, or whether they augur good or ill. 'I went into a café and there were three white tables; it seemed to me that this might mean the end of the world.' Ideas of an imminent catastrophe, of the approaching day of judgement, etc., are frequently mentioned in this connexion by patients who in fact are perplexed and helpless, but at the same time firmly convinced of the reality and significance of their experience.

Other critics of the primary delusion have pointed to the *characteristic mood* of the patient experiencing it and have insisted that the disturbance is primarily an emotional one. This 'delusional mood' ('*Wahnstimmung*') is sometimes a dominant aspect of the symptom; but it seems difficult to derive from it the varied and unexpected modes of thinking and behaving which are often entirely unconnected with the prevailing emotions of the patient.

Once the patient has accepted the validity of a primary delusion, there seems, in many cases, to be no end to the further *delusional misinterpretations* which may be based upon it. If they are logical, and to some extent, systematized explanations of the patient's situation or of other schizophrenic symptoms, there is no reason to range them with primary delusions as symptoms of the disease. In other cases, the primary delusions of significance, of clairvoyance, of reference, of symbolic meanings, etc., continue and become the main content of the patient's life. He learns in the course of time that others do not share his beliefs, but this does not shatter them. Pathological inactivity and weakness of volition may prevent him from acting in accordance with his convictions. But beyond this, there often seems to be some insight into the morbid nature of it all: the man who thought himself perpetually molested by means of the telephone and the wireless did not take his complaints to the Post Office or to the B.B.C., but consulted a psychiatrist.

A teacher improved from an acute paranoid schizophrenia after insulin treatment to the extent that she could resume her work as the English mistress of the sixth form in a grammar school. When she was seen five years after treatment, she still had an occasional recurrence of primary delusions in spite of her full insight: 'Things around me suddenly seem to fall into a pattern of meaning, with myself in the centre. Two girls came to school with their plaits cut off. I was convinced it referred to me. A man passes the house and I feel I should go down and speak to him. But I always realize after a short time that it is my imagination.'

Jaspers (1913a) has differentiated between *delusional perceptions, delusional ideas and notions* and *delusional awarenesss*. In the first of these, a normal perception is unaccountably endowed by the patient with some delusional significance which may be mystifying, apocalyptic, or merely peculiar. Special importance has been attached by Kurt Schneider (1952) to delusional perception which he distinguishes from other types of primary delusion. But its special diagnostic value does not rest on very clear evidence. In the delusional idea, a memory or passing thought suddenly generates a delusional conviction in the patient's mind. He may, for example, come to believe that he is descended from royalty or endowed with the gift of prophecy and these beliefs are then confirmed by memories now seen in a new light 'as if the scales had fallen from my eyes'. A king may have looked at a patient, or words with special intonation may have been spoken from the pulpit. The delusional awareness is particularly characteristic of florid and acute psychoses. The patient feels suddenly charged with knowledge of world-shaking importance, unrelated to any previous thought or perception of a relevant kind. The end of the world may be at hand, a plague or epidemic has begun in a town nearby, or the patient assumes the identity of a biblical character. On the existing evidence it is doubted whether any one form of primary delusion can be considered more specifically schizophrenic than another and the classification is perhaps over-elaborate. Distinctions of this kind however need to be borne in mind in the course of systematic comparisons of idiopathic with symptomatic schizophrenic disorders and other conditions of the schizophrenic borderland. Recent observations (Chapman, 1966) suggest that, in some cases of acute schizophrenia, primary delusions may be traced to disturbances of perception and cognition such as alterations in the size, distance and shape of objects, changes in colour or brightness/contrast; these are reminiscent of the disturbed perceptions encountered in association with organic disease of the parietal and temporal lobes. Abnormal concept formation has also been linked with disturbance of visual perceptual constancy (Weckowicz and Blewett, 1959). It is possible, therefore, that the perceptual process underlying primary delusions is not always a normal one.

(6) Hallucinations

It seems doubtful whether hallucinations as symptoms of schizophrenia should be ranged with the main disturbances of schizophrenia. They are often the most conspicuous sign of the illness and easy to elicit. Kraepelin insisted that auditory hallucinations were a diagnostically important sign of dementia praecox. But they occur in many types of mental disease. Those characteristic of schizophrenia are significant not so much as hallucinations as by virtue of their *combination with the symptoms mentioned above*: utterances which reproduce the patient's thought disorder, or contain neologisms; bodily sensations closely related to feelings of passivity or to catatonic movements; synaesthesiae with bizarre delusional content, behind which the hallucination proper remains indiscernible.

This has led various authors to psychopathological theories which deny the sensory nature of schizophrenic hallucinations. Schilder (1920), for example, emphasized the role of imagery in the 'fringe' of thinking, from which he derived the auditory hallucinations. Similarly Berze attributed their appearance to reduced mental control. C. Schneider (1925), equating the schizophrenic with the hypnagogic state, regards hallucinations as the inevitable outcome of the general condition. Their dissimilarity with normal sense perception was emphasized by Schroeder (1925), who thinks the *'verbal hallucinosis'* of schizophrenics is in a different category from other forms of hallucinosis.

The latter point is, to some extent, supported by the patients' descriptions; many localize the 'voices' in the head, speak of thoughts coming aloud or of thought echo (*écho des pensées;* de Clerambault, 1942).

Nevertheless, if the facts are allowed to speak for themselves, it is difficult to deny the primary nature of certain sensory abnormalities in schizophrenia. While they are sometimes clearly distinguishable from perceptions of reality, in other instances this is impossible. Their sensory character can be so striking that one patient hired a boat and went out on to one of the Swiss lakes in order to prove to himself that they were the product of his imagination. Schizophrenic hallucinations typically occur in a setting of clear consciousness, a very uncommon event in other psychoses.

Auditory hallucinations may be the first sign of a beginning schizophrenic illness, or they may be absent from the clinical picture for a long time. They may only appear on a single occasion, or may persist over years to overwhelm and direct the patient's behaviour throughout the illness. In fact, very few acute schizophrenic psychoses occur without hallucination at one or another stage of the illness. *Auditory hallucinations* may accompany every action of the patient with their comments, even repeating aloud what he is silently reading. In some cases, they consist of whistling only, or of inarticulate voices; or they consist of words which in spite of an honest effort the patient is unable to repeat, although they absorb his attention. Neologisms are often expressed by hallucinatory voices, and all other primary disturbances are reflected in schizophrenic hallucinations. Their 'unreal' appearance, even if recognized, does not reduce the patient's belief in their reality and importance. They are, in fact, frequently accepted with the same conviction as primary delusions.

Besides hallucinations of hearing, those of *touch, smell and taste* are observed and peculiar visceral sensations often related to the sex organs. Patients report feeling heat or intense cold on certain parts of their skin, or that they are sprayed with fine sand or hurt by bumps from behind. The flavour of food is interfered with, it is made tasteless or repulsive; certain smells indicate the presence of gases let into the room by hostile people; women complain of orgasm artificially imposed on them, etc.

Visual hallucinations are rare in schizophrenia, but not entirely unknown. Especially in acute delusional states, distortions of form and modification of colour are described similar to those produced by certain drugs, e.g. mescaline. In their early stages acute paranoid schizophrenics may take on an aspect resembling delirious states with some confusion and disturbance of consciousness; and then they may have visual hallucinations, e.g. of coloured lights or frightening faces, frequently experienced in fragmentary fashion. Such experiences are, in our observations, associated with a relatively favourable prognosis. The chronic paranoid schizophrenic after years of illness may also, though rarely, report visual hallucinations, without any sign of clouding of consciousness.

OCCURRENCE OF SYMPTOMS: GENERAL QUALITIES

Before discussing the occurrence of the principal symptoms, it seems appropriate to list the *mental functions generally undisturbed* in schizophrenia: consciousness remains clear; attention, orientation and memory are not affected by the disease; sensation, perception (except for hallucinations) are well preserved and so potentially is motility (except in catatonia). Intelligence, including acquired knowledge and ability to solve new tasks, may be found undisturbed even when the illness is fully established. The problem of schizophrenic deterioration will be discussed separately (see Outcome and Course). Special aptitudes in the artistic or intellectual field are often undamaged even after years of invalidism and seclusion; but it is, on the other hand, obvious that higher artistic qualities are easily affected by a disease interfering with expression and communication.

Although the principal symptoms described above may all be found in one patient at the same time or in the course of his illness, in many cases a preference is shown for one or for a small group of the symptoms, and the others are not seen. Thus, some develop thought disorder and shallowness of affect only, but never have delusions and hallucinations; some catatonics have for a long time stuporose episodes only, without psychological content except for some hypochondriasis in the free intervals or a few hallucinations in the introductory stage. There are paranoid schizophrenics without and with thought disorder. Volitional disturbance and loss of self may dominate the picture, perhaps with some delusional interpretations, etc., etc. *There is not one among the main symptoms which cannot be absent in a case of schizophrenia, provided the others, or some of the others, are present.*

The efforts, and their failure, to establish one fundamental disturbance from which the multiform symptomatology could be derived, have been mentioned before. In each theory is a certain core of truth, but none of them covers the facts with satisfactory completeness.

There are, however, some general, structural and ideational qualities of schizophrenic psychology, derived from the primary symptoms, by means of which it is sometimes easier to make a diagnosis than by the primary symptoms themselves.

Clearness of consciousness has been mentioned before. Except for a few very acute states, to be described in the section on clinical pictures, it is preserved throughout the illness. Because of it the patient can give a precise description of his experiences; and it facilitates the phenomenon of 'double orientation' (Bleuler), typically observed as a later development in chronic schizophrenics. They manage to live in two worlds at the same time, to fulfil the demand of reality and to follow their daily occupation, such as the humdrum life of a petty official, while at the same time secretly believing in the most fantastic delusions, e.g. of identity with Napoleon or Christ, and experiencing grossly abnormal sensations and influences.

This may, of course, be regarded as one of the instances of *splitting*. There are many others besides incoherence of associations and incongruity of the accompanying affect from which Bleuler first created the name of schizophrenia. Famous self-descriptions of patients (Schreber 1903; Jaspers, 1913; Staudenmeier, 1912) tell of subdivision of the patient's self into a number of dependent sub-selfs, parts of the personality which exercise some limited power over his life and actions, some exteriorized as ghosts or goblins, others located within his body and inhabiting certain organs. In less productive psychotics the quality of splitting may assert itself in many ways and be observed in all kinds of unexpected behaviour.

Another general quality of schizophrenia is its *remoteness from normality*. It is seen in the reaction of the non-schizophrenic towards the patient and his utterances, his ideas and actions. The words 'queer',' bizarre', 'absurd' ('*verschroben*', '*zerfahren*', '*verrückt*' are some equivalents in German) are used to convey it, but the inability of even educated patients to find the appropriate word for their feelings is rather more significant. Not only has the schizophrenic lost his faculty of empathy for the people around him, but the doctor tries in vain to imagine himself into the patient's frame of mind. He feels separated from his patient much more than from the subjects of any other type of psychiatric illness (see Diagnosis, p. 314), and schizophrenics living, for years, in the same ward of the same hospital are equally unable to understand one another. On the other hand, the patient may from the start, or certainly after some time, find nothing peculiar in his own behaviour and find his ideas and reactions quite appropriate and natural.

This latter phenomenon signifies a further general feature which as 'withdrawal' or 'autism' has by some workers been made a central factor in schizophrenic psychopathology. Detachment from reality is, in fact, an almost universal character of the schizophrenic, but it is rarely a deliberate withdrawal, and often not a withdrawal into a world of wishful phantasies and dreams. It is caused by the affective and volitional disturbances and leads in many cases to what has been called 'autisme pauvre' (Minkowski, 1927), a closed door behind which there is nothing. Some early schizophrenics realize their detachment and try to re-establish the lost 'rapport' with their environment, as can be observed during the course of treatment.

Finally the *content of schizophrenic ideas* can be shown to have some general characteristics—provided one remembers that many cases have little but the most trivial ideational content or none at all. The delusional interpretations, physical or spiritual, given by the patients for their strange experiences are, of course, largely influenced by the ideas of the era or of their cultural surroundings. The psychosis itself, however, seems to rouse the interest in spiritual, philosophical and other fundamental human problems. It is as if with the outbreak of the psychosis the patient's existence had become bottomless, and he had to find new bearings and a new system of values, earlier ones having been shattered by the event. Hence the attraction which the confidences of schizophrenics have for philosophically interested psychiatrists who see in the patient's attitudes slightly overdrawn examples of human reaction to an extreme situation of life (Binswanger, 1945). Features of primitive and archaic mentality have been discovered in schizophrenic philosophy and compared with the creeds and legends of primitive tribes, which in turn are supposed to be the products of early stages of mental evolution (Storch, 1922). This example of the regressive nature of schizophrenic ideas has provided psychoanalytic theory with apparent confirmation of the mechanisms of the unconscious (Freud).

The explanation may be no more than that through the medium of his illness the schizophrenic is confronted with the *basic first questions of life*. The illness also removes restraint and consideration for others and for the environment. Unconscious material is no longer 'repressed'. If the illness does not destroy the patient's capacity to think, he attempts to tackle these first questions according to his abilities. Unexpectedly to those who know him, he develops a concern with problems of religion, sex, power, or morals from which his delusional ideas take a typical content.

CLINICAL PICTURE

The four types of clinical picture usually distinguished, *simple, hebephrenic, catatonic and paranoid,* can readily be correlated with the six principal disturbances delineated in the preceding part. Loss of affective response is the leading symptom of simple schizophrenia. Thought disorder, emotional abnormalities and volitional weakness constitute, in varied distribution, the hebephrenic form. Catatonic symptoms predominate in the catatonic type, often accompanied by volitional and emotional disturbances. Primary delusions followed by secondary delusional interpretation determine the paranoid picture. Hallucinations may be present in all types except in the simple schizophrenic, in whom absence of any productive symptoms is a conspicuous feature.

These types were originally described as different diseases. Since Kraepelin's unifying step, it has been generally acknowledged that many patients pass from one type to the other in the course of their illness. Others exhibit from the beginning a *mixture of symptoms of all kinds*, and are only arbitrarily allotted to one or another group. On the other hand, it has struck many observers that certain features present from the start of the illness remain conspicuous throughout a lifelong chronic psychosis; this applies not only to individual traits of the pre-psychotic personality, or delusional explanations, or emotional reactions, but also to the *prevailing primary symptom*. Hence the theory of Leonhard and his school that schizophrenia comprises a number of systematic, heredo-degenerative diseases. The character of each is, according to this school, supposed to be preserved throughout the life of the patient—except in mixed cases of which there are many.

In spite of difficulties in apportioning certain cases to one of the four types, the subdivision has proved useful and of practical value. If the leading symptoms of the clinical cross-section are taken into account, assignment is possible and makes easier the problems of prognosis and mutual understanding between clinicians.

(1) Simple Schizophrenia

This type is, perhaps, the most difficult to diagnose because of the absence of all florid abnormal signs and of productive symptoms. *Shallowness of emotional response*, indifference or callousness combined with absence of will and drive are the principal symptoms. Catatonia, delusions and hallucinations are not found. Thought disorder may occur, but is often hard to detect and never prominent. The picture progresses over years leading slowly to destruction of the personality. In early phases, only an unexpected lack of consideration for the closest relatives and friends, or a reckless neglect of social obligations, may be conspicuous. The patient may even preserve a colourless amiability among strangers, but all deeper feeling seems lost. He may hold down an undemanding job, or engage in superficial relations with the opposite sex which come to nothing. He can make no decision and if he is not supported by indulgent relations, he drifts into poverty and lives in the lowest stratum of society as an unemployable idler, tramp, petty criminal or prostitute, etc. Many ineffectual, talentless and sterile dilettanti are simple schizophrenics, as also are some of the hangers-on of harmless sects and philosophies, or aiders and abettors of criminal gangs. Gross neglect and ill-treatment of children or of elderly relatives may be found to be due to an insidious simple schizophrenic illness in the culprit. If affective blunting is combined with a lesser degree of apathy the patient may live an antisocial existence for a considerable time.

We have observed a solitary solicitor who fell out with all his former friends because of his seclusiveness and aggressiveness. For a long time he spent his nights in a brothel with a prostitute, giving away large sums and munificent presents. He procured the money by fraudulent receipts which he presented to the authorities. At the same time, he continued his law practice with relative success. When his frauds were found out, his counsel asked him to see a psychiatrist. There was little doubt of the diagnosis of schizophrenia.

Single brutal crimes may be committed by an apparently harmless, solitary person, as, for example, a one-time 'promising' student who, however, never passed an examination. Of greater practical importance is the *effect of simple schizophrenia on marriage and family life*.

> The wife of a schizophrenic doctor gave us with great reluctance the following description of her married life: for years her husband treated her with extreme coolness and ruthlessness, asking for blind obedience and complete servility, although he did no work for the sustenance of the family but spent his time playing with pseudo-scientific plans. On the smallest provocation, he violently ill-treated his wife without any sign of remorse afterwards. He brutally demanded her submissiveness in sexual intercourse and refused measures of birth control in spite of the strained economic circumstances. The wife considered it her duty to continue this sordid companionship and refused any suggestion of separation.

The patients have no appreciation of their own shortcomings, no awareness of the progressing change in their personality. They do not complain of their isolated position in life and seem to find their social failure and everything they do and experience natural.

Vague hypochondriacal complaints bring some of these schizophrenics to the doctor, or to the practitioners of some quackery or nature cure. They may be met with in court or more often among the relatives of schizophrenic patients with more florid symptoms. But as a rule simple schizophrenics live outside hospital and shun contact with the psychiatrist.

The clinical picture usually develops insidiously without symptoms of the more florid type; and this is the classical schizophrenia simplex. In rare cases, a *short acute psychosis* with catatonic or hallucinatory symptoms is followed by a picture of schizophrenia simplex lasting over years; at this later stage it may be impossible to elicit anything about the initial attack which the patient hides or has forgotten. On the other hand, paranoid symptoms may suddenly or slowly make their appearance in middle life after decades of progressive emotional deterioration.

Some of these patients are difficult to distinguish from schizoid personalities who have never had a schizophrenia, especially from those of a callous and reckless type (see Chapter III, p. 156). Although in the majority of patients the break in the life-history at about adolescence is easily demonstrated, in others this is impossible. Insensibility already present in childhood remains the prominent character trait of the affected individual while he grows up. Educational and penal measures, such as child guidance, special schooling, and Borstal institutions, are of no avail. He seems a '*born criminal*' and destined for an asocial life. Lombroso may have conceived his idea of the 'delinquente nato' from the observation of such patients. If the schizophrenic gets into the company of professional law-breakers, he may become a most dangerous enemy of society, and spend most of his life in penal institutions. If he belongs to another stratum of society, he may be supported by his well-to-do family and tolerated as an idle eccentric. Many others land in poor-houses, or common lodging-houses, or receive public assistance as unemployables. Psychiatric examination of the inmates of such institutions has revealed a considerable proportion of schizophrenics, most of them without productive symptoms. Women of this type sometimes become prostitutes.

The relation of simple schizophrenia to 'moral defect' will be discussed in the section on differential diagnosis.

It is important to remember that the affective blunting so typical of the simple schizophrenic can also remain as the only mental scar after an acute schizophrenic psychosis of catatonic or paranoid type. The effect of the callousness of these *post-psychotics* on family life and on their relations with workmates and colleagues may be disastrous, especially if intelligence and volition are not seriously disturbed.

A woman who recovered from a short paranoid episode after insulin treatment tyrannized her husband and children to such an extent that their lives were filled with an uninterrupted dread of her irrational caprices and whims. Her husband, himself a professional man, had no say in the education of the children or any other matter of common concern. She decided when he had to go on his holidays and where he should spend them. Knowing of her illness he anxiously avoided irritating her; but whatever he said was sharply criticized and if he remonstrated he was reviled and reproached. At the same time, the patient was highly successful in her professional life, polite and amiable to visitors and without any remorse or recognition for the husband's patience and tolerance.

(2) Hebephrenic Schizophrenia

The emotional insensibility characteristic of the simple type is also frequently found in the hebephrenic together with the other 'negative' schizophrenic symptoms: disordered thinking, loss of volition and of the self. Hence some authors include the cases of schizophrenia simplex under hebephrenia; but as the simple schizophrenics conform to a well-defined clinical picture, and constitute a group which, though not large, is of special practical importance, their separation seems worth while.

Bleuler called the hebephrenic sub-group the great pot into which are to be thrown all cases not fitting into one of the three other types—simple, catatonic and paranoid. We think it preferable to place in this group all the cases of schizophrenia in which *thought disorder is the leading symptom*. This is a large group comprising the majority of schizophrenics whose illness starts before the age of thirty. They exhibit all the characteristic features of disturbed thinking, described in the chapter on psychopathology, in varying degrees from a mild vagueness to a complete disorganization of thought and speech.

An *insidious onset* is typical, especially if the illness starts between the ages of fifteen and twenty-five. There may at first be only a degree of difficulty of concentration in mental effort which does not hamper an unskilled labourer or an apprentice engaged in manual work, but is a definite handicap to a boy or girl at school. In a formerly promising pupil examinations prove insurmountable obstacles or are only passed after several attempts and with much help and cramming. The difficulties are often blamed on overwork in school or on unbalanced development in puberty; pedagogues and physicians are consulted who unfortunately do not suspect a serious mental illness and advise rest, change of teacher or school, endocrine preparations or psychotherapy. Hypochondriacal ideas fostered by popular literature may colour the picture, and are often centred around masturbation, menstruation or fear of severe illness such as cancer, tuberculosis or insanity. All normal problems of pubescence, physical and spiritual, provide the content of the oncoming psychosis—hence its name.

It has to be remembered that neurotic reactions at this age of intensive growth and development are in fact rare, and are certainly not frequently seen in the consulting-room. Even psychopaths rarely react with severe disturbances in this formative stage except under gross environmental mismanagement. Nevertheless hebephrenics can carry on, diagnosed as 'neurasthenics' and 'neurotics', as *regular and chronic visitors to surgeries* and to the out-patient clinics of general hospitals for a long time, until finally the frequent change of doctors or their fantastic complaints rouse the suspicion of a severe mental illness.

The vague and diffuse thinking of the hebephrenic makes him an aimless drifter in real life and may produce a *permanent state of dreaminess*. These patients are unable to concentrate on any reading, or to do any work unless they are supervised and directed at every step. They are attracted by pseudo-scientific or pseudo-philosophical ideas, try to solve the basic problems of life, consider themselves capable of great discoveries and inventions, but all without activity and often without any attempt to realize their pretentions. Probably the first case history published in English is to be found in Haslam (1809). After a two-years' apprenticeship with a merchant, the patient spent years reading books on all possible subjects, lying in bed, neglecting his appearance, idle and boasting. The following letter was written by a student of economics to his parents while he was in hospital:

'Dear Papi and Mami,
   I am glad as well as sorry not to have heard from you for a long time. I begin to confirm my suspicions along a totally different aspect of the nature of religions, nationalism or Imperialism. I admit I never even dreamt that it centered around the laziness, imperfection, or improper understanding of the tendencies in the nature of human fight and struggle against this religious approach which was partially forced on me?'

Acute states in which the thought disorder is marked may alternate with *periods of relative standstill* of the hebephrenic process. In the latter a maximum adaptation to simple work with relative adjustment to reality can take place. Thus, one finds chronic hebephrenics among unskilled labourers, maids, navvies, gardeners, dustmen, etc., doing a routine job with automatic precision. They may only be discoverable from their history, which is usually one of arrest and decline on the social scale—or when another attack brings out more severe symptoms.

With the loss of clear thinking, planning and anticipation of the future become impossible. System and order in life vanish and the sense of values is lost. Feelings and instincts gain the upper hand and rule behaviour. A flare-up of *sexual appetite* is not infrequent in the hebephrenic youth, leading to excessive masturbation or promiscuity. Girls throw themselves away on anybody who wants intercourse, with disastrous consequences.

In contrast to the superiority, the gravity and the pseudo-profundity of hebephrenic philosophers, and rather more typical of the clinical picture, are *silliness and hilarity*. Inappropriate laughter is the prevailing emotional expression, joking and punning is facilitated by loosening of the sequence of ideas. Some patients produce a patter of speech with a mirth in which the observer finds it difficult not to join. Mild hebephrenics have gained success on the stage as clowns or humorists by their ability to exploit this spontaneous silliness and the *bizarrerie* of thought associations.

Silliness is sometimes combined with '*Vorbeireden*', talking past the point—'a false response to the examiner's question where the answer, although wrong, indicates that the question has been grasped' (Anderson and Mallinson, 1941).

Hebephrenic laughter can, of course, be attributed to *schizophrenic disorder of affect*, and in fact most hebephrenics show some emotional symptoms as well as thought disorder.

They are mildly depressed, but without depth of mood even if they are not giggly; and the cooling off of their feelings for their relations and fellow human beings is rarely missed. Outbursts of primitive affect such as rage or terror are not infrequent in the earlier, more acute stages of the illness. There may be apparently adequate, but excessive, responses to real events, or completely incongruous and unexpected. In later stages the hebephrenic often shows a *bland serenity* which seems to indicate disdain of his environment, but, in fact, reflects vacuity of mind.

Hebephrenics may be over-active, and engage in an untiring search for an occupation or a philosophy; but the majority lose their drive and volition early in the illness, or after it has progressed. Mild *apathy* often precedes the thought disturbance. Seeing the dreamy, withdrawn hebephrenic who sits for hours staring into space and is only able to answer simple questions if addressed but unable to give an account of himself, it is difficult to say which of the two symptoms, thought disorder or passivity, is more responsible for his inadequacy.

Disturbances of the self take varied forms: thoughts may be put into the patient's head or withdrawn from his mind, he complains that his thoughts are broadcast to other people who know everything he thinks. He has times when thoughts race through his mind as if under pressure, in contrast to other times of complete emptiness and blankness. These symptoms may occur in the same patient, but more often not. Clear descriptions of the subtler passivity phenomena are not easily obtainable from the more severe hebephrenics because dissociated thinking and incoherence of verbal expression prevent a rational report. The phenomena, moreover, are so strange and complicated, that the language of day-to-day events is unfitted for their description.

Delusional explanations are more easily expressed and more lastingly retained. They are often proffered by the hebephrenic as the most disturbing of his symptoms. But in the typical case delusions are quickly changing and transient, as if they were broken up by the dominant fragmentation of thinking. Primary delusions may also be present transiently, but have little effect on behaviour.

Many hebephrenics show for a long time no signs of *hallucinations*, but in later stages of the illness they are rarely missed. When hallucinations appear, they are in close connexion with the disturbed thinking. Sometimes they are believed by the patient to cause his incoherent thoughts. The 'voices' interfere with his ideas, present contrasting ideas, repeat what he is thinking aloud or mock at his reactions and opinions. They contribute to his difficulty in concentration while reading, by repeating or contradicting what he has read.

Chronic hebephrenics in a more advanced stage of the illness are often completely absorbed by listening to amusing or flattering voices promising or describing successes in love, money-making and other worldly matters. It is difficult to say whether the patients believe in these imaginations; they certainly do not act on them.

Every psychosis with an insidious onset naturally derives much of its psychopathology from the *features of the patient's personality*. This is especially true of hebephrenia in which the symptoms, such as the decay of ability for formal thinking, weakening of will and purpose, and blunting of emotional response, are purely negative. Besides special traits of the personality, symptoms of a general kind, described as modes of *neurotic reaction* in an earlier chapter, may herald the schizophrenic process. They can colour the clinical picture for a considerable time until the more severe and typical symptoms of the illness become manifest. Hence the superficial view, held by certain workers in the field of psychiatry, that schizophrenia is an aggravated neurosis and may be regarded on the same plane, and treated on similar lines to a neurosis. Only from a considerable clinical experience can the diagnostic acumen be aquired to discern the schizophrenic signs behind the mask of neurosis. Even so, some cases will be misjudged, and hardly any psychotherapist is spared the disappointing experience of seeing a schizophrenic psychosis reveal itself during what seemed to be a hopeful course of psychological treatment.

Although differential diagnosis is discussed in detail elsewhere, a few common *disguises of hebephrenia* should be mentioned here. *Depressive reactions* are often the first sign in young patients of the loosening cohesion of functional response. They may be interpreted as the reaction of the personality to the sinister loss of foothold in the world of reality. If a youth appears depressed or sulky, this is only too easily explained as a reaction to conflicts at the critical and problematic time of adolescence when he has to deal with awakening sexual desire and to free himself of earlier emotional ties. As this is also an age of exaggerated emotional response and inadequate expression of feeling, it will obviously be difficult to recognize the nature of a depressive reaction as the initial sign of a schizophrenic illness. Diagnosis in such cases has often to be postponed till the persistence, monotony, lack of modulation of the affect itself, or its incongruity, or the flatness and stiffness of its expression, confirm the suspicion of a serious illness. If it is sought for, thought disorder is often disclosed early on.

Depersonalization and derealization are prodromal manifestations in other cases of hebephrenia disguising the real nature of the illness. Thinking in terms of normal psychology, nothing seems more appropriate than that the patient should be aware of the change in his mental life and should express the awareness of his loss of interests, activity and emotions in the terms of the depersonalization syndrome and his alienation from reality in those of derealization. It could be maintained—and has been maintained by theoretical thinkers, basing their view on a few chosen cases—that every schizophrenic passes at one stage of his disease through depersonalization, this being the psychological expression of what is actually taking place. In fact, the syndrome is far from frequent in schizophrenia. But when it occurs in early cases, it may for some time remain the sole indication of the progressing personality change, until it takes on a fixed quasi-delusional character, becomes flat and monotonous, or till other characteristic features of the schizophrenic illness make their appearance.

Obsessional phenomena, somewhat related to depersonalization, can usher in a hebephrenic psychosis if an obsessional personality is affected. Passivity can pave the way for obsessional and compulsive symptoms. The rarity of this combination may be seen from the work of Jahrreis (1926) who found only eleven patients exhibiting obsessional features among 1,000 schizophrenics.

A pre-psychotic obsessional personality has a favourable influence on the course of a schizophrenic illness (Stengel, 1945). A classical case of this type is Freud's patient 'Wolfsmann' who was psychoanalysed with apparent success at the age of twenty, but later developed a schizophrenic illness with hypochondriacal delusions (Brunswick, 1929). It is worth noting that the patient's symptoms, even at the time when he still considered him an obsessional, reminded Freud of those of Schreber, the paranoid schizophrenic, to whom he had devoted an earlier study.

(3) Catatonic Schizophrenia

The most frequent catatonic symptom is *stupor*. It varies in degree from a transient blocking of certain movements to immobilization of the whole patient in a fixed posture.

Semi-stuporose states are often seen as a catatonic admixture in otherwise mainly hebe-phrenic cases. In them the patient can still speak, and indeed carry out every kind of activity, but slowly or with frequent interruptions, as if he had to overcome an obstacle.

Typical catatonia is characterized by motor '*blocking*', distinguished by Kraepelin from motor retardation. The latter acts like a brake slackening the pace of all movements, while blocking interrupts or entirely stops the impulse which can flow at normal speed when the obstacle is removed. This analogy, taken from mechanics, is useful as a general description; but it does not help to explain the phenomena, the nature of which is in fact hardly understood at all.

Short interruptions in certain functions—suggesting absentmindedness—and transient immobility may rapidly become more general. The patient looks vague or perplexed; his interest in what is going on around (as expressed by eye movements) seems to vanish, until he becomes entirely unresponsive to any stimulus.

Other catatonic symptoms have meanwhile made their appearance. There may be *negativism* in the form of refusal of food, soiling of clothes or bed with urine or faeces, active resistance to any request, such as to dress, to wash, to leave the bed. Rigidity appearing the moment the patient is addressed or touched, though absent when he is left to himself, is perhaps the simplest form of negativism. General muscular rigidity lasting over days is very rare in schizophrenics. A common negativistic reaction may be seen in the patient who remains mute whatever is said to him, until the questioner turns his back when he answers or at least begins to answer. Or the patient leaves a full plate placed before him untouched, but steals food from another patient's dish. He refuses to use the toilet, but defaecates into the bed immediately afterwards. If kept in bed, he insists on lying in an un-comfortable position on the edge where he is in danger of falling; he may not actively resist when his position is corrected, but he returns to it when unobserved. The interpretation of negativism as a disturbance of volition has been discussed before (see Psychopathology).

Posturing is in general a symptom of more advanced cases of catatonic schizophrenia, but its less conspicuous forms can be observed in recent cases as well. Schizophrenics frequently hold their head a few inches above the pillow for hours, or sit balancing at the edge of a chair, apparently without fatigue or discomfort.

Together with negativism or alternating with it, *automatic obedience* may occur; while the patient at one time obstructs passive movements of his limbs by making himself stiff, shortly afterwards he may permit them to be moulded into uncomfortable postures which he then maintains, perhaps for many minutes. This symptom may or may not be accom-panied by waxy flexibility, a peculiar condition in which muscular tone is raised simultaneously in antagonistic muscle groups. Flexibilitas cerea proper is more common in certain encepha-litic states than in catatonia. The same holds true of echolalia and echopraxia; but they may occur as signs of automatic obedience in catatonics, emphasizing the neurological aspect of the disease.

Postural stereotypies may be taken on by the patient spontaneously and are often later explained as meaningful: stretching of the arms symbolizing Christ on the Cross, balancing on the toes signifying the balance between good and evil, a curled-up attitude under the bedclothes being likened to that of the foetus in the womb.

Transient *states of immobility* lasting from minutes to hours are sometimes reported as an early sign of catatonic schizophrenia. They may be accompanied by fear or hallucina-tions, but are often without psychological content or motivation, and the patient feels spellbound while completely awake.

The great variety of *stereotypies of movement* covers all possibilities from simple 'neurological' motor behaviour to complicated hyperkineses of a highly symbolical character. Some may almost be identical with extrapyramidal tics or cortical twitchings, such as the classical pouting ('*Schnauzkrampf*'), or the rhythmic turning of the head to one side or the 'ballistic' shaking of the arms. One of our patients grasped with eagerness anything she could reach and held on to it, squeezing relentlessly, apparently quite indifferent to whether it were a chair, a nurse's arm or a piece of paper. Others make movements which mimic gestures or facial expressions; frowning, for instance, is a very frequent symptom in early schizophrenics, and may perhaps signify an effort of concentration connected with thought disorder. Other expressive movements are a lifting of the upper lip as if in disgust, smiling with blinking of the eyes as if in embarrassment, shaking or raising of the head, hemming, coughing, etc. All these may mean what one would expect from one's knowledge of kindred normal movements, or just the opposite, or they may be entirely void of any psychological meaning.

Complex stereotypies are as a rule combined with spoken utterances—catatonic speech disorders will be discussed presently—but they may also occur in mute patients and have as ceremonious an appearance as the rites observed by obsessional patients. After each mouthful of food a patient opened and closed his eyes three times; another stamped the floor each time before he went through a door; a student, when putting down his slippers at the bedside at night, had to do this three times or any multiple number of three.

Stereotypies are sometimes a forewarning of an outburst of general hyperkinesis, but more often are the remnants of a phase of general agitation. *General hyperkinesis* may precede or follow stupor. Patients are restless and excited continuously, without rest or relaxation, and in the severest cases even without sleep. As a rule, however, catatonic symptoms, stupor as well as excitation, disappear like extrapyramidal motor disorders in sleep. *Sleep rhythm and depth of sleep* are often disturbed in all forms of schizophrenia, and especially in catatonia. The parasympathetic predominance throughout stupor, found by Gjessing, tallies with the clinical impression that the stuporose patient is always in a kind of half-way state between waking and sleep. The sleeplessness of the excited catatonic is a much more serious complication leading to exhaustion and possibly death, especially when the patient refuses food.

Schizophrenia sometimes begins with a sudden outburst of wild excitement. These cases, formerly called '*delirium acutum*', may begin out of the blue without any obvious premonitory signs, or they may follow a short period of physical discomfort. The degree of restlessness and excitation may exceed everything known in psychiatry, except perhaps some epileptic furors. The patient cries, hits, bites, breaks and destroys everything he can lay hand on, runs up and down, fights everybody and keeps moving day and night. It is impossible to establish any rapport with him, he continues to rage when left alone, independently of any stimulation. The impression is that of an uncontrolled, instinctive motor discharge. Horror or rage may be expressed in the patient's face, but often the expression is blank. Large doses of sedatives are needed to manage such patients; sometimes they can be persuaded to take some fluid or food when they wake up from sedation. Feeding by nasal tube is often necessary. In spite of all nursing care, acute catatonia of this kind frequently ends fatally. The hope, however, of some workers, such as Stauder (1934) and Scheid (1937) of establishing a specific pathology of 'acute lethal catatonia' has not been fulfilled.

Kleist has made a special study of hyperkinetic states and pointed out the similarity of certain motor components in the clinical picture with the *extrapyramidal hyperkineses* in encephalitis lethargica and in other diseases with a well-defined pathology. His precise observations and his attempts to differentiate the varied nature of the movements have contributed to our knowledge of motor behaviour in general. In fact, in general hyperkineses as in partial motor reactions, one finds every type of motor discharge from the simplest reflex-like twitchings to the most complex and highly skilled movements. Epileptiform fits sometimes occur. The repetitive and mechanical character of certain gestures and utterances reminds one of organic disturbances of subcortical origin. As a rule, however, catatonic excitation is psychologically not entirely meaningless. The patient certainly identifies himself with his behaviour—in clear contrast to the encephalitic who in some way succeeds in detaching himself from his motor symptoms.

Just as the hyperkinetic manic is versatile and adaptable, and expresses the heightened mastery of life felt by the manic patient, the hyperkinesis of the catatonic often *mirrors the incoherence* of his thinking or the vagueness of his ideation. His attacks may be impulsive and brutal, but they are seldom well prepared or cunningly planned. Hallucinations may be the cause of the bizarreness of certain gestures; delusions of a fantastic character may be found to be the motive power behind stupor, stereotypies or excitation. In fact, behind the visible catatonic signs all the other schizophrenic symptoms may be present and determine the variety of the clinical picture.

Since 'verbigeration', 'neologisms' and 'word salad' are terms used in the description of catatonia, this seems an appropriate point to discuss schizophrenic *speech disturbances.* Abnormal speech and speech-like utterance may be due to thought disorder or to affective disturbances such as outbursts of rage, fury or ecstasy. If the schizophrenic forms new words to describe his strange delusional, hallucinatory or emotional experiences or speaks in an incoherent style which corresponds to his impaired thinking, one can hardly assume a primary disturbance of speech (White, 1949).

Speech may be affected by catatonia as a mere part of its effects on motor behaviour in general. Immobility and negativism may be shown in mutism, and a state of excitation appear as verbigeration, iteration, etc. In the latter case it appears that the inner pressure to utter something is backed by no adequate fund of meaningful words and sentences.

In certain chronic cases the *distortion of language*, which may deteriorate into an un-restrained flow of gibberish appears as by far the most prominent symptom. These patients show no general hyperkinesis. They talk incessantly as if playing with the material of speech, and their productions have been compared with the playful disfigurement of language in the dreams of normal people (Kraepelin). It has been also shown that the schizophrenic may employ the normal ambiguities of language for his own convenience without regard to the 'social serviceability' of speech (Whitehorn and Zipf, 1943). More neurologically interested workers have likened the speech of schizophrenics to the jargon and logorrhoea of certain types of aphasia.

Patients have been observed who create their own *secret artificial language* and give a translation into ordinary speech. Other patients refer the origin of neologisms to hallucinatory experiences and insist that certain bizarre utterances are not their own, but other people speaking through their mouths. The fact that auditory hallucinations prevail in schizophrenia and, as one would expect, involve the same distorted words as the patient himself uses, has led to the idea of a primary speech disturbance as a symptom of schizophrenia and to the concept of 'schizophasia' (Bleuler). But, as Gruhle has pointed out, except for the cases in which a catatonic excitement implicates the speech mechanism as if by chance, and produces meaningless iterations, rhyming or ungrammatical jargon, the nature of all language anomalies in schizophrenia can be understood as the outcome of other primary symptoms.

Catatonic behaviour, which is a primary disturbance in acute schizophrenia, has a *tendency to persist* when the illness has come to a standstill. If it takes the form of catatonic habit formation, stupor or another form of reduction of contact and communication, this can be interpreted as part of the withdrawal from reality. If it is shown in hyperkinesis or some unpleasant stereotypy or grimacing, this theory is less plausible. Much can be done to correct such abnormal motor habits by directing the patient's mental and physical energy towards a useful occupation, giving him responsibilities on a small scale and opportunity to control his behaviour in the company of normal people. The considerable *influence of environmental factors* on the behaviour of the chronic catatonic is now generally recognized; and the organization of the patients' activities in chronic wards of mental hospitals into more normal and useful channels has improved the whole atmosphere and appearance of these wards.

In well-run hospitals catatonic stupor or excitement lasting for years is rare, and patients learn to control their mannerisms and utterances. One catatonic who used to stand for hours in a corner answering his hallucinations with bellowing noises lost this habit entirely after he was allowed to go to the neighbouring town entrusted with shopping errands. Only when he returns on winter evenings in the dark, he can sometimes be heard bellowing on the lonely road.

The clinical picture of catatonia would be incomplete without mentioning the *physical abnormalities* outside the motor field: sallow colour and greasiness of the skin, especially of the face; blue and mottled extremities which are always cool; a peculiar odour of the patient's sweat which is difficult to describe; excessive salivation; low pulse rate and low blood pressure; shallow respiration interrupted by sighs; relatively low body-weight, even when the food intake is normal or excessive.

Finally one must agree with those observers who emphasize the psychological aspects, that the catatonic symptoms in their milder form are representative of what one may call *the schizophrenic style*. Stupor expresses a shutting-off from the real world and from society; awkward and stiff movements signify the rigid and emotionally cool outlook of the schizophrenic's thinking and feeling; states of violent excitement correspond to his uncompromising mental attitude and fixed ideas. Features of this schizophrenic style are found in paintings and writings and other works of art produced by schizophrenic patients. They also find a validation and a justification when they are informed by genius, as in the works of van Gogh and Hölderlin (Lange, 1909; Jaspers, 1926). In some of these artists the flow of originality seems to be intimately related to the change in the vision of life wrought by the schizophrenic process.

(4) Paranoid Schizophrenia

Of all clinical types of schizophrenia, the paranoid type is the most homogeneous and the least variable. Schizophrenia simplex is often the precursor or the result of a catatonic or hebephrenic attack; and in other cases catatonic and hebephrenic symptoms frequently intermingle, or replace one another in the course of the illness, so that it is difficult to assign the patient to one or other clinical group. The paranoid form of schizophrenia, however, is relatively distinct from the others, and often *persists true to type* throughout its course. Primary delusions followed by secondary delusional interpretations are the leading symptoms, and, together with hallucinations, can remain almost the only disorder in a chronic psychosis lasting for years. Disturbances of thinking, feeling and volition, i.e. those symptoms which lead to deterioration of the personality, may be absent or inconspicuous, or only revealed under special circumstances. It is no wonder that critics of Kraepelin's concept of dementia praecox as a single large entity, have maintained that the paranoid psychoses were a distinct group.

The question as to why the symptom of delusion predominates in some schizophrenic patients while others are free is an interesting and important one. Although a conclusive answer is impossible at the present state of our knowledge, there is evidence that the paranoid type of reaction represents *the most frequent form in the middle-aged and elderly*, and therefore there is a suggestion that a later age of onset itself predisposes to a paranoid development. Patients who fall ill in later life can be regarded as having greater constitutional powers of resistance than those who are attacked young; and in fact in them the illness tends to take a more chronic and insidious course, with less destruction of personality. A full-blown paranoid development can only be seen while the personality is relatively intact, as gross symptoms of thought disorder and catatonic and volitional disturbances will interfere with its appearance. Kolle's finding of the late average age of onset of paranoia has already been mentioned. W. Mayer (1921), who followed up Kraepelin's cases of paraphrenia, thought that the late onset of the illness was responsible for the peculiarities of the clinical picture. Among 100 paranoid schizophrenics studied by Wyrsch (1942), eighty-one fell ill after the age of thirty, fifteen after the age of fifty; however, nineteen of his patients began their illness within the third decade. In his series of over 1,000 schizophrenics, carefully investigated genetically, Kallman (1938) found that the mean age of onset in the paranoid group was thirty-five, in all other types twenty-three years. Paranoid symptoms (though not primary delusions) are, moreover, rather characteristic of all kinds of mental illness in later life, especially in affective disorders at the time of involution, and in many senile and other organic psychoses of the elderly.

Coming on so late, and especially if it attacks a well-developed and imaginative personality, the psychosis may often produce a paranoid attitude which seems to be easily accounted for by the life situation. Moreover, in the majority of cases there is an insidious onset which gives time for features of the original personality to interweave themselves into the picture and for the close and *almost logical integration of the paranoid attitude with environmental circumstances.* Jealousy seems only too natural a reaction for the unhappily married husband; a secret passion for her chief might almost be expected from the spinster secretary; a self-conscious vigilance for remarks about his complexion is easily understandable in the masturbating youth. It is often impossible to determine the psychological point at which such understandable mild paranoid reactions crystallize into delusions. But when they appear as something entirely new and strange, and when they lack a clear connexion with the peculiarities of the patient's temperamental make-up, they should rouse the suspicion of a serious illness, however easily they may be explained by the life situation. The same is true for hypochondriacal ideas, for litigious activities and for fanatical devotion to political, religious and other missionary causes.

Delusional ideas in schizophrenia are often more or less logical, often free from direct emotional motivation, and always persist in a clear state of consciousness. These qualities have naturally attracted the interest of those who, dissatisfied with the theory that their basis is a psychological change derived without mediation from the pathological process,

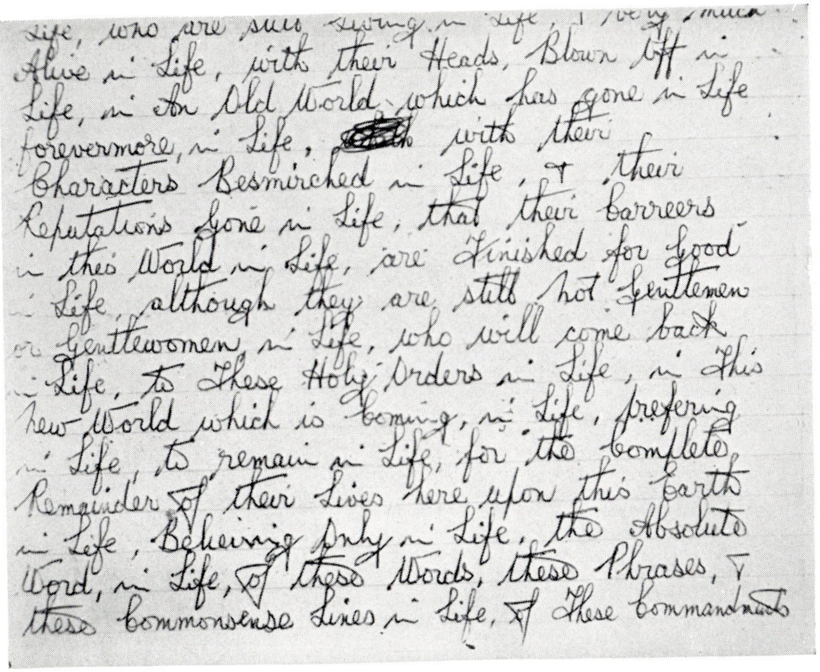

Life, who are still staying in life, & very much
Alive in Life, with their Heads, Blown off in
Life, in An Old World which has gone in Life
forevermore, in Life, ~~with~~ with their
Characters Besmirched in Life, & their
Reputations Gone in Life, that their Carreers
in this World in Life, are Finished for Good
in Life, although they are still not Gentlemen
or Gentlewomen in Life, who will come back
in Life, to These Holy Orders in Life, in This
New World which is Coming, in Life, prefering
in Life, to remain in Life, for the Complete
Remainder of their Lives here upon this Earth
in Life, Believing Only in Life, the Absolute
Word, in Life, of these Words, these Phrases, &
these Commonsense Lines in Life, & These Commandments

PLATE VII

Writing stereotype with repetition of phrases and punctuation mannerism
by paranoid schizophrenic patient, aged 52, ill for more than 10 years.

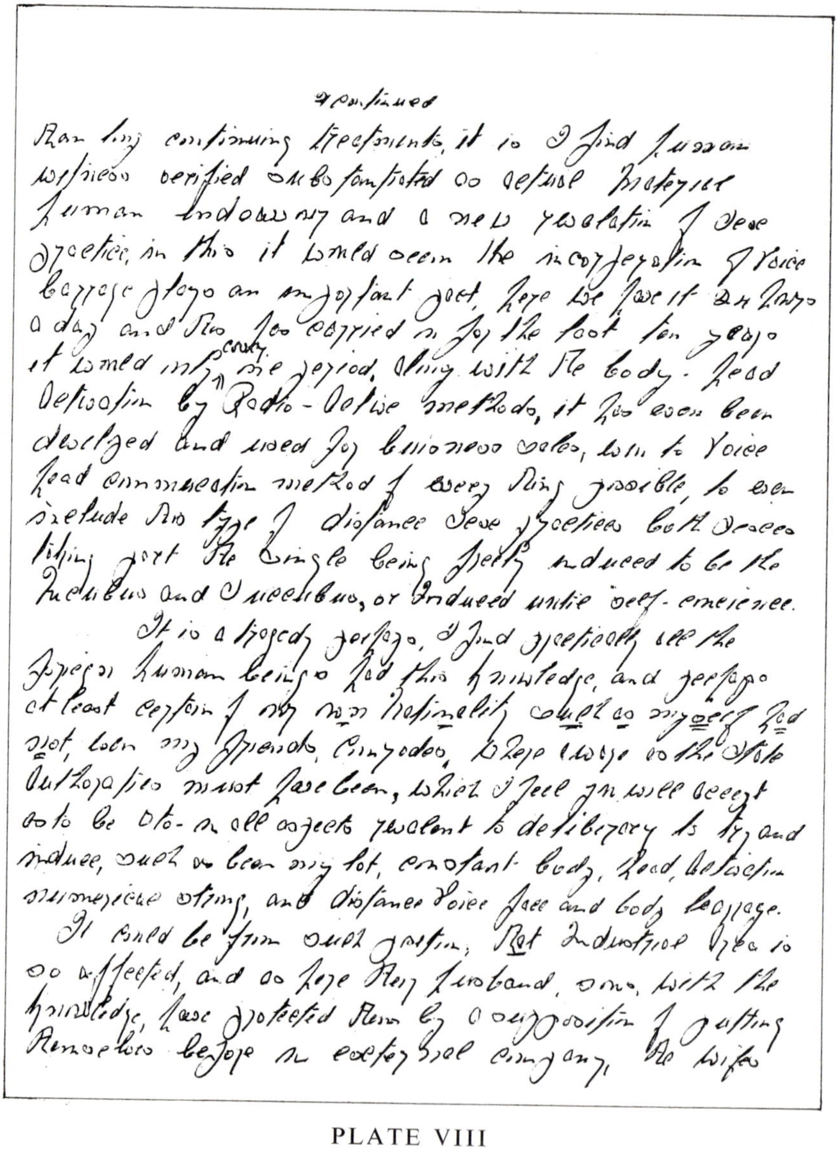

PLATE VIII

Part of a letter sent through the post showing schizophrenic thought disorder, with incoherence, tangentiality, neologisms and ill-defined, confluent paranoid delusional ideas. (A transcript of the extract is given on the facing page.)

TRANSCRIPT

2/ continued

than long continuing treatments, it is I find human
witness verified substantiated as actual material
human endouvair and a new revelation of sex
practice, in this it would seem the incorporation of voice
barrage plays an important part, here we have it 24 hours
a day and this has carried on for the past ten years
it would only cover one period, along with the body-head
Activation by Radio-Active methods, it has even been
developed and used by buisness sales, even to voice
head commucation method of every thing possible, to even
include this type of distance sex practice both sexes
taking part the single being freely induced to be the
Incubus and Succubus, or Induced until self-concience.

It is a tragedy perhaps, I find practically all the
foriegn human beings had this knowledge, and perhaps
at least certain of our own Nationality such as myself had
not, even my friends, comrades, where aware as the State
Authoraties must have been, which I feel you will accept
as to be Sts – in all aspects revalent to delibirary to try and
induce, such as been my lot, constant body, head, Activation
numerical strong, and distance Voice face and body barrage.

It could be from such position; that Industrial Area is
so affected, and so here their husband, sons, with the
knowledge, have protected them by a supposition of putting
themselves before in external company, the wifes

PLATE IX

Painting by a psychopathic subject. The artist communicates his anxiety and arrests attention in this painting of a night-marish world peopled with monsters, dismembered parts and slimy swamps. His vision is communicable and has a certain unity by contrast with the fragmented, private and inaccessible world expressed in the drawing by C. F. Hill (Plate X).

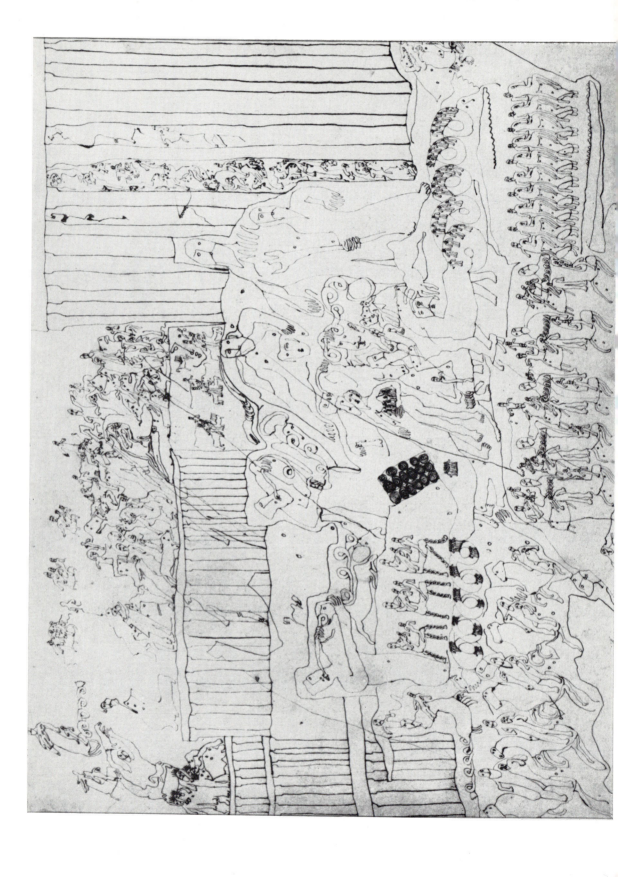

PLATE X

This drawing by the famous Swedish painter Carl Frederick Hill (1849–1911), who suffered from a psychotic illness during the greater part of his life, conveys in a vivid manner some of the characteristic features of the thinking and inner life of schizophrenic patients. There is a manneristic repetition of distorted human forms, parts of which are elaborated in stylised and meticulous detail in the lower part of the right-hand half of the picture. Fragments of the body, faces, hands are seen and there is coalescence and condensation of disparate human and animal forms as in the repeated centaur-like figures in the lower half. Some of the forms are reminiscent of the demon-like animals of Hieronymus Bosch. In moving from left to right in the small rectangle in the top left-hand corner condensed human-animal shapes are succeeded by an increasing chaos and dissolution of form.

PLATE XI

These two pictures by the celebrated Swedish painter Ernst Josephson (1851–1906) express only a single schizophrenic characteristic: experience of passivity. During the acute phase of the psychosis from which he suffered he believed that he was guided by great artists of the past. These two drawings bear the signatures Rafael Sanzio (*above*) and Velasquez through Ernst Josephson (*below*).

(The photographs for Plates X and XI were kindly supplied by Professor Cronholm of the Karolinska Institute, Stockholm)

have sought for *explanation along normal psychological lines.* Hagen (1870) held that delusional beliefs serve the patient as a prop in his perplexity and distress, and give his shattered existence some stability. Wernicke (1906) spoke of 'delusions of explanation', the patient's effort to solve the riddle of his strange experiences, his hallucinations, passivity feelings, etc. The patient seeks to explain them within the order of things as he knows them. Hence hypnosis, electricity, wireless and other familiar but little-understood phenomena are the recourse of the patient of today, while supernatural forces, fairies, werewolves, witchcraft and the devil himself served in ages past. There is little doubt that Hagen, Wernicke and others have much right on their side, and that the patient's delusions contain secondary elements which are derived from a partial adaptation to the morbid experience. Nevertheless these theories remain of a partial kind, and do not account for the primary delusion itself, nor elucidate its power over the patient and its fixity and rigidity.

Some of these qualities can be accounted for by *the directness of the original experience.* The patient is not equipped to distinguish a hallucination from a true perception, and must, as we all do, lend credence to his eyes and ears. The delusional experience arises very frequently in a pathologically altered mood which gives it an additional power of conviction. This delusional mood-state has already been referred to, and when it is well shown one is able to see the rudiments of delusional ideas, and half-way stages between them and altered perceptions.

A man of thirty-nine, asked whether he felt that people imitated him, replied: 'Yes. . . . I don't quite gather. I know one right and one left use both hands, but I can't follow the system that's working. The idea is meant in a kind way, but it's not the way I understand life. It seems to be people taking sides, as I understand it. If certain people agree with me they speak to me, and if not they don't. Everybody seems to be the doctor and Mr. H—— [his own name] in turn. The superiors here can't do as they like, they can't come up to speak to you as they like, because they have to take their turn of being superior and insuperior. To say things are all wrong means right in turn, but I don't appreciate it that way. If I go into the stores and say "Are my cigarettes here?" they say "No". But if I say "My cigarettes haven't come" they give them me.'

If the onset of a paranoid schizophrenia is observed in a man of fairly normal personality, the appearance of such a *delusional mood-state,* and still more of typical primary delusions, is easy to recognize. If the illness attacks a schizoid personality of the over-sensitive or suspicious type—a relatively small group among pre-psychotics—the first symptoms may be difficult to distinguish from habitual feelings of sensitivity and self-reference; and then only later and grosser symptoms, such as hallucinations, affective blunting or catatonic behaviour, may allow a definite diagnosis.

Fortunately for the problems of diagnosis, the greater number of paranoid schizophrenics *lack previous paranoid traits,* or even marked signs of a schizoid personality. Miller (1941) found only 50 per cent., of schizoid personalities in a large material. Before destructive changes have occurred, the paranoid schizophrenic is not an isolated shut-in eccentric; he often fights for his ideas, defends his rights, and joins groups or sects from whom he expects support for his cause, and only leaves them when he is disappointed.

L

Other patients hide their delusional ideas in the *early stages of their illness*, as if they realized their oddity. They continue in their work and in day-to-day relations with the people around them. This may go on for years, until, under some stress of circumstance, a whole system of delusions comes unexpectedly to light. As such a system has grown, encapsulated as it were in the patient's mind, and guarded against contact with reality, its content is often so bizarre that its nature is recognized at sight.

A company director, with a long and successful record, suddenly declared, during a dispute with his partner on business policy, that he was an illegitimate son of royal parents, that he had been watched by all his employees for many months, and that he had survived several attempts by his partner to poison him. These ideas had been ripening for years, and had become entirely fixed before he disclosed himself. Shortly afterwards he smashed his wireless set at home, and made a suicidal attempt which led to admission to hospital.

Paranoid schizophrenia may start suddenly, irrespective of such sudden ebullitions of a mind long diseased; and it is in these early and acute cases that the *primary delusion* is best studied (see p. 272). Some quite ordinary perception, such as an advertisement in the newspaper, or a talk over the radio, has an unexpected meaning for the patient, and, he feels, refers to him and to his life in past and future. A traffic accident he witnesses, the shining of car-lights through his bedroom window, the shapes of clouds in the sky, a glance between friends, take on a personal significance. He senses an impending revolution, the re-birth of Christ, adumbrations of a great destiny or of a threat to his life, from observations which he must have made often before, and which meant nothing to him till that day. From such an experience he dates his conviction that he is regarded as an outcast, is persecuted by the freemasons, the Jews or the government; or he feels called on to be a reformer, to spread the doctrines of a religious or political sect, to proclaim his mission as a new Messiah; or he may claim that he has discovered the secret of perpetual motion, has found some new scientific principle, can transmit power on a radio beam or has solved some other technical problem of incredible difficulty. Some patients at first discard these ideas as absurd, and only, as they continue to experience the feeling of a hidden meaning behind commonplace events, lose account of rational arguments and connect events in a quasi-systematic way. The effect of primary delusions may be supported by illusions and hallucinations, which may have been present from the start. While many hebephrenics have doubts about their auditory hallucinations and are willing to discuss the question whether they are real or not, the paranoid patient is certain and unwilling to admit any doubt.

Powerful *affective experiences*, apparently arising *de novo*, often strengthen the delusional belief. States of fear, bliss, rage, or feelings of overwhelming well-being and vigour, or its opposite, are often experienced in acute paranoid psychoses, as are also such mixtures of emotional and cognitive experiences as those of ecstasy, blessedness, damnation or direct intuitive insight into the deepest problems. Not all of these are without their capacity to awaken echoes in the normal, as is shown by many works of artistic or literary power which have been produced by schizophrenics of great innate ability. There are probably other primary affective disturbances for which no adequate description can be given in ordinary language. It is tempting to think, and has often been suggested, that all primary delusions are based on some affect; but an unbiased study of the clinical material shows that in many cases this theory fails to hold. It is characteristic of schizophrenic delusions that they do not correspond to the predominant affect, and that the patient's affective reaction to them is often incongruous.

There are obvious connexions between paranoid experiences and their associated affective states on the one hand and disturbances of the will and of the self on the other. They have a further connexion with the philosophical and religious preoccupations evoked by schizophrenic thought disorder. *Thought disorder is rarely absent*; and systematically coherent though they may be at first, paranoid delusions soon become illogical and self-contradictory even at a time when hallucinations have not yet appeared.

In the majority of cases, acute paranoid psychoses are *the beginning of a chronic illness*. One sees, however, short episodes which last only a few weeks and then seem to clear up entirely. During the remission the psychotic experiences may be forgotten, or, more frequently, they may become the focus or origin of a new orientation to life, as for instance in a religious conversion.

A young girl worked for several years as a parlourmaid in an industrial town. When the place was subjected to a heavy air raid during the war, she told her father with a smile that she was responsible for all the damage and for the death of many people. She moved with her family into the country and remained apparently normal for another four years, when she suddenly declared that President Roosevelt was going to marry her. This was the beginning of a chronic paranoid psychosis with catatonic features and hallucinations which led to admission to hospital.

Remissions after a longer paranoid psychosis are usually only approximations to a social adjustment. The patient is loath to give up his delusional ideas, although he may not act on them nor enlarge their range. On direct questioning, he becomes embarrassed or angry and uses subterfuges and evasions, thus disclosing their persistence. The state is very similar to that shown by the paranoid patient who, early in his illness, hides his thoughts and feelings while they are still fresh and unaccountable. There is a *degree of dissociation* which makes it possible for the paranoid ideas to be kept, one might say, in an isolated compartment of the mind, from which, however, they may break loose again under the stress of strong emotion or in a second attack of illness.

While there is little doubt that in these cases the psychotic process has come to a *stand-still*, one cannot be very sure whether the *process is continuing* or not in those chronic mental hospital patients in whom this isolation of morbid ideas does not occur. There are many who continue for years to suffer under the molestations of their persecutors, and are constantly distressed by the annoyances and the hostile attitude to which they are exposed. Anything unusual, the admission of a new patient to the same ward, a change of doctor or nursing personnel, the provision of a wireless set, a change in time or place of exercise, is related by the patient to himself and his delusional complex. This complex absorbs the whole of his attention and is his day-long concern; and the hallucinations and variations of emotion he undergoes add to his distress. The basic idea of the delusional system is usually taken from the early experiences of the illness, and remains in many cases unaltered for years. The patient, feeling himself wrongly treated, injured or tortured, is always tense and often seriously aggressive. The delusions remain a festering sore, do not become encapsulated, and bar the way to any social adaptation.

In other patients a far-reaching *integration* occurs *between the real and the delusional world*. They speak freely about their experiences, which are often as varied and fantastic as those of the distressed paranoid, but manage to maintain some equanimity. Though they believe that attempts are made to poison them, that dead relatives are resurrected and visit them at night, that the other patients in the ward are put there to remind them of their past, they take these things for granted, as part of the natural order of things, and keep their impassivity. They treat these spies in the guise of patients at their face value, and are fairly sociable with them, keep at work in the gardens or workshops, visit their relatives in the neighbouring town, and find nothing extraordinary about their lives. There is no clear line between the delusional and real world, and the scepticism of others concerns them very little. These patients may maintain an outward normality of personality and behaviour for a long time, although the beliefs they hold are as fantastic as any that we find. The content of their ideas may recall folk-lore or children's fairy-tales, or consist of elements of a melodramatic kind which seem to be taken from the penny-dreadful.

The group corresponds to what Kraepelin called *paraphrenia phantastica* and *paraphrenia confabulatoria*. The confabulatory group are those who falsify the whole of their past life in the sense of their delusions. They remember having lived in an aristocratic family as small children, being kidnapped and adopted, being married to a prince or princess, being deprived of their rights. This is but an extreme form of what may be seen elsewhere in much slighter degree. Many paranoid patients have a vague recollection, often dream-like in quality, of some single incident which fits in with their delusions, but which never occurred. Even normal individuals can have a similar feeling about the past, in this much slighter form.

There is a third group of paranoid schizophrenics who keep an almost impassable *gulf between the real and the delusional world*. They live a well-adjusted routine life, in hospital or outside, even earning their living as labourer or artisan or minor official. Nothing in their behaviour betrays their abnormality. They converse rationally about any topic, and may show natural emotional reactions, though restricted in intensity and warmth. A stranger may talk to them for hours without seeing anything unusual. Only if some special point is mentioned, the flow of delusions breaks out, as if a sluice-gate had opened. An entirely new person seems to be speaking. The force of feeling now revealed shows how attenuated the emotional expression had been before the paranoid ideas were touched on. The submerged hostility and resentment against his persecutors becomes manifest, as well as grandiose feelings of superiority, often expressed in a stilted language with neologisms and stereotyped phrases. In the course of years, these repressed affects lose their strength and may disappear. Later, even the relative coherence of utterance may go. It is doubtful whether the ever more stereotyped phrases in the end mean very much to the patient himself; but they can still be evoked by the right catchword.

This capacity of the patient to *split off a delusional complex* from the rest of the personality, which remains relatively well preserved, has served as a *model for treatment*. By strengthening all normal bonds between the patient and the outside world, encouraging all expressions of the preserved part of the personality, providing useful occupation and social contacts, one tries to counteract the influence of morbid ideas (see p. 326). The success attained may be considerable. If one meets in the outside world a paranoid patient who has reached a social remission through this healing process, one is often able to do no more than suspect the existence of a repressed delusional complex, perhaps from oblique references or from an unwillingness to discuss certain subjects. In support of one's suspicions there may be found some degree of aloofness from the pressing problems of existence, or a lack of empathy, or minor oddities of behaviour.

It was earlier mentioned that the over-sensitive and suspicious type of schizoid personality is sometimes attacked by a paranoid psychosis. It is equally important that a *personality change* in this direction can be the *sequela of an acute schizophrenic attack*, even in those without pre-psychotic paranoid traits. The two conditions can be so similar that they are very difficult to distinguish; and this has been the basis for the theory that markedly schizoid individuals have undergone a larval form of schizophrenia.

PARAPHRENIA and PARANOIA. When Kraepelin separated a group of cases under the name of paraphrenia (1920), because in these cases owing to the 'far slighter development of the disorders of emotion and volition the inner harmony of the psychic life is considerably less involved', Bumke announced the break-up of dementia praecox. However, follow-up studies by one of Kraepelin's co-workers (Mayer, 1921) revealed that more than half of 78 patients diagnosed as paraphrenic by Kraepelin himself developed into typical schizophrenics with other signs of the disease besides the delusions. The concept of *paranoia* appeared to suffer a similar fate. Kraepelin described this disorder as 'the insidious development of a permanent and unshakable delusional system arising from internal causes, which is accompanied by perfect preservation of clear and orderly thinking, willing and acting'. Hallucinations were absent and, although the disease ran a chronic course, deterioration of personality did not occur.

However Kolle (1931) selected 66 different cases which fulfilled Kraepelin's definition of 'paranoia', including 19 diagnosed as such by Kraepelin himself. In a follow-up study he found that in all but four of the cases primary delusions had subsequently developed. Moreover he inferred some genetic association with schizophrenia since the incidence of this disorder in the families of paranoiacs was higher than that in the general population. Following these enquiries, all forms of chronic paranoid psychosis unassociated with physical disease have been regarded by the majority of clinical psychiatrists as belonging to the schizophrenic group of disorders.

But it is doubtful whether refutation of the views originally expressed by Kraepelin about paraphrenia and paranoia was as conclusive as has been generally supposed. By modern standards, the old enquiries leave something to be desired. Neither study was controlled with comparable observations on schizophrenic subjects and it is difficult to evaluate Kolle's finding in the follow-up study (extending from 1 to 44 years) that 24 per cent. of patients with paranoia 'required permanent hospital care'. The degree of deterioration of personality as compared with that found in schizophrenia is not described. Moreover, although emphasis is laid on the genetical relationship with schizophrenia, the incidence of the latter among the relatives of paranoiacs was only half that recorded in the families of schizophrenics, a result comparable with recent findings in 'late paraphrenia'. An increase of this order in the expectation of schizophrenia among relatives has been described in other forms of paranoid illness, some of them almost certainly non-schizophrenic in character (Johanson, 1964). Nor does the view that all paraphrenics show progressive schizophrenic deterioration appear well-supported. In late paraphrenia, for example, the symptomatology is indubitably schizophrenic but detailed follow-up studies (Kay and Roth, 1961) have shown that deterioration of personality does not occur for many years and, when it does do so, is probably due to senile changes in the brain. From a clinical descriptive point of view this disorder therefore belongs with schizophrenia. But in its heredity and pattern of outcome it is not wholly uniform with it. This relative independence is also underlined by the presence of certain aetiological factors. Thus about 40 per cent. of late paraphrenics suffer from deafness and, while many have been life-long recluses, isolation is aggravated in these subjects in old age more often than in control groups owing to accidental factors such as bereavement.

Hence, when the question is raised as to whether a group of disorders belongs or does not belong to some other group, we have, in the present state of our knowledge, to specify what features membership of a clinical category entails, that is whether clinical, genetical, aetiological, prognostic or all of these criteria should show uniformity. These points are of more than academic importance. Much confusion may be traced to a failure to appreciate that, although schizophrenia may be regarded as a homogeneous entity from a descriptive and genetical point of view, this does not necessarily imply that it will prove to be uniform with respect to all such other criteria. Progress in enquiry in this field also demands this greater flexibility in approach; in other words, schizophrenic symptomatology should form the starting point of investigations into aetiology without any presuppositions as to whether this is single or multiple.

As far as chronic mainly endogenous paranoid psychoses without hallucinations ('paranoia') are concerned, there are also reasons for doubting whether the disorder pursues an undoubtedly schizophrenic course as often as Kolle claimed. Delusions of persecution or delusional convictions of jealousy or grandeur or of some disfigurement that is quite widely commented on, or that a smell emanates from the patient, sometimes appear in middle age in the absence of primary affective disturbance, and after trivial or no stress or minor physical illness. They can therefore be broadly regarded as endogenous paranoid psychoses. Yet although the symptoms persist in a high proportion of instances, 'first-rank' schizophrenic symptoms rarely develop and deterioration of personality is infrequent. Indeed, the symptoms not infrequently become encapsulated and the patient may achieve some sort of *modus vivendi* with them.

At the other extreme from the school that regards all chronic paranoid psychoses as schizophrenic is the group of psychiatrists including Gaupp, Kretschmer and E. Bleuler who have held that paranoia and similar disorders are psychogenic. Under the heading of *der sensitive Beziehungswahn* (1918) Kretschmer isolated a group of paranoid psychoses developing on the basis of a sensitive, tender and high-minded self-affirmative personality. With subtle psychological perception he traced the development of the delusional illness as the inescapable outcome of a patient's history and personal experience; his ideas, emotions, imagination and the content of his mental life were disclosed with delicate comprehension. Kretschmer has been criticized for forcing the facts into a Procrustean bed of preconception and of failing to ask himself why the patient's ideas acquired the convincing force of delusions. He may have overinterpreted his observations but he performed a valuable service in demonstrating that some chronic paranoid disorders had a relevant historical and personality background. The criticism of Kretschmer also implies a sharper line of demarcation between 'comprehensible' and 'incomprehensible' or 'true' delusions than can be accepted in the light of recent enquiries (Matussek, 1963). The concept of 'comprehensibility' and the distinction between 'development' and 'process' formulated by Jaspers have been and remain of very great practical and theoretical value in the field of psychiatry. Yet the distinction is not an absolute one (Roth, 1963) and applied in an all-or-none fashion the concepts can become rigid, unhelpful dogmas. Thus, apparently endogenous paranoid states commencing in middle age such as the delusional jealousy syndromes may, on detailed exploration, become partly understandable in the light of the personality background which often reveals marked sensitivity aggravated by inferiority feelings, physical blemishes or handicaps, a history of familial disruption or rejection and insecurity in childhood and life-long tendencies to some degree of enviousness and jealousy. On the other hand, the delusional and near-delusional ideas expressed by patients with 'psychogenic' paranoid reactions are not always wholly 'comprehensible' any more than we can wholly understand all the obsessions and rituals of obsessive-compulsive subjects as a natural extension of their pre-morbid patterns of behaviour.

Some of these points emerge clearly from a study of 52 cases of 'mild paranoia' by Johanson (1964). Six of the patients were diagnosed as schizophrenic but, in the remaining 46, constitutional and psychogenic factors, intoxications such as alcoholism and cerebral damage were combined in varying proportions. Although the symptoms tended to persist in some form over long periods even in the most reactive cases, the change from a simple paranoid to an indubitably schizophrenic picture was rare. The patients were selected from 930 first admissions to the University Department of Psychiatry at Uppsala. Cases with delusions associated with endogenous depression, a depressive content, or with clouding of consciousness were excluded. There were 12 patients with abnormal jealousy and two of these had had operations on the external genitalia. Acute or chronic physical disease or intoxication had made an important contribution to causation which was obvious and immediate in some cases and more remote in others. Three women developed their mental symptoms in connexion with childbirth or pregnancy, 5 patients had poor hearing, 2 defective eyesight and 7 had been born in a foreign country, 3 of them being refugees. Physical and social isolation may have therefore contributed. Twelve patients were under severe environmental stress when their symptoms began and deviation of personality was common. The morbid risk of schizophrenia among the siblings was low though slightly higher than in the general population, a finding which is repeatedly made in these borderland groups as for example in paraphrenia and alcoholic hallucinosis.

It is clear that the relationships of 'paraphrenia' and 'paranoia' and of certain reactive forms of paranoid illness to schizophrenia are complex and cannot be described in terms of all or none statements. The older view that these entities are wholly uniform with schizophrenia is no longer tenable. Thus although it was possible in Johanson's study to differentiate mainly endogenous cases from reactive ones, no sharp line of demarcation could be drawn; the incomprehensible delusions of the former were not sharply distinct from the delusional beliefs of the latter which could often be understood in the light of the life situation. All these groups of cases clearly have some symptomatological similarity to schizophrenic illness. But there is less hereditary loading with schizophrenia in the families. Moreover although the symptoms may persist for long periods, personality deterioration is rare. Exogenous factors such as alcoholism, brain injury and sensory defects, as also psychogenic factors, play some part in causation. It is clear, however, that such aetiological findings in the marginal groups cannot be regarded as wholly irrelevant for schizophrenia itself (McClelland et al., 1968). In short, Kraepelin's concepts of paraphrenia and paranoia may not have been as ill-founded as his contemporary critics believed. There is need for a re-examination of the relationship of all such marginal groups with schizophrenia. The results of comparative clinical, genetical, psychological and follow-up studies should help to define more clearly the boundaries of schizophrenic illness. They might also make some contribution to knowledge of its aetiological basis.

(5) Atypical and Mixed Clinical Pictures

The *neurosis-like pictures* which may be seen in early schizophrenia have already been mentioned. They are especially common in slowly progressing hebephrenia. P. Hoch (1949) was the first to point out the frequency of neurotic symptoms in early schizophrenics, and he tried to establish the existence of a special group of such cases. In certain circles this view has been found acceptable for the wrong reasons: when neurotic reactions failed to respond to psychotherapy an excuse was provided for their re-classification as schizophrenic, on grounds of non-response alone. When schizophrenia begins in an obsessional personality, it may for a long time remain disguised as an apparently obsessional illness, owing to the prominence of pathoplastic effects. In an earlier section (p. 287) we discussed the paranoid reaction which may appear as a prelude to a paranoid psychosis; and other causes of origin of atypical symptoms from pathoplastic factors were covered in the section on Precipitation. Among these we may mention again the delirious pictures shown when schizophrenia starts during an infective illness or after childbirth, and the colouring of the psychosis by psychogenic reactions derived from the special environment of the patient and the psychological situation. As examples of the latter, it is well known that the imprisoned criminal in the initial stages of schizophrenia sometimes shows a picture which closely resembles the hysterical reactions of prison life, until through this pathoplastic screen characteristic psychotic symptoms become manifest. H. W. Maier (1922) described what he called 'insurance hebephrenia', that is a mild schizophrenia initially taking the form of a compensation neurosis, a development which seemed to be favoured by the special conditions relating to insurance in Switzerland. The psychological content would at first be filled by the patient's fight for compensation; only in the course of time did his claims become more and more absurd, his complaints take the form of hypochondriacal delusions, and his arguments become illogical and finally incoherent.

Atypical features, derived from personality or environment, may colour the onset of any mental illness, and are only submerged as the more severe and characteristic symptoms become prominent. They are particularly frequent in schizophrenia, because it so often has an insidious onset and so many of its symptoms are of a psychological nature.

It might be expected that schizophrenia beginning about the *age of puberty*, either before it or after, would take on an unusual appearance. Here we shall only mention some of the commoner atypical features seen when the illness begins in early adolescence; the problem of schizophrenia in childhood will be dealt with in full in Chapter XI, p. 684. Affective abnormalities dominate the clinical picture: apathy, moods of whimpering, sulkiness and obstinacy, but also of 'naughtiness', impudence and rude mischievousness. These are, in short, the typical qualities of the teen-ager who has lost his balance; but in the early schizophrenic they lack the freshness and natural emotional colouring of normal children at this age. What looks like stubbornness may be a semi-stuporose state; and the contradictoriness of the feelings shown to persons in his circle may be a sign of ambivalence of emotional response and the cooling-off of normal sympathy.

The atypical feature of schizophrenia in dullards and *mental defectives* ('*Pfropfschizophrenie*') is the poverty of ideational content. Childish and silly conduct usually prevails, or there may be massive hallucinations of a primitive and monotonous kind, or a stereotyped hypochondriasis. Defective schizophrenics are not always shut in, and are often unaggressive. Their relative accessibility has been pointed out by many workers.

Atypical forms of schizophrenia at the time of the *menopause and involution* have attracted attention for many years; and some observers have even considered that they constituted separate diagnostic entities—'presenile delusional psychosis', 'late catatonia' (Kraepelin, 1909), 'involutional paranoia' (Kleist, 1913). Involutional depressives of a certain rigid type (Medow, 1922) are also probably atypical schizophrenics. A prevalence of paranoid and depressive symptoms is common in all mental illnesses of the higher age groups; and one would, therefore, expect such a colouring in a schizophrenia appearing at this epoch. Such features alone would not justify a separation of the late paranoid psychoses from the main body of schizophrenia; this was suggested much more by certain personality features common in these states, and the relative ease with which the delusional ideas could be related to the psychological situation, out of which they seemed to grow and by which they could be understood. The implications of this problem have been discussed in the preceding section.

What Kraepelin described as 'late catatonia' is more distinctive, a rare psychosis beginning with depression and hypochondriasis and rapidly progressing into stupor and negativism, leading to death. The relation of this condition to schizophrenia is very doubtful; it is perhaps, as Grünthal (1936) suggested, a special form of organic presenile dementia.

Alcoholism may veil the symptoms of schizophrenia. Many schizophrenics with mild symptoms take to drink, perhaps in order to overcome their increasing solitude and their failing contact with the people around them. Among chronic drunkards one finds a sprinkling, not only of early schizophrenics, but also of others, who have undergone some slight deterioration after one or more acute attacks. There is some evidence, recently called into question (Benedetti 1952), that chronic alcoholic psychoses, 'alcoholic hallucinosis' and 'alcoholic paranoia', have a genetical relationship to schizophrenia (see Chapter VII, p. 402).

An admixture of the symptoms of *affective psychoses* may produce a clinical picture of a mixed kind. The frequency of such states in the experience of the single observer depends on the criteria he uses for diagnosis. If the formulation we have proposed is adopted, their number will be found to be small, so that the extent of the literature concerned with the controversy they have aroused seems disproportionate to their practical importance.

If it is accepted, as in this book, that not only blunting of affective response, but also positive anomalies of affect are among the primary symptoms of schizophrenia, it is a matter for no surprise that *attacks of depression or elation* occur in schizophrenia, as well as the more characteristic affective disturbances, those of unmotivated rage, desolation, panic, ecstasy, etc. If, then, a patient showing characteristic schizophrenic symptoms also shows an endogenous mood change, either of depression or elation, the diagnosis of schizophrenia is not thereby weakened. To segregate him from other schizophrenics, as having a disorder of an aetiologically distinct kind, can only be a source of confusion, and leave one without the foundation of treatment or prognosis. No observer has been able to show that, over a prolonged follow-up study, the outcome of these states differs from that of the generality of schizophrenia. Again, the sufferer from schizophrenia is not deprived at once and completely of the power of normal emotional reaction; he is likely to suffer, and in suffering to become depressed. A depressive reaction is common in early schizophrenia, and contributes to the neurotic-like picture it may sometimes take. If, however, characteristic features of schizophrenia are also present, they are of very much greater diagnostic significance. In every such case, it will be found of help to examine carefully the *quality of the emotional change*.

When depression or elation are present, they rarely dominate the picture for any length of time. Judged by the general situation, they are often incongruous, and their expression often inadequate and stiff. The relationship between affect and motor behaviour holds in schizophrenia as elsewhere. In hyperkinetic phases a cheerful or elated mood is common, in an akinetic or semi-stuporose phase a mood of depression or distress. Nevertheless, the opposite may be observed, and then strongly suggests a schizophrenic aetiology. In nearly all schizophrenics these affective admixtures lack the natural and infective quality of the mood change in the manic-depressive group. The subjectivity of such a criterion is obvious, and is partly the reason why it is rejected by some psychiatrists. Those who do so are usually more interested in the patient's emotional response than in his other symptoms, or consider it of greater importance, or are concerned to relate every clinical finding to the patient's past experience, or, even, regard a diagnosis of schizophrenia as a counsel of psychotherapeutic despair. According to their views, they will diagnose the case as one of a 'schizo-affective psychosis', or as a 'mixed' or 'atypical' condition falling between and distinct from both types of psychosis.

The atypical group is further increased by those who consider any admixture of catatonic features as so important that they hesitate to diagnose manic-depressive disorder when they are present, especially in young patients (see Chapter IV, p. 221).

A third source of difficulty in distinction between schizophrenic and affective psychoses and for the creation of an intermediate class, is the existence of *periodic schizophrenic disorders*. Periodicity is, of course, a symptom most commonly shown by affective disorders; but, as will appear in the section on 'Course and Prognosis', about one-third of schizophrenics show some periodicity, in having one or more remissions, and sometimes this periodicity can be very marked.

From this discussion it will be clear that in clinical practice the frequency of 'atypical' and 'mixed' psychoses will vary with the criteria of diagnosis which are used. No system of diagnosis can be regarded as satisfactory which relegates a large proportion of all cases seen to a category of this kind, a group of cases united only by their exclusion from other groupings, and without aetiological, psychopathological or prognostic implications. One way of avoiding such a confession of failure has been taken by such workers as Kleist (1921) and Schroeder (1922). All those cases which fitted, in their opinion, neither into a schizophrenic nor into an affective classification they took together under the heading of '*degeneration psychoses*', a term from the French psychiatry of Magnan, but adopted by German psychiatrists to cover a number of infrequent but distinctive syndromes. From this point Kleist was led to differentiate still more narrowly and to break up the degeneration psychoses into small sub-groups based on single symptoms. It is not clear that any real advance has been made this way.

It seems to the authors a more promising approach to include 'atypical' or 'mixed' states into one or the other of the two main diagnoses; the number of cases which have to be excluded, if any due allowance is made for the variability of the clinical picture in schizophrenic and affective psychoses, is a small one. It cannot however be doubted that some patients still fall into this class. Thus Leonhard (1935) has shown that rare families are to be found, in which an atypical psychosis runs true to form through several members; and in such cases we may very likely be dealing with a heredo-familial disorder *sui generis*.

Rather more frequently, actual *combinations of manic-depressive and schizophrenic disorders* can be traced to a combination, in the patient, of schizophrenic and affective genetical factors coming from different sides of the family (Smith, 1925; Tuczek, 1933).

If account is taken of these, we are left with only one small group of atypical psychoses, *schizophrenic psychoses with clouding of consciousness*. Clearness of consciousness has been described as the characteristic background of all schizophrenic symptoms. Some of the rare exceptions to this general rule have already been mentioned: the peculiar dream-like state of early hebephrenics and catatonics, the catatonic stupors which seem to have passed in a mental vacuum, and leave no recollection behind, the acute catatonia which begins with a subacute delirious picture, even in the absence of any toxic or infective bodily illness. Such cases have puzzled many observers, and have been quoted in support of a theory which ranged schizophrenia with the symptomatic psychoses (Bumke). Finally there are states with multiple scenic hallucinations, in which the patient loses all contact with his real surroundings and acts like a dreamer ('oneiroid states'). They may last for weeks or months. They bear some resemblance to epileptic twilight states; and their fantastic content resembles that of the acute paranoid schizophrenia, but includes elements of a semi-realistic melodramatic kind, such as catastrophes, dangerous adventures, glimpses of heaven and hell. Psychoses of the oneiroid type have been found in more than one member of the same family, and there are also indications that they may be determined by a confluence of schizophrenic and affective genetical factors (Mayer-Gross, 1924). Meduna and McCulloch (1945) suggested that they should be considered together under the name of 'oneirophrenia' and supported this by reporting biochemical findings which have, however, not been confirmed by other observers.

SYMPTOMATIC SCHIZOPHRENIA

Until recently the very concept of symptomatic schizophrenia has been much disputed and is far from universally accepted. Many authors maintained that, though psychoses resembling schizophrenia could be observed in the presence of some specific pathogenic process such as cerebral syphilis, yet the experienced clinician would always be able to distinguish them; such psychoses were, in fact, to be regarded as merely offering a temporary illusion of schizophrenia, and their importance was practical, as a source of diagnostic error, rather than theoretical, as an indication of the pathological, physiological and psychological processes which were common to both schizophrenia-like psychoses and nuclear schizophrenias. The contrary view was maintained by others, who also considered that the large undifferentiable group of schizophrenic psychoses would ultimately be found to break down into aetiologically distinct syndromes. Needless to say there is also a school of thought which regards schizophrenia as a very vague region of the nosological map, a variety of modes of reaction with little in the way of common characteristics and but ill-defined distinctions from normality, affective psychoses and neurotic reactions. In recent years, however, there is accumulating evidence that some disturbances of central nervous mechanisms may result, at least for a time, in clinical pictures which are completely indistinguishable from schizophrenic psychoses; and moreover, that the schizophrenic appearances are not to be accounted for by any latent specifically schizophrenic predisposition.

AMPHETAMINE PSYCHOSES. Perhaps the best-established of the schizophrenia-like psychoses of known pathology are the psychotic states accompanying amphetamine intoxication, first described in some detail by Connell (1958) and recently discussed by Bell

(1965). The illness usually takes the form of an acute hallucinosis, perhaps with a delirious tinge showing in some impairment of contact with the environment, and may arise after the taking of a single large dose of amphetamine. The state of consciousness may be completely lucid; and, if the visual hallucinations and illusions which are usually prominent do not appear, the resemblance to a typical schizophrenic psychosis may be extremely close. One sees the prolific development of primary delusional experiences, extreme emotional reactions to them in which fear and suspicion are prominent, and secondary systematization and elaboration developing if the state continues for any time.

Resemblance to a schizophrenic illness is even closer in the psychoses which arise on the basis of chronic intoxication. The patient becomes depressed, tense and anxious, and begins to feel that something strange is going on. It is then gradually borne in on him that he is under the supervision of a gang, or that strangers on the street are talking about his past sexual life, or that he has been given a special mission. Auditory hallucinations especially of a persecutory kind, hearing one's thoughts spoken aloud, feeling one's thoughts interfered with and other passivity feelings are typical. While the psychosis lasts, it may be entirely indistinguishable from a schizophrenic one, although in the majority of cases there are exogenous features. Visual illusions and hallucinations, for instance, are common and may intrude at any stage. The subjective experience is nearly always felt to have a dream-like quality, so that the closest resemblance is to the 'oneirophrenic' group of schizophrenic states to which Meduna has drawn attention; a demonstrable degree of confusion or some impairment of memory for recent events may be found; although it is rarely severe or sustained, and the affective reaction is brisk and adequate.

Differential diagnosis is easy, by testing the urine for presence of amphetamine metabolites, once a suspicion of the nature of the illness has been aroused. In acute observation centres such urinary tests could well be done as a routine. Other qualities which distinguish the individuals who suffer from amphetamine psychoses from the generality of schizophrenics, are a history of psychopathically deviant behaviour in the past, rapid onset, and rapid recovery once the drug is withdrawn.

A fairly close parallel to chronic amphetamine psychosis is offered by the paraphrenic-like states and the chronic hallucinosis of alcoholic addiction. Although the clinical picture in alcoholic hallucinosis is dominated in a characteristic manner by the auditory hallucinations, the resemblance to schizophrenia is at times close. It is noteworthy that Connell found no evidence of an increased incidence of schizophrenia in the families of his amphetamine addicts; and that Benedetti (1952) found a low genetic loading for schizophrenia in the families of hallucinating alcoholics.

GROSS BRAIN LESIONS. Schizophrenic symptoms, and even schizophrenic-like syndromes have been repeatedly observed in connexion with gross brain lesions. Some of the aural phenomena observed in temporal lobe lesions seem to be psychopathologically indistinguishable from schizophrenic experiences. At one time, when general paresis was a common mental disease, clinicians recognized a mode of onset closely resembling an acute paranoid schizophrenia; usually the schizophrenic symptoms passed off rapidly under the influence of treatment, and later sequelae resembled those of an organic personality change rather than those of a post-schizophrenic state. Catatonic symptoms were also not infrequently noted with this disease. Schizophrenic symptomatology has also been reported many times in association with brain tumour.

Schizophrenia-like psychoses in the later history of patients suffering from severe traumatic lesions of the brain have drawn much attention. Although in many of these cases there was a history of post-traumatic epilepsy preceding the onset of the psychosis (and a schizophrenia-like psychosis seems to be particularly associated with temporal lobe epilepsy, see Chapter VIII p. 470), there are no noteworthy clinical differences between the psychotic pictures shown by the head-injured patients with and without epileptic attacks. Feuchtwanger and Mayer-Gross (1938) made a classic study of schizophrenic psychoses in soldiers with severe head injuries, mostly penetrating shrapnel wounds. They concluded that these psychoses were not significantly more frequent in the brain-injured than in the general population. This conclusion was probably not justified statistically. It is of interest that the incidence of schizophrenia among siblings of schizophrenics whose illness followed head injury is intermediate between that found in 'idiopathic' schizophrenics and the general population. Similar findings have been reported in paraphrenia and alcoholic hallucinosis. Hillbom (1960) in 415 cases of brain injury found no fewer than 11 patients with schizophreniform psychoses. Both Feuchtwanger and Mayer-Gross, and Hillbom, found that the predominant type of schizophrenic psychosis was of the paranoid-hallucinatory type. Hillbom comments that when focal psychological symptoms, such as primary delusions and hallucinations, occurred in clear consciousness there was always a lesional cause, usually in the temporal lobe. The literature on the relationship between head injury and schizophrenia was reviewed by Elsässer and Grünewald (1953); however the authors excluded all cases in which the psychosis followed more than 5 years after the head injury. This is unduly restrictive, since it seems probable that longer intervals are the rule. Recent work by Davison (1966) on combinations of schizophrenia with an organic diagnosis observed at the National Hospital, Queen Square, London, showed that such combinations occurred greatly in excess of chance. Diencephalic and brain-stem lesions seemed to have a preferential effect in causing schizophreniform psychoses, more so than hemisphere lesions. Once again the psychological disturbance most commonly took the form of paranoid delusions, and ideas of reference, with auditory hallucination as the next leading symptom. About half the cases showed the cardinal symptoms of schizophrenia, in Langfeldt's system, such as flat or incongruous affect and passivity feelings.

SYSTEM DEGENERATIONS. Of all the system disorders known to be associated with schizophreniform psychoses the best known is Huntington's chorea. Panse (1942) has provided us with an excellent and detailed account of 23 patients in which the original diagnosis was one of schizophrenia, and recognition of the organic pathology came only later, perhaps many years after. Here again the preferred form of psychosis was of the paranoid hallucinatory type, with catatonic states appearing rather rarely. There was no clinical psychiatric approach capable of distinguishing these symptomatic schizophrenias from genuine schizophrenia, according to Panse, though he noted that both the delusions and the hallucinations tended to be of a rather primitive kind, without the richness and complexity of schizophrenic symptomatology. Streletzki (1961) on the basis of Wendt's material of more than 5,000 cases, confirms the occurrence of paranoid psychoses of schizophrenic form in Huntington's chorea, especially in the early stages of the disease. The schizophrenic-like state usually wore off into an organic picture after a couple of years.

AGEING. A special position is occupied by late paraphrenia (Roth, 1955). Kay and Roth (1961) made a study of 99 such cases, and found that on clinical grounds alone the condition could not be distinguished from long-standing schizophrenia. The symptoms were remarkably consistent, rich and florid. 'Patients were "played upon" by means of electricity, radio, torture apparatus, etc.; spied upon constantly through the walls; dynamited through holes bored in the walls; squirted with poisonous fumes or liquid, subjected to noisy, indecent songs or commentaries, hypnotized or had their thoughts read; murdered by bolsheviks; raped every night, etc. Auditory, tactile and olfactory hallucinations were common.'

The condition could be clearly distinguished from senile and arteriosclerotic psychoses, and indeed did not appear to be in any way related to the grosser cerebral changes associated with ageing; expectation of life was normal as compared with the senile and arteriosclerotic cases who survived for only one-quarter of the life span enjoyed by the general population of comparable age. There was a remarkable preponderance of females (87:12). Female schizophrenics have a later age of onset than males (see p. 240) but the difference is hardly enough to account for this shift. The pre-psychotic personalities of these patients showed characteristic anomalies comprising emotional remoteness, coldness, difficulties in the emotional and sexual sphere, often combined with successful adjustment in occupational and intellectual activities. The incidence of schizophrenia in first degree relatives and in nephews and nieces was much greater than would be expected in a sample of the general population, but below the figures usually found in the relatives of schizophrenics: 5 per cent. of the sibs and 7 per cent. of the children of the paraphrenics were diagnosed as schizophrenic. It has been suggested (Kay and Roth, 1961; Roth, 1963; Kay, 1963) that the concept of schizophrenia should be enlarged to include clinically similar conditions however caused; and that, in this sense, late paraphrenia falls within its limits. These authors think that the genetical contribution to aetiology is more likely to be polygenic than dependent on any single specific gene.

'BENIGN' AND 'ATYPICAL' SCHIZOPHRENIA; 'PSYCHOGENIC' SCHIZOPHRENIA. The investigations of Schulz and Leonhard on the genetical background of 'typical' and 'atypical' schizophrenics were mentioned on p. 243. Related to them are the studies of Langfeldt who tried to differentiate two groups in terms of features of the clinical profile and the outcome. In Langfeldt's conception (1937), the most important hallmarks of schizophreniform illness are the presence of a precipitating factor, a relatively acute onset, clouded sensorium, a depressive, hysterical or paranoid colouring, and a symptomatology that is often psychologically understandable. One of the most convincing follow-up studies carried out to validate the concept of schizophreniform psychosis was that conducted by Langfeldt (1959) and Eitinger (1959). Of 110 patients diagnosed as suffering from typical schizophrenia by Langfeldt, only one was found to have recovered and four were much improved; whereas of 44 patients with schizophreniform psychosis, 88 per cent. had an excellent outcome. The follow-up period was 5–15 years. In another study by Welner and Strömgren (1958) on a group of patients suffering from schizophreniform psychoses, such as are commonly diagnosed as psychogenic psychoses by Danish psychiatrists, 72 of the patients could be followed for an average of 8·8 years; none developed into schizophrenics of the classical type. The incidence of schizophrenia in the sibs of these patients (1·3 per cent.) was not significantly higher than what might have been expected of a sample of the general population though the total of non-specific mental abnormalities in the sibships was higher. Welner and Strömgren concluded that these psychoses arose as a product of exogenous factors operating on an unspecific type of mental vulnerability. Clinically less well-sorted material, diagnosed in the Copenhagen Clinic 1924–26 as psychogenic psychoses was followed up by Faergeman (1945) for 15 to 20 years; 43 out of the 160 patients followed up proved in course of time to be suffering from schizophrenic psychoses of the usual kind, mainly in the group with paranoid syndromes.

Although a number of the descriptions of schizophreniform types of illness suggest a clinical picture clearly distinct from that of schizophrenia proper, evidence from detailed comparative studies does not confirm that very clear lines of demarcation exist. In a study already quoted (McClelland et al., 1968) an expanded material of 195 patients selected by the presence of the same six symptoms were given a formal clinical diagnosis after inclusion in the study (see p. 259); 132 were placed in a 'nuclear' group (the central 'idiopathic' variety based on the symptom syndromes of Kraepelin and Bleuler) and 63 in a 'non-nuclear' group, including those with cerebral damage, intoxication, patients who had an acute onset with clouding of consciousness not due to known organic causes, and those who showed delusional jealousy, isolated atypical hallucinoses, and psychoses with some schizophrenic symptoms in neurotic personalities. A multiple regression analysis of the two groups using 117 items relating to symptoms, personality and biographical data revealed that items connected with pre-morbid personality (e.g. lack of heterosexual interest and failure to marry) and chronicity of illness correlated most highly with the nuclear group and neurotic features and physical illness had the highest correlations with the non-nuclear group. Individual psychiatric symptoms of the current illness failed to separate the two groups. It would seem likely that classification into the 'schizophreniform' group may be decided to a considerable extent by biographical and pre-morbid personality findings of a favourable kind rather than by the features of the presenting illness. Results of this nature would also seem to indicate that the present system of classification, whereby various groups are wholly excluded from the concept of schizophrenia for reasons often not related to their symptoms, may limit the fruitfulness of research into this disorder.

The suggestion that schizophrenic or indistinguishably schizophrenia-like psychoses can be brought about by psychogenic causes has been supported strongly by M. Bleuler and the Zurich school (Ernst, 1956; Rohr, 1961). However, the best documented study has come from Basle where Staehelin's concept of the schizophrenia-like emotion-psychosis is in use; this is defined as a psychotic reaction to affective causes, characterized by schizophrenic symptomatology, rapid course and ready response to treatment. Labhardt (1963) has given a full account of 61 cases so diagnosed at Basle 1938–58. Eight of these cases proved on later investigation to be schizophrenic in the usual sense, but in the remainder a fairly consistent picture emerged.

The onset was acute and closely related in time with a major psychic trauma, perhaps after a prodromal stage of mounting difficulties and tensions. The picture was dominated by anxiety, auditory hallucinations and delusional ideas, the latter being of an overwhelmingly affect-laden kind, e.g. of impending death or world cataclysm. More specifically schizophrenic symptoms shown by a majority of patients included catatonic symptoms and formal thought disorder. Nevertheless there were differences from the usual schizophrenic picture. According to Labhardt the 'schizophrenic atmosphere' was totally lacking. Affect was invariably well preserved, and the patients not only made good affective rapport with the doctor, but usually became emotionally dependent on him very quickly. The picture had a dream-like or nearly delirious quality, though clarity of consciousness was well preserved in most patients at all stages; 14 out of the 53 patients showed some clouding at some stage.

The course of this illness was remarkable for its brevity, and the psychotic state cleared up within two weeks in 60 per cent. of cases; in less than 10 per cent. did psychotic symptoms continue after the fourth week. Response to treatment by tranquillizers combined with modified insulin treatment and with psychotherapy was most satisfactory. Relapse in later years into a psychogenic illness not necessarily schizophreniform in appearance was not infrequent.

Despite their clinical similarities, a genetical relationship between these 'emotion-psychoses' and schizophrenia does not seem to be probable. The family histories of Labhardt's patients showed no excess of schizophrenic loading; and the pre-morbid personalities of the patients were never schizoid but were either normal or neurotic in quality, anxious-sensitive, and over-conscientious personalities being the commonest deviation; hysterical traits of personality were rare, and in general Labhardt rejects the view that these psychoses are to be equated with hysterical reactions. The pathogenetic mechanisms, he believes, go much deeper. The stress required to produce these states is extreme, and 'existential', i.e. of a type to threaten the continued existence of the personality. These stresses operate significantly frequently on a basis of impaired physical health, e.g. after infections, surgical operations etc.; and before the onset of psychotic symptoms there had usually supervened a state of emotional exhaustion, possibly involving nutritional or electrolyte disturbance. Both Staehelin and Labhardt envisage the probability of disturbance of diencephalic and mesencephalic functions as playing a role.

This disorder almost certainly has some affinity with the acute short-lived psychotic reactions that follow calamitous stresses in vulnerable and neurotic subjects which have also been described in association with battle-stress and major disasters such as floods and earthquakes. In this condition also later stages of the illness have features of a more clearly psychogenic form. In the course of neurotic disorders and of severe phobic, anxiety and obsessional states in particular, stress of a life-threatening or onerous kind will at times be followed by an acute psychotic illness usually dominated by paranoid symptoms. Clouding of consciousness may or may not be present but an acute schizophrenic illness may be simulated. However, the diagnosis of 'nuclear' schizophrenia should be made with reserve in psychoses complicating an established neurotic disorder; these psychoses are usually transient and benign (Roth, 1963).

GENERAL CONSIDERATIONS. When we review the whole field, we must concede that psychotic pictures, clinically indistinguishable from acute paranoid schizophrenic illnesses may arise on a variety of bases, psychosomatic, neurotic, toxic, infective or lesional. Hebephrenic pictures are very rarely reported, and catatonic ones far from frequently. In all the aetiologically different types, the clinician has the impression that the mimicry of the nuclear schizophrenic state is incomplete; most authors remark that affective responsiveness is relatively well-preserved, but this might be an accidental feature caused by the illness impinging at a relatively late age on a well-matured personality, or due to recency of onset. In conditions such as the 'emotion-psychoses' which tend to be self-limiting, the schizophrenic symptomatology passes off into recovery to normality or neurotic disorder; in other conditions, such as the organic states, it passes on into more characteristically organic defects of personality and intellect. Apart from the late paraphrenias, it does not seem that there is anything in common between the genetical predispositions to 'idiopathic' schizophrenia on the one hand, and to symptomatic schizophrenia on the other hand. At the present time there would appear to be a number of important differences between the two forms of mental illness, both in aetiology and in course and evolution, if not unequivocally in symptomatology. These differences seem to be sufficient to persuade one to keep the two concepts distinct, and to try to distinguish them in clinical practice.

The *theoretical importance* of the symptomatic schizophrenias *cannot be belittled*. They offer the suggestion that disturbances affecting the same functional systems in the brain are involved in 'idiopathic' schizophrenia, or 'schizophrenia of unknown origin', as in the symptomatic state. The problem of discovering how it is that such symptoms as primary delusions and passivity feelings are produced by amphetamine intoxication, or by a temporal lobe lesion, is obviously a simpler one than finding out the mechanisms involved to the same end in the nuclear group of schizophrenias. Research into the symptomatic schizophrenias offers us accordingly relatively favourable prospects of advance not only locally but along a broad front.

OUTCOME

Residual States, Deterioration, Death

All authorities are agreed that one can never be certain that the illness has come to a definite standstill. A flare-up of acute symptoms is possible even after the clinical picture has remained stationary for years. Nevertheless the expression *'residual state'* is used for patients in whom characteristic forms of behaviour and ideation have taken root and are kept up, apparently for an indefinite time. The patient, living in an institution or outside, has come to an *arrangement with his illness*, he has adapted himself to the world of his morbid ideas with more or less success, from his own point of view and from that of his environment. Compared with the experiences during the acute psychosis, his positive symptoms, such as delusions or hallucinations, have become colourless, repetitive and formalized. They still have power over him, but nothing is added and nothing new or unexpected happens. Negative symptoms, thought disorder, passivity, catatonic mannerisms and flattening of affect rule the picture, but even they grow habitual with the patient and appear always in the same inveterate pattern in the individual case. There is a robot-like fixity and petrification of attitude and reactions which are not only due to poverty of ideas, but also to a very small choice of modes of behaviour. The patient has lost all flexibility, he has no future and his interest in present and past are narrowed and restricted.

Fixity of attitude, poverty of ideas and *narrowing of interest* are all the more striking in patients whose psychosis started with florid delusional experiences from which some kind of grandiose system originated. A patient who at one time believed himself the ruler of Central Europe, in his later years in hospital spent his time writing stereotyped figures on brown paper without order or system. He continued this all the day long without any regard for what was going on around him. If questioned, he insisted that it was his business to keep the accounts of his realm. At night he handed his papers to the nurse and never asked what happened to them. His only complaint was about the disturbing noises of other patients. It was not possible to talk with him about anything else, even to engage in the usual superficial conversation between doctor and patient; he seemed narrowed down to one attitude, his only remaining contact with the world around him.

Apart from certain general characteristics, residual states show numerous individual variations. Kraepelin distinguished *eight types of* 'Endzustand' according to the prevailing symptoms in the clinical picture: thought disorder mild or severe, with or without restlessness, catatonic features, hallucinations, loss of affective response, complete passivity or increased activity, and several combinations of these symptoms with paranoid features.

Withdrawal and autism can reach an extreme degree if it is not counteracted by regular occupation or other attempts to keep the patient in contact with reality. It would, however, be a mistake to assume that every withdrawn schizophrenic is lost in a world of wish-fulfilling fantasy. Kant (1943) examined 100 deteriorated patients, using Sodium Amytal to gain access to their mental life. He found many completely disorganized, petrified and empty of content.

In some paranoid cases, a certain *mitigation of hostility and resentment* takes place. This has been described as a 'second turning point' in the curve of the schizophrenic's life, the first being the onset of the illness. He becomes more accessible and regains, in a limited way, contact with the world of others. He gives up fighting and although he retains his delusional ideas, they are not taken so seriously. Patients in this stage may be found as tramps on the road, or as beggars and loafers in city streets. The 'second turning point' has been attributed to ageing; but it is doubtful whether this is the full explanation.

Encapsulation of delusional ideas, as described earlier (p. 292) is frequently seen in residual states. Patients vary very much in the degree to which they can maintain their original personality and adapt to a normal life. Whether they live a more or less sheltered life, inside or outside hospital, depends on this. In some cases, one sees a *longitudinal splitting*, as it were, in the current of life; both the reality-adapted and the delusional world go on alongside each other. On certain occasions, e.g. when meeting certain relations, or a return to certain localities, or during an interview with the doctor who treated the patient early in his illness, the delusional complex comes to the surface and florid symptoms reappear. The chronic schizophrenic is at the mercy of the psychological situation in which he finds himself, a quality which can be used to his advantage therapeutically.

In the pre-Kraepelinian era '*secondary dementia*' was considered the outcome of most psychoses now diagnosed as schizophrenia. Kraepelin spoke of different types of dementia, but himself pointed out that the deficiency was more in the field of emotion and volition, less in that of judgement or memory. In Bleuler's view the disturbance of intelligence could not be adequately described as stupidity or dementia. 'One has to keep in mind that, even in severe schizophrenia, all basic functions are preserved potentially. The schizophrenic is not plainly demented, but he is demented in relation to certain times, certain constellations and certain complexes. The disturbances in question can change from one moment to the next.' And it was the disturbance in affect, spontaneity and interest, rather than in intelligence, that was decisive. Berze's opinion comes closest to that prevalent at present when he calls the condition a defect in actualizing mental abilities.

The question whether *schizophrenic deterioration* leads to dementia can only be answered after defining this concept. If dementia is used, as it is in this book, as meaning impairment of intelligence, in contrast to impairment of personality, schizophrenia does not lead to dementia. Dementia of this kind is produced in organic brain diseases, mainly those of known pathology. These diseases interfere with the inborn intellectual abilities of the patient ('formal intelligence') as well as with his acquired knowledge. The same holds true in mental deficiency in which impairment of intelligence may be the only symptom.

In this sense the schizophrenic is not demented. Potentially his formal intelligence is preserved and so is his knowledge. Many apparently stupid chronic schizophrenics have surprised observers by occasional striking remarks showing that they not only grasped all circumstances of the situation, but judged it correctly and to the point. Even in the talk and writing of grossly incoherent hebephrenics the basic elements of their former intelligence are sometimes still manifest. It is, therefore, justifiable to regard the apparent dementia as the outcome of the *deterioration of the patient's personality*. In other words, the advanced schizophrenic cannot make adequate use of his intelligence because of his thought disorder and volitional, catatonic and delusional disturbances, and for these reasons alone. His intelligence may seem to have shrunk through lack of use, but this is a mere appearance caused by the fact that his mental activities have been narrowed down and have become fixed and rigid.

This statement is certainly adequate for the great majority of chronic schizophrenics. We cannot however say that it is sufficient for all. Some, who are often compared with burned-out ruins, come very close to the picture of organic dementia. Nevertheless, even in these patients, there may be more preserved than one can see. Buried abilities, and the capacity for a much more normal affective response, may be suddenly shown after years of stationary and apparently final deterioration, as for instance during an intercurrent infection. Observations of this kind are well known to physicians in mental hospitals.

Comprehensive *application of test batteries* as in the work of D. Shakow (1946) and other American psychologists has so far contributed little to the problem of schizophrenic deterioration. His findings, such as that the deterioration is selective, that 'conceptual organization' and voluntary behaviour are impaired or that the schizophrenic's reactions are personal, superficial and restricted in energy, confirm clinical observations.

Of some importance for the problem of deterioration in schizophrenia is the enquiry into pre-illness intelligence quotient conducted by Mason (1956). He was able to study 510 service men who broke down with some form of functional psychiatric disorder and who had been given the American Army General Classification Test on being accepted for service. A comparison with a group of normal controls showed that the schizophrenic group had been below average in intelligence before illness, whereas the manic depressives were above average. There is evidence from this and other enquiries that paranoid schizophrenics have the highest, and hebephrenic schizophrenics the lowest, mean intelligence quotient when this is recorded at the onset of illness. As the schizophrenic process develops there is a measurable intellectual deterioration, which is proportionate to the duration of the illness; this deterioration is most marked in the latter and least marked in the former type of schizophrenic illness (Trapp and James, 1937).

The illness itself is not lethal though it frequently leads to *suicide*. Among 716 admissions to a university clinic suicidal tendencies were present in almost 20 per cent. Many mysterious suicides in adolescence are due to an early schizophrenic attack. Sudden death in acute catatonia (see p. 285) has drawn the attention of workers hoping to find lesions indicating an underlying metabolic dysfunction (Stauder, Scheid). Critical examination of the post-mortem findings in such cases demonstrated as the immediate cause of death a concurrent somatic illness which could not be clinically diagnosed because of the patient's abnormal behaviour (R. Locher, 1941).

Many chronic schizophrenics died of *tuberculosis* at the time when conditions in mental hospitals favoured infection. The frequency of pulmonary tuberculosis which, according to Kraepelin, was four to five times that of the general population has decreased with more hygienic conditions; but it was still twice to three times that of non-schizophrenic patients living in the same hospital, as shown by Alström *et al.* (1943). The same authors found tuberculosis more frequent in catatonics than in other types and correlated it with a loss of weight which was due to the mental state, not to the infection.

Judged by their physique many schizophrenics look much younger than their years, especially if they live a sheltered life in hospital. Nevertheless, on the average they die comparatively early, from tuberculosis or some other intercurrent illness. From a relatively small sample of schizophrenics living inside and outside hospital, Sjögren (1948) has calculated that the average expectation of life for a schizophrenic is approximately three-fourths of the same figure for members of the general population of the district.

COURSE AND PROGNOSIS

For some authors schizophrenia implies, even by definition, a bad prognosis. In this book we have adopted a wider formulation, which is primarily symptomatic. All conditions which conform to the clinical picture we have described are covered by the definition, except those with a known gross pathology. It is therefore difficult to generalize about the course and prognosis, although it remains true that every condition grouped under the term schizophrenia is associated with a general *tendency towards disintegration of the personality*. An illness that may start at any time from puberty to late middle age, usually lasting for months, often for years, must necessarily show great variety in course. In this respect it does not differ from familial neurological diseases. E. Bleuler considered that its course was too irregular and variegated to allow the description of typical and atypical varieties; but he too accepted a tendency towards deterioration as a characteristic of schizophrenia. This tendency is, in our view, not diagnostically decisive, as some have maintained. Kleist (1943) and Langfeldt (1937), for instance, went so far as to say that the diagnosis must be revised if, after ten years or more, the patient was found to have recovered. From our point of view, the tendency towards an unfavourable outcome is a general attribute of the condition, or group of conditions, which we call schizophrenia, and is a partial justification of the use of a single term to cover such a wide variety of cases. The many exceptions to the general rule build no coherent picture which would suggest their segregation under another diagnostic heading.

The many studies of large series of patients which have by now been published give one some idea of the *average course and of the factors which influence it*. Unless he is treated by modern physical methods, the schizophrenic may either get steadily worse until, within a few years, he has suffered such deterioration that he will never be able to leave hospital; or the disease process may come to a standstill, leaving a personality defect of any degree from slight, and even sub-clinical, to grave. The defect is often not so severe as to bar the patient from life in the community, but as a rule reduces his ability to work and to enjoy a full life. The scarring of personality may remain stationary; or itself progress very slowly, showing that the disease process was never entirely halted; or a second attack of illness after few or many years may enforce readmission to hospital, perhaps this time for good. The illness may run in exacerbations and remissions from the beginning. The majority of catatonics take this course. Such fluctuations may continue throughout life, but this is rare. As a rule even if the patient recovers from his first and second attack, with the third his prospect of recovery becomes very small. The duration of attacks varies from several weeks to several years. Remissions may last a long time; if a remission has lasted for three years, the patient is probably safe for seven.

It is instructive to realize the difficulties, uncertainties and fallacies of the *follow-up studies* on which these general data are based. In discussing them, some light may be thrown on the problem of prognosis in an illness which is only recognized by psychological symptoms. And the student will become cautious in applying general findings to the single case.

Sources of error in follow-up studies may be objective and subjective. One is the nature of the material on which the study is based: a worker who takes his material from a hospital where more advanced cases are treated will arrive at a different estimate of prognosis from that reached by one who works in a clinic or observation ward. The willingness of the public to send their sick relatives into hospital, and the conditions and formalities of admission, must play an important role in the selection of case material. For instance the tables prepared by Danziger (1946) from the U.S. Bureau of Census on the schizophrenic's prospect of discharge from an American State Hospital will hardly be of use in other countries or with other material.

The *length of time covered by a follow-up study* itself involves sources of error; and studies covering not more than fifteen years are more reliable than longer ones. If a longer period is taken the problem of diagnosis arises; some patients may be included and others left out because the classification at the time of admission or discharge did not conform with the standard used at follow-up. Langfeldt (1937) has shown how important it is to rid one's material of doubtful cases. Even at present a very wide concept of schizophrenia is used in Switzerland under the influence of E. Bleuler's teaching. The frequency of the periodic course, reported in the study of M. Bleuler (1941*b*), may be due to the fact that he included among his schizophrenics some patients who elsewhere would probably have been diagnosed as having an affective psychosis.

The collection of *complete schizophrenic life histories* is a task of doubtful value for another reason: social remissions may extend over thirty or forty years, or even longer. We have observed a patient who after a catatonic illness at the age of twenty-two was practically well for forty-five years, founded his own business as a locksmith, married and had children. At sixty-seven he relapsed into a paranoid psychosis with catatonic, but also senile, features. These long remissions are rare, but not so rare that Wyrsch (1941) was not able to collect fifty-seven cases with social recovery lasting over fifteen years, from the material of two mental hospitals. The life of a single observer seems, therefore, hardly long enough to cover the life-expectations of his material.

The question of *degree of recovery* is another source of difficulty. Judged by their subsequent achievements, many schizophrenics are practically cured after their first or second attack. For this reason Kraepelin and others have frequently been blamed for being far too gloomy in judging the outlook. The reproach has some justification; but it must be realized that a recovery, complete for social and practical purposes, may not amount to complete restitution. 'In the single case', says E. Bleuler, 'the judgement that a cure has occurred depends on the psychological skill and, above all, on the time at the disposal of the psychiatrist for observing and examining the patient. Mental health cannot be diagnosed directly; one takes it for granted if one cannot find any symptoms in spite of a careful search. He who has no time for a thorough examination finds many patients recovered whom others would consider as only improved.' Bleuler also stressed the point that restitution of the *status quo* before the acute psychosis cannot be claimed as a complete recovery, if an insidious change had already taken place before the acute outbreak.

The implication of relatively *small defects* for the results of follow-up studies are obvious. A physician, a solicitor, a teacher or a creative artist may fail in their profession or their career owing to minor abnormalities in thinking, feeling or acting, which in an artisan, clerk or labourer are immaterial.

Of late, renewed attention has been given to prognosis because of the need for an accurate assessment of the newer forms of treatment. The following table of the results of such studies must be judged in the light of the remarks in the preceding paragraphs.

Author	Number of patients	Percentage of total remissions	Length of time covered
Cheney and Drewry (1938)	500	12	2–12 years
Kant (1941)	308	6·6	7½–10 years
Malamud and Render (1939)	177	14	5 years or more
Guttmann, Mayer-Gross and Slater (1939)	188	21·5	3 years
Rennie (1939)	500	24·5	9–20 years
Rupp and Fletcher (1940)	608	6·6	5–10 years
Silverman (1941)	271	10	15 years
Tangermann (1942)	418	18·2	5 years or more
Kelly and Sargant (1965)	84	31	2 years
Vaillant (1964)	103	40	18 months
Fröshaug and Ytrehus (1963)	74	31	2–8 years
Holmboe and Astrup (1957)	225	39	6–18 years

The figures call for a certain amount of comment. The results recorded in recent years appear at first sight to show a marked improvement on those registered 20-30 years ago. However, certain qualifications have to be made. A high proportion of those studied in recent follow-up surveys were on maintenance doses of phenothiazine drugs and it is too early to judge at the present time what proportion will remain permanently viable on this basis in the community. This point is lent some force by the fact that most recent follow-up studies have covered a relatively shorter time interval. However, the time factor did not appear to influence the older results to a marked extent. Thus in an earlier study of Mayer-Gross (1932) comprising 294 patients followed up for 16–17 years, the percentage of social recovery was 35, a figure identical with that found by Guttmann et al. (1939) in their follow-up after only 3 years.

Nevertheless an element of uncertainty attaches to the ultimate fate of remissions dependent upon continued administration of phenothiazines. The result reported by Kelly and Sargant (1965) showing 31 per cent. of schizophrenics to be symptom free and 67 per cent. to be living independently in the community has been criticized as being based upon selected material. However, Wing et al. (1964) have reported essentially similar results in 113 patients treated at three mental hospitals and followed up after a 5 year interval. Sixty-three per cent. of the men were employed, 24 per cent. unemployed but in the community, and 13 per cent. were in hospital. The results for women were slightly better and when the clinical and social outcome were combined 49 per cent. of patients were judged to be well and able to support themselves during the final 6 months of the five-year follow-up period. A further 7 per cent. were working but showing mild or moderate behaviour disturbance, 16 per cent. were unemployed but not severely disturbed, 17 per cent. were severely disturbed at some time during the final 6 months and 11 per cent. were in hospital during the whole of this period. These results are broadly comparable also with those of Vaillant, who found 36 per cent. to be social invalids and 13 per cent. back in hospital. His 40 per cent. of symptom-free patients was made up of 25 per cent. who were in full remission and 15 per cent. of patients who had no overt schizophrenic symptoms. Not all recent observers have reported favourable results. Johanson (1958) followed up, after a mean period of 14·1 years, 138 strictly defined cases of schizophrenia admitted between 1938 and 1942. Sixteen had died and 2 refused re-examination. Of the remaining 120 cases only one was considered to have made a complete recovery and in 8 further cases the prognosis was considered to be favourable. The majority of the patients had received varying combinations of convulsive therapy, insulin coma and prefrontal leucotomy. Further recent figures appear partly to reflect no more than liberal discharge policies; the findings by Wing et al. (1964) that 34 per cent. of 113 male patients were still actively deluded at the time of discharge and that 43 per cent. of the total had had to be re-admitted during the follow-up period of one year are a salutary warning. In a more recent one-year follow-up (Chester et al., 1969) of 196 patients of both sexes only 21 per cent. had remained completely well; 35 per cent. were in relapse or partial remission, 38 per cent. had been re-admitted during the year, and 6 per cent. undischarged or untraced (see also p. 339).

The prospects of a lasting *spontaneous remission* are greatest during the first two years of illness; after five years of continuous illness they become negligible. If a series of patients whose illnesses have lasted a year are followed up, about half are found eventually to remit; if the illness lasts two years, the proportion is still about 45 per cent. Thereafter it quickly declines. The number of remissions in the single patient in a series of relatively severe cases is reported by Lange (1922) as follows:

Number of remissions	1	2	3	4	5	6	7	8	10	more than 10
Number of patients	34	14	11	4	3	3	1	2	1	1

The evidence suggests that each succeeding attack of illness is more likely to leave permanent damage, and that after the third relapse the chance of a remission becomes small. Even if the course continues to fluctuate, periods of excitement alternating with periods of relatively quiet behaviour, the intervals are either too short or the improvement not significant enough to allow discharge from hospital.

Before considering the factors influencing the prognosis of the first attack, Manfred Bleuler's (1941a) investigation of 500 patients, observed *over the lapse of fifteen years*, must be mentioned. It gives in many respects a fuller picture of the course of schizophrenia than was available till then; and it relates the form of onset and course to the outcome. All but 5 per cent. of his patients belonged to one of the following types:

1. Acute onset leading to 'dementia', 5–15 per cent.
2. Insidious onset leading to 'dementia', 10–20 per cent.
3. Acute onset, arrest of illness and resultant defect, less than 5 per cent.
4. Insidious onset, arrest of illness and resultant defect, 5–10 per cent.
5. Periodic course leading to 'dementia', 5 per cent.
6. Periodic course leading to defect, 30–40 per cent.
7. Periodic course leading to recovery, 25–35 per cent.

These figures are the limits found in different localities and under varied conditions in Switzerland and the U.S.A., but include *hospitalized cases only*. Roughly speaking, one-quarter of his cases ended in 'dementia', a second quarter in marked personality deterioration, a third in mild defect and the fourth quarter recovered.

In this material most cases with an insidious onset deteriorated and recovery was exceptional; but only a quarter of the patients with an acute onset were severely deteriorated after fifteen years, and a quarter had recovered.

The results of this work tally in many points with the findings of other workers except for the inclusion of a *large number of periodic schizophrenics* with a relatively good prognosis. Possible reasons for this difference have been mentioned before.

Only follow-up studies conducted over a longer period than have been reported at the present time can tell whether the adjunct of psychotropic drugs and modern techniques of rehabilitation have produced any marked effect on the long-term pattern of schizophrenic illness.

Pointers of Prognostic Significance

These are rather difficult to adjudge as views differ on what constitutes a good and what a bad outcome. To take, for instance, the matter of *age*: the patient who falls ill before the age of fifteen, but also the immature youth up to the age of twenty, has a poor outlook, and frequently suffers rapid deterioration. After the age of twenty, the effect of increasing years is ambiguous. As the age of onset increases, the chance of remission slightly declines, but tendencies towards rapid deterioration are gradually replaced by tendencies towards chronicity with relatively good preservation of the personality. From the age of thirty-five on until the late involutional period the illness, even if chronic in course, generally leaves the personality intact. We know of no sure differences between the *sexes*, in the frequency of either deterioration or chronicity, but there is some suggestion that the female is more likely to remit (Rennie, 1939; Guttmann *et al.*, 1939). The same point arises in connexion with *type of onset*. An acute onset has long been known as a favourable prognostic sign, because of its association with remission; and Rennie found such an onset in seventy-one of 100 recovered schizophrenics. However, if he does not remit, the acute schizophrenic is likely to deteriorate rapidly; while the patient whose onset is insidious may have a smaller chance of recovery but a greater one of maintaining a relatively intact personality despite years of illness. A positive correlation between prognostic result and a supposedly significant clinical feature may disappear when other factors are taken into account. Polonio and Slater (1954) calculated the partial correlation coefficients between good result of treatment on the one hand, and five clinical features on the other: short duration, sudden onset, good personality, pyknic habitus and presence of a precipitating factor. The material was made up of nearly 500 schizophrenics, insulin-treated and controls, followed up for 5 to 10 years. It was found that the positive correlation between result and sudden onset and pyknic habitus became negligible when the other correlations were partialled out. Giving two points for short duration, and one each for good personality and present precipitation, produced a score which discriminated successfully between groups of patients with a score of 4 and 84 per cent. of good results down to those with a zero score and 13 per cent. of good results.

A well-integrated *pre-psychotic personality*, adjusted in the social, sexual and occupational sphere, has, as one would expect, a relatively good chance of return to normality after a psychotic breakdown; but sometimes he will be found to deteriorate rapidly, while the schizoid personality, with less margin of adaptation, takes a less fulminating course. Even on this point opinions are conflicting; e.g. Rennie found that 66 per cent. of his recovered schizophrenics had been of a schizoid type before their illness. Others have found that outgoing and cyclothymic personalities predominated among the recovered cases, and regard a schizoid make-up as of poor prognostic significance. The generally accepted rule that the outbreak of a psychosis in a schizoid personality is likely to lead to rapid deterioration and chronicity still holds true, though Manfred Bleuler's studies have shown that there are exceptions.

Bleuler found an interesting relation between outcome and *intelligence*. Among his recovered cases were more of above-average intelligence than could be expected by chance distribution, while among the severely deteriorated the opposite was true. Among the patients whose deterioration was uninterrupted there were a greater number of intellectually poorly equipped persons than among those with a periodic course. If, however, Bleuler's periodic patients included any considerable proportion of persons with a recurrent affective psychosis, their relative intellectual superiority would only be expected.

Precipitating factors, psychological and physical, if found to have played a part, seem to some extent to favour a better prognosis. Kant (1940; 1941 *a,b*) has studied the influence of psychological conflicts and mental strain and found them significantly more frequent in the history of recovered patients than with others, although in only a few cases these precipitating factors were of an objectively extraordinary nature. Patients whose illnesses were psychologically precipitated were found by Polonio (1957) to have a better prognosis than his control group (58 per cent. against 40 per cent.).

If a schizophrenic attack is precipitated by *bodily illness* remission is more likely, although about half of the post-puerperal schizophrenics have no tendency to spontaneous recovery. Thirty-five per cent. of Rennie's recovered patients had initial somatic disturbance as opposed to 22 per cent. in an undifferentiated group of cases.

Study of the patient's *heredity* helps in prediction because there is a considerable family likeness between schizophrenics of the same stock. It is, however, doubtful whether genetic loading itself has any bearing on prognosis. Rennie, for instance, found that fifty of his 100 recovered cases had a family history of psychosis while in 500 unselected cases the same figure was 40 per cent. only. In the recovered group, however, most of the psychotics among the relations had suffered from affective disorder. This has been confirmed by other workers. The literature has recently been reviewed by Vaillant (1963). Reports showed a positive family history for affective psychosis in about 36 per cent. of recovered patients, but in less than 10 per cent. of unrecovered patients. In short a hereditary taint of affective illness is a favourable prognostic sign.

This is in good agreement with the observation that in *atypical clinical pictures* an admixture of manic or depressive features can be taken as a good augury. The relatively benign nature of psychoses with atypical features has already been discussed in the section on benign and atypical schizophrenia on p. 302. Its corollary is the alleged malignancy of what have been called 'true process symptoms'. There is however, no very satisfactory measure of agreement on what these symptoms are. Some have emphasized the central importance of primary delusions, others the experience of passivity and influence phenomena and others still have regarded autism as the most specific feature. There is at the present time no satisfactory statistical evidence that any one of them, or any combination, has particular prognostic significance.

The prognostic significance of *individual symptoms* is altogether hazy. Kahlbaum's original view, that acute catatonic symptoms tend to be favourable, still holds; approximately one-third of these patients remit. On the other hand, it must be remembered that some of the most malignant as well as some of the more benign psychoses are found in the catatonic group. The retention of the capacity for genuine and adequate emotional response through the acute phase of the psychosis has been found by Collins (1943) to indicate a better chance of remission. The criteria of genuineness and congruity are naturally rather subjective. So is another favourable sign, the transient clouding of consciousness sometimes observed in acute catatonic or paranoid states. Nevertheless these symptoms may be helpful in prognosis, especially where other pointers are missing. According to Slater (1947), a 'dementing' course is relatively rare in paranoid schizophrenia, which tends above all to take a chronic course, and in cases where states of excitement are frequent; it is particularly associated with affective blunting and impoverishment (which indeed, of course, constitute the essential nature of the 'dementia'). On the other hand a remitting course was rare both in cases where there was much paranoid development and those showing affective impoverishment, relatively common where depressive features were prominent. These findings, although they fit in with our preconceptions, require confirmation.

To sum up: a good prognosis is indicated by acute onset, a well-integrated and adapted personality of above average intelligence, by the presence of precipitating factors of a psychological or physical nature, by a manic-depressive heredity or the occurrence of benign psychoses in the family, by catatonic and by atypical symptoms especially of the affective type and by a well-preserved emotional response within the psychosis. An insidious onset, or onset at a very early age, limited intelligence, marked schizoid features in the pre-morbid personality, early signs of emotional flattening, absence of an adequate external cause, and the existence of schizophrenic relatives whose illness has taken a deteriorating course, are of grave significance for the final outcome.

DIAGNOSIS AND DIFFERENTIAL DIAGNOSIS

Many attempts have been made to find a *single character* which would be *diagnostic of schizophrenia*, or a common denominator in terms of which all the psychological symptoms could be expressed and which would bring them into relation with one another. These attempts have taken two main directions, both of them of interest and value, and have ended either in the construction of theories, such as those of Stransky, Bleuler and Conrad, or in the singling out of individual features, to which an especial importance is given, as in the analysis of Jaspers. There is no single test, no one reliable and universal method, for the diagnosis of schizophrenia. We have still to rely on a totality of observations and impressions, and what in one case might be regarded as decisive might in another be discounted as explicable on extraneous grounds. Yet it is still true that in the majority of cases diagnosis is not difficult, and even the followers of different psychiatric schools find themselves in agreement about the individual case whose symptoms are at all typical.

Jaspers believes that this possibility of agreement is due to an 'intuition' of what is schizophrenic, which escapes our grasp however detailed our description. As a result of his analysis, Jaspers emphasized the value of the *observer's inability to feel with the patient* and to understand him. This is a quality we might expect to find where organic or pathological factors are at work, and where a phenomenon transcends the range of normal variation. Without too much difficulty we can understand the reactions of the neurotic. But it is impossible to think and feel oneself into the role of the schizophrenic who is experiencing such symptoms as primary delusions, passivity feelings and thought disorder; and it is equally impossible to understand the turn he has taken as a development of his personality, or account for his conduct by his previous life. According to Jaspers, the gift we all have for human empathy and the attempt that one human being makes to establish contact with another, encounter a more complete frustration with the schizophrenic than with the sufferer from any other psychiatric disorder. Kurt Schneider (1925), indeed, once held that the lack of personal rapport felt by the (non-schizophrenic) physician in examining a schizophrenic patient was one of the most reliable diagnostic symptoms.

Such a symptom is, of course, a subjective one. All the same, it is well not to ignore this, like other physiognomic impressions, when one meets for the first time a suspected schizophrenic. *The immediate impression* has its own value, and it can hardly be recaptured on later occasions. It is more often right than wrong, even though it may fade away, or come to be regarded as misleading, when attention is turned to detail, and to the ideas and the explanations that the patient provides.

Of equal diagnostic importance is the total *inability of many schizophrenics to have insight into either themselves or their environment* (see p. 276). The patient regards his peculiar behaviour as completely natural and rational. He does not even realize that others find difficulty in understanding it, and he cannot see the situation from anyone else's point of view. In his analysis Conrad (1958) emphasized this inability to change his attitude towards himself as a characteristic symptom of early schizophrenia. Tests may show that intelligence, grasp and judgement of indifferent material are well preserved, and that orientation and consciousness are clear; yet he cannot appreciate that his behaviour differs in quality from that of normal people, and from what was customary for him before the onset of his illness. Patients with purely affective disturbances never reach such a stage; and even the manic, lacking in insight as he may be, can be brought to see that others do not view his conduct in the same light as he does himself.

The problems of *early diagnosis* are well summed up in the following paragraphs quoted from Gillies (1949).

'When treatment was restricted to institutional care and occupational therapy, early diagnosis was scarcely important, but with the coming of the modern physical treatments, and the realization that the best results are obtained in early cases, it has become of the first importance to recognize the illness at its beginnings. When the onset is sudden and results in a catatonic stupor or frenzy, or in a florid outburst of delusions, then diagnosis will be easy, but doubt will arise when the disease has begun insidiously and has been present for months or years before the patient is taken to a doctor. Although the primary symptoms are almost pathognomonic, in their mild form they are difficult to detect and they may be masked by the patient's reaction to them.

'In adolescence the growing-up process tends normally to excite a rebellious, questioning attitude towards parents and teachers, and the gonadal changes often give rise to shyness, perplexity, slight depression, anxiety, hypochondriacal preoccupations with the body, and shame over masturbation. It is also normal enough for the adolescent to brood over the meaning of life, religion, and love. If these musings continue for long, or if they lead to a break with reality, they will not be transient phases of adolescence but will be due to schizophrenia.

'Early non-specific signs that may disquiet the relatives include day-dreaming, seclusiveness, undisciplined attitudes, violent temper, unfeeling criticism, lack of energy, and lack of interest in work and play. The patient himself may complain of these and also of self-consciousness, general uneasiness, apprehension, puzzlement, hopelessness, depression, moodiness, poor concentration, and of physical symptoms such as constipation, dyspepsia, poor appetite, abdominal pains, headaches, and poor vision.

'Although the schizophrenic tends to lose insight early, some patients will for long realize that they are mentally unwell and will complain that they have changed.

'It will always be wise to see the patient on several occasions before reaching a diagnosis, and certainly before ruling out the presence of schizophrenia, and it will be helpful to observe him in different settings or to obtain descriptions of his behaviour at work and at school as well as in the home. In their letters patients may show incongruities and illogicalities that are inconspicuous in their speech.'

Diagnostic Value of Symptoms

While the diagnostic significance of the schizophrenic ensemble, though considerable, is difficult to analyse, the *primary symptoms* can be grouped *according to their discriminative value.*

The presence of *thought disorder*, the predominant symptom of Bleuler's loosening of association, is a diagnostic sign of the first order, provided it is found in a setting of clear consciousness. In cases in which it is at all marked, it will not be missed in the first interview. Ordinary conversation may be interfered with by '*Vorbeireden*' (talking beside the point, or allowing the essential nature of an issue to escape), blocking of the stream of thought, drifting into irrelevant side-lines of thought, narrowing of concepts, vagueness, and all the other peculiarities which have been earlier described. It may be, however, that some emotional stress is required to bring them out, as for instance when the patient has to speak in front of several people rather than one, or to discuss personal matters of an unpleasant kind. In others still, the disorder can only be elicited if they are asked to make a mental effort, as in repeating the gist of a fable or explaining a proverb. In ordinary conversation question and answer tend to suggest one another so that they form a sequential chain; an emotional tension which is lacking in the test situation mentioned, is involved which does not necessarily demand any particular form of response and allows a greater latitude. So it is, too, that some patients will say that they can manage to take a normal part in conversation, but left to themselves find their thinking becomes woolly and confused. Thought-blocking may sometimes assume the appearance of a *petit mal*; but the need to distinguish one from the other rarely arises.

Because of its diagnostic significance, attempts have been made to investigate schizophrenic thought disorder, not only qualitatively but also quantitatively, and to measure its extent or prevalence. *Tests* have been constructed for *disorders of 'conceptual thinking'*. The Russian psychologist, Vigotsky, suggested a sorting-test of coloured wooden blocks, and concluded from his findings that there was loss of ability to think in abstract concepts and a regression to 'thinking in complexes' (Hanfmann and Kasanin, 1942). Hanfmann and Kasanin also used blocks, which could be sorted by colour, size or shape. They found that schizophrenics had difficulty in abstracting a quality which could be used for sorting, and once having found one such quality could not get away from it to discover another. The findings of these workers were confirmed by others, especially by Goldstein (1939), who applied a test battery similar to the one he used for his researches in organic brain lesions. The results in the latter showed considerable resemblances to those obtained with schizophrenics. He also speaks of an *impairment of abstract attitude*. The diagnostic value of all these tests is limited because they are applicable only to a minority of patients, those with pronounced and permanent thought disorder, and reveal only a part of the total and complex abnormality of function. Furthermore, results are affected by mental age and cannot be quantified, and for clinical purposes the tests have no advantage over the simple method of using stories and proverbs. Lovibond's method of giving the Goldstein–Scherer tests of thought disorder has recently been applied by McConaghy and by Lidz to the relatives of schizophrenics, with interesting results (see p. 266).

Diagnostically useful results can be obtained with the *Rorschach ink-blot test*, which however is not a test of thought processes only, but is also markedly influenced by affective factors and by mechanisms of projection. Two of the three signs considered by most workers in this field to be pathognomonic of schizophrenia, i.e. extreme variation in the form quality of responses and the so-called 'contaminated' answers, are obviously closely connected with thought disorder. Of the third specific sign, 'position answers', this is less certain. The reaction to the coloured blots is also rather characteristic, as well as the relative rarity of answers signifying movement. There is, however, no single and definite Rorschach picture which is typical for schizophrenia as a whole. In practical use, the main difficulty in the way of the diagnostic application of the test is the frequency with which patients reject cards, or refuse to supply any interpretations. On the other hand, in early and doubtful cases the ink-blot test, taken with other clinical signs, does help in arriving at a diagnosis (Skalweit, 1934; Klopfer, 1946).

In their studies of young adult schizophrenics and their families at the National Institute of Mental Health, Wynne and Singer (1963) have paid particular attention to communication patterns between family members and have proposed a scheme in which schizophrenic thought disorder is classified into amorphous or fragmented forms. Projective tests have been scored by unorthodox methods but under standardized conditions to elicit and express in objective form, patterns of interaction and communication within the family, to examine errors of attention and to test reality apperception (Singer and Wynne, 1965a). These workers have developed a number of categories of deviation in these areas, scoring such features as vagueness, intrusions, mispronunciations, difficulties in assigning meaning, and oddities of grammar, association and 'vantage point'. For these special methods of scoring the Rorschach and T.A.T. protocols inter-observer reliabilities in the order of 80–90 per cent. are claimed (Wynne, 1968). The method was developed over a period of fifteen years and it is claimed that it has made possible blind diagnostic predictions of a high order. Thus, without access to the patients or family members, and making use of data from protocols obtained by other psychologists, Singer was able to predict a correct global diagnosis in terms of schizophrenia, borderline schizophrenia or neurosis for the offspring of the majority of a group of 35 families, achieving a level of probability of <0·001. Similar levels were obtained for predictions of forms and severity of thought disorder, and for predicted matching of offspring to family (Singer and Wynne, 1965b). More recently Wynne has reported significant discriminations between the communication pattern scores of parents of schizophrenics on one hand and parents of neurotics and normals on the other, at a probability level of <0·0001 (Wynne, 1968). It is reported that the criteria for deviation in communication processes in the parents of schizophrenics, based on projective techniques, are also applicable to Object Sorting test responses (Wild *et al.*, 1965). The findings are of considerable interest and require independent evaluation. They could have arisen from the effects on patterns of communication, of having a schizophrenic or schizoid member within the family or could alternatively reflect a morbid influence that contributes in some measure to the causation of schizophrenic breakdown. The observations can be equally well explained in terms of genetic or environmental influences or their interaction. They should provide a valuable starting point for further research.

If *thought disorder* can be convincingly demonstrated, by clinical or other methods, its presence is highly significant, and may clinch the diagnosis. A negative finding is of much less value, and by no means excludes schizophrenia. *Problems of differential diagnosis* will also arise at times. The similarity of the formal results of schizophrenic and of organically determined thought disorder very rarely leads to diagnostic difficulties, because the two occur in otherwise very different ensembles. A disorder of thinking of a similar type to the schizophrenic may be seen in many conditions of clouded consciousness, in the epileptic and the hysterical twilight state, the subacute delirious state and in manic confusion. In these conditions the primary disturbance of consciousness is sometimes not easily recognized, and may be overlooked. Even then, however, the history of the illness and the total clinical picture usually decide the issue without ambiguity. Absentmindedness, such as one finds in normal persons, and the tendency to lose the thread of thought which may be shown by normal individuals when fatigued and by neurasthenic and other psychoneurotic patients, may both at times provide a suggestion of the schizophrenic. Such persons, however, can always supply an account of their inner experience at the time the phenomenon is observed, which will clearly distinguish it from the corresponding schizophrenic change, and show its different origin and mechanism.

Next in diagnostic importance and almost equal in value are *disturbances of volition and the self*. Positive passivity feelings such as feelings of an influence, not his own, affecting his thoughts, emotions or actions, feelings that thoughts from outside are being put into his mind, etc., are pathognomonic. If the patient complains of weakness, lack of energy, failing will power, etc., these symptoms may be mistaken for those of neurasthenia, exhaustion or mild depression. If, however, he makes no complaint but simply slackens in activity and gives way to what looks like laziness without seeing anything strange or unusual in his conduct, the suspicion of schizophrenia is very great. Some complaints of depersonalized or derealized patients may resemble passivity phenomena very closely; but depersonalization may be the prodromal symptom of a schizophrenic illness.

Excessive activity and hyperkinesis in schizophrenia are easily mistaken for manic excitement. Closer examination, especially if continued for some days or weeks, will show, however, the existence of elements irreconcilable with a manic state. Underlying thought disorder will show itself in the stream of talk, even reducing it to incoherence; or the over-activity will be accompanied not by elevated but by incongruous or inadequate affect; the movements themselves may show stiffness, monotony or a stereotyped repetitiveness. If manic excitation leads to clouding of consciousness, which may also accompany schizophrenic excitement, diagnosis on the basis of the present status may be impossible. The same is true of the hyperkinesis of epileptic twilight states. The differentiation of schizophrenic akinesis and hyperkinesis from similar phenomena associated with encephalitis lethargica will be discussed under differential diagnosis (p. 320).

The third place in the scale of diagnostic significance is taken by *primary delusions*. They are less valuable than the others already mentioned, not because they are less distinctive but because it is not so easy to be sure of their presence. This is especially so when the delusional ideas expressed by the patient seem to be closely connected with the psychological situation and derived from it. However, if the patient is intelligent enough and sufficiently clear in his mind, he may describe the sudden appearance of a delusional idea, which cannot be rationally explained by the circumstances at the time of its appearance, and which is experienced with an almost perceptual quality and the force of a sudden illumination. This phenomenon is practically pathognomonic. Similar phenomena are, however, sometimes to be met with in epileptic and other schizophrenic-like psychoses. Our difficulties mainly arise from the fact that paranoid schizophrenia frequently begins insidiously, primary delusional experiences are buried in the past, and the distinction from paranoid and hysterical reactions may then be difficult. Fortunately auditory hallucinations are often present from an early stage, thus aiding the diagnosis.

The commonest *emotional disturbance* is weakness or impoverishment of affective response: this is diagnostically most significant when it is seen as the numbing of feelings of sympathy and regard for other people. These feelings may die off in other organic mental diseases too, but, if so, there is always a parallel deterioration of intellectual ability and judgement, whereas in schizophrenia the latter remain unimpaired. Conversely, in G.P.I., epilepsy or early cerebral arteriosclerosis the emotional response may remain well preserved when signs of dementia are already manifest. Affective responses which are delayed, or incongruous, or which irradiate into inappropriate fields of mental activity, are also characteristic, especially when occurring in clear consciousness. Ecstasy and excessive and boundless emotions in acute paranoid states are hard to distinguish from similar experiences in epileptic psychoses. They only indicate schizophrenia when the patient himself gives a description of their unexpected and sudden appearance in a clear sky unexplained by circumstances, and unconnected with his preoccupations and interest. This is also the point at which they may be distinguished from the passionate outbursts of hysteria.

Catatonic symptoms, first considered as most significant by Kraepelin, have lost considerably in diagnostic value since they have been observed in many organic brain diseases. They are still rather typical in long-standing cases when stereotypies, mannerisms, 'word salad' and other positive symptoms are prevalent in the clinical picture. Stupor and other akinetic symptoms may be found in depressions and in hysterical psychoses and are then difficult to differentiate. Eleven out of thirteen cases diagnosed as 'benign stupors' by Hoch were found to be schizophrenics when followed up by Rachlin (1935). The psychological attitude of the schizophrenic towards his motor behaviour is, however, of some diagnostic help—his peculiar indifference, the dissociation between thought and conduct and the abstruse symbolism expressed in catatonic movements.

Finally, *hallucinations*, with some exceptions such as hearing one's thoughts repeated, are in themselves probably the least characteristic signs of schizophrenia. The predominance of auditory and especially tactile hallucinations suggests the diagnosis; but more pathognomonic than the hallucinations themselves are their participation in thought disorder, the inadequate emotional reaction of the patient, their influence or absence of influence on the patient's actions and their delusional interpretation. Among features classed by Kurt Schneider as being of the first rank in diagnostic importance were hallucinatory voices that conduct a commentary on the patient's actions; hearing thoughts spoken aloud or *écho de pensée*, broadcasting of thoughts, bodily feelings of influence, thought withdrawal, and other experiences of thought being directed as well as all forms of passivity feelings in relation to affect, instinct, and volition. As far as delusions are concerned, only the primary delusional perception was considered by Schneider as being peculiarly schizophrenic although few psychiatrists find any clear distinction between this and any other form of primary delusion. All other types of hallucination, emotional change and catatonic features were classed by Schneider as symptoms of the second rank.

Returning to the picture as a whole, the phenomenon of '*splitting*' remains an important diagnostic sign (see p. 276): dissociation of emotions from ideas, of expression from emotions, of conduct from intentions, of certain parts of mental life from the rest, taking either the form of 'double orientation' (Bleuler) or of encapsulation of a delusional system. All these differ from dissociations in hysteria in which the dissociation is, as a rule, transparent in its motive and thematic in its content and makes use of dysmnesic mechanisms. Hysterical dissociation is also more massive, while the schizophrenic form is shown in minutiae.

Differential Diagnosis

There is no short cut for differentiating schizophrenia from other mental diseases, for instance by way of a table of psychological signs from which a firm diagnosis could be established. One always has to consider the whole clinical picture; and the single symptom is only significant if assessed against its background, the past history, and all the circumstances and findings of the present. Tables of diagnostic symptoms have been made. But if they pretend to an absolute reliability, they contain only the rarer passivity phenomena, or combinations of these with thought disorder and hallucinations, as they are found in advanced cases (e.g. K. Schneider, 1942). They are of little use in early cases where diagnosis is most difficult.

Distinction is most easily made from the group of *psychoses with a cerebral pathology* (Chapters IX and X), because of the presence of physical signs, neurological and serological, in organic mental illness. In the latter the psychological changes proceed in the opposite order, defects of memory and intellect preceding disturbances of emotion. The affective relationship to environment is frequently well preserved at a time when signs of dementia are easily seen. This is the case in cerebral tumour, arteriosclerosis, presenile and senile dementia, as well as in post-traumatic and syphilitic conditions. General paresis in juveniles may sometimes be mistaken for hebephrenia; but it should be possible to find some specific physical signs, even if the serological findings are ambiguous.

Frontal-lobe tumours can give rise to difficulty until aphasia or physical signs, such as an extensor plantar response or papilloedema, appear. One is likely to be misled especially by the apathy, moodiness and impulsiveness which are caused by a prefrontal lesion, but also by the fact that early hebephrenics not infrequently complain of headache.

During and after the last epidemics of *encephalitis lethargica* it was often difficult to distinguish juvenile cases from early hebephrenic and catatonic states, especially if there was no history, or no reliable one, of the acute attack. In later stages, the Parkinson-like picture and the slowing-down of mental processes (bradyphrenia) without thought disorder made the decision easier. Loss of activity or restlessness, an impertinent manner, monotony of speech, obstinacy and other features are common to both conditions; akinesis may be taken for catatonic stupor. Thought disorder, however, never occurs in encephalitics, nor do they suffer from passivity phenomena and hallucinations. Oculogyric crises are unknown in schizophrenia.

Some disturbances of thinking and speech in *epileptic twilight states* can only be distinguished from the corresponding schizophrenic symptoms if one can establish the clouding of consciousness. This is often far from easy; and it is also difficult to distinguish the motor symptoms which in their stereotyped and repetitive character are sometimes identical with catatonic manifestations. Stupor and other akinetic states may be seen in epileptics, and it is then impossible to gain insight into the degree of clarity of the patient's mind. Primary delusions and hallucinations in some prolonged epileptic psychoses can be very like those in schizophrenia although the total picture differs in most cases: there is no emotional coolness, and the disturbance of thinking in the epileptic with its typical qualities of slowness and circumstantiality has nothing in common with schizophrenic dissociation. All these epileptic states can be distinguished from schizophrenia by adequate history taking and by the use of the electroencephalograph. Epileptic disturbances of consciousness are invariably accompanied by gross changes in the E.E.G. In the course of a long-standing epilepsy a chronic psychosis may arise which is usually paranoid in form and may be symptomatologically indistinguishable from schizophrenia. A fuller description is given on page 258. The history of epileptic attacks in the past, though not always the immediate past, should lead to careful investigation along electroencephalographic and neurological lines.

Some *chemical intoxications* such as mescaline, lysergic acid diethylamide and hashish can produce states indistinguishable from acute schizophrenia (see Chapter VII, p. 432). It is, however, doubtful whether they occur outside experimental conditions. Other drugs, such as cocaine, may lead to hallucinatory psychoses which have little in common with schizophrenic hallucinosis. On the other hand differential diagnosis from alcoholic hallucinosis can prove difficult. Some workers have attributed the condition to the action of alcohol on a latent schizophrenia. But Benedetti's recent studies have demonstrated its mainly alcoholic aetiology. Alcoholic hallucinosis differs from paranoid schizophrenia in the preservation of normal affect, and personality may be unimpaired for long periods. The clinical picture is dominated in a rather characteristic way by the auditory hallucinations which are often of a critical, accusatory or commanding character, but always intelligible and even banal. Determined suicidal attempts are particularly common. Active physical treatment with phenothiazines and E.C.T. almost invariably induces a remission in early cases and this often lasts until drinking is recommenced.

Most of the patients with paranoid psychoses following on chronic amphetamine intoxication have, at some stage, been regarded as schizophrenic. Differential diagnosis may be impossible clinically though it is easily made by testing the urine.

Differentiation from *symptomatic psychoses* can be extremely difficult. Some of the problems have been discussed in an earlier part (p. 259). As long as there is definite clouding of consciousness, the distinction will rest on this sign. In the subacute delirious state it is often hard to assess. It has been pointed out that the incoherence in this state differs from the schizophrenic dissociation by being less influenced by complexes, and being more uniform whenever tested. One does not get, as in schizophrenic thought disorder, a correct answer one moment and a confused one immediately afterwards; every utterance shows the disturbance if it is present at all. The results produced by the process of thinking may be similar, but the process itself seems to be disturbed in a different way.

Similar problems have to be faced in cases of confused *mania* and in certain mixed states of the *affective group*. Deceptive as the clinical picture at the moment of observation may be, the history of a preceding manic or depressive attack will help the diagnosis. Many efforts have been made to find an infallible criterion between the affective and the schizophrenic disorders. The effort has been in vain; and in consequence too much attention has been given to instances in which an immediate judgement was impossible, and the two disorders were regarded as 'combined'. For practical purposes, one should pay attention in the first place to emotional reaction and expression. If they are of one colour, and appear to come from the same mould, being either hilarious and elated, or cheerful and jocular, or angry and irritable, or despondent and sad, an affective disorder is more probable whatever the accompanying symptoms may be. If the warmth of personal *rapport* is preserved, this is a pointer in the same direction. Empathy is never entirely lost in the manic-depressive patient. Even in depressive stupor, an understanding glance, or tears, or a

M

blush may betray a fine thread of contact. Negativistic conduct, resistance or automatic obedience are ambiguous as diagnostic signs.

Involutional melancholia cannot always be differentiated from late catatonic and paranoid forms of schizophrenia. Hypochondriasis and delusion may be utterly grotesque and bizarre and their content may have little relation to the underlying affect. Nevertheless such ideas have little diagnostic significance as long as affective response is still present and conforms to its original colouring.

The only *psychopathic* syndrome in which a suspicion of schizophrenia arises, is that of the callous, emotionally cool psychopath, the 'moral defective'. It has been shown that personalities like this are sometimes found in families tainted by schizophrenia (Meggendorfer, 1921). Distinction from schizophrenia simplex is sometimes impossible, especially if no full history is at hand. If a change of personality is proven, even in early adolescence, the schizophrenic nature of the illness is beyond doubt. Early hebephrenia is sometimes mistaken for *mental deficiency*. Difficulties should arise only in patients who were defective before the schizophrenic illness occurred. Imbecile patients are frequently liable to affective storms in which hallucinations, incoherence and catatonic behaviour may be seen. Such states, however, pass off after days or weeks (very rarely months), and leave the patient exactly as he was before, while a hebephrenic illness always leaves a mark. If the patient was not originally defective, the school record alone should settle the diagnosis, even if the hebephrenia by causing loss of activity and disordered thinking has produced a picture reminiscent of imbecility.

Simulation of schizophrenia is very rare. Attempts can be seen in prison, and have been observed in soldiers, especially during the First World War. The expert will rarely be deceived unless by a malingered stupor, for instance in prisoners of war. A much commoner error is to mistake the silly hebephrenic for a malingerer, especially if he is detained for an alleged crime, or in compensation cases to misjudge schizophrenic loss of will power as laziness, and hypochondriacal complaints as a deliberate attempt to mislead the physician.

Dissimulation of schizophrenic symptoms is extremely common; indeed a good deal of the schizophrenic's capacity for social adjustment depends on it. It sometimes takes the interesting form, recognized and described by Bleuler, of the patient insisting that he has simulated his symptoms. A classical case of this kind was that of Rudolf Hess who by this unusual psychotic behaviour apparently prevented an array of international experts from reaching the obvious diagnosis (J. R. Rees, 1947).

TREATMENT
(1) Prophylaxis

(*a*) PERSONAL. As one would expect with our present ignorance of the causation of the disease, there is no possibility of preventing anyone from becoming schizophrenic. Entirely *irresponsible claims* have been made by enthusiasts for child guidance and by educationists with a dilettante's acquaintance with the doctrines of psychoanalysis. Nevertheless not a particle of evidence exists to show that any measure whatsoever can reduce the incidence of schizophrenia, whether it be by 'scientifically' regulated methods of upbringing, psychiatric supervision of the child–parent relationship, or by psychoanalysis or other psychotherapy of either the healthy, the neurotic or the introverted or otherwise endangered child or adolescent. The universal incidence of the disease in all races and cultures weighs heavily against any arguments that environmental and psychological factors of any specific kind play an important part in causing the disease; and so does the experience of the clinician who sees identical clinical pictures in patients from all walks of life and from the most diverse family and educational backgrounds.

On the other hand, a *realistic attitude* is not the same as one of fatalism and despair. There is no reason to think that the onset of schizophrenia could not be delayed, mitigated or even prevented, if we only knew how; and it is the physician's duty to do the best he can with such inadequate weapons as he has. It would be foolish not to make some effort to help the predisposed personality, as for instance by vocational guidance, by removing sources of frustration, and by directing the adolescent's energy and interest towards socializing activities and away from self-absorption ('presumptive prevention', Stevenson, 1946). More could perhaps be done to identify highly vulnerable subjects and schizophrenics in the earliest stages of their illness or in the stage of insidious, progressive alteration in personality that may precede the outbreak of a frank psychosis. Some features of the social and psychological profile of the most typical cases are already known; the subject is aged between 18 and 25, shy, remote, seclusive in personality, incapable of establishing contact with the opposite sex, usually single. A growing restlessness at his work, drift down the social and occupational ladder and increasing isolation are warning signals of imminent psychotic breakdown. Further observations could probably help to define more precisely such pre-morbid characteristics and make it possible to institute pharmacological treatment, psychological support and encouragement towards socialization at an earlier stage than is possible at the present time. One cannot be too sanguine about the results of such prophylactic measures but it would be logical and worth while to try them. Difficulties are often put in the way of such measures by the patient's own parents, who may be themselves schizoid and by their own peculiarities stultify the emotional development of their children. Analytic treatment should, as a rule, be avoided by the schizoid personality and still more so if there is any suspicion of an oncoming schizophrenia. The not infrequent outbreak of an acute psychosis during psychotherapy which has been begun in the prodromal neurotic stage has been mentioned before (p. 283).

(*b*) GENETIC. Our knowledge of the genetics of schizophrenia provides the basis for some conclusions about prophylaxis. These conclusions are, however, best expressed in terms of *probabilities*, and provide *no certainty in the individual case*. It is true that probabilities, if sufficiently overwhelming, justify mass action and the application of rules which, though occasionally unjust to the individual, are for the benefit of society as a whole. The Third German Reich passed a law for the safeguarding of racial health, which provided for the compulsory sterilization of sufferers from idiopathic epilepsy, manic-depressive psychosis and schizophrenia; and such patients had to be sterilized before they could be allowed to leave hospital, if they were still in the reproductive age. This law had no adequate scientific justification. This may conveniently be shown with schizophrenia as an example. The incidence of schizophrenia among the children of schizophrenics is between 10 and 20 per cent., depending on the type of psychosis. So it might be expected that sterilizing schizophrenics would prevent the birth of a substantial number of persons destined later to develop the disease. Schizophrenics, however, have a very low fertility, and, of such children as they do have, only a small proportion are born after the onset of the psychosis, that is after the schizophrenic has become recognizable as such. The great majority of schizophrenics are the children of non-schizophrenic parents. It follows that the sterilization of schizophrenics is almost useless as a prophylactic measure.

Zuring (1946) followed up a group of schizophrenics who had been discharged from hospital four to thirteen years before. They were all married, this being one of the grounds of selection, but only a few had married since leaving hospital. Of their 670 children, only 16 per cent. were born after the onset of the schizophrenia, and were therefore preventable. A rather more optimistic estimate is provided by Kallmann (1938); but he calculates that, at best only a third of the children of schizophrenics are preventable in this way. Schizophrenia is not a serious problem of eugenics, as owing to the low marriage and fertility rates associated with it the disease is racially self-limiting.

The problem of *voluntary sterilization* in the individual case is, however, a different one. For those who find their fertility a burden we can see no reason why permanent relief should not be provided, if it is desired. There is much to be said in its favour if the applicant has once had a psychotic illness. Family life, especially as an environment for children, cannot achieve normal standards of happiness and stability if one of the parents has any defect of personality, or lies under the shadow of a possible recurrence of serious illness. Zuring noted that though marriage adjustment was not unsuccessful in the group he studied, in more prosperous classes especially there were frequent disputes about the children. The problem, however, is one for the patient and his consort; and the doctor should not press his views in either direction.

Patients and their married or affianced partners often seek advice on the subject of *marriage and procreation*. The two subjects should be considered separately. Anyone who has once had a schizophrenic illness has a serious risk of recurrence, and no serenity can be promised for the future. For the patient himself, marriage with a woman who will face and share his risks with a full understanding of their nature, has much to offer. The woman (or man in the converse case) who would face these risks must be of quite exceptional personality. In general the young people who make such enquiries have no more than the amount of mutual devotion usual among affianced couples, and very rarely have any conception of what is involved in the prospects they are facing. It will be the doctor's duty to obtain the permission of the patient for a frank discussion of his case with his fiancée, and then to inform her of the probabilities of recurrence, and of the nature of the illness.

If the question of marriage is frequently not treated with the seriousness it deserves, the risks of procreation are as commonly over-estimated. The advice that is given will be based in the first place on *actuarial probabilities*, whose validity has been established by observation and does not depend on any theory of dominance or recessivity. The expectation given in the table on page 244 may be referred to.

It is generally agreed that the hereditary factor is manifested with a lesser frequency among the relatives of paranoid schizophrenics than among those of hebephrenics and catatonics. Kallmann, for instance, gives the incidence of schizophrenia among the children of the latter as 21 per cent., and among the children of paranoid and simple schizophrenics as 10 per cent.

These figures are sufficiently high to make *schizophrenic parentage a serious risk* for a child; and many people who are married to a schizophrenic will wish to avoid conception. In addition to the genetic risk there is also the disadvantage for the child of being brought up in a family in which there may be fundamental insecurities. With a less close blood relationship the genetical risk drops to near normal proportions. The risk for grandchildren of schizophrenics is so small that a healthy individual who has had a schizophrenic parent can regard it with equanimity. The same applies to the possible parents of children who would be nephews and nieces or more remote relatives of a schizophrenic.

Among these *relatives of schizophrenics*, the question of marriage may arise. A woman who is considering marriage with the brother of a schizophrenic may wish to know what risk she runs of her husband becoming schizophrenic. The incidence of schizophrenia among the sibs of schizophrenics has been assessed at various figures whose mean value is about 11 per cent. This might well be enough to deter a cautious woman. Individual circumstances, however, have to be taken into consideration. If the prospective husband has reached the age of forty, and is of a normal and not schizoid personality, the risk is a very much smaller one, and can indeed be practically regarded as negligible. If however he is a young man of twenty, and so has the whole danger period of life yet to survive, and still more if he is a sensitive schizoid, paranoid or unstable personality, the chance would have to be assessed at its full or even an increased value.

From this it may be seen that *no hard and fast rules* can be given when questions of marriage guidance and eugenic problems are raised. Individual circumstances will play a dominant part in deciding what advice is properly given.

(2) Psychological Treatment

If the patient is seen by a doctor within two years from the manifestation of the first symptom, and if the diagnosis of schizophrenia is established, it is nowadays a gross error not to press for his admission to a special unit or hospital where he can receive physical treatment. Even if the diagnosis is doubtful, he should come under psychiatric observation, in order to clear the issue and to begin treatment with drugs once there are sure grounds for doing so. Prolonged psychotherapy, even in mild cases, can no longer be justified. *Psychoanalysis* is, indeed, *contra-indicated* in any stage or type of schizophrenia; to apply it is, as Freud himself commented to L. Binswanger, a professional error ('*ein Kunstfehler*'). This statement has been supported by many critical workers in this field; but it has not prevented others from applying an analytic procedure. The analyst is constantly tempted to do so as, thanks to his incapacity for repression, the schizophrenic openly exposes symbolisms and mechanisms which have to be unearthed with difficulty in the neurotic. 'The transparence of the picture is again and again a temptation for the psychotherapist. We come to the conclusion that now all that is needed is to teach the patient our wisdom, and he will, like the neurotic under treatment, gain insight, adapt himself, and be saved. This conclusion, I think, is false' (Speer, 1927). Speer has also described how the disease process progresses, unaffected by the treatment; how the schizophrenic slips from the hands of the therapist; and how apparently good results are transient and chance affairs. Modifications of psychoanalytic procedure have lately been applied in more advanced cases, always with very limited results, not exceeding what intensive individual care can achieve without Freudian interpretations.

Experiments in analytical therapy were, in the authors' view, only permissible as long as no physical method of treatment existed. Schilder, in fact, gave as his reason for employing them the lack of any suitable physical therapy. For the early schizophrenic matters are now changed, and psychoanalysis can only now be justified as a *research procedure in the arrested case* with schizophrenic defect. Much of the psychoanalytic endeavour in schizophrenia during the past 15 years has been directed towards the treatment of cases described as 'borderline', 'latent', or 'ambulant'. The types of illness to which these terms refer have been most fully delineated in the papers on 'pseudo-neurotic schizophrenia' (Hoch and Cattell, 1959). These patients manifest a wide range of neurotic symptoms which extend from phobias, obsessions and depersonalization on the one hand to hysterical conversion symptoms and hypochondriasis on the other, all features showing a marked variability. There is severe anxiety, sexual and aggressive fantasies are given uninhibited expression and the course of the illness may be punctuated by attacks of psychotic disturbance lasting days, hours or perhaps only minutes. No satisfactory evidence exists that these patients are schizophrenics rather than disturbed neurotics who occasionally cross the 'reality line'. Techniques influenced by psychoanalytic thinking have also been applied in the treatment of chronic schizophrenics. Close and warm relationships are fostered between patients and nurses and communication at the patient's own archaic level is attempted in the hope that the patient can learn to differentiate better between self and non-self; the breakdown of this differentiation is regarded as the fundamental psychological disturbance. The more florid manifestations of catatonic and other types of schizophrenia which used to be so common in the old long-stay wards of mental hospitals can be influenced by such measures. But there is no evidence that they have any advantage over techniques in which a stimulating occupation, patient persistence and humanity are the only ingredients.

Unfortunately many schizophrenics are first seen by a doctor, or by a psychiatrist, when the illness has gone on too long and progressed too far for physical treatment to hold out much hope of complete restoration of the patient's personality. Some consult the psychiatrist for a *residual symptom after the acute attack* has passed. Others are discovered among the in-patients or out-patients of general hospitals, where they have been treated for a physical complaint. If any of them is tolerably adapted to his environment, is at work and lives a relatively normal life, it would be a mistake to interrupt his adjustment by admitting him to a special hospital. Yet many are in need of some help which can be supplied in an out-patient clinic or private consulting-room. Some of them are distressed by primary symptoms into which they still retain a degree of insight; the doctor can support their tendency to take an objective attitude, can help them to recognize the subjectivity of their experiences, and to maintain a socially acceptable adjustment to them. Many of these patients, again, are often lonely and search for some acceptance and understanding. Although it is a waste of time to argue with a paranoid patient about his delusions, he may still be persuaded to keep them to himself, to repress them as far as possible and to forgo the aggressive action they might suggest, and in general to conduct his life as if they did not exist. The latent schizophrenic loves regularity and routine; he is a creature of habit. Everything should be done to fortify this tendency and to direct it into useful channels. At the same time he should be encouraged to keep up his social relations, to mix with other people and to avoid brooding and philosophizing. Although schizophrenic subjects are emotionally remote and unresponsive, if time is spent and pains taken some degree of rapport may be achieved when the acute manifestations of psychosis have died down, particularly when some relatively healthy and normal components of personality survive. When contact has been made, many schizophrenic patients are prepared to attend an out-patient clinic regularly. A good deal can be done in such a setting over a long period, slowly to improve the patient's social contacts, develop his interests, encourage him to continue with medication, and help him to hold on to his job and to retain the support of his family at times when symptoms flare up. Hospitalization can also be arranged, if necessary, in good time without the crises which often precede admission and which slowly erode the patient's social resources.

Such is the *psychotherapy* which will be of greatest help with schizophrenia. It is unlikely that it will prevent the outbreak of another attack, but it counteracts the inclination to withdrawal and the downward drift in the social scale. Unlike classical psychoanalysis, it is a *therapy* not of dissection and uncovering, but *of covering and bridging over*. It takes advantage of the processes of healing and encapsulation of symptoms which naturally occur with spontaneous improvements and remissions, and aids and reinforces them. It is of particular value when some improvement has already been achieved through one of the physical treatments, or when it is combined with administration of the appropriate phenothiazine drug in adequate doses. The gap in continuity of mental life which has been left by the acute psychosis has to be bridged. The patient cannot be expected to dismiss the intense experiences of the acute psychosis as irrelevant and merely morbid, much as he wants to overcome their influence. His inner life has received a new orientation, and must be integrated anew; much tact and understanding and a good deal of personal sympathy are required to help him to do so. Not all schizophrenics are willing to keep in contact with the psychiatrist, but it is greatly to their advantage to do so.

HOSPITAL AND WARD MANAGEMENT. On the whole the managment of schizophrenic and other patients in the psychiatric hospital is turning away from the old pattern of custodial care and has been profoundly affected by the concept of the 'therapeutic community'. The basic notion is that a psychiatric institution should be a community— a place where people live and work—which in its whole social structure and way of life is therapeutic. That is, it helps those who are admitted towards recovery and discharge. Most mental hospitals in Britain have taken some steps towards this ideal.

'Notable advances have come in greater freedom for patients by open doors and recently by wide extension of informal patient status—by the organization of the full active day with occupational therapy programmes, industrial workshops and day and night patient facilities, by improvement and normalization of the patient's way of life, with increased visiting, more privacy, more personal belongings, greater mixing of the sexes, a more realistic working day and, to some extent, by self-government and the greater involvement of patients in the running of their lives, particularly with therapeutic social clubs and self-governing hospital activities' (Clark, 1964). (See also section on Social Treatment below).

The application of this concept at ward level for schizophrenic patients has been attempted on an experimental basis in many psychiatric hospitals. It has led to an imaginative and enterprising approach towards management and has stimulated much interest and enquiry in the rehabilitation of the chronic schizophrenic. It has also done something to render the attitude of professional staff towards their colleagues and patients more flexible and objective. There is, however, some danger that the concept of the 'therapeutic community' applied to the management of schizophrenic patients may become a catchword and lead to practices founded more in sentiment than in reason and evidence. Even in the case of neuroses and personality disturbances, the community organized within an institution should not drift too far from the realities of existence in the world at large unless clear reasons for some different kind of organization can be defined and carefully tested in practice. In the case of schizophrenic patients whose survival in society outside the hospital can at the best of times be precarious and can only be sustained with a good deal of support, supervision and treatment, the communal setting in which their treatment is to be provided can hardly be decided by abstract theories of social interaction. In creating this setting account has to be taken of the special limitations and needs of schizophrenic patients. For example, those who are concerned with fitting the schizophrenic into work in industry after discharge stress the importance of his work habits, personal habits and appearance approximating to those of his workmates. This will not happen spontaneously among schizophrenic patients. Helpful and imaginative direction and supervision are needed which will at the same time permit the widest possible scope for any initiative and enterprise shown by the individual schizophrenic patient and the ward community.

OCCUPATIONAL THERAPY. For those who had to remain *in hospital*, Bleuler found regular work of great help. He formed groups of patients who worked on the land, or in the gardens or in special workshops. He trained his nurses and attendants so to supervise the patient's activities that they gave him satisfaction and, if possible, some personal responsibility. Bleuler graded the patients according to their clinical state, and did everything possible to break the tendency to form undesirable habits. This method was taken up with great enthusiasm by Hermann Simon (1927), from whose hospital at Guetersloh *occupational therapy* made its way into institutions all over the world.

In English-speaking countries this form of treatment came to be entrusted to occupational therapists as an ancillary aid to the psychiatrist. The type of occupation practised for therapeutic purposes has in the past been dominated by rug-making, basket work, weaving and toy-making. This pattern has been much criticized in recent years. Occupational therapy in the form of such pastimes and hobbies has a more limited place in the hospital regime since the introduction of industrial workshops. But it is an exaggeration to say that they have no useful function. They provide diversion and recreation of a satisfying kind, they can be carried on in the ward, and therefore started in the early stages of the psychosis. It is important to stress the value of arranging this sort of activity so that the schizophrenic patient works in a *group*. This combats his tendency to withdrawal, mitigates his negativism, and gives him an opportunity to overcome other morbid tendencies. The simple schizophrenic may be stimulated to realize what has remained of his emotional life in the setting of the group; the hebephrenic learns to concentrate from the example of others; the catatonic finds an outlet for an excess of energy, or is awakened from stupor into action; the paranoid patient learns to repress his delusional world and is less under the influence of his hallucinations. These aims are not achieved to the same extent if the patient works a loom on his own, or withdraws into a corner with his rug. Supervision and individual attention from a kind and understanding therapist are, of course, indispensable to maintain the cohesion of the group and to support the patient who is in danger of slipping into 'autism'.

Therapists trained in the more artistic crafts are often led to stimulate the *production of free art* in schizophrenics. Schizophrenic drawings, paintings and sculpture are of great psychological interest to the physician who tries to understand his patient's inner life; and where this is active, and not merely empty, formalized and frigid, they are of interest to the artist and have a relevance to the theory and history of art (H. Prinzhorn, 1923). However, from the therapeutic point of view, drawing, painting and modelling which leave the patient free to choose his own subject and techniques are not to be encouraged. While the neurotic may relieve himself of emotional pressure and of the affects bound up with past experiences by artistic creation, the schizophrenic tends to slip further into his morbid fantasies. By drawing symbolical pictures he further relinquishes his contact with reality; his tendencies to avoidance of the world around are encouraged rather than impeded. 'Art therapy' of this kind is contra-indicated in schizophrenics, for the same reason as is psychoanalysis. It should, perhaps, only be allowed when the patient is himself a creative artist whose works have value in themselves, and even then for only a part of a day, the rest of which is spent in more social activities.

The methods of treatment which have been described above are in no way rendered obsolete by modern physical therapies. As will be seen, a number of patients do not respond to physical methods, or respond only transiently. Moreover the two methods of approach aid rather than interfere with each other; psychological and social care of the kind described has constantly to be applied in support of the physical procedure. Occupation and activity arranged for the patient in hospital and the work that he undertakes after his discharge into the community have to be envisaged as part of one continuous process of rehabilitation and re-socialization. This will be discussed in more detail in the section on social treatment (p. 337).

(3) **Physical Treatment**

Ever since psychiatry became a branch of medicine, attempts have been made to influence the severe and malignant disease we now call schizophrenia by physical means. *According to the theory prevalent at the time* or the predilection of the worker the most diverse experiments have been carried out, from transplantation of endocrine organs to operative resection of large parts of jejunum, from bloodletting and removal of septic foci to fever therapy—to mention only a few propagated during the last thirty years. Thanks to the irregular and often unpredictable course of the illness with its tendency to spontaneous remissions in the early stages and to unexpected improvements later, most workers have been able to claim a degree of success which, however, did not stand the test of critical and controlled examinations.

Because, as was described in a previous section, clinical appearances in schizophrenia are to some extent influenced by the psychological environment, any favourable results achieved by physical treatments have been attributed by some critics to the special care and attention given to the patients during the physical treatment. It has also been frequently objected that the best results are seen in early cases or in those which show other indications of a tendency to remission or a favourable course. Finally the empirical character of therapies such as E.C.T. and pharmacological treatment, has been the target of much criticism and an excuse for sceptical inertia.

The treatment of the acute stage of schizophrenia and of long-standing chronic patients has undergone a marked change in recent years through the introduction of 'neuroleptic' drugs which have replaced insulin coma therapy as the main component in the physical treatment of schizophrenia in most parts of the world.

Since its introduction into psychiatry by Delay *et al.* (1952) chlorpromazine has been repeatedly shown in the course of controlled therapeutic trials to be an effective substance in the treatment of acute and chronic schizophrenic illness. The most striking effects are exerted in anxious, hostile, paranoid, hallucinated patients; tension eases, restlessness subsides, hostile attitudes gradually abate and hallucinations commonly lose their affective charge, fade into the background and even disappear. Muteness, negativism and catatonic motor disturbances also frequently respond and rapport may be re-established in patients who have manifested catatonic symptoms over relatively long periods. Consciousness is not impaired and contact with the patient is maintained. Recent enquiries have clearly demonstrated that the effect of phenothiazine drugs is not confined to the symptoms of excitement, restlessness and aggressive behaviour and the term 'tranquillizer' applied to this group of drugs is probably a misnomer. In a controlled trial of phenothiazine treatment against a placebo (Goldberg *et al.*, 1965) it was shown that patients treated by the former method showed significantly greater improvement on an overall measure of clinical state and in 14 of 21 relatively independent measures of schizophrenic illness. The symptoms of apathy and motor retardation were among those that showed improvement, and irritability, slow speech and movements, hebephrenic symptoms, self-care, and indifference to the environment manifested significant amelioration only on drug treatment. There were other features such as incoherent speech, hostility, agitation and tension, ideas of persecution, and auditory hallucinations which showed significantly greater improvement with drugs. As the authors point out the first cluster of symptoms corresponds reasonably well to the group of features defined by Bleuler as 'fundamental' symptoms of schizophrenia. An important finding of this study was the efficacy of phenothiazine drugs in preventing the appearance of fresh schizophrenic symptoms. It is clear, then, that phenothiazine drugs cannot be regarded as being merely symptomatic therapies in the same sense as analgesic drugs.

Although improvement with phenothiazine drugs usually commences during the first 7–14 days of treatment, it may be delayed as long as five or six weeks. It is not possible to predict which cases will respond promptly and there is a proportion of patients who fail to improve with phenothiazine drugs but who make an excellent response when these are combined with electro-convulsive treatment. Patients in a catatonic stupor will often be slow to respond to phenothiazines and those in catatonic excitement may bring themselves to a dangerous point of exhaustion unless their symptoms are brought under rapid control with a few convulsions. Unless there are physical contra-indications, E.C.T. and phenothiazine drugs should be combined in the treatment of the majority of cases of schizophrenia. The response to chlorpromazine is variable and dosage has therefore to be individually determined for each patient. Anything from 150 mg. to over 1,000 mg. daily may be required to control the symptoms, although most cases are brought under control on a dosage of 200–400 mg. When improvement is established, the dosage may be reduced to a maintenance level which usually ranges between 100 and 300 mg. daily. But much higher doses may be required in rare instances. E.C.T. should be initiated at the earliest possible stage and, in very acute cases, up to 4 treatments can be given in the first week, reduced to two or three in the second week. Eight to 12 treatments will usually suffice to elicit an optimal response but up to 20 treatments may be required in highly resistant cases.

Although the neuroleptic drugs have diminished the importance of sedation in schizophrenia it is still essential to know how to deal with the emergency of an acute schizophrenic attack in the patient's home so that he can be transported to an observation ward or a psychiatric hospital. Some catatonically excited patients are dangerous and, if the patient refuses to take drugs by mouth and is generally uncooperative, the help of a Mental Welfare Officer should always be sought in an emergency. Unnecessary interference should be avoided until the moment the injection has to be administered or the patient needs to be transfered to an ambulance. The movements to bring the patient under control must be swift and concerted and the fewer the words spoken the better. An intramuscular injection of 100 mg. of chlorpromazine is very effective in the majority of cases, but if a particularly quick response is required 0·25 to 0·5 mg. hyoscine can be given. Its effect begins within 10 minutes and should make it possible to transport a young and physically healthy patient within less than 1 hour without risk. Morphine is best avoided. Paraldehyde should not be injected into a struggling patient or given by mouth to one suffering from paranoid delusions; in other cases, where behaviour remains uncertain and impulsive, an intramuscular injection of 6 to 8 ml. may be given. Barbiturates such as thiopentone

SOME DRUGS IN USE FOR THE TREATMENT OF SCHIZOPHRENIA
PHENOTHIAZINE DERIVATIVES

Chemical Structure

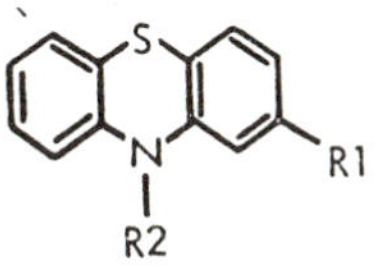

DIMETHYLAMINOPROPYL SIDE CHAIN

Drug	Trade names	Substituents
Chlorpromazine (Aminazin)	Thorazine Largactil Megaphen	R1 = Cl R2 = $(CH_2)_3.N(CH_3)_2$
Promazine	Sparine	R1 = H R2 = $(CH_2)_3.N(CH_3)_2$
Triflupromazine	Vespral Vesprin	R1 = CF_3 R2 = $(CH_2)_3.N(CH_3)_2$
Methotrimeprazine (Levopromazine)	Veractil Nozinan Neurocil	R1 = OCH_3 R2 = $CH_2.CH(CH_3).CH_2.N(CH_3)_2$

PIPERIDINE SIDE CHAIN

Drug	Trade names	Substituents
Mepazine Pecazine	Pacatal Lacumin	R1 = H R2 = $CH_2.CH_2$ 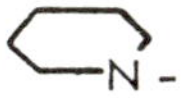 —⟨N – CH_3⟩
Thioridazine	Melleril	R1 = $S.CH_3$ R2 = $CH_2.CH_2$ $CH_3 - N$⟨⟩ 
Prochlorperazine	Stemetil Compazine	R1 = Cl R2 = $(CH_2)_3N$  ⟨⟩ $N.CH_3$
Perphenazine	Fentazin Trilafon	R1 = Cl R2 = $(CH_2)_3N$  ⟨⟩ $N.CH_2CH_2.OH$
Trifluoperazine	Stelazine	R1 = CF_3 R2 = $(CH_2)_3N$  ⟨⟩ $N.CH_3$
Thiopropazate	Dartal Dartalan	R1 = Cl R2 = $(CH_2)_3N$  ⟨⟩ $N.CH_2CH_2OCO.CH_3$
Fluphenazine	Moditen Prolixin Permitil Anatensil	R1 = CF_3 R2 = $(CH_2)_3N$  ⟨⟩ $N.CH_2.CH_2.OH$

FIG. 8

DRUGS OTHER THAN PHENOTHIAZINES

BUTYROPHENONES Haloperidol	Serenace Haloperidol	
RAUWOLFIA ALKALOIDS		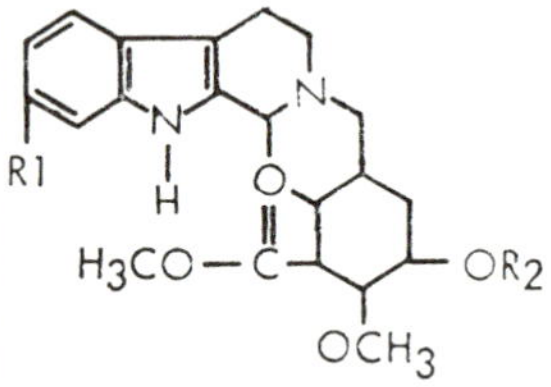
Reserpine	Serpasil	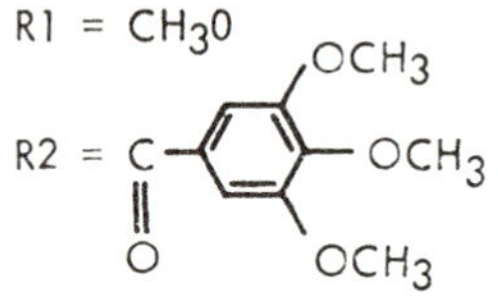 $R1 = CH_3O$ $R2 = $
Canescine (Deserpidine)	Harmonyl	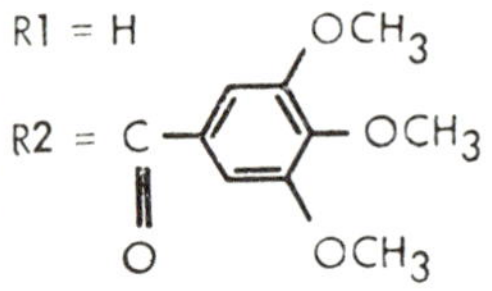 $R1 = H$ $R2 = $
Rescinnamine	Moderil	$R1 = CH_3O$ $R2 = $

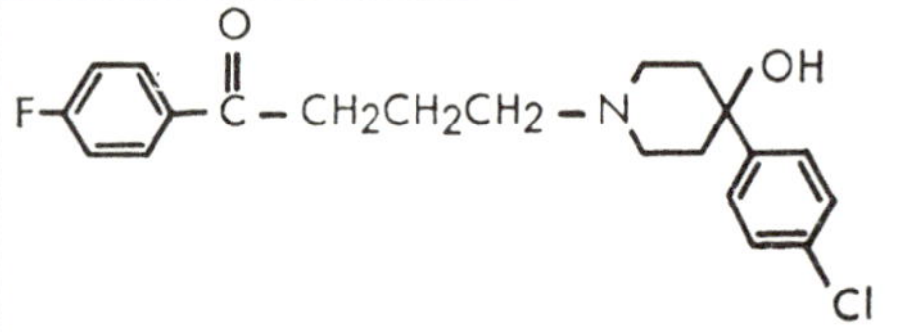

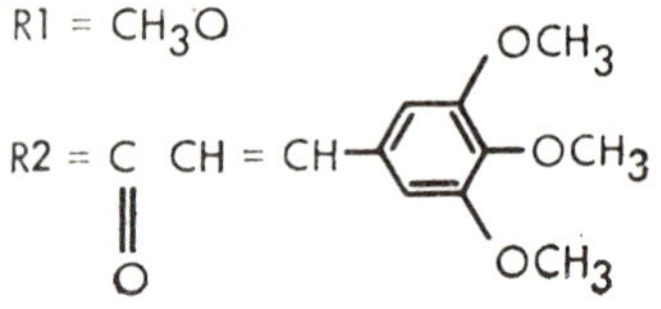

FIG. 9

and hexobarbitone sodium should not nowadays be administered by the intravenous route to acutely disturbed schizophrenic patients. It is far safer to give additional intramuscular injections of phenothiazine drugs if the patient's behaviour remains disturbed or uncertain after the initial measures.

The efficacy of phenothiazine drugs in acute schizophrenia has been firmly established. In one carefully designed controlled therapeutic trial of three substances and an inert placebo, 9 psychiatric hospitals participated (Goldberg *et al.*, 1965). The drugs administered to the 340 newly admitted patients included representatives of the three main groups of phenothiazine substances, namely chlorpromazine (Largactil) which has a di-methyl and aminopropyl side chain in the R2 position (Fig. 8), and fluphenazine (Moditen) and thioridazine (Melleril), both of which have a piperidine side chain in the R2 position. All three drugs proved effective but there were no differences between them. However, in patients with any suggestion of liver damage, it is preferable to use thioridazine in doses similar to chlorpromazine, or one of the low dosage phenothiazines such as trifluoperazine or fluphenazine.

As far as the choice of phenothiazines for long term use is concerned, it has been claimed that the more inert and withdrawn patients respond best to phenothiazines with a piperazine side chain such as trifluoperazine and prochlorperazine (Hollister *et al.*, 1960). It is also believed that over-active, excited, or aggressive patients respond better to high dosage phenothiazines such as chlorpromazine and thioridazine. There is, however, a good deal of overlap in the action of these substances and as already indicated the effects of the latter group are not confined to symptoms of restlessness and excitement. There is, further, an element of unpredictability in the response to drugs in that some restless and disturbed schizophrenic patients fail to improve on chlorpromazine but make an excellent response to one of the drugs with a piperazine side chain. These idiosyncrasies are not common but cannot be ignored in clinical practice and call for a certain amount of trial and error with different phenothiazine drugs in patients whose response appears unsatisfactory. For maintenance dosage with chlorpromazine and thioridazine, 150 to 300 mg. per day will usually suffice. In the case of the much more active phenothiazines of the piperazine group quite small doses (10 to 15 mg.) daily are adequate. But there are patients who can be stabilized only on much higher doses of phenothiazine drugs of any group and these require particularly careful supervision.

Although chlorpromazine has stood up to extensive trials and is on the whole a very effective and relatively safe preparation, certain toxic effects are common and the clinician has to be on the alert for them. Denber and Bird (1957), investigating 1523 patients who were given 300 mg. chlorpromazine daily, observed extrapyramidal symptoms (7·6 per cent.), skin rashes (4.6 per cent.), cardiovascular symptoms (1·8 per cent.), oedema (1·7 per cent.), jaundice (1·2 per cent.) and convulsions (1·1 per cent.). Blood dyscrasias in the form of agranulocytosis or aplastic anaemia are a rare but well-recognized complication and there is some evidence that they are commoner in females. Jaundice and skin rashes are unrelated to drug dosage and tend to occur in the early stages of treatment but not invariably so; they call for the immediate withdrawal of the preparation in question. There seems to be little association between these toxic effects and the dosage of phenothiazine drugs. Some undefined idiosyncrasy probably underlies most of them.

Although jaundice is a relatively rare complication and most patients recover within a few weeks of discontinuation of the drug, it occasionally progresses to a fatal necrosis of the liver. The jaundice generally has obstructive features and is due to a cholangiolytic hepatitis. The highly potent low-dosage phenothiazines more recently introduced, have the advantage that the hazards of jaundice and probably blood dyscrasia are far smaller. However, extrapyramidal symptoms including Parkinsonian manifestations and severe, painful, tonic spasms of the facial and back muscles occasionally leading to opisthotonos, sucking and chewing movements, facial grimacing and occasionally oculogyric crises, are all more common. In some patients 'akathisia' develops: this is a state of enforced motor restlessness, which renders the patient incapable of sitting still for more than a moment; he is forced to pace up and down in a restless manner and often experiences inner agitation.

The symptoms are rapidly reversed when the drug responsible is discontinued or reduced in dosage. Alternatively, the administration of an anti-Parkinsonian agent such as benzhexol in doses of 10 mg. thrice daily may effectively avert the side-effects.

Another substance which deserves brief mention is the substituted butyruophenone compound haloperidol (Fig. 9) which has a structure resembling gamma-amino-butyric acid. It has many properties of the major tranquillizers and has been found to be effective in chronic schizophrenia by Brandrup et al. (1961) who conducted a double-blind controlled study in 36 schizophrenic patients. The drug is sometimes effective where other preparations have failed, but extra-pyramidal and other side-effects may be very severe and it is best to proceed cautiously with doses of 0·75 mg. daily which may be increased slowly at intervals of a few days by doses of 0·75 mg. With the aid of anti-Parkinsonian drugs a dosage of 6 mg. daily may be tolerated but 2 to 3 mg. daily generally suffices for maintenance dosage. For rapid control in acute catatonic excitement a single intravenous or intramuscular dose of 5 mg. may be given.

Finally, a small place remains for rauwolfia-alkaloid (Fig. 9) in the treatment of schizophrenia. Its use is limited by the frequency with which it induces a depressive effect, and it is therefore particularly contra-indicated in schizophrenics with a depressive colouring. The side-effects also include sleepiness and lethargy, stuffiness of the nose, dizziness and diarrhoea as well as extra-pyramidal symptoms and hypotension. There is, however, a small proportion of schizophrenic patients that fails to respond to phenothiazines but improves on reserpine. The effect in the occasional patient with marked apathy and withdrawal can be striking. Dosage should commence with 0·5 to 1 mg. three times a day increasing until an optimal effect is produced. Doses as high as 9 to 12 mg. daily may prove necessary. It is claimed by some workers (Barsa and Kline, 1955) that a combination of chlorpromazine and reserpine is more effective in a proportion of schizophrenic subjects than either of the drugs singly, but this combination is now rarely used.

The introduction of neuroleptic drugs coincided with a period of renewed interest in the influence of social setting upon the behaviour of patients in mental hospitals and with development of the concept of the therapeutic community. This in turn reawakened interest in the achievements of the period of 'moral treatment' in the first half of the last century (Rees, 1957). The question as to the extent to which the increasing rates of discharge of schizophrenic patients from hospitals could be attributed to therapeutic enthusiasm and changes in administrative policy on the one hand, and to specific pharmacological effects on the other, has been studied by a number of investigators (Hordern and Hamilton, 1963; Hamilton et al. 1960, 1963; Bradley et al. 1959, 1964; Rothlin, 1961). The findings have proved interesting. A good deal of evidence has come forward to suggest that the effects exerted by drugs are in some measure dependent upon the general quality of care and the amount of stimulation received by the patient, as well as by the features of the social milieu in which treatment is provided (Meszaros and Gallagher, 1958). It seems clear also that intensive care and programmes of group activity can, over short periods, yield results which are comparable with those achieved by neuroleptic drugs alone (Cooper, 1961) and that 'moral treatment' can promote a significant reduction of symptoms (Hamilton et al., 1963). Some unexpected results have also emerged, for example, the finding (Hamilton et al., 1960) that drugs may exert an inhibitory effect upon the improvement that can be obtained in chronic schizophrenic male patients with occupational therapy. The precise implications of some of these findings are not clear.

There is little information as yet about the precise symptoms influenced by 'moral treatment'. In the case of neuroleptic drugs on the other hand, as already indicated, something more than an influence on isolated secondary symptoms appears to be involved and some experienced workers (Lehmann, 1964) consider that phenothiazine drugs hold the schizophrenic process in abeyance and should be regarded as 'psychotostatics'. We do not know either how long the effects of social and occupational therapy can be sustained, nor whether attempts to apply 'moral therapy' to schizophrenics discharged into the community would be either feasible or effective. The evidence that phenothiazine substances will frequently control many of the features of schizophrenic illness in most social settings, is now beyond reasonable doubt. Their beneficial effects endure over relatively long periods and seem independent of social class (Roth, 1964). There is evidence also that relapse and re-admission rates among patients discharged from hospital are significantly reduced by phenothiazine drugs (Gittelman *et al.*, 1964). The psychiatrist is unlikely to go far wrong if he seeks to provide for his patients both a stimulating environment and appropriate pharmacological treatment. The effect of pharmacological treatment and therapeutic enthusiasm has in most studies proved to be superior to therapeutic enthusiasm alone. On the other hand scepticism, with or without drugs, is unlikely to prove of value in treatment.

Thyroid medication has been introduced by Gjessing as therapy for periodic catatonia on the basis of his metabolic findings in long-term serial studies of such patients. Although Gjessing's pathological findings have been confirmed by others, some workers have not been as successful as he was in abolishing the periodicity; our own attempts have been unsuccessful.

PREFRONTAL LEUCOTOMY. There has lately been a sharp reduction in the use of prefrontal leucotomy as a treatment for schizophrenic illness: whereas in the years 1948–55 leucotomies for all forms of illness were carried out at a rate of approximately 1,000 a year (Tooth and Newton, 1961), Pippard (1962) found that in the year ending June 30th, 1961, 525 leucotomies had been performed. The change is probably due partly to the effectiveness of psychotropic drugs in the control of the chronically excited, aggressive, hostile schizophrenic patient. But some two decades of experience in the practice of prefrontal leucotomy had also taught us that in some of the most characteristic forms of schizophrenic illness it is of no value and may prove harmful. In cases of dulling of volition and emotion, whether due to an originally inadequate personality or the outcome of the disease itself there was never any rational indication for operation. But an affectless desolation of spirit may also underlie superficial over-activity or aggressive behaviour. The mis-identification of such conduct as the result of tension has sometimes led to unfortunate results. Some schizophrenics are liable to suffer more than other patients from organic lesions of comparable gravity. If operation is to succeed the patient must be able to adapt to the effects of the surgical lesion. However, if considerable deterioration of personality has taken place, this power of adaptation is lost and the result of adding an organic defect may be to bring about the total destruction of the patient's personality.

Recent years have seen a radical modification of surgical techniques and the orthodox operation in which thalamo-frontal connexions were approached through the lateral convexity of the frontal lobe is hardly ever used. Most of the modern procedures are aimed at the isolation of the medial or orbital surface of the frontal lobe. Thus bimedial frontal leucotomy (Paul, Fitzgerald and Greenblatt, 1956) involved division of the medial 2–3 cm. of white matter just anterior and medial to the frontal horn along a line extending from about 2 cm. in front of the coronal suture to the sphenoidal ridge. The blind rostral G operation (McKissock) aims at producing a more limited lesion mainly confined to the superomedial segment of the frontal lobe. More recently limited undercutting of the orbital cortex (Knight, 1964; Sykes and Tredgold, 1964), has been extensively used with considerable success in affective disorders, but experience of the operation in schizophrenic illness is very limited and results are far less favourable than in affective disorders. In recent years stereotactic operations (Herner, 1961) have made possible a far more precise location of the lesion and the use of radio-active yttrium (Knight, 1965) has enabled a more reliable and well-defined version of the operation to be developed. Modern operations have greatly reduced the hazard of serious personality damage from a leucotomy and, although the indications for surgery have dwindled, a very limited place for the operation in schizophrenic illness of late onset remains.

Operations undertaken for the management of patients with recurrent impulsive outbursts of violence and of periodic states of excitement or resistive and negativistic behaviour can now only be very rarely justified as the great majority can be readily controlled by a combination of convulsive treatment and neuroleptic drugs. Leucotomy cannot help the hebephrenic patient or the catatonic of early onset, and a frontal-lobe lesion will often appear even to accelerate the deterioration of personality. It is the paranoid and paraphrenic types of illness commencing after the age of 35 to 40 and the occasional case with catatonic features of late onset that nowadays provide the main indications for operation. If the operation is to have any chance of success, there should be evidence that the pre-morbid personality had some qualities of friendliness, warmth, drive, stability and effectiveness. Another good omen for a favourable outcome is provided by observations suggesting that some aspects of the pre-morbid personality survive in relatively intact form behind the psychosis. This can be judged to some extent from the quality of rapport, the extent to which feeling for and interest in relations and friends survives, the quality and degree of participation in social activities and hobbies. But in some patients only brief glimpses of the personality that survives can be obtained during the short-lived remissions induced by courses of electroconvulsive treatment combined with neuroleptic drugs. Patients with an illness of late onset dominated by paranoid features with a relatively well-preserved personality yield some of the best results. The paraphrenic whose illness began in late or middle life and the patient who is tormented by threatening and cajoling hallucinatory voices or spends his life writing letters to authorities protesting and complaining about alleged injustices will frequently do well. In place of the previous uncompromising rigidity we may see a return to normal and useful life after leucotomy.

The decision to operate on individual patients should be made only after a careful appraisal of the basic personality, the relative importance to be attached to the factors enumerated in the section on prognosis and those discussed above. The patient's prospects of adapting to post-operative frontal deficiency symptoms, and the social and occupational circumstances which will be faced in case of discharge, have also to be taken into account. There seems little justification for operating on a paranoid patient who has no home to go to and who has arranged despite his delusions, a tolerable life for himself within the hospital.

Schizophrenia is an illness of prolonged and varying course with the possibility of fluctuations and remissions, and the fear of relapsing into the 'masterly inactivity' of psychiatry in former periods should not lead us into an impatient over-activity. The time factor in psychiatric therapy is to be compared with that of orthopaedic rather than abdominal surgery. The ability of the patient to adjust to and even encapsulate the illness and

his response to treatment may take months or even years fully to disclose themselves.

An initial improvement after leucotomy is sometimes followed by relapse. This may
happen within a matter of weeks or months of operation, or after years in which case a
new lighting up of the disease process may be the explanation. It is then important to bear
in mind that treatments that have failed or led to short-lived remissions before operation
may prove more effective after it. A carefully-planned course of electroconvulsive treatment
combined with neuroleptic drugs is fully justified within two to three months of operation
and may be rewarded with an excellent result. If this should fail, signs of personality
damage are absent, and a review of the case confirms that indications for operation were
sound, a second operation should be considered. Where all the indications for operation
were favourable, failure is frequently due to an inadequate lesion or possibly one that is
incorrectly placed. But we have very little evidence at the present time that the anatomical
site of the cut should vary according to symptomatology or type of illness.

As far as results are concerned few recent figures are available for schizophrenia. In
Sykes and Tredgold's study out of 13 patients, 4 were discharged from medical care after
operation and in 5 the condition was unchanged. In Herner's enquiry (1961) the result was
said to have been good in 27 per cent. of 64 schizophrenics who had a stereotactic operation.

Of older series of patients studied before the days of neuroleptic drugs we may quote
that of Mayer-Gross. Of 95 patients in whom insulin treatment had failed and who had
had the orthodox Freeman and Watts operation, 32 were outside hospital, 10 as home
invalids at follow-up. In chronic schizophrenics, whose illness had lasted on an average
7·3 years, Oltman (1949) reported 37·4 per cent. as able to leave hospital and 56·7 per cent.
as showing significant improvement. However, an enquiry by Robin (1958) showed the
results not to differ from those in a control group.

(4) Social Treatment—Rehabilitation and Discharge into the Community

In the first two decades of this century E. Bleuler's gifts of astute observation, freedom
from preconceptions and disregard for traditional inertia led him to advocate (and put into
practice) regular occupation for the schizophrenic in hospital, early discharge as soon as
acute symptoms had subsided sufficiently to make it possible, and a social service by which
regular visits were paid to recently discharged patients and help was provided in the
readjustment of family life. These three features of care are once again the chief subjects
of changing policy, experiment, investigation and discussion in the social treatment of
schizophrenic patients.

In the last 25 years much has been achieved so that it is possible to say that 'a revolution
in management has completely changed the outlook in this the most malignant of the
psychoses'. Before 1939 nearly two-thirds of the patients admitted to hospital with this
diagnosis would still be there two years later—now less than 10 per cent. of these remain
after two years.

REHABILITATION OF THE LONG-STAY PATIENT. Real though this change is,
schizophrenia remains a chronic disease, as Wing (1963) points out, and even in a hospital
which has had a tradition of active treatment for the past 20 years and a well-developed
system of rehabilitation services covering the whole of the long-stay population, the

residual schizophrenic patients who had been in the hospital over 2 years amounted to 24 per cent. of the total patients in 1960 (Catterson, Bennett and Freudenberg, 1963). The proportion in the majority of mental hospitals is likely to be higher. This is the hard core of the problem of treatment and resettlement.

Only a small proportion of this group in any hospital retain florid symptoms which require constant vigilance. The majority need routine care only and the degree to which they remain passive and indolent would seem to be connected with the social environment provided by the hospital in a way that is difficult to explain except on the basis of direct cause and effect (Wing and Brown, 1961). Hospitals vary a great deal: at one end of the scale adaptation to institutional life becomes an aim in management and at the other end a full programme of rehabilitation (facilitated by the use of phenothiazines) is deployed. A complex system of ward organization and all grades of workshop are provided; the simplest suited to the very severely affected catatonics, and the rest graded to provide increasing stimulus and incentive till the patient has been trained in industrial work on a contract basis in the sheltered conditions of hospital, up to the stage where his working outside the hospital becomes a possibility (Early, 1960; Cooper and Early, 1961; Barton, 1966). The ultimate aim of the phased rehabilitation schemes in hospitals is resettlement of patients in the community, but progress is inevitably slow and, even where rehabilitation has been taken seriously, only something like 12 per cent. of long-stay patients are likely to hold down stable jobs and be discharged from hospital (Catterson *et al.*, 1963). Fit for *work* is not necessarily fit for *employment*. Most authorities are in agreement that before the schizophrenic has reached the psychiatrist and the hospital he has been losing what skills he formerly had. He is, even after rehabilitation, to some degree socially withdrawn, slow, lacking in skill, not very industrious or pleasant in manner. He also lacks initiative and the ability to take responsibility. These are severe handicaps in the open industrial market (Wing, Bennett and Denham, 1964).

ARRANGEMENTS FOR DISCHARGE INTO THE COMMUNITY. At the stage where emergence from the shelter of hospital is contemplated considerable flexibility in approach, so that the special requirements of the individual patient (whether long- or short-stay) are met, appears to offer the greatest possibility of success. The patient should, ideally, have the choice of living in and working out or working in and living out, during a transitional period. In Great Britain the facilities of day-hospitals, night-hospitals, hostels or houses specially provided by the local authority are some of the expedients recommended for the problem of accommodation; and Industrial Rehabilitation Units, employment in sheltered factories such as Remploy or by employers who know the problem and have supplied repetitive work to the hospital workshops, are suggested as employment at this stage. What is chiefly to be avoided is to launch the patient on the community suddenly in such a way that the support to which he is accustomed is withdrawn. For it is just at this stage that he most requires supervision and comprehensive after-care.

The Industrial Rehabilitation Unit where the schizophrenic patient works alongside physically handicapped people appears to offer special advantages. Within the hospital the impact of minor degrees of abnormality in behaviour on ordinary people may be lost sight of, and habits which are necessary in everyday life in industrial society are not regularly practised: for example travelling to work, good time-keeping, following workshop routines, getting on with workmates, and conforming to the standards of the social group in dress and manners. In the realistic setting of the Industrial Rehabilitation Unit the patient's assets and deficits in these respects and also all aspects of his ability to work are shown up so that his suitability for discharge to work outside can be assessed without incurring disaster. He has also the encouragement of working in a community where he sees other people overcoming their handicaps. It is, of course, essential that the mentally handicapped should constitute only a small proportion of the intake of these Units or their advantage is lost (Wing, Bennett and Denham, 1964).

THE POLICY OF EARLY DISCHARGE. The endeavour to avoid the secondary handicaps of institutionalization by early discharge has gone a long way. In one investigation the total length of stay during a 3-year period for patients admitted in 1951 was 17 months and 11·4 months for patients admitted in 1956. These trends probably illustrate the situation for England and Wales as a whole and have probably continued since 1956 to the present (Brown et al., 1961; Wing, 1964a) till the average length of stay is measured in weeks rather than in months.

The success of early discharge depends on the development by Local Authorities and the National Health Service of a system of community care within the immediate area of the mental hospital. Ideally it should comprise visiting the patient's family to prepare for his home-coming, a boarding-out officer to look after problems of accommodation, and hostels preferably for short-stay. It should include occupation centres, sheltered work-shops, and social clubs. There should be day-hospitals and centres, out-patient clinics and a team composed of psychiatrists, social workers, nurses, health visitors, district nurses and mental health officers centered on the psychiatric unit to prevent relapse by maintaining regular medication, securing attendance at day centres, and dealing with problems of finding work, supporting the families of patients, and emergencies generally. It is obvious that this is a joint clinical and social approach and depends for its working on breaking down the artificial division of responsibility and attitude between hospital-based and community-based staff, between the clinical orientation of the National Health Service and the social orientation of the Local Authority (May, 1964). It also depends for success on there being some headquarters such as a mental health centre, where information can be freely exchanged between staff and the organization of services without overlap or gaps and with the minimum of time-wasting effort can be undertaken. It must be emphasized that what we are reporting is based largely on the obviously desirable provision outlined and advocated by Wing and his co-workers and other writers concerned with this field. It is what should be the pattern but is not yet in being in anything approaching a complete form. Though there are pockets where development on these lines is well-advanced there is evidence to show that early discharge is out-stripping the provision of community services particularly in the large conurbations which account for half the population of the country.

In a study of male schizophrenic patients discharged from London mental hospitals in 1959, Wing and his associates (1964) found that at discharge 57 per cent. showed moderate symptoms and 17 per cent. severe symptoms. Fifty-six per cent. deteriorated in clinical condition during a year and 43 per cent. were readmitted to hospital. Of the 34 per cent. still actively deluded at discharge, 23 per cent. became worse subsequently. Fifty per cent. of patients for whom drugs were prescribed did not take them. In 59 per cent. of the patients' families, social relations were strained. One-third of the patients did less than three months' work during the year but nearly one-half worked for eight months or more. The majority made use of the services provided by out-patient departments and general practitioners, though there was very little domiciliary visiting. The writers say that these figures must be interpreted very cautiously in trying to formulate an overall picture. Mandelbrote and Folkard (1961) found considerably less disturbance in a Gloucestershire series where the community service was in process of developing but the information at their disposal was far less complete. In another study of three hospitals covering respectively a fairly compact industrial city, a mixed rural and urban area, and a predominantly middle-class suburban and commuter district, of 330 patients admitted in 1956, about half were socially reasonably well-adjusted 5 years later (Wing and Brown, 1961).

For the moment it must be assumed that schizophrenia still has a tendency to run a chronic course and that even patients now being admitted for the first time run a substantial risk of still being severely handicapped 5 years later. The community management of the patient whose disease runs an intermittent or chronic course—and who therefore ought to remain in contact with medical and social services for many years—is seen to be of central importance to the public health authorities. In the old days, these patients would have accumulated in mental hospitals; in future, they will accumulate in the community. Although many authorities are beginning to provide rehabilitation programmes lasting up to several months, few are willing to provide long-term services on the necessary scale. As matters stand at the present it appears to be true that the majority of schizophrenic patients remain in the community only at the cost of a great deal of strain and hardship for their families.

The final optimal balance as between long-stay hospital and care in the community will not be known till there have been some years of observation and experiment. In the best mental hospital of the old type the schizophrenic patients belonged to a community of a kind, and for some schizophrenics life in the outside community can only be purchased at a cost to society and to the patient himself. In the meantime it is vital that mental hospitals should retain their active therapy and rehabilitation programmes and not become reposi-tories for the hopelessly deteriorated.

THE PROBLEM OF ACCOMMODATION FOR THE DISCHARGED SCHIZO-PHRENIC PATIENT. Community care has been available from before the Second World War in the form of boarding-out. The best-known example is the colony of Gheel in Belgium, where many schizophrenics live distributed among the agricultural population, each as a member of a farmer's household. They are visited and supervised by a central body. A similar system is used by the hospital at Risskov near Aarhus in Denmark although it has declined in importance in recent years. These involve only a limited form of social integration for the patient which leaves him in a largely dependent role. In an industrialized society, the extent to which this approach can be applied is decreasing.

It is often easier to settle the discharged patient in work than in living accommodation. One of the benefits of early discharge is that the ties with the patient's family have not been severed; but whether he should be returned to the exact setting from which he entered hospital is a matter that requires careful appraisal in each case. There is some evidence to show that there is less chance of a stable adjustment when the patient returns to a household where there is a strong emotional involvement with some key person such as the mother or wife (Brown et al., 1958, 1962). These studies showed that patients tended to do better with remoter kin, in the households of carefully selected landladies, or in hostels, and that, wherever they were placed, they had a better outcome if they went out to work or were in other ways able to spend part of the day away from home. These are valuable clues to what may prove most beneficial to both patient and family but 'it would be most unwise, at this stage, to elevate such partial insights to the status of principles for preventive action' (Wing, 1964*b*).

The effect on the family receiving the patient again into its midst also requires careful consideration. If, as has been shown, something approaching half the receiving families function under considerable strain, it is obvious that some provision should be made to support them. Active family counsellors could do much by advising on management, and supervising drug administration. They could pass on information about the trend of events to other members of the team and decide what and when action was necessary. It would seem that a nurse who has known the patient in hospital might be the best person to fill this role, but it is obvious that any family counsellor is handicapped unless she can call upon the various agencies of a good community service.

CHAPTER VI

EXOGENOUS REACTIONS AND SYMPTOMATIC PSYCHOSES

(Psychoses accompanying infections, systemic, visceral and endocrine disease. Toxic-exhaustive psychoses. Psychoses in pregnancy and puerperium.)

BECAUSE of their physical causation psychoses of this type have always attracted the interest of the psychiatrist; but they have made up only a small proportion of his practice, because the mental complications of physical illness are *traditionally regarded as belonging to general medicine*. It is taken for granted by the physician that a patient with a temperature is somnolent in the daytime and delirious or restless at night, or that a child convalescing from one of the fevers is moody, over-sensitive and sleepless. Psychiatric advice is not sought when in a case of fulminating pneumonia languor and drowsiness are followed by a somnolence that deepens into coma and death. Ancient names like typhoid and typhus show us that at one time psychological symptoms were thought to be of diagnostic importance in general medicine; thanks to modern methods their significance has been largely lost. Little mention is nowadays made of the mental complications of infectious disease, even in comprehensive and up-to-date text-books. We can form no estimate of the absolute frequency of symptomatic psychoses, because we must include under this term the milder as well as the most severe mental symptoms; and the milder symptoms escape the psychiatrist and are ignored by the surgeon and the physician.

At one time psychiatrists believed in a characteristic mental picture for every physical disease, a belief that was long held and was for instance shared by Kraepelin. It was the remarkable achievement of Bonhoeffer (1910) to describe the *forms of exogenous reaction* and demonstrate their universality and independence of the nature of the underlying physical illness. This great work of clarification introduced order and simplicity into a field where confusion had previously reigned. It had, however, one undesirable effect in that since then interest in the finer discrimination of symptoms has dwindled. This is a matter for regret; for clinical observations which had been soundly established by critical physicians have been entirely forgotten, and the incentive for collecting and comparing new material in this field has failed.

AETIOLOGY AND PATHOLOGY

If there is damage to the brain by trauma or if an infection involves the central nervous system and causes meningitis or encephalitis the appearance of psychiatric symptoms is easily accounted for. But the degree of *involvement of the nervous system* and the severity of the symptoms are by no means always closely related. The brain maintains a functional stability which may show a considerable power of resistance to many general infections. Even in a case of tuberculous meningitis, marked mental symptoms may be absent if only a part of the cortical coverings is involved. On the other hand, post-mortem examination of the brain in cases of symptomatic psychosis often reveals to present methods of investigation no pathological findings which can account for the psychiatric symptoms. Even where the psychosis is due to a brain lesion, the extent of the cerebral finding is not often comparable with the severity of the mental symptoms shown in life.

Depending on the nature of the underlying physical condition, whether this is for instance an infection, a metabolic disorder or a traumatic lesion, different pathways for the production of psychiatric symptoms may be implicated. Some other difficulties may be illustrated by the theoretical explanations offered for psychoses accompanying infections. These may be classified as (1) rise of temperature, (2) vascular disturbance, (3) bacterial toxins, (4) toxic intermediate products of metabolism—singly, and in combination.

1. The severity of the mental symptoms frequently runs parallel with the fluctuations of the *fever* in infections, and delirium often subsides with a fall of temperature. On the other hand, psychotic symptoms may precede any rise of temperature, as in the so-called initial delirium of typhoid fever; or they may only appear after the temperature has returned to normal (post-febrile delirium). It is commonly held that fever is a defence of the body against invading micro-organisms; it is difficult to reconcile this notion with the idea that fever, by itself, may provoke symptoms which are a serious complication of any illness. Finally, it has not been found that the experimental production of fever causes any marked mental change; and we must conclude that there is no proof that the raised temperature seen in infectious diseases is a direct cause of mental disturbance.

2. In infectious and many systemic diseases, the regulation of *capillary function* is disturbed throughout the body. If this extends to the cerebral capillaries, the cortical cells cannot be properly supplied with oxygen and it may be expected that mental symptoms will ensue. This theory would certainly explain psychoses accompanying cardiac decompensation and the anaemias, but it seems doubtful whether it could be applied to the whole group of symptomatic psychoses.

3. The fact that many physically ill people show mental symptoms in the later and more severe stages of their illness suggests the idea that it is not the infection itself, but the *exhaustion* caused by it which has affected the central nervous system. The objection to this theory is that it is difficult to assign any precise meaning to the word 'exhaustion'; if it is used to mean a loss of resistance of the C.N.S. to noxious substances, it is merely a cover for our ignorance. It is probable that an infectious illness brings about a call on the body's reserves of nicotinic acid and other vitamins of the B group; and as has been shown by Sydenstricker (1943), acute deprivation of these vitamins can precipitate a symptomatic psychosis. The lack of nicotinic acid and of other vitamins which are important constituents of certain co-enzymes, interferes with the cellular metabolism and especially with the carbohydrate metabolism of the central nervous system. When infection increases the oxidative activity of the body while enzymes are wanting owing to a lack of chemical precursors, a deficiency syndrome ensues. These syndromes will be discussed in the special section of this chapter. The experiments and observations by American workers in this field and the lessons we have learned from reports on prisoner-of-war camps are striking advances and promise further elucidation. Nevertheless it would be going too far to claim that some form of vitamin deficiency is always operative in psychoses of this type:

4. There is much to be said for the theory that *toxic substances* produced by micro-organisms may adversely affect the function of the cerebral cells and produce mental symptoms. The close similarity of the forms of mental disturbance found in symptomatic psychoses with those seen in various types of chemical intoxication supports this view. Unfortunately we know so little of the chemical nature and pharmacological properties of these hypothetical toxins, that little help can be derived from it. Furthermore, all observers agree that symptomatic psychoses are almost unknown complications of diphtheria and tetanus, infections which give rise to the most powerfully acting exotoxins known, attacking the peripheral nerves and leading to motor and sensory symptoms. One would, therefore, have to assume a considerable specificity of action of the bacterial toxins, although they would produce a relatively non-specific mental reaction.

5. The accumulation of *toxic intermediate products of metabolism* is the cause of mental symptoms in uraemia and diabetes. It was long held that in the same way alcoholic delirium was caused by hepatic dysfunction; and the similarity of alcoholic delirium to the symptomatic psychoses generally suggested that the same principle was of even wider application. However, it is now generally accepted that Wernicke's encephalopathy is related to thiamin and other vitamin deficiencies whereas delirium tremens, in common with other delirious states, is a withdrawal syndrome of a special kind (see below). No general explanation of delirious states in terms of some disturbance of liver or kidney function is likely to be on the right lines (Wikler, 1957).

6. A discussion of the aetiology of symptomatic psychoses would not be complete without mention of the *constitutional factor*, although this is not likely to play either an essential or a very specific role. It is on *a priori* grounds probable that some people are more liable to mental disturbance than others, when placed under any kind of environmental stress; and this probability is to some extent borne out by experience. There are numerous clinical records of persons who became delirious every time they suffered from an infective illness, even though the infections were of different natures. A familial incidence of symptomatic psychoses is, however, rare. Formanek (1939) has reported the occurrence of endogenous psychoses in over 8 per cent. of the sibs of 117 subjects of symptomatic psychosis, a finding which suggests that a proportion of the propositi had been mis-diagnosed; but it is generally agreed that an attack of schizophrenia or manic-depressive psychosis may be lit up by a physical illness, and then may take on, at least at the beginning, a delirious quality (p. 259). Beck (1930) followed up 135 patients suffering from symptomatic psychoses. He found that if there was a familial tendency to endogenous psychosis, the clinical picture shown by the patient tended to have similar colouring; but that there were no features suggestive of an endogenous psychosis where the family history was negative.

A constitutional factor related to the *age of the patient* must be mentioned. Delirious states complicating an infectious illness are more common in children than in adults; emotional disturbances following infectious illness are said to be particularly frequent in adolescents and young people, and the Korsakov syndrome occurs most frequently as a sequela of a symptomatic psychosis in the middle-aged and the elderly.

Summarizing our discussion of aetiology, we may say that a symptomatic psychosis may probably be produced by *more than one type of pathogenic mechanism*. However, in the light of recent observations, it seems likely that all symptomatic psychoses in which a disturbance in the regulation of consciousness appears to be involved probably have a patho-physiological factor in common. Recent observations have demonstrated that the functions of awareness and vigilance are regulated by the reticular activating system of the mid-brain and diencephalon which has diffuse connections with the cortex of both cerebral hemispheres. That some interference with this system underlies delirious reactions is suggested by the nature of the associated electroencephalographic abnormalities which commonly take the form of bilaterally synchronous bursts of rhythmic slow activity. Moreover the gradual slowing of the E.E.G. in the course of ageing and the immature E.E.G. of children in which slow activity tends to predominate until the age of ten, may explain the special vulnerability of the two extremes of life to attacks of delirium. This explanation for the patho-physiology of states of clouding of consciousness is further supported by the fact that where these are caused by structural lesions, as in the case of intracranial tumour, raised intracranial pressure or apoplexy, the common factor appears to be a basal lesion or indirect pressure causing stretching and partial occlusion of the perforating arteries that supply the reticular formation from the circle of Willis. When mental function is disturbed, a very generalized syndrome results—most commonly some impairment of consciousness or cognitive function. To this, particular features may be added in the form of a depressive, manic or paranoid colouring, which in the past were commonly attributed to the constitution of the patient. Such explanations have proved too facile in a number of instances and there is now less readiness to accept them without statistical evidence.

Changes in the electrical activity of the brain are commonly associated with symptomatic psychoses particularly when they are associated with a disturbance of consciousness (Engel and Romano, 1944, 1959). In the mildest forms of clouded consciousness there may be slowing of the basic frequencies which would be difficult to detect unless the patient's previous E.E.G. pattern is known. Where the disturbance reaches the stage of mental confusion, the predominant frequency is generally within the theta range, although there may be a good response to visual attention and intellectual effort. In frankly delirious cases, slow activity is in the delta range and this becomes irregular and unresponsive. As coma develops the E.E.G. becomes dominated by generalized 1–3 cycles per second activity which is often bilaterally synchronous. However, the correlation between the disturbance in consciousness and the change in the E.E.G. is not as close as was previously thought. Thus both in barbiturate intoxication and in delirium tremens the record may be dominated by fast activity. Moreover, little abnormality may be detected in some cases of unequivocal clouding of consciousness. The E.E.G. and the psychological tests we employ to evaluate levels of awareness are independent measures, both relatively crude, for one type of disturbance of cerebral function. It is only to be expected that they should be incompletely correlated with one another. If correspondence were perfect one or other test would be superfluous.

Increasing attention has been paid in recent years to the occurrence of delirious states following the sudden withdrawal of drugs such as barbiturates, alcohol, and narcotic drugs in states of addiction. Delirium tremens is now widely regarded as being a withdrawal phenomenon. Sudden withdrawal of drugs of addiction may precipitate epileptic attacks and, at times, status epilepticus. The E.E.G. changes are of considerable interest in that bursts of spikes or spike and wave complexes may be seen even in cases without convulsions. In place of a typical delirious state, the effect of withdrawal may be to precipitate an acute paranoid psychosis with little or no disturbance of consciousness. The facts suggest a rebound phenomenon within the mechanisms concerned with the regulation of consciousness. Further enquiries into withdrawal-delirious states may, therefore, do something to clarify the physiopathology of this group of disorders.

CLINICAL PICTURE

General Clinical Features

When mental functions are interfered with by such organic causes as physical illnesses and intoxications, the nature of the symptoms depends not only on the nature of the basic disturbance, but also on the amount of interference with normal function and the rapidity with which it has come on. The specific symptoms associated with particular causes will be discussed under appropriate headings in this and the four following chapters; what it is important to note at this point is that these specific symptoms are always shown against a background of other non-specific symptoms, which show much constancy from case to case and are also largely invariant with respect to the personality. These general symptoms are of great diagnostic significance and in their totality define two recognizable syndromes, the acute and the chronic psycho-organic syndromes. In the chronic psycho-organic syndrome, which emerges when organic causes produce a disturbance of slow and insidious onset, we find the dementias and the organic personality changes. In the acute psycho-organic syndrome, with organic causes producing their effects rapidly, we find the twilight states and confusional states. The distinction between these two syndromes is based on quantitative differences, and is accordingly far from sharp. We find the symptoms of an early chronic psycho-organic syndrome among the prodromata of an acute psycho-organic syndrome; and the acute syndrome may leave behind it as sequelae changes characteristic of the chronic state. We also have to note the precipitation by organic causes of syndromes which clinically closely resemble the so-called functional psychoses, manic-depressive and schizophrenic. The chronic psycho-organic syndrome is described in detail in Chapter IX.

THE ACUTE PSYCHO-ORGANIC SYNDROME. (1) CLOUDING OF CONSCIOUSNESS. This is the cardinal symptom which is likely to appear when brain function is disturbed by a change which has come on rapidly and recently; and it is important that it should be recognized when present, even in its slightest degrees. Clouding of consciousness can be defined as a state of reduced wakefulness or a disturbance of awareness, and it can vary from the mildest diminution of functional capacities to the blanking out of consciousness in coma. The phenomena observed have a certain parallelism with the normal changes one may see in the subject who passes from complete wakefulness into the hypnagogic state, the state of light sleep and dreaming, and finally into deep sleep. It has to be understood that clouding involves all mental functions, including conative and affective ones; but that, as the cognitive functions depend on highly exact adjustments and adaptations, it is in this field that slight impairment of wakefulness is most readily observed.

Slight degrees of clouding of consciousness produce their effects at all stages from the receptive to the effector side of mental activity. The patient has difficulty in giving and in maintaining attention. He tends to be easily distracted; he is less master of himself than in the normal state, and he cannot dismiss from his mind the irrelevant sensory experience or the irrelevant idea. Perception is affected so that sense data are misjudged; illusions, especially visual illusions (the seeing of faces and figures in the pattern of wallpaper, for instance) are very much more likely to arise than in the normal state. There are corresponding difficulties in comprehension, shown at first only at the highest and most abstract levels. Perceptions received in such a state do not result in memory impressions of normal sharpness, so that subsequently the experiences undergone during a state of clouding may be impossible to recall—or may be recalled in a chaotic state, out of order or proportion, or tangled up with illusions. There is an equal difficulty in mobilizing the memory store; slight word-finding difficulties may be a distinctive feature. In general, however, focal psychological disturbances do not stand out from a level of mental functioning which is generally depressed. Called on to respond to a complex situation, the patient is likely to be slow, and to show some degree of perseveration in thought and speech. Judgements, also, will be less balanced and less adequate.

Conrad (1960) has made an interesting attempt to understand the psychological changes of clouded states with the aid of the principles of Gestalt psychology. Thus the difficulties in attention, comprehension, etc., can be described as difficulties in raising the figure from the background, in maintaining it against disturbing forces arising from the background, and in manipulating it. Gestalts are not sharply circumscribed and finely differentiated; figure-background differentiation is blurred, and is much less open to voluntary and goal-directed action. The patient loses his freedom to select the mode of figure-formation, and becomes the passive victim of forces which impose on him unwanted gestalts, e.g. illusions, which constantly change and shift. Conceptual thinking breaks down, and becomes cluttered with incoherent and fragmentary matter, often visualized and taking on a hallucinatory or pseudo-hallucinatory or delusional quality. Even the self and the environment are incompletely differentiated. Conrad likens the state of the patient to that of the man absorbed in the reading of a book, in a theatrical or film performance, or in listening to music; only by an effort can he come to himself, an effort which is beyond the powers of the patient in a state of clouding.

Accompaniments on the affective and conative sides are likely to be seen in mood changes and changes in behaviour. Many of these phenomena may appear as prodromata to the state in which consciousness is demonstrably impaired. One of the commonest conditions is a state of excitability and irritability. All thresholds are lowered, and the patient is intolerant of noise, likely to react with startle to a minor stimulus, restless, querulous, liable to complain largely of small matters.

The mildest degrees of clouding of consciousness may be difficult, even impossible, to recognize from a single examination. All the patient may show to the observer may be some slowness in responding and a tendency to lose the thread if called on to carry out an intellectual task. The difficulty in forming memory imprints, however, may be such that re-interviewed on the next day, the patient is found to have forgotten the themes of discussion of the day before, or even to have forgotten that that interview had ever occurred. In all states of clouding there is much fluctuation, from day to day and over the course of the day, If the state is a mild one, there will be long periods in which he is completely clear, and a repeated morning visit may find him again and again at his best. One should be alert then to reports of changes in behaviour towards the end of the day; one is more likely to detect clouding at such a time, or in circumstances of fatigue. One may see signs of motor unrest, the occurrence of illusions and misinterpretations of sense data, even hallucinations. Visual hallucinations are much more common than auditory ones, although auditory hallucination is the characteristic feature of the chronic hallucinoses which may also occur with symptomatic psychoses.

Other manifestations of organic interference with higher level mental functions are less specific. The patient may have no complaints, but is unlikely to feel well, and the vagueness of his malaise may suggest a neurotic rather than organic illness. Restlessness, anxiety, mild depression or dulling of spirits, emotional lability, edginess and irritability are all common. There is usually some disturbance of sleep, with difficulty in getting off, and a tendency to disturbed and vivid dreaming. Reversal of the normal sleep rhythm is a feature of encephalitis.

An increase in suspiciousness and the occurrence of delusional ideas is a feature of importance. These experiences may occur with suddenness and conviction, in a form indistinguishable from the primary delusional experience, in states of clouding so mild as to be unrecognizable as such. If delusional ideas well up in an impaired state of consciousness, they will be vague, fluctuating, chaotic, soon forgotten; if consciousness is clear they will be better defined and will be organized into the patient's experience of the total situation, with consequent rationalization and systematization. In such an event a very schizophrenic-like picture may be presented; and, after such an episode, the delusional idea may be retained without insight for a long time.

(2) DELIRIUM. In delirium consciousness is reduced to such a degree that the patient is disorientated for time and place. His attention is fleeting and the field of attention is narrowed. He is unable to grasp the situation for any length of time and to relate it to his recollections of the past. His thinking is disconnected and frequently concerned only with *imaginary experiences*. Besides these, there are *sensory and motor symptoms*. His perceptions of the reality around are confused by illusional falsifications and by hallucinations of dreamlike scenes, which are mainly visual but in which all other senses may be involved. He moves about in a superficially purposeful way, but shows in addition a general restlessness, trying to leave his bed to run away from his imaginary enemies, or to fight them.

In severer states, the hyperkinesis consists of fragments of purposeful actions only, and when clouding of consciousness passes this mark, movements are reduced to tossing, rubbing or trembling ('*muttering delirium*'). There is a corresponding disturbance of speech with iteration and perseveration, slurring and dysarthria. The mood of the delirious patient varies with his imagination, but fear and bewilderment usually prevail. The sleep rhythm is disturbed: during the day he seems dazed or drowsy, while towards evening sensory and motor signs come to the fore and are most marked at night.

Quiet sleep is often the first sign of the delirium subsiding, and a *terminal sleep* of over twenty-four hours is the usual end of the psychosis. As a rule *subsequent recollection* of the time of the delirium is fogged or completely obliterated, but isolated incidents may often be found to stand out in fairly clear relief. In unfavourable cases the motor excitation subsides as weakness increases, leaving finally nothing but an ataxic fluttering of the hands and muttering of the lips. The patient becomes entirely inaccessible and does not react even to painful stimuli, and finally sinks into a state of coma.

Among the *complications and variations* of the typical delirium are epileptic seizures, which may occur singly or in series. Bonhoeffer has also described *twilight states* very similar to those which occur in idiopathic epilepsy. In these the patient passes abruptly into a state in which severe clouding of consciousness is combined with extreme slowness of reaction, monotonous movements and occasionally outbursts of rage and fear. In the *infective hallucinosis*, also described by Bonhoeffer, hallucinations are prominent, while motor signs and disturbance of awareness are less conspicuous.

The pattern of a delirious state varies a good deal from case to case. Many authors have stressed the fact that each patient has an *individual pattern*, which appears whatever the physical cause of the underlying illness. Little is known of how individual predisposition on the one hand, and the quality and rapidity of action of the noxious agent on the other hand, influence the form of the delirium. Wolff and Curran (1935), studying 103 cases of delirium, found that the clinical picture was to a striking extent dependent on the previous personality of the patient. This referred not so much to the form of the psychosis as the content of delirious fantasies. These individual differences became blurred as the degree of mental disorder increased in severity.

Finally, '*residual delusions*' have been observed in rare instances, which have persisted after the delirium has subsided. These may take the form of an obstinately maintained belief in the reality of an impressive hallucination. Soldiers wounded in battle, during the period of their illness, have formed the idea that they had received a high decoration, and retained the delusion after all other symptoms had disappeared. In other battle casualties residual delusions have been repeatedly described which played the part of furthering an escape motive; but this type of explanation is by no means generally applicable. The mechanism of the residual delusion seems not unlike that of the experience known to many normal people, in which an exceptionally vivid dream maintains its quality of reality long into waking hours. It also resembles the persistence of belief in a schizophrenic delusion, after the active psychosis has remitted, even to the point where it is simply forgotten. Apart from specific delusions, a somewhat *paranoid attitude* is fairly common after recovery from a symptomatic psychosis; the hospital environment must in some cases be held partly responsible for producing this state of mind. Such an attitude, with vague feelings of reference, may be prominent and administratively disturbing, even when the preceding clouding of consciousness was so slight as to have escaped notice (see Chapter III, p. 148).

(3) SUBACUTE DELIRIOUS STATES (Confusional States). This is a diagnostic category which is not universally accepted. However, it seems desirable to distinguish the peculiar psychotic pictures one may observe in which states of clouding persist, without deepening into delirium, but with some degree of confusion and disorientation being present for long periods at a time. In typical cases awareness fluctuates between a lesser and greater degree of wakefulness. The *leading symptom* is *incoherence of thinking*, and this fragmentation extends to all mental processes, including perception and action. In more lucid moments the patient seems to realize the disturbance. He asks questions expressing his helplessness and perplexity—'Where am I?', 'What is going on here?', 'What does it all mean?'. After a few minutes, however, he slips back into the old confusion, in which actions are disjointed, purposeless, sometimes repetitive, and spoken sentences are fragmentary. Hallucinations, if present, are single, not in scenes.

Incoherence is the leading symptom in many acute psychoses. It is frequent in attacks of schizophrenia. In severe manic conditions incoherence and excitement may overshadow all characteristic signs of mania. Moreover, schizophrenic and manic psychoses may both be set alight by a febrile illness, and the clinical picture may then be coloured by symptomatic features such as clouding of consciousness. The resemblance between a subacute delirium and an acute catatonic schizophrenia may be so close that the possibility of mis-diagnosis may arise. The former is best distinguished by the *fluctuations of consciousness* and the relative accessibility of the patient in his more lucid periods.

THE DYSMNESIC SYNDROME. Disturbances of memory, including Korsakov-like states, after a symptomatic delirium are not rare. Not only does the patient have the usual blank recollection for the duration of the psychosis, but also a *difficulty in retaining recent events* and a vague or faulty orientation. Distant events are, however, well remembered.

There is a tendency to confabulate, even though this is not always marked. Abnormalities in the perception of time have been described, as in Korsakov syndromes of different aetiology. At this stage of the illness consciousness is clear, although delirious symptoms may recur at night. The condition may last a few days only and disappear quite suddenly, or recovery may be slow and imperceptible over weeks or months, depending on the progress of the physical illness. Signs of peripheral neuritis may or may not be found. Although it bears close clinical similarity to alcoholic Korsakov states, the prognosis is better, as eventual recovery is almost invariable.

Although it is sometimes seen in young patients, *post-infective dysmnesia* is mainly found in the middle-aged and elderly. Sub-clinical senile or arteriosclerotic changes have been held responsible, not always with good cause; and explanation by a hypothetically reduced resistance of the ageing brain is little more helpful though less likely to be wide of the mark.

POST-INFECTIVE NEURASTHENIA (DEPRESSION). This condition is treated neither by psychiatric nor by general medical text-books with the attention it deserves. It occurs after any severe physical illness, or during its later stages, and is a frequent sequela of such infections as influenza, typhoid, dysentery, Weil's disease and infective hepatitis. It may follow a period of delirium, but more often occurs independently. The symptoms resemble those of the first stage of delirium; malaise, headache, feelings of weakness and fatigue, hypersensitivity to light and noise, with a tendency to startle, frightening hypnagogic hallucinations, lack of concentration and listlessness. The patient is rather emotional, easily moved to tears, sometimes despondent, hopeless and depressed. He may also be disgruntled and suspicious, complaining of being badly nursed and neglected by his friends. In some cases *depression and retardation* are prominent, in others *anxiety and hypersensitivity*. Hypochondriasis is often marked; and some patients exaggerate their complaints in a hysterical fashion alien to their ordinary behaviour. On occasion symptoms of neurasthenia are mixed with those of a dysmnesic state; both conditions have been attributed to 'exhaustion' caused by the preceding physical illness.

The duration of post-infective neurasthenia is often unrelated to the course of the underlying disease, and depression and hypochondriasis may outlast all signs of bodily illness for months. Recovery may be gradual, or the sudden change-over to a feeling of well-being, which is so characteristic of recovery from severe bodily illness, may take place unheralded at any time. It will be plain that the clinical features of post-infective neurasthenia have much in common with the neurotic depressive and anxiety states which figure so prominently in contemporary psychiatric practice. The more depressive of these conditions responds well to antidepressive drugs, while the occasional case, in which the features are of a more endogenous kind, generally does well with electroconvulsive treatment. In the light of these facts, it is uncertain how far the physical illness can be regarded as sufficient cause of the psychiatric complications. Comparative enquiries into the clinical picture and pre-morbid personality of these patients, and follow-up studies of their pattern of outcome, should clarify the situation.

HYPOMANIC AND MANIC STATES. Excessive cheerfulness, over-activity and excitation accompanying or following physical illness are seldom mentioned as a form of symptomatic psychosis; but from our experience and from the cases reported in the extensive literature on the subject, we have little doubt that such conditions occur not infrequently and have the same causal connexion with the physical illness as the opposite affective condition. The reason that *euphoria* is not explicitly described, e.g. as a post-infective symptom, like 'neurasthenia', is because it rarely reaches a degree regarded as abnormal enough for a psychiatrist to be consulted or seriously disturbs the personal relations of the patient. He himself finds it only natural that he should be over-active and very refreshed after overcoming a severe physical illness. But observant physicians and friends and, in some cases, astute self-critics among the patients realize the abnormally strong and persisting euphoria.

Manic admixtures may also colour delirious and dysmnesic states and it has long been known that in certain fevers mania with extreme restlessness, distractibility, flight of ideas and delusions of grandeur can occur.

SCHIZOPHRENIA-STATES. Pictures closely resembling schizophrenia may occur in the course of mental illness resulting from physical causes. Perhaps the best established of these is the paranoid psychosis accompanying amphetamine addiction. A similar psychosis is produced by chronic alcoholic addiction and may show as an acute hallucinosis or less commonly as chronic hallucinosis or a state resembling paranoia. The schizophrenia-like psychoses accompanying chronic epilepsy, mainly with temporal lobe focal lesions, also resemble chronic paranoid schizophrenic states. The problem presented by these psychoses is discussed in the section on symptomatic schizophrenia on page 299.

Metabolic Disorders

VITAMIN DEFICIENCIES. The recent advances in our knowledge of the effects of metabolic and nutritional deficiency diseases, have added a great deal to our understanding of the aetiology and treatment of the psychiatric and neurological effects of vitamin deficiency. They have also shed a certain amount of light on the causation of symptomatic psychoses in general. It has been shown, for example, that the experimental withdrawal of vitamins from the diet of human volunteers exerts, within a relatively short time, certain specific effects on mental functioning (O'Shea *et al.*, 1942; Kreisler *et al.*, 1948). In certain of the deficiency diseases pathological findings in the central nervous system may be minimal or absent. Yet 'a biochemical lesion' has been indubitably conferred in these cases. This provides a good illustration of the fact that modern biochemistry has in this field of psychiatric research taken up the task that morbid anatomy has had to abandon (Mayer-Gross *et al.*, 1959).

PELLAGRA. In the earliest descriptions of the disease from Spain and Italy mental symptoms were mentioned along with disturbances affecting the skin, digestive tract and sensorimotor system. The pellagrine in Italy was a poor peasant who went mad. The disease is still endemic in Egypt and other Mediterranean countries, in the Far East, Africa, Mexico and the Southern States of the U.S.A. Its nutritional nature has long been recognized. It has been mainly found in poor communities living on cereals, especially maize, of low-protein value; complication by bacillary dysentery and other infections is very common. It has been suggested that the associated tendency to pellagra was one of the factors that set limits to the achievements of the great maize civilizations of South America. Pellagra is generally considered to involve a deficiency of several factors of the vitamin B complex. However, since it is rapidly relieved by the administration of nicotinic acid alone, pellagra is probably caused mainly by a deficiency in this vitamin. The association of maize with pellagra is in some respects unexpected in that whole maize contains more nicotinic acid than polished rice and pellagra is rare in the extreme among rice eaters. It would seem that the nicotinic acid in maize and other cereals is present in bound form from which it is released by treatment with alkali.

In advanced states of pellagra, 'central chromatolysis' in the Betz cells of the motor cortex, and in certain large and medium-sized neurones of the brain-stem and spinal cord, is the most consistent histological finding. In many cases degeneration of the posterior and lateral tracts of the spinal cord is also found.

The bodily symptoms take many forms, dermatological, gastro-intestinal and neurological, and may involve the special senses. The psychological symptoms, which have been described by many observers, are just as various. Characteristic seems to be an *intermittent quality of the mental symptoms*, which, like the skin lesions, tend to become worse in the spring.

Neither European nor American writers give any reliable estimate of the frequency of mental abnormalities among pellagrines. In all countries inadequate food intake is often due to mental deficiency or chronic psychosis, in subjects who may or may not be hospital inmates. Those sporadic cases seen in Britain and other lands where the disease is not endemic are usually drawn from such people.

A manic-depressive waitress employed in a huge, popular restaurant in town continued working in spite of her marked depressive state. Over many months she had no appetite and lived on plain tea and small bits of toasted bread. Her depression became worse and hysterical features appeared when, in early summer, a characteristic rash came out on her neck and hands, and she showed signs of neuritis and spasticity of the legs.

In cases of this kind, and in the chronic alcoholics who in U.S.A. form a great part of the pellagrines, it is obviously difficult to sort out the clinical features of the deficiency from the primary abnormality. Many divergent statements on symptomatology may be explained by these combinations. From the more critical descriptions which have been provided, it appears that mental symptoms may antedate physical signs by weeks and months. The most frequent early picture is one of *neurasthenia*, fatigue and lassitude, often with *depression* and suicidal tendencies. According to the personality of the patient, hysterical or anxiety symptoms may be prominent, or irritability and emotional tension. Rogina (1954) has described catatonic stupor, manic-delirious and depressive states among the psychiatric complications of nicotinamide deficiency. In its milder form the condition can easily be mistaken for a psychoneurosis, except for the very marked feeling of malaise and physical frailty.

Later on *delirium* and subacute delirious states seem to be by far the most common syndrome. They may also appear as an acute psychosis without prodromata. According to Italian workers, a marked *affective colouring*, especially of the depressive kind, is frequent in pellagrous psychoses. Mental symptoms of this severer kind seemed to be closely linked with physical signs and the attack may have a good prognosis; but relapses are frequent. Acute cases may take a fatal course if untreated. Dysmnesic states with general deterioration seemed to have been common among pellagrines in the past, but are apparently unknown since dietary therapy has been generally instituted.

In the *treatment* of the psychiatric symptoms of pellagra, nicotinic acid plays an important part. The patient is provided with a nutritious diet of high calorific value, with plenty of foodstuffs rich in vitamins of the B complex, such as milk, yeast, liver, egg, 'Marmite' yeast extract, etc. But in addition nicotinic acid or nicotinamide should be given in daily doses of 250–500 mg. during the first ten days, the dose being decreased later. Other compounds such as riboflavin and thiamin have to be given with caution because of the danger of disturbing the vitamin balance which in all cases of pellagra seems to be easily upset. Replacement therapy by large amounts of vitamins given orally and parenterally is justified on practical and empirical grounds; but theoretical support is more shaky than might be thought. Ellinger and his collaborators (1945) have shown that as much as 80 per cent. of the human requirement of nicotinic acid is manufactured by bacterial action and bio-synthesis in the gut.

THE ENCEPHALOPATHY OF NICOTINIC-ACID DEFICIENCY. This name was given by Jolliffe (1940) to a symptomatic psychosis characterized by clouding of consciousness, cog-wheel rigidity of the extremities and grasping and sucking reflexes. About half of his 150 patients had clinical evidence of pellagra and all were alcoholic. Some had serious organic disease such as septicaemia, phthisis, abscesses, etc.; many had polyneuritis and stomatitis. After testing these severely ill patients with different dietary régimes, it was found that large doses of nicotinic acid was the only medication that improved their condition and strikingly reduced the mortality. Prior to this report, Sydenstricker (1939) had reported a favourable response to nicotinic acid in a group of elderly patients with advanced arteriosclerosis whose prominent symptoms were unconsciousness and delirium; fifteen out of nineteen patients recovered. Most of the patients had been living alone on an inadequate diet, and were found unconscious and admitted to hospital in this condition; but none had signs of pellagra, nor a history of pellagrous complaints.

These observations have been confirmed, but the hope that symptomatic psychoses in patients not suffering from prolonged undernourishment could be relieved in the same way has not been fulfilled.

WERNICKE'S ENCEPHALOPATHY. Beriberi is now regarded as a thiamine deficiency. Although the peripheral nerves are frequently involved psychological symptoms are unusual. Fresh light was shed on the effect of this deficiency on the central nervous system by the study of what Wernicke in 1881 described as 'polioencephalitis haemorrhagica superior'. In three cases, two chronic alcoholics with delirium tremens and one young woman suffering from persistent vomiting, he observed ocular muscle palsies, spasticity and ataxia of the lower limbs and severe disturbances of consciousness. Post mortem he found congestion and haemorrhages in the grey matter of the brain-stem and hypothalamic region involving the mammillary bodies.

While the *pathology* was for a long time regarded as the outcome of a severe chemical intoxication, mainly by alcohol, identical findings were discovered as a terminal state in chronic illnesses such as intestinal carcinoma with vomiting and cachexia, pernicious anaemia, hyperemesis gravidarum. Alexander (1940) was able to produce in thiamine-deficient pigeons the lesions of Wernicke's syndrome identical in topographical distribution and histological appearance. Similar experiments have since been successful in foxes, dogs and cats. In human cases the illness is now not infrequently diagnosed *in vivo*; in some patients the level of pyruvate in the blood has been raised (Wortis *et al.*, 1942) indicating the disturbed carbohydrate metabolism which is due to lack of thiamine. Finally, the link between beriberi and Wernicke's syndrome seems to have been established in a series of fifty-two patients, observed by de Wardener and Lennox (1947) in a prisoner-of-war camp in Singapore. Of the patients who suffered from Wernicke's encephalopathy not less than 79 per cent. had also classical beriberi.

N

This evidence suggests that beriberi is produced by a slow and not very severe depletion of vitamin reserves, while Wernicke's syndrome is the expression of an *acute deprivation* superimposed on a pre-existing deficiency. The acute exacerbation is only likely to occur if some additional illness causes vomiting, diarrhoea and cachexia. This role may be played by dysentery, gastric carcinoma, toxaemia of pregnancy, chronic alcoholism and pernicious anaemia. Apart from lack of thiamine, other nutritional deficiencies are frequently involved as well.

About the *symptoms of early thiamine deficiency*, we are relatively well informed through controlled experiments in human volunteers carried out by several groups of American workers (Jolliffe *et al.*, 1939; Williams *et al.*, 1943; O'Shea *et al.*, 1942). Although some of the subjects were kept on a low thiamine diet for as long as 150 days and longer, it was found difficult to reproduce the neuritic symptoms of beriberi. Mental symptoms, on the other hand, were prominent, sometimes appearing after a few days. They were mainly of the nature of 'organic neurasthenia', depression, irritability, quarrelsomeness, general weakness, failing memory and confusion of thought, but included such bodily symptoms as anorexia, nausea, sleeplessness, constipation and dyspnoea on exertion. An increased sensitivity to noise and pain was also observed and a number of individuals were unable to carry on with their work. Mental inefficiency preceded by weeks and months the objective gastric and cardiac signs and peripheral neuritis.

It is obvious that symptoms so mild are apt to remain undiagnosed, especially if they occur in a chronic alcoholic or in the emaciated subject of carcinoma of the stomach or in a psychotic who starves himself.

The *fully developed picture* of Wernicke's syndrome with ophthalmoplegias and delirium or Korsakov syndrome is easily recognized, especially if peripheral neuritis and ataxia are also present. Mild intellectual deterioration is often missed, and the ocular symptoms may be transient. Ataxia and peripheral neuritis may be masked by a state of acute delirium and are difficult to establish in a patient severely ill with hyperemesis or intestinal carcinoma. Bender and Schilder (1933) subdivided their material, consisting of alcoholics only, into four groups. In the first group delirium, a variable rigidity, grasping and sucking reflexes were the leading symptoms; in the second, cerebellar and oculomotor signs; and in the third, catatonia were in the foreground; a fourth group showed polyneuritis combined with mental impairment.

The illness may be acute or subacute or appear as a terminal state. According to the localization of the lesions, involvement of the cranial nerves may vary or psychological signs may predominate. It is suggested that the *dysmnesic picture* results from foci in the mammillary bodies (see p. 487).

The following lists of symptoms and signs, giving their frequency in the fifty-two patients observed by de Wardener and Lennox (1947) are probably the most complete picture available at present:

Symptoms: loss of appetite, 88 per cent.; eye symptoms (wavering fields of vision on looking to the side, diplopia, photophobia) 63 per cent.; nausea and vomiting, 57 per cent.; insomnia, 38 per cent.; giddiness, 21 per cent.

Eye signs: nystagmus, 100 per cent.; external rectus fatigue and paralysis, 26 per cent.; complete disconjugate wandering, 8 per cent.; other signs (loss of visual acuity, papilloedema, pupil abnormalities, ptosis, complete ophthalmoplegia, retinal haemorrhages) each in 2 to 4 per cent.

Mental changes: emotional changes 67 per cent. (apprehension, 32 per cent., apathy, 32 per cent., excitement, 13 per cent.); memory loss for recent events, 61 per cent.; disorientation, 46 per cent.; confabulation and hallucinations, 25 per cent.; convulsions, 2 per cent.; sudden onset of advanced mental signs as first evidence of cerebral beriberi, 19 per cent. A recent study by Cravioto *et al.* (1961) suggests, however, that the typical triad of a disturbance of consciousness, some abnormality of extraocular movement and ataxia may be present in only a small proportion of cases. The commonest finding in the author's material was an organic mental syndrome dominated by a disturbance of consciousness which was present in 26 of 28 cases. In many subjects, no more than fragments of the typical Wernicke's syndrome, such as abnormalities of extraocular movement, ataxia and tremor were present, but extreme lethargy was common. An interesting observation was the frequent occurrence of hypotension, 20 of the 28 subjects having shown this abnormality at some stage of the disorder. As far as the pathological findings are concerned the dysmnesic picture was first traced to lesions in the mammillary bodies by Gamper (1927), a finding of some interest in view of the recent demonstration that lesions in other parts of the limbic system, as in the case of ablation of one temporal lobe, may produce a Korsakov-like syndrome (Penfield and Milner, 1958). In the study by Cravioto *et al.*, in addition to the typical vascular lesions of the mammillary bodies which were correlated with the organic mental syndrome, varying degrees of 'astrocytosis' were found, the thalamus being frequently affected.

The experimental evidence that Wernicke's syndrome is due to deficiency of thiamine has been successfully applied in *treatment*. The outlook in these cases was quite hopeless until recently. Thiamine given parenterally in daily doses of 50–100 mg. relieves the ocular palsies and has a striking effect on the milder psychological disturbances. Usually the whole B complex is given by injection; and from reliable reports, it seems that the mortality rate at least can be considerably reduced. Some structural changes are, however, likely to prove irreversible; and the mental or neuritic signs resulting from them will not benefit from this therapy.

VITAMIN B_{12} DEFICIENCY (Pernicious Anaemia and Related Conditions). While subacute combined degeneration of the spinal cord has been found, by different observers, in between 40 and 90 per cent. of patients suffering from pernicious anaemia, mental symptoms are rare. They were present in 4 per cent. of 1,498 cases of pernicious anaemia treated at the Mayo Clinic (Woltman, 1924). The number of cases seen by any single observer is small; and it is difficult to gain a general picture of the symptoms, and to decide how far they can be attributed to the physical disorder. Demyelination, closely resembling that seen in the spinal cord, and other histopathological changes have been found in the white matter of the cerebral hemispheres of psychotic patients.

An account has been given by Smith (1960) of mental illness occurring with B_{12} deficiency before the development of a recognizable macrocytic anaemia. Apart from the mental state, an abnormal E.E.G. might be the only positive finding. The psychiatric symptoms varied from case to case; headache, malaise and neurasthenic symptoms being prominent. The diagnosis was sometimes missed for so long that cerebral damage by demyelination occurred; and it was found that much larger doses of B_{12} were required for the treatment of such cases than was usually necessary in pernicious anaemia. As the E.E.G. is abnormal in some two-thirds of untreated cases of pernicious anaemia (Walton *et al.*, 1954) it may provide a valuable form of investigation in these early cases.

Psychological changes, such as neurasthenia, depression and irritability are sometimes precursors of the anaemia; somnolence and apathy may accompany it. In some cases manic states have been observed. But more common is a *paranoid psychosis with tactile hallucinations*, which can be traced to the paraesthesiae produced by the funicular myelopathy. Depression, which may be severe, and transient states of clouding may also occur. It may be difficult to differentiate these psychiatric syndromes from either an affective or a schizophrenic disorder. Later on in the disease exogenous features, such as disorientation, drowsiness and phases of delirium, may develop. The terminal delirious picture may be the result of Wernicke's encephalopathy, especially if the concomitant anaemia is not profound.

Loss of blood through *haemorrhage* does not produce mental symptoms other than loss of consciousness. This is true alike of post-partum haemorrhage and haemorrhage due to injuries received in battle, etc. Psychiatric symptoms indicate a complicating infection. Some *post-operative psychoses*, mainly of a delirious type, have also been explained by toxic factors and the products of breakdown of damaged tissues. Subacute delirious states after cataract operations are well known to the eye-surgeon, usually in middle-aged and elderly patients who have been kept blindfolded for some days. Arteriosclerotic or senile changes probably contribute, in elderly subjects, to these complex phenomena which are further discussed on p. 379.

EXHAUSTION AND STARVATION. The part played by exhaustion after *physical exertion* in the causation of severe psychological disturbance was formerly much overrated. Minor symptoms from this cause are well known, and can as a rule be easily understood from the psychological situation in which they occur. Explorers and mountaineers who are inadequately nourished become morose, irritable, hypersensitive and emotionally labile; they decline to speak, are slow in thinking and go about in a kind of dazed state of consciousness. If exertion continues without sleep, visual hallucinations and illusions appear, their content expressing anxieties or the fulfilment of wishes closely connected with the actual situation. After-images and hypnagogic hallucinations contribute to the symptoms and the picture is dominated by the affective state of the person or of the group. Most of these symptoms are due to the lack of sleep and to the anxiety caused by such situations as being marooned in difficult weather, or surviving after shipwreck (Critchley, 1943). In war-time a similar combination of physical and psychogenic factors results in what has sometimes been called '*battle exhaustion*' although the emotional strain may in most cases be more important than physical exhaustion. But it is worth noting that sedation and sleep is the really effective remedy.

If bodily exertion is required under conditions of *starvation*, the craving for food becomes the leading symptom. The effects of slow starvation have been studied by Leyton (1946) in German prison camps on prisoners whose rations of about 1,000 calories a day contained the bare minimum of vitamins to prevent clinical manifestations of deficiency. The subjective symptoms under this diet appeared in the following order: loss of the natural feeling of well-being, progressive mental lethargy, feeling of fatigue and sleepiness, difficulty in concentration and failing retention, although the power of recall of distant memories was well preserved. All movements, including gait, slowed down. At work the men were prone to accidents because they were too slow to move out of danger from a falling rock or tree. Apathy and a feeling of constant weakness prevailed, the only mental interest being food. *Hunger* increased during the first three weeks and persisted from then onwards unabated even after years of low diet. It occupied the whole thought and outlook, abolishing interest in books, games and any recreational pleasures, reducing self-control, the standard of cleanliness, personal appearance and moral conduct. The man would steal his best friend's rations and sell his overcoat for food or tobacco.

Almost identical observations have been reported by Danish workers studying their compatriots interned in Germany (Helweg-Larsen, 1952). In the United States experiments on 'semi-starvation' were carried out in 1945 in 32 volunteers who were kept on a diet of 1570 calories daily for 6 months. The principal features which appeared in all subjects during the experiment were again similar to those starving involuntarily: intense preoccupation with thoughts of food, irritability and depression, decrease in initiative, loss of sexual drive and 'social introversion', features which were absent or much less marked in the same subjects before and after the period of starvation (Schiele and Brozek, 1948).

The much more reduced nourishment in the Nazi concentration camps led to *cannibalism*; and an extreme degradation of behaviour in these camps has been reported by reliable witnesses. They tally with earlier reports of famines, e.g. in Russia after the First World War, when cannibalism was rife in large populations (Abel, 1923). Only in the last stage before death, does the apathy and stupor become so severe that the craving for food disappears.

These observations are of interest to the psychiatrist not only because of the distinctive *features of starvation* as compared with avitaminosis, but in view of the frequent observations of refusal of food in psychiatric patients suffering from anorexia nervosa, depression or schizophrenia. Here the powerful, basic instinct of self-preservation seems to be perverted or lost through the abnormal mental state and this may lead to symptoms of vitamin deficiency added to those of the original illness.

ELECTROLYTE DISTURBANCES. Water Intoxication (Cellular overhydration). Water intoxication may occur post-operatively if excessive quantities of 5 per cent. dextrose are given intravenously; it may occur in uraemic states if injudicious quantities of water are imbibed; and it can follow the administration of excessive quantities of vasopressin.

Initially there is anorexia, nausea and vomiting. The patient complains of lassitude and there may be mood changes. Convulsions are common and fully reversible focal neurological signs, particularly hemiplegia, may develop. Clouding of consciousness, deepening to stupor and finally coma, occurs and will be accompanied by other features of delirium. Muscle cramps and twitchings are seen occasionally. The serum sodium level is low.

Hypercapnia. An acute rise in the tension of carbon dioxide in the arterial blood to 100 mm. Hg. or more with a corresponding fall of pH of the blood to 7·1 or less occurs during the course of carbon dioxide therapy and is associated with loss of consciousness (Meduna, 1950). It is believed that the excess carbon dioxide interferes with intra-cellular enzyme systems leading to a disease of cerebral oxygen consumption.

A less dramatic development of hypercapnia is seen in cases of severe emphysema and status asthmaticus. Westlake *et al.* (1955) investigated 21 emphysematous patients and found that whenever the arterial tension of carbon dioxide rose to 120 mm. Hg. or more, psychiatric disturbances were always present. In some cases acidaemia played a part and it was noted that similar symptoms always occurred if the pH of arterial blood was below 7·2. Symptoms often appeared during the first 24 hours of oxygen therapy due to carbon dioxide retention increasing, as the dyspnoea was relieved.

The patients showed varying degrees of clouding of consciousness, the more severe cases lapsing into coma. They were confused, disorientated and sometimes auditorily and visually hallucinated. Headache was common as also were muscular twitchings and a coarse tremor.

In some cases there is a rise in intracranial pressure associated with papilloedema. This association with emphysema has been recognized for many years and at one time was thought to be due to the rise of venous pressure which so often accompanies this condition due to right-side heart failure. The correlation with the increase in venous pressure is not close and it is now realized that these phenomena are associated with carbon dioxide retention, and if the latter is relieved the rise of intracranial pressure and papilloedema subside.

Treatment is aimed at improving respiration by direct stimulation of the respiratory centre by the rapid intravenous injection of nikethamide 10–15 ml. every 2 or 3 hours. Oxygen is given at a rate of not more that 1–3 litres per min. so that an oxygen saturation of 80–85 per cent. is maintained in the arterial blood. Retained secretions should be aspirated by bronchoscopy, infection combated with antibiotics and bronchospasm relieved by cortisone.

WATER DEPLETION. The occurrence of water depletion in shipwrecked sailors and in men lost in the desert is well recognized, as also is their propensity for developing visual hallucinations and other delirious features. Factors other than water depletion, such as exhaustion and lack of food, may play a part in the production of this clinical picture. The condition is seen in purer form in patients suffering from severe dysphagia and particularly in cases of severe weakness resulting from physical illness. Thirst is intense, the mouth dry and there is weight loss proportional to the water deficit. The patient looks grey and ill. 'Serious people become sombre, while others normally cheerful exhibit a somewhat hollow vivacity' (Black *et al.*, 1944). Later a delirious picture develops and if the condition is unrelieved gives way to coma and death. The plasma sodium and chloride tend to rise, as does the blood urea, though more slowly.

Treatment calls for the administration of water in adequate quantity by mouth or if necessary per rectum. If intravenous medication is required, water should be given in the form of 5 per cent. glucose solution (Marriott, 1947).

SODIUM DEPLETION. Normally the body conserves sodium chloride more effectively than it does water, and salt deficiency therefore occurs only under special circumstances; they are fulfilled in any condition where there is excessive loss from the body of water and electrolytes and only water is replaced. This may occur in conditions of extreme heat, giving rise to severe sweating, in any condition giving rise to severe vomiting or diarrhoea and particularly after operations when patients are maintained on 5 per cent. glucose solution intravenously. A similar deficit may occur in Addison's disease due to excessive loss of sodium chloride in the urine.

Mild states of sodium depletion give rise to a neurasthenic-like state with lassitude, apathy and excessive fatigue. Such states are very common in tropical climates and a remarkable return of vigour may follow the administration of salt. Saphir (1945) has pointed out how closely sodium chloride depletion may simulate psychoneurotic states. Rather more severe cases show, in addition, headache of a hypotensive character, giddiness and a tendency to faint with muscle weakness of a myasthenic character. The most severe cases are anorexic, may suffer nausea and vomiting, appear dehydrated but make no complaint of thirst and experience severe muscle cramps. Clouding of consciousness occurs, the patient becomes disorientated, and may be deluded and hallucinated. If unrelieved, coma and finally death ensue. Hyponatraemia does not necessarily indicate sodium depletion, since it occurs in primary potassium depletion and also as a result of excessive water retention, often due to inappropriate secretion of antidiuretic hormone. Such hyponatraemia may be symptomless or may be accompanied by psychiatric symptoms of organic type. In the latter case, correction of the electrolyte disturbance, which is often complex, may lead to improvement in mental state. Treatment of simple sodium depletion involves the administration of sodium chloride by mouth or intravenously until both the urinary volume and the urinary and plasma sodium concentration are normal.

POTASSIUM DEPLETION. Potassium depletion occurs post-operatively in patients who have been maintained on intravenous fluids lacking in potassium. It may also occur as the result of dietary deficiencies in chronic diarrhoea as in ulcerative colitis, in some cases of Cushing's syndrome and following the administration of desoxycorticosterone, ACTH or cortisone. A cause which must be borne in mind in cases of obscure aetiology is self-induced purgation over long periods in neurotic and hypochondriacal subjects.

In many patients there may be marked lethargy and apathy. Depression, sometimes profound in degree and accompanied by suicidal thoughts, is frequent. Some patients on the other hand become tense, apprehensive and irritable, while a few show a typically delirious picture. Muscular weakness with depressed or absent deep reflexes occurs frequently, as do abdominal distension and muscle cramps. A low serum potassium supports the diagnosis but is by no means the rule. Typical electrocardiographic changes often occur.

Apart from dealing with the primary cause, treatment involves the administration of potassium salts by mouth or intravenously. Potassium chloride 600 mg. in the form of slowly released tablets ('slow-K') four hourly is a suitable oral dose.

PORPHYRIA. There are at least five genetically determined types of error of porphyrin metabolism (Waldenström et al., 1963) and the pattern within a given family tends to breed true to type. The two most important varieties are the Swedish type, or acute intermittent porphyria (the commonest form found in Britain) and the South African type, or porphyria variegata. Each of these disorders is determined by a dominant autosomal gene. As penetrance of the gene is incomplete, the disorder remains latent in a proportion of affected subjects although they have a demonstrable abnormality of porphyrin excretion. Following the studies of Waldenström, and later of Dean (1963), it is now generally accepted that the two conditions are genetically and pathologically distinct. The most prominent clinical difference between them is that, whereas skin lesions are prominent in the South African variety, they are invariably absent in the Swedish form of porphyria.

In the latter, the symptoms are episodic and take the form of acute abdominal pain, headache, vomiting often associated with a predominantly motor neuropathy and, in many cases, psychiatric symptoms. These may dominate the clinical picture with symptoms of clouded consciousness and paranoid, noisy and hallucinated conduct. A severe depressive colouring is a prominent feature in a proportion of cases. The general metabolic disturbance is severe and polyuria, hypertension and deep coma may develop during a crisis. In a suspected case it is important to establish or exclude the diagnosis as soon as possible, for the administration of barbiturates either for the control of psychiatric symptoms or in the course of anaesthesia administered for an exploratory laparotomy prompted by acute abdominal symptoms, may cause extensive paralysis to develop and the patient to succumb from respiratory failure.

The diagnosis is aided by certain characteristic features. The family history is often informative although the frequent latency of the condition may obscure its hereditary character. The disorder is seldom manifested before puberty, and appears most commonly in the third decade. It may, therefore, be mistaken for an acute schizophrenic illness. In addition to barbiturates, attacks may be precipitated by sulphonals, sulphonamides, allyl isopropyl-acetylurea (Sedormid) and aminopyrine. The literature relating to precipitation by drugs has been well reviewed by Weatherall (1954). In a recent study the psychogenic factors and instability of the pre-morbid personality have not been found appreciably to contribute, as has been formerly held, to the psychiatric disturbances associated with the disorder (Ackner *et al.*, 1962). The urine of porphyric patients contains porphobilinogen (PBG) and delta-amino-levulinic acid (ALA) and will usually turn dark on standing but may be almost normal in colour. The biochemical abnormality is due to an over-reduction of ALA from the condensation of succinyl coenzyme-A with glycine in the presence of a pyridoxal-containing enzyme. ALA is reduced to PGB by ALA-dehydrase and both compounds are excreted in the urine.

Dean (1963) has given a fascinating account of his enquiries into the South African form of porphyria or porphyria variegata. He has succeeded in tracing some of his families manifesting porphyria through fourteen generations back to a Dutch settler and his wife who married in 1688 and produced four children. It is from this family that the estimated 8,000 persons who have porphyria in the white and coloured population of South Africa have descended. Occasional examples of the South African variety may be found in northern countries; the skin lesions are then mild or absent. It has been suggested by Waldenström (1963) that freedom from exposure to intensive sunlight is responsible for this latency of the skin lesions.

LIVER DISEASE. Considerable attention has been given during recent years to the psychiatric and neurological complications of hepatic failure. Gradual failure of liver function is associated with a characteristic constellation of physical signs which include vascular spiders on exposed surfaces, loss of body hair, testicular atrophy in men and often gynaecomastia, and the characteristic heightening of the patchy mottling of the palmar surfaces and the soles of the feet. As these changes develop, however, certain anomalies of personality commonly unfold. Affect becomes blunted and somewhat incongruously jovial, self-control and finer aspects of social judgement become impaired (Murphy *et al.*, 1948), the picture being slightly reminiscent of a frontal-lobe syndrome. An insightless euphoria may be seen and periodic fluctuations to a featureless depression or to a grandiose expansive picture may occur. As hepatic function progressively fails, periods of drowsiness subsequently or a fluctuating, subacute delirium, make their appearance. The patient is restless, disorientated and visual hallucinations with fearful paranoid delusions are common. The only specific feature of this condition is its neurological aspect, particularly the 'flapping' tremor of the upper limbs (Sheila Sherlock, 1955). With the patient's arms and hands extended in front of him, a fine tremor of about 6 to 9 per second is apparent, upon which are superimposed rapid bursts of flexion and extension at the metacarpo-phalangeal and wrist joints, which have been compared with the flapping movements of a bird's wings. In severe cases, the shoulders and even the trunk may be affected, but with the patient at rest the movements may be easily missed. There is some generalized increase in muscle tone and plantar responses are extensor when the disease is well advanced. In the early stages there is progressive slowing and disorganization of the alpha rhythm in the E.E.G. but, as clouding of consciousness becomes more pronounced, theta activity becomes dominant. This activity at 5–6 cycles a second is most prominent in the fronto-temporal areas, but with the onset of coma, bilaterally synchronous bursts of slow waves at 2 cycles a second appear in the frontal areas. When delta activity dominates the E.E.G. the prognosis is grave and the disappearance of rhythmic activity is a preterminal phenomenon (Parsons-Smith et al., 1957).

The condition may occur in association with portal hypertension, as the result of a surgically induced porto-caval anastomosis, or with hepatic cirrhosis or other liver disease. The fluctuations from stupor or delirium to full awareness have been attributed (Walshe, 1951; Sherlock et al., 1954) to parallel fluctuations in the serum level of ammonium ion, and large quantities of protein in the diet may precipitate an attack of hepatic coma. However, there would appear to be no simple quantitative relationship between the serum ammonium level and the severity of the mental disturbance; the role of the ammonium ion in relation to the psychiatric symptoms remains uncertain.

The treatment of the condition consists of maintaining the patient initially on a protein-free diet for about a week, following which protein is gradually introduced up to a maximum of 50 grammes daily. Temporary sterilization of the gut with a broad-spectrum antibiotic such as oxytetracycline, helps to reduce toxaemia and to hasten the remission from the psychiatric and neurological disturbance (Sherlock, 1955).

CARDIAC AFFECTIONS. The ancient idea that the *heart is the seat of the soul* or of the emotions is closely connected with mental symptoms, was current among psychiatrists until about 100 years ago; they even believed they could base their view on post-mortem findings. What was once informed opinion has persisted in the beliefs of the common people. It has been kept alive by the normal occurrence of sensations in the cardiac region in any emotion which does not lead to immediate activity; and it is expressed in phrases in many languages, such as 'heartfelt', 'heartless', 'a broken' and 'a sinking heart'. The heart, as a part of the body image, enters into the symptomatology of many neurotic reactions. For some time, cardiac neurosis under the terms Da Costa's syndrome, D.A.H. or effort syndrome, was discussed among cardiologists as if it were a syndrome in its own right. Although under these and other names it was frequently diagnosed in the First World War, 'neuro-circulatory asthenia', as it came to be called, figured to an insignificant extent during the last war, owing to the better insight into the nature of anxiety neurosis of which it was the presenting symptom (Wood, 1941) (see p. 96).

Sensations are of little use *as a diagnostic guide* in organic heart disease. Gross disturbances of rhythm are in many cases not perceived at all, and those patients who complain of unpleasant feelings are usually found to be organically sound. If anything, there is an inverse correlation between subjective complaints and objective findings; but it is not absolute. Organic heart disease does not prevent the patient from developing neurotic symptoms related to the same organ—and if they reach a certain intensity they may produce feelings of impending death. Cardiac invalids in their enforced inactivity are naturally liable to keep an anxious watch on their cardiac action. And if their attention is focused on their hearts by an authoritative medical opinion, the permanent anxiety may cause an additional strain on the circulation.

Besides anxiety, depression sometimes accompanies chronic heart disease; hypomanic pictures may also be seen.

In *cardiac failure*, all these symptoms may increase, and new ones may be added. Fatigue on mental effort, lack of concentration, impairment of memory, sleeplessness, nightmares, and marked emotional lability are frequent, and are probably attributable to cerebral anoxaemia. Delirious states, usually with much anxiety, are rare; but if they occur, are a serious complication. The clinical picture is that of an exogenous reaction, and frequently clears up entirely as the patient's physical state improves, but may return with another attack. Cases of delirium have been reported in which the psychosis started after the heart failure had been treated successfully and the oedema had disappeared. Symptomatic depressions and dysmnesic syndromes do not seem to occur after cardiac affections.

Hypertensive and arteriosclerotic psychoses will be discussed in Chapter X.

URAEMIA. Whatever the cause of the uraemia which may be extra-renal or renal, whatever the mechanisms responsible for its different symptoms, *mental changes* play a prominent part in the clinical picture and are not infrequently the *presenting symptom*. This applies to the subacute condition in which irritability, headache, dizziness, drowsiness, etc., may be mistaken for neurasthenia, as well as to acute cases of renal uraemia often complicated by hypertension, cerebral oedema and acidaemia.

Mental symptoms in uraemia proper without gross hypertension are those of weakness, apathy, lack of spontaneity and sleeplessness. Localized twitchings of muscles may be present, as also dyspepsia and vomiting. Drowsiness and sopor follow in severe cases and may lead to coma and death without any or with only mild signs of delirium.

Irrespective of the blood urea, if there is *hypertension* the mental picture is more varied: epileptic fits and twilight states, delirium and subacute delirious states, periods of drowsiness alternating with attacks of crying or howling aloud and excessive restlessness are all frequent. Transient amaurosis and disturbance of hearing have been described; and there may be other signs of *increased intracranial pressure* such as severe headache, slowing of the pulse, sopor and signs of pyramidal lesions. The first sign of illness may be the abrupt appearance of a psychotic state. In chronic cases the clinical picture may simulate the expansive form of general paresis.

The diagnosis of an uraemic condition is not easy even if the psychiatrist confronted with the clinical picture of a *severe toxic psychosis* thinks of it as a possibility. The differential diagnosis is fully discussed in textbooks of medicine.

Endocrine Disorders

HYPERTHYROIDISM. Psychological disturbances are prominent when there is over-activity of the thyroid gland and some symptoms are present in every case of hyperthyroidism. The least controversial part of this subject is the psychiatric picture associated with *thyrotoxicosis*. The symptoms in most cases resemble those found in anxiety neurosis. There is marked anxiety and tension, the patient is unable to keep still or to concentrate, there is a distractible over-activity and exaggerated sensitivity to noises and other stimuli. There is also emotional lability, irritability and impatience. Minor neurotic traits are prone to become exaggerated and the formerly effective and relatively balanced individual may become unreasonable, demanding, and behave in a hysterical manner. The patient shows diminished tolerance for frustration, becomes less capable of sustained effort and craves for the stimulation of company without being able to respond to it as he would like. Syncopal attacks which are not uncommon in hyperthyroidism may exacerbate the anxiety and give rise to a phobic aversion to going out alone. There is often a quite strong depressive colouring but this fluctuates and there is no retardation. Sleep is light and frequently disturbed by anxious dreams.

The *differential diagnosis* between *thyrotoxicosis* and *anxiety neurosis*, which is a more common disorder, is a matter of great importance and recent studies by Wayne and his colleagues (Wayne, 1960) have shed useful light upon the problem. In an analysis of the symptomatology of 83 indubitably thyrotoxic patients and 99 non-toxic subjects, Wayne has shown that features characteristic of thyrotoxicosis, in order of their discriminating value in diagnosis are: excessive sensitivity to heat and preference for cold, increased appetite, loss of weight, excessive sweating, palpitations, tiredness and dyspnoea on effort. The signs in order of their diagnostic importance were: cardiac dysrhythmia, hyperkinetic movements, pulse rate of over 90 per minute, palpable thyroid, bruit over thyroid, lid retraction, hot hands, lid-lag and fine finger tremor. It will be observed that some time-honoured symptoms and signs come fairly low on the list and sleeping pulse rates were, for example, of little value. It is also clear that evaluation of certain of the symptoms of discriminating value inevitably involves an element of subjective judgement as well as skill.

In a recent enquiry (Gurney *et al.*, 1967) it was found that thyrotoxic patients could be differentiated from euthyroid patients with psychiatric disorder (initially referred for suspected hyperthyroidism) by a number of clinical features other than the physical manifestations of thyrotoxicosis. These include the presence of a psychological precipitant for the illness, hysterical symptoms in the course of the illness, panic attacks, a younger age of onset, a high neuroticism score on the Maudsley Personality Inventory, a neurotic personality as assessed by clinical examination and the presence of depersonalization. All these features were more common to a statistically significant degree in the euthyroid cases. Although physical signs and symptoms together with laboratory tests proved individually the best discriminators, separation between the two groups could be substantially improved by the addition of items derived from psychiatric observation. The observations were made without knowledge of physical diagnosis or laboratory findings.

Figure 10 shows the frequency distribution in the 135 patients of the weighted scores for the 12 best discriminating items (see table) derived from a discriminant function analysis. Although the hyperthyroid and euthyroid groups are largely distinct their scores overlap to some extent. It will be seen that this modified diagnostic index achieves rather better separation between toxic and euthyroid cases than a previous index based on physical items alone (Wayne, 1960) applied to the same group of subjects. It was of interest also that when 7 cases, where the diagnosis was considered doubtful, were scored with the aid of the weights derived from the discriminant function analysis, they mostly fell into the distribution occupied by euthyroid patients with psychiatric illness. Patients suspected of hyperthyroidism in whom the diagnosis remains uncertain even after full investigation are generally suffering from a psychiatric disorder.

Laboratory tests such as radio-active iodine uptake, protein-bound iodine, and thyroid antibodies in the serum will establish the correct diagnosis in the majority of cases. But there is a difficult borderland between anxiety neurosis and hyperthyroidism and such laboratory findings should not be allowed wholly to decide the issue in all cases as against the general clinical appraisal. For this a systematic analysis of the psychiatric as well as the physical findings is essential. Hyperthyroidism may be triggered by some psychological

SCORING SYSTEM DERIVED FROM DISCRIMINANT FUNCTION ANALYSIS

Item	Grade	Weighting system
Neurotic personality	marked	−2
	moderate	−1
	stable	0
Age	15–24	+2
	23–34	+4
	34–44	+6
	45–54	+8
	55 and over	+10
Precipitant	present	−3
	absent	0
Hysterical symptoms	marked	−1
	mild	−0·5
	absent	0
Increased appetite	present	+2
	absent	0
Palpable thyroid	present	+1
	absent	0
Unequivocal thyroid Bruit	present	+9
	absent	0
Exophthalmos	present	+3
	absent	0
Lid retraction	present	+2
	absent	0
Hyperkinesis	present	+2
	absent	0
Fine finger tremor	present	+3
	absent	0
Pulse rate	over 90	+8
	80–90	+4
	under 80	0

Euthyroid range   − 4 to +11·5
Doubtful range   +12 to +19·5
Toxic range   +20 to +40

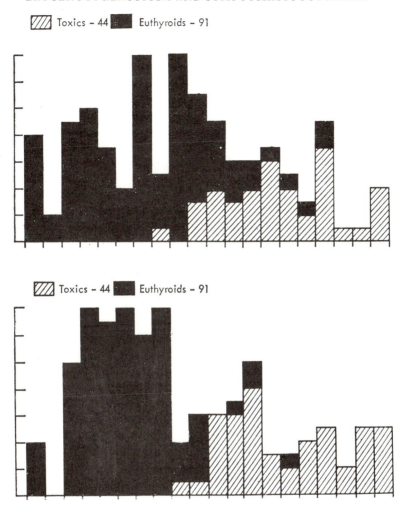

FIG. 10. Frequency distribution of toxic and euthyroid cases using (*top*) Wayne's Index and (*below*) Modified Index.

stress but this is less common and less impressively relevant than in the case of the neurotic disorders it resembles. The age of onset is higher and female predominance is greater than in anxiety neurosis. Hyperthyroidism is often described as a psychosomatic disorder and emphasis is laid on the importance of emotional conflict and imbalance in the previous personality (Mandelbrote and Wittkower, 1955) in the causation of the endocrine disturbance. The findings of some workers (Robbins and Vinson, 1960) who consider that the importance of personality factors has been overstressed, suggest, in fact, that the 'neuroticism' scores of thyrotoxic patients fall somewhere between those of normal and neurotic groups. The results of the enquiry described above were in broad agreement with these last observations. Although the hyperthyroid patients were a more stable group as judged by a number of indices, they did not differ significantly in respect of family history and previous record of psychiatric disorder from the euthyroid (largely neurotic) patients. These facts go some way towards explaining the sometimes relatively common clinical experience that thyroidectomy will fail to clear up the emotional disturbance in patients with proven hyperthyroidism (Carpelan, 1957). It seems likely that in a proportion of cases, at any rate, a predisposition to the development of neurotic symptoms contributes in some measure to the development of hyperthyroidism. Whether or not this has a relationship to the genetic factor in the causation of hyperthyroidism recently demonstrated by enquiries into the presence of thyroid antibodies in the serum of the relatives of thyrotoxic subjects (Hall, Owen and Smart, 1964) remains to be determined.

More serious forms of mental disorder were commonly seen in hyperthyroid patients before the introduction of antithyroid drugs and they frequently assumed the form of an acute organic psychosis. These pictures are less common at the present time and, when they occur, they may well be due to antithyroid drugs. Psychoses are more commonly of an affective nature nowadays and are often typically manic-depressive. An agitated depression is commoner than mania but severe manic conditions do sometimes occur. Schizophrenia-like illnesses have also been described (Kleinschmidt *et al.*, 1956) but the occurrence of this condition is regarded by Manfred Bleuler (1954) as fortuitous. The psychotic symptoms may subside with antithyroid treatment but this is by no means invariable and a depressive or schizophrenic illness may need independent treatment. Moreover, an acute psychotic reaction may develop after thyroidectomy or in the course of treatment with antithyroid drugs. Most of these disturbances respond to electroconvulsive treatment.

HYPOTHYROIDISM. Diminished activity of the thyroid gland may result from aplasia, hypoplasia, surgical removal of the gland, the action of antithyroid drugs or radio-active iodine or the inflammatory changes associated with Hashimoto's thyroiditis. Congenital aplasia or maternal iodine-deficiency are the basis of cretinism (see Chapter XII, p. 726). *Myxoedema* results from acquired hypothyroidism. It occurs most frequently between the ages of 40 and 60 and women are affected eight times as frequently as men. Although the highest incidence is in middle age, the illness may occur at all ages. In small children in whom myxoedema may be the sequela of measles or other infections, it is not easily distinguished from sporadic cretinism.

In addition to the changes in the skin, hair, heart and circulation through metabolism, mental changes are always present and are often the leading symptom; and the patient is frequently first seen by the psychiatrist.

The clinical picture has certain characteristic features. There is a progressive loss of interest and initiative and a pronounced slowing of all mental processes. The slightest exertion requires great effort and fatigue is quick to develop. The patient has difficulty in following a conversation, in reading a short newspaper article or carrying out the simplest intellectual task. She is slow in comprehension and action and takes a long time over the daily routine of washing, dressing and eating. Retention and recall of recent events is poor. Thinking easily becomes muddled and, in severe cases, a general intellectual deterioration develops in addition to memory defect. The colour and vivacity of the personality fade and this, together with a change in physical appearance, may render the patient unrecognizable. She may complain of her slowness and stupidity and say that there is a thickness or heaviness in her head, or that she feels she is in a fog. Later, distress is submerged in indifference and lethargy, and a sluggishness without emotion or desire supervenes. Every kind of activity is given up, and the patient just sits about, drowsy and inert. Charcot has compared the condition with hibernation (Zondek and Wolfsohn, 1944).

The severe forms of mental disorder associated with hypothyroidism provide a more controversial subject which has been well reviewed by Michael and Gibbons (1963). The psychiatric complications of myxoedema are rarely encountered in mental hospitals, yet Asher (1949) gathered 14 cases in an observation ward in London over a short period and Browning *et al.* (1954) were able to review 100 cases from the literature. A variety of psychiatric phenomena has been described, but the most common patterns of illness resemble those found in other chronic and subacute metabolic disturbances. Thus some degree of clouding of consciousness ranging from mild impairment to severe delirium is common but not invariable. Depressive symptoms are usually prominent and there is frequently a marked paranoid colouring with hallucinations of a persecutory and depressive kind. Anxiety, agitation and a bizarre hypochondriasis are other components described in some cases. Both Browning and Asher claim that adequate substitution therapy usually leads to complete mental recovery but this is by no means invariable.

The diagnosis is readily established from the clinical features in advanced cases but mild hypothyroidism is frequently missed. Laboratory investigations will usually decide the issue. The B.M.R. is always decreased to -20 to -40 per cent., plasma cholesterol is raised usually to some figure above 400 mg. per cent., and radio-active iodine studies show a poor uptake by the gland.

Thyroid treatment produces excellent results if it is begun early. Thyroxine needs to be administered with great caution as myocardial damage is almost invariable and, if the metabolic rate is increased too rapidly, heart failure or death from myocardial infarction may ensue. Treatment should, therefore, begin with no more than 0·1 mg. thyroxine daily. The dose should be increased gradually at intervals of two to three weeks.

CUSHING'S DISEASE (Pituitary basophilism). Clinical descriptions of Cushing's disease are generally dominated by the physical features, including the red moon-shaped face, hirsutes, wide purple striae on thighs, abdomen and buttocks, obesity, hypertension and mild diabetes. However, psychiatric disturbance is present in more than half the cases (Micheal and Gibbons, 1963) and is frequently prominent in the clinical picture. A number of the physical changes such as impotence, amenorrhoea, loss of libido, disfigurement and declining energy can be expected to prove distressing; but the psychiatric disorder is no mere reaction to the other components of the disease. Thus, although a retarded or anxiety-coloured depression is the commonest psychiatric disturbance, and elation is rare, 15–20 per cent. of cases are psychotic, and paranoid delusions and auditory hallucinations are occasionally reported. Sudden outbursts of restless, anxious or excited behaviour, or withdrawn and stuporous episodes are a common feature. The occasional appearance of psychiatric symptoms before the physical changes (Spillane, 1951) may be fortuitous although, in the few cases described, the picture conformed fairly closely to the psychiatric changes commonly associated with Cushing's syndrome. The diagnosis is made from the clinical picture combined with the characteristic biochemical changes; there is a markedly elevated urinary excretion of 17-hydroxycorticosteroids and the plasma level of cortisol is raised (20–50 micrograms per 100 ml.). The successful treatment of the endocrine disorder nearly always resolves the psychiatric illness.

ADDISON'S DISEASE. Psychiatric disturbances are almost invariable in Addison's disease, having been absent in only two of Cleghorn's 25 cases (Cleghorn, 1951) and three of the 40 cases studied by Bleuler (1954). The most common symptoms are apathy, depression, diminished drive and initiative and some fluctuation of mood. Elevation of affect appears far less common. A mild to moderate dysmnesic syndrome is present in the majority of cases. Addisonian crises are usually accompanied by an acute organic syndrome with clouding of consciousness, delirium and stupor (Michael and Gibbons, 1963). In the early stages of the disorder, the asthenia, loss of appetite and decline in weight and libido in a setting of moderate depression may lead to psychiatric referral. Pigmentation, hypotension, hypoglycaemia, and the biochemical finding of sodium loss, the retention of potassium and extra-cellular dehydration should help to establish the diagnosis. Treatment with cortisone usually terminates or improves the mental disturbance.

HYPOPITUITARISM. The view that chronic anterior-pituitary failure is associated with weight-loss still has a certain currency, although since Sheehan (Sheehan and Summers, 1949) published his classical description of the clinical picture of hypopituitarism, it has become clear that most of the cachectic cases of Simmond's disease formerly illustrated in text-books of medicine and physiology were almost certainly examples of anorexia nervosa. The psychiatric features have been well described by Kind (1958) who investigated 20 adult cases, selected with the aid of Sheehan's diagnostic criteria. Impotence in the male and loss of libido in the female were almost invariable and so was marked loss of initiative, somnolence and pronounced intolerance of cold. Mood disorder was present in every case with indifference, apathy and depression punctuated by outbursts of irritability. In severe cases there may be extreme inertia and inactivity associated with a decline in personal habits and standards. Associated with these changes are features of a mild chronic brain syndrome. An impairment of memory for recent events was present in the majority of Kind's untreated cases. The combination of apathy, mood-disturbance, lack of facial expression, memory impairment and loss of libido may lead to an erroneous diagnosis of primary psychiatric disorder. The physical crises may also be associated with confusional or delirious episodes, followed by stuporose or comatose states. Partial or complete loss of pubic and axillary hair, increased sensitivity to cold, amenorrhoea dating from post-partum haemorrhage, and a hypotensive episode, which is the cause of most cases, should help to establish the diagnosis. The majority of cases are relieved of their symptoms by the administration of cortisone alone in small doses. A small proportion of patients require thyroid in addition.

ACROMEGALY. In this disorder the physical changes are characteristic but an apathetic depression combined with some lability of mood is common even in the early stages. The mood change is to some extent a reaction to the disfigurement caused by the disease, the headache which may be sufficiently severe to cause sleeplessness, and the pain arising from the hypertrophied, distended extremities and joint changes. Muscular weakness and impotence or amenorrhoea are usual although accounts are sometimes given of considerable physical and sexual vigour in the early stages.

PSYCHOLOGICAL EFFECTS OF ACTH AND CORTISONE. These substances are extensively used in general medical practice for a wide range of disorders and the psychiatric complications which arise in a proportion of cases are therefore often encountered by the modern psychiatrist. The most common mood change is towards cheerfulness and euphoria but depression results in a small proportion of cases (Rome and Braceland, 1952), and other changes such as irritability, aggressiveness and lability of mood may be seen. Some alteration in affect can often be observed within a matter of six hours after commencement of treatment (Goolker and Schein, 1953). But this may be subtle in character and affect may not be overtly altered until treatment has been in progress for some days or even after it has been terminated. In about 5 per cent. of cases more serious mental disturbances develop. In these the clinical picture tends to ignore the frontiers conventionally established between organic and functional mental disease. Thus the psychoses may be acutely manic or depressive. But clouding of consciousness or frank delirium may be associated with the affective disturbance for part or whole of the illness. Moreover, paranoid or catatonic schizophrenia or an acute organic psychosis may be simulated (Michael and Gibbons, 1963). Recovery generally occurs when the hormones are withdrawn but this is not invariable. In persistent psychoses E.C.T. is generally effective.

Michael and Gibbons draw attention to the euphoria which tends to be induced by hormone administration in contrast to the predominantly depressive disturbance associated with Cushing's syndrome. Moreover, severe mental disorder is three to four times higher in Cushing's syndrome than in the course of treatment with hormones. The paradox is of some general interest in view of the mounting evidence for the existence of some association between depressive disorders and the activity of the adrenal cortex. The differences are probably due 'either to some totally unexplained factor or to differences in plasma levels of biologically active steroids or the chronicity of Cushing's syndrome'.

DIABETES. The predisposition to diabetes seems to be related on the one hand to the affective disorders, on the other to arteriopathy. French writers of the last century described a number of psychological symptoms in association with diabetes; but their findings could all be explained by the two relations mentioned, or by the non-recognition of cerebral syphilis in the pre-Wassermann period. Diabetic coma may be preceded by delirium. In hypoglycaemia, on the other hand, no delirious symptoms are seen; like anoxia it produces only a falling off in mental performance. Restlessness, irritability and foolhardy behaviour are early signs, and may then be followed by drowsiness, sopor and coma, sometimes with twitchings of the cortical as well as the subcortical type.

Hypoglycaemia may be induced by insulin, but may also occur spontaneously if caused by a pancreatic neoplasm. Its physical and mental symptoms have been studied extensively during the hypoglycaemic treatment of schizophrenia.

Patients with pancreatic insulinomata are not infrequently referred to psychiatric clinics on account of their anomalies of behaviour. There is a wide range of variation in the clinical picture and this may be one reason why, despite the extensive literature on the subject, the disorder continues to elude detection during life in a proportion of cases. The psychiatric disturbances are generally the most prominent ones (Todd et al., 1962) and there are certain general features which a high proportion of cases have in common. The psychiatric and neurological symptoms are transient, recurrent and episodic. They are particularly liable to come on when the blood sugar is reduced so that exercise or a period of some hours without food have often preceded an attack. This kind of history is not, however, elicited in all cases. In most instances the symptoms come on with a rapidity that is reminiscent of an epileptic disturbance and temporal lobe epilepsy is erroneously diagnosed in some cases. In other subjects there is a more gradual build up of symptoms commencing with weakness, perspiration, ataxia and anxiety combined with an extreme craving hunger for food. This often develops further into a state of disturbed consciousness in which the patient becomes disorientated and confused and may behave in a disinhibited, aggressive or childish manner that is out of character for him. Some patients become lethargic, apathetic, dazed and withdrawn and, when an attempt is made to rouse them, they may respond in a dysarthric and incoherent manner which at times suggests drunkenness; the extreme perspiration and pallor should, however, suggest the correct diagnosis. In some subjects, consciousness becomes severely deranged and they sink into extreme drowsiness and coma. Focal neurological signs such as hemiplegia, hemianopia or aphasia may be found. Their pathophysiology is uncertain but they are very likely due to areas of relative ischaemia. Focal signs may suggest a cerebro-vascular accident, but the changes are transient except where a prolonged or irreversible coma develops. Convulsions occur at some stage in about a fifth of the cases. The abnormal mental states are rapidly relieved by the administration of sugar and some patients gain weight due to the over-eating in which they indulge in order to fight off or terminate symptoms. After many attacks of prolonged hypoglycaemia permanent brain damage may result.

It cannot be emphasized too often that an ordinary glucose-tolerance curve does not exclude the condition. The diagnosis is suggested by the findings of a blood-sugar of under 50 mg. in the course of an attack and the relief of symptoms by intravenous 50 per cent. glucose. When observation of an attack has not proved possible, a 48-hour fast followed by exercise may provoke one. However, the use of insulin-sensitivity tests, the measurement of plasma insulin activity and a tolbutamide test may be necessary to establish the diagnosis. The removal of a benign tumour from the pancreas results in cure (Todd *et al.*, 1962) but the growth may be small and difficult to locate so that negative findings at operation do not always dispose of the diagnosis.

THE SEX GLANDS. There is probably a close relationship between the total endocrine balance and the pattern of personality; and in this balance the influence of the sex glands themselves must be considerable. Widespread and ancient beliefs go much further by suggesting a close link between sexual behaviour and insanity. There is little evidence in favour of this view. The single are statistically more prone to develop some forms of psychiatric illness than the married, and schizophrenic patients admitted to hospital before the age of 25, for example, are far less often married than the general population of comparable age. However, the explanation for this is probably that the defect of pre-morbid personality which is associated with schizophrenia has an adverse effect on the chances of finding a marriage partner. Pre-pubertal castration tends to be associated with disproportionate development of the skeleton owing to the delay in the closure of the epiphyses. There may also be an excessive deposit of fat about the pectoral regions, the thighs and abdomen, and, as secondary sex characters fail to appear and some gynaecomastia is commonly present, emotional complications frequently arise. However, in men who have attained sexual maturity, castration produces less marked effects. There is some diminution in facial hair growth and some adipose tissue may be deposited in the pectoral and trochanteric regions. There is some diminution in the size of the prostate, and potency and libido decline to some extent though they usually persist. The complexion becomes pasty; the patient complains of lack of initiative, fatiguability, and other neurasthenic symptoms. Hot flushes are often complained of. Voluntary castration of male sex perverts is generally followed by a severe reactive depression which tends to prove transient (Wolf, 1934).

MENOPAUSE. Cessation of ovarian function owing to surgical removal of the ovaries or damage to them for other reasons, gives rise to psychological symptoms similar to those experienced by many middle-aged women at the menopause. But they tend to be far more severe and disabling in those in whom the menopause has been induced or has occurred before the age of 35. There is marked emotional lability, diminished tolerance for frustration, irritability, fatigue on slight exertion, bouts of depression with weeping, palpitation and pre-cordial discomfort, insomnia and sometimes attacks of dizziness and syncope. The picture is in other words similar to that of an anxiety neurosis with predominantly somatic symptoms and a strong but fluctuating depressive colouring. These patients usually respond well to small doses of oestrogen and psychotherapy of a supportive and reassuring kind is also helpful.

The life situation with its obvious conflicts and disappointments is more important than the endocrine changes in most climacteric mental reactions. Many physical diseases, such as exophthalmic goitre, rheumatoid arthritis, hypertension and diabetes may start at this time of life, as well as involutional melancholia, paranoid schizophrenia and presenile deterioration. In the case of none of them is there any real knowledge to explain the relation to the menopause.

MENSTRUAL AND PREMENSTRUAL DISTURBANCES. The reciprocal relation between the *menstrual cycle* and mental symptoms has interested psychiatrists from an early date. The psychological state of the normal woman was seen to change at menstruation; and mental illnesses were accompanied by menstrual disturbances. These two observations led to theories and to schemes of classification, most of which have not stood the test of time. The frequent occurrence of *amenorrhoea* in neuroses and psychoses seems to depend on the emotional upset caused by the illness. Most workers found that amenorrhoea appeared most frequently in melancholia and in the catatonic excitement of schizophrenia. It is far more common in the schizophrenic than in the affective psychoses. Amenorrhoea is frequent in organic psychoses, general paralysis, disseminated sclerosis, and epidemic encephalitis. Early schizophrenics of the simple hebephrenic and paranoid type continue their cycle, but in later stages of the illness menstruation may cease. Menstrual anomalies in epilepsy have been found in 40 per cent. of cases. Attempts to restore menstruation by medication have no influence on the psychotic condition. The return of menstruation after a period of amenorrhoea may be a sign of imminent recovery; but after a stuporose or hyperkinetic attack of schizophrenia, restoration of menses may, like increase in body weight, augur not improvement, but progressive mental deterioration.

Hypersensitiveness, irritability, fatigue and sometimes mild depression often precede, accompany or follow menstruation in many physically and mentally well-balanced women. Recently the *'premenstrual tension state'* has attracted some attention (Greene and Dalton, 1953; Rees, 1953). It was originally described as a syndrome by Frank (1931). The condition, which is quite frequent in some degree, usually comes on in the latter half of the menstrual cycle and passes off with the onset of menstruation or shortly after. An enquiry by means of a questionnaire, in a number of general practices in different parts of England, (Kessel and Coppen, 1963) suggests that approximately 10 per cent. of normal women experience severe premenstrual symptoms. However, some workers consider that milder disturbances occur in a higher proportion of subjects. Symptoms may appear in the form of headaches, nausea, dizziness and palpitations, excessive thirst or appetite, hypersomnia and increased sexual desire. Nearly always there is marked emotional tension in the form of irritability, and often of anxiety or depression. There is a subjective sensation of being generally swollen, particularly in the breasts and abdomen. An increase in weight and fluid retention are often mentioned in the literature although Bruce and Russell (1962) were unable to find any evidence that water was in fact retained in the premenstrual period. Tension may be very severe and may be associated with headache which is typically migrainous in character in a proportion of cases.

Both psychological and physiological factors contribute to the causation of the syndrome. Thus Kessel and Coppen found a highly significant correlation between premenstrual symptoms and neuroticism in their general practice study. Menstrual symptoms in general were likewise found more commonly in neurotic women than in normal subjects in a later enquiry (Coppen, 1965a) and no less than 20 per cent. had had dilatation and curettage. The physiological mechanisms underlying the premenstrual syndrome are unknown, but various hypotheses have been advanced including disturbances in electrolytes, elevation of the oestrogen-progesterone ratio and changes in blood sugar. Good results are claimed for diuretics such as ammonium chloride given in doses of 1 gram capsule 6 times daily during the last 10 days of the cycle. Hormonal treatments are also recommended in the form of norethisterone which exerts a progesterone-like effect and is given in oral doses of 2.5–5 mg. daily during the last 10 days of the cycle. However, the relief of premenstrual tension rarely makes any impression upon an overall neurotic instability nor, as Rees (1953) pointed out, does improvement of neurotic subjects on psychotherapy necessarily bring relief for their premenstrual tension. A good description of the premenstrual syndrome has been given by Dalton (1964).

In those inclined to neurotic reactions and in unstable personalities, especially when exposed to other stress, *dysmenorrhoea* may become the main subject of complaint and self-pity and a reason for consulting the gynaecologist. As with many of the autonomic mechanisms which function best without interference from higher centres, a vicious circle is easily established, but is difficult to interrupt.

Menstruation has physiological and psychological relationships with sexual intercourse, marriage, and childbirth; it readily becomes connected in the mind with anxieties, desires and disappointments. It is therefore natural that it should become a *focus for hypochondriacal, obsessional and anxious preoccupations*, often made only worse by medication and by the local applications and operations intended for their relief. As in cases of backache, vaginal discharge, pruritus, and constipation, a relatively trifling somatic complaint becomes a genuine illness because of its psychological significance and its emotional repercussions. It is obvious that psychological help and guidance is the treatment of choice with as little in the way of physical interference as possible.

It is now known that *central control of menstruation* proceeds via the hypothalamus, the pituitary and the secretion of gonadotrophic hormone. It is, however, still unclear how the mental changes which normally accompany menstruation are mediated. Experienced workers believe that psychotic attacks often start at menstruation, and 35 per cent. of suicides in the female are committed at this time. Cooke (1945) has reported that 84 per cent. of crimes of violence by women occurred during or immediately after the menses; but Morton et al. (1952), in a study of prison inmates, found that 62 per cent. of crimes of violence had occurred in the premenstrual week, 19 per cent. at mid-cycle, 17 per cent. during menstruation, and 2 per cent. after the end of menstruation. McKinnon and McKinnon (1956) have found that deaths from accident or suicide in women were much more prone to occur in the premenstrual period than at other times.

There is, however, no *'menstrual psychosis'*. Rare cases have been described in the litera-ture· and have drawn much attention; most experienced psychiatrists have seen one or another patient in whom attacks of manic-depressive illness or of periodic catatonia were closely linked with the menstrual cycle. Ewald (1928) tried x-ray sterilization, oöphorec-tomy and total hysterectomy in one such patient without effect on the periodicity of the psychosis.

Although most of the mental abnormality which accompanies physical disease can be subsumed under one of the preceding syndromes, there are many more subtle observa-tions, some of them associated with particular conditions, and of clinical and theoretical interest.

Pregnancy and Childbirth

PREGNANCY. Although it causes large changes in metabolism and endocrine function, pregnancy does not bring any increased risk of mental illness. The number of psychoses starting in gravid women is not greater than in a control group of the same age. A study by Pugh *et al.* (1963) has shown this very clearly. They compared the number of married women aged 15 to 44 admitted to psychiatric hospitals in Massachusetts during 1950, who were either pregnant or had been delivered during the previous nine months, with the number to be expected if there were no relation between admission and parturition. There was a significant excess by this standard, but entirely in the post-partum stage, with an actual deficit of admissions during pregnancy.

In early pregnancy *emotional lability* and irritability are fairly frequent; and there may also be hypersensitivity of taste and smell, and *pica*, the physiology of which is difficult to explain and which may to some extent be psychologically determined. *Hyperemesis*, which is no doubt primarily a physical disturbance, is also affected by emotional factors. It is not easy to control if the mother is unstable or the child is unwanted. Under the same cir-cumstances reactive depressions may be serious and lead to suicide, for instance in illegi-timate pregnancy. On the other hand, many neurotic subjects become free of symptoms during pregnancy and afterwards regard that time as the best period of their lives.

A *feeling of unusual well-being* is in fact physiological for the healthy woman in the second half of pregnancy. Risks are, however, attached to the final stages. Towards the end of pregnancy *toxaemia*, hypertension and eclampsia may produce delirium and epileptic seizures, and call for a premature termination. Early termination may also be needed in chorea gravidarum, which is often complicated by a psychosis of the exogenous type.

In chronic schizophrenics pregnancy has little influence on the psychotic condition. The majority suffer no change in their indifference. However, as Baker *et al.* (1961) has shown, even inaccessible catatonic women can be brought to nurse their babies and mother and baby can be safely cared for together.

Affective disorders occurring during pregnancy have been successfully treated with con-vulsion therapy without untoward effect on the course of the pregnancy or on the child (Goldstein *et al.*, 1941; Thorpe, 1942).

CHILDBIRTH AND PUERPERIUM. When one considers that childbirth, in addition to its profound psychological implications, involves relatively sudden and far-reaching changes in metabolism and endocrine balance, and their frequent complication by physical exhaustion, loss of blood and sometimes infection, one would expect a much greater *incidence of puerperal psychoses* than is actually found. It is difficult to arrive at reliable figures for the incidence of puerperal mental disorder. Older figures (Engelhard, 1912) and those largely based on mental hospital material cite low rates of approximately 1·4 per 1,000 births. However, in the course of recent enquiries, increasing attention has rightly been paid to more mild and neurotic forms of puerperal mental illness. In a study by Jansson (1964), to which further reference will be made, all types of illness associated in a pre-defined manner with the puerperium were included. Jansson's cases formed 6·8 per 1,000 of deliveries in Göteborg over a five-year period of which 2·3 per 1,000 were admitted to the mental hospital and 4·5 per 1,000 to the psychiatric clinic associated with the general hospital. The mental disorders associated with childbirth formed 2·2 per cent. and 4·8 per cent. respectively of the admissions to two types of institution. There are marked variations in the reports of different workers as to the relative frequency of different forms of mental disorder in the puerperium. Thus, Brew and Seidenberg (1950) report 41 per cent. manic depressives, 51 per cent. schizophrenics. Boyd (1942), combining the diagnoses of 8 workers, reports an average of 40 per cent. affective, 20 per cent. schizophrenic, 28 per cent. symptomatic psychoses and also 11 per cent. neurotic or psychopathic reaction, whereas Polonio and Figueiredo (1955) report 48·3 per cent. exogenous or symptomatic psychoses, 27·8 per cent. schizophrenias and 15·5 per cent. manic-depressive psychoses.

Recent enquiries have shed interesting light on the situation in a number of ways. There has been a decline in the frequency of exogenous states of a toxic—or exhaustive—delirious kind, and this is sometimes attributed to the decreasing incidence of puerperal infections. But to some extent the change probably reflects a shift in diagnostic procedure. Thus Scandinavian authors, who have conducted some of the most careful and systematic enquiries into puerperal mental disorder, report a high incidence of cases with a clouded sensorium amounting, in Jansson's material, to 30·3 per cent. of the total and 60 per cent. of the mental hospital cases. But only rarely is any specific disease or sustained fever found in such cases with 'exogenous' features. More surprisingly, obstetric complications nowadays appear to have been no more common in patients with puerperal mental disorders than in those without psychiatric symptoms (Paffenbarger et al., 1961; Jansson, 1964). On the other hand minor physical disease, though not toxaemia, appears to be commoner during pregnancy among those with psychiatric complications, and peri-natal mortality also seems to be higher in this group.

Many of the difficulties of classification arise from the frequency with which confusional symptoms are combined with paranoid or schizophreniform features on the one hand and with depressive symptom clusters on the other.

Moreover, a greater overlap between depressive and schizophrenic symptoms is found than in the general run of psychiatric cases. This combination was reported in 11·8 per cent. of Jansson's material. This floridity and diffuseness of psychiatric symptoms is not confined to the psychotic disorders. It seems clear that the importance of neurotic illness in the puerperium has been underestimated in the past and Vislie's (1956) figure of 21 cases of psychoneurosis out of 67 cases of puerperal mental disorder corresponds to the findings of a number of authors in recent years. In these cases also transient clouding of sensorium may lend an atypical floridity to the clinical picture of proportion of cases. Thus there was a correlation between certain anxiety symptoms ('asthenic-emotional features') and clouding in Jansson's material; the combination of the two being reported in 9·2 per cent. of cases. The special importance of this last phenomenon is that it is liable to be mistaken for an endogenous or toxic psychosis. In anxiety and phobic states approximately 10 per cent. of cases in women commence in close association with childbirth and, in a small proportion of these, clouding of the sensorium is present at the onset (Roth, 1969). Clouding of the sensorium subsides in many cases and the diagnosis is then often simplified but by no means always resolved. Careful follow-up studies are required to provide a foundation for a satisfactory classification of puerperal mental disorders; the results would probably prove informative for the problems of classification in other areas of psychiatry.

In recent years there has been an increasing tendency to dismiss childbirth as an aetiological factor in its own right and to emphasize constitutional predisposition to breakdown as the principal underlying cause of puerperal mental disorder. Such views have received some support from the fact that mentally ill puerperal women do not appear to differ significantly in respect of personality, previous illness and other relevant variables from women with similar disorders unconnected with childbirth (Seager, 1960). Yet the symptoms appear in 35 per cent. of cases within one month after delivery, and the incidence declines very sharply after the two following months (Tetlow, 1955; Jansson, 1964). The study by Pugh *et al.* (1963) also showed that the excess of admissions to psychiatric hospitals occurred in the first three months post partum.

There is, in fact, statistical evidence to suggest that childbirth is in some measure specific as a stress. Thus, although previous psychiatric illness had been less common in Jansson's puerperal cases than in control subjects with mental illness, breakdown in close association with childbirth had occurred significantly more often among them. It is not in the indubitably schizophrenic or manic-depressive disorders but rather in the many cases with affective and neurotic symptoms which have been increasingly prominent in recent years, that childbirth appears of special importance in precipitating illness.

Some of the special stresses imposed by childbirth are known; others remain to be defined. Primiparae are more prone and particularly so if they are over the age of 30. Women with puerperal psychoses are significantly more often unmarried than those without psychiatric complications at childbirth (Tetlow, 1955; Jansson, 1964), and there are often other reasons in cases with puerperal psychoses why pregnancy may be unwanted. The happiness and fulfilment achieved in marriage will influence the attitude towards pregnancy. In dependent immature women the responsibilities of motherhood are anticipated with fear and apprehension which mount as the time for assuming their new role grows imminent. The fear that the child may be defective or deformed or that the patient will fail in her maternal role contributes to the stresses in obsessional and over-fastidious women. In other childish women the capacity for tenderness and affection is deficient and the child may be conceived as a rival helpless and dependent subject in the family, competing with the patient for the husband's affections. Pre-morbid personality deficiencies are found far more often among patients with puerperal mental disorders than among control subjects after childbirth. Such neurotic propensities are characteristic among patients with neurotic-depressive and anxiety reactions; they are uncommon in patients with schizophrenic psychoses and confusional states.

The majority of illnesses begin in the first three months after childbirth and a high proportion of them within four weeks. In the early stages, clouding of consciousness is common in the acute cases. There may be auditory or visual hallucinations, marked incoherence, restlessness and agitation, periods of confusion and stupor with episodes of lucidity. In the commonest type of acute psychosis to present in this manner, depressive features are already discernible at this stage, and they may be associated with paranoid, hypochondriacal and nihilistic ideas. Some degree of perplexity, phases of stupor and of other catatonic features are not uncommon but, where depressive features are prominent throughout, the picture usually becomes more unmistakably affective as the clouding of consciousness recedes. Auditory hallucinations closely linked with disturbances of thought, volition and motor activity are, however, more ominous even in the setting of clouding or a depressive colouring. However, a final decision about the nature of the illness should be deferred until the sensorium has cleared. In some cases a persistent though variable confusion, perplexity, and a wide-ranging and florid clinical picture render diagnosis in one of the generally accepted categories of psychotic illness impossible. When the illness develops less acutely, typical schizophrenic or affective psychoses may, of course, be seen.

In approximately 25–30 per cent. of cases the patient suffers from an acute neurotic illness, presenting with prominent depression, anxiety, irritability and restlessness. Phobic features may be present from the beginning or may develop as soon as the patient takes her first walk or makes her first shopping outing alone. In such neurotic disorders, as also in all those patients with markedly vulnerable personalities, or a previous history of neurotic breakdown, caution should be exercised in using electroconvulsive treatment. It may exacerbate anxiety and give rise to other unfortunate complications such as persistent depersonalization. In acute psychoses of predominantly depressive type, E.C.T. is the treatment of choice except in the milder cases in which a course of antidepressive drugs may be tried. However, in the presence of well-established delusions of guilt and persecution or other psychotic features they are unlikely to prove effective. In a predominantly schizophrenic psychosis, unless symptoms are clearly responding to drugs within a few days, E.C.T. should be used together with phenothiazines. In cases of acute neurotic breakdown the course may be a stormy and difficult one and weeks or months of skilful management making use of psychotherapy, antidepressive and tranquillizing drugs and abreactive treatment may be needed to bring the patient through the illness.

Overall, the outlook for puerperal forms of illness is a relatively favourable one. Few patients nowadays remain in hospital longer than a few months and the establishment of mother-and-baby units in many psychiatric hospitals has made it much easier to provide effective management for such patients in a hospital setting. Residual symptoms are of course common and further hospitalization is necessary in a proportion of cases. In Jansson's material 9·5 per cent. of the cases required admission to mental hospital for a further breakdown associated with childbirth over a mean follow-up period of 8 years 7 months. Moreover, 29·5 per cent. of the patients had been under care in a psychiatric hospital at some other time during the follow-up period. Needless to say, cases with indubitably schizophrenic features become chronic in a proportion of instances. But the acuteness of onset, the presence of clouded sensorium, the presence of an exogenous precipitant, as well as the common depressive colouring, are all relatively favourable features. These together with the long-term administration of phenothiazine drugs, account for the favourable results achieved nowadays in the best psychiatric hospitals. However, painstaking aftercare and supervision over a long period are essential if good results are to be achieved.

TERMINATION OF PREGNANCY.* The termination of pregnancy in subjects suffering from psychiatric disorder or with a history of previous attacks of illness is a common problem in psychiatric practice. It puts the wisdom and judgement as well as the clinical skill of the

_____

* This section was written before the Abortion Act came into force in April, 1968.

psychiatrist to a searching test. When the puerperium was considered a necessary and sufficient cause of the mental disorders associated with it, the issues were perhaps clearer than they are today. Now that it has become generally accepted that many patients with a puerperal disorder also suffer from ordinary endogenous psychoses and are vulnerable to other forms of stress, and that the outcome is often favourable, many considerations have to be weighed before decisions about termination are taken. Much emphasis has been laid on the improvement in outlook. Martin (1958) followed up 75 cases of puerperal mental disorder over an average period of $2\frac{1}{2}$ years and found that, of 27 cases in the affective group, only one had had a further puerperal illness and 3 suffered attacks of the disorder unconnected with the puerperium. All these patients responded well to electroplexy. Fifteen schizophrenic patients were followed up for a mean period of $4\frac{1}{2}$ years and 28 of 'schizo-affective' disorder for $4\frac{3}{4}$ years. In these two groups there was a total of three puerperal and three non-puerperal illnesses, all of them responding in a satisfactory manner to treatment.

The follow-up period of the study was, however, limited and in other enquiries in which excellent results have been claimed (Sim, 1963) there has been too little information about the course of the illness since first contact to assess the hazards involved. Even the relapse rates for puerperal psychosis recorded over short periods of observation can hardly be dismissed as a negligible hazard. Close observation (Baker, 1963) suggests that relapse is common in the first year after childbirth. Moreover, as already indicated, there is evidence to suggest that childbirth is more than an unimportant trigger but must, to a limited degree, be regarded as one of the causes of the mental disorders associated with it (Jansson, 1964). It has to be remembered also that, in the case of schizophrenia, little is known as yet about the outcome of treatment over long periods of observation. Further, in many patients, symptoms are held in abeyance only with the continued administration of phenothiazine drugs and much social and psychological support.

In each individual case the many facts to be weighed will include the detailed characteristics of the illness, the degree of association of previous attacks with childbirth, on the one hand, and with other causes on the other, the time that has elapsed since the last attack, the patient's and the family's attitude to the pregnancy, and the evidence of lasting schizophrenic defect in personality. In some cases, the psychiatrist will be driven to conclude that even a small risk of relapse into a psychotic illness would be unjustified and that pregnancy should be terminated. The risk of precipitating a schizophrenic or other psychotic illness by the operation for the termination of pregnancy can hardly be accepted as equal to those entailed in giving birth to and rearing another child, particularly where other family circumstances are unfavourable, or the mother's resources for coping with emotional problems are limited by persistent illness, personality damage or both.

Even if he takes an optimistic view of the *overall statistical prognosis* for puerperal psychosis, the psychiatrist may yet find a compelling case for termination of pregnancy in the individual patient. There are subjects, for example, in whom psychosis has consistently followed childbirth but rarely or never developed at any other time. This could of course, be due to an unlikely play of chance. But to act on this interpretation would be to gamble in an irresponsible manner with the health of the patient. A stage may be reached in a case such as this, particularly where the social setting is unfavourable, at which further pregnancy is likely to damage the patient's health. If he judges this to be the situation, the psychiatrist is fully justified in recommending termination of pregnancy.

Patients who have had a psychotic illness constitute only a small proportion of cases in whom the clinical psychiatrist has to take decisions about possible termination of pregnancy. The majority of such patients suffer from neurotic depressions, anxiety states and personality disorders. There has generally been a former neurotic breakdown, in some cases after a previous pregnancy. This has perhaps led to some degree of neurotic disability or residual symptoms, in the form of persistent anxiety, phobias, marked irritability, frigidity, often with domestic strife and an increasing fear of further pregnancy. Some patients are unmarried and these and others often express suicidal ideas or threats. These may contain an element of blackmail but often the personality background proves to be unstable and there is a history of impulsive suicidal attempts after exposure to frustration. In the majority of these cases the correct course is to provide psychiatric treatment and support and help the patient to accept the pregnancy. Where domestic and social circumstances are favourable and the patient's problems are handled with sensitivity and skill this will often succeed. In the remaining patients who cannot be brought to face pregnancy, the risk of suicide, or further breakdown, and of possible damage to the marriage and the family and the ultimate effects of these complications on their mental health have to be assessed. There is little substance in the view that suicidal acts are rare in pregnancy. After a review of the literature, Whitlock and Edwards (1968) concluded that pregnancy can be an associated factor in about 5 per cent. of all female suicides. In their own study of 30 pregnant women who had made suicidal attempts no evidence emerged that pregnancy provided any protection. Their finding that 7·2 per cent. of 483 women who had attempted suicide were pregnant agrees well with other Australian figures (Boxall and Chauvel, 1966) and observations in Great Britain (Harrington and Cross, 1959). Risks of this order can hardly be ignored. Suicidal hazards apart, the psychiatrist cannot overlook the manifold threats to the future welfare of mother and child that an unwanted pregnancy so often portends. Recent enquiries in Sweden (Forssmann and Thuwe, 1965) have shown that children born to mothers refused termination (between 1939 and 1941) and followed until the age of 21 were at a disadvantage compared with a matched group, in every aspect studied. More than a quarter were born out of wedlock, 60 per cent. had an insecure childhood, as judged by a number of criteria. They were more often educationally retarded, delinquent, subject to alcoholism, anti-social, unable to support themselves and mentally unstable. The women in question had been refused termination before the law in Sweden was broadened in 1946 to include social criteria as relevant to therapeutic abortion. The authors of the study concluded that the very fact that a woman applied for legal abortion meant that the prospective child ran a risk of having to surmount far greater social and emotional handicaps than the general run of children. One may add that the health and welfare of mother and family would not be likely to remain unaffected in the process.

Decisions about termination should always be taken in close consultation with the gynaecologist and the family doctor. If the psychiatrist's objection to termination arises from ethical or religious grounds, he should make this clear to the patient and her medical advisor and leave him free to refer her elsewhere. Termination may be followed by feelings of self-reproach and much emphasis has been laid on Ekblad's (1955) finding in the course of a follow-up of 479 cases of terminated pregnancy, that 11 per cent. expressed serious, and 24 per cent. mild self-reproach. However, social and economic hardship have long been among the indications for termination in Sweden and the situation in Great Britain is unlikely to be comparable when new legislation comes into force. In the authors' opinion psychiatric complications after termination are rare. The great majority of patients are 'well, co-operative and grateful' (Tredgold, 1964).

The legal position concerning termination is discussed in Chapter XIII.

SENSORY DEPRIVATION. During 1953–58 Hebb and his associates (Hebb, 1961; Heron, 1961) carried out research into 'perceptual isolation' which established the basic phenomena—that in states where subjects are denied one or another form of sensory stimuli, hallucinations and impaired cognitive functioning occurred. Hebb claimed that the hallucinations resembled those produced by mescaline and exposure to flickering light. Visual hallucination predominated and the imagery increased in complexity, duration and persistence as the period of deprivation was extended. He observed how the subject could describe the imagery while it was being experienced. Some elements were dream-like, some not. Much was vivid and as if in front of the eyes.

After a brief stay in the isolation chamber, subjects found they could not concentrate. They began to be uncertain whether they were awake and day-dreaming, or asleep and having dreams. In some instances they reported feeling dazed and confused.

Hebb and his co-workers withdrew from this field before the precise aetiology of the unusual mental symptoms they reported in their subjects was established. A great deal of subsequent research also failed adequately to explain the phenomena.

Ziskind who has worked on these phenomena since 1958 pointed out that it is their complexity that has impeded progress. Sensory deprivation is not a unitary condition since a variety of factors, including an unchanging environment, variable reduction of sensory input, as well as factors such as restricted motion, confinement and social isolation contribute in differing degrees under different circumstances. The manifestations of the phenomenon are also complex (Ziskind, 1964). Ziskind and his collaborators (1963, 1965) decided to concentrate on acute sensory deprivation in patients in an ophthalmological ward who (usually after surgery for cataract or detached retina) were required to have patches excluding the light from both eyes, to lie in one position for one or more days and were denied visitors post-operatively for two days. The subjects were retested at a later stage so as to eliminate any possible effects of the operation itself.

Ziskind sought to define very closely the symptoms which were observed. They occurred in clusters and in his view constituted a syndrome characterized by the following features:

(i) Visual imagery consisting chiefly of dream-like perceptual distortions. They were unlike dreams in being accompanied by some purposeful, well-coordinated movement which awakened the subject from sleep. They were not hallucinations as there was no lack of insight. Hypnagogic 'private cinema' phenomena were reported in some subjects.

(ii) Activity in contravention of instructions the patient had been given as an essential part of the treatment of their eyes. Removing the patches or changing the lying position was involuntary, and occurred in periods when the subject was half-asleep and probably experiencing sensory stimuli, such as discomfort. In some instances the accompanying dream content referred to internal stimuli.

(iii) Very transient confusion—a momentary disorientation in a half-awake state in patients without cerebral 'organic' or toxic manifestations.

(iv) More frequent periods of sleep than normal.

(v) Free-floating anxiety ranging from the mildest form to near panic.

(vi) Restlessness.

The first stage of their series of experiments confirmed these workers in the belief that the abnormal mental symptoms occurred in periods of reduced awareness and were aberrations of half-sleep, half-wakefulness. They were increased and prolonged by sensory deprivation and further supplemented and brought into prominence by the questioning of the experimenting team.

In the second stage they sought support for this opinion by increasing stimulation in their eye-patched patients. If sensory deprivation were the cause of the symptoms, an increase of stimulation should either remove or change them. Auditory stimuli and the continuous presence of relatives with the patients failed to produce conclusive differences in the incidence of mental symptoms. Constant monitoring of the subjects also revealed that mental symptoms varied with states of wakefulness.

In the third stage they put eye-patches on normal persons for ten-minute periods and roused normal subjects early in the morning. Both were given instructions to record the imagery they saw. The instructions were worded in a declining order of definiteness. The results demonstrated clearly that the more specific the instruction the more imagery was recalled. The authors interpreted this as indicating that normal imagery is present at all times and only requires deliberate focusing to bring it to notice.

The view that the hallucinatory and pseudo-hallucinatory experiences reported in the course of perceptual isolation experiments are due to intermittent reduction in the level of awareness is supported by the finding of E.E.G. changes both in the course of brief (Marjerrison and Keogh, 1967), and prolonged sensory and perceptual deprivation (Zubeck and Welch, 1963). The finding that the hallucinatory experiences and the impairment in cognitive functioning were associated with fleeting periods of sleep does not wholly exclude the contribution of reduced sensory input for this may play some part in the initiation and prolongation of the periods of reduced awareness. Although the 'hypnoid' syndrome described by Ziskind appears to differ sharply from the delirious states in that it is fleeting and unaccompanied by amnesia for the experiences, the difference may be quantitative rather than qualitative. Indeed reduction of sensory input such as that entailed in the aftercare of patients who have had operations for cataract may in brain-damaged or elderly subjects be associated not merely with fleeting interruptions of wakefulness but with a full picture of acute delirium. The states of acute confusion sometimes observed in elderly subjects with early brain damage when they are suddenly placed in the totally unfamiliar surroundings of a hospital ward probably have some affinity with these conditions since they are associated with interruption of the sensory cues from a familiar environment which are essential to maintain correct orientation in such individuals.

Ziskind emphasizes the 'brief duration and transience' of these hypnoid symptoms and suggests that it is this characteristic of the syndrome that has prevented its recognition in other situations where sensory deprivation has been examined. If his theory is accepted the hope that the study of sensory deprivation will throw light on psychosis is diminished. The practical implications, however, are clear both for hospital procedures, and in regulating the conditions of work in such occupations as long-distance driving or radar-scanning. Reduced awareness can be recognized as a hazard and 'circumvented by counteracting boredom and fatigue and by the intensification and multiplication of stimuli in several senses'.

The results of experiments in which sensory stimulation is interrupted or reduced for comparatively brief periods are not necessarily relevant when considering chronic states of isolation such as those obtaining in prisoners kept in solitary confinement or among immigrants cut off from social contact by the barriers of language and unfamiliarity with their environment. These conditions, together with deafness which also impedes social communication, are more complex situations than those created by short periods of experimental or clinical perceptual isolation.

DEPRIVATION OF SLEEP. This has certain affinities with sensory deprivation in that after prolonged wakefulness subjects manifest a tendency to 'lapses' in their psychological activity in the course of which changes in the electroencephalogram have been observed (Bjerner, 1949). Hallucinations and delusions, as well as lapses in consciousness may be reported after prolonged states of deprivation. Although there may be little apparent impairment in psychological performance during short tasks, there is a fall off in accuracy as the duration of the task is increased. The unevenness and inefficiency in the performance of sleep-deprived subjects are brought out particularly clearly in tasks paced by the experimenter (Williams et al., 1959). Prolongation of the reaction time to weak signals and the marked increase in the within-trials variance in performance scores have also been shown to be characteristic of the sleep-deprived state (Cohen et al., 1961). The latter is a particularly sensitive measure and might find application in the clinical investigation of subjects suffering from sleep disturbances or subtle impairments of awareness.

Advances in knowledge have perhaps been most striking in recent years in the fields of metabolic and endocrine disease. However, there have been developments also in relation to the clinical psychiatry of pregnancy and childbirth. It is perhaps the field of infectious disease that has seen fewest changes, probably owing to the decline in clinical importance of these disorders.

Infectious Diseases

Symptomatic psychoses due to infection have become rarer with the diminution of infections and the suppression of severe symptoms through preventive inoculation, chemotherapy and antibiotics.

Rheumatic fever and chorea: Rheumatic fever, an illness of unknown causation, which bears some relation however to the occurrence of a preceding infection with a strain of Group A beta haemolytic streptococci, has several psychiatric aspects. Cases with acute delirium and hyperpyrexia have now become very rare and some workers have doubted their rheumatic nature. Mental complications such as apathy, clouding of consciousness, emotional lability and semi-stuporose, sleep-like conditions, are still seen in the subacute form of the illness, especially in children. Almost all patients with severe mental symptoms also develop chorea.

Rheumatic children with and without cardiac disability are often handicapped educationally and emotionally. This is an important social and psychological problem because of the high incidence of the disease affecting up to four children in every hundred. Their schooling and readjustment has been made the subject of a vigorous public health programme in certain parts of the United States (Levitt and Taran, 1948).

Rheumatic chorea, probably an affection of the basal ganglia, aetiologically closely linked with rheumatic fever, shows psychological symptoms in almost every case. The first symptoms of chorea may be irritability, sulkiness, disobedience and misbehaviour in children, or the opposite, unusual placidity, lack of spontaneity, inattentive and absentminded behaviour. Psychopathic heredity or constitution has been claimed as predisposing to chorea, and schizophrenia has been found more frequent in the families of choreic children than in the average population (Guttmann 1936a). It has not been proved that a special type of personality is predisposed to chorea.

As soon as choreic movements become manifest, the diagnosis is easy; but akinetic cases with semi-stupor and mutism may be misdiagnosed as early schizophrenia. Rheumatic chorea has its maximum incidence between the ages of ten and fifteen, is extremely rare in persons over twenty, and is twice as frequent in girls as in boys.

Besides the hyperkinesis *emotional disturbances* are frequently present: depression or excessive hilarity; distractibility, absentmindedness, hypervigility, or lack of attention; insomnia and an anorexia which if combined with difficulty in swallowing may lead to a dangerous state of undernourishment. Delirium with continuous hyperkinesis is another serious complication. On the whole, mental symptoms go parallel with the choreic movements, while arthritic pains usually cease when the chorea begins. The illness lasts from six weeks to six months, but relapse occurs in one-third of the patients. There may be a neurasthenic-depressive aftermath, but hypomanic states have also been observed, all of short duration. More serious are *motor abnormalities*, such as twitchings, tics and compulsive utterances sometimes persisting into adult life. The latter, first described by Osler in 1894, may be involuntary grunting or 'barking' noises, but sometimes swear words or obscene utterances distressing to the patient and his audience have been observed (Creak and Guttmann, 1935).

Pulmonary tuberculosis: A symptomatic psychosis is very rarely seen in pulmonary tuberculosis, and when it occurs probably indicates either a secondary pneumonic infection, or the spreading of a miliary tuberculosis to the meninges. However, the mental state of the 'consumptive' has frequently been the subject of medical attention and the classical 'spes phthisica', though not now very frequently seen, has been attributed to a direct toxic effect of the infection on the brain. It is mainly observed in acute caseous tuberculosis. Other features, hypochondriasis, egocentricity, emotional lability, depression, may each or all be found, as also such hysterical behaviour as a demonstrative indifference to moral restrictions and a reckless disregard of reasonable medical advice. These symptoms are obviously the psychogenic reactions of neurotically predisposed young people to their special situation and their awareness that they are suffering from a severe and dangerous illness. In the sanatorium men and women in the prime of life used to spend months or years in enforced inactivity. Their illness, which in itself caused little discomfort, had a very doubtful outlook. The atmosphere of such a place possessed a morbid quality, and exerted a bad influence, especially on those with some psychopathic traits. The early symptoms of pulmonary tuberculosis often include a *general malaise and weakness* not infrequently wrongly diagnosed as neurasthenia. This may be followed by a false feeling of well-being; and as sexual drive is not impaired by the disease, concentration on sexual indulgence may become a problem. With modern developments in the chemotherapy of tuberculosis most of the complications, and those associated with sanatorium life in particular, have ceased to have more than historical importance.

Malaria: Malignant tertian malaria may start with an attack which is predominantly cerebral in localization. Delirium or drowsiness followed by coma are the main symptoms, focal signs such as paraphasia, hemiplegia, convulsions and chorea-athetotic movements can be seen; the patient may have to be restrained because of excitation and violent behaviour in epileptiform twilight states. Exogenous reactions tend to subside with the malarial attack

In these cases capillary blockage by parasitized corpuscles occurs in the brain leading to characteristic changes, and the formation of 'malaria granulomata' (Arieti, 1946). Many other mental abnormalities have been attributed to *chronic malaria* but with the wide prevalence of malarial infection in certain tropical regions, it is difficult to obtain a clear picture of the causal connections.

Trypanosomiasis: African sleeping sickness caused by *Trypanosoma gambiense* has long been known to involve the central nervous system producing sleepiness and simple dementia, sometimes with euphoria, carelessness and neglect similar to the clinical picture of general paresis. The resemblance of the cerebral findings to the latter was pointed out by Mott. The above symptoms are those of advanced cases. Early in the illness changes of personality and behaviour, especially in children and young people, are often the first sign of the infection; they may take the form of irritability, aggressiveness, querulousness, and be accompanied by intellectual deterioration. Paranoid features are frequent and the differentiation from schizophrenia may be difficult. Hypnagogic hallucinations and deterioration in habits may follow. The diagnosis can only be clinched by positive findings in the cerebrospinal fluid, or by the discovery of the organism in the blood. In an unselected group of 232 patients Tooth (1950) found mental symptoms in 84 per cent.

Typhoid and typhus: Among infections of bacterial causation, typhoid fever has always been known for its many mental complications. A hypomanic colouring is often found in the initial delirium, before there is much clouding of consciousness and euphoria may persist into the height of the fever. In the collapse delirium of typhoid, disturbance of sense of time has been observed, but it seems doubtful whether this is characteristic of enteric fever only. Severe dysmnesic conditions, depression and hypomania may follow during convalescence. Protective inoculation has modified the physical signs, but mental changes may be present in abortive cases.

Another infection with a characteristic cerebral pathology is the louse-borne typhus fever, of which widespread epidemics occurred in certain theatres during the last war. Subjective symptoms early in the disease are headache, irritability, giddiness and insomnia. After a short period of drowsiness, delirium with very vivid dream-like hallucinations commences, lasting over the whole period of raised temperature. States of panic with violence and restlessness, ideas of persecution and fantastic delusions are frequent. The clinical picture differs from typhoid fever in the much more serious and 'organic' mental symptoms. Excitation may subside and be followed by a stuporose state with catatonic and extra-pyramidal motor signs. 'Coma vigile', a severe akinetic state, is seen before the fatal end (v. Stockert, 1943).

Mental sequelae in those who survive typhus are especially frequent and may be severe, and in some cases mental deterioration may be permanent. Neurological findings have been related to vascular cerebral lesions. In the cerebrospinal fluid pleocytosis and increase of globulin are often present. In the cerebral grey matter nodules of endothelial proliferation are found in the small arteries surrounded by epitheloid cells; they give rise to thromboses and haemorrhages.

Other infections: Before the advent of the sulpha-drugs, transient delirious conditions were seen in *pneumonia* in 20 to 30 per cent. of cases. Delirium is rare in the initial phase, it usually comes and goes with the rise and fall of temperature. In alcoholics, pneumonia may release a typical delirium tremens. If there is delirium in pneumonia, the possibility of pneumococcal meningitis must be considered, especially in children. It is easily understood that during a widespread epidemic of *influenza* the absolute number of symptomatic psychoses is large. There is, however, no proof that influenza carries with it any special tendency to mental abnormalities. What has struck all observers is the frequency of depressive pictures during and after influenza; from larger series, however, it seems that delirium and subacute delirious states are at least as frequent. Depressive stupor may appear as early as the febrile period; and post-infective depression and neurasthenia may last for months after influenza and reach suicidal depth. Depression and even suicide are also a rather frequent complication of *infective hepatitis*.

In *septicaemia* the degree of mental involvement depends on the nature of the causative organism. Whereas the pyogenic streptococcus and staphylococcus aureus almost always produce mental symptoms, the anaerobic streptococcus leaves the sensorium free. The septicaemic patient is drowsy, slow, apathetic, often has a deceptive feeling of well-being, wants to get out of bed and seems without insight into the seriousness of his physical condition. *Clostridium Welchii* on the other hand with its powerful exotoxin, has no effect on the central nervous system and the patient suffering from gas gangrene remains remarkably clear and in contact with his surroundings. The same holds true for *tetanus* when painful spasms are experienced by the patient without any clouding of consciousness.

In *diphtheria*, the exotoxin of which so frequently involes the peripheral nerves, psychological symptoms are equally rare. When they occur, they indicate encephalitis or cardiac involvement. *Bacillary dysentery* and *cholera* also are not often complicated by delirious states, although in the later stages of cholera the so-called cholera–typhoid with exanthema and mental symptoms has been described as a serious complication.

Among the infections due to a filtrable virus *smallpox* is frequently accompanied by delirium with great restlessness which appears with the primary fever. It may subside after the eruption of the rash, but a severe delirious condition will return with the secondary fever.

COURSE AND PROGNOSIS

Broadly speaking, the course of a symptomatic psychosis is closely linked with the underlying physical illness. Some exceptions to this general rule have been mentioned under the headings of the individual illnesses. The prognosis is good if the patient survives: but it is well to remember that a psychosis is in itself a *serious complication of the physical illness*, interfering with medical treatment and making the nursing more difficult. A delirious patient may injure himself in his restlessness, or in a state of panic run into the open or jump out of a window. Suicide is a definite danger in post-infective neurasthenia where depression is marked.

DIAGNOSIS AND DIFFERENTIAL DIAGNOSIS

As a rule there is no great difficulty in recognizing the *clouding of consciousness*, which is the cardinal sign throughout the whole range of symptomatic psychoses, from the mildest to the most severe. Once chemical intoxication and head injury are excluded, and search for the neurological signs of organic disease of the nervous system has proved negative, every condition in which clouding of consciousness can be detected should be suspected of being symptomatic in nature. This means that every appropriate clinical and laboratory method must be used to *discover the underlying physical illness*, in order that treatment may be rationally applied. Great difficulties in the way of diagnosis may be met with: the full physical examination of a restless and uncooperative patient may be barely possible; a history may be unobtainable; in the early stages of illness laboratory findings are often inconclusive. But it is indefensible to abandon further physical investigation, and to make a facile diagnosis of schizophrenia or mania, when the clinical picture suggests a symptomatic psychosis. General physicians should be familiar with the main mental symptoms accompanying physical illness, and consult the psychiatrist when in doubt.

In most cases the specific cause of a delirious state is readily gauged from the history and physical examination. Among the more elusive causes are dehydration and electrolyte disturbances which may follow surgical operations. Potassium deficiency may also occur in patients who have suffered from prolonged diarrhoea and it is sometimes produced by prolonged and excessive purgation. Chronic subdural haematoma often causes fluctuations in consciousness during a delirious state, and malignant disease may also give rise to difficulties in diagnosis. In a small proportion of cases delirium may occur with or without peripheral neuropathy as the first manifestation of a primary carcinoma. Months or years may pass before the site or nature of this can be confidently identified: in one case seen by one of the authors, a confusional state of obscure aetiology thus preceded the local symptoms and signs arising from a carcinoma of the bronchus by nearly four years.

Accidental difficulties of diagnosis may be caused in a number of ways. For instance, the administration of sedative drugs, such as barbiturates, in the early stages of an attack of schizophrenia may cause clouding of consciousness and so awake the suspicion of a symptomatic psychosis. Antibiotics rashly given as soon as there is a rise in temperature, may obscure physical findings and, by their toxic effect on the patient, the mental picture too.

Other and less avoidable difficulties arise when an attack of schizophrenia or manic-depressive psychosis is *precipitated by a physical illness* such as an infection. This is quite frequent in puerperal cases. The existence of an endogenous psychosis may be suspected from the family history or from the previous history of the patient, and it is then well to reserve opinion on the prognosis. It is often impossible to differentiate a symptomatic from an endogenous psychosis as long as the physical illness persists, and judgement has to be postponed.

As has been mentioned before, the *subacute delirious state* may simulate an acute schizophrenic or manic attack, incoherence being a prominent feature common to both. It should be remembered that catatonic movements are found not only in schizophrenia, but also in other conditions of impairment of cerebral function such as delirious states and epileptic twilight states. Unless there is a previous history of epileptic attacks, it is particularly difficult to distinguish the epileptic twilight state from a symptomatic psychosis, in which seizures sometimes occur. Furthermore a symptomatic psychosis may mask the beginning of a chronic epilepsy, especially in children. In general, epileptic equivalents and acute schizophrenia do not show the fluctuations in clouding of consciousness with lucid intervals and return of insight, which are seen in symptomatic psychoses.

The differentiation of meningitis and encephalitis from a symptomatic psychosis depends on neurological and focal signs, but is often impossible in the early stages without examination of the cerebrospinal fluid.

TREATMENT

The treatment is in the first place that of the underlying *physical illness*, but is subject to some special difficulties and has to be modified to meet some particular requirements. The inability of the patient to co-operate, his inaccessibility and restlessness, often make rational treatment a formidable task, which may tax to the utmost the resourcefulness of the physician and the devotion of the nursing staff.

O

One of the first problems to face the doctor is the question whether the patient should be transferred to a *psychiatric hospital.* If the general hospital in which he is placed has a psychiatric unit, a delirious patient should be moved there, if only for the sake of the other patients in his ward. If the delirium is of the milder type, he can be treated in a single room adjoining a medical ward, but only if a special nurse can be provided round the clock; the danger of self-injury and suicide in these cases is often underrated. If no psychiatric unit is available, all difficult cases should be transferred to the nearest psychiatric hospital or observation ward.

If there is any reason to suspect nutritional deficiency, the patient should be provided with a balanced diet including milk, meat, eggs, vegetables, fruit juices, whole-grain cereals and bread. In such cases it is also worth while giving parenteral injections of vitamin B complex which may be conveniently administered in the form of 'Parenterovite forte' in doses of 7 ml. intramuscularly. According to some workers, nicotinic acid and nicotinamide are effective in some symptomatic states. But there is no very satisfactory evidence that the deficiency of this or any other vitamins plays a part in the aetiology of the small proportion of cases of confusional state of obscure aetiology seen in relatively affluent countries. However, if no satisfactory explanation can be found for the persistence of a state of clouded consciousness, nicotinic acid in doses of 300–400 mg. or nicotinamide in doses of 150–200 mg. daily by mouth may be given. It is hardly worth persisting with this form of treatment beyond 6–7 days if no response occurs. It is always important to combat dehydration by the administration of intravenous 5 per cent. glucose; vitamin B can be conveniently added to the intravenous infusion if required.

In a proportion of the cases the delirious state resists all therapeutic measures, there is difficulty in feeding the patient and the exhaustion caused by his continual restlessness gives cause for concern about his general health. A brief course of electroconvulsive treatment should then be considered. There are certain groups of patients in which this is specially indicated. There are those, for example, in whom some specific cause for symptomatic psychosis has been identified but has been brought under control without a change in the patient's mental state. Certain toxic delirious states and post-operative confusions fall into this group. It has to be remembered, however, that in elderly subjects, cerebral arteriosclerosis may be the underlying cause, and E.C.T. should be avoided in these cases as far as possible. There is another group in which mild clouding with a severe depressive colouring persists, or in which a state of stupor initially associated with clouding of consciousness and pronounced E.E.G. changes continues after there is reason to believe that the patient has regained contact with his environment. There is, finally, that group of cases in which the most painstaking search has failed to reveal any specific physical cause for the confusional state. In all these groups of cases the effect of two or three E.C.T. treatments can be dramatic and, at times, life-saving. The response is usually prompt and recovery often complete (Roth and Rosie, 1953).

Post-infective neurasthenia and depression may be severe enough to warrant the same supervision and the same type of treatment as an attack of endogenous depression (see Chapter IV, p. 228). In all patients showing the mental sequelae of physical illness, everything should be done to speed up bodily convalescence and at the same time to establish a psychological situation favourable to recovery. Skilled nursing of the confused patient is of the highest importance. He should, if possible, be cared for by the same day and night nurses throughout his period in hospital. His orientation and hold on reality are further helped by visits of relatives (see p. 602). The management of these cases has been transformed by the advent of phenothiazines, as restlessness is readily controlled by chlorpromazine or thioridazine in doses of 50–100 mg. three times daily; in restless or aggressive behaviour an initial intramuscular injection of 50 mg. chlorpromazine should be given. Cases which cannot be rapidly controlled in this way are uncommon and an intramuscular injection of 4–8 ml. paraldehyde is occasionally required to subdue restlessness and promote sleep. Morphine should never be administered to delirious patients. Quiet surroundings, shaded lights and other methods of reducing sensory stimulation can be helpful; but the fears and restlessness of a delirious patient often increase in total darkness.

CHAPTER VII

ALCOHOLISM, DRUG ADDICTION AND OTHER INTOXICATIONS

THE mental symptoms caused by intoxicants resemble those of the symptomatic psychoses. Although Bonhoeffer first described his 'exogenous reaction type' in relation to the mental symptoms of physical illness, it was soon found that the basic clinical syndromes were also seen after the absorption of *toxic substances with a special action on the central nervous system.* However, in addition to these general effects, almost every such substance or group of substances has a specific psychological effect, especially if it is administered in small and harmless doses. Some of these specific effects justify the use of certain drugs as medicines, and this will be discussed in this chapter.

Intoxicants may be absorbed *by accident,* as in coal-gas poisoning; they may make their way into the body in the course of daily work, as in *industries* where men are employed working with lead or mercury; or they may be given *as medicines,* as is the case with bromides and morphia. A special problem is set by those intoxicants which lead to *addiction* through their relief of tension or pain, their sedative or hypnotic effects and the social acceptance of their habitual usage, such as alcohol and opium. The use of such intoxicants is universal among different patterns of culture. The subject of addiction is of growing significance in modern psychiatry and, as it is the most important section of this chapter, will be dealt with first.

ALCOHOL AND ALCOHOLISM

Intoxication with ethyl alcohol is by far the most important branch of psychiatric toxicology. Its basis is a universal habit from which addiction springs with far-reaching consequences, both practical and social. The *good effects,* from the social point of view, of the consumption of alcohol in moderate amounts cannot be measured but can hardly be denied. To mention but one, the social converse of tired and over-strained people at the end of the day would be very much more difficult without it. The *ill effects,* on the other hand, are shown on a massive scale and can be expressed in cold figures, in the frequency of mental and physical diseases caused by alcoholism, the incidence of crimes due to drunkenness, the debasing effect on the social *niveau* of persons who spend an undue proportion of their income on intoxicating beverages. It is no part of our purpose here to discuss the enormous literature which has been accumulated on these aspects, apart from mental disease itself, except to say that there is, as yet, little awareness among the general public of the gravity of the problem of alcoholism and of the fact that it is a *disease.* The medical profession as a whole has become more conscious of the problem but knowledge about the incidence of alcoholism, about the premonitory features of chronic addiction, and the need for medical intervention at early stages in the development of heavy drinking is all too often on a superficial plane. Psychiatrists, more than other medical men, have emphasized the dangers of alcoholic addiction, and such eminent figures as Kraepelin, Forel, Bleuler and Abderhalden have been in the forefront of temperance movements. They had to contend with the influence of brewers and the 'trade' on the press, politics and public life, and above all the social acceptance of habits of drinking.

Incidence

It is the view of many observers that alcoholism is a problem of growing dimensions in all highly developed and affluent societies, but these are mere impressions. Precise facts about current prevalence and incidence of alcoholism and about changing trends in recent decades do not exist and would be very difficult to obtain. In England and Wales the numbers of persons admitted to mental hospitals with the diagnosis of alcoholic psychosis and alcoholism have risen from 439 in 1949 to about 2,760 in 1961. In Scotland also, admissions have risen from 732 in 1956 to 1,347 in 1961. This striking rise in admissions may reflect changes in the disposal of individuals identified by their practitioners as suffering from alcoholism, or variations in diagnostic practice rather than increasing prevalence. In 1961 admission rates in Scotland were 4 times higher than in England and Wales. One-third of first admissions of middle-aged men (43–54 years) to Scottish mental hospitals were suffering from alcoholism or alcoholic psychoses (Morrison, 1964), and male admissions for alcoholism were one-fifth of all admissions in Scotland. As compared with other psychiatric diagnoses where social class V has a massive preponderance, social classes I and II have much the highest rates of admission for alcoholism and alcoholic psychosis in England and Wales. In 1957 the peak admission rates were found in the 34–35 age group, while in 1952 the peak appears a decade later, in the 45–49 range. Persons are becoming addicted or being referred for treatment at an earlier age except in social class V where they tended to be older in 1957 than in 1952.

Those admitted to hospital represent, of course, only a small proportion of the total number of alcoholics. Parr (1957) conducted an enquiry into alcoholism in general practice and arrived at a figure of 11 alcoholics per thousand persons over the age of 20. The sex ratio which Parr estimated to lie between 7 : 4 and 2 : 1 with males preponderating is close to figures derived from hospital admissions, which show a ratio of approximately $3\frac{1}{2}$: 1. However, alcoholics consult their doctor only when forced to do so because of the symptoms of chronic intoxication or conflict with the law, and Parr estimated that practitioners were aware of the predicament of only one in nine of their alcoholic patients. Parr's overall prevalence figure would yield a total of about half a million alcoholics in England and Wales, which is higher than the 350,000 estimated on the basis of the Jellinek formula in 1951.

In a recent issue of the magazine of the World Health Organization the figure of over 5,000,000 alcoholics is cited for the U.S.A. This does not include the much higher proportion who can be regarded as 'problem drinkers' and yet amounts to 1 out of every 15 adults. Similar estimates are said to have been made for countries such as Canada, Australia and New Zealand. The number of 'excessive drinkers' estimated by the West German authorities is clearly not comparable but is quoted as adding up to 7,000,000.

As far as hospital admissions in other countries are concerned Jellinek has given the following figures: in the United States in 1950 the number of first admissions to hospital with psychosis was 106,707, and of these 5,450 were first admissions with alcoholic psychosis, i.e. 5·1 per cent. In Sweden the rate is higher: in 1949 there were 9,117 admissions, 783 or 8·6 per cent. being for alcoholic psychosis. In Finland the rate is lower, 190 out of a total of 7,614 admissions in 1949, or 2·5 per cent., and in Norway it was lower still, only 23 out of 1,723, or 1·3 per cent. In other countries information is more difficult to get. Jellinek has been able in France to find data only for a single Department, that of Gers, where in 1949 the alcoholic admissions constituted 17·6 per cent. of all admissions for psychosis. The very high value of this figure has to be considered in the light of the fact that, in France, the compulsory admission of a patient to a mental hospital may be enforced on the grounds of alcoholism which is rarely the case in this country or the U.S.A.

The *prevalence of alcoholism* appears to be markedly affected by *social and cultural* factors. In under-developed countries and among individuals living within a simple culture, drunkenness is generally agreed to be rare except for periodic celebrations of an orgiastic kind in which this, as also other forms of disinhibited behaviour, are permitted in a group setting. In highly-developed and affluent societies alcoholism is almost universal but wide variations in prevalence are found. There is no wholly satisfactory explanation for the observed differences although a number of hypotheses have been advanced. In France it is said that approximately a third of the adult population derives part or the whole of its income from the production or sale of alcoholic beverages (Kessel and Walton, 1965). There is a large measure of tolerance for wine drinking which is indulged in steadily during the working day by a relatively high proportion of the population. Drunken behaviour is rarely observed though chronic intoxication with consequent impairment of health is common. In Italy on the other hand it is claimed that drinking during working hours and alcoholism in general is much more strongly disapproved of with the result that, although wine production is of great economic importance, alcoholism is said to be relatively rare (Kessel and Walton, 1965). In the United States, the first year after the introduction of prohibition (1920) saw a marked reduction in the number of cases of drunkenness but the contraband indices of the prevalence of alcoholism showed a steep rise. It is of interest that the prevalence of alcoholism among Irish Americans is two or three times higher than that in any other section of the population (Hyde and Chisholm, 1944), while Jews, who number 15 per cent. of the population of New York State, contributed only 1 per cent. of all white first admissions to mental hospitals with alcoholic psychosis (Malzberg, 1960). The absence of strong taboos against alcohol amongst the Jews and their strong social cohesion has been advanced in explanation of this relative immunity (Pittman and Snyder, 1962) but there is little solid evidence in favour of such views; however, C. R. Snyder (1958) made the interesting finding that, as the Jew loses orthodoxy, the risk he runs of becoming an excessive drinker increases.

Chronic alcoholism and the more severe forms of alcoholic intoxication are frequent in all occupations concerned with the production and distribution of alcoholic drinks. The large *preponderance of male over female* admissions in all countries probably owes something to occupational hazard in that alcohol consumption is a widely accepted and consistent feature of the social activities closely linked with professional and business life. The person who opts out of the conventional ceremonies of conviviality and their rounds of drinks is at some risk of being regarded as an outsider.

The *age factor* is an important one. A large increase in total alcohol consumption within a given country may reflect an extension of the alcoholic habit to wider age or social groups rather than an increase in individual consumption; this was the explanation for the increase in total consumption in the U.S.A. during the last world war (Jellinek, 1947).

Admission rates for alcoholism and alcoholic psychosis in 1957 in England and Wales showed a substantial increase amongst those aged 20–24 which probably reflects the increase in alcohol consumption and drunkenness among young adults and adolescents that has recently been causing public concern.

Whereas the graver psychoses associated with alcoholism are shown at a mean age in the late forties, they are the result of drinking habits which have begun very many years before. Studies from U.S.A. (Jellinek, 1946), Sweden (Åmark, 1951) and Great Britain (Glatt, 1961a) agree in showing that the average length of drinking history in males before receiving treatment in their forties was 20–22 years. In women (Great Britain only) the period was shorter, averaging 13 years.

Effects of Alcoholic Consumption

Of the more important intoxicating beverages, beer contains 3–4·5 per cent. of alcohol wines 10–14 per cent., and spirits 30–40 per cent. in Great Britain. Higher concentrations obtain in the United States. Each of these can lead to addiction and to the severest forms of intoxication.

Alcohol is easily and rapidly absorbed from the intestine and passes into the bloodstream and thence into the tissues of the body. Maximum concentration of alcohol in the blood occurs between half-an-hour and two hours after ingestion. It is gradually oxidized, mainly in the liver, but 1 or 2 per cent. of the amount consumed is excreted by the kidneys and lungs. Although the quantity of alcohol in expired air is small, it correlates well with its concentration in the blood and tissues. The odour in the breath is derived mainly from other volatile constituents of alcoholic beverages and provides a poor guide to the amount of alcohol consumed. As it is readily metabolized, alcohol provides a rapidly available form of energy and it may supply as much as three-quarters of the calorie needs.

The *immediate action of alcohol* on the nervous system is that of a depressant, its effects first being shown in the higher centres. As the function of these centres is largely one of inhibition and control of lower ones, when their inhibitory action is reduced the total behaviour of the individual becomes more instinctive, more primitive and more spontaneous. Temporary release from inhibition causes the subjective experience of greater self-confidence, unjustified from a realistic point of view, as the efficiency of higher mental functions is reduced. The relief from worry, tension or shyness takes place at the expense of alertness, judgement and self-criticism. It is because shy and inhibited men become more sociable, tongue-tied people articulate and those laden with a sense of inferiority more assertive, that the consumption of alcohol has become such a prominent feature of social intercourse. However, there can be no doubt that in some people a change of mood towards depression, at times serious in depth, occurs, and such persons figure prominently among those who make suicidal attempts in a state of drunkenness. Others regularly become aggressive or violent to a dangerous degree. The supposed aphrodisiac effects of alcohol are illusory but it does lessen sexual inhibition.

The *reduction of efficiency* was established in famous experiments by Kraepelin and his pupils as early as 1892; subsequent investigators have repeated these experiments and have carried out others, with identical results. Alcohol in moderate amounts reduces motor control. Co-ordination of movements of eyes and fingers, marksmanship in shooting, accuracy in typesetting, typewriting, speaking, etc., are interfered with, and the movements are slowed and made more random. The increase of the random element in movement gives an illusion of increased speed and efficiency, not borne out by the results obtained. A similar impairment has been demonstrated in mental operations involving intelligence, memory, attention and judgement. Work in recent years has conclusively demonstrated that there is no threshold below which alcohol is without effect on skill and co-ordination, which are lessened even by small quantities. In an enquiry into the effects of alcohol on driving it was shown that bus drivers became increasingly inaccurate in deciding whether they could safely drive their vehicles between two marked points as their alcohol consumption increased. Their confidence in their ability to succeed showed a parallel increase (Drew *et al.*, 1958).

Besides the quantitative diminution in level of performance, there are *qualitative changes*, mainly in emotional reactions, which will be dealt with in the description of the clinical picture. The emotional reaction to increasing degrees of intoxication is to a large extent determined by the personality; but the extent to which the emotional reaction keeps this individual stamp diminishes as the degree of intoxication becomes progressively more severe.

However, it has been shown that *tolerance* varies considerably from individual to individual; and no scientific explanation has yet been found for the fact that the same amount of alcohol may produce signs of severe poisoning and even unconsciousness in one subject, and in another only a mild degree of euphoria. The fitness of an individual to carry out skilled tasks such as driving is therefore difficult to judge from blood-levels of alcohol alone. It has been suggested that differences in the rate of absorption from the intestine may be partly responsible but there is no evidence for this or any other explanation.

In the normal subject slight signs of intoxication appear when the *concentration of alcohol in the blood* reaches 0·2 per cent. by volume. Between 0·2 and 0·5 per cent. there are increasing degrees of intoxication, and above the higher figure there is danger of death. Bogen (1932) distinguishes a sub-clinical stage at 1–2 mg. alcohol per ml. of blood; when the concentration reaches 3 mg. per ml. the co-ordination of movement, speech and sensory perception are affected; and above 4 mg. per ml. there is apathy and stupor.

The *elimination* of alcohol, both by oxidation in the tissues and by excretion from lungs and kidneys, is slow compared with the rate at which it can be taken into the blood-stream from the intestinal tract. So it is that a drink taken a few hours after others may have a much greater effect than one taken in a state of complete sobriety. The disproportion between rates of absorption and elimination can also be responsible for the constant state of mild intoxication shown by the 'old soak'.

Although the depressant action of alcohol on the nervous system, first demonstrated by Schmiedeberg (1888), is fully established, there are no specific *pathological changes*. Oedema of the brain and meninges is found in casualties from an overdose. Subdural haemorrhages are frequent in chronic drunkards, and are usually attributed to falls on the head and similar injuries. Proliferation of small vessels and glia in the neighbourhood of the corpora mammillaria has been found by Gamper (1928) in chronic alcoholics as an almost regular finding, even in patients without symptoms of delirium or dysmnesic states.

Aetiological Basis of Alcoholism

A variety of *physical theories* of the causation of alcoholism have been advanced. No evidence has come forward that any specific metabolic, endocrine or allergic factor underlies alcoholic addiction. However, recent inquiries have opened up a number of important lines of enquiry into the biological aspects of alcoholism. As far as *genetic factors* are concerned it has been shown that strains of mice which prefer alcohol solutions to water reveal enzyme differences from those that do not. The former have a higher level of liver alcohol dehydrogenase than control mice and, under conditions in which alcohol is the only source of liquid, ingest more than controls (Hoff, 1961). No biochemical differences have to date been demonstrated in human subjects but there is a good deal of evidence that genetic factors make some contribution to the causation of alcoholism. Studies of the relatives of alcoholics by Bleuler and co-workers (1952) showed that the incidence of alcoholism in the parents and sibs of alcoholics was approximately two and a half times as great as in the parents and sibs of a control series of surgical patients. Åmark (1951) has shown that in male alcoholics there is a marked increase in familial incidence of alcoholism over normal expectation. Although the suggestion has been made (Kessel and Walton, 1965) that this may be due to emulation rather than inheritance, this is rendered unlikely by twin studies (Kaij, 1960) which have shown that monozygotic twins have a higher concordance rate for alcoholism than dizygotic twins. Moreover, there was an increasing concordance rate with increasing degrees of abuse in monozygotic as compared with dizygotic pairs. As far as the phenomenon of *increased alcohol tolerance* is concerned it has been found (Wartburg, 1965) that an alcohol breakdown rate of at least twice the supposed maximum of 7–8 grams per day obtains in the alcohol addict. The explanation may lie partly in catalase supplementing the alcohol dehydrogenase iso-enzymes. Dehydrogenase activity appears to be by no means limited to the liver, being also found in gut, kidney, lung and spleen. It would seem likely that the alcohol-dependent state of the chronic addict has some biochemical basis. In volunteers who had been drinking heavily for 7–12 weeks Isbell *et al.* (1955) observed that abrupt withdrawal was associated with syndromes ranging in severity from mild shakes to delirium tremens, alcoholic hallucinosis or epileptic fits.

It seems plain, however, that *social, cultural and psychological factors* make an important contribution and the interaction between alcohol and personality and between personality and social environment must be taken into account in approaching the problem of dependence. Some social and cultural factors are discussed on pages 390 and 394.

A variety of forms of *childhood deprivation* has been found in alcoholics. It has been shown for example (Hilgard and Newman, 1963) that the loss of a parent in childhood had occurred significantly more often in male alcoholics in the age group 20–39 than in control subjects. There is, however, nothing specific in the various forms of deprivation and childhood vicissitude that have been reported as they are to be found equally in association with other forms of psychiatric disorder such as neurosis and sexual deviation.

The same statement can be made in relation to reported findings as to the *pre-morbid personality* of alcoholic subjects. Vallance (1965) described 42 per cent. of 68 male alcoholics as having given a history of neurotic symptoms before the development of alcoholism and more than one-third he regarded as psychopathic. Feelings of personal inferiority and inadequacy, particularly in social situations, were common. This group was heavily represented among those who subsequently deteriorated. However, retrospective judgements on the pre-morbid personality of alcoholics are almost certainly unreliable. Personality is liable to undergo striking changes in the course of addiction. For example among 225 delinquent boys studied by McCord and McCord (1960) and followed up 20 years later, 11 per cent. were found to be alcoholic. Although they had been more self-confident and assertive and less troubled with neurotic symptoms than other boys, in later life they appeared abnormally dependent. Emotionally unstable, psychopathic persons and those suffering from specific neurotic symptoms are likely to be particularly at risk as far as alcoholic or any other form of addiction is concerned. Among such individuals a history of deprivation, hardship and unsatisfactory parent–child relationships is bound to be common. There is no evidence to suggest, however, that one type of personality, whether the 'oral', the dependent or the latent sexual deviant, is characteristic of alcoholics. Some alcoholics are indeed dependent and others are equally assertive and confident, some are gregarious and some extroverted, others are timid and shy when they embark on their career of addiction. Constitutional depressives make use of alcohol to conquer their reticence and pessimism. Obsessionals try to throw off the shackles of their compulsive thoughts; and the shy, the anxious and the socially awkward find that their anxieties are relieved and their social contacts eased under the influence of drink. Hysterics consume alcohol under the suggestive influence of the environment in which they find themselves, or when they crave stimulation and new sensations. There can be little doubt also that under specially stressful circumstances stable and well-adapted individuals may become addicted. In other words the basic personality of the alcoholic like that of the neurotic is probably a variant of the norm.

Among *social factors* that contribute to the initiation and persistence of alcoholic addiction are the approval given in many cultures to the man who can hold his drink; a substantial consumption of alcohol is prone to be regarded as a concomitant of manliness. As alcohol helps to overcome shyness and restraint, it often becomes one of the means adopted by the adolescent to advance towards manhood. Habituation is also encouraged by the fact that very often commercial and professional activity is conducted over a drink in a bar, at a luncheon or dinner or at a social gathering at which a good deal of alcohol is consumed. The ritual of each member of the company 'standing a round' is widely practised. As would be expected, certain occupations such as those of publican, hotel manager, barman and commercial traveller are at special risk. Other socio-economic factors associated with the perpetuation of drinking behaviour have been described by Vallance (1965) on the basis of a study of 68 general hospital patients. Physical illness or disability frequently exacerbated alcoholic addiction. In 15 per cent. of the cases employment appeared to have an adverse effect and this group was composed of business representatives and drink trade employees. Unemployment was more prone than otherwise to exacerbate the problem through idleness, and decline to cheap drinks or methylated spirits followed because of lack of money. Membership of an abnormal drinking group represented a serious obstacle to abstinence in that this demanded that the patient change his daily routine and whole way of life. On the other hand, the threat of losing a wife or of police action or of loss of employment will often slow down or terminate the bout of drinking and the patient can be prevailed on to accept admission. However, the loss of some supportive figure such as the wife, may lead to rapid deterioration.

This does not mean, however, that the search for specific physiological mechanisms underlying the consistent characteristics of addicts, perhaps concerned with perpetuation of the addictive state, need be fruitless. There are, for example, individuals who experience trouble with alcohol almost with the first drink (Hoff, 1961). These subjects are identifiable at a relatively early age and, in our experience, the phenomenon occurs in both sexes. These cases appear to merit special investigation. There are patients also in whom heavy drinking lasting many years appears to be tolerated without any harmful effects on work or social adjustment. After a period, however, a more or less abrupt decline in tolerance occurs, the patient becomes disorganized and often presents soon after for medical or psychiatric attention. It has been suggested that limited or subtle forms of brain damage may be related to this phenomenon as also to the increasingly frequent 'blackouts' of memory and perhaps the impaired ability to control alcohol intake (Hoff, 1961). However, psychological factors may also contribute to its causation.

Natural History of Alcoholic Addiction

VARIETIES OF DRINKING PATTERN IN ALCOHOLISM. It has been emphasized by a number of authors (Kessel and Walton, 1965) that a too narrow approach which focuses attention on the compulsive drinker to the exclusion of others who must be considered alcoholics requiring treatment, carries some dangers. The concept of alcoholism requires to be defined in broader terms. The following classification of alcoholism has been adapted from that established by Jellinek (1960) but departs from it in certain respects.

(A) THE ALCOHOL-DEPENDENT DRINKER. These individuals show a sustained psychological dependence upon the effects of alcohol for the relief of emotional distress or physical discomfort or to enable them to face, with some measure of composure, the everyday burdens of life. There is no loss of control and to some extent the ability to abstain is retained. Little or no progress may be observed over a number of years, obvious intoxication is uncommon and withdrawal symptoms rare unless interruption of drinking has been very sudden, as in the case of admission to hospital for injury or illness. However, tolerance is high in these subjects and large quantities of alcohol are consumed. Physical health is, therefore, gradually undermined and complications such as cirrhosis of the liver or peripheral neuritis are relatively common. These subjects are only rarely recognized as alcoholics by themselves or the family doctor looking after them. Treatment should, however, be instituted at the earliest possible opportunity, as mental and physical deterioration will ultimately occur in a high proportion of instances.

(B) THE WINE DRINKING ALCOHOLIC. This type of drinker was described by Jellinek as characteristic of wine-drinking countries. He can control the quantity of drink he consumes at any one time and he rarely needs to drink to the point of gross intoxication. However, he is *unable to abstain* even for a single day and, if he ceases to drink, he suffers craving and almost invariably shows withdrawal symptoms which may go all the way to delirium tremens after a few days. There is, therefore, both psychological and physical dependence on alcohol with increased tissue tolerance. Although few such subjects regard themselves as alcoholics, they are in a constant state of mild intoxication and the large number so affected constitutes a major public health problem in wine-drinking countries such as France.

(C) THE 'UNCONTROLLED' OR 'COMPULSIVE' ALCOHOLIC. In addition to increased tolerance to alcohol, physical dependence, craving and withdrawal symptoms in the case of deprivation, these individuals suffer from *loss of control*; they are unable to stop drinking after the first few drinks until their supply of money, or alcohol, runs out, or unconsciousness or accident terminates the session. They may have periods during which they abstain. This type of alcoholism is particularly common in Canada, the United States and Australia.

(D) THE SYMPTOMATIC ALCOHOLIC. In these cases the alcoholism is *secondary* to some neurotic, psychotic or organic disorder. The subject begins to drink in order to allay symptoms of anxiety, depression or schizophrenia or the early changes associated with cerebral disease. Patients suffering from phobic anxiety states which limit their activities or render them housebound not infrequently take to alcohol and this complication is particularly common *in males*. Physical dependence and addiction develop in time but the pattern of drinking is not distinctive in this group and may take a variety of forms. Treatment must be directed at the primary psychological disorder but this cannot properly begin until the alcoholism has been resolved.

(E) THE PERIODICAL OR 'BOUT' DRINKER. In this group there is alternation of brief bouts of grossly pathological drinking with long phases of normality during which the person is able to drink socially or to abstain altogether. The week-end drunk belongs to this group. No particular psychological stress is required to trigger off the phases of drinking which may commence with an almost explosive suddenness.

(F) CHRONIC ALCOHOLISM may be regarded as the final stage in which excessive drinkers manifesting different drinking patterns and underlying pathologies converge (Kessel and Walton, 1965). The chronic alcoholic manifests certain consistent physical and psychological changes. He suffers from continual nausea which usually leads to under-nutrition and this in turn contributes to the causation of the physical complications such as polyneuritis and cirrhosis of the liver which are common in chronic alcoholics. He shows rapidly diminishing physical tolerance and drunkenness may be produced by smaller and smaller amounts of alcohol. The reduced intake at one and the same time fails to satisfy craving but renders him more disorganized. Although he gains little or no pleasure from drinking he is compelled to continue with it and, if under financial pressure, may resort to drinking cheap wines or methylated spirits. The outcome is usually admission to hospital with one of the physical complications or with a psychiatric disorder such as delirium tremens or alcoholic hallucinosis, epilepsy or a paranoid psychosis.

Clinical Features

ACUTE INTOXICATION. The *immediate effect of the absorption* of alcohol into the circulation resembles that of any anaesthetic. After a short stage of 'excitation', due to the removal of the inhibitory influence of the higher centres, there is a reduction of psychological efficiency. Lack of muscular control, reduced attention, blunted sensory perception and slowness of thinking become obvious. Associations are superficial; there is considerable distractibility; retention is weakened, and memory for more remote events is patchy and unreliable.

Acquired inhibitions, self-control and reticence disappear, or are submerged under waves of emotion of a primitive type—hilarity and a feeling of good-fellowship, or, perhaps, sadness and self-pity, with weeping and a helpless clinging to the support of others. In the now considerably narrowed field of mental activity, performance comes easily and is uncritically regarded. This, together with the deceptive self-confidence, the absence of feelings of fatigue and the intellectual and moral irresponsibility of the drunken man, all contribute to a mood of pleasure and contentment. The *descent to a lower scale of values* brings personalities of all kinds to a lowest common denominator, an undifferentiated level of behaviour in which all are equal, and find companionship easy. It is true that, at this stage, hidden traits of the personality, ordinarily suppressed, may show themselves. But what emerges is often no true index of the personality, and seldom represents any of its better side.

In the early stage of intoxication, the deceptive feeling of warmth, due to dilatation of the capillaries of the skin, the insensitivity to physical pain, and the relative ease of movement, give a *feeling of superiority and strength*, which is important for the understanding of habit formation and addiction.

It depends mainly on the concentration of the alcoholic beverage, and the speed at which it is consumed, whether or not this stage of drunkenness persists for a long time, or is quickly followed by *symptoms of a deeper narcosis*: staggering gait, slurred speech, general ataxia, tremor, vertigo, vomiting and unconsciousness. On the mental side severer degrees of intoxication are often accompanied by increased irritability, outbursts of rage and violence after solitary brooding. For most of the events and actions in this stage the subject usually remains amnesic after return to sobriety. These symptoms may in some cases border on those of pathological drunkenness.

In *alcoholic coma* the temperature is subnormal, the breathing is slow and stertorous, and the pulse small. Pupils may be contracted or widely dilated; the deep reflexes are weak or absent. The skin is pale or cyanotic, and feels cold. There may be urinary retention, or incontinence. The smell of alcohol, or of the aromatic components of wines, beers and spirits, may rouse suspicion of the cause of the coma; but it must be remembered that an epileptic may have taken a drink before being overcome by a seizure, and head injuries are common after a drinking bout. More than once diabetics have taken alcohol, and then given themselves an overdose of insulin, producing hypoglycaemic coma. The importance of the *differential diagnosis* is obvious, and imposes caution. Admission to hospital is indicated; and there the stomach may be emptied by tube, and its contents and the blood be tested for alcohol, and other necessary examinations be made. That alcohol is the sole cause of the coma can hardly be verified without keeping the patient under observation until he has begun to come round.

ALCOHOLIC ADDICTION: GENERAL FEATURES. Those in the stage of *excessive drinking* who are dependent on alcohol but do not lose their ability to keep its consumption under control may be capable of reducing the amount they take once they are convinced that it is necessary, though they may be difficult to persuade that it is. Their social failures and increasing financial embarrassment may bring them or their relatives to seek help. Treatment begun early enough and on a co-operative basis can be successful. It may be found possible to put them on a drinking ration.

The kind and extent of change in personality which the excessive drinker passes through depend in almost equal measure on physical and psychological factors. In this first stage the drinker has not reached the point of self-deception. It is others, including possibly his doctor, whom he seeks to deceive about the extent of his drinking. His behaviour is determined equally by his impression that drink makes him function better in every sphere and by his guilt about this drinking. On the other hand, in this group there are men with such robust constitutions, steady temperaments and well-lined purses that even years of heavy consumption, which would ruin those less well-endowed, leave them unaffected in health or fortune. Knowing themselves to be well, and seeing themselves able to conduct their affairs and enjoy society without ill effects, they develop none of the guilt, the face-saving rationalization and self-deceptions which are the signs of deterioration in others.

The second group, whose alcoholism is a disease, are the main problem. For these there is no alternative to complete abstinence. These *compulsive drinkers losing control* over the amount they drink will always need psychological preparation before other treatment begins to convince them of the nature of their plight and to awake a desire for help in becoming permanently abstinent. Whatever their previous personality has been like, they are now given to self-deception. The addictive drinker makes daily resolutions to stop drinking which are daily broken till his self-esteem is undermined. This general weakening of volition makes him become irregular and inefficient at work. The need to conceal repeated social failure from himself leads him to ignore ordinary social standards, to become careless, slovenly, tactless and indulgent of fits of anger or suspicion. He may become cruel to his wife and shameless when drunk even in the presence of his children. The positive need for self-deception leads to an incapacity to see the truth about himself, however it is presented. If confronted with the facts, he makes light of them or denies them with great plausibility. He forgets the amount he has taken and thinks it less than it is. In so far as anyone or anything is to blame for his plight, it is not himself and he projects the blame for his inefficiency at work, the general disorder of his affairs, the disruption of his home and the alienation of his friends on to his wife, his colleagues, his past misfortunes or society at large. At some stage he may be induced, fortified by a preliminary drink, to come to a doctor, but his complaint will be of general nervousness or some physical symptom and he will not admit his enslavement to the habit, or even that he drinks to excess.

The *emotions of the alcoholic* are very much affairs of the moment. Early in the day before he has had time to drink, his mood tends to an *irritable depression*, his pre-morbid sense of humour now takes the form of a *flat or noisy jollity*, in which nothing is taken seriously. Alternating with cheerfulness one sees very often a *maudlin sentimentality*. Though he may have a spasm of depression and remorse occasioned by a momentary glimpse of reality, it will soon be drowned by a drink. Though his emotions may seem sincere, they are superficial. Even the flashes of self-depreciation are salves to the smart of wounded self-esteem. In the last stages, personal pride and dignity are given up completely, and he may accept the truth at this 'lowest point' as something that is past helping and now past caring for.

It is only seldom that heavy indulgence can be enjoyed for years without the appearance of *organic changes*. The personality of the alcoholic shows, as it were in a congealed state, the transient features of a mild state of drunkenness. His mental horizon is near and narrow, and his thinking proceeds in a rut. His talk is empty and abounds in clichés. Self-praise and complacency may be so extreme that the patient seems to have lost, as he may in fact have lost, all respect for truth and honesty. Judgement is confused, based on an inadequate grasp and distorted by emotional needs. The capacity for clear and logical thinking is reduced, though the patient feels himself to be alert and versatile. In later stages retention and memory are seriously disturbed.

When dealing with an alcoholic, it is always advisable to obtain as much *objective information* as possible from *independent witnesses*, especially if there have been family quarrels. Every step the physician takes to help the patient and his family should be based on unbiased information, which cannot be obtained from the patient alone. Wife and husband are not infrequently both drinking too much and equally untrustworthy in their presentation of their own cases and their defamations of the other. The psychiatrist should not permit himself to be hurried into defining his view and should defer action till he can be certain of the facts. This caution is especially necessary if jealousy is a feature, as it so often is, in the family life of the drinker. In attempts to give up drinking the alcoholic may have had *recourse to drugs*, either barbiturates or stimulants of the benzedrine group. He is likely to persist in taking these and the possibility of this added complication should always be borne in mind.

In those whose addiction at first takes a *periodic form* change in personality may take a different form from the usual one. These people are sometimes referred to as suffering from 'dipsomania'. At first the alternating bouts of indulgence followed by periods of hang-over and remorse are self-perpetuating. Then one bout tends to merge into the next and the final picture does not differ from the standard one.

There are others in whom drinking is *secondary* to primary mood changes and manic or depressive swings. In them personality changes which can be traced directly to alcohol are seldom prominent and the course of the condition will be largely what one would expect from the primary disorders.

In the *stage of chronic alcoholism*, neglect of nutrition may lead to physical illness and give the doctor his first opportunity to discover the facts. The decline of appetite, nausea and flatulence from which alcoholics frequently suffer are due to a chronic gastritis which subsides with the cessation of drinking. The mechanism by which liver disease is produced in chronic alcoholism is unknown. In the early stages the disorder is reversible but it later advances to cirrhosis which may be associated with jaundice, ascites and haematemesis. The associated malnutrition causes deficiency of B vitamins which make an important contribution to the causation of peripheral neuritis and the dysmnesic state of Korsakov's psychosis. Increased tremulousness is common and malaise and impairment of general health and vitality are invariable. The outstanding feature now is that tolerance of alcohol diminishes quite sharply. Craving is as great or even more pronounced but the alcoholic finds that he cannot drink as much as formerly. This reduced intake does not satisfy him and yet, at the same time, it reduces him to helplessness whereas in earlier stages of his illness he could take larger and larger amounts before he was prostrated.

DELUSIONS OF JEALOUSY. These are the signs of a *paranoid reaction*, which may have the most serious consequences for the family life of the alcoholic, and not infrequently leads to violence and even to murderous attacks. The combination of lessened potency, increased sexual desire when in an intoxicated state, weakened consideration and affection, may cause aversion in any wife. The slightest sign of reluctance on her part when approached by a drunken husband may arouse an uninhibited and insightless affective storm in which anger, resentment, suspicion and jealousy are given free rein. At the time there may be a scene of reckless savagery, followed in the sobriety of the next day by sentimental appeals for affection and forgiveness. Suspicions, however, persist and accumulate, and are finally not to be shaken off when sober. Impossible accusations are made, that his wife is committing adultery with strangers from the street, or with near relations and even her own children. He suspects her of an insatiable sexual appetite from which he only is excluded. He finds her behaviour strange. When he comes home, he sees her hurrying to the bathroom to put her clothes in order because her lover has just escaped through the window. He discovers seminal stains on the floor or in her laundry. He sees from the shadows round her eyes that she has been having sexual intercourse in his absence. She is cool and frigid to him, and this can only be because she is getting satisfaction elsewhere. He beats and kicks her, threatens to kill her, or terrifies her by actions less savage but more strange. The wife of one of our patients was frightened into seeking advice by waking up in the night to feel her husband, in the darkness, fingering her lips.

In many textbooks, including the previous edition of this one, the above syndrome is described as being particularly one of the complications of alcoholism. It has, however, become increasingly clear in recent years that alcoholism is merely one among many settings for the condition. In a recent statistical analysis of all cases of morbid jealousy recorded in the literature, Mooney (1965) found that alcoholism had been present in only 22·5 per cent. Langfeldt's (1961) material and Shepherd's (1961) included in Mooney's analysis make it clear that jealous reactions of a kind commonly linked with alcohol can appear on a non-alcoholic basis and Johanson (1964), reviewing a number of reports, comments that none shows a distinct causal connexion between alcohol and abnormal jealousy. Mooney observed, moreover, that among those with a pre-morbid disposition to jealousy there was no excess of alcoholics or heavy drinkers. Indeed neither in pre-morbid personality nor in the clinical details of the paranoid reaction does the alcoholic differ from others whose morbid jealousy is manifest in a setting free from alcoholic addiction. Traits of emotional instability, aggressiveness, irritability, feelings of inferiority arising from social, physical or personality handicaps are common. Although some subjects are unusually active sexually and may have been conspicuously promiscuous, others have had long-standing difficulties in sexual adjustment owing to impotence or other deficiencies. Feelings of sexual and general inferiority are common in these cases. In his classical paper on pathological jealousy, Jaspers (1910) divided these cases into those in whom the illness had understandable links with traits of jealousy in the pre-morbid personality and those in whom it appeared to emerge as a 'new process', the latter being examples of paranoid schizophrenia. The distinction was to some extent validated by Mooney (1965) who found that those in whom pathological jealousy seemed to arise as a 'new process' were more likely to be diagnosed as suffering from paranoid or depressive psychosis. However, there is no very sharp line of demarcation between the groups, and further enquiries in this field with the aid of modern techniques are needed. Langfeldt (1961) showed that alcoholism may be associated with a number of different jealous reactions. There can be a transient irruption of jealousy arising in a bout of intoxication and terminating with it, or more permanent jealous states may be present which can take the form of intensified normal jealousy or of a fixed delusional state. This last is relatively rare in cases of alcoholism. The causes of this variation in the symptomatology and course of the jealous reaction in alcoholic addicts are connected not so much with the amount of alcohol consumed as with other factors which produce similar variations in non-alcoholic subjects.

From the point of view of management there are a number of points of importance. A proportion of these patients are dangerous to their spouses, some 14 per cent. of recorded cases having made homicidal attempts. Where violence has been threatened, serious consideration must always be given to the possible need for compulsory detention of the patient. Apparent recession of morbid jealousy in the patient who is under treatment in the hospital is an unreliable guide to the future course of the disorder and long-term supervision is essential. A proportion of patients respond to long-term therapy with phenothiazines and the more acute and psychotic the disorder the more likely that a favourable response will be elicited.

In accordance with the new emphasis in relation to morbid jealousy, the subject has also been discussed in Chapter III. The valuable reviews of the subject by Langfeldt (1961) and Shepherd (1961) included detailed case reports of a large material.

DELIRIUM TREMENS. This is by far the most frequent psychosis in the chronic alcoholic. It is often of short duration; the patient rarely comes into a psychiatric hospital and in many cases is never seen by a psychiatrist. Sudden withdrawal of alcohol is now recognized as one of the ways in which delirium tremens may be caused. However, in

Sweden where delirium tremens was common after abolition of the alcohol rationing system in 1955, Lundquist (1961) found that abrupt withdrawal was the precipitating cause in only 12–13 per cent. of cases. Other contributory factors were infection, head injury, and poor nutrition. There can be little doubt also that in some subjects delirium tremens commences during a bout of heavy consumption of alcohol (Glatt, 1962). Vitamin deficiency may make some contribution to causation as it does in alcoholic Korsakov's psychosis, Wernicke's encephalopathy and pellagrous psychoses (Spillane, 1947).

Prodromata of a sub-delirious character are frequent. The patient is liable to anxiety attacks when lying down to sleep, or is awakened by nightmares, panic, sweating and feelings of oppression. There may then be illusions or hallucinations, at first appearing singly and in isolation, into which the patient has full insight. He may, for instance, see the shapes of men in a dark corner on the way home from the public-house, or see the pattern of the carpet in his room 'come alive'. Despite his awareness of the illusory nature of these experiences they are likely to arouse fear and restlessness. In a considerable proportion of cases the onset of delirium is heralded by a *single epileptic fit*, or two in short succession.

Once it has begun, the psychotic state grows rapidly worse. Its principal symptoms are those of delirium, and have been described in the previous chapter; but there are certain *characteristic features*. There is a coarse and persistent tremor of the hands, extending sometimes to the head, trunk and even to the tongue, which can usually be recognized as distinct from the extreme general restlessness which may mask it. There is also an uninterrupted pressure of activity, unlike what is seen in infective delirium. The combination of restlessness with ataxia and severe disturbances of equilibrium is a special source of danger to the patient, who may sway and fall and bruise himself or suffer a fracture, if supervision and control are inadequate. Clouding of consciousness varies in degree from case to case, and in the same patient from stage to stage of the delirium. If he is left to himself, he becomes absorbed in a dream world. This may be dominated by *habitual activities:* the baker imagines that he is kneading the dough, or moving loaves in and out of the oven, and can be seen going through the characteristic motions; and the barman pulls levers, draws imaginary corks, or distributes drinks. Fantastic scenes are equally frequent, especially at night. *Hallucinations* of quickly moving small animals such as rats and snakes have always been described as typical, together with the emotional reaction of terror they arouse. But the illusory animals seen in the bedclothes are as often huge as small; and though they may be threatening, others seem comical, humorous, or in sexual play with one another. Lilliputian groups of musicians may play drinking songs, or the patient's friends may appear in diminutive size, and drink and laugh for his amusement, their only curious feature being that they have no heads. The peculiar mixture of anxiety or even terror with cheerfulness and jocularity, which is sometimes seen, is typical of alcoholic delirium.

The attention of the patient can be aroused, and he can take part in a conversation. There is sometimes a *disturbance of speech* which shows itself not only in thickness and slurring of articulation, but also in dysphasic and paraphasic distortion of words. In conversation he will tend to ramble, and, if not re-stimulated, to drift from the point or to relapse into a dreamy state. He is *suggestible* to sensory deception in all fields, but especially in those in which he is hallucinated. He may read on demand from a blank sheet of paper, see animals when his eyeballs are pressed, or catch an imaginary thread of silk and handle it with his fingers.

Auditory hallucinations are rare, but they may occur as a part of the total situation, part real and part hallucinatory, experienced by the patient. On the other hand, *vestibular disturbances*, felt by the patient as falling walls, a moving floor, the entire room in rotation, are quite common. They may combine with rapidly moving visual hallucinations to convince the patient that he is on a journey, or involved in an adventure. The delusional ideas which appear in the delirious state are in conformity with the sensory experiences, and are as fluid and changeable as they are.

Most of the delirious experiences are forgotten afterwards; but some patients have a remarkably *clear recollection* of the fantastic scenes through which they have passed, though they rarely remember the extreme terror or other violent emotions which accompanied them. In his lucid state the patient may regard his past experience as entirely natural, and in reporting on it show no embarrassment and have a quick explanation for every oddity. The alcoholic virtuosity in self-excuse seems never to desert him.

Physically, there is often a slight rise of temperature, free perspiration, a coated tongue, and dry lips and sordes. The urine is scanty and may contain a small quantity of albumin. Pupillary anomalies and signs of peripheral neuritis are frequent.

Delirium tremens, if allowed to run its course, usually ends after three to seven days with a *terminal sleep* of up to twenty-four hours, after which the patient, though weak, feels he has fully recovered. The majority neither believe that they have been seriously ill, nor are easily convinced that the illness was connected with their alcoholic habits. A predisposition to similar attacks remains, and some old drunkards have survived a number of them. The main danger, besides that of fractures and injuries incurred during the phase of restlessness, is that of acute heart failure. Any physical complication, such as pneumonia, makes the outlook much more serious. Death may result from cardiovascular collapse, infection, hyperthermia or self-injury. Korsakov's psychosis or dementia may follow, usually after a succession of attacks.

Treatment of delirium tremens should always be undertaken in hospital. The patient requires immediate sedation with chlordiazepoxide 20–40 mg. which may have to be repeated every 4–6 hours. Dehydration and long-standing malnutrition have to be combated with liberal administration of fluids and a full, well-balanced diet with extra vitamins. In very severe cases intravenous vitamin B and ascorbic acid should be administered. It is convenient to do this in dehydrated cases with the aid of a glucose saline drip but fluid balance should be carefully evaluated and any electrolyte abnormalities rectified. In milder cases it is sufficient to give an intravenous injection of insulin 25 units and glucose 50 g. Prophylactic antibiotics are advisable particularly in severely undernourished subjects and, in the presence of cardiovascular collapse or hyperthermia, intramuscular or intravenous hydrocortisone should be administered. Recently evidence has been adduced (Flink *et al.*, 1954) to suggest that relative magnesium deficiency may be a factor in delirium tremens and intramuscular administration of 8 g. of magnesium sulphate daily for three days has been recommended. The therapeutic value of this measure is not established. Throughout treatment care must be taken to protect the patient from self-injury. If, despite all measures, he remains persistently disturbed and hallucinated, E.C.T. should be considered; it is often dramatically effective.

ALCOHOLIC HALLUCINOSIS. In this disorder hallucinations, usually of hearing, appear suddenly in clear consciousness. The aetiology of the phenomenon is obscure. In most instances it commences in a phase of withdrawal or relative abstinence following chronic drunkenness. The relationship to alcohol is, however, a complex one in that patients in whom hallucinations have been in abeyance in an abstinent period will often suffer relapse after even a short period of drinking.

The predominant symptoms are *auditory illusions and hallucinations*, on which a system of persecutory ideas comes to be based. Early on, the patient becomes aware of formless acoustic perceptions, such as crackling, knocking or roaring noises, the ringing of bells, or sibilant sounds like a half-heard whisper. Gradually these noises take on more form and become articulate. He hears the voices of friends and enemies, accusing him of drinking, of sex offences, of real or imaginary misdeeds in his past life. Other voices threaten to kill, mutilate or castrate him, accuse him of being a prostitute, a homosexual or a murderer or command him to do things against his will (Victor and Hope, 1958). These experiences naturally lead to delusions of interpretation. The patient believes he is surrounded by enemies, and is watched on every side; the police also join in the hunt. He finds no rest, changes his abode, dares not go to sleep at night, or to leave the house unarmed. He is eventually brought to medical attention by imploring his family or friends for protection, by an attempt at suicide, or by an extravagant act such as an attack on an imagined persecutor. The compelling quality of hallucinations in this illness is very great and the relatively frequent attempts at suicide are executed in a most determined manner. The patient will throw himself off a bridge or from a great height, shoot himself or slash his throat. Some patients, however, manage to hide their delusions and their fears for a long time, and even to keep at work in an accustomed routine.

When examined, the patient shows a *hallucinatory paranoid state* which bears much resemblance to similar schizophrenic states. The resemblance to schizophrenia is heightened by the clarity of the sensorium and the presence in a minority of cases of a phenomenon that closely resembles the delusional mood state. In rare instances affect is slightly incongruous or there may be marked perplexity. However, the illness is dominated in a characteristic way by the auditory hallucinations which have a simple, direct or banal character. Outward disturbances of behaviour of a schizophrenic kind are exceedingly uncommon. The mean age of onset tends to be higher in alcoholic hallucinosis and general adjustment in the social and sexual spheres tends to be better than in the young male schizophrenic. There will, moreover, be no schizophrenic thought disorder, discrepancy of affect, volitional disturbance, primary delusions or other typical schizophrenic signs, while there may be, apart from the indications of chronic alcoholic abuse, some sign of the organic pathology in difficulties in recollection, actual gaps in memory, and the inadequate performance of intellectual tasks. A further feature of interest is that, in a minority of cases, insight into the illusory nature of the hallucinations is present during the psychosis, or insight is recovered immediately the voices begin to wane (Victor and Hope, 1958). The general opinion among psychiatrists is that alcoholic hallucinosis is, in most instances, a benign and short-lived phenomenon but there have been few thorough long-term enquiries into the outcome of the illness. One of the most complete was that carried out by Benedetti (1952) who followed up 113 cases of acute alcoholic hallucinosis. Ninety patients recovered within 6 months. In the remaining 23, two patterns of outcome were observed. In 13 patients schizophrenic deterioration developed and, in these cases, Benedetti describes the development of disturbances of mood, grandiose delusions and tangential thinking. In the second group of 10 cases a progressive organic dementia had developed. However, in this latter group there were frequently such complications as liver disease, peripheral neuritis and other neurological disorders so that the relationship of the dementia to the hallucinosis is not quite clear. It is probable that after repeated attacks of alcoholic hallucinosis and continued alcoholic addiction, an organic syndrome does develop in a proportion of cases. In the study by Victor and Hope, 68 out of 76 patients recovered from their hallucinosis, but in 8 subjects hallucinations persisted for several weeks or months, and in four of these characteristic symptoms of schizophrenia developed.

The relationship of this disorder to schizophrenia is of both theoretical and practical interest. Most classical authors followed Bleuler in his view that the alcohol merely released a latent tendency to schizophrenic illness. There is very little evidence in favour of this view and Benedetti's familial study lent no support to it. In the light of the available evidence this would appear to be a symptomatic psychosis which may closely resemble schizophrenia, particularly in its chronic phase. The validity of this view is further supported by the effects of treatment. Where hallucinatory and delusional symptoms persist beyond a few weeks, a combination of electroconvulsive treatment and phenothiazine drugs almost invariably brings them under control. Maintenance treatment with phenothiazines for a period of some months, in addition to treatment for the alcoholism, is desirable in all cases.

After the withdrawal of alcohol in hospital, the delusions disappear, and full insight may be regained. Many patients, however, retain their delusional ideas for many months, slowly forgetting about them rather than developing a true insight. The intellectual changes also pass off, though sometimes not quite completely.

KORSAKOV'S PSYCHOSIS. The first complete description of a combination of polyneuritis with dysmnesic symptoms was given by Korsakov in 1887. He regarded the syndrome as the consequence of toxaemias especially likely to occur in chronic alcoholics. The disorder may develop insidiously or may appear as the residual sequel of one or a succession of attacks of delirium tremens. More commonly, however, careful history-taking reveals that the acute stage took the form of clouding of consciousness, confusion, drowsiness, inertia and indifference. There is disorientation in time and place and some misidentification of people and surroundings; but the hallucinatory experiences, delusions and the affect of fear associated with delirium are lacking. Impairment of memory for recent events is already conspicuous in a setting of a more generalized disorganization of mental functioning. Neurological examination during this phase will often reveal ophthalmoplegia, ataxia and, in some cases, peripheral neuritis and to this neurological component of the syndrome in the acute stage the name of Wernicke's encephalopathy has been given. As the acute symptoms subside the ophthalmoplegia improves but nystagmus and some degree of ataxia may persist over weeks or months. The confusion and restlessness may recur at this stage during the night; and, in the small proportion of patients in whom the illness began with delirium, visual hallucinations and fearful affect may then also return. Over a period of weeks, or more rarely months, these symptoms fade, the patient becomes more alert, his concentration improves and his speech becomes more coherent. It is at this stage that a severe defect of retention of memory for recent events presents as the main component of the syndrome.

The patient is alert, with good powers of apperception and attention, and in ordinary conversation may show no sign of abnormality. There is usually something noteworthy in the *affective state*, a flat sociable cheerfulness, a mild depressive state, or an increase in emotional lability. Behind the usually ready, or over-ready, emotional responsiveness, one can detect apathy, lack of spontaneity and a lack of persistence in emotional drives.

Comprehension tends to be slow, and in all intellectual tasks the patient tires rapidly.

All intellectual changes are, however, inconspicuous in comparison with the *disorder of memory*. This is largely restricted to an incapacity to retain recent experiences, sometimes not even for a few minutes. One may, for instance, talk to the patient, go out of the room and come straight back again, and then be greeted as if for the first time that day, no memory of the previous conversation being retained. The patient is invariably grossly disorientated, especially in time. Remote events, such as those which occurred before the onset of the syndrome, are usually well retained, and there is no incapacity in their reproduction. But as the days and weeks pass by, they leave no trace in the memory; and the patient, if he realizes he is in hospital, may think he arrived there only the previous day.

These gaps, long or short, in the storehouse of memory, are, characteristically, filled with *confabulated material*. Asked what he has been doing this morning, the patient relates how he has been out for a drive in the town, has been shopping, and has bought such and such objects, naming them, and being prepared to describe them in detail. In telling these falsehoods he believes everything he says; so that it seems that an idea which has entered his mind as a simple association with ideas that have gone before, is incapable of being distinguished from a memory. The patient is suggestible, and can be got to confabulate along any line proposed to him by the physician. However, confabulation is far from invariable and is rarely prominent in the chronic stage of the syndrome. It is becoming increasingly clear, moreover, that the intellectual deficit of Korsakov's syndrome is too complex to be wholly explained in terms of a defect of memory retention for recent events alone. Some impairment of memory for remote events is common and cognitive deficiencies often include an impairment of spatial organization and visual and verbal abstraction (Victor *et al.*, 1959). The patients also fail to order remote and recent experiences in their correct chronological sequence and this disorganization of the time scale of experience has been regarded as fundamental by some workers (Van der Horst, 1932).

Physically, in the early stages before hospital care has restored it, the state of the patient is poor, with signs of chronic malnutrition. Signs of peripheral neuritis shown in muscular weakness, sluggish reflexes, impaired sensation in the legs and a marked tenderness of the calves and Achilles tendons, for instance, are often present. The patients also may suffer from some other form of ill-health, such as chronic gastritis or myocardial or hepatic impairment.

The *prognosis* in Korsakov's syndrome is variable. In patients treated intensively from the early stages of the disorder, improvement may continue slowly over a period as long as two years. There may be marked improvement in the memory defect and the patient may be enabled to return to his original occupation. In other cases the patient has to take up work of a less skilled kind than he was previously capable of, and in some subjects permanent hospital care is required. Further deterioration in mental functioning is certain if the patient returns to his old alcoholic habits.

As far as treatment is concerned, intensive treatment with parenteral thiamine chloride (50 mg. daily) should commence as soon as a diagnosis has been made. This should be continued for a period of weeks and thereafter weekly injections should be combined with a varied diet and high potency oral vitamin B complex preparations such as Orovite (one tablet two or three times daily). It is advisable to continue treatment with vitamin B_1 for at least six months. If there is polyneuritis the affected muscles require support and massage and graduated exercises can begin when tenderness has subsided.

The Diagnosis of States of Alcoholic Aetiology

The difficulties which may arise in the diagnosis of *acute alcoholic intoxication* have already been referred to in describing coma. In all states which superficially resemble acute intoxication it is easy to be misled by jumping to conclusions after observing, for instance, a smell of alcohol on the breath. The patient may well have taken alcohol, while the apparently alcoholic intoxication is due to other causes—hypoglycaemia in a diabetic, confusion after head injury or an epileptic fit, intoxication by other drugs such as barbiturates, suicidal poisoning by carbon monoxide, etc. A full and reliable history and confirmation by physical examination are in all cases necessary; and these are often only to be obtained after the patient has been admitted to hospital.

The diagnosis of *alcoholism* is often made difficult by the patient's lack of truthfulness, which is itself a symptom of the illness. His relatives will often provide invaluable information but their history will not always be objective or dispassionate. Even the family doctor may not be entirely unbiased; for, though he may know that the patient is a heavy consumer, he may have long dismissed this fact from his mind, and fail to connect it with the patient's 'rheumatism', 'chronic bronchitis', gastric or cardiac 'neurosis', or 'neurasthenia'. The patient should be asked how much he drinks, though his statement should be taken as a minimum; but one should endeavour to get as precise an answer as possible, in terms of the actual amount consumed, or the total amount of money which is spent on it. Most heavy consumers, even though not so severely addicted as to be branded as alcoholics, minimize for themselves and their closest relatives the amount they take, and often show skill in so doing. Sometimes the patient's abuse is not discovered until after his death, when empty bottles are discovered in his room, or large bills are presented by purveyors. A diagnostic mistake of an opposite kind is not impossible; persons of hypomanic constitution are sometimes mistaken for alcoholics on the basis of their temperament alone. There will be little liability to error if the physician remembers the kinds of mistake which are possible, and bears the possibility of alcoholism in mind whenever he is faced with vague complaints of nervousness or digestive troubles by middle-aged patients, where there is no clear connexion with other causes.

For rational therapy, it is important to recognize those cases in which *alcoholism* is a *symptom* only, and the secondary consequence of a more fundamental disturbance. Manic-depressives, and persons of hypomanic and cyclothymic constitution, not infrequently mask their primary mood changes under alcoholic indulgence. Addiction to drink is, moreover, quite common in schizophrenics of the simple, hebephrenic or paranoid types. They are mainly those whose long-standing illness has come to a standstill. Some of them seem to take to drink to forget their hallucinatory experiences, others for the purpose of making some affective contact with their fellows from whom they feel remote, and still others to overcome shyness or social inhibition.

The differential diagnosis between alcoholic hallucinosis and alcoholic paranoid states with delusions of jealousy on the one hand, and schizophrenia on the other, was at one time the subject of much discussion. Since Bleuler's demarcation of schizophrenic symptoms, the diagnostic problem has become less difficult. One does not find the central and most pathognomonic signs of schizophrenia in conditions of alcoholic aetiology (see p. 275). But a proportion of cases do give rise to difficulties in diagnosis and one has also to remember that, in the mentally ill patient who takes alcohol, states of diverse pathogenesis can take on a characteristic but superficial *alcoholic colouring*. Early general paresis, arteriosclerosis and senile dementia, as well as all stages and forms of schizophrenic illness, can be masked by alcoholic euphoria, lack of inhibition, self-confidence and good-fellowship.

Prophylaxis

The *deleterious social effects of widespread drinking* have exercised such an influence on public opinion that various kinds of control have been instituted. These have taken the form of restriction of the hours in which alcoholic drinks may be sold, restriction and licensing of the places where they may be sold, public ownership or state monopoly applied to one or another branch of the drink trade, rationing systems, and taxation. Of all these the last has probably proved the most effective. In Switzerland it has been shown that the relationships between price, consumption and incidence of alcoholic mental disorder are close.

These experiences have led to a general agreement that the most important therapy of alcoholism is *prophylactic*; and prophylaxis has been the main plank in the programmes of temperance and anti-alcohol movements of all kinds. Propaganda issued by these bodies has been countered by advertisement and publicity schemes, and also at times by lobbying and by underground influence, engaged in by 'the trade'. The greatest success ever won by the teetotal movement was seen in the years of prohibition in the United States. That the experiment, despite the excellence of its motives, was a failure, owing to lack of general support, does not mean it was wholly without value.

In studies undertaken in America, Sweden and Britain the high percentage of alcoholics reporting the occurrence early in their drinking career of 'events', such as needing more drink to get the same effect, feeling more efficient when drinking, alcoholic amnesia, taking an early morning drink, solitary drinking and decrease in tolerance to alcohol, bear out the generally held opinion that such *premonitory signs* of alcoholism are important. Wider recognition of these prodromal signs would seem to hold out a chance to recognize and arrest alcoholism in its early stages (Glatt, 1961b). The British Medical Association in its annual meeting 1965 recommended an educational programme to enable these initial stages in alcoholism to be recognized and to persuade sufferers to come early for treatment. Specialists in alcoholism complain that some of the courts know nothing about the necessity for treatment of early cases of alcoholism that may appear before them. Compulsory abstinence in prison is not a 'cure'. There is a regrettable tendency on the part of general practitioners to shirk facing the evidence of incipient or actual alcoholism in their patients, and to treat the symptoms and not the patient.

Treatment

The treatment of alcoholism is in essence the *treatment of the habit*. This is an arduous undertaking, and if the physician is not prepared to give generously in time and trouble, then he had better hand the patient over to a colleague who is prepared to take pains. The personality of the therapist is itself important. Some maintain that it is only the doctor who has himself experienced what the addiction is like who can satisfactorily handle these patients. Certainly it is the extraverted rather than the introverted physician, the man who can respond warmly to his patient's dependence, the man of strong convictions, who gets the best results.

The first step is to enquire thoroughly into *the patient's history and present state*. Important though this last is, it should not monopolize attention so that underlying primary mental disorders of another kind are overlooked. One should also obtain an insight into the whole personality of the patient, the course of his past life, the causes which led to the alcoholism, and his present problems. The treatment should be *planned to fit the individual* case after a careful evaluation of these factors. This will usually necessitate the use of several forms of therapy.

It is as mistaken to concentrate only on dealing with the patient's alcoholism as a 'disease' in its own right to the neglect of his underlying social difficulties and personality as it is to do the reverse (Glatt, 1961c). *The alcoholic should be treated in hospital* even if he presents at an early stage of addiction. There is a case for choosing a hospital at some distance from his home because he needs to be removed temporarily from the environment which has had some part in producing his addiction and which has in turn been adversely influenced by his drinking. He should be treated in a psychiatric hospital in a specialized group within a general ward, in a ward set apart for alcoholism, or, best of all, in a specially staffed unit practising a variety of therapeutic techniques. The alcoholic patient feels ill-at- case in the general ward of a psychiatric hospital. In a specialized unit he is with others sharing his problem, and in the hands of staff who by attitudes and training are best equipped to benefit him.

WITHDRAWAL. The breaking of the habit should only be begun when, after admission to hospital, the patient's physical health has been as fully restored as possible. In the majority of cases, alcohol can be *completely withdrawn at once*. The patient should be confined to bed for a few days while withdrawal symptoms are still present. Minor symptoms may last longer than one realizes from a superficial examination, or from the patient's complaints; restless-ness, feelings of apprehension and depression in day-time and sleeplessness at night deserve careful attention and treatment. It is best to avoid barbiturates and paraldehyde which are all too prone to lead to habituation in alcoholics. However, in the acute phase of the with-drawal syndrome when the patient's severe anxiety and distress may demand immediate relief, they may be needed during the early stages. The prolonged action and slow excretion of chlordiazepoxide make it particularly suitable for covering withdrawal from alcohol. It is superior to phenothiazines for this purpose and, as its delayed action limits the danger of habituation, it has many advantages over older sedatives. The dosage should be guided by the severity of anxiety, tremulousness, insomnia and other features but as much as 200–250 mg. may be needed in 24 hours to control symptoms adequately. Sleeplessness may need to be treated with chloral hydrate in doses of 1·5–2 g. well diluted with water or milk, but this drug should be avoided if there is any evidence of hepatic or renal failure. When the withdrawal syndrome is subsiding chlordiazepoxide should be reduced at a rate guided by the patient's symptoms and signs. As soon as the patient is over the worst of the withdrawal effects, attempts should be made to stimulate appetite with the aid of 15–20 units of insulin each morning, half an hour before breakfast. A full diet should be given and a daily injection of one ampoule of high potency Parentrovite is advisable during the first 7–10 days followed by vitamin B by mouth for a number of weeks.

As soon as the withdrawal symptoms have subsided the patient should be encouraged to live an active life and take part in all activities of the hospital.

INDIVIDUAL PSYCHOTHERAPY. This may be the most important single factor in treatment. It depends greatly for success on the personality of the therapist and the relationship he is able to establish with the patient. The therapist should be adaptable and have made a careful appraisal of the patient's needs. He should also set his therapeutic target at a practicable and realistic level. He should be flexible and prepared to employ that combination of therapeutic approaches which appears best suited to the individual case.

Sessions of psychotherapy should be regular and designed to give the patient insight into those features of his personality, relationships and mode of living (and their interaction) which have contributed to his addiction. Its aim is to enable the patient himself, armed with these insights, to set right what has been amiss. If treatment of the addict is to be successful he must be advised that he is suffering from a disease which precludes his returning to normal drinking. Some patients find the simple statement 'I must face the fact that I am an alcoholic and must never touch a drop again' very helpful.

GROUP THERAPY. This treatment should begin during stay in hospital and be continued in weekly sessions as out-patient for at least a year. In the group process the patient benefits from the experience of his fellow patients, loses his sense of isolation and is fortified by seeing others accomplish the abstinence he thought impossible. He may acquire insight into the situations 'in which he repeatedly involves himself and which he characteristically mismanages so that he learns to deal with them more effectively. By examining his and other members' ways of reacting and by exploring the origins of these ways, he can in time modify his self-defeating patterns of behaviour' (Kessel and Walton, 1965). This statement is perhaps unduly optimistic but it does define the objectives in treatment even if they are attainable only in a proportion of cases.

AVERSION THERAPY. Alcoholism is one of the first conditions in which the ideas of Pavlov were applied in treatment. In recent years these ideas have undergone considerable development under the influence of the ideas of Hull, Watson, Miller, Mowrer and Eysenck who have been mainly responsible for the development of modern learning theory. Wolpe first applied these theories in a systematic way to the treatment of neurotic and allied disturbances. According to these theories alcoholism is a learned habit. The emergence of uncontrolled drinking is explained by the concept of reinforcement as formulated by Dollard and Miller (1950) who pointed out that sudden reduction in a strong drive will tend to reinforce any behaviour that leads to that reduction. In the alcoholic the drive that is reduced may be anxiety, fear or anger. With each bout of drinking the alcoholic habit therefore becomes more strongly reinforced. However, as Blake (1965) has pointed out, once having been stamped in like this the drinking habit may become autonomous. A stage is reached when alcohol is no longer related to a reduction of any identifiable disturbance of psychological equilibrium; rather, alcoholism, being by nature non-adjustive, now begins to generate its own peculiar tensions and disturbances of personal well-being. It is therefore possible that the conditioned response that is the alcoholic tendency may become extinguished while the drive—the fear or anxiety that originally motivated the drink—may remain unaltered. Relapse would therefore become probable. Metzner (1963) has therefore argued that aversion conditioning 'is only likely to be successful either (a) where the alcohol no longer reduces any drive except one that is self-generated, or (b) where the anxiety is simultaneously being extinguished by other methods'.

In practice this provides a strong argument for combining other forms of treatment with aversion therapy. In fact it is quite likely that the older aversion treatments such as those, for example, which employed apomorphine owed part of the success they achieved in the hands of some workers to factors incidental to the deconditioning procedures, which lacked rigour in their application. Thus, as Eysenck has pointed out (1959), the unconditioned stimulus was administered in this treatment in such a way that it preceded the conditioned stimulus. Such backward conditioning could not have been effective. More-over, the time relationships between the two kinds of stimulus are of great importance but almost impossible to control in a rigorous manner in the apomorphine technique. For these reasons, as also because of its unpleasantness and limited success, electrical aversion techniques have tended to replace the method based on the use of emetics.

The relaxation-aversion technique used by Blake (1965) has much to commend it. After psychiatric and psychological assessment the patient is given relaxation training which requires on the average 12 sessions each lasting approximately 20 minutes. This stage is directed towards relief of the underlying anxiety which, as already indicated, needs to be extinguished by methods independent of the aversion procedures. After the subject has reached competence in relaxation, 'motivation arousal' is introduced. The patient is in-structed while in the relaxed state to think about his drinking and the problems associated with it. He is questioned about the ideas and associations thus generated and the information reported is fed back for further conceptual activity at the next session. Arousal sessions take place daily and precede the first session of aversion training of the day. The 'arousal' pro-cedure often produces agitation and weeping. In the aversive conditioning stage the patient is told to sip the drink but avoid swallowing it. A shock of increasing intensity (starting randomly above the threshold reported by him in a pre-aversion test to be unpleasant) is delivered contiguously with his sip on reinforced trials. He is instructed to spit out the alcohol as a means of having the shock terminated. On non-reinforced trials the alcohol is ejected in response to a green light signal. It has been observed that the alcohol is ejected with the same eagerness on non-reinforced trials, even when the green light has ceased to be presented, as when a trial is reinforced by shock. Conditioning sessions extend over 4–8 days. The whole relaxation-aversion programme takes up an average of five hours per subject. On a six-months follow-up of 37 cases treated by this method (including neurotic, psychopathic and organic subjects) 54 per cent. were recorded as being abstinent, 38 per cent. had relapsed and in 8 per cent. there was no information or the patients had opted out of treatment. The results in a smaller number at 12 months were similar. Improvement was not confined to drinking habits, being also reflected in increased productivity, improved personal relationships and enhanced ability to handle ordinary psychological stresses.

DETERRENT DRUG TREATMENT. Certain alcoholic patients benefit by being placed on a maintenance dose of *Antabuse* (tetraethylthiuram disulphide, or disulfiram). The substance interferes with the metabolism of alcohol. It was formerly held to cause a marked increase of the blood acetaldehyde level though some writers have recently cast doubt on this explanation (Hebellinck, 1965). Its effect is to produce unpleasant symptoms which make it difficult for the patient to continue drinking. After a small quantity of alcohol is taken (following ingestion of the drug) dramatic toxic symptoms appear; they include flushing of the face, sweating, dyspnoea, headache and tachycardia. These symptoms are frequently followed by drowsiness, fall in blood pressure, and sometimes nausea and vomit-ing. Occasionally symptoms of peripheral cardiovascular failure have been observed. There is a rapid fall in blood pressure, the patient becomes pale and distressed, with sighing respiration and cold, cyanosed extremities. Should this occur an antihistamine drug should be given, in addition to the usual methods of combating shock. Antabuse in therapeutic doses of 0·5 to 1·5 g. daily rarely causes toxic effects, though a small minority of patients are sensitive to the drug and complain of lethargy and loss of appetite. Because of their variability of reaction to alcohol after taking Antabuse patients should always be given a *test dose* of alcohol (usually one ounce of whisky or gin) a few days after starting the drug, and while they are still in hospital. Antabuse should never be given to a patient without his full knowledge and consent.

Citrated calcium carbimide (Abstem) is claimed to have certain advantages over disulfiram. It acts more rapidly and sensitivity to alcohol is built up much more quickly. Side-effects after the ingestion of alcohol are less severe so that, though not so potentially dangerous, it may be less of a deterrent.

Such drugs are only a 'crutch' with which the patient may support his own will to abstain and their use should form only part of a general plan of treatment. The *careful selection of patients* for drug deterrent treatment is important. Drug deterrent treatments are of value in the management of the alcoholic who is *co-operative and genuinely desirous of overcoming his addiction*, but who knows that at times he has a craving for alcohol and is well aware that once he starts drinking he is unable to stop. It is psychologically easier for such patients to take their regular half-tablet every morning than to maintain throughout the entire day a firm resolution not to take a drink. Neurotic personalities with a strong desire to be helped often derive a feeling of security from taking these drugs, but those with little or no ability to control sudden impulses are not suitable. If there is a wife or other relative who can supervise the regular dosage after leaving hospital, the patient's chances of making a recovery from the habit are enhanced; but relatives must be warned of the dangers of giving the patient these drugs without his knowledge.

MANAGEMENT AND LONG-TERM CARE. Alcoholic habits play a positive role in the life of patients and supply them with an occupation for their hours of leisure, an anodyne for cares, and an easy companionship. The therapist has not done his work if, before discharging the patient, he has not made an effort to provide him with substitute activities. The association known as *Alcoholics Anonymous* provides many former alcoholics with a society of their own and with a valuable function in helping their own kind.

Active co-operation between this association and psychiatrists is increasing both here and in America. Rossi, Stach and Bradley (1963) report that patients formed and maintained their own AA group within the hospital from which they passed to association with others outside and Glatt's experience at Warlingham Park Hospital showed that AA groups in the neighbourhood of an alcoholic treatment unit would accept that there were other ways of treating patients than their own and would co-operate in the vitally important problem of after-care. However, despite its undoubted value, the organization is far from suiting all patients.

It is generally agreed that no part of the treatment of alcoholism is more important than *follow-up and after-care*. Vallance (1965) followed-up 68 male alcoholic patients who had been given 'first-aid' treatment only in a psychiatric hospital with an average duration of stay of 3·2 weeks and no systematic after-care. He found that 25 per cent. had improved at the end of two years but less than 5 per cent. were abstinent. Only 25 per cent. of the 50 per cent. who were offered the chance of coming back on out-patient visits availed themselves of this. In spite of such poor results the 'first-aid' approach has been the normal method of management in the United Kingdom, with some notable exceptions. In a follow-up study of patients who had been under observation with active after-care measures for periods varying from 2–3½ years it was found that just over one-third had recovered, and just under one-third had improved to a significant degree. This improvement was reflected not only in abstinence but at home, at work, and in interpersonal relationships in general (Glatt, 1961b).

Prognosis

There is considerable difficulty in comparing the results of follow-up studies because selection of patients and treatment facilities differ so widely between studies.

Davies, Shepherd and Myers (1956) studied 50 cases treated in a general psychiatric ward for 2–3 months. Therapy was geared to the individual patient's requirements. Group therapy was not employed but supportive out-patient treatment was provided and patients were established on treatment with disulfiram. Two years later 18 per cent. were found to be totally abstinent, another 18 per cent. had been abstinent most of the time and 42 per cent. had maintained their social efficiency despite light or heavy drinking. Glatt's result of 30 per cent. abstinent after treatment in a special unit including group therapy and very active after-care has been noted above. On the other hand, Rossi, Stach and Bradley (1963) following up 208 unselected male patients treated for 60 days in a state mental hospital in Minnesota, with little or no individual treatment and no after-care found that after 21 months 9 per cent. were abstinent, and 60 per cent. were drinking to a serious extent. The 30 per cent. who had returned to moderate drinking were traced again a year later and 90 per cent. of these were then found to be drinking with serious effects. There is general agreement that, among various forms of management, *prolonged and active after-care* carries the best prognosis. The danger of relapse is greatest in the first six months after discharge; as many as 90 per cent. of relapses occurring during this period. This finding has a bearing on planning after-care procedures and patients may be encouraged by the information that *six months is a hurdle* of prognostic significance. *Suicide* is also a serious risk, especially in these first few months after discharge from hospital. Kessel and Grossman (1961) found that 45 per cent. of patients in a Maudsley series of alcoholics who had committed suicide did so within the first year from discharge.

Age would appear to have prognostic significance. Glatt (1961b) showed that the prognosis in the age group 41–70 was significantly better statistically than in the age group 21–42. The most likely explanation is that late onset of alcoholism may often indicate a better basic personality than in young alcoholics. Alcoholics under 25 are much more difficult to treat and far more often have to be readmitted.

The *patient's desire to be cured and degree of involvement in his treatment* is of great importance in prognosis. Efforts should be made to orientate him to take an active role in his treatment. Equally it is important that he should accept the fact that he is an alcoholic and cannot become a controlled drinker ever again.

Once the alcoholic habit has been broken, the patient will have to adopt a new mode of life to ensure against a relapse. Certain kinds of behaviour, social engagements of certain types, for instance, will have to be given up; and from his knowledge of the patient's personality and of his emotional needs, the physician must assist his search for alternatives. Early relapse tends to take place in those who return to the same social milieu as before. They have changed in attitude to drinking but their former associates have not. Hence the importance of ensuring if possible that the discharged patient has contact with an association whose members take a pride in continued abstinence.

The alcoholic who has retained *close personal ties* with at least one person has a better chance of recovery. Hence the married do better than the single. For this reason there is a strong case for *involving the spouse in the treatment situation*. Loneliness is frequently given by women as a reason for excessive drinking and is often an obstacle to recovery. Alcoholism tends to develop later in *women* than in men but follows a more rapid course (Jellinek, 1952). They also make a poorer response to treatment than men.

Along with sex, *pre-morbid personality* is found to be the factor that probably has the most important bearing on outcome. Those of unstable or psychopathic personality and poor intelligence, those who have become addicted early in life or before they have registered much in the way of achievement, those with few positive qualities of personality and those who have become addicted without exposure to stressful circumstances all tend to do badly. The homeless vagrant alcoholic is a separate problem whose only hope of rehabilitation is in the provision of special centres and hostels. *Social class* in isolation from other factors is not of prognostic significance; it is important to encourage alcoholics from lower social classes to seek treatment. Existing hospital admission rates seem to suggest that at present they are not doing so.

In treatment, the clinician has to be satisfied in some cases with a limited degree of success and above all should exercise patience. An occasional lapse is not a reason for despair. In a number of patients, particularly women, unspectacular but steady progress over years may take place even though the immediate results following discharge may have been discouraging.

DRUG DEPENDENCE
Definition of Drug Addiction

A certain amount of confusion at present surrounds the definition of addiction. Most published work shows that the authorities in this field have been guided by the reports of the World Health Organization's Expert Committee which in 1952 and 1957 treated dependence upon various drugs as a single entity and distinguished between addiction and habituation.

Addiction they defined as 'a state of periodic or chronic intoxication produced by the repeated consumption of a drug. . . . Its characteristics include:

(1) An overpowering desire or need (compulsion) to continue taking the drug and to obtain it by any means.

(2) A tendency to increase the dose.

(3) A psychic (psychological) dependence and generally also a physical dependence on the effects of the drug.

(4) A detrimental effect on the individual and on society'.

Habituation was defined as 'a condition resulting from the repeated consumption of a drug. Its characteristics include:

(1) A desire (but *not* a compulsion) to continue taking the drug for the sense of improved well-being which it engenders. ·

(2) Little or no tendency to increase the dose.

(3) Some degree of psychic dependence on the effect of the drug, but absence of physical dependence and hence of an abstinence syndrome.

(4) Detrimental effects, if any, primarily on the individual'.

These terms were meant chiefly to separate physical from psychological dependence, a distinction which was found to be increasingly difficult to apply, as phases overlap and vary from drug to drug and patient to patient. The Expert Committee's report in 1964 introduces the single term *Drug Dependence* and stresses also that the drug dependencies are a group of illnesses with many features in common and not a single disease (W.H.O., 1964). However, as Glatt (1964*b*) has pointed out, the former distinction between habituation and addiction still has some uses in clinical practice, for instance, with regard to decisions about sudden or gradual withdrawal of a drug.

None of these definitions can be regarded as entirely satisfactory. The reason for this is partly to be sought in the fact that the subject of drug dependence is a highly emotional one and our attitude to it is influenced by social biases and preconceptions. Thus dependence on alcohol and tobacco incur nothing like the social disapproval that attaches to morphine or even barbiturates. Yet severe deprivation symptoms may follow withdrawal while the effects on mental as well as physical health may prove disastrous in the case of alcohol. Nor can the social effects be regarded as fundamentally different from those of drugs with a more sinister connotation since dependence on both alcohol and tobacco is spread to some extent by example and group pressure to conform among the young, the immature and the socially anxious and insecure.

Drug Dependence: General Considerations

The official Governmental attitude and the attitude of the medical profession in Great Britain towards the management of addicts has in the past been guided by the reports of two committees specially convened in 1926 and 1961. The treatment of drug addiction, following the advice of these committees, had hitherto remained an individual medical matter in Great Britain, in which the physician was entitled, at his own professional discretion, to provide narcotics to known addicts, with no absolute obligation either to notify the Home Office of the identity of an addict, or to take a second opinion, though both courses were specifically advised.

From the late 1950s the numbers known in Great Britain to the Home Office of those dependent on narcotics rose sharply from 359 in 1957 to 1349 in 1966. There was in addition much evidence to suggest that these numbers were an underestimate. It was also known that all but about 3 per cent. of the new addicts notified over this period had obtained their drugs illicitly in the first place, by buying them from others who had had drugs prescribed for them in excess of their needs. These serious developments demanded urgent reappraisal of the situation and led to the convening of the third Interdepartmental Committee under the Chairmanship of Lord Brain in 1964 and determined its terms of reference. Its recommendations centred on compulsory notification of addicts, provisions for treatment, and restriction of prescribing to licensed doctors serving in named treatment centres. Certain recommendations of the Brain Committee became law in April, 1968 (see Ch. XIII). The resultant changes in, and increasing knowledge about, the situation which will emerge are awaited with great interest.

The increasing numbers of addicts in their teens and early twenties is a very recent and disturbing development in Britain. By 1966 the proportion under the age of 20 was approaching 40 per cent. and well over 80 per cent. were under 35, whereas in 1959 there were no notified heroin addicts under the age of 20. In a field study aimed at early detection of heroin use, de Alarcón and Rathod (1968) found 14·8 per thousand of the group 15–20 years of age who were confirmed users and 27·2 per thousand when probable and suspected users were included. Ninety per cent. of their cases were male.

Aware that 'early diagnosis of heroin abuse is urgent, especially in the young who do not appreciate its seriousness', these workers employed five screening methods for detecting young users of heroin in Crawley New Town who had not been referred for treatment.

The 5 new techniques employed were: use of the Probation Service, the Police, information given by patients who were heroin users, a survey (in the general practices) of every patient aged 15–25 who had had jaundice in the previous two years and a search of records in the hospital casualty department for patients in the same age group who had been admitted for overdose of hypnotics or stimulants during those two years.

They evaluated these five sources of information and reached the conclusion that the most effective was information given by the heroin users already being treated for addiction in their unit. The second most productive source was the jaundice survey. Each method singly was of limited value but all five used concurrently supplemented each other and provided an automatic check on the information received. As a useful starting point for investigating the extent of heroin use in a given population they recommended the combined use of the jaundice and casualty (amphetamine) surveys which are easy to operate.

A second field study carried out in a provincial town aimed at gaining insight into social factors associated with heroin use (Kosviner *et al.*, 1968). They established such good rapport with subjects not receiving treatment that they were able to complete structured interviews covering social and family background, past and present social functioning, drug abuse, medical and psychiatric history, as well as the subjects' attitudes to treatment, to society, their families, friends and to themselves. The 31 subjects they interviewed were found to differ in many respects from samples studied in institutional and hospital settings and equally marked differences appeared within their sample. The authors concluded that the concept of a 'typical' heroin user should be abandoned and should be replaced by typologies of users after many different samples have been studied. For example, although the subjects studied by these workers had a distinctive social class structure, there is evidence to suggest that by 1966 the overall class distribution of addicts was closer to that of the general population than it had been a decade previously. Nevertheless, the questions that emerged from these studies appeared to be of general importance. Thus high social class backgrounds were associated with a tendency to abandon educational courses despite good opportunities. Was drug-taking a reaction to failure or an overt act of rebellion? What part was played by the drug-centred way of life, as distinct from the specific effects of the drugs, in perpetuating the state of dependence?

This and the study by de Alarcón and Rathod showed that studies of drug abuse in the community are feasible and that drug dependence is no longer restricted to large cities. However, it remains uncertain how far the 'users' identified in such enquiries consist of young people experimenting for a short time with the excitements offered by heroin. There is urgent need to define the characteristics of that hard core of subjects who graduate from cannabis and amphetamine to persist in frequent self-injection of heroin, often despite severe nausea and vomiting, and a need also to learn more about the state of mind they are presumably seeking.

Sedative Drugs: Barbiturates

Drugs with a sedative or hypnotic action are important tools in the hands of the psychiatrist, who has so frequently to treat symptoms of anxiety, restlessness, excitement and sleeplessness. These drugs are often the best means we have, both of relieving the grave emotional disturbances of the psychoses, and the less serious ones of acute and chronic neurotic states. Different types of drugs are needed for different purposes; and the clinician should make full use of the wide variety of drugs of short and long action to fit his treatment to the needs of the individual case. The treatment of 'symptoms' is often decried, though the part that it can play in relief of suffering, restoring social adaptation, and as an adjuvant to specific therapy cannot be over-estimated. Often symptomatic therapy is all that the doctor can offer. In prescribing sedatives the physician has two principal dangers to be wary of, those of *suicide* and of *addiction*.

Just as the injudicious administration of analgesics in bodily ailments may lead to habit formation and addiction, so also may addiction and acute or chronic intoxication follow the use of sedatives and hypnotics. The dangers are particularly great in psychiatric patients, who by their lack of mental stability are predisposed to lack of sense of self-control in taking medicines, to urges of self-destruction, or to victimization by the lure of an ano- dyne. Others take to drugs out of curiosity or desire for new sensations, and once enslaved cannot break free. The *risk of addiction* is certainly greater among the mentally than the physically ill.

The doctor should be particularly careful not to prescribe drugs of powerful action, such as barbiturates, as *placebos*. The general practitioner finds them a convenient means of stilling the demands of the chronic neurotic, whose complaints are beyond the reach of other remedies, and who does not respond to such simple psychotherapy as the doctor can give. Before the last world war, about 40 per cent. of the medicines prescribed to panel patients in Britain contained bromides; and though the use of bromides has now greatly diminished, barbiturates have tended to take their place. In 1957–9 barbiturates constituted between 19 and 20 per cent. of the total number of prescriptions for drugs of all kinds issued during those years.

When such drugs are given, the physician should have a clear idea of what he wants to achieve. Different drugs, different amounts, and different modes and periods of adminis- tration will be needed for *different purposes:* whether, for instance, it is desired to relieve general restlessness and tension, to mitigate some physical pain which, tolerable during the distractions of day-time, prevents sleep at night, to procure a deeper sleep and obviate early morning wakening, to protect the patient against an excessive sensitivity to noises and other sensory stimuli. Agitated depression, hypomanic excitement, states of epileptic or catatonic excitation, and other psychotic crises, all require handling along lines chosen to suit individual needs.

Barbiturates are *cortical depressants* which also have a similar action on the autonomic nervous system, probably through hypothalamic centres. They also have some depressing effect on the respiratory centre, and lower body temperature and the basal metabolic rate; but in therapeutic dosage these side-effects are unimportant. The theory proposed by Quastel and co-workers (1933) that their action depends on interference with the oxidation of glucose still holds the field.

Since derivatives of barbituric acid were first used as sedatives by Fischer and Mering in 1903, their variety and their modes of application have increased enormously. A special fillip was given by the discovery of members of the group suitable for intravenous admini- stration and for use in anaesthesia.

Barbiturates are a good example of drugs which can be in use for a long time before the danger of dependence becomes apparent. Goodman and Gilman (1965) state that abuse of barbiturates and other hypnotics exceeds that of opiates in the U.S.A. The con- vincing findings of Isbell *et al.* (1950) at the Lexington hospital first gave a warning which has been supported in Norway by Ancherson (1956) and Kåss *et al.* (1959). The discrepancy between registered addicts and hospital admissions may be considerable. Barely one-third of 230 odd registered addicts in Norway were dependent on barbiturates yet Kåss *et al.* showed that in Oslo alone medical departments have an average of one admission per day of barbiturate addicts. They suppose that the small number of reported cases may be partly attributed to the fact that many doctors and pharmacists have not hitherto considered dependence on barbiturate as a form of drug addiction, and to the comparative ease with which the drug may be obtained. Barbiturate addicts may also go undetected because they do not suffer from malnutrition as often as morphine addicts. In a study of 122 drug addicts admitted to the University Psychiatric Clinic, Oslo, between 1952 and 1962, Retterstöl and Sund (1964) found that 69 patients used barbiturates alone or together with other preparations and 40 were dependent on barbiturates alone. In Britain the number of cases admitted to hospital is small but available figures almost certainly underestimate the problem.

The symptoms of acute intoxication naturally depend on the amount of the drug and on its nature and speed of action. Most barbiturates are fairly safe, with the minimum lethal dose being about fifteen times the therapeutic one, but tolerance may be markedly diminished by liver or kidney disease or old age; while in porphyria, psychotic disturbances or peripheral neuropathy or both may be initiated by small doses.

Acute intoxication, however, is most frequently the result of a *suicidal attempt*, for which barbiturates have become increasingly the chosen means since the 1940s. Now these drugs, almost always obtained on prescription, are employed in well over 50 per cent. of attempts particularly by older women. The depressant action of the drug causes drowsiness and sleep deepening into coma. Pulse, respiration and peristalsis are slowed down, and there is a fall in body temperature with danger of shock. The deep reflexes disappear in comatose subjects. Death may follow from respiratory or renal failure consequent upon the diminished blood flow produced by arterial hypotension or from vasomotor collapse. The diagnosis of barbiturate-induced coma or stupor is readily made with the aid of laboratory techniques. Medium-acting barbiturates such as amylobarbitone, butobarbitone and quinalbarbitone which are broken down mainly by the liver and also excreted in varying degrees by the kidneys may be suspected as the cause of coma when barbiturate levels in the blood are in the neighbourhood of 1·8 to 2·1 mg./100 ml.; long-acting barbiturates such as phenobarbitone and barbitone are excreted unmodified by the kidneys and give rise to higher mean levels which lie between 8 and 15 mg./100 ml. (Cumming, 1961). An interesting E.E.G. finding in barbiturate coma which has as yet been little applied in practice is the generalized low to medium voltage fast activity which is found in even quite deep unconsciousness as distinct from the high voltage diffuse slow activity which dominates the record in coma induced by most other intoxications.

Among the *neurological findings* in acute or subacute intoxication, ataxia, asynergia, nystagmus and hypotonia are often seen, all being evidence of an effect on the cerebellum. These signs may also appear in *chronic intoxication*, in which the most characteristic psychiatric finding is a persistent hypomanic excitement interrupted by periods of irritability and restlessness. Some patients seem to be in a state of day-long drunkenness, tremulous and over-talkative; in others moodiness or sub-delirious symptoms prevail. The diagnosis may be difficult if the patient conceals what has occurred, as he may do if he has become addicted; or if there is a suspicion of an organic disease of the brain, such as general paresis, disseminated sclerosis or presenile dementia. In some patients addicted over long periods, nystagmus and ophthalmoplegia associated with profound though variable somnolence raise the suspicion of a mid-line tumour or encephalitis; and we have known such patients who have had extensive neurological investigations. There is some

P

resemblance between the symptoms of chronic poisoning by alcohol and by barbiturates. As some persons abuse both, differential diagnosis may be troublesome.

As far as the psychiatric aspects are concerned there is a high instance of *damaged and psychopathic personalities* among barbiturate dependent subjects particularly among those established on high doses. Childhood deprivation has often been severe; difficulties in sexual adjustment and in marriage are common. There is a sprinkling of patients with social misdemeanours; criminal tendencies and neurotic illness, prior to the commencement of addiction, have been common both in the patients and their families, although the familial incidence of drug addiction appears to be no greater than in control subjects (Retterstöl and Sund, 1964). There appears to be no specific kind of personality which is specially predisposed to become dependent on barbiturates as distinct from opiates, although Wikler and Rasov (1953) have suggested that drugs of the opiate group tend to be chosen for the satisfaction of primary cravings such as hunger and sexual instincts, whereas barbiturates, alcohol and cocaine are sought by those who wish to reduce inhibitions and aggressions. 'Regardless of conventional personality classifications which may be applied to them, addicts are individuals in whom the chief sources of anxiety are related to pain, sexuality and the expression of aggression.'

An important group among barbiturate-dependent subjects are those who first took to drugs after the commencement of a *neurotic illness* with severe symptoms of anxiety or phobic aversions leading to grave incapacity. With the aid of sedative drugs the patient is able for a period to maintain some kind of occupational and social adjustment. In these patients it is particularly important to direct attention to the underlying neurotic illness in the hope of being able to restore them to the relatively effective life-adjustment achieved before illness. The observation of Retterstöl and Sund that a proportion of subjects are initiated into their career of drug dependence by having had pain-killing and sedative drugs prescribed for pain and discomfort arising from neurotic depressions, is significant from the *preventive point of view*. As they point out, there is every reason with these patients to prescribe tranquillizing substances which are non-habit-forming. The follow-up study showed that the prognosis is not as hopeless as often supposed. After an average follow-up period of 6 years almost half of the 45 subjects regarded as habituated were found not to be using drugs and more than three-quarters were in the same employment as before admission. However, among those regarded as addicted only a fifth were not abusing drugs, an outcome which is hardly better than that among opiate addicts.

Careful history-taking is of particular importance in cases where the onset of addiction has corresponded with the abrupt commencement of a neurotic illness as treatment will often prove effective in some measure.

WITHDRAWAL SYMPTOMS. Isbell *et al.* (1950) found that when the drug was withdrawn after a period of chronic barbiturate intoxication, an acute withdrawal psychosis clinically resembling delirium tremens with anxiety and terrifying hallucinations, occurred in 3 out of 5 cases, two to three days after admission to hospital. Similar acute withdrawal psychoses have been reported by James (1963) in patients addicted to hypnotic drugs including barbiturates and, in association with other drugs having an hypnotic action on the central nervous system, by Hudson and Walker (1961) and Lloyd and Clark (1959). It is suggested that the tremulous withdrawal psychosis of sedative drug addiction and the delirium tremens of alcoholism are clinically identical. Major convulsions are relatively common after withdrawal and patients with emotional disturbance, in whom unexplained convulsions occur after admission to hospital, should be strongly suspected of barbiturate addiction. In some subjects withdrawal is followed by severe anxiety and tremulousness, physical weakness, anorexia, vomiting and postural hypotension. In a small minority of patients withdrawal leads to a paranoid reaction not always with definite impairment of consciousness.

TREATMENT. The abrupt cessation of barbiturates can have grave consequences and withdrawal should be covered with pentobarbital. A dose of 200–400 mg. six hourly may be needed and a mild degree of intoxication with nystagmus, moderate ataxia and slurring of speech is produced on these amounts. The aim is to eliminate tremor, insomnia and irritability and for this some subjects require as much as 2,000–2,500 mg. in 24 hours. Medication may have to be given at four-hourly intervals and varied according to the severity of clinical signs. When the dosage is stabilized, which usually takes some 48 hours, withdrawal at a rate of about 10 per cent. of the total dosage per day should be undertaken. However, the reappearance of tremor or postural hypotension necessitates additional doses of 200 mg. An unhurried regime must be pursued particularly in those subject to convulsions, and withdrawal may take anything from two to three weeks. For rehabilitation, contact with the family, diligent, systematic social and medical follow-up are essential.

Suicidal attempts with the aid of barbiturates are now commonplace and frequently encountered by family doctor and psychiatrist alike. Although modern techniques of *resuscitation* have reduced the mortality associated with coma from self-administered barbiturates to under 2 per cent., the situation always presents a serious emergency and, in the great majority of instances, the correct procedure is to arrange for the patient's transfer to a fully equipped hospital where a team of physicians and anaesthetists armed with full laboratory facilities, respirators and an artificial kidney can take over. If the patient is still conscious and wholly co-operative when seen, he should be asked to drink a tumblerful of warm water in which a tablespoonful of common salt has been dissolved, and a finger should be inserted into the pharynx to make him vomit. This can be done while arrangements are being made for his transfer to hospital. The stomach contents should be retained for analysis. It is unjustifiable to undertake gastric lavage at home in stuporose or comatose patients as it is impossible to protect adequately against aspiration of the gastric contents. Stimulants such as bemegride and picrotoxin play no part in modern resuscitation and should not be given. Some patients who are known to have made a gesture or demonstration with only a small dose may be allowed to sleep the effects off at home. But the patient's statement should under no circumstances be relied on and unless the amount that has been taken can be accurately judged (and this is rarely possible), he should be transferred to the care of a resuscitation team immediately. The artificial kidney has probably made a useful contribution to the treatment of patients with barbiturate poisoning. However, most patients recover satisfactorily without it and most experienced workers use dialysis only in a small minority of cases.

Amphetamine

Amphetamine sulphate was first introduced into clinical medicine in 1935, when it was discovered that, besides the sympathomimetic action that had been known for over twenty years, it causes marked *central stimulation*. It increases verbal and motor activity, elevates the mood and prevents drowsiness or sleep—hence its first clinical application in narcolepsy by Prinzmetal and Bloomberg (1935). It can be used to combat apathy, fatigue, depression and hunger, and is a useful aid when heightened confidence and decisiveness are needed.

These psychological effects did not fail to impress on early workers (Guttmann and Sargant, 1937; Guttmann, 1936*b*) that they might bring with them the *dangers of habit formation*, addiction and abuse. Their fears have proved to be justified, though to a degree which varies remarkably in different parts of the world. Abuse of amphetamines is rare in Norway, and in Switzerland it was rapidly curtailed when the drug was put on prescription; in Japan, South America and Sweden it has become a serious social problem.

In Great Britain, despite the increasing realization of the limited clinical value of the amphetamines, their use continues to be extensive. Analysis of National Health Service prescriptions in 1961 showed that 3 per cent. of the whole were for preparations of the amphetamines and phenmetrazine (*Brit. Med. J.*, 1961). It is likely that there is much *over-prescribing*. Kiloh and Brandon (1962) surveyed a population of 280,000 and estimate that this includes 500 persons with dependence on the drug. In another study of data supplied by 19 complete practices serving 79,300 patients, Brandon and Smith (1962) found that in a practice of 2,000 there would probably be 20 patients taking amphetamine at any time and at least four of these would be habituated. When the habituated group was examined, psychiatric symptoms predominated as the indication for prescribing the drug. The highest incidence of habituation was among patients over 65 years of age (24·5 per cent. of this age group). Seventy per cent. of this group were depressed. In Northern Ireland Hood and Wade (1968) showed that, in 12 per cent. of practices, amphetamines were not prescribed at all, while 1·3 per cent. produced 9 per cent. of the 11,400 prescriptions written in 3 months. This illustrates the ease with which amphetamines are obtained.

While adolescent *amphetamine-takers who obtain their supplies without prescription* are predominantly *male*, adults receiving the drug on prescription are predominantly *women*, especially middle-aged obese housewives. *Obesity* is the commonest reason for prescribing the drugs initially, although they do little to suppress appetite and there are increasing doubts about their value except perhaps for narcolepsy and rare cases of epilepsy.

Since supplies of heroin and cocaine were threatened by new legislation in 1967, increasing evidence of dependence on methylamphetamine, self-administered by intravenous injection, has appeared. States of euphoria with excitement which readily erupts into violence are commonly produced. Dependence occurs earlier than with heroin and deterioration in social adjustment is more rapid.

Scott and Willcox (1965) made a study of 474 (420 male and 54 female) young persons, the majority of whom were 14–16 years of age who had been admitted to Remand Homes during the first half of 1964. Evidence of amphetamine taking (by urine test) was found in 16–18 per cent. of admissions. They were able to distinguish two kinds of amphetamine-taker whom they defined as benign and malignant. The malignant taker increases the dosage and takes it throughout the week with adverse effects on general health and school or work record. They invariably had grossly unfavourable home backgrounds. The essential element in their personalities was a basic lack of confidence in making personal relationships, together with over-dependence on or over-identification with one parent. They appeared to live in a fearful, self-doubting manner. The writers concluded that amphetamine is particularly dangerous as an element in criminal propensities in the offender who is already inclined to feel persecuted. The relationship between crime and drug-taking was in parallel rather than causative, though each might facilitate the other. The benign group confined their indulgences to the week-ends, did not increase the dose, and both their home backgrounds and personalities were less abnormal.

According to an estimate by Bewley (1966) there were in Britain approximately 80,000 subjects habituated to prescribed amphetamines and a further 80,000 using amphetamines illicitly.

The development of physical dependence has been questioned but depression and attempted suicide are certainly common after abrupt withdrawal. Oswald and Thacore (1963) reported a method of detecting physical dependence by measuring the proportion of 'hindbrain sleep' detected by E.E.G. during withdrawal of amphetamine.

A considerable amount of experiment is taking place in methods of detecting amphetamine-dependence chiefly by analysis of urine. Most of these appear to make large demands on time, equipment and the experience of laboratory technicians. Beckett and Rowland (1965) describe a simple specific method based on gas-liquid chromatography for the analysis of amphetamine in urine.

M. Bleuler (1949) has described the self-assured confident mood of the habitual user of amphetamine, and the tendency to sexual excitement which is satisfied by the play of fantasy. The fatigue and other disagreeable feelings of the hangover force the patient to maintain and to increase the dose. His state of mind varies between restlessness and motor over-activity on one hand and fatigue and exhaustion on the other. Regular activities or work become impossible; and the patient may have to resort to lying or fraud to procure the drug. Addicts of morphia and the barbiturates not infrequently take amphetamine to counteract the depressant effect of the hypnotic, in the same way as opium addicts may take to cocaine. An aggressive psychopath, who has been given the drug to control his irritability, may become addicted to it. Others take amphetamine to relieve feelings of tension or depression to which they are liable, to enable them to get through work under pressure, or, especially women, for the initial purpose of controlling obesity.

The *great tolerance* which the habitual user may develop is remarkable. Out of thirteen cases collected by Knapp (1952), ten had reached a daily dose of 100 to 700 mg., without showing any physical disability and without developing hypertension.

AMPHETAMINE PSYCHOSIS. Attacks of psychotic illness are very common in subjects who are taking amphetamines in doses greater than 90–100 mg. and will sometimes occur on lower dosage. As the disorder frequently bears a close resemblance to schizophrenic illness, it is of considerable theoretical as well as practical interest. The euphoriant and disinhibiting effects for which the drugs are initially taken are gradually modified as the mood is lent an increasing colouring of anxiety. Ideas of reference and paranoid misinterpretation appear, the patient believing himself to be the object of special attention by strangers whom he later identifies as police agents, foreign spies or criminals. The psychosis proper develops soon after these premonitory symptoms with the sudden appearance of hallucinations and delusional ideas. These are characteristically observed in clear consciousness unless sedative drugs such as barbiturates have also been taken. Auditory hallucinations are common and, as they frequently consist of comments and tormenting criticisms relating to the patient's conduct, or accuse him of misdeeds and threaten him with violence and murder, they bear a strong resemblance to alcoholic hallucinosis. The hallucinatory voices often have an imperative quality, compelling the patient to obey. Their content may reflect complex grandiose delusions and among the delusions of influence there is often the belief that the patient is being hypnotized (Bell, 1965). The resemblance to an acute schizophrenic illness can in fact be very close. On the other hand, as Bell's study has indicated, visual hallucinations are relatively common and frequently express sexual and other problems related to the patient's previous life or personality. Although conversation may be almost unintelligible, true thought disorder is rare, and, when found, suggests that an independent schizophrenic illness is taking shape. A feature in which the illness perhaps resembles schizophreniform rather than schizophrenic disorders proper is the unusually strong colouring of depression or euphoria. When the patient is depressed the hazard of violent or serious suicidal attempts is considerable as in the hallucinosis associated with alcohol.

Amphetamine psychosis was first described by Young and Scoville (1938) and a full account of the syndrome has been given in a monograph by Connell (1958). Further material has been described by Beamish and Kiloh (1960) and Bell and Trethowan (1961). An important question is whether the amphetamines merely activate a latent propensity for psychotic illness or can be regarded as the main factor in the causation of this illness. On the whole the evidence supports the latter conclusion. Although many of the subjects are psychopathic or have serious personality defects, these do not fall into the schizoid or any other specific category (Connell, 1958; Bell and Trethowan, 1961). It seems likely that the personality disturbances are more closely related to the initial recourse to drugs than the psychosis as such. Moreover, in the great majority of instances, the psychosis subsides within a matter of weeks or a very few months after discontinuation of the drug. Where it persists for longer, a hidden source of amphetamine or the development of a schizo-phrenic illness should be suspected. From the therapeutic point of view persistent psychotic symptoms should be treated with phenothiazines and if necessary with electroconvulsive treatment which are usually effective.

Morphine

The intoxicating effect of the sap and fruit of the oriental poppy have been known for thousands of years; they were certainly known to the Greeks and Romans. It has been and still is a common practice in the Middle East, India and China, to smoke, eat or drink preparations of opium and its derivatives; in some countries it is as common as it is to take alcohol in Western regions. Where consumption is so very widespread, addiction seems to be relatively rare; and the daily smoker of a pipe of opium is no more an addict than is the daily drinker of one or two glasses of beer. About 10 per cent. of opium is morphine.

Although in some animals its effect is a different one, the *action of morphine in man* is mainly on the cortex, increasing its inhibitory effect on thalamic centres of sensation, and raising the pain threshold. No other analgesic is as potent as are morphine and some of its chemical relatives. Apart from its effect on pain sensation, it depresses sensation of all kinds to some degree, although itching may be increased. The highest cerebral functions are only slightly affected by ordinary doses, and the effect on mood is to cause contentment.

If it is taken by mouth, morphine is *quickly absorbed* through the intestinal mucosa, and is slowly oxidized in the liver. It is said that some morphine is re-excreted into the stomach after absorption. The average dose is destroyed or excreted in about three to five hours.

Opium contains *other important bodies* besides morphine; among these, or derived synthetically from them, are codeine, thebaine, dionine, diamorphine (heroin), dilaudid and dicodid. Their action on the nervous system varies. Some have a preponderantly narcotic effect, others affect particularly the spinal cord, or plain muscle. Any one of them may lead to an addiction, or be used by the morphine addict as a substitute. The addiction due to heroin, which may be snuffed as a white powder, is more dangerous than to morphine. Although the action of codeine on the pain threshold is much more feeble than that of morphine, it is useful for its analgesic effect. It is a common constituent of cough mixtures and headache powders; and it may lead to addiction in a predisposed individual, or, again, be used as a substitute for morphine by the addict.

The *parasympathetic nervous system is stimulated* by morphine, with the production of pin-point pupils, slow pulse, increased salivation and sweating, increased bronchial secretion, and retching or vomiting. The depressant effect on the respiratory centre may be so strong as to endanger the life of the patient. If asphyxia follows on acute morphine intoxication, the pupils are dilated, and the diagnosis may be more difficult. The spinal reflexes are increased, and the plain muscle of all sphincters is stimulated. Urinary retention is frequent in acute intoxication, and constipation is one of the chief complaints of the addict. The constipating and the miotic effect remains in chronic addiction, although the danger to the respiratory centre lessens. N-allylnormorphine (Lethidrone) has been found to be the most effective antagonist to morphine and all opiates (Unna, 1943).

The tendency of morphine to cause *addiction* depends on its analgesic and euphorizing effects, and also on the fairly rapid development of tolerance and liability to withdrawal symptoms. The personality and the circumstances of the individual are also important. The danger of addiction is great when the drug is used to relieve pain and discomfort in all chronic and recurrent illnesses. Most general practitioners, however, have one or two patients who regularly take their half-grain or so of morphine every day, under prescription, without showing a need for a heavier dosage. Nevertheless, the responsibility of the physician in managing the administration of morphine in chronic painful ailments is a heavy one.

The victims of addiction are often *abnormal personalities*. There is no one kind of personality that can be described as specially vulnerable but the inadequate, markedly anxiety-prone and psychopathic are commonly encountered.

Retterstöl and Sund (1964) examined the main diagnosis at admission to hospital of a group of 122 patients treated for drug dependence, 50 per cent. of whom were addicted. Just under half of the 'addicted' and a similar proportion of the 'habituated' took morphine. Narcomania and delirium by drug accounted for only 20 per cent. of diagnoses. Over 50 per cent. had a diagnosis of neurosis (21 per cent. of depressive type). The more endogenous psychoses did not appear to predispose the patient to drug abuse. There is also other evidence to indicate that there is little correlation between drug addiction and true schizophrenic or manic-depressive illness. These findings may be a pointer to the amount of chronic intoxication which goes undiagnosed for a time. When the original reason for taking the drug was enquired into, only 4 per cent. gave physical illness accompanied by severe pain, and the writers comment that, even so, physical illness is much less often the real reason for beginning dependence than the patients themselves claim it to be. Twenty-two per cent. of the 122 patients were considered to have a psychopathic personality; a preponderance of these were in the 'addicted' group.

The incidence of addiction to morphine and heroin is changing rapidly in Great Britain. Previously this country enjoyed the reputation of having relatively few addicts and little difficulty in controlling addiction-producing drugs. Members of the medical and nursing professions, together with patients who had been given morphine for the relief of pain, formerly constituted a high proportion of the total. In 1959 the number of known heroin addicts was 68; by 1964 the number had risen five-fold to 342. Bewley (1965) estimates that new cases reported double every 18 months. Only 4 per cent. of these had become addicted as the result of medical treatment. In 1963 for the first time there were more known addicts to heroin than to any other one drug. Now young people without therapeutic justification are increasingly becoming involved. In 1959 11 per cent. were under 35 and in 1964 nearly 40 per cent. (one addict being 15 years of age). All the addicts under 20 and most of those under 35 were taking heroin (Home Office, 1959–65). The majority of new addicts are between 18 and 35 years of age.

Despite this disturbing increase, the problem in Great Britain has smaller dimensions than in other countries. In U.S.A. one in 3,000 of the population was known to be drug dependent in 1958; in Canada, one in 6,000 in 1955 (10 per cent. of these were professional cases with easy access to drugs) and in West Germany the figure was 1 in 10,000 in 1953 (Lehmann, 1963). Reviewing an international literature on drug dependence, Retterstöl and Sund (1964) comment that drug-abusers seem to be a heterogeneous group of people with varying personal and socio-economic backgrounds. The studies they cite deal with a wide variety of material ranging from under-privileged youths in American urban centres to middle-class people in traditional European cultures.

The *clinical picture* shown by the addict is not very characteristic. *Physically*, he is likely to show the signs of a recent dose, miosis is usually present and he may have scars, or abscesses, at the site of carelessly given injections. There may be trophic disturbances of the skin, with loss of hair, brittleness of nails, etc. His appetite is poor, his health undermined by malnutrition, infection or liver damage following infective hepatitis.

The *chronic malaise* of the addict is temporarily relieved by a dose of the drug. He then feels released and calm, and can once again see the rosy side of life; anxiety, restlessness and depression are banished, only to return with the hangover. Succeeding doses of the same size tend to produce euphoria of a lesser degree and shorter duration. Some patients content themselves with this lesser effect; others, intent on maintaining the degree of relief, have to take more and more of the drug. The tolerance which can be gained may be very high: ten times the minimum lethal dose may be taken without ill effect.

Addiction does not lead to pronounced *mental changes*. There is no loss of intelligence, no dementia, and nothing is known of psychoses due to morphine alone. The great danger is *moral depravity*. As direct consequences of chronic abuse there are an increasing inactivity and laziness, the wasting of time in day-dreams, indecisiveness, and paralysis of the ability to make any strong and persistent effort. As a secondary consequence, due to the need to conceal the habit and to overcome social and other barriers in the way of regular supply, the patient is very likely to be led into fraud, the falsification of prescriptions, an all-embracing insincerity to family, friends, colleagues and doctors, dishonest manoeuvres of all kinds, and flagrant breaches of the law.

Before he comes to medical or psychiatric attention, the addict has probably made one or more *attempts at self-cure*, and has suffered an equal number of defeats. In his attempts at self-cure he may have made use of substitutes, and have become addicted to other drugs, alcohol, barbiturates, pethidine, or morphine derivatives such as codeine, dilaudid, etc. He has probably come to know well the symptoms of withdrawal, and whatever his professions, to be essentially unwilling to face them in all their nakedness. When admitted to a nursing-home or hospital, it is more likely than not that he will try to smuggle in a supply of the drug on his person when he arrives, and, not infrequently, through intermediaries afterwards.

WITHDRAWAL. Problems of withdrawal arise when the drug is one like morphine and heroin which produces *physical dependence*. This may be defined as a state of adaptation to the drug by the tissues of the addict so that (a) the continued presence of the drug is required for their normal function, and (b) its withdrawal produces a characteristic illness called the abstinence syndrome. This is far from invariable particularly in early cases.

The *withdrawal symptoms* are often severe. Euphoria, calm and content give way to depression, restlessness, and physical and mental irritability. Physically the habitual constipation changes to diarrhoea, and in addition there are anorexia, and perhaps retching and vomiting, trembling, yawning, sweating, pains in any part or all over the body, a profound malaise and anxiety. Almost invariably the patient is sleepless.

The *diagnosis* is almost always proffered by the patient himself. In cases of doubt, the pupillary changes when the patient is under the influence of a dose, and small injection scars in the skin at accessible sites, will prove helpful. When the patient is trying to conceal the addiction, a change in mood, with debility, tremor, apathy or depression at one time, followed, after an absence from the room, at a short interval by alertness and a cheerful humour, are characteristic of addiction to morphine, or perhaps cocaine or heroin.

TREATMENT. Immediate admission to hospital is essential as addicts are prone to drift away during a waiting period (Cameron, 1964). There is general agreement among those working in this field that the patient should remain in hospital for over four months and that the doctor who treats him should be in clinical control after discharge.

Osnos (1963) differentiates five stages in the treatment of narcotic addiction: (1) the pre-hospital phase when the patient is persuaded to enter hospital, (2) the withdrawal phase (with the purpose of total abstinence, usually by substituting drugs), (3) the rehabilitation phase with physical and emotional rehabilitation as its aim, (4) the transitional phase, with the object of making the patient able to manage his affairs outside hospital (this includes trial leaves of absence and the use of day or night hospitals), (5) the after-care phase which includes psychotherapy and co-operation with the patient's family, his doctor, employer and the social services. Freedman (1963) outlines a similar programme.

It is essential to ensure that there is no associated barbiturate dependence as the status epilepticus or acute delirium produced by sudden withdrawal of barbiturates may prove fatal. The safest and most satisfactory technique of withdrawal is methadone substitution. The amount administered should suffice to reduce to a minimum withdrawal phenomena such as dilated pupils, perspiration, vomiting, rhinorrhoea and restlessness. During the first 24–36 hours, the dose of methadone needed may be difficult to gauge. Fifteen to twenty mg. should be given in a flavoured aqueous solution as soon as withdrawal symptoms appear and further doses of 10–15 mg. should be administered to control fresh symptoms. After this initial stage, the dose needed for stabilization can be estimated from the daily dosage on which addiction had been previously established. One milligramme of methadone is equivalent to 3–4 mg. of morphine or 1·5–2 mg. of heroin. When the patient has been stabilized on methadone, gradual withdrawal should begin immediately and a 20–25 per cent. reduction daily is easily tolerated. Most patients can be comfortably withdrawn from opiates in this manner within 10–12 days. However, some malaise, weakness and insomnia may persist for weeks. If symptoms are severe, some relief is afforded at this stage by chlordiazepoxide in doses of 10–12 mg. three times daily. Methadone is itself addictive but has less devastating effects on health and adjustment than heroin.

The most difficult stage in the treatment is that of *rehabilitation* after withdrawal. The patient needs continued psychotherapeutic help and guidance and must be trained to support the vexations and anxieties of life without his drug, along the lines already suggested for the treatment of alcoholism. In the case of drug dependence, however, there is no equivalent of Antabuse and deconditioning therapy is not possible. *Prolonged after-care* is of the utmost importance and often frustrating, as the addict may be difficult to trace once he is discharged from hospital. Co-operative patients should be persuaded to return to hospital for overhaul every three months for one or two years. However, poor motivation for treatment and unwillingness to continue it are frequently encountered. Freedman *et al.* (1963) in a study of 490 heroin addicts admitted voluntarily to two special wards in a New York hospital, say that patients dropped out at every stage in their full programme of treatment and only 14 per cent. were attending the after-care clinic at the end of 22 months. Retterstöl and Sund (1964) quote 50 per cent. as having poor motivation for treatment.

PROGNOSIS. Retterstöl and Sund (1964), who have written a comprehensive review of follow-up studies, find that prognosis is difficult to evaluate on the basis of existing studies as they are founded on samples varying in degree of dependence, age, and socio-economic background, who have had different treatment for different lengths of time. It would appear to be best in patients who have had active after-care in an area where they are comparatively easy to trace. Kielholz and Battegay (1963) claim that the 40 per cent. permanent cure in their patients in Switzerland depends on this factor.

Few other studies show such good results. Columbia University School of Public Health follow-up of patients discharged from Riverside Hospital, New York, established for the treatment of adolescent narcotic addicts, showed that 91 per cent. of 147 patients who could be traced after two years had returned to regular daily use of drugs and only 24 per cent. had achieved one period of six months in the community without relapse (Freedman, 1963). Isbell (1963) speaking of U.S.A. states that at least 15–20 per cent. of narcotic addicts remain abstinent for five years after one adequate period of treatment. Retterstöl and Sund (1964) made a careful follow-up study of a group of drug-dependent patients whom they considered to be representative of those seen at any Norwegian psychiatric clinic, admitted because of nervous disorders rather than for cure of their addiction. They found that 70 per cent. of those addicted to morphine and 43 per cent. of those habituated to morphine were still taking the drug at follow-up which was, for the majority, after 4–5 years. Morphine addicts showed 50 per cent. readmission to hospital, the highest rate, and they were greatly in the majority among those readmitted several times. Thirty-five per cent. were unfit for work for over a year during the follow-up period. Clark (1962) did a follow-up study of 65 patients belonging to the medical or nursing professions admitted to Crichton Royal Hospital between 1949–1960. He separated out those addicted to drugs coming under the Dangerous Drugs Act and found that 14 per cent. of these had overcome their addiction, 61 per cent. had required further admission to hospital, and 18 per cent. had continued without interruption at their profession since discharge. The majority of patients had not had long periods of rehabilitation because few professional people will enter hospital if prolonged rehabilitation is in prospect and few will remain to complete it. He came to the conclusion that there was a considerable case for addicts with easy access to drugs to change their profession or transfer to a branch where access was not so easy. This recommendation echoed by many writers has a wider application. A change of social situation on leaving hospital probably improves the outlook for most addicts.

Mortality is high and tends to occur at an early age. Of 436 new addicts who became known to the Home Office during 1955–65, 39 had died by April 1965 (James, 1967). The male mortality of 27 per 1000 per year was twenty times the expected rate. Five of the males committed suicide and an open verdict was given on four more. Twelve deaths were due to an apparently unintentional overdose of the drug of addiction. Fourteen more male deaths were caused either by infections such as septicaemia and bacterial endocarditis consequent on using unsterilized syringes, or by accident such as falling from heights. The mean age at death of British-born male addicts was 30·3 years.

Cannabis

The psychological effects of *Cannibis sativa* (Indian hemp, hashish, marihuana) were known to the ancient Chinese and were mentioned in the herbal of the Emperor Shen Nung (about 2700 B.C.). It has been known in the Middle East for a thousand years or more that the flowering tops of the female plant of *Cannabis sativa* have a pleasant intoxicating effect. The drug is today used as a euphoriant in large parts of Asia and Africa. It may be eaten, drunk or smoked. For ingestion or inhalation, the drug is carefully prepared in ways which differ from region to region. In some African tribes the smoking of hemp is a part of certain religious ceremonies and community rites (Lewin, 1931). As the plant grows wild in the United States, and can be an unnoticed denizen of the back-garden, it is hardly surprising that its properties have been discovered there. The smoking of marihuana cigarettes has become common among professional jazz musicians, rebellious adolescents, some *avant garde* groups and university students.

The active principle of cannabis is supposed to be a resin or oil, of which pharmacologically very little is known. Various preparations differ greatly in their potency, and the descriptions of the results obtained by taking them have differed correspondingly. Recently the active constituent has apparently been isolated (Adams, 1942; Loewe, 1950); experimental investigations can now be carried out with more precision and with reliable results.

Most workers agree that the symptoms of intoxication are much the same whether the drug be ingested or its smoke inhaled. A more careful examination of reports (e.g. Allentuck and Bowman, 1942) suggests that apart from the dose, the *speed of absorption* is important symptomatically. The last-named authors describe the mild form of intoxication as follows:

'*Mental phenomena* arise two to three hours after ingestion, or almost immediately after inhalation of the drug. The subject admits to being "high". This state is characterized by a sensation of "floating in air", "falling on waves", lightness or dizziness in the head, ringing in the ears, and heaviness in the limbs. Euphoria is first manifested objectively in volubility and increased psychomotor activity, and later subjectively in a delicious and confused lassitude. Distance and time intervals subjectively appear elastic. In three to six hours after ingestion of marihuana, hunger, manifested mainly in a craving for sweets, and a feeling of fatigue and sleepiness become prominent. The individual may sleep from one to six hours and on awakening is "down"; that is, he no longer feels "high". The clinical phenomena may linger for another few hours.

'The mental status usually reveals a hyperactive, apprehensive, loquacious, somewhat suspicious individual. His stream of talk may be circumstantial; his mood may be elevated, but he does not harbour frank abnormal mental content such as delusions, hallucinations, phobias or autistic thinking. Attention, concentration and comprehension are only slightly disturbed, as is evidenced by the fact that the results in his educational achievement tests are only slightly lowered.'

Observers who have used larger doses and different modes of administration from smoking have described symptoms of a richer and more productive kind, reminding one of the psychoses: waves of exaltation alternating with fear or terror, feelings of unreality, or of double personality, distortion of shapes, exaggerated colours, illusions and hallucinations, a marked disturbance of the body image, disturbance of spatial order and of time, and various motor phenomena.

Beringer (1932) distinguishes three forms of the *thought disorder*, which as 'dissociation des idées', had already been observed by Moreau de Tours (1845):

1. Fragmentation of perceptive wholes through fragmentation of thought processes. A central point of reference is missing, and the subject is unable to link the parts with the whole. A street scene breaks up into its individual elements, a car, houses, people, a soldier, a policeman, etc.

2. A disturbance of memory by which everything experienced is forgotten at once. The present does not seem to arise out of the past. This is accompanied by perplexity and immobility.

3. Frequent and sudden interruptions of the stream of thought, the gaps only lasting a few seconds. These interruptions, though they last longer, resemble the absences of the epileptic and the thought blocking or thought deprivation of the schizophrenic.

Beringer also observed a great variety of *motor anomalies* including hyperkinetic and hypokinetic states. Much of the hypermotility seemed to be the expression of a general elation and to be in conformity with the euphoric mood, the over-active drive and abundance of ideas. But choreiform restlessness and twitching of limbs were also observed, which to the subject were psychologically unmotivated and described as highly unpleasant. Stuporose and catatonic-like states were less frequent, and hypokinesis usually corresponded with general mental passivity and lack of spontaneity. In fact, motor disturbances occurred at all levels of integration.

The frequent feeling of excessive hunger which is complained of at the end of the intoxication may be due to hypoglycaemia. It is noteworthy that Eastern people take cannabis either in sugar as sweets, or in a sweet drink.

It has been held, very debatably, that cannabis acts as a *sexual stimulant*. This idea has captured popular interest, and has been exploited in literary uses of the theme. It is unlikely that there is any specific effect; but in some men and more women it may have an aphrodisiac action by inhibiting higher moral control and releasing instinctive desires.

It is doubtful whether hashish is an *addictive drug* in the strict sense, though expert opinion varies. Probably there is no increased tolerance with continued taking, and no need to increase the dose to get the same psychological effect.

As one might expect, in those countries where its use is widespread, cannabis has been blamed for most abnormal mental conditions at one time or another. However, since cases of personality deterioration or dementia, attributed to abuse of hashish, have been more critically investigated, any causal connexion has become doubtful. The chronic *hashish psychoses* described by earlier observers have proved to be cases of schizophrenia complicated by symptoms of cannabis intoxication. However, Stringaris (1933, 1939), who studied the cannabis addicts in Greece, has described short delirious states with numerous dreamlike hallucinations. These *episodes* are well known among habitués. They may last several days, and have often the character of epileptic twilight states or fugues, with aimless journeys, outbursts of irritation, and subsequent patchy amnesia. Although Stringaris believes in the existence of a chronic hashish psychosis, he thinks it impossible to differentiate its symptoms from those of schizophrenia.

It is doubtful whether hashish by itself induces criminal behaviour; but like other addictions it lowers moral resistance, and it seems an appropriate drug to take as a stimulant of courage and recklessness before premeditated burglaries and crimes of violence. Crime-waves in New Orleans in 1930 and later have been thought to be connected with the widespread drug habit in that city and in the State of Louisiana but there is no clear evidence that this was the case. By 1937 every State in the U.S.A., as well as the Federal Government, had introduced some *prohibitory legislation*. Nevertheless, public consciousness was again aroused by discovery of the extent of marihuana-smoking by American school-children. Psychiatrists have maintained that the habit is altogether more dangerous in a Western culture than it is in the East, that marihuana-smoking is an introduction to more dangerous drugs, and Kosviner *et al.* (1968) found that all 30 of their heroin users who gave histories had begun with cannabis and amphetamine, 17 trying the former as their first drug. A report from Interpol (*Daily Telegraph* 17th Nov., 1964) states that the amount of hashish smuggled into this country increased six-fold during the period late 1963 to late 1964. The taking of hashish has proved in some cases to be a prelude to addiction to more dangerous drugs and its control needs to be rigorous. The drug is nearly always taken in company hence the spread of the habit.

It may be admitted that only weak, immature or psychopathic persons are liable to become victims; but we are all at some time immature, and the number of those who are weak or temperamentally susceptible is very great indeed. It is debatable whether hashish or alcohol is the safer intoxicant. But we are not in a position to choose between them, only to decide whether to add the problems of hashish dependence to those of alcoholism.

Cocaine

The history of cocainism begins in the eighties of the last century when Sigmund Freud (1884) introduced its use for the treatment of 'those functional states comprised under the name of neurasthenia' (Jones, 1954) and for covering the withdrawal of morphine in addicted patients. Although the use of the drug in psychiatric patients proved disastrous, Freud's observations paved the way for the introduction of local anaesthesia in ophthalmology and in medical and surgical practice generally. However, the habit of chewing the leaves of the South American plant *Erythroxylus coca* as a stimulant was found among the native Incas by the Spaniards when they conquered Peru in the sixteenth century. The chewer takes the leaves mixed with potash of lime, and may do so every day without apparent harm. About eight million people in South America are estimated to be coca devotees today, all of them of Indian race (Sollmann, 1948).

The medical importance of cocaine lies in its well-known properties as a *local anaesthetic*, and when used in this way any general effect is prevented by the simultaneous administration of adrenaline. The effects of the drug on the body as a whole have not found any useful medical application. It acts centrally as an excitant and euphorizing agent, and also stimulates the sympathetic, causing dilatation of the pupils, pallor of the skin, increase of pulse rate, sweating, and sometimes a rise of body temperature.

Addicts inject cocaine subcutaneously, or inhale it as a snuff, when it is quickly absorbed through the mucous membrane. In the body it is in part *metabolized* and destroyed, but some is also excreted unchanged in the urine. In large doses it produces hallucinations and a delirious state, in which there may be epileptic fits and eventual death from respiratory failure. The effect of a smaller but still intoxicating dose on a neophyte is subject to considerable individual variation. In general there is a stage of excitation lasting about an hour, which is followed by depression and lethargy. The need to overcome this aftermath probably lies at the root of habit formation. Withdrawal symptoms, such as insomnia, palpitations and feelings of oppression, are relieved by a dose, and so lead to dependence.

The effects which are desired by the addict are the immediate *elation*, with accompanying feelings of greater mental agility, greater precision of thought and action, immunity to fatigue, and greater muscular power. The addict in this state is excited and restless; he likes to talk, and mixes well in society. Now only he feels his best. He may make the impression of a brilliant conversationalist, witty and full of ideas. But his associations and his thinking are superficial, and his over-activity is restless and lacks direction.

To the morphine addict cocaine brings a welcome change by temporarily enabling him to surmount his solitariness and his passivity and lethargy. *Combined addiction* to both drugs is commoner than cocainism alone. Of the 171 known cocaine addicts in England and Wales in 1963, 168 also took heroin (Home Office, 1965).

Cameron (1964) in his study of heroin addicts found that 21 out of 23 whose records were complete usually took equal quantities of cocaine, i.e. 300 mg. in 24 hours. Many also took large quantities of barbiturates. However, there are devotees who take cocaine only on occasion during transient states of depression or when in difficult circumstances as a *drug of escape*, and never become true addicts. Cocaine addiction is a social habit like alcoholism, and especially when bought and sold as snuff, involves in certain circles of urban life the paraphernalia of elaborate customs. As the addict becomes more and more dependent on the drug, instability and weakness of will become marked. He cannot stick to a regular occupation, and what is left of his energy and persistence is devoted to procuring his supply of cocaine by any means, often very dubious ones.

The number of known addicts in 1959 in England and Wales was 30 and this figure had risen to 211 by 1964. There is evidence that cases of dependence on this drug are occurring in the provinces whereas previously they were largely confined to the metropolitan area.

On the basis of chronic addiction a number of *psychotic pictures* may develop. There are, first, *short-lived delirious states* characterized by a mixture of cheerfulness with fear. The desire of adventure and sensational excitement, typical of the addict in his normal life, colours the delirium and gives it content. Auditory and tactile hallucinations and illusions prevail, and delusional ideas are marked by paranoid suspicion.

The *cocaine psychosis*, which may persist over months, if the patient continues to take the intoxicant, is a *subacute delirious state* with some special features. The patient may continue with normal occupations and pastimes, but he appears moody and restless, at times irritable and anxious. He sleeps little, eats insufficiently, and looks pale and haggard. He is also troubled with paranoid ideas, into whose morbid nature he has a partial insight. Auditory hallucinations, illusions, especially at night, which take a delusional interpretation, are common. The affective reaction to these experiences may be extreme. The patient may wait in panic terror for his persecutors to enter his premises, to kill him or hand him over to the police; and as he is active and determined, he may then be very dangerous, and trivial causes may lead to catastrophes of violence or murder. Dream-like twilight states have also been described, in which the patient is at once frightened and amused by cinema-like visual hallucinations.

Tactile hallucinations are rather specific for the cocaine psychosis, although not always present. These, the '*signe de Magnan*', are possibly related to the effect of cocaine on the peripheral nerves. The patient feels small animals, worms, ants, lice, in the skin of his hands or all over the body; or he complains of electricity, or cocaine crystals entering his skin. He may not only feel but see; and the reality of the hallucinations may be so great that he pierces his skin with needles to try to pick out the foreign bodies.

The *diagnosis* of cocainism is often difficult because it is so often combined with addiction to other drugs such as morphine and alcohol. The most characteristic sign is the lesions of the mucous membrane of the nose which occur when cocaine is taken as snuff. The discovery of cocaine crystals in the patient's handkerchief may be the only but decisive clue. Cocaine delirium is very similar to delirium tremens, although the tremor of the cocaine patient is less coarse, his hallucinations are more personal and centre more on himself, and auditory experiences are more frequent than in the alcoholic. The subacute cocaine psychosis may resemble a schizophrenic episode. But the relatively good rapport with the addict, the natural liveliness of his affective response, and the absence of typical signs of thought disorder should facilitate diagnosis.

Prognosis and Treatment: When the long-standing addict of other drugs takes to cocaine, the complication is a serious one because it will quickly lead to his physical and mental ruin. Even when early admission to hospital can be arranged, and the patient is co-operative, the outlook is very doubtful. States of acute intoxication and episodes of excitement in chronic intoxication respond well to barbiturates. Delirium and subacute paranoid episodes pass off when the drug is withdrawn. Occasional users, and patients caught early in their addiction, especially if they take the drug nasally, pass easily through a withdrawal treatment; and the prognosis may be quite good if the patient's basic personality is fairly sound. What has been said about the treatment of morphine addiction applies here with equal force.

The *withdrawal of cocaine* should be immediate and complete, and no consequent danger need be feared.

Other Addictions and Intoxications

Towards the end of the last century sniffing *ether* or mixing it in drinks became popular in some parts of Central Europe and psychoses of a delirious type were occasionally seen following abuse of ether. These states are rare but ether addiction is occasionally the explanation for a delirium or hallucinosis of obscure origin in individuals such as doctors, or nurses who have access to anaesthetics.

There was a time when *bromide intoxication* was a relatively common cause of acute delirious states. They were usually florid in picture, and paraphasic speech disorder and confabulatory memory defects were present in addition to terrifying visual and auditory hallucinations and delusional misinterpretations. Occasionally states of addiction to bromide or bromide and chloral mixtures are seen; the presenting features may be milder, with slurred speech, ataxia, defects of memory and a moderate euphoria. However, since bromide is now so little used as a sedative or anticonvulsant, these conditions have become very uncommon. Among recently introduced drugs both *meprobamate* (Retterstöl and Sund, 1964; Glatt, 1959) and *glutethimide* (Bartholemew, 1961; Fry, 1962) have been found especially prone to lead to habituation and addiction.

That commonly prescribed drugs are associated with addiction has only recently begun to be appreciated. Growing awareness of the hazards may reduce the interval which elapses before the addictive properties of newly introduced drugs come to be appreciated.

James (1962) found that 12 per cent. of women admitted to an acute psychiatric ward in Perth were addicted to bromureide, barbiturates or glutethimide. Many of these patients suffered from chronic intoxication giving rise to depression, emotional instability, irritability, tension, social withdrawal and deterioration, incoordination, fits and episodes of clouding of consciousness. Bartholemew and James suggest that chronic intoxication with such drugs may be responsible for many *atypical psychiatric disorders which remain undiagnosed*. This point is certainly relevant for psychiatric practice in all advanced countries. It would seem highly improbable that prescriptions for barbiturates and non-barbiturate hypnotics would constitute 10 per cent. of all National Health Service prescriptions unless a large number of habituated and addicted patients were receiving these drugs. In the United Kingdom addiction to *pethidine* has increased by an average of almost 10 per cent. each year between 1961 and 1965. The total number of addictions to manufactured drugs other than morphine, heroin and cocaine had doubled in this interval (Interdepartmental Committee on Drug Addiction, 1965). *Dextromoramide and dipipanone* were mainly responsible for the increase, and about 1 in every 14 addicts known to the Home Office is taking one or other of these drugs which were not introduced until 1959.

It is surprising to find that certain morphine derivatives are freely available to the public without prescription. Thus *chlorodyne* contains 64 mg. of morphine hydrochloride and 3·6 ml. of chloroform in each ounce (28 ml.). Conlon (1963) has described three cases of addiction to this substance; each showed severe mental deterioration with evidence of peripheral neuropathy. The average daily consumption was at least 6 ounces. *Paregoric* or camphorated tincture of opium is another freely available source of morphine, 4 ounces (113 ml.) containing 1 grain (64 mg.) of morphine hydrochloride (Glatt, 1964*a*).

'*Glue sniffing*' has been prevalent for some time in the United States of America and has recently been appearing on this side of the Atlantic. The substances used contain various organic solvents including carbon tetrachloride and tricresyl phosphate. The patient described by Merry and Zachariadis (1962) experienced pleasant, vivid, hypnagogic hallucinations, and when he attempted to discontinue the habit a severe withdrawal state reminiscent of delirium tremens developed with intense fear, tingling and cramps in the hands and feet, abdominal pains, and visual hallucinations.

Bethell (1965) reviews fifteen cases of toxic psychosis following addiction to *sniffing petrol fumes* reported since 1951. The habit, which relieves tension, was continued for many years in a number of cases. When it came to light it was because of vivid, frightening visual hallucinatory experiences. The addiction can cause a sudden attack of unconsciousness and can lead to death due to renal and liver necrosis.

In view of the ever-increasing volume of sedative, analgesic and tranquillizing drugs being manufactured and consumed there is a growing need for more effective education of the general public, as well as medical students and practitioners, about drug abuse and the problems of addiction.

HALLUCINOGENS

Mescaline

This is one of the best studied of the drugs with central stimulating action which, because of their effect on imagery, have been called 'phantastica'. The pharmacologist Lewin found it in wide use as an intoxicant among Red Indian tribes in Mexico and in North America near the Mexican border. It was principally used to produce ecstatic states on special religious occasions. Lewin identified the mescal buttons which were chewed by the Indians as parts of a cactus plant (1888). The examination of early reports showed that the drug had already been mentioned in the description of this part of Mexico by Sahagun early in the sixteenth century, and that the 'prophetic' quality of peyotl, the native name of the prepared cactus, was probably known to Aztec medicine before the conquest of the country by Cortes.

The *chemistry* of the active principle in peyotl, 3, 4, 5-trimethoxyphenylethylamine, was studied and largely explained by Heffter in 1898.

Anthropologists such as Lumholtz (1894) and Mooney (1896) collected descriptions of the poetic and colourful mythos centring around the drug, and the elaborate ceremonies practised by the Indians when gathering, preparing and taking it. About the year 1900, thanks to the skill of exporters, the use of the drug spread from the Mexican frontier to several Indian tribes in the reservations of North America. An originally pagan rite, in which peyotl was regarded as god-like, came then to be incorporated into the Christian liturgy by Indian groups who had been converted to Christianity long before, but were still ready to revive old tribal customs, and to chew the mescal buttons at the time of festival gatherings. In these new circumstances the ecstatic and hallucinatory experiences embodied Christian symbols and were interpreted by the tribesmen according to Christian ideas.

Apparently it takes hours of chewing before the cactus itself produces the desired symptoms. It was, however, used in early experiments on themselves by Prentiss and Morgan (1896) and Weir Mitchell (1896), and was found to lead to experiences very similar to those obtained by the injection of mescaline. On the instigation of Kraepelin, Knauer administered mescaline to himself and his colleagues in 1911 (Knauer and Maloney, 1913); and since that time the experiments which have been made with the drug have led to a considerable number of reports. One of the more important of these is the monograph on mescal by Heinrich Klüver (1928).

The symptoms produced by mescal resemble those of cannabis in many respects; but the initial stage of mild excitement with cheerfulness and over-activity is absent with mescal, or not easily achieved. It has therefore never become a popular intoxicant for every-day consumption, and mescaline addiction is unknown. In the clinical picture the *predominance of visual experiences* is striking. Not only are there persistent visual illusions and hallucinations, but the real objects seen, their shape and colour, are experienced differently and with greater impressiveness. Visual images replace thinking, and express feelings and moods. The only competition in the dominance of consciousness comes from the tactile senses and alterations of the body-image. When Zador gave mescaline to a patient who had been blind since the age of two, he became hallucinated in terms of the body-image only. Generally speaking, mescal is the drug of the visionary, and it was probably for this reason that it lent itself so readily to religious use.

Within the field of vision, the drug interferes with the stillness and the movements of objects. The mechanism by which we normally see things as fixed and of persistent shape, though we alter our spatial relation with them, seems to break down in the intoxicated state. The process of perceiving and picturing our surroundings at an instantaneous glance is disturbed, probably slowed down, and something more nearly approaching a 'scanning' process takes its place:

'Looking at a pattern of triangles and dots on the cover of a book, I saw the triangles changing their shape, becoming higher and more pointed, wider and more obtuse; they came out of the paper as though plastic and then withdrew into it. At the same time the whole pattern was in movement. Also the dots were in steady movement away from one another and from the triangles. . . . The same persistent movement was seen in the changing visual hallucinations, but there were also periods of complete standstill. . . .'

Imaginary movement of this kind is obviously related to the creative play of imagination, such as has been described not only by artists of genius like Leonardo da Vinci and Goethe, but also by Johannes Mueller, the father of modern sensory physiology. The physiological rather than the imaginative basis of much of the experience comes out in many descriptions. One of Beringer's subjects reported as follows:

'On a whitewashed wall there is movement of grey and white lines apparently at different levels, horizontal and vertical, forming a lattice-work, moving from left to right; behind it, while the movement continues, a picture forms. One of the larger shady spots becomes a house, like a castle with windows, an entrance, a drive from the gate, a pond in front, the castle being mirrored in the water. Behind the castle come a mountain range, slow-moving clouds in the sky. The picture is in constant change, new lines becoming more marked and starting an entirely new design. The new design expresses itself ever more clearly, and when it has fully developed something different again is slowly started. Deliberate intention, independent of the basic material of lines, the will to imagine something entirely different, has no effect.'

Closely linked with the disturbed visual appreciation of movement, but not identical with it, are the frequent *disorders of time* experienced in mescaline intoxication. They vary a great deal from case to case; but a slowing-down of the passage of time, sometimes culminating in a standstill or complete timelessness, is often described. Continuing movement may be experienced as timeless—a vortex of kaleidoscopic colours turns without time. Some experiences of heightened insight seem of eternal duration. Time may be discontinuous and fragmented, as in the case of one subject who tried to imagine the way from the hospital to his home. He made only very slow progress. The different stages of the journey, which ordinarily took twenty minutes, seemed to go on without end. Moreover, the stages appeared disconnected, like a series of snapshots. The basic sense of a time continuum seemed to have gone.

Among the many striking phenomena of mescaline intoxication, the interrelation of sensory experiences in the form of *synaesthesiae* is of special interest. As visual perception prevails, the influence extends from other senses to vision: the knocking of workmen outside the room is accompanied by hallucinatory dots of colour in the air; with each stroke of a clock more red spots appear in a coloured pattern, etc. But synaesthesiae between other senses are also experienced. The following report from a usually matter-of-fact scientist illustrates, not only the peculiar quality of the synaesthetic perception, but also the inadequacy of ordinary language to describe it:

'One believes in hearing noises and seeing faces, but everything is one. I hear scratching, the sound of loud trumpets, I am the lattice-work. What I see, I hear; what I smell, I think. I am music, I am the lattice-work. I see an idea of mine going out of me into the lattice-work. This is not a metaphor, but the perception of something coming out of me. . . . I felt, saw, tasted and smelled the noise of the trumpet, was myself the noise. . . . Everything was clear and absolutely certain. All criticism is nonsense in the face of experience. . . .'

It is difficult to classify the *state of consciousness* during the intoxication which allows of such full self-observation and, at times, seems to foster detachment and self-scrutiny. At other times the same subject seems to have lost all clarity of consciousness, is drowsy and even close to sleep. The continuity of consciousness may be disrupted and fragmented. Single impressions are dissociated and without connexion at one time, and at another everything seems to flow in a unified stream of deep significance and importance, related in some way with the whole past life of the subject, who identifies himself with it. The breadth and capacity of consciousness may also be changed, constricted to a single small impression, as when one subject said that for him the whole world was contained in a fluff of dark wool on the doctor's white coat.

This summary is based on sixty experiments by Beringer (1927), in which mentally healthy subjects received 0·4 to 0·6 grams of the hydrochloric salt of mescaline. The hallucinations and kindred sensory disturbances were also studied in detail. It was found possible to relate the psychopathological phenomena of mescaline intoxication to those experienced in the psychoses. Many descriptions by patients of bizarre and improbable experiences are better understood in the light of mescaline observations—especially those reported in *early acute schizophrenia*. However, the similarity can be over-stressed. Many typical symptoms of this disease are never seen in mescaline intoxication, especially those of subacute and chronic schizophrenic states.

In view of this comparison, and of the predominantly religious use of the drug, it is of interest that the great majority of experimental subjects have been deeply impressed by the strange experiences they have had under mescaline. Some have felt that *a new and unknown mental world* had been opened up to them, and others that reality had been shown to them in new aspects, or that unknown sensory pleasures had been explored. Apart from the few who were disappointed and sceptical, by most the experiment was remembered as significant and important.

The *derealization and depersonalization*, which are of frequent occurrence in acute schizophrenia and severe anxiety neurosis (see p. 94), appear almost regularly after mescaline, even if only for a short period. Guttmann and Maclay (1936) suggested the use of mescaline in treating depersonalization, but when it has been tried no striking results have been obtained.

Although the symptoms of mescaline intoxication have been studied in great detail, little progress has been made in discovering the mechanism by which they are produced. Studies *in vitro* by Quastel and Wheatley (1933) showed that oxidation in the brain was inhibited by mescaline as it is by narcotics. Marazzi and Hart (1955) used the two-neurone transcallosal system to investigate the effects of various drugs on synaptic transmission in the cat brain. In these experiments an electric shock was applied in an area in the occipital cortex and an attempt was made to record the impulse in the contralateral cortex. This impulse would then have traversed one group of synapses. Mescaline injected into the ipsilateral carotid artery produced a marked inhibition of synaptic transmission, without any effect on conduction. It is of interest that the effects of mescaline are blocked by chlorpromazine in the transcallosal preparation. In experiments with 25 schizophrenic patients it has also been found (Denber and Merlis, 1955) that, following an intravenous injection of 0·5 g. of mescaline sulphate, alpha activity disappeared from the electroencephalogram in 21 patients. However, despite a good deal of experimental work and speculation, the mode of action of mescaline and other hallucinogenic drugs remains obscure.

Lysergic Acid Diethylamide (LSD 25) and Some Related Hallucinogenic Drugs

During the investigation of the constituents of ergot Hofmann (1955) discovered by chance a new substance with mescaline-like effect. Psychiatrists and pharmacologists were slow to grasp the significance of the discovery, but interest in it has gathered momentum.

It is readily synthesized in the laboratory and, as it appears to have a special fascination for some *avant garde* groups of students and intellectuals, its use is spreading.

The autonomic effects include rise in body temperature, hypoglycaemia, mydriasis and piloerection. Although the autonomic effects commence after 15–20 minutes, psychological changes are delayed for 40–60 minutes and are at their most intense after one or two hours. The experiences resemble those following mescaline but the mood-effects are probably more intense. There is a good deal of individual variation, but there is a strong tendency for a release and accentuation of pre-existing characteristics of personality although this does not describe all the effects of the drugs. The psychological effects of LSD in healthy volunteers have been studied by Anderson and Rawnsley (1954) and Von Felsinger *et al.* (1956), and of psilocybin by Delay *et al.* (1959). The main psychological effects of the two substances are similar. The predominant mood change is euphoria but it may be followed with dramatic suddenness, as will shortly be described, by profound depression and anxiety. There may be unmotivated giggling or laughter sometimes accompanied by tears. The subject may have a general feeling of physical well-being or a sense of oppressive malaise with depersonalization, and disturbances of perception. Visual hyperaesthesia is common; many subjects describe visual experiences of unparalleled purity, intensity, brilliance and novelty. There are also commonly illusions and, in some cases, hallucinations. Some subjects are overwhelmed by a sense of mystical significance in the experience and others make mildly hostile or paranoid misinterpretations of neutral events. In a few cases frank delusions are expressed. Among the physical effects, tremulousness, weakness, somnolence, giddiness, paraesthesiae and gastrointestinal disturbances predominate. Some subjects describe intense somatic discomfort or pain, feeling themselves crushed, twisted or stretched.

Both elation and ecstasy and a sense of desolation and despair are sometimes engendered. These traits are illustrated by some interesting self descriptions published by Janiger (1959). 'This moment, this ecstasy is the only time I am alive. Happiness is not something to be experienced some time in the future, on vacation, after retirement. It is now', and 'The designs were formal, symmetrical and exquisitely perfect but drawn in jewelled, illumined colours like melted precious stones. They formed patterns which dissolved swiftly to be replaced by other patterns, scintillating transparencies like filaments of amethysts and emeralds . . . I was overwhelmed by the beauty', but on the other hand one subject wrote, 'The world was drab and dead—when not positively creeping with fearful plots and conspiracies. I thought I was a dope fiend, an alcoholic and a leper. The whole experiment had been hell. There was no clear impression of anything except pain and I wanted it to end. I said over and over again, "I can't go through it, I can't". It came to me that I had stopped life in my childhood, stopped living and merely been existing the rest of my life'. It is not surprising that some of the experiments with LSD that have become fashionable among young men, particularly university and college students in the United States and elsewhere, have ended tragically in suicide. The fashion has probably been fostered in part by the literary 'drug movement' of recent years whose devotees have continued in the tradition of De Quincey, Coleridge, Poe, Baudelaire and Gautier. Among the modern habitués are to be found rebellious adolescents seeking a sense of 'belonging', those in quest of transcendental experiences or of escape into a world of phantasy, and the emotionally immature for whom an outré activity is an assertion of identity.

LSD 25 differs greatly from mescaline in chemical structure. It is effective in remarkably small amounts, viz. by oral administration of 0·03 to 0·06 mg. Its influence on the

subject's mood is perhaps more marked than that of mescaline, though the sensory phenomena are almost identical. The effect of LSD 25 on the E.E.G. is to change it towards a
pattern generally associated with arousal and vigilance. In man for instance there is a
tendency for the alpha rhythm to be decreased or abolished and fast activity at low voltage
to be substituted. This suggests an influence on the mid-brain reticular formation.

A number of attempts have been made to account for the properties of LSD 25; none
has so far proved wholly successful. One of the most stimulating and productive hypotheses
was that of Woolley and Shaw (1954b) who suggested that a number of naturally occurring
alkaloids such as LSD and the harmine and yohimbine groups owe their properties to the
fact that they are anti-metabolites or competitive antagonists of serotonin. This had
previously been found in considerable quantities in brain tissue by Gaddum, Page and
their associates. The common feature of all these substances which creates a resemblance
to serotonin is the indole-nucleus with a substituted amino-ethyl side-chain. However, as
Woolley himself has pointed out, there are a number of objections to the serotonin-
antagonist theory. There are other antagonists such as ergotamine that are not hallucinogenic, and serotonin fails to reverse hallucinogenic effects. Moreover, 2-brom-lysergic
acid diethylamide is quite as active as the parent compound in antagonizing the peripheral
actions of serotonin, but has neither its psychotomimetic nor its sympatheticotonic effects
(Rothlin, 1957). However, although interesting speculations about the mode of action of
many hallucinogens have not so far met with confirmation, the general interest aroused
in the metabolism of serotonin and other brain amines by the work of Woolley and others
has stimulated much valuable work in neurochemistry, particularly in relation to the
biochemistry of depression.

The much discussed view of Hoffer et al. (1954), that the toxic metabolite that is
responsible for schizophrenia might be an indole compound derived from adrenaline and
similar in structure to lysergic acid diethylamide 25 and other hallucinogens, has already
been discussed (see p. 254). In recent experiments Pollin and Goldin (1961) and Cardon
et al. (1961) gave intravenous adrenaline to schizophrenic and normal control subjects. Assay
of the tritium-labelled metabolites in the urine showed that practically none of the adrenaline
could have been metabolized via adrenochrome or its derivatives.

A number of workers have reported on the use of LSD as an aid in psychotherapy
(Sandison et al., 1954, 1957; Abramson, 1956, 1957). There can be little doubt that the
drug facilitates the recapture of past experiences that have often been long forgotten.
Intense abreaction sometimes occurs and a proportion of patients emerge from the
experience with memories that appear to have made a profound emotional impact. It has
also been claimed that, in the treatment of alcoholics, hallucinogenic compounds promote
heightened awareness of conflicts and personality problems and satisfactory results have
been described in 12 out of 24 patients treated (Smith, 1958). It is possible that LSD and
similar substances are a valuable adjunct in the psychological exploration of patients' past
experience and personality problems. However, to date there have been no controlled
trials to support the claims made on behalf of LSD. Individuals with latent propensities
for psychotic illness may be rendered overtly psychotic (Sedman and Kenna, 1965) and
lasting personality changes may occur. The mood of the patient remains uncertain after
termination of experimental sessions and suicidal attempts have not infrequently been
made by patients some hours after they had left the clinic or consulting room.

The first analysis by Stoll (1947) followed the pattern of the earlier mescaline experiments;
he classified the picture of intoxication as belonging to the 'organic psychosyndrome'

of E. Bleuler. The *importance of self-observation* in 'model psychoses' was, however, recognized, and the evaluation of self-observed experiences by both patients and normal subjects was reconsidered. Their value depends on two factors: the veracity of the subject and his sensitivity for bodily feelings and inner experience. The quality of truthfulness required is, in fact, of a different kind from that needed in external affairs. Moreover, the personal temperament has to be taken into account. Slightly hypochondriacal persons with a certain tendency to introversion are probably the best observers in this field. Probably the worst witnesses in this field are extravert hysterics. If self-observation is to be profitably used in the analysis of the psychological effect of drugs, a basic requirement is the development of an appropriate epistemology, using the knowledge gained by the phenomenological schools of psychology to compile a directory of common sources of error (Mayer-Gross *et al.*, 1959).

In this connexion one must not forget the *introspective origin of most psychological terms*. All our observations on the behaviour of animals, coming under such terms as aggression, fear and rage, are made by observers who have themselves experienced these feelings. It would be impossible to define or explain curiosity, desire of approval, or conflict, on external observation alone. Such concepts as reward and punishment, acceptance and rejection, could not be understood by anyone who had not been in the equivalent emotional situation. The behavioural psychologist, try as he may to avoid anthropomorphic interpretations, cannot do without such terms. Even if he re-defines them, he cannot divest his thinking of the halo of meaning which comes from their introspective origin. If, then, we cannot interpret animal behaviour without using a vocabulary based on psychological experience, we must recognize the fact explicitly.

Attempts to get *quantitative data* from a variety of psychological tests were made on a large scale by Abramson and co-workers (1955 and later). He used volunteers of several kinds, while Isbell (1956) experimented with narcotic addicts. The most interesting result was the appearance of a quickly developing *tolerance*; this became evident after three days of regular medication. When it had fully developed, four times the standard dose did not restore the original vividness of the symptoms. Tolerance was lost as rapidly when the drug was discontinued. Obviously, if the symptoms of the schizophrenic are a response to the elaboration in his metabolism of such a substance, it could not be one which produced such a degree of tolerance (Wikler, 1957).

The discovery of LSD has led to increased interest in other substances with hallucinogenic effects such as harmine, yohimbine, bufotenine, and psilocybin. Many of them were known and used for religious and ceremonial purposes by South American, Mexican and other native peoples over many centuries. Psilocybin, for example, is the active ingredient of teonanacatl, the sacred mushroom which has been in use over many centuries by the Chinatecs and Mezatecs of Southern and Central Mexico as a sacrament in religious ceremonies. A fascinating and scholarly monograph has been devoted by Heim and Wasson (1959) to the morphological characteristics and biological effects of the sacred mushrooms of Mexico and also the profound imprint they have made on the culture and archeology of the peoples who used them.

ANOXAEMIA

The brain is highly sensitive to want of oxygen, however caused. Some of the mental symptoms described in the preceding chapter as associated with anaemia or cardiac failure are probably due to inadequacy in the supply of oxygen to the brain. Carbon monoxide is an example of a poison whose sole immediate action is to cause oxygen lack, which it does by combining with haemoglobin and preventing its oxidation. But even the barbiturates probably owe their action on the nervous system to interference with oxidative processes in the brain cells. The 'anoxic' poisons, which include carbon monoxide, cyanide, carbon bisulphide, barbiturates and anaesthetics such as ether and nitrous oxide, show a consistent tendency to attack certain sites in the brain. These are the cerebral cortex, the basal ganglia and particularly the globus pallidus, the Purkinje cells of the cerebellum, the Sommer sector and the cerebral white matter. The site of the lesions depends to some extent on the dosage of the poison. Thus in cyanide poisoning, massive doses cause lesions mainly in the cerebral and cerebellar cortex, whereas repeated small doses produce bilateral necrosis of the basal ganglia or of the cerebral white matter or both (Hurst, 1944).

But the poisons also show some degree of specificity. The psychological action of drugs has lately become a subject of very general interest, because it may provide a scientific approach to the aetiological problems of psychiatry (Wikler, 1957). Necrosis of the globus pallidus is particularly characteristic of carbon monoxide poisoning, which rarely causes the widespread degeneration of Purkinje cells that often follows anoxia due to anaesthesia (Meyer and McLardy, 1950). However, lesions of the globus pallidus are the most consistent change produced by the anoxic poisons. They may be produced, in addition to carbon monoxide, by potassium cyanide, ether, dinitrobenzol, and by morphine intoxication when this leads to respiratory failure. They have also more recently been described in barbiturate and in carbon bisulphide poisoning. The reasons for the vulnerability of the globus pallidus are not fully understood. It has been suggested (Alexander, 1942) that damage in this region is due to thrombosis of the anterior choroidal artery, which also supplies the cornu ammonis, another structure specially vulnerable to anoxaemia. This is the cerebral vessel with the longest subarachnoid course; it is prone in consequence to become thrombosed during circulatory disturbances. Among the oldest investigations of hypoxia was that conducted by Boycott and Haldane (1908) in a decompression chamber. They showed that a marked decline in mental powers tended to occur with loss of judgement and irrational behaviour as their alveolar oxygen pressure fell below 45.

In *altitude sickness*, which has been fully studied in aviation medicine, the principal symptoms are psychological. It can be observed in mountaineers, although the slow ascent makes adaptation relatively easy. In its dramatic form it occurred in aviators, before the time when oxygen apparatus came to be regularly used, during the rapid ascent to altitudes above 12,000 feet. Considerable individual differences in susceptibility have been found; but above 20,000 feet, when atmospheric pressure is reduced to less than half, and the arterial blood is only 82 per cent. saturated, symptoms become universal.

Perception, thinking and motor responses are impaired without the subject being aware of the inadequacy of his performance. 'The skilled photographer takes eighteen photographs upon the same plate, the pilot makes for a wrong destination or goes to sleep. . . . On return to land a muddled and confused memory of what has happened during the flight is all that remains. Lesser degrees of this condition have led to great errors in judgement, foolhardiness, apparent cowardice and irresponsibility in military aviation. So insensibly does this mental paralysis come on and so deep may be its effect before its presence is realized, that in Tissandier's balloon ascent in 1875, all three aeronauts, though provided with oxygen apparatus, were paralysed beyond movement before realizing the necessity for using it, and two of them lost their lives' (Collier, 1947). Besides lethargy and sleepiness, frontal headache and vomiting are frequent symptoms.

Another example which shows the *loss of interest and initiative* caused by anoxaemia is that of Longstaff. The purpose of his expedition to the Himalayas was to try, by means of the theodolite, to find the highest point by ascertaining the height of the various peaks. He lost interest in his observations and failed to check his results carefully and critically when he was at great heights, so that the figures were of no value upon his return. He failed, therefore, in the main object of his expedition. A third incident happened to Barcroft who related it in his monograph. He had planned to incarcerate himself for a week in a low-pressure chamber. On the fifth day his wife called to see him and asked him about the barometric pressure. He stated that he had been at a simulated altitude of 18,000 feet and was now at 15,000 feet but, 'after all, it made no difference'. His wife realized at once that his judgement of what was important had vanished, and the experiment was ended at that point (Van Liere, 1942). These observations must be qualified however in that it is now known that man can acclimatize to some extent to low oxygen tensions. West *et al.* (1962) have reported that mountaineers, acclimatized at 19,000 feet, could exercise until their alveolar oxygen pressure fell to 25–35 and experienced only severe dyspnoea without adverse mental effects.

Four *stages of anoxia* have been distinguished (Henderson and Haggard, 1927). About one-fifth of atmospheric air is composed of oxygen, which therefore exerts a pressure of 20 per cent. of an atmosphere. When this is reduced to between 16 and 12 per cent. sensory and motor functions may still be unimpaired, but attention and clear thinking require greater effort and muscular co-ordination may be somewhat reduced. If the pressure of oxygen drops further from 14 to 9 per cent., a state resembling alcoholic intoxication is induced; the subject becomes talkative, quarrelsome and emotional, or he may complain of headache and numbness of the limbs. Muscular co-ordination is faulty, but even now perception, memory and judgement may still be well preserved. It has, however, been observed that bruises or burns incurred in this state may remain unnoticed. There is often a feeling of fatigue and a slight respiratory abnormality of the Cheyne-Stokes type. At the third stage, when pressure is reduced to 6 per cent., nausea and vomiting are frequent, as also is an ascending paralysis of the limbs. The subject becomes insensible to stimuli and completely indifferent to his surroundings. At this stage consciousness must be clouded, for after recovery the subject is completely amnesic for this period. If the oxygen pressure drops below 6 per cent., twitching and epileptiform convulsions occur, respiration ceases and the heart stops after six to eight minutes.

Finally it may be of interest to call attention to the ten most common psychological alterations in behaviour which McFarland (1932) reported. These observations were made on members of the International High Altitude Expedition to Chile. In order of frequency, they were as follows: (1) greater effort to carry out tasks, (2) more critical attitude toward other people, (3) mental laziness, (4) heightened sensory irritability, (5) sensitiveness on certain subjects, (6) dislike of being told how to do things, (7) difficulty in concentrating, (8) slowness in reasoning, (9) frequent recurring ideas, and (10) difficulty in remembering. Tune (1964) has reviewed the literature dealing with the effects of hypoxia on sensory function and psychological performance. There is evidence to indicate that there is impairment of critical flicker-fusion threshold, visual sensitivity and auditory acuity, and deterioration in performance in pursuit meter and tracking tasks, in problem-solving and immediate memory tests.

The *cerebral lesions* following prolonged anoxia have been discussed above.

If anoxia is accompanied by *asphyxia* producing a simultaneous accumulation of carbon dioxide, consciousness is lost in the stage at which respiration becomes irregular and shallow.

Such combined effects may be observed after *suicidal attempts by hanging*. Even if the patient is found and resuscitated soon after his act, the prognosis for recovery is usually doubtful; irreversible cerebral damage results from anoxia of only a few minutes' duration. The resuscitated patient may survive for days or weeks, but suffer from choreo-athetotic hyperkinesis, epileptic fits and severe dysmnesia. It has been pointed out (Hutchinson *et al.*, 1964) that the effects produced by a low arterial pO_2 are less marked than would be expected from observations on subjects in a decompression chamber. The reasons for this are that in this latter situation there is hyperventilation, owing to the low pCO_2 which causes cerebral vasoconstriction, thereby potentiating the effects of hypoxaemia. In respiratory failure, however, there is cerebral vasodilation owing to hypercapnia, and this exerts a protective effect by increasing the cerebral tissue oxygen tension for a given level of peripheral arterial pO_2.

Carbon Monoxide Poisoning

Carbon monoxide is produced wherever carbon or its compounds is burnt and combustion is incomplete; combustion outside the body practically always is incomplete, unless the fuel is burnt at a high temperature with a forced draught. Carbon monoxide, produced from slow-combustion stoves, inadequate chimney ventilation, the exhaust gases from petrol engines, blast furnaces, explosions in mines, etc., is the cause of many *domestic and industrial accidents*. Ordinary coal gas contains between 4 and 9 per cent. of CO but some mixtures may contain up to 20 per cent.

As it has 300 times the affinity of oxygen to haemoglobin, it displaces oxygen in the red cells and the main symptoms it produces are those of oxygen lack. The amount of carboxyhaemoglobin formed depends on the concentration in the atmosphere, the duration of exposure, and the respiratory rate of the person exposed. An increase in the temperature, humidity, and carbon dioxide content of the air, or a decrease in the oxygen content, however, will stimulate respiration and hence the amount of CO absorbed will be increased. The formation of carboxyhaemoglobin causes a corresponding reduction in oxyhaemoglobin, but the toxic effects are not entirely due to the anoxaemia brought about by this reduction in the oxygen-carrying power of the blood. The oxygen supply to the tissues is further reduced, because carboxyhaemoglobin interferes with the dissociation of oxyhaemoglobin, and the diminution of the available reduced haemoglobin interferes with the transport of CO_2. Carbon monoxide may also react with other chemically related pigments such as pseudo-haemoglobin, myoglobin, or cytochrome, but it is not certain whether the function of these pigments, or of those found in the brain, is affected by the poison.

The gas has neither smell nor taste, nor can it be seen. People are unaware of its presence, and this is the source of danger. They will often go on working and staying in the room where there is an escape of gas without realizing that, if they feel headache or nausea, it is for that reason.

The *symptoms* produced closely resemble those of a slowly oncoming anoxaemia; lowering of efficiency and of self-control, without insight, leads imperceptibly to loss of consciousness without any intermediate delirium. The driver in a closed motor-car, poisoned by the leakage of exhaust fumes, may behave recklessly or irresponsibly like a drunkard.

Interesting examples are reported by Haldane. An inspector of mines who had been affected by carbon monoxide gas came out of the mine and shook hands cordially with the bystanders, but when the doctor in attendance offered him his arm, he regarded this as an insult and challenged him to a fight. Another case was that of Sir Clement le Neve Foster, who was chief government inspector of mines in Great Britain; he inspected a mine in which a disaster had occurred and became himself a victim of carbon monoxide poisoning. He has given a dramatic account of his experience. He could have walked away from the danger zone, which he himself knew; but he lost his initiative, so that, instead of so doing he sat down and wrote farewell messages, in which he repeated the word 'good-bye', sometimes misspelt, a number of times.

The psychiatrist is chiefly interested in the patients who are *revived after an accident* or attempted suicide. In only about half the cases is there recovery without serious sequelae. The others develop chronic symptoms which may follow directly on the acute intoxication, or after a *free interval* of one to three weeks. Then once again the patient becomes disorientated, his consciousness is clouded, he seems absentminded, confused and amnesic. He complains of headache, giddiness and often of lancinating pains in the extremities, due to neuritis. Not infrequently a Parkinson syndrome develops, with akinesis, rigidity and a mask-like facial expression.

Psychotic pictures of the acute psycho-organic type have been observed, and have a relatively favourable prognosis; recovery may occur even when they have lasted for months. Symptoms of aphasia, apraxia and agnosia are more frequent and have a less satisfactory outcome, because the focal vascular damage to the cortex which has caused them is irreversible. It is important to bear in mind the *late mental symptoms* which can follow carbon monoxide poisoning, when assessing the prognosis in earlier stages.

Treatment of acute poisoning is by the administration of pure oxygen with the aid of an efficient mechanical respirator. It is usual to add 5 per cent. CO_2, but this is contraindicated in cases of respiratory failure. In severe cases hypothermia probably helps to reduce the risk of permanent neurological damage. If respiration has failed, artificial respiration should be administered by the mouth-to-mouth breathing technique and continued in the ambulance until the patient arrives in hospital where a mechanical respirator can be substituted. An exchange transfusion of blood may prove necessary. Cold and all physical exertion should be avoided to minimize tissue demands for oxygen. *Morphine must never be used* as it is a depressant of the respiratory centre. Whatever is done, the danger of a permanent lesion, even if life is restored, is considerable.

The mechanism by which transient and permanent lesions are caused is bound up with the *action of carbon monoxide on the capillaries*. They seem to be especially sensitive, and impairment of their function leads to oedema of the surrounding tissues, haemorrhages and focal necroses, notably in the central nervous system.

Chronic carbon monoxide poisoning has been thought by some workers to result from the cumulative effect of intermittent exposure to carbon monoxide in industry. There is no good evidence that this disorder has an objective physical basis and it will not be further discussed.

INDUSTRIAL INTOXICATIONS
Lead

Like other heavy metals, lead acts on the central nervous system only if a cumulative effect is produced by *absorption over a long period*. Lead is used in many industries, and there is a widespread risk of daily intake of small quantities. Prophylactic measures against the lead poisoning of workers have been taken in all civilized countries and have proved effective. Lead in paint is an important source of danger; droplets may be inhaled in paint-spraying, or when spraying fruit with lead-containing insecticides, and lead on the hands of the work-man may contaminate his food. Lead compounds are easily absorbed from the mucous membranes, either of the respiratory or the alimentary tracts.

Encephalopathic symptoms are rare but may come on in a relatively short time after absorption of the volatile compounds, tri- and tetra-ethyl-lead. The typical picture is that of a confusional state with signs of meningeal irritation, focal signs such as aphasia, transient paresis and convulsions terminating in coma if untreated. In more slowly developing cases the patient manifests a retarded depression, dullness, failure of concentra-tion and memory, headache, deafness, transient speech defect and visual disturbance. The diagnosis may be established with the aid of haematological studies which show a hypochromic anaemia together with punctate basophilia of the red cells. The concentration of lead in the blood is above 1 milligram per 100 ml. The treatment of lead intoxication has been revolutionized by the introduction of chelating agents. The agent generally used is calcium disodium versenate (ethyline diamine tetra-acetate). The lead displaces the calcium and the resulting chelate, which is much less toxic than ionized lead, is excreted by the kidneys. Four to eight daily intravenous injections of 3 g. of calcium EDTA in 600 ml. of 5 per cent. dextrose in distilled water are given over a 2-hour period, and as much as 13 mg. lead may be excreted daily in the urine (Hunter, 1959). Lead intoxication has on rare occasions been found associated with childhood autism or psychosis. Children are said to be especially susceptible, and to react with convulsions and other cerebral symp-toms which, on passing, may leave permanent defects behind (Byers, 1943).

Cyanide

Potassium cyanide is widely used in industry (photography, electroplating, etc.), and hydrocyanic acid gas is generally used for the control of pests and vermin. Furthermore, cyanides are often used for suicide, having the advantages of rapid and certain action. In some States of the U.S.A. hydrocyanic acid gas is the chosen means of executing criminals condemned to death.

When large doses are taken, the patient loses consciousness almost at once (within ten seconds) and dies in convulsions in five minutes. With a smaller but still lethal dose, the symptoms are vertigo, headache, palpitations and drowsiness, followed by severe dyspnoea, loss of consciousness and convulsions. Death is due to asphyxia caused by paralysis of the respiratory centre. Besides its immediate action on the medullary centres, cyanide also interferes with enzymatic oxidative processes in all the tissues of the body.

Fumigation by cyanide gas, as used for the killing of rats, involves dangers for human beings. Unless the odour is observed, the first sensation may be the deceptive one of warmth, caused by vasodilatation. This may be followed by nausea, vomiting and dyspnoea, and later by respiratory paralysis and convulsions. Treatment is the same as for carbon monox-ide poisoning.

Mercury

Workers in the mercury industry, such as those who mine the ore, or who are engaged in the manufacture of mirrors or thermometers, and technicians in laboratories may in the course of time absorb enough of the metal to develop symptoms, as protection against the inhalation of mercury vapour is difficult. The intestinal and excretory systems are the first to be affected; but emotional and other nervous symptoms are frequent. Early ones are fatigue and lassitude; and tremor, irritability, restlessness and insomnia may occur later.

Psychoses seem to be rare, and the picture is rather that of a *neurasthenic reaction* with some excitability, or, in other cases, with timidity, self-consciousness and generalized physical complaints. In acute poisoning, therapy with dimercaprol (BAL) may be life-saving but its value is uncertain in chronic intoxication.

Manganese

Prolonged exposure to dust or fumes in industrial processes involving manganese leads to severe neurological symptoms of the type seen in Parkinson's disease. Degeneration of cells in the large basal ganglia, caudate and lenticular nuclei, and in the thalamus, have been held responsible for these signs; but the lesions may extend to many other parts of the central nervous system. *Psychological disturbances* are often present at the same time: emotional lability, uncontrolled laughing and crying, and impulsive affective outbursts, preceded at an earlier stage by general apathy, languor and sleepiness. If the patient is removed from exposure early, he should recover from the psychological disturbances, but the neurological changes persist (Fairhall and Neal, 1943).

Arsenic

Arsenic and its derivatives are widely used in industry; they are constituents of weed and vermin killers, and were formerly used in the making of paints. Although the main effect of chronic poisoning is on the mucous membranes, the skin, and the haemopoietic system, there is also an effect on the nervous system. From this property is derived the *addiction* of peasants and mountaineers in Styria and some other countries to *arsenious oxide*. Relatively small amounts are taken, once or twice a week; but to maintain the feeling of well-being the dose has to be increased. Addicts become more and more tolerant, and stand severely poisonous doses which would kill a normal person. Although chronic arsenic poisoning may cause peripheral neuritis and neurological symptoms, psychoses are not known to occur.

Other Industrial Poisons

The symptoms of poisoning with *methyl bromide and methyl chloride*, used in the manufacture of refrigerators, are similar to those associated with carbon monoxide. The signs of organic damage may appear some time after the acute intoxication has cleared up, and then only slowly regress (de Jong, 1944). Lesions of the central nervous system causing aphasia, amblyopia and epilepsy have been described.

A number of *solvents*, used in various branches of industry, have a narcotic effect if taken in a large single dose, but if absorbed in smaller amounts over a long time cause pathological changes in the nervous system and nervous and mental disturbances of a serious kind. *Carbon disulphide*, which is important in the rubber industry, but is now also used as a solvent in rayon manufacture, is comparable in its action to chloroform. Chronic poisoning is not infrequent among workers constantly in contact with it. Early symptoms are headache and paraesthesiae in the limbs, vertigo and insomnia. At a later stage signs of organic mental deterioration, loss of memory, apathy, impotence, epileptic attacks, and sometimes transient delirious psychoses (Kraepelin and Lange, 1927) have been observed. *Benzene*, which is widely used as a solvent, may be responsible for severe anaemia, and have effects on the peripheral and central nervous system.

CHAPTER VIII

THE EPILEPSIES

EPILEPTIC seizures are a common event in many forms of psychiatric illness. They are frequent and sometimes diagnostically significant in certain organic cerebral diseases which will be discussed in chapters IX and X of this book; they also may complicate symptomatic psychoses and chemical intoxications and constitute an important item in the practice of child psychiatry (Chapter XI, p. 672). Moreover, induced epileptiform convulsions have become a widely applied therapeutic tool of the psychiatrist. Hence his considerable theoretical and practical interests in the epilepsies. However, in no field of psychiatry is the overlapping with the interests of the neurologist as great as in that of the convulsive disorders. In a treatise on clinical psychiatry it would be inappropriate to discuss at length those features of the disease which are mainly neurological. However, the psychiatric aspects of the epilepsies are so important and their role in the clinical picture and in the treatment of the patient so prominent that the psychiatrist is often first called to deal with the case. Neurological text-books often pay inadequate attention to the psychological symptoms which are our main concern in this chapter.

DEFINITION

'Epilepsy is a paroxysmal and transitory disturbance of the function of the brain which develops suddenly, ceases spontaneously, and exhibits a conspicuous tendency to recur' (Russell Brain, 1951). The disturbance may be very localized and be shown, for instance, in the twitching of a single muscle group or in a single sensory experience in one of the special senses. In such cases there is often no general alteration of consciousness; these cases of focal epilepsy are the subject matter of neurology rather than psychiatry. Disturbance of brain function may, however, be general, and may then be of any degree. At one extreme there is a total loss of consciousness, which may last from a fraction of a second to many minutes; at the other extreme there may be only slight impairment in the power of attention, or a minor mood change.

The symptoms are as varied as the underlying aetiological factors. More and more in historical development has epilepsy, originally regarded as a disease entity, become a symptom of many diseases; however, there still remains today a not inconsiderable number of patients suffering from *'idiopathic'* epilepsy, i.e. from *epileptic symptoms for which no cause is yet known*, other than a presumed constitution, genetic or acquired.

PHYSIOLOGICAL BASIS

The essential quality of an epileptic manifestation is the occurrence of *spontaneous neuronic excitation* at some focus. This may or may not then spread to other neurones. The discharge may be narrowly confined as in the focal epilepsies and the clinical appearances remain focal. It will then be experienced as a transient sensory or motor phenomenon unless it occurs in a silent area of the brain, in which case it will be without clinical effects. The electroencephalograph has in fact shown that many epileptic discharges are subclinical and not felt subjectively, or shown objectively in any alteration of behaviour.

This local discharge may spread and ultimately produce excitation of the subcortical centres concerned in the production of the *generalized electrical disturbances in the brain*; an epileptic seizure or some abrogation of consciousness then follows. It is the ease with which such a diffuse disturbance is generated in the brain that probably constitutes the fundamental difference between the 'idiopathic' epileptic and the normal individual. With adequate stimulation, such as that produced by the passage of a 50-cycle alternating current through the head or by sufficiently severe metabolic stress, a major epileptic fit may be produced in any human being. But whereas the ordinary individual's vulnerability is only made manifest under such extreme conditions, in the idiopathic epileptic the mechanisms regulating generalized cerebral discharge break down spontaneously, possibly under the influence of the everyday metabolic and other stresses which in most people produce no adverse effects.

The *difference between symptomatic and idiopathic epilepsy*, on the other hand, would appear to lie in the fact that in the former the epileptic seizure commences at some focal source in the cortex, and the centres concerned with the detonation of a generalized electrical discharge are activated secondarily. In idiopathic epilepsy these centres, which are probably situated in the upper mid-brain and thalamus, are the primary site of discharge, and there is no 'irritative' cortical focus. Although a specific acquired cause cannot always be demonstrated, it is probable that all cases in which the epileptic fit seems to commence at such a focal source have a similar patho-physiology. It is for this reason that the Moutreal School (Jasper and Kershman, 1949) has made a fundamental distinction between focal abnormalities where these take the form of a spike or sharp wave or well-localized slow wave discharge and abnormalities which are bilaterally synchronous and in which the epileptic discharge is therefore probably 'fired' simultaneously in the two hemispheres from some subcortical midline centre. The distinction between these two types of abnormality has considerable practical significance, since establishment of a diagnosis of focal epilepsy by clinical or physiological evidence or both implies the presence of an acquired local lesion which may be amenable to treatment.

The facility with which a diffuse epileptic discharge may be generated in the brain varies from case to case. This has been ascribed to a *constitutional factor* which plays its part in the pathogenesis of even the symptomatic epilepsies. The existence of such a factor has been demonstrated by Conrad's finding that the monozygotic (MZ) twins of symptomatic epileptics had an enhanced expectation of epilepsy, and by Lennox's observation of identical electroencephalographic patterns in MZ twins, even where one twin had a symptomatic epilepsy and the other was clinically normal. On the other hand, an epileptic predisposition may not become manifest until the occurrence of some minor injury or stress; thus one of a pair of MZ twins who were acrobats in a circus was mildly concussed in a fall and began to suffer from major fits about three months later; both twins had generalized electroencephalographic abnormalities of a similar kind.

The nature of the appearance and spread of an epileptic discharge in the central nervous system appears to be intimately related to changes of a chemical and electrical nature at the cell membranes. The membrane of the nerve cell is encrusted with synaptic knobs, which are the endings of the axons of other neurones. From them chemical transmitter substances are discharged which alter the permeability of the sub-synaptic membrane, and so promote ionic flux between the interior of the cell and its environment. As the result of the electrolytic exchange, electric potentials are set up at the cell membrane. If the resting potential difference across the membrane falls below a certain critical value there is de-polarization (excitatory post-synaptic potential or E.P.S.P.) and an impulse is propagated down the nerve fibre leaving the cell. Whereas some connexions from other cells to the surface of the membrane release a chemical transmitter substance that reduces the potential difference across the membrane and tends therefore to promote a nerve impulse, other connexions, probably by releasing a different chemical transmitter, increase the potential difference across the cell membrane (inhibitory post-synaptic potential or I.P.S.P.) and so cause the cell to fire. In normal conditions large groups of cells do not discharge synchronously, or are prevented from doing so. On the other hand it is characteristic of epilepsy that massive and synchronous discharges do occur. Whether these massive discharges are due to a positive excitation of the cells or to the temporary failure of some mechanism which prevents synchronous discharge is not clear. Either is possible.

Transfer of excitation normally takes place via the synapses and in an orderly way. It is characteristic of epilepsy that the spread of excitation occurs otherwise than along the neuronic pathways involved in physiological responses, so that the events which follow have a disorderly and catastrophic character. The spread may proceed from one area of the cortex to another via relays in deeper structures, or laterally by the subcortical network. However, the abnormality of the epileptic probably lies not in the brain cells as such but in the highly exaggerated tendency towards the synchronization of the activity of distinct groups of cells. *Greatly increased voltage or hypersynchrony* is therefore the most constant feature of the electroencephalogram during a seizure. According to recent work this hypersynchrony would appear to be due to the progressive recruitment of massive dendritic potentials possibly mediated by electrotonic field effects on the dendritic membrane (Ward, 1961).

Gastaut and Fischer-Williams (1959) have reviewed the evidence relating to the spread of abnormal nervous activity in experimentally produced focal epilepsy. From the cortical focus this charge is conducted to the lower part of the brain-stem and thence to the thalamus from which a generalized cortical discharge is then generated through the diffuse projection system. When an extensive area of cortex is involved in a hypersynchronous discharge, the sharply defined mental processes of normal awareness are no longer possible and consciousness is lost. This in turn undermines cortical control of the brain-stem and, as a result of this disinhibition, a discharge arises from the lowest part of the brain-stem initiating the tonic phase of the epileptic fit. The continuous hypersynchronous activity of the cortex now begins to be interrupted by discharges from the caudate nuclei which produce rhythmic interruptions of cortical electrical activity; these correspond to the jerking of the clonic phase. The activity of the caudate nuclei gradually checks cortical activity until cortical control over the medulla is re-established and the convulsive movements gradually die down. In the centrencephalic type of seizure it is suggested that there is a state of hyperexcitability in the thalamus which can thus initiate the course of events described without preliminary discharge from a cortical focus.

The facility of spontaneous excitation or of spread of discharge in the nervous system is greatly affected by *metabolic changes*, most particularly by a change in the alkalinity of the blood. Hyperventilation, by reducing the amount of carbon dioxide in the blood, renders it more alkaline, and in some epileptics this will be sufficient to cause a fit. In other cases, where the spread does not go so far, hyperventilation is so successful in bringing out abnormalities in the electrical rhythm of the brain that it is a device regularly applied by electroencephalographers in the diagnosis of epilepsy. The facilitation of spread is also caused by other changes such as *lowering of the glucose level* in the blood, and the production of a state of *hydraemia*, as by drinking large volumes of fluid. An inverse relationship to the level of attention of the subject is well recognized and is of some importance. Many epileptics suffer attacks only during sleep and many diurnal attacks occur only in moments of boredom or relaxation. Circumstances which increase concentration usually preclude the onset of an attack so that fits are unlikely to occur in dangerous situations. The induction of sleep by means of seconal or pentothal is well known to provoke epileptiform activity in the E.E.G. It is possible that still other changes may have an effect, a conclusion which is suggested by the fact that some female epileptics are particularly liable to fits at a given stage in the menstrual cycle, that epileptics of both sexes tend to have a time of the day or night at which fits are most likely to occur, and that longer rhythms in the recurrence of fits, even annual ones, can be identified. It is in connexion with these longer rhythms that somewhat fanciful theories have been raised to connect the occurrence of fits with the phases of the moon, with season and weather, with sunspots and variations in terrestrial magnetism.

The *electrical changes* which go on in the brain have recently proved susceptible to investigation by the electroencephalograph, which permits their infinitesimally small reflexions in the scalp itself to be picked up and amplified. Direct electroencephalography is also possible by the implantation of wire electrodes in the brain. During an attack of petit mal, the electroencephalogram generally shows a highly specific pattern of activity, the so-called '*wave and spike*' rhythm (Fig. 11). Both components of this complex, which recurs

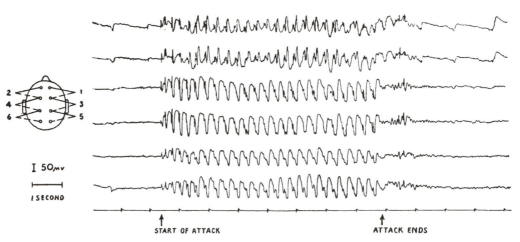

Fig. 11.—E.E.G. during an attack of petit mal, showing typical wave and spike pattern, the complexes occurring at a frequency of 3/sec. Highly intelligent woman of 34 years, whose attacks had commenced at 13. No treatment of avail until she was put on troxidone at the age of 32. In the two years since she has been completely free from attacks, and carries on a normal life.

with a frequency of about three per second, are strictly synchronous in the two hemispheres, and it has been shown experimentally (Jasper and Drooglever-Fortuyn, 1947) that the source of this disturbance may be a deep midline structure; the intralaminar nucleus of the thalamus. The frequent occurrence during the attack of bilateral facial movements such as blinking and faint twitching is in accord with such an origin for the electrical disturbance. In a *major fit*, a crescendo of waves at 8–12 c/s is seen followed by a variable admixture of sharp waves and slow waves. The epileptic discharge involves wide areas of the brain in both types of seizure, but the major fit involves a more profound and sustained abrogation of cortical function. A psychomotor attack is often associated with runs of rhythmic slow waves which vary in frequency in different individuals from three to seven per second; 'sharp' waves are observed in many patients, especially from the temporal lobes.

Epileptics also show *disturbances of normal rhythm* at times other than during the actual occurrence of a fit. These abnormalities are shown by some 60 per cent. of epileptics in seizure-free periods, and the proportion of abnormal records rises to 80 per cent. with the use of special methods of activation such as barbiturate sleep and the injection of subconvulsant doses of Megimide. Some of these disturbances, such as an excess of fast activity or runs of medium- and low-voltage slow waves, are non-specific in that they are present in about 10 per cent. of clinically normal individuals, and must therefore be interpreted with caution. Paroxysmal disturbances of rhythm of the kind shown in Fig. 12 can be seen in the epileptic with greater frequency as the time for an attack approaches; after a major fit, and especially after a series of major fits, the normal rhythm will remain disorganized for a time.

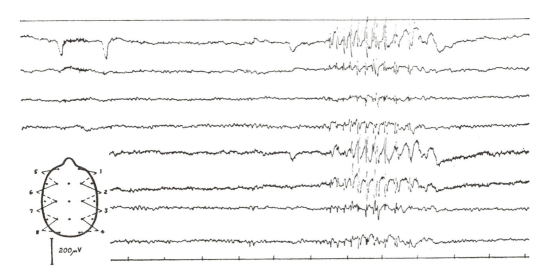

Fig. 12.—Interseizure pattern in male aged 21 years with infrequent grand mal attacks. Suffered from petit mal attacks in childhood. E.E.G. shows bilaterally synchronous and symmetrical paroxysms of frontally predominant irregular spike and wave activity.

Apart from the advance in our understanding which study of these electrical changes provides, they can give information of practical value. They can, for instance, be used to localize the origin of the fit where a tumour or cicatrix is suspected.

INCIDENCE

The relative incidence of centrencephalic and focal epilepsies is differently estimated by different authors. All are agreed that the great majority of epilepsies appearing in the first twenty years of life are centrencephalic, while after this age the proportion due to focal causes rapidly increases. Conrad (1937*a*) in his collection of 553 institutionalized epileptics, diagnosed over half as 'idiopathic' and a further quarter as cases in which hereditary and other factors had each played a role. Only about one-fifth were regarded as purely symptomatic.

The age-adjusted prevalence of epilepsy of all types in the general population has been estimated in a small rural town in the U.S.A. as 3·76 per thousand (Kurland, 1959). In hospital populations in different countries epileptics make up from 3 to 10 per cent. of the total of admissions for mental disorder. An investigation sponsored by the College of General Practitioners (1960) showed that, in England, epileptics numbered about 5 per thousand of the population, and that the prevalence remained steadily around this figure in all age groups.

The incidence is about the same for the two sexes. Infantile convulsions are essentially attacks of epilepsy provoked by febrile illnesses and metabolic upsets in infants whose immature brains appear to be highly susceptible to this form of development. In some cases attacks continue spontaneously throughout life but in the majority increasing maturity is associated with a rise in the threshold to the epileptic process so that no further attacks occur. About *40 per cent.* of epileptics have their first fit between the ages of *one and ten years*, and a further *30 per cent.* between the ages of *ten and twenty years* (see Chapter XI, p. 672). In a survey conducted by Pond, Bidwell and Stein (1960 *a,b*) in fourteen general practices it was found that approximately one-sixth to one-quarter of epileptics suffered from conspicuous psychiatric disorders, and about 10 per cent. were admitted at some time to mental hospital, usually for short periods of investigation and treatment. Amongst the young adult male epileptics in this survey, the number originating in social class V was considerably in excess of expectation. This may reflect a greater tendency to seek medical attention for epilepsy and its complications in the lower social classes or it may suggest a greater hazard of social and psychological maladaptation among epileptics in those classes. It may, however, arise from the greater hazard of malnutrition, infection, violence and poorer obstetric care. The clinical histories of this group of patients showed that they were severely handicapped by the number and severity of fits as well as by their intellectual and personality problems, so that finding and retaining employment was difficult.

AETIOLOGY

Gross interference with brain function, with the appearance of epileptogenic foci and a facilitated spread, may occur during the course of *systemic diseases* such as infections and fevers, intoxications such as uraemia and eclampsia, and interference with the amount or quality of the blood supplied to the brain, as in cardiac decompensation. The main clinical interest attaches to the primary cause, and the fits themselves are relatively unimportant.

Any *local damage* to the brain may set up a focus of abnormal discharge; the symptomatic epilepsy which results in this way is found in infections such as meningitis, cerebral syphilis and, rarely, encephalitis; it is also seen after local vascular damage as in cerebral arteriosclerosis and cerebral thrombosis. *Birth injuries* to the brain especially if combined with asphyxia are fairly commonly followed by epilepsy. Those cases of temporal lobe epilepsy which are associated with areas of gliosis, particularly in the region of the uncus and hippocampus, are believed to result from birth injury of a characteristic kind. Earle, Baldwin and Penfield (1953) gave the name *incisural sclerosis* to this condition and claimed that it accounted for the lesion in two-thirds of their series of cases of temporal lobe seizures.

They consider that during the passage of the infant through the birth canal there is a sharp rise of intracranial pressure which leads to herniation of the hippocampal regions through the incisura of the tentorium cerebelli. The vessels supplying these areas will be dragged through also and if they become compressed against the free edge of the tentorium, the territory of their supply will be infarcted, the nerve cells will die and later be replaced by glial tissue. However the studies of Meyer and his co-workers (Cavanagh and Meyer 1956; Meyer, 1956) suggest that birth trauma is not an exclusive cause of incisural sclerosis; anoxia at birth or at a later age, encephalitis of infancy, minor head injuries, oedema of the brain in the course of acute fever, and the cyanotic stage of infantile convulsions being probably capable of producing an identical effect. Epilepsy is a common sequela of head injury in the adult. Hillbom (1960) reported that 20 per cent. of 2,047 patients with closed head injuries developed epilepsy (diagnosis certain) and a further 11 per cent. developed epilepsy (diagnosis not certain) and attacks of undetermined nature. Landolt (1960) regards the temporal lobe as particularly liable to damage in closed head injuries, both directly and by contrecoup. Epilepsy is even more common if there has been penetration of the dura; Russell (1951) reported an incidence as high as 43 per cent. Cerebral tumour has been regarded as a common cause of epilepsy appearing in adult life. But a study of 141 patients with an onset over the age of 20, and a follow-up of not less than three years, gave an incidence of tumour in only 11 per cent. (Raynor et al., 1959).

A special interest attaches to *reflex epilepsy*. Flashing lights prove to be an effective provoking agent of epileptic seizures in certain susceptible individuals who may suffer attacks of epilepsy at the cinema or whilst watching television. It is this group too who may develop epileptic phenomena whilst driving along a tree-lined avenue in the setting sun. Flicker produced by stroboscopic lamps is used as a method of provoking epileptiform discharges in the electroencephalogram. Pond (1961) quotes Sherwood's description of self-induced epilepsy in a group of children who discovered that they could provoke brief but atypical petit-mal attacks by flickering their fingers before their eyes while they stared at some bright light. A few cases of *acousticogenic epilepsy* have been reported in man, and it has been shown that a musical stimulus can be an adequate cause of a fit. The subject has been well reviewed by Poskanzer (1962) who described an interesting case in which a focal epileptic seizure was invariably initiated by church bells sounding within a discrete frequency range. In animals, especially the rat, it is extremely easy to produce acousticogenic fits, even by such a trifling stimulus as shaking a bunch of keys. The *significance of constitution* is shown here, as the mouse, in contrast to the rat, does not have fits of this kind, and is extremely resistant to attempts of all kinds to cause convulsive seizures. In the rat, again, some strains are much more susceptible than others. Other forms of reflex epilepsy are shown in man in those cases where the cause of the fit can be traced to irritation, e.g. by pressure on a neuroma of a peripheral nerve. An essential aetiological factor is afforded by a constitutional tendency towards the easy spread of the electrical discharge throughout the brain.

A peculiar form of human epilepsy is *myoclonus* epilepsy which was first described by Unverricht. The family studies of Lundborg (1912) have shown it to be due to an autosomal recessive gene. There is some evidence to suggest that a storage process is involved and that the metabolic error is in glycogen metabolism (Edgar, 1963). There are, however, sporadic cases of myoclonus combined with epilepsy which do not appear to have a familial basis.

All these are forms of epilepsy which are based on a gross pathology, or which for other reasons are to be regarded as *symptomatic* in nature. When all such cases are excluded, there still remains a very large group of patients, in whom no local or general pathology can be shown, who show specific hereditary relationships, a constitutional basis, and frequently a course and development which entitle them to description under a single heading—that of *idiopathic epilepsy*. It is possible that, as some workers think, this group will go out of existence entirely when the causal agents producing epilepsy become better known. There is no doubt that the number of patients assumed to be suffering from idiopathic epilepsy has been reduced; but it is probable that it will be a long time before the concept can be abandoned.

Heredity

Many workers, investigating the parents, sibs and children of epileptics, have estimated the expectation of epilepsy in each of these groups as 3 to 6 per cent. The incidence of epilepsy in the general population has, in most countries, been found to be about one-tenth of this.

Support for the genetical contribution to the aetiology of epilepsy has come, above all, from the study of twins. The classic work in this field was that of Conrad (1937 *a,b*). Among monozygotic twin partners of epileptics twenty out of thirty were themselves epileptic; but if only the 'idiopathic' epileptics were taken, the concordance was 19/22 or 86 per cent. Closely comparable figures have been found by Rosanoff, Handy and Rosanoff (1934), by Lennox (1947, 1951, 1954) and most recently by Inouye (1960). In Conrad's material, which was published in detail, there were striking resemblances within twin pairs in age of onset, type of fit, and course and outcome; a good deal of clinical similarity within pairs is also reported by Inouye, least marked in the exogenous cases.

Investigations into the incidence of epilepsy in the first-degree relatives of epileptics have been carried out in recent years by Conrad in conjunction with his twin studies, by Alström (1950), Ounsted (1952), Lennox (1951) and Harvald (1954). Alström differed from other workers in finding relatively low expectations of epilepsy among first-degree relatives; 1·3 per cent. in parents, 1·5 per cent. in sibs, and 3·0 per cent. in children. Moreover, the expectations among relatives were much the same whether one proceeded from probands with epilepsy of unknown causation, or of probably or certainly known cause. He failed to confirm a raised incidence of psychopathy, criminality, etc., among the relatives of epileptics, which had been found by Conrad. The interesting aspect of Ounsted's work, based on 337 epileptic children, was the high incidence of epilepsy (11 per cent.) in the sibs of the probands, and the lack of any sharp distinction between clinical types of epilepsy, the strength of the hereditary factor seeming to vary quantitatively. He quoted the opinion of Russell: 'It is simpler to think of all people as epileptics, and regard the matter as one of threshold.'

Harvald's careful study made extensive use of the E.E.G. He started with 237 epileptics of whom 203 were diagnosed as 'cryptogenic'. The incidence among first-degree relatives of the cryptogenic cases was about equal for parents and children at 4·2 per cent. E.E.G. abnormalities were commonest among the relatives of probands with marked non-focal abnormalities (males 10 per cent., females 18 per cent.) and were rarest in the relatives of probands with focally abnormal E.E.G.s. Harvald considered the hereditary factor was most probably multifactorial and additive in nature, though in individual families a single dominant or recessive gene might be responsible. He would be inclined to suppose that the hereditary predisposition showed itself partly in a tendency to produce spontaneous cerebral paroxysmic discharges, and partly in a tendency for spontaneous discharges to spread with more than average facility. Only the former of these two tendencies would be recognizable on the E.E.G.

In recent years, accordingly, the opinion has tended to prevail that the genetical basis of the hereditary component in epilepsy was polygenic (multifactorial) in nature. In his recent review of the field, Koch (1963) has taken this view. On *a priori* grounds the hypothesis seems a most convincing one. The capacity to produce an epileptic discharge is part of normal human physiology. On that basis alone it is likely to have a normal adaptive function. In addition, as we shall see (p. 462) there is strong clinical support for the view that, in certain psychophysical states of the brain, ictal discharges have a homeostatic effect and help to preserve normal psychological function. It would seem then that variation in the ease with which a spontaneous discharge is produced, and its tendency to spread, must be quantitative, and therefore multifactorially based. However, we can be sure that the epilepsies are aetiologically heterogeneous, with exogenous factors playing a major role in some cases, a minor role in others. Room is left for the operation of single genes in some syndromes.

A possibility of this kind has been brought close by the work of Metrakos (1963) which was focused on the E.E.G. investigation of parents and sibs of patients with centrencephalic epilepsy, compared with the relatives of normal controls. The hereditary syndrome was found to be, not the occurrence of overt seizures, but the existence of a centrencephalic type of E.E.G., a constitutional trait which could well be combined with psychiatric normality. The manifestation of this trait was age-determined. Under the age of $2\frac{1}{2}$ only one out of 16 sibs of centrencephalic probands showed the trait; between the ages of $4\frac{1}{2}$ and $16\frac{1}{2}$ the trait was shown by 65 out of 146 sibs, i.e. 45 per cent.; and at later ages the incidence of the trait tapered off until after the age of $40\frac{1}{2}$ it was found in only one of 40 persons. Metrakos proposes the hypothesis that the centrencephalic trait is a manifestation of a dominant autosomal gene, with penetrance very low at birth, rising rapidly to nearly 100 per cent., and then dropping gradually to zero. This hypothesis is important and suggestive, but awaits confirmation.

ASSOCIATIONS

Although the epileptic is subject to psychotic manifestations which will be described on a later page, there is no close association between epilepsy and the endogenous psychoses. Needless to say, epileptic fits may readily occur during the course of such organic psychoses as general paresis or cerebral arteriosclerosis, but this is of comparatively little clinical interest. Whether there is an association between epilepsy and schizophrenia, positive or negative in sign, or of zero magnitude, has been a greatly vexed question of much historical interest. It was on the assumption that the combination of the two psychoses was rarer than the product of their separate frequencies that Meduna was led to try the therapeutic effect on schizophrenia of convulsions induced by the injection of camphor. There is, however, no ground to think that fewer than 0·5 per cent. of schizophrenics have at some time had epileptic fits, or that fewer than 0·8 per cent. of epileptics develop a schizophrenic psychosis. Despite its eventual useful results, Meduna's innovation was probably theoretically ill-founded.

On the other hand, it seems probable that certain schizophrenic psychoses can bring about epileptic fits. Epileptic fits appearing in chronic deteriorating schizophrenia are far from uncommon, and may be found in many mental-hospital records. In more recent schizophrenias, abnormal and epileptiform E.E.G.s are found in a significantly high proportion of cases, especially in an acute phase (Hill, 1948). Clinical and E.E.G. phenomena of an epileptiform type are particularly associated with catatonic states. The converse relationship, the tendency of some basically epileptic conditions, especially temporal lobe epilepsy, to produce schizophrenia-like psychotic states, is fairly well established (Landolt, 1960; Slater, Beard and Glithero, 1963), and these symptomatic schizophrenias are discussed on page 470.

The association between *epilepsy and mental defect* is a closer one. It cannot be wholly explained by the finding that organic injuries and processes in the infant and the child may be the cause of both epilepsy and mental defect. There is, almost certainly, some causative factor in common between idiopathic epilepsy and mental deficiency. From his investigations Lennox (1942) showed that the incidence of epilepsy in the relatives of epileptics differed in the three classes of epileptics, those mentally defective from birth, those normal at birth but subsequently deteriorated, and those who had been born normal and had remained of normal intelligence. In the first group it was 6 per cent., in the second 3 per cent. and in the third 2·4 per cent. Other figures he provides also support his hypothesis of a genetical relation between the two conditions. However, it appears to be the case that, in testing the intelligence of epileptics, the more random the sample the more closely does the mean intelligence approach the normal average. Low intelligence is much more frequent in the symptomatic than in the idiopathic case.

A genetical relation between *epilepsy and migraine* is also fairly well established. The numerous investigations quoted by Kinnier Wilson (1935) show a raised incidence of convulsive disorders among the relatives of the migrainous, and a similarly raised incidence of migraine among the relatives of the epileptics. The factual evidence seems to be unequivocal, although Wilson himself was inclined to doubt its cogency. Selby and Lance (1960) found the E.E.G. to be abnormal in 30 per cent. of 459 patients with migraine who were studied in a headache-free interval. Camp and Wolff (1961) describe the abnormalities as consisting usually of episodic diffuse 4–7 cycles per sec. activity, but patients with focal mental disturbances commonly showed theta or delta foci usually localized to the appropriate region.

By far the most important psychiatric association of epilepsy, as well as the one most difficult to interpret, is with *psychopathic personality* (see Chapter III, p. 139). As in the case of the association with schizophrenia, accidental factors enter the situation. Epilepsy itself, after some years of duration, frequently causes an alteration of character; this is described on a later page. But in addition, many epileptics, even before the onset of overt fits, show disorders of personality, particularly more or less frequent episodes of aggressiveness, impulsiveness and moodiness, which may be regarded as mild psychomotor equivalents. Such behaviour may become habitual. Even more importantly, psychopathy of personality seems to be frequent among the relatives of epileptics. Conrad (1937a), investigating institutionalized epileptics, found in a large collection of their children a criminality rate four times that found in the general population, and a raised incidence of suicide, especially of forms of suicide which indicated an act committed in a sudden change of mood. He found no indication of an excess of persons with personality traits of pedantry, bigotry, or perseverative qualities ('*Klebrigkeit, Haften*'). The distribution of occupations indicated a shift towards the lowest level of unskilled workers. The psychopathic types who were present with increased frequency were the explosive and those of unstable mood. They, however, were so frequent that Conrad concluded that their presence in the families of epileptics could be regarded as a point of diagnostic significance for hereditary idiopathic epilepsy. Alström was unable to support Conrad's findings; and Pond (1957) has thrown a good deal of doubt on the existence of any close association between epilepsy on the one side, and psychopathic personality, suicide and crime on the other.

Finally, the association between *epilepsy and hysterical symptoms* should not pass without mention. There are some features in common between a hysterical disturbance of consciousness or a hysterical fit and the corresponding epileptic phenomenon. Yet there are seldom any serious difficulties in diagnosis. A more interesting fact is that epileptics are at times liable to disturbances which closely resemble hysterical ones, and even to undoubtedly hysterical mechanisms. It is probably true that, as with many chronic organic conditions, the long persistence of an epilepsy can encourage the changes on which a hysterical alteration of personality, and an enhanced susceptibility to hysterical symptoms, can arise.

CLINICAL MANIFESTATIONS

Epilepsies may be divided into the two broad groups, generalized and focal. In the former, described by the Montreal group as centrencephalic epilepsy, extensive areas of both hemispheres are simultaneously activated by the epileptic discharge from some midline centre, probably in the thalamus. In the latter, the epileptic discharge is initiated from a localized epileptogenic area, from which the spread may be limited or extensive. In either group the seizures may be major or minor.

Generalized or Centrencephalic Epilepsy

In the major seizure there is no aura, the convulsions are generalized from the first, and the E.E.G. shows no focal abnormality. The clinical features of the minor seizures are those of the petit mal triad. The E.E.G. in these cases shows the bilaterally synchronous 3/sec. wave and spike pattern.

Although the major seizure may come unheralded, there are often prodromata which may precede the attack by hours, rarely by days. They are in the form of mood changes (see p. 466), restlessness, headache, and even gastrointestinal and autonomic changes and skin eruptions.

The convulsive stage begins suddenly without aura. The patient sometimes emits a high-pitched scream and falls to the ground if erect. Immediately his whole musculature goes into a powerful tonic spasm. This is often slightly asymmetrical, causing the head and eyes to be rotated to one or other side, while the trunk is turned slowly in the same direction. The upper limbs are held close to the body, the elbows straight and wrists flexed, the fingers driven into the palms, with thumbs adducted. The lower limbs extend, with inversion of the feet and flexion of toes. The trunk muscles are involved in the generalized spasm, respiration ceases, and the face becomes livid. The pupils dilate and become inactive; the eyes are insensitive to touch.

After some 10–30 seconds a partial relaxation of the musculature occurs followed at once by a return of the spasm. Violent jerks then convulse the body in increasingly rapid succession and blood-stained froth exudes from the mouth. Emptying of the bladder or bowel, and less often of the seminal vesicles, may occur. The intervals between the jerks lengthen, and cyanosis intensifies. The clonic stage is brought to an end with a final violent jerk and after a few moments of flaccidity, breathing is re-established. The patient then passes insensibly, or after a few minutes of returning consciousness, into a deep sleep. Deep reflexes are usually absent, and there is often an extensor plantar response during the fit and for a short period after it.

In the fit itself, whether major or minor, complete abrogation of consciousness is expected by the clinician and is the most typical occurrence. A fact, however, which is often forgotten is that in some forms of epileptic seizure *total loss of consciousness need not occur*. Quoting Gowers, Symonds (1948) has said that the effect of an epileptic attack on the stream of consciousness may vary from complete interruption of its flow to a mere ruffling of the surface. French clinicians, especially Marchand (1948), have made a special study of epileptic attacks with preserved memory and with almost undisturbed clearness of consciousness. This is relevant to any consideration of the *psychiatric manifestations of epilepsy*; for in these we also find all shades of disturbance, most frequently, but by no means always, complete unconsciousness; in almost every case there is some evidence of impairment or alteration of consciousness. However, partial or complete preservation of consciousness is a feature of the focal attack, especially the temporal lobe attack, rather than of any seizure associated with centrencephalic epilepsy.

If there has been complete abrogation of consciousness, there will of course be amnesia for the events of the fit, often extending slightly in a retrograde direction. Even if loss of consciousness has not been complete, there can still be a complete amnesia, or on the other hand recollection may be partially or totally preserved. The commonest sequela is for the patient to fall asleep. *Sleep* may be unusually deep, and may itself be the cause of accidents. *Headache* is another very common sequela, and may persist even after waking from the post-epileptic sleep. As a rule, once the patient has wakened from sleep, consciousness is fully recovered. If sleep does not occur, however, or if it is postponed, phenomena of psychological interest may be seen. *Some degree of confusion* can nearly always be elicited. The patient will be disorientated, and even may not be clearly aware of his own identity. Rambling and disjointed talk may be observed, perhaps with definite paraphasias. The patient is likely to be restless, to want to get up and go out without any ascertainable purpose, or to fidget with the objects around him in a manner reminiscent of 'occupational delirium'. *Post-epileptic automatisms* may be of very varying degrees of complexity, from the short burst of purposeless running, to apparently conscious and well-controlled behaviour. The patient may, for instance, unbutton his trousers to micturate at the side of the road, or may pick up an object in a shop and walk out with it, regardless of the impression made on bystanders. *Explosions of irritability* and anger are not infrequent, and the patient may make violent aggressive attacks on the people around him. The emotional storm and aggressiveness may amount to such a degree as to justify the name of *epileptic furor;* and epileptic patients are in these episodes the most dangerous of all those in the disturbed wards of a mental hospital. For those who have had experience of the therapeutic convulsion, the phenomena observed after an electrically induced fit may be significant for the diagnosis of the underlying illness. Thus, there is very often an emergence of concealed symptoms; and the depressed patient may reveal himself as paranoid, hostile, and in the course of a few minutes, an unmistakable schizophrenic.

The minor form of generalized epileptic seizure is *petit mal*, which was recognized in ancient times and named the 'absence' by Calmeil (1824).

It is the most subtle form of epileptic attack of short duration and lasts only from one to a few seconds. There are no premonitory symptoms. 'The subject loses consciousness entirely and remains immobile; he does not hear or see; he is completely "absent" from his surroundings (eclipse of consciousness). His glance is fixed and vague; his face pale. If the attack occurs while he is doing something, he stops; if he was speaking, he becomes mute. The muscular tone, in this simple form, is not modified or only slightly diminished. Sometimes, the subject holds his breath. One does not note any twitching or disorder of language, but sometimes there is trembling and a few drops of saliva trickle from the mouth' (Marchand and Ajuriaguerra, 1948). The E.E.G. has shown that two other types of attack are closely allied to this typical form of petit mal. In the *akinetic seizure* which usually lasts only a few seconds, there is a sudden loss of muscle tone as a result of which the head slumps forward and the patient may fall to the ground. Almost immediately afterwards he seems fully conscious and is able to get up. Another type is that of *myoclonic seizure* common in children (Fig. 13). These three kinds of attack have been named by Lennox (1945) the *petit mal triad*. Not only do they all show *wave and spike activity* but the seizures are also frequent, brief, sensitive to changes in acid-base balance, oxygen lack and alterations in blood-sugar in each case. All are resistant to the usual anticonvulsants but respond to troxidone (see Treatment, p. 478).

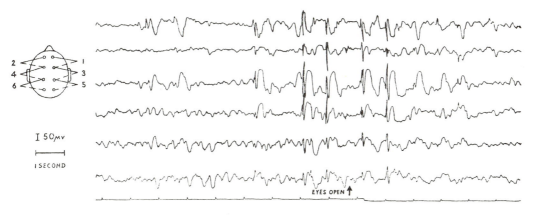

FIG. 13.—E.E.G. in a boy of 5 subject to attacks of myoclonus and also of grand mal. The spike and wave complexes are slower and less regular than those in Fig. 11. The record is asymmetrical, the discharges being of higher voltage on the right side. These features in the spike and wave discharge are often associated with an organic aetiology. In his myoclonic attacks, the child would jerk his shoulders, head and neck, and look dazed, or fall to the ground as a result of sudden clonic contraction of all four limbs. Unexpected noises would make him turn round and round, and he was also subject to attacks of compulsive running. In typical myoclonus complexes would be faster and symmetrical.

PETIT MAL STATUS. This is a condition sui generis, and is one form of twilight state. The E.E.G. shows continuous spike and wave complexes, and the mental state is one bordering on stupor. The patient sits or lies apathetically where he is, making no attempt at spontaneous activity. He can be partially aroused, but is extremely retarded, lifeless in affect, and dull of comprehension; both speech and action show marked perseveration. In most cases there is very little in the way of mental content during these states, and when the patient comes round he has nothing to tell. However, this is not always the case. One of our patients was subject to twilight states lasting a few days to a week about once every three months, in which he would see Christ descending from his cross surrounded by his angels, and would hear the voice of God. All that his wife observed was that he would become slow and sit in a corner in a dull and unresponsive state. While in hospital for investigation the patient passed into one of these phases. Though dull and very retarded, rational responses were to be obtained; but the interview of one day was forgotten by the next day. During the whole of this state there was a continuous recurrence of petit mal rhythms.

The great majority of cases of idiopathic epilepsy have absences on one or another occasion. Sometimes the patients deny having absences because they have no realization and recollection of them. Attacks of petit mal may be the only symptom of epilepsy as, for example, in *pyknolepsy* of children, which consists only of absences occurring daily in large numbers (see Chapter XI, p. 673).

Focal Epilepsy

In the major attacks of focal epilepsy one or more localizing features are found: transient psychological, sensory or motor symptoms, constituting the '*aura*' which normally lasts a few seconds; focal symptoms, such as twitching of some part of the body, sniffing, chewing or lip-smacking movements; a focal paroxysmal discharge in the E.E.G. preceding the generalized hypersynchrony of the convulsion.

When the aura occurs by itself it may be regarded as a minor focal seizure. Motor phenomena are common: clonic jerkings of a limb with or without a Jacksonian march, vocalization, masticatory movements, or adversion of the head and eyes. Visceral sensations may show as a simple epigastric sensation, or a 'rising sensation' beginning in the epigastrium.

It is important to be familiar with the variety of phenomena which may constitute the aura preceding the epileptic seizure because the aura may be for a long time *the only symptom* of the illness. By its fleeting nature and short appearance it is liable to be overlooked till one day the first major fit appears and clarifies the diagnosis. Similarly, when the major fit is suppressed by medication, the aura may remain as the only symptom of the epileptic illness.

The difference between the aura and the transient seizure is one of degree, although as the aura is very short and consciousness is not wholly lost it is often remembered whereas the seizure is not. An interesting experience, related to the aura, is the patient's conviction that he sometimes can suppress the oncoming seizure by voluntary effort. This is frequently reported and appears to have some objective foundation.

The *localizing value of the aura* for indicating the focus from which the epileptic discharge arises is very important. In 222 out of 259 patients with focal epilepsy, Penfield and Kristiensen (1951) determined the localization of the initial epileptic discharges. In 125 cases the aura was reproduced by stimulation of the appropriate area of cortex and in 97 patients the localizing significance of the aura was confirmed by finding localized lesions or by the results of electrocorticography. Observations and stimulation experiments by Penfield have suggested that an aura of hallucinations or 'dreamy state' may point to a focus in the temporal lobe, that imposed and impulsive thoughts point to the posterior part of the frontal lobes and that the recollections of special situations of the past point to the lateral and superior surfaces of the temporal lobes.

TEMPORAL LOBE ATTACKS. By far the most common form of focal epileptic discharge shows up on the E.E.G. in the region of the temporal lobes, on one or both sides, and either on the convexity or through sphenoidal leads. Clinically, this is associated with 'psychomotor' attacks, which can be contrasted with the 'psychoparetic' attacks of generalized epilepsy. The condition is a common one, and bulks increasingly largely in out-patient clinics with samples of epileptics of increasing age. Characteristic of the condition is the immense variability of the picture from patient to patient, and the fixity and stability of what is experienced by the individual patient in every one of his attacks. Only gradually over the passage of years do the symptoms change much in any one patient. The nature of the E.E.G. changes which take place during an attack has not been fully established. Landolt (1960) has described normalization of the E.E.G. as the usual change. This is certainly seen in the early stages of many attacks although in others a gradual progressive extension of rhythmic slow activity over the greater part of the cerebral cortex runs parallel with the development of the attack. The temporal lobe epileptic syndrome is of great significance to psychiatry, not least because of the frequency with which it is associated with psychotic states. These are discussed below.

The psychomotor attack (temporal lobe attack, twilight attack) is a disturbance of mental functioning, not always amounting to impairment of consciousness, of short duration, usually accompanied by motor automatisms, vegetative symptoms and disturbance of behaviour and speech; hallucinatory experiences and abnormal mental experiences of other kinds are common, and certainly are much commoner accompaniments of this type of epilepsy than of any other. An ictal focus in a temporal lobe will be demonstrable with sufficiently careful and repeated investigation.

Of these vegetative symptoms the most distinctive when it appears as an aural symptom is a peculiar sensation in the epigastrium which is felt to rise towards the throat at which point consciousness is usually lost. Such phenomena are often associated with foci in the region of the Sylvian fissure and Island of Reil. The epigastric and rising sensations are frequently accompanied by an emotion of dread which may, however, be independent or accompany other abnormal mental phenomena. Also very distinctive are the *déjà vu* and the *déjà vécu* experiences; these are often coupled with other falsifications of memory or imposed recollections e.g. of the first epileptic fit, or the panoramic memory of the patient's whole life appearing in a flash (Wilson, 1935). Other experiences closely linked with these are the uncanny feelings of change in the outer world or in the self, derealization, *depersonalization* and disturbances of the body image. If these mental experiences are very vivid, they may take on the character of an illusion; visual illusions are the commonest, and may consist in seeing people as distorted, flattened, or elongated or as only half figures. *Forced ideas* experienced like passivity phenomena in schizophrenia have been described; for instance the idea of eternity or infinity may suddenly present itself to the patient, or a storm of indescribable thoughts may race through his mind. An *affective aura* is common and the description given of this aura by the Russian writer Dostoievsky suggests commencement of excitation in a temporal lobe focus: ' . . . a feeling of happiness which I never experience in my normal state and of which I cannot give the idea . . . complete harmony with myself and with the whole world'. Sudden feelings of despair, guilt, anxiety and terror may form the content of the aura in other cases. Premonitions of death, of the end of the world, basic religious or philosophical doubts, suicidal and aggressive urges also have been described.

Illusions and hallucinations are relatively common. Visual hallucinations may be unformed or present as figures or scenes complete to the last detail. Auditory hallucinations may present as primitive sounds of buzzing, drumming or jangling bells; these occur with foci in the first temporal gyrus and are often accompanied by vertigo. If the focus is more posterior the hallucinations take the form of voices, snatches of song, or fragments of music.

From the uncal region arise olfactory auras often of an unpleasant character and the rare gustatory aura is associated with discharges in the same region.

Vestibular experiences, which may be regarded as either illusions or hallucinations, are distinctive of a temporal lobe focus; if felt as vertigo, it is said that there is usually no nausea. Olfactory and vestibular experiences are most suggestive of a temporal lobe, auditory sensations are less so; and there is no way of distinguishing temporal lobe from occipital lobe visual illusions and hallucinations.

In these attacks clouding of consciousness is variable in degree. Where there is no more than an experience of *déjà vu*, or forced thinking, there may be no lowering of the level of consciousness at all, though one might say that its span is narrowed. Hallucinations may also occur in an apparently completely lucid state. In psychomotor attacks of a duration of a minute or so there is likely to be partial abrogation of consciousness with motor automatisms, such as masticatory movements of the jaws or tongue; or the patient may exhibit semi-purposeful movements, fumbling in his pockets, passing his hand over his face, perhaps trying to light a cigarette without a match, or wandering vacantly across the room as if looking for something. He may appear anxious and behave in a resistive manner; there is no response to commands. A subsequent amnesia is common but on the other hand recollection may be partially and even totally preserved. It is common for the patient with psychomotor epilepsy to have also more or less frequent attacks of grand mal; these are often followed by post-epileptic automatism. A fuller description of the mental picture in temporal lobe focal damage will be found in the following chapter (p. 494). Meyer-Mickeleit (1953) who collected seventy-two cases of temporal lobe epilepsy found the majority to be patients of higher age, many of them suffering from symptomatic epilepsy due to trauma, tumour and encephalitis. There was, however, also a small number of patients in whom the epilepsy was familial and no organic causation could be elicited. Barslund and Danielsen (1963) have described three pairs of monozygotic female twins, in which each member of the pair suffered from temporal lobe epilepsy, with further cases in the family in every case. It would be unsafe to suppose that every case of focal epilepsy was of exogenous causation.

SIMULATION OF TEMPORAL LOBE ATTACKS IN NEUROTIC ILLNESS. It has been known for some time (Antoni, 1946) that the central features of the 'dreamy state', namely symptoms of depersonalization and derealization and closely associated *déjà vu* experiences, may be simulated by a patient suffering from emotional disturbances. The resemblance becomes especially close where there are other features present which were described by Hughlings Jackson as characterizing epilepsy, namely 'paroxysmal' nature of the attacks and 'defect of consciousness'. Some degree of overlap between the symptomatology of temporal lobe epilepsy and neurotic disturbances is likely since dissociation or dimming of consciousness is prone to occur in states of extreme fear and transient bouts of emotional disturbance will at times appear paroxysmal and thus raise the possibility of 'ictal anxiety' or 'ictal depression'. In the phobic anxiety-depersonalization syndrome the problem of differential diagnosis from temporal lobe epilepsy arises in a proportion of cases partly owing to the relatively frequent attacks of syncope in this condition but also because transient bouts of panic, visceral discomfort, depersonalization and *déjà vu* experiences are common.

Harper and Roth (1962) compared the clinical features of 30 patients with temporal lobe epilepsy and 30 suffering from the phobic anxiety-depersonalization syndrome. There were similarities and differences between the two disorders. Thus depersonalization, *déjà vu* experience, distortion of perception, hallucinations, paroxysmal attacks of fear and disturbances of consciousness of some kind were found in both types of disorder. Episodic mood disturbances (mainly in the form of acute panic in the neurotic cases) showed no significant difference in frequency in the two conditions. Moreover six of the epileptic patients had phobic symptoms similar to those of the neurotic cases. As was to be expected, self-injury and incontinence of urine or faeces were significantly commoner in, though not wholly confined to, the epileptics. Thus an anxious patient would occasionally faint with a full bladder and then void urine. Episodic disturbances of speech and automatic behaviour were largely confined to the epileptics while emotional triggers for attacks were far commoner in neurotics.

A number of the more important differences in the family and previous medical and personal history of the two groups are tabulated below; the difference in the aetiological basis of the two conditions is clear. The emotional disturbance, 'agoraphobic' symptoms and unreality feelings dominated the picture in the neurotics and disturbances of consciousness were rare and not disabling whereas, in the epileptics, fits were the central feature of the illness, emotional disturbance being less conspicuous. The pre-morbid personality of the neurotic cases was significantly more often marked by features of immaturity and dependence. Moreover, all the epileptic cases were readily identifiable by the consistent and orderly march of events in the course of a temporal lobe seizure in contrast with the far more inconsistent and variable course followed by attacks culminating in panic, syncope or bouts of neurotic depersonalization. Finally, as can be seen from the table on the next page, in the majority of epileptics the E.E.G. was abnormal whereas most of the neurotics had normal records. More detailed E.E.G. studies would almost certainly have widened this gap. Yet the small group of cases of phobic anxiety-depersonalization states with abnormal E.E.G.s are of some importance in clinical practice for, although the

THE PREVIOUS HISTORY IN 30 CASES OF THE PHOBIC ANXIETY-DEPERSONALIZATION SYNDROME (P.A.D.S.) COMPARED WITH 30 CASES OF TEMPORAL LOBE EPILEPSY (T.L.E.)

	P.A.D.S.	T.L.E.	*	P(df = 1)
Family History				
Family history of epilepsy	3	5	n.s.	
Family history of neurosis	10	2	s.	<0·05
Previous Medical History				
Severe birth trauma, prolonged anoxia or head injury with loss of consciousness	—	16	s.	<0·01
Meningitis, encephalitis, mastoiditis	—	6	s.	<0·05
Migraine	12	2	s.	<0·01
Personal History				
Phobias in childhood	18	8	s.	<0·02
Other neurotic traits in childhood	17	10	n.s.	
Failure or maladjustment at school	4	4	n.s.	
Unstable work record	9	4	n.s.	

* Statistical significance of difference.

abnormality is never specifically epileptic, it is on occasion sufficiently striking to suggest possible organic disease. Only rarely does a differential diagnosis between neurotic disturbance and temporal lobe epilepsy give rise to great difficulty. But in cases in which the issue remains in doubt after detailed clinical and laboratory investigation and a period of observation only *specifically epileptic abnormalities in the E.E.G.* should be allowed to decide the issue in favour of temporal lobe epilepsy. Many such patients suffer from neurotic illness.

THE ELECTROENCEPHALOGRAPHIC FINDINGS IN 23 CASES OF THE PHOBIC ANXIETY-DEPERSONALIZATION SYNDROME (P.A.D.S.) AND 30 CASES OF TEMPORAL LOBE EPILEPSY (T.L.E.)

	P.A.D.S.	T.L.E.
Normal	16	1
Mild non-specific abnormality	5	3
Abnormal, probably pathological	2	11
Epileptic	—	15

States of Longer Duration and Epileptic Psychoses

These are most conveniently classified into those which occur in a state of clouded consciousness, and those which occur in clear consciousness. The distinction, however, is to some extent an arbitrary one, as a minimal clouding or change of consciousness is much more common than can easily be demonstrated clinically.

In the first group we have petit mal status (p. 457), psychomotor attacks and automatisms, twilight states, fugues and furors, and confusional states with paranoid ideas. In the second group we have epileptic mood changes, epileptic personality changes and chronic paranoid psychoses. The more important of these sub-groups will be separately considered, but it must be remembered that they tend to merge into one another. Thus mood changes are particularly common in epileptics showing personality changes; and patients with chronic paranoid psychoses, even those which most closely simulate a schizophrenia, usually show some sign of personality change or intellectual impairment.

The electroencephalographic relationships of all these conditions are still not completely clarified. Petit mal status is the only one to have a characteristic E.E.G. The other types of disturbance occurring in clouded consciousness show less specific E.E.G. changes, though the E.E.G. is nearly always abnormal, and shows more generalized slow-wave activity than in the same patient in a lucid state. The connexion with focal abnormality in one or both temporal lobes is probably close: psychomotor attacks and automatisms are almost certainly caused by temporal lobe epilepsy, and probably also most twilight states. The causation of confusional states with paranoid ideas, often religiose, is not known, but is again attributed to temporal lobe epilepsy by Pond (1957).

PSYCHOMOTOR ATTACKS AND AUTOMATISMS, TWILIGHT STATES AND FUGUES. An important principle has been enunciated by Landolt (1960) on the basis of observations which are confirmed by many others (Kammerer, Alajouanine, etc.). This is the concept of 'forced normalization'. Extending over the duration of certain types of twilight state, it is found that ictal frequencies disappear from the E.E.G., and, in comparison with the previous and succeeding dysrhythmia, the E.E.G. becomes relatively or completely normal. It has been suggested that the excessive excitement of these twilight states is related to hyperactivity of the waking centre in the reticular substance of the brain-stem. It is supposed that there is a reciprocal functional antagonism between temporal lobe structures and the reticular substance, and that activity in the latter tends to inhibit ictal waves and epileptic attacks. The suggestion accords well, of course, with the frequency with which epileptic attacks occur in the half-waking state or in sleep, and the great rarity with which they occur in states of heightened attention and awareness. The hypothesis is supported by experimental evidence (Magoun, 1958) which goes to show that stimulation in the neighbourhood of the reticular substance in the brain-stem tends to desynchronize spontaneous brain electrical activity, and also diminishes the recruiting response. It is thought, then, that normalization of the E.E.G. is a response on the part of the healthy brain to the occurrence of ictal frequencies themselves, or to the less specific dysrhythmic frequencies set up by them in neighbouring structures. It is, in fact, an adaptive process that goes too far.

It has now become usual to discuss under these names all the states formerly described as 'equivalents' of epilepsy, i.e. short attacks or more prolonged states in which *psychological symptoms* are present, either alone or together with motor disturbances and anomalies of the vegetative nervous system. Thanks to findings of the electroencephalograph, these conditions, which had been rather neglected by the students of epilepsy, are now in the centre of interest and better understood; but there are still many doubts as to the importance of localization and unsolved problems as to the clinical significance of electroencephalographic findings. The following attempt to reconcile clinical observation and physiological findings, must necessarily be incomplete because everything in this field is still in flux.

The school of Penfield (1952) has produced an impressive body of evidence to suggest that when automatic behaviour is prominent or prolonged at whatever stage of the epileptic attack, the origin of the initial discharge is narrowed down to certain sites in the cerebral cortex. When attacks begin with discharge in the motor areas or one of the sensory areas outside the temporal cortex they will lead to a generalized motor seizure with loss of consciousness, but rarely to simple automatism. The occurrence of the latter at any stage suggests either a temporal (Fig. 14) or occasionally a frontal source. The occurrence of olfactory, visual or auditory hallucinations, forced thinking, depersonalization or chewing movements further restricts the possible sites from which the attack could have originated; such seizures have usually *started in the temporal lobe*. The recollection of a well-defined aura after automatism is further evidence in favour of this site of origin. When automatism is seen after an attack of petit mal or grand mal, it is usually less sustained and organized than in temporal lobe seizures. It thus appears that one of the commonest forms of epileptic automatism, or at least the one which has attracted most attention, is the *'temporal lobe seizure'* (Jasper *et al.*, 1951) or 'twilight attack' (Meyer-Mickeleit, 1953) (see p. 458). The non-paroxysmal episodic disturbances to which epileptics are subject can be classified (Landolt) into five types:

1. Petit mal status, which has already been described; this is typical of generalized epilepsy.

2. The post-ictal twilight state. This may follow all kinds of epileptic attacks, both the major attacks of generalized epilepsy and focal attacks of all kinds, including the temporal lobe psychomotor attack. It is particularly likely to occur after a succession of attacks, or

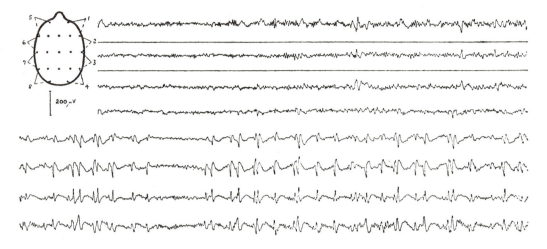

FIG. 14.—Interseizure pattern in female aged 37 years. Daily attacks of psychomotor epilepsy comprising epigastric aura, adversion, fumbling movements, salivation and clouding of consciousness lasting for 1–2 minutes and followed by gradual return of clear consciousness. E.E.G. shows very frequent sharp wave discharges, focal in the left midtemporal region, but extending both anteriorly and posteriorly on the left side.

after one or more attacks consequent on a reduction of medication. The E.E.G. shows generalized slow waves, especially in the frontal regions, which may persist for minutes or for days. There is clouding of consciousness, with diminished awareness and reduced powers of comprehension, but often great irritability and sensitivity to minor stimuli, which may precipitate outbursts of rage or other primitive reactions, such as aggressive defensive acts, running away etc. Stereotyped and repetitive movements are common, perhaps against a background of general unrest; these movements such as trying to cover oneself up, may have the appearance of spontaneous meaningful acts.

3. Twilight states accompanying bursts of bilateral synchronized theta rhythms, which according to Cobb (1950) are likely to be an expression of a lesion in the neighbourhood of the third ventricle, and according to Jasper (1941) may go with a temporal lobe lesion. These dysrhythmic bursts may be asymptomatic.

4. States of clouding resulting from an excess of drugs. These should be easy to recognize if there are any neurological signs such as ataxia, dysarthria, nystagmus, etc. Psychologically there is difficulty in comprehension, and general slowing and dullness, with or without sleepiness, perhaps interrupted by impulsive acts. In the E.E.G., there is usually a generalized slow dysrhythmia with or without spikes.

5. Twilight states with acute psychotic symptoms, delusional ideas, hallucinations, illusions, compulsive acts, disturbances of affect. There is no obvious diminution of consciousness, though the patient may be disorientated, and there may be a subsequent amnesia. According to Landolt, there is forced normalization of the E.E.G., ictal frequencies disappearing entirely from the record. This form of twilight state is particularly associated with temporal lobe epilepsy, and indeed might be regarded as a prolonged psychomotor 'equivalent'. However, it may also occur in cases of generalized epilepsy.

Among the episodic non-paroxysmal states one should also include the mood changes, which are perhaps the commonest of all. Landolt states that during them also the E.E.G. normalizes itself. They could, perhaps, be regarded as twilight states in which consciousness is unimpaired and there are no disturbances of perception, attention etc. They are discussed below.

The twilight states of epileptics, however caused, tend to conform to a picture which resembles a symptomatic psychosis, but has features of its own. The picture is a widely variable one, but for the individual patient takes on its own stamp. While the attack lasts, there is no major or minor fit, though a general convulsion may terminate the episode. The duration varies widely; a post-ictal twilight state seldom lasts more than an hour or two, while a psychotic state may go on for a week or even longer.

The disturbance of consciousness may be of slight degree, and be shown in little more than some dullness and slowness in comprehension and reaction. Even when it is of this minor nature the next day there may be an amnesia for the whole day including the psychiatric interview at which these findings were elicited. At the other extreme are delirious states with disorientation and complete unawareness of the environment and unresponsiveness to it. Some twilight states, especially petit-mal status, are marked by *psychomotor retardation*, which may be extreme. Even when the patient appears to be lucid, it will take him seconds or minutes to catch the meaning of questions put to him and a long time to frame some response. Movements of limbs or body, carried out spontaneously or at request, will be slowed to a fraction of the normal speed. Expressive movements of the face and gestures are also slowed. Other signs seen are *perseveration* and iteration in speech.

Hallucinations are a characteristic feature and are often extremely florid. Visual hallucinations predominate, and are often coloured (there is said to be some preference for the colour red), highly complex, and endowed with movement. Whole scenes, e.g. of an apocalyptic nature, may be enacted before the patient's eyes. They may call forth the liveliest emotional responses, e.g. of terror, and yet there may be little sign of it in outward behaviour.

As has been said, the psychomotor retardation may be broken up by explosions of affect, which most typically take the form of attacks of *panic* or outbursts of *aggressiveness*. Crimes such as murder or rape, or both, may be committed in rare instances especially in the post-ictal state. Such discharges of emotion seem to be in a truer sense psychomotor equivalents as, like the major fit itself, they generally run a short course of a few hours, after which the patient is likely to fall into a sleep, from which he wakens eventually with a complete amnesia for the episode. The quieter twilight states, without such explosions, may last much longer.

While the essential feature of a twilight state is the dream-like, absentminded behaviour and the experiences which the patient undergoes, the *fugue* is a condition in which the patient wanders away from his surroundings in an automatic state. The fugue is, therefore, one type of epileptic twilight state.

Marchand and Ajuriaguerra (1948) give some idea of the *frequency of fugues* in epileptics; in 1,000 patients they found them in 6·4 per cent. of the cases; they were about twice as frequent in men as in women. A fugue may replace the terminal sleep after a seizure; but it may, in the course of the illness, in a special case, even precede the first major fit.

The patient may walk off, cycle away, or may take a train or other public vehicle. But walking and other actions are often disturbed and his behaviour may be disorderly. The patients are careless with money, appear *drowsy and absentminded* and are considered drunk by the people who meet them. The abnormality of behaviour is usually clear on careful history-taking; but difficulties will be caused when conduct has taken on a criminal quality. In these cases, unless it can be clearly demonstrated that the patient is epileptic, it may not be possible to rebut the theory that the most grossly abnormal behaviour, of the most characteristically epileptic kind, with a subsequent amnesia, has not been done out of wickedness. The air of apparent purposiveness which accompanies some of the more complex post-epileptic automatisms can be very deceptive.

While from the clinical point of view there is little doubt of the epileptic nature of fugues with disturbances of behaviour and amnesia, the *'orderly' fugue* has always been debated and its epileptic nature has been questioned. The fugues in classical descriptions lasting over days and weeks in which the patient finds himself waking up in a strange country after travelling by various conveyances without becoming conspicuous by his demeanour, have been suspected of being a *hysterical* symptom, a hysterical 'vigilambulism'. The French literature contains many of these cases which are especially doubtful in their aetiology if they show no other symptoms of epilepsy; but some of the cases have been very well observed by critical physicians and belonged to families in which there were other cases of confirmed epilepsy.

MOOD CHANGES. These are probably the most common mental symptoms in epilepsy, but unfortunately often missed by the neurologist; if mild changes are taken into account, the majority of epileptics show something of this sort. The change may be in one or more of several directions. A prodromal mood of depression may be entirely relieved by the occurrence of the fit; and the same is sometimes true of a mounting state of irritability which has *preceded the fit*. On the other hand moods of depression (and more rarely of elation) and of irritability are common for some days *after the fit*. These mood changes are associated with the electrical changes. Where there is much post-epileptic dysrhythmia, post-epileptic depression and irritability can be expected; on the other hand pre-ictal moods are seldom accompanied by E.E.G. abnormalities. In appropriately chosen epileptics such findings may suggest the replacement of spontaneous by artificial fits (see Treatment). The occurrence of a minor fit, unlike that of a major one, seldom alters the mood state in either direction. One may correlate this with the finding repeatedly made with electroconvulsive therapy, that a minor seizure is of no therapeutic effect in the treatment of depression.

The epileptic is liable to *sudden variations of mood*, independent of seizures, which on occasion can resemble to some degree the mood-swings of the manic-depressive. As in the latter, they may take the form of elation or even ecstasy, or of profound depression. There is, however, one marked distinction. The epileptic mood is of *sudden onset*, and from its first beginning builds up to the full extent in the course of a few hours. One of our patients was subject to depressions of such severity that, although he himself recognized their abnormality and their temporary nature, he was hard put to it to avoid suicide. If he felt that suicide was imminent, he would try to prevent it by inflicting on himself the most extreme forms of pain, e.g. by laying a red-hot poker against his cheek until a deep burn had been caused. Furthermore, unlike the manic-depressive mood, the epileptic mood usually passes off in a few hours, or at most a few days. Suicidal attempts in epileptics are not as frequent as one would expect from their prevailing depressive mood. Among 880 out-patients, Marchand found only 5 per cent. who had attempted suicide. However, the problem of suicide and attempted suicide in epileptics deserves re-examination. There is no doubt that suicidal attempts made in epilepsy, as in other conditions in which some degree of disturbance of consciousness is present such as alcoholic and arteriosclerotic psychoses, tend to be particularly serious and determined. It is not rare in clinical practice to encounter the epileptic who makes repeated attempts on his life and finally succeeds in killing himself.

Depression and elation are by no means the commonest epileptic moods. More common are moods of *irritability*, even of violent anger with senseless aggression. These may occur without any apparent clinical disturbance of consciousness, although consciousness is probably in fact altered. One of our patients, after a series of such recurrent moods, and after an evening of increasing irritability, walked away from his wife, took an aimless bus-ride, followed a girl who dismounted from the bus, and sprang on her from behind in a dark passage. He was apprehended, and might well have gone to prison, as he had never had an overt fit. His electroencephalographic record, however, was abnormal, and treatment by amphetamine caused rapid cessation of the mood states. After temporal lobectomy there is a clear correlation between decrease in aggressiveness and diminution in the number of fits but neurotic disturbances will persist after the fits have been controlled (James, 1960). The indications of some slight disturbance of consciousness during the mood are strengthened, in some cases, by a subsequent *amnesia*; in others it may be shown by a lack of orderliness and rationality of conduct, e.g. wandering away inadequately dressed or without money. Under the old term '*poriomania*' are included fugue states and repeated wanderings, which may be a marked feature in some individuals.

Each patient is likely to have his own individual pattern. Some epileptics are liable to mood changes in which they start a drinking bout ('*dipsomania*'): they may continue thus for several days, consume enormous quantities of alcohol without ever getting completely drunk, and eventually fall asleep to waken later in a state of lucidity. Other patients, during the course of one of their moods, are liable to a great number and variety of *paranoid experiences*. The mood itself has a suspicious character and any and every event in the outer world is liable to misinterpretation. The whole state may be terminated by a major fit.

PERSONALITY DETERIORATION AND DEMENTIA. There is no evidence that the *pre-epileptic personality* differs in any special way from the norms of the general population. Such anomalous traits as can on occasion be demonstrated to have antedated an epilepsy, such as tendencies to irritability, anger, explosive emotions, or slowness and circumstantiality, are interpretable as being themselves manifestations of a masked epilepsy. Some authors (e.g. Bumke, 1924) maintain that many epileptics are by nature simple, good-humoured, conscientious though limited folk, and show in fact a personality deviation of a non-psychopathic kind. Nothing is proven on this point.

It is however certain that *personality changes* may take place *after the onset of the epilepsy*. Not more than a *minority* of patients show this change, and they are in greater part the severe and long-standing cases. It is important to keep this in mind when the physician is asked about the social prognosis of an epileptic illness in a young patient. The great majority can live a useful and tolerably well-adapted life without any gross mental abnormalities. The cause of the mental change is still in doubt. It has by some been attributed to prolonged *medication by anti-convulsant drugs*. This is not a satisfying explanation and has been rejected by the most experienced and critical observers in this field, even though epileptics who have been treated in a stereotyped way in chronic wards by large doses of drugs will often show a considerable improvement in their behaviour when the dosage of drugs is more carefully controlled. It is more probable that it may arise from the *ill-effects of the fits* themselves. It is for the most part the epileptics in whom fits occur with the greatest frequency, and those who have had a great number of major convulsions, who show the severest alterations of personality.

From experience of the *artificial convulsion* produced by electricity in persons of non-epileptic constitution, we know that *changes in intellectual function* are produced roughly proportional to the number and frequency of the fits. After six or more convulsions at weekly intervals many patients complain of some subjective disturbance of memory. And after more intensive treatments given in a short time, very gross impairments of memory, and amnesic gaps of many months, some of retrograde character, have been observed. Parallel findings have been made with the electroencephalograph. After a major convulsion cerebral rhythms are disturbed as a rule for a period of hours. The degree and duration of the disturbance increases very much if treatments are administered in quick succession. The danger of an increasing change is not entirely eliminated by keeping the frequency down to once a week; with higher frequencies the risk is disproportionately greater. Ottosson (1960*a*, *b,c*) has shown that, whereas the therapeutic effect and slowing of the E.E.G. were related to seizure intensity and independent of shock strength, memory changes were closely related to the amount of electrical energy administered in inducing the fit.

Experimental work by Scholz (1951) confirmed the earlier findings of Spielmeyer which pointed to cerebral damage, especially of the cornu Ammonis, caused by vascular spasm and other disturbances of the blood supply during and after the major fit. Scholz also takes into account the observations of Jung (1949) and Ruf (1952) according to which the great increase in cerebral metabolism during the fit leads to cerebral anoxia and correspondingly to damage to nerve cells. Altogether, it seems that it is not so much the single fit, but rather a number of convulsions following one another at short intervals, as in status epilepticus, which lead to exhaustion of the cells and to abnormalities of circulation causing permanent cell damage. Cavanagh, Falconer and Meyer (1958) found Ammon's horn sclerosis in 25 out of 36 cases of temporal lobe epilepsy with diffuse and disseminated lesions. It is of interest that none of the 14 cases with focal discrete lesions was found to have Ammon's horn sclerosis.

In an earlier study Cavanagh and Meyer (1956) found that status epilepticus had preceded the onset of psychomotor seizures in 11 of 17 cases with Ammon's horn sclerosis. It is highly probable, therefore, that recurrent convulsions, perhaps by transient anoxia or by producing acute cerebral oedema, cause organic damage to the brain. This may then show itself in a focal epilepsy, intellectual impairment or affective and temperamental changes.

Penfield and Jasper (1954) point out that extensive epileptogenic lesions are particularly liable to be associated with intellectual and personality deterioration in both adults and children. It is as if the diseased areas of brain exert a generalized malign influence on the function of the brain as a whole. Excision of the damaged regions frequently leads to an improvement both in intelligence and in the personality. There is some evidence (Liddell, 1953) suggesting that personality changes are more likely to occur if the temporal lobes are affected.

The *personality change* is easily recognized when it is seen in a well-marked degree. Both intellectual and affective components combine in a characteristic clinical picture. On the intellectual side are *retardation, perseveration*, narrowing of the field of attention, and *circumstantiality*. Both thought processes and their expression are slowed, and are described by many clinicians as having a 'sticky' or 'viscous' quality. It is as if the sufferer were struggling in a medium which resisted his movements. There is no lightness or ease in his processes of association, and the ideas that come to him are those within easiest range. For this reason one will see him pad out his sentences with clichés until they are of ponderous length, while the idea behind, though rational enough, is of the most commonplace kind. His utterances are heavy-handed and pompous, and lack any trace of wit. The deficiency of ideas is made up by prolific detail; circumstances, even of little relevance, are described to the last minutiae. Well-worn and hackneyed phrases abound, no doubt because they come easiest to hand; but the patient often seems to have a particular preference for those of the most orotund kind. In intellectual tasks the patient will often show a measurable retardation, although the task itself may be completed well enough in the end. Actual achievement is, however, not infrequently impaired by some disturbance of memory or of powers of retention. The following self-description of the epileptic's difficulties in thinking and expressing himself is worth noting for both form and content:

'I am writing this after the interview. On being asked a question, I do not think my trouble is loss of words. I believe I get an immediate and correct answer, but also other possible answers and details to the question. As a result, I possibly forget my original answer, have difficulty in choosing from the answers, or make up a poor answer from the answers and details available.'

Perseveration can be seen in the way in which the patient will stick to his theme, despite attempts to divert him. Asked a question on another topic, once he is well embarked on some trivial narration, he ignores the question and continues on his way, or goes back and repeats the last sentence or so in almost identical words.

The greatest difficulty is experienced in getting the patient to *respond to changes in the situation*, in either its rational or its affective aspects. Moods as well as ideas tend to persist unduly and in conduct there is a remarkable obstinacy. Nevertheless one seldom sees such a degree of perseveration as can be found on occasion in the brain-injured patient, who, for instance, repeats the answer to one question to several different and succeeding ones.

To a certain extent the perseveration can be regarded as an *adaptive phenomenon*. Owing to his slowness the patient will get nowhere unless he sticks to a single task until it is finished. We note, therefore, in many of these patients what Goldstein has called '*organic orderliness*'. In tying himself down in detail, in having a daily routine worked out to the last particular, the patient is protecting himself against circumstances which will otherwise utterly confuse him. The other side of this tendency is shown, however, in a difficulty, doubtless organic, in distinguishing between the essential and inessential, and an incapacity to express abstractions and generalities, except in the familiar cliché.

The *narrowing of the intellectual field*, shown in ideas, in interests, in associations, and in the possible subjects of attention, results in an increasing *egoism*. The patient becomes completely absorbed in those matters which are of immediate concern to himself. His own affairs and those of his nearest family comprise the whole of his world; beyond them his horizon does not reach. This itself is often reflected in an extreme *hypochondriasis* of a peculiar stamp. It is far from unusual to find that the epileptic patient has kept a careful diary of his fits, of his doctors, his treatments, and even, in one of our patients, an elaborate graph extending over many years and over many sheets of graph-paper. Many patients have wearisome details to report about the actions of their bowels, their pulse, their sleep, or the frequency of sexual intercourse.

The deteriorated epileptic, no less than other epileptics, is liable to *explosions of affect*; and in some, the tendency to such an *emotional instability* seems to increase with time and with the extent of the personality change. According to Minkowska (1937) the concept of the 'epileptoid' character is bipolar including 'viscosity' and 'explosivity'. There are also more constant and lasting affective changes. Most frequently these take the form of a mulish moroseness and rancour. Slights are felt to the quick, and malice is borne for months or years. In an epileptic ward gossip, lying and slander will all too easily reign. Any slight on dignity is especially felt; but a more general paranoid quality is common, and may at times amount to paranoid delusions of a more lucid and systematized kind than those engendered by the prolonged or repeated twilight state. Chronic epileptic patients are capable of actions of the most malicious and petty spite, and of combining them with self-justification and self-praise:

A curious feature, and one for which there is no plausible explanation, is the tendency to turn towards *religion*. What results is a 'religiosity' which consists largely in interlarding conversation with oily and sanctimonious religious phrases and platitudes, that are devoid of sincerity or inner feeling. The same unctuous quality may extend to conversation on other than religious topics, which the patients conduct with a sticky over-politeness, and into which they drag an air of sentimentality or pathos.

These empty displays of emotion do not, however, exhaust their repertoire. Profounder and more genuine mood states may at times be seen, such as moods of solemn elation or of profound despair. Although these moods may be unaccompanied by any sign of altered consciousness, they are reminiscent of those seen in twilight states.

In the more advanced stage of *epileptic dementia* there is not only an incapacity to deal with what is new, but a gradual loss of the old and well-established patterns. Memory deteriorates, as do the faculties of attention, comprehension, judgement and recall. The poverty of thought becomes more marked; irrelevant words and phrases are interjected in greater abundance; logical consequence is almost absent until at last a state of incoherence is reached which may sometimes resemble a schizophrenic end-state. If there are also paranoid experiences and impulsive affective outbursts the resemblance may indeed be very close.

CHRONIC PARANOID PSYCHOSES. The first explicit recognition of this interesting syndrome seems to have been made in print by Pond (1957); he described the main clinical features, and associated the condition with temporal lobe epilepsy. The psychotic state, he found, only came on after years of epileptic fits; and though clinically the state closely resembled a schizophrenic psychosis, there was no deterioration to a hebephrenic-like state. These psychoses had, however, attracted notice for many years previously (e.g. Krapf, 1928; Glaus, 1931; Gruhle, 1936). It was thought to be a matter of high importance to decide, if possible, whether these schizophrenia-like psychoses were true cases of schizophrenia, occurring in epileptic subjects as a matter of coincidence; whether perhaps the schizophrenia-like symptoms could be regarded as a reactive delusion formation on the basis of epileptic personality change; or whether, as Gruhle believed, the schizophrenia was symptomatic, and the direct consequence of the epilepsy.

A systematic study of 69 patients suffering from these disorders was made by workers at the National Hospital (Slater, Beard and Glithero, 1963). Evidence was available to show that they occurred with much greater frequency than could be accounted for by random association of epilepsy with schizophrenia. The pre-psychotic personality of these patients fell within the normal range, with some suggestion of an epileptic personality change in cases in which the epilepsy began early. There was a very definite relation between the age of onset of epilepsy with mean at 16 and the age at which the schizophrenia-like psychosis first began with mean at 30. Enquiry into the past history showed that a high proportion, 40 per cent., of the patients had experienced birth traumata, closed head injuries, middle ear disease, encephalitis, etc. (conditions liable to cause a brain lesion); and in 80 per cent. of cases there was evidence of temporal lobe epilepsy. Eleven of these patients had been submitted to temporal lobectomy, the pathological lesions found including a variety of conditions, neoplasms, a dermoid cyst, circumscribed tuberose sclerosis and atrophic lesions. A family investigation showed no increase in schizophrenic illness above average expectation in the parents and sibs of these patients, though the incidence of epilepsy in these relatives was somewhat higher than expected. A follow-up study carried out at a mean interval of eight years after the onset of the psychosis showed a tendency towards remission of the schizophrenia-like state, but also a tendency to pass on into an organically impaired state of a kind commonly seen in the late stages of chronic epilepsy. In summary, then, the evidence from many sources converged towards the view that these psychoses, closely though they might resemble schizophrenic ones at some stage in their development, were from the aetiological point of view chronic epileptic conditions.

The clinical similarity to a schizophrenic illness was often so complete that most of these patients had been repeatedly diagnosed as schizophrenic by competent clinicians. Delusion formation of a typically schizophrenic kind was found in nearly all, and 75 per cent. of the patients experienced typically schizophrenic hallucinations in clear consciousness. Violent disturbances of affect, depressions, and ecstasies were fairly common. These psychoses might start acutely, for example, after a short series of fits, or after several episodes of abnormal experiences (twilight attacks) but most commonly insidiously. Though the course of the illness was sometimes towards improvement, and sometimes fluctuating, the most common tendency was towards chronicity. The course was often stormy, sometimes with interruptions by twilight states with confusion, but usually settled down into a state of partial mental and social incapacity.

On examination in hospital, more often than not there were some signs of slight organic impairment, consonant with the personality change. Thus there might be slight signs of an expressive dysphasia, of learning difficulties, or some impairment of recent memory. Tendencies to circumstantiality, pedantry, repetitiveness, and concreteness of thinking processes were common; and sometimes there was in addition actual incoherence. In some cases the thought disorder was clearly of an organic type, in others it resembled that of the schizophrenic. One patient described his feelings in the following terms, which show dysphasic and perseverative tendencies as well as a schizophrenic-like use of such concepts as 'memories' and 'religion':

'Well, the trouble was that those queer feelings, you see, those turns, you see, like I definitely do know through my own experience which I stopped by, I take it for granted that some sort of religion is trying to work out purposes which are definitely known. Well the sort of purpose which, for example, now I have been trying to listen to the wireless and I was trying to listen to that and unable to get the memories through. I take it for granted that it is some sort of religion. Well, I take it for granted, well, as I say, I am not superstitious. I take it for granted that it is God, see, and my memories, I do definitely notice that, because my memories for some time I have been listening and a lot of memories, you see, well when people ask me several questions, you see, like I have been unable to answer them. I am unable to think of my memories right.'

In these patients the affective responses were often warm and well preserved; indeed, the main clinical difference from a schizophrenic state might well be the good emotional rapport. However, in course of time the affect appears to become flatter, and may even take on a quality of distance, superiority or sardonic reserve which again recall the schizophrenic. Outright hostility was seen in only one patient after many years of hallucinosis.

Both the mode of appearance and the nature of the delusions, primary and secondary, of these epileptic psychoses closely resemble schizophrenic phenomena: feelings of passivity, of being mysteriously observed or influenced by unnamed others; being drawn by rays; being spied on, and having articles at home tampered with; having thoughts read and echoed. Scent is sprayed on the patient in the bus. The veins have gone bad. One patient said her mother was not her mother, but was wearing a mask; another wondered whether her husband was her husband, or her uncle transformed. Paranoid ideas and a paranoid mood are often expressed in queer allusive terms: 'It is different from what it used to be, it's the modern world.' 'It is something to do with the will.' A grandiose element is not uncommon. One patient said 'I come from God's family from the beginning of time, that is why I, the man, should not have children'; and again, 'I am the Ark of God'; and again, 'The brain is a TV camera for the Great Power, the sun, moon and stars, the great electronic brain emitting messages; so if there is destruction of life on earth, the spirit will go back to God and man will be a lump of uranium in darkness'.

An equally schizophrenic quality attaches to the hallucinations. These are mainly auditory, though hallucinations of vision, taste and smell are also seen. One patient received auditory hallucinations from his stomach and intestines, or from his 'mind', or his 'determination': 'this is your common sense speaking to you', the voice might say. Another patient reported that he was followed into the cinema, and people would sit in front of him and say 'Margaret'; he knew what they meant. Another said that voices came from the walls, and spoke of them as 'this wording'. People were reading her thoughts and 'digging at her privacy'. Other patients taste things put into their tea, or smell 'a holy smell'.

Catatonic phenomena in the lucid state are fairly common in the form of very schizophrenic-like grimaces; sitting or standing and staring for minutes together and sudden impulsive acts, such as thrusting both hands through glass panels have also been observed. One patient in a twilight phase spent the night in a repetition of stereotyped ritualistic exercises; he would interrupt them to reply to questions from the doctor, and explain the spiritual significance of what he was doing, but immediately returned to them again.

The nature of the relationship between these psychoses and the underlying epilepsy presents unsolved problems. In the material reported no sign could be found that the occurrence of the psychosis was related to the severity of the epilepsy, the number of fits sustained, the quantity of the drugs consumed, or the degree of control of fits by drug therapy. However, the psychosis did seem to be connected with the site of epileptic discharge, and the length of time for which it had been going on. In a few cases the psychosis was coupled with a centrencephalic epilepsy; but it is difficult to believe that evidence of temporal lobe pathology in eighty per cent. of cases is without aetiological significance. The time relations also suggest that epileptic processes must have continued for some time, perhaps without any openly recognizable seizure, before the psychotic process can begin. Both physiogenic and psychogenic hypotheses can be framed to account for at least part of the phenomena.

Pond (1962) has suggested that, if twilight attacks occur repeatedly without subsequent amnesia, the patient is faced with a mass of abnormal experience which has somehow to be organized, for example, in ramifying delusional interpretations and by a confusion of reality and autistic thinking. The main objection to this hypothesis is that though it accounts for much of the delusional symptomatology, it leaves other important phenomena unexplained: the volitional disturbances, the thought disorder, the hebephrenic symptoms, and the hallucinations occurring in clear consciousness during the long inter-ictal intervals.

An alternative explanatory hypothesis is offered by Symonds (1962) which emphasizes the epileptic process as a continuous one, a background disorder on which the fits and the E.E.G. changes are raised as epiphenomena. This background disorder would be the proximate cause of the psychosis. The schizophrenia-like aural symptoms of temporal lobe epilepsy suggest that the temporal lobe includes within its boundaries circuits concerned with the physiological basis of the psychological disorder we call schizophrenia. It is not the loss of neurones in the temporal lobe that is responsible for the psychosis but the disorderly activity of those that remain.

These views are very similar to those of Landolt. He has found himself, and quotes other authors to the same effect, that schizophrenia-like psychotic states occurring in epileptics are predominantly associated with an ictal focus in a temporal lobe. However, the appearance of a psychotic state is not directly related to ictal discharges occurring in that region. Such discharges can continue several times a second for years without producing any psychological disorder. Furthermore, bilateral temporal lobe foci seem no more likely than unilateral foci to predispose to the occurrence of a psychosis. It would seem then that the psychosis is a response on the part of normal brain tissues to functional disturbances, showing perhaps as non-specific E.E.G. abnormalities, in parts of the brain connected with the local lesion. The nature of this adaptive response by the normal parts of the brain to the local disturbance takes the form, according to Landolt, of forced normalization; and it is only *when the ictal frequencies are suppressed* that the psychosis is liable to appear. At the basis of this adaptive response Landolt suggests that there is a relationship of functional antagonism between the temporal lobe system and the waking centre of the reticular substance of the mid-brain. These views, again, fall in line with those of Hill (1948) who regards ictal phenomena as essentially homeostatic, and playing a part in preserving the integrated function of the brain as a whole. They are also in accord with the observed effects of convulsions induced for therapeutic purposes; the associated E.E.G. changes have been shown to be essential for sustained clinical improvement in depressive illness and the features of these E.E.G. changes and some of the clinical changes that run parallel to them suggest the operation of diencephalic regulating centres concerned with homeostasis (Roth, 1951).

In all these theoretical interpretations no important part is played by actual destruction of cells. Deficit syndromes, such as are found late in the history of patients who have suffered from destructive lesions, when temporary disturbances have settled down, do indeed bear little relation to the acute and florid symptoms of the twilight attack or the schizophrenia-like psychosis in its early stages. However, late on in the life history of these psychotic patients one finds irreversible changes in personality, of the organic type, and often some degree of dementia; and at earlier stages there is often evidence of a severe degree of neuronic fall-out. In the case material reported by Slater *et al.* (1963) more than half the patients examined by air encephalography showed cerebral atrophy, mainly atrophy of the central white matter. In 19 out of 56 cases examined there was dilatation of one or both temporal horns, either alone or as part of a general ventricular dilatation. As death of cells must be occurring, it seems likely that the background disorder postulated by Symonds is related to the physiological disturbances caused in their own and in connected systems by the dying neurones. If this were the case one would have a natural explanation for the lapse of years between onset of epilepsy and onset of psychosis which is actually observed, and for the finding that the schizophrenia-like psychosis seems to be an intermediate stage in the long life history of the epileptic background disorder, which either recedes or tends to pass into a quiescent deficit state.

If theoretical comprehension of the relationship between the schizophrenia-like psychosis and epilepsy is difficult and problematic, one enters on a still more speculative field in trying to account for the relationship between this symptomatic schizophrenia and schizophrenia of the usual kind. The fact that the incidence of schizophrenia in the parents and sibs of these epileptics was no higher than in the general population suggests that any normal brain can react in. this schizophrenic way, provided that a disturbance of the right kind can be set going in the right functional systems. There is no schizophrenic symptom which cannot be seen in epilepsy; and the clinical distinction between a schizophrenic patient and a schizophrenic epileptic patient can only be established by demonstrating the existence of an epileptic disorder in the latter. In the one we have a genetically determined condition, and in the latter a phenocopy. Landolt observes that his finding of forced normalization applies not only to epileptic but also to schizophrenic psychoses. E.E.G. examination of patients suffering from endogenous psychoses may well have proved as disappointing as it has because it has been conducted only during psychotic phases; repeated examination extending into phases of psychological normality might have yielded more information. The occurrence of ictal discharges and of manifest seizures is a feature of the later history of a substantial proportion of patients suffering from schizophrenic syndromes of the usual kind. One is forced to consider whether the nuclear schizophrenias also may not be organic processes, affecting the same functional systems of the brain as those involved in epileptic schizophrenia.

Despite their similarities, the differential diagnosis between paranoid schizophrenic psychoses and epileptic psychoses should not be difficult. The epileptic psychosis is an integral part of the epileptic development as a whole, growing out of the pre-existing personality change and with its content derived from aural and semi-confusional epileptic experiences. Cases in which the patient is properly regarded as suffering from coincidental but independent epileptic and schizophrenic disorders must be relatively few; and one would think that the double diagnosis should not be made when the epilepsy long antedated the paranoid psychosis and persisted into it.

DIFFERENTIAL DIAGNOSIS

The differential diagnosis of epilepsy is perhaps one of the most complex problems in medicine, and one in which mistakes are frequent and may be fateful for the patient. The psychiatrist will be consulted when, as is often the case, mental symptoms occupy the foreground of the clinical picture. However, the differentiation of the absences and other paroxysmal symptoms from other psychiatric phenomena is not always easy. Anxiety attacks and vasomotor attacks may simulate epilepsy.

The differential diagnosis of a major epileptic fit from *grande hysterie* is now a problem of some rarity. As Kinnier Wilson has remarked, the ability to feign an epileptic fit, which was at one time so widespread among soldiers, tramps and beggars, is now a dying art; and the hysterical imitation of a major attack has become correspondingly unusual. In the hysterical fit there is no true loss of consciousness; reflexes are not altered; the movements do not follow the typical tonic and clonic stages, but are of a voluntary and *expressive kind*. However, the behaviour of a patient immediately after a minor temporal lobe seizure, laughing or crying, resistive and only mildly confused, may be closely similar. In the rare hysterical twilight state, there is fairly full awareness of the environment, and consciousness is not dulled, though its field may be narrowed; behaviour is of an emotionally understandable kind. There are **none** of the E.E.G. changes in the hysteric that will be seen in the epileptic state. However, a full and reliable history is often necessary before a definite opinion is reached. The mistake of taking the epileptic to be a hysteric is much commoner than its converse.

The differentiation of the epileptic psychosis from the *symptomatic psychoses*, or even from *schizophrenia*, may on the other hand be at times very difficult. However, the dullness and retardation of the epileptic twilight state can be very characteristic; and the subjective experience of a massive and complex or scenic visual hallucinosis, described by the patient on recovery of full consciousness, is almost equally so. If typical fits occur, there will probably be no great difficulty in diagnosis. The short recurrences of deliria, with intervening periods of lucidity in which there is no loss or gross abnormality of affect, will distinguish these epileptic psychoses from all but a rare and restricted group of schizophrenics. A therapeutic test may provide some help and the electroencephalogram is an important source of evidence in some cases. But only on rare occasions will the latter decide the issue by itself when a careful history and detailed clinical examination have left it in doubt; this statement holds for differential diagnosis of all kinds of epilepsy. Special caution must be exercised in the evaluation of abnormalities of a non-specific kind (see p. 449).

A problem which has puzzled generations of psychiatrists is the differentiation of the masked epileptic, subject to psychomotor equivalents, from the *impulsive, aggressive and emotionally unstable psychopath* (see Chapter III, p. 139). In some cases the differentiation is, even theoretically, of dubious value. The electroencephalograph may not decide the issue, as the unstable psychopath of the type described himself often comes from a family the other members of which are epileptic, and he may himself have an abnormal electroencephalogram. The case may be considered for all practical purposes as one of epilepsy, if there are typical epileptic findings, e.g. of spike and wave rhythm or a spike or sharp wave focus, either in the ordinary record, during sleep, or after some physiological stress such as overbreathing, or intravenous metrazol in subconvulsant doses. The cases in which a differential diagnosis is most urgently called for between epilepsy and this kindred psychopathy, will be those in which a *medico-legal problem* arises. If the alleged crime is a serious one, such as murder, the most careful consideration will be required. All circumstances of the crime should be studied, in order to establish, if possible, whether it took place in a state of lucid or disordered consciousness; the past history will be examined for the indications of previous epileptic attacks or psychomotor equivalents; and a detailed electroencephalographic investigation should be arranged.

The differentiation of syncope and the transient bouts of panic, visceral discomfort, anxiety, depersonalization and perceptual distortion that may occur in some forms of neurotic illness from attacks of temporal lobe epilepsy may prove difficult; the subject is discussed on page 460.

Once it seems probable that the patient is suffering from an epileptic disorder, every effort must be made to discover a proximate cause for the epilepsy, if it exists. An important part of this enquiry consists in localizing, if possible, the focus of origin of the fit. If this is centrencephalic, the epilepsy is likely to fall into the cryptogenic class, in which genetical factors play the major role. If a cortical focus of origin can be found, one can assume that this is the result of a local lesion. Clinical judgement, based on history, neurological, psychiatric and electro-physiological examination, is then needed to decide on the pathological nature of the lesion, the diagnostic procedure continuing, perhaps, into electrocorticography on the exposed brain in the operating theatre. A disabling epilepsy, based on a sharply circumscribed focus in the anterior part of the non-dominant temporal lobe, will have to be seriously considered for neurosurgery. In the localization of the focus electro-physiological investigation plays a most important role. If a consistent focus of random spike or sharp wave discharge is located on one side, it may be assumed that there is in the neigh-bourhood an area of cortical damage. However, local slow waves and even bilaterally synchronous patterns such as spike and wave activity may at times be found in focal epilepsy, although at the beginning of a seizure the abnormalities are seen to be local. Detailed localization studies in expert hands, usually based on repeated examination, can provide a fairly reliable opinion as to whether there is a cortical focus of origin for the attacks. Whether the lesion so indicated is diagnosed as atrophic or neoplastic will depend on more general clinical considerations, supported by other special investigations such as air encephalography or arteriography.

The position with regard to psychiatric symptoms as an indication of localization of the epileptic discharge has as yet not been adequately clarified. Gibbs *et al.* (1948) noted that personality changes occurred rarely in idiopathic epilepsy but frequently accompanied psychomotor epilepsy, being associated with disturbances of the anterior portions of the temporal lobes. In Liddell's (1953) cases—the entire epileptic population of Runwell Hospital—23 out of 47 showed temporal lobe foci on electroencephalography. The use of more sensitive techniques such as sphenoidal recordings and electrocorticography could only increase the proportion of patients showing temporal lobe abnormalities.

TREATMENT

Although nobody has been able, so far, to cure a case of idiopathic epilepsy, sympto-matic therapy by drugs makes it possible to suppress the manifestations of the illness or to modify them in a large number of cases. As the *medicinal treatment* has to be continued over years, the treatment should be simple and not too costly. To treat an epileptic success-fully by drugs, and to help him in his individual symptoms, is often a delicate and difficult task. In some cases the electroencephalogram will suggest that a specific drug should be tried but in most patients the optimal treatment can only be discovered by trial and error. A short time of observation in hospital is often very helpful in finding the right régime.

The *mental state of the epileptic* often prevents the full benefit of symptomatic treatment. His peculiar optimism, perhaps due to the revival of consciousness after the fit, and the tendency to hypochondriasis and self-observation characteristic of all chronic disablement, induce him to omit his regular medicine for a trial, to change his doctor or to try some new cure advertised with high promise. The question of full confidence in the physician has a special aspect for an epileptic, especially if he shows the first signs of personality change. The psychiatrist who is used to similar vicissitudes in the patient–doctor relationship with his other patients, is specially suited to deal with this problem in the treatment of epileptics. The aim of treatment, and its optimal results, would be to suppress all epileptic symptoms, especially the major fits. There is, however, a considerable proportion of epileptics in which this ideal cannot be attained. In such cases one has to strike a balance between the number of fits that can be tolerated and the results of over-medication. Some unfortunate patients land on a moving staircase, and the pharmacological escalation can carry them to dizzy heights over the course of years. Such is the intolerance of the out-patient registrar for an epileptic fit in one of his patients that, if one happens, even if this is after months of successful treatment, the dose of drugs is at once increased, or a new drug is added without omitting one of the old ones. The doctor should be aware, not only of the dangers of over-medication, but also of the risk of controlling paroxysmal disturbances at the expense of impairing the health between attacks. We agree with the view that ictal phenomena are in part at least an adjustive phenomenon, a safety-valve as it were; and that the total suppression of attacks in some cases, perhaps especially the focal epilepsies, may bring with it an increased incidence of epileptic moods, twilight attacks and epileptic psychoses.

Pharmacological Treatment

Barbiturates

Phenobarbitone is the most generally useful remedy, especially for major seizures. Its effect on petit mal is rather unpredictable, as also its effect on psychomotor equivalents, epileptic behaviour disorders and mood states. For some of these phenomena it is found helpful, usually when combined with amphetamine; but it sometimes increases irritability. Phenobarbitone is particularly indicated in patients whose attacks are infrequent or mainly nocturnal. As none of its side-effects is serious it is also worth while beginning treatment with this preparation. Phenobarbitone should be commenced with a dose of 30 mg. night and morning and increased slowly to a maximum of 180 mg. a day. Phenobarbitone is considerably less depressing than bromides, it makes many patients cheerful and gives them confidence, but after prolonged treatment toxic symptoms may develop. These include headache, lethargy, impotence, and muscular incoordination. Retardation and intellectual slowing may be marked and the mood may be depressed. Many epileptics with mood changes or other psychiatric manifestations are found to tolerate phenobarbitone badly, and are then best treated with other drugs such as hydantionates.

When the dose adequate for the suppression of fits has been discovered, medication should be rigorously maintained. Women during menstruation and pregnancy should continue the drug. Even in febrile illnesses the medicine should not be entirely stopped, but the dose can be reduced. Sudden interruption of phenobarbitone carries the great danger of repeated seizures and status epilepticus or delirious psychoses. If phenobarbitone causes undue drowsiness or other side-effects, methylphenobarbitone (Prominal) may be tried. The effective dose is twice that of phenobarbitone.

Hydantoinates

Although phenobarbitone may give adequate control of the fits it is often necessary to combine it with one of the hydantoinates. Phenytoin sodium (Epanutin) is the first choice, the dose being built up successively from 0·1 g. twice daily to 0·3–0·6 g. daily. The therapeutic and toxic doses are quite close to one another. Hydantoinates are particularly effective in the treatment of major attacks and rather less useful in psychomotor epilepsy. They often aggravate petit mal seizures and should therefore be avoided in cases where these are the major disability. Mild gastric disturbances, sleeplessness or a feeling of unsteadiness may occur transiently. More serious is a frank ataxia, sometimes with diplopia, and this is an indication for reducing the dosage. Hypertrophy of the gums may occur after prolonged intake of the drug, particularly in younger patients. Serious toxic effects necessitating the abandonment of this form of medication are pyrexia, polyarthropathy, macrocytic anaemia or an exfoliative dermatitis.

Methoin (Mesontoin) has a similar action to phenytoin sodium and is given in the same dosage. It does not give rise to hypertrophy of the gums but it is more liable to give rise to blood dyscrasias.

Oxazolidines

Troxidone (Tridione), the anti-epileptic introduced by Lennox, is specific for epileptic attacks associated with the spike and wave dysrhythmia which includes petit mal, pyknolepsy and some cases of myoclonic epilepsy. It may also be found useful in some cases of epileptic mental disturbances. The commencing dose is 0·3 g. three times daily, and total dosage should not exceed 2·1 g. a day. There is the danger of developing the grave complication *agranulocytosis or aplastic anaemia* in a proportion of cases. Visual glare is a common toxic symptom. Regular blood-counts should be carried out every month in all patients on treatment, the examination to include haemoglobin estimation, a total white cell and differential count. If the polymorph count should fall to 2,500–3,000, weekly examinations should be made and treatment terminated should the count be found in the neighbourhood of 1,500. Patients should be instructed to report immediately any falling-off in general health and in particular the development of sore throats. Paramethadione (Paradione) has similar effects to troxidone but is less toxic and may be tried if the latter produces undue side-effects.

Phensuximide (Milontin), a drug of the succinimide group, is also effective in petit mal in doses of 0·5 g. three to six times a day. It has little effect on grand mal attacks and may in fact aggravate them.

Pyrimidines

The only drug of this group in use is Mysoline (primidone). It is administered in an initial dose of 0·25 g. daily, increasing every few days by 0·25 g. to the limit of tolerance which lies between 0·75 and 1·5 g. daily. It has a wide range of usefulness being valuable in grand mal and focal seizures and quite effective in temporal lobe epilepsy. However, although toxic effects of a disabling kind are confined to a minority they can on occasion be very severe and often commence early in treatment. They include dizziness, nausea, vomiting, drowsiness and ataxia.

Treatment of Psychiatric Complications

The epileptics who will most frequently come the way of the psychiatrist are those in whom there are serious *psychiatric complications*. If major or minor fits are occurring as well, then treatment will be directed in the first place towards reducing them to a minimum. If that can be done, there will probably be a corresponding reduction of mental disturbances. Treatment will be to a considerable extent empirical; and it will be of great help if it can be controlled by regular electroencephalographic examination. There are, however, frequent cases in whom clinical improvement is not accompanied by any marked change for the better in the E.E.G.; and there are others in whom an electrophysiological improvement is not accompanied by a clinical one. If the mental disturbance is the main or only disability the same principles will be followed, i.e. the empirical adjustment of treatment so as to secure maximum relief.

In patients with prominent symptoms of aggressiveness, restlessness, agitation, marked paranoid features and hostility, *phenothiazines* can prove of very great value in treatment. Chlorpromazine (Largactil) or thioridazine (Melleril) in doses of 50 mg. two to four times a day may radically change the picture and improve the patient's social adjustment. Phenothiazines are also of great value in the management of acute epileptic psychosis and severe mood changes. In very tense and apprehensive patients chlordiazepoxide may bring about striking improvement. Some patients who suffer from episodic mood states and exacerbations of irritability will respond to amphetamine sulphate but this usually needs to be combined with anticonvulsants.

The treatment of an *epileptic twilight state*, once it has started, is often difficult. Antiepileptic drugs are more successful in preventing the recurrence of such states than in influencing them once they have appeared. If the state develops into a wild and dangerous excitement, a treatment similar to that adopted in status epilepticus will be called for.

In twilight states and other epileptic psychoses of acute onset there is an important place for *electrical convulsant therapy*. The treatment is particularly effective in psychoses with a strong depressive colouring and/or delusional and hallucinatory symptoms of a florid kind particularly where the disorder has evolved rapidly in a relatively undeteriorated personality. There is a limited place for convulsive therapy in the acute exacerbations of more chronic epileptic psychoses although these can almost invariably be satisfactorily managed with the aid of phenothiazine therapy. As already indicated, the danger of successful suicide is always considerable in severely depressed epileptic patients and there should be no undue delay in having recourse to electrical convulsant therapy where antidepressive drugs fail to elicit rapid improvement. There is a group of cases in which fits or mental disturbances occur at infrequent but regular intervals preceded by some days of altered mood or malaise. These patients probably suffer during this prodromal state from a cerebral dysrhythmia which may itself be terminated at times by spontaneous convulsions. If this is the case the artificial convulsion may beneficially replace the spontaneous one. Finally in patients who have a spontaneous convulsion at strictly regular intervals it has been claimed that an artificial convulsion may protect against a spontaneous fit (Kalinowsky and Kennedy, 1943). This could be socially valuable in some subjects but further evidence about the efficacy of the technique is needed.

Treatment of Status Epilepticus

This complication is serious and calls for emergency measures. The first thing to be done is to give a deep intramuscular injection of 10–12 ml. of paraldehyde followed by 5 ml. every half hour until the fits cease. Paraldehyde is probably the most effective anticonvulsant in status but the intravenous route of injection formerly used carries hazards and is best avoided except in the most severe cases in whom a 10 per cent. solution of paraldehyde in 500 ml. of water can be given by intravenous drip. An alternative to paraldehyde is 200 mg. of sodium phenobarbitone intravenously, a further dose of 100 mg. being given in $\frac{1}{2}$–1 hour. In prolonged status the patient should be nursed in a quiet, darkened room; the head should be flat and turned sideways to prevent mucus and saliva from running into the trachea. The lower bowel should be emptied by an enema; this may be followed by an enema containing 60 grains of chloral hydrate, an old-fashioned but useful anticonvulsant. Altogether, the risk from exhaustion and cardiac failure is considerable. Nourishment may need to be maintained by tube-feeding.

Neurosurgery

Although excision of grey matter at the supposed site of the focus of epileptic discharge has been undertaken as a treatment for epilepsy for some 80 years and used extensively during the past 25 years, its precise value remains uncertain. Encouraging results have been published from a number of centres but, in the majority of cases, the only form of comparison made in the assessment of outcome has been that between the state of the patient after operation and before it. Hence, although a large number of operations have been carried out, the scientific evidence about the degree of success achieved is limited.

Penfield and Paine (1955) reported the results of temporal lobe excision in 67 cases of temporal lobe epilepsy operated upon between 1940 and 1950, those with neoplasms being excluded. Added to two previous follow-up studies this gave a total of 217 cases subjected to surgery. The attacks ceased after operation in 41 per cent. and the results were regarded as satisfactory in a further 35 per cent. The operative mortality was 1·5 per cent. All these cases were disabled in varying degrees before operation and Penfield regarded surgery as having been worth while in 75 per cent. This series did not include patients with any psychiatric disorder that would preclude their being nursed in a general hospital.

The Maudsley group used three criteria in deciding upon surgery (Falconer and his colleagues, 1955); psychomotor attacks which do not submit to drug therapy; the presence of spike-discharging focus chiefly in one temporal lobe (the presence of an independent but much less vigorous focus in the opposite lobe was not considered a contra-indication); and the occurrence of a personality disturbance resistant to treatment. The anterior two-thirds of the temporal lobe was resected in one piece in all cases.

The outcome of the operation could be predicted from a number of clinical, psychological and E.E.G. criteria which correlated well with pathological findings (Meyer, Falconer and Beck, 1954; Cavanagh, Falconer and Meyer, 1958; Falconer and colleagues, 1958). Pathologically the cases could be clearly separated into two groups; those with focal and those with diffuse lesions. The latter group was characterized by onset of epilepsy in infancy, a high incidence of abnormal birth or birth trauma and frequent family history of epilepsy. There was often radiological evidence of slight atrophy of one hemisphere together with atrophy of one half of the cranial cavity or middle temporal fossa. In the focal cases the clinical and historical features were in an opposite sense and radiological findings were insignificant or absent. More than half the diffuse cases had sclerosis of Ammon's horn and it was in this group that aggressive outbursts were most common (53 per cent.). The most striking improvements in respect of fits were seen in the focal cases associated with tumours and hamartomas (73 per cent. markedly improved). The next best results were obtained in that sub-group of the diffuse cases in which Ammon's horn sclerosis was found. Improvement in personality (42 per cent.) and working ability were seen as well as reduction of fits (62 per cent.). In all groups, cases with aggressive tendencies or no personality disturbance tended to do well while hysterical or paranoid features carried a poor prognosis.

Hill (1958) considers that 50 per cent. of cases of temporal lobe epilepsy have abnormal personalities and 25 per cent. suffer from psychotic episodes. Furthermore the psychiatric disability is often far more serious than that resulting from the fits and it is important to know the effects of surgery in this group. Hill finds that the degree of improvement of fits and of behaviour is closely related and that if the fits are controlled by suitable medication then the psychiatric disorder alone is not an indication for operation. Northfield (1958) has operated upon 16 cases with psychiatric disturbances, mainly abnormal personalities with overt aggression. Eleven of these were in mental hospitals before operation. The results are described as good in 8, fair in 2, with no improvement in 6. The improvement in regard to the fits and the psychiatric symptoms was roughly parallel but in individual cases behaviour might be much improved although the fits persisted. Similar results are reported by Serafetinides and Falconer (1962) in a group of 12 patients with epileptic psychosis in association with an anterior temporal lobe focus. Five of these patients were completely fit-free after a temporal lobectomy, 5 more greatly benefited, and the remaining 2 patients were improved at least 50 per cent. as regards their epilepsy. Confusional episodes showed themselves as directly dependent on the epilepsy and ceased after operation; paranoid states improved after operation to some extent; schizophrenia-like states became somewhat less florid.

Of 50 cases operated upon by Falconer (1958), 45 showed personality disorders. Following operation, 24 remained free of attacks for two to seven years and in 14 the degree of improvement was assessed as at least 50 per cent. In general the improvement in the psychiatric state was of an equivalent degree, particularly in those showing aggressive tendencies.

From these results it might seem that operation has a firmly established place in the treatment of temporal lobe epilepsy. But as Bates (1962) points out in a critical evaluation (*The Surgery of Epilepsy*), marked variation with time in the incidence of fits makes it difficult to assess what can be truly attributed to surgery. Moreover, widely differing techniques have led to very similar results and there would appear to be little doubt that histologically normal tissue is at times removed on the strength of electrocorticographic observations made during operation. This raises questions about the specificity of the effect of excising an area of cortex that is identified as an epileptogenic focus. These facts have led some surgeons to experiment with less extensive procedures than temporal lobectomy. Turner (1958) has explored the effects of an operation aimed at isolating the anterior portion of each temporal lobe by division of fibres in the roof of the anterior horn of the lateral ventricle. Other workers (Desrochers *et al.*, 1961) have attempted to replicate the success of hemispherectomy in reducing the incidence of fits by ablating the prefrontal lobe of the minor hemisphere. The rationale of the operation is that reduction of the total mass of cerebral tissue may limit the spread of epileptic discharge from a focus. Judging from the early results, these procedures appear to have some promise.

The authors broadly follow the view of Hill that there is a definite though limited place for surgery in patients with a unilateral focus particularly where this is in the minor hemisphere and where epilepsy cannot be controlled by other measures. In such patients amelioration of positive psychiatric disturbance runs parallel with decline in the incidence of fits. However, more scientific evidence about the precise effects of temporal lobe surgery is urgently needed.

Social Aspects

The social aspects of the treatment of epileptics are of the greatest importance, and not sufficiently well recognized by the general public. In medical practice an excessive preoccupation with the need to bring the convulsions under complete control has perhaps tended to obscure some of the social and psychological aspects of epilepsy which go far to decide whether or not the patient can lead a normal and effective life in the community. In Pond and Bidwell's (1960*a*) survey of epilepsy in 14 general practices, psychological difficulties often closely linked with a disturbed environment, were found in 29 per cent. of the patients and this was almost certainly an underestimate. About half of the patients of employable age had had difficulties with their jobs and this was particularly marked in the younger age groups and in the lower social classes. In these, mental backwardness or psychological difficulties rendered social adjustment difficult. About 10 per cent. of the patients were more or less unemployable. Psychological, medical and social team work based to some extent on centres such as those recommended by the Cohen committee (1956) are needed for the effective care of epileptics in the community. For the present there are few centres where facilities along these lines are available.

R

There remains even nowadays a strong public prejudice against and fear of the disease, and not until this has been eradicated will it be possible to provide treatment in the fullest sense for epileptic patients. Many epileptics suffer grave disadvantages in obtaining and keeping employment, although the character and frequency of their attacks do not in themselves unfit them for paid employment. Too often they are taught in schools for physically defective children or together with children of retarded intelligence. If the fits are infrequent in school hours, and the child is of normal intelligence, it is much better for him to attend an ordinary school.

As far as possible, also, the epileptic should be allowed to follow *a normal career* and to take up the occupation of his choice. Certain occupations, such as car-driving or those which involve close proximity to dangerous machinery, heights, fire or water, are obviously out of the question. For those in whom attacks are frequent, uncontrolled by medication, or whose mental state renders a normal social life impossible, some form of *colony life* or a protected existence will be required. Finally, those patients who are liable to be dangerous to others, or who undergo deterioration, or are subject to frequent psychotic episodes, will need mental hospital treatment.

A word should be added on *the physical and mental hygiene* of the epileptic's daily life. He should live regularly, sleep at least seven hours and get up and go to bed at fixed times. Sudden changes of régime should be avoided. Meals should be taken regularly and special precautions against hypoglycaemia are advisable; the patient should carry a bar of chocolate if there is a likelihood of a missed meal. He should be warned against unwonted or prolonged physical exertion and spirits on an empty stomach are likewise strongly contraindicated. Otherwise the epileptic should live a full life and take an active part in social activities. Long-term supervision by a sympathetic physician who is prepared to devote time to supporting the epileptic through his many difficulties and the assistance of a social worker experienced in the problems the epileptic encounters in the community are of inestimable value.

The physician is occasionally called on to answer questions about *marriage and procreation*. It can, of course, only be advantageous for the epileptic to marry a normal individual who will be able to help in his care; but the prospective spouse should be made fully aware of the partner's disability, though of course the physician will take care to secure the patient's permission for disclosure of such confidential matters. Severe or uncontrolled epilepsy can be a serious handicap in marriage. If either parent, but especially if the mother is liable to have epileptic attacks in the home, the child cannot receive the harmonious and secure environment which should be his birthright. Furthermore, if the epilepsy is one which has persisted from early years into adult life, it will nearly always have had some deleterious effect on the personality, an effect which will have repercussions on the child. On the other hand, 'epilepsy' covers a wide range of disabilities and fits can nowadays be brought under more effective control than was the case 20 years ago. The risk of epilepsy to the child is not in itself prohibitive. If one of the parents is normal not more than 3·2 per cent. of the children are likely to be epileptic (Alström, 1950; Lennox, 1960). In centrencephalic epilepsy and in cases with early onset the risks are slightly higher. It is the psychological fitness of the patient for marriage and parenthood rather than the occasional convulsion or absence that should decide what advice is given. There are mature and courageous epileptics who can surmount their handicap and make a conspicuous success of their personal and social lives. Where the social circumstances are favourable for rearing children, where the patient's attacks are controlled or nocturnal, and he shows resourcefulness, emotional resilience and intelligence, marriage and parenthood should not be discouraged.

CHAPTER IX

MENTAL DISORDER IN TRAUMA, INFECTION AND TUMOUR OF THE BRAIN

THE psychological disturbances produced by demonstrable damage to the brain have certain distinctive features differentiating them from those associated with 'functional' disorders such as schizophrenia and manic-depressive psychosis. In this book 'organic' refers to disorders caused by a demonstrable cerebral lesion or physical disease outside the brain, while 'functional' is used to denote psychiatric disturbances unassociated with cerebral pathology or identifiable somatic disease. The authors are aware that this use of the terms is open to certain objections on logical and semantic grounds. However, no satisfactory alternatives in nomenclature or classification have yet been suggested.

The fact that the line of demarcation between the organic and functional territories is not a very sharp one deserves emphasis. Thus the symptom complexes of the 'functional' groups may be found in the presence of established cerebral disease and clear-cut organic mental symptoms may be lacking in such cases. Depressive, schizophrenic, manic, hysterical, phobic and obsessional symptoms have all been described in association with cerebral disease. The association has been perhaps most clearly exemplified by the schizo-phrenia-like disorders that have been described in association with chronic epilepsy (Slater and Beard, 1963), amphetamine addiction (Connell, 1958; Beamish and Kiloh, 1960) and head injury (Hillbom, 1960). There is also a close relationship between depressive states and anxiety neuroses, commencing in the senium, and physical disease (Kay and Bergmann, 1966). To some extent these cases manifest characteristics of both classes of disorder. Thus, although the partly organic causation of symptomatic schizophrenias has in some cases been established beyond reasonable doubt, the symptoms frequently respond favourably to the administration of phenothiazine drugs. A further example is the response to convulsive treatment that is commonly made by the depressive, manic or catatonic states that may follow severe or exhausting physical illness; it will be recalled that Bonhoeffer (1910) classed these syndromes with the 'symptomatic psychoses'. Again the acute psychoses of epileptics may be associated with abnormalities in the electroencephalogram yet the psychiatric disturbance is often promptly terminated by the application of electroconvulsive therapy.

There are other clinical phenomena which render the boundary line indistinct. Thus symptoms highly suggestive of structural brain disease or brain dysfunction may present in the absence of any known organic aetiology. Clouding of consciousness may occur in association with acute mania and more rarely in severe agitated depression. It has also been described in association with the schizophreniform psychoses (Langfeldt, 1937, 1960). Again a picture resembling dementia is occasionally found in patients without evidence of brain disease and it seems likely that many of these subjects suffer from atypical affective psychoses (Kiloh, 1961). The overlap between the functional and organic groups of disorders is important from both a practical and a theoretical viewpoint. So far as clinical practice is concerned, the absence of organic clinical features does not wholly exclude the possibility of co-existing organic disease of which, indeed, the functional disturbance may be an early manifestation. On the other hand, organic syndromes, as in the case of the pseudo-dementias, may show a favourable response to treatment. Where organic disease and depressive or schizophrenic syndromes co-exist, the course pursued by the functional disturbance and its response to treatment will be independent in some cases of the course followed by the organic disorder; the latter may progress while the former remits until submerged by advancing dementia.

From the theoretical viewpoint, the overlap is of great importance for psychiatric classification and for scientific enquiry in the field of psychiatry as a whole. There is insufficient evidence to make possible any definitive judgement on the significance of this overlap. The explanations advanced have ranged between two extremes. On the one hand it has been suggested that the association of schizophrenic and other functional syndromes with organic disease is fortuitous and due to the release of latent schizophrenic illness, for example, by a cerebral lesion. In the case of symptomatic schizophrenia, this explanation has been rendered unlikely by the work of Slater and Beard who have found that the morbid risk of schizophrenia among first degree relatives of their patients with epileptic paranoid psychoses to be negligible. Other studies point in the same direction (see Chapter V, p. 299). At the other extreme it has been proposed that these conditions may be regarded as organic psychoses of a special kind. This explanation is reflected in our present nomenclature which describes many of these disorders in terms of the associated organic disease as 'epileptic psychosis', 'alcoholic hallucinosis', 'toxic psychosis'. In its simple form this viewpoint is invalidated by the fact that functional syndromes appear only in a minority of cases of cerebral disease, although this minority has been shown to exceed chance expectation in some instances. The true explanation probably varies for different phenomena but there is evidence, no more than suggestive at the present time, that it is likely to be found somewhere between these two extreme viewpoints. Much more research will need to be done to clarify the situation.

In the meantime, suggestions have been advanced to resolve the difficulties created in psychiatric classification by the element of ambiguity that attaches at present to the terms 'functional' and 'organic'. This is in turn closely related to the fact that psychiatric taxonomy is based both on a descriptive and an aetiological principle which leads to contradictory results in the area of overlap discussed here. The suggestion made by Essen-Möller (1961) is that for each psychiatric patient both a descriptive and an aetiological diagnosis should be separately specified. Unfortunately, in our present state of knowledge of aetiology, this is not likely to be practicable. An alternative suggestion (Roth and Kay, 1969) is that for each psychiatric patient a descriptive diagnosis should be supplemented by a statement about any organic disorders present. In this way knowledge about the precise contribution of cerebral and physical disease to the causation of psychiatric disorders could be slowly accumulated. A similar practice with regard to factors of possible psychogenic significance, particularly in relation to neuroses and personality disorders, would have much to commend it although it would demand the resolution of some difficult problems.

It must be emphasized that what may be called the overlap between the organic and functional territories is relatively small. It does not invalidate the broad distinction that has been drawn between the two groups of conditions.

PSYCHOLOGICAL CHANGES PRODUCED BY ORGANIC BRAIN DISEASE

Brain diseases tend to produce certain general patterns of deficit in mental function irrespective of their localization. The outfall of abilities represents, however, only one aspect of the clinical picture. In acute states there are widespread disturbances of affect and autonomic function, an upset of the sleeping-waking controls, and positive rather than deficit symptoms, such as hallucination. In the chronic states mechanisms of other kinds come into play. The work of Goldstein (1930, 1937 and 1942) has shown that the personality of the brain-injured patient struggles to overcome its defects, and to maintain its integrity in certain characteristic ways. In any full investigation of a case of organic cerebral disease it is essential, therefore, to study not only the pattern of intellectual impairment, but also the general behaviour of the patient.

The Acute Psycho-Organic Syndrome

This has been described in detail on pages 346–349. None of the phenomena described in those pages are incompatible with acute disturbances of cerebral function arising from cerebral trauma or disease, though they may also be produced by general systemic disturbances such as infections. Clouding of consciousness is the cardinal change, and may be of any degree of severity, or so slight that it shows itself only in deficient attention and subsequent difficulties in recall of sense impressions received in the clouded state. In the initial stages of development of diseases of the brain and particularly in cerebral tumour and arteriosclerosis, episodes of clouding of consciousness may be short-lived and produce evanescent changes in behaviour whose character may go unrecognized if the possibility of a change in level of awareness has not been considered; an important clue at an early stage of the disease may thus be overlooked. Ageing seems to bring with it a heightened predisposition to states of clouded consciousness, and this may complicate relatively slight damage to the brain. The diagnosis is particularly difficult when there are mild degrees of clouding with some *difficulty in grasp, a tendency to vagueness and incoherence in thought, fluctuating disorientation*, and restlessness. The dangers are that a picture of this kind may be wholly missed, or that though he recognizes it, the clinician may assume in subacute and chronic cases, particularly in old people, that clouding and other reversible defects are due to a progressing dementia. Careful history-taking can obviate most mistakes of this kind, but in difficult cases some help may be obtained from the electroencephalogram, which shows a reasonably good correlation with the level of awareness (Engel and Romano, 1944; Romano and Engel, 1944), whereas in an established dementia due to degenerative disease, little may be seen apart from a rather slow alpha rhythm.

The Chronic Psycho-Organic Syndrome

A chronic state of impairment of the mind and personality may be left behind by an acute illness in which there has been brain damage, or it may arise slowly and insidiously in the intact individual as a result of progressive changes. In either case there may be temporary exacerbations in which symptoms of the acute psycho-organic syndrome may be seen, which then pass off to leave the more lasting state here to be described. It must be remembered, however, that there are possibilities of restitution of function even when there has been permanent damage to the brain; so that the signs and symptoms of a chronic syndrome do not necessarily imply its permanence. These signs and symptoms are shown in the three fields of affectivity, memory disturbance, and other defects of intellectual function.

AFFECTIVE CHANGES. In many organic states these changes may be seen at a very early stage, before there is any detectable impairment of memory or intellect. At such a stage they are very likely to be misinterpreted, perhaps as indications of a neurotic reaction, so that the organic cause of the change in personality is diagnosed only after unnecessary delay. Nevertheless, these changes have characteristic qualities, both in their mode of development and their appearance, which may suggest the desirability of investigation along physical lines. If the patient, or still more the relative of a patient, gives a history of a change in personality affecting the habitual modes of behaviour of a stable well-adjusted man in middle or later life, this alone will be enough to suggest looking beyond psychogenic causes to the possibility of underlying physical ones.

Most characteristic is an increased lability of affect. The patient reacts excessively to minor frustrations or disappointments, though the affective reaction may be quick and short-lasting; this alone, if the change is a marked one, lends to the emotional responses a quality of childishness. The patient has less insight into his emotions, and less control over them. Impulsive acts, which may take on an antisocial character, such as a sexual offence or larceny in a shop, are made more probable; and such an act by someone of unimpeachable respectability may be the first sign of organic brain disease. The superficiality of affective reactions may be combined with increased suggestibility to produce hysterical and dissociative symptoms. Such symptoms occurring in mature and stable personalities should always be made grounds for further enquiry along organic lines. In the advanced case, the patient's incapacity for control of the physical expression of his emotions may be shown in pathological laughing or crying. The emotion itself may be so slight as to be hardly felt, and yet because, say reference is made to his long-dead mother, the tears well up into the patient's eyes. The emotional reactions to which such patients are particularly predisposed are those of irritation and anger; a grouchy, morose or querulous irritability, which flares up on the slightest or on only imagined cause, is common in these patients, and a frequent source of difficulty in their management. A tendency to paranoid suspicion is also fairly frequent and may lead to delusions of reference or persecution.

Lasting mood changes may also appear early in the development of a chronic organic syndrome. Of these the commonest is a depressive state, often with a good deal of hypochondriacal colouring. Depressive, hypomanic or paranoid states may be so florid that the psychiatrist mistakes them for an endogenous psychosis. Later on in the course of the illness, these brisk emotional reactions tend to flatten out into a state of affective impoverishment. The patient is then left in an apathetic state, unable to take any interest in his old hobbies or in the affairs of his family, querulous, dull and increasingly egocentric. The loss of drive leads to incapacity for decisive action, so that the patient may haver and dither about the most trifling matters, and show an equal incapacity for persistence in a consistent course of conduct. Symptoms of an obsessional type may appear to complicate the picture, but can usually be readily recognized as of secondary nature. With further advance of the illness, a stage of affective dilapidation is reached. Emotions, which had once been over-brisk and labile, are now dull, shallow and blunted.

DISTURBANCES OF MEMORY. The dysmnesic syndrome has been briefly described in the chapter on Exogenous Reactions and Symptomatic Psychoses (p. 349). An essentially similar state is often seen after severe closed head injuries, or damage from sub-arachnoid haemorrhage or encephalitis, or accompanying such diseases as general paresis, cerebral arteriosclerosis and cerebral tumour. The most prominent defect of memory functions is usually shown in retention, and this may be so marked that all other aspects of memory disturbance fade into relative insignificance. The clinical picture will then approximate to the Korsakov syndrome. This syndrome is most commonly seen in association with alcoholism (see p. 404); but the specific memory defect, i.e. an incapacity to retain recent impressions, the filling of amnesic gaps with confabulated material, accompanied by a disorientation in relationships of time and space of which the patient himself seems to be unaware, is a common sequela of subcortical centrencephalic damage such as may occur with carbon monoxide poisoning or head injury.

It is of interest that a permanent dysmnesic syndrome has been produced in a number of cases by bilateral resections of the medial aspects of the temporal lobes. The hippocampal gyri appear to be of greatest importance in this respect and the disability is proportional to the posterior extent of the lesion (Scoville and Milner, 1957). Similar results have followed where the excision has been limited to the dominant temporal lobe (Milner and Penfield, 1955) but in these cases it was probable that the opposite temporal lobe was atrophic. The belief that bilateral lesions of the mammillary bodies give rise to a dysmnesic syndrome has been held for some considerable time and further support for this view has been provided by Williams and Pennybacker (1954). It is significant that the hippocampal regions of the temporal lobes have a strong projection to the mammillary bodies and that one of the well-recognized temporal lobe auras is the phenomenon of panoramic memory. It is unlikely that the temporal lobes are the repositories of the individual's store of memories in the manner suggested by Penfield (1954).

Failure of retention is usually only part of the total disturbance of memory. Experiences which are retained are often not readily recalled on request, and may only emerge with the aid of a clue. Recognition is always better preserved than recall. Recent memories are often badly preserved, while the patient is still able to produce memories of the remote past with normal facility. Part of this difficulty in forming stable memory traces may be due to a generalized intellectual impairment, shown in difficulties of comprehension and reduced attention with greater distractibility. In course of the progress of disease, the memory stores themselves become depleted; and if this goes far a demented state is reached, with a washing away of the very identity of the personality. While relatively long-term memories are preserved, and there is no affective flattening, even a severely brain-injured patient will retain a facade of his old personality, which may be completely convincing to the casual visitor.

Recent enquiries into the Korsakov syndrome by Talland (1965) have shown that the dysmnesic syndromes are far more complex psychological disturbances than has been generally supposed. Although the subject's capacity to register new information is severely impaired, most patients manage to assimilate and learn some simple instructions and respond to their environment in a surprisingly appropriate manner. More unexpected still is the success some patients achieve in carrying out more or less complex instructions which have to be followed for relatively long stretches of time. Reasoning and judgement show no anomalies, but concept formation which demands fresh learning is usually defective. The capacity to recall past memories is severely impaired as well as the ability to assimilate and recall new information. There is a marked susceptibility to interruption, and inability to resume tasks after such a gap is regarded by Talland as a major source of the Korsakov patient's disability. He considers the basic defect of these patients to be one of conation. They lack the capacity for the sustained intellectual effort involved in matching and testing of new information with that already stored; this is essential for the acquisition of new learning. The recall of remote memories also requires some search of the memory store and testing for fit. Here again intellectual effort dies away before it can come to fruition. It is suggested that lesions of the hippocampal memory system are associated with impairment of initiative, memory and new learning because this part of the brain is probably connected with 'programming behaviour' (Pribram, 1963). General intellectual ability may remain intact in the dysmnesic syndrome, an I.Q. of 116 having been recorded (Zangwill, 1964).

DISTURBANCE OF OTHER INTELLECTUAL FUNCTIONS. Intelligence itself always suffers when there is a memory defect, though its impairment may not be easy to demonstrate. The patient becomes less able to deal with new ideas, and will reject them in favour of his set ways of thinking; his own capacity to produce anything new or fresh also diminishes. Thought is impoverished, and in progressive disease is bit by bit reduced to banalities and clichés. There is a particular difficulty in handling abstract ideas, while the capacity to deal with the concrete is retained; details are better handled than ideas of a general kind. One sees a better performance if the patient is discussing matters which closely concern him, and are tied up with an affective response; this goes hand in hand with a reduction of interests to an increasingly egocentric range. At the highest level, both judgement and insight are likely to suffer early. Later there is a loss of intellectual flexibility and the capacity to respond adequately to changes in the situation. Still later one finds clinically observable deficiencies in comprehension, and overt disturbance in powers of attention. In a relatively advanced stage there appear general retardation and tendencies to perseveration.

The circumscribed defects of function which accompany localized lesions in the brain, which are discussed later in this chapter (pp. 492–499), are also frequently demonstrable against a background of generalized intellectual impairment in pathological states affecting the brain as a whole (e.g. general paresis, presenile dementia, arteriosclerosis). One can, for instance, often show that the man who, on superficial examination, appears to be suffering from a severe and generalized intellectual impairment, is in fact capable of thinking at a higher level but is hampered by word-finding difficulties. Dyslectic, dyspractic and dysgnosic symptoms may also at times stand out in some prominence in cases where there is no doubt of some degree of failure of a generalized kind.

When we come to consider the variation with age in the effects of brain damage, we encounter an interesting contradiction. Damage to the speech areas in the dominant hemisphere in a young child may be followed either by no impairment of speech function or by a dysphasia that recovers with time, whereas destruction of the same area in an adult will give rise to much more serious damage of an irreversible character. In contrast to this, damage to the frontal lobes in an adult will generally cause no demonstrable intellectual defect despite severe changes in personality, whereas similar damage in a young child will give rise to a permanent defect in relation to certain types of intellectual activity.

GENERAL BEHAVIOUR. No one has contributed so much to our understanding of the way in which the brain-injured patient adapts himself to his difficulties as Goldstein has;

and Goldstein's ideas are fundamental to a modern view of the problem and to considerations both of diagnosis and treatment (Goldstein, 1930, 1937 and 1942).

The sick man unconsciously attempts to readjust his life so as to be able to meet all demands made upon him by the environment as well as he can. When exposed to situations with which he cannot cope, he is likely to become anxious, agitated, sullen, angry and evasive. His pulse may rise, he will appear restless and tremulous, and may burst into tears. This *'catastrophic reaction'* is not simply the patient's response to an awareness that he has failed in his task for it develops simultaneously with his performance not after it, nor is the patient usually able to offer any explanation for his distress. In order to prevent this 'catastrophic reaction' from occurring, the patient restricts his environment in such a way that he is unlikely to be exposed to situations which might provoke it. He may become solitary and withdrawn, and makes himself relatively impervious to those stimuli from the environment which he dreads. He may, on the other hand, take refuge in the kind of purposeless over-activity appearing as 'occupational delirium' that is observed in many cases of dementia.

The possessions of the patient are frequently disposed in a stereotyped and meticulous manner, although it is difficult to discover any logical reason for the arrangement chosen. This *'organic orderliness'* may also show itself as a compulsive tendency to order the property of others, and to make impossible demands on the orderliness of any children there may be in the house.

Goldstein has pointed out that the brain-injured person tends to suppress all knowledge of his disability. This suppression seems to be more easily achieved by the patient in whom some function is wholly destroyed, than by the individual whose disability is incomplete; the rule holds good not only for perceptual defects such as blindness and deafness, but also paralysis of limbs and disturbances of speech. There is often a better adjustment to the disability in the case with a complete than in one with an incomplete hemiplegia, and more emotional disturbance is commonly present when sight is severely impaired than in the totally blind. It would seem that a new equilibrium based on *adaptation to a shrunken environment* is difficult so long as the impaired function can continue in partial use.

Lesions cause not merely an arbitrary loss of ability, but a systematic disintegration which shows certain general features irrespective of the type of function affected. Thus there is a *rise in the threshold of excitement*, so that stronger or more prolonged stimulation is required to elicit a response. Once excitation has occurred, however, it irradiates excessively and lasts abnormally long. This law provides some insight into the nature of such phenomena as the 'affective slumber' seen in some early cases of dementia (e.g. Alzheimer's disease). Intense stimulation is prone in these cases to evoke an exaggerated emotional response, or a prolonged bout of tense purposeless hyperactivity. The perseveration of aphasics and the logoclonia and pallilalia of some cases of presenile dementia may also be explained by these changes in cerebral excitability. Such phenomena are of practical importance, since they often create problems of some difficulty during the training of persons disabled by brain damage.

The patient appears abnormally *susceptible to external stimuli*. But he is distractible rather than inattentive. His attention may, in fact, be very difficult to divert in some circumstances, and he is often aware of this subjectively as an inability to shift his attention voluntarily from one part of the environment to another. He is thus distractible in some situations, and 'tied to the stimulus' in others.

Another source of difficulty to the patient with cerebral damage lies in his inability to distinguish between *'figure' and 'background'* of phenomena in perception. As a result, while attempting to solve problems, or even in normal surroundings, the patient experiences the uncertainty and instability of a normal person confronted with 'ambiguous' figures. The metaphor of 'figure and ground' widely used in Gestalt psychology may also refer to the brain-injured man's difficulty in distinguishing essentials from non-essentials (Critchley 1953).

Goldstein has described two types of attitude towards the world: (1) A relatively primitive and *'concrete'* attitude in which thinking is determined by and cannot proceed beyond some immediate experience, object or stimulus. (2) The *abstract* attitude which involves a relative detachment from the given experience, and in which thought and action are directed by some general concept that embraces the immediate situation as one of a certain class of phenomena.

Goldstein cites the following as characteristic of the abstract attitude: '(1) Assuming a mental set voluntarily. (2) Shifting voluntarily from one aspect of a situation to another. (3) Keeping in mind simultaneously various aspects of a situation. (4) Grasping the essential of a given whole, breaking up the given whole into parts, and isolating them voluntarily. (5) Abstracting common properties, planning ahead ideationally, assuming an attitude to the merely possible, and thinking or performing symbolically. (6) Detaching ego from the outer world.'

Some activities can be successfully executed only through the adoption of the abstract attitude, but for other tasks, the concrete attitude is the appropriate one. The normal individual can assume either, and is able to shift voluntarily from one to the other. The individual with a brain lesion is relatively *incapable of assuming the 'abstract' or 'categorical' attitude*, and cannot *shift at will from one attitude to the other*. It is a matter of everyday observation with such patients that the greater the need for detachment from a concrete task for the successful solution of a problem, the greater the likelihood of failure. Thus, there are patients with parietal-lobe lesions who are able to use scissors, to open a door with a key, or to smoke a cigarette, but asked to mimic the movements required for any of these tasks they are completely at a loss.

Some brain-damaged patients while unable to read may yet be capable of identifying letters or words if they are underlined. It is phenomena such as these which make it useless to score the patient's performance purely in terms of success or failure. A severely disabled patient may contrive to achieve some task in some very roundabout manner. If the final result only is taken into consideration, his disability will be overlooked. It is, therefore, of great importance to try to learn how he achieves his task in detail.

Although performance in 'sorting' and related tests of the abstract attitude yield results of clinical interest, it is doubtful whether the effects of brain damage can be described in terms of a unitary functional disturbance. Nor is loss of the abstract attitude specific for brain damage (Zangwill, 1964).

DEMENTIA. Dementia refers to a global deterioration of mental functioning in its intellectual, emotional and cognitive aspects. Intellectual decline is the central feature but affective and personality changes are nearly always closely associated and in the early stages of some dementing processes as, for example, in Pick's disease and arterio-sclerotic psychosis, the deterioration may be confined to these emotional aspects. However, dementia should not be used to describe personality changes unless intellectual deterioration can be confidently predicted at a later stage. Some structural alteration in the brain is probably always present in dementia but this is not necessarily irreversible.

In the process which we call dementia, the clinical picture is usually dominated by intellectual disintegration, but feeling and striving are always affected. The general features of the syndrome show a fairly consistent pattern which is varied in the individual case according to the pre-morbid personality, the age of onset, the nature of the cause, and any local preponderance in the early lesions. The impairment of memory for recent events, which is the earliest change, may be effectively compensated for a considerable time by a surprising ingenuity in concealment, adherence to a rigid daily routine and the use of a notebook. This adjustment breaks down as intellectual grasp weakens and thinking becomes slow, laboured and ill defined. Attention is now aroused and sustained with difficulty, the patient tires easily, particularly with any unaccustomed task, and he is prone to become lost in the middle of an argument or sentence. Poverty of thought supervenes in a once richly stored, flexible mind: it shrinks to a small core of ever-recurring, rigidly held ideas and re-evoked memories of the remote past, which may for long remain vivid and clear.

The impairment of memory and poverty of grasp may give rise to *delusions* of a characteristically transient, ever-changing and unorganized kind, commonly concerned with fears of being robbed, deprived, influenced. Emotion, at first labile, grows increasingly shallow and blunted with the progress of the disease. The death of a life-long partner or dearly loved friend is passed over in indifference, though some trivial inconvenience arouses violent anger. Finally the reaction to all situations is one of *fatuous, euphoric equanimity*. Judgement and self-control are impaired, so that sexual assaults on young children or exhibitionism may bring formerly blameless characters to the attention of the police. Personal habits deteriorate and the patient's appearance and home get so neglected that he has frequently to be removed to hospital from conditions of unbelievable filth. With the disorganization of thought, speech becomes more and more incoherent and contact with the patient increasingly tenuous, until all that is left is a gabbling, fatuous, incontinent shadow of his original self.

In accounts of dementia the main emphasis is generally laid on the intellectual defects because these are its most consistent manifestations. But the *other facets of personality* are usually also affected. Nor is the intellect always the first to deteriorate; some processes of progressive deterioration such as those in general paralysis, alcoholism and epilepsy may first present with a picture of decreasing initiative, blunted emotion or impaired judgement in which deficiencies in formal intelligence may be impossible to demonstrate.

Although the term 'dementia', as it has been defined above, applies only to irreversible processes, all of the symptoms associated with it, even the most characteristic ones, may be seen in conditions which can be halted or reversed, such as cerebral tumour, pernicious anaemia, general paresis, and myxoedema. Furthermore, the deficit symptoms left behind by a permanent but static cerebral lesion may be relieved of their disabling effects by processes of psychological adjustment; re-training and self-training may in fact radically alter the clinical picture. It is therefore important not to be misled, when observing the symptoms characteristic of a dementing process, into thinking that irreversible and progressive changes are necessarily occurring.

For some time *psychometric tests* have been widely used to identify dementia (in particular its cognitive aspects) and to measure its severity. When considering this problem of intellectual deterioration it must be first decided whether or not the psychiatric group in question shows deterioration from its pre-illness level of cognitive functioning. Although the aetiology of the intellectual impairment cannot be concluded from the psychologist's assessment, deterioration can be assessed.

Among the long-established methods by which psychologists have investigated intellectual deterioration are the Babcock-Levy test of efficiency of mental functioning

(1940), the Shipley-Hartford test of deterioration (1940), the Hunt-Minnesota test of organic brain damage (1943), the Wechsler Deterioration Indices (1944, 1958) and subsequent indices derived from these scales.

Underlying these procedures are two basic assumptions: (1) that vocabulary tests in normal people have a high correlation with other tests of general intelligence (2) that the test yielding the smallest mean difference between normal and psychotic or brain-damaged groups is a vocabulary test. Consequently the present level of vocabulary of a patient is a good measure of his pre-illness general intelligence. The discrepancy between the present I.Q. and the vocabulary score provides an indirect measure of deterioration. It should be noted, however, that vocabulary itself may deteriorate slightly with illness (Shapiro and Nelson, 1955; Payne, 1960). Further, none of the tests has been adequately standardized, nor correctly validated.

The Wechsler scales are based on the assumption that certain sub-tests of intelligence hold up and others decline with age, and that deterioration produce by psychosis or brain damage can be identified with deterioration consequent on normal ageing, except in respect of speed of onset. In practice the deterioration indices and the verbal-performance discrepancy scores calculated from the Wechsler Adult Intelligence Scale have not proved effective in differentiating brain-damaged from non-brain-damaged psychiatric patients (Bolton, Britton and Savage, 1966). A new kind of test was introduced by Shapiro and Nelson (1955) when they suggested that diminution of present learning ability is an important component in the impairment of intellectual functioning among psychiatric patients. They devised a test which entailed the learning and retention of the meaning of five previously unknown words. In their Modified Word Learning test Walton and Black (1957) carry this technique a stage further by administering the Terman-Merrill vocabularly test until the subject is unable to recall the meanings of ten consecutive words. The meaning of these ten words is then communicated to the patient and the process repeated until he is able to give a definition of at least six of the words. Rote learning is avoided by changing the wording used to explain meaning. In the earlier studies (Walton et al., 1959) it was claimed that over 80 per cent. of organic subjects could be correctly identified without any misclassification of subjects free from cerebral disease. However, in a more recent investigation, Orme et al. (1964) classified 81 per cent. of organic subjects correctly but only 69 per cent. of those without organic lesions. A similar result was registered by Bolton et al. (1967). They were able to identify correctly 71 per cent. of organic and 100 per cent. of normal subjects. However, only 77 per cent. of schizophrenic and 71 per cent. of affective subjects were correctly classified. The Paired Associate Learning test devised by Inglis (1959) makes use of a slightly different principle and has also proved a valuable adjunct in the diagnosis of organic disease.

PSYCHOLOGICAL EFFECTS OF FOCAL BRAIN DAMAGE

It is often asserted that localization of function in the brain is an abstraction since the cerebrum works as a whole. It may be admitted that the mosaic picture of cerebral function drawn by some extreme exponents of cerebral localization does not do justice to the facts. The cerebrum works as a totality and knowledge of its functions can hardly be built up from observations of the effects of lesions alone. Yet lesions in one part of the brain indubitably exert different effects from those produced in other parts as far as speech, movement, sensation, motor skill and orientation in space are concerned. Although the derangements in pattern of behaviour produced by localized brain damage are perhaps of a less specific kind, the syndromes associated with frontal lobe and temporal lobe damage provide valuable guides to the localization of the responsible lesion.

However, recent enquiries have altered our views about the specificity of the effects of localized lesions. The enquiries of Teuber and Bender (1948–51) have shown, for example, that non-specific effects co-exist with specific ones in the same groups of patients with localized lesions. Localized occipital lesions, for example, may produce highly specific and localizable effects in the form of scotomata, but there are also diffuse changes revealed by tests of flicker fusion, dark adaptation and motion perception in the whole of the visual field. Moreover, the older views about the independence of 'higher' and 'lower' aspects of sensation, according to which the ability to discriminate objects placed in the hand, or astereognosis, was regarded as independent of disturbances of primary sensory function, appear to require revision. According to these workers discrimination deficits of this nature are almost invariably associated with more basic sensory defects, and these may also affect seemingly unimpaired parts of the patient's body, such as the contra-lateral hand. Patients with visual object agnosia are also found to manifest more elementary disturbances of visual perception. Again, analysis of a patient with a visual-spatial agnosia associated with route-finding difficulties (Weinstein et al., 1956) has shown that a defective performance in route-finding tests was closely associated with impairment of two-point discrimination. The agnosia was thus associated with a defect of somaesthesis and therefore lacked the specificity for a single modality of sensation that was implicit in the classical concept of agnosia. However, neither the 'higher' nor the 'lower' level defect suffices to explain the total deficit of function manifested by the patient. Recent observations have also cast doubt on the sharpness of the distinction formerly made between dysphasia and intellectual impairment. Dysphasic patients tend to show poorer performance than other subjects with brain damage in non-verbal as well as verbal tests. Moreover, there is quite strong evidence that patients with lesions of the left hemisphere, without clinical dysphasia, are liable to prove inferior in performance to subjects with equivalent right hemisphere lesions on tests of verbal intelligence and memory (Piercy, 1964).

These fresh observations are of considerable interest from a theoretical point of view. From the practical clinical viewpoint they imply that the symptoms of impairment in higher levels of function in perception, speech, intellect and general behaviour must be interpreted with greater flexibility and reserve than in the past. Nevertheless, the effects of lesions remain in some measure specific, and when these are integrated with information derived from the clinical history, clinical examination, the E.E.G. and radiological evidence, they can make a valuable contribution to the localization of lesions.

PREFRONTAL REGION. Lesions in front of the precental gyrus produce a *change in personality* that has become widely familiar since the operation of prefrontal leucotomy has been practised.

The patient's behaviour becomes unrestrained and tactless, and his mood changes to a uniformly *fatuous jocularity* which finds expression in ill-timed bawdy and puerile jokes ('*Witzelsucht*') quite out of keeping with his usual behaviour. His feelings are blunted so that he behaves with a callous unconcern for his family. Boastfulness, grandiose behaviour and megalomaniacal ideas reflect an expansive trend that is reminiscent of general paralysis; the similarities are due to frontal preponderance of the changes produced by the latter. Deterioration of memory and intellect is not necessarily present, but imaginative or original qualities in thought tend to be suppressed, and spontaneity and initiative are diminished. The patient is inattentive, distractible, and his work increasingly slapdash and inefficient. Sometimes there is a uniformly *dull apathy, indifference and slowness* of thought instead of euphoria. In all cases drowsiness, lethargy and retardation tend to become increasingly prominent in progressive lesions, and are reflected in a vacant stupidity of the facial expression. The patient becomes careless in dress, eats gluttonously and may urinate in public without shame or embarrassment. With rapidly expanding frontal-lobe tumours states of *extreme aspontaneity* may be seen and sometimes conditions sharing many features with catatonic stupor. The grasp reflex and forced groping are particularly common with pictures of this kind produced by prefrontal neoplasm. Generalized *convulsions* occur in about half the cases; with tumours on the convexity, turning of eyes and head towards the opposite side may help in localization. Expressive *dysphasia* appears when the tumour invades Broca's area in the posterior part of the lateral surface. In the case of meningiomas other symptoms may aid localization. Those arising in the olfactory groove give rise to unilateral—and sometimes bilateral—anosmia, often with a ipsilateral primary optic atrophy. If raised intracranial pressure is also present the opposite eye may show papilloedema.

Tumours involving the anterior two-thirds of the *corpus callosum* produce a mental picture that is indistinguishable from the frontal lobe syndrome. Retardation and intellectual disturbance is, however, often exceptionally severe, and *apraxia* on one or both sides and asymmetrical pyramidal signs are often associated. All these features are in fact due to invasion of the adjacent regions of the frontal lobes. Surgical experience has shown that the corpus callosum itself can be severed without obvious impairment of cerebral function.

A small proportion of *temporal lobe* tumours produce a similar personality change and as Bleuler (1951) has pointed out this change may also occur in the case of growths in the diencephalon. From the latter, frontal lobe tumours may sometimes be distinguished by the patient's total lack of insight; in diencephalic growths the patient is more likely to be aware of his deficiencies.

TEMPORAL LOBE. The ictal phenomena produced by a temporal lobe focus have been described on page 459.

In 1938 Klüver and Bucy published their classical observations on the effects of bilateral temporal lobectomy in monkeys. The changes included visual (and at times other forms of) agnosia, increased oral activity, marked changes in emotional sexual behaviour, and eating habits. The changes in emotional and sexual conduct, were especially noteworthy. The monkeys became tame and showed no anger or fear reactions, even when exposed to live snakes or other objects which normally evoked extreme excitement. There was also a striking intensification of hetero-, homo- and autosexual conduct. These studies stimulated a great deal of investigation into the functions of the limbic system or old olfactory brain in the higher mammals. There is now a good deal of evidence that very little of the rhinencephalon serves olfactory functions in man and that the greater part of the limbic system is concerned in some way with the regulation of affective life in the individual. The striking affective and temperamental changes often seen in the presence of lesions of the temporal lobes, whether or not associated with epilepsy, are thus explained.

Emotionally the patients become more unstable, irritable and aggressive. Outbursts of an explosive kind, and acts of violence, may result. In long-standing cases there are often hypochondriacal preoccupations concerned with some part of the body-image. These may have their origin in depersonalization experiences during the seizures. It is now well established also that bilateral hippocampal damage gives rise to defects of recent memory leaving remote memories largely intact. The degree of deficit varies in proportion to the extent of the hippocampal damage produced bilaterally (Scoville and Milner, 1957). In the occasional case in which a similar syndrome has followed unilateral lobectomy there has probably been a pre-existing lesion on the opposite side. In relation to other deficits reported following temporal lobectomy, operations on the two hemispheres appear to have differing effects. Thus Meyer *et al.* (1955) have reported defective performance in tests of verbal intelligence learning following left lobectomy without any corresponding effects in patients who have suffered removal of the right temporal lobe. Kimura has also shown that patients who have had a right lobectomy show a significantly poorer performance than those who have had a left lobectomy in certain tests of auditory perception and musical aptitude (Kimura, 1961). Little attempt has been made so far to apply these observations in clinical practice but within the next few years we shall doubtless see the application of such findings in the localization of lesions in the cerebrum.

Visual field defects may occur in temporal lesions. They are due to the involvement of the lower fibres of the optic radiation as they turn posteriorly along the lateral aspect of the inferior horn of the lateral ventricle. The defect is therefore a superior quadrantic homonymous hemianopia which is usually more extensive on the side of the lesion. *Aphasia* occurs in about half the cases, and is usually nominal in character, but marked *syntactic defects* may occur similar to those in parietal lobe lesions to be described presently. In patients who speak an *incomprehensible jargon* the condition may be wrongly diagnosed as a psychotic illness, especially as the associated emotional disturbance may appear incongruous and inexplicable. Elderly subjects may be regarded as suffering from dementia with superimposed acute confusion. Mild contralateral pyramidal signs are generally present, the most common being weakness of the lower face. Emotional disturbances may be prominent between fits in temporal lobe epilepsy (see p. 464) and schizophrenia-like psychoses may develop in chronic cases. Impotence (Johnson, 1965), fetishism (Mitchell *et al.*, 1954) and transvestism with fetishism (Epstein, 1961) have been reported in association with temporal lobe lesions.

PARIETAL LOBE. Lesions of the parietal lobes produce defects in the highest levels of sensory integration. While the appreciation of tactile and painful stimuli may be superficially unaltered their localization and discrimination is no longer possible; the sense of position in space and of passive movement are impaired, and the ability to identify objects in the affected hand by their shape, size, weight, and texture alone, i.e. *stereognosis, barognosis,* is defective. The threshold for the perception of stimuli is raised and rendered variable, and excitation of a relatively large area may be required before the nature of the stimulus is identified. Associated with these defects there is usually an inability to distinguish a stimulus, that seems by itself to reach consciousness, when it is competing with some rival form of stimulation on the unaffected side of the body. This phenomenon was originally described as '*inattention*' for tactile stimuli by Oppenheim (1885) and was among the defects studied by Weizsäcker and his school, and embodied in their concept of '*Funktionswandel*'. Recently it has been named '*extinction*' for visual and tactile stimuli (Bender 1945, Bender and Furlow 1945). It is not essentially different from the phenomenon of suppression of perception of one stimulus by some prior stimulus on the same side if separated by only a short interval from it, or from the failure to discriminate between simultaneous stimuli close to each other in space.

The prime deficits associated with parietal lobe damage may be summarized under a number of headings.

IDEOMOTOR AND IDEATIONAL APRAXIA. The distinction between these two forms of defect is uncertain. The former is generally taken to refer to inability to imitate or execute gestures although the patient is aware of what is required of him and motor weakness is limited or absent. Ideational apraxia refers to the unskilful and uncoordinated use of common objects such as scissors, key, or cigarette. The balance of the evidence suggests that these defects are prone to appear in the presence of left parietal lobe lesions and rarely in right hemisphere lesions (Ajuriaguerra et al., 1960). Left-sided apraxia appears to be associated with lesions of the corpus callosum, which are held to interrupt a pathway from a principal co-ordinating centre for skilled movement in the left hemisphere to a subsidiary centre in the right hemisphere.

SOMATAGNOSIA, SPATIAL AGNOSIA AND DRESSING APRAXIA. The two parietal lobes appear to differ in the role they play with respect to somatic and spatial perception. Patients with right or minor hemisphere lesions may show inattention to the left half of the body and, if it is weak or helpless, as is often the case, the disability may be denied. When evidence to the contrary is forced on the patient's attention he may disown the affected limbs and advance grotesque explanations for his inability to move them. This phenomenon is often associated with neglect of the left half of visual space and such patients therefore show preference for right turnings; as a result, they may fail to find their way in familiar surroundings (Brain, 1941; Roth, 1949). These are the phenomena of agnosia for the left half of space and anosognosia for hemiplegia. Commonly associated with these disturbances is difficulty in dressing or 'dressing apraxia' derived from a failure to pay due attention to both the left and right half of the body and the corresponding parts of the garment concerned. Cases of anosognosia for hemiplegia and related defects have often been published in the past without evidence relating to the general intellectual status of the patients concerned. This has fostered the view that the deficits may be manifest in the presence of a wholly intact sensorium and intelligence. In fact, careful examination usually reveals disturbances of attention, memory retention and orientation and some subjects are frankly clouded in consciousness. However, the cognitive and intellectual deficits are rarely severe enough to explain the associated disorders of spatial and somatic perception.

The somatagnosic disturbances that appear in association with left-sided lesions differ in that they usually involve both sides of the body. However, the great majority of these defects consist of finger agnosia and left/right disorientation. This difference between the right and left hemisphere lesions in their effect on somatic perception has been recently confirmed by Hécaen (1962) in an extensive study of left and right hemispheric lesions.

GERSTMANN'S SYNDROME. Finger agnosia and left/right disorientation are components of Gerstmann's syndrome which was originally attributed (Gerstmann, 1927) to a lesion of the angular gyrus in the dominant hemisphere. The other components of the syndrome are agraphia and acalculia. The view that these deficits are highly correlated with one another has been submitted to a good deal of criticism in recent years. Different components of the syndrome may occur in isolation or in combination with other deficits. Skill in constructional tasks, visual memory and reading ability appear just as closely correlated to the components of the Gerstmann syndrome as its constituent deficits to one another (Benton, 1961). The only constituents which have stood up to close scrutiny have been right/left disorientation and finger agnosia which do appear to be correlated with each other and with a lesion in the major parietal lobe.

CONSTRUCTIONAL APRAXIA. This refers to the failure to reproduce or copy simple patterns or designs with the aid of pencil, blocks or matches. The separate parts of the pattern are incorrectly articulated and the final result is chaotic. Attempted drawings of common objects such as a bicycle or a flower show the parts disproportionate and incorrectly linked with one another, and the planes confused. Most of the evidence suggests that this deficit is more pronounced and common with lesions in the right than lesions in the left hemisphere (Piercy and Smyth, 1962). The possibility that the two hemispheres subserve different visual spatial tasks has been raised but not adequately evaluated for the present.

AGNOSIA. Reference has already been made to the doubts recently raised about the concept of agnosia in its classical sense. The field is in need of clarification which will doubtless come with further experimental studies. Some workers (Piercy, 1964) consider that, while there is evidence for diffuse sensory deficits in cases of visual agnosia, for example, these are insufficient to explain the agnosic defect observed. There is some evidence also for differentiation of function between the two hemispheres in respect of agnosic defects. Thus in an enquiry by Hécaen and Angelergues (1963) it was found that, whereas visual-spatial agnosia, associated with difficulties in spatial orientation and route-finding, was commoner with lesions of the posterior part of the right hemisphere than the left hemisphere, agnosia for faces, objects and pictures was commoner with posterior left hemisphere lesions.

OCCIPITAL LOBE. In the relatively rare tumours of this lobe a homonymous hemianopia occurs early in most cases. A loss of colour vision may come before a loss for white objects. Localized epileptic discharges originating in this area give rise to visual hallucinations, usually of a crude character, the patient describing flashes, stars or zigzags of light. When more highly organized hallucinatory experiences are reported, they usually suggest extension of the tumour forwards into the parieto-temporal region. In tumours of the dominant hemisphere, alexia is common. Papilloedema tends to occur early in occipital lobe tumours. A lesion in the occipital or occipito-parietal regions will not necessarily produce complete blindness in the affected parts of the visual field. Much more subtle defects may be seen whose elucidation requires careful study. There may be deficiencies of visual attention, colour perception, object recognition and localization in space of which the patient does not directly complain. Or objects in the affected parts of the field will be recognized by themselves, but will not be identified or even seen, when some competing stimulus is given in the unaffected parts of the field. Psychiatric changes in the sense of a chronic psycho-organic syndrome rarely occur with occipital lesions until there is a more generalized disturbance of brain function, e.g. by rise in intracranial pressure or by extension of the tumour.

LESIONS OF THE THIRD VENTRICLE, MID-BRAIN AND THALAMUS. The tumours in these different sites have been grouped together because the effects they produce on personality have certain common features. Moreover, the derangements of consciousness which may result from interference in these sites have certain characteristic qualities.

The *change in personality* consists of a diminution of initiative, a change to childish, fatuous jocularity, and deterioration of personal habits which have much in common with the frontal lobe syndrome. As already pointed out, however, the patient with the diencephalic lesion differs in that he is much more aware of the change that is thus being imposed upon him.

Cairns (1952) has given an account of the various kinds of *disturbance of consciousness*. They may be episodic or sustained in character. The former take the form of paroxysmal seizures with hyperextension, head retraction and in some cases the full posture of decerebrate rigidity (tonic fits). Loss of consciousness is almost invariable with the decerebrate rigidity, but occasionally tonic spasms may occur with retention of full awareness. Bouts of momentary unconsciousness with muscular hypotonia which resemble minor epilepsy are also seen, and provide some confirmation (as do the other manifestations of deranged consciousness from localized diencephalic lesions) for the observations of Penfield, Jasper and their associates (Penfield and Jasper, 1947; Jasper and Drooglever-Fortuyn, 1947; Jasper, 1949) that the primary site of disturbance in petit mal seizures is the thalamus.

In the sustained bouts of unconsciousness the patient appears to be normally asleep, his musculature relaxed, his breathing quiet. An attempt to rouse him may produce a few seconds' wakefulness but he will fall asleep 'even while talking or eating'. If a conversation can be maintained for a period, it will be evident that the patient is *clouded, disorientated and inclined to confabulate*. When the degree of unconsciousness is less profound, the patient's eyes are open, and painful stimuli may evoke some reflex response. This condition has been named '*akinetic mutism*', a name which gives an inadequate description of the patient's state of obnubilation, his failure to register what goes on around him, and the total amnesia for the 'mute' period, after recovery.

In all tumours in this neighbourhood, headache, vomiting and papilloedema are common. In *colloid cyst of the third ventricle* attacks of delirium or clouded consciousness and paroxysmal bouts of violent headache tend to have a sharp onset and terminate as suddenly. The headaches may be relieved by sudden changes in posture. Attacks of sudden weakness in the lower limbs, causing the patient to fall to the ground, may be mistaken for hysteria, especially as neurological signs are often absent. In other cases an erroneous diagnosis of cerebrovascular disease may be made.

Attacks of unconsciousness produced by diencephalic lesions may occur at an early stage when physical signs are scanty. They may therefore have considerable diagnostic significance. The electroencephalogram is occasionally of value in localizing the lesion as during attacks it shows highly rhythmic generalized paroxysmal slow waves synchronous in the two hemispheres.

CONSISTENT DIFFERENCES IN EFFECTS OF LESIONS OF THE TWO HEMISPHERES. Though there are no deficits which are associated exclusively with lesions of one or other hemisphere, certain fairly consistent differences have been demonstrated with the aid of experimental enquiry. Thus dysphasia, bilateral apraxia and finger agnosia, with defect in right/left orientation, almost invariably result from left hemisphere lesions in right-handed individuals. There is evidence also (McFie, 1960) that left hemisphere lesions generally produce greater intellectual deficits than those of corresponding lesions in the minor hemisphere. On the other hand, inattention to the contralateral side of the body, agnosia for the left half of space (in left-handed individuals), anosognosia for hemiplegia and also constructional apraxia and visual-spatial agnosia are more commonly produced by right than left hemisphere lesions. There is also the suggestion that, whereas removal of the right temporal lobe gives rise to subtle perceptual deficits in both visual half fields, left temporal lobectomy produces defects restricted to the opposite visual half field. An excellent review of the effects of cerebral lesions on intellectual function has been published by Piercy (1964) and this section has been much influenced by his views. Critchley's book on the parietal lobes (Critchley, 1953) reviews the subject in all its aspects. Allison's book, *The Senile Brain*, contains a wealth of clinical observation and should be consulted in relation to methods of examination for focal and general deficits.

INJURIES OF THE BRAIN

Mental disease due to brain trauma is only rarely a cause of admission to mental hospital, but psychiatrists are participating to an increasing extent in the work of general hospitals where they are often confronted with the problems connected with brain injuries. With the increasing mechanization of modern life, injuries to the head are becoming relatively common.

Aetiology and Pathology

On the whole severe fractures tend to be associated with extensive brain damage; but this may be present without fracture, and conversely the brain may escape injury though the skull has been fractured.

In the *severe cases of head injury* which prove fatal there are generally extensive areas of haemorrhage and laceration in the brain; the subarachnoid space is filled with blood, and the meninges are torn. The lesions are most severe at the site of the blow, at the point of *contre-coup*, and at the poles of the hemispheres; the tips and outer surfaces of the temporal lobes are particularly prone to be severely damaged. Microscopic examination reveals punctate haemorrhages and perivascular spaces filled with blood in widespread areas of the brain and the brain-stem. There are scattered areas of oedema and subsequently patches of severe demyelination appear which are probably secondary to injury and swelling of neurones. It is probable that in severe injuries which do not prove fatal, pathological changes of a similar though less severe kind are present and are responsible for the organic symptomatology which follows. However, *concussion*, the general paralysis of cerebral function that immediately follows a blow on the head, cannot be due to such anatomical changes. The available evidence suggests that this condition is independent of any coarse organic brain damage or contusion.

Recent work has not confirmed Trotter's widely accepted modification of Kocher's theory according to which the loss of consciousness is due to a sudden cerebral anaemia produced at the moment of impact. The investigations of Denny-Brown and Ritchie Russell (1941) suggest that the phenomena of concussion result from the direct effect of the *force which stretches and deforms the neurones, causing a reflex paralysis* of respiratory and vasomotor functions and loss of such lower level reflexes as the corneal and pharyngeal. This effect has been shown not to be dependent on the presence of the fore-brain or the integrity of the vestibular pathway. It has been suggested by Jefferson (1944), however, that the traumatic stupor is due primarily to the effect of the force on a *mid-brain centre* concerned with regulation of the level of consciousness and not to neuronal paralysis in the brain as a whole.

Thus the changes in pulse and respiration rate, blood pressure, and the pupillary, corneal and pharyngeal reflexes may be simply accounted for in terms of brain-stem paralysis. Moreover, it has become increasingly apparent in recent years from clinical and neurosurgical observations that a focal lesion in the posterior hypothalamus or upper mid-brain will often produce a state of unconsciousness, whereas extensive cortical excisions or lesions fail to do so. Further support for Jefferson's views has recently been provided by the work of Magoun and his school (Moruzzi and Magoun, 1949; Lindsley, Bowden and Magoun, 1949) who have shown that the reticular formation in the brain-stem has some specific role in the regulation of the level of awareness.

The work of Holbourn (1943) has shown that damage is most likely to result from blows which impart *shear strains to the brain* rather than those that compress it. Being a relatively incompressible substance in an enclosed space the brain can make only a swirling movement; this is restricted by the falx and tentorium and by bony projections within the cranium such as the sphenoidal ridge; it is at these places (e.g. the temporal poles) that damage is usually greatest. Holbourn has demonstrated that in models the maximum shear strains occur at sites corresponding to those at which brain damage is most often observed at autopsy.

It seems a little doubtful whether a theory involving structural changes can account for the *mildest forms of concussion*, in which unconsciousness is instantaneous but of only momentary duration. Furthermore we have to consider concussion of the brain in relation to the well-established cases of concussion of the spinal cord. In view of the excitability by mechanical means, such as vibration, of all nervous tissue, and the sensory phenomena which are experienced in degrees of concussion in which there is only dazing but no abrogation of consciousness, a physiological pathogenesis has, at least, to be considered. Whatever the cause of the initial loss of consciousness, a specific role in its perpetuation must be attributed to changes in the brain-stem, and probably in the upper mid-brain.

Mental Symptoms in the Acute Stage

There is no clear line of demarcation between the symptoms produced by simple concussion and those occurring when some contusion is present in addition. However, in general, as unconsciousness increases in duration above one to two hours, there is a growing likelihood that some degree of coarse brain damage has been sustained. It is customary to divide the symptoms in the acute stage into those seen in *mild, moderate* and *severe* cases (Symonds, 1949).

It must be emphasized that this classification of Symonds, which equates severity of the injury with the length of the period of unconsciousness, applies to closed head injuries. Cases with very severe open head injuries—particularly when due to high velocity bullets—may show no impairment of consciousness.

In a *mild case* the patient may not lose consciousness completely but may continue what he was doing in a slow, dazed and confused manner. On the other hand consciousness may be completely lost for a few seconds or minutes. Consciousness usually returns slowly so that a period of confusion follows in which the patient appears dazed and may be resistive. There will be a complete amnesia for this period, for the accident and for a brief interval before it. Headache and drowsiness are common sequelae but within a few hours mental symptoms will have completely abated in the majority of cases.

In the *moderate case* there may be unconsciousness for as long as several hours, and before awakening the patient passes through a stage of clouded consciousness which may be followed by a period in which he is in a dysmnesic state. These stages last from a few hours to two to three days. On coming out of a coma the patient is resistive and perplexed, and misinterprets his environment, perhaps imagining he is in a foreign country or in prison and identifying the doctors as spies or gaolers. He is disorientated, though frequently expressing an apparently delusional compromise between the true and some preferred but false orientation (Paterson and Zangwill, 1944). Thus a Lancashire man may be apparently aware that he is in hospital in London but insist that Manchester is a couple of miles away. Occasionally episodes of aggressive behaviour occur in which crimes of violence may be committed. This stage of clouded consciousness may take the form of an acute delirium particularly in the old and alcoholic and in cases complicated by severe loss of blood and secondary infection. The patient experiences terrifying visual hallucinations and delusions; he is in the thick of battle surrounded on all sides, armed gangsters are approaching with threatening gestures, other patients are spies, dope-pedlars or prostitutes in disguise. These delusions are ever changing and unsystematized since they originate in sensory falsifications and poverty of grasp. The picture as a whole is labile, fear, excitement and aggressiveness giving way with rapidity to a dazed, dreamy state or to a bland euphoria. Thought is vague and incoherent. There is a marked defect of retention, and suggestibility is heightened, the patient being easily induced to produce grotesque confabulations. The florid features of the stage of clouded consciousness or delirium subside, hallucinations and delusions cease, and eventually a fatuous, inert state may supervene in which a memory defect for recent events is evident. In this post-traumatic dysmnesic state (see p. 487) restlessness or mild delirium may at first develop at night but the patient returns to normal within 48–72 hours. In moderate cases the deep and superficial reflexes are absent immediately after consciousness is lost. They return after a short interval and the plantars are then extensor but in the majority of cases this is a fleeting phenomenon. On lumbar puncture, blood-stained fluid is obtained on the first five to six days, and it is frequently under raised pressure.

In cases of *severe* head injury the period of unconsciousness may last hours, days and even weeks. An essential feature of these cases is brain-stem involvement which may show structural damage, displacement and compression, oedema or a combination of these factors. The coma may be profound from the time of injury or may deepen rapidly for a period in those cases where intracerebral and subarachnoid bleeding are prominent. In the most severe cases, flaccidity, thermolability and a falling blood pressure with gasping respiration indicate a progressive medullary failure and imminent death. A somewhat better prognosis is present in those cases who develop hyperpyrexia, a decerebrate rigidity with tonic fits, tachycardia, stertorous breathing and distended neck veins. These features are largely due to the effect of anoxia which results from obstruction of the bronchi and bronchioles by blood clot and vomit and from the damage to brain-stem centres. These two factors combine, interact and a vicious circle is set up; if appropriate treatment is not instituted death is likely to occur within twenty-four hours (MacIver *et al.*, 1958).

It is inappropriate in a psychiatric text-book to enter on the subject of treatment of acute brain injuries. Modern treatment has reduced mortality in severe cases from 80 per cent. to 40 per cent. and less, but is best made the responsibility of an emergency neuro-surgical service.

In recent years, the syndrome of '*blast concussion*' has been seen in subjects exposed to large explosions. The damage to the brain as well as to other organs is due to the sudden sharp rise in venous pressure resulting from compression of the chest by blast. Extravasation of blood occurs from the ruptured venules throughout the brain and elsewhere. Petechial haemorrhages—sometimes confluent—are usually present over the chest, upper limbs and face. The subject becomes deeply unconscious. Considerable retrograde amnesia is generally present after arousal but does not seem to be invariable, and a hazy memory for the actual explosion may remain. Immediately after the explosion there is often a period of clouded consciousness followed by apathy or lability of affect (Anderson, 1942a). Anterograde amnesia extending from the moment of the accident varies in duration according to the severity of the condition. On recovery, patients complain of agonizing headache, which slowly decreases. They exhibit marked motor unrest, anxiety, tremulousness and intolerance of noises (Cramer et al., 1949). Neurological examination rarely reveals physical signs suggestive of coarse damage to the brain.

The Convalescent Stage

In patients without surgical complications this may be held to extend from the moment of recovery of consciousness to the time of return to work or duty. During this stage it becomes necessary to assess the severity of the brain injury and the likely duration of the patient's stay in hospital. Ritchie Russell (1934) was the first to suggest that the severity of 'concussion' might be gauged from the *duration of the post-traumatic amnesia*. This is best measured from the time of the injury to the beginning of continuous awareness and has proved of great value in practice; but, as Guttmann (1946) has pointed out, there are limitations to the method, which must be borne in mind. Thus if an attempt is made to assess the duration of amnesia when the clouding of consciousness has not completely cleared, the result will be grossly misleading. Avoidance of this source of error requires considerable clinical experience, for the patient may appear to be behaving in a purposeful and organized manner and is apparently fully conscious to the untrained eye, but in fact he is slow and laboured in thought, has impaired retention and is more or less disorientated. Clouding of consciousness leaves behind no sharply defined period of amnesia, for patchy memories survive here and there; it must be borne in mind, therefore, that the first memory that the patient may reproduce does not define the duration of post-traumatic amnesia. Sedation with drugs and alcoholic intoxication may further complicate the problem of assessment, while in some patients hysteria or plain falsifications add to the difficulties of evaluation. There may also be an absence of definite landmarks to provide aid to the patient in the description of the period of his amnesia. Finally, there is probably the most important source of error in severe cases, that is, that during the Korsakov phase the patient fails to retain memories and his amnesia consequently extends to include this period.

However, Russell's method of assessing the period of post-traumatic amnesia gives on the whole a reliable picture of the severity of brain injury, and there is a considerable measure of agreement among different authors that it provides a fairly reliable method of predicting the period for which the patient is incapacitated from his work. Thus for a post-traumatic amnesia lasting less than one hour, absence from work for a period of four to six weeks is required: if the amnesia lasts one to twenty-four hours, six to eight weeks; if it lasts one to seven days, two to four months; and four to eight months will be needed if the post-traumatic amnesia has lasted over a week. This is, of course, only a rough and general guide.

The *electroencephalographic changes* run parallel with the clinical state in the acute stage.

The E.E.G. taken some hours after the injury occurred is made up of generalized irregular slow activity at $\frac{1}{2}$–3 c/s. A gradual diminution of slow activity proceeds *pari passu* with the return to clear consciousness. In many head injuries focal damage occurs and if this is so, as the generalized slow activity becomes less obvious, focal slow activity in relation to the site of the injury becomes apparent. During the convalescent stage, the electroencephalogram remains disturbed in a proportion of cases. There is evidence to suggest that the incidence of abnormality in the electroencephalogram is directly related to the severity of the injury, the duration of post-traumatic amnesia and the persistence of symptoms (Williams, 1941*a* and *b*). However, no reliable indication as to the likely duration and severity of disability can be obtained from the electroencephalogram alone; the results must be related to the clinical findings. In certain circumstances during the convalescent stage, the information provided by the electroencephalograph may be particularly useful. Thus if symptoms or signs suggestive of a neurological lesion persist, in the absence of electroencephalographic abnormality, it may be assumed that irreversible cellular damage has occurred and an unfavourable outcome is rendered more likely (Williams, 1941*b*).

Most of the defects and disabilities to be described in the next section, dealing with the chronic stage, will already be apparent in the convalescent period. These should not be considered as chronic states until a period of convalescence corresponding to the duration of post-traumatic amnesia (as described above) has elapsed. This is of course an arbitrary definition of chronicity, and it is well known that in some cases improvement continues for periods of eighteen months or longer. But where symptoms continue to be severely disabling beyond the periods described they are likely to be of prolonged duration.

The Chronic Stage

By far the commonest defect in the chronic stage is the symptom-complex of headache, giddiness, insomnia, irritability and impaired concentration, commonly known as the 'post-concussional' or 'post-contusional' syndrome. Its aetiology is not known for certain, but it is probable that in the great majority of cases both functional and organic factors play a part in causation. In the classification that is given, this condition has therefore been described as a functional-organic defect.

The disabilities may be considered under the following headings:

(1) *Organic defects*
    (*a*) Post-traumatic dementia and personality change
    (*b*) Post-traumatic epilepsy
    (*c*) Chronic subdural haematoma

(2) *Functional-organic defect*
    The post-concussional or post-contusional syndrome

(3) *Psychoses*

POST-TRAUMATIC DEMENTIA AND PERSONALITY CHANGE. Reports of earlier years (e.g. Cedermark, 1942) showed a low incidence of serious psychiatric sequelae after head injuries. Some of the follow-up studies covered only a short time interval, and some of them paid more attention to neurological sequelae than to psychiatric ones. The most recent prognostic study is that carried out by Hillbom (1960) in Finland on 415 men intensively investigated out of a total of 3,552, who sustained brain injuries during the wars of 1939–1944. Serious psychiatric sequelae were of course much more often associated with penetrating injuries and severe brain injuries than with mild closed injuries. Post-traumatic epilepsy also worsened the outlook. Noteworthy psychiatric disturbances occurred in 30 per cent. of all cases followed up, and were found in as many as 25 of the 56 cases with closed post-concussional and post-contusional injury. Amnesic and dementing syndromes were noted only in the moderately and severely injured men. Psychoses occurred in 15 per cent. of the severely injured, in 7 per cent. of those with injuries of moderate severity, and in 3 per cent. of the mildly injured; they were most commonly short-lived and of the typical psycho-organic reactive type. However chronic psychoses, approximating to schizophrenic paranoid-hallucinatory psychoses, occurred in nine cases, all of them severely or moderately severely injured. Other types of psychotic illness observed were characterized by depressive or hysterical traits, with episodic confusion, hallucination, etc. Severe post-traumatic neuroses occurred in 11 per cent. of cases, mainly of the 'neurasthenic-hypochondriacal-depressive' type, and were equally associated with all grades of severity of injury. The frequency of personality change severe enough to cause social difficulties was closely associated with gravity of injury, being seen in 22 per cent. of the severely injured and 7 per cent. of the mildly injured. All types of psychiatric after-effect were substantially commoner with left than with right-sided lesions, being present in 47 per cent. of the former as against 30 per cent. of the latter.

The general features of the post-traumatic syndrome correspond with those of the chronic psycho-organic state already described (pp. 485–492).

The commonest change is a combination of *forgetfulness, impaired concentration and diminished spontaneity in thought*. In a typical case the patient gives a clear and consistent account of his difficulties. Forgetfulness is a constant feature. A housewife reports that she goes out shopping and completely forgets what she has gone to buy. A business man turns up for an appointment and at a crucial moment is unable to recall the purpose of his visit. The patient cannot take in what he reads, his thought is slow, laboured and circular. Mild conditions of this character are probably not as uncommon as they seem in statistical data, but they prove a substantial disability only in the case of professional and intellectual workers. There is an exaggerated susceptibility to the effects of tobacco and alcohol, a phenomenon common to all organic brain disorders.

The following is a sample of dysphasic talk from a woman of thirty-eight who had suffered from cortical venous thrombosis after E.C.T. It shows difficulty in word- and phrase-finding, the use of meaningful but inapposite clichés and words (Stengel, 1964a), the breakdown of syntax, and a tendency to perseveration. She was asked how she liked it at the convalescent home, and replied:

'Everybody sits together to eat, men and women. And it is rather a big place. And the amount they gave me to eat, I couldn't eat it. I tried to be good-looking, guide-looking ... All that was given me to eat I would sit down and eat properly, do it squarely. The material for food they gave you, it all seemed to be well after time; it was old. Every other woman, they've got an enormous food or feed, and they've eaten the lot. So I thought perhaps it was something else gone wrong with you.'

Severe dementia and personality change are much more uncommon. Usually this change has many features in common with the *frontal lobe syndrome*, and there is much to suggest that severe injury of the prefrontal region is often responsible although when the lesions are confined to this area intellectual deterioration is usually absent or minimal. The patient's mood ranges from jocularity to euphoria, he is talkative and disinhibited and inclined to be tactless and expansive. Left to himself, he becomes inert, apathetic and somnolent; his diminished concern for relatives and friends betrays a blunting of feeling. Insight for these changes is poor or lacking. Another pattern of post-traumatic personality change is that towards a querulous, morose mood with episodes of aggression and explosive anger. Features of these two types of change, the euphoric-disinhibited, and the morose-aggressive, may of course be combined in the same patient. A group of patients manifesting excessive fear and anxiety described by Paterson (1944) have in our experience a far better prognosis and are unlikely to be wholly organic in aetiology.

The syndrome of *punch-drunkenness* seen in boxers, is a special form of chronic encephalopathy due to repeated small injuries to the brain which are cumulative in their effects. The average interval between taking up boxing and the onset of the condition in a series of twenty-one cases was sixteen years (Critchley, 1949). Once established it progresses relentlessly even though boxing be given up. It begins with unsteadiness of the lower limbs, leading soon to a reeling, drunken gait, followed by slurring of speech and deterioration of memory and intelligence. Any combination of pyramidal, striatal and cerebellar signs may be present but striatal rigidity and tremor are particularly common, so that the resemblance to post-encephalitic Parkinsonism may be close. Fits are common and delinquency arising from the personality and intellectual deterioration may be the presenting feature of the condition (Guttmann and Winterstein, 1938; Critchley 1957).

The brain is said by many authorities to have greater *powers of recovery in children* than in adults, and this certainly seems to hold as far as sensory-motor functions and speech are concerned. Even gross injury to the brain may be followed by complete recovery in function. After destruction of the area concerned with speech in the major hemisphere below the age of five, a new speech centre arises in the minor hemisphere and total recovery of speech generally occurs. Yet severe and permanent personality change is a not uncommon sequela to brain damage in children, and its incidence would appear to be as high as organic personality disorders of a comparable character in adults. Guttmann and Horder (1943) found a qualitative change of behaviour of this character in two out of a series of sixty children. It would appear that when severe personality change occurs it has many features in common with that following encephalitis lethargica. An excellent account of the clinical picture of these cases has been given by Blau (1936). The injury is usually sustained between the ages of 3 and 10 but several years may elapse before the child comes under psychiatric observation. His destructive and asocial behaviour, disobedience and intractable aggressiveness have by then made him intolerable in the home or at school. The prognosis is poor and severe cases have to be institutionalized. Follow-up of sixty-three children with severe head injuries demonstrated that the pre-traumatic personality and family setting were more important for the psychiatric outcome than the nature and severity of the head injury (Harrington and Letemendia, 1958).

In the assessment of post-traumatic intellectual defect some help may be derived from *tests for deterioration* such as the Babcock, Shipley-Hartford and Brody scales. But the results should never be allowed to override an all-round clinical assessment.

POST-TRAUMATIC EPILEPSY. The frequency of this complication varies with the type of injury. In gunshot wounds of the head Sargent (1921) reported an incidence of 4·5 per cent. in 18,000 cases, while in a similar material Wagstaffe (1928) found 9·8 per cent. post-traumatic epilepsy in 377 cases and Ashcroft (1941) 34 per cent. in 317 cases. Hillbom

(1960) found an incidence of 44 per cent. in 1,505 cases of open injury, and 20 per cent. in 2,047 closed injury cases; a further 10 per cent. were uncertain, but possible epilepsy could be added to both these figures. Among civilian cases the incidence would appear to be considerably lower. During an observation period of ten years only 1–2 per cent. of Ceder-mark's cases had had fits. Eleven of 407 civilians studied by Penfield and Shaver (1945) developed seizures after leaving hospital within a follow-up interval of 2–13 years. It would seem probable that in civilian practice 2–4 per cent. represents the incidence whereas in military casualties a considerably higher figure can be expected. *Penetration of the dura* is a very important aetiological factor and this may also be partly responsible for the discrepancies in the findings of different workers. A constitutional predisposition to epilepsy probably plays no significant part (Hillbom, 1960). In Hillbom's cases, 24 per cent. of the epileptics had their first attack more than five years after the injury, and 9 per cent. more than ten years after.

The *prognosis of post-traumatic epilepsy* depends on the interval between the injury and the first seizure. Most of the patients whose fits occur within a few days of trauma do not develop recurrent seizures, whereas epilepsy commencing months or years afterwards rarely subsides spontaneously. In Penfield and Shaver's material only 4 out of 14 cases (28·5 per cent) with early epilepsy were found to have experienced later attacks. The majority of patients have their first seizure within two years but it is not until 8–10 years have elapsed since the injury that the risk becomes really small, and epilepsy after intervals of as long as twenty years has been recorded.

The commonest *form of attack* is grand mal, but psychomotor epilepsy may occur in association or independently. The aura and the march of events at the commencement of the fit betray the presence of focal injury in a proportion of cases; but in many, the attacks are indistinguishable from those observed in idiopathic epilepsy. Radiography may reveal an area of cortex adherent to the dura or the presence of a 'traction diverticulum'; in this the lateral ventricle is pulled towards the side of the lesion by traction of the scar tissue. The electroencephalogram, especially if methods of activation are used, may reveal a spike or sharp wave focus.

The medical treatment of traumatic epilepsy should be governed by the same principles as those discussed in relation to idiopathic epilepsy. Penfield and his school (Penfield, 1936; Penfield and Steelman, 1948) carried out excision of the cortical site of focal discharge and claimed good results. In this country, surgical treatment of focal epilepsy is still in an experimental stage. The criteria that have been developed for selecting suitable cases and the results obtained have been discussed on page 480.

CHRONIC SUBDURAL HAEMATOMA. This is a late sequela of head injury, symptoms usually appearing after a latent interval of weeks or months. It is due to the slow accumulation of blood in the subdural space, probably originating in rupture of the tributary veins of the dural sinus. The blood proteins in due course break down into smaller molecules which exercise a higher osmotic pressure so that the fluid continually tends to increase. The self-perpetuating process leads to the end result of a collection of disorganized blood ranging in consistency from a coffee-brown clot to a yellow fluid. In most cases the haematoma lies over the fronto-parietal region and it may be bilateral. It is enclosed in a thick capsule which has a complicated structure. Apart from head injury the condition may be produced by intracranial aneurysm, blood diseases and carcinomatosis, but trauma is by far the commonest cause. Cerebral arteriosclerosis is probably a predisposing factor.

The condition generally follows a *relatively slight injury*. Because of the trivial nature of the trauma and also because of the likelihood of subsequent memory disturbance, the patient is often unable to recall the injury. Such cases usually occur in old age. In infancy —the other period of life in which subdural haematoma is fairly common—the condition usually follows a difficult labour. Headaches and drowsiness may follow almost immediately but may be delayed for weeks or months. It is characteristic of the disorder that somnolence, retardation, memory defect and clouding of consciousness show striking *fluctuations in severity* from one day to the next or even within hours. A patient who appears to be sinking into coma in the morning may be alert and talkative the same evening. Even when consciousness is clear, the patient may be severely retarded; he lacks spontaneity and shows an empty, vacant, apathetic mood. Subdural haematoma may produce the full picture of dementia or occasionally an acute delirium with motor excitement. Headache is usually intense but it also fluctuates. As the haematoma is extensive, localizing signs are poorly defined. A slight hemiparesis or monoplegia, inequality of pupils, paralysis of conjugate upward deviation and a mild dysphasia may be present. Epileptic fits may occur, more often in children than adults. Physical signs may, however, be absent, the patient presenting merely with headache and a fluctuating mental disturbance. Papilloedema is present in about half the cases but is late in onset. The cerebrospinal fluid pressure is usually slightly raised and sometimes shows a rise in protein or actual xanthochromia but the fluid may be normal or under low pressure. The *electroencephalogram* is frequently of value in establishing the diagnosis, showing either an area of silence corresponding to the distribution of the haematoma, or a localized region of slow activity. With ventriculography and angiography most cases may be identified with certainty. It is usually possible to evacuate the haematoma through burr holes but where the contents are firmly clotted a more extensive operation is required. In a high proportion of cases *total recovery* is achieved with treatment.

THE 'POST-CONCUSSIONAL' OR 'POST-CONTUSIONAL' SYNDROME. Both names have been used for the condition, although the former is probably more correct, since slight injuries with very transient and trivial effects on consciousness may produce it. It is a common complication of head injury; about 55 per cent. of patients exhibit it at some stage in convalescence, and according to Guttmann (1946) 20-30 per cent. become chronic.

The patient's complaints present a characteristic and consistent pattern; he suffers from severe *headache, giddiness, difficulties in concentration, and anxiety*. The headache is severe and throbbing in character, worse when lying down, and exacerbated by physical or mental effort and any stress or excitement, but improved by rest and quiet. It is particularly prone to occur in severe injuries. The giddiness is not a true vertigo, since it is not associated with a subjective sense of rotation. It is rather a sense of instability on change of posture (Symonds, 1942). Entangled with the patient's description of dizziness there is a symptom which is in effect distinct. This is the blackout, a combination of momentary haziness of vision and instability probably syncopal in character. The patient's mood is one of fluctuating anxiety and depression and he responds to mild stress, or to situations which formerly would have left him unmoved, with exaggerated fear and apprehension. There is insomnia, difficulty in concentration, irritability and intolerance of noise. The patient complains that he is incapable of sustained physical or mental effort as within a short time he becomes tense and tremulous, his concentration fails and he is overcome by fatigue. He may become petulant, quarrelsome and difficult. Hypochondriacal self-preoccupation may magnify his disabilities in his own eyes and impede attempts to keep him actively occupied.

There is much evidence that *neurotic predisposition and psychological environmental factors* play the major role in the causation of a prolonged disturbance of this kind. In Denny-Brown's careful survey (1945) an intimate relationship was demonstrated between the occurrence of the post-concussional syndrome and a neurotic disposition. In Service patients Symonds and Russell (1943) observed that their chronic cases, admitted to hospital after failure of treatment elsewhere, showed a far higher invaliding rate than acute cases with a similar duration of post-traumatic amnesia. They found the explanation for the unsatisfactory progress and poor prognosis of the chronic group in a far higher incidence of constitutional predisposition to mental disorder. Lewis (1942) compared the clinical picture of the post-concussional syndrome with that of common neurotic disorders and found a very close resemblance.

Psychological factors of a more recent kind also contribute in a variety of ways. As constitutional predisposition is of importance in causation, many of the subjects affected are already suffering from mild symptoms of anxiety or depression often associated with difficulties in their life situation, before the accident occurs. The head injury exacerbates the affective symptoms formerly held in check, and precipitates neurotic breakdown. The accident is also prone to generate fears that many patients find it difficult to formulate. The head looms large in the body image, and the impressiveness of unconsciousness and confusion, and ignorant beliefs about its implications, combine to produce a typical attitude of self-scrutiny in these patients which has been called 'head consciousness'. Some patients are also worried by the knowledge that they have suffered a brain injury, and post-concussional patients who experience severe tension often have persistent fears that they will 'lose control' or 'go mad'. It is all the more important in the management of these patients to avoid behaving in a way that is likely to suggest that the patient has sustained serious damage; *iatrogenic symptoms* are frequently implanted by prolonged bed rest and an abundance of impressive investigations.

That *compensation* is an important factor in many cases is illustrated by the fact that post-traumatic neuroses are far more common in industrial accidents than those sustained in amateur sports. They are also more common in the insured than in the uninsured person. Hope of financial gain contributes to a variable extent to causation, but it is seldom fully conscious; real malingering is a rare condition. It is sometimes assumed that a latent interval between injury and commencement of symptoms is due to litigation but it may occur in cases where this factor does not enter. The significance of compensation as an aetiological factor can only be assessed in relation to the individual patient's personality and life-situation; its importance has probably been over-emphasized.

In his Milroy lectures to the Royal College of Physicians, Miller (1961) has produced evidence to suggest that deliberate simulation or malingering is the explanation of many chronic disabilities following accidents, that are, at present, regarded as being neurotic in nature. In a series of 200 cases of head injury referred for *medico-legal* examination, 'neurotic' complaints were noted twice as often in industrial as in road accidents and there was an inverse relationship between frequency of 'compensation neurosis' and severity of injury. Thus gross psychoneurosis was found in 31 per cent. of patients without radiological evidence of *skull* fracture, in 9 per cent. of the patients with simple fracture and in only two out of 25 subjects with compound fracture of the skull. In a follow-up study of fifty cases he found, moreover, that only two remained disabled by psychiatric symptoms two years after the compensation issue had been settled. That an *element of conscious simulation* commonly enters into the production of hysterical symptoms is generally accepted. The difficulty of evaluating the results reported by Miller arises from the fact that cases referred to a neurologist are unlikely to be a representative sample of individuals disabled after accidents; they may well *contain an over-representation* of those in whom the nature of the disability is subject to dispute. The almost invariable recovery within two years of settlement of compensation is striking, but the experience of those working with 'compensation neuroses' in psychiatric clinics is unfortunately nothing like as encouraging.

Despite the role of constitutional predisposition, there is much evidence to suggest that other factors must also contribute to the causation of post-concussional symptoms. Thus Guttmann (1943), in a survey similar to that of Lewis, found that the post-concussional group when compared with neurotics showed significantly less predisposition to neurosis as expressed in personal history, character traits and home atmosphere. Moreover, the clinical picture in all patients has so many fundamental points of similarity that it would seem unlikely that psychological causes can wholly account for it. The nature of this factor is at present unidentified. The headache has been attributed to high cerebrospinal fluid pressure which is in fact not uncommon, but the symptom is certainly not dependent upon it. Other changes which have been incriminated are ventricular dilatations and adhesions between meninges and cortex, on very slender evidence in each case. The giddiness is unlikely to be due to labyrinthine injury, which produces a distinct syndrome. The inverse relationship observed by Miller between severity of head injury and the evidence of 'gross psychoneurosis' requires further investigation with careful attention to the contribution of age and severity of psychological deficit to the differences observed. Some subtle organic basis for the syndrome is likely, particularly where injury has been severe and pre-morbid personality was free from neurotic tendencies.

To sum up: the available evidence seems to suggest that underlying the post-concussional syndrome there may well be some subtle but specific modification in brain function which is potentially reversible though of varying severity in different cases, but that the duration and severity of the disability are dependent to a large extent on the patient's predisposition and the influence of psychological and environmental stresses.

PSYCHOSES. It is not common for an affective or schizophreniform psychosis to come on after head injury, and until recently the conjunction was regarded as coincidental. At the most it was considered that the injury brought out the predisposition which would very likely have ultimately become manifest without it. However, recent observations and re-evaluation of older findings have put the matter in a different light. Thus Feuchtwanger and Mayer-Gross (1938), on the basis of head injury statistics, thought that the frequency of schizophrenia in head-injured patients did not exceed that in the general population. However, if all subjects with indubitably schizophrenic symptoms had been reckoned, irrespective of whether or not some organic features (e.g. convulsions) were recorded, the incidence would have exceeded chance expectation. Moreover, Hillbom (1951, 1960) has drawn attention to the occurrence, a long period after injury, of schizophreniform and affective psychoses, these states being preferentially associated with temporal lobe injuries. 14·8 per cent. of the severely injured developed psychoses and in 9 of the 33 cases the similarity to schizophrenia was close. One must conclude from the published material that schizophrenia-like psychoses can be directly brought on by head injury, with or without the accompaniment of epilepsy. If such psychoses are regarded as symptomatic schizophrenias, of purely organic pathogenesis, their exclusion from the syndrome of endogenous schizophrenia is based on other considerations than insufficiency or atypicality of schizophrenic symptomatology.

Differential Diagnosis

The changes in behaviour attributable to an unquestionable organic causation are not difficult to distinguish. The patient's behaviour undergoes a qualitative change foreign is some essential features to his personality. Changes in circumstance have little effect and insight is lacking. Emotion is blunted and a blend of euphoria with outbursts of anger following minor frustration are common. Conspicuous hysterical or paranoid symptoms are often a caricature of features of his pre-morbid personality. Tactlessness, lack of judgement, and serious intellectual and mnesic damage are also characteristic.

A difficult and commonly occurring problem of diagnosis is that of estimating the *relative contribution of organic and psychological factors* in a post-concussional syndrome. Between the two extremes of conditions largely organic and those largely psychogenic in aetiology, which account for a very small proportion of cases, there is the vast majority of patients in whom the two factors contribute in varying proportions. There are certain features which favour an emphasis on organic factors in assessing the case, but others an emphasis on the pre-morbid personality and patient's psychological and social difficulties. In the illness of largely organic aetiology the injury has usually been severe and there is often objective evidence of some degree of consistent impairment of memory and intellectual efficiency. The symptoms show little response to change in surroundings. There is frequently a gross intolerance of heat and alcohol, and hysterical symptoms, including exaggeration in behaviour and description of disability, are absent. In cases that are predominantly psychogenic, on the other hand, the symptomatology is less consistent and the patient may be distracted from his disabilities by changes in his surroundings or circumstances. Hysterical features are often in evidence. Finally, psychological factors which may go some way towards explaining the perpetuation of symptoms are often discoverable.

The *electroencephalogram* may give some aid in making a correct assessment since cases of predominantly organic aetiology will often show focal abnormalities, while in those of largely psychogenic origin the E.E.G. will be normal or show diffuse changes (Heppenstall and Hill, 1943).

The less severe the accident, as judged from the length of post-traumatic amnesia, the greater the instability of the personality as judged from the history of his previous adjustment to life, the more florid and demonstrative the symptomatology, the greater the secondary gain from illness, and the more understandable the whole disability in terms of psychological factors, the more likely it is that the condition is one to which psychological rather than organic factors make the greatest contribution. The converse is also true. Organic damage to the brain is not excluded by the absence of neurological signs, nor does the presence of some electroencephalographic abnormality or some anomaly in the air-encephalogram justify the conclusion that the disability is necessarily due to cerebral disease. It must be emphasized that the two patterns described represent extremes which are rarely seen in practice, and they are given as a guide to the evaluation of the relative significance of the organic and psychological and social components.

A reasonably correct estimate of the relative contribution of the various factors is not merely of academic interest, nor is it important only for the problems arising in connexion with compensation. The *physician's ability to gain the confidence* of his patient will depend a good deal upon the extent to which his assessment corresponds with the true state of affairs. This is bound to influence the lines of psychological treatment and rehabilitation in the convalescent and chronic stage, and an exaggerated emphasis either on the organic or on the non-organic aspect, based on a false estimate, will quickly lead the patient to conclude that the doctor does not understand his case. Treatment is thus likely to be seriously hindered.

Prognosis and Treatment

Where there are signs of organic personality change and, still more, dementia, the prognosis must be guarded. No *final assessment* of the degree of damage should be made until 12–18 months after injury, as improvement may continue for this length of time. Intellectual tests may fail to reveal dementia, yet when the patient has returned to his work, his impaired judgement and irresponsibility may prove him wholly unsuited to his previous occupation. However, a defect that wholly incapacitates an intellectual worker may not prevent an unskilled labourer from earning his living. Organic dementia is a far more common sequel in the middle-aged and elderly than in young patients.

In the post-concussional syndrome proper, the prognosis depends to a very large extent on the *stability of the patient's personality*, his intelligence, his need and desire to get well, and the possibility of dealing with his personal problems. These factors are far more important in deciding the issue than the severity of the injury. Some 50–60 per cent. may show an abnormal electroencephalogram in the chronic stage. The degree of abnormality runs approximately parallel with the severity of injury, but shows little correlation with the outcome, which is not surprising, since the basic personality, the most important factor in prognosis, finds little expression in the electroencephalogram.

Rehabilitation should begin the moment the patient recovers consciousness. It is important to give explanation and reassurance at this stage and to instil a positive and optimistic attitude. The patient is in a highly suggestible state, and fears are easily implanted which are later difficult to eradicate. The patient should not therefore be asked about symptoms of which he does not spontaneously complain.

Within a few days of recovering consciousness the majority of patients can be got out of bed. A carefully planned programme of rehabilitation should be drawn up in each case. This should allow for a gradual increase in the patient's physical and mental activities. His day should be unobtrusively filled with tasks that interest and stimulate him without overtaxing his strength, particularly in the early stages when long periods of rest should be allowed for in cases of severe injury.

However, a well-ordered régime of occupational therapy, games and exercises will not by itself prove adequate for the successful rehabilitation of brain-injured patients. The management of these cases calls for *a high degree of psychiatric skill* and understanding. Unconsciousness, confusion and the threat to his life are prone to arouse in the patient feelings of anxiety, insecurity, and apprehension about the future. The ordinary difficulties of life assume exaggerated proportions and pre-existing neurotic conflicts are often exacerbated. It is therefore essential to gain the patient's confidence at an early stage of treatment, to investigate his assets and limitations as a personality and to become acquainted with his problems and difficulties. Much of what we know of the course and outcome of cases of head injury indicates the necessity for such a psychiatric approach which demands an intimate rapport with the patient. But only rarely will anything more be required in the way of psychotherapy than sympathetic explanation, guidance and advice based upon a correct assessment of the relative importance of the different factors that contribute towards the patient's total disability.

Treatment is most effectively managed at a hospital which has well-run departments for *occupational and recreational therapy*, and facilities for games and physical exercises. As patients are frequently worried and uncertain about their ability to return to their previous employment, or even to earn their living, it is particularly important that occupational therapy should be directed towards resumption of normal working life or rehabilitation in some other occupation. In such circumstances basket- or rug-making create boredom and frustration whereas work in a *well-equipped workshop or garage* will help many patients to regain confidence and provide opportunities for assessing their chances of successful readjustment.

Graduated exercises and organized games are of great value not only in cultivating fitness but also in restoring physical self-confidence which so often suffers. Lectures, group-discussions and debates, and, in selected cases, group treatment along psychological lines, have proved their value at rehabilitation centres in recent years; they combat the morbid self-scrutiny which so readily develops in the disabled, foster a more positive attitude towards life and help the patient to adopt an *objective and philosophical attitude* towards residual disabilities. Persistent dysphasia will necessitate referral to a specialist in speech therapy. Considerable advances have been made in the methods used in the re-education of these patients during the past thirty years (Goldstein, 1942).

In a small proportion of patients with head injury the history will reveal that they have been repeatedly involved in accidents. It may be found for example that a lorry driver, despite adequate experience on the roads, has sustained a succession of injuries in the course of a few years. Every effort should be made to persuade such *accident-prone individuals* to change their occupation to one less likely to expose them to risk.

As soon as possible, both the patient and his relatives should be given a clear statement as to the likelihood of residual disabilities; in the majority of cases the prediction of a favourable outcome will be fully justified. Some patients will be unable to return to their former occupation; *a course of re-training* may then be necessary, during which the family will need financial support. In these and other problems of resettlement, the help of the psychiatric social worker and the rehabilitation officer of the employment exchange is invaluable. Where compensation is involved, negotiations should be brought to as speedy an end as possible.

There is a considerable range of variation in outcome for head injury of a given severity which is doubtless determined in large measure by constitutional differences among patients, but also to some extent by the intelligence, energy and psychological understanding with which they are treated.

ENCEPHALITIS

Acute and subacute encephalitis are not rarities in clinical practice. In a four-year period (1964–67) 120 patients suspected of encephalitis were seen at one neurological institute and the diagnosis of encephalitis was confirmed by biological and other findings in 20. In a further 48 a presumptive diagnosis of encephalitis was made. The remaining patients were found to have other disorders. Although it is widely assumed that the post-infectious encephalitides of measles, varicella, rubella and mumps figure prominently among such cases, in a number of recent enquiries (Miller and Ross, 1968) the majority of patients investigated in detail proved to suffer from an infection with the virus of herpes simplex. The clinical manifestations include fever, headache, vomiting, drowsiness, motor dysphasia, visual field defect, increased reflexes, purposeless repetitive movements, nystagmus, ataxia, facial weakness, deafness and convulsions (Gostling, 1967). In addition, psychiatric disturbance may be prominent and clouding of consciousness, delirium or coma may be seen. The histological picture is commonly that of acute necrotizing encephalitis and these cases may present as a temporal lobe tumour or abscess (Bennett *et al.*, 1962). Early diagnosis is important as the mortality rate is high, particularly in adults and rapid treatment with antiviral agents probably improves the chance of survival. The diagnosis is made with the aid of examination of the cerebrospinal fluid which contains increased protein and lymphocytes, the E.E.G. and the demonstration of virus or of the histological appearances of encephalitis in brain biopsy.

The importance of this group of observations is that some workers suspect subacute inclusion encephalitis of being a related disorder or at least of being of viral origin. It also seems highly probable that rapidly developing dementia of obscure aetiology in middle and late life will receive increasing attention with the aid of modern techniques of investigation, as being possibly caused by a virus infection.

Rabies deserves mention, since the first symptoms after the prolonged incubation period are generally those of a rather characteristic mental state of *depression, anxiety and apprehension*. At night the patient becomes delirious and experiences terrifying delusions and ideas of reference. During this stage the only physical symptom may be some pain and stiffness in the lower part of the body. When the typical pharyngeal spasms and the phobic horror of water appear, hallucinations and delusions of a florid kind are prominent and may lead to violent excitement. Prophylactic treatment with vaccine commenced soon after the bite of a rabid animal aborts the infection in the majority of cases.

Subacute Encephalitis

Two forms of subacute encephalitis described in recent years, the subacute *leuco-encephalitis of van Bogaert* (1945) and the *inclusion encephalitis of Dawson* (1933, 1934) are both of some psychiatric interest in that mental abnormalities are prominent in each, and many of the patients described had been treated in mental hospitals for the psychiatric disturbance (Brain, Greenfield and Russell, 1943; Corsellis, 1951).

Both conditions usually attack children or young adults, and almost invariably prove fatal. In subacute leuco-encephalitis the onset is insidious, with fever, lethargy and nocturnal delirium. The patient becomes slow, apathetic and forgetful, and a progressive dementia supervenes. However, pictures resembling catatonic schizophrenia (Malamud, Haymaker and Pinkerton, 1950), depressive illness (van Bogaert, 1945) and childhood autism have all been described. Aphasia and apraxia are common, but most characteristic are the *jerky, involuntary movements* occurring every few seconds. Their extrapyramidal origin is confirmed by the presence of rigidity of lead-pipe character. The electroencephalogram shows highly characteristic bursts of slow-wave activity at fairly regular intervals of seven seconds either at the termination or immediately after the muscular spasms. A very useful diagnostic feature is the paretic curve in Lange's test which has been a finding in the

S

cerebrospinal fluid of the majority of cases. In the terminal stage which supervenes in six to twelve months, the patient is comatose and in a posture of decerebrate rigidity. As Corsellis (1951) has pointed out, the inclusion encephalitis of Dawson is in many ways similar in its clinical features; there are the same involuntary jerking movements, progressive dementia, rapidly fatal course and decorticate posture before death, and the findings in the cerebrospinal fluid also resemble those in the encephalitis described by van Bogaert.

PARKINSONISM

Postencephalitic Parkinsonism

These rare cases are unlikely to come the way of the psychiatrist in the acute stage, which is characterized by the triad of somnolence, often accompanied by reversal of the sleep rhythm, delirium and the neurological signs of involvement of the mid-brain, such as an ophthalmoplegia.

In about a quarter of the cases complete recovery occurs; in the remainder, chronic disabilities may develop in one of a number of different ways. The patient may be left with disabling sequelae in the form of rigidity, slowness or tics, which are gradually aggravated in the course of years and develop into the full picture of postencephalitic Parkinsonism. In some patients a clear interval of a year or so may be followed by a number of relapses with Parkinsonism as the end-result. Alternatively there may be a latent interval of five to as long as twenty-five years before the symptoms of the chronic stage make their appearance. In many cases of chronic encephalitis lethargica no history of an acute illness is forthcoming and it seems that the most severe sequelae may occur with the mildest of initial infections. The causal organism is probably active in the brain in the chronic stage.

The *chronic condition* presents a typical picture. The patient's face acquires a mournful, immobile staring expression, the lower jaw drooping and saliva dribbling out of the corner of his mouth. There is a marked poverty of motor activity; associated movements as in walking disappear and when seated the patient remains rigidly confined in one position. A forcible effort of will has to be made to start any movement, but once initiated it tends to continue outside his control. In walking this gives rise to the phenomena of propulsion and retropulsion. It is as if spontaneous, secondarily automatized, behaviour of the body were suspended, to be replaced by a rigid, will-directed, self-conscious and caricatured version of it. The rigidity is of the extra-pyramidal cogwheel or lead-pipe kind. There is weakness and slowness of movement which affects the small muscles with particular severity, to produce micrographia and slurring monotony of speech. In addition to the pill-rolling tremor there may be choreiform and myoclonic movements or multiple tics affecting the face. Respiration is generally increased in rate and the rhythm is disorganized, with intervals of stereotyped sighing and yawning. Hypothalamic involvement may give rise to obesity, impotence, attacks of flushing and polyuria.

It seems likely that the concept of 'critical periods' has some application in regard to the form taken by the sequelae of an attack of acute encephalitis lethargica. If the acute illness occurs in the first years of life, mental defect is likely to ensue. In childhood the grosser psychopathic disturbances are likely to result, whereas in adults the illness is likely to have neurological sequelae only.

The ocular factors seen in the acute stage often persist and in many cases *oculogyric crises* develop. In these the eyes and often the head are deviated upwards and are maintained in this position for seconds, minutes or even hours. Less frequently the eyes are deviated laterally, obliquely or even downwards. Eyelid flutter on attempted eye movements and blepharospasm are not infrequently associated with oculogyric crises. Emotional factors play an important part in the precipitation of the condition and an attack in a single patient may serve to initiate spasms in a whole ward of post-encephalitics.

The element of *compulsion* present in such phenomena and in the disorders of movement is also to be found in many of the *psychological features of the illness*. Many of the mental symptoms occur in intimate association with the spasms, involuntary movements or tics. Most commonly it is the oculogyric crises which are associated with some incessantly reiterated word or thought, some grotesque obscenity or meaningless sequence of words or syllables. The patient may feel himself compelled to sing or whistle some melody, contrast opposites or add up figures in endless succession. He may be seized with a terror-stricken doubt that he cannot resolve. Of rarer occurrence are ideas of an overtly paranoid kind, and hallucinations.

Compulsive movements may occur in association with myoclonic or tic-like symptoms, or independently. Other examples of similar phenomena are a tendency to perseverate with the terminal syllable of a word (pallilalia) or the end-fragment of a gesture or movement. Some patients feel an irresistible compulsion to echo what is said to them or to describe what they see. All these compulsive phenomena seem to be intimately associated. The impairment of volitional control manifest in the involuntary movements, and the rigidity that shackles the patient, seem to find expression in the obsessive-compulsive symptoms. This close association between the compulsive features in thought and motor behaviour and their derivation from regions in the upper brain-stem and hypothalamus is of great interest for the theory of compulsive symptoms.

We have seen many patients who bore their severe disabilities with surprising fortitude. Nevertheless, the organic lesions and the hopeless character of a patient's disability may have serious *effects on his personality*. His life becomes egocentrically restricted, his emotions dilapidated, monotonous and stereotyped. Although he may look alert and intelligent the patient's thoughts are generally repetitive, circular and narrowly confined, often to a hypochondriacal self-scrutiny. He lives from day to day in a small world bounded by the individuals who are the objects of his importunate and demanding behaviour. Insight into these changes may be extraordinarily shallow in spite of the lack of evidence of intellectual deterioration on formal tests in most cases. Many patients are plunged into despair by the defeat of their hopes, the disfigurement wrought by the disease, the emptiness and sterility which afflict their minds. Depression is relatively common, and successful *suicide* has been frequently recorded (Harris and Cooper, 1937). It is therefore important to keep an eye open for the development of a depressive symptom-complex. This is seldom wholly to be accounted for in terms of reaction to disability, and may respond favourably to treatment by induced convulsions or antidepressant drugs.

In distinguishing post-encephalitic Parkinsonism from paralysis agitans there is the earlier onset of the former with an occasional history of an acute illness with somnolence and double vision. Rigidity is often present without tremor in the post-encephalitic type. Ocular signs and particularly oculogyric crises, sialorrhoea and grotesque disturbances of posture are virtually diagnostic of the post-encephalitic variety of Parkinsonism. Personality change and compulsive features are much more common following encephalitis, and the condition progresses with greater rapidity.

Paralysis Agitans

In this condition personality changes are less prominent than following encephalitis lethargica, possibly because the disease supervenes in patients who are older and have therefore had the advantage of an integrated pattern of behaviour for a much longer period than in the case of encephalitic Parkinsonism. While tremor is more common, other involuntary movements such as facial tics, myoclonus and bradykinesia are far less often observed whilst oculogyric crises never occur; the obsessive-compulsive symptoms are likewise less frequent. The *genetical and psychiatric aspects* of the condition were studied by Mjönes (1949). The genetical findings are compatible with inheritance through a dominant autosomal gene of approximately 60 per cent. penetrance. In Mjönes's cases about 40 per cent. of affected individuals had mental symptoms. He could find no evidence for the view often expressed that previous to the onset of the physical symptoms there are certain consistent personality traits in those who suffer from paralysis agitans, namely inflexibility, meticulousness, emotional rigidity and immaturity. During the illness the psychiatric complications may be subdivided into three groups of symptoms, the first two being combined in varying degrees in different cases and the third developing in a small proportion of cases in the terminal stages of the illness: (1) The general personality changes are similar to those seen in adult cases of post-encephalitic Parkinsonism. The patient becomes egocentric, exacting and hypochrondriacal; he complains a great deal in a querulous, demanding manner, and is depressed by his affliction; (2) A variable amount of intellectual change of organic type may be present. Thought is retarded, memory for recent events impaired; there is a lack of concentration, and ready fatigue. The changes in emotion and behaviour are aggravated by the advent of these organic features; (3) Senile dementia proper has for long been regarded as a relatively common complication of paralysis agitans. The incidence in the material studied by Mjönes was in fact rather greater than that in the normal population but the numbers were too small for any definite conclusion to be drawn.

Treatment

In the chronic stage the patient should be helped to lead as active a life as possible by means of *physiotherapy*. In early cases, a course of retraining may help him to occupy himself and even partly to earn his living for a time. The rigidity is helped by *drugs of the belladonna group*, the most effective being tincture of stramonium, given in doses of 10–90 minims (0·5–5 ml.) three times a day, the doses being gradually increased and maintained at a level just short of the stage at which difficulty in accommodation is experienced. Side-effects such as dryness in the mouth may be counteracted by pilocarpine gr. 1/12 (5 mg.) twice daily, while dexamphetamine 5–10 mg. in the morning and at noon is of help to come cases in overcoming slowness, inertia, depression and the oculogyric crises. The synthetic drugs benzhexol (Artane) and ethopropazine (Lysivane) are being found helpful; the former is administered in a dose of 2 mg. on the first day and this can be gradually increased to a total of 5 mg. three times daily, while the latter is given in doses which gradually increase from 50 mg. to 400 mg. daily. Artane (benzhexol) is the most consistently helpful drug of the new preparations. Its therapeutic effects are improved by the simultaneous administration of antihistaminic drugs, but it is advisable to give a stimulating substance such as phenindamine tartrate (Thephorin) in the morning and noon, and diphenhydramine hydrochloride (Benadryl) 50 mg. at night. When the symptoms of a typical depressive illness occur after encephalitis lethargica, the condition often responds quite dramatically to convulsant therapy, although it may be partly reactive to the disabilities imposed by the organic illness. The more depth there is to the depression and the more typical the depressive and hypochondriacal ideation, the greater the likelihood of improvement.

Important advances have been made in recent years in the surgical treatment of Parkinsonism. With the aid of stereotactic apparatus, a limited and precisely placed lesion can be made in the basal ganglia by electrical coagulation. In successful cases, tremor and rigidity may be abolished or mitigated on the side opposite the lesion. Serious complications are relatively rare, and the mortality is less than 3–4 per cent. in modern series. The operation is particularly suitable for *unilateral* cases. Evidence of cerebral arteriosclerosis, hypertension, *generalized* ill health, intellectual deterioration or other evidence that the reserve capacity of the brain has been encroached upon by structural disease, are strong contraindications to operation. General vigour and intellectual preservation are more important than chronological age in deciding the result of surgery. Young subjects with rapidly progressive disease are unsuitable.

In 1960 Ehringer and Hornykiewicz made the interesting observation that there was a marked reduction in the concentration of dopamine in the globus pallidus and striatum of patients suffering from Parkinsonism. This has stimulated therapeutic trials with methyldopa in Parkinsonism and favourable results have been claimed in some preliminary observations by Marsh, Schnieden and Marshall (1963) who reported improvement in tremor following treatment with doses of 1–1·5 g. daily. There are, however, conflicting observations and further studies are in progress.

HEPATO-LENTICULAR DEGENERATION (WILSON'S DISEASE)

This condition is due to the presence in duplex state of a recessive gene causing an abnormality of copper metabolism. Normal production of coeruloplasmin, the copper-carrying protein of the blood, is defective; copper, circulating in the serum in a more loosely bound state, is rapidly eliminated by being laid down in the tissues. The tissues in which this occurs are, most importantly, the liver, the basal ganglia and the periphery of the cornea. The disease caused by degeneration of the corpus striatum and associated with a cirrhosis of the liver, begins between the ages of five and twenty-five, and is characterized by tremor in association with bizarre athetoid and spasmodic movements or a torsion dystonia. Bulbar symptoms occur early; rigidity is a later development. The patient has difficulty in swallowing, and speech becomes unintelligible. Irritability, explosive behaviour and spasmodic laughter and crying occur, and there is a progressive organic dementia in the great majority of cases. The diagnosis is suggested by the familial nature of the disorder, the presence in some cases of signs of liver disease (although these may be trivial), and in a small proportion, the identification of the Kayser-Fleischer ring, a zone of coloured brown pigmentation in the outer extremity of the cornea. Treatment of the condition, which is moderately successful if begun early and may hold progression of the disease at bay for years, consists in mobilizing the deposited copper from the tissues by administration of penicillamine or dimercaprol (B.A.L.).

SYPHILIS OF THE CENTRAL NERVOUS SYSTEM

Half a century ago general paralysis of the insane constituted a high proportion of mental hospital admissions and accounted for an appreciable part of the chronic population of such institutions. However, with the development of increasingly effective methods of treatment, cerebral syphilitic infection is becoming relatively rare. Yet the study of syphilis of the central nervous system remains of great scientific interest for the light it throws on the nature of the relationship between cerebral and mental disease.

Psychological Reactions to Infection

When a patient becomes aware that he has been infected with syphilis, he may develop an intense depression of a reactive kind. In rare instances there may be severe feelings of guilt and unworthiness, and nihilistic paranoid and hypochondriacal delusions similar to those of an endogenous depression.

In our civilization knowledge that the infection has been contracted is always a severe trauma because of the *social stigma* that attaches to the disease and the widespread ignorance as to the effects of the illness and the chances of recovery with treatment. Patients need careful handling, and often help, in order to overcome a crisis in their marital relations, which may prove disastrous both for themselves and their families. It is therefore important to have *psychiatric advice* readily available at venereal disease clinics; and there is an advantage in having a psychiatrist permanently attached to the clinic in order to ensure continuity of psychiatric treatment for those cases that require it. The services of a social worker are invaluable in negotiating the difficult and delicate social situation that is often produced. A clear statement as to the nature of the illness, the plan of treatment, the likelihood of cure and the possibility of after-effects helps the patient to adjust to the situation. The handling the patient receives after he has become infected often decides the establishment or prevention of a lifelong neurotic disability.

Mental Changes in the Primary and Secondary Stages

Even before the appearance of the primary sore, spirochaetes may reach the nervous system and lymphocytosis and some increase of pressure may be found in the cerebrospinal fluid in a small proportion of cases. It may be for this reason that the condition which has been called '*syphilitic neurasthenia*' sometimes occurs at this stage. The patient complains of headache and difficulty in concentration, tires very easily and shows marked irritability. There is a general malaise, with vague bodily discomfort, possibly pains in the limbs, constipation and a sense of fullness in the abdomen. These symptoms improve with anti-syphilitic treatment. A similar picture may be observed in the secondary stage. However, in some cases an acute febrile illness, with somnolence and delirium, may make its appearance at this stage and in rare cases it evolves into a fulminating and fatal meningo-encephalitis. Lumbar puncture will always reveal the diagnosis. The fluid is under increased pressure and there is an increase in cells and of the globulin; the Wassermann reaction is negative in the fluid but positive in the blood of an untreated patient. With early treatment complete recovery is obtained.

It is important to remember, however, that in the early stages neurosyphilis is often asymptomatic. In the past the frequency with which the nervous system was affected was probably under-estimated, but since routine cerebrospinal fluid examinations have been carried out, neurosyphilis is known to supervene in a much higher proportion than the five per cent. of patients formerly quoted. Underlying this *asymptomatic infection* there is probably a mild degree of leptomeningitis. In the 'early asymptomatic neurosyphilis', which Hahn and Clark (1946) found within two years of the primary infection, the Wassermann reaction in the blood is positive, in the cerebrospinal fluid it may be either negative or positive; there is an increase of protein and cells, and the Lange curve is luetic, meningitic or, rarely, paretic in type. This condition generally responds to penicillin treatment. Where it resists treatment or is discovered more than two years after infection, the danger of general paralysis is considerably greater. There is some evidence that an unusually tenacious or resistant meningeal infection is a pre-paretic condition.

Meningo-Vascular Syphilis

The symptoms of this stage of the disease appear within a few months to a year of infection but may be delayed for as long as five years. The *pathological changes* underlying the condition are those of a *chronic syphilitic meningitis, endarteritis and periarteritis*. The organism and the toxins it produces attack the large and small cerebral and meningeal vessels to produce an infiltration of the adventitial and middle coats and hypertrophy of the intimal layer. The lumina of the vessels may become obliterated by intimal proliferation, or by thrombi. Occlusion of large vessels in this way will produce areas of cerebral softening. Surrounding the vessels there is an area of infiltration with lymphocytes, plasma cells and fibroblasts. As a result of these inflammatory changes in the meninges and the obliteration of meningeal vessels, areas of syphilitic necrosis surrounded by a zone of fibroblastic proliferation are produced. These are the *gummata of the tertiary phase* and they may be of variable size. Areas of inflammation extend from the meninges to the brain, and multiple small cerebral gummata are relatively common. They are rarely large enough to produce pressure effects like those of a tumour. The lesions in the meninges, vessels and brain are usually all present in varying degrees; but one type of change may be predominant.

CLINICAL PICTURE. The disease generally develops with rapidity, and mental abnormalities are frequently prominent. After a period of general malaise, headache, fatigue, and disturbed nights, the patient becomes slow and forgetful, and loses his grip on his work. His thoughts become retarded, he is inclined to grow careless over detail, and his concentration fails. The patient often has a considerable measure of *insight* into the impairment of his capacities, and the tension, anxiety and uncertainty in behaviour which are to some extent secondary may lead to a diagnosis of *anxiety state*. He may on the other hand be complacently devoid of insight and offer foolish and irrelevant explanations for his deficiencies.

As the disorder develops, episodes of *clouded consciousness and delirium* may supervene, and attacks of acute manic excitement occur in some cases, probably for the most part in predisposed individuals. Associated with these mental changes there are *physical signs* which vary according to the distribution of the lesions. The pupils may be abnormal, usually showing a failure to react to light, and they are generally unequal, but the 'pin-points' of the typical Argyll Robertson pupil are less common than in tabes. Oculomotor paralysis is commonly associated. Facial weakness and palsy of other cranial nerves are more uncommon. Papilloedema is rare, but visual impairment with field defects of a homonymous or bi-temporal kind may occur from involvement of the chiasma by basal meningitis. When the convexity of the brain is affected, Jacksonian seizures or generalized fits, hemiplegia, monoplegia, aphasia, apraxia and other signs of local cerebral involvement are generally found. Convulsions may leave behind a residual hemiplegia or an aggravation of pre-existing physical signs. In cases that have suffered a partial hemiplegia on both sides, pseudobulbar palsy with 'emotional incontinence' will be encountered.

A characteristic feature is that both the mental changes and neurological symptoms in the early stages of the disease show marked and unexpected *fluctuations in severity* in a way that mimics the clinical picture of chronic subdural haematoma. The disease can manifest itself in such an infinite variety of ways, ranging from some slight pupillary abnormality on the one hand to diffuse cortical symptoms with dementia on the other, that in differential diagnosis the whole field of neuropsychiatry would need to be considered if it were not for the fact that the *cerebrospinal fluid* is nearly always diagnostic. The pressure is usually normal, but may be increased; the Wassermann reaction is generally positive in the blood and also as a rule in the cerebrospinal fluid, although it may be negative in predominantly vascular cases; there is a cellular reaction of 30–150 cells per cubic millimetre, mostly of mononuclear leucocytes; the protein is increased and the globulin fraction likewise. Lange's test yields either a luetic or paretic curve. If the latter is the case, the problem of differentiation from general paralysis arises. It is important to make this differentiation because where the disease is meningo-vascular the prognosis is far better. In meningo-vascular syphilis the interval since infection is much shorter, the condition develops more acutely, the patient generally has more insight, and his personality as a whole is more often preserved; tremor is uncommon and neurological signs indicative of focal cortical lesions are much more often present.

Parenchymatous Syphilis

Though meningo-vascular and parenchymatous syphilis are rarely seen in pure form the distinction between them is valid and valuable. Many attempts have been made to explain the specific localization of the spirochaetal infection in tabes and general paralysis. It has been suggested that this is due to infection by a *neurotropic strain of the spirochaete*. A certain amount of evidence does in fact point in this direction. It is common to find in tabetics and general paralytics that the primary, secondary and tertiary manifestations of the disease are either trivial or absent. Moreover, many examples of conjugal parenchymatous syphilis are on record, and the children of general paralytics frequently manifest an infection which is confined to the central nervous system. It has also been observed at times that several cases of general paralysis have originated from a single source. However, in the case of certain primitive peoples said to be free from parenchymatous syphilis it has been found that the Europeans they infected were by no means exempt from tabes or general paresis, and this rather invalidates the theory of a neurotropic strain. Moreover, conjugal infection does not by any means always result in a similar kind of disease. Finally, somatic syphilitic lesions, though rarely diffuse in general paresis, are not uncommon; syphilitic aortitis is found in the majority of patients at autopsy, while arteritis of vessels and syphilitic fibrosis of internal organs is sometimes seen. On the whole, the evidence would appear to be against the view that a specific strain is responsible for the features of parenchymatous syphilis.

To test the theory that intensive treatment with mercury and arsenicals has changed the symptoms of syphilis and contributed to the apparent increase in 'metalues' of the central nervous system, a Russo-German expedition went in 1928, to the Burjato-Mongolian Republic in Central Asia. Among the inhabitants syphilis was endemic, 25 to 50 per cent. of the population being affected. The members of the expedition examined 475 serologically positive patients and found 42 cases of general paresis and tabes, i.e. 8.9 per cent. Yet, no treatment by the drugs indicated was in use among the natives (Beringer, 1934).

The distinction between tabes and general paralysis, on the one hand, and meningo-vascular syphilis on the other, is probably explained by the theory of McIntosh and Fildes

(1914–15). It is suggested that in the latter the neurones suffer secondarily, the primary infection being in mesodermal tissues, particularly the blood-vessels. In tabes and paresis, on the other hand, the spirochaetes traverse the blood-vessels and attack neurones directly.

GENERAL PARALYSIS. The principal features of this condition were recognized towards the end of the eighteenth century, and its relationship with syphilis was the subject of embittered controversy until the discovery of the Wassermann test early in the twentieth century. Even then the *relationship between infection and mental disorder* remained obscure until Noguchi demonstrated the presence of spirochaetes in the brain in 1911.

PATHOLOGY. Post mortem in an advanced case the meninges are found to be thickened and adherent to the brain to such an extent that any attempt to separate them leads to tearing of the subjacent cortex. The brain is very shrunken, the gyri reduced in size and the sulci wide, the changes being specially marked in the *frontal, temporal and parietal regions*. The ventricular surfaces are sprinkled with minute, whitish granulations. Microscopically, the pia arachnoid is found to be diffusely infiltrated with leucocytes and plasma cells, and the cortex is so disorganized that the different laminae are no longer recognizable. In many areas the cells have disappeared or are in various stages of degeneration. There is a gross microglial proliferation forming a dense feltwork immediately below the meninges. A similar neuroglial feltwork may be seen subjacent to the ventricular ependyma. There is a vast increase in the number of microglia cells which are also enlarged in size and may be seen sometimes arranged in rows of 'rod cells' at right-angles to the cortex. Turnbull-blue preparations show iron-containing pigments deposited in the bodies of these cells, as also in the walls of cortical vessels. Lymphocytes and plasma cells pack the perivascular spaces in addition to infiltrating the meninges. The presence of *spirochaetes* can be demonstrated in the brain.

CLINICAL PICTURE OF THE ADULT FORM. A period of five to twenty-five years elapses between the *primary infection* and the appearance of the *first symptoms* of general paralysis; the usual interval is ten to twelve years. The disease generally commences between the ages of thirty and fifty. It is two to three times more common in men than in women, and in women it tends to appear later in life than in men. A carefully-taken history will frequently reveal that for some time the patient has had a number of ill-defined symptoms such as headache, giddiness, insomnia, restlessness and weakened drive and vitality. By the time the patient comes under observation the picture is usually that of a *chronic psycho-organic syndrome* which has been in progress for a period of months and often has certain suggestive features. Temperamental and personality changes, of a type associated with lesions of the frontal lobe, often occur early, even before any intellectual change. The patient's memory for recent events is impaired first, and his thought becomes retarded and laboured. He has great difficulty in grasping a situation, and in discussion he drifts around the point with vague irrelevancies. His behaviour at work becomes disorganized and unpredictable. He is late for appointments, turns up at the wrong place, gives mutually contradictory orders. This stage develops episodically into one of clouded consciousness in which he may lose his way in a familiar district, wander into the street without his clothes on, or find his way into a lavatory for the opposite sex. In more rapidly evolving cases an acute delirious episode may usher in the condition. At an early stage of the disease behaviour grows more coarse, *tact and judgement deteriorate* and *the moral and ethical control* of behaviour are *undermined*. A cultured and refined individual may be observed to eat his meals in a gluttonous and revolting manner; his personal appearance becomes slovenly; he is rude and obscene at his home and in the presence of his friends, and brutal to subordinates. A well-known lawyer, asked to propose a toast at a dinner, regaled the assembled company with a recital of bawdy songs. A surgeon began an operation for appendicitis by making an incision from the interclavicular notch to the symphysis pubis, having in a dazed and vacant state assumed that he had come to do a post-mortem. A politician, seated on the platform at the annual congress of his party, was observed to pick his nose assiduously throughout the proceedings.

The effacement of the moral and spiritual components of behaviour and the commission of serious errors of judgement may occur before any serious intellectual deterioration, in a strict sense, has occurred. This therefore is a dementing process in which *dilapidation of emotion and social misdemeanour* may be the precursors of the later disorganization of intellect. It is all the more important to remember this because in the regular routine of his life a patient with established disease may continue for a considerable time without drawing attention to himself, although a sudden change of environment may serve dramatically to reveal the inroads made by the disease. A school-teacher who had been observed to grow 'anxious, depressed and a little forgetful' was sent for a three weeks' holiday by himself in France, which he was visiting for the first time in his life. There he contracted a bigamous marriage, ordered three motor-cars, and was finally arrested after a particularly brutal assault on a man in a night club. He was by then incoherent in thought and the nature of his mental illness was obvious.

Affectively, the patient is not moved either by the good or ill fortunes or even the death of those nearest and formerly dearest to him. The response to all situations is a vacant, stupefied equanimity, perhaps enlivened in the company of others by a childish and fatuous elation. A *simple* or *euphoric dementia* is the picture in about two-thirds of cases. Superimposed upon it in a proportion of patients is an attitude of *expansiveness* in a setting of generous and condescending good humour. The patient boasts a state of superhuman physical fitness, his athletic feats are likely to break world records, his wealth is reckoned in millions, his estates limitless; his intellectual prowess is the envy of Einstein, his imaginative and artistic gifts are beyond description, while Casanova's memoirs are likely to become forgotten when his own amorous adventures have been recorded. This picture is not generally associated with an affect of true *manic elation;* the playfulness of the ordinary manic and the infectiousness of his mood are often lacking. The expansive paralytic is childish and naïve, and his behaviour has a more pathological flavour than the grandiosity of the manic. A typically manic picture is relatively rare, but *depression* is more common. The nihilistic and hypochondriacal delusions in the depressive form may be of the most grotesque kind, although perhaps what makes them so noteworthy is the fact that they are seen in a setting of disproportionately shallow disturbance of mood. Moreover, some degree of dementia is present in most cases, and the paralytic patient is far more suggestible than the depressive and more easily distracted from his gloomy preoccupations. However, a typical depressive picture may occur.

In the *paraphrenic form* of the disorder, grandiose ideas of boundless power and wealth are associated with delusions of persecution, and hallucinations. The patient may consider himself pursued by the agents of foreign powers or by the representatives of Jews and Freemasons who are plotting to deprive and rob him. He feels himself under the influence of electrical machines, the rays of which are directed upon him. His movements are hampered, the voices of his persecutors upbraid him in profane and obscene language and threaten him with violence. While certain themes are consistently discernible, the paranoid ideas are rarely well systematized, and the patient shows less affective reaction and distress than does the ordinary paraphrenic.

Presentation with an acute onset was commonly seen when the disease itself was common—an apparently typical depression, or hypomania, or perhaps an acute delirium. These states responded rapidly to treatment, and the degree of recovery eventually attained was often very satisfactory. Presentation as a Korsakov state may also occur.

By the time the patient's mental abnormalities have drawn attention to his illness, the *clinical signs* are usually unequivocal. It will be found in the majority of cases that he is poorly orientated and that his memory for recent events in particular is grossly impaired. If asked to sign a form his writing sprawls across the page, words and letters are omitted and misspelt. He is quite incapable of making simple calculations and will dismiss his failure with a childish evasion. *Physically*, he will be found to be in poor health, with a flabby musculature and a slouching gait. There is a characteristic coarse tremor of the face, lips and tongue. If asked to pronounce words such as 'Methodist Episcopal, Royal Irish Constabulary, Biblical Criticism' he shows a gross dysarthria and as he trips over his words the tremulousness round his mouth grows worse and radiates to other muscles of the face. His movements are clumsy, and in finger–nose and heel–knee tests, considerable incoordination will be observed. In rather more than 50 per cent. of cases the pupils are small, unequal and irregular in outline and fail to react to light although the reaction on accommodation is preserved; the deep reflexes are exaggerated. The plantar responses are generally normal at an early stage, but one or both may be equivocal or extensor. The patient may come under observation because of an *epileptic fit*. This is generally a major convulsion with loss of consciousness, though psychomotor attacks occur commonly. Any variety of aura may be seen in different patients. In other cases, apoplectiform attacks are seen early in the disease; there is sudden loss of consciousness, and focal cortical symptoms such as hemiplegia, apraxia or a homonymous hemianopia may remain for a period of hours, days or weeks after the seizure. Recovery is usually complete, but a residual hemiparesis or dysphasia may remain.

In *taboparesis* general paralysis is combined with tabes and sensory changes of the latter condition are present as well as loss of deep reflexes and sphincter disturbances. In the *Lissauer type* of general paralysis the signs and symptoms of severe focal cortical involvement present themselves, and aphasia, apraxia or hemiplegia may suggest a space-occupying lesion.

In the *untreated case* which was a familar sight in the mental hospital of half a century ago the progress of general paralysis was marked by increasing dementia, physical enfeeblement, and degradation of habits. The delusions, the grandiose fabrications, and the depressive ideas gradually died away to leave the patient in a state of apathy and inertia in which his mutterings would dimly recall fragments of his former delusions. His awareness of his whereabouts grew more and more dim, and ultimately he failed to recognize relatives and friends. In the terminal stage, a shrunken and dilapidated shadow of his former self, he led a purely vegetative life, punctuated here and there by paroxysms of childish rage if crossed in some trivial matter concerning his food or comfort. His gait was now slow, laboured, broad-based and slouching. Very soon he had difficulty in getting about or even standing without support. At the end, he was bedridden, and it required only a sudden movement to fracture his humerus or femur. Toxaemia from bedsores or a hypostatic pneumonia finally carried the patient off. However, with the advent of *malaria therapy* and later of penicillin, this picture is no longer seen, and had become a rarity even by the 1930s. In the great majority of cases modern treatment arrests the progress of the disorder and prevents the pitiful state of physical enfeeblement that was the lot of most patients in the pre-malarial days.

The *cerebrospinal fluid* exhibits diagnostic changes. The Wassermann and Kahn reactions are strongly positive both in the blood and cerebrospinal fluid. There is an excess of cells of about 10–50 per cu. mm., protein is increased and there is a rise in the globulin content of the fluid. Lange's colloidal gold curve is of the paretic type, e.g. 5555544332.

Clinically, the condition may be confused with cerebral tumour, particularly with a prefrontal tumour. It may be also difficult to distinguish the condition from cerebral arteriosclerosis, presenile dementia and alcoholic deterioration, but the physical signs are usually pathognomonic and the cerebrospinal fluid findings serve to establish the diagnosis with certainty.

It is *among the old*, however, that the diagnosis is most easily missed; the condition may present as an apparent case of senile dementia. Where a dementing process commences relatively early in life in an individual who is physically well preserved, G.P.I. should always be borne in mind as a possibility. A detailed physical examination and investigation of the cerebrospinal fluid are essential in all such cases if general paralysis in old age is not to be overlooked.

JUVENILE PARENCHYMATOUS SYPHILIS. This represents a very small proportion of cases of congenital syphilis, the incidence being reckoned about ½–1 per cent. In juvenile paresis symptoms generally commence between the ages of ten and fifteen. The clinical picture, while similar in general features to that of the adult variety, differs in the relative infrequency of positive symptoms. Thus the expansive, depressive, or the acute delirious forms are rare, the picture generally being one of *simple dementia* which commences insidiously and progresses slowly. Delusions, if present, are of a childish and naïve kind. Juvenile tabes starts at a somewhat later age and may not commence until adult life. In both juvenile tabes and paralysis, optic atrophy and pupillary abnormalities are frequent, but dilatation and fixation are commoner than the Argyll Robertson pupil.

Prognosis and Treatment of Neurosyphilis

General paralysis may be prevented by the energetic treatment of syphilis in the primary stage. Examination of the cerebrospinal fluid should be carried out in every case of primary syphilis and treatment continued until all signs of active infection have disappeared. The danger of general paralysis is particularly great where the cerebrospinal fluid changes are severe in the early stages of infection or persist longer than two years after it. A *yearly cerebrospinal fluid examination for five years* is indicated in such cases, and any sign of recrudescence of activity, such as a rise in cells or protein, should be energetically treated.

The introduction of penicillin has revolutionized the treatment of neurosyphilis. *Penicillin* is now the treatment of choice in all kinds of syphilitic infection of the nervous system, and with minor exceptions there is very little evidence that the addition of other forms of treatment improves the outcome. Details of treatment should be sought in neurological textbooks.

CEREBRAL TUMOUR
Incidence

The investigation of Walther-Büel (1951) has shown that *70 per cent.* of cases of cerebral tumour show some *psychological disturbance.* In a considerable proportion of these the disturbance will be among the early manifestations of the growth. The modern mental hospital and the clinics it serves are catering to an increasing extent not only for the serious psychotic illnesses but for a representative cross-section of all diseases complicated by prominent mental symptoms, and problems such as those presented by tumours are likely to appear to an increasing extent in psychiatric practice especially where its scope extends to the work of a general hospital.

Some impression of the frequency with which cerebral tumours occur in medical practice may be obtained from autopsy data. Several surveys have reported figures which agree fairly well with the incidence of 4·6 per cent. found by Braatelien and Gallavan (1950) in their large series of 1,168 consecutive autopsies in a mental hospital. Only 41 of the 54 tumours found were judged by these authors to have been of sufficient size to play a part in deciding the clinical picture. It is instructive to note that in 22 cases the growth had been unsuspected; senile and arteriosclerotic psychosis accounted for more than half the erroneous diagnoses.

Since the *different kinds of tumour* vary in their tendency to produce mental symptoms, some knowledge of their relative frequency is of importance for the psychiatrist. Gliomata have been found the commonest form of tumour in most surveys, accounting for 40–50 per cent. of the total. By far the commonest type of glioma is the spongioblastoma multiforme which by itself accounts for some 20–25 per cent. of growths. Meningiomas, making up 20–25 per cent., are reported next in frequency. Metastatic, pituitary, acoustic, congenital (craniopharyngiomas), granulomatous (gumma and tuberculoma), and blood-vessel tumours are rather less common (Walshe, 1931; Cushing, 1932; Cox, 1934; Symonds and Cairns, 1950); in most of the more recent surveys metastases have proved to be the most frequently occurring growths in this latter group. Surveys in the U.S.A. suggest that pituitary tumours are more common there than in this country.

In Cushing's classical survey (1932), two-thirds of cerebral tumours occurred *between the ages of twenty and fifty,* and incidence reached a peak between forty and fifty. In adult life most tumours are found above the tentorium, in children below it. There is a slightly higher incidence in males, which is in contrast to the greater tendency for women in general to develop growths. The commonest sites for growth would appear to be frontal, cerebellar, temporal, parietal, and pituitary, approximately in that order.

There are certain points of psychiatric significance which require to be made with respect to these data. It will be seen that two of the three commonest sites for tumours in general, the frontal and temporal lobes, are relatively *silent areas,* in which invasion by tumour may be expected to result in focal signs at a late stage; *psychological anomalies* and the symptoms and signs of increased intracranial pressure are likely to precede neurological focal signs by a considerable interval of time. Spongioblastoma multiforme, the commonest cerebral neoplasm, tends to occupy a frontal site and is especially prone to present with signs of intellectual deterioration and personality change. Again, meningioma, which is the second commonest kind of tumour, compresses the brain without invading it, so that focal signs, except in the case of suprasellar and sphenoidal tumours, are likely to be late in appearing, trivial, or absent. The patient here, too, will often present with a history of personality change, epileptic fits, or episodes of clouding of consciousness and symptoms due to raised intracranial pressure before he reports the effects of focal interference.

General Features

The psychological changes produced by cerebral tumours are of two kinds; those occurring with tumours in general, and those produced by focal invasion of the brain. The former will normally be found in association with the somatic symptoms and signs of *raised intracranial tension*, such as headache, vomiting, epileptic fits and papilloedema.

SOMATIC SYMPTOMS. The *headache* is paroxysmal and has a typically 'bursting' character. It tends to appear on awakening in the morning, but gradually extends in duration to last for an increasing period during the day. It tends to be intensified by straining, coughing or any muscular effort, and is usually relieved somewhat by lying down. It may be associated with tenderness of the scalp and of the cervical spine. Occasionally, when occurring more consistently in one part of the head, it points to the localization of the growth.

Vomiting is again prone to occur in the early morning, especially when the headache is at its height and may have an abrupt explosive character. Nausea may be absent, but more usually it is very much in evidence. *Epilepsy* tends to occur in about one-third of cases of tumour, and is often the earliest symptom in the two commonest varieties—glioblastoma and meningioma. If the aura points to some locality in the brain, or if there is a Jacksonian spread of epileptic disturbance in the initial phases of the fit, the possibility of an underlying organic lesion should be fully investigated. The later in life epilepsy appears, the more likely it is that it is symptomatic (see Chapter VIII, p. 450); after the age of forty a considerable proportion of such epilepsies of late onset are due to cerebral tumour.

Papilloedema is commonest in tumours so placed that they obstruct the free flow of cerebrospinal fluid from the ventricles to subarachnoid space, i.e. those of the cerebellum, mid-brain and third and fourth ventricles. It is rarer in tumours of the pons and the pituitary. In tumours of the prefrontal and temporal regions papilloedema may be at an early stage the only abnormal physical sign. Patients with a severe degree of papilloedema may experience attacks of blindness lasting a few seconds or longer. Other manifestations of raised intracranial pressure, seen more rarely, are a feeling of unbalance when standing, tenderness over the area of distribution of the fifth nerve, and at an advanced stage, paralysis of the sixth cranial nerve, and extensor plantar responses.

PSYCHOLOGICAL SYMPTOMS. The main types of reaction are clouding of consciousness, the dysmnesic syndrome, dementia, and, more rarely, a depressive, schizophrenic or neurotic picture.

In the large material studied in Bleuler's clinic (Bleuler, 1951), *clouding of consciousness* was observed in 37 per cent. of cases. Usually the change is not severe. The patient shows deficient grasp, is slow, inert, sleepy and inattentive, his mood is rather facile and he is partly disorientated. Rapid fluctuations in this picture are prone to occur, particularly in the case of tumours such as the colloid cyst of the third ventricle that are likely to produce intermittent hydrocephalus. There may be either rapid recovery to full alertness or a sudden change to acute delirium. Sometimes a rapid change for the worse will be due, in a case with marked increase in intracranial pressure, to herniation of the uncus of the temporal lobe below the tentorium cerebelli; it may then be associated with hypothalamic symptoms such as flushing, hyperpnoea, hyperpyrexia, and fall of blood pressure. There will also be a spastic hemiparesis from compression of the brain-stem against the opposite tentorial edge, pupillary changes due to pressure on the third nerve, neck rigidity and a rapid descent into coma.

While it remains true to say that clouding or loss of consciousness may be produced by a tumour at any site and is therefore a feature of cerebral tumours in general, the *pathophysiology* of this symptom is not certain. Recent work has shown, for example, that tumours in the brain-stem and diencephalon may be associated with attacks of clouded consciousness or coma where a general rise in intracranial pressure is safely excluded as a cause (Jefferson, 1950; Cairns, 1952). It is possible, therefore, that in many cases this general symptom is produced by pressure on the diencephalon, and where other evidence of raised intracranial pressure is lacking it should be interpreted as a phenomenon of local interference in this region.

The *dysmnesic syndrome* has already been described (Ch. VI, p. 349 and Ch. IX, p. 487). In Bleuler's material this condition was found in 38 per cent. of cases of cerebral tumour, and he has recently re-emphasized the view that it is due to diffuse damage or interference with brain function. Admittedly the syndrome is often seen in cases of long-established cerebral tumour, but localized lesions near the floor of the third ventricle may suffice to produce it (Gamper, 1931; Meyer, 1944; Schürmann, 1951); so also may bilateral, and rarely even unilateral temporal lobe lesions (Scoville and Milner, 1957; Dimsdale *et al.*, 1963. The significance of the dysmnesic syndrome therefore depends upon the presence of other evidence of increased intracranial pressure. If this is clearly present the dysmnesic syndrome has little localizing significance; if it is absent and the clinical evidence points to a basal or temporal lobe neoplasm, the presence of the dysmnesic syndrome confirms it.

In long-established tumours the patient may appear *demented*, but a spongioblastoma multiforme may produce a picture of dementia even when of short duration. Moreover, even meningiomas may cause dementia (Sachs, 1950) and elderly patients with cerebral tumour are particularly prone to manifest it. The frequent absence of papilloedema in the old may make diagnosis difficult. The possibility of a tumour should always be borne in mind in any rapidly developing dementia, particularly if the *patient's physical state* is strikingly discrepant with it. A sustained increase in intracranial pressure tends to lead in young people to reversible clouding of consciousness, which on long duration is likely to evolve into coma, whereas in the middle-aged and old it is a dysmnesic syndrome that tends to result from raised pressure, and in the long-standing cases the end-result is dementia (Walther-Büel).

Depressive, schizophrenic, hysterical and other neurotic states do occur with cerebral tumours but they are rare. Bleuler observed them in less than 5 per cent. of his material, and he found evidence to suggest that most of these patients had a constitutional predisposition which was thus merely rendered overt by the tumour. This explanation is not necessarily the correct one since there is reason to believe that functional psychoses are particularly prone to become manifest in an organic setting when the cerebral disease in question pursues a chronic course over a period of years and when cerebral damage is of limited extent. These conditions are satisfied in only a small proportion of cases of cerebral tumour. When depression occurs in a case of cerebral neoplasm, the patient's complaints of sadness or gloom are often in striking contrast with a flat, empty affect that arouses little response in the observer. Hysterical symptoms may be florid and unaccountable, occurring in individuals who had until recently shown a stable adjustment to life, or in middle-aged persons for whose breakdown no convincing psychological reasons can be discovered. The neurotic illness in those whose life-history fails to throw any light on the cause should always arouse the suspicion that some organic disorder such as a cerebral tumour has been overlooked.

Diagnosis

The cases of cerebral tumour most likely to present in psychiatric practice are those with relatively few localizing signs or with an atypical mode of evolution or clinical picture. The psychiatrist is therefore often confronted with a problem of especial difficulty. Yet when a tumour has been overlooked and the case is examined in retrospect the mistake is often seen to have been an avoidable one. An endogenous depression may have been diagnosed in a patient whose mood conveyed no positive sadness, only an empty, inert apathy. Or a neurosis was perhaps found in a patient whose previous adjustment to life made it a rather unexpected development and the activating causes held responsible were inadequate or irrelevant. *Careful history-taking will prevent most mistakes* of this kind, and a thorough physical examination in every psychiatric case is an essential safeguard.

The symptoms of *raised intracranial pressure* must be differentiated from psychoneurotic symptoms which may mimic them. Headache due to raised pressure which has already been described differs from psychogenic headache in that the latter tends to be vertical, is not aggravated by coughing or straining, shows marked variations in severity, and is usually associated with an anxious affect and other signs of neurosis. However, neurosis of late onset, and hysterical symptoms in particular, call for careful exclusion of cerebral disease including tumour.

Both general paralysis and meningo-vascular *syphilis* may mimic a cerebral tumour closely, but may usually be distinguished by the presence of typical pupillary changes, absence of signs of raised intracranial pressure (except in rare cases of meningo-vascular syphilis), by the positive Wassermann tests in the blood and cerebrospinal fluid, and also by changes in cells and the Lange curve which are very rare in tumour.

Arteriosclerotic psychosis shows a markedly fluctuating course with a much slower evolution of the clinical picture than in tumour of the brain. In its early stages there may be periods of complete remission between episodes of mental disturbance which, with rare exceptions such as the third ventricle cyst, are not imitated by neoplasms. The patchy dementia of cerebral arteriosclerosis is rare in tumour, and when present, the *well-preserved insight*, typical of the former condition until an advanced stage, will be lacking in most cases. The history, signs and symptoms of focal vascular occlusion may help, and in most cases of cerebral arteriosclerosis evidence of raised intracranial pressure will be absent. In the malignant form of hypertension, however, there may be papilloedema, severe headache and vomiting, and it may not be possible to exclude a neoplasm until *air studies* have been carried out.

Senile and presenile dementia usually show a slower and more gradual development than tumour, and evidence of raised intracranial pressure is lacking; but no reliance can be placed on these features alone. In middle or old age a spongioblastoma multiforme or even a meningioma (Sachs, 1950) may present with the picture of a progressive dementia, and papilloedema may be late in developing, or absent. A history of dominant inheritance of the dementing illness will help in *Pick's disease*, and the characteristic blend of parietal lobe symptoms in Alzheimer's. The electroencephalogram in the degenerative disorders will show considerably less abnormality than would be expected of a tumour producing an equivalent degree of dementia and focal features will be lacking. But angiography or air studies will be required to decide the issue in some cases. *Intracranial abscess* usually develops acutely, and a primary source of infection is generally present.

Cerebral tumour or metastasis occasionally presents as a depressive illness particularly when it is in the temporal or frontal lobes. Some organic features are usually present and general health has often undergone deterioration by the time psychiatric symptoms appear. But this is not invariable and special vigilance should be maintained in depressions that develop organic features in the early stages of a course of E.C.T. or relapse rapidly after the end of the course despite typical endogenous features in the psychiatric picture.

A problem of some difficulty may be presented by cases with *stupor*. It may be very difficult to distinguish clinically between a depressive stupor and stupor due to a tumour invading the third ventricle, and in these cases the electroencephalogram will be a considerable help, since in the latter it will be grossly deranged, showing high-voltage generalized rhythmic slow waves. Catatonic stupor has more specific features such as negativism, waxy flexibility, echopraxia, etc., which are rare in diencephalic tumours, but the electroencephalogram will be an additional aid in differentiation.

In *epilepsy of late onset* a detailed investigation should always be carried out, to exclude the possibility of tumour, since a substantial proportion of such cases do in fact have a neoplasm.

Aids to Diagnosis

Where a suspicion of cerebral tumour has been aroused by the history and examination, ancillary methods within the reach of most psychiatric centres will help to decide whether or not the patient requires detailed investigation in a neurosurgical unit. X-rays of skull and chest, and an electroencephalogram, should be done in all cases. Lumbar puncture is more rarely required and is contraindicated if a space-occupying lesion is suspected.

(1) X-RAYS. An ordinary X-ray of the skull may show erosion of bone locally, or in cases with chronic rise of intracranial pressure, the generalized patchy rarefaction which has been called the *beaten copper skull*. A tumour in one hemisphere may displace the pineal gland towards the opposite side, or erosion of the clinoid processes may have occurred as a result of a pituitary or suprasellar tumour or as a secondary effect of raised intracranial pressure. The site of a tumour may be betrayed by the presence of calcification in it. In all middle-aged and old patients suspected of cerebral tumour an *X-ray of the chest* should be done as this may reveal a *primary growth* that has not betrayed its presence by chest symptoms. Alternatively an active chest infection may be found which favours a diagnosis of abscess rather than tumour.

(2) THE ELECTROENCEPHALOGRAM. About 70–80 per cent. of tumours produce abnormalities in the electroencephalogram. In cases with high intracranial pressure these will take the form of high-voltage generalized slow rhythmic waves. When the pressure has been reduced by intravenous 50 per cent. sucrose a more focal abnormality may be revealed. This generally takes the form of high-voltage irregular slow waves which have a focal source over the site of the tumour. In deep tumours the slow waves are of lower voltage without superficial focus and often with a frequency of 4–7 waves per second. Secondary tumours generally produce a very severe abnormality, often with more than one focus of slow waves.

(3) THE CEREBROSPINAL FLUID. Where definite evidence for raised intracranial pressure has been obtained, or there is strong evidence in favour of a tumour, it is unjustifiable to carry out lumbar puncture. The danger is that the withdrawal of cerebrospinal fluid may give rise to a cerebellar or tentorial pressure cone which may occur even when there is no indication of raised intracranial pressure. This complication frequently proves fatal. Lumbar puncture is only justified where there is a strong presumption in favour of some other condition such as presenile dementia or arteriosclerotic psychosis, though

a remote possibility of tumour exists. It is essential to allow the fluid to escape very slowly and to remove no more than 2–3 ml. In the presence of a tumour some rise of pressure will generally be found by manometry, and in some cases a rise in protein will also be present. The cell content of the fluid is usually normal except in cases of tumour that impinge on the meninges.

A lumbar or cisternal *air encephalogram* involves a quite unjustifiable risk in hospitals not attached to a neurosurgical unit. The modern techniques of percutaneous *angiography* and *ventriculography* will establish whether a tumour is present with a high degree of certainty. The former has, to an increasing extent, replaced air studies in recent years.

Treatment

Modern surgery in cerebral tumour carries a mortality of about 10 per cent. In many cases of meningioma complete removal of the tumour is possible with little or no cerebral damage, and a total recovery may follow. Sometimes the tumour may prove too large, and even where wholly removed, recurrences occasionally occur. The removal of gliomata usually leaves behind severe residual defects except occasionally in prefrontal tumours where a total excision of one frontal lobe may be possible, which will leave behind little or no personality change. Tumours of the brain-stem are not amenable to surgery apart from decompression.

Where coma suddenly develops in a case of suspected cerebral tumour it may be necessary to bring about *dehydration of the brain* as an emergency measure. This should be done by warming a 25 per cent. solution of magnesium sulphate to body temperature and injecting 8 oz. slowly per rectum. Alternatively, to achieve more speedy dehydration 75–100 ml. of 50 per cent. sucrose may be injected intravenously.

No time should be lost when it has been decided that a patient probably has a cerebral tumour. He should be transferred without delay to a unit that can deal with any emergency that may develop.

DISSEMINATED SCLEROSIS

In this country the condition is one of the commonest organic diseases of the nervous system, with an *incidence* of about 5 per 10,000 persons. It appears to be far more common in Northern European and in Mediterranean countries and is a rarity in Africa. In the U.S.A. the incidence is approximately equal to that in this country. It attacks principally young adults, and there is a slight preponderance of women. There is evidence that a genetic factor makes a contribution to causation in some cases (Curtius, 1933; Pratt, 1951).

It has been claimed that there is a specific type of personality which is prone to acquire the disease, but a careful investigation (Pratt, 1951) has failed to confirm that the pre-morbid personality differs significantly from that of other patients with neurological illness. However, at the time of onset of the disease *changes of behaviour* may be evident. The patient may become moody, restless, demonstrative, and worried about himself. Inextricably entangled with these mental changes there may well be fugitive physical signs which are likely to be attributed to 'hysteria'. This is particularly prone to occur because already at this stage the patients may show a tendency to smiling and laughter with excessive facility which appears to be inappropriate in the circumstances and may be reminiscent of the '*belle indifférence*' of hysterics. The patients at this stage, with their ever-changing, ill-defined physical symptoms and their preoccupation with themselves, are often *suggestible*, and hypnosis or psychotherapy may exert a dramatic effect, thus providing a further spurious confirmation for a diagnosis of 'hysteria'. Yet in such cases a detailed neurological examination may already reveal some pallor of the discs and increase in the deep reflexes.

The onset of the disease is frequently associated with some *minor infection, trauma* or other illness. Some patients also say that an *emotional upset* occurred just before the onset of the illness, or before an exacerbation of the established state. There appears to be an objective basis for these accounts, and the association may be a real one. However, it is very unlikely that such stresses can play more than a subsidiary role.

Later, the facility of emotion may develop into a characteristic state of euphoria. While aware of his illness, the patient will often show an inadequate and shallow emotional response to it. This is all the more peculiar in that it may exist even though the patient has an astute insight into the nature of the condition. This *emotional state* may be associated with a tendency to over-activity and an unwise expenditure of his diminished physical resources. The mood may at times be so elated as to acquire a manic quality. Kraepelin suggested that in such cases the organic illness might have released a cyclothymic predisposition. The euphoria is by no means invariable; the patient may show instead a deep and inconsolable depression with a hostile, irritable and querulous flavour. A more rare phenomenon is the feeling of intense physical well-being which is experienced by some patients—the so-called '*eutonia sclerotica*'. They may boast of an immense physical energy and vigour even though the illness may already be well established.

As the disease progresses, intellectual changes appear. The patient becomes forgetful, particularly for recent events, his concentration fails, he is distractible and complains of a diminished capacity to direct his train of thought. In cases of established disease some degree of *intellectual deterioration* is common. But only rarely is this severe; the affective changes are generally far more pronounced. The affect of excessive cheerfulness is later complicated by attacks of incontinent laughter or weeping. Increasing eroticism and sexual desire may develop in a setting of total physical impotence. In patients who are not very demented these developments may bring acute distress. In the terminal stages, the intellectual defects combined with a shallowness of emotion, in some measure, protect the patient from grasping in full the state of physical and mental disintegration to which he has been reduced. In rare cases schizophrenic pictures have been described in association with the disease.

Disseminated sclerosis may sometimes take on a very *acute form*, commencing with fever, delirium and the simultaneous appearance of multiple lesions. It is extremely difficult to differentiate this condition from acute disseminated encephalomyelitis, and it is probable that the two disorders are variants of the same process, the difference being attributable to the speed of evolution.

Disseminated sclerosis may commence late in life and it then frequently heralds the onset of a rapidly progressive intellectual decay. There is some evidence to suggest (Einarson *et al.*, 1944) that these conditions are related to Schilder's disease.

Diagnosis

Differentiation from a hysterical state may be difficult in the early stages of the disease. Careful physical examination is, of course, obligatory, but does not always settle the issue. Even where the symptoms are highly suggestive one cannot rely on finding definite signs of organic disease. Where no convincing psychological causes emerge on careful investigation of an apparent case of 'hysteria' in a young patient, and especially where the history of previous development fails to provide any evidence of a neurotic maladjustment, the possibility of early disseminated sclerosis is always worth considering.

There may also be difficulties in differentiating disseminated sclerosis from cerebral tumour and from neurosyphilis. However, the scattered nature of the neurological lesions and the history of a fluctuating course with clear-cut remissions usually serve to establish the nature of the condition. These features will also serve to distinguish it from such conditions as Friedreich's ataxia, subacute combined degeneration of the cord, and spinal tumour. The cerebrospinal fluid may provide some help in diagnosis; the pressure is normal and there may be a slight increase in mononuclear cells in rare cases. A paretic Lange reaction is seen in about half the patients but the protein is not raised and the Wassermann reaction is negative.

Treatment

The task of the physician is to keep hope alive and provide moral support in a prolonged struggle with an incurable affliction. There is no specific treatment for disseminated sclerosis, but the *psychological handling of the patients* is of the greatest importance. It is a mistake to try to fob off the patient with evasive explanations of the condition. There are patients who clearly wish to be told the truth and the diagnosis should not then be withheld. Others make it equally plain that they wish to cling to illusions and their peace of mind should not be disturbed more than is necessary.

A *positive and optimistic attitude* is a great help to the patient, provided that no unduly extravagant expectations have been aroused. The knowledge that the disease is characterized by remissions which may last a considerable time is a source of hope and comfort to patients, particularly during the early stages of illness. They are rarely without gratitude for the hopes thus sustained even when they are ultimately confounded by a further attack of the illness. It is important to help and encourage the patient to *organize his life* so that it is adjusted to his disabilities. A clearly defined routine of activities is probably more important than any other factor in keeping patients going in a reasonably happy and contented frame of mind. It is unwise to tell the patient that no treatment does any good; there are few patients who can face facts such as these. It is better to administer two or three times a year a course of intramuscular vitamins of the B group or a course of liver injections without, however, allowing the patient to hope that they will cure him. *All heavy exertion should be forbidden*, but every attempt must be made to keep the patient in productive employment for as long as possible. In sedentary workers it is often possible to achieve this with relatively little reorganization, during the early stages of illness at any rate. Manual workers will, however, need re-education for new occupations. Re-educational exercises may also help many patients to cope better with their incoordination.

It is important to remember the *patient's family*, who sometimes endure greater misery and hopelessness than the patient himself, especially where it is the breadwinner who is stricken by the disease. If the psychological aspects have been well handled and a skilled social worker has been employed to attend to the problems of rehabilitation and to the maintenance of morale in the patient's family, it is astonishing what ingenious and determined compensatory efforts may be evoked in some cases.

CHAPTER X

AGEING AND THE MENTAL DISEASES OF THE AGED

INTRODUCTION

DURING the past half century the number of persons aged 65 and over in the population of Great Britain has almost trebled; they now constitute 12 per cent. of the population, numbering six and a half million. It is anticipated that by 1981 those between the ages of 65 and 74 years will increase by one-third and those 75 years and over by more than 40 per cent. The ageing of the population in highly industrialized and relatively affluent parts of the world creates complex social, economic and medical problems and health and welfare services are being compelled to an increasing extent to direct their attention to issues that bear some relationship to senescence (Logan, 1965). Among these, mental illness is one of the most important, for the probability of developing it increases steeply after middle age. This is clearly illustrated by the variation of first admission rates to hospital with age (Fig. 15). In consequence the percentage of admissions constituted by those aged 65 years and over has been rising rapidly in recent years in many countries. As chronic patients of all kinds are surviving also for longer periods, the population of mental hospitals is ageing. In England and Wales those aged 65 and over make up about 37 per cent. of those resident in mental hospitals and residence rates during the past ten years have increased among those aged 75 and over although they have fallen in all other age brackets. A similar situation prevails in U.S.A. where in 1963, 30 per cent. of the population of long-stay mental hospitals were in this age group. Moreover, almost 40 per cent. of the patients in geriatric wards show psychiatric symptoms as severe as those of many aged mental hospital patients (Kay et al., 1962). Hence psychiatric disturbances figure prominently in all kinds of institutions for the aged and probably constitute the largest single cause of chronic infirmity in senescence. As a number of surveys of the aged in the community at large have shown in recent years (see p. 543) there is a high prevalence of both functional and organic psychiatric disorders among elderly people. In Newcastle upon Tyne there were nearly three times as many people aged 65 and over with a relatively severe psychiatric illness living in the population at large, as there were in all forms of hospital and residential accommodation.

An important advance in recent years has been the demonstration that many disorders formerly attributed to senile degenerative or arteriosclerotic changes in the brain are largely or wholly independent of such changes and often make a favourable response to treatment. However, the degenerative processes are the underlying causes of the most severely chronic, disabling and intractable psychiatric illnesses of the aged, and in more subtle ways they lend some colouring to a number of cases of relatively benign character. The relationship between somatic and psychiatric disorder is in fact closer in old age than in earlier parts of the life-span. Biological, physical and social factors operate respectively as causes, modifying influences and as effects of mental disorder in old age.

THE PHYSICAL AND BIOLOGICAL ASPECTS OF AGEING

Ageing is associated with a decline in physical and mental health and vigour whose severity and rate of progress is subject to much variation. There is a decline in muscular strength; movements are slowed; the gait is more halting and the facial expression loses some of its mobility. As the subcutaneous connective tissue degenerates the skin becomes wrinkled. Hair grows more sparse and loses its pigment. The acuity of vision and hearing are impaired. There is a tendency to a gradual decalcification of the bones with the result that the vertebral column tends to develop deformities and stature shortens.

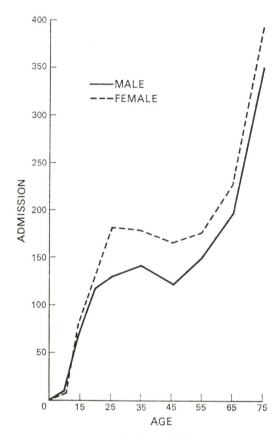

FIG. 15. First admission rates per 100,000 population at risk by age and sex in England and Wales 1960 (Registrar General, 1964).

This decline in physiological efficiency is probably related to the decrease in the number of cells or functional units that occurs with advancing age (Shock, 1964). The loss is of special significance when it affects organs and tissues such as the kidneys, musculature and central nervous system which have a finite cell population and which, in the adult, cannot replace a fall-out by regeneration.

Changes in the structure and biochemical composition of the brain are of special interest for senescence and the psychiatric disorders related to it. Important enquiries in this field have been conducted by Bürger (1957), who reported on the findings in a total of 2,187 men and 1,489 women. The average weight of the brain reached a peak between the ages of 20 and 30 years and thereafter showed a steep decline, the pattern being similar in both sexes. At the age of 70 the rate of decline became very steep and at this age there were also important changes in biochemical composition, a steep increase in water content being accompanied by a parallel decrease in dry weight. These changes were partially reversed at the age of 80 in that some decline of water content and increase in dry weight were noted. The oxygen uptake of the entire brain probably decreases with advancing age (Himwich and Himwich, 1959).

The concentration of a wide range of chemical constituents of the brain including total protein, lipids, nitrogen and phosphorus all showed a fall according to Bürger's enquiry. This commenced in middle age and continued after the age of 70, but desoxyribonucleic acid (D.N.A.) and sulphur increased. These changes were probably associated with proliferation of glia which are less rich than neurones in protein and lipids. It has been suggested on the strength of these biochemical findings that the process of senescence might have its starting point at about the age of 70. It is of interest in this context that, in subjects coming to post-mortem in general hospitals, mean counts of senile plaques also show a sharp increase at about the age of 70 (Tomlinson, 1968b). These counts have recently been shown to correlate with measures of psychological functioning carried out in elderly subjects before death. This subject will be further discussed in the section dealing with senile dementia.

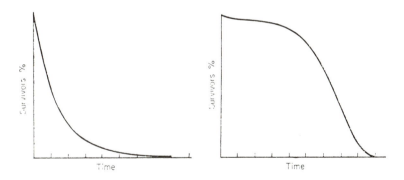

FIG. 16. Survival curves (Comfort, 1965).

Other histological changes are gradual loss of Nissl substances, shrinkage and pigmentation of cells and a decline in the cell population (Andrew, 1956). Alzheimer's neurofibrillary change and granulovacuolar degeneration have been shown to occur also in a number of psychologically normal subjects (Gellerstedt, 1932).

Until the advent of the modern era of gerontology the changes of senescence tended to be regarded as a part of human inheritance for which it was unreasonable to entertain any hopes of mitigation. Progress in gerontology has tended to push the shape of the survival curve of populations from the logarithmic form, characteristic of populations in which the chances of dying were mainly accidental and did not therefore vary with chronological age, to the more 'square' form, characteristic of populations with a high standard of living (Fig. 16). As social and medical progress produces this increasing 'squareness' in the survival curve

(Comfort, 1965) it reveals with increasing clarity the effects of senescence. If specific causes of death such as cancer, cardiovascular and infectious disease could be wholly eliminated, the age at death which would then be due largely to senescence would probably be distributed more normally about a mean of 75–80 years without any marked extension of the total life-span. The nature of the factors underlying this inherent tendency to declining vitality and death has aroused much speculation. It has been suggested, for example, that ageing is due to the increasing disorganization that arises from the accumulation of somatic mutations in subdividing cells during the life-span. This view is rendered plausible by the similarity between the effects of radiation in experimental animals which tend to show premature greying, loss of vigour and changes in fat deposition and 'ordinary' senescence. However, this theory is unacceptable for several reasons. Among these is the fact that although there is no mitotic division in the CNS it shows striking changes during senescence. Another theory attributes senescence to the fall-out of irreplaceable cells from certain organs such as the central nervous system, the musculature and the kidneys. This view accords with a great deal of morphological and physiological observation.

Whatever the precise mechanisms of the ageing process, genetic factors play an important part in controlling its rate. The influence of genetic factors on the life-span was first clearly demonstrated by Raymond Pearl (Pearl and Pearl, 1934); and, in studies of twins, Kallmann and his co-workers (Kallmann and Sander, 1948; Kallmann, 1951) have shown that differences between the life-duration in monozygotic pairs of twins were only half as great as those found in dizygotic twin pairs. Moreover, the causes of death tended to be strikingly similar in the former. However, the genetic factors involved appear to be of non-specific type and it seems probable that multifactorial genes similar to those associated with variation in graded characteristics such as stature, intelligence and temperament are involved. Genetic factors almost certainly play a part in the causation of diseases of middle and old age such as hypertension and diabetes, which are prone to produce a picture of premature physical and mental senescence in their advanced stages. Natural selection can be expected to give rise over the generations to a progressive accumulation of harmful genes in the post-reproductive part of the life-span. For genes are eliminated only by virtue of their impairment of fitness (the capacity to produce offspring). Deleterious genes which impair fitness would tend to have their age of manifestation postponed. Once the process of postponement has reached the end of reproductive life, natural selection can no longer operate to eliminate the gene, or challenge its reintroduction by fresh mutation. The post-reproductive period is therefore an evolutionary backwater in which mutations detracting from full health and vigour have probably been deposited over the generations. It follows that any genes that influence the length of the life-span and health and vigour in old age cannot have been directly selected since these effects are manifest after the end of reproductive life. They are therefore probably closely related to fitness in earlier life.

However, environmental factors almost certainly play a part in modifying the effects of heredity. In a number of lower animals, the life-span can be increased and reproductive capacity improved if growth is retarded by restricting the number of calories in the diet. There is a well-established association between overweight and a diminished expectation of life in the human subject. The most important disorders found in higher frequency among the obese are cardiovascular and renal diseases, diabetes mellitus, cirrhosis of the liver and gall bladder disease. The association with hypertension and arteriosclerosis is particularly striking. The former develops in the obese at two and a half times the rate it does in those of average weight and the incidence of atherosclerosis is also greatly increased.

PSYCHOLOGICAL CHANGES WITH AGEING

The psychological changes associated with ageing were well described by Burdach (1819) some 150 years ago.

'Generally speaking, his (the old man's) susceptibilities are diminished both in range and degree. He is indifferent to much that interested him keenly in earlier life. His emotions are calmer, and less frequent. His power of assimilating new ideas and of doing unaccustomed things is lessened. He easily forgets what he has recently experienced or what he himself has said or done. He takes longer to think anything out and, like his power of intellectual assimilation, so his intellectual productivity is diminished. New and substantial creations which call for exalted flights of the imagination are no longer produced and, while there are instances of very old men who have produced intellectual achievements of great perfection, these latter were partly works of ripe judgment and deliberation rather than creative imagination . . . .'

Scientific enquiry has during the past half century placed our knowledge of the psychological changes associated with senescence on a more objective basis. But in many respects it has done little beyond filling out with detail and expressing in a more precise form the phenomena clearly described by Burdach. He had already noted the decline in ability to assimilate fresh concepts and to behave efficiently in novel situations. Objective tests have confirmed this and have also demonstrated that ageing impairs the capacity for abstract thought. The relationship between ageing and creativity is perhaps more complex than is implied in the old description. Leonardo da Vinci, Titian, Dürer, Michelangelo, Voltaire, Goethe, Verdi, Renoir and Picasso provide some examples of artistic genius that continued to flower in old age, sometimes in novel and unexpected ways. However, among experimental scientists and mathematicians, in whom originality can be judged by more generally agreed standards, the most important discoveries are recorded in early life. Intellectual achievement may continue into old age but is usually derived from ideas first conceived in earlier life.

Observations in recent years have refined our understanding of the impairment that occurs in the capacity for learning and assimilating recent experiences. Thus immediate memory span for digits is little affected in aged subjects, whereas the ability to retain and recall some recently acquired skill or knowledge undergoes marked impairment. The failure of old people to learn is attributed by Welford (1962) to the increasing tendency for short-term memory traces to be disrupted by distraction during the period of 'holding'. As a result the process that results in more permanent registration in the brain cannot operate effectively. Welford considers that, when such registration is achieved, memories survive well, and that old people probably learn more readily and effectively than is commonly supposed. The slowness to which Burdach refers has now been defined as a general slowing of sensory motor performance which is only partly attributable to changes in the sensory or locomotor system. 'Slowness of performance among older people is not due so much to inability to see or hear or execute actions as to taking longer to recognize what is observed and to choose and control responding actions' (Welford, 1963).

These observations open up the possibility of creating conditions under which the elderly can learn effectively. Where a task demands speed, strength and frequent resetting of attention from one group of stimuli to another old people are at a disadvantage and acquire a skill much more slowly than younger persons. On the other hand, once new learning is assimilated, their special assets of persistence, stability and judgement may enable them to achieve a productivity that is comparable with that of younger individuals.

Welford (1962) has sought to account for the slowing in performance shown by elderly people in terms of changes in the central processing mechanisms concerned with signals and the responses made to them. He points out that the outfall of neurones and the possible decline in their functioning efficiency will tend to weaken the strength of the signals that are evoked by stimuli in assemblies of cells. On the other hand, there is a good deal of evidence for an increase of neuronal noise in the ageing brain; the discrimination of signal from noise will thus tend to become less efficient. Among the compensatory mechanisms adopted by the elderly person to enable him to minimize his deficiencies are load-shedding or narrowing of attention so as to concentrate on tasks most likely to need vigilance. There is also the tendency to develop routines of judgement and action to deal with total situations that are treated as one for purposes of identification, decision-making and appropriate response. The disadvantage is that where situations are undergoing rapid change, such set attitudes will tend to give rise to inappropriate decision-making and action. On the other hand, where the scene is shifting at a slower pace the advantages of long experience and the ability to take an overall view will tend to bring out 'the wisdom of old age' (Welford, 1963).

Many tests for measuring the intellectual deterioration of old age have made use of the tendency for vocabulary to remain relatively impervious to decline. Vocabulary tests can, therefore, be used as a measure of original intellectual endowment and the ratio of scores on performance tests over that registered on vocabulary tests can thus be used as an index of deterioration. The existence of verbal performance discrepancy in this sense has been confirmed by many studies of deterioration in old age although recent enquiries have necessitated considerable modification of the original Babcock principle in that verbal ability has itself been shown to be subject to deterioration (Roth and Hopkins, 1953; Orme, 1957). This has stimulated the development of other methods for differentiating between intellectually deteriorated and normal subjects (see also p. 554).

These and other observations about the cognitive abilities of the aged appear to be in general accord with the concepts of Cattell (1943) who advanced the hypothesis that there were two types of adult mental capacity, the 'fluid' and the 'crystalline'. The former is based on the ability to perceive new relations and the latter upon long-established habits in a particular field which no longer require 'insightful perception for their successful operation'. The first declines with senescence while the second is relatively unaffected by it and may sustain intellectual achievement in old age.

Ageing tends to be associated with a move towards introversion and this increasing inwardness is fostered by retirement and the gradual disappearance of the old man's contemporaries. The greater emphasis on custom and tradition and the rigidity of the aged can be exaggerated and they are certainly subject to variation.

There is a tendency for the emotions to cool and for sexual interest to decline with ageing. The decline is less steep than was formerly supposed (Kinsey et al., 1948, 1953) and recent surveys have tended to suggest that in the absence of physical ill-health or infirmity, a relatively high proportion of old people remain sexually active; those with strong sexual interest in early life manifesting particularly sustained libido in old age. The decline of physical and mental vigour, the appearance of physical signs of ageing in women, the fading of beauty and the end of reproductive life may cause depressive reactions but very rarely does this occur in the mature, previously well-adjusted personality. The same statement can be made about unrealized ambitions, shrinking opportunities and the departure of children from the home. However, the progressive decline of physical health and vitality and the accumulation of losses, deprivations and vicissitudes as age advances give rise to emotional disturbances in a relatively high proportion of the elderly. Physical illness and infirmity are one of the most important causes of anxiety and depressive neuroses in old age. The subject will be discussed at a later stage (p. 569).

THE INCIDENCE AND PREVALENCE OF MENTAL DISORDER IN OLD AGE

The rate of first and total admissions of old people into mental hospitals has been rising rapidly in many of the economically advanced countries of the world in recent decades.

Some indication of the trends is provided by figures from the United States. Between 1904 and 1950 the number of persons of 55 years and over in the population multiplied by four, but the number of first admissions in this age group to mental hospitals showed a nine-fold increase. It was not until the last three decades that a similar trend has become clearly apparent in England and Wales; the advent of the National Health Service and the consequent loss of beds formerly catering for elderly patients in public assistance institutions and in general hospitals has caused a general worsening of the situation. The rise in first admission rates for elderly people in psychiatric hospitals is considerable even over a period of ten years. The number of people aged 65 and over in the population of England and Wales rose by about 1 per cent. between 1951 and 1960 but the first admission rates show a rise of 31 per cent. for males aged 65–74 and 39 per cent. for those aged 75 and over. The rise for women is over 41 per cent. in both age groups. In numbers of patients this represents an increase of 5,657 between 1951 and 1960. In the one year 1959–1960 alone, the number rose by 1,495.

When the resident population in psychiatric hospitals is examined similar disproportion emerges. In 1949 approximately 11 per cent. of the general population were aged 65 years and over but the percentage of those resident in psychiatric hospitals in this age group was 27·6 per cent. By 1960 the corresponding figures were 12 per cent. in the general population and nearly 37 per cent. in the psychiatric hospital population. In their point-prevalence survey of elderly people in the mental hospitals of the north-east region of Scotland, Kidd and Smith (1966) demonstrated that a large part of the patients had been in hospital for a very long time; more than half for five years or more and half of these for more than 20 years. Patients admitted in old age make a smaller contribution to the load of chronic elderly patients than do already chronic patients who are admitted to geriatric status in increasing numbers. In a follow-up study conducted 16 months later they showed that of those who had been in hospital under two years, 16 per cent. had been discharged, 34 per cent. had died and 50 per cent. remained in hospital, whereas, of the patients who had been in hospital longer, 2 per cent. had been discharged and 20 per cent. had died (Kidd and McKechnie, 1967). The authors point out that one hope of lessening the future geriatric case load in a psychiatric hospital is the rehabilitative effort now being directed to younger chronic patients. Special investigation into what had determined length of hospital stay revealed that social causes were as important as clinical factors.

Socio-economic factors have probably contributed to the rise in admission among the aged. Decrease in the stigma which attaches to admission to psychiatric hospital and evidence of the effectiveness of physical treatment in psychiatry may also play a part. It is true also that psychiatrists are now dealing with a far wider range of psychiatric disorders in old age including the functional depressive and paranoid illnesses and that these swell the ranks of those entering mental hospitals. It now seems unlikely that the rise in admission rates is due to an increase in the frequency with which organic disorders are occurring in old age. A survey by Lin (1953) in Formosa, where old age presumably remains a privilege reserved for the robust and resilient, reveals an incidence of senile arteriosclerotic psychosis that is almost identical with that found in more highly developed countries. Moreover, an investigation by Sjögren and Larsson (1959) in Sweden, where the registration of mental illness is exceptionally precise and reliable, shows that the incidence of senile psychosis had not undergone any change in the previous 25 years.

The relative incidence of the various mental disorders of senescence is only roughly indicated by hospital admission rates. The Registrar General's analysis of the three major groups of psychoses diagnosed in patients aged 65 years and over admitted *for the first time* to psychiatric hospitals in England and Wales in 1960 shows the following distribution (rates given per million):

	65–74		75 and over	
	M	F	M	F
Schizophrenia	30	84	23	68
Manic-depressive reaction	529	756	268	299
Senile psychosis	582	781	2,054	2,723

Comparison of these figures with the percentage distribution by diagnosis of the resident population 65 and over in the psychiatric hospitals serving the north-eastern area of Scotland in January 1965 illustrates the fact that ageing chronic schizophrenic patients make a contribution almost as large as senile psychoses to the geriatric population of psychiatric hospitals.

	Percentage	
	M	F
Dementia	32·8	44·2
Manic-depressive	13·0	18·4
Schizophrenia/paraphrenia	43·7	30·5
Other (including mental deficiency)	10·5	6·9

Hospital figures, however, give only an incomplete picture of total incidence and distribution. Since the pioneer work of Sheldon (1948) and Hobson and Pemberton (1955) a number of surveys based on random samples of old people living at home in urban and country areas or in general practices has appeared (Primrose, 1962; Miller, 1963; Kay et al., 1964; Watts et al., 1952; Williamson, 1964; Parsons, 1965; Bremer, 1951; Essen-Möller, 1956; Gruenberg, 1961; Nielson, 1963). The studies undertaken in Great Britain agree in making clear that the three to five per thousand people over 64 who became psychiatric in-patients in the course of a year in England and Wales represent only a fraction of the actual prevalence—possibly only one in ten.

ESTIMATED TOTAL PREVALENCE RATES FOR THE MAIN
PSYCHIATRIC DISORDERS PER 1,000 POPULATION AGED 65 YEARS OR OVER

	1 Institutional cases, per 1,000	2 Cases living at home, per 1,000	3 Total prevalence per 1,000 with standard errors	Approximate ratios: column 2 to column 1
Senile and arteriosclerotic dementia	6·8	38·8	45·6 ± 11·0 ⎫	
Other severe brain syndromes ..	0·8	9·7	10·5 ± 5·0 ⎬	6
Manic-depressive disorder ..	0·7	12·9	13·6 ± 6·4 ⎫	
Schizophrenia, chronic	(0·2)†	9·7 ⎫	⎬	(12)
Paraphrenia, late onset	0·9	0·0 ⎭	10·8 ± 5·6† ⎭	
Psychoses, all forms	9·4	71·1	80·5 ± 14·7†	8
Organic syndromes, mild forms ..	5·3	51·8	57·1 ± 12·6 ⎫	
Neuroses and allied disorders (moderate/severe forms)	1·9	87·4	89·3 ± 16·1 ⎬	23
Character disorders, including paranoid states	0·5	35·6	36·1 ± 10·5 ⎭	
All disorders	17·1	245·9	263·0 ± 24·5	14

† Long-stay mental hospital schizophrenics not included.

These writers' estimates of the prevalence of the main psychiatric disorders of senescence diverge to some extent and their assessments of the frequency of less disabling forms of mental disorder even more, owing to differences in the criteria applied. However, some measure of agreement emerges on the prevalence of dementia. Parsons' figure of 4·4 per cent. approaches agreement with that of Hobson and Pemberton and others as does his estimate of 7 per cent. prevalence of psychotic illness (see the table on p. 543).

Beginning in 1960, a survey of 297 subjects aged 65 and over, living at home and selected at random from districts of differing social and economic status, was carried out in Newcastle upon Tyne (Kay *et al.*, 1962, 1964a,b; Garside *et al.*, 1965). Some of the results of this survey are shown in the table above. Among those living at home, 10 per cent. (38·8 + 9·7 + 51·8 per 1,000) were considered to be suffering from an organic brain syndrome; senile dementia 4 per cent., an arteriosclerotic brain syndrome 4 per cent., other brain syndromes 2 per cent. Half these persons showed severe and half a milder degree of deterioration.

Severe or moderate functional psychiatric disorders, including character disorders, were found in 15 per cent. (12·9 + 9·7 + 87·4 + 35·6 per 1,000) and chronic schizophrenia in 1 per cent. All late paraphrenics were in hospital but about 1 per cent. living at home exhibited strongly paranoid attitudes. The total prevalence of affective disorders and neuroses (not reckoning character disorders) was 10 per cent. (87·4 + 12·9 per 1,000) but mild disorders which are not shown in the table were found in a further 16 per cent. Five per cent. suffered from a neurotic or an affective illness of at least moderate severity which had arisen late in life, constituting an entirely new development in the medical history.

As the table shows, the number of cases drawn from the same areas and actually in hospitals and welfare homes was small compared with those living at home. All cases in institutions added up to a rate of 17 per 1,000 of the estimated population at risk out of a total prevalence more than 15 times as great. Less than one-fifth of the cases with severe brain syndromes were being cared for in the mental hospital or psychiatric unit which served the area. In this and other studies (e.g. Nielson, 1963) patients living at home with severe brain syndromes were as seriously ill as those under hospital care. The table on p. 543 shows that with mild cases omitted from the Newcastle figures the prevalence of broad categories of mental disorder in old age is closely similar in a number of countries with roughly comparable living standards.

There appears to be a fairly wide measure of agreement that *neurotic illness* is common in old age. Kessel (1960) and Kessel and Shepherd (1962) showed that, although after the age of 60 the referral of neurotics to hospital falls steeply, the prevalence of neurosis in *general practice* remains surprisingly constant throughout adult life at about 10 per cent. among men and 15 per cent. among women.

In surveys based on general practice it has been repeatedly found that apathy, resignation and disability itself prevent the elderly person from calling in medical aid. Even severe illnesses are untreated and many milder disabilities go unrecognized. This is particularly true of psychiatric illness. In the Newcastle survey only one subject had been referred out of 32 persons considered to be in need of psychiatric out-patient treatment. Parsons (1965) found that, out of 9·2 per cent. of a domiciliary sample markedly handicapped by a psychiatric condition present at the time of visit, approximately half were unknown to the family doctor.

This failure to report illness probably arises most often when the elderly live alone. Thirty-three per cent. of the Newcastle sample aged 70 and over were living alone. Some supervisory contact was obviously needed but only approximately 4 per cent. of the whole sample were receiving it. Even when there is supervision, depression is only too likely to go unrecognized as it so often masquerades as irritability, or paranoid symptoms, or comes to the doctor's notice as subnutrition or in the form of minor hypochondriacal complaints. These latter may be investigated repeatedly without the true cause coming to light till attempted suicide or a state of severe agitation call for emergency admission to hospital. Equally in affective disorder occurring in old age, exaggerated hypochondriacal complaints may effectively camouflage serious physical illness.

SUICIDE IN LATER LIFE. In the past 50 years male suicide rates have been decreasing in most countries. The elderly have benefited least from this all-round decrease and rates among women have been rising, especially among those in higher age groups.

There is a good deal of epidemiological and clinical evidence to favour the view that those who commit and those who attempt suicide are two distinct but overlapping populations (Stengel and Cook, 1958). Thus the incidence of attempted suicide decreases with age whereas the frequency of consummated suicide increases; the incidence of depressive illness is lower in cases of attempted suicide than among successful suicides. The overlap between the two populations is particularly marked among the elderly whose attempts are often of a more serious kind.

The question arises whether there are any factors related to suicide in the aged that could be used as a basis for prediction and preventive action. Recent enquiries have, to some extent, defined the medico-social profile of the aged person who carries out suicidal acts. The proportion judged to be suffering from a *depressive illness* ranges from about 48 per cent. (Capstick, 1960) to 70 per cent. (O'Neal *et al.*, 1956). This disparity probably arises from

THE PREVALENCE OF THE MAIN PSYCHIATRIC SYNDROMES OF OLD AGE, ACCORDING TO VARIOUS AUTHORS

Percentages

	Sheldon (1948) (N = 369) 65+	Bremer (1951) (N = 119) 60+	Essen-Möller (1956) (N = 443) 60+	Syracuse (1961) (N = 1,592) 65+	Primrose (1962) (N = 222) 65+	Nielsen (1963) (N = 978) 65+	Kay (1964) (N = 297) 65+
Senile and arteriosclerotic psychoses ..	3·9	2·5	5·0	—	3·6 } 4·5	3·1	4·6 } 5·6
Other organic syndromes ..	—	—	—	—	0·9 }	—	1·0 }
Major functional disorders	—	4·2†	1·1	—	1·4	3·7†	2·4
Psychoses, all forms.. ..	3·9	6·7	6·1	6·8	5·9	6·8	8·0
'Mild mental deterioration' ..	11·7	—	10·8	—	—	15·4	5·7
Neuroses and allied disorders (moderate/severe forms)	9·4 } 12·6	5·0 } 17·6	1·4 } 12·0	—	10·4 } 12·6	4·0 } 8·7	8·9 } 12·5
Character disorders	3·2 }	12·6 }	10·6 }	—	2·2 }	4·7 }	3·6 }

† Includes 'constitutional' and 'psychogenic' psychoses.

differences in diagnostic procedure; persons classified under the heading of 'neurotic or personality disorder' amount to 41 per cent. of cases in some series (Gardner *et al.*, 1964). However, in many of the latter subjects a diagnosis of psychiatric illness as well as relevant personality disorder can be made. *Physical illness* commonly accompanies suicidal behaviour; Sainsbury (1962) found it among 35 per cent. of elderly persons committing suicide.

He also found that *living alone* (39 per cent.) and *bereavement* (16 per cent.) were more often associated with suicide in the elderly whereas disturbed personal relationships were a common setting for it in younger age groups. *Lack of employment* contributed in 21 per cent. of his elderly suicides and Gardner *et al.* (1964) also found disturbed employment records and downward mobility in occupational status. Further investigation is needed into these social factors to disentangle cause and effect. This is also true of the observation that the single, separated, divorced and widowed predominate among elderly suicidal subjects, especially males. It is possible that both adverse social circumstances and the subsequent suicide derive, in a number of cases, from lifelong personality difficulties and the cumulative problems these create. No factor operates in isolation. Social factors increase the chance of depressive illness among those predisposed by physical illness or long-standing difficulties in personality: these often contribute to a further decline in the old person's social condition, increasing his loneliness and forcing him into an environment in which his hold on life proves to be tenuous. Suicidal attempts by the elderly should be taken seriously as they are usually very determined. Those who survive such attempts are in particular need of psychiatric help.

GENERAL AETIOLOGICAL FACTORS

In the different mental disorders of old age, genetical, social, cerebral degenerative processes and physical ailments contribute in varying proportions. The role of hereditary factors is discussed later in relation to the different forms of illness. Cerebral degenerative change, the principal causal factor in the senile and arteriosclerotic psychoses but occurring also in normal senescence, is described in the relevant parts of this chapter and its contribution to "functional" types of disorder under "classification" on page 548. The role of physical illness in the different forms of mental disorder is dealt with on page 586 and the contribution of sensory defects mainly in connection with paraphrenia on page 581. There remain some general social and personality factors whose contribution is most clearly seen in the large group of affective and neurotic disorders but which may be regarded as relevant in some degree within the whole span of normal and pathological ageing.

Social Factors

ISOLATION. Until recent years it has been widely regarded as the lot of a considerable proportion of the elderly in many countries. However, the belief that young people shirk their responsibility towards their elderly relations, leaving them isolated and friendless has proved to have little foundation. Recent research has shown that the pattern of contact of elderly people with their families is closely similar in Britain, the U.S.A., Denmark, West Germany and Austria (Townsend, 1964). There was little evidence from these enquiries of progressive atrophy of social relationships among the aged. Although relatives of the elderly may live in different households, they are often sufficiently close to permit continuing contacts and a reciprocal flow of services of great value to young and old alike. In addition to these close ties most old people have been found to have an extensive network of friends and acquaintances among neighbours, shopkeepers and other old people. Retirement and ill-health usually lead to a restriction of social participation but with some compensatory intensification of ties with near relatives and some lifelong friends. Some 80 per cent. of old people were regarded as being in this sense in contact with their families. It is this measure of family cohesion and the willingness of younger members to look after ailing relatives which make the present institutional provision for the aged just viable in England and Wales. Four and a half per cent. of people aged 65 and over at present resident in some kind of institution are enough to cause serious over-crowding and long waiting-lists especially in urban areas. Should any kind of social change cause part of their burden to be relinquished by the family, the pressure on the health and welfare services might be four to five times as great as it is (Townsend, 1957).

Progressive severing of ties with the outside world is more common than the pattern of continued gregarious activity and active social participation early gerontological research tended to uphold as the healthy pattern of adjustment in old age. Disengagement from a social role into more limited and intimate relationships within the family is probably the normal pattern among the aged in our society (Cumming and Henry, 1961). It tends to be accentuated by illness, disability and widowhood. However, the fact that it is a widespread phenomenon does not necessarily imply that it is always conducive to healthy adjustment in old age. The needs of old people vary and we cannot judge at the present time how far cultural norms reflect circumstances that meet their needs and aid health and happiness.

The concept of isolation is often employed in a vague way and its use requires scrutiny and more precise definition as well as further study. In the Newcastle study (Kay, Beamish and Roth, 1964b; Garside, Kay and Roth, 1965) it was found that respondents' complaints of loneliness were not co-extensive with the number of their daily contacts with other people. A similar observation was reported by Lowenthal (1964a). Nearly half the functionally-ill subjects who had many contacts described themselves as lonely, while of those with few contacts only about one-third complained of loneliness. This contrasted with the normal subjects whose subjective feeling of loneliness was closely related to the number of their contacts. 'Isolation' was statistically correlated not so much with paucity of social contacts as with functional symptoms of anxiety and depression, with pre-morbid personality traits of moodiness, concern about health and a history of previous mental disorder together with a longstanding tendency to be unsociable. In other words, complaints of loneliness were symptomatic of an underlying psychiatric disorder prone to generate the feeling of being neglected.

The functionally-ill subjects had been on the whole less in contact with other people than the normal subjects and there was much evidence to suggest that this had arisen from a lifelong tendency to form fewer relationships with other people than was the case among normal subjects. In 10 per cent. of functional subjects the number of everyday contacts had declined during the year before they were interviewed as compared with 2 per cent. of the normal group. In the functional nervous disorders and in the tendency to have few contacts we may be seeing different consequences of a predisposition shared to some extent by both; the one tends to augment the other, giving rise to a vicious circle.

The relationship between actual isolation and psychiatric disorder is highly complex and the term 'isolation' comprises a variety of circumstances. At one end of the scale are the lifelong isolates for whom solitary existence is a way of life (Lowenthal, 1964b). These are isolated because of abnormalities of personality which have arisen in early life. Among them are to be found a small proportion of mentally abnormal and rootless persons whose oddities of personality are so severe that the possibility arises that they have evaded

T

breakdown by avoiding all involvement in interpersonal relationships. Many paraphrenics belong to this group. Others are tough, resilient individuals, who are neither lonely nor psychiatrically ill. They raise the question of whether we should interfere lightly with the long process of progressive self-isolation that is found in certain elderly people. At the other extreme there are those who have become isolated in late life owing to the development of illness, physical or mental: the latter being the more likely to cause the dropping off of social contacts, as it is less well tolerated. Between these two extremes are those who have long experienced difficulty in establishing personal relationships but whose adjustment has depended on being able to maintain a limited number. In old age, when these few relationships are likely to be disrupted by bereavement, illness or other accidental factors, psychiatric breakdown may result. A sweeping programme to deal with isolation as a uniform problem would be inappropriate: a flexible approach is required both in prophylaxis and in remedial measures.

Although isolation is the fate of only a minority of old people and the causal connexion between it and psychiatric illness is in doubt, it is well established that those who lack family support are prone to become institutionalized. In Great Britain it has been shown (Townsend and Wedderburn, 1965) that far more old people in institutions are unmarried, 33 per cent., compared with 10 per cent. of those in private households; more of those married or widowed lack children (26 per cent. compared with 16 per cent.), more lack brothers and sisters (40 per cent., 22 per cent.) and more of those who have children have only one (39 per cent., 26 per cent.) and they tend to have sons rather than daughters. Such facts are of importance for health and welfare services. Increased geographical mobility by separating the generations is likely to institutionalize a proportion of that marginal group of old people who, with the help of their relatives maintain a precarious adjustment in the community, and thus through time cause serious embarrassment to these services. The need to anticipate this situation by means of integrated provision for the elderly that places strong emphasis on domiciliary care and support is becoming increasingly appreciated.

BEREAVEMENT. The Newcastle study showed bereavement to have little correlation with psychiatric illness as a whole. This may have arisen partly from a definition of bereavement which did not concentrate on very close ties or because the subjects who had lost a key relative had swiftly been moved to institutional care. However, in a large sample of 483 San Franciscans aged 60 and over who were admitted to psychiatric hospital for the first time at this age, Lowenthal (1965) found that, while 38 per cent. of the sample were widowed, only 5 per cent. underwent this stress in the year preceding the onset of their first psychiatric illness and only 8 per cent. in the five-year period prior to onset. Loss of spouse did not differentiate between the psychogenic and the organic groups into which the subjects were divided. The connexion found to exist between bereavement and psychiatric illness in earlier age groups (Parkes, 1964) may not be equally operative among the aged. The subject deserves further study.

RETIREMENT. Circumstances connected with retirement have often been cited as causes of unhappiness and emotional breakdown in old people. The elderly man in particular is left with unlimited time on his hands and his diminished earnings restrict his activities. Whereas the elderly woman, particularly in working-class families, remains the centre of the household, the elderly man after retirement loses prestige when he relinquishes his role as breadwinner. In few parts of the world does the old age pension suffice for adequate nutrition, comfort and security nor does it cover the whole of the aged population. However, recent enquiries have shown that retirement has been previously exaggerated as a cause of ill-health; this frequently precedes and is often the cause of cessation of work in old age. When elderly men who are still working and those who have retired for non-health reasons are compared there is little or no difference in respect of medical attention and mobility (Richardson, 1964). Kay, Beamish and Roth (1964b) found that being unemployed for at least 5 years before interview distinguished between those who were normal and those who were psychiatrically ill at a high level of significance. However, as it did not differentiate between the functional and organic groups the connexion with psychiatric disability is more likely to be consequential than causal.

However, the increasing proportion of old people surviving 15 years or more beyond the age of retirement raises important questions about the role of the aged in modern society. In many civilizations and tribal societies of the past, as Sir James Fraser among others has taught us, the aged were the law-givers, the counsellors, governors and spiritual guides of the community. Such gerontocracies were, on the whole, slow-moving, rigid and resistant to change. However, the aphorism in which Kant attributed 'cleverness', 'sagacity', and 'wisdom' to the three ages of man ushered in by the twentieth, fortieth and sixtieth years appears in the light of psychological research to have some substance. Some judicious balance between the influence of young and old in society is required so that old age can become more than an eventless interregnum between retirement and death (Roth, 1966, 1967).

POVERTY. This is a widespread cause of distress among the aged. Fifty-two per cent. of old people in Great Britain have been found to be either wholly dependent on the state or to have less than £1 per week of non-state income (Townsend and Wedderburn, 1965). In a city sample in Edinburgh 22 per cent. were found in such straits that their basic financial needs were not being met (Williamson, 1964). Yet clear evidence that either social class or poverty affect the incidence of mental disorder in the aged was lacking in the Newcastle community survey and in those of other workers.

It is possible that, where social adversity is present in old people who become mentally ill, it acts along with predisposition to illness rather than being itself the cause of it. That it produces unhappiness and distress is not in question.

Predisposition

The feelings of loneliness of which many old persons with functional disorder complain and the narrowness of their social life have been shown to be associated with long-standing difficulties in human relationships. It has been shown that such individuals have in the past been more moody, more prone to anxiety and to worry about their health and to have had narrower interests than normal subjects. Vispo (1962) found similar differences between the pre-morbid personalities of a group of elderly subjects with functional disorders and those of a group of normal controls. This predisposition may be presumed to originate in early environmental and genetical factors.

Two other aspects of their earlier life distinguished the functionally disabled from the normal subjects in the Newcastle study. These were a previous history of psychiatric illness and the loss of a parent before the age of 15. The difference from normal subjects in the latter respect was, however, barely significant statistically and the suggestion that insecurity in childhood may predispose to a neurosis in late life needs further evaluation.

In the organic group of subjects *reduced mobility and capacity for self-care* stand highest among the features distinguishing them both from normal subjects and from the group with functional disorder. Moderate or even severe physical disability is usually either a direct consequence of focal brain damage or due to *peripheral sensory defects*, which are significantly more common in this group. Sixty-two per cent. suffer some degree of deafness (21 per cent. moderate or severe) and 42 per cent. from defective eyesight (28 per cent. moderate or severe). It is possible that these defects of sight and hearing play a part in the production of mental symptoms by reducing contact with the outside world; for the association of sensory defects with organic mental states seems to be too strong to be wholly explained by the *advanced age* of the subjects.

The importance of the connexion between psychiatric and physical illness in the aged (see p. 586), along with the more equivocal role which is now emerging for factors such as 'isolation' which have previously had prominence, has *implications for the orientation of the services* for the aged, which are now being developed. It is at least arguable whether programmes directed mainly at socializing isolated old people will have much effect in preventing psychiatric illness. The medical services should therefore remain firmly at the centre of plans for prophylaxis and treatment. To sum up, recent sociological and medical research has, on the whole, provided a much more hopeful picture of old age than had been formerly prevalent. The majority of aged people are active, and in contact with their families. The commonest forms of illness are associated less with current adversities such as isolation and bereavement than with long-standing predispositions to emotional instability and difficulties in human relationships in the moulding of which socio-familial factors may in the remote past have had a share.

The most immediate and pressing need is to apply existing knowledge to the amelioration of definite psychiatric disorder and to the physical illnesses which are frequently associated with it. There is much evidence to suggest that a great deal of psychiatric disorder and of functional illness in particular goes unrecognized at the present time. This happens in the community and in medical and surgical wards of hospitals alike.

CLASSIFICATION AND DIAGNOSIS OF MENTAL DISORDER IN THE AGED

Special Problems in Classification

During the past two or three decades our views on the aetiology and classification of mental disorder in old age have undergone fundamental revision. The modern era in geriatric psychiatry began at the beginning of this century with the differentiation of senile dementia, arteriosclerotic dementia and the presenile psychoses from one another and from other organic psychoses, such as neurosyphilis. The early clinical accounts of the psychiatry of old age were largely confined to these disorders and, until recent years, psychoses with dementia formed the only subject to which text-books directed attention when dealing with mental disorder in old age. The fact that psychoses of a relatively benign nature do occur among the elderly has been recognized for a considerable time although the nosological position of these conditions was left in uncertainty. Clouston (1904) referred to simple melancholia as differing in no way from the corresponding disorder in early life. Kraepelin (1909–13) found that 7 per cent. of cases of manic-depressive disorder began after the age of 60 years and Bleuler (1916) referred to the depressive form of senile psychosis.

However, affective and paranoid disorders were regarded for the most part as forms of senile psychosis which led eventually to deterioration of personality and intellect, and the precise relationship of these conditions to the functional psychoses of early life was hardly considered. Differences in attitude to the classification and diagnosis of these illnesses persist and the wide disparity in the rate of first admission for senile and arteriosclerotic psychoses in the U.K. and the U.S.A. (Roth, 1959b) is very likely due to the fact that a wider range of mental disorders of senescence are diagnosed as organic psychoses in the United States than in this country. When the introduction of electroconvulsive therapy (E.C.T.) for elderly patients (Mayer-Gross, 1945) began to make it plain that some depressive and, to a lesser extent, paranoid syndromes responded to this treatment, the practical importance of the distinction between clinical varieties of mental illness in the aged became clear. The view that irreversible pathological changes of senile degenerative and arteriosclerotic nature provided the whole explanation for such disorders began to be called into question.

Follow-up studies soon provided further evidence that a fresh approach to the aetiological basis of some very common forms of mental disorder in old age was needed. A number of enquiries in Great Britain and the U.S.A. (Post, 1951; Robertson and Browne, 1953) showed that there were striking differences in outcome and in mortality in particular, between groups showing predominantly functional and predominantly organic psychiatric symptoms. The hypothesis that the mental disorders in old age comprise a number of distinct nosological entities with relatively little overlap was tested explicitly by Roth and Morrissey (1952) and Roth (1955). Patients were classified on the basis of psychiatric features into five groups: affective disorder, late paraphrenia, acute or subacute delirious states, senile psychosis (i.e. senile dementia) and arteriosclerotic psychosis, and these groups were found to differ sharply in pattern of outcome at six months and two years after admission to hospital (Figs. 17 and 18). Follow-up studies 7–8 years after admission to hospital revealed the differences between the groups still to be clearly evident although mortality due to ageing had to some extent blurred them (Fig. 19). The hypothesis that the groups were distinct from one another was further supported by the result of formal psychological testing (Hopkins and Roth, 1953; Roth and Hopkins, 1953) and by studies of the prevalence of physical illness (Kay and Roth, 1955). The causes of death were also found to differ in the different groups. Whereas vague causes of death such as myocardial degeneration, bronchial pneumonia, and 'old age' were commonly cited in cases of senile and arteriosclerotic dementia, in the case of affective and paranoid psychoses in old age, death was ascribed to clear-cut and specific physical illnesses such as cardiac disease, cancer, peptic ulcer, and hypertension in a far higher proportion of subjects (Kay, 1962).

Affective disorders in these early enquiries covered a broad spectrum. It had been thought initially that most subjects presenting with a depressive illness in old age would suffer from an endogenous depression. It has, however, become increasingly plain that, even in mental hospital practice, at least half of the patients suffer from depressions of a neurotic kind, reactive to a considerable extent to environmental stress and to physical illness. Population studies have revealed the subject of neurosis in old age to be of even greater importance. The majority of cases fall into the categories of neurotic depression and anxiety neurosis which overlap to a marked extent. Observations in coming years will doubtless serve to establish a valid classification of these important disorders in the aged.

In an investigation into outcome in 236 patients admitted with mental disorder after the age of 60 years, an almost complete follow-up was achieved in that the subjects were traced without exception (Kay, 1962). The relative independence of depressive and paranoid

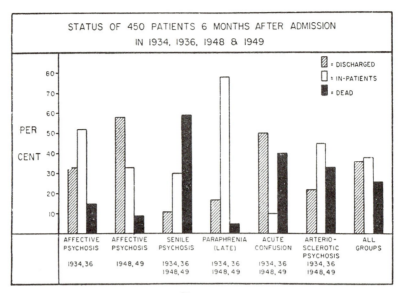

FIG. 17.

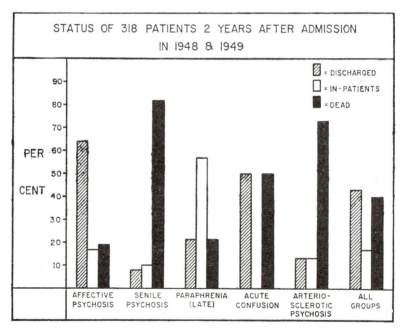

FIG. 18.

FIGS. 17 and 18. Pattern of outcome of patients aged 60 and over admitted to mental hospital and differentiated according to presenting clinical picture. The proportions of discharged, dead and in-patient were ascertained by means of a follow-up study. (For 'senile psychosis' read 'senile dementia'.) Pattern of outcome of patients admitted in 1934–36 with predominantly affective symptoms differed from outcome in later years and has been shown separately in Fig. 19.

groups from dementias of late life was confirmed. While the duration of life among patients with senile dementia and arteriosclerotic psychoses was only one-fifth of that predicted for the average population of Stockholm of corresponding age, the late paraphrenic cases were found to have had an almost normal life-span. The affective cases with onset late in life had survived for about seven-tenths of the normal life-span but the increased mortality was due in the main to various kinds of somatic disease; dementia and signs of cerebral disease very rarely developed. In the paranoid cases also the final clinical picture had as much in common with schizophrenic personality change as with organic dementia, which was observed as a rule only at a very advanced age after many years' illness.

The higher mortality of patients with affective disorder of late onset is of clinical importance. A number of these subjects do in fact show mild memory impairment or transient confusion in the course of their illness but this is due to the associated physical illness and not to the development of focal or diffuse brain disease. Cerebrovascular infarction may play a part in the onset of illness in up to 10 per cent. of cases of late affective disorder and it may also provoke a further attack in many depressive subjects with a history of illness in earlier life. However, the risk of developing cerebrovascular disease after an interval of many years following the onset of a depressive illness in old age is probably no greater than in the population at large. Furthermore, part of the deaths that occur in elderly subjects in the first two or three years after developing a depressive illness are probably due to causes other than cerebrovascular disease.

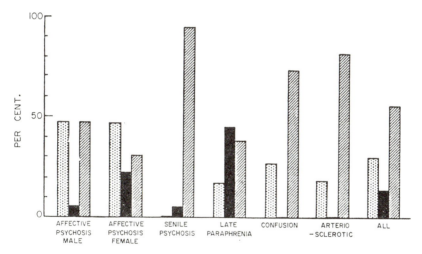

FIG. 19. Pattern of outcome in 1955 of 322 cases admitted at 60 years of age and over with mental disease in 1948 and 1949. The status of the patients is shown in terms of discharged (dotted column), in-patients (black column) and dead (hatched column). (For 'senile psychosis' read 'senile dementia'.)

In patients with late paraphrenia, cerebral disease accounts for the onset of illness in no more than 5 per cent. of cases. However, in approximately 6–8 per cent. with organic psychoses, depressive or persecutory delusional symptoms are prominent and long-sustained in the early stages. In a proportion of these patients there is strong evidence of a predisposition to functional symptoms which is caricatured with the advent of organic change in the brain. Long-term observations suggest that we deal here with two relatively distinct groups of symptoms due to different processes. For, while the affective or paranoid features tend gradually to die away, the organic symptoms continue to advance. Treatment of the functional symptoms may also prove effective while the organic symptoms are un-changed.

General Principles of Diagnosis

The facts outlined in the preceding section have important implications for the clinical assessment and diagnosis of mental disorder in old age. It is clear that the overlap between organic and functional mental disorder in old age is relatively small. It has probably been underestimated in early life and exaggerated among the aged. Painstaking history-taking and detailed psychiatric examination are all the more important in that it is on these findings that the treatment adopted as well as the prognosis will be largely based. Minor neurological signs abound in the elderly and may include rigidity, diminished reflexes, doubtful plantar responses, nystagmus, minor irregularities of the pupils, and impaired vibration sense. Unless such findings can be indubitably related to some episode suggesting a cerebrovascular acci-dent, they should have little bearing on the prognosis of illness and should not be allowed to influence the choice of treatment. Minor defects of memory and retention and disorientation for time and place are commonly found also in healthy old subjects. A careful history will reveal in most such cases that the patient has suffered from a limited non-progressive cognitive defect over a considerable time. The advent of a severe emotional disturbance can be expected to aggravate such benign deficits but the change will prove reversible in the majority of instances. The weight that is given to any unequivocal evidence of cerebral damage that may be present will depend upon the psychiatric picture and the result of care-ful physical examination and history-taking. A long-established neurological lesion, due perhaps to an old head injury or meningitis, need not place limitations on the choice of treatment and will not detract from an excellent result in cases with depressive or paranoid symptoms. When there is hemiparesis due to a recent cerebrovascular infarction, the prog-nosis will of course be far less favourable. But if organic features are absent from the psychi-atric picture, depressive symptoms should respond well. Some amelioration will occur for a limited period also in patients who are showing signs of dementia.

In old age, in other words, it is particularly important to formulate a separate sympto-matological and aetiological diagnosis in every case. In the majority of instances they will show concordance but in an important minority of cases, discrepancies will be found. Cerebral disease may be discovered in association with a 'functional' psychiatric picture and the association may not be wholly fortuitous. In these patients the neurotic, depressive or paranoid symptoms will often respond to treatment, at any rate for a period, while the organic disorder progresses.

In other instances a depressive illness with some degree of clouding of consciousness proves to have no organic basis. Alternatively the clinical picture of dementia will in rare instances be simulated (p. 569). The outcome in such cases is favourable.

Although there is little overlap between affective disorder and *cerebral* disease in old age, the connexion between extra-cerebral somatic disease and affective and neurotic disorders in old age is a close and important one. Thus male subjects with affective distur-bance have a relatively high mortality and this may be wholly explicable in terms of the chronic physical illnesses they often manifest. On the other hand depressive or anxiety symp-toms will usually respond to some extent to treatment and it should be begun as early as possible. It is not known whether treatment of the commonly associated emotional distur-bance affects the mortality in these cases.

A psychiatric disturbance may be the most prominent feature where the physical disorder evolves in a 'silent' and insidious manner. Thus myocardial infarction may occur painlessly and give rise to an acute confusion; broncho-pneumonia may be apyrexial and give rise to the same picture of extreme apathy and inertia with less marked cognitive defect. Silent 'coronaries', silent pneumonias, urinary infections, mild uraemia due to prostatic obstruction, myxoedema, pernicious anaemia and diabetes are perhaps the most commonly missed physical disabilities. None of these is a rarity in psychiatric practice and a careful physical examination is essential in every case. It is probably advisable to carry out haemoglobin estimation, total red and white cell count, sedimentation rate and an examination of the urine as a routine. When there is pyrexia of unknown origin or obvious physical illness for which the reason cannot be defined, an x-ray of the chest, an electrocardiogram and an E.E.G. are advisable.

The development of psychiatric illness can be equally silent. Depression may be manifest as apathy and inertia or may grow insensibly out of the feeling of general debility and malaise that physical illness brings. Physical discomfort may be complained of and depression may be denied. The emotional state of the patient has to be judged from his facial expression, motility, and general behaviour. The content of thought should be examined in detail if the findings suggest affective disorder, and suicidal ideas should always be carefully enquired after. Chronic physical disease with associated depression carries a risk of suicide but so does an anxiety-laden and obsessive preoccupation with some somatic symptom that lacks a definable organic basis.

Careful history-taking often yields the most valuable information elicited during enquiry. However, many old people are slow and reticent and great patience is required if an accurate account of the illness is to be obtained. It is essential whenever possible to secure an objective witness. The duration and the rate of development of symptoms provide valuable clues. The dementias of old age evolve over a period of years and, with organic symptoms, a history of no more than weeks or even months should direct attention to such possibilities as a space-occupying cerebral lesion or neurosyphilis, an acute toxic or infective process, hepatic disease, a urinary infection, cardiac failure or perhaps a bronchogenic carcinoma. For even cerebrovascular disease will only rarely, after a first infarction, prove to be the explanation for a rapidly progressive dementia. This will more usually arise after the reserve capacity of the cerebrum has been encroached upon by several cerebrovascular accidents. Closer examination of an apparent organic dementia of very short duration will often reveal it to be a subacute delirious state or perhaps an affective disorder presenting as a pseudo-dementia. The dementing process is sometimes claimed by the relations to date from some dramatic event such as a surgical emergency or a bereavement; on closer investigation, a slowly progressive decline in memory, grasp and practical competence will be found to have preceded this event by some years.

Any emotional disturbance developing for the first time in senescence is often regarded as being of endogenous origin on the assumption that an unstable personality would nearly always have revealed itself in some form of breakdown long before senescence. In recent years it has become clear, however, that depressive anxiety and phobic neuroses are common among the aged and, in a small proportion of cases, the stresses of old age usher in the first illness. In the affective disorders of old age systematic enquiry into the pre-morbid personality is of the greatest importance for accurate diagnosis. An attempt has to be made to define the vulnerable spots in the personality that may have been impinged upon by the stress of decline in physical health, bereavement or isolation. In an elderly person the vulnerable area will often be of limited extent and difficult to define. These patients prove to be relatively stable when compared with those who have succumbed to illness in the earlier stages of life. They differ, however, from those who have resisted even the vicissitudes of old age in having certain deficiencies of personality (perhaps well-compensated for in earlier years) or by having suffered greater tribulations than the general run of old people.

Special Methods of Investigation

PSYCHOLOGICAL TESTS. A history of progressive impairment in the ability to cope with everyday tasks, of declining memory for recent events and of failure in intellectual powers in general will betray cerebral disease in most cases. Any suspicions thus raised can be further evaluated with the aid of simple psychological tests. However, in some cases of acute or recently developing cerebral disease, the disturbances of consciousness and of intellectual functioning may be intermittent. If any suggestion of possible cerebral disease arises during clinical examination, admission to hospital for observation over a period is imperative. Here it may be observed that the patient is prone from time to time to lose his way in the building, to show intermittent disorientation or perhaps to become restless, confused or hallucinated at night. If the history in such cases is of short duration, investigation should be pressed ahead until an aetiological diagnosis can be arrived at; there is always a specific cause in these patients and it may be treatable. In patients with organic deficits of recent and rapid onset, disturbance of consciousness may be mild and short-lived. A careful search for focal deficits such as aphasia, agnosia and apraxia should be carried out, making use of the techniques of examination described in Chapter II. Such tests have of course little or no value for subjects with well-established dementia in whom focal deficits are submerged 'in a sea of mindlessness'. The early stages of an organic process will sometimes betray themselves in the course of examination in the form of mild nominal dysphasia or perseveration, a fleeting show of perplexity or an unexpected and inappropriate euphoria.

For a full investigation of possible intellectual deterioration the help of a clinical psychologist should be sought. However, a number of relatively simple tests have proved of great value in recent years and are applicable in the clinical situation. Questionnaires seeking information about important dates in the patient's earlier life, the names of leading figures and the dates of historic events have been found in a number of enquiries to differentiate with some measure of reliability between patients with cerebral disease and those who are suffering from functional disorder (Hopkins and Roth, 1953; Shapiro et al., 1956). One such questionnaire has been reproduced in full on page 556. Such tests can of course be further elaborated and have been shown (Cosin et al., 1957) to discriminate fairly successfully between demented and non-demented subjects. They provide an index of impaired orientation and memory for recent events and are useful as a screening tool. However, they do not discriminate reliably between different types of organic disturbance. Subjects with a very mild or fluctuating confusional state will often score highly while patients with an amnesic syndrome, whose intelligence may be relatively well-preserved, will do badly.

There are a number of better validated tests, whose effectiveness has been established in recent years and which can be readily applied in clinical practice.

(1) THE PAIRED ASSOCIATE LEARNING TEST (Inglis, 1957). This has been shown to be sensitive to memory impairment but to be largely independent of intellectual functioning. It is therefore particularly useful for the further investigation of those patients in who am

Form A		Form B	
Stimulus	Response	Stimulus	Response
(a) Cabbage	Pen	Flower	Spark
(b) Knife	Chimney	Table	River
(c) Sponge	Trumpet	Bottle	Comb

specific defect of memory is suspected. The test consists of two alternative sets of three stimulus words that are paired with response words which have to be learnt by the patient.

The patient is given instructions similar to those for the paired associate items of the Wechsler memory scale. The three pairs of words are then presented to the patient, leaving an interval of about 5 seconds between pairs of words. After a further interval the patient is given a stimulus word, 'What went with flower?'. If the reply is wrong the examiner supplies the correct association. The stimulus words are presented in this manner until the patient gets three consecutive correct responses for each stimulus word or until each stimulus word has been presented thirty times. The score consists of the total number of repetitions carried out to achieve learning and ranges from the highest score of 3 points for learning at the first presentation to the lowest of 93 points for failure to learn after 3 times 30 additional trials. Although it tests memory defect alone, grossly demented patients can be identified by their very poor performance on account of the very severe defect of memory that is almost invariably associated.

(2) THE MODIFIED WORD LEARNING TEST (Walton and Black, 1957; Walton, 1958). In this test the patient is given the vocabulary part of the Terman-Merrill (Form L) test until the subject is unable to give the meaning of ten consecutive words. The subject is then told the meanings of these ten words. Thereafter each of the ten words is read in turn to the subject who is asked to provide meanings for each of the words so far as he is able to remember them. The criterion of successful performance is the correct definition of any six of the ten words. If the subject fails to reach this criterion the meanings of all ten words are repeated although the wording is changed to avoid rote learning. The final score is obtained by subtracting from 11 the number of times that the list of ten words and their definitions have to be repeated. Thus success after the first presentation secures 10 points while a further repetition secures nine points.

In a recent enquiry (Bolton *et al.*, 1967) the Walton-Black test was found to be effective in discriminating between organic subjects on the one hand and normal subjects and patients with functional disorders on the other. However, only 80 per cent. of organic cases and about 70 per cent. of cases of schizophrenia and affective disorders were correctly identified so that the test provides only one aid to diagnosis.

OTHER ANCILLARY AIDS IN DIAGNOSIS. Improved techniques of neurological investigation in recent years have included more refined interpretations of pneumoencephalographic records. Moderate and severe cerebral atrophy can usually be identified by radiological means. However, the earlier stages of cerebral degenerative disease may be associated with little change in the angiographic or air-encephalographic pictures. Moreover, since enlargement of the ventricles and of the subarachnoid space occurs in the course of ordinary senescence suggestive or even more pronounced changes will at times be found in healthy

PSYCHOLOGICAL TEST PROFORMA

Orientation Test

Name	1
Age	1
Time (hour)	1
Time of day	1
Day of week	1
Date	1
Month	1
Season	1
Year	1
Place—Name	1
Street	1
Town	1
Type of place (e.g. home, hospital etc.)	
Recognition of persons	2

(cleaner, doctor, nurse, patient, relative; any two available)

———

———

Memory Test

(1) Personal

Date of birth	1
Place of birth	1
School attended	1
Occupation	1
Name of sibs or Name of wife	1
Name of any town where patient had worked	1
Name of employers	1

(2) Non-personal

Date of World War I	1*
Date of World War II	1*
Monarch	1
Prime Minister	1

(3) Name and address (5 minute recall)

Mr John Brown

42 West Street, Gateshead	5

———

———

Concentration Test

Months of year backwards	2	1	0
Counting 1–20 forwards	2	1	0
Counting 20–1 backwards	2	1	0

* ½ for approximation within three years.

old people. Hence in those aged 65 and over the radiographic investigation will only rarely add anything of importance to the information derived from an all-round clinical appraisal. In the aged this technique should therefore be employed mainly to exclude a space-occupying lesion and not to confirm the presence of a cerebral atrophy which already appears highly probable from history-taking, clinical examination and simple diagnostic aids.

In the investigation of *presenile* dementia, however, air-encephalography plays a more important part in that the presumption must always be in favour of some specific and possibly eradicable cerebral or other organic cause when dementia develops in middle age. There is also a limited place for air-encephalography in the patient of more than 65–70 years in whom dementia comes on rapidly and in whom focal symptoms, in a setting of mild to moderate intellectual deterioration, are present but cannot be attributed with certainty to cerebrovascular disease.

Certain radiological findings would make cerebral atrophy a probable diagnosis. Gross enlargement of the lateral ventricles associated with increased size of the third ventricle, pools of air on the convexity or over the insula without distortion or displacement of the ventricular system indicate atrophy with a high degree of probability. A phenomenon that is of some limited value in diagnosis is that, whereas in most patients the introduction of air during air-encephalography is followed by a severe headache, those with marked cerebral atrophy often experience little or no discomfort during or after the procedure. Whatever the findings of radiological examination they should not too readily be allowed to override the results of overall clinical assessment (Plate XII).

THE E.E.G. IN OLD AGE MENTAL DISORDER. Although the E.E.G. in old age mental disorder shows no high degree of specificity, there are certain broad differences between the various types of illness which make it a valuable adjunct in the differential diagnosis of mental illness. As at other ages, abnormalities are far commoner among the 'organic' than among the 'functional' psychoses (McAdam and McClatchley, 1952; Obrist, 1954) and the degree of overlap with respect to *gross* anomalies is relatively small.

The dominant rhythm is within the alpha range in the majority of functional cases, but below it in a substantial proportion of organic psychoses. But a considerable minority of affective and paraphrenic cases share this feature with the organic group and its discriminating value is therefore low. On the other hand, delta activity of moderate or high voltage is almost invariably indicative of an organic psychosis, being found only in a very small minority of functional cases. Although a relatively high proportion of organic patients show little or none, delta activity when present has an almost unequivocal significance and is an objective sign of value, particularly in acute florid psychoses, or when the patient is mute and inaccessible. Moreover, in some organic patients in whom delta activity is absent or of low voltage the dominant rhythm is in the theta range.

It is, however, probably in relation to differential diagnosis within the organic group that the E.E.G. finds its most useful application. In senile dementia the appearance of the E.E.G. tends to be normal although the dominant rhythm is often a slow alpha or even in the theta range (Fig. 20). The presence of any more conspicuous abnormality speaks against a diagnosis of senile dementia. Prominent delta activity is relatively common in both arteriosclerotic psychosis and delirious states, and during the acute stage of delirium high voltage rhythmic delta activity, often most prominent in the frontal regions, is to be found in the great majority of cases. This tends to prove transient in arteriosclerotic psychosis, subsiding quickly to a pattern with slow dominant rhythm with or without minor asymmetries. In delirious states associated with extra-cerebral disease, however, it tends to persist longer as well as occurring rather more often, and is, therefore, particularly characteristic of this group. In reversible deliria, it eventually subsides leaving a relatively normal record. When high voltage rhythmic bilaterally synchronous delta activity is present, an intensive search must be carried out for some specific illness of relatively recent development. Figures 21 and 22 illustrate this particular point.

The only chronic progressive cerebral degenerative disorders which sometimes show

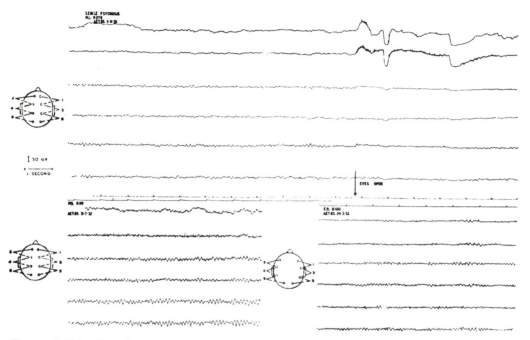

FIG. 20. E.E.G.s from three cases of advanced senile dementia. The E.E.G. shows a regular slowish alpha rhythm, frequency 7–8 c/s in the upper record and 8 c/s in each of the two lower records. All three patients were over 80. A similar pattern is found in advanced arteriosclerotic psychosis.

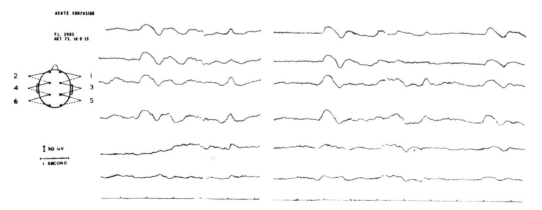

FIG. 21. E.E.G. from a man of 73 with a seven-week history of confusion beginning with an attack of lobar pneumonia. Restless, disorientated, deluded and doubly incontinent. The E.E.G. shows paroxysmal bursts of slow activity most prominent in the anterior parts of the head.

high voltage slow activity are a number of cases of specific presenile dementias, particularly Alzheimer's disease (Liddell, 1958) (Fig. 23). The slow activity shows a poor response to sensory stimuli, diminishes during drowsiness and the fast activity response to barbiturates is poor (Letemendia and Pampiglione, 1958). It is of considerable interest that the E.E.G. of

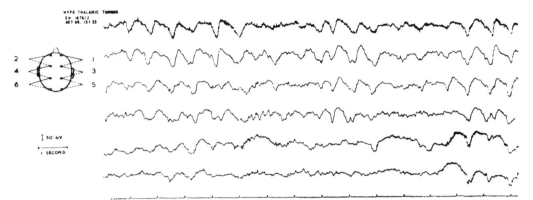

FIG. 22. E.E.G. from a woman aged 69 during an attack of acute delirium. History of two years' lassitude, gain of weight, excessive thirst and hunger, and impairment of social judgement. After one year, repeated, frequent attacks of delirium, later with memory and intellectual impairment between attacks. No papilloedema or other neurological signs. Ventriculogram attempted, but the air could not be made to enter the left ventricle. But ventricular c.s.f. had only 50 mg. protein and, in the absence of papilloedema and shift of the septum, a space-occupying lesion was thought unlikely. At post-mortem, craniopharyngioma $2\frac{1}{2}$ cm. across, distinct from, but indenting the third ventricle, was found. The E.E.G. shows high voltage, rhythmic, paroxysmal, frontally predominant, bilaterally synchronous slow waves at $1\frac{1}{2}$ c/s.

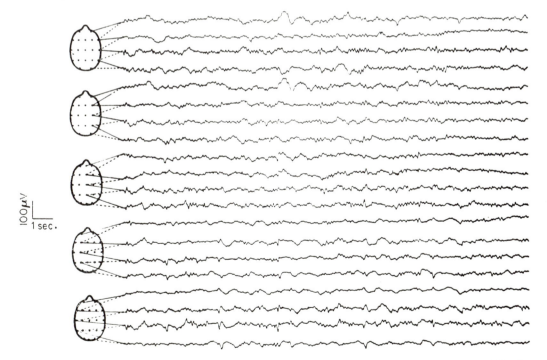

FIG. 23. E.E.G. from a case of Alzheimer's disease. Male aged 59 years. Irregular theta and delta activity in all areas. Note complete asynchrony between right- and left-sided channels.

these specific cases provides a contrast to that found in cases of non-specific, simple presenile dementias without any focal signs. In one study (Roth, Green and Osselton, 1960) nine cases of simple presenile dementia all showed a relatively normal E.E.G; whereas in ten of twelve cases of Pick's disease, Alzheimer's disease and Jakob-Creutzfeldt's syndrome, the E.E.G. contained a great deal of medium or high voltage delta activity without any specific features. The first group are thus in this respect similar to senile dementia, the latter distinct from it. A grossly abnormal E.E.G. calls for revision of a diagnosis of senile dementia. In some of these cerebrovascular lesions contribute; others are specific presenile dementias of late onset.

GENERAL MANAGEMENT AND AFTERCARE OF OLD PATIENTS

PROPHYLAXIS. Research is showing more and more clearly which are the *vulnerable* amongst the ageing—the bereaved, those with sensory defects, those with physical illness or disability which makes movement difficult, those who live alone, those who have had earlier phases of psychiatric illness, those who are over 70 and those with the faint prodromal signs such as memory defect which may be pointers to later psychiatric disorder. The advantages of these vulnerable persons being known and visited regularly are obvious.

ASCERTAINMENT. Ascertainment and intervention at an early stage before a crisis situation arises is the best form of prophylaxis. The compiling of *registers* of those of pensionable age combined with screening for vulnerability and the use of health visitors attached to practices to do *routine visiting* have been strongly recommended.

The Royal College of Physicians of Edinburgh (1963) advocates among other provisions the setting up of *consultative clinics* to which cases can be referred. Experience in Oslo, where, of those informed by letter of the services available at *Old Age Welfare Centres*, only 26 per cent. used them, shows that the existence of clinics and centres, however much publicized, is not a complete solution. The Oslo study of a sample of non-attenders showed that many preferred their known family doctor to any other service and that 'one of the main problems was lack of insight on the part of these old people into their situation, and inability to come to decisions' (Beverfelt, 1962). This writer came to the conclusion that visiting by social workers was necessary.

'Self-reporting' even to the family doctor is also unreliable. Various studies (Parsons, 1965; Williamson *et al.*, 1964) show the large proportion, particularly of psychiatric illness, which does not come to the attention of the family doctor and the frequency of 'crisis' admission to institution or hospital, with all its attendant disadvantages, is another index of unascertained disorder.

The early ascertainment of senile dementia could possibly result in delaying the grosser manifestations. Cosin *et al.* (1958) have shown that occupation and social stimulation would improve the behaviour of senile dements. The effects were short-lived but better results might have been achieved had the subjects' deterioration been less advanced.

RETIREMENT AND THE USE OF LEISURE. In spite of the evidence (see p. 537) that the elderly are capable to some extent of being retrained and capable of adaptation to change in working conditions (Welford, 1962) they tend to be passed over, because retraining has to be arranged for them at a special pace. Any quickening of the process by which production processes become obsolescent is likely to have a detrimental effect on the older workman. Heron and Chown (1961) comment in their study of the ageing semi-skilled workman engaged in the manufacturing industry that the administration of business at present favours a compulsory retirement age at 65 and will probably continue to do so, even though those who work close to the older man are aware of the difference between one elderly person and another in skill and ability and of the special qualities of conscientiousness, and responsibility characteristic of the older workman. If these two trends continue, working people should be helped to approach retirement with an understanding of what it involves and with a degree of preparation for it.

The part played by retirement in precipitating psychiatric illness is difficult to assess. Ceasing to work, with the loss of social contacts and a feeling of no longer making a significant contribution, is inextricably bound up with other factors such as declining energy and fitness and loss of income. Lowenthal (1965) and Kay, Beamish and Roth (1964b) found no clearly causal relationship between the length of time the elderly person had been retired and the onset or existence of psychiatric symptoms. On the other hand Sainsbury (1962) found that lack of employment was a factor contributing to 21 per cent. of suicides in a group aged 60 and over and for 15 per cent. economic stress had been operative. Neither was as important a precipitant as living alone or physical illness. When suicide figures for all age groups are examined it is found that whereas male suicides reach their peak at the post-retirement age 65 to 70 years, women, whose working life is not so abruptly changed at this age, do not show the same marked increase. If social class is taken into account another difference emerges. The risk of suicide decreases on retirement in higher socio-economic groups and *increases* in *lower* ones. Precise interpretation is impossible but the facts may reflect the influence of better economic circumstances in the former group and of their equipment by education and opportunity to have more varied interests.

Perhaps having some kind of employment is a more important factor than remaining in the accustomed job at the familiar place of work. Investigations have shown no large numbers of retired persons expressing a wish to re-enter the labour market. This is especially true where work has been laborious or monotonous. Bucke (1962) throws light on the subject of the *leisure-time activities* of the elderly. She quotes Townsend (1957) to show what a small proportion of those of pensionable age take part in group activities, such as attendance at clubs. Before 1939 one-quarter of elderly people were retired but in 1962 only one-fifteenth of persons of pensionable age were known to be in full or part-time employment. The 'club' movement in Great Britain has grown as the actual need has increased yet does not attract a large proportion of the elderly. But club attendance is not in itself an index of mental health and, in any case, provides only for the fully mobile. Those who are equipped to enjoy activities of their own choice pursued alone or with a few congenial companions do not need clubs.

One of the reasons why the present generation of the old have fewer developed leisure-time activities is that most of them grew up in a society which placed emphasis on the moral as well as the utilitarian value of work and lived through periods of low-wages and long working-hours with neither money nor leisure left over after the day's work. The present rapid development of means of recreation used by the young and middle-aged is not familiar to them. There is some evidence to show that those not yet retired have centred their lives less exclusively on their work and for only a few is the place of work the focus of the social relationships that mean most to them. The problem of leisure-time activities for the old is, therefore, possibly one that will diminish in succeeding generations. But the present need to provide meaningful activity for the aged remains, allied with the need to increase their financial security. Hobbies and social activities are expensive.

The idea that the robust elderly could with reciprocal advantage be employed to some extent in the expanding services for the less mobile elderly is in debate, but unquestionably some elderly persons feel happier when they are making some useful contribution to the life around them and a few opportunities are available such as the 'night help' service in Wolverhampton and Birmingham.

EDUCATION. Efforts have been made in many countries, mainly in the U.S.A., to provide education and counselling in an attempt to aid the ageing person to achieve a balanced, healthy and well-adjusted life after retirement. A number of leading industrial organizations provide counselling services, and, in a number of communities, adult education classes or university courses in preparation for retirement have been sponsored. Perhaps ideally these educational programmes should be available in earlier stages of life (Roth, 1959b). Dietary habits and attitudes to exercise, for example, have an important bearing on the general health of aged people but are difficult to change in late life.

COMMUNITY PROVISION. Shenfield (1962) makes an interesting comparison between the general trends of community provision for the old in U.S.A. and Great Britain. In the former it takes the form of 'creative leisure' programmes which 'place emphasis on group activities, and high value is given to the capacity to adjust in the group and get on well with others. . . Some work habits appear to be being carried over into organized leisure programmes, with their set schemes, goals of achievement and demands made upon members... The American projects appear to be based on a middle-class concept of ageing'. In Great Britain (and in some European countries), on the other hand, interest has spread out to the whole field of ageing 'from an original historical concern with the plight of the elderly poor, and a considerable part of welfare services are still directed to the needs of this group'.

This is especially true of the *domiciliary services*. A wide range of these is being developed though they are not uniformly available. Some have always been the concern of the local authorities; others have been the creation of voluntary societies. A very comprehensive study of these and other services is given in Tunstall's *Old and Alone* (1966) and by Bell (1965).

District nurses can advise and help relatives in caring for the bed-ridden, and laundering services are available in some areas. For the frail the *home-help* service and *meals-on-wheels* can make possible continued life at home. Visiting *physiotherapists* can do much for patients with hemiplegia and arthritis where home circumstances are good and there is a medical condition capable of improvement (Adams *et al.*, 1958). A visiting *chiropody* service has obvious advantages in helping to maintain mobility. The sphere of both the 'home-help' and the *Health Visitor Service* is progressively being extended to take in the elderly. Moreover the community at large is being alerted to a responsibility for *friendly visiting*, shopping services and such minor amenities as bringing library books to the elderly at home and making holidays and excursions available and cheap. The contribution of all such services to the continued mental health of the elderly is clear, as also their usefulness in maintaining at home the large numbers with subacute psychiatric disabilities.

Residential homes provided by the voluntary societies and local authorities are surveyed in Townsend's *The Last Refuge* (1962). They are intended for patients still ambulant and alert yet too frail to maintain themselves at home and with no relatives available to take care of them, yet investigation of residents of these homes has revealed (Kay *et al.*, 1962) that two-thirds were suffering from some degree of psychiatric disorder and 13 per cent. were classed as permanently disabled by physical illness. On the other hand, reports from geriatric units reveal that patients remain as long-stay patients for domestic reasons after their acute illness is over. Similarly, *misplacements* occur, as between geriatric wards and mental hospitals (Kidd, 1962*b*). In Kay's study at least half of the patients in geriatric wards showed mental symptoms as severe as those of many aged mental hospital patients, while 18 per cent. of mental hospital patients suffered from physical disability rated as 'severe', and 37 per cent. were 'house-bound' so that geriatric ward care might equally well have been recommended. Obviously, screening procedures and a closer integration of the tripartite services involved in the care of the aged are needed but, in the absence of these, a more flexible and efficient system for mutual consultation between staffs would facilitate arrangements for *transfer* of patients from hospital wards to residential homes and vice versa so that they might be under the care of staffs specially trained to give them the kind of treatment which they most need.

Unsuitable housing stands high among social conditions which may have an adverse effect on mental and physical health (Edge and Nelson, 1964). The old, because of financial stringency and a propensity to cling to the familiar, tend to remain in or gravitate to housing with low rentals and therefore lacking in basic amenities or, at least, inconvenient for the frail or disabled. A circular issued jointly by the Ministries of Health and Housing (1961) advises local authorities on the provision of a variety of types of housing for the aged. In particular, partial-dependency housing is of value in maintaining elderly people in normal living conditions where they can retain self-respect, independence of action and some of their own possessions—all essential to their morale. The whole situation of an old person can be improved by modifications in his home such as, for example, the addition of indoor sanitation, hand-rails, ramps and adapted gas-cookers, and an approach can be made to the housing authority with this in view. So much of disability is chronic in the elderly that the more hopeful therapeutic approach is often to try to modify his environment.

From whatever angle community services for the elderly are approached, whether providing for their leisure or giving supportive services, it should be remembered that the old are not an undifferentiated mass of the population or, with the best of intentions, they may come to be treated as a minority problem group. Indeed, services should be to some extent organized with them and not just for them so that their contribution may be used and their own wishes understood and respected.

THE WORTHING EXPERIMENT. The term 'community service' is used in a different sense by Sainsbury, Costain and Grad in their studies of the psychiatric services of Worthing and district, initiated in 1957. These services were designed in the first place to reduce the previously high rate of admission to mental hospital. They are based on a day-hospital centre with out-patient clinics and domiciliary visiting by psychiatrists. The resources of the local public health authorities are scarcely exploited at all. A psychiatrist at the centre deals with all requests for patients to be seen and sees them all outside the hospital before deciding whether to treat them by admission to mental hospital or at home. Grad and Sainsbury (1963, 1966) made a number of studies of the effects of this service using a hospital-based service of traditional type in a similar area as control. They have shown that with the use of these relatively limited resources the proportion of patients admitted to hospital was lower in the community-based service, and that the total amount of time spent in hospital by those admitted was reduced. In the Worthing service the mean number of weeks spent in hospital by patients aged 65 and over was only 7 as compared with 11 weeks in the traditional service.

Desirable as it is for patients, especially elderly ones, to be maintained in their familiar surroundings, the extent to which their families suffer as a consequence is an important consideration. The circumstances of 410 families were examined and it was found, at first assessment, before referral to mental hospital or 'community' service had been made, that nearly two-thirds of these families had well-marked problems and it was the elderly patients and those with organic psychoses who restricted other family members in numerous ways and caused the most severe burden. At follow-up two years after referral (Grad and Sainsbury, 1968) the traditional service was found to have provided greater relief to the families of patients treated within and outside hospital alike. However, neither in the case of the severely burdened group generally nor in the families of the aged in particular was there a significant difference in the relief afforded. It was in the 15–64 age group, comprising mainly neurotic patients, that the 49 per cent. of Worthing families whose burden had been eased contrasted with 90 per cent. in the traditional service. Many families prefer to bear the cost in hardship entailed by keeping patients at home and there was evidence that more intensive social work in Worthing could have mitigated it. Domiciliary visiting by the psychiatrist, close contact with general practitioners and more intensive follow-up and social case work would greatly enhance the possibilities of community care for the elderly and other psychiatric patients.

NURSING AND REHABILITATING GERIATRIC PATIENTS. Geriatric nursing has, at first sight, the appearance of being unrewarding as full recovery is less often achieved than in other groups of patients. As Kidd and Smith (1966) point out, a large part of the 30–40 per cent. load of geriatric patients to be found in most psychiatric hospitals is made up of ageing chronic patients. Fifty-six per cent. of their elderly patients had been in hospital for over five years and 28 per cent. for over twenty years. The fact that these patients' ties with home are so often irreparably broken and that more than half are aged 75 and over means that they must be accepted as a permanent load on the hospital. A large number are frail and suffer from a wide range of disabilities often severe and multiple. This places heavy demands on both medical and nursing staff and such nursing calls for very special gifts. At one time, when hospital wards were often situated in work-house buildings, the old and infirm lay in bed year after year without proper examination, let alone treatment. The pioneer work done by Marjory Warren, Cosin and Howell showed what cheerful surroundings, active treatment and planned rehabilitation could do in preventing patients from being bed-ridden and in making them ready for discharge. During the past twenty years their ideas have been widely accepted and put into practice.

In mental hospitals, too, patients were formerly allocated to wards according to age and irrespective of diagnosis. Overcrowding, understaffing and the absence of occupational facilities frequently led to these patients being confined to bed. Even those suffering from recoverable diseases were reduced to misery and apathy.

Nursing the elderly psychiatric patient should have the positive aim of restoring activity and ability for self-care. Prolonged bedrest spells the loss, possibly forever, of muscle tone, co-ordination and confidence to stand upright. It also spells stiff joints, pressure sores and hypostatic pneumonia. Therefore the kind of care which is needed by the acutely ill patient should be continued no longer than is necessary, and the tendency to become dependent should be gently corrected so that rehabilitation can be begun to restore fully the measure of self-reliance of which the patient is capable.

As physical disability is so often present in conjunction with residual mental symptoms, when the time for rehabilitation is reached, *close co-operation between physiotherapy and occupational therapy* staff is needed (Macdonald, 1960). It is advisable that these treatments should be specifically prescribed by the doctor for each patient, taking his particular state into account so that harm is not done by giving exercise indiscriminately. The programme of activity should be reviewed at frequent intervals to fit it to the patient's gradually restored capacity and ensure that it is varied enough to keep him interested. Patients with 'functional' and 'organic' disorders naturally require different regimes and the first introduction of each patient to rehabilitation procedures should be carried out with patience and a permissive attitude so that his natural diffidence is overcome and he is not frightened by too much too early. Beresford-Cooke (1964) outlines an excellent scheme of occupational therapy and shows how it can be closely related to what the patient will most need on return home. For example, the patient can be shown how to plan and cook nourishing meals and how to lay out a limited budget. Training in the use of disability aids can be given while the patient is working.

For men for whom discharge is not envisaged or for patients having day-care, it is sometimes possible to arrange paid work of a simple kind. This is not suitable for short-stay patients in hospital as it might tend to prolong their stay. Where this is successfully practised the staff are enthusiastic about its results. Financial incentives produce a greater interest in life, incontinence diminishes and appearance and personal habits improve.

SPEECH THERAPY for aphasic patients is a form of psychotherapy; to restore the possibility of communication relieves their sense of isolation and their fear of death and may give them energy to tackle the heavy task of physical rehabilitation. This form of therapy is perhaps best undertaken in a combination of group and personal sessions.

AFTERCARE is an important component of all psychiatric treatment and particularly so in geriatric medicine. On account of general frailty and chronic disability elderly patients are socially more dependent. Weeks of expert hospital care may be wasted if they are discharged into conditions which are not conducive to their continued well-being. The resettlement of partly recovered patients is not an easy procedure. They are not always eager for discharge even after rehabilitation designed to prepare them for it. Dependence develops quickly. Regular pre-discharge conferences for older patients where doctor, ward sister, psychiatric social worker and health visitor can plan aftercare have been found helpful by Woodside (1965). Some person attached to the geriatric unit, who has seen the patient in hospital and discussed his case with the hospital doctor, can help him and the medical social worker to arrange the patient's discharge home and can follow him up. She can rally relatives and neighbours, verify that the welfare services arranged by the medical social worker have been mobilized and act as liaison with the patient's family doctor. Adverse changes which have occurred during the patient's absence in hospital can be reported and rectified. A visit during the first few days after discharge, which are critical for the patient's adjustment, will often prevent failure, and during subsequent visits the visitor can watch progress and arrange readmission if conditions have deteriorated. Nisbet *et al.* (1966) have found in a city area that a district nurse who is one of the geriatric unit team most adequately performs this function. In more dispersed hospital catchment areas, health visitors attached to practices could make a prompt visit part of their routine.

Two more types of follow-up care are increasing in urban areas; attendance at *day-hospitals and day-centres*. For attendance at both, adequate ambulance services are necessary as, apart from those who live alone, it is the house-bound who will benefit most from these services. Patients attending day-hospitals are closely followed up by the psychogeriatric physician and rehabilitation by physiotherapy, for example, begun in hospital can be continued. At the same time the patient continues under the general care of his local practitioner. The day-hospital is an excellent meeting ground for the three sources of service which cater for the old—hospital, family doctor and local authority services.

Attendance at the day-hospital can begin towards the end of an in-patient period and can be continued after the patient returns home. It is of particular value for the patient suffering from a chronic emotional disturbance who improves on admission to hospital but deteriorates on each return home (Macmillan, 1960). Equally, demented patients can be maintained until hospital beds are available for them. If the day-hospital is part of a general or psychiatric hospital, continuity of care is easier (Whitehead, 1965) and the undesirable segregation of the elderly is avoided if the day-hospital is not specifically for geriatric cases. Woodford-Williams (1962) describes the effect of attendance on a 'day-hospital' group of physically ill patients as compared with a group remaining at home. They were less depressed, of higher morale, less reserved and more self-confident. Their physical deterioration was noted earlier yet their independence was not undermined.

Old people referred to *day-centres*, which have been increasing in numbers during the past ten years, benefit from regular meals, recreational facilities and company. Their progress can be watched and reported and other forms of help they need can usually be readily arranged. Regular visits by a geriatrician and good liaison with the hospitals increases the usefulness of centres. Macmillan (1960) has found that paranoid patients, whose symptoms are often a reaction to loneliness, can remain at home if they are persuaded to attend a day-centre where they are resocialized and can be put in touch with other social services they may need. The day-centre provides old people living alone with a regular routine and with the sense of belonging to a group (Macmillan, 1963). Indeed it is necessary to form small groups within day-centres to encourage old people to get over their apathy.

These three forms of care—at home, in day-hospitals and in day-centres—not only benefit the patients and particularly those who live alone, and obviate unnecessary re-admission to hospital, but they also *relieve the families* who have undertaken to look after their elderly relatives. The evidence of continued interest in the patient on the part of the hospital and the knowledge of where they may turn for help in domestic crises or difficulties provide relatives with much needed support. Relief during the day frees households to function more normally, especially where there are children or where all the adults go out to work. Ten to eleven per cent. of relatives in Kidd's Belfast study (1962a) had had to give up employment to look after their elderly and 22 per cent. complained of the financial burden involved before they asked for the patients' admission to hospital.

Temporary admission to hospital can also relieve relatives. For bed-ridden patients who severely drain the emotional and physical resources of relatives, a periodic form of admission can be used. For less severe cases, shorter periods of admission at longer intervals or timed to coincide with the family's holiday arrangements will be enough. This ensures regular treatment for the patient and keeps him securely based at home. In this way the source of the mounting feeling of rejection and guilt in relatives described by Macmillan (1960) can be avoided. Once incontinence and nocturnal wanderings, which may be aggravated by emotional disturbance, have arisen they may lead to increasingly strained relationships with the family. Indeed, once the family have made their rejection explicit, it is almost impossible to change their attitude and the patient becomes a permanent hospital case instead of a temporary one. A visit by the social worker to explain that the period in hospital is a temporary one and to arrange a discharge date often proves essential to ensure the patient's return home.

The elderly almost without exception are happiest remaining in the familiar surroundings of their homes and among their families and chosen companions, so that every effort that can be made to look after them there in spite of subacute disability is beneficial. But to maintain elderly people at home, when their psychiatric disability allows, must depend in the long run on a service ranging from an occasional supervisory visit to home-help and nursing care. Domiciliary services are described at greater length on p. 562. The situation of the frail old person can change overnight from being quite manageable to being critically overstrained if there is an accident or sudden illness or if some key relative or neighbour is removed by mishap or illness. Before the elderly in-patient is discharged it is therefore advisable for the psychiatrist, through his social worker and with the consent of the practitioner, to call in the appropriate service provided by the local authority or voluntary agencies. In spite of treatment in hospital followed by aftercare, psychiatric disorders like other illnesses in old age tend to become chronic and recurrent. Colwell and Post (1959), in a follow-up study of one year's discharges from a geriatric unit devoted to recoverable illness, showed that only 29 per cent. of discharged patients did not receive any further psychiatric attention apart from checks during the following two years. Twenty per cent. had further out-patient support and 31 per cent. had further in- as well as out-patient treatment. The load on aftercare services is therefore likely to be heavy. That the available community care is not always adequate is also shown in this study. One-third of all the patients went through periods during which community action would have benefited them or should have brought them more promptly back into psychiatric treatment. Thirty-seven per cent. of the group studied had been continuously disabled after discharge and 42 per cent. of these may not have been under supervision or psychiatric treatment for considerable periods while both they and their families were in need of help.

AFFECTIVE DISORDER IN OLD AGE

Depressive Illness

Depression has long been recognized as a characteristic mood of senescence and old descriptions have often referred to the melancholy, dolorous, crabbed mood of the aged. Cicero described old men as 'morose, troubled, fretful and hard to please', although he was before his time in attributing these features to 'faults of character' rather than to age. Burton's celebrated treatise abounds with references to the melancholy of the aged and depressive illness is clearly recognizable in the picture drawn of some of those burnt at the stake for witchcraft in the Middle Ages. Thus North observed of women tried at Exeter that 'the evidence against them was very full but their own confessions exceeded it. They appeared not only weary of their lives but seemed to have a great deal of skill to convict themselves'—an apt vignette of psychotic depressives and their guilt-laden self-accusations.

The medical importance of depressive illness in old age and the vast extent of the problem both in hospital practice and in the community at large has come to be appreciated only in the past 20 years. Current psychogeriatric practice presents a wide ranging variety of affective disorders in addition to the classical endogenous depressions.

At the present time it is probably unprofitable to attempt more than a broad sub-division into two main types of depressive illness in old age. The first conforms to the classical picture of endogenous depression and its affinities are with the manic-depressive psychoses. The clinical features comprise the usual profile of retardation, guilt and self-depreciation, hypochondriacal ideas or somatic delusions. The depression is at its worst in the morning and the sleep disturbance is characterized by early morning wakening. In the other group, the neurotic depressions, the emotional disturbance is generally less profound. It is often reactive to physical illness, social hardship and vicissitude. A clear diurnal variation of mood is absent, and there is initial insomnia or fitful sleep throughout the night. The prevalence of physical illness is greater in the latter group.

Among depressions of the aged those who have also had attacks of affective disorder before the age of 60, have been shown to have a hereditary loading for affective disorder among their first-degree relatives similar to that recorded in the case of manic-depressive psychosis, that is, approximately 10 to 12 per cent. On the other hand, among depressions of late onset genetical factors have proved to be of lesser importance and morbid risks of approximately 4 to 4·5 per cent. have been recorded in relatives (Stenstedt, 1959; Kay, 1959). This latter figure reflects the greater importance of extrinsic factors. It has been known for some time that approximately 6 to 7 per cent. of manic-depressives fall ill for the first time after the age of 60. However, three-quarters of late cases have been found to have experienced clear physical or social stress prior to onset, as compared with one-half among early onset affectives and only one-quarter of paranoid cases (Kay, 1959).

In the sections that follow we shall not deal with the detailed features of these types of affective disorder which have already been fully discussed in Chapter IV. We shall describe instead the special colouring that is given to depressive illness by senescence and the differ-ing physical and psychological settings in which it may occur. The sub-headings that follow do not refer to distinct but to overlapping varieties of illness and represent in effect a summary of the reasons that frequently cause the depressive illness to be overlooked. The distinction between endogenous and neurotic depression will therefore be ignored. However, the cases to be described under the first three headings would, in fact, mainly conform in their detailed clinical profile with the picture of endogenous depression; those in the fourth and fifth (accounting for the majority of cases) with that of neurotic depression. 'Organic' depressions are very variable in picture.

(1) ATYPICAL DEPRESSION. The clinical picture described under the heading of involutional depression with extravagant and bizarre ideas of guilt, self-denigration and marked retardation or agitated and importunate behaviour is not uncommon in old age. It may be associated with the Cotard syndrome of nihilistic ideas about the body in which the patient believes it to be decaying or disappearing as a result of disease. How-ever, a less dramatic picture comprising apathy, inertia, withdrawal into solitude and quieter self-depreciation is rather more common. The patient's passive appearance, emotional unresponsiveness and the laconic replies to questions are prone to be attributed to old age rather than to illness; careful history-taking combined with painstaking clinical analysis may be needed to lay bare the nature of the condition.

Among depressed old patients presenting with a picture of marked apathy there are some in whom subnutrition is a factor in the situation. Fowlie et al. (1963) found 20 per cent. of elderly subjects with undernutrition to be suffering from a depressive psychosis; the incidence being well beyond chance expectation. Anorexia is of course a common symptom of depressive illness but the under-nutrition that results can itself cause further apathy and inertia and a vicious circle is prone to be created in this manner.

Although suicidal attempts are not made so frequently by patients with atypical depression as they are by those with associated physical disease or pain and discomfort, some of the former are to be found among consummated suicides because the nature of the underlying illness is prone to be overlooked.

(2) PSEUDO-DEMENTED DEPRESSION. The illness is specially prone to be mistaken for a progressive dementing process in those cases in which the patient is markedly retarded and where memory-defect and cognitive impairment appear to be present. In a number of these patients both clinical observation and careful psychometric investigation may suggest marked intellectual deterioration. For these and other reasons, the simulation of dementia can be very close as Kiloh (1961) has pointed out. The correct diagnosis will be revealed by the relatively short history of presenting symptoms, the occurrence in some cases of previous depressive attacks, the presence of a family history of depressive or manic-depressive illness and the patchy character of the intellectual impairment. The majority of these cases also make a prompt and striking response to electroconvulsive treatment.

(3) DEPRESSION WITH CLOUDING OF CONSCIOUSNESS. Approximately 10 per cent. of cases of depression in old age have a short-lived confusional phase which subsides within a relatively short time to reveal the underlying affective disorder. The stage of clouding of consciousness is associated with a considerable risk of determined suicidal attempts. These patients are liable to be diagnosed as suffering from cerebrovascular disease. The explanation for the clouding may be found in some associated febrile or metabolic disturbance, but physical illness is not present in all cases and when it is found it is often chronic and seemingly quiescent and its association with the clouding unclear. Under-nutrition can also become one of the factors contributing to confusional symptoms in the early stages of depressive illness and the nutritional status should be carefully investigated in such patients.

(4) PHYSICAL ILLNESS AND DEPRESSION. A depressive illness may fail to be identified as such because of associated physical illness for which the mood disturbance may be regarded as appropriate. The physical illness is often chronic and disabling and for this reason attempts at treating the psychiatric symptoms may be regarded as fruitless. However, the emotional disturbance often remits despite chronicity of the physical disorder and there is, therefore, a strong indication for treating it.

The majority of patients discussed in this section show the neurotic type of illness, the clinical features being dominated by a variable blend of depression and anxiety, irritability, attention-seeking behaviour and an abundance of somatic complaints with a history of previous neurotic personality traits. However, a small proportion of cases are indubitably endogenous or manic-depressive and the need to treat the psychiatric disorder, whatever the nature or progress of the physical condition, applies particularly in these cases.

Hypochondriasis may seem to be a misnomer when applied to patients suffering from some physical disease. However it is frequently very difficult in elderly subjects to judge whether complaints of somatic pain or discomfort arise from physical or psychiatric disorder or both. Physical illness is prone to creep on in a silent and insidious manner in old age and what may appear to be hypochondriacal symptoms in a setting of mood disturbance may conceal underlying physical disability. On the other hand true hypochondriacal complaints may simulate angina pectoris, cardiac dyspnoea, gastrointestinal disease, cerebrovascular or intracranial disease, and the patient may be submitted to prolonged and fruitless investigation. De Alarçón (1964) found hypochondriacal symptoms in the sense of 'physically unjustified body complaints' in 64 per cent. of 152 consecutive admissions with depression in patients over the age of 60. Complaints referred to the alimentary tract were by far the most frequent; 32 per cent. complaining of constipation, the symptoms often having a delusional, nihilistic colouring; 19 per cent. had head symptoms and 8 per cent. cardiovascular symptoms. Twenty-five per cent. of the patients with hypochondriacal symptoms had made serious suicidal attempts, a much higher proportion than in the remaining cases. Suicidal tendencies had been particularly common among those in whom hypochondriasis was the dominant symptom. It is evident, therefore, that a high suicidal risk attaches to persistent physical complaints whether these are truly hypochondriacal or associated with actual physical disease (p. 542).

(5) 'REACTIVE' DEPRESSIONS. This group overlaps to a considerable extent with that described in the preceding section. In both a high proportion have long-standing neurotic personality traits although in those who break down *de novo* in old age these are limited and have been well-compensated over the greater part of the life-span. The presenting features are similar, a variable depression strongly coloured with anxiety, irritability; some fluctuations in response to environmental change and initial insomnia. Physical stress does not separate out a distinct group for it frequently constitutes an emotional burden and potentiates the effects of adverse environmental circumstances.

Depressions reactive to environmental hardships, physical illness or both make up the greater part of functional disorders of old age seen both in psychiatric and general practice. The environmental and personality setting may obscure the illness in a number of ways. As it often follows closely upon one of the many hardships from which old people suffer, the depression may be regarded as merely one facet of the hard fate the patient shares with many other old people rather than an illness. Yet these conditions often respond, and at times to a surprising degree, to appropriate treatment. The presence of some long-standing personality problems and a history tending to react with dejection to life's defeats and disappointments may lead to the depression being regarded as one chapter in a long, long story and to neglect of that part of it which may be treatable. Old age is prone to uncover, in some persons, Achilles' heels successfully concealed during the ascendant part of the life cycle. Some men retain their emotional equanimity only so long as authority, prestige, physical health and vigour are theirs. The hypochondriasis of men who have invested a great deal of effort in physical fitness and have to adjust to physical limitation or illness for the first time in old age is particularly prone to be overlooked. These are men who have often been outgoing, energetic, assertive and successful during the greater part of life. Women on the other hand, may achieve superficially satisfactory adjustment so long as sexual attractiveness and the social domination it permits are theirs. When it wanes there is often a flight into neurotic symptoms with a colouring of depression.

(6) ORGANIC DEPRESSION. In these cases depressive symptoms occur as episodes in the course of a progressive cerebral degenerative process or as part of a well-advanced metabolic disease such as myxoedema or pernicious anaemia. In their most characteristic

form the depressive symptoms are of a fluctuating, fragmentary kind. Organic psychiatric features, in the form of some degree of clouding of consciousness or memory defect, may be prominent but in some cases they are present in subtle form or wholly absent. An irregular alternation with a euphoric mood may be present. The depressive bouts are dangerous in that they are prone to be associated with determined suicidal attempts. The presence of indubitable signs of cerebral infarction should not be regarded as a contra-indication to treatment of the depressive symptoms which may respond temporarily at any rate in a dramatic manner. In cases where nothing can be done to alter the course of the cerebral disease, relapse is frequent until dementia becomes far advanced and careful follow-up is indicated.

Mania

Attacks of mania or hypomania constitute about 5–10 per cent. of cases of affective disorder in old age. In approximately half the cases this is a recrudescence of illness that had already been manifest in early life; in the other half the first attack occurs in the senium. The onset is often abrupt and there are the usual features of hyper-activity, over-talkativeness and flight of ideas. However, comparison with the clinical picture in younger manic patients reveals certain differences in the elderly subjects. Instead of the usual infectious gaiety there is more often an empty, euphoric and insouciant quality which is prone to suggest the permanently damaged affect of a psychosis of organic origin. Speech and thought lack the spontaneous sparkle and versatility found in younger patients and are commonly threadbare and repetitive. Hostility and resentment at being hampered in carrying grandiose and extravagant intentions into effect are often marked. The paranoid colouring is often sufficiently prominent to raise the suspicion of a schizophrenic illness and sometimes a firmly knit and consistent delusional system takes shape. However, hallucinations are rare and the over-activity and talkativeness and the quality of the affect of the pre-morbid personality should help to establish the correct diagnosis. The patients are quickly exhausted by their illness and are frequently admitted in a frail and debilitated state. As a mild intellectual impairment is commonly present, the possibility that the condition is symptomatic of an underlying senile or arteriosclerotic process has to be carefully examined. Most manic syndromes of fairly rapid onset in old age are functional in character and, although the illness quite commonly pursues a chronic course, in our experience progressive intellectual deterioration is rare.

TREATMENT OF MANIA. Many attacks of mania in old age are relatively mild and chlorpromazine in doses of 200–300 mg. daily together with skilful nursing may suffice to bring an attack under control. A recent advance in the pharmacological treatment of mania in old age is the introduction of the butyrophenone haloperidol (Serenace) which brings some otherwise refractory cases under control rapidly. It can be given in a dosage of 5 mg. intramuscularly or in exceedingly restless and disturbed patients, intravenously and a total of 20–25 mg. can be administered in the course of 24 hours. Within four to five days this can generally be reduced and maintenance dosage can ultimately be brought down to 3–4 mg. daily. The disadvantage of the drug in some subjects, particularly those with some measure of cerebral damage, is that they are prone to develop severe extrapyramidal symptoms. In patients with chronic manic illness lithium carbonate now has an established place. Provided that cardiac and renal failure and hepatic disease have been excluded a trial with this preparation is well worthwhile where other treatments have failed. Patients should be kept under close supervision and vigilance should be maintained for toxic effects such as abdominal pain, nausea, vomiting, headache, giddiness and ataxia.

Prognosis of Affective Disorder in Old Age

In a six-year follow-up of 100 consecutive cases of depressive symptoms Post (1962a) found only 19 who had achieved a recovery both of satisfactory quality and sustained for long periods. In 35 patients the illness had been longer, recovery was at times incomplete but on the whole the previous level of social adaptation had been retained or recovered. In 28, although the recovery was incomplete, there was little decline in social status while in 18 the illness had never mitigated and the patients' social predicament had undergone a steady deterioration. Yet the majority of elderly depressives derive some temporary or lasting benefit from treatment. A programme of social aftercare and maintenance treatment with antidepressive remedies enhances the degree of relief and the quality of the adaptation achieved by the patient. The chronicity of residual disability in about half of Post's cases sounds a gloomy note. However, even in early and middle life, the degree of success achieved in a broadly defined group of depressions when results are assessed some months after treatment is disappointing, relapses being relatively common (Kiloh, Ball and Garside, 1962; Carney et al., 1965). It has to be borne in mind also that the significant part of the invalidism of the elderly depressed patient often arises from underlying chronic physical illness which frequently shows little change for the better.

Treatment

The majority of elderly subjects with a depressive illness can be treated nowadays on an out-patient basis or in a day-hospital setting. However, the undernourished, neglected, markedly apathetic, retarded and inert cannot be relied on to take medication. For such patients and those who are largely isolated or potentially suicidal admission to hospital should be arranged. As physical illness is such a frequent contributory factor, a detailed physical examination should be made in every case and, in patients who complain of feeling frail or physically ill, x-ray of the chest, full blood count and E.S.R. should be carried out and careful temperature and pulse counts should be kept after admission to hospital. Undernourished and emaciated patients should be given two or three days' rest in bed and 10–14 days' course of modified insulin to stimulate appetite. The addition of vitamin preparations is beneficial. It is undesirable in the milder cases to embark immediately upon pharmacological or other antidepressive treatment. Removal from a home environment that may have been (as in the case of a bereavement) a source of painful association or a constant reminder of the problems and anxieties from which the patient has fought to extricate himself may itself mitigate these symptoms to some extent. In a hospital environment with nurses and other members of staff who are skilled in making the old person feel wanted, in rehabilitating their sense of worth and self-respect and arousing their interest, striking improvement may be seen within seven to ten days of admission in the milder depressive states.

ANTIDEPRESSIVE DRUGS. Antidepressive drugs are the first treatment of choice in the majority of cases of depression, the exceptions being the patients who present an immediate suicidal risk, the severely agitated and others discussed below in relation to the use of E.C.T. Imipramine hydrochloride (Tofranil) is the most effective substance in indubitably endogenous cases and it can be given in doses of 25 mg. three times daily and be raised within four to five days to 50 t.d.s. and even to a total of 250 mg. daily, side-effects permitting. Derivatives of imipramine such as desmethylimipramine appear to carry no advantage although opipramol (Insidon) has been claimed by Kent and Weinsaft (1963) to be helpful in the depressions of old age in doses of up to 150 mg. daily. In depressions of a neurotic type or where there is a strong colouring of anxiety it is preferable to use amitriptyline hydrochloride (Tryptizol). This can be started at the same dosage and a total dosage of 150 mg. daily usually suffices although on occasion 200 mg. daily has to be given. With imipramine the main side-effects are dryness of the mouth, constipation, excessive perspiration and sometimes some difficulty in initiating micturition. In the case of Tryptizol drowsiness can be troublesome but other side-effects are usually trivial.

Evidence for the efficacy of imipramine and amitriptyline is available from a number of controlled therapeutic trials (Ball and Kiloh, 1959; Kiloh, Ball and Garside, 1962; Hordern *et al.*, 1963). Extensive clinical experience has shown also that these are safe preparations for use in old depressed subjects. Special vigilance has, however, to be maintained since these drugs tend to produce hypotension which could have unfortunate consequences in individuals with a past myocardial or cerebral infarction or cardiovascular or cerebrovascular insufficiency. Sudden changes in posture ought to be avoided as far as possible by patients taking these drugs.

Evidence for the efficacy of monoamine oxidase inhibitors in the treatment of the depressions of old age is more uncertain. The most careful and thoroughly controlled therapeutic trial of recent years, that conducted under the aegis of the Medical Research Council (1965), showed imipramine to be an effective preparation, its efficacy being comparable to that of electroconvulsive treatment. However, one of the most widely used monoamine oxidase inhibitor drugs, phenelzine (Nardil), proved less effective than a placebo. The trial was designed so as to evaluate the efficacy of antidepressive treatment in a precisely defined group of depressive cases. The criteria used were in fact those which would have admitted most endogenous cases but excluded a substantial proportion of subjects with neurotic and reactive depressions. Hence, although there is little purpose in giving monoamine oxidase inhibitors to patients with endogenous depression, in neurotic depressions they are worth trying if amitriptyline or one of its derivatives has failed to elicit a response. The drugs of choice in old people are isocarboxazid (Marplan) 10 mg. t.d.s., or phenelzine (Nardil), 15 mg. t.d.s. which can be reduced to one or two daily doses after 10–14 days. It is highly preferable to start treatment in elderly subjects with amitriptyline or a derivative. If this fails, an interval of seven to eight days should be allowed to elapse before embarking upon treatment with a monoamine oxidase inhibitor.

It is particularly important to warn old people against the dangers of eating cheese, yeast extracts, broad beans etc. while taking MAOI substances as an abrupt rise of blood pressure could prove catastrophic (see p. 201).

ELECTROCONVULSIVE THERAPY. In patients who present a grave suicidal risk, those becoming exhausted with inanition and in persistently deluded and severely psychotic subjects it is undesirable to await the effects of antidepressive drugs over a period of weeks; most such patients should be given a course of E.C.T. as soon as possible. In endogenous depression it can be relied on to induce excellent remission in some 85–90 per cent. of cases. In neurotic depressions the results are far less satisfactory. However, although antidepressive drugs are greatly preferable in these cases and the effects of E.C.T. are often temporary, there is a place for this treatment in the minority of neurotic depressions with strong suicidal risk or in those tormented or becoming exhausted by their symptoms.

E.C.T. should be administered two to three times during the first week and thereafter twice weekly up to a total of six to eight treatments the number being decided by the change in the clinical picture. Only rarely should a course of more than 10 treatments be given and in cases in which even a small measure of relief is not being produced after four to five treatments a favourable response is unlikely. It is unwise to press ahead after six or seven treatments, particularly where there are signs of mounting anxiety or in patients who develop marked memory impairment. Some degree of impairment of memory is almost invariable but it slowly recovers in the course of a few weeks. In the elderly convulsions must always be modified by muscle relaxants and an experienced anaesthetist should always co-operate in treatment. It is a remarkably safe procedure and there are few contraindications. It is unwise to treat patients with a recent myocardial infarct or a severe respiratory disease but patients with old infarcts and a history of cardiac failure or cerebrovascular accident in the past have been treated with safety and success with the aid of modern relaxants and anaesthesia.

Electroconvulsive treatment does constitute a risk in the exceedingly frail subject and the individual with some degree of cardiac decompensation or marked hypertension, albeit a small one. This has to be balanced against the risk to life caused by the patient's state of increasing exhaustion, inanition and suicidal potentialities and also against the hopeless misery he has to endure. It has been shown that in carefully selected cases excellent results may be achieved in spite of heart disease, hypertension and arteriosclerosis.

PREFRONTAL LEUCOTOMY. Although total and lasting remissions can be achieved in only a proportion of patients with depression in old age, in the majority a satisfactory degree of symptomatic improvement and level of adaptation is rendered possible by anti-depressive drugs or E.C.T., social supervision and regular clinical aftercare. There is, however, a minority in whom all forms of treatment fail or only fleeting remissions can be obtained or relapse recurs after increasingly short intervals. Where social support by the family is inadequate these patients are faced with the prospect of indefinite confinement in mental hospital and may have to spend the rest of their lives there. In these patients leucotomy deserves consideration although it involves some hazards. These have to be balanced against the danger to life from suicide, and the progressive deterioration arising from the interaction of physical and mental ill-health. The usual criteria apply (see Chapter IV) except that, in view of the limited span of life ahead of the patients, efforts at treatment with more conservative measures cannot be sustained as long as in the younger subject. However, if attempts to achieve satisfactory remission with the aid of antidepressive drugs, an immediate course of E.C.T. and adequate aftercare are attaining no success in a period of two to two and a half years, leucotomy should be carefully considered. Those with a markedly neurotic, unstable or aggressive personality and those with a lifelong history of maladjustment should be excluded. It is also unjustifiable to recommend leucotomy in a patient who is never going to be able to return to either independent or family-supported life in the community. There are, however, several special contraindications in aged subjects. Those with evidence of cerebral disease should not be considered because of the hazard of severe personality change and rapid intellectual decay after the operation. Severe hypertension is a contraindication that carries a hazard of haemorrhage into the operative area which may prove fatal or lead to some severe organic syndrome. However, other associated physical disease need not be an absolute contraindication provided it is not so serious as to carry a markedly decreased life expectation. A history of manic attacks precludes operation. Excellent results can however be achieved in suitable elderly subjects (Thorpe, 1960; Freeman, 1962; Sykes and Tredgold, 1964). The frontal lobe syndrome may be pronounced in the first weeks or months after the operation but this tends to prove transient and need give no concern unless there is associated evidence of haemorrhage into the leucotomy cut producing a lesion far greater than that intended. Modern operations have improved the prognosis in elderly subjects as in other groups but in the aged there is much to be said for open operations of the retro-orbital undercut or bimedial leucotomy and particularly the technique of stereotactic placement of radioactive yttrium (^{90}Y) which has been described by Knight (1964).

PSYCHOTHERAPY. Aims in psychotherapy for the aged have necessarily to be limited. It is futile to expect that fundamental changes in attitudes will be achieved. The feelings of loneliness of which old people complain and the difficulties in inter-personal relationships experienced are frequently found to have been rooted in the past and to be derived from lifelong personality traits. A study of the neurotic disorders of elderly people brings home the element of truth in the statement Dostoevsky puts into the mouth of Stavrogin, 'One sees yet again that the whole of the second half of human life generally consists of the habits acquired in the first half'. However, within limits, skilful handling of the situation can improve it. Isolation, even if bred of ingrained proclivities, will tend to aggravate pessimism, intolerance, and feelings of envy and dissatisfaction. A process of resocialization can be begun in hospital and continued afterwards with the aid of day hospitals, day centres or clubs, or, if these measures are inappropriate, by the friendly interest of a member of the voluntary or local authority services.

The preference for the past and a tendency to reminiscence should be combated by engaging the patients' interest in out-going hobbies, social activities and the assumption of some limited responsibility for others where opportunity for this offers. The more vigorous of the elderly are admirably suited for providing help and support, whether on a voluntary or paid basis, for their less fortunate contemporaries. Engaging positively in such activities is one way of countering that tendency to 'undue absorption in the past', stressed as one of the dangers of old age by a man whose life well into advanced old age has been marked by quite exceptional vigour, activity and dedication to future generations (Bertrand Russell, 1956). 'It does not do to live in memories, in regrets for the good old days, or in sadness for friends who are dead. One's thoughts must be directed to the future and to things about which there is something to be done. This is not always easy; one's past is a gradually increasing weight. It is easy to think to oneself that one's emotions used to be more vivid than they are and one's mind more keen. If this is true it should be forgotten, and if it is forgotten it will probably not be true'.

The objectives of treatment can be defined in the course of preliminary exploration. In the general run of cases they will be concerned with social and economic difficulties, declining social contact, adjustment to physical handicaps, conflict within the family such as rejection by children and failure to gain satisfaction from available activities and pastimes. The only possible means of accommodating some of the vicissitudes that the old person faces is through an attitude of acceptance and resignation. Some anxiety-laden issues such as the problem of increasing physical decrepitude and death are faced by the more intrepid with remarkable stoicism and fortitude. In others such issues are clearly dissociated and it is often best to leave them so.

Though in many cases complaints will arise from hardships which are difficult to alter, such as chronic physical illness, bereavement, and financial hardship, careful history-taking will often reveal that some difficulties and dissatisfactions originated at a definable time in the past. Depression coming on in a relatively silent and unobtrusive manner will in fact frequently accentuate the patient's real difficulties and treatment to relieve the depression will result in the patient viewing his situation in a better light. Such complaints may also be the reflection of a long-standing defect of adaptation following an earlier depressive disorder. Psychotherapy should be supportive and reassuring and mainly confined to current problems and reinforced as far as possible by practical measures aimed at ameliorating the worst features of the patient's environment.

Removal to hospital is, for the elderly psychiatric patient particularly, a bewildering and frightening experience. This is especially true of the demented whose clouded intelligence cannot grasp what has happened, slows down orientation to new surroundings and often prevents his expressing his feelings in comprehensible language. He reacts to the new situation with restlessness, anger or aggression which may be misinterpreted. Methods which would be effective in establishing rapport with younger patients do not apply. The patient's emotional faculties are often better preserved than his intellect and he may feel that by being sent to hospital he has been rejected. What he needs is a new sympathetic relationship and it will best be established by approaching him with an attitude of interest, concern and tolerant acceptance of his confused, difficult or hostile behaviour. His antipathy to his new surroundings will die down and, with the right management, he may begin to identify himself with the new group of people amongst whom he finds himself. For this reason it is often advisable to induce him at an early stage to join in activities with others (Goldfarb, 1962).

AFTERCARE. As such a high proportion of depressions in old age leave residual symptoms of a disabling kind or are followed by some measure of maladjustment over a long period, regular and systematic supervision and aftercare are an indispensable component of management. A programme of long-term care has to be worked out in close consultation with the psychiatric social worker. As the proportion of patients suffering from depression who come under observation increases, collaboration between staff in psychiatric hospitals and the community health services catering for the aged will become even more essential than it is at the present time, to ensure that all those who require support to enable them to remain viable in the community receive it. This will ensure also that relapse into depressive symptoms is noted and psychiatric treatment instituted at an early stage.

The general principles of management of mental disorder in the elderly are discussed more fully on p. 560.

NEUROSIS IN OLD AGE

The neglect of the subject of neurosis in old age probably arises to some degree from a number of related and widely held assumptions. It tends to be taken for granted that those who suffer from frequent neurotic breakdowns or persistent neurotic symptoms first manifest in earlier life continue to manifest their disability in essentially unchanged form into senescence. It is also assumed that those who have passed through the full range of stresses that the greater part of the life-span can present are unlikely to succumb for the first time in old age. In the absence of a previous history of neurotic illness there may, therefore, be a tendency to see a connexion between breakdown in late life and the early stages of degenerative change in the brain or to find in it evidence for the presence of an endogenous psychosis. Investigations of emotional disturbance among the elderly undertaken during the past few years have shown the situation in a new light (Kay *et al.*, 1964*a*; Bergmann, 1966).

Too little is as yet known about the natural history of neurotic illness commencing in early life which continues during the later phases of the life-span but there is good reason to believe that certain anxious, inflexible persons with high levels of aspiration find a measure of serenity when they are relieved of some of the more onerous responsibilities of adult life. Equally there are those whose Achilles' heels have been well-concealed for the greater part of life but who are incapable of maintaining emotional stability when exposed to the hardships that await many in old age. The majority of those who present with neurotic breakdown in senescence have in fact had early episodes of illness. However, in a number of subjects, emotional breakdown appears in old age as an entirely new development.

In Bergmann's domiciliary study of neuroses of recent onset in the aged, moderate or severe depressive symptoms were the most common, being found in approximately 60 per cent. of the 72 patients; diffuse tension of at least moderate severity came a close second, being found in about 54 per cent. of subjects. Phobic and obsessional symptoms were less frequent, the proportions being about 18 per cent. and 11 per cent. respectively. In a report on 1,250 admissions, Sjögren (1964) described 323 of the patients as suffering from a psychoneurosis. He placed 193 patients in a dysphoric group manifesting predominantly feelings of depression, loss of self-esteem and a 'moderate degree' of hopelessness. The other subjects were classed into a hypochondriacal sub-group (108 patients) and a sensitive sub-group (22 patients) of persons who conformed to the sensitive-delusion syndrome of Kretschmer. This was a different population from Bergmann's in being made up entirely of admissions to a psychiatric hospital but here too patients with depressive symptoms predominated. Many investigators have emphasized the growing awareness of ageing, social and economic difficulties and decline in health as being important factors in the causation of breakdown (Diethelm and Rockwell, 1943; Clow and Allen, 1951; Busse *et al.*, 1960). As many of these patients convey an impression of achievement and stability during much of their earlier life, it is perhaps understandable that the main weight of emphasis in causation has been placed on such situational factors.

However, one feature that differentiates such old people from subjects who have retained emotional stability in old age is a long-standing predisposition to respond adversely to certain kinds of stress. They tend to have been less sociable, to have had fewer contacts and to have been more moody, anxious and concerned about their health than normal old people (Vispo, 1962; Garside *et al.*, 1965). Bergmann found that abnormal personality traits differentiated between neurotic subjects in old age and normal individuals more significantly than any other variable. A tendency to react to stresses with marked psychic and autonomic tension symptoms was one of their most conspicuous traits and had in most instances been lifelong. In old age the response to stress was no longer a passing fear of difficult predicaments but an all-pervading sustained and disabling anxiety, often with a strong colouring of depression. Other subjects showed a markedly obsessional personality and for them ill-health constituted a threat to perfectionist standards of well-being and effectiveness.

Physical illness and disability, especially among men, emerge clearly from each of the Newcastle studies as an important factor in causation. However, as is the case with bereavement

U

and with reduction of social contacts, physical health does not constitute an adequate cause of psychiatric illness. Its effectiveness in the disruption of emotional stability appears to depend to a considerable extent on a pre-existing vulnerability.

Viewed in retrospect, the lives of many of those who break down in old age look rather like a protracted game of chess in the early stages of which some of the more powerful figures have been eliminated from the game thus restricting the possibilities of effective action and survival for the remainder. In comparison with healthy old people (Kay *et al*. 1964*b*) neurotic subjects had more often lost a parent during childhood, and emotional disturbances in early life had been commoner for inherent or environmental reasons or both. Marriage had often taken place later or not at all and there was a higher incidence of divorce or separation. In adult life there had been more restricted participation in social activities and among men, more frequent failure to procreate. As life progressed the chances of successful adjustment became further narrowed and by middle age a proportion had suffered breakdown.

It is not surprising that in the old age period a higher proportion are found to be living alone; they pay fewer visits to friends and relations and make fewer contacts. They retire earlier, have poorer amenities at home and a lower income than healthy old subjects. It should be stressed, however, that such indices of early maladjustment emerge only when comparison is made with a very stable group of subjects, namely those who have remained free from neurotic symptoms even when exposed to the vicissitudes of old age.

There is some tendency for lifelong personality traits to become caricatured in the course of ageing. Those who have been preoccupied with their health are prone to become rather hypochondriacal, those who have been suspicious of being isolated become overtly paranoid. Anxiety wanes in a proportion of subjects but it tends to fasten upon others in old age while those who have been habitually moody and despondent are prone to grow more pessimistic and depressed. The markedly egocentric, the coldly psychopathic, the drifters and alcoholics and those always dependent or parasitic on others cease to hold their place in the community and are found to be over-represented in residential accommodation provided by the public authorities. Deviant tendencies successfully held in check over much of the life-span may be released for the first time in old age. Exhibitionism and genital play with children and occasionally sexual assault on the young comprise over 12 per cent. of the offences for which old people are prosecuted, homosexual and heterosexual assaults against adults being much less common. The early stages of cerebral degeneration are responsible for some of these misdemeanours but, in the majority of cases, psychological deterioration is minimal or absent. Hirschmann (1962) has studied some of the factors which contribute to this form of sexual deviation. The elderly succeed in establishing relationships which are the preliminaries to sexual offences because children react to the figure of grandfather with confidence, affection and submission. The tendency to seek out children is all the greater because the old man is less likely to experience rebuff or humiliation than in encounters with adult women. Although few of the patients studied had had a previous record of offences, many had been subject to sexual difficulties of an inconspicuous nature in earlier life. Help along psychotherapeutic lines proved of value in a proportion of cases. The waning of sexual desire or potency is rarely if ever a primary cause of emotional breakdown in elderly people and, when it is presented as a symptom of relatively recent onset, functional illness or psychosis of recent development should be suspected. In other cases, metabolic, somatic or cerebral disease is responsible.

Typical hysterical conversion symptoms seldom if ever arise *de novo* in old age and when they appear abruptly they are indicative either of a functional psychosis or of rapidly developing organic, most commonly cerebral, disease. One of the authors has seen three cases during the past five years in which dissociative phenomena or conversion symptoms appeared in this manner out of a relatively clear sky; two of the patients recorded proved to have cerebral metastases from a bronchogenic carcinoma and in a third an embolus from a recent myocardial infarction was almost certainly responsible. In the first two cases several months had passed before the cerebral lesion manifested itself in neurological signs and psychiatric organic symptoms.

The same statement can be made of typical obsessive-compulsive neuroses. Isolated obsessional features are not uncommon but are almost invariably symptomatic of an underlying anxiety state in anxious-anancastic individuals or of an endogenous depressive illness in similar personalities. Treatment should accordingly be directed towards the underlying affective disorder.

Treatment

Although neurotic illness in the elderly person may present an unpromising prospect for treatment, long-term observation suggests that symptoms are often relieved even where the patient's physical health is deteriorating. The distress occasioned by bereavement and loneliness is not easily mitigated but depressive and anxiety symptoms will usually respond to psychiatric help in which treatment with simple psychotherapy and drugs each have an important part to play (see Psychotherapy on p. 574).

Antidepressive and tranquillizing drugs have an important place in the treatment of some of the more neurotic reactions. Amitriptyline is probably the drug of choice in all subjects with depressions showing clear endogenous features and those in whom the depression is very profound or sustained although there is reason to believe the condition is essentially neurotic in character. Small doses of 25 mg. four times daily frequently suffice and it is very rarely necessary to go beyond a total dosage of 150 mg. daily. Monoamine oxidase inhibitors are generally successful in the treatment of patients with a depression of unequivocally neurotic type, those in whom the illness is associated with very marked anergia and those whose disorder is complicated by physical illness. Despite the sedative tranquillizing properties of amitriptyline, some old people complain of symptoms of restlessness, agitation, and insomnia while on it. In the presence of such side-effects a diagnosis of endogenous depression requires reconsideration as a high proportion have in fact a depression of neurotic type. Among monoamine oxidase inhibitors, two that can be used with comparative safety among elderly people are phenelzine (Nardil) and isocarboxazid (Marplan), the former in doses of 15 mg. t.d.s., the latter in doses of 10 mg. t.d.s. It is advisable to administer in addition a drug with tranquillizing effects such as diazepam (Valium) in a dose of 5 mg. two to three times daily. A careful watch needs to be maintained on the blood pressure in elderly subjects, particularly in individuals who have previously sustained a myocardial infarction or a cerebrovascular accident. Insomnia, constipation and difficulty in initiating micturition are other side-effects that may prove troublesome where a drug of the imipramine group is being given. If there is any reason to suspect prostatic enlargement, imipramine and its congeners should be avoided as retention of urine may result.

The opportunity of regular contact is beneficial even if at infrequent intervals of four to six weeks when current difficulties can be unburdened and discussed, reassurance and kindly support can be given. Opportunities for widened social contact in some type of organization appropriate to the patient's social background and personality can also help to ease distress. Spontaneous remission or recovery occurs in some elderly people when they are observed over long periods, although many remain chronically depressed and anxious. Skilled psychiatric treatment helps to blunt the edge of distress and to speed improvement on its way. Psychotherapy in elderly people is discussed more fully on p. 574.

LATE PARAPHRENIA

It has been known for a considerable time that schizophrenia-like illnesses occur in old age. In a review article published in 1943, Bleuler expressed the view that 15 per cent. commenced after the age of 40, some 5 per cent., after 60 years. However, the tendency in clinical practice has been to regard these disorders not as schizophrenias but as pathoplastic effects released by cerebral disease. Roth (1955) drew attention to a group of patients whose first illness occurred in senescence, in whom paranoid delusions and hallucinations often with unclear schizophrenic features, were the most prominent features of the illness, and who tended to be diagnosed as suffering from senile or arteriosclerotic psychoses. He called this condition *late paraphrenia* to draw attention both to the schizophrenic nature of the illness on one hand and to certain distinctive aetiological and clinical features on the other. In contrast to schizophrenia in early life the disorder is mainly confined to women in whom it is by no means rare, accounting for some 8–9 per cent. of all female first admissions over the age of 65.

The term 'late paraphrenia' has been the subject of some controversy since it was first introduced in 1952. The concept of paraphrenia, introduced by Kraepelin, came to be widely abandoned after investigations into the outcome and hereditary basis of paraphrenia and paranoia (Mayer, 1921; Kolle, 1931) showed that there were no adequate grounds for regarding them as distinct from schizophrenia. Yet it is precisely in relation to these two criteria of outcome and genetic basis that late paraphrenic cases have failed to conform to the pattern now generally accepted as uniform in schizophrenias of early life, paranoia and paraphrenia alike. Thus deterioration of personality does not occur in late paraphrenia, except after such long periods of observation that senile degenerative change is a more likely explanation than a schizophrenic process. As far as heredity is concerned, although the psychoses found among the first degree relatives of paraphrenics are mainly schizophrenic, the morbid risk for this disorder is substantially lower than that which has been recorded in most enquiries into schizophrenia (Kay, 1959; Kay and Roth, 1961).

Hence, in the light of the two criteria that have been held in the past to invalidate the concept of paraphrenia, recent observations have not favoured the critics of Kraepelin. In respect of clinical symptomatology, however, these cases belong with schizophrenia: the frequency of schizoid traits in the pre-morbid personality, the excess of unmarried individuals and the low fertility of those who marry, are other points of affinity. Moreover, although a number of aetiological factors have been shown to contribute none of them is associated with a clinically distinctive group of cases. About a third of late paraphrenics are deaf and a proportion are blind; approximately 5 per cent. suffer from cerebral disease but lack organic psychiatric features. In some cases severely stressful circumstances are associated with the onset of symptoms and in others these have been absent. Yet the course the illness follows is uniform in all these groups. The late paraphrenias therefore show in a particularly clear manner that symptomatic and idiopathic schizophrenias may be regarded as a unity at least from the clinical, therapeutic and prognostic points of view.

The observations of Post (1966) lead to essentially similar conclusions. He divided a group of paranoid states of late life into the three syndromes of paranoid hallucinosis, schizophreniform and schizophrenic psychosis. However, no clear differences in aetiology or response to treatment with phenothiazine drugs emerged between the groups. Post concludes that 'late schizophrenic illnesses should be regarded, to differing degrees, as partial or incomplete schizophrenias'.

Aetiology

Hereditary factors almost certainly contribute to the causation of late paraphrenia in that, in approximately one-fifth of patients, at least one member of the family has suffered from an indubitably schizophrenic illness. Late paraphrenia resembles schizophrenia also in the low marriage rate and low fertility rate of affected subjects, these features being probably associated with the abnormal pre-psychotic personality. However, the full genetic predisposition underlying schizophrenia of early onset is apparently lacking since the expectancy of schizophrenia among first degree relatives of late paraphrenics is substantially lower than among the first degree relatives of ordinary schizophrenics. Exogenous factors play a correspondingly greater part than in schizophrenia of early life. As many as 40 per cent. of paraphrenics suffer from impairment of hearing of marked or moderate degree and over half have defects of hearing and/or vision. The view that cerebral degeneration is an important factor in causation is rendered improbable by the finding that these patients have a lifespan almost identical with that of the comparable age group of the population at large (Kay, 1962). Moreover admission rates show little change in age groups above 60 years, which also argues against any important connexion with cerebral degenerative change. However, in about 5 per cent. of cases an indubitable cerebral lesion is present.

The patients are often found to be living in a state of extreme isolation from others. However, despite their frequently schizoid or bizarre personalities and the effects of this on their adjustment, their isolation cannot be regarded as wholly self-induced. They have been found to have fewer surviving siblings, smaller families, fewer surviving children and a higher incidence of deafness and other sensory defects; and all these may have contributed in part to their isolation in old age. In a minority of cases, the domestic upheavals following the death of a husband or the loss of a child with whom a special bond existed had been followed by a period of emotional disturbance from which the paranoid illness developed. Thus, while family ties are relatively few, where they do exist, their disruption may be one of the factors that initiates the illness.

From an aetiological point of view there are then in the late paraphrenias a number of factors—genetic and constitutional, psychological, somatic, cerebral, social—in varying combinations probably acting additively to produce the same clinical picture. These features and the important threads of continuity that can be traced as between pre-morbid personality, the circumstances surrounding breakdown and the features of the illness are in some ways more reminiscent of the course of events in neurotic illness than of that we tend to associate with schizophrenia in early life (Roth, 1963). For these reasons and because of the low morbidity risk for mental illness among the relatives of late paraphrenics the condition is more suggestive of the effects of polygenes than of the specific monohybrid type of inheritance that is generally held to underlie schizophrenia in early life (Kay and Roth, 1961). This view would be compatible with a substantial contribution to causation by exogenous physical and psychological factors.

Pre-morbid Personality

Abnormalities of personality found in a large proportion of the patients are probably the main causes of the failure to marry, the low fertility and social isolation and are also related to the actual psychosis. Personality traits of a paranoid or schizoid type (jealousy, suspiciousness, arrogance, egocentricity, emotional coldness, extreme solitariness) are characteristic of many late paraphrenics; others are described as explosive or sensitive or found to belong to obscure religious sects. In comparison with affective groups, paraphrenics have been described more often in terms such as, 'narrow', 'quarrelsome', 'religious', 'suspicious' or 'sensitive', 'unsociable' and 'cold-hearted' and less often 'kind', 'thoughtful', 'affectionate', 'sociable', 'even-tempered', 'nervous', 'worrying', or 'dependent'.

An example which exhibits both the strong and the vulnerable features of personality of paraphrenic patients is provided by a single woman of 83 who lived with her sister. She was strong-willed, independent, energetic, versatile and capable, also kind and fond of children. Gifted with a sense of humour, she was never moody or over-anxious. She belonged to a religious sect called the Brides of Christ, and led a life regulated by its principles by which marriage and sexual intercourse were absolutely forbidden. Six weeks before admission she began to believe that the child living in the upstairs flat was being tortured and calling to her for help, and rapidly built up a delusional system in which the child became her adopted son.

Even when a marriage had been contracted, it was often unhappy or barren, or the patients were described by their children as cold and unloving mothers. Marriages had often taken place late in life, were unusual in character and marked by difficulties in sexual adjustment and by pronounced jealousy. Of 39 female paraphrenics studied at Graylingwell Hospital (Kay and Roth, 1961), 11 were married, among them one whose husband had been admitted to mental hospital many years previously, and two whose husbands shared their wives' delusions, and another who lived with her ageing taciturn husband in an isolated rural cottage. A fifth had remarried shortly before her psychotic breakdown. Four out of these five marriages were childless. The fact that the personality of most of these patients had been unfavourable to the formation of close and affectionate attachments even long before illness and was a major cause of their isolation was confirmed in an additional study (also Kay and Roth, 1961) carried out in Stockholm. One-quarter of 48 women had had illegitimate children but only two had married the father. Among patients with affective disorder, on the other hand, the much smaller number of women with illegitimate children legitimized their union almost without exception. This reflects the sharp differences in emotional make-up between paraphrenic and affective cases, apparent almost half a century before the patients are burdened with old age.

Clinical Picture

The disorders range from one extreme at which an important reactive factor can be discerned to the other at which organic factors indubitably contribute in causation. However, the points of similarity between the different groups are more impressive than the differences and lines of demarcation are even more difficult to draw than in schizophrenias of early life.

There is a small group of disorders that bear some resemblance to paranoid reactions. The persons affected are lifelong paranoid personalities who become increasingly embroiled in conflict with those in their environment. They are often described by their relatives in such terms as 'not ill but exaggeratedly themselves' and 'I always expected this' (meaning hospital admission) 'to happen'. The patterns of behaviour characteristic of the pre-morbid personality and those associated with illness do not seem clearly distinct from one another and hallucinations are rare. Yet observation over a period shows these disorders to pursue a chronic course. Hence the term 'paranoid reaction', in the sense of a potentially reversible response to vicissitudes by an over-sensitive or suspicious personality, hardly seems applicable. Moreover, the patients have important features in common with the remaining cases: many of the basic features of paraphrenic personality, the contribution made by physical factors to causation in some cases, the course of the illness prior to the introduction of neuroleptics and the favourable response to phenothiazine drugs elicited nowadays. While these cases may deserve some separate consideration in research, it is doubtful whether they should be distinguished from late paraphrenia in practice.

At the other extreme are cases with some evidence of cerebral disease but again with no distinctive features; in particular psycho-organic features are lacking.

In the majority of cases two stages may be defined in the development of the illness. The first takes the form of accentuation of previous personality traits. The patient becomes more irritable, suspicious and dejected. Character traits of bad temper, hypochondria or hostility may come to the fore. Sleep is restless; the patient becomes tired, weak, loses weight and the doctor may be visited frequently because of nervousness or vague pains. She may seclude herself, refuse callers and develop ideas of reference in relation to those living near. A friend, relative or neighbour may come under her suspicions and the police may be pestered with complaints, or strangers bombarded with anonymous letters. The next stage is initiated in a more abrupt and dramatic manner with the onset of auditory hallucinations, consisting of threatening, commanding, accusing or cajoling voices, jeering commentaries, screams, or shouts for help. The patient may hear obscene words spoken and songs performed; loud bangs, rappings, shots or explosions may be complained of. 'Messages' are received from a distance and acted upon. Thoughts are repeated aloud. God, spirits, distant or deceased relatives or, more often, jealous or hostile neighbours are held responsible. At this stage the patient's disturbed behaviour almost invariably brings her under medical observation or to the attention of the police, and admission to hospital occurs within a matter of hours or days.

The hallucinosis is often more disturbing at night, particularly in very old patients, although clear evidence of disturbed consciousness is lacking. Men, boys or animals are seen to enter the bedroom walls, faces appear on the ceiling, bad smells, fumes or the stench of rotting corpses are described, and 'electric' feelings or vibrations in the perineum or abdomen are complained of. Patients complain vehemently that their bodies are being cut or stabbed, the 'backbone split in two'. In other cases intruders are detected on the roof or famous personages are seen to pass by outside. In some patients both delusional and hallucinatory experiences wax and wane in a conspicuous manner, behaviour being correspondingly very disturbed or almost normal. Delusions frequently arise in a characteristically schizophrenic manner, abruptly and out of a clear sky. The patient may suddenly accuse a man who has never shown the slightest interest in her of interfering with her at night or actually entering her bed. Some simple words of greeting exchanged by neighbours mean that they plan to rob and murder her. Thereafter life is made intolerable by threats which are heard through the walls, there are rumblings in the cellar where her persecutors are digging a tunnel to gain access to the house; she smells foul fumes or a constant odour of burning all of which are stratagems for getting her evicted. On the radio she hears the voices of impersonators who slander her by oblique remarks. Her enemies communicate with each other by shining lights from windows. The patient locks and barricades the doors and windows of her room and tries to shield herself from noxious agencies by the use of newspapers or an umbrella.

In the place of such systematized persecutory delusions there may be erotic, hypochondriacal or grandiose delusions in that order of frequency and in varying combinations. They tend, however, to be relatively restricted to those in daily personal contact with the patient. In about one-third of the patients there are feelings of mental or physical influence. The patient feels drugged or hypnotized, has her thoughts read, 'her mind and body worked upon' by ray machines or electricity. She complains that she is spied upon and that she can get no privacy in thought or act. There are strange sensations in her genitals and she believes that by occult means she is being raped. Catatonic stupor is rare but impulsive and aggressive behaviour may occur in connexion with auditory hallucinations.

The grosser forms of affective change as seen in schizophrenia of early life are not found, but some emotional blunting, mild incongruity or euphoria are fairly common in illnesses that have lasted any length of time. In the earlier stages emotional responses are congruous and consist of fear, anger or depression and, occasionally, excitement. When there is a marked colouring of depression, the mood is much more variable than in manic-depressive psychosis, the changes often occurring with rapidity. Retardation and self-accusation are uncommon.

Incoherence of talk and neologisms may occur, but only exceptionally and in cases of long duration. The patients are generally lucid; verbosity, circumstantiality, or irrelevance are found in some 30 per cent. of cases and might be put down to senile deterioration, but for their persistence and lack of change over many years.

Cognitive defects are uncommon, disorientation is present in occasional cases, amounting to no more than uncertainty about the date of the month, or the name of the hospital. In a small proportion more marked defects of memory may be present but, provided no other evidence of cerebral disease is found, they are not necessarily of ill-omen.

Course and Outcome

The illness tends to pursue a chronic course and, prior to the introduction of phenothiazines, some patients showed increasing affective blunting and incongruity and many, particularly the deaf, became withdrawn, mute, incoherent and inaccessible. Nevertheless, pronounced deterioration in personality and habits was unusual and the majority remained clean, tidy and generally well conducted. Since the introduction of phenothiazines, the psychosis is controlled in a more effective fashion and deterioration is uncommon. Nevertheless, minor symptoms can frequently be elicited and disturbed spells with abusive and hostile behaviour may continue at rare intervals, although they can be quickly brought under control by an increased dosage of drugs. In about a fifth of the cases changes suggesting senile dementia or focal signs of cerebral disease eventually develop. However, this does not occur until many years have elapsed, being, for example, particularly rare within the first five years of illness. Whether some part of the deterioration after many years' illness is schizophrenic in character is usually difficult to determine. The fact that the overall expectation of life within the group is very close to that of the general population of comparable age suggests that much of the cerebral disease observed in paraphrenic cases after years of illness is coincidental and due in part to the advanced age to which many of these patients survive. For example, systematic examination of the certified causes of death of a group of cases studied in Stockholm showed that 10 per cent. died of 'cerebral haemorrhage' and allied causes. Figures corresponded exactly with the frequency of deaths from this cause in the general population of Stockholm aged 70 years and over (Kay, 1962).

Treatment

The prognosis for survival amongst the schizophrenic disorders of the aged is considerably better than in senile and arteriosclerotic psychoses; in fact patients with late paraphrenia have a virtually normal expectation of life (Kay, 1959). Thus two years after admission to hospital, 20 per cent. of paraphrenics are found to have died, whereas more than 80 per cent. of patients with senile dementia are dead (Roth, 1955). In the past a high proportion of these patients spent the remainder of their lives in mental hospital. There is little doubt that the majority of them were regarded then as suffering from a form of senile dementia and that the possibility of treating them was rarely considered. However, the advent of modern pharmacological treatments for schizophrenia has transformed the outlook also for late paraphrenic cases. Post (1962) has reported on the outcome of treatment in 63 patients who were divided into three groups. Twelve were not treated with tranquillizing drugs at any time, 16 were given short courses of drugs in small doses and 35 were given extended courses of phenothiazines with a dosage high enough to produce side-effects. Of the 29 patients found to be free from psychotic symptoms at the end of two years, 27 were in the group that had had extended courses of phenothiazines in high dosage and only one each in the other two groups. Withdrawal of drugs led to relapse in a high proportion of cases. In a later report (Post, 1965) treatment was found to have failed in only three of 28 subjects on full treatment whereas 16 out of 23 inadequately treated patients continued to exhibit marked mental symptoms throughout the whole follow-up period. Mild symptoms and paranoid attitudes persisted in a proportion of cases. Eight out of 28 fully treated patients had exhibited such features over a three-year period as compared with 20 of the 23 inadequately treated subjects.

It would seem then that the majority of patients with chronic paranoid psychoses in old age respond to phenothiazine drugs given in high dosage over a long period. As Post points out, although insight is rarely achieved, the favourable response can be sustained indefinitely in nuclear or symptomatic schizophrenias alike and even in the less typically schizophrenic paranoid syndromes. Where treatment along pharmacological and other lines has failed, and the personality is relatively well-integrated and social circumstances are favourable, leucotomy has a limited but useful place.

A high proportion of late paraphrenic patients have long-standing difficulties in interpersonal relationships and many are isolated. There is scant hope of changing the pattern of their lives in old age but careful follow-up and painstaking social work are of great value in long-term management. It is essential to ensure that drugs are being taken, that recurrence of symptoms comes to notice at an early stage and that the channels of communication with the community at large are kept open as far as possible. The psychiatric social worker or mental welfare officer can make a valuable contribution in a number of ways; among other things they can do a great deal to mobilize support for the patient by interesting relatives and friendly neighbours.

Differential Diagnosis

There may be difficulty in distinguishing paraphrenia from affective disorders showing marked paranoid features. This is especially so in cases where the mood is depressed and ideas of reference and persecution relating to the neighbours are present. In paraphrenia self-reproach is generally absent and the behaviour of various persecutors is regarded as unjustified. A depressive colouring does not contraindicate a diagnosis of schizophrenia (in late or early life) provided that clinical features specific for the latter are present. Where delusions are prominent and extend well beyond the themes of self-reproach and deserved contempt and punishment, a diagnosis of endogenous depression should be made with reserve; such patients move progressively closer to paraphrenia in their later course.

A further problem is to differentiate these cases from paranoid states associated with senile and arteriosclerotic psychosis. In senile psychosis the delusions are vague, loosely connected and unsystematized, and quite evidently arise from poverty of grasp; there is gross deterioration of personality and intellect. In arteriosclerotic psychosis paranoid ideas sometimes occur and may be more closely knit than in senile psychosis; but unlike late paraphrenia, the condition shows marked fluctuations. There is, moreover, obvious dementia, and neurological signs of cerebrovascular disease may be present. Finally the delusions and hallucinations of delirious states occur in a setting of clouding of consciousness and not, as in paraphrenia, in clear consciousness.

PHYSICAL ILLNESS IN MENTAL DISORDERS OF OLD AGE

Physical illness is common in all forms of mental disorder in old age (Kay and Roth, 1955; Roth and Kay, 1956), but it is prone to be overlooked. The patient often cannot give a history of his illness and there may be no relative able to do so. The doctor, anxious to secure one of the scarce mental hospital beds for his patient, may be inclined to stress the mental abnormalities of the patient to the exclusion of physical illness such as heart disease or hypertension, although they may be present and relevant to the psychiatric disorder. Finally, physical illness in the aged tends to be ill-defined and diffuse, and the symptoms are often inconspicuous; the whole picture is, therefore, prone to be attributed to the decrepitude of senescence.

Physical disease has been shown to be significantly more common in subjects in whom a functional psychiatric illness begins for the first time in old age than in those in whom there has also been a previous breakdown. It is found in association with psychiatric disorder more commonly in males, the sex difference being particularly striking in the case of affective psychoses.

In a recent four-year follow-up of 297 subjects aged 65 and over in the general population (Kay and Bergmann, 1966) the respective courses pursued by physical and psychiatric illness were examined and it was found that two-thirds of the survivors in the neurotic affective group had deteriorated physically and one-third remained more or less the same; none had improved. Psychiatrically, however, almost a third of these survivors (all women) had either recovered or improved and they belonged to the group whose physical illness had proved intractable. In other words, although the physical illness probably contributes to the emergence of the affective disorder, the two conditions can subsequently pursue an independent course. The psychiatric condition is, therefore, always worth treating in its own right. Excellent results can be obtained in such cases with antidepressive drugs or electroconvulsive therapy. Physicians as well as psychiatrists should therefore be alert to the possibility of psychiatric complications which may retard recovery following physical illness or surgical operation and treatment should not be withheld for reasons of physical health or age.

In the same follow-up study, patients with a functional disorder were found to have a high mortality. Among males the mortality rate of 50 per cent. was markedly in excess of the expected rates in a comparable sample of the general population. In the women the mortality was 26 per cent. but, although this was also excessive, it did not differ significantly from the expected rate (Fig. 20). Organic cases showed the usual excess mortality.

The excess mortality may have been due to the fact that those with functional illness were also more seriously ill physically than the normal subjects in the sample. It remains to be determined whether the prognosis for life can be improved by active treatment of the depressive symptoms but it is important to treat them and in this way ameliorate the lot of these doubly incapacitated subjects.

In delirious states, a specific physical illness is the cause of the condition in the great majority of cases and this is frequently susceptible to treatment. A contribution to the clinical picture of arteriosclerotic psychosis is made in some cases by associated cardiac or urogenital disease or respiratory infection. But in senile dementia physical illness outside the brain is uncommon and if present, is generally mild and intercurrent. The cause of death in these patients even after post-mortem examination is difficult or impossible to define. This obscure mode of death also holds to some extent for arteriosclerotic psychosis, since only a minority of patients finally succumb as the result of a cerebral catastrophe.

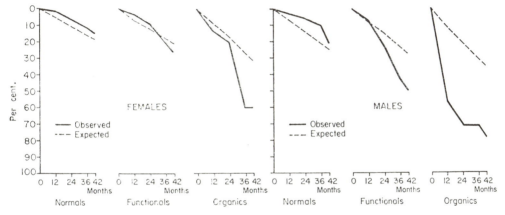

Fig. 24. Observed and expected percentage of deaths at four-year follow-up of a random population sample of subjects aged 65 and over (Kay and Bergmann, 1966).

Hence in the affective, paraphrenic and delirious cases which carry a relatively good prognosis, the somatic disease present tends to be clear-cut, and in the event of death, a specific cause can be recorded; whereas in the conditions with the highest mortality, namely senile dementia and arteriosclerotic psychosis, the illness present during life and the stated cause of death are far more often ill defined, 'senility' and 'myocardial degeneration' being very common statements on the death certificate. It would seem then that the most potent cause of mortality among the aged with psychiatric illness is cerebral degeneration. When this is present, old people are liable to die of trivial causes such as mild intercurrent infections, or perhaps after a fall complicated by fracture in some or bruising in others.

Psychoses due to Cerebrovascular Disease

THE NATURE AND AETIOLOGY OF HYPERTENSION. Cerebral infarction which gives rise to the clinical manifestations of arteriosclerotic psychosis is closely related to high blood pressure. Well over half the subjects who suffer from cerebral infarction have associated hypertension (Dickinson and Thomson, 1961) while cerebral infarction is a common complication of and cause of death in hypertensive disease. Population studies have shown that the incidence of one of the disorders tends to be closely paralleled by that of the other in contrast to myocardial infarction which appears to vary independently. Thus among the Japanese the incidence of cerebrovascular disease and of hypertension in adult life is exceptionally high (Schroeder, 1958) whereas coronary artery disease is relatively rare; the same pattern has been found among the Bantu (Walker *et al.*, 1960).

Since hypertension, with or without cerebral infarction, frequently brings the patient to the psychiatric clinic by one route or another, the controversy that has been in progress in recent years on the nature of the disorder is of some interest. Observations on the distribution of measurements of blood pressure among a large sample of patients attending hospital clinics for disorders connected with disturbances of blood pressure (Hamilton *et al.*, 1954) and in a random sample of the population at large (Miall and Oldham, 1963) have led Pickering and his associates to conclude that variation in the distribution of arterial tension is continuous and that the difference between essential hypertension and normal arterial pressure is not qualitative, but one of degree. The increase in blood pressure levels associated with age is regarded as a normal effect of senescence and not a result from the development of the disease 'high blood pressure' in a group of patients separate from the normal population. According to this concept, then, hypertension may be regarded as the extreme variant of a graded characteristic rather than as a specific disease. Pickering (1955) considers that blood pressure, like height and intelligence, is transmitted by multifactorial genes over the whole range of variation. The degree of resemblance between propositi and first degree relatives is represented by a correlation coefficient of approximately 0·2 for systolic pressure.

Platt (1959) has questioned the validity of these conclusions. Making use of the observations of Hamilton *et al.* (1954) and of Søbye (1948) he found that the blood pressure measurements of the sibs of middle-aged hypertensives showed a bimodal distribution. A similar bimodality was apparent in the distribution of blood pressure among the sons of parents who had died in middle life; this contrasted sharply with the continuous distribution of blood pressure among the sons of parents who survived into old age (Morrison and Morris, 1959). These findings tended to suggest the existence of two populations, one of whom had inherited the tendency to high blood pressure and another to which it had not been transmitted.

However, with the small numbers analysed, the break in the distribution curve could not be regarded as statistically valid. As against the Pickering view, it has been pointed out that the degree of resemblance between first degree relatives is much smaller than for height and that the comparison with stature falls down for other reasons (Acheson and Fowler, 1967). Nevertheless, certain points would be generally agreed. It is accepted that a certain part of the variation in blood pressure is continuous and probably due to polygenes and that blood pressure tends to rise with chronological age. It is generally agreed also that whether or not essential hypertension is a consequence of normal variation, the ratio of actual to expected mortality increases progressively with rising blood pressure.

Further observations which could help to resolve this controversy would have practical as well as theoretical importance. If essential hypertension is indeed due to one or a few major gene differences it would be reasonable to search for specific biochemical correlates of the genes in question in the hope that they would prove susceptible to modification. If, on the other hand, no one genetic or other factor is dominant in aetiology, and polygenes are the underlying hereditary causes, environmental factors might be important as in the case of other phenomena under the control of multifactorial genes. The search should then be focused on the environmental, physical and psychological factors which contribute to the elevation of blood pressure. A survey conducted by Miall and Oldham (1963) in the

Rhondda Fach and the Vale of Glamorgan suggests that variation in blood pressure may be due to environmental factors which are non-familial. Among these factors obesity and the onus of physical work as indicated by occupation are already identified. The marked differences in the prevalence of hypertension among genetically identical populations exposed to different socio-economic conditions (Cruz-Coke, 1964) suggest that future research may reveal additional environmental factors and clarify the importance of psychological characteristics such as emotional stress which are regarded by some observers as important.

In hypertension without cardiac failure the cardiac output and venous pressure are not significantly raised. Since the level of the blood pressure varies with cardiac output and peripheral resistance, it follows that the hypertension must result from *constriction of arterioles*. This is shown by the fact that even in long-established and severe hypertension it is possible temporarily to reduce the blood pressure to normal levels by the use of powerful vasodilator drugs.

The problem as to why this arteriolar spasm should occur in hypertension is not at present solved. That *emotional disturbance* plays some part seems possible. It is well known that it may produce changes in blood pressure. It would appear, moreover, that prolonged emotional stress and sustained unresolved tension play some part in the initiation of hypertension; for in the early stages of the disorder strong *emotional stress* frequently operates, and persons working under great pressure or shouldering worrying responsibility seem specially prone to develop hypertension. Persons whose blood pressure is much affected by emotional and other influences are ultimately prone to develop hypertension, even if it is possible initially to reduce it to normal levels by sedation, rest, or removal from a disturbing environment. However, while emotion can play some part in the production of a given reading, an additional factor is required to account for the *disease hypertension*. This additional factor may be a heightened susceptibility to arteriolar constriction and it is this susceptibility that may be under the control of the hereditary factors operating in hypertension. There is a *high familial incidence of raised blood pressure* and its complications in essential hypertensives, but it is unusual to obtain a positive history in cases secondary to renal disease (Platt, 1947).

Obesity certainly, and the menopause probably, have some association with hypertension but their role is not understood. It has also been claimed that more specific *psychological mechanisms* than those already mentioned are important in causation. The hypertensive patient, it is suggested, has incompatible unconscious impulses towards dependence and passivity on the one hand, and aggression on the other. This gives rise to a tendency to compromise and 'keep the peace'. A real or fancied threat to the life of the patient or a parent figure is claimed to play a further part in precipitation (Wittkower, 1949). In the personality profiles of Dunbar (1943) some of the psychological conflicts described were of a similar nature. However, the evidence in favour of the view that some specific pattern of personality predisposes to hypertension is very slender.

CEREBRAL ARTERIOSCLEROSIS. In England and Wales vascular lesions of the central nervous system are the cause of death in 11·8 per cent. of the men who die at the age of 45 years or over and in 18·1 per cent. of women. These figures give some rough indication of the size of the problem but they probably represent a fraction of those cases in which cerebrovascular disease causes only psychiatric symptoms. These percentages distort also the sex incidence which is almost equal with only a very slight excess among males (Registrar General, 1966). Morbidity statistics from general practice (Research Committee of the Council of the College of General Practitioners, 1962) reveal that patient consulting rates per thousand at risk at the age of 65 and over are 30·4 for men and 28·5 for women in this group of complaints.

AETIOLOGY. It would seem that atherosclerosis may be produced at will in experimental animals by raising the plasma cholesterol level. In man, although the habitual intake of cholesterol in the diet bears little relationship to the serum cholesterol level, any large variation in dietary fat gives rise to corresponding changes in the level of serum cholesterol (Keys *et al.*, 1950; Keys, 1952). That the aetiology of atherosclerosis is in some way linked with high cholesterol and a fat diet is suggested also by the fact that during the 1939–1945 war, dietary restrictions in most European countries were associated with sharp falls in the mortality rates from the disorders associated with atherosclerosis, while the rates in the U.S.A. increased throughout this period (Malmros, 1950). Moreover, atherosclerosis is very common in conditions associated with a raised serum cholesterol such as diabetes mellitus, nephrosis and myxoedema. A diet low in animal fat has, therefore, been suggested as a rational form of prophylaxis against atherosclerosis. However, nutrition is likely to prove, at the most, only part of the story. It cannot explain differences in the distribution of atheromatous change which predominates in the cerebral circulation in some, in the coronary circulation in others. The view that atherosclerosis arises from filtration of lipid material from the blood into the arterial wall (which appeared to be supported both by observations of experimental atherosclerosis and the association between high blood cholesterol and some forms of atherosclerosis in man) has been contested in recent years. Duguid (1955) considers that the initial lesion, which is specially prone to commence near the original branch vessels, is a deposit of fibrin and thrombus on the surface of the arterial wall. Formation of a covering layer of endothelium buries the mural thrombi in the intima and the process advances by the addition of fresh surface deposits of fibrin and thrombus. Successive layers become organized, the intima becomes sclerosed and thickened and the lumen of the vessel is progressively narrowed. Pickering (1965) considers that this proliferative process is the only one that advances to occlusive arterial disease. However this view is not yet generally accepted, as some occluded atheromatous arteries appear to consist very largely of massive deposits of lipid substance. It appears likely that a variety of factors may be concerned with the aetiology of atherosclerosis although the process of encrustation discovered by Duguid enters frequently into the pathogenesis of occlusive arterial disease in man. Genetic factors are of some importance in adiposity and very likely also in atherosclerosis. In coronary heart disease, physical inactivity would appear to be a factor (Morris *et al.*, 1953) and additional causes may well emerge in relation to cerebrovascular disease.

Essential hypertension is frequently associated with atheroma in the cerebral blood vessels, but the nature of the relationship between the two phenomena is far from clear. The correlation between high blood pressure in man and atheroma of cerebral vessels is not a very consistent one. Although most authorities consider that cerebral atheroma is secondary to hypertension, Dickinson (1965) has recently advanced the hypothesis that the causal relationship is in the reverse direction. In other words, 'essential hypertension, by this hypothesis, is the normal adaptation of the body to an increase in cerebrovascular resistance which cannot be, or has not been, overcome by compensatory vasodilation and opening up of collateral channels'. He considers that the main cause of the increased cerebrovascular resistance in high blood pressure is atheromatous constriction or occlusion of the larger vessels supplying the hind brain.

Rothschild (1947) has put forward the view that the severity of symptoms in arteriosclerotic psychosis depends on the degree of integration and the *assets of the personality*—narrow, inadequate, ill-adapted people suffering severely even from small lesions. Williams *et al.* (1942), on the other hand, has found the personality of cerebral arteriosclerotics relatively normal in comparison with that of patients with senile psychosis. The premorbid personality and constitution survive to influence the total picture, much later in arteriosclerotic than in senile psychosis, and discrepancies between clinical and pathological findings are not unexpected. But the failure to demonstrate a correlation between the degree of structural and clinical change by present-day methods does not mean that none exists.

MORBID ANATOMY. There is little association between peripheral and cerebral arteriosclerosis; even retinal arteriosclerosis bears little relationship to the condition of the cerebral vessels. A much more intimate association is usually found to exist between the condition of the *renal and cerebral vessels* and this has its counterpart in the tendency for the symptoms of derangement in the two organs to be combined. There is frequently considerable difficulty in assessing to what extent sclerosis of vessels observed at post-mortem has been responsible for symptoms or even for cerebral lesions; normal-looking vessels may be surrounded by areas of softening while diseased arterioles may supply healthy cerebral tissue.

The *lesions in the blood vessels* may take one of three forms: (1) In atherosclerosis which affects the large vessels there are patchy areas of degeneration owing to the irregular deposition of lipoid-containing cells in the subendothelial tissue. The yellowish plaques are similar in appearance to those in the wall of the atheromatous aorta; (2) Arteriosclerosis usually occurs in the small cortical arterioles. The affected vessels show a generalized thickening owing to hyaline change. This commences beneath the intima and gradually extends to the whole wall; the nature of the change is not understood; (3) Arteriocapillary fibrosis affects the smaller vessels and capillaries which are surrounded and gradually narrowed by a fine mesh of connective tissue. The three types of change are usually combined but may occur independently.

The simplest *classification of the cerebral changes* associated with vascular disease in the brain is that due to Greenfield (1938). (1) The first and commonest type of change includes all cases with softenings and haemorrhages in the cortex and subcortex. He suggests that the pathogenesis of Binswanger's subcortical encephalopathy (as well as of the type of change in which there are multiple haemorrhages in the subcortex) is due to the poorly developed anastomoses between the long vessels that supply the white matter. (2) The second type is the verrucose or granular atrophy of the cortex commonly associated with renal arteriosclerosis and hypertension. In this condition both nerve-cells and fibres are affected in an irregular, patchy manner, and there is a secondary overgrowth of neuroglia. (3) The third form is generally associated during life with hypertension. There are no naked eye changes but microscopically numerous widely scattered areas of focal rarefaction are visible, the result of intimal hypertrophy of the small cortical vessels. There is little glial proliferation.

CLINICAL PICTURE: EARLY SYMPTOMS OF HYPERTENSION. Essential hypertension is symptomless until a relatively advanced stage of the illness at which the symptoms of heart failure, renal failure and cerebrovascular disease make their appearance. Both in the medical and psychiatric clinic the symptoms in the early stages are encountered more frequently in men, and in a substantial number they are iatrogenically induced. A careful history will usually reveal that the symptoms originated shortly after the diagnosis of 'high blood pressure' was communicated to the patients, or within a short time after an unfavourable verdict in an examination for life insurance. The symptoms complained of vary but commonly include difficulties in concentration, insomnia, easy fatiguability, palpitations or constant awareness of one's heartbeat, anorexia, dyspnoea on exertion, precordial pain and feelings of anxiety. There is difficulty in falling asleep, nocturnal restlessness, frightening dreams and early awakening in a restless, anxious mood. Moreover, vague feelings of precordial discomfort, frequent palpitations, constant fatigue, a sense of pressure in the head, and an indefinable loss of the sense of well-being combine to evoke an attitude of anxious self-scrutiny. The patient loses his freshness, liveliness and spontaneity and becomes slow, dilatory and inefficient. Aware of the change in himself and oppressed by the compulsive examination of his symptoms, he is inclined to become moody, depressed, irritable and aggressively over-sensitive to criticism. The symptoms are in fact identical with those of an anxiety neurosis although, in a middle-aged or elderly subject, a depressive colouring is common.

The frontal headaches often complained of in the early stages of the illness are generally also functional and not organic in origin. However, occipital headache, which commences on waking and lasts for a few hours, is more specifically related to essential hypertension although it is not commonly a very early symptom. The headache is possibly of vascular origin although its precise pathophysiology is unknown. Dizziness and nose-bleeding are also related to the hypertension, and may likewise appear fairly early in the course of the disorder. These complaints may become entangled with others that are to a large extent psychologically determined.

Many of the symptoms bear little relation to the severity of hypertension as assessed from fundal changes, presence of cardiac enlargement and the height of the blood pressure, and often begin soon after the diagnosis has been communicated to the patient. It is only when cardiac, renal or cerebral complications begin that most of the symptoms arising specifically from raised arterial tension make their appearance.

Though insight and the personality in general are well preserved even after some years of illness, if the neurosis is not resolved these patients may become difficult, withdrawn, rigid, stubborn and intolerant, their vigour and initiative decline and their work and social adjustment suffer. In an intelligent and co-operative patient of stable personality the neurotic symptoms can often be alleviated with the aid of simple psychological measures (see p. 597).

Attacks of *hypertensive encephalopathy* are usually ushered in by a considerable rise in blood pressure with vomiting, amaurosis, epileptiform convulsions, and mono- or hemiplegia. There may be drowsiness or sopor and this may deepen rapidly to coma. Recovery is usual although there may be a period of clouded consciousness before full awareness returns. At one time attacks of delirium or twilight state were seen in the course of severe hypertension with hypertensive encephalopathy. Such complications have however become very rare since the introduction of effective hypotensive drugs. There is little evidence that cerebral angiospasm can be the cause of these attacks. Cerebral oedema is found in some of the cases post-mortem. In others a small occlusion with oedema round the infarcted area, which subsequently subsides, is responsible.

Hypertensive encephalopathy may also leave behind some *residual neurological lesion* such as a partial hemiparesis, dysphasia or a field defect. These changes generally subside within hours or days, but after several attacks some permanent neurological disability may result.

Hypertensive crises associated with a suprarenal medullary tumour have certain specific features. Onset is particularly sudden, and attacks may be brought on by exercise or a sudden change of position. There is perspiration and intense pallor in addition to headache and vomiting. Palpitations, a sense of constriction in the chest, and anginal pain, are associated with a *terrifying feeling of impending death*. Breathlessness and a sinking feeling in the epigastrium are common. Localized vasoconstriction may produce coldness and pallor in the fingers. The blood pressure may rise to 250–300 systolic over 140–160 diastolic. Glycosuria may occur, and sometimes continues between attacks. The crisis comes to an end suddenly within minutes, but if prolonged further, cardiac arrhythmias may develop. The suddenness of onset, the acute fear often aroused by the attacks, and their brief duration, may suggest a neurosis with bouts of panic, or anginal attacks associated with coronary artery disease. The attacks are caused by the liberation into the blood of large quantities of a pressor substance similar to adrenalin.

ARTERIOSCLEROTIC PSYCHOSIS. This condition usually begins in the sixties or seventies, but occasionally as early as the middle or late forties. Hypertension is present in about half the patients and conspicuous symptoms generally make their appearance following a number of cerebrovascular accidents. However, enquiry will often reveal that the patient's memory has been failing and he has been restless, 'very emotional' and inclined to wander at night, for some months previously. He will have complained of headaches, giddiness, palpitations or momentary 'blackouts'. Memory and intellectual impairment may be preceded by a caricature of one or more conspicuous personality traits, a growing suspiciousness, pathological jealousy or valetudinarianism, or a previously well controlled tendency to sexual deviation becoming manifest. As the change is gradual, patients rarely come under observation unless prosecution or the family's anxieties about testamentary capacity bring them to notice. Lasting intellectual deficit rarely develops until clinical evidence of focal infarction has appeared. It is rare also for a single stroke to be followed by dementia unless massive infarction has resulted, although dysphasia can prove a serious handicap. The man who is perhaps the most celebrated contemporary composer continues after a number of cerebral infarcts with his creative and intellectual powers seemingly undimmed. Dementia usually makes its appearance after a succession of strokes, and when a single small infarct is followed by rapid deterioration, some additional degenerative process or causal agent is almost invariably present, commonly senile dementia. Memory for recent events is affected first but general intellectual ability soon becomes impaired. The patient has difficulties in concentration, is slow to grasp situations particularly if they present new problems, and is laboured, repetitive, and inefficient even in the execution of habitual tasks. His outlook becomes narrowed, his emotions cool, drive and initiative are diminished, and the long-established routine of his daily work makes a progressive encroachment on his former interests, hobbies and friendships. Yet *judgement and the basic personality may be well preserved*, and until a late stage of the disease the patient can retain *remarkably good insight* into the nature of the change that is overtaking him. The impression is often one of patchy destruction which leaves the general framework of the personality intact. This is unlike senile dementia in which the personality tends to be demolished at a relatively early stage, only isolated islands of behaviour being discernible which are reminiscent of it. The patient reacts to his awareness of progressive decline with *despondency* and *pessimism*, but if moved to either tears or laughter he rapidly loses control and a bout of unrestrained weeping or laughter results. This *emotional incontinence* and the overflow of mirth and laughter into tears are again more characteristic of arteriosclerosis.

The intellectual disturbances progress at a slower rate than in senile dementia, but a more distinctive feature is the *marked fluctuation* in the course of the illness. At a relatively early stage when there is little beyond a mild restriction of memory for recent events, acute delirious episodes similar to those described in the case of hypertension may begin quite suddenly. In such an attack the patient may be wholly out of touch with his surroundings, but the clouding of consciousness may be overlooked, and a superficial examination may convey the impression that he is severely demented; yet in a few days or weeks he will emerge from his attack quite as suddenly as he went into it. Careful examination after such an episode will reveal some *residual impairment* in most cases; but remissions sufficiently complete to enable the patient to leave hospital for many months, are not uncommon in the early phases of the illness, and there may be many such episodes before dementia becomes too profound for him to live outside hospital. There is also a fluctuation in the severity of the condition from hour to hour in many cases. Totally disorientated and inaccessible on one occasion, the patient may be found to be comparatively lucid and in good contact a few hours later. Very often clouding of consciousness is most severe during the night, and may lead to nocturnal wandering during which the patient endangers the household by turning on gas-taps or starting fires. After several delirious episodes dementia is obvious, the patient being slow, forgetful, deteriorated in habits, emotionally labile though often still capable of making a good impression for short periods.

Depression is noticeable at some stage in almost a third of cases; but a mood change of the intensity and persistence usually seen in endogenous depression is not frequent, occurring in about 5–10 per cent. of cases. Most depressive episodes are short-lived, and they often appear in a setting of clouded consciousness. The mood change is shallow, and emotional incontinence endows it with a characteristic quality. Depressive delusions are stereotyped and grotesque. Determined *attempts at suicide* are likely to be made in delirious episodes with a strong depressive colouring, but so unstable is the picture that a few hours later when the patient has been admitted to hospital he is often euphoric, fatuous, and oblivious of what has happened. If a much more severe and sustained affective change appears, resembling the picture of a typical endogenous depression or manic illness, a family history of affective disorder or a history of previous attacks of affective illness is frequently obtained.

Somatic symptoms such as headache, giddiness, tinnitus, general malaise and precordial discomfort are common. The last of these is particularly worthy of attention, as coronary artery disease may complicate the condition. The physical symptoms may give rise to anxiety and hypochondriacal self-scrutiny, the patient becoming tense, restless and importunate; this is particularly likely when hypertension is associated with arteriosclerosis.

Neurological lesions make their appearance sooner or later. They take the form of attacks of transient or permanent hemiparesis, aphasia, or field defects. Consciousness may be retained during fleeting disturbances and even during those leaving a permanent disability; they are caused by cerebral thromboses. In cases associated with hypertension, cerebral haemorrhage may give rise to deep coma and a fatal outcome. *Epileptiform seizures* occur in 15–20 per cent. of cases usually in the form of generalized convulsions or, less often, Jacksonian or other focal seizures. Occasionally attacks of unconsciousness occur without convulsive movements, but accompanied by a hemiplegia which may disappear after recovery. The aetiology of such seizures is unknown but they may be caused by small cerebral thromboses. A Parkinsonian syndrome develops in a small proportion of cases. It is quite common to elicit minor neurological abnormalities such as sluggish pupils, inequalities in the tendon reflexes, and an extensor plantar response even when no definite disability is complained of. Focal neurological signs nearly always precede intellectual decline and psychiatric disorder often by some years. Personality changes may appear sooner but, in isolation, can rarely be confidently attributed to cerebral arteriosclerosis.

The *fluctuating course of the disease* is maintained until a late stage, but each attack adds to the severity of the residual change. The picture of total disintegration of the personality, inaccessibility, and a uniform apathy or euphoria, seen in senile dementia, does not appear until a very late stage, and even when fatuous, forgetful and incontinent, the arteriosclerotic patient may remain recognizably his former self.

Pathologically there is some degree of overlap between the senile and arteriosclerotic forms of degenerative disease. Hence it is not possible to assign every subject with a progressive dementia in old age associated with degenerative disease to one or other group of conditions. However, the pathological evidence suggests that the overlap is likely to be due to the fortuitous coincidence of two distinct pathological processes, both relatively common among the aged. Recent pathological studies (Blessed *et al.*, 1968) suggest that there is probably a tendency to over-diagnose arteriosclerotic psychosis. Thus in some patients the dementia pursues a progressive and unremitting course for a number of years followed by a solitary cerebrovascular accident with transient effects or a single epileptiform convulsion. A diagnosis of arteriosclerotic psychosis is then made. At post-mortem in such cases it is quite common to find only small infarctions, which are frequently present also in the brains of healthy old subjects of comparable age. It is probable that in such cases the illness was due in the main to senile dementia, and that the very limited vascular changes found expression in minor focal symptoms and signs only because the reserve capacity of the brain had been encroached upon by senile degenerative change.

In recent years increasing emphasis has been placed on the importance of extracranial arterial disease as a cause of cerebral infarction. Yates and Hutchinson (1961), in an investigation of 100 cases suffering from cerebral ischaemia, found evidence of cerebral infarction in 35 cases. However, whereas only 19 of these showed 'significant stenosis or occlusion' of intracranial arteries, 'significant stenosis or occlusion' of extracranial cerebral arteries was found in all but 3 of the 35 cases. The carotid and vertebral systems were simultaneously narrowed in many cases and these findings suggested that if one of the four main vessels was affected there was an approximately 80 per cent. chance that one of the remaining vessels would also be affected to a significant degree. These authors found moreover that infarction due to carotid disease tended to affect the ipsilateral, frontal and parietal lobes, whereas vertebral-basilar disease was usually associated with lesions in the brain stem, cerebellum and occipital lobes. Combined disease of carotid and vertebral arteries was likely to give rise to extensive infarction of one cerebral hemisphere and both cerebellar hemispheres. Yates and Hutchinson also stressed the importance of general systemic factors such as anaemia and hypotension in the production of cerebral ischaemia. Thus, among their 22 cases with severe coronary atherosclerosis, 13 were found to be associated with cerebral infarction. All these observations have tended to focus attention on the extracranial vessels and systemic factors in the causation of cerebral infarction. The possibilities of surgical treatment for chronic cerebrovascular disease seemed hopeful; and since the successful excision of the stenosed portion of an internal carotid artery, reported in 1954 by Eastcott, Pickering and Rob in the case of a patient who had suffered from a succession of 33 attacks of blindness and contralateral hemiparesis, there have been a number of reports of successful operations. However, recent observations tend to dim the optimism generally felt ten years ago. Schwartz and Mitchell (1961) reported that the frequency of stenosis in the extracranial vessels in an unselected series of necropsies does not differ from that observed by Yates and Hutchinson. Dickinson and Thomson (1961) reported that carotid stenosis was just as likely to cause infarction in the contralateral as in the ipsilateral hemisphere, suggesting that by the time clinical symptoms of cerebral ischaemia make their appearance, widespread atherosclerosis has probably reduced the vascular reserve of the brain. There have been a number of other studies to suggest that disease of extracranial vessels only rarely exists independently of intracerebral disease (Stein *et al.*, 1962). In the aged, disease wholly confined to the extracerebral vessels is particularly rare and careful dissection of the intracerebral arterial system will generally reveal the local site of the occlusion corresponding to a region of infarction.

The indications for surgery in the treatment of cerebral ischaemia appear therefore much more limited in the light of recent findings than they did a decade ago. Among the more favourable cases are those with incipient strokes, as in the syndrome of occlusion of the internal carotid artery first described by Moniz (Moniz *et al.*, 1937) in which successful intervention has been recorded in a number of instances. The condition is characterized by repeated transient attacks of paresis in one or both limbs on the opposite side of the body, or alternatively there may be dysphasia or localized parasthesiae. The premonitory symptom in a number of subjects is a fleeting monocular blindness of abrupt onset on the affected side (Fisher, 1951), which may recur within short intervals. These short-lived symptoms may be due to embolism from a fresh platelet-leucocyte-fibrin thrombus (Russell, 1961). Many workers would regard such forewarnings of incipient stroke as an imperative indication for treatment with anticoagulants (Adams, 1965). Other authorities hold that in an attempt to improve cerebral blood flow such measures should be combined with a surgical approach to any accessible vessel showing stenosis or occlusion. However, the indications for surgery are uncertain at the present time. Whether or not it improves the outlook in cases with incipient stroke or actual occlusion remains to be determined with the aid of controlled trials.

The *prognosis* in arteriosclerotic psychosis is somewhat more favourable than in senile dementia. Six months after admission a third of our patients were dead, a quarter discharged and the remainder were still in hospital (see Fig. 17, p. 550). After two years, however, the outcome is only a little better than that of senile psychosis (i.e. dementia) the mortality having climbed to 70 per cent.

DIAGNOSIS. Hypertensive patients are frequently referred for a psychiatric opinion because in the early stages their symptoms may be largely neurotic in origin or coloured by emotional disturbances. Detailed investigation to exclude hypertension due to such conditions as a diseased kidney, coarctation of the aorta, Cushing's disease and phaeochromocytoma, will usually be carried out in conjunction with the general physician. If, as is often the case in the early stages of essential hypertension, the emotional disturbance is the main cause of disability, a balance must be struck between a plethora of anxiety-provoking investigations and masterly inactivity. The understandable desire to establish a confident prognosis must not be allowed to dictate the management of the patient. In many early cases the hypertension is discovered fortuitously and the blood pressure readings may prove normal at subsequent examinations or return after rest to near normal levels. Although this labile blood pressure may herald a sustained hypertension, care should be taken to prevent the anxieties of the doctor being communicated to the patient. The patient can be helped with any emotional difficulties that may be contributing to the lability of his blood pressure, or if necessary be given advice to modify his diet and his pattern of daily activity in an attempt to deflect the usual course of the illness without being made aware that his blood pressure is reaching a pathological level.

Patients who develop *severe hypertension under the age of forty*, or who on examination prove to have albuminuric retinitis, present a problem of particular urgency. The prognosis in such 'malignant' cases is grave; untreated they die within 12–18 months. The introduction of hypotensive drugs has substantially improved the outlook, particularly where treatment can be initiated at an early stage of the disease.' Even where mental changes are to some extent established in a case of cerebrovascular disease associated with hypertension, the psychiatrist should not be content with a diagnosis of arteriosclerotic psychosis until the *cause of the hypertension* has been investigated· and the possibility of a primary disease has been eliminated.

Arteriosclerotic psychosis needs to be differentiated from such conditions as cerebral tumour, general paralysis, presenile dementia and subdural haematoma. The *differential diagnosis* has already been discussed in connexion with these diseases. The distinction from senile dementia is based on the presence of cerebrovascular lesions, a markedly remitting or fluctuating course, the preservation of the personality, a large measure of insight until a relatively late stage, explosiveness or incontinence of emotional expression, and epileptiform attacks; all these features are characteristic of arteriosclerotic psychosis and make the condition a *fairly well-defined clinical syndrome*, whereas cerebrovascular lesions are absent in senile dementia and the other features are rare. The usefulness of this clinical distinction between the two disorders is not affected by the observation that the two types of pathological change are often associated to some extent in the brain, so that one is strictly justified in speaking only of the preponderance of one or other type of process.

TREATMENT. A high proportion of cases of hypertension come to notice on account of symptoms related to hypertensive cardiovascular disease such as restlessness, anginal pain, cardiac failure or a cerebrovascular accident. But many cases are detected during some routine medical examination; and many of these patients, on learning of their 'high blood pressure' begin to complain of headache, giddiness, forcible or possibly irregular action of the heart, which fill them with fear and foreboding, general nervousness and irritability. Occasionally these symptoms arise in the absence of previous knowledge of hypertension. But in the majority of instances, they must be regarded as *iatrogenic*, as essential hypertension may remain symptomless for many years. In either case, it seems probable that patients who present themselves at an early stage are a selected group in which those with a lower threshold for the development of neurotic symptoms are over-represented. In many other cases, the psychiatrist is asked to see the hypertensive patient on account of some *side-effect produced by drugs*, a depressive or anxiety state, a suicidal attempt or perhaps a confusional episode due to one of the hypotensive drugs; it must be stressed that some undesirable side-effects almost invariably attend the treatment of hypertension with drugs and few patients feel really well while taking them.

If essential hypertension is first seen at an early stage in a patient of 50 years or more, it will be found to progress only slowly or, especially in women, not at all. Complications are, in any event, unlikely to arise for a considerable time. On the other hand, the long-term effects of the disorder are often malign and its complications in the cerebral, coronary, renal and retinal systems make it a leading cause of death. The first task of a physician or psychiatrist is to gain the patient's full confidence and to make a careful assessment of the sort of person with whom he is dealing. This will help him to decide which of these facts should receive the main emphasis in his discussions with the patient. The dominant, over-active, expansive individual will need to be told that he has a reduced expectation of life, but one which may be influenced within limits by the restraint and good sense he brings to bear in the conduct of his life. In the majority of the reasonably mature, stable and intelligent, something of the nature of the condition should be revealed, although it is as well not to be drawn into details as to the level of blood pressure. Moreover, the all-prevalent fears about 'high blood pressure' must be allayed by explaining that the condition often runs a benign course for many years, sometimes remits spontaneously and complications are far from inevitable. Over-anxious, unstable, inadequate and hypochondriacal patients are best left in blissful ignorance as long as possible; the knowledge that they have hypertension may turn them into chronic psychiatric invalids. It is a common psychiatric experience nowadays to encounter the individual in whom a formerly symptomless hypertension has been transformed into a crippling disability by ill-judged pronouncements and sombre warnings. Many patients with essential hypertension probably suffer more from their neurotic anxieties about the disease than from any disability which it inevitably causes.

The majority of patients with emotional disturbances derive benefit from *clear guidance*, *sympathy*, *understanding* and simple psychological help consistently given over a long period.

Among the patients who present with symptoms of hypertension in early or late middle age are many who make *excessive demands on themselves*, are filled with a restless, irritable discontent with life, or who have not yet adjusted their ambitions to an objective appraisal of their capacities. Psychological treatment is of value in such patients, particularly if they are intelligent and have sufficient maturity to co-operate in an exploration of their life-history and personality, aimed at shedding light on their motivation and conflicts.

It may be necessary to advise an anxious hypertensive who is pushing himself too far, to *restrict his responsibilities* and reduce the tempo of his existence. Provided the advice given is sensibly attuned to the personality and takes reasonable account of his economic needs, the patient will usually benefit from it. The aim must be to get him stabilized so as to reduce the likelihood of emotionally induced fluctuations in his blood pressure. If the patient can by a combination of medical and psychological measures be tided over until late middle age the prognosis may be improved.

The *general management of the patient* should be undertaken in collaboration with a general physician. Many patients are obese and derive a great deal of benefit from reducing their weight. This can often be achieved by a restriction of calories to about 1,500 and reduction of salt intake for short periods at a time as in the rice diet introduced by Kempner. Few patients can, however, tolerate salt depletion for long periods, nor should this be attempted as there is some danger of uraemia, particularly in severe hypertensives. An adequate amount of sleep, at least eight hours a night, should be insisted on, and excesses in the consumption of alcohol and tobacco eliminated. A rapidly excreted barbiturate such as sodium quinalbarbitone may be required to counter insomnia.

It is generally agreed that non-progressive, uncomplicated essential hypertension does not call for treatment by means of hypotensive drugs which have found their most successful application in rapidly progressive or malignant hypertension and in cases complicated by cardiac failure. However, in carefully selected patients, headache is relieved, nocturnal dyspnoea improves, left ventricular hypertrophy is reduced, recurrence of cardiac failure delayed, and life may be significantly prolonged by means of these drugs (Leishman, 1959). Where there is reason to suspect coronary or cerebral atheroma or where marked impairment of renal function is present, great caution is required in the use of hypotensive drugs.

Little can be done at present to alter the course of arteriosclerotic psychosis, except where it is associated with hypertension that is itself open to remedy. Severe restlessness and agitation frequently respond to chlorpromazine in doses of 150–400 mg. daily and in some cases the clinical picture is transformed in a favourable direction. Cardiac, respiratory and renal disease are relatively common in arteriosclerotic psychosis and tend to be overshadowed by the cerebral disease (Kay and Roth, 1955) yet it may be disease outside the brain that is partly or even wholly responsible for the delirious features. It may prove susceptible to treatment with corresponding improvement in the psychiatric picture. After acute delirious episodes an attempt should be made where possible to *discharge the patient* back to his family. He may well be able to carry on at home for a considerable time and it is probable that old patients deteriorate more rapidly if kept in hospital away from their folk. Discharge should not be deferred too long, otherwise it may prove difficult to resettle the patient outside hospital. It helps these patients to be kept active, and whether in hospital or outside in the community; before the disease has caused severe dementia a skilled *social worker* may be able to find the patient part-time work, get him introduced to a club for old people, and help to keep his hope alive by paying him periodic visits.

Where a fully-fledged depressive condition complicates arteriosclerotic psychosis, the *agitation and undernutrition* which result are a danger to life, and the question of *electroconvulsive treatment* must be considered. No rules can be laid down which will hold in every case. The treatment carries some risk where there is evidence that occlusion of a large vessel has occurred. But whether or not there is evidence for a previous occlusion, after weighing the risks, the correct decision may be to administer treatment. The results in selected cases are surprisingly good, although the dementia is of course unaffected and the effects may prove to be shortlived. The treatment must be carefully spaced so as to minimize the memory impairment. Convulsant therapy should only be contemplated in the case of a prolonged and severe affective disorder. It is quite unjustifiable to employ the treatment for the more commonly occurring transient depressive episodes, or, in the present state of our knowledge for the delirious episodes of patients with cerebrovascular disease. The advent of antidepressive drugs such as imipramine has provided a very satisfactory alternative to E.C.T. in the treatment of depressions of organic aetiology in old age.

The hopeless prognosis that used to be attached to patients who have suffered from strokes has given place in recent years to a more positive outlook (Adams, 1965). Almost two-thirds of 729 hemiplegics treated over a four-year period regained independence (less than half with use of hemiplegic hands). One-quarter became invalids and the rest died within two months owing to complications. The patients who had died or who became chronic invalids were older than the remainder but there were no significant age differences between grades of recovery. An interesting and unexpected finding was the higher proportion of patients in the recovered group whose lesions were on the dominant side. Among factors influencing the outlook for residual disability Adams lists intellectual impairment, the time that elapses after onset before efforts to restore activity begin, persistence of treatment as long as improvement continues, the willingness or ability of the patient to co-operate and the support on which the patient can count at home. These factors were more important than the extent of the paralysis, sensory deficit, impaired postural control, poor physical condition, hypertension or limited exercise tolerance. 'Mental barriers to recovery' tend to interfere with rehabilitation in a small proportion; they include defective comprehension or neglect of limbs, denial of disability, disturbance of body image, space blindness, apraxia, perseveration, memory impairment, synkinesia, loss of confidence, true depression and emotional lability and catastrophic reaction (Adams and Hurwitz, 1963).

Anticoagulant treatment has been recommended in recent years for progressive cerebrovascular disease. On the whole the available evidence suggests that it has no place in therapy of the great majority of cases of psychiatric and neurological disability associated with this disorder. It may on the other hand improve the prognosis of cerebral embolism arising from rheumatic heart disease and of vertebral-basilar artery insufficiency.

Delirious States

The pattern of outcome of delirious states described above (and represented in Figs. 17, 18 and 19, pp. 550, 551) refers mainly to disorders in which evidence for structural cerebral disease is lacking. A delirious state may arise in association with limited cerebral disease such as a metastasis or early GPI, but these are rare cases and the psychiatric picture is usually more complex. Theoretically delirium could be the first manifestation of cerebrovascular disease but in practice the latter rarely proves to be the explanation of a state of clouded consciousness that comes without warning. In most cases the process is well advanced (before delirium occurs) as evidenced by subtle focal signs and general intellectual or personality change. The principal causes of delirium in old age are cardiac failure, chronic respiratory disease, often with cardiac failure, acute respiratory infection, surgical operations, dehydration and electrolyte disturbances, anaemias, malignant disease, alcoholism and overdosage with drugs, and vitamin and nutritional deficiencies. Causes prone to be overlooked among the aged are the effects of a sudden fall of blood pressure associated with a painless myocardial infarction, the 'silent' pneumonia of the aged, slowly developing prostatic obstruction and on occasion pulmonary tuberculosis. If physical investigation is thorough only a small proportion of cases remains in which *no specific cause* for the attack of clouding can be discovered. Even in these cases an unidentified toxic factor or deficiency may be suspected.

A high proportion of the infective, toxic, epileptic, anaemic and post-operative cases recover but amongst patients with multiple disorder or carcinoma mortality is high. However, cardiac, respiratory and cardio-respiratory cases, which constitute a relatively high proportion of delirious cases treated in psychiatric hospitals, show approximately equal percentages of deaths and discharges; and this pattern of outcome is not wholly explained by differences in the apparent degree of severity of the illness on admission. Prompt medical treatment may tilt the balance in favour of recovery; the onset of delirium in the course of physical illness in an old person should be regarded as a possibly fatal complication.

The clinical picture has already been described (Chapter VI, p. 348) and only those features need be discussed here which have special bearing on the problems of differential diagnosis in the aged. Clouding of consciousness or delirium may complicate the acute initial stages of a rapidly evolving *affective or paranoid psychosis*; it may also appear in the course of a *progressive dementing illness*. In old age a small proportion of cases with a depressive, manic or paraphrenic symptom-complex show clouding of consciousness in the acute phase; it is perhaps in acute mania that this complication is commonest. Where the history in these psychoses does not reveal pre-existing dementia, clouding of consciousness does not necessarily worsen the prognosis for the attack or signify that there is an organic cause for the illness. But a careful investigation of this possibility should always be carried out by detailed neurological examination and a search for possible toxic and infective factors.

The differentiation from acute disturbances occurring in the course of progressive dementia produced by organic cerebral disease such as senile dementia and arteriosclerotic psychosis can be difficult. The terms 'delirious state' and 'clouding of consciousness' are prone to be used loosely in relation to these states. If the dementia is at an advanced stage, the patient will have been totally disorientated and out of contact with the environment even before the acute attack, and it may be difficult or impossible to determine whether any decrease in the level of awareness has occurred. In most cases of senile dementia admitted to hospital the change described as delirium is merely *a state of contentless hyperactivity or incoherent excitement* without demonstrable change in level of consciousness. However, where the dementia is of a much more patchy and partial kind, as in arteriosclerotic psychosis, the term 'delirium' is appropriate provided there has been a definable change in the patient's orientation and grasp of what is occurring around him. The history and clinical picture will frequently permit of a differential diagnosis between an acute deterioration in behaviour in an advanced dement in whom very little improvement towards a clearer state of consciousness can be expected, and a case of delirium complicating an illness of relatively recent onset.

However, in old people a history is frequently not obtainable, and it is important to be able to judge from the clinical picture alone whether or not the patient is likely to show recovery to a more normal level of awareness.

The patient who has been mentally well until recently, and has then developed an acute toxic-infective state, will usually be *well preserved in general appearance* and his *rapport*, despite the clouding of consciousness, will for brief intervals be surprisingly good except in the most severe and florid delirious attacks. Defects of retention and recall will be confined to recent events, whereas in the long-established dement the memory defect will nearly always extend much farther into the past.

A fluctuation in the level of awareness is very characteristic of the acute toxic-infective deliria of old age. During the evening one old man of seventy-one imagined himself in a railway station, saw trains racing past him emitting deafening whistling sounds, hailed railway porters and shook his fist at other passengers. The following morning he was more alert, and though partially disorientated, showed a measure of insight into the hallucinatory character of his experiences of the night before. The same evening he was again acting as if in a railway station. This fluctuation is no longer to be discerned in an established dement and one will not obtain the impression, as in the acute delirious state, that the patient is capable of living, within short intervals, at different levels of consciousness.

As a rule, the well-preserved patient with an episodic type of illness will respond to questions by giving *positive answers*, whereas most senile dements and deteriorated arteriosclerotics will respond in vague terms or disclaim all knowledge even though their answers may show that they have understood what has been asked. The delirious patient will make positive misinterpretations of events and individuals round him, which he will fit into the context of the environment in which he lived immediately before the acute episode. The nurses are children, the doctor the son of a neighbour, the ward orderly a policeman dressed up, another patient perhaps a spy sent to keep an eye on him by an unfriendly relative. There is therefore a *richness in the content of thought* of a clouded patient which is in sharp contrast to the negative, empty and featureless thinking of the established dement.

A characteristic feature of true clouding of consciousness is the *inconsistent orientation* of the patient. His assessment of his whereabouts will vary from one hour to the next and is likely to be prompted by some isolated feature of the surroundings which he seems incapable of relating to its wider setting. This restriction in the perceptual field, the defect of retention and probably the patient's preference for some other environment permit the co-existence of two or more totally incompatible orientations. The patient will not be entirely unaware of the discrepancy but will tend to reconcile his conflicting statements by some fanciful rationalization. A highly intelligent schoolmaster in hospital in Sussex in a subacute delirious state insisted that his Cheltenham home was just a few streets away. As the delirium clears the patient gradually returns the preferred environment to its correct geographical position. But soon after he has regained full orientation he will frequently insist that only a short while before he had been in the preferred surroundings. These misidentifications and rationalizations are not seen in acute disturbances occurring in a severely demented patient.

The differences are not absolute. They will be helpful in distinguishing between acutely delirious patients on the one hand, and on the other hand dements brought into hospital in a state of acute excitement. There may be very little in the clinical picture at a single examination to distinguish between clouding in an early arteriosclerotic psychosis and delirium due to extracerebral disease. But in the former there will nearly always be focal signs and often some evidence of lasting intellectual or other deficit and, over a period of weeks or months, patients with this condition may be found to drift in and out of a state of clouded consciousness. After the clouding recedes, permanent defects of memory and intellect will generally be found. On the other hand when patients with delirium recover they do so with little or no defect. If they die evidence of cerebral disease is nearly always present (Blessed *et al.*, 1968).

In investigating the possible cause of a delirious state it must be remembered that when associated with an acute infection such as pneumonia, the condition may not start until the convalescent stage, perhaps one or two weeks after the febrile illness has subsided. Careful history-taking is therefore essential if some specific cause is not to be overlooked. A simple but valuable criterion is the duration of illness. In the majority of cases the history is one of a few weeks or months in a delirious state, whereas a progressive dementia associated with cerebral degeneration has usually been in progress for years before medical attention is sought. This is of importance in that fulminating physical disease will occasionally so alter the clinical picture that fluctuations of consciousness are not evident and the patient may appear inaccessible or stuporose, thus raising a suspicion of cerebral disease. When the condition proves to be of no more than a few weeks' duration, there is presumptive evidence for mental disturbance that is essentially delirious in character, and a careful search for a specific physical cause is indicated.

TREATMENT. This has been discussed in detail in Chapter VI (p. 385). The section on disturbances of electrolyte balance (p. 357) is particularly relevant for delirious states in the aged as their impaired homeostasis renders them specially susceptible. The 'silent' pneumonia and 'silent' myocardial infarction deserve yet one more mention because of their great importance in the elderly. If intensive investigation should fail to establish a specific cause for a delirious state and recovery does not appear to be occurring spontaneously, it is justifiable and sometimes highly effective to administer a course of antibiotics. Tranquillizing drugs are of great value in the control of restlessness and excitement in delirious patients. Their use is discussed in the section on the organic psychoses of old age. The activation and rehabilitation of these patients in convalescence calls for clinical and nursing skills of a high order. They may prove decisive in returning the patient to the community; without them permanent hospitalization may be inevitable.

Senile Dementia

The expectation of mental disorder shows a steep increase with advancing chronological age and beyond 75 years a large part of this increase is accounted for by disorders associated with degenerative changes in the central nervous system for which no remedies are known at the present time. Of these disorders senile dementia is the most common. Larsson, Sjögren and Jacobson (1963) have estimated that the aggregate morbidity risk for this disorder up to the age of 70 is 0·4 per cent., to the age of 75, 1·2 per cent., and up to the age of 80, 2·5 per cent. For higher ages the estimates were probably less reliable, but the risk calculated up to the age of 90 was 5·2 per cent. In a survey of a random sample of elderly people aged 65 and over in an urban population, Kay et al. (1964a) found a total of 4·2 per cent. of elderly subjects to be suffering from senile dementia, 2·9 per cent. of this being made up of mild cases.

Senile dementia is associated with progressive disorganization of all aspects of personality functioning; there is memory impairment, disorganization of general intelligence, lability followed by blunting of the emotions, reduction in initiative and deterioration of personal habits. The relationship to this phenomenon of the much more limited decline of intellectual efficiency and the personality change associated with advancing age has been much debated. Simchowicz (1910), who gave the senile plaque its name, considered that senile dementia was an accentuation of the normal processes of senescence. In the half century that has intervened much evidence for and against this view has been presented. The question requires independent consideration from the clinical standpoint on the one hand, and from aetiological and pathological points of view on the other.

As far as the clinical aspect is concerned the problem to be resolved is whether the gradual process of intellectual decline that culminates in senile dementia can be differentiated from the mental changes associated with 'normal' ageing. According to Kral (1962) there are two types of memory dysfunction in aged persons. In 'benign senescent forgetfulness' memory impairment is variable, and the failure of recent recall is patchy, being confined to some isolated aspect of an experience which is otherwise correctly reproduced. In the 'malignant' type of forgetfulness, on the other hand, the whole of a recent experience appears to have been forgotten or is inaccessible to recall. There is also some psychometric evidence (Botwinick and Birren, 1951) to suggest that there may be qualitative as well as quantitative differences between senile dements and normal old subjects. However, only surveys in representative samples of the general population can decide whether normal and pathological ageing can in fact be regarded as distinct phenomena. In a recent survey, elderly subjects judged clinically to be suffering from benign forgetfulness were found over a four-year period to have suffered a mortality significantly above normal expectations suggesting that a progressive organic disorder was associated (Kay et al., 1966). The pathological evidence to be discussed below also suggests that the apparently sharp distinction between the normal subject and the senile dement may arise from a 'threshold' phenomenon; an abrupt alteration in the pattern of mental functioning when pathological change exceeds a certain intensity. However, recent genetical observations (Larsson et al., 1963) appear to be in conflict with such a view (see below).

Senile dementia and arteriosclerotic dementia are the two main forms of cerebral degenerative disease associated with ageing and some relationship between the two processes has often been suggested. However, their sex distributions differ, arteriosclerotic psychosis showing a preponderance of males. Recent neuropathological studies suggest that there are probably two relatively distinct processes with some degree of overlap (Corsellis, 1962; Blessed *et al.*, 1968); this could be expected to occur by chance in such common conditions.

AETIOLOGY AND PATHOLOGY. It has long been suspected that a hereditary factor plays a part in the causation of senile dementia (Meggendorfer, 1926). Kallmann's twin studies (1948, 1951) have strongly confirmed the importance of heredity; whereas only 8 per cent. of the dyzygotic twin pairs were concordant for senile psychosis, monozygotic twins were concordant in 43 per cent. of the pairs studied. In the major study by Larsson, Sjögren and Jacobson (1963) the incidence of all forms of mental disorder in the parents, sibs, spouses and children of 377 probands with senile dementia was investigated. These workers found that, whereas there was no enhanced morbidity risk for other psychoses, sibs, parents and children of subjects with senile dementia showed a morbid risk for this condition 4·3 times greater than that in a corresponding segment of the general population. As 'intermediate' forms between senile dementia and normal ageing were absent among the unaffected sibs and children of their probands they concluded that a major autosomal gene with partial penetrance was likely to be at work. However, this finding can be explained also in terms of pronounced threshold effects in the evolution of the underlying pathological process; the transition from the clinical picture of normal psychological senescence to senile dementia might occur abruptly and within a relatively short period of time. Their observations on the life expectation of this condition confirmed those of other workers (Kay, 1959); this was only about 50 per cent. of that to be expected for persons of comparable age in the general population.

Abnormal personalities have frequently been held to be particularly susceptible to the development of senile dementia. It has been found for example (Oakley, 1965) that senile and arteriosclerotic dements are significantly more obsessional in personality than a comparable group of old people without mental disorder. Such results, however, may be affected by the special selection of those with personality defects for admission to hospital. Thus the period of survival of senile dements with loosely-knit paranoid delusions or depressive colouring to their illness is longer than that of individuals whose illness is uncomplicated in this manner (Kay, 1962). However, this is very likely due to the earlier admission to hospital of these patients probably because the personality features released and caricatured by the organic process tend to bring them into earlier and sharper conflict with their environment. In the course of community studies those affected by senile dementia do not appear to conform to any special personality pattern; all types of personality appear to be susceptible.

A similar selectivity probably explains the correlation of senile dementia with adverse socio-economic circumstances that has often been inferred from hospital admission figures. In their Swedish population study Larsson *et al.* found that while crude indices of isolation such as single status were associated with an increased rate of hospitalization there was no evidence that social or other environmental factors had in any way contributed to the aetiology or development of senile dementia. An identical statement could be made about the role of somatic disease. In the 30-year period between 1931–35 and 1956–60 which had seen rapid social changes in Sweden there had been no significant increase in the morbid risk for senile dementia. They concluded that the condition was essentially genetic in origin.

The brain in senile dementia shows a variable amount of atrophy, the sulci are widened and the ventricular system dilated. Microscopically there is a profuse outfall of nerve cells although the cytoarchitecture of the cortex is fairly well-preserved in most cases. The remaining neurones show shrinkage and chromatolysis. Some mild proliferation of the microglia is usually present. Silver stains reveal the presence of senile plaques, neurofibrillary change and granulovacuolar degeneration. The absence of neurofibrillary change has been reported in clinically typical senile dementia but this is rare. The anterior frontal layer may be more severely affected than the motor area and the posterior parts of the cortex. Plaques and neurofibrillary change may be present in the grey matter in the neighbourhood of the third ventricle and also the basal ganglia and thalamus (Grünthal, 1927).

It has long been known that identical pathological changes were at times to be found in the brains of normal old people and that occasionally plaque formation was just as intense in the normal as in the demented individual. Such observations led Rothschild and his coworkers to suggest that the clinical effect produced by a given lesion depends upon the capacity of the personality to compensate for the brain damage present. Consequently little correlation could be expected between the quantitative severity of pathological change and the clinical disturbance (Rothschild, 1956).

However, Corsellis (1962) in a study of 300 cases that had come to post-mortem in a mental hospital showed that there was close agreement between the psychiatric diagnosis of the clinical disorder manifest during life and the nature and severity of the pathological changes found in the brain after death. Thus the great majority of those who had been diagnosed as suffering from organic psychoses showed senile or arteriosclerotic changes of moderate or severe degree in the brain. On the other hand, only about a quarter of the subjects with affective, schizophrenic and paranoid illnesses showed vascular change, atrophy, neurofibrillary change and senile plaque formation to a moderate or severe degree; to some extent this overlap was due to the development at an advanced age of organic pathological changes in subjects whose initial illness had been of a 'functional' kind.

The nature of the relationship between the psychological and pathological changes in cases of senile dementia and those found in normal elderly subjects has been recently investigated in the course of an enquiry in which a large number of psychiatrically ill subjects and persons admitted to hospital on account of physical illness alone were tested with the aid of two psychological measures designed to describe their level of intellectual functioning and their competence in everyday activities in quantitative terms (Roth et al., 1967; Blessed et al., 1968). A high proportion of those admitted with physical disease showed neither psychiatric disorder nor any obvious psychological deficit on clinical examination. In those patients who came to post-mortem detailed pathological studies were carried out and this included a mean plaque count computed in each case from a total of 60 microscopic fields sampled from 12 sections of cerebral grey matter. There was a highly significant correlation between both the psychological measures and the mean plaque count found ($r = 0.77$ and 0.58; $p < 0.001$ in each case). The relationship between dementia scores and test scores and the mean plaque counts in 60 brains are shown in Figs. 25 and 26; there is a broadly linear relationship between the psychological and neuropathological measures. The results suggest that the occurrence of senile plaques (and associated pathological changes) in patients with a wide range of psychiatric disorders and normal elderly subjects alike, arises from the fact that the cerebral degenerative process the plaque represents is closely related to a psychological change that cuts across diagnostic distinctions to some extent: the deterioration of intellectual and personality functioning that is in some measure universal in old age. Among patients diagnosed as suffering from an indubitable senile dementia the association between plaque formation and intellectual impairment showed the same trends but was much less pronounced. This may have been due to the difficulty of measuring differences in psychological performance within a population with relatively severe deterioration, as also of quantifying the pathological change in the presence of intense plaque formation. It seems likely that the differences between well-preserved, mildly impaired and unequivocally demented subjects are of a quantitative nature, though the possibility that senile dements are qualitatively apart in respect of some pathological change that remains to be discovered cannot be excluded. Plaques are found in 80 per cent. of well-preserved subjects over 70 years old who die from acute illness or accident. A certain amount of the degenerative change measured by plaque counts may therefore be accommodated within the reserve capacity of the cerebrum without causing manifest intellectual damage. In other words the clinical picture of senile dementia may become manifest when

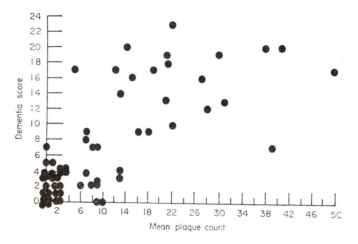

FIG. 25. The relationship between dementia score and mean plaque count in 60 brains post mortem.

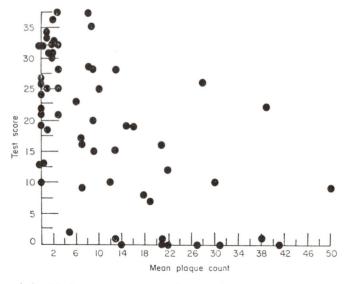

FIG. 26. The relationship between test score and mean plaque count in 60 brains post mortem.

a certain threshold is passed by the degenerative process. All the pathological changes described in association with senile dementia—plaques, neurofibrillary change and granulovacuolar degeneration—have been found to a limited extent in well-preserved old people. Neurofibrillary change in healthy old subjects is often found confined to the hippocampal region (Gellerstedt, 1933; Tomlinson *et al.*, 1968*a*), and this is of some interest in view of the evidence linking the limbic system with memory functioning. However, there is no evidence that damage strictly localized in this area or in any part of the brain produces measurable intellectual deficit. This appears to be invariably associated with diffuse changes.

Plaques provide only one index, and a crude one, of the underlying degenerative changes in the cerebrum in old age. Their association with the outfall of neurones has long been suspected and recent electronmicroscopic studies by Liss (1960) have confirmed that plaque formation is always secondary to neuronal degeneration. Plaques found in authenticated cases of Alzheimer's disease have also been reported by Kidd (1964) and Terry *et al.* (1964) on the basis of electronmicroscopic studies, to consist of degenerated nerve cell processes, intracellular amyloid and reactive microglia and astrocycosis.

The independence of arteriosclerotic and senile dementia has frequently been called into question both on clinical and pathological grounds. The findings of Corsellis (1962) showed that the processes were distinct to a large extent, overlap between the two kinds of change being found in only about 20 per cent. of the brains studied. It has also been shown (Blessed *et al.*, 1968) that the mean plaque counts in subjects with unequivocal cerebrovascular disease did not differ significantly from those in normal subjects suggesting that the overlap between the two processes arose from fortuitous coincidence of two disorders which were both common in old age.

CLINICAL PICTURE. Few cases begin under the age of seventy and there is a *preponderance of females* (in contrast to arteriosclerotic psychosis, which is commoner in males) which may arise partly from the much higher rate of survival of women into advanced age. The onset is gradual and the disease may seem at first to be an acceleration of the normal process of ageing. The patient's memory usually becomes affected first; he is unable to retain or recall recent events though his *memory* for remote experiences seems intact. An old lady speaking of the village where she had spent her childhood remarked 'I can remember it as clearly as if I had seen it yesterday'—she had (Pratt, 1953). There usually appears at the same time some *diminution of vitality*, a narrowing of interest, a *blunting of emotion* and a tendency to petulant and irritable behaviour. Soon the patient's sleep is disturbed, and he potters about the house turning out cupboards, putting lights on and off, perhaps wandering out into the street. An acute infection, a fracture, or a sudden change in circumstances may at this stage precipitate an *acute delirium* with severe restlessness, auditory and visual hallucinations, and paranoid suspicions which may lead to a violent assault. Recovery from such an episode is never complete and leaves behind in most cases a dementia far more severe than the history shows to have been present before it.

The prognostic significance of the *memory impairment* that is found so commonly in normal elderly subjects is at present uncertain. Parsons (1965) described considerable impairment of memory, often independent of any generalized dementing process in over half of the women aged 80 years and over investigated in the course of a community survey. It was rather less common in men surviving to this age. The view that many memory impairments in elderly people are of a benign nature has been given more detailed expression by Kral (1962) who emphasized the patchy character of the benign forms of memory impairment and the tendency in old people so affected to forget relatively unimportant details such as the name or place as distinct from the experience itself which is subject to recall and can often be correctly reproduced. These interesting observations require confirmation with the aid of systematic enquiries among aged subjects over a long period. Evidence for the affinity of, at any rate, some forms of 'normal' memory impairment in old age with senile dementia is the great increase in mortality over the normal expectation in individuals with memory defects (Kay *et al.*, 1966). The possibility that memory defect in an elderly subject, particularly when it shows some signs of progression, is a premonitory sign of senile dementia should always be considered. Such a finding demands detailed physical and psychiatric investigation for it may, of course, reflect instead the early stages of decompensation in the course of cardiac or cardio-respiratory disease.

Although the illness begins in an insidious manner and its evolution proceeds evenly it usually *advances with rapidity*, and two or three years after the first symptoms have made their appearance the patient may be quite changed; slow, blunted, apathetic, and physically feeble and shrunken. Memory grows rapidly worse, possessions are mislaid and others are blamed for losing or stealing them. Gaps appear in the memory for the events of the day; at first the patient is adept at confabulating to fill them, or dissimulating with a kind of affectation of ignorance when examined. In the early stages of the disorder a façade of mastery and full grasp of the situation may be successfully maintained particularly in those of high intelligence and privileged socio-economic status. When combined with the excellent preservation of long-established social responses the presence of a mild or moderate degree of dementia may be effectively concealed. Attempts at formal psychological testing may be sidetracked or a lifelong lack of interest and power of concentration in the course of such activities may be laughingly protested. If the subject co-operates her performance may be marked by extreme orderliness or stereotypy, irritability or impatience which may be interpreted as attempts at warding off a full 'catastrophe reaction' (p. 139). Yet the picture of *'presbyophrenia'* in which a defect confined to memory impairment is seen in a setting of a well-preserved demeanour and a cheerful, talkative, extroverted manner, is rare. The manner is there often enough, but it generally conceals much more than an impairment of retention; on closer scrutiny such patients are usually found to be grossly demented, their friendly, sociable exterior being a deceptive façade. In some patients this social façade is preserved and physical health and vigour seem unaffected for two to three years, a picture more common in women than in men, whose personality disintegrates at a more rapid rate. Yet the illness is rarely seen in its early stages at the clinic in either sex; a history of 2–3 years' symptoms at the least is usually obtained.

With the advance of the disease more and more of the past is blotted out; the death of a marital partner, brothers, sisters, parents, are forgotten. *Islands of memory* stand out but deal mainly with events that have made a vivid and profound impression, experiences during a battle or crisis, or some profoundly moving episode in early life. The patient may imagine he is living in the remote past, even in childhood; he may have wholly forgotten his marriage, or a woman may declare that she is expecting a child. General intellectual defects appear at an early stage. Difficulties in grasp and concentration render thought hazy and fragmentary; essentials are overlooked, and unimportant details seized upon. The patient *tires easily* and *cannot follow an argument*. His difficulties are particularly severe with what is new and unfamiliar. In the early stages he may attempt to adjust himself by an inflexible adherence to routine. In many patients, however, the march of the disease is too rapid for this form of compensation to prove effective for long. There is slowness, perseveration and

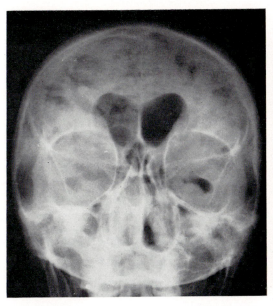

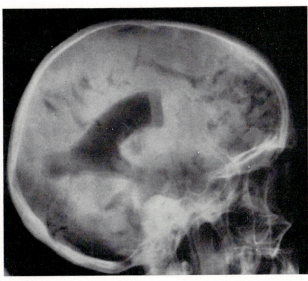

1. Antero-posterior brow-up view showing dilatation of both lateral ventricles and widening of the third ventricle. The sulci over the frontal poles are wider than normal.

2. Lateral brow-down view showing dilatation of the posterior parts of the lateral ventricles without displacement. The widening of the sulci over the convexity is generalised. The fourth ventricle is normal.

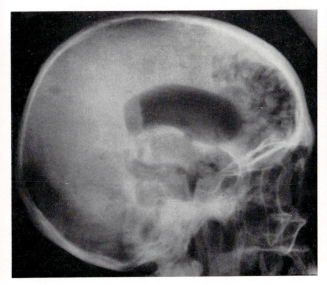

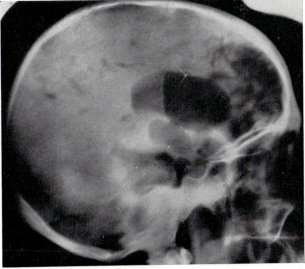

3. Lateral brow-up view showing the same features as 1. The aqueduct is not dilated.

4. Mid-line sagittal tomography showing the dilated sulci on the medial aspects of the cerebral hemispheres. The anterior recesses of the third ventricle are not dilated, thus excluding an obstructive cause for the ventricular dilatation.

PLATE XII

Air encephalogram of female, aged 45, with presenile dementia showing radiological appearances of cerebral atrophy.

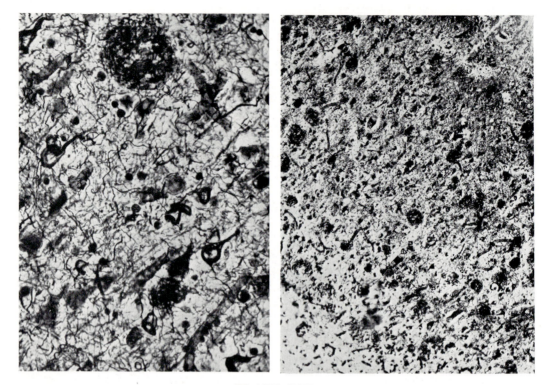

PLATE XIII

Alzheimer's Disease. Section from cornu ammonis impregnated by Hortega's silver carbonate technique. The characteristic histological features are well shown; loss of nerve cells, senile plaques, Alzheimer's neurofibrillary change, microglial activity and residual gliosis are all present. Plaques and neurofibrillary change are evident even under low magnification.
(*Left* ×280, *right* ×70.)

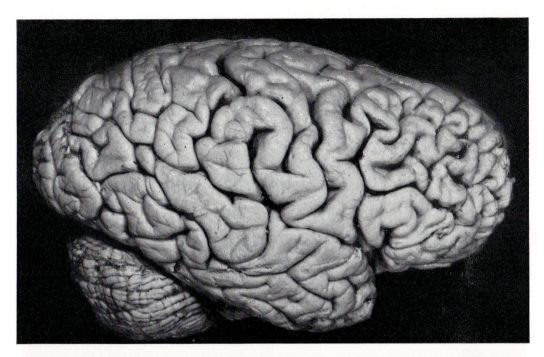

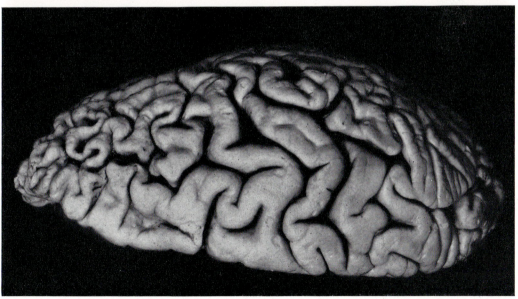

PLATE XIV

Pick's Disease. There is marked atrophy largely confined to the prefrontal regions.

PLATE XV

Dressing apraxia in a case of Pick's Disease. *Right*. Inability to start putting on jacket. *Below*. Inability to continue after being helped into one sleeve.

confusion even with the most familiar and habitual tasks. Speech becomes at first verbose and repetitive, filled with stereotyped phrases and platitudes, and the train of thought is easily lost. As thought becomes fragmented, speech grows more incoherent, replies to sentences are inappropriate and soon consist of fragments of sentences, perseverated phrases and eventually just an unintelligible babble of words. A progressive blunting of emotion accompanies these changes. At first he responds more slowly and less strongly; later a vagueness and flatness of emotional response appear; and ultimately there is a complete apathy or a childish euphoria that finds its expression in the piercing cackle that often resounds in wards for the senile.

In the earliest stages a *depressive colouring* may be seen, with fear of punishment, everlasting torment, and extravagant delusions of guilt and depravity. The mood, however, is shallow and lacks the resonance of ordinary depression; the depressive ideas and affect are transient and fragmented, the full symptom-complex of a depressive psychosis is rarely present. Within a few hours of an outburst of depressive self-accusation, the patient may be euphorically oblivious of it. Even such short-lived depressive episodes are rather more characteristic of arteriosclerotic psychosis, where insight into the patient's failing powers may survive until a relatively late stage.

Delusions have the same protean character, arising as they do from lack of grasp, failure of orientation and an inability to interpret the environment. Patients think the articles they have mislaid have been stolen; the furniture in the ward is their property, the nurses are their children, the doctor is an old friend or neighbour. Any attempt to persuade them to relinquish the rubbish they have hoarded will be interpreted as assault and robbery.

Some impairment of *control of the sphincters* occurs early, and *habits rapidly deteriorate* so that many patients have to be extricated from conditions of unbelievable filth when removed to hospital. Other ways in which the patients often draw attention to themselves are by starting fires, screaming from windows at imaginary persecutors, walking the streets at night in a delirium. The combination of disinhibition, loneliness, absence of normal means of gratification, and impairment of finer sensibilities, may lead in the early stages of the disease to *perverted forms of sexual behaviour;* in such ways the patient may come into the hands of the police. But the emergence of this sort of behaviour in old age for the first time is not always associated with demonstrable deficit, and some cases of this kind present medico-legal problems of considerable difficulty.

Many cases of senile dementia are brought to hospital following an acute *flare-up of a delirious kind.* The mortality in this type of case is exceedingly high (Roth and Morrissey, 1952; Roth, 1955). But even apart from such exacerbations, most cases of senile dementia brought to mental hospitals or observation wards are at a relatively advanced stage of the disease. The history on admission is usually of $1-2\frac{1}{2}$ years' illness. Sixty per cent. are dead within six months of admission, while eighteen months later some 80 per cent. have died. Death occurs from an intercurrent infection, following an injury or fall, from what appears to be a process of *vegetative extinction* with falling weight, declining activity, and lowering of temperature and blood-pressure. It is relatively uncommon for well-defined or specific diseases to be found at post-mortem and nebulous causes of death such as 'senility' or 'myocardial degeneration' are usually given on the death certificate.

Senile dementia may be regarded as a terminal generalized disorganization of the personality in all its aspects; but at present we neither know its causation nor understand its pathophysiology.

X

DIAGNOSIS. The differentiation from conditions such as tumour, and general paralysis, has been dealt with elsewhere. Arteriosclerotic psychosis is differentiated by its more acute, remitting or fluctuating course, the presence of cerebrovascular symptoms and signs, and the better preservation of the personality (see above). Alzheimer's disease is distinguished by its earlier onset, focal symptoms and the discrepancy between physical and mental ageing.

TREATMENT. The section on the general management of old patients should be consulted (p. 560). Early cases may be cared for at home, but if the patient is very restless, violent or noisy, admission to a mental hospital should be arranged. In the treatment of confused, restless, aggressive or impulsive senile patients, phenothiazine derivatives are of proven value. Quite small doses such as chlorpromazine 25 mg. three to four times daily may suffice and can be given without causing drowsiness and apathy that would interfere with the patient's activities during the day. During episodes of severe restlessness much larger doses may be required. Nocturnal restlessness is usually controlled by chlorpromazine, 100 mg. orally or 50 mg. intramuscularly at 12-hourly intervals; this may need on occasion to be supplemented by 2–4 ml. of intramuscular paraldehyde at night. In patients who are undernourished or are known to have lived on a very poor diet, intramuscular vitamins, particularly of the B group, should be administered intensively during delirious episodes. With skilled nursing and rehabilitation the restlessness of many patients with senile dementia abates, their personal habits improve, and their interest, initiative, and ability to occupy themselves may show partial recovery. Many such patients can return to the care of their relatives who should be encouraged at the time of admission to expect discharge from hospital after a period of treatment.

However, the effects of even intensive programmes of social activity and occupational therapy along simple lines are transient (Cosin *et al.*, 1958). Many medical remedies devised down the ages for arresting or reversing the progress of senile deterioration have likewise proved useless. The attempts made in recent years to improve memory functioning in demented subjects by administering ribonucleic acid was stimulated by the suggestion of Hydén (1955) that the structure of the substance would make it potentially capable of storing ten to fifteen or more bits of information. Cameron and his associates (Solyom and Beach, 1961; Sved and Wainrib, 1962; Cameron, 1963) after some years of experimentation used RNA in a 10 per cent. buffer solution which they have administered intravenously to subjects manifesting intellectual deterioration. It is claimed that the treatment produces a change towards normality in the E.E.G., and improvement in performance in a number of psychological tests which include the Wechsler memory quotient and a counting test. The best results are claimed in subjects with memory disturbance due to cerebrovascular disease, followed by patients with presenile dementia of the Alzheimer and Pick type; the response in patients with senile dementia being the least favourable. In all forms of illness the early stages of memory deterioration have responded best. These findings await independent confirmation. In the absence of carefully controlled clinical trials the efficacy of intravenous RNA remains in doubt.

DEMENTIA IN MIDDLE AGE

Under the heading of 'Presenile Dementia' there are usually included *degenerative disorders of the nervous system* that give rise to dementia during middle age. The main diseases bear the names of Pick, Alzheimer and Jakob-Creutzfeldt. But it will also be convenient to discuss in this section Huntington's chorea, a genetically determined degenerative disease of the nervous system which causes dementia in youth or early middle age and therefore has many features in common with the other diseases mentioned.

Dementia in middle age may be due also to disorders whose aetiology is known, such as neurosyphilis, cerebral tumour and myxoedema. The identification of these 'secondary' dementias and their differentiation from the 'essential' dementias has already been considered in the appropriate sections of this book.

The Significance of Presenile Dementia

The concept of presenile dementia was introduced by Binswanger (1898) and afterwards clarified and established by Kraepelin (1909). The latter believed that the diseases were merely severe and early varieties of senile dementia determined by the same aetiological factors but occurring at this period of life in more malignant form. Similar views have found further expression in the writings of a number of authors who have regarded these disorders as *caricatured versions of ageing* of the nervous system. The concept of *'abiotrophy'* introduced by Gowers (1908) has been used to unify all the disorders in this group under a single heading. It has been suggested that they may be attributed to a precocious ageing of the central nervous system due to limited viability of the cells concerned. There would be some advantage in a hypothesis along these lines if it promoted a clear line of attack on the aetiological problems of the group. But unfortunately it does not even serve as a basis for classification, since it exaggerates the similarities and overlooks the differences between the different members of the group. Thus apart from the pathological differences which are themselves striking, Pick's disease appears to be determined by a single autosomal dominant gene, in Alzheimer's disease a multifactorial mode of inheritance may well operate (Sjögren, *et al.*, 1952), while in Jakob-Creutzfeldt's disease no clear-cut genetic causation has been found.

An integrating concept along somewhat similar lines proposed by Jervis (1945) evades the difficulty posed by the heterogeneous pathological and genetic basis of the different disorders in the group. He suggested that the basic process common to senile as well as to all the presenile dementias is atrophy of nerve cells and fibres with some reaction of glia. The differences between the various clinical disorders are due to the variety of genetic or of exogenous factors which may be superimposed on the *basic process of senescent atrophy*, leading to its manifestation in a premature and distorted form. The more conspicuous pathological changes such as senile plaques could also result from such 'secondary' factors. The 'secondary' factor in the case of Pick's disease would presumably be a single autosomal dominant gene. In Alzheimer it might be either some exogenous toxin, as would appear to have been the case in some of the published examples of the juvenile forms of the disorder, or a large number of genes each of small effect. An early version of this theory was the concept of *systemic atrophies* introduced by Spatz (1938), who classified under this heading a wide range of disorders including Pick's disease, Huntington's chorea, Jakob-Creutzfeldt's disease, olivo-ponto-cerebellar atrophy and spinal degenerations such as familial spastic paraplegia and amyotrophic lateral sclerosis. Alzheimer's disease was excluded because of the positive tissue reactions in addition to atrophy, namely senile plaques and fibrillary changes.

More limited concepts have been advanced (Newton, 1948; Sjögren et al., 1952), linking the intellectual changes of senescence, senile psychosis and Alzheimer's disease with a single pathological process developed to different degrees of severity. The evidence from

Sjögren's investigation that *multifactorial inheritance* probably operates in Alzheimer's disease makes this theory particularly attractive, since one would expect the manifestations of a process so transmitted to be quantitatively graded. The evidence that a quantitative gradation in the severity of the process associated with the formation of senile plaques and neurofibrillary change underlies the distinction between normal psychological senescence and senile dementia has been discussed elsewhere (p. 605). The relatively abrupt transition from the picture of normal senescence into a demented state that is at times observed in the evolution of senile dementia appears to be at variance with this view (although it can be reconciled with it). Alzheimer's disease appears to lie even more distinctively and qualitatively apart from normal senescence. Moreover, on the basis of their recent observations of senile dementia Larsson *et al.* (1963) have concluded that the hereditary basis of senile dementia is probably a major dominant gene of partial penetrance. Among the lines of evidence that led to this conclusion was the absence within the families of patients with senile dementia of psychological disturbances that could be regarded as intermediate or transitional between normal senescence and senile dementia. Nor was the incidence of Alzheimer's disease increased.

Moreover, the pathological picture of Alzheimer's disease is not specific, for similar changes have been described in amyotrophic lateral sclerosis and cerebellar atrophies (Jervis, 1945) and in post-encephalitic Parkinsonism (Greenfield and Bosanquet, 1953). In the family described by Worster-Drought *et al.* (1940) in which presenile dementia was associated with spastic paralysis the disorder clearly had some affinities with Alzheimer's disease in important respects although it was distinct clinically from the majority of cases of this disorder. It is possible therefore that in the changes regarded as characteristic both for senile dementia and Alzheimer's disease we deal with the end-result of a number of conditions whose only common feature is that they all give rise to neuronal destruction.

On the other hand with existing methods of observation, there is certainly little at the present time to suggest that within the senile dementias (which constitute the overwhelming majority of cases with Alzheimer type of pathological change) we are likely to be dealing with a heterogeneous group of conditions. Furthermore, the application of quantitative techniques places these matters in a different light. In cases of cerebrovascular disease the senile plaques in cerebral grey matter are no more abundant than in normal elderly subjects, which indicates that not all forms of neuronal destruction lead to plaque formation. The clinical features of Alzheimer's disease are admittedly different from those of senile dementia but pathologically no sharp distinction exists. Moreover, as Sjögren *et al.* (1952) have suggested, 'threshold phenomena' may explain the clinical differences between normal senescence, senile dementia and Alzheimer's disease; as the accumulation of pathological change reaches certain levels, qualitatively distinct phenomena may make their appearance. These could also be expected to show some variation with the age at which the condition becomes manifest. Further, although among patients studied in hospital the transition to senile dementia may appear retrospectively often to have been abrupt, field studies yield a different picture.

The picture of normal senescence often evolves gradually into senile dementia and there is more overlap between the clinical features of 'senile' and 'presenile' dementia than the literature would lead one to believe. Unitary theories that regard both senile dementia and Alzheimer's disease as variants of the pathology of senescence have therefore a good deal to be said in their favour. However, in the present state of knowledge in this difficult field views have to be expressed with reserve and final conclusions must await further systematic observation.

The term 'presenile' has come in for a certain amount of criticism. It has been pointed out that not all cases begin within the period from forty to sixty which is usually implied by 'presenile'. For example, a number of cases of Alzheimer's disease are on record which began quite early in life, others being described as commencing in ripe old age. The confusion as to the precise significance of the term 'presenile dementia' has probably arisen partly from the fact that the occurrence of senile plaques and neurofibrillary changes does not serve to delimit a single clinical entity. For the time being, the disorders in this group can *only be defined* with any consistency *in clinical terms*. When specific cerebral conditions such as cerebral tumour and cerebrovascular disease have been excluded as causes, a case of organic dementia, with focal symptoms and signs, occurring in an individual in whom there is a disparity between the degree of physical and mental deterioration, is conveniently regarded as belonging to the group of 'presenile dementias'.

If the conditions that produce highly specific neurological signs such as Jakob-Creutzfeldt's disease and Huntington's chorea are now set aside, the remaining disorders will mainly fall into two fairly clearly defined groups: Pick's and Alzheimer's disease. Most of the cases defined in this way will be found to have commenced between the ages of forty and sixty. In other words, the most consistent features validating the concepts of presenile dementia are the presence of clinical signs indicative of focal preponderance of the degenerative process and discrepancy between physical and mental ageing. For presenility would be useless as a purely chronological concept. Some individuals are 'senile' before sixty, others 'middle-aged' at seventy. It has to be added that there is a substantial group of cases without focal signs and there is some reason to believe these 'simple' presenile dementias may be distinct from the groups with more specific features (see p. 625).

Alzheimer's Disease

The number of cases of this disease published since the condition was first described by Alzheimer in 1907 does not adequately reflect the incidence of the disease. Sjögren (1952) has calculated a morbidity risk of 0·1 per cent. for Pick's and Alzheimer's disease together, and he estimates that they account for about 8 per cent. of the total number of presenile and senile psychoses. He further estimates that some seventy-five new cases must appear in Sweden each year. Alzheimer's disease is certainly much more frequent than Pick's disease.

AETIOLOGY. The general problem of aetiology of the presenile group of diseases has already been dealt with. There is no doubt that genetic factors make a contribution to causation, but there is some doubt whether the form this takes is polygenic, or as a major autosomal dominant gene, with some diminished penetrance. Some authors write of a 'familial' form of Alzheimer's disease, to distinguish it from the clinically and pathologically indistinguishable cases that occur sporadically without any known family history of the disease. It seems that workers such as Sjögren et al. (1952) and Constantinidis et al. (1965) who have carried out systematic studies of unselected series tend to accept multifactorial inheritance. But on the other side is to be set the considerable number of reports of isolated families in which Alzheimer's disease, fully confirmed pathologically, was clearly manifesting as an autosomal dominant (van Bogaert et al., 1940; Essen-Möller, 1946; Wheelan, 1959; Zawuski, 1960; Bucci, 1963; Feldman et al., 1963; Heston et al., 1966). The latest of these (Heston) describes a family in which 19 persons over four generations were affected by progressive dementia with Parkinsonism and long-tract signs; case histories are provided for 18 persons, and one biopsy and 3 autopsies provided data about the brain tissue in four cases. In this family every affected person had an affected parent; in sibships there was a 1:1 relationship between affected and normal; the male/female ratio was not significantly different from equality (10:8). It seems probable that in the majority of cases Alzheimer's disease appears on a polygenic basis; while distinct from them are the cases in which it is caused by a dominant gene. From an inspection of the pedigrees, it seems that in the latter case the major gene affects males and females with approximately equal frequency (31:31 in the papers noted), while in the multifactorially determined cases females preponderate.

MORBID ANATOMY. Macroscopically the brain is atrophied, the sulci wide and the ventricles enlarged. The cortex is attacked with special severity. All areas are generally affected, although the prefrontal and temporal areas are often more markedly shrunken than other regions, without, however, showing the sharply demarcated atrophy seen in Pick's disease. On microscopic examination there is an outfall of cells affecting particularly the outer three cortical layers; the remaining cells show degenerative changes. Secondary gliosis may fill the gaps left by neuronal atrophy. The two characteristic features in the histological picture are the *argentophil plaques* and the *neurofibrillary change* of Alzheimer. All these changes, including the atrophy, generally affect the thalamus, basal ganglia and cerebellum as well as the cortex, and may attack the mid-brain and substantia nigra (Sjögren *et al.*, 1952).

The plaques, which may occupy most of the cortex in an advanced case, are seen with a silver stain as irregularly shaped masses up to 100μ in diameter. Numerous club-shaped filaments seem to radiate outwards from a dark centre. Degenerated microglia and nerve-cells are mingled with the substance of the plaque, while in the periphery deformed astrocytes may be seen. There is considerable variation in size and form; stars or circular-shaped masses may fuse to form gigantic plaques of irregular shape. Among atypical plaques are the perivascular or 'pseudo-plaques' seen in the familial presenile dementia described by Worster-Drought, Greenfield and McMenemey (1940). The derivation of the senile plaque is obscure. One view is that in the course of ageing the brain colloids change from a highly dispersed to a less dispersed state and tend to precipitate out. The process takes place in the 'ground substance', plaques and neurofibrils being secondary phenomena. The neurofibrillary change consists of an irregular thickening of the fibrils which become bent and twisted into spirals and tangles. The change usually extends over the entire cortex and it is probable that the severely affected cells are functionless (McMenemey, 1940).

More recent histochemical investigations may have opened a new chapter in our knowledge of these changes. Divry (1947, 1952) has shown that the plaques, the fibrillary changes of nerve cells and the senile vascular change described by Scholz, all show an identical histochemical reaction which may be brought out by staining with congo red and examination under polarized light. He considers that the change common to these structures is a form of amyloid degeneration. There is a certain amount of evidence to suggest that the amyloid-like substance emanates from the walls of capillaries and arterioles (Morel and Wildi, 1952).

In two cases of typical Alzheimer's disease, Corsellis and Brierley (1954) employed histochemical techniques and found a substance in the centre of the plaques, the walls of blood vessels and in interstitial tissues which was probably a mucopolysaccharide.

CLINICAL ASPECTS. The disease usually begins with an *impairment of memory* for recent events and a *failure of efficiency* in the usual activities of daily life. Belongings are mislaid, appointments forgotten. A tidy, meticulous man begins to walk about in a daze, his trouser-buttons undone; an efficient housewife lets the soup evaporate, chars the joint and serves the vegetables uncooked. Orientation for time and place are lost or impaired at first for short periods, and the patient becomes incapable of finding his way in familiar surroundings. Later, *orientation for time* and place completely disappears, but knowledge as to own identity is late to be affected. The patient shows a purposeless hyperactivity in an emotional setting of perplexity and agitation as if he were baffled and distraught at the change that had come over him. His behaviour has a futile, repetitive and stereotyped quality that is characteristic. He is constantly packing and unpacking his belongings or sorting them into piles, opening and shutting doors and windows, incessantly polishing furniture and brass or reciting again and again in a voice devoid of expression some verses learned in childhood. Sometimes aspontaneity and loss of drive rather than restlessness is the predominant feature, and Sjögren has found it in fifteen of his eighteen cases at this early stage. He points out the similarity to the lack of initiative shown by patients with frontal-lobe lesions. Incontinence of urine is a further point of similarity.

The illness may develop very slowly. It may, for instance, produce some forgetfulness and lack of judgement in a business man who is still able to put up a tolerable façade. Only when his repetitive story-telling and facile over-activity create difficulties at his work or render him a social nuisance is medical advice sought. Many Alzheimer patients have no insight into their deficiencies and take it lightly if friends and relations do not pay attention to what they say. One patient we observed, deteriorated quickly after a long preliminary period of repetitive hyperactivity progressing over several years. Rather suddenly he became like a child, entirely dependent on his wife who used to send him to the grocer's with a shopping-list and money to buy the household requirements which he was unable to remember. At that time, his gait was already rather stiff and his demeanour greatly altered.

The *emotional disturbances* at the commencement of the disease are variable. When depression is present it has a curiously fleeting, unstable character. Depressive or suicidal thoughts are uttered one moment, a short while later the patient is lost in his hyperactive rituals, perplexed, bewildered or euphoric. A typically sustained, depressive state, leading to actual difficulties in diagnosis from involutional depression, is very rare but is occasionally seen. In such cases there is a danger of suicide, for the patient may have some insight into his illness. Auditory and visual hallucinations and paranoid ideas are occasionally present; but fantastic and childish fabrications and confabulations, forgotten almost as soon as expressed, are commoner. A rather characteristic *change in muscle tone* may be observed at an early stage in the disease. Though it affects both the gravity and antigravity group of muscles it is neither cog-wheel nor clasp-knife in quality. At first both weakness and rigidity are curiously ephemeral, but with progress of the disease the rigidity becomes permanent and then usually has extrapyramidal characteristics. It is probably the relative severity of lesions in the basal ganglia and frontal lobes that determines the type of rigidity that is found in a given case. A facial weakness of upper motor neurone type is a common finding and in the early stages may prove to be valuable in differential diagnosis.

The second stage may be said to begin when *dysphasic symptoms* make their appearance. These are caused by involvement of the temporo-parietal region, and since other parietal-lobe symptoms such as apraxia and agnosia are commonly associated, a complicated interplay of psychological deficits results in which it is impossible to distinguish separate disabilities.

Both expression and comprehension are affected in speech, which is rapidly disrupted; sentences become ungrammatical, incomplete and poor in substantives (Stengel, 1943). There is a senseless repetition of words or sentences, echoing of phrases (echolalia), interminable reiteration of last words of a sentence (pallilalia), and reiterative utterance of parts of words (logoclonia). To the question, 'When did you come into hospital?', one patient said, 'Last week-ik-ik-ik-ik-ik-ik'. She would also reiterate for minutes at a time nonsense syllables such as 'pip-ip-ip-ip-ip-ip-ip'. Writing and reading are affected very early in the condition and sometimes before there is any noticeable disturbance of speech they tend to show the same defects. At this stage *inertia* is prominent, the patient appearing emotionless, dull, apathetic, his attention difficult to arouse. A very strong stimulus may, however, suddenly make him much more accessible, or it may evoke tense, anxious, purposeless hyperactivity. An alteration in the *patient's gait* now becomes markedly apparent; he walks in a slow, stilted and stiff manner, the smooth freedom of the normal gait being decomposed into forced, deliberate, puppet-like movements. He is unsteady on his feet, and, if he encounters an unexpected obstacle, may become locked in position or fall down. The body is carried stiffly and swinging of the arms is reduced, although they are not held in an attitude of flexion. Later on in the disease the gait may acquire the character of the '*marche à petits pas*' which is more reminiscent of Parkinsonism. *Convulsions* are common in Alzheimer's disease, and occur in about a quarter to a third of cases.

When dementia is well advanced, the patients may manifest the '*signe du miroir*', sitting for long periods in front of a mirror and talking to their own reflection: a fascination with the strange, easily evoked moving image of themselves in dements who have lost all memory of their personal identity.

In *the terminal stage* of the disease, the patients show a profound *dementia*, and decline to a vegetative existence. If they are not speechless their talk is a meaningless jumble of words. Contractures and bedsores, forced grasping and groping, and a sucking reflex may appear. The patient is without movement or expression, and there may be forced crying and laughing, or periods of high-pitched shrieking. An interesting phenomenon is the extreme emaciation sometimes observed at this stage, despite the fact that the patient continues to eat ravenously almost to the last.

As senile plaques and neurofibrillary changes tend to be diffuse in Alzheimer's disease, *cerebral biopsy* has been used in recent years to establish diagnosis (Green *et al.*, 1952; Smith *et al.*, 1966). Material obtained at biopsy can be used for the preparation of frozen sections and can also be embedded for preparation of sections stained by the usual techniques.

Sim *et al.* (1966) have recently compared the clinical features in 35 patients with Alzheimer's disease confirmed by means of cerebral biopsy with those in 21 patients with presenile dementia in whom cerebral biopsy proved negative for Alzheimer's disease. While impaired memory, generalized disturbance in the activity of the E.E.G. and apraxia tended to occur early in the Alzheimer cases they appeared late in the other group of subjects. The reverse situation was found in respect of epileptic fits, incontinence, neurological signs, confabulation, personality changes and psychotic symptoms. The differential diagnosis from Pick's disease is discussed on p. 619. The diagnosis of dementia in middle age is discussed at the end of this section.

Treatment is limited to sedation during phases of agitation, maintaining the patient's nutrition, preventing bedsores, and keeping him occupied as long as possible.

Pick's Disease

AETIOLOGY. In this condition, *progressive dementia is associated with cortical atrophy* which is generally more circumscribed than that observed in Alzheimer's disease. It was first described by A. Pick in 1892, and in the four following decades a series of papers (Onari and Spatz, 1926; Stertz, 1926; Braunmühl, 1930) established the disorder as a clearly defined nosological entity. Its independence is supported by a much more distinctive pathological picture than in the case of Alzheimer's disease, and by the evidence that it is caused by a dominant autosomal gene. The main evidence for this is supplied by the definitive work of Sjögren, Sjögren and Lindgren (1952). In Pick's disease, as in the multi-factorially determined form of Alzheimer's disease, there is a considerable preponderance of women. Torsten Sjögren thought that, either there was a lowering of penetrance of the gene in the male, or that there might be a sex-linked inhibiting factor, operating in the female only when homozygous. In a recent report (Schenk, 1959) a family is described in which, followed-up over twenty years, a total of 6 males and 14 females became affected. An interesting observation, and one which provided some support for the independence of Pick's from Alzheimer's disease, was the distinct geographical distribution of the cases in Sweden. The majority of cases of Pick's disease came from near Stockholm, whereas Göteborg supplied most cases of Alzheimer's disease.

MORBID ANATOMY. The *atrophic change* in this condition is *selective*, affecting most severely the outer three cortical layers. The changes are maximal in the frontal and temporal areas, and extension of the process to the parietal lobes is unusual. The affected convolutions are shrunken and have a rough, slightly discoloured appearance. Although the commonest finding is symmetrical fronto-temporal degeneration, atrophy may be confined to the frontal lobes, may be unilateral or may affect the temporal areas only. The histological changes are much more extensive than would appear from macroscopic appearances. The affected areas show a considerable outfall of cells, while those remaining may show varying stages of degeneration with advanced chromatolysis. Normal cells can be in close proximity to neurones showing severe atrophic changes. 'Ballooning' of the nerve cell with enlargement of the cell body, disappearance of Nissl's bodies and extrusion of the nucleus are typical of Pick's disease. The other change commonly found consists of the appearance of argentophil inclusions of a fine granular texture in the cell body. These changes show a much more irregular distribution than the atrophy itself, and their mode of formation is unknown. The atrophic areas show a glial proliferation which may be very pronounced. Senile plaques and Alzheimer's fibrillary changes do not occur, and changes in the blood vessels are very common.

CLINICAL ASPECTS. The most striking changes in the early stages of the disorder are the blunting of emotion and diminution of drive and general coarsening of the character. Affect becomes fatuous and euphoric and this, combined with the diminution of self-restraint and impairment of insight, gives rise to tactless, uninhibited, insensitive behaviour. The patient manifests a brutal frankness with colleagues and friends, begins to tell risqué, lewd stories and behaves in an unfeeling or cruel manner towards his family. All this will usually be out of character for him. His conversation becomes banal, repetitive and inappropriate and his manners deteriorate. Attempts by his family to criticize or correct the patient's behaviour elicit no response. One of our patients, a forty-year-old man, began to pinch his daughter's cheeks and to twist the curlers she put in her hair in the evenings until she screamed in pain and pleaded with him to stop. The patient responded to this with roars of laughter. He had previously been a model father and husband.

The patient's memory and intellectual functions may be relatively well-preserved in the early stages and delusions and hallucinations are rare, but loss of insight is almost complete. The features described, together with the vacant facial expression and fatuous smile are often reminiscent of general paralysis of the insane. The changes in character and the blunting of emotion are prone to lead to difficulties in relation to the patient's work at an early stage. Personal relationships tend also to be undermined and bouts of alcoholism, sexual adventures or other types of anti-social conduct may bring some patients to the attention of the police. From a study of three cases of Pick's disease, Robertson *et al.* (1958) described egocentricity, stereotypy, perseveration and restlessness, an absence of self-criticism and self-restraint, a placid or euphoric mood as being among the most prominent clinical features at early stages of the illness.

The patient loses all liveliness in thought and behaviour and grows inert, apathetic, lacking spontaneity, or becomes foolish and fatuous, constantly laughing and joking, repeating again and again some silly platitude or singing loudly some fragment of a song. Fondness for silly jokes was the first sign noticed by the relatives in one case we have observed. He was a fireman on a railway engine and amused himself and his mates by jumping up and down the footplate whenever the engine was standing in a station. He later became the good-natured clown and 'butt' of the ward in hospital. Another patient in whom the temporal lobes were mainly affected showed a typical sensory aphasia combined with the *'gramophone symptom'* (Mayer-Gross, 1931). Every time a physician or one of the staff came near him, he would repeat with correct expression and diction an elaborate anecdote, seeming himself to be highly amused by it, and could not be stopped until he had told the whole story. After a short interval he would repeat his anecdote as something quite new. Comprehension of speech was almost completely lost. An increased urge to talk, together with poverty of ideation and loss of retention, had produced the symptom. An empty and apathetic mood and euphoric, jocular garrulousness may be seen on different occasions in the same patient.

A *speech defect*, either an amnesic or sensory aphasia, may occur but less commonly and at a later stage than in Alzheimer's disease; the two types of defect are often combined. At first the patient merely omits words or uses them in a vague and peculiar fashion. Soon he experiences difficulty in finding the names of objects, and speech becomes filled with grotesque paraphasias and agrammatisms; sentences are left incomplete, tenses are confused, words and phrases repeated in a meaningless way. Speech rapidly deteriorates to an *incoherent jargon*. In some cases the patient becomes totally mute; alternatively, he may be silent for long periods or show a strong disinclination for speech. Pure motor aphasia is extremely rare in Pick's disease. Reading and writing tend to show defects that correspond with those occurring in speech. Apraxia and agnosia resulting from parietal-lobe destruction are seen in a proportion of cases of Pick's disease but are much rarer than in Alzheimer's disease.

The dementia progresses rapidly, with increasing disorientation and loss of contact with the surroundings, impairment of initiative in thought, speech and movement. The course may be punctuated here and there by brief outbursts of restlessness. In Sjögren's material disturbance of gait was very rare in Pick's disease, and the change in muscle tone characteristic of Alzheimer's disease was also unusual. The two cases of Pick's disease showing alterations in muscle tone proved at autopsy to have no histological changes in the basal ganglia, and Sjögren has therefore concluded that the anomalies of gait, tone and posture observed both in Pick's and Alzheimer's disease, being independent of changes in the basal ganglia, are unlikely to be extra-pyramidal in nature; he attributes them to *frontal and temporal atrophy*, a pathological change common to most cases of both conditions. Where frankly Parkinsonian features have been recorded in Pick's disease as in the case described by Akelaitis (1944) who showed cog-wheel rigidity, propulsion and masklike expression, the basal ganglia have been found to be involved. Robertson *et al.* (1958) have described three cases of Pick's disease, the diagnosis subsequently being confirmed by pathological studies. Each patient showed a hyperalgesia reminiscent of the thalamic syndrome though pathologically the thalami proved to be unaffected. This feature disappeared within a year of admission to hospital as the dementia advanced. The hyperalgesia was considered to be of diagnostic importance.

As the process advances, emotional blunting becomes extreme, and the only change of affect seen is one from monotonous apathy to fatuousness or euphoria. In the terminal stage the picture is identical with that described in Alzheimer's disease.

In *differential diagnosis* from Alzheimer's disease, it is useful to remember that amnesic aphasia, agraphia and apraxia, while occurring in Pick's disease, are all considerably less frequent than in Alzheimer's disease. Despite some reports to the contrary it is to be doubted whether logoclonia ever occurs in Pick's disease. On the whole, the picture in Alzheimer's disease tends in the early stages to be dominated by *parietal-lobe symptoms* and in Pick's disease by *frontal-lobe symptoms*, while the vague resemblance of the former to senile dementia and the latter to G.P.I. is also of value in differentiation. The *disturbances of gait and muscle tone* typical of Alzheimer and rare in Pick would appear to be particularly reliable in distinguishing between them, and the occurrence of *epileptic seizures* is also uncommon in Pick's disease. Treatment, as in Alzheimer's disease, is limited to symptomatic measures.

As far as aetiology is concerned it has been suggested (Malamud and Waggoner, 1943) that Pick's disease is a systemic degeneration of the *phylogenetically youngest areas* of the brain. However, primordial fields such as the temporo-polar and orbito-frontal are frequently affected and microscopically the changes in the cortex are found to be diffuse. In Bagh's large material (1941, 1946) the insula, a phylogenetically old area, was always severely involved, while lesions of the caudate nucleus and substantia nigra were also quite common.

Jakob-Creutzfeldt's Disease

This is a presenile psychosis originally described by Jakob (1921, 1923) and subsequently given its present name by Spielmeyer partly as a tribute to a report of a similar case by Creutzfeldt in 1920. The changes are diffuse involving the deep or superficial layers of the frontal and temporal cortex, the basal ganglia, the cortex of the cerebellum, the optic thalamus, the substantia nigra, and the anterior horn cells. Histologically there is atrophy of the ganglion cells, with fatty change and secondary gliosis. The corticospinal tracts are degenerated and there may be hyperplasia of the adventitia of bloodvessels and perivascular infiltration.

As to aetiology, a positive family history is rare but in a few cases the disease would appear to have been genetically transmitted. In one described by Meggendorfer (1930) the mother and seven uncles of two affected sibs had succumbed to paralysis. In Worster-Drought's case (1933) there were nine affected individuals over three generations.

The clinical picture has been fully described by Jansen and Monrad-Krohn (1938). It is a disease of middle or late life but most cases begin in the fifth decade. In the *prodromal* stage there is ready fatiguability, apathy, some impairment of memory, and unpredictability of behaviour, which may be noticed by family and friends. In some cases dysarthria, dysphagia and uncontrolled laughter and crying develop. Epileptiform convulsions are fairly common. The patient complains, at this stage, that his limbs are weak, his gait may be ataxic, and a defect of speech becomes evident. According to a review by Jervis (1954) speech disturbance is consistently present, other neurological symptoms varying a great deal in their intensity. The disease runs a subacute course, and in the *second* stage, neurological disturbances become widespread, with gross ataxia, growing spasticity of the limbs, and often extensor plantar responses. In the early stages of development of the motor paralysis severe anxiety and depression may be prominent but an acute organic psychosis frequently evolves as the disease advances. This is marked by auditory hallucinations and delusional ideas, variable clouding of consciousness or a frankly delirious picture. Dementia develops with rapidity, and the patient soon loses contact with his environment owing to inertia, failure of attention, and a marked defect in the registration and retention of recent experiences. A tendency to confabulation is prominent in some cases. In this phase of the illness extrapyramidal features such as grotesque choreo-athetoid movements, tremor, and cogwheel rigidity, usually become prominent. In the final stage, speech is an incoherent jumble, gross spasticity and paralysis develop, sphincter control is lost, and death supervenes in a state of extreme emaciation. The exact *clinical picture depends on the areas of the central nervous system which have been attacked* by the disease. Dementia may be the most prominent feature, spasticity and tremor being relatively slightly developed, or the converse may hold. The disease usually proves fatal in one or two years, and no treatment avails.

More recently a number of cases have been reported of a rapidly progressive form of presenile dementia associated with extrapyramidal changes (Jones and Nevin, 1954). This condition, previously described by Heidenhain in 1928, has been regarded as identical with Jakob-Creutzfeldt's disease by many workers. It is, however, regarded as distinct from it by Nevin (1967) who cites in evidence the non-familial character and later age of onset of the disease, the more rapid course with death within 3–6 months, the frequent involvement of the visual cortex resulting in visual failure, the myoclonic movements and the distinctive spike and slow wave discharges in the terminal phase. He also considers the detailed pathological changes in subacute spongiform encephalopathy as differing in many respects from those of Jakob-Creutzfeldt's disease.

Differential diagnosis from other diseases is not difficult because of the characteristic combination of neurological and mental changes. Post-encephalitic Parkinsonism will occasionally suggest itself as an alternative diagnosis. But although the mental development of children may be arrested in this disease intellectual deterioration is very unusual, compulsive symptoms are common, pyramidal signs rare; the converse obtains with respect to all these features in Jakob-Creutzfeldt's disease and sialorrhoea and pupillary changes do not occur in this condition. Differentiation from other forms of presenile dementia may be difficult, but the rapid course and the early severe motor involvement should suggest the diagnosis.

Huntington's Chorea

A very comprehensive review of what is known about Huntington's chorea has been provided by Myrianthopoulos (1966). It seems that the disease was first described in America by Waters in 1848 and others, before George Huntington gave his famous account of it in 1872. Huntington was the third in a family of doctors, and the condition was probably first recognized by his grandfather in 1797. However, Huntington's paper, *Hereditary Chorea* provided the classic description. American workers traced the condition back to migrants from England who landed in Boston Bay and subsequently settled in Long Island. Vessie (1932) described a pair of brothers who emigrated from Bures, a small village in Suffolk, to America, to produce there eleven generations of choreics.

There have been extensive studies of the epidemiology of this disease; prevalence rates vary much from country to country, and even in different parts of the same country. In England the prevalence in Cornwall (56 per million) and Northamptonshire (65 pm) is at least three times as great as in London or East English counties. The highest prevalence in the world is reported in Tasmania (174 pm) much higher than in Victoria (45) and Queensland (23). In the U.S.A. (Minnesota and Michigan) the figures cluster about 50 pm. The lowest world rate, 4 pm, has been found in Japan.

AETIOLOGY. The disease is transmitted by a *single autosomal dominant gene*, and about half the offspring of an affected person can therefore be expected to develop it (Sjögren, 1935). There would appear to be a manifestation rate of almost 100 per cent., and hardly ever does the condition skip a generation. Rosanoff and Handy (1935) have recorded five pairs of twins coming from families affected by the disease. Three of them were monozygotic, and in each instance both twins were affected. Of the two binovular pairs, one was concordant and the other discordant. Haldane (1941) has produced evidence to suggest that there may be sex-linked modifiers which tend to raise the age of onset in males. There would appear to be a phenotypic variation of the condition with age (Pohlisch, 1941); the *mean age of onset* is about thirty-five, when choreic symptoms are predominant. Striate rigidity tends to dominate the picture in the twenties, while in the sixties intention tremor is the leading disability.

In recent years a search has been made for biochemical anomalies which may be associated with the main gene difference and could perhaps provide a genetic marker for the carrier state.

In one study (Cowie and Seakins, 1962) two sons of a mother with Huntington's chorea were found to have raised levels of serum alanine while two other sibs gave normal values. Delinquency may have been an early manifestation for Huntington's chorea in the two affected brothers. Unfortunately no follow-up investigation of this family could be undertaken. McMenemy (1961) describes three cases of chorea, one of them a certain case of Huntington, another with a suggestive clinical picture. In all three cases the serum theta-globulin level was raised and there were abnormalities in the gamma-globulin fraction.

In a controlled investigation (Cowie and Gammack, 1966) of fourteen cases of Huntington's chorea qualitative differences in electrophoretic pattern were not found between the two groups but there was a statistically significant elevation of gamma-globulin in the patients manifesting Huntington's chorea. This finding awaits further exploration. If confirmed, it may prove of value in identifying the carriers of the major gene before the disease is manifest.

MORBID ANATOMY. Macroscopically there is nearly always an extensive and severe chronic meningitis in which the dura may be involved. The *brain is atrophied*, the fronto-Rolandic areas being most markedly affected. A secondary hydrocephalus with gross dilatation of the ventricular system is a prominent feature. There is a marked outfall of cells in the *third and fourth cortical laminae* and the *caudate nucleus* and the *putamen* are atrophied. The globus pallidus and thalamus are usually normal. Histologically the small striatal nerve cells are seen in various stages of degeneration. It is not uncommon to see hypertrophy of the vessel coats, and round-cell infiltration producing cuffing of vessels is sometimes found. There is some degree of variation in the distribution of the changes. The thalamus, substantia nigra, red nucleus and cerebellum may all be involved. No clue has been obtained so far as to the way in which the dominant gene that causes the condition exerts these pathological effects.

CLINICAL PICTURE. Our views on the age of onset have had to be revised since the work of Wendt (1959), which has avoided statistical sources of error by which earlier studies were affected. While earlier workers found a mean age of onset of about 35 years, both for men and women, Wendt shows that a more correct estimate is 44 years (males 44·25, females 43·69), with a standard deviation of about 11 years. In the great majority of cases the illness begins between 25 and 55; but the illness is not unknown in children, the earliest onset reported being 3 years, and it can also come on as late as 70.

Subjects of Huntington's chorea should not marry without full knowledge and agreement of their partners, and should not produce offspring. It is therefore of vital importance to *identify the manifestations of the disease* at the earliest possible phase of their development. There is some evidence that the pre-morbid personality of a person destined to develop Huntington's chorea tends to be more abnormal than that of individuals in the same family who are not carrying the responsible dominant gene. Thus alcoholism and criminality have been frequently recorded as having preceded the appearance of the characteristic neurological and psychiatric symptoms by a considerable interval. Other precursors are impulsive and unpredictable behaviour, outbursts of explosive rage and violence, gross callousness, and sexual promiscuity. The fact that these traits may also be found in some members of Huntington families who are not predestined to develop the condition does not destroy their predictive and eugenic value particularly when they are shown in extreme form. In an investigation of the pre-psychotic personality of 44 cases, Minski and Guttmann (1938) described 9 cases as normal, 8 alcoholic, 2 criminal, 4 violent-tempered, obstinate, inefficient and careless, 3 calm, placid, sober and kindly, 9 reserved, shy and sensitive, 4 querulous and erratic, 2 melancholic and highly strung, and 3 quick-tempered. They also reported the interesting observation that choreic cases tended to resemble in physique and facial expression parents or ancestors who suffered from the disease in contrast to other sibs who tended to resemble the healthy parent.

The *tendency to suicide* was described as a cardinal feature of the condition by Huntington himself. Many cases are on record of both successful and failed attempts at suicide by members of a Huntington family who were themselves unaffected by the disease. Sometimes this occurs very early in life. The tendency to suicide shows a marked familial trend, and a grave view should be taken of any suggestion of suicidal rumination in any member of such a family. Reference to the high incidence of suicide among families affected by the disorder was made in a study of Huntington's chorea in Cornwall (Bickford and Ellison, 1953).

Although most descriptions give the neurological symptoms and signs as the first manifestations of the disease process, detailed investigations suggest that *psychiatric anomalies usually precede* them by a considerable interval. The patient may become irritable, moody, ill-tempered, and show a morose and truculent discontent. He is over-sensitive to slights and may express ideas of reference or paranoid delusions. The picture may on the other hand be one of apathy, slowness, and increasing slovenliness. The condition occasionally makes its appearance soon after severe physical stress such as an operation or acute infection, or following a psychological trauma such as the death of a near relative.

The *involuntary movements* usually commence in the face, hands and shoulders, but it may be some abnormality in the gait that draws attention to the patient. At first the changes are so subtle that the patient just seems excessively clumsy and fidgety. But the restlessness soon acquires its characteristic jerking quality, abrupt movements are seen in the proximal parts of the limbs, and a constant writhing contortion gives the face a grotesque expression. Voluntary movement is accompanied by a widespread irradiation of jerking and muscular contractions. A characteristic feature when the disease has been present for some time is the way in which, in order to conceal the choreic movements, these are exploited to serve volun-tary actions of a quite unnecessary kind. Thus from a forward jerk of the upper limb the arm will be brought back to smooth hair with the hand, or a sudden lurch of the upper trunk will be utilized for brushing a speck of dust from a trouser-leg. A clowning quality is in this way sometimes conferred on the involuntary movements. One of our patients, admitted to hospital at the age of twenty-seven, had been for years a popular member of the local amateur dramatic club: he played comical roles with great success because of his funny movements—which were, of course, the first signs of his choreic illness.

As the disease progresses, voluntary *movement is disorganized* to an increasing degree, the diaphragmatic movements become erratic, breathing grows jerky, and speech acquires an abrupt, staccato quality, with rapid modulations in tone and tempo. Facial expressions are fleeting in character, and a momentary grin suddenly gives place to an expression of squirming distaste. Sooner or later the patient manifests the *apathy and inertia* which are the commonest features of the dementing process in this disease. Thinking becomes mud-dled; he complains of feeling dull, stupid and forgetful, and in conversation shows a striking and characteristic *distractibility* which may be regarded as the counterpart in the sphere of thinking of the ever-changing pattern of somatic movements. This is an example of the influence of motility on patterns of thought to which attention was first drawn by Kleist (1908). Against this background of slow, muddled thought, ill-directed attention and loss of initiative, there are often to be seen attacks of acute restlessness and irritability, and the patient if disturbed or interfered with is inclined to be spiteful, quarrelsome and violent. A fatuous, euphoric or facile affect is the commonest mood-change, but there may be a shallow, ill-sustained depression, particularly where some degree of insight is retained. As the disease advances, the patient becomes increasingly disorientated and inaccessible, insight is destroyed, and the picture tends to become one of fatuity uninfluenced by any change in the environment.

There is little specific in the *dementing process* once it has reached an advanced state, but early in the disease *memory* may be surprisingly *well retained* even when dementia is well established, a feature which sets this disorder aside from many other dementing processes. Moreover, the marked distractibility in a setting of an ever-changing pattern of involuntary movements may be regarded as characteristic of the condition.

Positive *psychotic disturbances* are not uncommon in the disease, although in view of Hughes's statement (1925) that for every case of Huntington's chorea in hospital there are four at home, it is probable that they are over-represented in mental hospital material. The commonest psychosis seen is a shallow, ill-sustained *depression* which is noteworthy because of the frequency with which it leads to impulsive suicidal attempts. It is rare for a depressive symptom-complex to occur by itself at an early stage so as to lead to difficulty in diagnosis from depressive psychoses; in the majority of cases the depression appears when the dementing process has been already established in some degree, or involuntary movements have placed their stamp on the disorder. Ideas of reference frequently develop as a result of the attention the patient attracts with his involuntary movements. In Minski and Guttman's material, however, three cases showed a *paraphrenic picture* with increasing muteness, deterioration and inaccessibility. In his very thorough study of a large case material, Panse (1942) found that the most commonly made mis-diagnosis in a case of Huntington's chorea was one of schizophrenia (general paresis being the next most frequent). He gives a graphic account of a number of these cases, and shows that for years before there are any detectable neurological signs the patient may have shown a schizophrenic syndrome, as a rule of a paranoid kind, and in every way typical. We have to accept Huntington's chorea as one of the possible causes of a 'symptomatic schizophrenia'.

Epilepsy and *mental defect* appear to be common in Huntington families, but the relationship between these phenomena and the genetic basis of the disease is not at present clear. It is possible that the association is due to assortative mating.

Among the variations of the clinical picture which it is important to bear in mind in diagnosis are the cases in which dementia occurs *without choreiform movements* (Curran, 1930). This may occur in individual cases even where chorea was a prominent feature of the disease in previous generations. On the other hand, chorea may be the sole manifestation of the disease, and in Bell's series (1934) as many as one-third of the cases are reported as free from mental symptoms. Cases are also on record in which instead of increasing involuntary movements a progressive rigidity developed, culminating in a picture very similar to Parkinsonism, with rigid, immobile features, and an absence of involuntary movements.

The average *duration* of the disease is some ten to fifteen years, and death usually takes place before the age of sixty, but in some families a much slower rate of progress is observed, with a total duration that extends over several decades.

DIAGNOSIS AND TREATMENT. By far the most important problem in Huntington's chorea is to identify the carriers of the responsible gene at the earliest possible stage. Special attention should therefore be paid to the features of the *pre-morbid personality* which have been outlined above. There is a possibility that, as suggested by Patterson *et al.* (1948), the electroencephalograph may detect the condition in an early state. In our experience a very flat low-voltage record may be found very soon after the onset of the disease, and has been seen to appear *de novo*, at a time when there were no other symptoms or signs, in an individual who subsequently became choreic.

The condition must be differentiated from senile chorea, which is not necessarily associated with dementia and is not familial. Sydenham's chorea is a much more acute disease occurring in younger individuals, and there is no family history. Achoreic Huntingtonians may be confused with patients suffering from such conditions as G.P.I., tumour, presenile and senile dementia only when there is no family history of the typical picture of the disease. Sporadic cases of the condition do in fact occur, and detailed investigation is required in such patients where the picture is atypical, to exclude the possibility of disorders that may respond to treatment.

In the control of involuntary movements there is a limited but useful place for phenothiazine drugs. It is well worth trying the effects of thioridazine in doses of 50 mg. t.d.s. or trifluoperazine 5 mg. t.d.s. (Oliphant *et al.*, 1960). Considerable relief is gained in some cases but pseudo-Parkinsonism may prove a troublesome side-effect. Stereotactically placed lesions (Wycis and Spiegel, 1956) may serve dramatically to reduce the involuntary movements and in early cases, particularly where intellectual deterioration is not yet in evidence, the operation may be worth while considering. Bilateral pallidal or thalamic lesions are well tolerated and may enable the patient to feed himself and to perform simple tasks.

It should not be assumed in every case of mental illness occurring in a Huntington family that the disease is due to the specific gene. *Neurotic and psychotic illness* seems to be *common* in these families, even in individuals unaffected by the disease. Until signs of the progressive disease have unequivocally declared themselves, a neurotic or psychotic disorder should be treated on its own merits. In a case of established Huntington's chorea, every attempt should be made to keep the patient in some form of occupation as long as possible. This may involve frequent adjustment of the nature of the work to match the patient's decreasing capacity, but that this can be carried out, at any rate in rural communities, is shown by the way in which a large number of these patients can continue in spite of their disease in some form of agricultural employment. There is some suggestion that they deteriorate at a more rapid rate when they are institutionalized. In the case of an acute psychosis or dangerous outbursts of destructiveness and violence there may of course be no alternative to hospitalization.

Other Forms of Presenile Dementia

SIMPLE PRESENILE DEMENTIA. It is doubtful whether the well-known categories of Huntington's chorea, Pick's, Alzheimer's and Jakob-Creutzfeldt's diseases account for all cases of dementia occurring in middle age. It is, for example, not uncommon to see cases of rapidly progressive dementia commencing between the ages of forty and sixty without either neurological signs or the focal symptomatology specific for these disorders. The gross discrepancy which is often to be observed between the degrees of general somatic and of intellectual ageing sets many of these cases aside from senile psychosis proper. It was probably considerations of this kind that led Gillespie (1933) to suggest the additional entity of *simple presenile dementia*. He was willing to concede the possibility that these cases represent an early stage of the more specific forms of early dementia but there would appear to be little doubt that there is a group of cases that remain free from focal neurological and psychiatric features throughout their illness. Where such patients come to post-mortem they should be investigated in detail to decide upon the nosological status of such conditions. Some of these cases will doubtless prove on pathological examination to be examples of Alzheimer's or Pick's disease. As distinct from the specific group conspicuous E.E.G. abnormalities are uncommon in the 'simple' presenile dementias.

EPILEPSY OF LATE ONSET AND 'CORTICAL ATROPHY'. It has been generally held for a considerable time that epilepsy appearing relatively late in life is more often than not symptomatic and that a substantial proportion of such patients prove on investigation to have cerebral tumours. However, many such patients investigated in recent years have proved to have no space-occupying intracranial lesion. Air studies, on the other hand, reveal appearances that are frequently considered indicative of 'cortical atrophy'. These changes are also shown in many cases investigated for dementia, and where the picture does not readily fit into a known clinical category the case may be labelled with the radiological change observed in lieu of a diagnosis. '*Cortical atrophy*' has thus in recent years gradually come to assume the status of a nosological entity, though its claims to this distinction are dubious. For the studies of Heinrich (1939) have shown that considerable enlargement of the ventricles and subarachnoid spaces may occur in the course of normal ageing and that there is a range of variation in the appearances at any given age. Unless account has been taken of such facts when the air studies have been assessed, the diagnosis of enlargement may be associated with no sign of dementia. It may well be for this reason also that some authors have found 'cortical atrophy' in schizophrenic, paranoid and other psychoses (Delay, 1944, 1945; Mallison, 1947). Moreover, even where there are good reasons for concluding from the air studies that 'cortical atrophy' is present, this should not preclude further investigation; it may be due to senile, presenile or arteriosclerotic psychosis, an old head injury, or encephalitis, among other causes. (See also p. 629.)

However, even when due regard has been given to these disorders there remain cases whose *aetiology is obscure* and whose nosological status is uncertain. Thus some cases of epilepsy appearing in middle age undergo progressive dementia without exhibiting the clinical picture corresponding to cerebral arteriosclerosis or Alzheimer's disease, nor can any other specific cause be discovered. There are other cases of this kind in which dementia occurs in association with gradually developing focal neurological signs. Thus Jackson (1946) described patients with 'cortical atrophy' commencing between thirty and fifty who were intellectually dull, and showed defects of memory. He observed also pyramidal signs, reduced sensory perception, and in a third of the cases a visual field defect. Epileptiform attacks of Jacksonian kind were common, and eventually led to a mono- or hemiparesis. Mallison (1947) described a premature state of intellectual and emotional decrepitude ('*Versagenszustand*'), the leading features of which were a caricature of pre-existing personality traits, unaccountable though short-lived bouts of depression, apathy, impairment of concentration, and reduced vitality. Such cases, which do not fit into the accepted clinical categories are not uncommon in the experience of psychiatrists and neurologists.

It is too early to suggest a classification of these 'non-specific' atrophies. But in considering the differential diagnosis of dementia at this time of life, the existence of such atypical disorders needs to be borne in mind.

SECONDARY DEMENTIAS. Dementia in middle age may be secondary to syphilis, cerebrovascular disease, trauma, cerebral tumour, myxoedema, alcoholism, and chronic neurological disorders such as subacute combined degeneration of the cord. These conditions have already been described in the appropriate chapters of this book.

Investigation and Differential Diagnosis of Dementia in Middle Age

The most important problem is to differentiate between the primary and the secondary dementias.

A *careful and detailed history* is as always the key to success in diagnosis. It is all the more important here because the patient is often unable to give much help; the picture of a severe or advanced dementia tends also to create a prejudice in favour of an irreversible disorder, the previous history of which may be felt to be merely of academic interest. Information should be sought from relatives or friends; but one should not neglect to obtain any account the patient may still be able to give of his past history and illness.

The *family history* may suggest that one is dealing with a case of Huntington's chorea, Pick's disease or Alzheimer's disease, or possibly one of the cerebellar atrophies. In the first of these diseases the family history alone will often be sufficiently specific for the diagnosis to be suspected.

Study of the patient's past history and personality may reveal a previous suicidal attempt by gassing himself and thus suggest carbon monoxide poisoning. It may lead one to suspect that one is dealing with a case of punch-drunkenness, or may uncover psychopathic or hysterical traits that raise the possibility of pseudodementia.

The *history of the development of the illness* will help to identify neurological disorders such as encephalitis, disseminated sclerosis and severe epilepsy, which tend in later life to manifest some degree of disintegration of personality. It may reveal chronic alcoholism and thus throw light on the picture of a forgetful, plausible, confabulating and rather fatuous middle-aged person whose relatives bring him to hospital because of their increasing concern over his progressive inefficiency, deterioration of habits, or callousness.

The majority of *primary degenerations* evolve in a slow and gradual manner. A sudden onset of symptoms is exceedingly rare, although it has been occasionally recorded, for example in Huntington's chorea. On the other hand, what usually brings the case of heart failure, uraemia, arteriosclerotic psychosis, and many cases even of early cerebral tumour, to hospital, is an episode of clouding of consciousness leading perhaps to restlessness or acute excitement, hallucinations and delusions. This distinction between the gradually progressive course of the primary dementias and the acute, florid, step-like changes in the condition of the secondary group, is useful, but its value is only relative; investigation will reveal that in the latter there has quite often been a period of gradual intellectual decline before the acute episode. This is particularly true of arteriosclerotic psychosis. Moreover, general paralysis and not infrequently cerebral tumour may present with a history of gradually progressive dementia without any spectacular fluctuations. Acute episodes of restlessness or of clouding of consciousness may on the other hand occur in Alzheimer's disease, Huntington's chorea and epilepsy of late onset.

Since it is particularly important not to overlook those diseases occurring at this time of life which may be halted by treatment, namely *general paralysis, cerebral tumour* and *subdural haematoma*, in no case should one fail to inquire after syphilitic infection, a recent blow on the head or such symptoms as headache, vomiting or disturbance of vision. Yet one more condition responsive to treatment, which it is easy to overlook, and which may present with dementia, is *myxoedema*. Pathognomonic symptoms are often lacking in the early stages; for the gradual distortion of facial expression and the increasing slowness of speech and movement over a relatively short time may pass unnoticed by the patient, and even the relatives may fail to mention them if no inquiry is made (see Chapter VI, p. 366).

In an obscure case, particularly with an inaccessible patient, it is important to inquire whether he has had any bout of prolonged substernal pain with or without collapse, or any pain in the chest on effort. A *coronary thrombosis* may be followed by severe mental symptoms as the result of *cerebral anoxia*, particularly where there has been a series of cardiac infarctions. Loss of consciousness with some epileptiform jerking not uncommonly occurs at the commencement of the attack, and often leads to a diagnosis of cerebral thrombosis or haemorrhage; the myocardial infarction may thus be overlooked. Attacks of severe collapse followed by confusion, leaving behind no residual neurological signs, and unassociated with any other evidence of cerebrovascular disease, should therefore be viewed with suspicion. Myocardial infarction as a cause of mental symptoms is particularly prone to be overlooked in hypertensive patients whose systolic pressure may drop to a normal level following a coronary thrombosis. When an acute confusion complicates a case of *chronic heart failure* this is often a terminal phenomenon, but even here it may be some complication such as a superimposed pneumonia which is the cause of the mental symptoms. A careful history is particularly necessary when a patient with heart disease begins to dement. One of our own patients aged sixty with chronic heart disease began to show increasing forgetfulness, inertia and eventually slovenly neglect and complete loss of contact with his surroundings. His history revealed that some six weeks previously he had had a large number of dental extractions. At post-mortem there were multiple cerebral emboli and large vegetations on the mitral valve due to subacute bacterial endocarditis.

On *examination* the *facial features* may betray to the discerning eye the presence of myxoedema; the dry skin, frontal baldness, scanty eyebrows, pinkish nose and cheeks, and vacant ape-like expression are unmistakable. The moon-shaped face and plum-coloured complexion of Cushing's disease, and the empty, fatuous grin and pinpoint pupils of the general paralytic can provide hints which can be followed up during examination.

When a *detailed physical and psychiatric examination* has been carried out, the diagnosis will seldom be left undecided. The specific neurological symptoms and signs in Huntington's chorea, Jakob-Creutzfeldt's disease, and cerebellar atrophy, which have been described above, will permit identification in most cases of these diseases. Signs of raised intracranial pressure or focal neurological lesions may suggest the presence of a space-occupying lesion. Evidence of heart failure and uraemia should now be sought, and a primary carcinoma should always be looked for if an intracranial neoplasm is suspected, although in patients who become cachectic from the progress of malignant disease, dementia seems not uncommon even where no cerebral metastasis is present.

Wassermann and Kahn reactions in the blood should be examined as a routine in all cases. Where the diagnosis remains in doubt after full clinical examination, x-rays of the skull and chest should be taken; they may provide hints as to the presence of a tumour and information as to its primary source.

An *electroencephalogram* may provide further evidence in favour of cerebral tumour or chronic subdural haematoma (see Chapter IX, p. 506, 529). It is also an aid in the identification of cases with prolonged bouts of clouding of consciousness in whom a dementing process may be suspected. In such delirious episodes there may be diffuse, high-voltage, slow activity, whereas in an established dementing process little may be seen beyond some slowing of the alpha rhythm. If there is a disturbance of the electroencephalogram of an acute and temporary type, judgement should therefore be reserved—unless the presence of a dementing condition can be inferred with certainty on clinical grounds.

An examination of the *cerebrospinal fluid* should practically always be made, unless it involves a risk, as for instance when there is a possibility of cerebral tumour or of raised intracranial pressure. This will lead to the identification of cases of neurosyphilis, and may provide valuable evidence in patients with chronic subdural haematoma. A rarity which should be mentioned here is aneurysm of the anterior cerebral artery (McMenemey, 1941). This may undergo such enlargement that it produces pressure on both frontal lobes, and a frontal-lobe syndrome may be seen in a setting of dementia. As a result the cerebrospinal fluid may show some xanthochromia or raised protein from an old leak.

Air studies may provide valuable information, but they should always be carried out at centres where neurosurgical help is readily available, except in the very rare cases in which cerebral tumour can be confidently excluded as a possibility. Even when the investigations have been carried out at a neurosurgical unit, however, the psychiatrist may be called upon to integrate the radiological evidence with other data about the case and for this he needs to know something about *the contribution air studies can make* to the investigation of cerebral atrophy. The problem usually arises in relation to cases with affective or schizophrenic symptoms that, because of atypicality, an unexpected resistance to treatment, or a suggestion of deterioration in personality or intellect, raise the possibility of an early presenile dementia. The x-ray investigations are only one source of evidence, and the findings should not be allowed to override an all-round clinical assessment. But certain findings make cerebral atrophy highly probable. Gross enlargement of the lateral ventricles associated with enlargement of the third ventricle and pools of air on the convexity or over the insula, without distortion or displacement of the ventricular system, always indicate atrophy. A further useful point in diagnosis is that although most patients get severe headache when air is placed over the convexity, those with atrophy often suffer little or no discomfort during or after air encephalography. But, headache does not exclude atrophy. There are many cases, however, in which an unequivocal opinion cannot be given on the radiological appearances alone. It must also be remembered that there is evidence to suggest that the ventricles and subarachnoid space normally undergo a progressive enlargement with age.

The most important application of air studies is, however, in the diagnosis of cerebral tumour. When the cause of dementia remains uncertain after all investigations short of air study have been completed, most types of 'secondary' dementia will have been eliminated as possibilities. But it is often impossible to be certain that cerebral tumour has been finally excluded even though the evidence may be strongly in favour of one of the primary dementias. Such doubts can only be resolved by means of air studies and in some cases carotid angiography, and the patient should be transferred to a neurosurgical unit for these investigations.

The differential diagnosis between the primary dementias has already been discussed. Most cases met with in practice will prove to be examples of Alzheimer's disease; Pick's disease being a rarer condition. 'Simple' presenile dementia and epilepsy of late onset followed by dementia for which no specific cause can be discovered, are less common disorders although not rarities. They are perhaps seen more often in neurological than in psychiatric departments.

It is possible that the situation in relation to presenile dementia will become slightly less gloomy in coming years. Recent reports on low pressure hydrocephalus (Hakim and Adams, 1965) suggest that rare instances of chronic subacute delirious state or dementia in middle or late life may respond to treatment. It is also possible that chronic viral infection may be the explanation of some other rare cases. However, it is too early for a satisfactory evaluation of the promise of these recent developments.

CHAPTER XI

CHILD PSYCHIATRY

INTRODUCTORY

The development of child psychiatry during the last half century, and its well-established position today, make it desirable that its place and range should be clearly defined in a system of clinical psychiatry, such as this book. It cannot be expected that the whole of psychiatry, as applied to children, should be expounded in this chapter; but the commoner and more important clinical pictures and symptoms will be discussed, as far as their incidence and their appearance in the child differ from similar manifestations in the adult.

On the whole, children presenting 'nervous' or psychological complaints have been infrequent in the physician's clientele until lately; and, as Capon (1950) has pointed out, the famous text-books on diseases of children have taken scant notice of psychological illness. One of the reasons for the *indifference of medical men* was that many problems, which are now considered as psychiatric, were dealt with by educationists by pedagogic means. Just as mental deficiency, before being recognized as a field of medicine, was regarded as an educational problem, its constitutional nature and physical implications being ignored until a later stage of scientific development, so the role of psychiatry in the study and treatment of other developmental failures has only recently been acknowledged. Even now, vociferous claims are still made that the emotional maladjustments of children need treatment by education only, either of the child or his parents. But the fact that such maladjustment is so frequently associated with disorders of bodily function makes a medical approach imperative. It is only with the aid of medical training and experience that one can assess the relative importance of symptoms, and differentiate psychologically determined disorders from those caused by physical disease.

Two other factors have contributed to the recent recognition and expansion of child psychiatry: the belief that the origin of the neurotic and psychotic illnesses of adult life is to be found in the experience of early childhood, and the hope, based on that belief, that the psychiatric treatment of children may prevent the psychiatric illnesses of adults. This belief arises from the teachings of Freud and relies for evidence on the interpretation of data provided by adult neurotics during psychoanalytic treatment. Its simple mechanistic character, out of harmony with the detailed observations of modern developmental psychology, has been criticized in Chapter I. The recent discovery by biologists that there are critical stages in the adaptation of young animals, such as birds and sheep, has been cited to support the theoretical existence of similar critical periods in the development of the human infant, but so far without convincing observational evidence.

The hope of *preventing* by psychiatric supervision or treatment in early life a large part of *adult maladjustment or illness* is even less substantial. All that the present state of our knowledge justifies is the hope that in some cases, which we may eventually learn to identify, the chances of illness or abnormality will be materially reduced by sane and healthy up-bringing. The data available, such as follow-up studies from child-guidance clinics and their comparison with untreated control series (Cambridge-Somerville Youth Study, 1951), are insufficient to support the belief that these cases constitute any large part of the total prob-lem. Juvenile delinquency, though admittedly a yardstick of doubtful validity, has been found to be equally prevalent in areas with highly developed child-guidance services as in those without them. It is, however, probably too early to reach any definite conclusions about these results. Furthermore, psychoses, such as schizophrenia, have, in spite of all the assurances of psychoanalytical writers, been found to be uninfluenced in their incidence by early upbringing, home life, and childhood experience. The claims of uncritical enthusiasts that, if only sufficient child psychiatrists and children's clinics could be made available, most mental-hospital beds would become redundant, can be dismissed as wishful thinking.

Whitehorn, in his introduction to Kanner's text-book (1948), draws attention to the contrast between our small knowledge and eager expectations: 'In recent years in America the pressing demand for psychiatric services for children has brought so great an absorption of effort, into day-to-day operation of clinical services as to endanger somewhat the free exercise of that inquisitive, investigative spirit which seeks continually to understand better the nature of the problems presented and the forces which operate for therapy and pre-vention.' We are just as much beset by dogma today as was the case in 1948.

The hope of preventing, on a large scale, the psychological and social failures of adults by the psychiatric treatment of children, may well prove illusory: there are no present grounds other than optimism for thinking otherwise. Even so, as will be seen in this chapter, there is a wide field of *suffering among children and distress among their relatives*, where the psychiatrist can do valuable work. While serious psychoses and severe neuroses based on constitutional psychopathic abnormalities are rarely seen in children, or develop at that time of life to a stage where recognition is easy, more superficial *reactive conditions* are common and are almost more varied than in the adult. This is where the main emphasis falls in child psychiatry; and, thanks to the pliancy and fluidity of the developing organism, these conditions are in many cases easily influenced and remedied. This is the justification of the atmosphere of confident optimism which prevails in children's clinics, which is not so easily engendered in adult psychiatric work.

The fact that the child is so easily influenced by environmental changes of all kinds, and that so many of his symptoms are psychogenic, has made child psychiatry an especially suitable field for interpretation in terms of the *Meyerian school of psychobiology*. From this may arise the influence and success of the Johns Hopkins Department of Child Psychiatry under *Leo Kanner*, who also wrote the clearest, most comprehensive and least doctrinaire text on child psychiatry, to which this chapter owes much.

INCIDENCE: CHILD PSYCHIATRIC SERVICES

Because of the nature of the study—for instance, a very well-behaved child may by some workers be considered abnormal on that account alone—*no reliable figures* for the incidence of psychiatric abnormality in children are available. The numbers attending clinics vary with the provision of practising psychiatrists and psychologists and their skill, and, even more, with the attitude of teachers and parents towards the clinic and to psychiatry in general. Widespread public concern about juvenile delinquency, and eagerness to secure the welfare of children, have not removed prejudice, as vociferous against the psychiatric treatment of children as of adults.

Child psychiatry began as an *offshoot of the study of mental deficiency*, which is still its largest problem both in size and social importance. The first book in English on the subject, by Ireland (1898), deals almost exclusively with intellectual retardation. In this country, under influences described in Chapter XII, mental deficiency has developed along an independent line. *In Europe*, 'Heilpaedagogik' included the study of retardation both of emotions and of intellect. Educationists founded progressive schools and organized special classes in collaboration with medical specialists.

In the United States the forerunner of the child guidance service was a psychological clinic at the University of Pennsylvania, established by Lightner Witmer in 1896. William Healy founded a clinic in Chicago, mainly for the purpose of studying juvenile delinquents. He used psychologists, social workers and doctors; and this was the beginning of the multi-disciplinary or team approach to psychiatric work with children. Since then 'the team', consisting of psychiatrist, psychologist and social worker, forms the nucleus of most clinics in English-speaking countries. Healy later transferred to the Judge Baker Foundation in Boston, and in 1912 the Boston Psychopathic Hospital opened its doors to children. *In Britain* development took place a good deal later. In 1939 there were 30 child psychiatric or child guidance clinics in Great Britain; in 1958 there were over 350 such clinics, though a large number of them were only part-time. Opinion in this country has veered towards the view that child psychiatric clinics should if possible stand in close liaison with children's hospitals, or with the paediatric departments of general hospitals.

In Britain, the scarcity of trained psychiatrists, the avidity of educationists and psychologists to tackle all manner of children's problems, and the parsimony of local authorities, have in many places delayed the setting up of fully staffed clinics. Blacker (1948), when trying to plan the psychiatric services required for the country, distinguished between *child-guidance centres* and *child psychiatric clinics*, the former with a non-medical staff or with a visiting psychiatrist only, the latter under psychiatric direction. Presuming that 1 to 2 per cent. of all school-children are in need of clinical advice and treatment every year, Blacker estimated that ten centres and three to four clinics have to be set up for every million of the population, in which 200,000 children between the ages of three and sixteen will be found. There is, however, in this estimate no provision for mental defectives, nor does it make allowance for children below the age of three. More recently (1960) the Royal Medico-Psychological Association has estimated the need to be one clinic team per 200,000 total population.

As a provisional measure, until more medical personnel are available, this project may be acceptable, but even then for the larger cities only. In smaller towns and country districts, where only one clinic can be set up, the cheaper 'centre' will be preferred by local authorities. The psychiatrist is often excluded from the direction of the centre, though, as will appear in this chapter, his part is an essential one.

Views on the organization of *in-patient treatment* for children differ widely, even in the United States where child psychiatry has made such vigorous strides in the last twenty years. 'Stefansburg' in Zürich, the oldest child psychiatric unit in Europe, having been founded by E. Bleuler, is today run entirely by teachers as a boarding-school, although under the direction of a child psychiatrist. It has no nursing personnel, and is completely removed from the hospital atmosphere. Many medical schools in Germany, Scandinavia and the U.S.A. have small children's in-patient units, connected with psychiatric or paediatric hospitals. They form a part of the hospital, and have visiting teachers only. Holland, on the other hand, has only a few out-patient clinics for children. Maladjustment is regarded as an educational problem and, apart from these clinics, is left to teachers who do their work in a great variety of schools. Britain has at present about one dozen in-patient units for children, each of twenty to thirty beds; they are parts of psychiatric hospitals and are under the direction of psychiatrists.

PSYCHIATRIC EXAMINATION OF THE CHILD

The psychiatrist experienced in observing and examining the unwilling, uncooperative resistive or stuporose patient should, one would have thought, be able to observe and examine the child, even if at the first meeting with the doctor he be shy, resistive, sulky or mute. This is not entirely true; there are parallels in the two situations, but also differences. *The child's inaccessibility* may indicate no severe mental disturbance, though in the grown-up this is as a rule a sign of a serious, often psychotic, disorder. As the child's resistance is superficial and transient, the physician must try to overcome it. He must make allowance for the special sensitivities of children, make use of play and other techniques to get information, and be aware, especially with small children, of the part played by non-verbal communication, gesture, mime and expressive utterance. As Kanner has said, 'a sustained discussion of himself is not a part of a child's way of living'; and yet, as the same author emphasizes, the initial contact of physician and child may be 'a crucial event'. One should try to have a talk with every child over six. The amount of information one can obtain is sometimes astonishing, and if the child will talk at all his observations are often remarkably pertinent. Too little use is generally made of the ordinary interview between doctor and patient in child psychiatry, special indirect methods being exclusively relied on.

It is clearly important, in order to understand the case, to get an *'objective' history* from one or both parents, a guardian or teacher. None of these informants can give more than a partial account, so that it will be all the better to exploit every suitable source of information available. Parents are emotionally involved in the abnormality or failure of their child, and feel personally responsible. What their report lacks in objectivity it may make up by supplying clues to the aetiology. The psychiatrist will listen quietly to the mother's story and give her her head, however biased she may seem, before he finally puts his questions.

Because of the importance of what may then emerge, many psychiatrists doubt the wisdom of leaving to the social worker *the first interview with the mother* who brings her child to the clinic. There is plenty of exploratory as well as remedial work after the initial examination, for which the assistance of the social worker is essential.

Indirect methods of exploration of the child's mind may be verbal, as when he is asked to talk about his dreams, his waking fantasies and imaginary companions, or to say what his choice would be if he were given the fulfilment of three wishes by a fairy. More important are the non-verbal methods, such as watching the child drawing, finger-painting, modelling, or at play. The *play technique* has been elaborated and studied more than all the others. Play may be controlled and the situations so arranged as to reveal the child's outlook and reaction to his special situation; or it may be free and uncontrolled. The method of combining treatment with examination in play therapy has been largely developed by psychoanalysts. Their views on the procedure, and especially on the use of interpretation, vary widely (e.g. Anna Freud, 1928, and Melanie Klein, 1937).

It is debatable how far play techniques should be applied by the *non-medical psychologist* of the team. He certainly has to use these and similar indirect methods if the child refuses to co-operate in the usual tests. His original field is the cognitive abilities and scholastic prospects of the patient, as far as they can be ascertained by psychological test methods in the widest sense. This is important work; large numbers of intellectually subnormal children are brought to the clinics because of their backwardness, or because of other complaints closely connected with it. Beyond the crude results of tests of personality and maturation as well as of intelligence, the experienced psychologist can contribute observations made on the child during testing which may provide clues for the total assessment and treatment.

MENTAL DEFICIENCY

This numerically highly important part of child psychiatry is the subject of a later chapter, where the recognition of mental deficiency in infancy and early childhood, the evaluation of test results, the clinical picture, social and educational consequences, and treatment, are fully discussed. The student is referred to this part of the book which, as far as it concerns itself with mental deficiency in childhood, is to be regarded as part of the present chapter. It is a regrettable shortcoming, in our view, of a book on child psychiatry such as Kanner's that he excludes from consideration the main problem of the great numbers of intellectually subnormal children, glossing over their abnormality by blaming the intellectual requirements of 'the culture which surrounds them'.

It is a truism that high-grade defectives may be 'as . . . stable or unstable, secure or insecure, placid or moody, aggressive or submissive as any other member of the human species'. But they also show, more frequently than the average or above-average child, *signs of maladaptation not explained by their intellectual defect alone.* This needs an explanation. Moreover, the symptoms of emotional and conative abnormality take on in the feeble-minded and the dull a special colouring which makes it often difficult to discover their nature. In the majority of cases it is for these symptoms, and not for his lack of scholastic achievement, that the child is sent to the psychiatrist. Every child psychiatrist, therefore, should be familiar with the high-grade defective and his peculiarities, and the innumerable ways in which his life is influenced by his defect.

PSYCHONEUROTIC REACTIONS AND PERSONALITY DISORDERS

There is no difference in principle between the psychiatric formulation required for a discussion of psychopathic behaviour in the child and that needed for the adult. The general section on terminology, aetiology and pathology, as well as the special forms of reaction and personality, described in Chapter III, should, therefore, be consulted for a proper appreciation of what follows. The occurrence and manifestations of psychiatrically abnormal reactions at different periods of life have been mentioned there in each instance. It was also emphasized that, in the authors' view, these reactions and deviations of personality represent variants of normal behaviour and personality equipment.

This tallies well with the point often made in recent writings on child psychiatry, that the most frequent 'abnormalities' of child behaviour are, in fact, *normal stages in development*, which have, in our patients, been extended in time or in significance. This applies to such symptoms as enuresis, hesitation in speech, indulgence in rocking movements before going to sleep, magic rituals reminiscent of obsessional behaviour, etc. Lapouse and Monk (1958) studied a representative sample of children between the ages of six and twelve;

in a high proportion the mothers reported behaviour characteristics commonly thought of as pathological, and there was evidence that the mothers were underestimating the amount of 'abnormality'. The authors thought that these characteristics might well be no indication of psychiatric disorder, but merely a transient developmental phenomenon in essentially normal children. The frequency of psychiatric symptoms, singly and in combination, was also studied in children selected from birth registrations by McFarlane, Allen and Honzik (1954), with comparable findings.

Similar reservations must be made about certain *personality features*, which are common and normal in childhood but, when carried on into adult life, represent psychopathic traits which can be interpreted as due to delayed maturation. Submissiveness, weakness of will-power in the face of temptation, impulsiveness in action which is guided only by affect, lack of foresight and living under the impact of the present, are normal in childhood, when full allowance may be made socially for them. In the adult the same allowance cannot be made; one has the problem of psychopathy, and special measures are required. Clearly, psychopaths of these kinds could not have been recognized as such during childhood.

Another peculiarity of psychiatry in children is due to the *lack of any clear-cut expression* of mental abnormalities. In the unformed and developing organism, constitutional variations do not show themselves in the well-known, relatively definite, psychological forms with which we are familiar in the adult. They produce instead failures of general adjustment which take their content and colour from the environment. Hence the prevalence of relatively *simple and transparent modes of reaction*, closely connected with the stage of development through which the child is passing; that such things may be the precursors of serious deviations of personality, can only be discovered later. This is not always so. Mothers and elderly relatives sometimes make remarkably accurate prognostications, from evidence which seems insignificant to the expert. This may be because they are able to draw upon a full, if intuitive appreciation of the situation, and the recollection of what was shown at the same stage of development by others of the same family stock who have now grown up.

If one considers, from the point of view of the biologist, the helplessness of the newly-born infant, the long duration of his childhood, and the variation in pace of development both between different children, and between the physical, intellectual, emotional and sexual aspects of the same child, one is not surprised to find that obstacles and difficulties may arise at every stage. The functions of sleep and waking, intake of food and excretion, speech and skilled movement, sexual and emotional behaviour, have to be integrated, and may be disturbed in the process. They may become centres of symptom formation. Such disturbances, though often only localized and partial, may also be *signs of a general impairment of development*, which later may provide the predisposition for a severe neurotic illness. Anomalies, such as enuresis, sleep-walking, prolonged dependence on the mother, are found a good deal more often in the early histories of adult neurotic patients than in control cases; if a number of them are accumulated in the same individual they may be the indications of a neurotic or psychopathic predisposition (Mayer-Gross *et al.*, 1949).

On the other hand it is to some extent characteristic of the symptoms of children to be shown and to remain as isolated abnormalities, indicating a difficulty of integration *at a certain stage* and *in a special field*; and in this case they are of little value in predicting later mental maladjustment or disease. As a rule they disappear without trace, as happens with most episodes of truancy or thumb-sucking; and others which persist through life, such as a stammer, or food-fads, or nail-biting, do so without impairing adjustment in other fields.

The clinician who has to treat the disturbed child will allow only a relative importance to single symptoms. In order to arrive at a plan of treatment and a prognosis, he has to gain a *picture of the child as a whole*, to weigh features of strength against ones of weakness, assets against deficiencies or forms of dysfunction.

The Parent–Child Relationship

The child is more responsive than the adult to the emotional atmosphere of the environment in which he lives; and for the child too young to go to school, the home makes up the whole of that environment. The relationship between the child and his parents and other members of the family therefore assumes a central importance. If the relationship is amiss, one may expect unhappiness for the child and an increased probability of neurotic symptoms or behaviour disorders. Thus Bowlby (1951) has attributed a central importance, for the healthy mental development of the child, to the existence of 'a warm, intimate and continuous relationship with his mother in which both find satisfaction and enjoyment'.

MATERNAL DEPRIVATION. It has been maintained, and sometimes still is maintained, that separation of mother and child, or changes from one to another mother-figure in the crucial first three years, or failure to form a satisfactory relationship with a mother-figure, may lead to a permanently distorted development of the personality. This is commonly known as the hypothesis of Maternal Deprivation, on which a very large amount of work has been done during the last twenty years since it was first formulated by Bowlby. In more specific terms it is supposed that the extreme susceptibility of the child to the effects of maternal deprivation is shown during the first year or two years of life, after which this susceptibility diminishes. Support for this view is derived from ethological studies of bird and mammalian life, which indicate that in the young of some species 'imprinting' effects occur which may finally determine a behaviour pattern; thus the young gosling can be trained to accept a human being as the mother-figure. So far, however, no evidence has been found for the importance of such processes in the human infant.

Bowlby's first work on the subject of maternal deprivation was based on forty-four juvenile thieves (1946); he concluded that the specific abnormality of personality development which resulted from maternal deprivation was a deficiency in forming adequate interpersonal relationships; what eventually emerged was an affectionless, psychopathic child, adolescent and adult. There was an enhanced probability of delinquent behaviour and, among delinquencies, thieving was especially likely. Deficiencies of development, however, could occur not only in the temperamental but also in the cognitive field; psychologists have found that maternally deprived children, e.g. those brought up in institutions, have lagged behind their peers especially in verbal intelligence. The whole field has been reviewed by a number of authors in a W.H.O. booklet edited by Ainsworth (1962), and has also been subjected to a very useful critical review by O'Connor and Franks (1960).

However, criticism has not been lacking, not only from outside but also from within. Bowlby himself (1958) was led by his re-examination of the relevant facts to conclude that 'statements implying that children who are brought up in institutions or who suffer other forms of serious privation or deprivation in early life commonly develop psychopathic or affectionless characters (e.g. Bowlby, 1944) are seen to be mistaken.' The validity of the maternal deprivation syndrome, standing on its triple footing of (1) a specifically susceptible age span, (2) a specific psychic trauma, and (3) a specific distortion of personality development, has been devastatingly attacked by Barbara Wootton (1959), also in Ainsworth (1962); in fact, at the present time little of the original structure can be said to remain. There is practically no evidence that a limited experience of maternal deprivation occurring at any age produces irreversible effects. The earlier retrospective case studies of delinquent children with serious personality disorders found a significant incidence of severely depriving early separation experiences. But later prospective follow-up studies of children who have suffered early prolonged and severely depriving separation experiences showed a small incidence of delinquent outcome.

Hilda Lewis (1954) studied 500 children, boys and girls, admitted to a reception centre because of neglect (111), being uncontrollable (90), loss of parental care (78), pilfering (50), etc. Psychiatric disturbance in these children was associated with (1) a neurotic or psychopathic mother, (2) mother lacking in affection, (3) father lacking in affection, (4) prolonged stay in public care, (5) illegitimacy. It was found that a mentally disturbed mother tended to produce a neurotic reaction in the child. Unsocialized aggressive behaviour was more likely if either the mother or the father were not affectionate, or if the child had been in public care. However, separation from the mother as such did not seem to be particularly important; unless it had occurred before the age of two years, and had been lasting, it bore no statistically significant relation to the normality or otherwise of the child's mental state at the time of admission. No clear connexion was evident between separation from the mother and any particular pattern of disturbed behaviour. Neither delinquency nor incapacity for affectionate relationships was significantly more frequent in the separated children. Children long exposed to the dislike or indifference of their natural mothers gained rather than lost by separation, provided they passed into kind and sensible hands.

In many of the studies supposed to show the effects of maternal separation or deprivation, the subjects were living in a deprived state, e.g. in a 'broken home', at the time of the study; this would not suggest the importance of a critically susceptible stage in the child's life at an earlier time. The specificity of the psychic trauma has also been eroded, since much of the work has been done on institutionalized children, who may represent a genetically biased selection, and who may well have suffered from other deprivations (e.g. nutritional) than that of maternal love. Wootton says that the main result of much work has merely been to show that deplorable patterns of upbringing are prevalent in institutions. Thirdly, the specificity of the response has become blurred. Little by little a great range of behavioural anomalies has come to be associated with forms of maternal deprivation more and more loosely defined.

As an example, Hewitt and Jenkins (1946) made a study of the so-called conduct disorders. They examined 500 case histories of problem children referred to the Michigan Child Guidance Institute, using the routine case records of children of 11 and 12 years and a mean I.Q. of 94. Forty-five traits were taken from the case histories, and correlations were calculated. A cluster analysis then showed three clusters of intercorrelated traits, and related to them by significant correlation coefficients there were three clusters on the parental side. Parental rejection went with unsocialized aggressive behaviour on the part of the child; parental negligence with socialized delinquent behaviour of the child; parental repression with over-inhibited behaviour by the child.

Attempts at a better formulation of the maternal deprivation hypothesis have led to a subclassification into sensory, social and emotional components. This standpoint has been taken up by Laurence Casler (1965a,b; 1968), who notes the accumulation of evidence, both on the human and animal level, that impoverishment of sensory stimulation, e.g. along tactile and vestibular pathways, and 'perceptual deprivation' may have significant consequences for development. This formulation too, however, requires more rigorous definition.

It must be noted finally that doubts have crept in whether there is any statistically reliable association between a delimited period of separation from the mother and any subsequent abnormality. Douglas and Blomfield (1958) reporting on the National Survey of the later development of a population sample of children born in 1946, noted that 52 per cent. of the legitimate children were separated from their mothers at some time between birth and the age of six. Comparing the separated and non-separated children there was no significant difference in the incidence of neurotic traits, if the children remained at home. If there was a separation both from mother and from home, one symptom showed up more frequently in the separated than the non-separated children—bed-wetting.

The effects of maternal separation and maternal deprivation have recently been reviewed by Yarrow (1964). He concludes that the evidence is convincing that harmful effects result from marked deprivation of sensory, social and affective stimulation, such as the child frequently has to suffer in institutional life; but much of the evil effects of separation from the mother have been caused by unfavourable features of the environment into which the move was made.

However as Wootton has pointed out, research into the effects of maternal deprivation has been of value in mitigating the conditions under which children had been reared in institutions. It has also encouraged more enlightened attitudes in children's hospitals and exerted beneficial effects on the practices of organizations responsible for the care of illegitimate and homeless children for whom it is now usual to arrange adoption or foster-home care with the least possible delay.

THE BROKEN HOME. If the specific postulates of the theory of maternal deprivation are abandoned, we are left with a formulation of a much more general kind, to which there are few who would take exception. This is the homely truth, in the words of Barbara Wootton, that children 'need to be dependably loved, and that without such dependable love, they are likely to become frightened, unhappy or mentally retarded'. There seems to be no reason to suppose that it has to be the child's blood-mother who supplies this love, or that a kind, loving and sensible aunt, granny or foster-mother cannot fulfil the need. The maternal deprivation theory, deprived of its specificities, merges into the theory of the 'broken home', which also has been held responsible for a multiplicity of psychiatric and psychosomatic disorders in children, and perhaps particularly for juvenile delinquency.

The studies made on the significance of the broken home in the aetiology of behaviour disorders in children are, if anything, even more numerous than those made into maternal deprivation; but the results obtained are much more consistent. In the field of delinquency, especially delinquency in girls, the evidence supporting the view that the broken home plays an important role, is strong and consistent. This theory too has been sharply criticized by Barbara Wootton, but mainly on the grounds of being insufficiently precise. The definition of what constitutes a 'broken home' is indeed a matter of considerable difficulty. One may choose a wholly objective definition, which does not do justice to the psychological circumstances; or one may choose something more psychologically apt, at the cost of introducing a subjective element. However, on either basis, the findings made for example in the field of delinquency, are consistent.

Among the objective definitions of a broken home one of the best is that of Carr-Saunders, Mannheim and Rhodes (1942). They classified homes into four types:

'(A) Normal family consisting of husband and wife, who are parents of the case, and children (including the case) living at home.

(B) Normal family, as in (A) with the addition of others, relatives, e.g. grandparent(s), or non-relatives (lodgers).

(C) Other families, with two heads of the household (male and female), e.g. uncle and aunt of the case, or step-father and mother of the case, or father and mother cohabiting but not married, etc., and children (including the case) living at home, and others, relatives or non-relatives.

(D) Families with one head of the household only, e.g. widowed mother of the case, and children (including the case), and others.'

These authors applied these standards to nearly 2,000 delinquent boys, equally divided between London and six provincial cities, and matched them with an equal number of control boys of the same age from the same schools. In London 25 per cent. of the delinquent boys came from families of types C or D, as against 13 per cent of controls, in the provinces 32 per cent. as against 18 per cent. in controls. In their report on delinquent girls Cowie, Cowie and Slater (1968) noted that 58 per cent. of the girls in a year's intake to a classifying school came from homes of types C or D. Other authors have used slightly different definitions, but agree in finding a higher 'broken home' incidence in boy delinquents than in controls, and a higher incidence in delinquent girls than in delinquent boys.

Objection can be made to the reliability of these findings in the field of delinquency, because many of the samples studied may have been selected, in part at least, by the magistrates or other social agencies for the very fact that the home background of the child was known to be broken; this would be a reasonable cause, for instance, for deciding that institutional care was called for. However, the raised incidence of broken home is still found when one retreats further and further away from any possible effect of administrative selection. Thus it has been found, not only in children who have been committed to care, but also in samples of those convicted, regardless of committal; in samples of those charged, regardless of conviction; in samples of those against whom a complaint has been made, regardless of whether they were charged or not; and finally in samples of those, selected from the general population, who have, in the anonymity of the research enquiry, provided their own statement of delinquent or aberrant behaviour (Cowie et al., 1968).

If we ask what kind of breaking of the home is of particular aetiological significance, forms of breaking which involve emotional tensions and stresses show up in relative prominence; merely being orphaned, for instance is much less dangerous for the child than living with his natural parents when they are constantly quarrelling. The disturbing effect of such emotional stresses is shown predominantly at the time; if the child can be removed from such an unsatisfactory environment he responds very well to treatment or rehabilitation. Really lasting effects usually result only from years spent in a psychologically traumatic background.

It must be admitted that we know very little of the specific effects of unfavourable aspects of the home environment; nor do we know whether there are, as some believe, any particular danger periods in the development of the child when unfavourable circumstances will have their maximum effects. In practice we have to make the best use we can of ideas which may seem to be mere commonplaces. The child in his dependence needs love and attention, and, in order to feel secure, some consistency in his environment. He can be expected to thrive when his parents are themselves well adjusted, affectionate and placid. It seems that excessive strictness may tend to produce neurotic patterns, and excessive indulgence and permissiveness tend rather towards delinquency; worse than either is an unpredictable variation from one attitude to the other which leaves the child bewildered and deprived of all security. Any sudden change in the environment, and particularly one in which there is a sharp fall in the level of affectionate protection, may produce an emotional crisis, especially in the insecure or over-sensitive child. Going to school, admission to hospital or being left to stay with relatives may act in this way. Neurotic tendencies in the parent may evoke or reinforce neurotic traits in the child. Dissensions between the parents, and exhibitions of strong emotions of anger or fear, seem particularly likely to arouse insecurity and anxiety. What is remarkable, clinically, is that the mental health of children from unfavourable homes is as good as it is. Even from such homes the majority of children develop normally; and gross disturbances of behaviour or neurotic states may be shown at times by children from happy and sensible homes.

Some special modes of reaction have been held to be particularly dangerous for the child. A mother may seek compensation for her unhappy marriage by building up strong emotional ties with her son. Unable to face the prospect of his separation from her, she may block or delay any step he takes towards greater independence, and so encourage in him the development of a dependent and inadequate personality. Another pattern which is frequently held accountable for neurotic symptoms, is seen when the mother comes to be regarded as the source of all love and tenderness, and the father is a remote figure whose relationship with the children is largely that of a disciplinarian. Plausible as it is that such constellations may cause neurotic symptoms in the child, there is no sure proof and we do not know how frequent and how important they are. Similar doubts apply to suggestions that only children, and the first and the last child in a sibship are specially endangered. One might expect that such children would be more prone than others to be domineering or demanding, or to remain babyish, dependent and lacking in self-reliance. We do not know that this is so.

Adverse home circumstances are not, of course, the only causes of failure of adjustment in childhood. We cannot even say of any particular symptom or syndrome that it must be caused in this way. Nevertheless such circumstances are common, and where they are found they may be assumed to be playing some part, and to be making the adjustment of the child so much the more difficult. This will be true in conditions in which the primary cause of abnormality is to be sought elsewhere, such as in cases of epilepsy. If the unfavourable environmental factors are then ignored, treatment of the primary condition will probably be less successful than it otherwise would be. In other cases, the adverse environment may prove to be the main or even the only significant cause of maladjustment, and should be the focus of the therapeutic attack. One must, however, be wary of jumping to conclusions, of assuming merely because of the existence of a neurotic symptom in the child that the environment must be at fault, in total disregard of the lack of any positive evidence that it is so.

It is quite common even for highly intelligent parents to show very little insight into the nature of the situation within the family that contributes to or causes the child's behaviour disturbances. In such cases the psychiatrist is frequently able to give help by relatively simple measures. In addition to providing specific treatment for the child's illness, his aim must be to educate and encourage the parents to adopt an objective attitude towards the problem that confronts them. He too, should remember his own inadequacies and the uncertainty of all his insights. As Lauretta Bender has remarked (1962): 'For fifty years, child psychiatry has been identified with the child-guidance movement, emphasizing the use of psychotherapy in child guidance clinics directed at the child–parent relationship in all behavioural problems of childhood. Evaluated follow-up studies comparing children after prescribed treatment in child guidance clinics with children who "defected" in treatment after the initial diagnostic interview, have shown no difference in the outcome.'

Isolated Symptoms

DISORDERS OF SLEEP. Investigations into the physiology and psychology of sleep, which have recently been reviewed by Oswald (1962) and Kleitman (1963), are of great interest and importance to the psychiatrist and neurologist. Kleitman's work, with a bibliography of over 4,000 titles, gives a comprehensive account of a vast range of phenomena. There is of course no human function in which there are not differences between the sleeping and the waking states, not to speak of such intermediate conditions as the hypnotized state, somnambulism and somniloquy; and the examination of changes between sleeping and waking, along biochemical, physiological and electro-physiological lines, leads to theoretical problems many of which are unresolved as yet. Nevertheless recent advances have been so great that earlier theories of historical importance, looking for the regulation of sleep in humoral changes, or in reflex irradiating cortical inhibition, now find little support. The predominant view is that wakefulness is the positive phenomenon, sleep itself being thought of as a passive state, needing no special mechanisms for its onset. Waking is controlled by a subcortical centre, most probably in the mesodiencephalon. In the infant the spontaneous rhythm generated by this centre involves short cycles recurring a number of times in the day, with about twice as much time spent sleeping as waking. With the maturation of the individual, largely as a result of processes of learning and habituation, the waking centre comes gradually under cortical control. This finally results in a single twenty-four hour cycle, in which the proportions are reversed, and twice as much time is spent waking as sleeping.

INSOMNIA AND RESTLESS SLEEP. Disturbances in the development of the normal pattern are only rarely due to a fault in the central component. Lethargic encephalitis and narcolepsy, in which a lesion of the sleep centres may be suspected, are rare until after the age when the sleep rhythm has been differentiated, in school-children or adolescents. On the other hand *peripheral causes of disturbance* may be important. Any kind of physical illness which can cause pain or other forms of sensory stimulation, alimentary disorders, or the breathing difficulties caused by adenoid vegetations, may disturb sleep. Children who are getting an inadequate amount of sleep are generally fidgety and restless or liable to outbursts of temper; but it is doubtful whether lack of sleep is the cause of such symptoms or only an associated manifestation.

Lively active children sometimes show unusual patterns of *motor behaviour in sleep* such as tossing, jerking or talking, crying out or screaming without waking up, and grinding the teeth. They are mostly of little significance, but may at times be indications of emotional difficulties. To the same group of anomalies belong certain *rhythmic movements shown before going to sleep*, especially head-rolling, 'jactatio capitis nocturna'; in rare instances motor phenomena of these kinds may be seen when sleep is very deep. As a rule these symptoms disappear when the child grows up. If there is other evidence of emotional upset, and no physical cause can be found, an environmental stress can be looked for: disharmony between the parents, the excessive strain of competition with an elder brother or with school-fellows, or the anxious solicitude of the parents for the child to excel.

Y

Sleeping difficulties often arise from or are made much worse by the fact that *parents* easily become disturbed about any minor anomaly that is shown. The *emotional tension rises at bed-time*, and dramatic scenes ensue. Kanner refers to three typical ones: 'Refusal to go to bed, with arguments, excuses and delays; rituals, crying, calling, playing after the child has gone to bed; waking at night, calling for mother or father until the child has been "calmed" or taken into the parents' bed.'

These children often show other signs of defective training in feeding, excretion, etc., which the physician may only discover after asking about them. The parents themselves may be irregular and erratic in their sleeping habits; and by direct suggestion, in conversation about late nights, or grumbles about the noisiness of the neighbourhood, they may be the immediate cause of the symptom they deplore. Treatment can only start when the nature of the situation has been understood, the parents are made aware of it and are prepared to collaborate. It consists in giving the regular and consistent habit-training which should have been provided from the earliest age.

SLEEPWALKING. Sleepwalking is quite common; it has been estimated that about 1 per cent. of the general population are occasional sleepwalkers, and up to 6 per cent of children having any type of sleep disturbance. Sometimes it has been found to run in families. Physiologically it is looked on as a partial break-through of the sensory and motor block (de-afferentation and de-efferentation) by which the cortex is normally isolated during sleep; and clinically the state is more akin to waking, with symptoms of hysterical dissociation, than to the normal sleeping state. As an isolated symptom, it is rarely brought to the attention of the physician, and he usually meets it only when there are also other neurotic complaints. His main duty will probably be to point out its insignificance.

Children who cry out or talk in their sleep often sleepwalk too; and there is a connexion between somnambulism and night terrors. For all these symptoms a subsequent amnesia is the rule; but unlike the child with night terrors, the typical sleepwalker shows *little sign of affect*, walks slowly and deliberately, and engages in no dramatic action. Although perception is reduced or narrowed, he seems to find his way and avoid objects, and is rarely in danger. Accidents, even severe ones, can however occur; and if the sleepwalking pattern obviously involves risks, accidents must be guarded against.

If sleepwalking occurs frequently and persistently, it may well be an expression of a conflict in the child's life, such as a division of loyalties between parents, siblings or friends, or the first unrequited love for a grown-up. If, with treatment, the symptom is not resolved, it may be easily influenced by suggestion.

NIGHTMARES AND NIGHT TERRORS. These two forms of reaction to fear in sleep, though similar, should be kept distinct. Nightmares can be experienced at any age, and are in essence no more than frightening dreams. Night terrors are peculiar to children, mostly between the ages of three and eight years, and are not seen after puberty.

If the child has a nightmare, usually a dream of a threatening kind of men or animals, he wakes up, lies awake *remembering the dream*, and calms down quickly from his fear. The night terror has been described by Roger (quoted by Kleitman): 'Suddenly, while fully asleep, after a short period of agitation and one or two groans, the child sits up in bed, eyes wide open and facial expression one of terror. Pale, covered with perspiration, he extends his trembling arms, as if to protect himself against an approaching enemy.' The child is in a twilight state, usually cannot be wakened, and is not accessible to calming words of reassurance. He still sees whatever it is that terrifies him, and sweating and other physical evidence of fear continue, perhaps for half an hour, until of his own accord he falls into a deep and peaceful sleep. There is complete amnesia for the attack as well as for the dream content.

Nightmares are relatively harmless and pass off, either of their own accord or after attention to a precipitating cause. One of the commonest causes, in adults as in children, is distension of the stomach by food or by gas, pressing on the neighbouring structures. Alternatively it may be found that the child has been reading over-exciting stories in the evening, or that he tends to twist the sheets round him in his sleep causing restriction of the limbs, or to creep with his head under the bedclothes.

Night terrors are more serious. They may interfere with the life of the whole family, and prove intractable to simple methods of adjustment. For this reason they have often been taken to be signs of an illness with a physical basis. Epilepsy, hypoglycaemia, and carbon dioxide intoxication due to respiratory obstruction from adenoids, have at times been blamed, and may in rare cases be responsible. On the basis of the E.E.G.s of seven patients with night terrors, Maria (1956) concluded that it was a form of psychomotor epilepsy. Grand mal attacks, occurring in deep sleep without convulsion, have been observed with the aid of the E.E.G.; if then the subject were forcibly awakened, the convulsion would occur.

More usually, however, night terrors are regarded as a neurotic reaction to a conflict situation. In eleven case histories quoted in Homburger's text, they occurred in the children of alcoholic fathers who came home late at night, and in the children of quarrelling parents. They have also been found in children with psychopathic traits, including delinquent tendencies. Night terrors may also be a symptom in a child of anxiety neurosis, which is discussed below.

Other interesting departures from normal sleeping patterns are shown in the heavy sleep of many brain-injured and hyperkinetic children, and the depth of the sleep in which enuresis often occurs. Psychotic children, on the other hand, often sleep lightly; and they may wake up in the night, and babble away and play oblivious of the dark, and generally occupy themselves as they do during daylight.

DISORDERS OF FOOD INTAKE. The digestive system is one of the first to respond to any disturbance of the child's well-being. Refusal of food and food-faddism, nausea and vomiting, abdominal pain and constipation, may equally be the symptoms of a psychogenic upset or those of an infection or general systemic disease. When one of the psychological variants of these symptoms occurs, it is not infrequently a *sequel of physical illness in the past*. Then the child enjoyed the special care and attention of the mother, and after physical recovery he may continue with the same symptom as long as it retains her attention. If one wishes, one may interpret this as the result of the child's wish to dominate through his symptoms, or as the persistence of a conditioned pattern of behaviour so long as the requisite stimuli are applied. It may also be, however, that the physical illness has left a somatic weakness behind; or that there is a constitutional instability of the vegetative nervous system, which shows up both in the physical and the psychogenic upsets of the alimentary system.

In paediatric and child-psychiatric circles there has been a radical change in the approach to *infant feeding and weaning*. The rigid schedules that once obtained have given way to more flexible feeding regimes; and with this the number of children with feeding problems coming to children's psychiatric outpatients clinics has diminished to a trickle. Some now claim that most of the feeding problems which used to fill the clinics were iatrogenically induced.

In some cultures emphasis has been placed on the value of breast-feeding to the infant. Largely on the basis of psychoanalytic concepts, it has been held to be necessary if child and mother are to achieve a mutually satisfying relationship. Of this there is no proof. The subject has been reviewed by O'Connor and Franks (1960), since when there has been no new work of importance. In the United States, where parents are very open to psychological guidance, the frequency of breast-feeding has dropped dramatically, though at the time of writing there are hints of a change in the opposite direction. Practice in child-feeding seems to be much affected by non-medical and non-psychiatric influences, and tends to be a matter in which there are changes of fashion from time to time.

The decision whether to breast-feed or bottle-feed, and when to wean, depends a good deal on social considerations, on the mother's ideas on the subject, on her attitude towards breast-feeding and her relationship to the child. Similar factors affect the question whether the feeding regime will be well organized, or flexible and permissive. It may be well, for instance, to advise the rather indecisive and inadequate mother with little self-confidence to have a definite feeding schedule, whereas the child of a perfectionistic and obsessional mother is best not exposed to such a regime.

REFUSAL OF FOOD AND FOOD FADDISM. In our last edition we wrote that these problems were very common, and were presented by a quarter or more of the children attending psychiatric clinics and paediatric clinics. This seems to have been to a large part caused by the anxieties of mothers to rear their children by the best scientific standards. Now that scientific standards have been made more flexible, and approach closer to the folk ways of unsophisticated peoples, the problems are receding again.

Children show a great variety of feeding preferences and habits, and the regime to which they adjust should itself be adjusted to their individual desires and needs. A generation ago the paediatrician Davis (1928, 1935) showed in experiments on self-selection of diet in young children, that they were well able to choose the diet which best suited them and thrive on it, without any adult direction. His experimental subjects were 'omnivorous' and governed not only by caloric needs but also by preferences which changed from time to time in an unpredictable way. If today the psychiatrist is asked to advise in a case of food-refusal or food-faddism, he will look for the source of anxiety in the feeding situation as the prime cause of refusals and difficulties, and will probably pass off the food-fad as a temporary and harmless affair. We have found that if force, bribing, cajoling and similar tactics are abandoned, and nutritional perfectionism allowed to lapse, food-refusal and anorexia, the one-time dreaded *crux paediatrica*, disappear.

NAUSEA AND VOMITING. Nausea and vomiting are in children readily provoked by any mental upset, and also by any disturbance of physical health. They may be the early signs of a serious physical illness, such as meningitis or cerebral tumour. Vomiting may also be a physiological mode of self-protection against over-eating.

Once it has been established as an *easily released mechanism*, vomiting may appear in the child in any situation of unhappiness, frustration or excessive excitement. The child who dreads going to school may vomit earlier in the morning. Vomiting at meal-times is generally part and parcel of a variety of feeding difficulties; one-third of Kanner's children who had such problems were also liable to vomiting and gagging. Vomiting at night may occur with over-fatigue, or with over-excitement at a game or party. The cause in small children is usually not far to seek, and once found can soon be remedied. In school-children something more may be required. The cause may not be so obvious, and may for instance be found in a forcing of the pace by ambitious parents or teachers, or an unhappy relationship with a school-fellow. Even after the basic trouble has been put right, some active step, such as a few but impressive suggestions from the doctor, may be needed to terminate the abnormal pattern.

Cyclic vomiting, lasting two to five days and recurring after weeks or months, represents a definite clinical syndrome. The causation is not fully understood, but there is always severe ketosis and usually acidosis during attacks. These may be precipitated by events with an affective colouring, and the patients often have emotional problems of some seriousness. Cyclic vomiting may be the *precursor of migraine* in the adult. It never outlasts puberty. The attacks are usually brought under control by the administration of glucose in small, frequent doses, and sodium bicarbonate gr. 15–30, 4–6 hourly, to combat acidosis.

Abdominal pain, colic and constipation in children have been thought to be psychogenic, without much proof; but considering how sensitive the child's digestive tract is, psychological causes may well be the important ones in some cases.

With rather more justification, *rumination* and *pica* have been regarded as evidences of mental abnormality. Rumination, the returning of food from the stomach into the mouth without nausea, may be an apparently pleasurable habit, which may lead to loss of weight and serious consequences. It can be combated by symptomatic treatment and fully engaging the child's attention elsewhere between meals. Pica, 'perverted appetite' in children below one year of age, is mainly found in neglected and retarded children who are inadequately nourished. The tendency of the baby between four and nine months to put into his mouth everything within reach, may last longer in backward children. There are, however, no cravings for special substances, as in the pica of pregnant women. Normal nourishment and proper care easily cure the habit, even though, as in severely retarded children, it extends to the swallowing of its own faeces.

DISORDERS OF EXCRETORY FUNCTIONS. Encopresis, involuntary defaecation in children, not directly attributable to any organic lesion, is a sign of a serious disturbance and is relatively rare. Enuresis, on the other hand, is so frequent that one-quarter of the children seen in clinics all over the world are brought there because they are enuretic. The symptom rightly takes up considerable space in books on child psychiatry.

ENURESIS. The real *number of enuretics* is probably much higher than appears from the statistical data available in clinics. Parents are reluctant to disclose the child's bedwetting, because, in their mind, it is a sign of unsuccessful training and their own fault. The majority of patients are brought to the psychiatrist between the ages of eight and eleven, when all attempts at training have failed. The greater frequency of enuresis in boys than girls, which has been reported by most observers, may be in part unreal, an appearance caused by greater reticence about the habits of girls. However, it is probably in part genuine; the female may in fact be somewhat more easily conditioned than the male. In children under five in the National Survey (Douglas and Blomfield, 1958) there was a higher incidence of enuresis in the lower socio-economic classes. Kanner also found enuresis more frequent in families of the lowest income groups and in children of dull or lower intelligence. Hallgren (1957) noted that cessation of night-wetting might be delayed by mental retardation.

Hallgren's monograph on enuresis is important with regard to both epidemiology and aetiology. He started from 229 propositi from psychiatric departments in children's hospitals, and investigated 173 secondary cases among siblings and parents, and 530 unaffected siblings and parents. He found much individual variation in the time at which wetting ceased. Children suffering from both nocturnal and diurnal enuresis cease to wet, as a rule, later at night than by day; on average boys stop later than girls, and children with primary later than children with acquired nocturnal enuresis. Nocturnal enuresis is associated with diurnal frequency and urgency of micturition. Hallgren found heavy sleep to be associated with nocturnal enuresis, but the relationship did not seem to be a simple causal one. Physical disorders were not prominent in the aetiology; but emotional disturbances were commoner in enuretic children with nocturnal and diurnal enuresis than in the non-enuretic, and this type of enuresis might appear as a result of disturbances of the child's emotional security.

Hallgren concluded that nocturnal enuresis was aetiologically heterogeneous. There are probably non-genetic cases, but very probably also a nuclear group in which the liability to enuresis is primarily genetically determined, gene manifestation being modified by environmental factors. In familial cases, the morbidity risk was about 40 per cent. in fathers and brothers, and about 20 per cent. in mothers and sisters. On the other hand there was no evidence that diurnal enuresis, occurring alone, was due to any genetical difference. The mode of inheritance was probably polygenic, or if related to a major dominant gene, subject also to polygenic modification. Enuretics and their relatives were not found to be liable to any raised mortality or decreased fertility.

Similar conclusions were reached by Barbour et al. (1963). A positive family history of the condition was frequent, and abnormalities in the E.E.G. were present in 84 per cent. of all cases. The majority of the children came from stable homes, and most of them did not show any marked emotional disturbances. The authors regard enuresis as a developmental functional retardation, for which no single cause or factor could be held responsible.

Toilet training is usually completed by the age of three. It has been made the focus of interest by *psychoanalysis*, for which it has a central *importance in the development of personality*. It is 'the ego's first conscious struggle for the mastering of an id impulse'. One may admit that the passing of urine or stool into the chamber by a baby is, under the stringency of present-day washing facilities, a present to the mother which is received with a smile of approval. But why this nursery event should be surrounded by a mass of sophisticated interpretation, taken from adult psychology, is difficult to see. Toilet training is a mode of adaptation which normally in man, as in animals, proceeds of itself, and is only disturbed when the integration which is needed on various nervous levels is interfered with by constitutional, physical or situational factors. A critical review of both Freudian and learning theory in relation to enuresis has been provided by O'Connor and Franks (1960).

There are several stages in the *development of central regulation*. This is well illustrated by experiments in which children at the early age of four to five months were conditioned to cleanliness by linking the feeling of the cold brim of the chamber with urination. Of those who were successfully trained, 70 per cent. lost the automatic response once more between the ages of nine and fourteen months. 'The child had then to learn intellectually what was expected of him and gain conscious control of his sphincters' (Hellmann, 1949).

Physical factors, which at various times and by various authors have been regarded as playing some part in the causation of enuresis, include spina bifida, local irritation of the genitals, small size of bladder, adenoids, abnormally deep sleep, and epilepsy. In individual cases each of these may prove to be important, but none of them is of significance in the bulk of cases. *Parental attitudes*, especially maternal over-protection, are probably somewhat more important. Mothers who go on putting diapers on their children to an abnormally late age, or who otherwise encourage dependence and immaturity, are asking for trouble. In slum dwellings, urban or rural, where there are inadequate lavatory facilities, clean habits may never be developed. Some of the children of relatively advanced age, who in Britain during the war were evacuated from danger areas to new homes, surprised their hosts in this way. *Regression to earlier behaviour patterns*, and not only the loss of toilet habits but the resumption of baby talk, may occur during a physical illness. Among the affective influences which may start enuresis in formerly clean children the arrival of a new baby is well known.

The *clinical picture* and the course of enuresis involve all kinds of variations. There may be any combination of daily and nocturnal wetting, although regular nightly enuresis is by far the most common. A very few children wet only occasionally, or in spells, though the latter rhythm may be seen prior to recovery, under the influence of regular waking by parents or by other therapeutic measures. Enuresis may not always end with entry into adult life, even when the best measures have been taken. *Grown-up bedwetters* may be found sleeping in common lodging-houses because they cannot find lodging elsewhere.

Before treatment can be embarked upon, an intelligent appraisal of the relative importance of the different factors in causation is called for. Enuresis may represent only one symptom in a normal child or one link in a complicated life situation which needs disentangling. *Treatment* should then proceed along general lines. The child must be encouraged to give free expression to his difficulties without fear of ridicule or disapproval, the parents helped to understand their role in the situation and the ways in which their attitude to the child calls for modification. Punishment is of no avail and the parents should be persuaded to repudiate it. A small reward for each 'dry night' is, on the other hand, a valuable aid to treatment. In a high proportion of cases, however, the domestic situation and the child's psychological difficulties will not by themselves account satisfactorily for the condition; they will, for example, be no longer active as causes. In such circumstances it is fully justifiable to employ measures aimed at terminating a bad habit. The reduction of fluid intake, and waking before the parents retire for the night or before wetting can be expected to occur, will often be of some help. Ephedrine in doses of 15–60 mg. a night, or amphetamine from 2·5 mg. to much more, have proved effective in some cases, probably not altogether owing to suggestion. The latter is probably better avoided. An autonomic blocking agent, such as propantheline 15 mg. and posterior pituitary snuff, are also efficacious in some cases. The antidepressant imipramine has been found to be helpful (Noack, 1964; Mariuz and Walters, 1963; but see also Fisher *et al.*, 1960). Throughout treatment the role of the doctor, as Kanner has pointed out, should be that of a protector, upholding the self-confidence of the child and encouraging him in his efforts to cure himself .

A method of treatment based on the principles of conditioning used for some time but revived and popularized by Mowrer (1950) achieves success in a considerable proportion of cases. The method is aimed at producing awakening as soon as distension of the bladder has occurred and before reflex relaxation of the sphincter has initiated urination. The instrument used consists of a pad of some thicknesses of an absorbent fabric which separates two large pieces of metal screening. When urine flows onto the pad it penetrates the fabric and produces electrical contact between the metal screens thus completing a circuit which causes a bell to ring; the child wakes while in the act of micturition and is then able to get out of bed and finish voiding his bladder. In due course distension of the bladder, through frequent association with awakening, proves adequate to arouse the child; and eventually this happens even after the unconditioned stimulus, that is the ringing of the bell, has been discontinued. The child is now awakened by distension alone and is able to anticipate the onset of urination.

It is not only, as has been suggested, because of their large numbers that enuretics cannot be treated by a prolonged course of *psychotherapy*. If enuresis is an isolated symptom in an otherwise well-adjusted child, psychotherapy on analytical lines usually does no good, reinforces the child's feeling that there is something special the matter with him, and may destroy his spontaneity or add to his unhappiness. In these circumstances, the symptom nearly always passes off of its own accord, as a part of the process of maturation, and sometimes does so prematurely as a result of a change of environment, such as a holiday with friends.

ENCOPRESIS appears hardly ever as an isolated symptom, but as a rather ominous one in a maladjusted child with a number of neurotic traits. It is a more difficult problem to deal with than enuresis, and causes much more distress and anxiety to parents.

Vaughan and Cashmore (1954), and later Anthony (1957) along very similar lines, distinguish three ways in which the problem may appear. (1) What may be called the un-trained soiler comes from a family in which there is poor training and in which the child is, in effect, trained to be 'dirty'. Family standards and the general social level are low. The way to deal with the problem is to institute ordinary bowel routine and habit training. (2) The over-trained soiler is related by Vaughan to prolonged conflict between mother and child, in which the child is using bowel success or failure to resist the mother's high standards. The denial of the call to stool leads to retention constipation and overflow, or misplaced and mistimed evacuation. There will be alternating periods of soiling and retention. Vaughan claims that this is usually a product of a compulsive home environment; there has usually been a period of early achievement of bowel control, but later breakdown. Soiling starts at the age of five or six, and tends to occur on the way home from school. It ceases at nine, ten or eleven; and then the child starts to steal. (3) Encopresis may also appear as a psychological response to stress. These children just produce a passive overflow in response to chronic stress. They soil when stress or tension is high in the home, and do not soil when the home atmosphere relaxes. The children are often clear of the symptom in hospital, but relapse to soiling on return home.

Encopresis was found by Rogers (1953) to be closely related to hostility and aggressiveness in the child towards the mother, and may indicate a bitterness of feeling and an irreconcilable attitude which make the case a difficult therapeutic problem.

CONSTIPATION. This is best not defined as infrequent bowel movement or lack of a daily stool, but confined to those cases where a clinical problem arises, i.e. when the evacuation of hard faeces becomes difficult. Local abnormalities always have to be looked for, and the possibility of an anal fissure should be remembered. The passage of one large hard painful stool may cause the child to become afraid of going to the lavatory. After that his efforts to hold back a bowel movement, which he fears may be painful, increase the constipation. Pinkerton (1958) describes the bowel negativism aroused in children by either over-fastidious or over-anxious mothers who make the mistake of taking 'issue over a function which they cannot dictate because the child retains its own voluntary control. . . . Resistance to defaecation by the young child can be so determined and so protracted that it may produce major physical repercussions, including radiologically demonstrable megacolon'. He claims that fissure-in-ano, a more frequent complication, does not precede the constipation but is caused by it and is an organic complication in a disorder which is psychogenic in origin. It may deflect attention away from the emotional basis of the constipation and so prevent its resolution.

The application of learning theory to the treatment of single symptoms in children, especially phobias, enuresis and encopresis, has been discussed by Eysenck and Rachman (1965*b*) at theoretical, experimental and clinical levels. Operant conditioning is seen as likely to become a treatment of choice. Operant behaviour affects the environment and generates stimuli which feed back to the organism; conditioning therapy consists in modifying the feed-back stimuli so as to reward, or better reinforce, one mode of response rather than another.

DISORDERS OF SEXUAL DEVELOPMENT. The basic problems of this field are discussed in Chapter III, in which the section on 'the sexually perverse' (p. 160) deals with many questions related to child psychiatry. It also contains a critical appreciation of Freud's pioneer work.

As a general introduction to the preventive aspect of this part of child psychiatry, we propose to quote in free translation from Homburger (1926). Homburger follows in many points the views of Freud, and gives useful advice on the *upbringing of children with regard to sex*. This consists mainly in commonsense rules; but they are addressed to doctors who, as he points out, often have to deal with mothers who are themselves unstable, uncertain, too tied up with repressions to respond naturally to the situation, or too simple to think of a way out close at hand.

From the time of infancy the child should be protected against *untimely sexual excitement*. The mother who is free of psychopathic traits instinctively gives her child the fondling and hugging he needs, but in no excessive measure. She does not yield to the temptation of comforting her own weakness at the expense of physical or emotional claims on him which may be harmful. However, we must be aware that many mothers have little insight and little control. Equally harmful, though today we may be over-estimating the harm it can do, is an excessive reticence and an unwillingness to give or to receive the expressions of love.

As the child grows out of infancy, caresses by bodily contact should begin to become less frequent. By play, occupation and companions, the interests of the child should be *directed away from his own body* as the main source of pleasure. He should not be indulged with petting and cuddling whenever he finds something to dislike, or fails in an effort and is disappointed.

Homburger disapproves of any cultivation of the coquettishness and graceful display of children, especially girls; he thinks that it may do no harm as long as it is naïve and unselfconscious, but that it may awake vanity, wantonness and premature sex interest later. The child should not be the witness of the parents' connubialities, and should not share their bedroom. On the other hand, the atmosphere of warmth and love in a happy marriage, the tenderness and mutual respect shown by his parents, helps him to *emotional security* and balance. Ambiguous references to sex and conversations with shady double meanings should be avoided in the presence of children, in whom an unhealthy curiosity may be aroused thereby.

An important and sometimes difficult task for parents is the development of the *sense of shame*. It may be that this is an artefact of our culture, and certainly in some other cultures it plays a less momentous role. Nevertheless the child has to be brought up to be happily adjusted to our prevailing customs and ideas of decency. The usual practice is to link ideas about sex with the distinctions drawn between what is clean and unclean, neat and ugly; and the fact that the same organs are used for sexual and excretory purposes makes this easy. This is quite unnecessary and may prove positively harmful. Children learn in an automatic way that certain modes of behaviour are or are not possible in company, and by their imitativeness and tendency to conformity usually accept general practices without question, in the same way as they learn to refrain from handling their food with their fingers.

Finally, when the first quasi-sexual feelings make their appearance in affections for other people, the child who has learned to *limit his desires* for food, possessions or pleasures in other fields, will readily accept limitations here.

MASTURBATION. Here again we refer the reader to the corresponding part of this book in Chapter III (p. 163). Children who masturbate are rarely referred to the physician unless the habit is excessive. There are *two periods* in which masturbation is relatively frequent. The infant plays with his genitals as with other parts of his body, unaware of the sophisticated ideas of his elders; and in infant boys penile tumescence may be observed. Sometimes this seems to arouse pleasurable feelings, which induce repetition of the play. Tumescence also occurs in times of restlessness, crying and fretting, and if the child then handles his genitals, it may be interpreted as a mode of relief similar to thumb-sucking. There is no need then to be alarmed, or to fear that it will lead to masturbation. Diverting the child's interest to play with other objects is all that is usually needed.

What has been described is commoner in boys than in girls; but in older children of three or more masturbation seems to be equally frequent in both sexes. It may be induced by local irritation or a skin infection, by tight clothes, or certain forms of playful exercise, such as climbing or riding astride a rocking-horse. Sometimes the child has been 'seduced' by older children or an irresponsible nanny, but more frequent is the apparently accidental discovery of the manipulation and its pleasurable effects, then felt by the child to be a *soothing relief* for moods of anger or frustration.

If the cause can be found and removed, the habit ceases. This is not always easy, and the full co-operation of the parents may be required. They will themselves almost certainly need enlightenment, and reassurance about the harmlessness of the dreaded 'self-abuse'; and the child will benefit by diversion of interest. In any case, it will almost certainly prove a passing phase.

If masturbation presents itself as an isolated complaint *in puberty*, the knowledge alone of its almost universal occurrence in the male may be sufficient to allay the parents' and the patient's fears. It is desirable that the patient should guard himself against the development of a habit, or persist in his efforts to gain control over it, both as a valuable form of self-discipline and as an insurance. The confirmed masturbator often has difficulties in making an easy and successful adjustment to adult heterosexual life.

There are, however, rare instances, usually in a highly psychopathically tinged milieu, in which a child masturbates at every moment when he is unobserved, and bears the tired and guilty expression attributed by common belief to the *habitual masturbator*. In pubescent boys this may be combined with premature or perversely directed sexual development; and the abnormal, eccentric or asocial behaviour of the parents may reduce any chance of social therapy. It is this type of case which the psychiatrist is asked to see when the family doctor and social agencies have exhausted their resources. Then only by admission to a hostel or department of child psychiatry, can one hope for improvement, which may then be relatively easily achieved thanks to the complete change of environment.

Homosexual activities in childhood are sometimes the object of parental distress and medical attention. They are often no more than experimental sex play between boys, one of whom is older and more mature. In any case the degree of sexual development attained by a given age varies very much. The play often takes on the character of a group activity, involving a number of boys who practise masturbation at a secret meeting-place. Other manifestations of childish homosexuality are the strong affections and passionate devotions felt, in all seriousness and depth, by girls and boys towards a class-mate or teacher.

All this is common and without lasting significance, except in the single instance when it releases an aberrant predisposition and becomes the *'key event' of a lasting homosexuality*. The patient then seems to be sidetracked from the developmental highroad, and to proceed no farther towards adult heterosexuality. We have no means of knowing the relative importance of environmental and constitutional causes in determining the deviation, or whether the Freudian notions of mother-fixation and castration-anxiety in boys and penis-envy in girls have much importance. Genetical factors are not to be ignored (see Chapter III, p. 170) and may be the only significant ones in a group of patients at one end of a scale, at the other end of which environmental causes equally preponderate.

In concluding these remarks on the sexual behaviour of children, two points need to be underlined. The first is that we do not have sufficient knowledge of the factors that govern sexual development, physically and emotionally. There is a great degree of *variability in the pace of development*, which sometimes seems to be but poorly correlated with maturation in other respects. If all forms of maturation occur at equal and harmonious speed, there seems to be a much better chance of the child passing through the difficult time of pubescence without the storms and suffering that others endure. We know little even of the frequency of these inequalities in rate of maturation, or of their influence on the adult personality. Here, as in so many other fields, opinions are determined by preconceptions rather than factual knowledge.

The second point for emphasis is our lack of knowledge of the *effects of education*. There is no general agreement about the way in which education on sexual matters should be given to children, the persons who should give it, or the age at which it should be made available. In our own view, the most sensible thing to do is to answer the questions of children whenever they are put, with frankness and without concealment, but in a way to satisfy that degree of curiosity which is actually shown. There is no need for the parent to belabour the child with unasked-for information. An acquaintance with the biological background of development and reproduction might well be part of the general science course at schools.

DISORDERS OF SPEECH. As speech is one of the highest forms of neuronic integration one should expect that imperfections would be relatively frequent. A common form of imperfection is *stammer*, a symptom which is of considerable significance for the development of the personality. There are, however, other rarer speech symptoms, such as delayed onset of speaking, transient or 'elective' mutism, disorders of articulation, such as lisping, lalling, etc., baby-talk, and aphonia, all of which are usually psychogenic in origin, or involve a psychological element in causation. Whenever one is faced with a disturbance of speech, one should remember the important part played by accurate *hearing* in the correct development of speech. If there is any doubt of the patient's acoustic abilities, a specialist should examine the child, audiometrically as well as otherwise.

Stammering (or stuttering) in most cases begins during the period of intensive speech acquisition during the third and fourth years of life. At that time the child's world and his interests are rapidly extending, and his vocabulary grows, or should grow, correspondingly. One need think nothing amiss if he then hesitates, or needs some time, to find the right word; physiological stammer has been spoken of as occurring at this age. Other important times are the age of first attendance at school, and puberty; the group of stammerers who date their handicap from this last age is relatively small.

At all these times it is clear that special demands are being made on speech. In the *young child*, acquisition of speech is the highest point of cortical integration yet reached, and follows or coincides with the ability to eat solid food and to make full use of the hands. The co-ordination of function at many levels of the nervous system, which is necessary for speaking, may easily be disturbed. *Speaking at school* is, for many children, speaking in front of an audience of strangers for the first time, and an element of anxiety is often prominent in disturbances which then first appear. The widening of the mental horizon at *puberty*, and the occurrence of more differentiated emotional reactions, for which adequate modes of expression may be lacking, makes this another danger period. As in the small child, the stammer which starts at puberty is a hesitation due to a need for words while there is a superabundance of thoughts.

In a survey of all the children in the last two years of their primary schooling (age range 9–11 years) in Newcastle upon Tyne, Andrews and Harris (1964) carried out a principal component analysis of data relating to 80 stutterers. Three factors emerged corresponding with the three most common settings for stuttering. The first is composed of items illustrating the child's poor ability on tests of intellectual functioning, of his retarded and abnormal speech development and of his failure to learn to fit in with others. The items concerning the mothers and home show evidence of a poor school and work record in the mother, but more importantly, failure to create a stable home and marriage as a satisfactory background for the child. The second factor appears to be primarily descriptive of the severe syndrome. Overactivity, irritability and articulatory ataxia seem to be associated with a rapid increase in the severity of the stutter and hence in its persistence. These features are reminiscent of changes commonly associated with brain damage in children, which appears to be associated with an increased incidence of stuttering. These cases will tend to merge in their clinical features with those in which definite though minimal brain damage plays a part. The third factor describes able, anxious children who have difficulty in developing or retaining fluent speech under the double handicap of genetic endowment and parental pressure on them to succeed. In this representative sample these cases formed a much smaller group than in some other series. A genetic study showed that the risk of stuttering among the first degree relatives of probands was 3 to 4 times higher than the risk in the general population. This was difficult to explain on the basis of non-genetic factors alone and familial cases almost certainly have some hereditary basis. This may consist of a common dominant gene and a multifactorial background with sex limitation. Alternatively inheritance may be wholly polygenic (Kay, 1964). The risk of developing the condition was highest in the male relatives of female stutterers and lowest in the female relatives of male stutterers.

One may presume that in some cases, probably a small minority, the organic tool of speech is itself at fault. Such a defect might be caused genetically, or by damage to the speech centres during foetal or early infantile life. Because an excess of left-handed people has been found in stammerers and their relatives, blame has been laid on the transient rivalry for *cerebral dominance* between the two hemispheres. Nothing certain is known about these physical factors. Minor organic faults, or disturbances of dominance, are as a rule compensated for and overcome during the normal process of growth and development. But if at any time unfavourable emotional tensions develop, due perhaps to anxious perfectionist parents, a bullying brother or a disciplinarian teacher, impairment of certainty and control may lead to a stammer. Acute factors, such as a sudden fright, have been held responsible; but the general pressure of the life-situation and anxiety are more often the decisive psychogenic factor.

The idea of Homburger (1926), that stammer is always a symptom of an *anxiety neurosis*, probably goes too far. Often enough, anxiety tendencies develop as an effect of the speech handicap. A stammer may, however, be the sign of a general abnormality of personality, and be associated with anxious and obsessional traits. Nevertheless it occurs, as West (1943) has pointed out, in all kinds of personalities, in all strata of society, in rich and poor, in city and country dwellers, and is independent of physique, blood-groups, race, language and nationality. There is, however, a *differential sex incidence*. Stammering is definitely more common in boys (the sex ratio varies from 2:1 to 10:1, according to age), and no explanation has yet been found for this. That girls acquire speech earlier, make use of it more easily, quickly and purposefully than boys, may perhaps provide a clue. The reports of anthropologists that stammer is not found in primitive groups, such as the American Red Indians, where there are different methods of child-rearing, cannot be accepted without reserve.

Whatever the original mental make-up of the stammerer, his psychological growth is unfavourably *influenced by his symptom*. He becomes insecure in his relations with parents and playmates and others, and by his 'speech consciousness' is driven into isolation and barred from the enjoyment of school and play and social activity. If he tries to take part, he develops all too easily a state of tension which makes his speech worse and his social incapacity more extreme; and this may then become habitual. The very knowledge that the stuttering only appears in certain situations, and that he and his parents have nourished the hope of mastering it by an effort of will, necessarily increases his insecurity and frustration. At the time when the stammerer is seen by the psychiatrist, all kinds of popular remedies have usually been tried, and the stuttering pattern is firmly established.

Early treatment is also often delayed by the widespread belief that the child will outgrow his handicap one day. If he does, it is a rare and exceptional event. Such comforting beliefs have been kept alive by tales of famous orators who have been stutterers. Treatment should be begun as early as possible, as in many cases not only the child, but also the parents and teachers have to be included in the therapeutic plan. The doctor will have to combat their distress and anxiety, their perfectionism, and the inclination to coercion. The patience, tact and resourcefulness of the therapist will be fully extended if he is to bring about the *change in emotional atmosphere* surrounding the child, which is necessary before personal and direct therapy can yield results. This preliminary work cannot be left to the *speech therapist* or the educational psychologist; and even the choice of cases in which technical assistance alone will suffice must be made by the psychiatrist. Educational treatment by the speech therapist should be but a *part of a general psychotherapy*. Its purpose is to enable the child to relax and to use his speech apparatus, including respiration, freely and unconcernedly, whatever his audience. It should enable the stutterer to understand that the situations in which he stutters are not necessarily a cause for anxiety, and that he can come to face them with less and less emotional disturbance. This learning of new and more realistic attitudes is often most easily achieved in a group. It is made easier if at the same time the *symptom of stuttering* is being treated so that the patient has sufficient control of his stutter to be able to communicate with comparative fluency.

A useful technique for achieving this is *syllable-timed speech*. This is a form of speech from which all the stress and syllable contrasts are removed. The patients are taught to speak syllable by syllable, stressing each evenly and saying each in time to a regular even rhythm. This requires about 100 hours' practice given intensively over a short period and at first this artificial form of speech must be used consistently in all situations. Speed and fluency quickly increase to normal levels without stutter. Through time a return to the stress contrasts of normal speech takes place spontaneously. This technique has produced promising results particularly in pre-adolescent children but controlled enquiries into its efficacy are needed (Andrews and Harris, 1964).

PSYCHOMOTOR DISORDERS: HYPERKINESIS AND TICS. Winnicott, in his *Clinical Notes on Disorders of Childhood* (1931), has a special chapter on *fidgetiness*. He compares and contrasts cases in which the 'restlessness is part of the child's nature' with others in which it follows an attack of *chorea*. His description of common fidgetiness is worth quoting and even today has not been superseded:

'Such a fidgety child is a worry, is restless, is up to mischief if left for a moment un-occupied, and is impossible at table, either eating food as if someone would snatch it from him, or else liable to upset tumblers or spill tea. . . . Sleep is usually restless. . . . These children are over-excitable, or "nervy" rather than nervous (of things, people, the dark, being alone). However, these children are often happy, though irritable if restricted in activity. Picturing such a child one remembers countless children of between five and ten years old, thin and wiry, quick in the uptake, and eager.' Similarly, in a German text-book of diseases of children the condition is described as follows: 'Restlessness and instability of voluntary musculature of which the child is not conscious is a purely nervous anomaly, though psychic influences tend to increase it. Such a child is fidgety, it cannot sit still, plays with its fingers or its clothes, grimaces, turns its head right and left, licks the corner of its mouth. This behaviour is intensified by emotion and is often reminiscent of early chorea. Often the tongue cannot be kept still when put out; on closing the eyelids a slight tremor is noticeable, and the spread-out fingers exhibit a moderately fine tremor' (Goett).

In Winnicott's view, common fidgetiness is related to anxiety; and there is no doubt that emotional factors can increase the motor overflow in children. Nevertheless all children are hyperkinetic in comparison with adults, and restlessness may be little more than abundant vitality. 'General motor unrest' may be either a *constitutional peculiarity*, or may in some cases signify a *developmental delay*; if it is the latter, we may suppose that the child did not develop the feeling for kinetic economy at the normal time, which in the majority of children is before the age of five. A caricatured form of overactivity was first described by Kramer and Pollnow (1932) in the *hyperkinetic syndrome*. This is described and discussed on p. 690.

One outlet for constitutional hyperactivity is the *tic or habit spasm*, so much more fre-quently seen in childhood than in later life. Boncour (1910) found 23 per cent. of tiqueurs among 1,759 children between the ages of two and thirteen. Girls and boys seem to be equally affected, and the variety of movements and their combinations in the same patient are numerous. Kanner includes the following in his *list of multiple tics*: clearing the throat, twisting the mouth, and wrinkling the forehead; turning the neck and opening the mouth in a child who had previously been blinking; making a noise in the throat, blinking, twitching the neck muscles and at times mouth and nose; twitching the hands, jerking the head and blinking; jerking the arms, jumping and grimacing.

Any sudden, quick, frequently repeated and purposeless movement may be called a tic. As a rule the child says he cannot help doing it. Tics may be an isolated symptom, but more often present in a picture of *general psychopathic maladjustment* and neurotic difficulty. Some say that it points to mental loneliness, or is an expression of the child's defence against the unpleasant, or of disgust or aversion from persons or things, or of negation or disapproval. In some cases the tic is actually expressive of such emotions, and can be easily recognized. But in other cases any *psychological explanation* is forced and artificial, and may be wrongly applied to movements fully explicable neurologically and of organic origin. Whether the tic be psychopathologically or neuropathologically determined, its automatic and repetitive character indicates a disturbance of function at the level of the thalamo-strio-pallidar centres.

Suppression of the tic by voluntary effort results in feelings of uneasiness or anxiety, similar to those felt by other children in suppressing compulsive symptoms. True compulsive symptoms are relatively rare at this time of life.

By following up a number of children attending at a child-guidance clinic for motor restlessness or for tics, Guttmann and Creak (1940) found mild *residual motor symptoms* in a considerable proportion; these were of a nature only to be found by the careful observer, and on the whole the prognosis of psychomotor abnormalities in childhood is good.

While tics in childhood may be substitutes for more highly differentiated activities such as compulsive rituals, they are also related to such primitive manipulations as *thumb-sucking* and *nail-biting*. These and other *habitual manipulations* of certain parts of the body can, however, be distinguished from tics. They have not the sudden onset and short time-pattern of the tic; unlike tics they are not repeated in the photographically identical form; and they are more obviously purposive in providing pleasure. Subjectively they are felt to be under volitional control, and they always involve two parts of the body at the same time, one of which is usually the hand.

Thumb-sucking can be regarded as a normal habit: Bühler (1927) found it in 83 per cent. of all infants. Babies have been born sucking their thumbs, and, as Gesell (1937) has shown, it is associated with *hunger* in the first months of life, and later with the relief of pain or irritation due to *dentition*, playing a part 'in the developmental economy of teething'. The persistence of thumb-sucking after the age of two or three has, because of its unhygienic and hedonic aspects, been the cause of anxiety to parents. Fears are aroused that the teeth may be malformed, that an intestinal infection could occur, that it is a sort of masturbation, or that it adumbrates indulgence in oral pleasures later in life. All this is without factual justification. In the otherwise well-adjusted child no concern need be felt, and the way to therapy is indicated by Kanner's dictum: 'If a child's hands are pleasantly occupied with some interesting activity, he does not and cannot suck them at the same time.'

Parents seldom bring their child to the doctor because he bites his nails, and *nail-biting* is usually discovered incidentally. About a quarter of the nail-biters seen by Kanner showed motor restlessness and sleep disturbances, and 19 per cent. suffered from tics. Nail-biting has been interpreted as a 'motor discharge of inner tension', and may spread among whole classes of school-children disciplined by a particularly severe teacher (Bowley, 1943). In psychopathic children, nail-biting is the most difficult symptom to treat, persisting even when the apparently causative emotional difficulties have been removed, and other symptoms have passed off.

DISTURBANCE OF SOCIAL BEHAVIOUR. The things children do, which their elders consider morally wrong, are usually covered by the term 'delinquency'. Kanner has pointed out how unfortunate, and often how meaningless, the use of this term is. Truancy and other forms of running away, stealing, lying, cruelty, and aggressive behaviour, are often shown in isolated episodes, or as single symptoms, in otherwise well-adapted children. They may also be shown by the children who exhibit the psychopathic symptoms which we have already described in earlier pages. Like those symptoms, antisocial trends may be reactions to an unfavourable environment, or be the result of a delay in development which is itself either constitutional or environmental in origin.

Piaget (1932) describes two stages in the development of the child's respect for the moral behests of society. The first of these is *blind obedience*. The child at this stage feels that the precepts of the adult are powerful and objective realities; they are, in fact, 'reified'. At this time parental example and the tone of the environment will obviously be decisive.

The reification of precepts may only be achieved after some delay, but even more so the *second stage*, in which *mutual respect and co-operation* are required. This is ordinarily achieved at the age of seven or eight. Then environmental influences, such as low social standards in the home, play their part; but emotional differentiation and the maturation of intelligence are equally important. In the single case the disentangling of the complex causation of delinquent behaviour will be difficult, although the successful therapist may find relatively easily a practicable way out of what appeared to be a maze. As long as our knowledge of normal standards is so incomplete, Burt's concept of the 'multiple causation' of delinquency, physical, mental and social, can be accepted as a working hypothesis.

There is much to be said for the point of view presented by Nye (1958), namely that one should not think of delinquency as having been caused, but think rather that there has been a failure in its prevention. Delinquency in itself is normal from the psychopathological point of view; and to prevent the child and adolescent from developing along delinquent pathways positive action is required. Nye classifies the social controls which prevent delinquent behaviour as twofold: the internal controls which are built up within the personality of the developing individual by equipping him with a conscience and standards of behaviour, and the direct controls which impose some punishment for infractions of the rules of society.

On this basis the causes of delinquency should be investigated along the lines suggested by learning theory and conditioning processes, and the contribution of pathological processes should be small. This is largely true, although the capacity of the developing individual to respond successfully to training may be interfered with in a number of ways. Any brain damage may impair this capacity, so that delinquent behaviour is more common in defectives and epileptics. The extent to which the common syndrome of 'minimal brain dysfunction' may interfere with social development has not been adequately explored. Some evidence has been produced by Stott (1957, 1959) that congenital factors and perinatal damage may contribute to delinquency.

Perhaps more important are the constitutional factors involved in the normal processes of maturation. Particularly if there is some disparity in the degree of maturation, physically and emotionally, a pattern of delinquent behaviour may arise. In many youths with a delinquent history the electroencephalographic record shows evidence of delayed maturation of cerebral function. The work of Glueck and Glueck (1950), in which two series of delinquent and non-delinquent children were carefully matched for age and intelligence, showed the significance of *constitutional factors* of both physical and temperamental kinds. Physically, the delinquent boys were rather more robust than the controls, bigger, stronger, more muscular and more masculine. In temperament they were more adventurous, assertive, impulsive, independent and insubordinate. It appeared that positive assets of the personality might constitute a danger to the individual, as much as deficiencies such as inadequate self-control.

The *social causes* of delinquency are undoubtedly the most important. The work of the Gluecks suggests that the delinquency of childhood and adolescence may be partly, at least, a form of seeking for danger, adventure, independence and self-assertion for which inadequate outlets are provided in many cultures, especially in large towns. A similar suggestion arises from the age incidence of delinquency and the sex distribution. Delinquent behaviour is many times commoner in boys than in girls, and rapidly rises in frequency from about the age of ten, over the years of adolescence, to diminish again steadily thereafter. These are the years in which there is a great increase in the flow of energy and animal spirits, which can all too easily take a socially obnoxious form.

Probably for both sexes but certainly for girls, by far the largest factor in securing development along socially adjusted lines can be traced to the parental home. The influence of the 'broken home' has been discussed on p. 638. It seems probable that the role of the mother is even more important than that of the father, and if she is unstable or emotionally disturbed, or defective in intellect or personality, or if she is subjected to excessive external stresses, or finally if her attitude to her child is lacking in love and care, the future adjustment of the child is prejudiced. In their study of delinquent girls Cowie, Cowie and Slater (1968) found evidence to suggest that the psychopathic mother had a bad effect on her daughter more by way of being a source of tension and difficulty, than as a transmittter of unfavourable constitutional components of personality. In this study as in many others, delinquents were found to come from families of more than average size, where the mother was likely to be overpressed. It was the earlier rather than the later members of the sibship who had the greatest predisposition to delinquency, again very likely because the elder children would be more likely to slip out of control when there were younger ones in the house to claim the mother's first attention. One child in a sibship would be endangered if another child had already become delinquent, and the danger was the greater the closer the two came to one another in sibship order. This is one of the many findings which suggest the significance of psychological contagion in spreading delinquency. Suggestive of neglect outside the home is the poor educational record which has been generally found among young delinquents, both girls and boys. In the sample of girls mentioned, nearly all were found to be educationally retarded to some degree; using Burt's standards over half the girls were 'backward' or worse in reading and more than three-quarters of them were 'backward' in arithmetic, although the mean I.Q. of the whole group approximated closely to normal (96 per cent.). One of the interesting findings of this survey was that pathological factors, such as mental subnormality, neurosis, abnormality of personality, epilepsy, manic-depression and schizophrenia, played a material role, affecting nearly one in three; this is therefore psychiatrically a more abnormal group than a corresponding group of boy delinquents would be. Nevertheless mental abnormality was the exception, and the majority of these girls had been motivated into delinquency by environmental forces sufficient to overwhelm a basically normal psychological make-up.

In American studies crime and delinquency have been frequently related to the social disorganization which is characteristic of certain areas of large cities. Investigations in this country (Sprott, 1956; Mays, 1952; Spencer, 1955) have shown, however, that there are wide variations in the social climate prevalent within a given locality. Streets which are side by side as in Sprott's investigations, may constitute different sub-cultures with corresponding variation in the incidence of delinquency. In those contributing a large proportion of delinquents, there is a pattern with the familiar constituents of over-crowding and large families, inadequate facilities at home and a tendency for the children to seek recreation in the streets where their play and activity are not supervised by the parents and they readily fall in with the tradition of ganging. Discipline tends to be laxer and more inconsistent and it is part of the accepted social tradition for children to commit certain illegal acts such as shoplifting and petty larceny. 'Delinquency is thus embodied in a way of life, is part and parcel of the juvenile code and pattern of behaviour to which the majority tend to conform' (Mays, 1956). In the same neighbourhood there is often a clustering of problem families, mental defectives or persistent truants, yet social communication between the families is relatively free. In an adjacent street occupied by individuals who come from the same income group, there may be found the 'respectable' pattern of life in which great pains are taken with the upbringing of children, discipline is stricter, money is less liberally given, ambitions run higher and leisure time is spent in the home and more strictly supervised. In such streets situated in the same locality, delinquency will be a rarity. In Spencer's studies in Bristol this pattern was associated with a desire for privacy and isolation and also, it is claimed, with a higher rate of neurosis.

The twin studies which have been carried out in the field of delinquency tend to emphasize the importance of environmental forces in the aetiology. This is shown particularly in the high concordance rates found among same-sexed dizygotic twins, often closely approaching the concordance found among monozygotic twins. Rosanoff, Handy and Plessett (1941) studied four groups of same-sexed twins, totalling 269 pairs, 162 male pairs and 107 female pairs, 137 MZ and 132 DZ. Their results are shown in the tabulation below with the concordance rate (C.R.) given as a per cent:

	N		C.R. (%)	
	MZ	DZ	MZ	DZ
Childhood behaviour difficulties:				
pre-neurotic and pre-psychotic types, males	19	19	77	12
,, ,, ,, females	10	22	80	34
pre-delinquent types, males	8	9	100	56
,, ,, females	14	19	100	42
Juvenile delinquency, males	29	17	100	71
,, ,, females	12	9	92	100
Adult criminality, males	38	23	76	22
,, ,, females	7	4	86	25

It is noteworthy that the highest concordance rates among DZ pairs are shown in the juvenile delinquent group. Relatively high rates in DZ pairs have also been found among adult criminals by Kranz (1936) and by Stumpfl (1936); in both these reports the DZ rate came fairly close to the rate in MZ. Kranz's figures were 65 per cent. for MZ pairs and 53 per cent. for male DZ pairs, and Stumpfl's were respectively 61 per cent and 37 per cent.

Stumpfl found that genetic factors played a smaller part in the causation of occasional than of persistent criminality; and his results were such as to stress the significance of family tradition and the effect of parental example on the standards and behaviour of children.

Yet another pointer to the great significance of the cultural milieu is the large upsurge of juvenile as well as adult delinquency after a social upheaval such as is caused by war. The detailed analysis by Wilkins (1960) of persons found guilty of indictable offences 1946–1957 with birth years from 1925/6–1948/9 showed the greatest crime proneness in those who went through their fifth year (the year immediately preceding school attendance) during the war. This implies that disturbed social conditions may have their greatest effect on children at this time in their lives. Delinquency rates in young people have risen steadily since the war; and according to the 1961 Criminal Statistics for England and Wales, more than 120,000 persons between 8 and 17 years of age were found guilty of offences. Girls up to the age of 17 contribute only about one-sixth of the indictable crime.

In recent years delinquency has become more and more a subject for sociological rather than psychiatric or even psychological research. More and more emphasis has come to be laid on the specific features of the social environment in which the adolescent boy grows up (Cohen, 1956; Cloward and Ohlin, 1961; Downes, 1966). Some of these theories, such as the theory of cultural transmission (Shaw and McKay) and the theory of differential association (E. H. Sutherland), which have been reviewed in the book by Cloward and Ohlin, are clearly capable of explaining part at least of the facts. It would be regrettable to dismiss them because they do not, alone, give a solution to all the problems. Cloward and Ohlin were specifically concerned with the theory of delinquent gangs. These they relate to three types of subculture: a criminal subculture, in which there is integration at all age levels, and the young learn from the older; a conflict subculture, in which the background is chaotic, and the boy finds his avenue to success by showing his 'guts' or 'heart', and developing his 'rep' (reputation); and the retreatist subculture, among which are to be found the drug-takers as well as other types of delinquents who have failed to find status. There has been much less tendency in Britain than in the U.S.A. for the development of highly organized gangs; but the formation of a rather more fluid group, with a leader and followers, is a not uncommon event among schoolchildren.

The antisocial activities of children are of course much narrower in range than those shown by adults, and in many cases are rather simply motivated and easy to understand. Children may steal to make impressive presents to their companions, or tell lies to make themselves important. Pseudologia in children is fairly common, and may be engaged in in good faith, as it were, without any conscious intent to deceive, on the basis of a vivid imagination and a love for stories. Truancy and running away always need to be taken seriously. Truancy shows a strong correlation with more antisocial forms of delinquency which occur with the onset of adolescence; and it is a sign that the child is already breaking away from conventional standards and is getting out of control. It has its own unfavourable consequences, since the child who is absenting himself from school is likely to fall in with wrong companions. Running away from home is practically always a sign of a serious conflict situation, and of the child's unhappiness and need for help.

There are no large differences between pre-pubertal boys and girls in the forms of delinquency most favoured, and no very large sex difference in their frequency. With the onset of adolescence, however, sex differences soon increase. Although in both sexes there is an upward slant in the curve of incidence, it is much steeper in the male than the female; by the age of sixteen or so the male preponderance is very large, and has been estimated in different samples as anything from 5 : 1 to 14 : 1. In 1965, 4,633 boys as against 764 girls went to Approved Schools in England. The pattern of delinquency in the two sexes has also become quite different. While boys of sixteen are mainly convicted of crimes against property, some of them of a very serious kind, the total range of criminality open to them is almost as wide as that of the adult. Girls of sixteen, on the other hand, are most usually charged with non-indictable offences (being in need of 'care or protection'), consisting in such behaviour as promiscuity, wandering around at night, and thumbing lifts from lorry-drivers over the country. Only one out of every four girls is charged with an indictable offence, and in almost every case it is petty larceny.

Depressive and Neurasthenic Reactions

These are apparently rare in children, at least in the form seen in adults. It may be, however, that the *timidity and shyness* of the small child, or the complaints of forgetfulness, *dreaminess and inability to concentrate* of the young school-child, correspond to the re-active depressions of the adult. Suicide in children can occur, though very rarely under the age of fifteen. Debility, tiredness, weakness and over-sensitivity, when observed in children, often have a physical basis. If that has been excluded by proper investigation, a psychological cause is probable and often not difficult to elicit.

'Hospitalism' may be mentioned here, a concept on which attention has been focused by the work of Goldfarb (1943) and Spitz (1945) in the United States. Children who are brought up in institutions, or who spend large parts of their early lives in hospital, are *deprived of emotional contact* with a mother or mother-substitute. It has been held that in consequence they are rendered liable to an enormous range of abnormal reactions; failure to gain weight, sleeplessness, frequent stools and persistent infections; listlessness, apathy, unhappiness and depression; unsocial behaviour, hostile aggression and insecurity in adapting to the environment. It is doubtful how much of these, if they do occur to excess, are attributable to lack of maternal love, how much to other deficiencies in the environment. In so far as emphasis is laid thereby on the importance of maternal love and care, the conclusion is a banal one.

Although the danger of hospitalism has probably been overdrawn, the lack of maternal or even individual care and attention *in orphanages and institutions* produces in a number of children an easily recognized clinical picture well-known to the child psychiatrist: the child makes great demands for affection on any adult put in charge of him, such as teachers, foster-parents, etc. Often these demands cannot be met without detriment to the interests of other children in the group. The child, on meeting with rebuffs to his excessive demands for affection, reacts with asocial behaviour, such as making a noise in class or otherwise drawing attention to himself. Further repressive action may lead to lying, stealing, tale-bearing and other underhand antisocial acts, often associated with enuresis and even encopresis.

It is obvious that the treatment and above all the prevention of such disorders lies in not having large groups of children under one roof. Large homes may be economical in the first instance, but they are very much against the interest of the child and his development into a useful member of the community. A good foster-home or adoption at an early age seems the ideal preventive solution and also represents the therapy at a later stage.

The child showing the severer form of disorder may go through the same stages in reverse when he recovers.

Fear Reactions and Anxiety

Anxiety states in the child take a different form from those usual in the adult. In the adult specific phobias are less common than diffuse and undirected anxiety. In the child the converse holds, and fears are more commonly related to a distinct object or situation, these specific reactions constituting the phobic states whose treatment constitutes a considerable part of child psychiatry. Children are naturally fearful, and the younger they are the smaller the cause which will provoke a fear reaction. This fearfulness is biologically useful, and is the basis on which much adaptive learning takes place; only low-grade defectives lack the capacity for fear.

As with some other forms of stimulation which for the adult are wholly disagreeable (e.g. vertigo), children can derive keen pleasure from experiencing fear in a relatively mild degree. The physical accompaniments of anxiety, the toning up of the nervous system, the prickling of the skin, the shiver down the back, even the sinking sensation in the belly, both attract and repel. Games in which children dare one another into foolhardy risks have an insistent appeal, especially for boys; and much enjoyed also are adventure stories and stories of witches and ghosts, even though they may have to be paid for by disturbed dreams. Some children who have been carefully shielded from horrific folk-lore seem to be able to derive similar notions out of their own capacity for fantasy.

Some children are more 'nervous' than others. It seems probable that part of this individual variation is derived from constitutional differences, but a large part can be put down to the child's psychosomatic state; and this will depend on age and maturity, physical robustness or alternatively minor ill-health, and past conditioning. Much of a child's general anxiousness can often be traced to simple contagion from an anxious parent, or to a home situation full of tension or conflict.

We owe an excellent account of the phobias of children to the psychologists Eysenck and Rachman (1965*b*), who base their presentation largely on the work of Wolpe. The psycho-pathology is reduced to nine statements, each of which can be, and has been, tested experimentally and checked against clinical observation:

'1. Phobias are learned responses.

'2. Stimuli develop phobic qualities when they are associated temporally and spatially with a fear-producing state of affairs.

'3. Neutral stimuli which are of relevance in the fear-producing situation and/or make an impact on the person in the situation are more likely to develop phobic qualities than weak or irrelevant stimuli.

'4. Repetition of the association between the fear situation and the new phobic stimuli will strengthen the phobia.

'5. Associations between high-intensity fear situations and neutral stimuli are more likely to produce phobic reactions.

'6. Generalization from the original phobic stimulus to stimuli of a similar nature will occur.

'7. Noxious experiences which occur under conditions of excessive confinement are more likely to produce phobic reactions.

'8. Neutral stimuli which are associated with a noxious experience or experiences may develop (secondary) motivating properties. This acquired drive is termed "the fear-drive".

'9. Responses (such as avoidance) which reduce the fear-drive are reinforced.'

On this theory it is quite possible for a phobia to arise after a single causal experience; but it is probable that most phobias develop after a series of traumatic experiences, and may readily do so even when the shock or the noxiousness of these experiences is quite mild.

In the development of a phobia an important part is played by the psychological vicious circle which is initiated with the appearance of the 'fear-drive' as a motivating force. The natural response to the noxious situation is to seek escape; relief is obtained when escape is made; an attempted escape is serially reinforced as the mode of response with each experience of the feared situation; the situation which produces this response becomes more and more generalized. 'The fear is *generated* by a painful experience (or experiences) and is *sustained* by the operation of the acquired fear-drive.' It is to be noted that, if there is no possibility of escape, rapid adjustment takes place to a fear-producing stimulus which is learned by experience to be harmless; thus children, even more readily than adults, after a change of environment, accustom themselves to sudden aircraft or street noise. Eysenck and Rachman emphasize, on the other hand, the important part played by 'confinement' or restriction of the possibilities of effective adaptive response, in furthering the development of a neurotic (non-adaptive) response.

It has been observed that the responsiveness of the child to fear-producing situations changes in the course of development. To begin with the infant is frightened by 'any intense, sudden, unexpected or novel stimulus for which the organism appears to be unprepared' (Jersild, 1957). As the child learns to adjust to such immediate stimuli, e.g. sudden noises, he becomes open to upset from more complex situations, and from anticipatory anxiety. Six-year-old children are relatively immune to the loud noises which frighten the toddler, but are susceptible to imaginary bogies. Imaginary fears are particularly difficult to deal with therapeutically, since the effective stimulus is not easily evoked at will, in a therapeutic situation.

By sensible management much may be done to prevent phobias from developing. Everything that is part of the child's known and trusted environment helps to provide a feeling of security; this applies to parents and sibs, and especially to the mother. Any novel phenomenon, normally liable to arouse fear, will be tolerated best if as many as possible of the reassuring elements are present; and the child may be progressively desensitized to it by its repeated presentation in such conditions. The social contagiousness of fear or its antithesis, security and freedom from fear, should also be borne in mind; children are much less frightened by a stimulus that is new to them if they are in the company of other children who know it and are unafraid. In many situations the security or the anxiety of the mother who is accompanying the child is of critical significance in preventing or facilitating the appearance of an anxiety reaction. Such principles are made use of in the practice of a hospital dental outpatient clinic mentioned by Eysenck and Rachman. No treatment is given on the child's first visit, and time is given him to get used to the place; the first time that anything is done it will be a painless dental inspection. In an anxious child who is slow to become desensitized, it may be as late as the fifth visit that actual treatment begins.

A rational approach to the problems of treatment may also be based on the principles of learning theory. Simple reassurance and explanation are by themselves ineffective treatment of the child's fears, and the main aim must be to desensitize him. This will be done by singling out the object or phenomenon or situation which seems to be the centre of the child's fears, about which any other fears have grown by a process of generalization, and then subjecting the child, in an otherwise totally reassuring situation, to successively stronger doses of the feared stimulus, beginning with the very smallest. Thus a child with a bee phobia, so severe that he could not go into the garden, was presented first with small photographs of bees, then with larger ones, then with coloured photographs, then with a dead bee in a bottle at the far end of the room, then with the dead bee brought gradually closer, the dead bee out of the bottle, the dead bee on his coat, increasing manipulation of the dead bee, etc. (Jones, quoted by Eysenck and Rachman).

During this process of desensitization the mechanism of reciprocal inhibition will be made use of. The noxious stimulus is presented together with other stimuli of such a kind as to inhibit an anxiety response. In adults this is often a state of relaxation, perhaps drug-aided or perhaps the result of a course of relaxation exercises. In the child the presence of the affectionate reassuring parent, or of other unafraid children may be so used; but a particularly valuable reciprocal inhibitor is feeding. Just as the stimulation of an anxiety response will destroy appetite and inhibit feeding, so will the presence of appetite and the feeding response inhibit a tendency to anxiety, if it is only sufficiently mild. Care must be taken with this regime since, if it is hurried, anxiety may inhibit eating and the child's state be actually worsened.

Much attention has been paid to *school phobia*, which can be taken as a common and typical example of child phobias, and one which has proved rather difficult to treat. Hersov(1960*a,b*) and other writers have distinguished between truancy as a conduct disorder and school phobia as one aspect of a neurosis which involves mother as well as child. Hersov concluded that the familial setting and personality of children suffering from school phobia were different from those of truants and control children, but his finding that school phobics achieve a high standard of work at school has not been confirmed by others (Chazan, 1962). Further investigations in this field may make clearer the personality of the typical school-phobic but for the present it is safer to assume that children generally are liable to such a development regardless of personality, if the circumstances favour it. Circumstances in school are often of such a kind; and children learn to dread being shown at a disadvantage with their peers, which any failure at a test, or any departure from school conventions or childish norms of behaviour may involve, or any scolding or reprimand by the teacher. As a rule there are so many attractions for the child in school life that such minor traumata are fully compensated for, but the balance may easily tip the other way.

The theoretical view-point has often been taken that school phobia is a phobia not so much of school as of separation from the mother or that it is symbolic of some deeper unconscious fear, connected with infantile sexuality as conceived in psychoanalytic terms. It is not easy to set out detailed objective evidence to support such views and such evidence has not been forthcoming to any adequate extent. In one of the few more objective studies using controls Hersov discovered separation anxiety (among other features) in 36 per cent. of his 50 cases of school refusal. In 22 per cent. the fear arose directly from some aspect of school life. Chazan found that 17 out of 24 school-phobics were to some degree backward and were having difficulty with school work.

Eysenck and Rachman (1965*b*) take the commonsense view that a child's fear of school should be taken at its face value until clinical investigation (including a school visit) fail to reveal some disturbing factors in school. Then, if separation anxiety presents as the alternative cause, this can be tested, to some extent, by discovering how far the child is liable to anxiety when separated from his mother on other occasions such as when going on an excursion without her. The distinction between 'school phobia' and 'separation anxiety in a school situation' is important because the two states require different procedures in treatment.

In the appreciation by Eysenck and Rachman of reports on the treatment of this neurosis, it seems that methods, based on learning theory and applying the usual methods of desensitization and deconditioning, have proved among the most successful.

'Hysteria'

Many of the features of personality which we call hysterical in the adult are normal in childhood; and hysterical symptoms, both somatic and psychic, are common at that time. With a few exceptions, such as 'double personality', all the very various forms of hysteria have been observed in children and are still often seen. The decline in the incidence of 'grande hysterie' in adults, which began some decades ago, seems to have been followed by a similar fall in incidence in children, at least in this country. In the United States the picture is apparently different. There seems to be little purpose in comparing the incidence of hysteria in children and in adults, because of the 'contagious' nature of hysterical symptoms and their dependence on the 'Zeitgeist'. *Mass hysteria* has been frequently observed in school-children. As late as 1943, Schuler and Parenton reported on an 'epidemic' of hysterical twitching and trembling in a girls' school in Louisiana.

According to Kanner, hysterical blindness, paralyses of single limbs, astasia-abasia, aphonia and mutism are not uncommon in children; sensory symptoms, circumscribed anaesthesia, localized pain ('topalgia'), and globus hystericus are observed; seizures with dramatic motor behaviour and postures such as arc-de-circle are no rarity. Amnesic symptoms are less frequent, and if they occur are less involved and complex than in the grown-up.

Child hysteria is often *monosymptomatic*, and its purpose easy to see through. The child uses his symptoms unconcernedly to achieve what he wants, and all the single psychopathic symptoms mentioned earlier in this chapter may be used in this way. French workers have pointed to the massive nature of child hysteria. The hysterical child lives completely in his illness, which involves all his contacts with reality, and no loophole is left by which he can secure freedom of action to terminate the state voluntarily.

On the other hand hysterical symptoms in the child are often very *transient*. Their impact on the child and on his further development may be negligible.

Hysterical fugues and twilight states are relatively rare in children; more frequent are episodes of *day-dreaming*, which may be carried on over months and be accompanied by the telling of fantastic tales and 'mythomania'. The possibility of hysterical *psychotic states* in children, such as stupor and Ganser states, should not be forgotten. In recent years psychiatrists seem to have ignored their occurrence, and have been inclined to classify all psychotic behaviour in children as schizophrenic (see p. 668).

Anorexia nervosa has been observed in children. Lesser *et al.* (1960) followed up fifteen girls who suffered from it at ages from 10 to 16, and found that, the younger the patient, the more easily the symptom was resolved. The underlying personality might be hysterical, when the prognosis was best, but might also be obsessional or schizoid.

However transient they are, and however insignificant they may appear to be for the child's development, hysterical symptoms in children as in adults may be indications of an underlying *hysterical personality*. The first manifestations of such a make-up can sometimes be seen at an early age, in the form, for instance, of a peculiarly unchildish emotional indifference, intense selfishness, or a delight in histrionics. We repeat Homburger's description of the hysterical character, with additions from Kanner:

'True love and attachment, gratitude, loyalty, naïve fulfilment of duties, truthfulness, reliability are substituted by artificial, feigned, consciously, or not quite consciously, falsified sentiments and performances which are invented, and carried out largely to produce the impression of one's own excellence which is fully or partly believed and more or less efficiently acted. . . .

'There is a marked desire for ostentation, a studied coquettishness which shows itself when confronting a teacher, visitor or physician, when asking a passer-by for the correct time, or when reciting a poem. At home, in school, among strangers, in the street-car, the child finds or creates opportunities to attract attention by fair means or foul. There is a display of assumed poise, "putting on airs", ready judgements which are either enthusiastic endorsements or disdainful disapprovals. . . .

'The expressions of love, hatred, anger, pain, despair, repentance are carried to extremes, being out of proportion to the importance of the exciting cause in their boundless massiveness and violence.'

It would, however, be a mistake to treat such traits in a child as static and unchangeable and prognosticate gloomily of the future. There will be a change in the course of growing up, and in any case the adaptability, affective detachment and capacity for self-display may with right training be made features of advantage.

Irritability

Irritability in children is very frequently connected with physical illness. All mothers know the fretfulness which is due to insufficient sleep, fatigue or hunger, which is associated with malnutrition, digestive disturbances, the prodromal stage of an infection or convalescence from it. Irritating skin conditions such as scabies or oxyuriasis and other forms of physical discomfort make children irritable. Irritability is also more than normally likely to be shown by some brain-injured and epileptic children.

Child psychiatrists believe that there is a 'negativistic' stage of development which is passed through during the toddler period. It should be regarded as normal, unless it is unduly prolonged in duration or so marked that it has unfavourable consequences; it has been 'explained' (if what is offered is any better than a tautology) as the period when the child discovers that he has a mind of his own and so becomes self-assertive, or alternatively as a manifestation of rebellion against parental training. Trouble arises if a perhaps too perfectionist mother sees it as a breach of authority and makes a major issue of it.

In children under the age of three, irritability is likely to show itself in a *temper-tantrum*, the dramatic outburst of anger characteristic of infancy; at a later stage sulkiness and discontent are more probable. Such outbursts are readily understood when they occur on isolated occasions and for an adequate cause, and may then be looked on as a natural form of expression of an appropriate mood. When temper-tantrums become habitual, especially after the earliest years, the psychiatrist will look further afield. The liability to outbursts of temper depends on the 'emotional explosiveness' prevailing in the family in which the child lives. Kanner found that the families of two-thirds of his tantrum children were unrestrained in expressing their feelings. A persistent difficulty or frustration in the life of the child may also be responsible; jealousy of a sibling, excessive strictness or over-protectiveness of one or other parent. In such cases worth-while results will only be obtained by a *comprehensive treatment of the whole family situation*, psychologically and socially.

Aggressiveness, destructiveness and *cruelty* in children may spring from the same source and be a part of a temper-tantrum. But it would be a mistake to regard every act of destructiveness, every ill-treatment of human beings or animals, as deliberately destructive or aggressive. Awkwardness in manipulation, curiosity and inquisitiveness, inadequate understanding of the situation, and lack of realization that others also may suffer pain, may in the small child lead to actions which are not meant to hurt and are not aggressively motivated.

On the other hand, destructiveness with a definite aggressive intention, which is directed specifically against some person or thing, may occur, and not only in acute outbursts. Some such acts are carried out surreptitiously, after premeditation, and with the *enjoyment of vengeance*. When this is seen, as a rule a model for the child's behaviour is not far to seek in his environment. Many of these children have been severely disciplined and beaten by parents or teachers.

In some cases aggressiveness and cruelty in a child flares up transiently as an outlet for primitive instinctive feelings or for an accumulated resentment. Parents are deeply shocked and worried, but as a rule an event of this kind is no sign of psychopathy. The doctor should have no difficulty in distinguishing between an episode of this sort in a warm and well-balanced youngster, and a similar act differently motivated by the *emotionally cool and callous*.

The personality of this kind is an extreme variant, but all transitional shades can be seen. The callous psychopath of adult life, as described earlier (Chapter III, p. 157), has almost always distinguished himself by his behaviour in childhood, and such children are recognizable at an early age. Coldness to parents, brothers and sisters and playmates, possessiveness, egoistic greediness at meals and aggressiveness at play, a passion for mockery, insult and bullying, recklessness and indifference are prominent features. Most characteristic are the spiteful or cruel acts carried out in a mood of coolness and without manifest enjoyment. These children are untouched by any reproof, are beyond the reach of a friendly approach, and receive admonition with impatient indifference or sulky rancour.

Homburger points out how many difficulties these children present when they enter adolescence, and how many of them become dangerous criminals. But, as he says, one should not over-estimate the frequency of the rare and extreme irreconcilable '*enemy of society*'; in most such children an element of callousness has had its effects magnified by an unfavourable environment. Very often there is hostility between the parents, who are no warmer or more affectionate than their child, and between him and them there is a hopeless estrangement. The task of the psychiatrist of *finding a point of emotional contact*, of softening the child's obdurate attitude, and restoring natural relations with other human beings, though difficult, may be most rewarding. Whatever psychopathological theory of interpretation he subscribes to, the psychiatrist should regard this as his main task in most disorders of behaviour in childhood.

Obsessional–Compulsive States

Compulsive symptoms, as defined in Chapter III, are relatively complex psychologically and one would therefore hardly expect to find them in the small child. The full development of verbal expression in the patient is necessary before the observer can be sure of the nature of the symptom; but the symptom itself may have existed from an earlier time. Compulsive symptoms as early as two or three are no rarity, and were described by observers of the last century. From that age on such symptoms become more frequent, and the stage of development of the child under ten favours their appearance. At this time the child is insecure about values and supports himself by rigid standards of right and wrong; insurance against doubt and insecurity may also motivate the repetition in an exact stereotype of any daily activity, repeated questioning of anything or everything (*'folie de doute'*), or the repeated touching of objects. Childish games often have a magical quality, which also appears in compulsive behaviour. Groups of children perform rituals and ceremonies reminiscent of tribal taboos. The new and unpractised tool of thinking is also used playfully at this age—in counting and arithmomania, playing with contrasts and the opposition of antitheses, or the universal extension of a single concept such as the possibility of error.

The average child overcomes these tendencies with little difficulty; but the timid, tender or sensitive child, the serious-minded and intellectually precocious, those who lack naïveté or self-confidence, may founder in a quagmire of compulsive symptoms. *Perfectionist parents or teachers* may help to make matters worse, and possibly also be a prime cause of the trouble. But in some cases the psychological environment has played no part, as when the condition begins in a state of exhaustion or during convalescence after a severe infectious illness. In a mood-setting of morose restlessness, the child begins to doubt everything: 'are these really my parents', 'am I their child', 'does mother love me', 'am I really good?' The contribution of genetical factors has been discussed in Chapter III.

The *obsessional personality* may show itself at an early age, and in the severer cases the first symptoms will have been seen long before puberty. Relatively few of these patients, however, are seen by the psychiatrist during childhood or youth. The young people themselves do not consider their mild compulsive symptoms as anything but props and aids to support: and the parents, if they notice anything amiss, are very likely themselves of the same type, and unwilling to think such things are morbid. Many adult obsessionals have tolerated their symptoms since childhood without speaking to anyone about them, until a crisis compels their disclosure.

The effect of severe compulsive symptoms on the *development of the child* should not be minimized. Aware of an eccentricity, he is often shy, solitary and secretive, and withdraws from company or attaches himself to few or to a single person. He is likely to become restricted in outlook, and may appear stupid or dull. If the compulsive symptoms can be relieved, he may then for the first time be able to make free use of his intelligence, and his behaviour becomes natural.

Severe compulsive symptoms, appearing in puberty, barring the patient from company and increasing his adolescent restraint to the point where he becomes almost inaccessible, should arouse the suspicion of a *schizophrenic illness*. Compulsive symptoms are fairly common at the onset of a hebephrenic schizophrenia. This, however, may be no more than a coincidence, without causal relation (see Chapter V, p. 283).

Even the severer and more disturbing compulsive symptoms, being commoner in children than in adults, and less frequently connected with a thoroughly abnormal personality make-up, are relatively *accessible to treatment*. Psychotherapy, which should include not only the uncovering of repressed material but also a positive direction of the child's outlook and the suggestion of useful and practical occupation of mind and body, will generally lead to good results. Without offering much resistance, the obsessional child produces, in drawings or in play, evidence of the experiences which are connected with the origins of his illness; but conscious discussion of these alone, without active support, relieves him as little as it does his parents. Kanner states that he has never seen recovery from childish obsessional states without an *active therapy*, which may have to include treatment of the mother and re-arrangement of home life. One would, however, expect spontaneous remission of the milder states to occur with maturation, as well as a periodic fluctuation like that observed in adults.

The relationship of disturbed and neurotic behaviour in childhood to adult psychiatric disorder is a subject of considerable interest and importance. A recent enquiry of O'Neal *et al.* (1958, 1959, 1960) sought to establish the outcome in 227 children with behaviour problems thirty years after they were initially seen in a child guidance clinic. The subjects were found to have a significantly higher rate of psychiatric disorder than a matched control group. Both the seriousness of the initial state and the sex of the patient influenced the outcome. Those referred on account of delinquency yielded a relatively high proportion of sociopathic personalities (34 per cent.). Those referred for antisocial tendencies without being diagnosed as delinquents showed a high proportion of psychotic disturbances (20 per cent.). It is of interest that the highest proportion of patients found to be without psychiatric disability as adults (42 per cent.) came from the group initially referred for neurotic complaints. There was a higher proportion with psychiatric disability among women than among men. Findings in some respects similar were registered in a recent enquiry by Pritchard and Graham (1966). Their investigation shows an impressive association between the three childhood categories of 'delinquency', 'behaviour disorder' and 'neurotic disorder', and the adult categories of 'antisocial personality', 'inadequate personality' and 'neurotic disorder' respectively.

THE PSYCHOSES OF CHILDHOOD

In this area the psychiatrist finds himself, at the present time, facing a wilderness lacking any generally recognized landmarks, and himself deprived (often of his own act) of the conventional aids to navigation. The psychoses of childhood have become equated with 'childhood psychosis' and that in turn with 'childhood schizophrenia'. About these conditions very little is known for sure, in respect of aetiology, pathology, clinical features, course and outcome, or treatment. In an over-enthusiastic holistic approach some clinicians have even abandoned the attempt to distinguish these conditions from the mental deficiencies and congenital abnormalities. In this section we shall accordingly begin by delimiting the contribution of syndromes which can be identified with equivalent states in adults; and only thereafter discuss the syndrome which, in our view, is best named 'childhood autism'.

Affective Psychoses

Although manic or depressive psychoses do not as a rule make their appearance before adolescence, single cases at an earlier age have been observed and have been reported in the literature. Barton Hall (1952) found six cases of affective illness among 1,000 patients between the ages of five and sixteen of whom, however, only two were manic-depressives, the others being reactive depressions. A history of fluctuations in school performance, indicating fluctuations in mood, is not infrequently obtained from adult cyclothymics, but in the child this is difficult to assess. An endogenous mood change in the child is most likely to take the form of mania or hypomania, and will then probably be regarded as childish liveliness and overflow of energy. The cyclothymic child will then only be taken to the psychiatrist when he is in a depressive phase, and that appears to be very rare. However, one of these alternating cases has been described, in which the first depressive phase was noticed at the age of two (Schachter, 1952). Hyperactive children may remain so indefinitely, only in adult life being classifiable as hyperthymic, or showing the basic predisposition for the first time in a recognizable form with a depressive illness, perhaps not until middle age.

Because of the generally cheerful, outgoing and positive temperament of childhood, suicide and suicidal attempts, although rare, attract attention. In the U.S.A. 49 deaths by suicide were registered in the age-group from four to fourteen in 1940, 1,462 in the age-group fifteen to twenty-four. Successful suicide is more frequent in boys than in girls, and in white than in coloured children (Despert, 1952). In England and Wales for the last fifty years the suicide rate in boys from ten to fourteen has varied around 2 and 3 per million, 0 to 2 per million in girls. Attempted suicide may be commoner in girls than boys. Toolan (1962) studied 102 cases of suicide and attempted suicide, 18 of them in children under the age of 12 and 84 in adolescents aged 12 to 17; in this series there were 81 girls to 21 boys. Toolan categorized the cases under a number of diagnoses, including 35 labelled as schizophrenic reaction, but nevertheless considered that the basic disorder was a depressive reaction.

Severe mental abnormality plays little part in these early suicides. Most of the well-studied cases have proved to be impulsive acts connected with disappointed love, frustrated ambition or fear of punishment; the motive of vengeance, or punishment of the parents, has very often played a part. It is not until after puberty that suicidal attempts without motivation begin to occur, and then they are often the first symptom of a schizophrenic illness.

Schizophrenia

Autistic syndromes in childhood, including so-called childhood psychosis and childhood schizophrenia, are discussed on p. 678. Schizophrenia is probably no more frequent than manic-depressive psychosis in children, but the diagnosis is more often made. Recently almost all psychotic conditions seen before puberty have been called schizophrenic, although most workers agree that a number of the cases so called have an organic pathology.

Another group of cases often labelled schizophrenic are severe hysterical reactions to an emotional loss, an affective trauma or a deprivation of support and home. These *hysterical psychoses* may occur in children of an introverted and solitary disposition, and the features of personality which have predisposed to the reaction colour it clinically and make its diagnostic recognition difficult.

The relationship of schizophrenia of adults to the so-called schizophrenic psychoses of children is further complicated by the existence of features in the behaviour of the *normal child* which are reminiscent of *schizophrenic symptoms* (Wildermuth, 1923): withdrawal from reality, day-dreaming, playful preoccupation with imagery and fairy-tales, repetitive stereotypies of movement, the silly jokes and puns enjoyed by children, tinged with illogical and 'archaic' thinking, catatonic posturing, negativism in the 'first negative period' (*Trotz-phase*), i.e. the third or fourth year of life. All these are transient phenomena of development, but may appear as symptoms of any psychological disturbance occurring at that stage, and then be regarded as suspicious of schizophrenia.

Schizophrenic-like symptoms, especially catatonic ones, are also found in *low-grade defectives and idiots;* either they correspond to the developmental stage at which the mental life of the patient came to a halt, or they are signs of cerebral pathology. The existence of these cases has led to the idea that a proportion of mental deficiency is caused by schizo-phrenia. This theory has been discussed, together with the question of '*Pfropfschizophrenie*', in other chapters (Chapter XII, p. 703, p. 730, Chapter V. p. 296).

The real incidence of schizophrenia in childhood is very low indeed. Until the recent fashion for designating as schizophrenic any strange withdrawn state in a child, this state-ment would not have been disputed. Unfortunately, since we have had this fashion, the terms 'schizophrenia', 'childhood schizophrenia', and 'childhood psychosis', as applied to children, have been deprived of all meaning, in aetiology, pathology, and even very largely in prognostic and clinical descriptive senses. Modern statistics accordingly are unable to provide us with any useful information about the prevalence in childhood of schizophrenic illnesses falling into the same biological continuum as the schizophrenic illnesses of adults. If we are to judge by the diagnostic principles on which any reliable epidemiology has to be based, we must turn to older reports. One from the Zurich clinic (Schnabel, 1921) showed only four children under the age of twelve in a total of 16,000 admissions. Lutz (1945), a pupil of Bleuler, reviewing the literature critically, found reports of thirty patients under the age of ten, in only fourteen of whom the diagnosis of schizophrenia was certain. He contributed six new cases of his own observation, and estimated that less than 1 per cent of all schizophrenics fall ill as children.

It seems probable that reasonable standards of diagnosis were applied by psychiatrists of the New York State Hospitals during the period 1948–52. Kallmann and Roth (1956) report that during that period the proportion of patients under the age of fifteen constituted only 1·9 per cent of all schizophrenics admitted, and 0·6 per cent of all admissions. They collected 52 twin and 50 singleton propositi, the mean ages of onset being for male twins 9 years, female twins 11 years, and for the singly born 7 and 10 respectively. Kallmann and Roth checked the diagnoses, and say that they were on the conservative side; they did not include children with psychoses complicating mental deficiency. This clinical material is clearly much older than the infants and young children who are labelled as schizophrenic in current child psychiatric practice. The important finding that emerges from the work of these two authors is that, in its genetical relationships, schizophrenia in childhood behaved in much the same way as in adults, the chief points of difference being the high male preponderance (74 males to 28 females), and the relatively early age of onset in secondary cases in sibs. The incidence of schizophrenic psychoses in the parents (9 fathers, 9 mothers) and in the sibs (13 brothers, 5 sisters) was at a level comparable with Kallmann's findings in adult schizophrenia. The concordance rate in the 17 MZ co-twins was 88 per cent. (15 affected), and 23 per cent. (8 affected) in the 35 DZ co-twins.

It is unfortunate that Kallmann and Roth did not provide any account of the clinical condition shown by these pre-adolescents. Since the diagnosis was verified by the genetical relationships and the after-history, it would have been instructive to know how far the psychotic symptoms resembled or differed from those of childhood autistic states. As matters stand, the 'diagnosis' of childhood schizophrenia has become so contaminated that it is best to use it only with extreme reserve. Owing to its liability to confusion with early childhood autism, the term should never be applied to children under the age of five. After that age it should be used, and then tentatively, when early development has been normal and is then interrupted by an acute or insidious psychotic change, for which no organic basis can be found, and which shows symptoms of the same type as those typical of adult schizophrenia.

From the older literature it would seem that paranoid schizophrenia does not occur in children; hebephrenic pictures predominate, with catatonic symptoms appearing perhaps suddenly after a slow and indefinite change in personality has been going on for months. The progressive nature of the illness may show itself not only in 'regressive' phenomena, enuresis, encopresis, temper-tantrums and emotional outbursts, and other infantile forms of behaviour, but also in increasing incoherence of thinking and speaking, in affective incongruity and cooling, and blunting of all the finer reactions to other persons.

Symptomatic Psychoses and Psychological Reactions to Physical Illness

Psychological anomalies accompanying physical illness are probably more common in children than in adults; but this impression may be due to the greater frequency of infections in childhood. One might have expected that paediatrics would have contributed more than it has done to our knowledge of the origin of symptomatic psychoses, such as delirium. We do not know why many children so easily have states of *clouding of consciousness* with an infection, either with or without rise of temperature, nor why they are especially liable to *epileptiform fits*. Both symptoms may be related to the immature state of the brain. One might imagine for example that the blood–brain barrier, which in the adult shields the brain from a circulating poison, is less developed in the child. Symptomatic psychoses in children are often very transient, sometimes lasting only for an hour or two. In other instances they may persist for days, but even then usually terminate without any serious sequelae.

On the other hand, the subacute delirious state with no marked clouding seems to be unknown in children, as also is the dysmnesic syndrome. Post-infectious depressive conditions and paranoid reactions, such as are observed in adults (p. 349), are also rarities. *Moodiness, touchiness, irritability* and restlessness after an infection are, however, common and may be a childish equivalent. In some cases these organic reactions may be mistaken for psychogenic ones.

The *reaction to physical illness* of very young children is of psychiatric interest, because of the tendency to regress to an infantile level of behaviour and to unlearn the habits which made him independent of the intensive motherly care, which has to be given again during the physical illness. As experienced physicians have always known and taught, children in hospitals and sanatoria who suffer from a chronic disease have to have their emotional and intellectual development carefully watched. The opposite is also quite common, the *promotion of development by a physical illness;* through suffering, rest and isolation the child becomes more mature, or even precocious, in his reactions, more adult and easier to live with.

The *interplay of psychological with physical* factors is often difficult to disentangle, as for instance in rheumatic chorea (see Chapter VI, p. 381). The hysterical mass infection of a whole school class by one choreic girl whose movements had a graceful quality which appealed to the others has been observed. Post-choreic motor and other abnormalities may be a mixture of organic and psychogenic symptoms. In the growing and developing organism they are accessible to skilful handling of the psychological component and to adaptive management. Later on they will become fixed habits, so the opportunity of early treatment should not be missed.

In this connexion the child's reaction to *mutilation and disablement* (Guttmann and Mayer-Gross, 1940) should be mentioned. In childhood and youth a state of continuous physical change and functional adaptation goes on, and mutilation only means a change in the direction of development. This is why congenital and early-acquired lesions are so easily overcome. In any home for cripples miracles of adaptation can be seen, and remarkable performances by cripples in sport have been published by several workers (Walthard, 1926; Jokl and Guttmann, 1932). The psychological adjustment to mutilation is easy in childhood, because there is no memory of a time when it did not exist. The adaptation of **crippled** children largely depends on a suitable psychological atmosphere, so much so that neurotic 'cripple reactions' can nearly always be traced to faulty handling.

A distinction must, however, be drawn between cases with *peripheral* and with *central damage*. Lesions of the central nervous system, which disable the infant, such as birth trauma, asphyxia and infantile encephalitis, may cause at the same time a personality disorder which is often wrongly regarded as a psychological reaction to the physical handicap. The causative link is proved by the fact that certain *types of central lesion* are *associated with* certain *types of personality*. For instance, the friendly and sociable character of the athetotic child is well known; Bender (1940) described the 'clinging' personality of children with cerebellar lesions. Poliomyelitis, when it involves the brain-stem, may affect the personality; and this may partly explain the feeble reactions and resigned attitude of paralysed poliomyelitic patients. Finally any intellectual impairment, due to a cerebral lesion, will also affect the level of adaptation.

Among the unfavourable *social and psychological* influences, it should be remembered that pity, sympathy and over-protection may breed self-pity, excessive dependence and a craving for the role of 'mother's best baby'; for such unhealthy privileges the child will fight by all means including importunate conduct, manipulation and hysteria. Hard conditions on the other hand may stimulate ambition and determination, and adversity may strengthen the cripple's character. The problem in treatment is that of striking a balance in management so as to provide a kindly but invigorating environment and suitable incentives for achievement and independence. Negligence and lack of interest or affection may not only fail to achieve the best, but may arouse in the cripple resentment, hatred and aggression. Adler's ideas on 'organ inferiority' and its psychological consequences can often be helpfully applied, but cover only one aspect of the problem. The great variability of response can only be explained by taking into account a multitude of factors. Of these the predominant attitudes of the family are some of the most important, being connected with the constitutional make-up of the child and colouring his environment.

ORGANIC CONDITIONS OF OBSCURE AETIOLOGY
Epilepsy

As more than one-third of epileptics have their first convulsion before the age of ten, epilepsy is an important *illness of childhood*. In fact, many more children are treated in the paediatric division (in-patients and out-patients) of Johns Hopkins Hospital, Baltimore, for convulsive disorder than for rheumatic fever or tuberculosis (Bridge, 1949). According to the same author, about one in fifteen children in a mixed sample of patients in a paediatric service had convulsive disorder at one time or another. Not all these convulsions, however, were signs of epilepsy. Peterman (1946) gives the following table indicating the 'background' for the initial convulsion in 2,500 children below the age of seventeen:

Acute infection	33·4 per cent.
'Idiopathic' epilepsy	26·3 ,, ,,
Cerebral birth injury or residue	14·2 ,, ,,
Miscellaneous known causes	13·4 ,, ,,
Spasmophilia or tetany	7·4 ,, ,,
Cause not established	5·6 ,, ,,

The same writer related *age* to the nature of the convulsions: of the convulsions seen in infants under one month, three-quarters were due to birth injury or developmental anomalies.

Tetanic convulsions occurred after the age of one and below the age of three and this was also the age for seizures associated with infection and fever. As age advanced, the diagnosis of epilepsy was made in an increasingly larger proportion of cases. The survey made by the College of General Practitioners (1960) showed that the prevalence of epilepsy was approximately 5 per thousand, at all ages.

Fever convulsions and similar accidental seizures in young children do not differ from major epileptic fits in appearance. Differentiation is only possible by the after-history, which shows that even repeated convulsions, each coinciding with an infective illness, do not necessarily indicate a later epilepsy. 'A normal electroencephalogram after the age of six can give added reassurance' (Bridge). However, as Bridge has pointed out, none of the follow-up studies of children with febrile convulsions carried out so far has been entirely satisfactory. There is some overlapping: infection and fever not infrequently release for the first time a tendency to fits which persists.

Frequent brief seizures of minor epilepsy recurring uniformly over a period of days, weeks and even years have been given the name of *pyknolepsy* (Adie, 1924). During the attacks the child remains standing or sitting, or continues to play; he looks absentminded, distracted or inattentive. The hands do not lose their grip, and there are only subtle changes in the expression of the face during the absence.

In recent years it has been demonstrated that the electroencephalogram of these children shows the wave and spike pattern which is typical of minor epilepsy when it commences later in life. Pyknolepsy would thus appear to be merely petit mal commencing in childhood. However, Walter (1950) has described cases of pyknolepsy which would appear to differ from most cases of minor epilepsy in childhood in their exhibiting bilateral occipital foci of delta waves between attacks and in showing during seizures a wave and spike pattern which is confined to the occipital lobes. He has claimed that these cases respond to stimulant medication, as for example with liberal doses of amphetamine sulphate. Children with minor seizures exhibiting such an electroencephalogram are exceedingly rare, and it is doubtful whether the effect of a stimulant is specific or proven in these cases. In the great majority of patients with petit mal in childhood troxidone is the treatment of choice (see p. 478).

Intelligence is generally low in children whose fits date from the first years of life, since the fits are the result of severe brain damage. In contrast, those in whom the onset occurs during school age (from 4 years) usually have normal intelligence though the focal epilepsies may be associated with a lower I.Q. In general, children who have frequent fits (especially grand mal) have more impaired ability than those with few, probably because the greater number of fits arise from more brain damage and also because major seizures with anoxia can in some instances lead to further brain damage. Although the majority of epileptic children develop intellectually at the normal expected or a slightly lower rate, a few deteriorate. Chaundry and Pond (1961) found that drugs were not the cause of this deterioration. Even young children can tolerate doses up to adult level and combinations of several drugs may be needed (Pond, 1965).

Psychological equivalents are relatively rare in children, although epileptic moods and fugues may occur. The epileptic nature of a transient mood may pass unrecognized, or be falsely interpreted. Irritability and moodiness before the fit, dreaminess and withdrawal afterwards, are part and parcel of the epileptic attack; they should not be treated as a behaviour disorder arising out of the special situation of the epileptic child.

However, as Pond (1965) points out epileptic children are brought most often to seek

z

psychiatric aid for symptoms that arise from *social difficulties* consequent on having attacks. These children are bewildered by their disability, shunned by other children and frequently misunderstood. They need a great deal of support and the nature and extent of their limitations should be explained to their parents. The epileptic child needs an environment that is neither over-anxious and over-protective, nor one that rejects him because of his affliction. He much more often suffers from being frustrated by too much restriction than from the dangers involved in allowing him to lead a reasonably normal life. There is a clear danger in such sports as swimming but there is no doubt that interesting activity reduces the tendency to fits and over-protection itself sometimes leads to the tendency towards violence or sexual malpractice which it is designed to prevent. The largely mistaken idea that epilepsy is necessarily connected with serious deterioration in personality and dangerous tendencies still lingers in the popular mind.

Measures to promote the psychological stability of the epileptic child and awareness of his dependence on the familial context are very important and sometimes neglected considerations. In adolescence, when familiar patterns of life at home and school (with their supervision) are broken by going to work and forming new relationships, particular care is needed.

The problems of temperamental abnormality associated with epilepsy, which have been discussed in Chapter VIII (p. 467), apply equally to child and adult.

An important respect in which there are differences of emphasis between adult and childhood epilepsy is in the *psychological effects of drugs*. In children phenobarbitone has little sedative effect, and will only make the child drowsy if given in large amounts. Amphetamine, on the other hand, is not an excitant, and usually calms down the restless hyperkinetic child, improving his behaviour and adaptation (Bradley, 1937). One of the recent advances in the treatment of epilepsy in children has been the introduction of succinimides such as ethosuximide (Zarontin) or the diones in the treatment of petit mal and generalized myoclonic seizures. Ethosuximide is given in doses of 250 mg. twice daily, increasing gradually to a total dosage of $1\frac{1}{2}$–2 g. per day according to need. The side-effects are relatively mild, consisting of skin rashes, drowsiness and photophobia. The field of pharmacological psychiatry in the child deserves closer study.

Encephalitis

The immature brain reacts to encephalitis lethargica in a very different way from that of a fully-grown individual. After the acute lethargic phase, young children rarely have a latent interval. Instead they go through a period in which over-activity, aggressiveness and an intractable, malicious spite make them quite intolerable in the ordinary household. The child's restraint is completely in abeyance and his behaviour may bring him to the attention of the police. A characteristic picture is of an alert child in a state of restless vigilance, distracted by any passing event, and inclined on impulse to commit acts of wanton cruelty or destructiveness. It is as if the nervous organization subserving social behaviour had become disorganized, leaving him at the mercy of the untamed instinctive drives. The child's behaviour is qualitatively transformed, and reasoning with him to try to get him to modify his conduct is usually quite futile, as is also any attempt to discipline him in the ordinary way. About half of these children develop Parkinsonism, and as they do so their behaviour becomes gradually more subdued. Similar gross behaviour disturbance may occur in older children and adolescents and is likely to persist into adult life. It is this group of patients that one finds in mental hospitals and to a smaller extent in mental defective hospitals, where they often give rise to administrative problems out of proportion to their numbers.

Only the mildest cases can be treated in their own homes. The most important principle in treatment is that they should be found a useful outlet for their continuous fund of restless energy. In institutions, occupational treatment in agriculture combined with games and plenty of physical exercise may produce considerable amelioration in the less malignant cases. Improvement takes several years, and is recorded in about half the children sent for treatment.

Milder symptoms of hyperkinesis, tics and all manner of repetitive movements, have frequently been seen in young encephalitics, and include yawning, coughing, sniffing and peculiar breathing abnormalities. Oculogyric crises, on the other hand, are rare in children.

It is well to remember that *any encephalitic illness* can cause a complete *transformation of the child's personality*, perhaps with severe aggressiveness and antisocial tendencies. Encephalitis after measles, chicken-pox, mumps, whooping cough and vaccinia may produce after-effects very similar to those of lethargic encephalitis. As a rule the outcome is more favourable, but mental changes may persist, as they may after other neurological lesions.

Early Dementias

Apart from familial amaurotic idiocy, which is discussed according to convention in the chapter on mental subnormality (p. 726), there are other rare conditions in which a normally-born and well-developed infant begins early or late in childhood to show signs of *organic deterioration*. Except for Schilder's disease and Wilson's disease, their pathology is poorly understood and their aetiology unknown.

Early dementias have been known since 1908, when Heller described the first cases of what he later named *dementia infantilis*. Heller's patients, of whom thirty had been reported by 1930, fell ill during the third or fourth year of life and became hyperkinetic, irritable, moody, anxious and sometimes hallucinated. All that they learned in previous years is rapidly lost, speech and the comprehension of speech, skill of movement and control of sphincters. Grimacing, tics, bizarre postures, similar to those of low-grade defectives, are seen; but the facial expression remains relatively normal until late in the illness. Sancte de Sanctis, described under the name *dementia praecoccissima*, a rather similar syndrome, usually classified as an early form of dementia praecox; but these cases probably, like the subjects of Heller's disease, include a mixture of organic dementing processes of various aetiology.

In certain cases in which a progressive deterioration first shows itself in school performance, the process seems to have been started by an infection, with or without signs of encephalitis. If epileptic seizures occur, they are likely to be held responsible for the dementia, though they may both be symptoms of a single underlying process.

It has become increasingly clear during the past 15–20 years that the various 'dementias' of childhood named after Heller, de Sanctis and Weygandt are not distinct from but merge with Kanner's syndrome. Thus, although psychoses that begin after two to three years of normal development do not strictly conform to the criteria for diagnosis of autism as employed by the Johns Hopkins investigators, there is no evidence that in terms of clinical picture, family background and prognosis, such children differ from cases of typical autism (Rutter and Lockyer, 1967). Further, although the profound regression described by Heller as occurring between the ages of 3–5 years carries a grave prognosis, these cases do not invariably do badly. Finally, evidence of brain damage is not confined to the syndrome described by Heller; it is found in a proportion of cases of typical infantile autism (p. 685).

Focal Symptoms

In children, the term *aphasia* was and still is loosely applied to cover a variety of congenital speech defects. In 1930 Ewing showed that in a small number of children who had been diagnosed as aphasic, the inability to learn to speak was due to a defect of hearing involving the range of sounds needed for speech perception. Delay in speech development may also have other causes; and as long ago as 1897, Freud, in his monograph on infantile cerebral paralysis, distinguished cases in which speech had not been acquired or in which there had been delay in acquisition from those with a true aphasia, i.e. a disturbance of the speech faculty already attained. Some authorities have doubted whether true aphasia occurred in children; but Guttmann (1942) showed, in a material of thirty patients aged fourteen and less, with hemisphere affections (tumour, abscess, injury, thrombosis) that aphasia occurred with the same regularity as in adults, when speech centres in the dominant hemisphere were involved. In most cases the symptoms were rather less complex than in the adult, the main one being a diminished speech production. Recovery was surprisingly rapid, especially from aphasia of the purely motor type. In temporal-lobe aphasia the excess of speech production seen in adults was not found in children below the age of ten. The focal lesion had little or no influence on the intellectual growth of the child later on.

Developmental aphasia has become a focus of interest since clinicians became aware of its similarities with early childhood autism. The late and difficult learning of a vocabulary, the prominence of echolalia, the distortion of words, the use of parts of words for the whole, the appearance of neologisms, reversal of word order, all these are common to both syndromes. However, the total effect on the personality and intellectual functions of the child is less in the case of simple aphasia; general intelligence is less likely to be shifted downwards from normal; and the outlook is better, since from about the age of six onwards aphasic children respond increasingly to educative training.

Infantile hemiplegia is also a condition which can be variously caused. It may appear after a febrile illness, e.g. at about the age of eighteen months, and be due to multiple vascular lesions, predominantly in one hemisphere but affecting also the other. In this case no specific remedial measure is likely to be of much avail. But in an important group of cases the cause lies in asphyxial complications at birth and thrombosis or embolism of the middle cerebral artery on one side. In this type the damage done is local and surgical treatment is often effective. A full discussion of the pathological, clinical and therapeutic aspects has been provided by Carmichael (1953). As the infant grows older the parents become gradually aware that he is unable to move one arm or one side of the body as well as the other. Severe retardation of growth in intelligence and of development in general is usual, and epilepsy is very common. The epileptic patients also often show severe disorders of temperament and behaviour: the child is irritable and aggressive, liable to temper tantrums with or without psychogenic precipitation, and he is not infrequently hyperkinetic, interfering, mischievous or spiteful.

The *diagnosis* of widespread but one-sided damage to the brain may be established by clinical findings and by the aid of electroencephalography, arteriography and pneumoencephalography. Partial excisions of the most grossly damaged parts of the cortex often prove insufficient; but remarkably good results may be obtained by *hemispherectomy*. In this operation the basal ganglia are left as far as possible untouched, but the entire overlying cortex on the affected side of the brain is removed. This seemingly heroic operation has been found to produce in these cases much less serious consequences on the debit side than might have been expected. An increase in the degree of the hemiplegia, for instance, often does not follow. The good results are shown most commonly by a diminution in the frequency of the epileptic fits, down to their complete disappearance, marked improvement in temperament and behaviour, so that active education may at last be engaged on, and not unusually some improvement in the intelligence quotient.

Reading disability is an example of the multiple causation in the child of a focal disturbance which in the adult is due to a specific cause, in this case a lesion in the lingual gyrus of the dominant hemisphere. It is probably not by chance that the first case of 'congenital word blindness' in the medical literature was published in this country (Morgan, 1896), and that all the more important work on the problem has been concerned with English-speaking children. The texts of Homburger and Tramer do not even mention the subject. While figures of 12 per cent. of poor readers are given in the U.S.A., and Watts and Vernon (1950) even found 24·4 per cent. of 'backward readers' among fifteen-year-old males in this country, it is doubtful whether the condition plays any comparable role in countries with other languages. One of the few reports available (Hallgren, 1950) estimated the incidence in Sweden at 10 per cent. It seems very probable that phonetic spelling and writing, as in the Latin languages, makes learning to read a much easier task.

In his work on specific dyslexia, Hallgren (1950) studied 116 probands and a further 160 cases among their parents and sibs, examining 270 of these cases personally. He found an association between specific dyslexia and speech defects, and also a raised incidence of left-handedness in affected persons; but affected children in the general population were not mentally retarded, or affected by nervous disorders. A genetic basis in an autosomal dominant gene, as the preponderant specific cause in the majority of cases, was thought to be highly probable.

As reading forms the start of the school career of each child and is of paramount importance for his educational progress, difficulty in reading will be found to underlie *most learning difficulties*. Stogdill (1965) stresses the importance of close investigation of reading difficulty in individual children at an early stage. He points out that faulty perception, visual or auditory or both, is an important factor though many others play a part. He gives a closely observed account of the perceptually-handicapped child on which the following description is based.

Auditory perception difficulties. Some children are slow in attaching meaning to the word they hear or in distinguishing between sounds in words, especially the short vowels. For example, they will confuse 'till' and 'tell'. When confronted by written symbols they have difficulty in recalling the sound equivalent. When speaking they may substitute one sound for another or reverse sounds or syllables. Their understanding of what they hear will be found to vary from day to day.

Visual perception difficulties. When writing some children persist in reversing letters or groups of letters. Most have outgrown this by the age of six but some continue and their difficulty is so marked that they 'mirror-write' or invert complete lines of written material. When reading they confuse words which look similar or omit words and phrases. This is often mistaken for carelessness and inattention.

Other features of the perceptually handicapped child. On examination these children, whether their difficulties are mainly auditory or mainly verbal or both are likely to give the impression of general immaturity. They may have difficulty in distinguishing right from left and show poor orientation in space and time. Their results in either verbal or performance tests will give an I.Q. which is lower than their potential intelligence warrants. The perceptually handicapped child will be slow to develop a body image (a drawing of himself will reveal this) because he has failed to learn from the usual clues—visual, auditory, kinaesthetic and tactile—to locate objects in space relative to himself and to other objects and to grasp the relationship of different parts of his body to each other. Consequently he has difficulty in perceiving spatial relations, motion and direction.

Relating parts to wholes is necessary in learning to generalize and to form concepts. So the perceptually handicapped child will be slow in classifying objects, perceiving differences in quantity and in relating cause and effect.

He will be easily distracted, unable to distinguish between significant and unessential stimuli and try to react to everything at once so that his *behaviour* may be restless and uncontrolled. He will have difficulty in grasping the whole of a given task and retaining in his mind the sequence required for its completion. 'Anything that can be pushed, pulled, twisted, folded or bent may elicit a motor response' and this failure to control impulse involves danger. His slowness in completing what he is given to do is often mistakenly set down to laziness or day-dreaming. In fact, slowness arises from disorganized thinking, perseveration, and a rigidity which inhibits him from moving on to the next stage in what he is doing. A sudden explosive fit of crying or outbreak of motor activity may be precipitated by the prospect of a new or more difficult assignment. He may be emotionally labile generally and his emotions may often be expressed in aggression.

His *standard of performance* will vary. What was accomplished easily one day will present as a new difficult task the next. He will alternate between appearing bright and competent on one occasion and unaccountably slow, incapable and unable to concentrate on another.

Some children who present this picture at six or seven have almost caught up with normal children by the time they are nine or ten and other members of their family may show a similar history. Their handicap has been explained as a development lag. In other cases (as also in the family history) there is persisting failure to develop language functions continuing into adult life. Stogdill suggests that this is a recognizable clinical entity which has been called 'primary language disability syndrome'. Because these children have many features in common with children who have a definite history of brain damage, their disability has been set down to subtle brain damage although there is no history, or physical laboratory finding that would support such a diagnosis. More cautiously it is sometimes described as 'minimal brain dysfunction'. In a proportion of cases of persisting difficulty in reading, it seems likely from the work of Kinsbourne and Warrington (1963) that we are faced with a developmental Gerstmann's syndrome (see p. 496). A large number of mild difficulties with reading are explained by emotional factors and recourse to cerebral damage seems unnecessary. However, although the concept of 'minimal brain damage' or dysfunction as a cause of some language difficulties has as yet no firm factual foundation it provides a plausible hypothesis deserving much further exploration.

Early recognition of the difficulty is very important, as it may very largely be surmounted by specific educational methods, especially oral teaching by the method of auditory repetition, and the repetitive association of visual patterns with sounds (Critchley, 1964).

Early Infantile Autism (Kanner's Syndrome)

Kanner's classic paper 'Autistic Disturbances of Affective Contact' was published in 1943; his account of the syndrome, which he later named early infantile autism, was based on eleven cases. Since then the number of cases observed and reported on by Kanner and his collaborators has increased to well over a hundred. Very unfortunately, while on the one hand insisting on the uniqueness and specificity of the syndrome, they have classified it as one of the forms of childhood schizophrenia (Kanner, 1948; Eisenberg and Kanner, 1956). This *semantic confusion*, giving to the term 'schizophrenia' on the one hand a purely descriptive connotation and on the other hand allowing it some classificatory value (as if it had aetiological, diagnostic and prognostic significance), has been the foundation on which a veritable psychiatric Tower of Babel has grown. Conditions of the most heterogeneous kinds have been discovered by a variety of workers to be related to Kanner's syndrome, and they too have been regarded as forms of childhood schizophrenia. If, as a consequence, childhood 'schizophrenia' comes to bear no resemblance to schizophrenia of the adult, this gives no one cause for doubt or hesitation; as the child is so different from the adult, one should not expect childhood schizophrenia to bear any resemblance to adult schizophrenia! An eminent English authority on the subject once said to us, 'it seems to me that everything is schizophrenia, and schizophrenia is everything'. The reader will not expect the authors of this textbook to share that view.

Kanner's syndrome has many *characteristic features* and is fairly well circumscribed. During the first few months of life no abnormality is detected; at a later time there are likely to be difficulties in establishing normal routines of eating, sleeping and elimination. There may also be long spells of implacable and apparently unmotivated screaming, or —a more characteristic phenomenon—the child may be abnormally quiet. The earliest typical symptom to appear at about the fourth month is that the baby does not lift up its arms when about to be picked up; held against the mother's body, the baby does not mould himself to her, and the mother complains that he is not cuddly. Kanner emphasizes as pathognomonic the child's aloneness, and his need to impose on the environment an unchanging sameness. Speech never develops normally, and there is a failure to use language for the purpose of communication. Speech shows pronominal reversal, echolalia, affirmation by repetition, literalness. The desire for sameness is enforced by the development of routines; and if an attempt is made to get the child to deviate, it is met by rage and aggression, or by panic. Kanner and Eisenberg believe that, despite a retardation in speech which may be so extreme that the child never learns to talk, he still has good cognitive potentialities. Memory is good, and may be unusually so, especially for learning by rote.

In the first hundred cases there were 80 boys and 20 girls. Other observers, who have accepted Kanner's syndrome without dilution, have also found approximately a 4:1 ratio of male and female. There is no easy explanation for this, though a similar *sex ratio* has been found in other congenital disorders of development.

As a rule the children are good looking, even beautiful, often with graceful movements. A very striking and remarkable feature is the *look of intelligence* they have, say at about the age of five, so different from the dull, vacant, apathetic gaze of most seriously retarded children. To the newcomer in this field, his first sight of one of these children, absorbed in his own singular occupation, whose bright alert gaze slides past or through him, is not to be forgotten. It is perhaps this appearance as much as anything that led Kanner to think his children had good potentialities, potentialities unfortunately that are rarely realized.

Eisenberg (1956) reports the *outlook* as being highly *unfavourable*. A follow-up of 63 of Kanner's first 100 cases after a period of 4 to 20 years, showed that only 3 had achieved a good result, functioning well at academic, social and community level, though still perhaps somewhat odd persons. In 14 cases the result was fair, the patients (at an average age of 15) being able to attend schools at a level commensurate with their age; they had some meaningful contacts with other people, but retained 'schizoid' traits of personality sufficiently marked to cause trouble. The remaining 46 patients were hospital or family invalids. The nature of the outcome was closely related to speech development. About half of these children remained speechless, and of them only one out of 31 had a fair result. This very gloomy report should not be regarded as final. There is every indication that better results are already being obtained with modern training methods.

The guiding light of child psychiatry has long been the idea that the *causes* of the psychological disorders of childhood are to be sought in abnormalities and disturbances of the child–parent relationship. If this idea is to be used as a working hypothesis, rather than as irrefutable dogma, it suffers from the deficiency that there are no normal standards by which to judge. Accordingly any and every child–parent relationship, once put under the dissecting microscope, is found to be amiss; and one and the same mother will be told that she is, say, too distant and also too involved, by different experts at the same time, and by the same expert at different times. Looking to the child–parent relationship for a clue to the causation of early infantile autism, Kanner made two observations, of which one is probably significant and the other is not. In the first place, he found that the parents of these children were with remarkable consistency highly intelligent and highly educated people, both of them usually having a college education, and the fathers often professional men of distinction. Kanner's other private patients fell well below this standard. This result has been put down to a sampling error, since parents brought their children to Kanner from all over the United States and it may well have been the most intelligent and the best informed who sought him out. However the result has been confirmed. Selective bias would seem to have been avoided in the study made by Wing, O'Connor and Lotter (1967), who attempted a complete ascertainment of autistic children in all the children in the county of Middlesex aged 8, 9 or 10 on 1st January 1964. They found that 60 per cent. of the fathers of children in the core group (Kanner's syndrome) were in social classes I and II, compared with 18 per cent. in the general population of England and Wales; 21 per cent. of the mothers and 29 per cent. of the fathers were university graduates; and both mothers and fathers had intelligence quotients significantly higher than expected when tested on the Mill Hill vocabulary scale.

Kanner and Eisenberg believe that the parents of autistic children constitute a deviant group in personality also; as yet, this observation has not been confirmed. The parents were reported as being detached, humourless, obsessive personalities, treating their child with mechanical perfectionism, in an atmosphere of emotional refrigeration. It was rather held against them that they were able to provide such excellent and objective accounts of the development of their child. They also noticed that the incidence of mental illness in relatives was very low; only one of the first 200 parents had experienced a psychotic episode, and only six had had clinical psychiatric disorders; in the 400 grandparents and 373 known uncles and aunts there were only twelve cases of mental illness (Eisenberg and Kanner, 1956).

The general picture of Kanner's syndrome has been confirmed and further described by a number of other workers. Our knowledge has been advanced, particularly by Rimland (1964) and by the Maudsley group (Wing, 1967), to the point where it seems fairly safe to *classify the condition among organic disorders*.

Rimland has given an excellent account of the literature, as well as elaborating his own views on the pathogenesis. He stresses the evidence for the persistence of *islands of normal and superior ability* above the general depression of function caused by the autism and the

PLATE XVI

Childhood autism. The two upper photographs show the aloof child
in immobile postures; the lower ones show posturing and perplexity
in perceiving while scrutinizing and exploring parts of the body.

speech handicap. The child may show a phenomenal ability to recall the exact state of the environment; one block experimentally turned, in a jumble of blocks the child had left on the floor, was noticed at once on his return to the room, causing screams of rage until the original placing had been exactly restored. Remarkable rote memory for poems and names, timetables, shapes of wheels of motorcars, etc., are recorded. Spatial ability as tested by the Seguin formboard is well preserved. The children are often good at jigsaws, and may assemble the puzzle as well or better with the pieces face down as face up to show the picture. One may speculate that the children find difficulty with a complex visual gestalt, so that an excess of information proves a hindrance rather than a help. In general the children are agile and graceful, and show good, sometimes exceptional, manual ability and finger dexterity. Musical interest and exceptional musical ability are shown quite frequently; in one of Kanner's earliest cases the boy eventually became a composer. Mathematical ability is also common. Rimland comments that *idiots savants* have excelled in calculation, music, art, mechanics, mental calendar manipulation and memory; most of these are on the list of the autistic child's abilities and interests. It may be that some of the *idiots savants* of mental institutions that have been reported from time to time represent the end-states of what had been autistic children.

Kanner's belief that children with infantile autism were initially well endowed but suffered damage, which is supported by Rimland, has come under criticism. Bender (1959), for instance, points out that the better the psychometric examination of a retarded child, the more likely it is that islands of relative normality will be found by subtests of one or another kind. However Mittler (1967) found that there was much more variability between subtest results in children with early childhood autism than in matched controls of mentally subnormal children of equivalent I.Q.

Rimland considers a psychogenic aetiology of the syndrome to be very unlikely. There are cogent objections which can be made to the arguments on which this theory of causation is based; and apart from that there are many features of the condition which fit much better with specific organic causation: the onset 'from the moment of birth' (Kanner), the large male preponderance, the 100 per cent. concordance in MZ twin pairs*, the similarity of the syndrome to the known consequences of organic brain disease, and its uniqueness and specificity with an absence of gradations between infantile autism and normality. Rimland believes that infantile autism is a form of cognitive dysfunction; the function which is particularly affected being the ability to relate new stimuli to remembered experience. This can be compared with the Eisenberg-Kanner theory (Eisenberg, 1956) that, like the brain-damaged, the autistic child is unable to organize perceptions into functional patterns, but that this inability is not on a perceptual basis, as in the brain-damaged, but at a higher level where purpose and meaning are lost. Eisenberg says the the primary psychopathologic mechanism is a disturbance in social perception; affective contact is lacking. In his view there can be no anatomical locus for such a disability, which is a reflection of the failure of cortical integration of the affective and cognitive components of behaviour. It will be seen how the views of a leading proponent of the psychogenic school approximate to Rimland's conception. A priori, there is no particular reason why the somewhat loosely defined dysfunction postulated by Eisenberg should not be associated with localized damage or maldevelopment in the brain.

* Kamp (1964) has described an autistic syndrome, not regarded as identical with Kanner's syndrome, in a four-year-old girl, one of a pair of MZ twins, her twin sister being normal. In fact, the clinical similarity with Kanner's syndrome is a close one.

Rimland develops a somewhat speculative hypothesis that the brain-system specially involved in infantile autism is the reticular formation of the brain-stem. He quotes the work of Keeler to show how one possible mode of pathogenesis could account for some of the curious features of the syndrome.

Keeler (1958) reported on five blind children with retrolental fibroplasia who had been referred because of an almost typically autistic syndrome. She then examined 35 other children with retrolental fibroplasia in an institution for blind children. They had not been referred to a psychiatrist, but they all showed a similar autistic syndrome, though to a lesser degree, so that they were educable. On the other hand, 18 children blind with purely ocular defects, and 17 blinded after birth by local conditions, did not show the syndrome. Retrolental fibroplasia is very probably only part of a more general damage. Children who suffer from the condition have usually been premature infants who were nursed in an oxygen tent; and it is thought that certain immature tissues are especially susceptible to oxygen poisoning, from even a slightly raised oxygen tension in the alveolar air. Rimland points out that there are infrequent cases of children with retrolental dysplasia who have only been submitted to oxygen at atmospheric tension, and who therefore can be presumed to have much greater than normal susceptibility. Autistic children may have had just such a raised susceptibility, and have been poisoned by oxygen at atmospheric pressure, the tissues that suffer in their case being in the central nervous system. Such a hypersensitivity of central nervous tissue might (perhaps!) be expected of children of two parents both highly intelligent, who are, as it were, 'homozygotic' for high intelligence. Ill supported as it is by any concrete evidence, this hypothesis (if one were to generalize hyperoxia to a much wider range of noxae) would suggest the possibility of a number of lines of research.

The work of the Maudsley group, in the book edited by J. K. Wing (1967), represents a comprehensive attack from a number of sides on the important problems offered by Kanner's syndrome. Wing gives good reason to enlarge the confines of the syndrome, and while reserving the name of Kanner's syndrome for the nuclear group of autistic states starting during the first year of life, if not from birth, he brings in an approximately equal number of cases nearly but not quite so typical, in some of which development in the earliest months seems to have been normal, the first symptoms being shown after the first year and sometimes as late as the fourth. Clinically these children were not easily to be distinguished from the others, and they are all brought together under the title of 'early childhood autism'.

The *prevalence* of this condition was estimated by Wing, O'Connor and Lotter (1967), in a survey of all children aged eight, nine and ten in the County of Middlesex on 1st January 1964, as constituting approximately 4·5 per 10,000 of their age group. One could estimate that in the whole of England and Wales there would be about 3,000 such children of school age, a figure which is comparable with the 1,422 blind children and the 3,356 deaf children.

Wing believes that the basic disability is that the child has difficulty in making meaningful patterns out of both auditory and visual stimuli; handicapped in the 'distance' senses, he is likely to make as much use as possible of the 'close' senses of touch, taste and smell (and hence perhaps also derive his special liking for kinaesthetic and vestibular stimulation). These difficulties lead to the speech disorder, and together impair his relationships with the environment and cause the odd behaviour, the autism, and the emotional disturbances. Not only is the condition of variable severity, but in every child the pattern of disabilities and retained abilities varies too.

Autistic children have difficulty in making use of auditory information; they will show 'auditory avoidance' (e.g. by covering the ears) especially to loud noises and to speech. Other sounds may be liked, and music is generally enjoyed; many children can sing when they cannot talk. The visual perceptual difficulty is of a similar kind. The more complex and variable the object, the less easily is it comprehended; a child may not recognize his own house at a distance. Human beings, who offer insuperable difficulties to the child by presenting him with both visual and auditory stimuli of a highly complex and changing kind, are met by visual avoidance, by covering the eyes or turning the head away. The child prefers to use peripheral to central vision, and looks past objects or people. Some children play with their fingers at the periphery of vision.

Speech may not develop at all, or may begin and be lost, but most usually begins about the age of five and develops very slowly. Echolalia, almost universal, is shown both in an immediate form (e.g. by repeating the question), and delayed (repeating a phrase from something he has heard, hours or days later, again and again). 'Pronominal reversal', the child using 'you' for 'I', or speaking in the third person, is probably a simple consequence of echolalia; it has been fancifully interpreted as evidence that the child has lost sense of its own identity. Dysphasic phenomena, of kinds which occur in the normal child but only over a limited period, are invariable: using parts of words for the whole, using the wrong one of words commonly coupled ('brush' for 'comb'), using words in a metaphorical sense or portmanteau words. 'No' is learned sooner than 'yes'; and all the small words, prepositions and conjunctions, etc., offer particular difficulty. Wing discusses for comparison the symptoms shown in developmental aphasia, as described by Orton (1937) and Ingram (1959), and concludes that in effect there are no differences of significance. There is no reason to avoid using the term 'aphasic' in describing the speech of autistic children; but one should recognize that they suffer from other disabilities as well. In fact, they show a variety of focal anomalies of the kinds one associates with cortical parietal and temporal lobe lesions, aphasia and agraphia, dyslexia, visual agnosia, dressing dyspraxia and other apraxias, etc. Wing agrees with Rimland in thinking that cognitive disabilities are at the heart of the problem, and that the autistic behaviour is secondary to them.

Wing has no hesitation in rejecting the psychogenic hypothesis when discussing the aetiology. Children who are brought up in a totally deprived setting, e.g. a poorly run institution, do not seem to run any special risk of developing childhood autism. In all the literature on severe maternal deprivation (Bowlby, Ainsworth, Spitz and others) there is no claim of an association with Kanner's syndrome. Despite the statements of Kanner, Eisenberg and many others, there is no scientifically acceptable evidence that the mothers (or the fathers) of autistic children are unduly cold or abnormal, not to say pathogenic. Given the right slant one can see the gifted, conscientious, efficient and reserved as over-intellectual, obsessional, mechanical and cold. It is exceedingly rare for the mother of an autistic child to have a second with the same disability (unless they are monozygotic twins); the other children she will have will be normal.

One may equally dismiss the idea that there is any relationship between Kanner's syndrome and schizophrenia. There is no very close similarity between the clinical symptoms of early infantile autism, or early childhood autism, and schizophrenia; the disturbances of thought and language, for instance, are quite distinct. Adult schizophrenia does not occur with any more than random frequency in the kinship of autistic children, and Kanner's syndrome does not occur in the kinship of schizophrenics. Adult schizophrenics never give a history of an autistic syndrome in childhood; and cases of Kanner's syndrome do not grow up into adult schizophrenics. The after-history of these children is in fact characteristic of gradual and partial adjustment to a severe and lasting but stationary disability.

The treatment of Kanner's syndrome may be briefly touched on. Medical treatment is useful only for assistance with some of the symptoms, such as the screaming attacks; phenothiazines and antidepressants have been used. It should be remembered that the most distressing symptoms, such as screaming and self-isolation, are at their worst in the early years, and tend to diminish after the age of five or six.

Psychotherapy along conventional lines has proved entirely useless. A permissive unstructured environment is not suitable for these children, and they need a well-planned routine with little deviation from day to day, in order to provide the much needed sense of security, and to combat their own tendency towards morbid routines and obsessive rituals. An exceedingly *carefully adjusted and very gently progressive educational regime* is required, no advance being made until the foundation for it is fully stabilized. Operant conditioning, for instance as described by Lovaas (1967), would seem to be both theoretically and practically a promising line of training. This has to be taken extremely slowly in order not to overload the child with stimuli more complex than he can grasp; the first steps may be to teach the child to imitate, something that the normal child does spontaneously. Results obtained by training methods are certainly more encouraging than those reached by analytically oriented psychotherapy. The development of speech is, of course, favourable for further improvement; but it has been shown that the child's measured intelligence (these children are rarely untestable, if the right tests are used) is the best indicator of what one may finally expect. With right handling the autism consistently improves; and though intellectual functions do not progress with equal steps, they respond to the point where, by the age of ten or so, education in a normal school may be possible.

Other Autistic States ('Childhood Schizophrenia')

It is the practice among many child psychiatrists to regard 'childhood schizophrenia' as compatible with mental retardation, organic brain disease, and even such aetiologically distinct syndromes as phenylketonuria. It is clear that the term 'schizophrenia' so used can have no aetiological significance at all, and must be a purely descriptive symptomatic one. But 'schizophrenia' has been preempted by adult psychiatry to name a concept with aetiological, diagnostic and prognostic significance; and it is not legitimate for child psychiatrists to take over the word for a completely different use.

There is no evidence that 'childhood schizophrenia' has any relationship whatever with adult schizophrenia. We have the statement of Bender (1961) that from 66 per cent. to 89 per cent. of the children 'diagnosed as schizophrenic' at Bellevue were later cases of adolescent or adult schizophrenia. No substantiation of these figures is provided, and no clue as to what is meant by any of the three kinds of schizophrenia, childhood, adolescent or adult. Bender has defined schizophrenia as 'a total psychobiological disorder in the regulation of maturation of all the basic behaviour functions seen clinically in children', which would seem to mean just about everything. Bender and Faretra (1961) reported very high incidences of pregnancy and birth problems in all three classifications of 'schizophrenic', 'organic' and 'behaviour disordered' children. There was a history of one or more of the following abnormalities in respectively 63 per cent., 80 per cent. and 56 per cent. of children in the three groups: abnormal delivery, respiratory disorder being maintained in an incubator, jaundice, Caesarean section, twins, neonatal abnormalities. Bender (1961) has also reported on 51 patients considered 'schizophrenic' in childhood who had also some form of convulsive disorder; 31 of them were regarded as essentially organic, while in a further 9 epilepsy was thought to be combined with schizophrenia. It would seem clear that an organic causation is very much in the picture for Bender's conception of schizophrenia; and it is to be supposed that her report of 1961 means no more than that organically damaged children observed at Bellevue in 66–89 per cent. of cases gave evidence of being organically damaged in later life.

The *heavy incidence of organic damage* in children labelled as schizophrenic has been observed by others. Creak (1963a) comments that many so-called psychotic children appear to have sustained minimal brain damage; and Creak and Ini (1960) noted that in their series maternal age was 1·6 years older than the average for the general population. In her follow-up study (1963b) Creak reported that, of her series of 100 childhood psychotics, two had died in hospital in their later twenties, each of them with the pathological findings of a neurolipidosis; in addition there were 12 cases of epilepsy, in seven of which onset of fits followed the onset of psychosis.

It should perhaps be emphasized that a substantial minority of children presenting initially with autism of the Kanner type subsequently prove to have brain damage. In a recent 5–15 year follow-up study of a group of 63 psychotic children (the majority with abnormalities from early infancy) evidence of brain damage was obtained during the follow-up period in a quarter of the cases; none had shown equivocal neurological abnormalities when first examined. The children were often of normal intelligence and the picture was typical in all other respects of infantile autism (Rutter *et al.*, 1967). Creak's material was probably made up to a considerable extent of clinically typical cases. The nature of the material reported on by some other authors is less certain. Malamud (1959) reports 6 cases in which the diagnosis of childhood schizophrenia had been made, who were later shown clinicopathologically to have degenerative brain disease.

Goldfarb (1961) compared 26 seriously disturbed 'schizophrenic' children with a control group of 26 normal children. The so-called schizophrenic children proved inferior to the others in perceptual tests involving figure-ground discrimination, psychomotor behaviour, speech and capacity for abstraction. Though gross organic lesions had been eliminated before the start, it was still possible to classify the disturbed children into an organic and a non-organic group on clinical psychiatric grounds. This distinction was validated by independent examination showing 'soft' neurological signs, and by histories suggestive of early brain damage. The organic 'schizophrenics' outnumbered the others. This work has been further validated, as regards the significance of perinatal factors, by Taft and Goldfarb (1964).

The evidence suggests, then, that the majority of children, whose autistic symptoms lead to their classification as 'schizophrenic', are either brain-damaged or develop some progressive organic process. For any progress to be made in this field, such cases should be carefully sorted out, and what then remains could be made the subject of special study. Further investigation of aetiological factors should be kept distinct in the organic and non-organic groups.

Information on *aetiological aspects* so far available is very slight. Bender (1963) reports a heavy familial incidence of 'schizophrenia': 40 per cent. of 143 'schizophrenic' children had one parent 'schizophrenic', 10 per cent. had both parents 'schizophrenic', and 8 per cent. had a 'schizophrenic' sib. No clinical information of any kind is provided about the so-called schizophrenias of either probands or relatives. Pollack and Gittelman (1964) have reviewed available publications on the siblings of children with childhood 'schizophrenia'. Apart from the well-known paper by Kallmann and Roth (1956) these communications seem to be of very poor quality, without clinical data and usually without age distributions. The authors conclude that only five studies systematically evaluated the status of the sibling; among singleton siblings there was a concordance rate of 8 per cent. As noted earlier, Kallmann and Roth's series were pre-adolescent cases, and not children; if they had been eliminated the findings would have been even less impressive. The report by Creak and Ini is more reliable, and shows a negligible incidence of psychosis in the families. The series of 102 cases included those children whose deviation in development was judged to be different from simple mental defect. As noted earlier, the maternal age was found to be raised. One father and 1 mother had had schizophrenic illnesses (no clinical data), 2 fathers and 2 mothers had had epileptic attacks at some time, and in addition there were 3 mothers with depressive episodes, 1 father with an anxiety-depression and one father with dementia following head injury. In the 79 families with more than one child there were 2 with one other psychotic and 4 with a mentally defective child, all male.

Psychogenesis is very widely regarded as providing the primary causation of childhood psychosis. All the available evidence goes against this. Creak and Ini, for instance, found no support for the view that 'parental personalities and child-rearing attitudes are a principal cause of childhood psychosis'. Klebanoff (1959) studied the attitudes to their children of 15 mothers of schizophrenics, 15 mothers of brain-injured and retarded children, and 26 mothers whose children were adjusting normally. The highest degree of disturbance in attitude was found in the mothers of the encephalopathic children whose disturbances were clearly not of psychogenic origin. Klebanoff concludes that there is some evidence of a reactive disturbance in the mothers of schizophrenic children, but no suggestion of a primary one of aetiological significance. The experienced child analyst Mahler, reviewing a broad experience with the mothers of 'schizophrenic' children (1961), rejects the concept of the 'schizophrenogenic mother'; she notes that while many mothers are clearly disturbed, many others belong in the large group of 'ordinary devoted mothers'.

In so far as they have a bearing on psychogenesis, the available reports on intensive psychotherapy for psychotic children are of some interest. Brown (1960), starting with 73 children with 'atypical development' (a new name for 'childhood schizophrenia'), ranging from $1\frac{1}{2}$ to $5\frac{1}{2}$ years, reports on a follow-up when the group were aged 6 to 17 years; many of the children and their parents had received intensive psychotherapy. The author reports that 'surprisingly enough' no treatment variables were significant. Boatman and Szurek (1960) experienced the same disappointment. Their work, carried out over a period of twelve years, was designed to test two hypotheses: that the psychotic disorders of childhood are entirely psychogenic, and that the schizophrenic disorder could be reversed if the psychotherapy were sufficiently intensive. The hypotheses were tested on 100 pre-adolescent children. Of this total, 20 showed major improvement in the course of therapy, 3 of them having severe difficulties later. The remainder failed to show any significant improvement. With regard to the first hypothesis, the authors failed to find any particular kind of traumatic event, parental neurosis, or parent–child interaction which was unique in the families of psychotic children. As regards the second hypothesis, the reader will conclude that, at the best, intensive psychotherapy achieves results which are about as favourable as no treatment at all, and probably a good deal less favourable than planned education.

Minimal Chronic Brain Syndromes
(Minimal Brain Damage, Minimal Cerebral Dysfunction)

At the time of birth every infant is subjected to a period, short or long, of asphyxia. Brain cells are extremely sensitive to *anoxia*, and cannot survive more than a few seconds of total deprivation of an oxygenated blood supply. The asphyxial period through which the infant passes on the way to being born is estimated as being quite commonly of two or three minutes' duration, and during this time the oxygen tension of the blood must be dropping rapidly. Four or five minutes of asphyxia are not regarded as dangerous; and even after as long a period as twenty minutes infants have been known to survive without obvious signs of brain damage. Nevertheless it seems probable that during the process of birth there is some destruction of neurones in every case, and the fact that normally there is no indication of brain damage can be attributed to the large reserve capacity of the brain and its powers of adaptation. This capacity must show a good deal of individual variation, and it may be that well-endowed brains are better able to compensate for neuronic loss in the birth process than are the less well-endowed. This may, perhaps, be one reason why there is a raised incidence of the known brain damage syndromes of infancy in social class V. The birth process, of course, stands out as the time of all times when the risk of brain damage to the infant is critically enhanced. But both intra-uterine life and the neonatal period up to the end of the first year are also times of danger in which a variety of noxae may take effect.

The brain's capacity to adapt functionally to any localized damage is of a very high order over the whole of this danger period, and only begins very gradually to diminish as childhood succeeds infancy. Even in advanced adult life it is still shown, for instance in the powers of recuperation in both speech and motility of the middle-aged man after a hemiplegia. Adaptation depends very largely on the transfer of functional control from the damaged side to homologous structure-systems of the opposite hemisphere. The most remarkable evidence of adaptation by transfer has been provided in the course of study of infantile hemiplegics subjected to hemispherectomy (p. 676). McFie (1963) quotes the case of a patient operated on by McKissock who had her entire right cerebral hemisphere removed at the age of twenty; ten years after the operation she had a moderate physical handicap, but had an I.Q. of about 105, and had married and had 3 children. McFie comments, 'experience with hemispherectomy suggests that injury to either hemisphere at birth or in the first year results in *all* psychological functions becoming established in the intact hemisphere'.

As a working hypothesis one may advance the suggestion that brain damage, e.g. from anoxia, suffered by the newborn child, unless of an extremely massive kind, will only become manifest in so far as homologous structures in both hemispheres are affected; under other circumstances adaptation will occur. This would introduce a large fortuitous element into the relationship between the insult and the functional disability such as accords well with clinical observation.

Objections have been made to the term '*minimal brain damage*' on the grounds that it implies that there has been an episode which has produced anatomical change (when, it is said, there is often no history of an injuring process), and that there is commonly no evidence of actual damage, what is observed being a disorder of function. To these objections one might reply that every child goes through an episode which is likely to produce anatomical change; and in any case one need expect no parity between the amount of anatomical change and the degree of dysfunction it causes, since everything will depend on the accidental circumstance whether there is bilateral homologous localization. The international study group held at Oxford in 1962 (MacKeith and Bax, 1963) came to a majority conclusion that the term 'minimal brain damage' should be abandoned; though no adequate alternative could be found, there was some acceptance for the term 'minimal cerebral dysfunction'. This seems to us less satisfactory. 'Minimal brain damage' could be used clinically to cover disabilities which were believed to have been produced by physical causes (rather than emotional or psychogenic ones), which were stationary and non-progressive, which could be expected to improve with maturation, and which would need specific remedial education, training and physiotherapy. The term 'minimal cerebral dysfunction' does not lend itself for the categorization of any clinically significant group of cases.

The importance of *perinatal stress factors* in the causation of a great variety of syndromes has been underlined by the work of Pasamanick and his colleagues. For example Kawi and Pasamanick (1958) matched the prenatal and hospital birth records of 205 boys with reading disabilities with those of 205 controls; 16·6 per cent. of the former as against 1·5 per cent. of the latter had been exposed to two or more maternal complications, especially pre-eclampsia, hypertension, bleeding during pregnancy. By similar work they have connected maternal risks with risk to the child of epilepsy, cerebral palsy, mental deficiency, tics and childhood behaviour disorders. Knobloch and Pasamanick (1959), comparing at 40 weeks 500 prematurely born with 492 full-term infants, found higher incidences in the former of indications of brain damage of all four classified degrees of severity: possible minimal damage (13·5 per cent.: 10·4 per cent.), minimal damage (16·3 per cent. : 10·0 per cent.), possible cerebral palsy (6·1 per cent. : 1·0 per cent.), overt abnormality (2·1 per cent. : 0·6 per cent.). Pasamanick postulates a 'continuum of reproductive casualty', showing its effects all the way down from foetal and neonatal deaths to the minimal brain syndromes under discussion here.

However, it is not only environmentally determined noxae, prematurity, hypoxia, infections, vascular accidents, etc., which may produce specific non-progressive disabilities and dysfunctions; *genetical causes* also enter the picture. It is a commonplace that there is a very wide range of individual variation in general intelligence. There is probably an equal and largely independent variability in other nervous functions (passing motor, speech and reading milestones, eye-hand coordination, deftness and agility, etc.). Accordingly some children may be unduly hyperkinetic, or unduly clumsy, or otherwise at a disadvantage solely as a consequence of normal variation. However, since genetical and biochemical variations

Area of Cerebral Function	Possible Overt Manifestations	Borderline Manifestations
Motor	Cerebral palsies	Minor choreoathetosis or tremor Isolated hyperreflexia Excessive clumsiness
Mental	Mental deficiency	Mild or minimal retardation Overactivity, impulsiveness, distractability, short attention span, low frustration tolerance, tantrums Perseveration, concrete patterns of thought, difficulty in abstraction, dyscalculia
Sensory	Cortical blindness or deafness Visual field defects Astereognosis, impaired 2-point discrimination, etc.	Impaired memory for shapes or designs Impaired spatial concepts Visual or tactile inattention (extinction)
Convulsive	Epilepsy	Abnormal E.E.G. without seizures

(From Paine 1962)

show their effects at a particular stage in maturation, affecting both sides of the brain equally, we have in addition the dysgenesias in which certain systems of the brain suffer delayed maturation or inadequate development. From such causes may arise some of the developmental dysphasias, agnosias, and dyspraxias, which may show up in sharp contrast to otherwise normal functioning in the child of average or good intelligence, or may prove a disability of critical significance in the child who is not otherwise well-endowed. It seems difficult to cover these disorders under the term 'brain damage', so that we have preferred to group both genetically and environmentally determined cases together as '*minimal chronic brain syndromes*'. All that is meant by 'minimal' in this connexion is that the degree of disability should be less than obvious and such as to need careful examination for its detection and specification. It follows that all 'minimal chronic brain syndromes' are related to syndromes of major severity, but likely to be encountered very much more frequently. These relationships may be conveniently shown in Paine's tabulation (1962), shown above.

Other Brain Syndromes

We may now briefly discuss some of the *loosely definable individual syndromes* with the qualification that, in the case of any given child, symptoms from more than one 'syndrome' will very probably be seen. Some child psychiatrists would indeed say that individual variation, in the way in which symptoms are combined, is so great that organization into syndromes goes beyond the observational basis.

MINIMAL CEREBRAL PALSY. The paediatrician Elisabeth Köng (1963) estimates the social problem caused by this syndrome as one of some magnitude. In many school classes there is a clumsy child, who writes slowly and badly, who does not concentrate well, is slow in his reactions and is awkward at gymnastics. Children like this are misjudged by their school-teachers, their comrades and their parents, because of their normal appearance, and are handled in the worst imaginable way, ridiculed, scolded, exhorted and over-taxed. Psychologically they are aware of not doing well, and are liable to anxiety over failure, to stuttering, shyness, self-isolation, and to overcompensate for their inferiority complex by various forms of behaviour disorder. Clinical examination will reveal minimal spasticity, minimal athetosis or minimal ataxia. It is most important that parents and teachers should be informed about the nature of the disorder, as a minimal cerebral palsy, if they are to make the necessary allowances for the child's difficulties.

These difficulties are shown more widely than in the motor field alone. Hansen (1963) examined 55 Danish and 19 English ten-year-old children suffering from a variety of conditions of this kind (spastic hemiplegia, spastic diplegia, ataxia, athetosis and combinations) and found that in all neurological types there were additional focal psychological disabilities. Of these 74 children, 31 had difficulties in reading and writing, 26 had dyscalculia, 27 had right/left confusion, 18 finger agnosia and 26 constructive apraxia. The average I.Q. for the Danish children was 90, and in no case below 80; the average for the English children was lower.

Illingworth (1963), at the Oxford symposium, reported on 27 children, chosen from a total of 500 with cerebral palsy, who had normal gait, minimal neurological signs on careful testing, and no history of any causative postnatal disease. These children caused concern in their parents by their clumsiness, by falling, bruising themselves, being slow and awkward. At school many of them got into serious trouble (e.g. for 'bad writing'), and might be made very unhappy and disturbed. I.Q. scores tended to be below average, but some were superior, and one was 138.

Focal psychological deficit as a cause of backwardness in learning to read and write was brought out in a study by Kinsbourne and Warrington (1963). Gerstmann's syndrome, in which finger agnosia, right/left disorientation, dysgraphia and dyscalculia are combined, is regarded by these authors as most probably a disorder of the unitary function of ordering objects (fingers, letters of words, etc.) relatively to one another. Applying finger tests to normal schoolchildren, they found a normal growth curve, with the proportion of successes increasing from the age of $4\frac{1}{2}$ to reach a 50 per cent. level at $5\frac{3}{4}$ and 95 per cent. at $7\frac{1}{2}$. In a series of children referred for examination because of backwardness at reading or writing, some failed these tests though they were of normal intelligence and old enough to pass. The spelling mistakes they made were of the 'order' type; they showed selective impairment on subtests of the WISC with a high spatial loading; they did badly on tests of mechanical arithmetic; they confused right and left. In fact they showed all the features of Gerstmann's syndrome in a developmental setting.

THE CHOREIFORM SYNDROME: THE HYPERKINETIC SYNDROME. This was first described by Prechtl and Stemmer (1962), and has been generally accepted. While taking the E.E.G.s of some overactive children who had been referred because of poor school performance, the authors noticed that there were chorea-like twitchings of the limbs and head, showing up on the E.E.G. as muscle artefacts from the cervical and temporal muscles. A group of 50 such children were more fully studied. The children showed slight jerky movements, occurring quite irregularly and arhythmically in muscles of the tongue, face, neck and trunk, and sometimes in the limbs as well. Case histories showed that two-thirds of the patients had had one or more obstetrical or postnatal troubles, and in more than three-quarters the history was at least suggestive of perinatal complications. The syndrome was regarded as a form of minimal brain damage, falling into the category of cerebral palsy.

Prechtl's syndrome appears to be clinically related to the hyperkinetic syndrome first described by Kramer and Pollnow (1932). This is a condition of persisting motor unrest which makes its appearance between the ages of two and four years, in association with cerebral damage or epilepsy. The children are slow to develop intellectually, although intelligence ranges from high average to low-grade defect. There is marked distractability, a tireless unrelenting exploration of the environment, and a tendency to put objects into the mouth, and suck, bite, or chew them (Ingram, 1956). The child is often very aggressive, especially to his brothers and sisters, who may be brutally attacked without provocation; as a rule he is fearless and unaffected by threats or punishment. Parents complain of the cold unaffectionate character of the child; where the condition has followed cerebral damage occurring in childhood after a period of normal development, the change in the affective side of the personality is very striking. Intractable aggressiveness, destructive behaviour and distractability often make ordinary education impossible; prolonged hospitalization, and then upbringing in a school for the maladjusted, are often needed. Epilepsy is a complication in about half the cases, and E.E.G. abnormalities, often localized in the temporal region, are relatively common (Ingram, 1956); but objective evidence for a brain lesion may be lacking, apart from the hyperkinesis. Many patients respond to chlorpromazine, 25 mg. three times daily, or primidone 125 mg. twice daily (Ounsted, 1955). Others respond to amphetamine and can tolerate large doses. In many cases there is spontaneous improvement between the ages of seven and ten.

The temperamental changes produced by cerebral dysfunction may be emphasized or masked by other constitutional factors, e.g. the genetical make-up, and by the social environment. Studies of brain-damaged or epileptic children have repeatedly shown how much individual variation may be attributable to such causes, and how the damaged child, perhaps even more than the normal one, reacts or over-reacts to the tensions in his environment.

OTHER CHRONIC BRAIN SYNDROMES. In his address to the Oxford symposium, Ingram (1963) classified the symptomatology of such syndromes into three grades. In the first one had to deal with defined clinical syndromes with constant evidence of abnormality, for instance, the three syndromes discussed above. In the second group come defined clinical syndromes with inconstant evidence of brain abnormality. Here we have the focal learning defects, specific developmental aphasia, dyslexia and dysgraphia, and specific clumsiness. In the third group we have the symptoms for which brain abnormality may be an inconstant direct or indirect contributory cause: distractability, variability of behaviour, impulsiveness, irritability, anxiety, emotional immaturity.

The classification provided by Wrigglesworth (1963) on the same occasion is instructive for its detailed and systematic construction. Its main headings are: (A) Minimal cerebral palsy (pyramidal, choreo-athetoid, ataxic). (B) Minimal sensory dysfunction (e.g. partial deafness, peripheral visual defects, etc.). (C) Minimal perceptual dysfunction (higher level disturbances of auditory, visual, spatial and linked functions). (D) Minimal intellectual (conceptive) dysfunction (which we all have). (E) Minimal behavioural dysfunction (hyperkinetic, hypokinetic, perseverative and fluctuating). (F) Minimal conciousness dysfunction (epileptic phenomena). (G) Other neurological dysfunctions (cerebellar, sympathetic/parasympathetic, lower motor neurone). From this it may be seen how wide is the world of pathology which we have only just begun to explore.

CLINICAL CYTOGENETICS

Since these pages went into proof, there have been remarkable new advances in clinical cytogenetics, which suggest that individuals of XYY constitution, i.e. males with an extra Y chromosome, are specially at risk for delinquency in adolescence and criminality in later life. Jacobs, Brunton, Melville, Brittain and McClemont (1965) reported an XYY constitution in 7 men from a series of 197 patients with criminal records detained at a State mental hospital under conditions of maximum security. Further studies, particularly by the Edinburgh group of workers, Court Brown and Jacobs on the cytogenetic side, and Price and Whatmore on the clinical side, have confirmed the association of this chromosome constitution with a generally normal male physique but usually of high stature (six feet or more), quite often a minor degree of mental subnormality, and a more than average risk of becoming delinquent and particularly becoming delinquent at an unusually early age. For a clinical discussion Price and Whatmore (1967a, b) may be consulted. The provisional results (unpublished) of work done in association with the MRC Psychiatric Genetics Research Unit at the Maudsley suggest that a raised incidence of sex-chromosomal aneuploidy may be found in delinquent girls and women also. Our knowledge in this field is growing rapidly, and it is at present much too early to interpret its significance.

CHAPTER XII

MENTAL SUBNORMALITY

(*Amentia, Oligophrenia*)

DEFINITIONS AND CLASSIFICATIONS

MENTAL subnormality is used in this book to denote a condition of retarded, incomplete or abnormal mental development, present at birth or in early childhood, and characterized mainly by limited intelligence. We use the heading 'mental subnormality', in place of the earlier term 'mental deficiency', as the Mental Health Act of 1959 has superseded the Mental Deficiency Act of 1927, and new definitions have been imposed by legal authority. The new definitions are by no means an improvement on the older ones. Mental subnormality (which is included under the all-inclusive concept of 'mental disorder' together with the psychoses, neuroses and psychopathies) is graded into two degrees. 'Severe subnormality' is a state of arrested or incomplete development of mind which includes subnormality of intelligence and is of such a nature or degree that the patient is incapable of leading an independent life. 'Subnormality', not further qualified, means a state of arrested or incomplete development of mind (not amounting to severe subnormality) which includes subnormality of intelligence and is of a nature and degree which requires or is susceptible to medical treatment or other special care or training of the patient. Severe subnormality covers the idiots and imbeciles of the older terminology, and subnormality (unqualified) roughly corresponds to the feeble-minded. The old category of moral deficiency has been replaced by 'psychopathic disorder', and relates to a group of patients which has been discussed in Chapter III. In the present chapter we shall continue to make use of accepted medical gradings, into low-grade and high-grade defectives, idiots, imbeciles and the feeble-minded.

Mental deficiency as used here implies a *definition of intelligence.* Some definitions are very general and comprehensive, as the following by Jaspers (1945): 'Intelligence is the total of all mental endowments, talents and skills useful for adaptations to the tasks of life.' Others enumerate many detailed functions: 'Intelligence is the ability to learn useful information and skills, adapt to new problems and conditions of life, profit from past experiences, engage in abstract and creative thinking, employ critical judgement, avoid errors, surmount difficulties, and exercise foresight' (Page, 1947).

Both are unsatisfactory because they do not exclude abilities such as sense perception, attention, retention and memory which can remain intact in cases of impairment of intelligence. W. Stern's definition of intelligence as 'the general ability to adapt to new situations by means of purposeful thinking' has been widely adopted.

All definitions refer to the role of human intelligence in biological adaptation. Its spontaneous and slow growth during the long childhood of man, who is so much poorer in preformed instincts ready at birth than many animals, is another important factor to be considered in mental deficiency. The mental defective is handicapped in his adaptation because his equipment is below standard at birth and its growth is more or less stunted during childhood.

It will be shown in the section on genetical aspects that in the large majority of cases the subnormal development can be regarded as a variation of the normal. These cases, following the classification of E. O. Lewis (1939), are distinguished as subcultural aments from the smaller group of pathological aments, in whom a special pathology is found or suspected.

For practical purposes it is customary to classify defectives into *feeble-minded, imbeciles and idiots*. Though it is useful, the division is arbitrary because the gradation from one level to the next is continuous. The Mental Deficiency Act 1913 defined idiots as 'persons in whose case there exists mental defectiveness of such a degree that they are unable to guard themselves against common physical dangers'. Imbeciles are 'persons in whose case mental defectiveness, though not amounting to idiocy, is yet so pronounced that they are incapable of managing themselves and their affairs, or, in the case of children, of being taught to do so'. The feeble-minded were defined as persons who, though their defect does not amount to imbecility, require care, supervision and control for their own protection, or for the protection of others; or, who, in the case of children, appear to be permanently incapable of receiving proper benefit from instruction in ordinary schools.

The subdivision, originally devised for administrative use only, gained in value by being linked with the mental age and *intelligence quotient* as ascertained by *intelligence tests*. Idiots have an I.Q. under 20, imbeciles under 50 and the feeble-minded from 50–70. While little difficulty arose in the lower grades of idiocy and imbecility, for the much greater number of feeble-minded 'mentally subnormal' the upper limit is somewhat doubtful. Some think the I.Q. of 70 too high because a number of children between an I.Q. of 60 and 70 can still make some progress in ordinary schools; others consider it too low because the next group between 70 and 85, classified usually as 'dull', may prove difficult to educate together with normal children. Another concept, important in this context, is that of educationally 'backward' children which comprises those who although of average or better mental endowment show some delay in their development and in adaptation to ordinary methods of schooling, but finally reach normal standards.

To the student of psychiatry concerned with cases of this kind, it must seem remarkable how relatively well the examination of intellectual endowment by psychological tests indicates the biological and social abnormality with which he is concerned. These test methods originally designed to test the educability of normal children, have proved to be most valuable not only in the rough classification of the cases, but also, if used with discrimination, in *diagnosis and prediction*. The test method and its practical application have been much criticized because they have not fulfilled the excessive expectations and claims of earlier workers. The educational bias present in many tests has incurred the disapproval of medical men. Psychiatrists have objected to psychometric tests because they apply the scale of development of the normal child to the abnormal defective who cannot be measured by the same standard (Bleuler). As a clinician one has certainly to be on one's guard not to over-value one sign or one method of inquiry and to know its limitations. But with these reservations in mind, intelligence tests have proved a very useful tool for mastering both the theoretical and practical problems of mental deficiency.

INCIDENCE

Thanks to the work of E. O. Lewis on behalf of the Mental Deficiency Committee (Wood Committee, 1929) fuller information on the incidence of mental defect in England and Wales is available than on any other psychiatric condition in any country. He tested representative samples of all school-children in various parts of the country and ascertained by all available means the adult mental defectives in the same areas. In a total population of over 600,000 he found over 5,000 defectives of whom 5 per cent. were idiots, 20 per cent. imbeciles and 75 per cent. feeble-minded. The total incidence of 8 per 1,000 must be regarded as a minimum for England and Wales; the average incidence in urban areas was significantly smaller (6·7 per thousand) than in rural areas (10·4 per thousand). There is a definite preponderance of male over female defectives in this investigation as was found in an earlier assessment of the English Royal Commission in 1904.

An investigation by Mayer-Gross (1948) in a rural district of Scotland with a population of 56,000 where the whole school population had undergone an intelligence test, showed a mental-deficiency rate of 27 per thousand school-children and 15·6 per thousand of the population, a considerably higher incidence than that found by Lewis twenty years earlier. This inquiry also ascertained the dull and backward group (I.Q. ranging from 70–85) which amounted to about 6 per cent. of the school-children and almost 3 per cent. of the total population. These figures have also to be regarded as the minimum for the population.

The greater incidence in rural areas especially of higher-grade mental deficiency—Lewis estimated that 50 per cent. more of those cases are found in the country than in cities—is probably due to the rapid depopulation of these areas in Britain during the last sixty years. One result of this migration to the industrial towns is that rural areas 'have lost the more virile and intelligent men and women, and have been left with a poor stock which has been inbreeding for two or three generations and has produced an unduly high proportion of feeble-minded children' (Lewis).

Precise estimates of the prevalence of mental subnormality have been attempted in London and Middlesex (Goodman and Tizard, 1962), Salford (Kushlick, 1961) and 'Wessex' (Kushlick, 1964–6) and similar rates for *severe abnormality* were found in the three studies, amounting to about 3·7 per 1,000 in the age group 10–19 in which all affected persons are likely to be known. The rates for urban and rural areas proved to be similar in these more recent surveys. Comparable figures have been obtained in other countries. A rate of 3·6 per 1,000 at 5–17 years of age was found in Onondaga County (1955) and of 3·3 (ages 10–14) in Baltimore (Lemkau *et al.*, 1943). In a rural district of Sweden, Åkesson (1961) reported 5·8 per 1,000 for all ages.

Estimates for *mild subnormality* are more difficult to make as all cases are not reported. In the Salford survey the highest administrative prevalence rate of 8·6 per 1,000 was found among those aged 15–19, the age at which the majority of the mildly subnormal are first classified as such when they are notified as in need of supervision on leaving school. For *all ages* the rate was 2·06 per 1,000 and a total of 4·4 for *all grades* at *all ages* was found. The rates in the 'Wessex' survey were lower. However, a high proportion of defectives, especially of the lower grades, die early in life, and it has, therefore, been considered likely that 5 per cent. of all children born are aments. The usual preponderance in males is probably due to the greater variability of the male, which is itself due to genetical causes. Psychometric data are available from the Scottish Survey of 1949. This showed that of 1,215 eleven-year-old children given individual tests (Terman-Merrill) 3 per cent. had I.Q.s below 70, equivalent to 1·4 per cent. on the Stanford with its smaller standard deviation. On this test there was no preponderance of males at low I.Q. levels. However, in the group tests performed on approximately 38,000 boys and 37,000 girls, very low scores were given by 8 per cent. of the boys as against 5 per cent. of the girls.

AETIOLOGY AND PATHOLOGY

Genetical Aspects of Mental Defect

Mental deficiency is a biological phenomenon resulting from a variety of causes, of which the greater part are still unknown; even the known causes, genetical and environmental, are very many. In a large number of cases it is difficult to separate the effects of the two types of agency, as the condition is caused by a concatenation of factors. The complexity of these problems is well set out by Penrose (1949a); and in his review he pays regard to such varied aspects as germ plasm injury, mutation and selection, dominant, recessive, sex-linked and additive genes, irregularity of manifestation, maternal genetical influences, the maternal environment, intra-natal and post-natal environment, and the methods of differentiating between the effects of nature and nurture.

It is a paradoxical circumstance that we have learned more about the genetical aspects of mental subnormality (over the greatest part of its range) from the investigations of psychologists, who have not concerned themselves with that problem at all, than from the efforts of psychiatrists and medical geneticists, who have made it a subject of close study. As Huxley (1942) has pointed out, medical men have been obsessed by the notion that such a character as mental defect must be inherited by simple Mendelian rules, as a unit character, either present or absent. They have also devoted a great part of their attention to those forms of mental defect which are accompanied by evidence of pathological change, such as mongolism, and have neglected the merely dull and backward. The psychologists were governed by no such preconceptions. They were concerned simply with discovering reliable tests of intelligence, with measuring the growth of intelligence in childhood and adolescence, with discovering how it varied from individual to individual, and in recent years, with the problems of education and training.

Psychological investigations have shown that we cannot think of human beings as either mentally defective or normal (as indeed forensic psychiatry requires), but that we must think of them as varying along a continuous scale from idiocy at one extreme to genius at the other. When more or less random samples of the population, such as school-children, have their intelligence measured by intelligence tests, an average value is found to which most of them approximate; extreme values are rare in proportion to the degree to which they vary from the average. If, in fact, the numbers of persons of a given intelligence are plotted on the scale of intelligence from high to low values, a hump-backed curve, the 'normal curve', is obtained (see Fig. 23). The essential qualities, or parameters, of this curve, which from the mathematical point of view are sufficient to describe it completely, are the mean, and the standard deviation. The mean gives the average value round which the majority of people cluster, the standard deviation expresses the way in which they are scattered on either side of this point (more precisely, the square root of the average value of the square of their deviations). For instance the average school-child has an intelligence quotient, measured on the Binet scale, of 100, with standard deviation of 16. This means that within half a standard deviation of the mean, from I.Q. 92–108, we can expect to find

34 per cent. of all such children, and within two standard deviations, from I.Q. 68–132, all but 5 per cent. These proportions are determined by the fact that we have to do with a *normal distribution*. They bring home to us the fact that the distinction between the normal and the defective is one of degree, and not necessarily one of kind.

DISTRIBUTION OF INTELLIGENCE

(Revised Stanford Binet Scale, 3,268 London School Children; from Sir Cyril Burt)

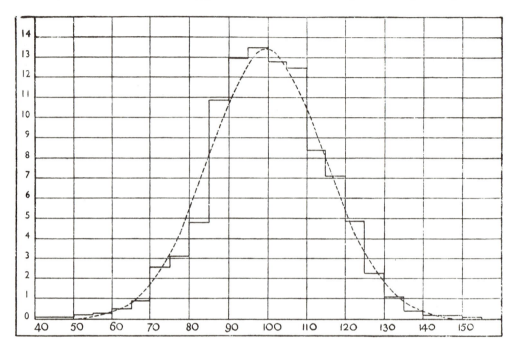

Intelligence Quotient

Fig. 23.—The histogram shows the distribution of the observed test results. Their mean and standard deviation determine the normal curve which has been superimposed. It will be seen that the fit is excellent, and that the observations are in consequence adequately accounted for by normal variation.

The curve is symmetrical, and equal deviations to either side of the mean are equally frequent. Approximately 52 per cent. of the scores fall between 90 and 110, 84 per cent. between 80 and 120, 97 per cent. between 70 and 130. An important feature which is not very obvious is that, at each successive degree of deviation from the mean, the frequency becomes an increasingly smaller fraction of that which went before. This is shown, where towards the centre frequencies are high, by the increasing steepness of the curve. It is masked towards the extremes where frequencies are getting small absolutely, but will be seen if the heights of successive ordinates are compared with one another.

The followers of Spearman and his school tried to formulate the best tests they could for the measurement of intelligence. The tests were refined again and again in the effort to get away from learning and educational standard down to native wit; and as they accumulated in number they were checked more and more against one another, rather than against any outside standard, such as the reports of teachers. There was, of course, a considerable consistency in the achievements of any one individual from test to test. This meant that, if the results of two tests on the same group of persons were compared, a high positive corre-lation coefficient was found. If three or more tests had been given to the same group, every arrangement of them in pairs gave a correlation coefficient, and all the coefficients taken together could be subjected to a specially developed mathematical technique, that of *factor analysis*. This method enabled one to separate out a general factor, common to all the tests; and in the mathematical notation of the time this general factor was called *g*.

By itself, *g* would not account for all the intercorrelation between test results which was found; but what was left over was attributable to special factors, peculiar to the several tests, or sometimes to groups of them. Spearman proposed the hypothesis that the general factor corresponded with intelligence. Some tests were found to be highly saturated with *g*, i.e. to correlate highly with other satisfactory tests, and were therefore efficient standards for the measurement of intelligence (in Spearman's sense); others were less efficient, being more greatly influenced by a special factor. Spearman was led to the view that intelligence was essentially unitary in nature, thereby opposing the school of Thorndike, who regarded intelligence as the sum of a great number of special abilities. The success of the mathe-matical methods he used was thought for a time to establish Spearman's views as correct; but this is now no longer agreed. Nevertheless the conclusion gained wide acceptance, that the most important part of a man's native abilities could be measured on a single scale. The *g* rating of school-children of a given age was found to be 'normally' distributed; and the normal curve used to describe the distribution could be represented in the simplest terms, with two axes only, one for levels of frequency and the other for values of *g*.

This was a working hypothesis which proved for a long time of great practical usefulness. But as more and more tests of intelligence were invented, and some were found better than others for predicting success at certain occupations, it came to be recognized that there were also '*special abilities*'. Two of these which are generally recognized are 'verbal' and 'mech-anical' ability. It is a common experience to find that some men have a special ability in the handling of words; they may thereby give an impression of having a greater degree of general intelligence than they really possess. It is equally usual an experience to find that some highly intelligent men are complete fools at handling tools, bits of mechanism, and the like. There are probably a number of other special abilities, mathematical, musical, etc., which have not yet been subjected to adequate psychological analysis and measurement. We arrive then at the view that to describe a man's abilities, it is not enough to consider his position on a scale of general intelligence. Variation is not in one but in many dimen-sions; and general intelligence itself probably consists of a large number of special abilities which are psychologically, and perhaps genetically, closely related.

THE GENETICAL BASIS OF NORMAL VARIATION. These facts about the distri-bution of different values of intelligence tell us nothing in themselves about the causes of this variation, whether genetically or environmentally determined. All that the normal distribution suggests in itself is that the causes of variation are very numerous and of individually small effect, and that their effects may counterbalance one another or may act cumulatively if in the same direction. Both environmental and genetical factors may work in this way; the '*genes of small effect*' are now well known to biology, and on the environmental side, such factors as a more or less satisfactory home life, the intellectual stimulus of clever brothers or sisters, different qualities of education, and the degree of satisfac-toriness of nutrition during childhood might all be thought to have an effect on the intelligence of the growing child. For evidence of the genetical basis search has been made further afield.

The *native ability* of a man tends to resemble that of his close relatives, particularly his parents and his brothers and sisters. As we are dealing with a metrical quality, we can measure the degree of resemblance and put it in the form of a correlation coefficient. Careful work by Fraser Roberts (1940) shows that the correlation coefficient between the intelligence of sibs is slightly in excess of $+ 0.5$, which is the expected value if half of the determinants of intelligence level are shared by both members of the pair of sibs. This is of course the case with the genes. A man receives half his genetical equipment from his father, half from his mother; so will his brother, but the halves need not be the same. On an average a quarter both of the father's and of the mother's genes will be held in common by both of the pair of sibs, amounting in all to half the total genetical equipment. Consequently two brothers tend to resemble one another genetically about as closely as father and son, though it may be a little more or less. If, however, the pair of brothers happens to be a pair of uniovular twins, the relationship is a much closer one and amounts to genetical identity. In uniovular twins the correlation coefficient in intelligence is very much greater than $+ 0.5$, and by most workers has been found to exceed $+ 0.9$ (e.g. Newman, Freeman, and Holzinger, 1937). The evidence that this provides is important and suggests that genetical equipment has a principal share in determining human variation in intelligence.

A *general theory of the genetics of intelligence* and of mental deficiency was first enunciated in a clear and precise way by Fraser Roberts (1939). Fraser Roberts compares intelligence with stature, and points out that over the greater part of the range, in intelligence as in height, there is continuous variation; but at the lower end of the scale there are pathological variants. When we consider height, there are the dwarfs, cretins, achondroplasics and others. When we consider intelligence the pathological variants are the idiots and imbeciles. Their occurrence in numbers too high to be accounted for by normal variation alone is reflected in the fact that the curve of distribution departs from normality. Above an I.Q. (Binet) of 45 per cent. by far the greater part of variation is attributable to non-pathological causes, in their genetical aspect to multifactorial genes, 'the host of normal genes, busily engaged in their task of guiding the normal human being along his normal developmental path'. Below this level of intelligence, variation is principally caused, in so far as it is caused genetically, by chromosomal defects or by single abnormal genes, each of which, by itself, is capable of rendering normal development impossible, despite the effect of all the other genes. Feeble-minded persons are therefore only to be regarded as abnormal against the background of a complex civilization; but within that environment they are responsible for serious social consequences. Imbeciles and idiots are abnormal in a more fundamental sense; but on the other hand, though a social burden, they are relatively few in number, are mostly maintained in institutions, and give rise to only inconsiderable effects of a socially undesirable kind. Fraser Roberts considers that these single genes of large effect must be as a class very numerous, but each of great rarity. Probably no one of those already known, such as the genes for phenylketonuria or amautoric idiocy, accounts for more than 1 per cent. of low-grade mental deficiency. Many of them may be genes of only occasional expression.

This theory fits all the observed facts, and is particularly valuable because it relates our understanding of the genetics of mental deficiency to general biological genetics. By far the greater part of evolutionary change is believed to be due to the accumulation in a given strain of multifactorial genes of individually infinitesimal effect. An increase in fitness, measured by the number of offspring, due to a given gene, need only be as small as 1 per cent. to cause the diffusion of this gene throughout the species. Most of the measurable qualities, such as size, coloration, fertility, longevity, etc., are controlled by multifactorial genes. Furthermore, genes exert their influence in more than one direction. Probably the genes of small effect, which help to determine the intelligence of the adult, have effects on growth more generally, and thereby influence stature and health. There are small but positive correlations between intelligence and both these qualities.

Similarity between *members of the same family* is shown more strongly in a quality which is controlled by multifactorial inheritance than in one controlled by single gene inheritance. The parents of imbeciles and idiots are nearly always of normal intelligence; the parents of the feeble-minded are generally of dull though not moronic intelligence. Fisher (1927) estimated that only 11 per cent. of the feeble-minded of one generation are descended from the feeble-minded of the last generation. This is to be attributed to the relative frequency of the classes involved. The feeble-minded are relatively few, and despite their higher liability to produce defective children, produce an absolutely smaller number of defectives than the more numerous class of persons of dull intelligence. The same phenomenon is shown at the other end of the scale. The majority of persons whose intellects would qualify them for the stamp of genius come from the marriages of parents who are themselves gifted, but do not attain that rank.

AFTER BIRTH OF PROPOSITUS PROPORTION OF SIBS

Observed No. of Families		Normal I.Q. 85+	Dull I.Q. 70–84	Simpleton I.Q. 50–69	Imbecile I.Q. under 50
Propositus Dull					
Parents N × N	101	87·0	9·5	1·9	1·6
N × D	40	67·0	26·4	6·0	5·5
D × D N × S	11	53·3	33·3	10·0	3·3
D × S	6	25·0	33·3	33·3	8·3
S × S	2	20·0	—	80·0	—
Propositus Simpleton					
Parents N × N	219	91·9	4·6	2·1	1·4
N × D	86	68·6	18·8	10·4	2·2
D × D N × S	62	53·1	23·7	18·7	4·5
D × S	31	36·3	24·2	25·3	14·3
S × S	9	13·0	21·7	39·1	26·0
Propositus Imbecile or Idiot					
Parents N × N	486	90·4	5·2	1·6	2·7
N × D	70	60·8	18·9	10·1	10·1
D × D N × S	40	53·6	18·8	19·6	8·0
D × S	16	53·5	11·6	25·6	9·3
S × S	12	34·2	15·8	39·4	10·5

In giving a *genetical prognosis* to parents who have borne one defective child, it is wise to be guided by empirical findings rather than by theoretical considerations—that is unless a firm diagnosis of some specific form of deficiency can be made. The expectations of mental defect among the sibs of a defective of known grade are given in the table above, quoted from Penrose (1949). From this one may read, for example, that if two normal parents have produced a child who is a simpleton, then there are 8 chances in 100 that any further child they have will be of dull intelligence or lower.

On this table Penrose comments that if birth injury or encephalitis can be diagnosed in the propositus, the probability of any later child born being defective approaches that for the general population (say 0·2 per cent.) with the degree of certainty of the diagnosis. If parents are consanguineous, the prognosis becomes worse than that shown in the table; there is then a greater chance of the defect being due to a simple recessive gene, which would involve a 25 per cent. chance of re-occurrence.

MUTATION; RADIATION DANGERS. Pathogenic genes are normally eliminated from the population by selective processes; their loss is made good by fresh mutation, but the resultant of the two processes is, usually, a low gene frequency. It is possible that this gene frequency could be increased by an increased frequency of mutation. In recent years there has been growing concern about the dangers of irradiation to health, and in particular to the state of the germ plasm which could have far-reaching effects over many generations. In a report by the Medical Research Council (1956) on the hazards to man of nuclear and allied radiations, it is pointed out that there are grounds for believing that a doubling of the mutation rates would in one generation, amongst other effects, increase the frequency of low-grade mental deficiency by three per cent. The Council recommends the restriction of the use of any source of ionizing radiation, on however small a scale, to essential purposes.

INBREEDING; ASSORTATIVE MATING. Inbreeding means the mating of related individuals; assortative mating usually means the mating of individuals who resemble one another in some particular. Related individuals carry a proportion of their genes in common, a proportion that increases with the nearness of the relationship; in the case of parents and of sibs this proportion is one-half; in the case of first cousins one-eighth. Since for any quality that we like to think of there is quite likely to be some genetical basis, assortative mating also implies the mating of people who resemble one another genetically. Both these processes increase the variability of a race by making unlikely combinations of genes more probable. In the long run, if the race is subjected to intensive natural or artificial selection, its homogeneity is increased, as the elimination of unfavoured genes is speeded up. It is by intensive inbreeding that races of cattle, mice and racehorses have been standardized. The most intensive form of human inbreeding that occurs in civilized countries is the marriage of first cousins, which in this country is only about 0·7 per cent. of all marriages. But the marriage of more distantly related persons must be very common. In some isolated communities, such as Iceland, or in remote hamlets in other lands, nearly every inhabitant has an ascertainable relationship to nearly every other, and almost any marriage that occurs will be between blood relatives. In a still more distant degree we are all relatives of one another, and the concept of inbreeding has to be considered more widely. As Dahlberg (1941) has pointed out, the choice of possible mates is limited for every one, by geographical, religious, social and other boundaries, which despite occasional trespass generally hold good. The community may be divided into loosely inbreeding groups or 'isolates'. These isolates are tending to break down. Increasing facilities of transport widen geographical limits, which are also extended by migration. Social-class distinctions are less rigid than they were. And religious prohibitions on intermarriage are less generally regarded. According to Dahlberg, the frequency of cousin marriage is declining in most European countries, and fell for instance in Bavaria from 0·87 per cent. in 1876–80 to 0·20 per cent. in 1926–33.

The *tendency of like to mate with like* probably remains undiminished. In whatever respect married or engaged couples have been investigated, they have been found to resemble one another more than chance would allow. The correlation coefficient between the intelligence ratings of married pairs was found by Jones (1929) to be + 0·55. This means in effect that husbands and wives tend to resemble each other in intelligence about as closely as brothers and sisters.

This human tendency is of considerable importance from several points of view. For instance the tendency of spouses to resemble one another increases the expected degree of resemblance between their children. This might lead us, as Hogben (1933) points out, to over-estimate the importance of heredity in accounting for human variation in intelligence. From a wider aspect, it is important because it tends to speed up selective processes. If, as seems probable, the more intelligent members of the community are producing fewer children than the less intelligent, then a similar selection affects the children of two intelligent or unintelligent parents; whereas if clever men tended to marry stupid women, selective tendencies would tend to balance one another.

DIFFERENTIAL FERTILITY. While the fertility of idiots and imbeciles is very low, the fertility of the feeble-minded approaches normality, and that of the dull and backward is probably high. In a large and unselected group of school-children Fraser Roberts (1939) found that the more intelligent the child, the fewer brothers and sisters he had. There was a correlation coefficient between intelligence and number of sibs of − 0·22. Fraser Roberts considers this figure is an under-estimate, as many of the less intelligent families were incomplete, whereas most of the more intelligent families were complete. The association between dullness and fertility of the parents was independent of the occupation of the father, and poor but intelligent families were as infertile as equally intelligent members of more prosperous classes. The effect is such a big one that Roberts estimated that if the tendency continued unchecked, the average intelligence of the population would fall by three points on the Binet scale from one generation to the next. Criticisms of these conclusions, and similar ones reached by other workers, have been made on the ground that infertile families, by being in a position to provide a better environment for such children as they do have, will tend on that account alone to have more intelligent children. All the evidence has been summarized and discussed in an impartial spirit by Burt (1946). Burt reached the same conclusion as Roberts, but estimated a fall of about one Binet-scale point per generation. An important survey (Scottish Research Council, 1949), which was made on Scottish school-children at the instance of a Royal Commission on Population, failed to bear out these gloomy prognostications. No fall in intelligence over twenty years could be established. It is however possible that a fall in native intelligence has been balanced by the stimulus of better education. The problem is still an open one.

ENVIRONMENTAL INFLUENCES. The operation of the genes in controlling development cannot be considered in an environmental vacuum. The child who is born with normal hereditary equipment can still be reduced to imbecility by *birth trauma* or by an attack of posterior basic meningitis in early childhood. Tredgold (1947) states that environmental causes of this kind are responsible for about 5 per cent. of defectives. This figure, however, would almost certainly give a very inadequate idea of the importance to be attached to environmental influences as a whole.

Of greater importance than gross pathological lesions of the central nervous system brought about by some outside agent and resulting in mental deficiency, are the influences exerted on intelligence by less drastically operating causes, such as *nutrition in childhood*, *education*, etc. It is extremely difficult to reach any accurate measure of the effectiveness of such factors as these. Hogben (1941) has pointed out that all investigations designed to measure comparatively the effect of environment and heredity in determining the intelligence of children are carried out in a relatively homogeneous environment, and so tend to underestimate environmental effects. He points out that in twin investigations, both members of the pair are brought up in the same family and educated at the same school; the environment is more alike for them than for pairs of unrelated children taken at random. Siblings reared apart have been found to show a markedly lower correlation coefficient than sibs reared together.

The difficulty may be surmounted by examining monozygotic (MZ) twins who have been separated from infancy or very early years. Newman, Freeman and Holzinger (1937) estimate that the correlation coefficient between intelligence ratings of MZ twins reared together is Binet + 0·91 and Otis 0·92, while for MZ twins reared apart they are + 0·67 and + 0·73 respectively, i.e. considerably lower and only exceeding by a little the correlation coefficients of same-sexed sibs reared together. A more recent study has been made by Shields (1962) of 44 MZ pairs of twins brought up apart, with a control series brought up together. The intra-class correlations were the same in the two series ($r = +0·8$); but the mean intra-pair difference in points was somewhat greater in the separated series. The findings suggested that differences in early environment were likely to lead to differences between MZ twins in respect of intelligence, especially on verbal tests. The differences between separated and control series are less marked than in the American study of 1937.

This is probably the only satisfactory experiment at the present time designed to measure the relative effects of environment and heredity on normal intelligence. There are a number of large-scale investigations on *mentally defective twins*, among which may be mentioned those of Rosanoff (1931), Smith (1930), and Juda (1939 *a,b*). With the exception of Rosanoff, whose work is in some ways unsatisfactory, these investigators agree in finding a very high degree of concordance in regard to mental defect in uniovular twins; approximately 90 per cent. of twin pairs are concordant, when exogenous causes for defect are excluded. Both Juda and Smith agree that even when neurological abnormalities are found, the twins are still frequently concordant, and often show in addition to concordance in presence and degree of mental defect, a concordance in neurological picture. This indicates that neurological abnormalities cannot necessarily be regarded as pathognomonic of an exogenous factor, such as birth injury. Work which to some extent runs in the opposite direction is that of Brander (1935), who on a basis of ten twin pairs was inclined to emphasize the importance of minor birth injuries, which, obviously, may not infrequently affect both members of a pair of twins.

Summarizing, we may say that measurements of the relative effects of heredity and environment in bringing about first variation in normal intelligence and secondly mental defect are still lacking. The genetic contribution to mental defect is established, but environmental influences certainly play a not inconsiderable role, even in so-called idiopathic mental deficiency. A noteworthy phenomenon of recent years has been the fundamental and extensive advances in our knowledge of aetiology which have come from the genetical side; and that it is from that side that such order and system as we have has come.

The Association of Mental Subnormality with other Syndromes

Mental deficiency may be one of the clinical manifestations of a great variety of pathological processes or abnormal developments of early life, particularly of those whose central effects are on the nervous system. Thus it is more than normally frequent in such syndromes as Friedreich's ataxia, dystrophia myotonica and neurofibromatosis. Marked deficiencies of the sensory apparatus, as in deaf-mutism, may be associated either with inadequate development of the central nervous system in general, or, functionally, by interfering with the processes of learning, may lead to mental retardation. Some rare genetically determined disorders of skeletal development, e.g. hypertelorism and Marfan's syndrome, are commonly but not invariably accompanied by defective mental development.

The suggestion has repeatedly been made that the mentally defective are preferentially liable to a number of other conditions. Juda (1934) found about six times as high an incidence of *epilepsy* among the relatives of defective school-children as among the relatives of normal children, but about equal incidences of schizophrenia, and about six times as high an incidence of manic-depressive psychoses among the normal. Myerson and Boyle (1941) found *manic-depressive psychoses* heavily represented in certain socially important and able families in New England. This work confirms findings in Germany (Luxenburger, 1933) that manic-depressive psychoses have a socially superior distribution, schizophrenia is evenly distributed through the population, and only epilepsy of all the organic psychoses is likely to be associated with mental defect. Careful work on a large American twin series (Kallmann, Barrera, Hoch, and Kelly, 1941) failed to show any association between mental defect and *schizophrenia*. Schizophrenia and mental defect are both common psychiatric conditions and as a matter of experience are not infrequently found in the same patient. The occurrence of schizophrenia in a defective may result in somewhat atypical symptoms and the syndrome was at one time dignified with the name 'Pfropfschizophrenia'. Brugger (1928) investigated the relatives of a number of these cases, and found no suggestion that there was any genetic or other causal relationship. Larsson and Sjögren (1954), however, found in their psychiatric survey of a large Swedish population an incidence of oligophrenia among schizophrenics which was well above normal expectation. The question remains open.

The association of epilepsy and mental defect seems on the basis of published work more probable. Certain rare syndromes, such as epiloia, tend to produce both mental deficiency and a tendency to fits. Any organic damage to the brain may, obviously, result in both states. Idiopathic epilepsy, occurring in early years, may itself cause organic damage to the brain, and so bring about a secondary state of mental defect. There is no suggestion, however, that the defectives who are the tail-end of the normal distribution are specially liable to epilepsy. Conrad (1937b) found that in a very large collection of epileptic families 6 per cent. of the children of the epileptic propositi were dull and backward, imbecile or idiot, and 10·5 per cent. were of stunted intelligence ('beschränkt').

The relationship of mental deficiency to *neurosis and abnormality of personality* is a still more debated topic. E. O. Lewis (Wood Report) in a survey of the incidence of mental defect in England and Wales, came to the conclusion that a large proportion of defectives came from families among other members of which there was an excessive incidence of crime, prostitution, vagrancy, pauperism, and other syndromes of social significance. His finding led to the formulation of the concept of the 'Social Problem Group'. Arguments for and against the existence of this group in a biological sense, and discussions of its nature, have been collated by Blacker (1937). The possible explanations of the findings of the Wood Report are many. It may be that unhealthy family traditions corrupt manners and morals, and that inadequacy of intelligence aids in the process. It is also possible that a sordid and impoverished environment in early years may have an unfavourable effect on bodily health and the growth of intelligence, so laying the foundation for mental abnormalities of all kinds. Finally it is likely that any physiological or psychological disability that reduces the capacity for social adaptation will be found in excess among the denizens of the least prosperous hundredth of the community, and will be found to converge in individual families as a direct result of assortative mating.

Evidence against the view that mental defect is associated with personality deviations of all kinds was provided by investigations concerned with the military neurotic casualties of the 1939–45 war. *Neurotic soldiers* as a single group showed no significant deviation in mean intelligence from normal ones, although they showed a significantly higher variability in this quality. This suggests that persons of less than average intelligence are more than normally liable to some forms of neurosis while those of superior intelligence are more than normally liable to other kinds of neurosis (Slater, 1943; Eysenck, 1947). This has indeed been confirmed. It has been found that in a group of neurotic soldiers, anxiety neurotics, reactive depressives and hysterics showed average intelligence, but obsessional neurotics scored significantly better, irrespective of the type of intelligence test chosen (Slater, P., 1945).

We may, therefore, conclude that dull intelligence carries with it an enhanced tendency to some forms of neurotic reaction and psychopathic behaviour. There is also some reason to think that hysteria may be commoner among defective and dull individuals than among the normal, but the evidence is conflicting. Beyond this we are not at present able to go, nor to say what are the forms of neurotic behaviour to which the unintelligent are liable. It is quite likely that there are genetic factors which are common to both types of constitution, and tend to cause both a reduction of intelligence and a tendency to neurosis or psychopathy. Their effect is, however, probably negligible in comparison with the social and environmental agencies which, by putting an emotional strain on the unintelligent, increase his liability to disorders of behaviour.

Aetiology and Pathology other than Genetical

While insight into the genetic causes of mental deficiency has made remarkable progress during the last twenty years, the contribution of environmental factors has proved more difficult to elucidate.

SOCIAL ENVIRONMENT AND EDUCATION. Ever since Itard reported on the education of the 'wild boy' of Aveyron (1789) a poor social environment, or neglect in upbringing and education, have been regarded as causes of mental deficiency. At the beginning of the nineteenth century when Guggenmoos in Austria and Séguin in

France founded the first institutions for defectives, philanthropic interest was kindled by the hope of overcoming backwardness through proper education. Since the introduction of general and compulsory schooling, the main argument for the significance of the environment in causing mental deficiency has been the finding that a large majority of the pupils of special schools and the inmates of institutions came from the lower strata of the population. This has been confirmed by numerous workers in many countries. Against this fact it was pointed out that the backward children of the wealthy are placed in private schools and homes, and that their number is relatively small because of the smaller size of families in the better-educated classes. However, Isserlis (1923) was able to test the intelligence of a mixed group of school-children and found it was highly correlated with the quality of their home environment, whether measured by the economic status of their parents or by the care they received at home or by their clothing. Children brought up in a 'neutral' environment such as orphanages (Jones and Carr-Saunders, 1927) or adopted children (Freeman, Holzinger, and Mitchell, 1928) have been examined from this point of view—without conclusive results.

The issue is clouded by the frequent *familial incidence of backwardness* and mental deficiency. The low economic and cultural status of the home may be due to the low intelligence of one or both parents, rather than itself being the direct cause of mental deficiency in the child. Assortative mating between defectives and consanguineous marriages in rural areas may be additional factors. Sjögren (1932) has collected evidence on the frequency of mental defect caused by consanguinity in an isolated rural population in Sweden. The greater frequency of mentally subnormal and defective children in rural than in urban districts of England disclosed by E. O. Lewis (Wood Report) has been attributed by the author to the migration of the more intelligent inhabitants into urban districts where they found better-paid work in industry.

Increasing attention has been devoted in recent years to defining the precise nature and extent of the contribution made by social environment to the causation of mental subnormality. Unexpectedly large changes of intelligence quotient have been found to occur in feeble-minded children observed over a period of time, those who had suffered very bad home conditions showing greater improvement than those exposed to a less adverse home environment (Clarke, Clarke and Reiman, 1958). Changes of this order, which had been as high as 16 points over a period of 6 years in the group from very bad homes, had been observed by earlier workers but recent investigators have verified both that the changes were real and that they were probably due to removal from adverse environmental conditions such as cruelty and neglect in early childhood. Clarke (1958) considers that the most severe degrees of deprivation, which are found in about 40 per cent. of the certified feeble-minded, retard intellectual development by at least an average of 14 points. These and other findings are of considerable importance in view of the fact that the great majority of patients in mental deficiency hospitals, and of pupils in schools for the educationally subnormal, are drawn from the lowest segments of society. They are therefore more often unwanted, liable to receive less love, attention and stimulation, and less encouragement in their initial attempts at exploration and self-expression and their nutrition also would more often be unsatisfactory (Sarason, 1953). There can be no question that heredity sets limits to the intellectual development of the individual but the range within which environment can operate to cause him to fall short of, or to achieve his full potentialities may be wider than originally thought. It is possible, as has been suggested by Clarke that, when they have been exposed to cruelty and neglect, subcultural defectives function near the lower end of the range of intellectual potentialities prescribed for them by heredity whereas normals function under ordinary conditions more closely to their upper limits.

The phenomenon of pseudo-feeblemindedness suggests something of this nature in that in these children intellectual endowments which appear permanently set at a feeble-minded level change markedly when the children are removed from their adverse environment.

Whatever the effect of environment and education on the result of intelligence tests, society should aim at providing optimal conditions of home and schooling for that part of the population which is intellectually less well endowed. There is no doubt that considerable improvement in this respect is possible in all countries.

BIRTH HAZARDS. Babies are 'at risk' of interference with normal mental development, if they are prematurely born as estimated by dates, or are small though not necessarily born before time, or are actually injured at birth. This fact has gained much attention recently, and has been the basis of prospective studies, such as those of Prechtl (1960) and Illingworth (1960). Prematurity, as shown by low birth weight, has been particularly implicated since the work of Asher and Roberts (1949), who found a number of children with a very low birth weight in an institution for the mentally retarded and in a school for the educationally subnormal. However, as low birth weight is associated with a number of physical defects, especially cerebral palsy, which might be independent causes of impaired mental development, the influence of prematurity as such has not been fully established. This question was investigated by McDonald (1964), who traced the after-histories of 1,066 infants admitted to 19 premature baby units in Britain in 1951–52, and tested them psychometrically when aged six to nine. Excluding children with cerebral palsy, blindness and deafness, it was found that the mean I.Q. (corrected for true age) of the 625 singletons was 102, that of the 267 twins was 98 and that of the 13 triplets was 92. This suggests that prematurity as such has no very dangerous effects.

Besides prematurity, difficult and prolonged labour, abnormal presentations and instrumental deliveries have been strongly suspected of constituting additional risks.

Investigations of a relatively large post-mortem material from patients, whose defectiveness dated from birth injury and early infections, disclosed the importance of asphyxia. The border territories of the large cerebral arteries were found to be specially vulnerable (J. E. Meyer, 1953). Children with genetically determined under-development of the brain or malformation of the head are probably less resistant to the physical stress of labour, and therefore more prone to trauma. 'The diagnosis of trauma from the examination of physical signs many years after the causal injury . . . is not easy—even if the case comes to autopsy. Without a complete family investigation and personal (including maternal) history, correct evaluation of trauma as a cause of defect is impossible' (Penrose, 1949c).

Strauss (1947) attempted to differentiate high-grade defectives with brain injury from congenital cases with the help of mental tests and behaviour studies. His work, based on Goldstein's theories and observations in brain-injured adults, refers to a group which included not only birth injuries, but other types of early damage to the brain through infections, etc. He finds this 'exogenous' group of defectives different from the 'endogenous', congenital group in respect of mental and physical growth, reaction to change of environment, test performance, neurological findings, etc. Strauss was also the first to make practical use of his findings by developing special methods of instruction and training for the brain-injured group, the size of which he estimated as being from 20 to 25 per cent. of the 667 children with an I.Q. of 50–80 trained in the institution where he worked. Tredgold on the other hand estimates that at the outside the cases due to birth injury number between 4 and 5 per cent. of all defectives; but he also points out that traumatic cases, if compared with other aments, show differences in behaviour, especially in their emotional reactions, and are also more frequently liable to epileptic symptoms.

The existence of focal neurological signs is not reliable evidence of localized trauma. Symmetrical symptoms, such as diplegia, suggest the effects of more general causes such as anoxia or genetical factors. It is now generally recognized that the motor disabilities of Little's cerebral palsy (spastic paralysis and athetosis), whatever their cause, can be present in persons of average intelligence, and that congenital athetosis in particular can be associated with superior mental equipment. The motor handicap may merely deprive the child of the opportunity to use his abilities. The belief that birth injury may lead to mental defect or personality disorder without neurological symptoms is still only a hypothesis.

FOETAL INFECTIONS. The classic example of a foetal infection which may cause mental defect is congenital syphilis. The *Treponema pallidum* is transmitted to the foetus by intra-uterine infection from the mother. The great majority of these infants are stillborn or die soon after birth. In those who survive, the Wassermann reaction is positive, but only for some months or years. The testing of unselected groups of defective children for a positive reaction is, therefore, not an adequate method of ascertaining the part played by syphilis in the causation of amentia. Clinical signs of intra-uterine syphilis, such as Hutchinson teeth, rhagades, keratitis and deafness, are often absent, even where the Wassermann reaction is found to be positive. The condition is now regarded as rare; Berg and Kirman (1959) found 0·6 per cent. of patients admitted to a hospital for defectives had a history of syphilis.

If the defective's mother or father has been treated for syphilis and there is a history of miscarriages or stillbirths in the family, and of paralysis of limbs or eye muscles and a positive Wassermann test in the child, it is highly probable that the mental defect is caused by syphilis. All degrees of mental defect from the mildest to the severest can be associated with infantile syphilis; and sense deprivation may be an additional handicap. Paralysed patients are often low-grade defectives or idiots. On the other hand, children with a positive blood test may show no signs of mental enfeeblement. Congenital syphilis, therefore, does not always affect the C.N.S. and it has been suggested that the immunity or susceptibility of the foetal brain to maternal infection may be due to hereditary factors.

In *congenital toxoplasmosis* the organism which is transmitted from mother to foetus is a protozoal parasite; the mental defect which results is usually severe (Penrose, 1963).

A much commoner accident of pregnancy is the infection of the foetus by the virus of *rubella*; the foetus is at risk if the mother suffers from rubella during the first three months of pregnancy. The commonest lesions produced in the infant are physical defects such as heart lesions, cataract, deafness; mental deficiency, if it occurs, is likely to be severe. Recent studies in this field have been made by Lundström (1952, 1962) and Manson, Logan and Loy (1960). A follow-up (Sheridan, 1964) of 259 children of mothers who had had rubella in the first 16 weeks of the pregnancy showed major physical abnormalities in 15 per cent. of the children, and minor abnormalities in a further 16 per cent.; but the distribution of intelligence in the children was normal, and it was thought that no evidence had been obtained that mental subnormality is a common sequel of early maternal rubella.

MATERNAL-FOETAL INCOMPATIBILITY. Among the agents which may damage the child *in utero* or at birth are blood agglutinins which enter the blood stream of the child from that of the mother. If mother and child are of different blood groups, the mother may become sensitized to the agglutinogens of the child and herself produce antibodies which are capable of destroying the blood corpuscles of the child. It is possible that such a reaction between mother and child may take place with the ABO agglutinogens; but in the case of maternal–child incompatibility in respect of the rhesus factors it is established. Newly born children, poisoned by receiving into their blood stream a dose of maternal Rhesus agglutinins, may develop erythroblastosis and later on kernicterus, with damage to the basal ganglia. A proportion of these children may be mentally defective, as well as suffering from specific neurological abnormalities. Rhesus incompatibility is not regarded as a numerically important cause of mental deficiency (Penrose, 1963).

POST-NATAL ENCEPHALITIS. Encephalitis occurring in post-natal life following infectious diseases such as measles, scarlet fever, whooping cough, mumps, as well as infantile polio-encephalitis may produce mental retardation and personality deviations. Bacterial meningitis was found by Berg (1962) to be responsible for about 3 per cent. of defectives admitted to the Fountain Hospital.

In children the personality changes following encephalitis lethargica differ considerably from the sequelae of this illness in adults (see Chapter XI). As a rule, they do not impair the intellectual abilities of the patient although they may interfere with education and the proper use of intelligence.

The aetiology and pathology of special forms of mental deficiency will be dealt with in the clinical part (p. 719).

CLINICAL FEATURES

Early Diagnosis

The physician is frequently asked to judge the developmental prospects of small children. Over-solicitous parents may be alarmed by some minor retardation in early development; others will display a blind spot for the most obvious signs of defect. Much tact and sympathy are needed when informing the mother that her child is defective; her reaction to the diagnosis may be such as to spoil her attitude towards the child and his up-bringing. When an infant is to be adopted, the exclusion of mental deficiency is vitally important for the prospective parents. Whereas the appearance of the sucking reflex is delayed, and there are anomalies in movements and in the sleep rhythm, as well as abnormalities in physical appearance in most imbeciles and idiots, yet high-grade defective children may display no abnormality immediately after birth or within the first few months. By careful observation, experienced mothers or nurses may discover a delay in the appearance of expressive movements like laughing or crying, in developing the power to hold up the head, or in crawling. Inadequate behaviour at feeding and persistence of foetal posture between the sixth and twelfth months are also ominous. But children offered for adoption are often not well observed and cared for, and the material for forming a judgement may be lacking.

Data for developmental diagnosis have been accumulated for small children (Gesell, 1941; Schwab, 1925; Bühler and Hetzer, 1927) and have been set out in tables which should be consulted in doubtful cases.

In the following tabulation (extracted by permission from Illingworth, 1960) a very partial selection has been made; for instance the large amount of normative data relating to reflex behaviour have been omitted. It is not suggested that what remains represents an adequate scale for the measurement of development, for which the original authority should be consulted. What is shown here is intended to provide an impressionistic picture of psychological development.

TABLE OF NORMAL DEVELOPMENTAL DATA

Age	Development
4 weeks	Hands predominantly closed; grasp reflex. Watches mother's face when she talks to him and he is not crying; opens and closes mouth; bobs head up and down.
	Supine, regards dangling object brought into line of vision, but not otherwise when in midline; follows it less than 90 degrees. Quiets when bell is rung.
8 weeks	Hands frequently open; only slight grasp reflex. Smiles and vocalizes when talked to. Vision: fixation, convergence and focusing; follows moving person; supine, follows dangling toy from side to point beyond midline.
12 weeks	Hands loosely open; no grasp reflex. When rattle is placed in hand, holds it for a minute or more. Squeals of pleasure; 'talks' a great deal when spoken to. Supine, characteristically watches movements of his own hands; follows dangling toy from side to side; promptly looks at an object in midline. Turns head to sound.
24 weeks	Sits supported in high chair; held in standing position, almost full weight on legs. Holds bottle; grasps his feet. Palmar grasp of cube; drops one cube when another is given. Drinks from cup when it is held to lips. When he drops a toy, looks to see where it has gone to and tries to recover it. Smiles and vocalizes at mirror image. Shows likes and dislikes. May show fear of strangers and be 'coy'. Displeasure at removal of toy. Play: laughs when head is hidden in towel. Imitates cough or protrusion of tongue.
40 weeks	Crawls by pulling self forward with hands. Sitting can go over into prone, or change from prone to sitting. Can pull self to sitting position. Sits steadily with little risk of overbalancing. Can stand holding onto furniture; collapses with a bump. Goes for object with index finger. Beginning to let go of objects (release). Looks round corner for object. Responds to words, e.g. 'Where is daddy?' Pulls clothes of another to attract attention. Holds object to examiner but won't release it. Repeats performance laughed at. Waves bye-bye; plays patacake.
1 year	Prone, walks on hands and feet like bear. Walks, one hand held. Beginning to throw objects to floor. Holds arm out for sleeve or foot out for shoe in dressing. May understand meaning of phrases, 'Where is your shoe?' May kiss on request. Apt to be shy. Has two or three words with meaning; knows meaning of more words.
18 months	Goes up and down stairs, holding rail, without help; walks up stairs, one hand held; pulling toy or carrying doll; seats self on chair. Beginning to jump, both feet. Cubes, builds tower of 3 or 4. Throws ball without fail. Pencil spontaneous scribble. Manages spoon well. Takes off gloves, socks. Points to 2 or 3 parts of body; obeys two simple orders; names one common object. Turns pages of book 2 or 3 at a time; points to picture of car or dog; shows sustained interest. Speech-jargon; many intelligible words. Sphincter control; dry by day, occasional accident.
2 years	Picks up object without falling; runs; kicks ball without overbalancing. Turns door knob; unscrews lid. Washes and dries hands. Cubes: tower of 6 or 7. Puts on and takes off shoes and socks. Points to 4 parts of body; obeys 4 simple orders; names 3 to 5 common objects. Book, turns pages singly. Speech: asks

for drink, food, toilet; uses 'I', 'me', 'you'; joins two or three words in sentences. Talks incessantly. Play: wraps up doll; puts it to bed. Watches others play, and plays near them, but not with them.

3 years

Jumps off bottom step; goes up stairs one foot per step, and down stairs two feet per step. Rides tricycle. Can help to set table, not dropping china. Dresses and undresses fully, if helped with buttons and advised about correct shoe, back and front. Cubes: tower of 9; imitates building of bridge. Play: dresses and undresses doll; speaks to it. Now joins in play. Copies circle on a card; imitates cross; draws a man on request. Knows some nursery rhymes. May count up to 10. Is constantly asking questions. Uses pronoun.

There is a very great deal of variability from individual to individual, and no far-reaching conclusions should be based on retardation which is only partial or lacking in consistency, and which is not persistent over a long time. Illingworth points out that such functions as smiling, grasping and chewing develop over a fairly limited span of time; while a normal child may start to sit unsupported at any time between the fourth and twentieth months, to walk unsupported at any time between the eighth month and the fourth year, and to speak in sentences at the twelfth month, or start to use single words at the age of four years or so. The understanding of speech is more reliable than motor speech as an indicator of normal development. Variations in the degree of development in some aspects of behaviour as compared with others are also seen. There are also slow starters, and other children who show pauses in development for some months at a time, who catch up with normal standards later.

Disorders of Development

Development may be *restricted* in range and in speed through abnormal genetic equipment, or through pathological factors interfering in the foetal or neonatal stage. In the subcultural defective, restriction in range and time go together: a relatively small range of mental activities is acquired in a much longer time than it takes a normal child to reach the same goal. The difference from the normal average becomes greater with progressing age. Hence the difficulty of predicting mental capacity in early infancy.

Development may be *delayed in partial functions*, such as sitting, standing, walking, speaking, cleanliness and especially the control of micturition. At the same time, general mental development may proceed at a normal pace. The significance of partial delays of this kind can only be assessed by observation of the child's total behaviour over some time. His reaction in typical situations, e.g. when eating, expressing affection or hostility towards the people around him, or in playing with children of the same age, and the progressive acquisition of more complicated patterns and attitudes may indicate normal development in spite of partial shortcomings.

General delay of development may be caused by gastrointestinal disturbances and infectious disease in infants. They may even cause a relapse into earlier forms of behaviour which the child had already outgrown. However, progress is resumed when physical health is restored and the child rapidly makes up for the lost time.

The same holds true for prematurely born children. They are naturally delayed in their early development, for a month or two, and some exhibit marked retardation for several years. Nevertheless, as a rule they do not differ from their contemporaries when they reach puberty.

Most observers agree that the child does not develop mentally and physically in a smooth and steady way, but rather by alternate phases of rapid progress and relative arrest.

This may be the case throughout the whole field of mental and physical development, as well as in partial attributes like physique, motor skill, intelligence or emotional behaviour. This uneven progress may explain the cases of early *acceleration of development* sometimes observed in children in whom at the age of four or five progress slows down to normal. Others remain precocious till puberty, which is in fact the testing time when it can be seen how far the prodigy fulfils his early promise. Many precocious children become average in their achievements. Intellectual forwardness is frequently not in harmony with the development of personality or with sexual development and leads to difficulties in adjustment. (See sections on psychopathic personality and child psychiatry.)

Development may be *thwarted* by chronic physical illness such as rickets, osteomyelitis, tuberculosis, cardiac invalidism, etc. If the child remains in a stage of baby-like dependence, or relapses into behaviour long outgrown, the suspicion of mental enfeeblement may be raised. In such cases the oversolicitousness of mothers or nurses, and lack of education and of contact with other children may be responsible, and the counter-measures are obvious.

Lastly, normal development can be *arrested* by diseases of the brain such as cerebral trauma, encephalitis following childish infections, neurosyphilis, epilepsy and encephalitis lethargica. The history of typical cases shows normal development up to the time of the accident or illness. This is unfortunately the history given by most mothers presenting a backward child to the physician. It has never occurred to the inexperienced or unobservant mother that the child's early development was not normal and, anxious to find a cause for his inability to play, his prolonged baby talk, his restlessness or lack of adaptation in company with other children, she attributes the trouble to some accident or illness. If, however, she has had previous children who developed normally, she will be able to make comparisons and her report may be reliable.

The Feeble-Minded (Moron)

It has frequently been pointed out that the personalities of high-grade defectives vary as much as those of normal persons, and this certainly is correct. Because they differ so much each case should be studied by the teacher and treated individually. It is, therefore, an over-simplification to subdivide the feeble-minded into two groups of the placid and restless, the stable and unstable, although this subdivision is useful in certain contexts: an equal or greater number lie between the two extremes.

The *clinical picture* cannot be described by simply subtracting different degrees of the 'ability of adaptive thinking' from the normal personality. The defective during his childhood and when he is grown up, is a whole person and has characteristic positive features besides his defects.

The defective child, even before school age, lacks the curiosity, spontaneity and interest of the normal child. In consequence a great number of these children are placid, quiet, and good in the home in spite of their slow development and backwardness. Many remain placid and passive throughout life; credulous and weak-willed, they are led as easily into good as evil paths. Although the sensory organs are usually intact, the feeble-minded individual is slow to perceive and to understand the objects around him, and apperception even if quick is unselective. He is unable to distinguish the essential from the non-essential and is mainly impelled by the strongest stimulus, the loudest noise, the brightest light or colour, etc. Whatever he has perceived he holds on to and his thinking frequently centres in these concrete sensory impressions. *Abstract ideas*, if they are formed at all, are narrow, badly formed and close to actual experiences: 'Freedom is when there is no school'; 'Religion is if one goes to church'. In a typical case the patient realized that 'justice' could mean punishment, but was unable to bring into the concept the idea of well-deserved reward (Bleuler). Like the small child or the member of a primitive race, the defective often cannot understand the abstraction of numbers: he may have learned to count buttons or marbles, and yet be unable to count his own fingers.

The *inability to free himself from a habit* of behaviour is well illustrated by a patient, observed by Kraepelin, who learned to cook in a hospital kitchen. When she returned to a private house and had to cook for three or four persons she prepared the meal using the same number of eggs as she had learned to use in the hospital. The stubbornness and inaccessibility to reason of defectives belongs to the same order of anomalies. Many are very conservative and extremely orderly as they have been taught to be in the colony or school, even when under different circumstances these habits are entirely out of place. 'Defectives are petty, they cling to details, are dependent, inconsequential, egotistic and inclined to over-value their own person. They have little self-control, may follow any impulse and are easily induced and led by others' (Hoche).

On the other hand, it is noteworthy that certain *mental functions* are relatively *undisturbed*: besides retaining intact senses, the feeble-minded suffer from no primary disturbance of retention and memory. Their attention, if roused, is usually normal; they can concentrate and persist in what interests them, although some are extremely distractible and others easily tired. They have potentially normal emotional responses, although often restricted to primitive and simple feelings which they express in a direct and crude fashion. Sexual development is sometimes delayed, but the accompanying affect is normal. Finally, many high-grade defectives have a certain insight into their shortcomings, and although they can rarely express this in words, they make an effort to appear intelligent. One of our patients collected old medical journals from the dustbin of the hospital and carried them in his pockets although he hardly looked at them and was unable to understand what he read.

Speech, often late in development, is poorly articulated; modulation and expression are often lacking, and the vocabulary is small. Part of the speech difficulty so frequently seen may be due to *inadequate muscular co-ordination*, which is also commonly shown in reduction of manual dexterity. Many dullards and high-grade defectives are ungainly in bodily balance and clumsy in walking. They are smaller in stature and of lower weight than the average of the population and are said to have a lower resistance to physical disease. How far the last is due to a real physiological abnormality or to neglect in upbringing and careless and imprudent behaviour is difficult to decide. '*Stigmata of degeneracy*' were at one time regarded as important physical signs of all degrees of amentia, but many have been found in equal frequency in the normal, and they are now not employed for diagnostic purposes.

THE DEFECTIVE AS A SCHOOLCHILD. The majority of subcultural defectives come from the least prosperous economic classes. The mother can pay little attention to the mental growth of her child, because she is over-burdened with a large family or has herself to go to work. So it is that most of the cases are only discovered in school, i.e. at the age of five or later.

Many high-grade defectives are easily handled children; they do not differ from the average in appearance, are well behaved and affectionate, and adjust well to a kindergarten atmosphere. At a later stage when it comes to reading and writing, the child's failure is sometimes put down to anything but backwardness: to lack of effort, distractibility, poor nutrition or insufficient sleep. In fact, emotionally maladjusted children may be sent to the psychiatrist sooner than the intellectually backward. It is often difficult to convince parents of the *advantage of special education*. They dread the transfer of their child from the ordinary into a special class or school; and the older he is, the more reluctant they are to make the change. It is, therefore, desirable that mental defect should be recognized and diagnosed as early as possible. The Education Act, 1944, provides for free psychological and medical advice for every child from the age of two. The family doctor should make every possible effort to see that full use is made of this provision. If it is properly applied it should save the teacher much useless trouble, and much suffering to the child.

At the same time there is an increasing awareness that selection of those who need the facilities of a special school cannot be satisfactorily made on the basis of the intelligence quotient alone. Some children being educated at these schools are found to have an intelligence quotient well above 70, while others with an I.Q. in the feeble-minded range are able, under favourable circumstances, to benefit from education at an ordinary school. A decision to send the child to a school for the educationally subnormal should therefore be made only after a careful appraisal of the personality and social background as well as the intelligence of the child. There would be considerable advantage in more flexible arrangements for interchange between the two types of school. If account is taken of his special difficulties, the high-grade defective may be a happy and well-adapted schoolchild and he can be helped to develop into a useful individual. Fortunately, the old occupational and diversional types of activity at special schools are giving place to an increasing extent to programmes, making use of modern educational techniques, directed towards the task of developing the child into a confident, self-respecting and adjusted member of society. Maturation in a defective child takes place at a slower rate than in children with normal intellectual equipment and this necessitates a longer period of social education and play imparted by methods of the kind used in nursery schools. When the time arrives for initiating formal education (and it is preferable to start this at a later age than in normal children) the guiding principles should be a slow pace of work, frequent repetition, ample concrete illustrations and learning through the incentives which can be provided by practical tasks such as cookery, shopping and handwork. In this way many children can learn simple reading and writing, the handling of money and the composition of a simple letter which go far in deciding their chances of employment. The group setting in which the child strives to attain such goals, that have always to be kept within his reach, is important for inculcating the rudiments of group responsibility and discipline (Hilliard and Kirman, 1957) as well as for educational purposes. The chances of subsequent social adjustment and economic independence are largely determined by the success achieved in the course of education.

AFTER LEAVING SCHOOL. The field for employment of the high-grade defective has changed during recent years. Labouring, in which he traditionally found a place most readily, is now a shrinking occupation. Agriculture is becoming increasingly mechanized and rationalized so that he finds less scope there. Similarly defective women are more difficult to place in private or hotel domestic service because of household appliances which are a substitute for servants and require intelligence in their use. This is a tendency which will increase with time. On the other hand the simple repetitive processes which are at present increasing in urban industry are within the ability of the trained defective and light industry is spreading into areas previously exclusively rural. Many defectives, in addition, are capable of learning a trade and continuing to be employed as tradesmen. It is more with these types of employment in view that the feeble-minded should be trained in future. A number of recent studies is discussed by Hilliard and Kirman (1957) which go to show that about half the defective children with I.Q.s of less than 70 are found to be satisfactorily employed on follow-up. The same conclusion is reached by Gunzburg (1960). It has been found in a follow-up study of feeble-minded patients (Stanley and Gunzburg, 1957) over a period of about three years that between one-quarter and one-third may fail in their first job in industry, but that the majority, even under traditional methods of training and placement, succeed perhaps in their second, third or even fourth job. A high proportion of the feeble-minded should accordingly be capable of achieving social and economic independence. Satisfactory employment depends on carefully directed vocational training and a favourable state of the labour market. Because he is slow and inadaptable the defective's fate is closely linked with economic conditions and community attitudes. When applying for work for which he has been rendered fit, he is apt to be rejected by employers and he is the first to be dismissed when the number of workmen has to be reduced. Much has still to be accomplished in overcoming prejudice and in developing co-operation between manufacturers on the one hand and the staffs of training centres and social workers in charge of placing defectives on the other. Machinery of modern type, suitably adapted, could be lent to training centres to facilitate realistic training and some of the most stereotyped and simple processes can be carried out as industrial subcontract work under sheltered conditions. Given training and opportunity the feeble-minded person can be a reliable and untiring workman (O'Connor and Tizard, 1956).

In the case of the adult feeble-minded person who has failed to obtain or keep employment, or who suffers from the effects of a long period of institutionalization, a special programme of training (in a centre or hospital "school") directed towards surmounting particular shortcomings that stand in the way of social integration will be helpful (Gunzberg, 1958). It should be mainly concerned with the acquisition of simple social skills such as finding his way about an unfamiliar district, the use of the telephone, information about jobs and how to secure them and guidance about health and medical treatment. The ability to conduct simple social transactions such as the purchase of tickets and putting money in a savings bank can be learnt if practised frequently in the real situation.

Support from home, from membership of a social club, or from a religious group is of great assistance in his social development, stability and integration.

Only if one is aware of the mentality and social conditions of the numerous defectives living in the community, can one understand and deal appropriately with the *difficulties and conflicts* which bring them into contact with physician and psychiatrist. The usual stumbling-blocks of life, sex and marriage, physical illness and accident, delinquency and crime, evoke specific reactions from the high-grade defective.

SEX AND MARRIAGE. Tredgold's distinction between the stable and the unstable feeble-minded is of some importance in this context. It is based on emotional response and motor behaviour; the distinction is essentially the same as that drawn between the 'torpid' and the 'erethic' defective in Continental psychiatry. This was found useful clinically, especially in considering personal and social conflicts. Stable defectives are placid, dependable, unemotional, easily led to good or evil; unstable defectives are restless, easily roused to emotions, have marked likes and dislikes and are unpredictable in their reactions.

During puberty and with sexual maturation these emotional differences become more manifest. While the stable defective *girl* may fall to the first seducer at an early age and have an illegitimate child, she will remain in her employment and try to make good; the unstable girl becomes increasingly restless and throws herself into sexual adventures. She becomes promiscuous, neglects her work and gives up all ties with her family. These girls spread venereal disease, become victims of tricksters and ruffians and end in remand homes, poor-houses and other institutions. 'Many women of this type have considerable mental ability, but they are so prone to attacks of excitement, violence, sulkiness or moroseness, so fickle and undependable that it is quite impossible for them to retain any situation' (Tredgold).

Males of the stable type often seem under-sexed or late in sex development. For the stable defectives only, one can agree with Goddard who, 'after years of study of the problem' came 'to the conviction that the sexual instinct in these people is under-developed rather than over-developed'. 'Feeble-minded people are not nearly so promiscuous in their sexual relations as we might at first expect . . . a great many of them live together in wedlock and true to each other' (Goddard, 1914). Instability in the male defective becomes more marked when his sexual urges mature. Refused by the average girl, he may pursue his aim by indecent exposure or by violence, crudely assaulting elderly women and not infrequently children. Bestiality with domestic animals is a frequent outlet for the sexual drive of the rural defective (Kinsey *et al.*, 1948).

The unstable defective often continues his or her *promiscuity* even after finding a partner for marriage. Women carry on as prostitutes, and become a moral and hygienic menace to the street or village where they live. The number of mental defectives among professional prostitutes has been found to be about 30 per cent. by observers in different countries (Bonhoeffer, 1903; Schneider, 1926; Tage Kemp, 1936). Even among the more stable group the effect of mental deficiency on married life, housekeeping and the upbringing of children is often evident. Cases of *cruelty and neglect* of children are frequently accounted for by the mental deficiency of the mother. Her inability to keep an orderly home leads to domestic quarrels and constant strife if the husband is of somewhat higher intelligence. The defective husband, on the other hand, may become a burden to a wife of normal intelligence, a burden which proves socially overwhelming when added to the others she has to bear—home duties, the care of children, and not infrequently a job of her own. If both are defective they may live in dirty and verminous conditions, disgusting to the neighbourhood.

The contribution of mental deficiency of one or both marriage partners to *unhappy family life*, broken homes and child neglect is not sufficiently realized. Figures for this country are not available. In Ramer's (1946) follow-up of 600 Swedish pupils of special schools who otherwise adapted favourably, the divorce rate was two and a half times as great as in the normal control group. Only 50 per cent. of the special school group were married, against 64 per cent. of the controls.

ILLNESS. Defectives are often rather tolerant of pain and injury. They take little notice of the knocks and bruises they receive by their careless handling of tools, and festering wounds seem not to worry them. Conversely, like small children, they may respond with howls and yells and signs of panic to relatively trifling pain during surgical treatment.

They like to be cared for and indulge themselves in playing the patient. Escape into some indefinite ailment leading to medical treatment easily becomes a habit with the feeble-minded man. He likes to frequent surgeries and clinics. If he has some physical handicap —as so often is the case—he makes every use of it to dodge work and the frequent difficulties of family life. Some may become prone to accidents, especially if their occupation is technically above their intellectual grasp. The contribution to absenteeism in industry which is made by those of subnormal intelligence is considerable. Russell Fraser (1947) found the average absence from work due to all causes, including sickness, proportionally greater in the group of low intelligence both in men and women. The incidence of definite physical illness showed also an inverse relationship to the level of intelligence.

DELINQUENCY AND CRIME. It seems probable, although there is no reliable evidence on this point, that mental defectives are more than normally liable to be involved in delinquency as children and adolescents and in more serious offences as adults. The principal reason for this belief is the finding that lowering of intelligence sets the child at risk. This is shown by the estimates that have been made of the mean levels and distribution of intelligence in samples of delinquents and offenders. Thus Burt (1948) found a mean I.Q. of 89 for 197 delinquent boys and girls. The subject has been reviewed by Woodward (1955). She concluded that early studies were unreliable, and that even the best and most recent work was unable to eliminate cultural effects which might suggest a relationship which did not in fact exist. Modern work has, in fact, yielded higher mean I.Q.s for delinquents than older studies; and there is a suggestion that in recent years the risk of delinquency has become more nearly the same for children of normal and those of retarded intelligence. No systematic studies of the intelligence of adult criminals have been carried out to the knowledge of the authors during the last twenty years.

The social prognosis with regard to delinquency is affected by the emotional stability of the defective. The more stable and passive may drift into membership of gangs; and feeble-minded children are sometimes used by parents for shoplifting and pilfering. Thefts in big stores and shops are a common offence, especially among girls, and appear to constitute a somewhat greater temptation for girls of dull intelligence. In the study by Cowie et al., (1968) of a year's intake into a girls' classifying school a significant excess of cases of larceny was found among the girls of I.Q. 70–79; but among the girls of I.Q. below 70 there were very few offenders and almost all the 'delinquency' was of a sexual nature. Practice in the Courts suggests that offences are more likely in girls during the premenstruum, one of the many phenomena associated with the increased state of emotional tension at that time. Katharina Dalton (1960) has demonstrated very elegantly the association is schoolgirls of misbehaviour with menstruation.

Impulsive crimes, committed by unstable subnormals, are often more difficult to understand. The best known are acts of wilful damage such as haystack-firing and other forms of arson. Dullards in dependent positions such as those of labourer or farm-hand, apparently discharge, by such acts, their resentment against workmates or employers to relieve the emotional tension due to their personal situation. Mutilation of cattle has been observed, and also murder. Jaspers (1909) described dull and defective girls who killed young children in their charge. One of them pushed an infant into a deep well. She gave 'home-sickness' as the motive of her crime: she disliked being in service with strangers and wanted to stay at home with her parents.

It is difficult to make an estimate of the *proportion of criminals who are defective,* whatever method is employed. If the concept of mental defect is restricted to the certifiable defective and if the provision of institutions for disturbed defectives is adequate, the number of subnormals found in the prison population will be relatively small. This explains the result of an inquiry of Norwood East (1938) who found only 0·42 per cent. certified defectives among the receptions in prisons of England and Wales during ten years. Experienced observers (Parker Wilson, Pailthorpe, Tredgold) estimate that not less than 10 per cent. of criminals are defective. As one would expect, the proportion is higher among recidivists.

Severe Subnormality

IMBECILITY. Although the terms 'feeble-minded', 'imbecile' and 'idiot' no longer have any legal sanction, they still have some practical usefulness. Nevertheless, the demarcation between imbeciles and the feeble-minded on one side and idiots on the other is far from sharp. In terms of I.Q. imbeciles are regarded as extending from 50 to 20, with idiots below that level; and in terms of social adequacy they are those who do not need to be constantly looked after and protected from common dangers, but who are incapable of managing their affairs or of being taught to do so. They are four times as numerous as idiots, and make up about one-fourth of the 'mentally subnormal'.

As one would expect, low-grade mental deficiency can be *diagnosed more easily* and earlier after birth than can the higher grades. This is due to the frequent combination of imbecility with physical abnormalities and malformations, marked squint, paralysis of one or several limbs, peculiar forms of face or head, and many developmental anomalies: delay in response to stimulation, lack in spontaneity, marked postponement of the usual milestones, such as sitting up, walking, speaking and cleanliness. Fretfulness and restlessness of the infant may presage imbecility of the excitable type. The child is unable to play with ordinary toys, is destructive and cannot join in the play of children of his age.

Because of the difficulty of bringing up such a child in the family, his unresponsiveness in school, often even in a special class, and, on the other hand, because of the relative ease with which he can be trained in an *institution*, parents should be persuaded to place his education in expert hands. The imbecile should go through an institution, at least at one stage of his life, and should remain under the care and supervision of the authorities. Subnormal children are found to benefit from care in small 'family' groups instead of large institutions in the same way as normal children (Tizard, 1960b; Tizard and Grad, 1961).

Earl (1936) has studied and given a lively description of *the behaviour of imbecile children* of school age in an institution and has emphasized the great influence of the environment on these children. He found that most of them were lacking in drive. They are in need of constant stimulation and their persistence in any task is small. Conversely a small group, showing over-activity which could be attributed to lesions in the basal ganglia, are handicapped by their restlessness and distractibility. To direct this over-activity into useful channels is a special educational task.

A second feature is the imbecile's *emotional infantility*. He craves for caresses and protection like an infant. Judicious petting is the most potent stimulus to success in a task or to improvement in behaviour. 'Emotional expression is uninhibited, laughter and tears are quickly roused and as quickly banished; pleasure is expressed by movements involving the whole musculature—the hands are rubbed together, the head rotates, while the whole body squirms in an ecstasy of joy'. 'In play, boys of 10–15 capable under instruction of quite complicated games, will revert in their free play to the aimless psychomotor activity, the rapid changes of objective, of a child of two'. Earl points to the need for a simplified environment for these children. Different results in different institutions depend on the skill of the training staff. He also finds a lack of team spirit among defectives and inability to co-operate in play groups. 'The imbecile is not antagonistic towards his fellow children; he does not shun their company, but he does not want their comradeship. He is indifferent rather than seclusive.' Mood-swings may, however, occur without any external cause, as many low-grade defectives suffer from *epileptic fits* and epileptic equivalents. Tredgold estimates that 42 per cent. of imbeciles are epileptic, a figure which he himself considers as probably too high because it refers to institutionalized patients only and includes cases with rare fits or small series of fits at an early age.

Status epilepticus or an accident in an epileptic seizure is a frequent *cause of death* in imbecility. Even if there is no known pathology, the expectation of life is less than average; and imbeciles and idiots are supposed to have a reduced resistance against infection and other disease.

Adult imbeciles with their lack of inhibition and their suggestibility are sometimes *misused for criminal purposes* by others, who may induce them to steal or to receive stolen goods, to start fires or to commit brutalities and other acts of revenge. If the imbecile acts alone, the offence is often carried out without prevision, and in such a simple manner that he rarely escapes detection. Sexual exposure and attacks on small children or elderly women are, apart from stealing and vagrancy, the most frequent offences of defectives of this grade.

The training and education of the severely subnormal as well as the feeble-minded have received a good deal of attention in recent years. It seems clear that the extent to which knowledge and skill can be imparted, even in the severely handicapped, has been under-estimated until recent years. Gunzberg (1958a) has discussed the education of children who are not admitted to school. Training, he considers, should aim at making a severely handi-capped child more readily acceptable to the family and at reducing tensions and anxieties within it. He must be trained to dress, keep himself clean and to feed himself acceptably. A careful investigation will reveal where the emphasis should be laid in training in each child. Attention should be mainly devoted to enabling the child to move more freely in his limited environment and to cultivating those abilities which will prove useful later, such as signing his name, recognizing printed words such as street names, bus destinations, common warning signs and the recognition and handling of coins.

In 1929 the Wood Committee's report pointed out that 'if we were to place greater emphasis upon activities of the mental defective that can be directed into useful channels, we should need to concern ourselves less about their care and supervision and control'. However, occupational and recreational therapy, which was the main formal activity provided for the mentally handicapped in institutions in the past, did little to promote the socialization that is so readily fostered by the ability to work. The custodial outlook failed to provide adequate incentives or to foster work habits and has thus been responsible for deterioration of the capacity for social adjustment in the more severely mentally handicapped.

IDIOCY. The practical distinction of idiots from imbeciles by the inability of the former to guard themselves against common physical dangers has little scientific significance. Idiots represent the lowest grade of mental deficiency, and there is no clear dividing line between them and the severer cases of imbecility. Their I.Q. is estimated to be below 20, but in many instances the usual tests of intelligence are not applicable.

About 5 per cent. of the total number of defectives belong to this category. Incidence is greatest in childhood and decreases with age owing to the high mortality rate. E. O. Lewis found 0·4 male and 0·29 female idiots per 1,000 of population of each sex.

Theoretically there should be a small number of defectives of the lowest grade in whom the intellectual deficiency is the only variant. They do not seem to survive if they exist at all. The lower on the scale the patient is placed mentally, the greater is the extent to which *anatomical and physiological abnormalities* are found combined with the defect. The majority are stunted in growth, deformed and misshapen in the form of their head, the proportions of head or limbs to trunk. Congenital aplasia of certain parts of the central nervous system are found resulting in severe neurological symptoms, such as hemiplegia or diplegia. In addition, there are frequently central lesions usually attributed to early trauma or infections such as porencephaly, or to microgyria, hemiatrophy, etc. Many idiots are bed-ridden all their lives, or cannot walk and only sit on a chair. Their movements are poorly co-ordinated, and a choreiform or athetotic hyperkinesis or tremor may be the only motor performance of which they are capable.

Some cannot feed themselves and those who do are so voracious that they are in constant danger of choking. Others, like small children, put everything they can get hold of into their mouth and swallow it, earth, grass, stones, leather or pieces of cloth and other material torn from their clothes or bedding. Other features which are reminiscent of infancy are *persistent rhythmic movements* such as rocking the trunk or shaking the head. They may chew their fingers, or indulge in repetitive cries or other noises, or have outbursts like temper-tantrums. Incontinence and playing with urine and faeces are frequent. Most idiots are speechless, a few learn to articulate monosyllables like pa, ma; most utterances are purely emotional expressions comparable to the cries of animals. By grunting and yelling they can express their primitive feelings and wants.

One of the most striking symptoms of low-grade defectives and idiots is the *blunting and perversion of sense perception*. Without anatomical lesions of the peripheral sense organs, they may be impervious to optic, acoustic, tactile or olfactory sensations. They may not distinguish between different tastes, and eat and drink everything. At the same time, they have a morbid craving for strong sensations, especially pain; they pull out their hair, hit and wound themselves incessantly with apparent delight so that they have to be restrained.

Although some idiots can be taught regular habits and cleanliness, most of them need constant care and supervision such as can only be provided in an institution. There is very little they can learn and it is hardly possible to direct the movements of the hyperkinetic into useful channels. Few families will take the responsibility of keeping them at home; and when that has been done, restless idiots have sometimes been treated in the most inhuman fashion.

Fifty-six per cent. of idiots suffer from epileptic fits (Tredgold), and many die in status epilepticus. When they become ill or suffer an injury, their uncooperative behaviour makes medical or surgical treatment very difficult.

Special Forms of Mental Deficiency

The specific syndromes which are liable to be accompanied by mental deficiency, mild or severe, may be classified in the following tabulation:

1. Chromosomal Abnormalities:
   (a) of the autosomes,
   (b) of the sex chromosomes.

2. Genic Abnormalities:
    (a) due to dominant genes,
    (b) due to recessive genes.
3. Environmentally Determined Abnormalities.

It is not possible within the scope of a single chapter to give a comprehensive account of the many individual syndromes which fall into this classification. Instead of attempting this we shall discuss single examples of these groups of disorders, choosing those which are of most importance or interest.

AUTOSOMAL CHROMOSOMAL ABNORMALITIES

MONGOLISM. Mongolism is by far the commonest of the clinical syndromes associated with mental subnormality, and has been reported as occurring in nearly all ethnic groups. According to Penrose (1949*b*) about one in every 700 births is of a mongol. The figure estimated by Carter and McCarthy (1951) for the incidence of mongolism in live births is somewhat higher at one in 666; and a further correction, making allowance for cases escaping diagnosis in the neonatal period, has been suggested by Zappella and Cowie (1962), bringing the figure to one in 557 live births.

The *incidence* of mongols among the inmates of mental deficiency institutions has been estimated at about 5 per cent.; but as 25 per cent. die between birth and the age of five, the number of mongols born seems difficult to gauge. Of those who survive to the age 15–19, they were found to account for just under one-third of all severe subnormality in the survey of the 'Wessex' region, a mixed urban and rural area (Kushlick, 1965). Mongolism is, unlike subcultural mental defect, equally frequent among the rich and the poor. There is no difference in sex incidence.

The importance of heredity in mongolism was long suspected from the evidence of twins. In all reported monozygotic pairs, both members of the pair were mongols; in nearly all dizygotic pairs, one of them only. Furthermore, it was noticed that there is a small but significant excess of mongols among the sibs of mongols, with an incidence of about one in 100 births. Mongols are not infertile and, of the children reported in the literature as born to mothers who were themselves mongols, about half were mongols and half were normal. There was, however, one very striking phenomenon associated with mongolism, which was thought to provide an argument against genetical theories of causation, i.e. the late mean maternal age of 37 years. After the mother has reached the age of 30, the likelihood of mongol birth is multiplied some twenty or thirty times, to reach its peak between the maternal ages of 45 and 49. As Penrose has shown (1934), other correlated findings, such as high paternal age and a late position in the birth order, probably do not have any direct influence of their own. Even today the explanation of this phenomenon remains speculative.

For many years a conflict raged as to whether environmental or genetical factors were of the greater significance in the aetiology of mongolism; and until quite recently there was a predominance of opinion in favour of environmental causation, supported by the late maternal age effect and the view that the condition was brought about by defects due to ageing in the reproductive system of the mother. Mechanical faults, such as insufficiency of endometrium for implantation of the ovum, were cited as likely causes.

Rapid advances in cytological techniques in recent years have, however, thrown entirely new light on genetical causation, following rapidly on the discovery that man has 46 chromosomes and not, as was long thought 48. A small extra chromosome was discovered in tissue cultures from the connective tissue of three patients with mongolism by Lejeune,

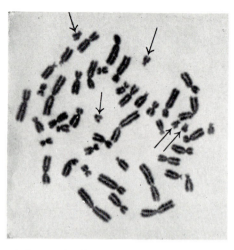

1. Down's Syndrome 47,XY,G+ (five instead of four chromosomes in group G marked by arrows).

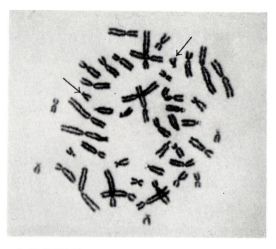

2. 47,XYY (the two Y chromosomes are marked by arrows).

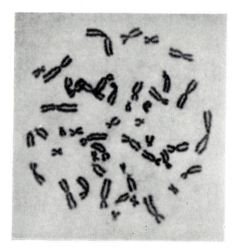

3. Klinefelter syndrome, 47, XXY (the two X chromosomes cannot be identified without radioactive labelling techniques).

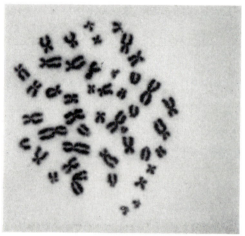

4. Turner's syndrome, 45,X (the single X chromosomes cannot be identified without radioactive labelling techniques).

PLATE XVII

Karyotypes of four subjects with chromosomal abnormalities.

(Photographs kindly supplied by Dr Jacob Kahn and Mr Nigel Dernley)

Gautier and Turpin (1959); and similar observations were made by other workers (Jacobs *et al.*, 1959; Ford *et al.*, 1959). Since then it has become fully established that a fundamental characteristic of mongolism is the triplication (or the equivalent of triplication) of one of the small acrocentric chromosomes. It is estimated that in over 90 per cent. of mongols the diploid number is 47 instead of the usual human complement of 46 chromosomes, owing to the presence of this small extra chromosome. In the remaining 10 per cent. of cases the chromosome number is normal, but there is still an excess of genetical material, since the greater part of the extra chromosome is fused on to another chromosome, producing an abnormally large chromosome, by the process of translocation. Translocated chromosomes may be transmitted through families for several generations without the emergence of a mongol child. Carriers of these abnormal chromosomes are apparently phenotypically normal, but their diploid number is 45 so that they are 'balanced' in respect of the quantity of chromatin they are carrying. This would be an obvious source of multiple appearances of mongolism in one sibship; but in fact the translocation mechanism is by no means always seen in families with two or more fairly closely related mongols. It seems reasonable to suppose that there are other less obvious genetical mechanisms, possibly acting at genic level, which may play a part in the familial occurrence of mongolism.

Although the great cytogenetical discoveries of recent years have demonstrated the causal relationship between mongolism and triplication or its equivalent of one of the small acrocentric chromosomes, the origin of this chromosomal anomaly on the one hand, and the means by which it brings about the profound developmental changes of mongolism on the other, are great problems which remain to be solved. The evidence collected by Benda (1947) in support of the view that mongolism is a form of pituitary hypo-function starting in foetal life, and related to the endocrine balance of the mother in pregnancy, may have a place for consideration in reviewing these problems. Benda's hypothesis drew considerable attention at the time; but now it stands as only one among many sets of observations, endocrinological, biochemical and clinical, that may help to elucidate these fundamental issues.

The *signs of mongolism* are all present from birth and do not become more marked as the child develops; on the contrary grown-up mongols may show less pronounced features. Penrose (following an idea of Anton who spoke of 'slack-baked' children) suggested the name 'foetalism' because many of the signs can be regarded as remnants of foetal existence and the whole picture as one of development retarded mentally and physically. Benda speaks of the mongol as an 'ill-finished child'.

The ensemble of *physical signs* is very characteristic and the remarkable resemblance of mongols to one another has been pointed out by many workers; each single character, however, may be absent in one or another case.

The skull is small, rounded and brachycephalic with flattened face and occiput. The face is moon-shaped without the prominent cheek bones of the Mongol race. The palpebral fissures of the eyes are narrow and have a downward and inward slope. An epicanthic fold is frequent, especially in infants, and so is convergent squint. The conjunctivae are often inflamed and there is a tendency to chronic nasal catarrh. There are characteristic abnormalities of the facial bones in the x-ray picture. The nose is short and squat and the nasal and oral cavities small. The tongue is often large and protrudes from the mouth; by the third year of life it shows numerous transverse fissures. The cheeks are rosy and the hair is coarse, wiry and sparse. The hands are soft and flabby, the fingers easily hyperextended, thumb and little finger are too small and the palm creases are abnormal. The feet often show a cleft between the first and second toes. Delayed dentition and ossification of the epiphyses, umbilical hernia, laxity of ligaments and under-developed genital organs in the male are other characteristics. Epileptic fits and other symptoms of epilepsy are not observed in mongols.

Intellectually most mongols are imbeciles or idiots, the majority belonging to the former. Only a few are feeble-minded. While often placid and inert in infancy, they later develop a peculiar distractibility and curiosity. All the usual milestones, sitting, walking and talking are delayed. They are lively, observant, like to mimic and imitate, and look bright and cheerful. They have a striking interest in music and a sense of rhythm, and love dancing and clowning. They remain good-tempered, affectionate and sociable and are, therefore, frequently kept in the family where they are well liked, spoiled and petted by all who have to deal with them. This is one of the causes of difficulty in ascertaining the incidence. The same mental characteristics are found in institutionalized mongols. Those with less intellectual defect can be employed in very simple routine duties, but are rarely of much use in manual work because they lack dexterity and have little physical strength.

Few mongols survive the age of fifteen; the majority succumb to tuberculosis and other infections of the respiratory system, and others die from congenital heart lesions which are a frequent complication of mongolism, or of duodenal atresia (Bodian *et al.*, 1952).

Other autosomal chromosomal anomalies, all of them associated with severe mental deficiency, have been discovered. Trisomy among the chromosomes of the 13–15 group was first described by Patau *et al.* (1960). The abnormalities are very diverse including cleft palate, heart and eye defects. Trisomy 17–18 was described by Edwards *et al.* (1960) associated with cranial dysmorphia and a heart defect, as well as brain abnormalities including a defective falx. The latest and the most romantically named of these syndromes has again been described by Lejeune and his colleagues (1964) under the name of 'cri du chat' syndrome, because of the mewing cry of these infants. Mentally there is severe defect, physically a craniofacial dysmorphia. The chromosomal basis is a deletion of half of the short arms of chromosome 5.

SEX CHROMOSOMAL ABNORMALITIES

KLINEFELTER'S SYNDROME. A syndrome was described by Klinefelter *et al.* (1942) which, when adequate cytological investigation became possible, was found in about half the cases to be associated with duplication, once or even more times, of the X-chromosome in the male. These males are sterile, and the principal physical anomaly is an atrophic state of the testes, accompanied by gynaecomastia and other indications of feminization. The condition is relatively common. According to Penrose (1963) the pooled results of a number of sex chromatin examinations of the buccal mucosa of newly-born infants indicate a frequency of one in 400, 18 out of 6,801 males showing female sex chromatin. Among male mental defectives the frequency of the XXY sex chromosome constitution is estimated as being about one in 100 so that the extra X-chromosome probably does interfere to some extent with normal mental development. The same is thought to apply to XXX females. However, the level of intelligence is subject to variation and cases with average or superior intelligence are on record. A number of reports have appeared recently of a schizophrenia-like syndrome occurring in patients with Klinefelter's disease (Biesele *et al.*, 1962).

TURNER'S SYNDROME. Turner's syndrome, brought about by deletion of the Y-chromosome leaving only a single X-chromosome, i.e. XO chromosomal constitution, is associated with female bodily sex, with inadequate genital development and sterility, but not usually with mental retardation. Despite the dwarfism and other deformities, psychological abnormalities appear more uncommon than in the Klinefelter syndrome.

ABNORMALITIES DUE TO DOMINANT GENES

EPILOIA. Dominant genes which produce severe abnormality early in life are extinguished by selective processes before they can be transmitted to the next generation. In such cases they will only be seen when first produced by mutation; and it may be extremely difficult to establish that such a condition is based on a genic abnormality. However, in the course of countless generations, a genetic stock adjusts itself to the occurrence of disadvantageous mutations by the accumulation of genes of minor effect which mitigate the severity of the effects produced by dominant mutations. The modifications which take place in the course of evolution may take a number of different lines. The degree of dominance of the mutant gene may be reduced so that it is shifted towards recessivity over an intermediate stage of reduced penetrance; its time of manifestation may be shifted towards later ages of life; or its effects may become milder. So it is that the effects produced by pathogenic dominant genes tend to be milder and more variable, and often later in onset, than those of recessive genes.

Among the conditions caused by dominant genes are a number of *skeletal conditions* such as hypertelorism and acrocephaly; only a proportion of these patients are mentally defective, and the degree of defect is variable. The same applies to the commoner condition of *epiloia* (tuberose sclerosis). Relatives of hospital patients suffering from this condition are often found to be showing part only of the syndrome, e.g. the skin condition of adenoma sebaceum, or an epilepsy of occult origin. Nevertheless, the gene so frequently causes a severe degree of mental deficiency, with consequent infertility, that direct inheritance from parent to child is exceptional. Gunther and Penrose (1935) estimate that a quarter to a half of all cases are due to fresh mutation.

Among defectives not more than about 0·5 per cent. suffer from epiloia. The main symptoms are mental deficiency from birth, epilepsy and adenoma sebaceum of the face, forming the typical 'butterfly rash' over nose, cheeks, chin and forehead. The most important pathological change is the presence of multiple nodules of glial tissue with undifferentiated nerve cells with a widespread distribution, including the cerebral cortex. There are often other anomalies of the skin, fibromata and naevi, tumours in kidney, heart, retina and other organs. The degree of mental defect is usually fairly severe; and progressive deterioration may occur. Psychoses with catatonic symptoms have been described.

Huntington's chorea may occur in childhood, and Jervis (1963) has described four cases with onset at 3, 5, 6 and 9 years. A review of the literature covering 2,394 cases revealed 7 with onset before the age of five, and 13 with onset between five and ten. Appearing so early, the condition leads to an intellectual deficit resembling defect rather than dementia; and it may be that a number of cases in Huntington families have been missed on this account. Jervis draws attention to the absence of choreic movements and the occurrence of epilepsy in childhood cases.

ABNORMALITIES DUE TO RECESSIVE GENES

Unlike dominant genes, recessive genes are protected from weeding out by natural selection to a degree proportional with the rarity of the gene; for if the gene frequency is p, then the proportion of all genes in circulation, which are being carried by homozygotes and so exposed to selection, is $2p^2$, while the proportion which are being carried by the heterozygotes, who do not show the abnormality and so have normal chances of survival and procreation, is $2p$. A rare condition with an incidence of 1 in 40,000 would be associated with a gene frequency p of 1 in 200 and a heterozygote frequency of 1 in 100 which would mean that little more than 1 in every 200 mutant genes would be extinguished between one generation and the next. Malignant recessive conditions are rare; but once they have attained a certain degree of rarity there is no strong natural tendency for them to become rarer still. So it is found that the effects of recessive genes are often early in onset, severe in degree, and clearly defined in clinical manifestation with little variation. Clearly marked syndromes are the rule, very much more than in dominant conditions. To this class of anomaly belong the major part of the known inborn errors of metabolism, each with its specific enzyme deficiency. It has been estimated by Paine (1960) that approximately 5 per cent. of all patients in institutions suffer from a metabolic abnormality of this nature. Moncrieff (1960) has reviewed the field and attempted a classification grouping the conditions broadly under four headings—the cerebral lipidoses, the amino-acid anomalies, the carbohydrate anomalies and the disturbances of water and electrolyte metabolism. Although they are genetically determined, the resulting enzyme defects leading to an accumulation of substances toxic to the developing brain, Moncrieff pointed out that acquired toxic conditions such as lead poisoning can give rise to similar results. He also stressed the importance of detecting these conditions since early treatment may prevent the development of subnormality. A number of syndromes has been defined in this group but the commonest and best studied so far is phenylketonuria.

PHENYLKETONURIA. Phenylketonuria is typical of the inborn errors of metabolism, and both the genetics and the biochemical basis have been worked out in some detail. The subjects are defectives of usually imbecile level (a few have been described falling within the normal range of intelligence), with no very distinctive clinical picture. The condition was, in fact, discovered by Fölling (1934) by means of the test for phenylpyruvic acid in the urine. The principal features are the *blond, or inadequately pigmented, appearance;* and, not infrequently, the presence of extrapyramidal signs such as *hyperkinesias, muscular hypertonus and chorea-athetotic movements.*

The genetical basis was completely worked out in a classic paper by Jervis (1939). Estimates of the frequency of the condition are subject to wide margins of error, but in the United Kingdom and in the U.S.A. it is likely to be in the neighbourhood of 1 in 25,000. Phenylketonurics constitute only about one per cent. of institutionalized defectives. The gene responsible is recessive, and the parents of phenylketonurics are of normal intelligence; there is a high incidence of cousin marriage, about 10 per cent., among them.

The enzymic deficiency is an incapacity to hydroxylate phenylalanine $C_6H_5.CH_2.CHNH_2.COOH$ into tyrosine $HO.C_6H_4.CHNH_2.COOH$. As the normal metabolic pathway is blocked a slow and relatively inefficient alternative is made use of by which the attack is on the side-chain instead of the benzene ring nucleus, and phenylalanine is converted into a number of ketonic acids, principally phenylpyruvic acid $C_6H_5.CH_2.CO.COOH$. This last is eliminated in the urine and gives a green colour reaction with ferric chloride.

The disastrous effects of this incapacity on the developing organism are not felt while the metabolic activities of the mother can accommodate those of the foetus. The first appearance of phenylpyruvic acid in the urine does not occur until some three weeks after birth. This has given rise to the hope that normal development can be ensured by putting the infant, once his condition has been recognized, on a diet with barely minimal amounts of phenylalanine (Medical Research Council, 1963). This amino-acid cannot be eliminated altogether without killing the child, but the amount taken can be safely made very small. Early results indicate that, by this treatment, development can in fact be made nearly normal. It is thought that none of the side-products of the metabolism of phenylalanine along the subsidiary pathway are of themselves toxic, but only the excessive accumulation of phenylalanine itself in the tissues, especially in the brain. Once the physical development of the brain is complete at six years, return to a normal diet may be possible.

The genetical and biochemical story has been made practically complete by the demonstration (Hsia *et al.*, 1956) that the heterozygous carrier of the gene, such as the parent of a phenylketonuric, can be distinguished from both the normal and the abnormal homozygotes. The relationship between one gene and one enzyme can be quantified into one gene one dose of enzyme. The heterozygous individual is, in fact, able to hydroxylate phenylalanine, but only about half as well as the normal individual, a relative incapacity which can be established by a loading test. After the administration of a dose of phenylalanine, the concentration in the plasma rises to about twice the normal value and is so maintained for some hours. The finding is of theoretical interest in showing the nature of gene-enzyme relationships, and in providing research possibilities; and also of practical value as providing the basis for genetical advice to close relatives of phenylketonurics.

OTHER AMINO ACIDURIAS. The conditions associated with amino aciduria have been reviewed by Woolf (1961). Many but not all of these are associated with mental subnormality.

Maple syrup disease. In this condition, first described by Menkes, Hurst and Craig (1954), there is a high level of leucine, isoleucine and valine in the blood and urine. The condition appears to be determined by an autosomal recessive gene (Lane, 1961). It has been suggested (Mackenzie and Woolf, 1959; Menkes, 1959) that there was a block in the oxidative decarboxylation of the branched chain L-keto acids (leucine, isoleucine and valine) which accumulate in the blood and are excreted in the urine with the equivalent L-hydroxy acids. There is severe subnormality with cerebral degeneration and many affected infants fail to live more than a few months. However, early administration of a diet low in the three relevant amino acids has been shown by Holt and colleagues (1960) to prevent cerebral degeneration.

Hartnup syndrome. The main features of this condition, described by Baron *et al.* (1956), are a pellagra-like syndrome with subnormality and an episodic cerebellar ataxia. It is inherited as an autosomal recessive and shows a tendency to improve with increasing age. Patients without mental subnormality have been described by Hersov and Rodnight (1960). The amino aciduria is complex, the most prominent abnormal constituents of the urine being tryptophan and other indole derivatives. Milne *et al.* (1960) have shown that the basic defects lie in the absorption of the amino acids both from the bowel and from the renal tubules. As the amino acids are retained longer than usual in the gut, they are more than usually subject to bacterial action. Tryptophan is particularly subject to breakdown in this way so that excess quantities of indole and indolylacetic acid are formed and excreted in the urine. The pellagra-like state results from nicotinic acid deficiency secondary to loss of tryptophan. In treatment it has been suggested that nicotinamide is helpful (Woolf, 1961) and that alkalinization of the urine is also of value as it encourages excretion of indolylacetic acid (Milne *et al.*, 1960).

GALACTOSAEMIA. In this condition, which is inherited as a Mendelian recessive, there is a metabolic inability for conversion of galactose to glucose owing to absence of the enzyme T-galactose-uridyl-transferase. The infants appear normal at birth but within a few days vomiting begins and thereafter failure to thrive, hepatomegaly, ascites and oedema make their appearance. Death results from wasting and malnutrition, while survivors are stunted in stature and mental retardation and cataracts are common. Diagnosis is readily made by the demonstration of galactose in the urine and high blood levels of galactose. Elimination of milk and all products liable to contain galactose from the diet may enable the child to develop normally.

LAURENCE-MOON-BIEDL SYNDROME. This condition can be attributed to a recessive gene, and its results are very constant. It produces backwardness from infancy, usually of the less severe type, retinitis pigmentosa leading to defective vision, and polydactyly of upper and lower extremities. In addition obesity and hypogenitalism are often present. Incomplete forms, with extra digits or toes or with obesity and hypogenitalism have been found among the relatives.

Because of the similarity with dystrophia adiposo-genitalis (Fröhlich's syndrome) which sometimes also is associated with mental deficiency, dystrophy of the pituitary has been suspected as the immediate cause; but no certainty exists about this.

FAMILIAL AMAUROTIC IDIOCY (TAY-SACHS'S DISEASE). This is a degenerative disease of the central nervous system due to a recessive gene. The disease may start in the first few months after birth. These were the cases first observed in children of Jewish parents by Tay (1881) and Sachs (1887). Similar pictures with an identical pathology have since become known starting in late infancy, adolescence and later, and occur in Gentiles. Juvenile amaurotic idiocy is genetically distinct from the infantile form, but also due to a recessive gene. The child is normal at birth and develops perfectly until the onset of the disease. The main symptoms, arrest of mental development, muscular weakness and amaurosis appear together. There is a characteristic ophthalmoscopic finding in the macula lutea, a whitish oval patch with a central dark red spot formed by the fovea centralis. Mental enfeeblement and apathy together with the bodily symptoms progress rapidly in the typical case and the child dies within two years.

In later forms, the ophthalmological picture varies, but the cardinal signs are the same, though the disease sometimes takes a more protracted course.

Besides the genetics, the histopathology of Tay-Sachs's disease has attracted much attention. The accumulation of lipoid substance in the cells of the cortex and other centres has been explained as due to a congenital enzymatic abnormality similar to that in phenylketonuria.

Other conditions associated with mental deficiency, which in individual pedigrees have been found to be dependent on recessive genes, include microcephaly, cerebral diplegia, and deaf-mutism and cretinism; but in all these syndromes non-genetical cases probably predominate.

CRETINISM. While endocrine *aetiology* can be suspected in mongolism, the relation between the thyroid and cretinism has been known for over seventy-five years. Cretinism is now an extremely rare condition in Great Britain; and many experienced observers have stated that the number of cretins has decreased everywhere during the last few decades.

The incidence appears higher in regions of the world where endemic goitre exists. In this type the goitrous thyroid does not function; in other sporadic cases the thyroid gland is absent.

The cretin appears a *normal child at birth*, in contrast to the mongol, and the first signs of abnormality appear at about the sixth month of life. The child does not grow, has a yellowish-grey colour and seems slow in his reactions and apathetic. He may not even suck, does not smile, his respiration is snoring and his cry peculiar. The skin of the face is loose and wrinkled. A puffiness appears in the eyelids, lips, hands, and feet and in the back of the neck. The body temperature is subnormal and the mental and physical development is stunted. Cretins have a full crop of wiry black hair in contrast to children suffering from acquired myxoedema, whose hair is thin and sparse (Benda).

It is important to recognize these signs, especially the *yellow puffy skin* and the *lethargy*, for diagnostic reasons, because replacement therapy with thyroid, which is so often successful, cannot be started too early. The differentiation from mongolism is sometimes difficult—mixed cases have been described—especially in the infant, but it is relatively easy when the symptoms of cretinism are fully developed.

Mentally the cretin is quiet, harmless and passive; he smiles 'with a childlike benignity which spreads after a latent period very slowly over his countenance' (Means, 1937); he shows nothing of the liveliness, responsiveness and curiosity of the mongol, but is in the majority of cases intellectually better equipped.

ENVIRONMENTALLY DETERMINED ABNORMALITIES

HYDROCEPHALY. Environmental causes of mental deficiency were discussed on p. 701. Hydrocephaly is one of the commoner syndromes which may result from such causes, particularly intracranial infections. It may be caused by blocking of the outlets for the cerebrospinal fluid from the ventricles or by the failure of absorption. It frequently leads to mental deficiency, especially if it occurs at an early age. It may be due to congenital syphilis or other forms of meningitis; but many workers believe that it may be caused by developmental abnormalities. In the growing child the head gradually enlarges while the hemispheres are stretched, flattened and undergo atrophy.

Paralysis of the limbs, deafness and blindness are frequent complications and so is epilepsy. Hydrocephalic defectives in whom the process has come to a standstill are often only feeble-minded, and easily trained for simple work. Internal hydrocephaly may be also present in microcephalics. Moderate degrees of hydrocephaly are compatible with normal intelligence.

Other deformities of the skull are sometimes seen in defectives, but their relation to the mental state is doubtful. This is especially true of oxycephaly ('steeple-head', 'tower skull') which may lead to blindness and is sometimes combined with synostosis of fingers and toes. In some families oxycephaly follows a simple dominant inheritance.

RHESUS INCOMPATIBILITY. This may be ranked among environmentally determined deficiencies, as there is no genetical abnormality in either mother or child, but merely an antigenic incompatibility between them. The genetical basis was discussed on p. 708. In the individual case, in which it is shown that the blood-groups of mother and child are incompatible, a probability arises that mental deficiency in the child has arisen from this cause, but a good deal more evidence would be required for convincing proof. Perhaps it is because of the occurrence of cases in which the association is purely coincidental that the clinical picture associated with rhesus incompatibility is rather unclear. According to Crome, Kirman and Marrs (1955) the typical picture is a combination of bilateral athetosis and deafness with mental retardation, but there is much variation. Even the triad described, as well as atypical varieties with ataxia and hemiplegia, may also be caused by other agencies. Apart from the bodily handicaps, the degree of mental impairment varies from idiocy to normal intelligence; and it may be that mental deficiency without neurological signs can be produced. The pathological findings include widespread loss of nerve cells in the cerebral cortex and degenerative changes in the globus pallidus.

All the nine children studied by Crome and his co-workers had been formerly classed as ineducable, although in three of the cases they concluded that this judgement had been erroneous. They point out that the education of these patients demands painstaking individual attention, both to the deafness and the motor handicap.

DIAGNOSIS AND DIFFERENTIAL DIAGNOSIS

Psychiatrists often fail to diagnose mental deficiency in those high-grade defectives who show symptoms of a neurotic or psychopathic reaction. The combination, even if it be assumed to occur only by chance, is naturally not infrequent. Suspicion may be aroused by atypical features; and these, though previously inexplicable, at once fall into line when the role of intellectual endowment is remembered and the patient is asked to do a systematic test.

The diagnosis of mental deficiency in infants and children up to the age of three has been described in another section (Clinical Features, p. 708). After the age of three, *mental testing* is possible with standardized tests. The significance of the test results is not entirely unequivocal, except in the lowest grades of deficiency, which are in any case easy to recognize clinically; and the physician should always take into account all other data, especially the history of the patient. The psychiatrist should be familiar with the methods of testing intelligence, and be able to evaluate their results critically. For the tests themselves, the reader may be referred to special manuals, such as those of Terman and Merrill (1937) or Cattell (1948). Tredgold in his text-book gives E. O. Lewis's Serial Tests, i.e. a version of the 'Standard Revision' of Binet and Simon's scale, modified for English children. Griffiths (1954) has devised a series of tests based on the observation of behaviour of young children, which as well as being used as a measure of the abilities of normal children under the age of two years can also be applied to the assessment of mental defectives.

In all doubtful cases, and particularly where the results are being affected by some form of emotional disturbance, the psychiatrist should test the patient himself. The observation of the subject during his performance often provides valuable information. Not only his failures and successes, but also the way by which he has reached them, his reaction to each problem and to his own solution, can throw light on the prognosis and the possibilities of training. Intellectual abilities and deficiencies cannot be considered as if they were locked up in a water-tight compartment. For practical purposes the *interplay of emotional and conative factors* with what remains of intellectual endowment is much more important than the bare result of the test.

If the test is to give a picture of the real capabilities of the subject, he must co-operate willingly and fully. *Neurotic children* are often anxious, and do not do their best, in a situation which reminds them of school. Other children, too, may easily become fatigued, and give random answers. Yet others are so eager to oblige and to answer quickly, that their results are worse than they would have been if sufficient time had been taken. Results may be interfered with by defects of vision or hearing, or, when given in written form, by special disabilities in reading and spelling. Linguistic gifts and disabilities may distort the results of a test which is intended to measure general intelligence; but, on the other hand, tests designed for the purpose are of great value in *diagnosing a special defect* of reading ability, and other such disparities. Any mild infection, or the asthenia or depression which follows an infective illness, impairs results. In the adolescent or adult there are many psychotic conditions, such as depressive, manic or schizophrenic states, or a slight and scarcely recognizable clouding of consciousness, which may make the patient appear much duller than he usually is; the diagnosis of mental enfeeblement should never be based on a test given to an acutely psychotic patient. Test results can be very deceptive if uncritically used on persons awaiting trial for a delinquency, as a hysterical pseudodementia often enters the picture.

With the most commonly used methods of testing, mental *deficiency may be missed* in persons whose verbal abilities cover, in the test situation, the capacity for error which in day-to-day life is caused by their lack of judgement and adaptability. As most of the usual tests are verbal ones, borderline defectives who have had a good deal of individual attention and education attain scores which do not correspond with their general efficiency. With them, *non-verbal tests*, such as Penrose and Raven's Progressive Matrices, Kohs Blocks, or the Porteous Maze Test, are helpful.

A similar problem of diagnosis is presented by the over-educated dullard whose other advantages have brought him into a position which his natural abilities are not sufficient to enable him to maintain. The disability has been called by Bleuler *'proportional defect'* (*'Verhältnisblödsinn'*), because of the disproportion between the task and the ability to carry it out. In its widest application, the concept can be associated with phenomena of great social importance; in every walk of life we find positions which demand high talents and which are held by people of mediocre and insufficient ability. From the psychiatric point of view, however, it is well to confine the concept to persons of less than average intelligence who have been tried too high, and whose limited attainments are out of proportion to what they expect of themselves and is expected of them by others. They fail and break down in their occupations, in their marriages, and in their conduct of social relations, and they may be exploited and ruined by the shrewd and unscrupulous with whom they come in contact. Their recognition is not difficult if a reliable history and school record are available and an intelligence test is given. They are rarely mentally defective in the legal sense; and when their ambitions can be rectified and they can be placed in an occupation commensurate with their powers, they may become contented and reliable members of the community without the need for special care. Difficulties, however, often arise through the lack of insight or of co-operation of the relatives.

Memory, in both its aspects of retention and recall, is not necessarily impaired in mental defectives. As a rule, if the patient forgets past events, or allows an immediate task to slip from his mind, it is probably because he did not understand what it was he had to do, or took no interest, or was unable to apply himself to the effort of recollection.

In some cases, however, an *extraordinary mnesic ability* exists alongside mental deficiency of high or medium grade. The disproportion between memory and general intelligence may attract attention, even if the former ability does not exceed that found in many normal persons. If a retentive memory is combined with some verbal facility, these defectives may escape detection for a long time; and they can do useful work as clerks, messengers, doorkeepers, etc. If they grow up in institutions, they may make a speciality of remembering the calendar, the hymn-book, or the system of numbers.

Many single cases of this type, the so-called '*idiot savant*', have been described, and some of them have even performed in public. The attention of experts and lay writers has been attracted from time to time by the problems raised by the preservation and even development above average of isolated faculties against a background of an otherwise inadequate intelligence. Most of those who have reported these cases have seen only one or two, and the literature on the subject is rather anecdotal. However, a group of ten 'talented aments' has been studied with psychological tests by Rothstein (1941); and Goldstein *et al.* have investigated by experimental methods an eleven-year-old calendar calculator with an intelligence quotient of 50 per cent. (Scheerer, Rothman and Goldstein, 1945).

In infancy and childhood, mental deficiency is usually easily distinguished from other psychiatric abnormalities. During puberty and adolescence *organic encephalopathies* may simulate a congenital amentia, if no history is available. In juvenile general paresis, the neurological findings and the cerebrospinal fluid will decide the issue, although the Wassermann reaction may be negative for a long time. Traumatic dementia and epilepsy may have to be considered; but they rarely lead to any severe degree of intellectual defect without causing some neurological abnormality. Epilepsy, however, may accompany congenital defect of any degree. At puberty, an early *schizophrenia* with apathy, semi-stupor or thought disorder can sometimes be mistaken for mental deficiency, especially if schizoid personality features of early development have prevented an adequate school career. The problems of schizophrenia in childhood are discussed in Chapter XI (p. 669). The repetitive stereotyped movements of low-grade defectives have sometimes been regarded as catatonic signs, and are probably caused by cerebral mechanisms similar to those involved in schizophrenia; but the total mental picture presented by the defective has nothing in common with that of the catatonic schizophrenic.

There is a group of children suffering from physical disabilities often mistaken for or complicated by mental subnormality, and the special needs of these children with double handicaps are frequently overlooked. Two categories of such children should be mentioned:

(1) those whose physical and mental handicaps co-exist and may have a common cause (e.g. subnormal children who are also blind or deaf);

(2) those having physical handicaps which, if not diagnosed promptly and treated wisely, may be mistaken for and actually lead to mental subnormality (e.g. some partially deaf or spastic children who are often mistaken for imbeciles or idiots) (W.H.O. Report, 1954).

PROGNOSIS

Neither the subcultural defective, nor those who are defective from one of the syndromes with a definite pathology, can be raised to normal intelligence by medical measures. It is misleading to hold out hopes that a defective child will reach normality at puberty or later, or that the growth of intelligence can be accelerated by special diets, endocrine preparations or psychotherapy. Valuable time is lost by taking such children to all kinds of specialists, and even quacks, instead of giving them the systematic training and education which may make them happier and more useful members of the community. 'Relatively few persons are so defective that they cannot be improved to some extent, even if only in habits of cleanliness and the curtailing of destructive or dangerous propensities. . . . Some defect, however mild, will always remain, rendering competition on an equal footing with the normal population impossible' (Tredgold, 1947).

Despite the truth of these generalizations, it is often difficult to forecast the development of a defective child. *Imbeciles and idiots* can, as a rule, be diagnosed as such at the age of three, and the extent of their limitations predicted within narrow limits. Even if they are not, as is often the case, handicapped physically by paralysis or sense deprivation, and even if they grow up under the most expert and systematic education, they will always remain dependent on others and in need of care. Epilepsy makes the prognosis much more unfavourable, even if it responds to anti-epileptic treatment.

In the *feeble-minded* group the prognosis is less certain, because so much depends on character and temperament. Affective relations and habits of emotional response are strongly influenced by the environment through which the patient passes as he develops from a child. Just as the diagnosis should not be based on the intelligence quotient alone, neither can one's views on the outlook. One must observe the child in his natural surroundings, see his behaviour to his parents and to his playmates, and when left by himself, and have reports on his behaviour at school. With all the facts one can muster, there will still be room for guesswork. Before formulating more than a provisional prognosis, the response to training will have to be seen. If there are no psychopathic features, and the child lives in a good home with understanding parents, and can be given individual attention by skilled teachers, he can be trained to a useful existence and to enjoy most of the pleasures of life. Unfortunately many of the feeble-minded grow up under the worst rather than the best conditions, and contribute accordingly to social distress and misery.

It is worth remembering that the mental development of the defective comes to a *standstill* earlier than that of the average child. What he has achieved in his formative years will hardly be improved upon, but neither need he deteriorate below the standard he then attained nor lose the social responses he has acquired.

The prognosis of the special forms of mental deficiency with definite pathology has been discussed in their respective sections. It is doubtful whether the prognosis of mental deficiency after birth injury or meningitis is any better than with subcultural defect. It will, of course, depend very largely on the amount and site of the cerebral damage. Nevertheless, neurological findings are certainly no reliable indication of the possibilities of mental development.

TREATMENT

Prevention

In the preceding section, an attempt has been made, not to present mental deficiency as a hotchpotch of medical curiosities and pathological freaks, but rather to outline the psychiatric and social problems of a group to which, in this country, it is officially estimated that 8 per cent. of the school population belong. Even if the number of subcultural defectives is not increasing, it is too high for their contribution to social failure and human wretchedness to be neglected, for their own sake and for the sake of the community.

In fact, however, it is quite likely that the proportion of defectives in the population is increasing. The effects of differential fertility and of assortative mating, as set forth in the section on the genetics of mental defect, are added to by the emigration overseas, unequalized by the counter-balancing immigration, of the more virile and intelligent. If humane and rational measures which would counter the increase of mental deficiency are possible, they should be taken.

In Denmark, a country very similar to ours, provided with a fully developed health administration, *preventive measures against the unrestricted procreation of high-grade defectives* have been taken. A Sterilization Board has been set up, to which a recommendation for the voluntary sterilization of a defective may be made when he is unfit adequately to educate his children or provide for them by his own work. Genetical reasons for sterilization are not mentioned in the Danish law, but, according to Nørvig, play an important part in the considerations of the Sterilization Board, for 'discharge (from the institution) of a fertile individual with hereditary mental deficiency is hardly conceivable'. Furthermore, the Danish Marriage Law makes marriage of a defective dependent on the permission of the Ministry of Justice. The Ministry is advised by a Medico-Legal Council, and may make previous sterilization a condition of the permission to marry (Nørvig, 1948). These laws have been in force since 1934; however practice has varied much with time, and has radically changed since the last war (see p. 758).

The eugenic prevention of mental deficiency undoubtedly remains the chief hope for the future, and in no other way can we expect any large-scale effect. The way this is to be obtained is, however, by a *re-orientation of public attitudes* and values rather than by any semi-compulsory or even voluntary measures directed only to a small section of the entire community. Those who are average or better in general health and intelligence should feel themselves under some obligation to provide the next generation with a quota of children sufficient to secure survival of their own hereditary equipment, an equipment which is, as it were, not their own private possession but in trust for the race as a whole. Those who fall below average standards should feel absolved of any such duty, and helped to secure themselves against their mostly unwanted fertility. While private wishes would be allowed their normal paramouncy, such a feeling dispersed through the community would have its effect in changing a dysgenic into a eugenic differential fertility, and the problem of sub-cultural defect would in principle be solved.

Although it is true that this is the only way, short of a tyrannical interference in private life, in which a mass effect of the desired kind could be produced, the *voluntary sterilization of defectives* would have a minor part to play. It appears to the authors that the main justification for the sterilization of defectives is twofold. Defectives scarcely ever have the qualities required to provide a normal child, not to speak of a defective one, with the environment needed for a happy and healthful development; and defectives, though often anxious to avoid procreation, seldom have the self-control and intelligence to cope with the usual contraceptive techniques. There can be little doubt that if high-grade defectives were relieved of their power to reproduce (and to produce families often of unusually large size, living on the border of destitution), much would be done to reduce the incidence of unhappy homes and of unhappiness in childhood life.

The *education* and the *vocational direction* of the high-grade defective also have their preventive aspect, as it is on the results of attempts in these directions that one can decide whether the patient is going to be able to adapt to normal social life. This is as true of the children with an intelligence quotient of 70 and above, who under the Education Act of 1944 are to be educated in an ordinary school, as for the children with an I.Q. of 60 to 70 who may attend a special school.

It is the duty of the *School Medical Officer* to determine whether a child is educable or not in a school provided by the Education Authority. His decision must be based on the teacher's report on the child's progress, on a physical examination and on test results. If it is decided that the child is so educable, the matter is taken out of medical hands, although psychiatric advice could certainly lighten the burden on the teachers and improve practical results in some cases. The greatest handicap for teacher and child is, in our experience, the impossibility of individual guidance and education in a class with a very large number of children. The backward child naturally does not respond in such an environment, and the teacher is discouraged. Headmasters and higher education authorities take little interest in the training and education of these children. Satisfactory results are more easily obtained in special schools.

If it is decided by the School Medical Officer that the child is 'unsuitable for education at school', the local education authority must notify the local health authority and must give the parent twenty-one days' notice in writing of its intention to do so. During this period, the parent has the right of appeal to the Minister of Education with whom the final decision now rests. A child so excluded from school normally attends a training centre from the age of 5 upwards and there is statutory authority to enforce attendance, though again the parent has the right of appeal on the ground that the child is receiving equivalent training elsewhere (Mental Health Act, Section (12)). At any time the local health authority can give notice to the local education authority requesting reconsideration of the child's suitability for education.

Such children usually attend a training centre until the age of sixteen, after which age their welfare becomes the responsibility of the local health authority, who may provide help by friendly supervision or by some form of community care. If these methods of helping the patient are inadequate or unsuitable, resort may be had to care either by guardianship or by admission to hospital (Tredgold and Soddy, 1963).

Treatment and Training

These two terms are, as yet, largely synonymous, but there are some exceptions. Medical and dietetic treatment is possible in cretinism and phenylketonuria, success depending very much on early diagnosis. There is also a place for *surgical treatment*. A great number of operations have been contrived in the attempt to relieve hydrocephaly and cranial deformities with which mental defect is commonly associated, such as acrocephaly; but on the whole these have not met with much success. A small number of defectives with epilepsy and behaviour disorder have been found to suffer from a temporal lobe epilepsy which could be treated by temporal lobectomy. Results are not always very satisfactory, as Hilliard and Kirman (1957) have pointed out, since lesions in the brain may be more widespread than electroencephalographic findings suggest. The much more drastic operation of hemispherectomy has been justified in some epileptic defectives in whom clinical investigations show wide destruction of the cortex of one hemisphere, usually following a vascular accident at birth. In favourable cases, the operation has brought about cessation of fits, great improvement in behaviour disorder, and even some improvement on intelligence tests (Carmichael, 1953). Symptomatic treatment by surgery for the relief of contractures in spastic mental defectives, and other orthopaedic procedures, play an important part in the welfare of many patients.

The treatment, training and rehabilitation of the mentally subnormal, outside special schools, is the task of hospitals and training centres. The special requirements in education and training of the various grades of defectives have been outlined in the sections devoted to them (pp. 711–719). Some more general matters remain to be considered.

There is an urgent need for further research to determine the methods of training most suitable for achieving social effectiveness in mentally handicapped persons. The situation appears most unsatisfactory in relation to the severely subnormal whose education was excluded from the main provisions of the 1944 Education Act. According to some experts (Tizard, 1960) the effect of this has been unfortunate in that the activities of *occupation and training centres* both in hospitals and in the community have been little affected by advances that have taken place in the teaching of normal children, especially in nursery and infant schools. Education in this field is therefore 'neither enriched by the fresh currents of thought that continually revitalize educational practice; nor do doctors or teachers appreciate the complexity of the problems that their colleagues meet in these muddy backwaters' (Tizard, 1960a). The staffs of these centres are in many cases still untrained.

For the present there is a good deal to suggest that judging a child to be unsuitable for education on the basis of an I.Q. of 50–55 alone is unsatisfactory as it takes little account of the uneven pattern of development in both intellectual capacity and social maturity of subnormal children. The assessments should ideally be undertaken by an educational psychologist assisted by several people with direct knowledge of the child so that account can be taken of his personality. Periodic review of the child's progress and regular psychological assessment are important.

The methods employed in *hospitals and institutions* make allowance for the slowness of mental development, the lack of spontaneity, interest and attention, and the relative sensory inaccessibility of these patients. Their motor handicaps, clumsiness and lack of co-ordination of movement are also given special attention and training. They learn to help in the work of the institution and develop in an atmosphere of shelter and care which does much to rectify the adverse effect of the poor home background from which a considerable number of them are removed.

If flexibility and the possibility of movement is what is required within the range of educational and training facilities, stimulus of the patient is what is needed in the institution according to specialists in this field. It is to be hoped that the increasing emphasis placed by the Mental Health Act on community care will in the course of time find expression in practice in the shape of ample facilities for training, sheltered and other employment and training hostels within the community for all those who can be rendered viable there. This shift of emphasis from hospital to community care is bringing about a change in outlook and practice.

Residence in an institution, because of the quite necessary supervisory arrangements, may tend to deprive inmates of the need to make decisions, to use initiative and to organize their own activities; so whatever, within reason, will bring the inmate more into contact with life outside is desirable (Report of a Working Party set up by the Paediatric Society of the S.E. Metropolitan Region, 1962.) A more liberal use of parole, in spite of its risks, and a fuller use of opportunities to send inmates out to 'daily work' either in actual employment, or in training centres, make them more aware of what the community expects of them.

On the whole their capacity may tend to be underestimated and ultimate discharge and employment should be kept before them as a goal. To this end, better work habits such as punctuality, more sustained application and concentration should be inculcated. Their fear of the unaccustomed should be countered by planned changes of work, once any skill has been mastered. The incentives of payment, progress charts and the granting and withdrawal of privileges have been shown to have a beneficial effect. To those most likely to leave the institution, training in how to lay out their money and what it costs to live should be given and, to avoid breakdown, they should have adequate preparation for leisure, including being linked with organizations that will give them support and an outlet for the desire for friendly relationships which is so strong in the feeble-minded. During the initial period of settlement outside the institution, which is crucial for the patient's future, follow-up by social workers is of the greatest importance (Gunzburg, 1958b).

With all this, emotional instability, inability to endure the stresses imposed by community life or prolonged institutionalization in adult cases will give rise to failure in the attempts to settle a proportion of mentally subnormal patients. It will be essential to make regular realistic appraisals of the position in each case so that patients who are not surviving can be returned to the shelter of institutional life for short or indefinite periods. There is some danger that, through inadequate supervision, resocialization may give rise to an excessive rate of failure and thus run ahead of what the community can tolerate at the present time, or indeed can reasonably be expected to shoulder.

Some of these children grow up *at home*, and mothers may ask the psychiatrist for advice about their upbringing. The task requires much time, patience and devotion as well as a good deal of insight and self-control from the mother. The common mistake is to continue to treat the child as a baby, to wash, dress, feed him and attend to his toilet, until he is of school age, without any serious attempt at training. Training in such personal habits can only be achieved by a greater expense of time than that required by the mother's attending to these functions herself, more time in fact than many mothers can afford, especially if there are other children; and it is a process of wearying slowness. Health visitors and social workers should be able to provide much needed help and explanation, and the doctor can encourage the mother by warning her of the various difficulties she will have to face. The National Society for Mentally Handicapped Children, 5 Bulstrode St., London, W.1., gives help and advice through over 300 Local Societies. If the difficulties are so great that the child himself or his brothers and sisters are suffering, the mother should be encouraged to hand over his care to other and better-equipped hands.

CHAPTER XIII

ADMINISTRATIVE AND LEGAL PSYCHIATRY

THE fact that a mentally disordered person may perform acts to which the normal logic of human behaviour does not apply, and that he may need protection against himself, and society need protection against him, has led in all countries of the world and from the earliest times to the existence of special laws and special administrative arrangements for the psychiatric patient. In the most primitive cultures the insane, often under the protection of some form of religious taboo, were allowed to roam at will. As the state of civilization became more complex this was no longer possible, and arrangements had to be made for their custodial care, often against their will. This deprivation of liberty added an element of disgrace to the superstitious awe with which mental disorders were popularly regarded. Throughout their long development from ancient customs, laws and administration have been profoundly affected by these influences, and the 'stigma' of insanity is with us to this day. In every country the legal and administrative system has been of slow growth and closely connected with tradition; to its nationals it may seem to be the only natural system, and the arrangements made by other countries may seem dubious and surprisingly inappropriate. In very few States have law and administrative practice been fully brought up to date with our present level of scientific knowledge and understanding.

In this country the situation has been transformed by the Mental Health Act of 1959, which has brought all forms of mental disorder within the compass of one statute, all previous Acts being repealed. In essence what the Act has done is to put the mentally ill and the mentally subnormal on an equal footing with the physically ill. Their admission to hospital is without formality, given the patient's consent; and they may go to hospitals of any kind, without any legal restriction. An end has been made of designating hospitals for the care of the mentally ill, as well as of special supervisory authorities. These truly revolutionary changes were made on the basis of a report by a Royal Commission (1957) and to a large extent embody enlightened modern psychiatric opinion.

The mental hospitals, as they were called, continue their existence as hospitals within the National Health Service regional system, and are administered, except for their internal affairs, by the Regional Boards. Each hospital has its own catchment area which it is supposed to serve; but it is free to admit patients from anywhere. Admission is usually arranged, either from the outpatient clinics run from that hospital as a centre, or from other community services which it provides, or directly by the patient's general practitioner, perhaps after a domiciliary consultation with a consultant psychiatrist.

The Act has also greatly encouraged the development of psychiatric units within general hospitals. It seems probable that the number of such units, of from 60 to 200 beds, will continue to grow; in time all urban areas should have such a service, and the first admission of the psychiatrically ill patient will most usually be to such a unit. Most importantly of all, the setting up of psychiatric inpatient units in general teaching hospitals has been encouraged, with all that that means for the progress of academic psychiatry. The rapprochement between psychiatry and general medicine has resulted in the setting

736

up of a number of professorial chairs of psychiatry both in the principal provincial universities and in some London teaching schools. These university departments of psychiatry are closely associated with the general hospital and medical school on one side, and one or more of the regional psychiatric hospitals on the other side. By this means progress has been stimulated in two directions: the medical student is encouraged to take an interest in the psychiatric aspects of the medical and surgical cases with which he is daily concerned; and again the junior clinical psychiatrist is brought into contact with up-to-date teaching, with research, and with the advances in medicine which have their repercussions in psychiatry.

Other consequences of the new organization of psychiatry cannot yet be fully envisaged. There is no doubt that one of them has been the widely prevalent ambition to transform the old style mental hospital into a much more dynamic 'therapeutic community', and to provide a wider range of community services. These developments are discussed on pp. 327 and 804.

Under the Act of 1959, 'mental disorder' is taken to mean mental illness, arrested or incomplete development of mind, psychopathic disorder, and any other disorder or disability of mind. 'Severe subnormality' means a state of arrested or incomplete development of mind which includes subnormality of intelligence and is of such a nature or degree that the patient is incapable of living an independent life or of guarding himself against serious exploitation, or will be so incapable when of an age to do so. 'Subnormality' means a state of arrested or incomplete development of mind (not amounting to severe subnormality) which includes subnormality of intelligence and is of a nature or degree which requires or is susceptible to medical treatment or other special care or training of the patient. 'Psychopathic disorder' means a persistent disorder or disability of mind (whether or not including subnormality of intelligence) which results in abnormally aggressive or seriously irresponsible conduct on the part of the patient, and requires or is susceptible to medical treatment. Some of the disadvantages of these definitions are referred to in Chapters III and XII.

The Mental Health (Scotland) Act of 1960 differs from the English Act in some respects. Only two forms of mental disorder are statutorily recognized, i.e. 'mental illness or mental deficiency however caused or manifested'. 'Psychopathic disorder' finds no mention in the Act, and the term 'mental deficiency', one is glad to note, has been retained.

The Northern Ireland Mental Health Act, 1961, differs again. In this Act 'mental disorder' means 'mental illness, arrested or incomplete development of mind and any other disorder or disability of mind'; psychopathic disorder is not specifically included, but there is nothing to preclude the admission to hospital of those whose aggression or irresponsibility requires or is susceptible to medical treatment. In the Northern Ireland Act a 'person requiring special care' is the equivalent of the 'subnormal' of the English Act; and the category is not divided into degrees of severity. The Northern Ireland Act follows the precedent of an earlier Act of 1948, which was advanced for its time, in vesting to a great extent the care of the mentally subnormal in the Northern Ireland Hospitals Authority through 'special care management committees'.

The guiding spirit of all these Acts is the same, namely to make the admission of a mentally disordered patient to hospital, and his care there, as far as possible as entirely informal as is the case with purely bodily illnesses.

In other countries practice varies very widely. In *Belgium*, informal admission to mental hospitals is universally available, and if the patient wishes to leave at once, without notice given, he is free to do so. In *Germany*, *Austria* and *Switzerland* voluntary admission is not governed by any formality, but the extent to which use is made of it varies from region to region. In *Spain* also voluntary admission is without formality, and increasing use is being made of the facility; there are many clinics which accept patients only on this basis. In *Holland* mental hospitals are divided into open and closed parts; no formalities are required for admission to the open wards of a patient who gives consent or who offers no opposition to admission. According to Rylander (1961) *France* must have been one of the earliest countries to create the possibility of informal admission with 'services ouvertes', first with an open ward in the general hospital of Tunis, and then with the Henry Roussell Hospital as the open section of the great hospital of Ste. Anne in Paris.

VOLUNTARY TREATMENT

As has been said, in the United Kingdom the legal provisions relating to admission to a mental hospital and treatment there on a voluntary basis, were swept away by the Mental Health Acts of 1959–61. For the most part other countries employ a system of voluntary treatment which still requires some formalities, both with admission and with discharge. An account of these variations has been compiled by Rylander (1961).

In most countries the patient has to make written application, except in *France* where this is done for him by a relative, friend or social worker. A parent or guardian has to apply, or to confirm the patient's application, in the case of children or minors, the age limit varying from 15 (Finland) to 21 (South Africa, Sweden, Australia); in New Zealand no patient under 21 may be admitted on a voluntary basis. In some countries (Norway, Mexico, Sweden and Yugoslavia) the patient's application must be countersigned by witnesses. In most countries a medical certificate is not required; but it is mandatory in Brazil, Denmark, Ireland and some of the provinces of Canada.

In the *U.S.A.* all States with the exception of Alabama provide for the possibility of voluntary admission, but the procedure varies from State to State. It appears that in some States voluntary admission is in practice restricted to paying patients, and that in some others no voluntary admission is possible because of the overcrowding of hospitals. The proportion of voluntary patients in State mental hospitals is low. Although the general public accepts psychiatric treatment without attaching any stigma to it, and even has an over-developed psychiatric health-consciousness, there is still fear of the State hospital. The early treatment of neurotic and psychotic illness and of addiction is conducted almost exclusively in university psychiatric clinics and private clinics and sanatoria. Patients and their families are prepared to spend almost all their resources to avoid the 'asylum', and can cover the financial risk involved only very inadequately by means of insurance.

In *Germany, Austria and Switzerland*, voluntary admission to psychiatric clinics and mental hospitals is not governed by any formalities; but the extent to which use is made of the facility for voluntary admission varies from region to region. In general it is required that the patient should understand what he is doing, and that he should state in writing his willingness to be admitted and to conform to hospital discipline. The patient's understanding of what he is doing is strictly judged; if there is any doubt of it, the admission is not regarded as voluntary, even though the patient may explicitly consent. In *Holland* mental hospitals are divided into open and closed parts. Admission to one of the closed wards occurs only on the authorization of a justice, and in urgent cases on the authorization of the burgomaster of the municipality where the patient happens to sojourn. Admission to the open wards of a willing patient, or one who does not oppose his admission, requires no official sanction. The disadvantage of the system is that two sets of admission wards, for the open and closed departments, are required and other administrative arrangements have to be duplicated. In anticipation of new legal regulations the authorities countenance the mixing of both categories. A ministerial committee is now preparing a modern law on the care of mental patients, including mental defectives and mentally disturbed old men and women (personal communication, Dr. P. van der Esch).

In some countries voluntary admission is practically unknown; and as a general rule, such is the fear of the mental hospital that the patient will not enter it voluntarily even where the law permits. In *Greece* it is practically impossible to admit a patient to hospital before his relatives have found him an intolerable burden. In *Italy* treatment in a mental hospital has to be noted in the patient's personal identification papers in the same way as a court conviction; and as one is obliged to present these papers when applying for a job and on other official occasions, this regulation has prevented and still prevents the admission of many early cases. A modern mental treatment Act has been prepared but, as far as our information goes, has not yet reached the statute book. Writing in 1961, Rylander noted that voluntary admission was coming more and more into practice, with England and Scotland leading the field. The proportions of all admissions which were on a voluntary basis were in England (1952) 70 per cent., Scotland (1952) 67 per cent., Sweden (1956) 48 per cent., France (1952) 31 per cent.

In admitting himself to hospital voluntarily, the patient would naturally expect to retain the power to discharge himself. As a rule it is required of him to give notice before leaving, the stipulated interval varying from 24 hours (Australia) to 21 days (Norway). If the patient cannot, in his own interests or in the interests of society, be allowed his freedom, some form of legal commitment has to be gone through, either to the hospital in which he is, or to another.

In Norway and Denmark the hospital doctors have greater rights to detain the patient even against his will, once he has been voluntarily admitted, than they have elsewhere. In *Norway* the patient has to give three weeks' notice of his wish to leave; in *Denmark* he may be detained if the superintendent considers his treatment is incomplete or if he is dangerous, but the superintendent must then report the case to the Ministry of Justice which may or may not confirm his decision. A curious provision in Denmark is that the patient may also be detained if it is considered that discharge will cause serious inconvenience ('ulempe') for the patient. Examples of 'inconvenience' are the troubles which manic patients can bring on themselves, such as economic disaster, venereal infection and illegitimate pregnancy. Any patient who is obviously unable to take care of himself and who has nobody to support him sufficiently may be detained on these grounds. It is an anomalous feature of Danish law that 'ulempe' is a sufficient cause for detaining the patient, but no legal cause for his commitment to hospital.

New regulations came into force in *Sweden* in 1967. This time was chosen to coincide with the transfer of responsibility for the care of the mentally diseased from the State to the county councils and the local governments of large boroughs. Since practically all the care of physically and mentally disordered persons is therefore under the same administration, it is considered desirable for the same regulations to apply, regardless of whether an illness is classed as mental or physical. The law implies that admission to hospitals or clinics for mental nursing can be arranged without formality when a patient himself applies for treatment, or when he does not object to treatment. A patient admitted in this way cannot be detained in hospital against his will. However if a patient, admitted according to free forms of admission, is considered at discharge to be a danger to another person or to his own life, he can be detained by decision of a local discharge board. The reason for this has been to avoid the situation that a dangerous patient, as soon as he leaves the hospital, must be taken care of by the police or other body authorized to apply for mental hospital treatment in opposition to the patient's own wishes. It is expected that voluntary application for treatment will become the rule.

According to the study by the American Bar Foundation (Lindman and McIntyre, 1961), in most of the States of the *U.S.A.* authorizing voluntary admission, the patient may be detained for a fixed period, and even then kept still longer while compulsory indeterminate hospitalization proceedings are initiated. In only six States must the patient be released forthwith on application; in others delay before release may be from 48 hours to 30 days. Some States require of the patient submitting himself for voluntary admission that he should bind himself to stay for a minimum period of time, e.g. four months. In some State hospitals the power of the voluntary patient to obtain his release by application may be a dead letter since he may be ignorant of it, and there is no requirement that the voluntary patient shall be advised of his right to request release.

Probably one of the most serious bars to voluntary treatment in the United States is the uncertainty of the legal position in which the voluntary patient may find himself. He may, in fact, lose some of his most important civil rights, e.g. to secure his own discharge, to engage in correspondence, to receive visitors and to drive an automobile. Some States provide that the fact of hospitalization alone is sufficient to establish legal incompetency; only four States specify that the mere fact of hospitalization is insufficient to establish incompetency; and in the others there are no statutes, or for other reasons the legal situation is undecided. Lindman and McIntyre say that an examination of the relevant statutes does not reveal any significant difference between the rights of voluntary and involuntary patients in regard to correspondence, visitation, mechanical restraint and the exercise of civil rights.

The liberalization of law and administrative practice has everywhere been closely connected with the progress of research and treatment. In Britain, the ready admission and the ready discharge of patients has at times been superciliously referred to as the 'principle of the revolving door'; but through this same revolving door there has been an inflow and an outflow not only of patients but also of ideas and communications, which have brought the general public into touch with what goes on in a psychiatric hospital and has brought the hospital psychiatrist at last into contact with the community. The advances made by treatment, and the therapeutic energy and enthusiasm which have been so aroused, have especially contributed to a revolution in public attitudes. Furthermore, there can be no doubt that the open-ended flexibility of practice is greatly in the interest of the patient. When he is ill and unable to cope, there is one place where he can rely on help; and while there he remains a free man, under no constraint to stay.

PROCEDURE GOVERNING COMMITMENT

England and Wales

Commitment procedure under *the new Mental Health Act* abolishes the judicial authority and the various methods of reception, such as temporary procedure or certification. The unwilling patient is admitted to hospital at the petition of the nearest relative or a Mental Welfare Officer, and on the recommendation of two practitioners who have both recently seen and examined him. One of these must be a practitioner approved for the purpose by a local health authority as having special experience in the diagnosis or treatment of mental disorder; and the other shall if possible be a medical man who has previous acquaintance with the patient. They have to testify and give as the reason for admission that he is suffering from mental disorder of a nature and degree which warrants his detention in a hospital in the interest of his health or safety or for the protection of others. The patient can either be admitted for observation for a maximum period of 28 days (Section 25), or for treatment (Section 26). In the absence of relatives, a 'mental health officer' can apply for the patient's admission, 'mental health officers' replacing the officials formerly named 'Duly Authorized Officers'. There is, for *cases of urgency*, an emergency application based on one medical recommendation only, if possible the family doctor (Section 29). This order expires after 72 hours, at the end of which time the patient must be discharged if he has recovered. If still ill, he may have recovered to the point where he consents to remain in hospital informally. But if he is still ill, and unable or unwilling to remain informally, he may be compulsorily detained for observation under Section 25, for which a second medical recommendation will be needed.

Detention for observation cannot be prolonged by a new application for further detention for observation; and if further detention is needed, it must be detention for treatment under Section 26 (or the patient must be received into guardianship (see p. 752)). In the great majority of cases these compulsory detentions are soon allowed to lapse if the patient is willing to stay in hospital informally.

Admission under Section 26 authorizes the hospital to detain the patient for a period up to a year. The recommending doctors, in supporting the application of the relatives, have to specify whether the patient is to be admitted on account of mental illness, severe subnormality, subnormality or psychopathic disorder; and they have to support this with the clinical grounds on which this opinion has been reached, and the reasons why compulsory admission is thought to be necessary. Admission under this section of persons suffering from psychopathic disorder is only possible for those under the age of 21.

Sections 60 and 61 of the Act empower courts to make a 'hospital order' or 'guardianship order' in respect of certain offenders or children or young persons found to be in need of care or protection or beyond control. The court has to be satisfied on the evidence of two doctors, at least one of whom is specially approved, that the subject of the order is suffering from one of the specified forms of mental disorder of the required nature or degree; there are no age limits for subnormal or psychopathic patients under this section. Further requirements are that a particular hospital is willing to admit the patient, or that a local authority or other approved person is willing to receive the patient into guardianship; and that the circumstances of the case are such as to make this the most suitable procedure. Superior courts, but not magistrates courts, may add a 'restriction order', where this is thought necessary for the protection of the public. Patients admitted to hospital under a court order are in much the same position legally to those admitted under Section 26 except in respect to discharge.

Patients detained in hospital under Section 26 may be discharged on the order of their nearest relative, but not patients detained under Sections 25 or 29. The nearest relative has to give 72 hours' notice of his intention to the managers of the hospital; but this may be negatived by a report from the responsible medical officer that the patient would be dangerous to himself or others if discharged. The responsible medical officer is, as a general rule, the consultant psychiatrist in clinical control of the case. In the ordinary way, of course, discharge is at the instance of the medical officer in charge of the case, and is exercised by the managers of the hospital. Patients suffering from psychopathic disorder who are detained under Section 26 must be discharged on reaching the age of 25 years. Power to order discharge is also held by Mental Health Review Tribunals, when determining applications under the Act or references from the Minister. Patients detained in hospital (or received into guardianship) under a court order cannot be discharged on the order of the nearest relative, but the relative has the right to apply to a Mental Health Review Tribunal once a year. Furthermore, persons suffering from psychopathic disorder, who are detained in hospital under a court order, are not required to be discharged on reaching the age of 25, even if under the age of 21 when the hospital order was made; discharge at 25 is mandatory with patients in this clinical category detained under Section 26. If the court has made a restriction order, while the order is in force neither the patient nor his nearest relative may make application for his discharge to a Review Tribunal; but the Home Secretary may refer the patient's case to a Tribunal at any time.

Mental Health Review Tribunals have been appointed for each of the 15 regional hospital areas in England and Wales. The legal members are appointed by the Lord Chancellor and have such legal experience as he considers suitable; the medical members are appointed by the Lord Chancellor after consultation with the Minister of Health; and the lay members are appointed by the Lord Chancellor after consultation with the Minister, and have had such experience in administration, such knowledge of social services, or such other qualifications or experience as the Lord Chancellor considers suitable. One of the legal members is appointed by the Lord Chancellor as Chairman of the Tribunal.

Patients under guardianship, or detained in hospital after admission under Section 26, may apply to a Tribunal on specified occasions; applications may also be made once a year by the nearest relative. The Minister has power to refer a patient's case to a Tribunal at any time. When they have considered the application, the Tribunal have the power to discharge the patient, and also to reclassify him; broadly speaking, discharge will be ordered if the patient is not then suffering from mental illness, psychopathic disorder, subnormality or severe subnormality, or if it is not necessary for him to be detained or to remain under guardianship in his own interests or for the protection of others.

Application to a Tribunal is made in writing on a prescribed form. A copy of the application is sent by the Tribunal to the responsible authority. At the time of consideration by the Tribunal, which may or may not be a formal hearing, the responsible authority, the patient, the nearest relative, and certain other persons have the right to be seen by the Tribunal and/or to make written representations. The Tribunals also have power to obtain any other information they think necessary. A medical member of the Tribunal will in all cases be required to examine the patient or take such other steps as he considers necessary to form an opinion on the patient's medical condition. Hospital authorities will usually be represented by the responsible medical officer, who should be ready to answer any questions put to him about the patient's suitability for discharge and his home circumstances. Other persons, e.g. social workers, may be brought as witnesses when necessary. The Tribunals are expected to wish to meet at the hospital where the patient is detained.

Scotland and Ireland

In *Scotland*, under the Act of 1960, there is no provision whereby patients can be admitted to hospital for observation for 28 days; but the emergency admission may last for seven and not for only three days as in England. In the case of compulsory admission to hospital and to guardianship, the application must be submitted to and approved by a sheriff.

No provision has been made in the Scottish Act for Mental Health Review Tribunals, their place being taken by the sheriff to whom appeals may be made. An independent central body known as the Mental Welfare Commission has been set up 'to exercise protective functions in respect of persons who may by reason of mental disorder be incapable of adequately protecting their persons or their interests'.

In *Northern Ireland* the application for compulsory admission by the nearest relative or person with authority to act is founded on only one medical recommendation which must, if possible, be given by the patient's medical practitioner, or by a medical practitioner who has had previous acquaintance with the patient. This permits detention for 21 days, at the end of which time he must be discharged unless he elects to remain on informal status, or unless a psychiatrist of approved status and experience on the staff of the hospital has made a report to the managing committee (between the 14th and the 21st day after admission) to the effect that the patient is suffering from mental disorder of a nature and degree which warrants detention in hospital for his own health or safety or the protection of others. Detention for six months from the date of initial admission is thereby authorized. Authority to extend that period requires a further report to the management committee by the 'responsible medical officer', which then authorizes detention for a further twelve months.

If in the two months immediately preceding the end of that period it is deemed necessary to continue detention, medical examination and report by *two* medical officers is required, one of whom has made neither the medical recommendation for admission, nor the medical recommendation to continue detention at a later stage. After this, detention may be renewed at two-yearly intervals on the report and recommendation of the responsible medical officer. It is to be noted that the Northern Ireland Act lays greater emphasis on the statutory control of detention than on pre-admission formalities. Particular attention is directed, by the procedure described, to the crucial stage of the illness eighteen months after admission, which so often seems to mark the Rubicon between acute and chronic states of mental illness.

Arrangements regarding admission to hospital of persons concerned in criminal proceedings are very similar to those in England. In the same way, procedure with regard to the Mental Health Review Tribunal for Northern Ireland is based on that for similar English Tribunals, except that members are appointed by the Lord Chief Justice.

In *Eire* (*Southern Ireland*) a statute of 1945, amended in 1961, codified all previous legislation and introduced some novel measures. The law is administered by a section of the Department of Health under the direction of the Inspector of Mental Hospitals. Treatment as a voluntary patient has to be by application accompanied by a doctor's recommendation. Committal procedure resembles the English procedure before the 1959 Act, except that the functions of the judicial authority are discharged by the hospital's medical superintendent.

The important difference between the law in Eire and in England is in Temporary certification. The Temporary certificate has to be by the hand of the Medical Officer of the district in which the patient lives, who states that the patient is suffering from a mental illness, that he requires for his recovery not more than six months' treatment, and that he is unfit for treatment as a voluntary patient. The period of six months may be renewed up to a maximum of eighteen months. Furthermore it is possible to arrange for the *Temporary treatment of an addict*, if the Medical Officer certifies that he is an addict, and that he requires for recovery at least six months' preventive and curative treatment. The definition of an addict for the purpose of the Act, is that he is a person who, (*a*) by reason of his addiction to drugs or intoxicants is either dangerous to himself or to others or incapable of managing his affairs or of ordinary proper conduct, or (*b*) by reason of his addiction to drugs, or intoxicants, or because of his perverted conduct, is in serious danger of mental disorder. The temporary certification of addicts has not been a great success and is not widely used.

Scandinavian Countries

In *Norway* the commitment procedure still rests on the principles laid down in the Mental Diseases Act of 1848, an Act so liberal and humane that only minor changes had to be made in the new Mental Health Act of 1961. The matter is primarily one for the family, and only becomes a public concern when relatives are not available, or when they are unable or unwilling to take the necessary steps. No court order is required and the certificate of the family doctor and the consent of the relatives are sufficient. Owing to the great distances commonly involved, the family doctor will usually act entirely on his own responsibility. It is becoming increasingly common, however, for a psychiatrist to be consulted, and in and near the larger cities this is now the rule.

The public health authorities or the police will normally only be involved if the patient refuses to go to hospital and is obdurate to persuasion, or if he has no relatives to authorize his admission. In the larger towns these authorities have their own psychiatric service.

Once the patient has arrived in hospital, the medical superintendent has to satisfy himself that the admission documents are in order and that the admission is 'in the interest of the patient or necessary for public order or for the purpose of averting substantial danger to himself or others'. After admission the patient loses practically none of his legal rights, the only one of consequence being that he may not marry. If he has financial affairs which he cannot handle because of his mental condition, a guardian may be appointed by the court. Temporary admission for observation is possible in doubtful cases, with a maximum duration of three weeks. No special legal arrangements are needed in a case of urgency; in such a case the doctor can arrange for the admission of his patient by telephoning the medical superintendent, and then bring the documents with the patient to the hospital. Direct admission to a psychiatric hospital is usual, but it may be through an observation ward. Observation wards are increasing in number, and they receive non-voluntary patients under the three-weeks' observation clause.

The grounds on which the patient may be sent to hospital, though widely defined, are taken to cover only psychoses (in the Act defined as 'serious mental disorder'). Drug addicts, alcoholics or psychopaths can be certified in this way only if psychotic symptoms are present. A person with a delirious reaction or other very temporary disorder is not considered psychotic, and can be admitted for three weeks' observation only.

If the patient protests, and if the legal basis for compulsory admission seems weak, he may sometimes be charged with an offence, and he will then be dealt with under the criminal law. A situation like this may arise when the psychotic symptoms consist exclusively of delusions of jealousy, and the diagnosis rests on a decision on points of fact which can be determined more safely by testimony in court. Court procedure may also be desirable if the patient has been accused of a criminal act, when the question of his guilt and the risk of future crimes should be decided by a court.

Once the patient is in hospital he may be detained indefinitely without the need for recertification, provided that the condition which necessitated his admission still prevails. If the patient believes he is unjustly detained, he may appeal to a local Board of Control, appointed for each hospital by the King, which consists mainly of laymen with a judge as chairman. In principle the hospital takes all decisions about treatment, but it is customary to obtain the consent of relatives in the case of surgery.

There are no formalities governing discharge, and once he is discharged from psychiatric care the patient lies under no civil disabilities. Seamen are not allowed to ship out, unless approved by special medical authorities.

In *Sweden*, a patient may be taken to hospital against his will if it can be certified that psychiatric care in hospital is absolutely necessary, and the patient (1) is obviously unaware of his situation and may be greatly relieved by treatment or greatly impaired by lack of treatment, or (2) is a threat to the personal safety or physical or mental health of others, or to his own life, or (3) is unable to take care of himself, or (4) has manifested seriously disordered behaviour. The Act makes a mental abnormality, which is not mental disease or mental retardation, equivalent to mental disease. Application for commitment can be made by husband, wife, near relatives, guardians, the chairmen of certain social boards, the police, commanding officers in the armed forces, or doctors at hospitals not providing psychiatric treatment. Applications for hospital treatment must be accompanied by a medical certificate. This certificate reports information and observations showing that mental disease is present, and that hospitalization for psychiatric treatment is absolutely necessary. For the certification of the first of the grounds of commitment enumerated above the certifying doctor must be a specialist in psychiatry; otherwise a certificate may be issued by any practising doctor or other person licensed to act as a doctor. Judicial authority may also order that a person who has committed a crime is to be confined for psychiatric treatment. As a rule the crime must have been committed under the influence of mental disease or mental retardation grave enough to be classified as mental disease.

The head physician of the hospital must examine the patient for the necessity of hospital treatment within ten days of commitment. When there is no need for him to be detained against his own wishes, he must be discharged immediately by the head physician. Patients detained for treatment after court proceedings can be discharged by the local board only. If the patient demands his discharge and it is refused by the hospital authority, he may appeal to the local board. This board consists of three members: a lawyer who is also chairman, a psychiatrist not attached to the hospital where the patient is detained, and a third person with experience of public administration. There is also a central board to deal with appeals from the decisions of local boards.

Patients who are compulsorily detained in hospital may also be compelled to accept treatment; proceedings can be taken to ensure the fulfilment of the purpose of detention, or to protect the patient himself or protect others. This is thought necessary to ensure the possibility of psychiatric treatment and later discharge, and to prevent the stay in hospital from becoming purely protective confinement.

In *Denmark*, commitment to hospital is governed by an Act of 1938. A dangerous patient may be admitted to hospital against his will on the certificate of a single doctor. If the patient is not dangerous, the certificates of two medical men are required (one of them being a State Medical Officer). They must certify that admission is necessary because the possibility of recovery would otherwise be considerably reduced, and they must give evidence for their opinion. Admission of the patient against his will can be enforced by the police (and the doctors). He then has the right to protest immediately to the Ministry of Justice; and by a law of 1953, if he objects to the Ministry's decision, he can appeal from it to the courts.

Switzerland, Germany and Austria

In *Switzerland* the care of mental patients and the laws and regulations relating to them are the affair of the individual cantons, and the Federation as a whole is not concerned. The cantons differ in minor respects among themselves, but the canton of Zürich, which is the most populous, may be taken as an example. In Zürich admission to hospital is governed by a law of November, 1962. Patients who know what they are doing may be admitted voluntarily at any time without further formal procedure. A private medical man, with a licence to practise in the canton, may order the admission of a patient to hospital if he is in need of care or treatment, or if he endangers the security of himself or others. The concurrence of the guardian or nearest relative is also necessary. The patient must be admitted within fourteen days of medical certification. Certain officials, e.g. justices and the Public Prosecutor, may also order the admission of a patient. The poor-law authorities are also legally entitled to act in this way, but in practice are not permitted to do so without medical support. Once the patient has been admitted, the medical director of the hospital must be satisfied that it is proper for him to remain, but he is not required to set down his opinion in writing, or to renew the certificate.

Patients who are admitted by private physicians with the consent of their relatives can be discharged when the medical director of the hospital judges that it is proper. If the patient asks for discharge and discharge is not granted, he can then ask for a special commission to decide the matter. This commission is nominated by the cantonal government, and includes a psychiatrist as a member. Relatives may remove patients, even against medical advice; but if the patient is thought dangerous the medical director refuses discharge, and it is then open to the patient and his relatives to ask for a special commission. Patients can be and are certified and admitted to hospital, who suffer from ephemeral deliria, or from an addiction to alcohol or drugs with serious consequences, or who are severely psychopathic though not psychotic.

No particular formalities are required for discharge, although much use is made of trial periods at home. After his discharge from hospital the patient suffers from no legal disability; and indeed in hospital he keeps his civil rights, frequently even the freedom of movement, unless special provisions (e.g. for guardianship) are made. He may legally refuse to undergo any special form of treatment.

Commitment procedures in *Germany* and *Austria* before Hitler were not very different. During the Nazi régime in Germany and in most countries occupied by the Nazis, admission to and detention in mental hospitals was widely misused for political purposes: for the removal of politically unwanted persons as well as for the protection of the persecuted. Hence the return in Western Germany after the war to strict and rather bureaucratic commitment procedures including two doctors' certificates, one by an officially recognized physician, and a judicial decision. The magistrate himself may interview the patient and hear evidence on the case. University psychiatric clinics in these countries frequently fulfil the function of observation wards in England, and a large number of the patients admitted to them are brought in directly by relatives, doctors and the police. The great variety of clinical material seen in this way at university centres is valuable for both teachers and students.

An interesting feature of the law relating to mental disorder in Germanic lands is the extensive use of precautionary measures relating to social incapacity on psychiatric grounds. While the appointment of a Receiver or Curator bonis only arises under special circumstances in Britain, in Germany the concept of *capacity to manage affairs* ('*Geschäftsfähigkeit*') is of wide practical application at least according to the word of the law. Patients can be declared by a judge to be incapable of managing their affairs not only on grounds of mental disorder or mental deficiency, but also because of alcoholism, psychopathy and other conditions. Such a certificate is not bound up with the need for hospital care, and the patient who has been deprived of his civil rights in this way ('*entmündigt*') remains under the care of the guardian ('*Vormund*') whether he is in hospital or out of it; in fact, the idea of guardianship in these cases is to give him protection from misuse of his rights and abilities, by others as much as by himself, when he is outside the guarding walls of the hospital. The certificate of incapacity on grounds of alcoholism can be given when the patient 'because of alcoholism is unable to manage his affairs, or lays himself or his family open to the danger of becoming necessitous, or endangers the safety of others'. In practice, this legal order has always been found difficult to apply. In a less formal way German law also provides for the care of personal belongings and minor business interests ('*Pflegschaft*') while the patient is incapacitated.

The Mental Health Act of 1959 introduced *reception into guardianship* side by side with hospital admission. The local health authority takes over the guardianship, on medical recommendations similar to those made for hospital admission. Guardianship confers on the guardian 'powers as if he were the father of the patient and the patient were under the age of fourteen'. This measure takes account of the many mental patients who live in the community and need some protection, such as that which is made available in some Continental countries (see below).

Other European Countries

The arrangement in *Holland* by which mental hospitals are divided into open and closed departments has already been mentioned. Admission to and discharge from the closed wards is governed by a law of 1884. Admission is only possible *on the authorization of a judge*, and he acts on the basis of an application from a near relative together with a medical certificate stating that the patient is mentally ill and admission to a mental hospital is necessary or desirable. The public prosecutor can demand admission if there is no relative to act in this way, or if the patient is dangerous or likely to disturb public order. The admission of a criminal patient may be ordered by the criminal court. The principal medical officer of the hospital has wide powers over the discharge of criminal and non-criminal patients alike. When however a criminal patient, by order of a criminal court, apart from a sentence to prison and/or apart from his stay in a mental hospital, has at the same time been placed 'at the disposal of the government' (comparable in English parlance to 'H.M.'s pleasure') his discharge from hospital by the medical officer may not be the end of the matter. If the Minister of Justice considers that the medical discharge from the hospital has been over-hasty with regard to public order and security, he may order the detention of the patient in an asylum for psychopaths. Apart from medical discharge, the non-criminal patient may be discharged to the care of the relatives if they take responsibility, with the same restrictions respecting public safety as in other lands. Regular medical reports have to be written on certified patients; and the liberties of the subject are supervised by the public prosecutor and by medical inspectors for mental health (registered psychiatrists in full-time government service) superintending the field of mental health. If the patient or his relatives wish to make representations about his detention or treatment, they will make them to the inspector or to the public prosecutor. The certified patient in hospital loses practically all of his ordinary civil rights. Guardians are provisionally appointed for the management of his affairs, the guardianship ceasing on his discharge from hospital.

Arrangements in *Belgium* are governed by laws of 1850 and 1873. In ordinary cases the medical practitioner delivers two signed copies of a certificate, which if unused expires in fifteen days. The nearest relative has also to sign an application for commitment, and the commitment itself is ordered *by the mayor or his representative*. The grounds of admission are essentially social and not medical, and relate to the possibility of danger to the patient himself or to the public peace. Patients suffering from temporary illnesses, alcoholics and drug addicts, can all be dealt with in this way, but usually not psychopaths of other kinds unless public order has been disturbed. The discharge of the certified patient from a mental hospital has to be ordered by the President of the Civil Court, and he may hear evidence. Relatives cannot secure the discharge of a patient without application to him, and any complaint the patient has to make about his detention will go to him also. Theoretically, the certified patient suffers no loss of civil rights, but of course he is largely unable to exercise them. His position in the matter of refusing treatment is unclear in law. Directors of mental hospitals content themselves in practice with the permission of relatives to initiate treatment. Institutions for the care of mental patients are supervised by a physician who is General Inspector appointed by the Ministry of Health. Direct control is exercised by the King's Prosecutor in each of the judicial districts of the province.

In *France* commitment to a mental hospital is governed by a law of 1838. This law was modern and liberal for its time, but in recent years has been increasingly felt to be unsatisfactory. Repeated attempts have been made in the past thirty years to introduce amendments, but none have reached the statute book. Commitment may be by *placement volontaire* or by *placement d'office*, about nine-tenths of all admissions being the former. The application for *placement volontaire*, despite its name, cannot be made by the patient himself but must be made by a relative. It is supported by a medical certificate describing the symptoms of mental disorder and stating that the patient needs care according to the provisions of the law of 1838. The application is to the *Préfet* (civil authority), who orders the admission. For the *placement d'office* no medical certificate is necessary; this procedure is a police affair and is not used unless the patient is dangerous or is liable to disturb public order. Alcoholics and psychopaths can be admitted to hospital against their will by the *placement volontaire* and, although the legal justification for this is unclear, alcoholics are often kept in hospital after the end of any acute form of mental upset while their addiction is treated. Admission of a psychopath is only feasible if he has caused some form of social disturbance. Apart from medical discharge, relatives can require the discharge of the patient from hospital, unless he is transferred from a *placement volontaire* to a *placement d'office*. The *Préfet*, or his delegate, makes inquiries about all patients in hospital every three months, and in addition the *Procureur de la République*, an official of the central government, visits hospitals twice a year.

In *Spain*, as has been noted, informal voluntary admission is very common. The second most widely used method of admission is on the certificate of a doctor, not necessarily a psychiatrist, who certifies the existence of the illness. The nearest relative asks for the admission. This method of admission does not affect the legal rights of the patient. Government officials and judicial authorities may also order admission, but always with accompanying medical certificate. These formalities hold for admission not only to mental hospitals but also to the psychiatric departments of general hospitals. Psychopathic and addictive states can be covered. The medical officer of the hospital has to ratify the admission. If the patient objects to admission, he must have recourse to a judge, who may then order a special investigation. Relatives may obtain the discharge of a patient, even against medical advice, provided he is not dangerous; there are no formalities governing discharge. While in hospital the patient loses none of his civil rights, and he may refuse treatment if he is sufficiently intact to exercise a free choice. If it is necessary to deprive a patient of his civil rights, legal procedure and a judge's declaration of incapacity are required.

A law of 1945 greatly modernized legal and administrative practice in *Portugal*, so that the country might have become one of the most advanced in Europe in this respect. The law envisaged that psychiatric treatment included prophylaxis, treatment and child welfare, and it had provisions relating to ambulatory treatment, hospitalization, domiciliary treatment, and the placing of patients in private families. The implementation of law in practice, however, was a slow and difficult process. In the meantime there has been a further mental health Act of 1963, which changed the projected organization once again. Regional health centres should each be provided with a clinical unit, a dispensary and out-patient clinic, and social services. The distribution of local community mental health activities, which had been too much concentrated in the main cities, should thereby be much improved. However, up to the time of writing, no mental health centres are yet in existence. The law of 1963, moreover, against the advice of the psychiatrists, introduced more administrative and legal control, essentially with the idea of protecting the certified patient. It seems to have made it rather more difficult for psychiatrists to maintain their high proportion of voluntary admissions to hospital.

Certification is on the statements of two doctors not on the staff of the hospital to which the patient goes, but rather on the staff of the dispensary. Supervision of the liberties of the individual rests in the hands of the Institute of Mental Health, with authority exercised in this matter by a judge. Complaints by the patients are referred to him.

United States of America

In the *United States*, every State of the Union has its own law, and these laws vary very widely indeed. No State can be regarded as typical of them all. A thorough review of the law relating to the mentally disabled has been prepared by the American Bar Foundation, under the editorship of Lindman and McIntyre (1961). In the field of commitment procedure, it discloses a state of affairs unparalleled in the western world. It seems clear that America has become the victim of her history, and that it has now become extremely difficult for the community, for the patients and for psychiatrists, to escape from the legal straitjacket in which they have become tied. The first asylums for the mentally ill were established about two hundred years ago; and for about one hundred years after that the commitment of patients to hospital was effected with such ease and informality that abuses were possible. Campaigns to secure decent care for the mentally ill highlighted these deficiencies with the result, which we may think typical of America, that reform was sought through changes in the law rather than changes in practice and administration. Commitment laws were now enacted which specified the use of judicial procedures, laws which were dominated by 'almost single-minded concern' with the possibility of wrongful commitment. To this day, the pattern has remained much the same, although in some

States hospitalization by medical certification and temporary and observational procedures have been provided for.

The obsessive fear of even the barest possibility of wrongful commitment was no doubt largely caused by the extreme deprivation of human rights which was likely to befall the patient once he was admitted. This was the situation which called for reform, and which reform has barely begun to touch. Involuntary hospitalization was for an indeterminate period, and State laws permitted the retention of the patient in hospital on the original documents without calling for re-certification after any stated period. The medical superintendent was able to resist the efforts of the responsible relatives to secure the patient's release; and the only means to achieve this might be by means of a writ of *habeas corpus*. Even this might be defeated by keeping the patient incommunicado. In the 1930s in two New York State hospitals, the medical superintendent intercepted letters from the patient to his attorney, knowing that they related to *habeas corpus* proceedings. The court subsequently held that this constituted an unreasonable restraint, and the legal position in New York has now been changed by statute. However, according to Lindman and McIntyre, in more than a quarter of the States there is no provision affirming the patient's right to receive and send correspondence; and in more than half the States there is no provision covering the receiving of visitors. As has been noted earlier (p. 740), the voluntary patient is generally subject to the same loss of civil rights and liberties as the involuntary patient.

The therapeutic conditions inside the hospitals call for no less concern. Mechanical restraints are still being applied in some hospitals. The patient can be submitted to such measures as convulsive therapy, psychosurgery and sterilization without his own consent or the consent of his relatives. Electro-shock is sometimes applied for disciplinary as well as therapeutic purposes, and there is no effective relief if damage is done. Lindman and McIntyre note that it is difficult for the patient either to protect himself from injury, or to recover damages for negligence or gross negligence. Overcrowding of hospitals is widespread and severe, and yet in one survey as many as 70 per cent. of the inmates 'did not need to be in a mental hospital'. In a 1965 study of Texas mental institutions it was found that of the 134 patients in one ward, 45 had never been diagnosed; no one knew what, if anything, was the matter with them. Similar conditions were found in other Texas hospitals, and about 30 per cent. of the patients had received no diagnosis.

It is against this background that American commitment laws have to be understood. Thirty-seven jurisdictions provide some form of judicial hospitalization; this means that a judge or jury determines whether a person is mentally ill to such an extent as to require hospitalization and, if so, the court orders him to be hospitalized for an indeterminate period of time. The decision may or may not be based on the advice of medical experts. Thirteen jurisdictions authorize the use of a jury to decide the question of hospitalization. The criteria for hospitalization may be (1) that the patient is dangerous to himself or others, or (2) that he is in need of care or treatment, or (3) both of these, or (4) no criteria may be spelled out. The State of Massachusetts is unique in providing that mere social nonconformity may be sufficient, anyone being regarded as mentally ill who is 'likely to conduct himself in a manner which clearly violates the established laws, ordinances, conventions or morals of the community'. Involuntary hospitalization is also available for mental defectives, epileptics (18 States), alcoholics (36 States), drug addicts (34 States). The mental defective is, typically, a 'person whose mental abilities have been arrested by disease or physical injury occurring at an early age, who requires care, treatment, detention and training'.

No I.Q. rating is specified. The procedure involved in judicial involuntary hospitalization calls for an application (in 18 jurisdictions by *any person*), notice, hearing, right to counsel, right to trial by jury; not all States allow for each and all of these formalities.

Nonjudicial involuntary hospitalization is possible in 31 States, and in 12 it is the only procedure. In some States there is a hearing by a commission or board, and there may be one or more doctors on the board. Involuntary hospitalization for an indeterminate period, without the patient's consent and over his objection, on the basis of medical certificates, is available in 9 States; approval or endorsement by a judge may also be required, but the need for hospitalization is determined by the physicians. Non-protested admission is a procedure by which an individual may be hospitalized for an indeterminate period, on the basis of one or more medical certificates, provided he does not object; this is in use in 14 States. During the last twenty years, in 34 States legislation has been introduced providing for temporary or observational hospitalization. In 16 States, the aim is to care for a patient for a limited time, in no case longer than six months, at the end of which he must be released; in the remaining States the procedure is used in connexion with judicial hospitalization proceedings, as a preliminary intended to provide the court with the means of making an informed judgement. Powers of emergency detention are usually delegated to the police; in 12 States judicial approval is required, and in 16 States a medical certificate.

Lindman and McIntyre report the conclusions and recommendations reached by the American Bar Foundation on the present state of affairs. Most of the recommendations are, as one might expect from a legal body, directed towards a tightening up of the law. In addition, independent proceedings for the temporary or observational hospitalization of the mentally ill, the allowance of sufficient time to observe and diagnose before the hearing, and special provisions for emergency detention, are all recommended.

MENTAL DEFICIENCY

In England and Wales, the Mental Health Act, 1959, made a no less fundamental change in the law relating to mental deficiency than in that relating to mental illness. It is envisaged that in almost all cases it should be possible for patients to receive care in the community, from their own families and from the local health authority, without being subjected to legal controls. These will be necessary only in a small minority of cases to control the patient's place of residence or his everyday life for his own welfare or for the protection of others. In the ordinary way patients suffering from mental deficiency are admitted to hospital, and receive any other service required, without formality. This applies, for instance, to the great majority of children taken into hospital for investigation, for treatment or for long-term care.

If legal controls are required they will usually be provided under Sections 33 and 34 of the Act, by which the patient is received into guardianship. On exactly the same model as certification under Section 26, application is made by the nearest relative or a mental welfare officer, and is supported by recommendations from two doctors, one of them specially approved by a local health authority. The application is made on the grounds that the patient is suffering from mental disorder, namely mental illness or severe subnormality (the patient being of any age) or subnormality or psychopathic disorder (the patient being under the age of 21 years); that his disorder is of a nature or degree which warrants his reception into guardianship; and that it is necessary in his interests or for the protection of others that he should be so received. From this it may be seen that not only mentally subnormal, severely subnormal and psychopathic patients may be placed under guardianship, but also patients suffering from mental illness. This provision may therefore be very suitable for the patient who has made a partial recovery from a schizophrenic illness, and is well enough to live in the community, but is in need of protection. A duty is laid on local health authorities to make arrangements for the care of persons suffering from mental disorder who are resident in their area, and for their after-care. It is a necessary part of this duty for the authority either itself to undertake the duties of guardian, or to arrange for another person to do so, in cases where guardianship is necessary for the proper care of the patient.

Application may be made by the nearest relative, or by a mental welfare officer with the consent of the nearest relative. The person named as guardian in the application may be a local authority, or any other person (including the applicant). Any private person named as guardian must give his consent. The duties of the guardian include the provision of occupation, training or employment of the patient, arrangements for his recreation and general welfare and for the promotion of his physical and mental health. The powers of the guardian are described as equivalent to the powers of a father of a child under the age of fourteen.

In Northern Ireland and Scotland, the situation is very much as it is in England. However in Scotland application for reception into guardianship must be submitted to a sheriff; and it is the sheriff who exercises the functions of the Review Tribunal.

BOARDING-OUT AND GUARDIANSHIP

Up to the time of the Act of 1959, there had been little provision in England for the patient who had made a partial and incomplete recovery from a psychosis, but whose further stay in hospital was no longer called for on clinical or social grounds. The provisions for guardianship, which have been outlined above, should be sufficient for dealing with this problem; but at present no statistics are available to show how many patients are under the guardianship of local health authorities, or other persons such as relatives, and how many of them are classifiable under each of the four officially recognized categories of mental disorder.

In Scotland the position is different, and the boarding-out of chronic patients, with relatives or with unrelated guardians, has been extensively used for the past hundred years, especially in certain rural areas. At the end of 1963 there were about 1,250 mental defectives under statutory guardianship, and less than 100 mentally ill persons. In addition there were just under 6,700 mental defectives and rather more than 2,300 mentally ill persons in the community, receiving regular visits from local authority staff.

In other countries also, far-reaching arrangements are often made. In *Switzerland*, for instance, *family care* of patients who have made a partial social remission is supported by the canton, and the patients are visited by medical and nursing officers who have been appointed to this work. The patients may live and work, not only in their own homes or with relatives, but also in the homes of any respectable citizens who are willing to take them and who can be regarded as sufficiently responsible by the canton. Similar arrangements exist in *Belgium*, especially at the famed colony at Gheel in the province of Antwerp, where the tradition of family care is a very long one, and the local inhabitants, mostly engaged in farming activities, are thoroughly accustomed to this office. In *Denmark*, the mental hospital at Aarhus used to supervise about the same number of patients boarded out among the rural population of the area as were cared for as in-patients of the hospital. The number of boarded-out patients has decreased rapidly since the war, and the proportion now is less than ten per cent. In *Sweden*, mental defectives and people who have not recovered completely from psychoses but are still partially incapacitated are often maintained in family care. The organization of family care is divided into districts, each with its chief psychiatrist and nurses who travel around in it. One of the special features of Swedish hospital organization is that small homes situated in rural areas are used for the care of chronic psychiatric patients who can keep themselves clean, are easily cared for and able to do some work. They are placed in groups of a few up to about 30 in farm-houses where they form a community under a head nurse. They learn to take some pride in helping to run the home and the farm. Every second week the psychiatrist or the nurse visits the homes, which are owned by the county councils. The same arrangement holds in *Norway*, where about half of all the patients under public care are boarded. The large proportion, however, seems to be due to the fact that hospital accommodation is inadequate. Some of the patients boarded-out would be better maintained in hospital in-patient care. Supervision is in the charge of the officers of the mental hospital, or of local public health officers.

Apart from the countries mentioned above, grant-aided family care is unknown. Even the continued supervision of chronic mental patients returned to their own families is lacking or haphazard in most lands, although in England and the United States it is beginning to grow. In 1956 in the *U.S.A.* over 7,000 patients were living in family care at public expense. It is not easy to assess the *factors which make boarding-out relatively easy* in some areas and almost impossible in others. The small amount of cash the peasant's wife receives for keeping a former patient in her household seems to be attractive enough in Denmark, where through the universal co-operative arrangements of buying and selling little money goes through her hands. The importance and the meaning which Christian principles have for a rural population are also not to be under-estimated.

Further development along these lines is probable, and necessary in the future, if only to check the over-crowding of many hospitals. A vigorous attack on the *resocialization* of those who are only *partially incapacitated* in the chronic mental-hospital population is now being conducted at many hospitals. It is anticipated that the long-stay population of psychiatric hospitals will be reduced, with important changes in hospital routine resulting. The supervision of chronic patients in the community is, however, not always as thorough as might be hoped. We are still in the process of discovering how far rehabilitation can go, how far families are able to support the burden of a mentally ill member, and how far hospital facilities are needed to provide the help of an asylum for the otherwise helpless.

Recent attempts in Britain to bring psychiatry into closer relation with the community, for instance by the employment of social workers in larger numbers, by domiciliary visits from psychiatrists and treating patients in their own homes, were stimulated by earlier work along these lines in *Holland*. In the largest cities a central office of the local authority supervises both hospital admissions and former and prospective patients living in the community. In the country outside those largest cities social psychiatric services, with psychiatrists and mental nurses trained in social work, supervise the mental patients as long as they are in the community; and they are intermediary in most cases when admission to or discharge from a mental hospital is arranged.

THE ORGANIZATION AND ADMINISTRATION OF
PSYCHIATRIC SERVICES

In almost all countries the main parts of the *psychiatric services are decentralized* to a large extent; as a general rule, they are financed and managed by the local authorities of cantons, provinces, districts, etc., with some supervisory control from the central government either from its department of justice or department of health, or sometimes both. In some countries the central government may have one or more hospitals under its direct control, more particularly hospitals for criminal psychiatric patients.

In Britain the *National Health Service Act of 1946* and the corresponding Scottish Act of 1947 completely re-organized hospital administration, taking the hospitals away from the county and borough authorities who till then had administered them, and placing them under the control of the Ministry of Health and the Department of Health in Scotland. This is an entirely new development, and warrants some description. A fuller account than is possible here has been provided by Maclay and Wilson (1950).

Three sets of authorities are involved in the administration of psychiatric services in England and Wales, separate but similar organizations existing in Scotland. The first of these is the *Mental Health Division of the Ministry of Health*, which has the duty of co-ordinating mental health services in different parts of the country with each other and with other medical services, and supervising the work of the *Regional Hospital Boards*.

These latter are the second set of authorities involved. The country is divided into fourteen areas, each with its central office, medical officers and psychiatrists, committees and permanent officials. The Regional Hospital Boards are responsible for the satisfactory working of the hospitals and out-patient clinics and other services under their jurisdiction, for planning new building or development, appointing medical and other hospital officers, supporting research, etc. Some hospitals, e.g. those to which a medical school is attached, which are under the control of the universities, and 'disclaimed' private hospitals, are not managed by the Regional Boards.

Finally, despite the very great extent to which mental-health work has been brought under central control, the *local authorities* are still responsible for the welfare of patients living in the community and for the *after-care* of those who have been discharged from hospital.

The psychiatric services also have relationships with other government departments. As a result of war-time experience, at most employment exchanges, which are administered by the Ministry of Labour, there is a *Rehabilitation Officer* whose duty it is to obtain the most suitable employment possible for persons partially disabled, whether by injury, disease or mental abnormality. This officer consults and is consulted by hospital almoners and social workers working under medical direction in hospitals and clinics. The work done by these officers has been found of the greatest value by psychiatrists, who have been aided by them, and by the national full-employment policy, to get neurotic and post-psychotic patients back into useful employment in a way which was never possible before the war.

The responsibility for the conduct of *psychiatric clinics for children* is shared between the *Ministry of Education* and the *Ministry of Health*. At most child-guidance clinics there is a close integration of the work of psychiatrists, psychologists, social workers and school teachers. At many centres there are regular conferences at which these workers meet. The merits and disadvantages of present child-guidance arrangements have been discussed in Chapter XI, p. 631.

It is probably still too early to say to what extent this organization of psychiatric services will need modification in the course of time. The tendency towards *administrative decentralization* is clearly expressed in the 1959 *Mental Health Act*. It details the provisions to be made by local authorities in the form of accommodation and centres for discharged mental patients, appointment of mental health officers, taking over guardianships, etc. It also tries to dovetail provisions for the education of subnormal children by the local authority with other legal acts referring to children, such as the Children and Young Persons Act (1933) and the Childrens Act (1948). The Mental Health Review Tribunals are intended to be of local character; the Mental Health Division of the Ministry of Health has become essentially a supervisory and co-ordinating body.

THE MENTAL PATIENT IN CIVIL LAW

The wide field in which mental disorders and incapacities may affect civil rights, responsibilities and duties cannot be covered in this text in any detail. The subject has recently been reviewed by Rylander (1961). In some countries, e.g. Canada, the Netherlands and some of the States of the U.S.A., most civil rights are suspended when the patient is committed to a mental hospital. As one authority (Overholser, 1954) has noted, it is quite unjustified to confound commitment with an adjudication of incompetency, which has serious consequences, and is a hardship for many patients. In nearly all other countries, commitment of the mentally ill patient does not deprive him of his civil rights, and the question of competency is dealt with after admission when an issue arises which requires a special decision.

In England before the 1959 Act a person certified insane was presumed to be incapable of making a valid contract, unless the medical superintendent of the hospital certified that he knew the nature of what he was doing. Since the passing of the Act, the patient committed to hospital lies under no legal disability of any kind, since all that the doctors have certified is the patient's need of in-patient care. Whether or not the patient is able to make a valid contract now depends, therefore, on his actual state of mind. As Henderson (1950) has pointed out, the general theory of contracts requires free and full consent of the contracting parties, and the consent must be an act of reason accompanied by due deliberation. Overholser has said that a reasonable degree of mental alertness and contact with reality, together with a reasonably intact memory, must be demonstrated to permit the mentally ill individual to make a valid contract. In France, Switzerland and Austria the criterion used is the capacity of the patient to form normal motives and to be guided by them. In France the contract entered into by a patient certified insane is not void, but it must be annulled if the patient is shown to be suffering from 'démence'; in Austria it must be shown that the patient was competent; in Italy also the certificate of the psychiatrist is required to show that, with regard to the act in question, the patient had full understanding and volition.

In countries where the acts of the insane do not have to be validated, they may nevertheless be invalidated if evidence is brought for that purpose. In Sweden it must be proved that the act was made under the influence of mental disorder, and in Switzerland that the patient was not capable of forming normal motives or of acting according to them.

The rules regarding testamentary capacity tend to run along parallel lines to those governing contractual capacity, but to be interpreted within wider limits. In Switzerland a lesser degree of 'Urteilsfähigkeit' is required for testamentary capacity. In Sweden the formulation of the law is the same in the two cases, but the courts are more reluctant to declare wills void than the contracts made by mentally disordered persons. In the U.S.A. the testator should be clear that he is devising his property, know what it is and know who are the natural objects of his bounty.

In England and Scotland it is essential that a will, disposing of property after death, to maintain its validity should be made by 'a person of full age and sound disposing mind, executed in due form'. 'A sound disposing mind' is not necessarily synonymous with perfect sanity, as there are persons who are mentally ill who may even be certified patients in a mental hospital, and yet are capable of making a satisfactory will (Henderson and Gillespie, 1950). What is required is that the patient, at the time he makes his will must be able to recall (a) the nature and extent of his property, and (b) the persons who have claims upon his bounty; and (c) his judgement and will must be so unclouded and free as to enable him to determine the relative strength of these claims.

Marriage and Divorce

Mental illness and mental deficiency may be a bar to the patient's marrying; it may be grounds for a petition for the annulment of a marriage, either by the patient or by his partner; and it may be grounds for a petition for divorce by the partner. The law relating to all four types of legal process varies from country to country.

In *Switzerland* no mentally ill person ('*Geisteskranker*') can contract a valid marriage. Mental illness ('*Geisteskrankheit*') is a much wider concept than insanity, and may exclude from marriage persons who are not insane in the British sense, but who may even be capable of making a valid business contract. Furthermore the person who is about to marry must have the judgement and the insight into the nature and significance of marriage to understand all the problems and duties which are involved. These high requirements have been somewhat lowered in practice. In *Germany* and *Austria* anyone who is incapable of managing his own affairs ('*geschäftsunfähig*') is incapable of marriage. Feeble-minded persons, psychopaths, addicts and persons who have suffered a serious brain injury are commonly regarded as '*geschäftsunfähig*', and can be placed under guardianship. If that has been done, they can only marry with their guardian's consent.

In *Sweden* insanity and mental deficiency are bars to marriage. For those who are capable of setting up and maintaining a home, it is possible to get the King's permission to marry, after they have submitted themselves to sterilization. An application for nullity can be made by either partner, by the mentally disordered person not later than six months after recovery, by the healthy partner not later than six months after first learning of the other's mental disease or defect. An application for divorce may also be made by the healthy partner if the mental disease of the other has lasted for three years. In *Finland* and *Norway* psychosis and imbecility are absolute bars to marriage.

In other countries mental abnormality has to be severe to invalidate a marriage, although subsequent actions for nullity on slighter grounds may be possible. In England a marriage is void *ab initio* if either party at the time of the marriage is suffering from insanity to such an extent as to be incapable of understanding the nature of the ceremony, or to have insane delusions about it. The Matrimonial Causes Act of 1950 makes a marriage voidable if one of the parties was at the time of unsound mind, or a mental defective, or subject to recurrent fits of insanity or epilepsy. Only the sane party may seek relief, and must have been ignorant of this state in the partner at the time of marriage, and must have instituted proceedings within a year. In the United States, in nine States, eugenic considerations are involved, since mentally disabled persons are permitted to marry when sterilization has been performed, or when the woman is over forty-five years of age. The argument is that mentally disabled persons, whether their condition is due to hereditary causes or not, are unfitted to be parents. Britain and Sweden are among the few countries allowing a petition for annulment by the healthy spouse. In practically all countries a mentally incapacitated person may petition for the annulment of his marriage on the grounds that his consent was not valid. In *Greece*, where there is no restriction on the marriage of the insane and defective, annulment of marriage on these grounds is not possible.

In countries where the influence of the Roman Catholic Church on the civil law is strong it is not possible for either party to a marriage to obtain a divorce on grounds of the mental disorder of one of them. This is the case in *Belgium, France, Italy*, the *Netherlands* and *Spain;* in *Portugal* a civil marriage can be dissolved, but not a Catholic one unless the religious authorities agree. In most countries, however, the spouse of an insane individual can obtain a divorce if the illness has lasted a certain time and is deemed incurable. Generally three years is the period stipulated, but in England and Scotland it is five years.

In *Britain*, since the *Matrimonial Causes Act of* 1937, it has been possible for the wife or husband of an insane person to obtain a divorce on the grounds of the incurable insanity of the partner. It must be shown that the patient has been continuously under care and treatment for at least five years, even though for part of this time the treatment may have been received in a voluntary capacity. By incurable is meant that the patient is incapable of recovering by any means whatever to such a state as to be able to resume the ordinary responsibilities of marriage, even though he may be able to live outside the walls of an institution.

Sterilization

In many countries of the world an operation designed for the sole and exclusive purpose of causing sterility is not specifically permitted by law, and so may be felt to involve legal risks. Specific statutes legalizing sterilization have been passed in Denmark, Norway and Sweden, and in a number of States of the U.S.A. In *Britain* the legal position has never been clarified beyond doubt, but there is little reason to think that an operation which is asked for by a patient and agreed to by the spouse would cause any undesirable legal repercussions. Practice has changed a good deal in recent years, to a considerable extent due to the pioneering work of Dugald Baird in Aberdeen, so that the welfare of the patient, including her social welfare (for it is nearly always the woman who asks to be sterilized) has come to be the primary consideration. The freedom with which psychiatrists ask for this operation, and with which surgeons carry it out, varies very much from individual to individual. Sterilization on medical considerations usually causes no difficulty whatever, e.g. where it is desirable to relieve a woman of the chance of pregnancy if that involves a risk to life or to mental or physical health. Sterilization solely for eugenic reasons is unusual, but has certainly been done without any unfavourable legal consequences to the surgeon or to the medical advisers. The importance of social grounds is increasingly widely recognized, but very variably interpreted. Thus a general practitioner, with or without the support of a psychiatrist, should find no great difficulty in arranging for the sterilization of a middle-aged mother of many children, overburdened by her large family. But it might not be so easy to arrange for the sterilization of a defective girl of promiscuous habits before allowing her to leave the institution for life outside, desirable as that might be for her future health and happiness.

In the three Scandinavian countries voluntary sterilization on medical, social or eugenic grounds has been permitted by Acts of Parliament. The *Norwegian* law was passed in 1933, the *Swedish* one in 1941. In these countries it is quite possible to recommend sterilization before permitting a mentally disordered or defective person to marry, or to leave a hospital for boarding-out. Psychiatrists in these countries have no doubt that the law is humane and permits greater freedom to partially incapacitated people to enjoy a more nearly normal life. Most sterilizations are being performed on mothers who are worn out and do not want more children, and who for a variety of reasons cannot use contraceptives. In *Denmark*, however, ever since the German occupation during the war of 1939–45, public opinion has been extremely sensitive to anything which can be construed as an attack on personal liberty. It has occasionally been claimed that the law does involve a hidden compulsion; and sterilization is used on a much smaller scale than before the war. Some authorities think that this tendency has gone too far. The genetical consequences may become apparent in due time. It has been calculated that the number of new cases of mental deficiency in Denmark is at the present time about 50 per cent. of what it would have been but for the application of the sterilization laws to mental defectives in the past; and it may be that for the sake of human liberty an increasing number of oligophrenics will have to bear the burden of their incapacities in years to come.

In *Switzerland*, also, sterilization has been widely used in many cantons, in a way similar to that obtaining in the Scandinavian countries. The availability of sterilization, and the security it gives to a married couple, have encouraged some relaxation of the law forbidding the marriage of the mentally disordered and the defective. The effective consideration is not so much that, by sterilization, the risk of passing on a morbid inheritance is obviated, as that by its means potential children are guarded against the risk of being brought up in an inadequate or even tragically unsuitable home.

In *America*, Minnesota and Vermont are the only States which permit sterilization solely on a voluntary basis; all the other 26 States which have statutes provide for the compulsory sterilization of the mentally disabled. In these States the inmates of State institutions are liable, and six States provide also that persons outside such institutions come within the law. In 27 States mental defectives are specified as liable to sterilization, and nearly all States also identify the mentally ill as being within the statutes. In 18 States epileptics are also included; and in some States other groups also, such as 'hereditary criminals', sex offenders and syphilitics. However, in many States, the number of persons actually sterilized annually is very small; and according to Lindman and McIntyre, it is claimed that most of the operations are carried out with the consent of the patient.

It appears that opposition to sterilization is growing in the States, particularly where Roman Catholic influence is strong; it is said that Catholic opposition has contributed to the defeat of such legislation in several States. Lindman and McIntyre not only criticize the formal aspects of the law, e.g. for lack of due process, but they also question their scientific basis and call for its re-examination.

A few words on this aspect would seem to be called for. It is very doubtful indeed whether compulsory sterilization should ever be enforceable by law. It is an interference with the subject which, when inflicted without his consent, is likely to offend against deep feelings and be felt to be humiliating. Furthermore, the existence of laws permitting compulsory sterilization is a barrier in the way of developing a sensible attitude in society towards voluntary sterilization. If the law were to make voluntary sterilization available to the individual who wished for it, on sound medical or social grounds, this would add to the liberties of the subject; it would indeed in many cases be of great help and service to the individual himself, without taking any account of following generations. From the point of view of the next generation, many will think that a child born into a civilized community should have at least an average chance of growing up in a happy healthy family. If one of the parents is feeble-minded, or schizophrenic, or liable to frequent epileptic attacks, the chance that the child has of enjoying normal care, love and security at home must be materially lessened. In comparison with this consideration, the genetical risks to the unborn in such cases would appear to be relatively unimportant.

Castration

The operation of castration has not been authorized by law in any other than the three Scandinavian countries; and in them it cannot be carried out against the will of the individual. It can be applied to the insane or the mentally defective, or to aggressively psychopathic persons with deviant sexual inclinations. The purpose is both to prevent sexual crimes, and to alleviate the mental suffering of the individual under the pressure of his sexual aberration. It is claimed that the aggressive psychopath who asks for and submits to the operation benefits by a considerably increased chance of settling down into normal life, and freeing himself from the tendencies which bring him into conflict with society. However, very few operations have been carried out in recent years.

Termination of Pregnancy

Throughout the world, a movement towards the liberalization of the law and practice in relation to abortion is gathering strength. This movement is principally inspired by a widening of what is thought possible on humane grounds, and by the idea that women themselves should be able to exercise a larger measure of control over their own destinies and the destinies of their families than has hitherto been thought right in patriarchally oriented societies. This shift in ideas has also been strongly influenced on the one hand by the conservative effects of Christian religious beliefs, and on the other hand by the revolutionary force of ideas engendered by the world-wide population explosion. As an example of what is demographically possible one can point to Japan, where the widespread availability of abortion, and its very low cost to the individual in monetary terms, has been a more potent force than propaganda for contraception in enabling the population size to be brought to equilibrium. In such countries as Japan psychiatric indications for termination of pregnancy will not need to be put in evidence; in such countries as Italy and Spain such indications, however urgent, would not be permitted to prevail against the total interdict on destroying the life of the embryo. In Britain the liberalizing tendency gathered momentum over a period of about two years to the point at which, against extremely dogged resistance both in Parliament and without, the Abortion Act of 1967 was passed. The Act came into force in 1968; its provisions are discussed below.

In Europe the countries that lead the advance are *Denmark* and *Sweden*. In these lands special laws legalize the termination of pregnancy on medical grounds, if the pregnancy is expected to cause serious impairment of the woman's health or risk to her life, on eugenic grounds, and on humane grounds in the case of pregnancy from rape or incest. Psychiatric medical grounds for termination include psychotic states, reactive depressive conditions with risk of suicide, and psychasthenic or neurasthenic conditions. Social circumstances are also to be taken into account in recommending termination on medical grounds. Women who have had too many children, or who cannot have more children without being adversely affected, may also have the pregnancy terminated on grounds of 'weakness' or 'weakness foreseen'.

Ekblad (1955) carried out a follow-up study of 479 women in whose cases pregnancy had been terminated on psychiatric grounds; the modal age was in the quinquennium 26–30, and 65 per cent. were married, 27 per cent. single. Nearly 60 per cent. of these had had symptoms of chronic neurosis or abnormal personality even before the pregnancy. None of them was suffering from an endogenous psychosis at the time of the abortion; psychasthenia and anxiety neuroses were the commonest diagnoses (36 per cent.), but no fewer than 201 out of the total of 479 were regarded as normal personalities. The commonest indication for abortion was that of weakness. The risk of illegal abortion or suicide was greatest in the women who had been deserted by their male partner, especially among the unmarried women. About a quarter of the women felt some self-reproach after the abortion, and about one in nine of them (54 in all) felt serious self-reproach or regretted it. If one regards this as a depressive reaction to the termination, then it was a very mild one, reaching a point at which working capacity was impaired in only 5 cases. It is noteworthy that the psychiatrically normal women were the ones least likely to show this unfavourable reaction afterwards: the greater the psychiatric indications for a legal abortion, the greater also was the risk of psychic sequelae. Ekblad concluded that termination of pregnancy could often be properly combined with sterilization, which would obviate the risks of repeated pregnancies and repeated legal terminations; where the women strongly desired sterilization it would have the least risk. In a later work (1961) Ekblad showed that sterilization was an extremely safe procedure psychiatrically in women over the age of 30 who already had one or more children.

The situation in *England*, *Wales* and *Scotland* has been transformed by the Abortion Act of 1967; the Act does not apply to Northern Ireland. The Act came into force in April 1968 for the rest of the United Kingdom. At the time of writing, the Minister's Regulations under the Act are yet to be made. The medical viewpoint on the provisions of this Act have been clearly explained in a memorandum from the Medical Defence Union, published in the *British Medical Journal* on the 23rd March, 1968, to which we now refer.

The Act is permissive only. Abortion remains a criminal offence under the Offences Against the Person Act of 1861; but exceptions are now created by which a registered medical practitioner will not be guilty of an offence when he takes steps to terminate a pregnancy in certain circumstances, as follows:

Section 1 (1). Two registered medical practitioners must form in good faith the opinion set out in the next succeeding paragraph and certify it in accordance with the regulations made under Section 2 of the Act.

The opinion must be to one or more of the following effects:
(a) that the continuance of the pregnancy would involve risk to the life of the pregnant woman greater than if the pregnancy were terminated; or
(b) that it would involve risk of injury to the physical or mental health of the pregnant woman greater than if the pregnancy were terminated; or
(c) that it would involve risk of injury to the physical or mental health of any existing children of the pregnant woman's family greater than if the pregnancy were terminated; or
(d) that there is substantial risk that if the child were born it would suffer from such physical or mental abnormalities as to be seriously handicapped.

Section 1 (2). In determining whether the continuance of a pregnancy would involve risk of injury to the physical or mental health of the pregnant woman or to the physical or mental health of any existing children of her family greater than the termination of the pregnancy the practitioner may take into account the pregnant woman's actual or reasonably foreseeable environment.

Section 1 (4). An abortion may be performed by a practitioner who is of the opinion, formed in good faith, that the termination is immediately necessary to save the life or to prevent grave permanent injury to the physical or mental health of the pregnant woman. In such a case a second medical opinion is not required by law, nor is there any restriction on the place where the operation may be performed. The regulations regarding certification and notification apply.

Any treatment for the termination of pregnancy, but not preliminary examinations, must be carried out in a National Health Service hospital or in a place approved for the purpose by the Minister of Health or by the Secretary of State for Scotland. The fact of the termination must be notified in a prescribed form to the Chief Medical Officer of the Ministry of Health or to the Chief Medical Officer of the Scottish Home and Health Department.

The Medical Defence Union memorandum gives useful opinions on a number of knotty points. Under Section 1 (1) 'any existing children' includes a single child, legitimate or illegitimate, or adopted, or a step-child, if part of the pregnant woman's family; nor must the child be under 21. A practitioner would, for instance, be entitled to take into account the existence of a severely handicapped adult child living with the mother, or indeed of any child who is dependent on her for health and well-being. 'Substantial risk' and 'seriously handicapped' are phrases not defined in the Act. They are undefinable, and it is probable that the courts would be at pains to avoid trying to define them. The question which would be asked is 'Was the doctor's opinion that there was or was not a substantial risk of serious physical handicap one which could not in good faith be formed by any reasonable doctor?' The risk, then, has to be a real risk and one which a practitioner acting responsibly and with reasonable care would not be justified in disregarding.

Under Section 4, the Act lays down that no person shall be under any legal duty to participate in any treatment authorized by the Act to which he has a conscientious objection, unless the treatment is necessary to save the life or prevent grave permanent injury to the physical or mental health of a pregnant woman. This does not absolve a practitioner from his general duty to his patient. If the doctor thinks that, were it not for his conscientious objection, it might be lawful to recommend or perform abortion, or if he feels that his conscientious objection makes it impossible for him to form an opinion on the question, then he should refer the patient to another doctor. It would be quite possible for a doctor to have a conscientious objection to abortion in one set of circumstances, e.g. 1 (1 d), and not in another set. It might also be right for a doctor to feel a conscientious objection in the circumstances of an individual case, though not generally.

The memorandum gives clear directions on the subject of consent. The written consent of the patient should always be obtained. If the patient is married and living with her husband the proposed abortion should be fully discussed with him if time and circumstances permit. If the reason for the proposed termination is risk of injury to the physical or mental health of any existing children of the family, a discussion with the husband would normally form part of the doctor's consideration of the 'actual or reasonably foreseeable environment'. If the pregnancy is to be terminated because its continuance would involve a risk to the mother's life or her physical or mental health it is not essential in law for the consent of the husband to be obtained. More difficult is the case in which the husband refuses to agree to an abortion which the doctor thinks justified under 1 (1 c or d). Such a refusal may not be thoughtless or selfish, and may arise from deeply felt convictions. In such a case it would be well to take further advice from colleagues; but in the end it will be the doctor's duty to make the decision. If in good faith he then terminates the pregnancy in spite of the husband's refusal, he will be most unlikely to find himself in serious trouble in the courts.

If the patient is single no consent is required from the putative father. It is not considered necessary in law to obtain the consent of the parents to terminate the pregnancy of an unmarried girl who is aged between 16 and 21; but it is thought that it would be prudent to get their consent if the girl were living with them. The doctor *must get the girl's authority before he seeks the consent of her parents*. Parental consent would certainly not be necessary if the girl had left home with her parents' agreement and was leading an independent life. *When the girl is under 16 her parents should always be consulted, even if she herself forbids the doctor to do so.* The written consent of the parents should be obtained, but their refusal should not be allowed to prevent a lawful termination to which the patient herself consents and which in the doctor's opinion is clinically necessary. Conversely, termination should never be carried out in opposition to the girl's wishes, even if the parents demand it.

Psychiatrists will wait with the keenest interest to see what the Minister's regulations will be, and how the new Act will work out in practice. It is most unlikely that there will not be a considerable easing of the pressures of fear and guilt which have in the past motivated the medical profession to a rigid conservatism in this field. However, changes in practice are not likely to be revolutionary. Beds in National Health Service hospitals are probably not going to be made available in sufficient numbers to cope with the numbers of terminations which will now qualify under the terms of the law, and with the demands which will be made by women seeking relief from a pregnancy which seems to them a disaster. Gynaecologists are not going to be willing to see their hospital practices disrupted; nor does it appear that, up to the time of writing, there has been more than a trickle of applications by nursing homes to be put on the Minister's list of places approved. One may see the number of illegal operations carried out annually being only slowly eroded. Nevertheless much good may be done. If the change in attitudes which can be expected has only the effect of bringing women with an unwanted pregnancy to proper medical consideration in the earliest weeks of the pregnancy, instead of at the last possible moment, the stress and even panic which till now has so often prevailed will give place to an emotional atmosphere more propitious for humane and reasonable decisions. When, in the fullness of time, the chemical methods of termination have been perfected and surgery is no longer needed except in unusual circumstances, this compromise Act can be expected to show its beneficent potentialities more fully.

CRIMINAL RESPONSIBILITY

England and Wales

In British procedure the psychiatric state of an offender is likely to be taken into consideration at almost every stage of the administration of justice. It will first arise *during the course of police inquiries*. If the offence is not a very serious one, and the offender is manifestly mentally ill and if furthermore the police can assure themselves that such arrangements are being made for the treatment of the offender that public safety and order are not jeopardized, it will frequently happen that no legal action for his punishment will be taken. On occasion even such offences as a theft, assault or a sexual misdemeanour, attributable to mental illness which has led to admission to a mental hospital, are not followed by prosecution. This is a discretionary function which, if not strictly based on law, is yet beneficial in action; and it merely means that law officers from the Director of Public Prosecutions down to senior police officers of local districts are open to the influence of commonsense. For law officers to permit the incident to be handled in this way the offence must be a relatively unimportant one; and in all other cases a prosecution will be begun, though it will not always lead to trial.

In *magistrates' courts* psychiatric issues are handled in a way very different from the treatment they are given in higher courts. In these courts of summary jurisdiction it is most unusual for sentences longer than six months to be imposed. It is, therefore, hardly surprising that the magistrate is not able, as is a jury in a higher court, to find that the accused was guilty of the act charged but was insane; for such a verdict would lead to the classification of the accused as criminally insane, and his detention as a criminal lunatic for an indeterminate time. It is, however, quite possible for the magistrate to find the accused not guilty on the grounds that he did not really know what he was doing. Alternatively, if the magistrate believes that the accused should be dealt with as an insane person, he can take appropriate action.

The Mental Health Act 1959 eased the path of judicial authorities in dealing with offenders along psychiatric lines. If the offender is convicted and is liable to imprisonment, the court may authorize his admission to hospital and detention there, or place him under guardianship. The court must be satisfied by the evidence, written or oral, of two medical practitioners that the offender is suffering from mental illness, psychopathic disorder (at any age, and not only under 21), subnormality or severe subnormality, and that it is of a nature or degree which warrants detention in hospital or guardianship; and the court must be of the opinion having regard to all the circumstances that the most suitable method of disposing of the case is by means of an order under the Act. A magistrates' court may make such an order without recording a conviction, if the accused is suffering from mental illness or severe subnormality, and the court is satisfied that he did the act or made the omission complained of. One of the two practitioners whose evidence is taken into account must be a practitioner approved for the purpose by a local health authority as having special experience in the diagnosis or treatment of mental disorders. A suitable hospital has to be found whose managers are willing to receive the offender as a patient, and he has to be conveyed there within 28 days.

This does not exhaust the powers of the magistrate. He can also, in appropriate circumstances, give a short sentence of imprisonment and at the same time order that the prisoner's mental condition be brought to the attention of the prison medical officer. If the man is insane, it is open to the prison doctor to certify him and arrange for his transfer to an ordinary mental hospital. The prison medical officer is also able to certify, and to transfer to a mental hospital, persons awaiting trial as well as those who have already been convicted.

Finally it is common practice for the magistrate to remand an accused person for a *medical report*, and when this report is to hand, to be influenced thereby in the sentence he gives. He may, for instance, forgo the award of punishment, but put the accused on *probation* on the undertaking that he will receive *medical treatment*.

At higher courts, such as an assize court, the mental disorder of the accused may be brought as a plea in bar of trial, and it is open to the representative of the accused to contend that his client is unfit to plead. For this to be sustained, the jury must be satisfied by the evidence, e.g. that of the prison officer who has had the man under observation, that he is unfit to understand the evidence, or to instruct his counsel, or suffers from some similarly fundamental disability. If this is found, then the jury may find that the accused is 'under disability', and the court will then order him to be admitted to such hospital as may be specified by the Secretary of State. The patient is then dealt with as if he were subject to a hospital order under Section 60 of the Mental Health Act, together with an order under Section 65 restricting his discharge without limitation of time.

It is to be noted that the requirements of the law are strict, and that only persons who are very grossly mentally disordered fall within them. Persons in a severe state of psychotic depression, or suffering from a delusional psychosis without gross disorganization of the personality, would not ordinarily be regarded as unfit to plead, if it were not that in practice the interpretation of the law, both by medical witnesses and judges, is much more liberal than the law itself. *Mental defectives* may also be found unfit to plead; idiots and imbeciles would certainly be deemed unfit, and many in the lower grades of feeble-mindedness would also escape trial in this way.

As a matter of practice, if the fitness of the accused to plead is put before the jury it is not usually in dispute. The opinion of the prison medical officer is as a rule accepted by the prosecution, the defence and the court itself without question. The report of the medical officer is made available to the defence, who then call him as a witness. It is not open to the prosecution to produce this evidence, but if they do not contest it, the judge will direct the jury to return a verdict accordingly. However, there was a remarkable case in 1950 (Rivett) in which two juries, under the guidance of the judge, found the accused fit to plead, although two medical practitioners on the first occasion, and three on the second, gave evidence that he was insane and unfit to plead. He was subsequently found guilty of murder, and was finally executed after a statutory inquiry had been held.

The third stage in the administration of justice at which the insanity of the accused may be considered is *at the trial* itself. The defendant may then enter a plea that he was not guilty, and support it by evidence of insanity. If the evidence is accepted, the jury will bring in a special verdict that he is not guilty by reason of insanity. This verdict may be reached when it has not been offered as a plea by the defence. An appeal to the Court of Criminal Appeal can be made, on grounds of law or fact (the Criminal Procedure (Insanity) Act, 1964). The law assumes that every man is sane until proof is brought to the contrary, and the onus of proof is therefore on the defence, who must show that at least a balance of probabilities is in favour of insanity. Furthermore it must be shown that the accused was *insane at the time the offence was committed.*

The degree of insanity required to sustain such a defence has been laid down. The way in which this was done is unique in the history of English common law, as the definition was not made by a Court of Justice in a specific case, which could then be quoted as a precedent, but by *Rules laid down by Judges* who were called on to consider purely theoretical issues. These Rules are generally called the *McNaughton Rules*, as they were occasioned by the trial in 1843 of a deluded murderer of the name of McNaughton*. Public interest in the case led to a debate in the House of Lords, and the House of Lords subsequently put five questions to the judges, whose answers constitute the Rules. This unusual procedure has undoubtedly been a stumbling-block in the way of progress in forensic psychiatry from 1843, when the Rules were framed, to the present day. For it crystallized a contemporary opinion, and isolated it from the continuous process of growth and development to which the common law is otherwise subject.

Those of the Rules which are now operative, when expressed in non-technical language,

---

* This is the spelling of McNaughton's one and only known signature (Morton, 1956).

affirm that the accused shall only be regarded as insane to the point of escaping responsibility for his criminal act, if he was labouring under such *a defect of reason, from disease of the mind, as not to know the nature and quality of the act, or if he did know it, not to know that what he was doing was wrong.* The precise meaning of these phrases has also been made clear by high authority. The accused must not have understood the physical nature of the act, e.g. he must have thought that in striking his victim with an axe he was chopping a piece of wood. Alternatively in not knowing that what he was doing was wrong he must (by disease of the mind) have been deprived of the knowledge that his act was against the law of the land.

These rules are, of course, exceedingly strict, so strict in fact that few people other than idiots, imbeciles and the delirious or grossly demented would be covered. In practice, however, *interpretation is as a rule much more liberal.* Judges may not even mention the Rules, or may fail to apply them strictly, if there would be little doubt on the evidence that the jury would regard the accused as insane. On the other hand, if the accused were more probably psychopathic than psychotic, and especially if his crime had aroused strong feelings of reprobation and horror, the trial judge might lay down the law as expressed in the Rules in a very precise and strict way, and hold the medical witnesses firmly to the point.

This *variable attitude on the part of judges* has led to curious anomalies. It has meant that there have been differences between judge and judge and from case to case, which are not in accordance with the spirit of justice. The personal reaction of the judge to the case before him, through its effect on the examination of medical witnesses, has probably influenced too much the verdicts of juries and the fate of prisoners. How far this reaction may deviate from one which a psychiatrist could welcome is shown, for instance, in the evidence given by the Lord Chief Justice to the Royal Commission on Capital Punishment in 1950. Referring to the trial of Thomas John Ley, Lord Goddard stated the strictly legal view-point clearly and uncompromisingly. He maintained that a man might be insane, and yet so wicked in his madness as to be properly sentenced and executed. A delusion might excuse a criminal act, if the act were legally excusable had the delusion been true. The significance of the delusion as evidence of an insanely distorted mind was not felt to be important.

Whereas insanity on arraignment is commonly found in cases where the accused has committed a less serious crime, a plea of not guilty on grounds of insanity is rarely made except in trials for murder. Nevertheless as murder is rare and other serious crimes are much more common, the number of such pleas in other cases is probably greater than in murder cases. Now that capital punishment has been suspended in Britain for a trial period of five years, changes in practice with regard to the defence plea of insanity will probably occur.

Although the McNaughton Rules speak of 'disease of the mind', they had always been held to cover also persons whose reason was impaired by mental deficiency. A different interpretation, however, was made by the judge in the trial of *Straffen* (in 1952), a feeble-minded killer of small girls, who had once previously been found unfit to plead and been confined in Broadmoor. He succeeded in escaping from this institution, and during his few hours of liberty strangled a young girl. Public opinion was deeply aroused about this case, and a full trial was a psychological necessity for the nation as a whole. His fitness to plead was therefore never questioned before trial. During the trial expert evidence of his mental deficiency was given and was not disputed by experts appearing for the prosecution. All medical experts, however, were compelled to agree that the accused was not suffering from a disease of the mind, in the accepted psychiatric usage of that term, and that he was not insane. After a very full discussion of the psychiatric aspects of his case, he was found guilty and sentenced, though subsequently reprieved.

At the present time, accordingly, it is difficult to know how far the mental defective is covered by the McNaughton Rules. Indeed the entire legal situation must be regarded as in flux, since the Mental Health Act of 1959 destroyed the entire concept of certifiable insanity, with which the medico-legal concepts of responsibility have been so integrally connected.

The way in which these various provisions relating to the legal treatment of the insane criminal in the case of murder, and the extent to which mental abnormality enters into such violent and unusual crimes, may be exemplified by *Home Office statistics* for the years 1900–48. During this period there were 7,318 murders known to the police, and in 1,635 cases (22 per cent.) the suspect committed suicide. Persons arrested for murder numbered 4,077; but only 3,061 were committed for trial at Assizes. Of these 654 were acquitted or not tried, 412 (13 per cent.) were found insane on arraignment, and a further 783 (26 per cent.) were found 'guilty but insane'. A further small proportion, about 4·5 per cent., having been sentenced to death, were certified insane in prison and respited to Broadmoor.

Sufficient mention has been made of the effect in criminal law of insanity and mental deficiency. It remains to consider lesser degrees of psychiatric abnormality. In England the position was radically changed in crimes of homicide by the *Homicide Act of 1957*. The principal effect of this Act was to classify murder into two classes, capital murder and murder, liability to the death penalty being restricted to the former. In addition the Act enlarged the concept of provocation and made special provision for suicide pacts, in reducing murder to manslaughter. However, the most important provision from the psychiatric point of view was to introduce into the English system the Scottish concept of *diminution of responsibility*. The clause in the Act runs:

(1) Where a person kills or is a party to the killing of another, he shall not be convicted of murder if he was suffering from such abnormality of mind (whether arising from a condition of arrested or retarded development of mind or any inherent causes or induced by disease or injury) as substantially impaired his mental responsibility for his acts and omissions in doing or being a party to the killing.

(2) On a charge of murder, it shall be for the defence to prove that the person charged is by virtue of this section not liable to be convicted of murder.

(3) A person who but for this section would be liable, whether as principal or as accessory, to be convicted of murder shall be liable instead to be convicted of manslaughter.

(4) The fact that one party to a killing is by virtue of this section not liable to be convicted of murder shall not affect the question whether the killing amounted to murder in the case of any other party to it.

Now that the capital penalty has been suspended for five years it is not clear how widely this section will be applied. It is possible that some killers who are brain injured or grossly psychopathic or of low intelligence will be dealt with under its terms.

In crimes other than homicide, no question of impaired responsibility arises. It is possible that the mental abnormality of a psychopath might be taken into consideration by the judge when passing sentence, especially if there is a prospect of medical treatment preventing a second offence. Judges, however, bear in mind the fact that psychiatric treatment is possible in prison as well as out of it.

Evidence of *neurotic illness*, of anomalies of personality and of emotional disturbance in the accused is quite frequently given in magistrates' and higher courts on behalf of persons accused of crimes of all degrees. The evidence is given with a view to *mitigation or variation of sentence*, and is not infrequently supported by a guarantee that the accused will, if given the opportunity, seek *medical treatment*. Thus a woman accused of shoplifting may bring evidence of suffering from a hysterical illness or from a menopausal emotional lability, or a homosexual accused of an act of indecency may find psychiatric support for a claim that his abnormality can be treated and the community thereby insured against a repetition of his act. Persons whose alcoholism or addiction to other drugs have brought them into trouble are very often excused punishment on agreeing to undertake medical treatment.

On these and similar occasions the medico-legal responsibility of the accused is not called in question. Magistrates and judges are, in practice, not ill-disposed to *medical evidence* along these lines if it is sensible and realistic. This attitude to psychiatry has become increasingly favourable in recent years, and modifications in the administration of justice in the last few years have enabled the referral of persons convicted of the less serious offences to hospitals and psychiatric clinics in increasing numbers. Once that referral has been made, a firm grip is usually taken of the case by social agencies; and probation officers and psychiatric social workers maintain a liaison, and collaborate with the hospital psychiatrist who assumes control.

Another point at which noteworthy advance has occurred is in the attempt to understand and to reform the *young offender*. Since 1905 juvenile courts have been set up, under magistrates specially appointed to the task. They are well equipped with social workers and can call on help from Child Care Committees, educational authorities and child-guidance clinics. Sessions are held in private in an informal atmosphere, and the entire emphasis is on the reformative rather than the deterrent and punitive aspects of treating the offender.

Scotland

Law and practice in Scotland is much the same as in England, with some important exceptions. If an accused person is insane, he will almost certainly be found so *before trial*, on arraignment, so that psychiatric defences in the trial, and the special verdict of 'guilty but insane' are comparative rarities. If such a defence is raised at trial, the McNaughton Rules are not often cited by judges as the definitive criterion of insanity, although by the normal process of development of the common law the spirit of those Rules informs the summing-up.

In the Scottish law relating to homicide the doctrine of diminished responsibility developed slowly in the common law, but is now firmly founded. If it can be proved that the accused is suffering from some condition which, though not rendering him legally insane, affects his powers of understanding or self-control, then it is possible to reduce the crime from murder to the lesser offence of culpable homicide. For this the sentence is for any period of detention up to life, and is usually one of seven to ten or more years. The convicted prisoner spends his term of imprisonment in an ordinary prison, and is not sent to a psychiatric institution. Scottish lawyers are convinced that the concept of diminished responsibility has enabled a greater measure of justice to be done in homicide cases. The psychiatrist, however, is inclined to doubt the wisdom of a system which removes from society for only a limited term what are probably among the most dangerous members of the community; and it would seem to him that an *indeterminate sentence* would be more realistic. As the law operates, psychopathic personality is not covered except in rare cases; the conditions which are most usually taken into account in this way are mild organic defects of the nervous system, such as may have been produced by alcohol, old meningitis or encephalitis, head injury, etc. Other patients who have escaped the death penalty by these means have also included mild paranoid states, and even persons suffering from severe neurotic conditions.

The provisions in *Scottish law* relating to *mental deficiency* differ somewhat from the English ones. Mental deficiency cannot be pleaded 'in bar of trial', and, theoretically, it cannot be pleaded 'in bar of sentence', i.e. to obtain the special verdict of 'guilty but insane'. In practice, however, it seems that the grossest degrees of deficiency would be accepted by the court as excusing from responsibility, and mental deficiency is often a strong element in a plea of 'diminished responsibility'. If such a plea were sustained, the judge could order, in lieu of punishment, that the prisoner be detained in an institution for mental defectives.

United States of America

As both law and practice vary widely in the United States from State to State, it is difficult to say much about the Union as a whole. Judges, counsel and jury seem to have a rather greater respect for psychiatry and the psychiatric witness in America than in England, although the attitude of psychiatrists to criminal responsibility and insanity also differs widely from centre to centre. In many States there are two (or even three) *degrees of murder*, only the first being met with a capital sentence; and in these States psychiatric evidence frequently has the effect of reducing the degree of the crime of which the accused is convicted, rather than leading to a verdict of 'guilty but insane' or its equivalent. Similarly, in the case of lesser crimes than murder, psychiatric evidence may be produced in order to secure a *mitigation of sentence*. In many, if not all, States the tendency is to find all insane persons unfit to plead, so that insanity is considered at a stage of the trial before the legal battle has started in earnest. This preliminary elimination has the effect of reducing the importance of legal tests of criminal responsibility.

The *powers of the jury* are much wider in the United States than in England, and the power of the judge to direct them correspondingly less. It seems, in fact, perfectly possible for the jury to ignore the directions of the judge entirely; and in most States the judge has to be careful in summing up merely to instruct the jury in the state of the law, leaving it to them to apply the law to the case under consideration. The legal definition of the various degrees of murder is vague, and to juries largely incomprehensible, so that they reach their verdicts probably largely influenced by thoughts of what would and what would not be an appropriate punishment.

After they were formulated in England, the McNaughton Rules came to be adopted in the United States as well, since American common law is itself an offshoot of English common law. In 30 States they are the sole criterion of criminal responsibility, and in all other States (with the exception of Vermont, New Hampshire and possibly Montana) and in the armed forces they are used in conjunction with other tests. However, the interpretation of the Rules often differs from that obtaining in England. In England it is no defence for the accused to have committed his act, as he believed, under the direct instruction of the Almighty if he still retained the knowledge that it was against the law of England; in America they set a less extreme value on the sacrosanctity of their laws, and concede that the Almighty's express commands might be deemed to take precedence.

An important additional test, which is nowhere relied on as the sole criterion of criminal responsibility, is in use in fifteen States and in the military and the federal jurisdiction, coupled with the McNaughton right/wrong test. The test applies to a defendant who may know the nature and quality of his act and may be aware that it is wrong, but who, nevertheless, was irresistibly driven to it by an overpowering impulse resulting from a mental condition; normal passions, such as blind anger or jealousy, do not qualify as a 'mental condition' in this sense.

A most interesting development has been the introduction of what is called the 'Product Rule'. In 1871 the New Hampshire Supreme Court rejected the McNaughton Rules as inadequate, stating that the verdict should be not guilty by reason of insanity, 'if the killing was the offspring or product of mental disease in the defendant'. New Hampshire was alone in the use of this formulation until 1954 when the United States Court of Appeals for the District of Columbia in the case of *Durham v. United States* held that 'an accused is not criminally responsible if his unlawful act was the product of mental disease or mental defect'. This corresponds very nearly to the strong subjective sense that psychiatrists have of what responsibility should mean; and it has an advantage over the irresistible impulse rule, in that it covers acts which are the result of slowly rather than suddenly formed resolutions, such as the acts of the melancholic and the paranoiac. Further precision has been given to the formulation by stating that the criminal act was the product of the mental disease or mental defect 'if the act would not have occurred except for the disease or defect; and that is so whether the disease or defect was the only cause of the act, or the principal one of several causes, or one of several causes'.

The American Bar Foundation (Lindman and McIntyre, 1961) discuss the McNaughton and these other formulations in an exhaustive and critical way. In general it seems to be agreed that the primary defect of the McNaughton test is that it rests 'on an entirely obsolete and misleading conception of the nature of insanity, since insanity does not only, or primarily, affect the cognitive or intellectual faculties, but affects the whole personality of the patient, including both the will and the emotions'. The McNaughton Rules are minimalistic; the great majority of patients in mental hospitals, even the grossly insane, know what conduct is proscribed by the rules of the hospital, and know that breach of the rules may result in the forfeiture of some privilege. Chief Judge Biggs of the U.S. Court of Appeals gave in a written judgement the opinion: 'The law, when it requires the psychiatrist to state whether in his opinion the accused is capable of knowing right from wrong, compels the psychiatrist to test guilt or innocence by a concept which has almost no recognizable reality.' However, conceptual and semantic difficulties arise in connexion also with the irresistible impulse rule and the product rule. There is likely to be no final escape from these sources of confusion, until rules of all kinds are given second place to the practical requirements of handling the offender in a way which, as a first priority, protects the public, and, as a second priority, provides him with the means of rehabilitation.

Partial responsibility is recognized in the United States only in the sense that in some States it has been definitely laid down by the courts that mental abnormality, short of that which exempts from responsibility, may negative deliberation and premeditation, and may thus reduce the crime of murder from first to second degree. Nine States have definitely rejected the concept, two have partly rejected it, six have accepted it, and in the remainder decisions are doubtful. However, in all States, regardless of the existence of a doctrine of diminished responsibility for murder, evidence of the psychiatric abnormality of the accused can be produced in trials for non-capital offences for the consideration of the judge when passing sentence.

The *administrative arrangements* which are made to obtain psychiatric evidence in those cases where it is relevant also vary widely and interestingly. In most States the *duty of obtaining such evidence* lies *with the court*, which may require a psychiatric examination of the accused on its own motion, or that of prosecution or defence. In New Hampshire the accused may be transferred to the State Hospital for examination at any stage of the trial. In several States, of which Massachusetts is one, official psychiatrists are appointed by the State to examine and report on accused persons in custody, and their evidence, being manifestly impartial, is treated with a respect which is not necessarily given to a medical witness hired by the defence.

In the *State of New York* an even more comprehensive system obtains. Here all prisoners accused of serious crimes, i.e. not only murderers, in whose case there is any doubt of psychiatric normality, are transferred for observation to Bellevue Hospital. All the necessary investigations are then made there under expert psychiatric supervision. In due course a very curious form of *psychiatric 'trial'* takes place in the Hospital, in public, with the representatives of the press being present. Witnesses can be sworn, and counsel for prosecution and defence can intervene and put questions. The decision on the psychiatric issues is made by the medical board, consisting of the senior staff of the Hospital, and is reported to the trial judge, who almost invariably accepts the findings without further inquiry. The psychiatrists who compose the board take a realistic rather than a theoretical attitude, and one which is in conformity with the general sense of current psychiatric opinion. They would, by and large, for instance, regard anyone suffering from a psychotic state, organic or endogenous and functional, even such a temporary one as a delirious reaction, as relieved of responsibility, but would not consider that psychopathic personalities or persons whose disturbance is of a neurotic kind were non-responsible.

As in England, the psychiatric aspect of a case can also be taken into consideration by the executive in considering the exercise of clemency. Again practice varies widely throughout the States. In some States the Governor regards himself as bound by the findings of his advisers; his advisers are the *Pardons Board*; this Board meets in public, and is often extremely sensitive to public fears of undue leniency; and the decision of psychiatric non-responsibility is made on the basis of the McNaughton Rules.

Scandinavian Countries

Forensic psychiatry in these countries presents an entirely different picture from the one described in the English-speaking world. In *Sweden*, for instance, medical opinion prevails in the courts, apparently without ill effect to the community, to an extent which would be impossible in England. In Stockholm there is a *Professor of Forensic Psychiatry*, and in the whole of the country there are fifteen *forensic psychiatric clinics*. Evidence on the psychiatric aspects of a crime is given in the courts by specialists in the service of the State, or those who have been called upon for a particular trial. Psychiatrists act as counsellors in the courts, i.e. as subsidiary judges and aids to the trial judge himself.

The courts may ask for a psychiatric examination of the accused, not only if it is suspected that the crime was committed in a mentally abnormal state, but also if *medical evidence* is needed to help decide *what penal treatment would be the most appropriate*.

No legal definition of psychiatric non-responsibility is used as a yardstick. Quite simply, the perpetrator of a crime is excused from punishment if the crime was committed under the influence of psychosis, or mental deficiency, or another mental abnormality of such a fundamental nature that it must be considered to be on a par with a psychosis. Thus the severer sequelae of brain injuries, encephalitis, etc., and very severe forms of psychopathy will be so considered, especially if they have already in the past interfered with a normal social life, for instance causing repeated admission to a mental hospital. The very concept of non-responsibility is hardly taken into account, the real grounds for excusing a man from punishment being that, in his case, *punishment is an irrational method of treating him*, his proper treatment being, whether therapeutic or solely custodial, best left in medical hands. The administrative method of dealing with such cases is not different from that employed for other patients who are a social danger, but have not committed crimes, and admission to psychiatric hospital or out-patient department is the mode of disposal.

Just as the concept of non-responsibility is in desuetude, so also is the concept of diminished responsibility. Nevertheless *psychiatric findings* can be *taken into account* in mitigating sentence, and may have the effect of reducing a term of imprisonment, if the psychiatric evidence is such as to suggest no added danger to the public. Minor degrees of enfeeblement of intelligence are often taken into consideration in this way; and youths of dull intelligence may be given a suspended sentence and put on probation or recommended for treatment in a youth institution.

In harmony with their generally rather severe attitude towards *alcoholism*, the Swedes have not liberalized the attitude taken to crimes committed in a state of intoxication so much as in other psychiatric fields. Delirium tremens or any other alcoholic psychosis is treated exactly as any other psychotic state; but where it is a case of simple intoxication, the crime is regarded as on a par with crimes committed in a sober state. This is the position in England and America, where it is considered that if a man is responsible for making himself drunk then he is responsible for any crime he commits in a drunken state. The same attitude prevails in Norway and Denmark. Psychotic alcoholics in addition to those suffering from pathological intoxication are regarded as not responsible.

What has been said about the general attitude to the psychiatric aspects of crime in Sweden is also largely true of *Denmark and Norway*. In Denmark there are now four clinics of forensic psychiatry. Medical opinion almost always prevails in the courts, but its effect may be to substitute for punishment a period of *subjection to safety measures*. This may tend to reduce the enthusiasm with which the defence will be inclined to seek for a psychiatric examination. The psychotic subject is not sentenced to any form of punishment, but will be sent to a hospital. The greatest freedom is allowed in Norway to the medical staff of the hospital, who may discharge the patient from hospital care on their own decision without consulting the Department of Justice. In Norway, psychopaths are regarded as responsible for their acts, but may be subjected to 'safety measures' in lieu of, or in addition to, any punishment. These safety measures include various forms of supervision, up to and including detention in an institute, the requirement to live, or not to live, in any given district, or to take some special type of work, or to board with a given family, or to forgo alcohol. Both in Denmark and Sweden there are *special institutes*, under medical direction, for the custody and treatment *of criminal psychopaths* (see Chapter III, p. 183). Denmark makes considerable use of *indeterminate sentences*; but in Norway the 'safety measures' are imposed for a stated time, mostly three to five years.

In Denmark the concepts of responsibility and non-responsibility are still recognized to some extent, but medical opinion, as expressed in court by psychiatrists (officially appointed to carry out this function) largely decides the issue. Legal tests of the McNaughton type are not applied, and all that is necessary is to show insanity or 'a condition comparable to

this', or weakmindedness to a higher degree. There is no concept of diminished responsibility. If, however, it is shown that the accused is mentally underdeveloped, or that his mental
faculties are weak or disturbed (which includes sexual abnormality), the court will decide,
on the basis of medical evidence, whether he is fit for punishment, or should serve his
sentence in an institution, e.g. for psychopaths. In the case of minor abnormalities punishment may be mitigated, or even altogether spared. It may also be replaced by security
measures such as are used in Norway and Sweden. Provisions exist for the review of any
sentence passed. A man who is interned in the psychopathic institute at Herstedvester or at
Horsens for an indeterminate term, may by his progress under occupational therapy,
discipline and psychotherapeutic help, graduate by degrees to assigned work at a farm
outside the walls, and eventually to freedom. At this institute, which is under medical
direction, a considerable use is made of castration for sexual offenders, but not as a punishment.

Capital punishment does not exist in Scandinavian countries, which means that conflicts
between the legal and medical viewpoints in an acute form and with maximum publicity do
not occur. Furthermore in cases of homicide there is less temptation, than in countries
where there is a death penalty, to run a defence of insanity where the psychiatric case is
weak, but no other line of defence is likely to succeed.

Other European Countries

No other country in Europe is burdened with a formulation of the McNaughton type,
and the decision whether the mental abnormality of the accused was of sufficient degree to
relieve him of the liability to punishment is in effect left to the jury to decide on the medical
and other evidence. In Holland, where juries do not exist, the decision is left to the criminal
court. The court may substitute punishment partly or completely by medical treatment,
or by expert nursing and re-education. In such cases the patient is placed for an indefinite
time at the disposal of the state authority, either conditionally or unconditionally.

Formulations vary from country to country. In the *Netherlands* no punishment is
imposed on the person 'who commits an act for which he cannot be held responsible
because of backward development or unsound mind'. In *Belgium* the phrase used is 'a
state of insanity or severe feeblemindedness or severe mental unbalance, rendering him
incapable of normally controlling his actions'; the insertion of the word 'normally' by the
Act of 1964 into the provisions of the old Social Defence Act of 1930, is regarded as a wise
addition. If the accused is found not responsible, the sentence is for an indeterminate
period; the duration of commitment depends on the evolution of the illness as judged by a
Commission of Social Defence, a body consisting of a magistrate, a lawyer and a psy-
chiatrist-anthropologist. If there is reason to think that this Commission proposes to
release the abnormal offender too soon for the safety of society, the prosecutor can appeal
to a higher Commission. This new provision by the 1964 Act has been found very necessary,
because previously some Commissions were over-lenient, and many crimes were committed
by recidivists who had been set free again and again.

In *Switzerland* a person is non-responsible who through disease of the mind, idiocy
or serious disturbance of consciousness ('grave altération de conscience') was unable to
appreciate at the time of the act that it was wrong, or to act according to his appreciation.
In *France* the statute reads, 'There is no crime or misdemeanour when the accused was
in a state of insanity at the time of the act or in the event of his having been compelled by a

force which he was unable to resist.' France is the only European country to make use of the concept of irresistible impulse.

In *Germany* the criminal code laid down as long ago as 1871 states that: 'an act is not punishable when the doer was at the time of committing the act in a state of unconsciousness or morbid disturbance of mental activity by which a decision of free will was excluded.' The awkward concept of free will was found unsatisfactory, and in 1934 the paragraph of the code was altered to 'when the doer at the time of the deed was, because of disturbance of consciousness, because of morbid disturbance of mental activity, or because of mental weakness [a term which includes mental deficiency and mental deterioration] unable to have insight into the impermissible nature of his act or to act according to this insight'.

In general, acute *alcoholic intoxication* is excluded from similar alterations of consciousness produced by other causes, and provides no relief of responsibility. Germany is unusual in providing that when a man gets drunk and commits a crime in a state in which he can be held to be irresponsible, he can be punished for drinking. The court can then order his detention in an institution where he can be given withdrawal treatment and be rehabilitated and educated to an orderly life. *Switzerland* is another exception, and medical witnesses tend to take the attitude that alcoholic intoxication is, forensically, equivalent to similar states of different aetiology. If the state of intoxication is a mild one, then there is some degree of diminished responsibility; if it is severe, then there may be total abrogation of responsibility. There has, however, to be some concession to the popular opinion that alcoholic intoxication is a normal state, and that alcoholically intoxicated persons are normally responsible; for this reason the criteria applied tend to be rather stricter in alcoholic than in other intoxications.

In *Switzerland*, the forensic *conception of insanity* or mental disorder is rather wider than in most other European countries. The psychopath who commits a crime in a hysterical twilight state may be regarded as totally non-responsible. Public opinion, at least in the Canton of Zürich, tends to move even ahead of medical views; and it is not infrequently the case that whereas the medical expert in his report has stated that the prisoner is responsible, the court declares him of diminished responsibility.

In nearly all European countries the concept of *diminished responsibility* is recognized, and has the effect of diminishing the severity of punishment. In Germany, for instance, rather illogically, the degree to which punishment may be mitigated is to that level which would be appropriate if the crime had been attempted but not actually committed. In some countries the mitigation of sentence is compensated for by the imposition of safety measures, but this is not always the case. In Belgium, we are informed, it is possible for a dangerous psychopath to be set free sooner than an ordinary criminal, which is felt to be a defect in the penal system. Even where special administrative measures are not taken for dealing with the juvenile criminal, *youth* is accepted as a factor which diminishes or even abolishes responsibility. In the German formulation this is expressed in a way which makes youth·largely equivalent to mental illness or mental defect: the young person between the ages of fourteen and eighteen is not punishable if, at the time of the act, he was unable, according to his mental and moral development, to understand that the act was unlawful or to direct his will according to this understanding.

In most countries, *psychiatric evidence* is obtained *at the instance of the court*; impartial experts are appointed to examine the prisoner, and it is rare for conflicts of medical evidence to arise. In Belgium, however, separate experts are commissioned by the prosecution and the defence, by the latter with the aid of a special fund if necessary, and battles in court on the English model may arise. This may also occur in France. In Germany, Austria and Switzerland, the usual practice is to order the admission of the prisoner suspected of mental abnormality into a hospital which is often a University Psychiatric Clinic for an observation period not exceeding six weeks. It is the duty of the Professor of Psychiatry (or the Director of the Hospital, if it is not a university centre) and his medical staff to observe and investigate the case, and report back to the court. The system is clearly of great advantage to psychiatry, as it not only assures for the court the expert opinion of the best authority, but also accustoms the students at an early stage to the consideration of forensic psychiatric problems, which are often of great clinical interest.

NEW LEGISLATION IN RELATION TO DRUG ADDICTION IN THE UNITED KINGDOM

Two of the recommendations made by the Brain Report (1965) required legislation and the appropriate sets of regulations became law on April 16th, 1968.

One of these (Supply to Addicts) gives effect to the recommendation that the *prescribing* of heroin and cocaine should be restricted. The regulations prohibit medical practitioners from administering, supplying or prescribing *heroin or cocaine* to a person addicted to any drug (or from authorizing anyone else to do so) except under a licence issued by the Secretary of State.

The regulations do not interfere with the right of any medical practitioner to give heroin or cocaine to any patient for the relief of pain due to organic disease or injury. This means that a practitioner without a licence may treat an addict with heroin or cocaine if it is to relieve pain arising from organic disease or injury but in no other circumstances.

The Secretary of State proposes to grant licences to consultants and to medical staff of named grades under their supervision who are on the staff of institutions where there are facilities for in-patient or out-patient treatment of addicts. A licence will be valid only for the purposes of prescribing at *named hospitals*, and in those places only the licensed doctor may authorize (in writing) a nurse, other doctor or registered pharmacist to administer and supply, but not prescribe, heroin and cocaine. He may not authorize doctors at other hospitals or general practitioners to give these drugs to addicts, even in 'emergencies'. The regulations are carefully framed to prevent exploitation by addicts attempting to obtain drugs in excess of their requirements.

A person is to be regarded as addicted to a drug for the purpose of the regulations 'if, as a result of repeated administration he has become so dependent upon it that he has an overpowering desire for its administration to be continued' (Ministry of Health and Home Office, 1968).

When the regulations were drawn up it was foreseen that situations might arise where a doctor without a licence was in doubt whether a person he attended was to be regarded as addicted for the purposes of the regulations; for example, he might be undecided whether the drug was required for the relief of distress arising from dependence or from other illness or injury in an addicted subject. Accordingly the Minister put into operation the Interdepartmental Committee's recommendation that a *panel of doctors* 'representing a wide variety of medical and surgical interests should be formed to advise doctors who are in doubt' (Ministry of Health, 1968). The members of the panel as now constituted are widely spread geographically and are to be consulted individually.

The other set of regulations (Notification of Addicts) requires all doctors to *notify* particulars of addicts whom they attend to the Chief Medical Officer of the Home Office. The notification is to be by letter and the particulars to be supplied are set down. It is to be sent to the Home Office within *seven days* of diagnosing the patient as being an addict. Medical Officers treating heroin addiction use a special form H.S. 2A/1 for the purpose of identifying heroin addicts.

This statutory notification is designed to prevent duplication of supplies of heroin or other dangerous drugs to heroin addicts. Therefore, when a patient attends for treatment of heroin addiction who is not known to the hospital staff, the first step is to ask the Home Office to check whether this patient is already receiving supplies from another hospital with licensed staff. If this should be the case, the notifying doctor should get in touch with the other hospital and the two doctors should agree whether there are sufficient reasons for transferring the patient. (The Home Office *must* be informed of all changes in the situation of an addict such as transfer.) During the time it may take for this procedure to be completed it is recommended that the addict should be treated with a substitute drug.

It should be noted that, although the Act restricts the prescribing of heroin and cocaine only, it requires that *addicts dependent on any of the drugs* listed in the 1965 schedule of dangerous drugs *be notified*. These preparations include opium alkaloids and their derivatives, semi-synthetic derivatives and surrogate of opium, a wide range of substances structurally distinct from, but with a pharmacologically similar action to morphine (e.g. methadone, pethidine, phenoperidine); cocaine and ecgonine derivatives; and extracts or tinctures of cannabis. The Ministry has issued a memorandum (F/D 121/20) on the new regulations outlining the facilities now available and giving advice on the treatment of addicts when clinics are closed. In the Metropolitan area a special telephone service has been set up to provide information to doctors and hospitals, right round the clock, about the out-patient services available at any particular moment.

The addicts' routine of a daily visit to the pharmacist to collect a daily dose is not suitable for one group which used to be typical and has now become exceptional. These are the few elderly therapeutic addicts. These should be referred by their general practitioner to a licensed doctor who can arrange for a pharmacist to dispense heroin at suitable intervals, not exceeding a month, on prescriptions issued by the hospital.

CHAPTER XIV

SOCIAL PSYCHIATRY

INTRODUCTION

THE possible importance of social factors in the causation of mental illness has been recognized for many centuries. In discussing 'the knowledges that respect the mind', Francis Bacon emphasized study of the relationship between society and the individual as one of the four main lines of investigation requiring development: 'philosophie or humanitie . . . have two parts: the one considereth man segregate or distributively; the other congregate or in society.' Pinel, in the late eighteenth century, was well acquainted with the higher incidence of mental disorder in the single as compared with the married; and in 1842 Samuel Hitch, one of the founders of the Royal Medico-Psychological Association, mentioned cooperation in 'collecting statistical information relating to insanity' as one of the purposes of founding the association. Esquirol (1838) expressed the view that revolutionary social change and the 'bouleversement dans la position sociale de beaucoup des individuels' had contributed to the causation of insanity.

During the past few decades both investigators and clinicians have given increasing attention to the social factors related to psychiatric illness. The term social psychiatry has gained currency as a description of a number of related and overlapping disciplines and activities, whose ultimate aim is to identify the social factors that contribute to the causation of mental disorder, and so to prevent psychiatric illness or reduce its prevalence.

In this field the epidemiological approach concerns itself with investigation of the frequency with which definable forms of psychiatric disorder occur in carefully delineated populations. Once reliable measures of prevalence and incidence have been established, attempts can be made to relate them to measures, as precise as the situation permits, of the way of life or 'culture' of communities or groups. They can be related also to indices of social change and classical sociological variables such as social class, mobility, isolation, kinship and economic status. The help of social scientists has been essential in these endeavours and their cooperation with psychiatrists in investigation and clinical work has become an increasingly common feature of the psychiatric scene, particularly in the United States and to some extent also in Great Britain and Scandinavian countries.

Activities on the smaller scale of the mental hospital community and the immediate social environment in which its patients live have also increased at a rapid pace, particularly since 'open door' policies began to develop about 20 years ago. Energy and enthusiasm are given to the prevention of permanent institutionalization and of the artefacts of apathy, inertia and dependence partly created by it, to the development of 'community care' as an alternative to hospitalization, to the coordination of all health and welfare services concerned with the treatment, support and after-care of psychiatric patients, and to the comparative assessment of different forms of care, so as to achieve optimal use of existing facilities. As a result there has been much more interest in the environment of the psychiatric patient as an important instrument in treatment as well as a possible factor in the causation or perpetuation of illness.

As Ødegaard (1962) has pointed out, although the psychiatrist is more concerned with individuals, he must be prepared to investigate groups and populations if he is to arrive at knowledge that is reliable and objective. 'The very uniqueness of each psychiatric observation makes deductive reasoning from individual cases rather hazardous and the need of some statistical control is always felt—or ought to be felt. Psychiatry is forced to study groups and populations *because* it deals with individuals—not *in spite of* this fact.' The logic of this is compelling. Moreover, if the psychiatrist has to study populations to arrive at general laws applicable to the individual case, his samples should be as free as possible from the bias conferred by the many forms of selection that operate before patients arrive at the clinic.

Reid (1959) puts the case for the application of epidemiological method in even more forceful terms '. . . since many mental diseases are "crowd" diseases, as in typhoid fever, the epidemiological methods developed there for the study of infectious diseases apply equally in the investigations of the individual's reaction to his surroundings and of the varied patterns of mental disorder'. Here it could be objected, however, that the statement assumes much that needs to be established with the aid of empirical investigation. One must doubt the extent to which infectious 'crowd' diseases such as typhoid fever can provide satisfactory models for mental illness. There is little in what has yet been brought to light in this field to encourage the view that the host of environmental relationships that obtain in relation to infectious disease are replicated even approximately by the interaction between the individual and his social environment in the generation of mental illness.

Perhaps the best known attempt to describe the causation of a psychiatric phenomenon in wholly sociological terms was the classical study conducted by Durkheim (1897) on suicide. Durkheim considered that the suicide rate reflected patterns of social relationship within communities and that individual mental disorder had little bearing upon it. To substantiate this viewpoint he cited the example of the Jews who showed a high prevalence of mental disorder but a relatively low incidence of suicide. Durkheim held that the essential cause of suicide was to be sought in a weakening of the link between the individual and the social group to which he belonged; whenever the links that united individuals into groups with common religious and other beliefs and aspirations were loosened the suicide rate tended to rise. This could result from conflict between different cultural groups within society, as in the case of racial or immigrant minorities separated from the host communities in which they live, or from social disorganization and economic hardship which frustrate the individual's aspirations leading to 'anomic' suicide. Alternatively the loosening of family or social controls might foster a morbid individualism which tended in its turn to cause 'egoistic' suicides. There was also the 'altruistic suicide' such as that of the aged Eskimo whose separation from his community arose from his awareness that he was a burden to others. Durkheim's investigation was an epoch-making one but he was unaware of many of the pitfalls that beset the investigator in this kind of study. In particular he was too ready to make inferences from statistical correlations to causes; he made little attempt to disentangle causes from consequences and was oblivious of the complex ramifications of the sociological variables he was investigating. However, despite these limitations, some of his findings have been amply confirmed and, in a study of suicide in London carried out by Sainsbury (1955), the pattern of incidence, which proved to have been strikingly consistent over three decades, was very much as Durkheim might have predicted it. For example, significant correlations were found between suicide and indices of social isolation, social mobility and the divorce and illegitimacy rates. Suicide remains the outstanding example of a psychiatric phenomenon to which disturbance of social relationships makes a contribution. Interesting information has also been coming to light recently in relation to the social dimensions of attempted suicide. However, among the causes of suicide the relative importance of mental illness, physical disability, social and economic factors and personality disorder remains to be determined.

Community studies of mental disorder have proved helpful in setting problems in better perspective and in defining more clearly the lines along which investigation should proceed. The relative importance of a whole range of possible factors may be wrongly estimated when focused by the distorting lens of hospital selection and admission procedures. Thus aged people admitted to hospital are very often unmarried, isolated or recently bereaved and their symptoms often appear to be related to these vicissitudes. However, enquiries in a representative population have shown that the extent to which the old person is in contact with others, together with other aspects of his social predicament, his physical and mental health, are strands within a complicated matrix of causes and effects which also include genetic predisposition, pre-morbid personality traits, biological changes with age and economic factors. Isolation emerges as having little relationship with illness and often reflecting a style of life fashioned by lifelong personality traits. (Kay *et al.*, 1964*b*; Garside *et al.*, 1965).

Extension of enquiries into the community can help to round off the clinical picture of disease, and the completed picture may serve to reveal features of predictive value; in old people simple memory defect of 'benign' or 'normal' type proved in one community study to be correlated with a significant excess in mortality (Kay *et al.*, 1966). In other cases enquiries may have helped to define earlier stages in the development of illness or may show a psychiatric problem to be of unsuspected dimensions. It is clear for example, that only a small fraction of the neurotic illness prevalent in the community can be dealt with by hospital psychiatric services (Shepherd *et al.*, 1966). Our present rather scanty success in pinning down social causes of specific mental disorders has been put down to the many practical obstacles: the difficulty of securing agreement about diagnostic criteria among different workers, the problems of defining what constitutes a 'case' among the neuroses and personality disorders, and the crudeness of the classical sociological variables of class, income, mobility, and isolation. There is also the problem of enlisting the cooperation of people in the community at large; they cannot be as strongly motivated as sick people to provide information that is detailed, precise and candid.

The problems do not differ except perhaps in degree from those faced by epidemiologists in any field of enquiry. Psychiatrists differ in their diagnostic practices; but variations in procedure, convention and nomenclature and semantic difficulties are responsible for this, and not the inherent indefiniteness of the phenomena they are studying. Recent enquiries have shown that with the aid of operational definition of terms, preliminary discussion and detailed instructions to secure consistency in examination and inference, a satisfactory measure of agreement can be achieved in relation both to diagnostic decisions and judgements on individual clinical items (Wing *et al.*, 1967). To some extent such achievements ought to be capable of translation into the epidemiological field.

The crudeness of the tools available for evaluating social variables seems to be a more important limitation. It is a plausible view that social change occurring at too rapid a pace to permit gradual adaptation is a cause of some forms of mental disorder. However, if the example of rapid industrial change is taken (and this could be described in terms of a move from agricultural to industrial employment which is a relatively objective index) the immense complexity of the problem and the difficulty of defining relevant variables for investigation in relation to mental disorder become apparent. Increasing affluence and changes in pattern of life go hand in hand with rising social and geographical mobility, a move into urban environments with less cohesion than rural ones, and a decline in the strength of traditional and religious supports. Economic advancement may bring increased security and leisure often at the cost of increased monotony and boredom. Large numbers may achieve freedom from want from the cradle to the grave but their lives may lose at the same time most of the ingredients that make for challenge, adventure and the need to strive to overcome obstacles. Nor can such a process be described in sociological terms alone. Populations isolated and inbred over many generations migrate and interbreed with one another, and genetic constitutions adapted to one way of life are perhaps being exposed to a different one. Moreover, comparisons between rural and urban populations in such a setting may yield misleading results; the former will be survival populations, the latter swollen by recent migrants. Nor will either be comparable with its own rates at a previous time in respect of the prevalence or incidence of psychiatric disorder.

A further difficulty is created by the possibility that it is perhaps a predisposition to some forms of illness rather than mental disorder as such that is to a variable degree influenced by social and familial factors. The transition into illness often occurs in an abrupt manner and this may be decided by stresses that have a large element of randomness in their incidence. Exposure to the latter apart, the neurotic person may not differ from a multitude of others who remain well. However, as there are no reliable measures of vulnerability or of the personal experiences that have fashioned it, the problem of uncovering social contributory factors presents difficulties. These may be among the reasons why explanations of mental disorder, drug addiction, alcoholism and suicide as being forms of escape into oblivion from the alienation, competitiveness, materialism or aimless vacuity of modern industrial society appear so plausible, and yet so little success has been achieved so far in defining social contributions to causation in psychiatry. The results have perhaps been most striking in relation to suicide and delinquency. In the case of most forms of mental disorder studied, however, sociological and epidemiological enquiry has defined social correlates that have proved to be consequences rather than causes of illness.

The association between sociological and clinical variables defined by epidemiological research therefore rarely permits an unequivocal interpretation. More frequently, the work of the social psychiatrist only helps one to define problems which then have to be investigated by other techniques, usually the more detailed, flexible and extended enquiries of a clinic. The reciprocal feed-back between the findings of social and clinical psychiatry and the combined investigation of biological and sociological variables may yield results superior to those achieved by either type of enquiry independently.

The epidemiological approach has brought greater methodological rigour into the field of psychiatry as a whole. The insistence on careful design of enquiries and on precise definition of terms, the development of objective and reliable indices for the phenomena under investigation which have been characteristic of the best of epidemiological work have contributed to self-criticism and discipline in clinical and scientific work.

In the view of some observers, however, the possibilities of applying the findings of social psychiatry in theory and practice already go well beyond what has been envisaged in this outline.

'There are thus two ways of regarding illness. One way sees it as a series of episodes. Health is interrupted by encounters with bacteria, banquets, fast-moving vehicles, or what you will; from each of these we recover, with or without the help of a doctor, until we meet one which proves to be the last. The other way sees these episodes as imbalances in the process by which individuals and societies maintain themselves as dynamic systems and thus as failures of regulation. This view focuses attention not so much on the need to correct the imbalance as on the need to fortify the regulator which allowed it to occur. I will call it a "systemic view", since the word systematic has collected a wider meaning. A systemic view is more sophisticated than an "episodic view"; life—individual or collective—should be more than bumping from one episode to another.

'None the less, both views are needed. The hospital isolates the episode, each beginning, not with onset, but with admission and ending within weeks or days in death or discharge—discharge, not recovery of health, still less restoration to the community of the well. Public health stresses the systemic view; it is a continuous exercise in regulation' (Vickers, 1965).

However attractive one finds this view, one must remember that more facts are needed. The hypothesis that mental disorder can be regarded as the expression of a failure of regulation of interactions between the individual and society has to be separately tested in relation to each form of mental disorder. However, there are hazards run by the psychiatrist who spends his time dealing with individuals, for he may fail to take adequate account of the environment in other than a very immediate and limited sense. Baroness Wootton (1959) has emphasized this in relation to the problems of delinquency and mental subnormality: 'By tracing the springs of antisocial behaviour to the individual rather than to the social environment we are, after all, only following what has long proved itself to be the path of least resistance . . . always it is easier to put up a clinic than to pull down a slum, and always it is tempting to treat the unequal opportunities of the slum and of the privileged neighbourhoods as part of the order of nature.'

No attempt will be made in this chapter to cover the whole subject of social psychiatry. What will be attempted is a survey of those areas most relevant to clinical work, and those in which growing points show promise for the advance of clinical knowledge. In this wide region it is easy to get lost without the help of reliable guides. The following texts are suggested as likely to prove helpful to the as yet uninstructed reader:

Mental Health in Modern Society (1948): ed. T. A. C. Rennie and L. E. Woodward; Commonwealth Fund: Oxford University Press. *Mental Health and Mental Disorder, a Sociological Approach* (1955): ed. Arnold M. Rose; Norton, N.Y. *Explorations in Social Psychiatry* (1957): ed. A. H. Leighton, J. A. Clausen and R. N. Wilson; Tavistock Publications, London. *Causes of Mental Disorders: a Review of Epidemiological Knowledge, 1959*: Milbank Memorial Fund, 1961. *The Burden on the Community: the Epidemiology of Mental Illness; a Symposium* (1962): Nuffield Provincial Hospitals Trust: Oxford University Press. *Stirling County Study of Psychiatric Disorder and Sociocultural Environment* Vols. I–III (1959–63) A. H. Leighton and collaborators; Basic Books: New York. *Suicide in London* (1955) P. Sainsbury. Maudsley Monograph I. Institute of Psychiatry: London. *Attempted Suicide: its Social Significance and Effects* (1958) E. Stengel, N. G. Cook and I. S. Kreeger. Maudsley Monograph 4. Institute of Psychiatry: London.

STUDIES OF PREVALENCE AND INCIDENCE

Reliable figures for the prevalence and incidence of psychiatric disorder are a basic requirement for the planning of psychiatric services in any population. They are also necessary for many forms of biological and epidemiological enquiry. Incidence figures reveal the operation of the underlying causal agents more directly than prevalence rates which are influenced also by the many contingencies that affect the duration of an attack of illness. It is only in recent years that population studies of psychiatric illness have employed an adequate standard of rigour in estimating the rate at which disorders occur and their relation to social variables.

The figures recorded vary with the criteria applied for the assessment of psychiatric disturbance. In the Stirling County study (Leighton *et al.*, 1963) in which the presence of 'significant psychiatric symptoms and the functional impairment they produced' were assessed, 20 per cent. of the population were judged to be suffering from psychiatric disorder leading to significant impairment of functioning; and in the Midtown Manhattan Study (Srole *et al.*, 1962) which employed similar criteria, 23 per cent. were thought to be suffering. Four-fifths of the population surveyed in both these enquiries showed some symptoms of emotional disturbance. Other American population studies applying more conventional psychiatric criteria arrived at lower figures such as that of Lemkau (1941–43; Baltimore) who found 60 per thousand. Pasamanick (1959) in the same city estimated 93 per thousand.

The first large-scale British investigation conducted on a 12·5 per cent. sample of the population of 46 general practices in Greater London produced findings that came close to the lower American figures. For formal psychiatric illness the prevalence rate during the 12 months' period covered by the survey was 102 per thousand persons at risk, while the total prevalence rate (which included identified emotional disorders associated with physical illness and psychosocial problems) was 140 per thousand. The inception rate was 52 per thousand. Shepherd *et al.* (1966) concluded that between a tenth and a fifth of the total population were mentally ill or emotionally disturbed. Women predominated in a ratio of nearly 2 to 1. After the age of 25 years age-specific prevalence rates changed little for males; those for women were highest in the middle years (25–64) and declined gradually after the age of 65. Inception rates reached their peak for both sexes between 25 and 45 then declined, suggesting that the increased prevalence in middle age was due to an accumulation of chronic cases rather than to any large augmentation by new illness. In more than half the cases the disorder was classed as chronic, that is, as having persisted continuously for more than one year.

In a number of respects the picture of prevalence was at variance with that derived from studies of hospital admissions. Thus there was no clear association with social class, nor did one see the excess of single people characteristic of hospital populations. Over 60 per cent. of the patients given a formal psychiatric diagnosis were classified as neurotic, psychoses accounting for less than 5 per cent. The finding in this study that not more than about 10 per cent. of cases identified are referred to psychiatrists agrees with that in several other enquiries (Rawnsley and Loudon, 1962; Kessel, 1960; Taylor and Chave, 1964). It is clear that in the future development of mental health services the family doctor should play a more prominent part in the treatment of mental disorder and that the alternative of extension and proliferation of psychiatric services is neither logical nor practicable.

Two findings of possible aetiological significance emerged from this study. The first was the association between emotional disorder and a high demand for medical care; there was evidence to suggest that this arose from a real association between mental ill-health and physical illness rather than a high demand for care due to the patients' attitude to health. In the case of mental disorder in old age the association is now well established on the basis of both clinical and pathological population studies (Roth and Kay, 1956; Kay and Bergmann, 1966). The second observation was the association between a high psychiatric morbidity rate and a high mobility rate as indicated by a high patient turnover in practices. The meaning of this association is obscure, however, as it may have reflected either the stresses entailed in changes of environment or the greater mobility of emotionally unstable individuals or both.

In the Stirling County study (Leighton *et al.*, 1959–63) the investigators set out to test the hypothesis that the state of social integration of the environment would affect the mental health of the people living in it. They, therefore, looked for communities that would contrast sharply in respect of integration to test the prediction that psychiatric disorder would be significantly more common where disintegration prevailed. To measure integration they used such criteria as broken homes, few and weak associations, inadequate leadership, few recreational activities, hostility, inadequate communication, poverty, secularization and cultural confusion.

The main conclusion was that 'disintegrated' communities show a striking increase in the risk of mental disorder as compared with 'integrated' ones. This was associated with a shift in the sex ratio. Women in the county as a whole showed a higher prevalence rate of psychiatric symptoms whereas, in disintegrated communities, men were found to have a higher risk of psychiatric disorder than women. The findings could not be explained in terms of a drift of individuals in low occupational positions into the disintegrated communities. People of lower social and economic status in integrated communities proved to be at much less risk than upper class individuals in disintegrated ones. There appeared to be less risk of psychiatric disorder among persons who were firm members of a local well-knit group than for 'non-conformists', but the trends were no more than suggestive. 'It is not poverty, or lower social status or limited education *per se*, that makes the difference to mental health but rather a whole group of factors that tend to be associated with these and that create a social environment that lacks features that are vitally important to mental health.'

Some association between indices of social disintegration and a high prevalence of psychiatric symptoms appears to have been established in this study. However, as community studies of the prevalence of symptoms have yielded such very high figures and as some of the findings cannot be interpreted in an unequivocal way, their significance for the social causation of psychiatric illness is not clear. Dohrenwend (1957) claims 'that social disorganization impinges on such needs of the individual as those for physical security, sexual satisfaction, the expression and securing of love, the securing of recognition and the expression of creativity, thereby producing psychological stress and disruption' but in the absence of further evidence, this and similar hypotheses cannot be regarded as upheld if 'psychological stress and disruption' are intended to mean mental disorder.

In the important prospective study conducted by Hagnell (1966) to follow up the survey conducted by Essen-Möller and his colleagues in 1947, very few associations between social factors as registered in the 1947 study and mental disorder in the current investigation were found. There was a relatively high incidence of mental illness in females drawn from the families of skilled workers. However, as in a number of British enquiries, there was no association between incidence and income. Complaints of headache, dizziness and poor sleep were highly correlated with the later development of mental disorder and so were migraine, fatigue and nervousness in women. The personality dimensions of Sjöbring proved to be poorly correlated with mental disorder but absence of abnormal personality traits was linked with a favourable outcome.

Hagnell recorded life-time expectancies for psychoses of 1·7 per cent., for neurosis 13·1 per cent., and for mental deficiency 1·2 per cent. However, if the criteria applied in the Stirling County study had been used, the figure for total prevalence of mental illness would have been 25–40 per cent. The special value of this enquiry derives from the fact that almost the whole population was interviewed and in every instance by Hagnell himself. Moreover, the follow-up enquiry made it possible to examine the predictive value of a number of indices of personality structure, social status and symptomatology.

The hypothesis that defective integration of the individual with the community exerts an adverse influence on mental health has also been tested in some enquiries undertaken in new housing estates. Attention has often been drawn to the poor neighbourliness and deficient social cooperation of such communities; and in the thirties Taylor coined the term 'suburban housewife's neurosis'. Martin *et al.* (1957) reported an increased prevalence of psychiatric disorder in the population of a new housing estate as indicated by utilization of psychiatric out-patient services, mental hospital admissions and the results of a survey conducted by personal interview. However, there are a number of possible interpretations of such findings. More recent enquiries have not on the whole confirmed the view that living in new housing estates carries a higher risk of developing neurotic illness. Hare and Shaw (1965a) compared mental health in two districts of Croydon, a new housing estate on the outskirts and an old, poor, densely populated district at the centre. Measures of psychiatric status, social factors, physical health, physique and personality were evaluated. No differences were recorded in neurosis rate for the two areas and the authors concluded that the amount of ascertained psychiatric illness is unaffected by residence in a new housing development. In this enquiry as in a number of others a clear association between poor mental health and poor physical health emerged. The authors also found an association between mental ill-health and a past history of concussion and certain infectious diseases. Moreover in a supplementary enquiry (Hare and Shaw, 1965b) a clear association was established between ill-health in parents and family size. This was more marked in the mothers than in the fathers. The authors concluded that these associations were very likely due to the impairment of parental health by the strain of caring for a large family. They also produced evidence for a tendency for ill-health to run in families (Hare and Shaw, 1965c). Thus when the health of either parent (in terms of the indices used) was poor, the health of the children tended to be poor. When either parent had neuroses the children tended to have high consultation rates. Neurosis in the father but not the mother was linked with high rates of behaviour disorder in the children. Between parents there was a strong association for rates of ill health and also for neuroticism though not at all for extraversion. The authors advance the tentative suggestion that 'assortative mating' takes place for the personality factors of neuroticism (MPI) but if one spouse develops a neurotic illness the other may do so through interaction. They also conclude from their findings that there is a group of persons comprising some 10–15 per cent. of the population who are particularly prone to ill-health of all kinds and make a correspondingly high call on the facilities of the health service.

On the other hand, in *Mental Health and Environment*, Taylor and Chave (1965) carried out an enquiry in the different setting of a new town where attention had been given to community development. They investigated in-patients, out-patients, those in whom a diagnosis of mental illness had been made by their general practitioner, and those who had reported psychiatric symptoms in the course of a household interview. The findings here were compared with those registered in an LCC housing estate, a decaying London borough, and national figures. There was no less neurosis in the new town nor any smaller incidence of 'sub-clinical' neurosis. The incidence of psychosis was diminished and the authors were prepared to attribute this to the new setting. They suggested also that, for purposes of prognosis, constitutional neurosis should be differentiated from an environmental variety but it seems unlikely that the distinction does more than select for special emphasis the extreme ends of a continuum.

It is on the definition of clear social determinants of mental illness that any programme of preventing psychiatric disorder must ultimately depend. Yet, in all, the evidence in favour of clear social determinants of mental disorder in these enquiries has not been impressive. This may of course have been due in part to the relative bluntness of the tools at the investigator's disposal at the present time.

SOCIO-ECONOMIC FACTORS

Migration: Social Class and Related Factors

One of the major pitfalls that awaits the investigator in the field of social psychiatry is the risk of confusing social vicissitudes arising from pre-morbid personality traits and initial psychotic symptoms with the causes of illness. The work of Ødegaard over a period of 30 years (1932–63) has been particularly helpful in resolving a number of ambiguities of this nature. Social selection will confer a special handicap or initiate some specific form of social behaviour in disabled individuals, such as choice of a certain occupation or exclusion from the married state, and this may lead to the erroneous conclusion that illness has been engendered by social mechanisms. Thus the excess of single people among schizophrenics appears to be very largely due to the disadvantages imposed by the pre-morbid personality. The relatively high incidence of mental disorder among migrants is mainly attributable, as Ødegaard showed in his classical study of Norwegian immigrants to the U.S.A. (Ødegaard 1932), to the special tendency of the unstable to emigrate; and urban-rural differences are decided in some measure by the drift of individuals with psychopathic traits.

In a later study of internal migration in Norway, Astrup and Ødegaard (1960) found that first admission rates were significantly lower for those moving into other areas in their own country than for those who remained where they were born. Particularly low rates were associated with short-distance migration as well as with migration from rural districts into cities, with the exception of the capital. Migrants to Oslo, particularly women, had higher rates than the city-born. The authors regard 'selective' migration as the most likely explanation for their findings, 'selection' differing according to the type of migration. 'Internal migration is less final and irrevocable than emigration . . . Often it is a natural and well-prepared step in the progress of a young person who has acquired some special training.' The environmental stress of migration, however, would be expected to bear much more heavily upon the overseas migrant who has to adjust to a radically different social situation, who has to break contacts with family and friends and is unable to make elaborate preparations. The authors suggest that the difference between overseas and internal migrants with regard to mental health may, therefore, be taken as lending some support to the 'environmental' hypothesis.

A different kind of mechanism is at work where social pressures push the individual over the borderline from mental health to maladjustment or illness, a mechanism which Ødegaard (1962) describes by the term 'social stress versus protection'. There are few examples of this phenomenon in relation to mental disorder which can be quoted with confidence; Ødegaard mentions here the higher incidence of crime in the slums (where the individual is exposed to adverse circumstances in excess) than in fashionable suburbs.

Ødegaard (1956) has found that low social prestige, low income and a low level of training are correlated with a relatively high incidence of mental disorder. This was borne out by comparisons of groups within the same occupation. Rates for mental disorder were higher in farm labourers than farmers, in seamen than officers of the merchant marine, higher in labourers than artisans and technicians, and higher in trade employees than owners and managers. Some of these differences may have been statistical artefacts. For example, when civil status is taken into account the difference between farmers and farm labourers becomes insignificant. However, as selection into certain occupations and for marriage may have the same basis in personality and run in the same direction, the elimination of variation in marriage rate may in some instances obscure an important difference. In the other occupations the pattern was not changed when marital status was taken into account.

Another example of social selection was provided by the differences in trends over time. Over the period 1926–1950 morbidity had increased markedly among farm labourers and decreased in public service. The former occupational group had declined to a considerable extent whereas the latter had expanded. The differences may suggest that those who join expanding occupations may be relatively stable mentally while the reverse may hold in a declining industry.

As far as diagnosis was concerned the variation between occupational groups was made up to a notable extent by schizophrenia. Manic-depressive psychosis on the other hand, showed a relatively uniform distribution. Results similar to this or with an excess of manic-depressives in the higher socio-economic groups have been recorded in many other studies. The importance of social circumstances was brought out particularly clearly by Ødegaard's (1957) comparison of female domestic servants and single women at home. They did the same sort of work but the former showed markedly higher morbidity rates. The deciding factors most probably were different status and home of origin. The standard of living and social prestige of domestic workers in Norway is rather higher than in countries like England or the U.S.A., and many girls from solid farming homes still take such posts for a period as a regular part of their experience and training. However, the servants had been drawn mainly from the labouring classes; two-thirds had left home before the age of 18; 86 per cent. had had only primary education. The operation of social stress was clearer than in any other group studied but detailed investigation served to illustrate the problems rather than to solve them.

In a study (Ødegaard, 1963) of 5,000 secondary school leavers who could be followed for a thirty-year period with regard to mortality, marriage rate and professional career, 117 (2·3 per cent.) were found to have had hospital admission with psychoses at some time. Males with secondary education had had admission rates slightly lower than those of the general population whereas females had higher rates particularly below 25 years of age and over 45 years. The same trend was found in overall admission statistics where women with higher education (teachers, trained nurses) showed higher morbidity. In this group the diagnostic distribution was different. Manic-depressive psychoses were twice as frequent as in the general population. Schizophrenia was in excess only in women. The lower rates for males generally were therefore caused by the scarcity of organic psychoses. In women schizophrenia and manic-depression shared responsibility for the raised rates.

In an enquiry into the prevalence of treated mental disorder in New Haven, Hollingshead and Redlich (1954, 1958) found marked differences in the prevalence of schizophrenia in the different social classes. Social class V, the lowest, contributed 45 per cent. of the total number of schizophrenics ascertained although it formed only 18 per cent. of the general population; classes I and II, constituting 3 per cent. and 8 per cent. of the population, contributed 0·7 per cent. and 2·7 per cent. respectively. The authors found that treatment varied according to the social class from which the schizophrenic subject was drawn and concluded that the differences in prevalence reflected differences in 'the responses patients in the several classes make to the treatment process'. However, subsequent enquiries have shed much doubt on whether the undoubted excess of cases in social class V in any way reflects a causal association between adverse social circumstances and schizophrenia. For example, the findings of Morris (1959) and Goldberg and Morrison (1963) clearly established that the fathers of young schizophrenics did not differ in respect of occupation from a sample of the normal population. On the present evidence, the large excess of schizophrenic subjects in the lowest socio-economic groups of the community probably arises largely from a drift down the social scale. This appears in turn to be due to occupational failure in the early stages of illness or a consequence of pre-morbid deficiencies in personality.

Martin (1962) has made useful and perceptive suggestions aimed at refining the sociological criteria being currently employed. He has pointed out that in the first decades of the century, poverty, malnutrition, overcrowding, insanitary housing conditions, inadequate medical care, and unskilled employment were highly correlated with one another and in such a way that the pattern of their relationship could be expressed by a single factor conveniently labelled 'social class'. However, as the result of recent social changes including the marked reduction in the size of the wholly unskilled class and increasing social mobility, no single simple scale such as the Registrar General's classification can provide an adequate index of our class structure. The time has come for social scientists to study the distribution in the population of other social economic variables—levels of education, income, methods of child care, values and attitudes, social standing—and to show in what way they are related to occupation. These and other related variables might also prove useful in investigating the social component of psychiatric disorders particularly in the field of neuroses and personality disorders.

Social Isolation

The possible contribution of social isolation to the causation of a number of forms of mental illness has been studied by many workers during the past two decades. In their classical study 'Mental disorders in Urban Areas' Faris and Dunham (1949) showed that schizophrenic patients tended to come predominantly from the densely populated parts of cities where social disorganization prevailed and where social isolation (Faris, 1934) was therefore likely to be operative. The results of subsequent enquiries have, however, called into question the validity of the social isolation hypothesis. The careful and critical retrospective study by Kohn and Clausen (1955) was concerned with small groups of 45 schizophrenics and 13 manic-depressives admitted for the first time to mental hospital. It yielded no evidence in favour of social isolation in adolescence as a factor contributing to cause either schizophrenia or manic-depressive psychosis. Gerard and Huston's study (1953) in Worcester, Massachusetts, suggested that isolation was the result of self-segregation; and Hare's enquiries in Bristol (1956) on the whole favoured the same conclusion.

In relation to the aged, recent enquiries have led to similar conclusions (see p. 544). In enquiries conducted in both the United States and Great Britain very little relationship has been found between isolation and mental illness in elderly people (Lowenthal, 1964a; Kay et al., 1964b; Garside et al., 1965). Those among the aged with mental illness who were living in relative isolation had become segregated mainly as a result of lifelong tendencies to unsociable, solitary behaviour.

Hence, in some of the most important settings in which social isolation has been inculpated as a cause of illness, it has proved on careful enquiry to be an effect rather than a cause; this describes the present overall consensus of opinion in relation to schizophrenia and other mental disorders found among immigrants and the aged. Social under-privilege, economic handicap, low occupational status appear also, for the present, largely to reflect social selection rather than social stress.

However, this is not to be taken to indicate that the social factors in the causation of psychiatric disorder have been disposed of. As Ødegaard pointed out, after concluding that his findings failed to support the influence of social stress in the aetiology of psychoses, the epidemiological method may be too coarse, the correlation between occupation and real personal problems may not be sufficiently high, and major psychoses treated in psychiatric hospitals may be less adequate material than, for instance, neuroses or psychosomatic conditions.

War and Peace

It has been known for more than a century that changes in psychiatric morbidity are associated with war. Esquirol noted the decline of insanity in periods of war; and during the Second World War statistical data from France (Abély, 1944a, b), Great Britain (Registrar General, 1953), Denmark (Svendsen, 1953), and Norway (Ødegaard, 1954) all provided evidence for a sharp decline in mental hospitalization during the first years. The possibility of statistical artefacts is difficult to exclude. However, Svendsen's analysis provided some convincing evidence to suggest that the decline was likely to be real. For example, there was a marked decrease in the hospitalization of patients with attempted suicide which generally constitutes an imperative cause for admission. Ødegaard could not find evidence that the change in rate of hospitalization was due to an increased delay of admission after the onset of illness. In Denmark and Britain the rate of hospitalization rose sharply immediately after the war.

The factors underlying the changes and trends are obscure. A similar decline occurs in suicide rate and was, for example, associated with each of the revolutionary upheavals and wars during the last century. In this case, the suggestion has been made that it is the increased social integration promoted by war that constitutes the operative factor. In other words the individual becomes less egoistic and acquires a sense of purpose through pledging himself to a cause and merging his identity with that of the community in which he lives. If this could be established it would be an example of social integration enhancing mental health. However, the evidence for the present is wholly of a demographic nature; and no observations are available on the effect of major social upheavals and wars on vulnerable individuals such as those prone to make repeated attempts at suicide or to suffer from recurrent attacks of mental disorder.

SUICIDE

Demographic and Social Aspects

Suicide is now included in the first ten causes of adult deaths in industrialized communities. The rates were comparable until a few decades ago with those for pulmonary tuberculosis but in the United States and Great Britain they have now out-run them by 50 per cent. and closely approach the rates for death by road accidents. It seems likely that, even in countries where vital statistics have been carefully recorded for a long time, the published suicide rates tend to understate the truth. Dublin (1963) estimates that the number of suicides in the United States is probably higher by a quarter to a third than that given. The expected figure there for 1965 was 19,000 and is more likely to be 25,000. The same is probably true in Great Britain where the total in 1961 was 5,216.

When the national suicide rates recorded by the World Health Organization for the year 1961 are examined, wide differences appear between country and country. For example, the Republic of Ireland and Egypt show the lowest rates of 3·2 and 0·1 per 100,000 respectively and West Berlin and Hungary the highest at 37·0 and 25·4. The rates for Sweden and Denmark are the same at 16·9 and that for Norway considerably lower at 6·8. The factors lying behind these differences are difficult to disentangle. If it is the opprobrium attached to taking one's life in countries where religious faith is strong which keeps the recorded rates low in Ireland, the rates in Roman Catholic Hungary and Austria, which are among the five highest in the world, are difficult to explain. In part the answer would appear to lie in differences in the reliability of national figures. Following an examination of coroners' records for the city and county of Dublin (population 718,332 in 1961) McCarthy and Walsh (1966) computed a rate of 4·5 per 100,000 in contrast to the official rate for the same region and period of 2·2 per 100,000. The leniency of coroners had probably been at work.

An attempt has been made to account for differences between Scandinavian countries in terms of differences in character structure that are according to Hendin (1964) culture-specific. He suggests that in Denmark, aggression and competition are frowned upon, dependency and passivity are encouraged and, when threatened, suicide results. In Sweden, early separation of mother and child are common, relationships are kept at a superficial level and suicide tends to be connected with failure at work for men or in marriage for women. In Norway, emotional expression is more unbridled and people are less ambitious; good mother-child relationships prevail but independence is also fostered. Many interesting hypotheses involving differences in culture patterns have been advanced but in no case can they be said to have been substantiated.

There are, however, some consistencies. The rates for *men* are invariably higher than those for *women* and where *negro* and *white* populations are looked at separately in the same country the negroes show a lower rate than the whites. For example in the United States and S. Africa, the rate for the white population is more than three times higher than that for negroes. There is a widespread tendency for rates to rise with *age*; and this is probably part of the explanation for the comparatively high incidence in highly developed and prosperous countries where expectation of life is longer and there is evidence that younger age groups have moved out. It is noteworthy, however, that the brunt of the 5 per cent. increase in the total suicide rate in the United States in the past 10 years has been borne by males aged 15 to 19 years. For them the rate has risen by 44 per cent. in contrast to a decrease in the rate of 15 per cent. between the ages of 65 and 74 years.

When annual national suicide figures are examined for a period of years other features emerge. In both the United States and this country the rates in the present decade resemble those at the beginning of the century. During the interval there has been in both countries a similar pattern of fluctuation. The peaks at about 1910 and 1930 correspond with periods of *economic depression* and the lowest rates coincide with the two world wars. That economic insecurity is probably related to suicide is further illustrated by Dublin (1963) who separated out the suicide rates for wage-earning families in the United States from the rest. Though their rates show the national pattern of fluctuation for periods of economic depression and war, the fluctuation is less pronounced than in the population as a whole, and over the 50 years between 1911 and 1960 their rates fell by 60 per cent. During this period the economic position and security of this group improved, and the stresses to which immigrants and first-generation families were subject at the beginning of the century may also have a bearing on the high rate at that time. However, as Dublin warns, there is no simple causal relation between economic factors and suicide.

The fact that the incidence of suicide in both men and women is lower during *wars* is variously explained. Those who see in homicide and suicide equally the expression of uncontrolled aggressive impulse suggest that it receives an outlet in war. Others relate the phenomenon to Durkheim's (1897) finding that suicide is associated with whatever weakens the link between the individual and the social group to which he belongs. In war a sense of common purpose draws communities together (see p. 787).

The *sex difference* in incidence, though marked and widespread, is not a constant factor. Dublin describes how in the first decades of this century the rate among girls up to 19 years of age was higher than for boys. The figures for the two sexes crossed in the 1920s and the rate for young women is now less than one-third that for men. Throughout Europe and the United States at present many more men than women commit suicide; the usual proportion being about 2 or 3 men for every woman. Norway, Finland and Eire show an even more marked disparity. However, in many countries the trend in recent years has been to reduce these differences between the sexes. For example, in Great Britain the gradual rise in the total suicide rate since 1951 is almost wholly due to a rise in the female rate. In other words, the female suicide rate has now risen above the level it reached before the Second World War while the male rate has remained below it.

The fact that the suicide rate reaches a peak in *old age* in most of the countries for which statistical data are available is important at a time when the proportion of the aged in the population is increasing. In Great Britain the rates for men rise steadily with age to being about 45 per 100,000 at the age of 70 and over. The curve for women reaches its peak (at over 20 per 100,000) in the age group of 60–69 and then falls to just over 10 at the age of 80 years and over. The picture in U.S.A. is somewhat similar except that there women reach their maximum of 10 per 100,000 in their fifties.

In Europe on the whole, there is a marked difference in incidence between *urban and rural* areas. In countries like Denmark, Sweden and Austria there is a large gap in incidence between the large cities and the rest of the country while in England and Wales there is a rough correspondence between city size and suicide rate. But in the United States the picture is by no means so clearly defined. The gap between urban and rural areas has narrowed over recent years to only 7 per cent. (Dublin, 1963). It would seem that where urban rates are still very high, other factors are influencing the situation, as for example, the rapid movement of population in cities like Los Angeles and San Francisco and the concentration of older people in St. Petersburg and Miami, in Florida. In a study by Stengel and Cook (1961) of two cities in northern England, it was found that in the smaller city with a very high suicide rate, decline in local industry had caused a considerable movement of younger people to other areas leaving an unusually high proportion of the aged behind without family support.

Suicide has been found to vary in incidence in economically advanced countries between the several parts of large cities. This emerged plainly from Sainsbury's study of London

(1955); areas characterized by a 'rootless', drifting, anonymous population, by large numbers of bed-sitting rooms and cheap hotels had the highest rates. Areas with a long-settled working-class population drawn together by close ties of kinship and acquaintance, though characterized by habitual poverty and poor living conditions, were comparatively free from suicide. In certain respects the social and demographic setting of attempted suicide as defined by Kessel and his co-workers (1965) in Edinburgh was similar. However, in one important respect it differed. There was there no significant correlation between the rates of attempted suicide and the proportion of people living in single-room households or in hotels. Studies of Chicago (Shaw and McKay, 1942) and of Vienna (Fuchs, 1961) show that suicide is found in distinct city areas also associated with over-crowding, loneliness, alcohol and drug addiction and criminality. It is to such areas that maladjusted persons are likely to be attracted. The *socially disorganized milieu* in which they find themselves probably hastens their deterioration and removes any immediate restraint upon suicidal acts.

Since Kraepelin's journey to Java (Kraepelin, 1904) the view that the peoples of *under-developed countries* rarely suffer from depression, and suicide is uncommon, has gained wide currency. However, in the absence of careful and objective studies such claims have to be regarded with reserve. In New Britain suicide by hanging appears to be common (Hoskin and Friedman, 1968); there is a high incidence of suicide in the neighbourhood of Okapa in New Guinea where Kuru is rampant (Mathews, 1967), and among the Kaiadilt group of Australian aborigines now living in Mornington Island (Cawte, 1968).

Social and Individual Factors

SOCIAL CLASS AND OCCUPATION. The Registrar General's analyses of occupational mortality show that a high incidence of suicide is associated with Classes I and II and V in that order. Doctors and dentists, with their ready access to poison and awareness of disease, are among the group with the highest rates, more than double the rate for their equivalent in the general population. Breakdown by age shows that after retirement Classes I and II benefit but Social Class III, which has amongst the lowest rates at earlier ages, has a higher rate and joins Social Class V which has a high rate throughout the life-span. Sainsbury (1962) makes a similar observation (see p. 561).

In the United States the situation is not the same. There, little difference appears between the first four classes and the significantly high rates are in Class V. What was previously said about rural rates in U.S.A. is reflected in the high suicide mortality among agricultural workers there. The narrowing gap between urban and rural areas may also reflect the movement of population into cities leaving behind a survivor population with a relatively high proportion of the aged and unfit. Those who work on the land enjoy relative immunity in England and Wales, where the highest rates are found among the unoccupied. It would appear that it is not low income but insecurity of employment, abrupt changes of economic status and personal predisposition that are operative.

MARITAL STATUS. Marital status shows interesting differences within the social class framework. Though the rate for men in Social Class I is 40 per cent. and that for married women 63 per cent. above average, there is almost no difference among single women between the ratios in the various classes. While the high proportionate mortality by suicide for men in Social Class I is no longer maintained after 65 it continues for their wives. Overall, marriage and a large family appear to protect against suicide; separation and divorce, especially the latter, seem to increase the hazard. To what extent such findings reflect social selection and how far stress is operative is difficult to judge without specific enquiry.

Even in the case of aged suicides where *isolation* is so prominent a feature, the relationship is likely to be far more complex than the simple isolation hypothesis implies. Rates among university students separated from the family appear to be higher than among those who live at home and also exceed the rates in the general population. Here again, separation is unlikely to be more than one among many contributory factors.

The Medico-Social Profile of the Suicidal Subject

The precise relation between suicide and *mental disorder* is difficult to establish because a high proportion both of persons with psychiatric disability and those who complete the suicidal act have not been under psychiatric supervision or treatment. Recent studies suggest that family doctors are having their attention drawn to the presence of some emotional disturbance in an increasing proportion of their patients who commit suicide. Yet such records as exist often make no reference to psychiatric abnormality even at the present time.

In the enquiry conducted by Seager and Flood (1965) in Bristol it was possible to match coroners' records for 1957 to 1961 with any hospital records available for those who had previously received treatment. Over the five-year period reported there were officially 325 suicides from a population of 810,000, an incidence of 8 per 100,000. Physical illness of a disabling kind was present in 20 per cent., a family history of mental illness in 10 per cent., a previous suicidal attempt in 16 per cent., and previous psychiatric breakdown requiring psychiatric treatment in 30 per cent. There was evidence of mental illness of some kind in over two-thirds of the cases. Of the two groups into which suicides could be divided the smaller consisted mainly of women with a previous psychiatric illness or suicidal attempts; in the larger group suicide had been an early and often the only indication of morbidity. The majority in this group were males, and physical illness, loneliness and alcoholism or a threat of court appearance had been common. Twenty-three per cent. had seen a doctor within a week of their suicide and 41 per cent. within four weeks.

In Sainsbury's earlier study (1955), which included an examination of 400 suicides of all ages dealt with by a London coroner between 1936 and 1938, he estimated that 37 per cent. had been mentally ill and a further 17 per cent. had had abnormal personalities. The view that this was an understatement has been most strikingly confirmed by the recent more intensive Chichester studies (Barraclough *et al.*, 1968; Sainsbury, 1968a, b). A psychiatric diagnosis of depression was made in no less than 80 per cent. of cases. Among social, demographic and clinical features the following were identified in these studies. There was an over-representation of the upper social classes, the elderly and the male sex. Forty-eight per cent. were living alone, 40 per cent. had lost a parent by death before the age of 16, 24 per cent. had moved home within a year. Loneliness was rated as important in 40 per cent.; recent bereavement in 12 per cent.; and 60 per cent. had seen their doctor preceding death. Twelve per cent. had a history of suicide in a close relative, 28 per cent. had made a previous serious attempt, 40 per cent. had a serious physical illness, 28 per cent. were on drugs such as reserpine and guanethidine which had probably contributed to their depression.

The association between mental illness and suicide is further suggested by the observation that suicide rates and rates of admission to mental hospital show a peak in the early summer in both hemispheres (Swinscow, 1951). There is also a great deal of evidence to suggest that the incidence of suicide among the relatives of persons suffering from affective disorders is considerably larger than in the general population (Stenstedt, 1952).

To sum up, suicide arises from a wide variety of causes; some within the individual and some in his surroundings. Personality, mental and physical illness and social factors contribute in varying proportions; suicide arises from their interaction. A good summary is given by Stengel (1964b): 'Suicide rates have been found to be correlated with the following factors: male sex, increasing age, widowhood, single and divorced states, childlessness, high density of population, residence in big towns, a high standard of living, economic crisis, alcohol consumption. Among factors inversely related to suicide rates are female sex, youth, low density of population (though it must not be too low), rural occupation, religious devoutness, the married state, a large number of children, membership of the lower socio-economic classes, war' . . . 'None of these factors should be looked upon in isolation as determinant. Each may be impinged on by another in differing times and places. A picture which grows more complex and shifting the closer it is examined presents itself. Personal characteristics and social forces interact.' A growing body of evidence suggests that in the majority of cases the final common pathway towards which those different causes converge is a depressive illness which could have been expected to respond to treatment. This is manifest in individuals who had often exhibited their susceptibility to affective disorder earlier in life. In the middle aged and aged physical illness is an important contributory factor.

ATTEMPTED SUICIDE

The earlier literature on suicide and attempted suicide reveals that these two phenomena tended to be regarded as one, directed at death, which succeeded in some cases and failed in others. During the last two decades the follow-up investigations of Dahlgren, Schneider and Stengel and the series of papers from the last named and his associates in London and Sheffield have been followed by an increasing number of reports from a variety of settings. The point made by Stengel and Cook (1958) that these are two separate if over-lapping populations is now widely accepted. Kessel (1965) following a very detailed survey conducted in Edinburgh now goes further by saying that attempted suicide is not a diagnosis and not even a description of the behaviour of great numbers of cases coming for treatment under this heading even when the behaviour is clearly a deliberate act of self-injury and not accidental.

The *incidence* of self-injury is not easy to establish, as it was and still is liable to be disguised or not recorded for religious and social reasons. Few enquiries into incidence have been carried out; three notable ones are those of Farberow and Schneidman in Los Angeles (1961), Stengel in Sheffield, and Kessel in Edinburgh. The frequency of 8 attempted suicides for every consummated suicide reported by Farberow and Schneidman in Los Angeles probably comes nearer to the truth for urban communities in this country than the ratio of 6 to 1 quoted in the Ministry of Health Circular H.M. (61) 94. Even this lower ratio produced an estimate of 30,000 per annum in England and Wales. This indicates a great volume of acute distress.

The circular quoted above was issued in 1961 after attempted suicide ceased to be a legal offence. It states that attempted suicide is to be treated as a medical and social problem only and concludes from this that it becomes all the more important for hospitals to be ready to give proper care. Hospital authorities are asked to do their best to see that all cases of attempted suicide brought to hospital receive psychiatric investigation before discharge and that psychiatric advice should be quickly available to the casualty officer. Community treatment, care and help instead of (or after) hospital treatment and the need for out-patient supervision in some cases are emphasized. This as Stengel (1963) points out is a formidable extension of the load on psychiatrists.

The Medico-Social Profile of those Attempting Suicide

That those who are admitted to hospital for attempted suicide are a population distinct from suicides is evident from its composition by *sex and age*. Women preponderate usually by a ratio of 2:1 and there is evidence that the comparative proportion of women to men is rising. Bridges and Koller (1966) who review the results of a number of studies, find that, in the majority, 20–29 years is the commonest age. A third of their subjects were in this group and 17 per cent. 19 and under, so that nearly half were under 30.

Notable features of the Edinburgh study are the high rates for teenage girls (one in every five hundred that age) and for women in their early twenties. Kessel (1965) suggests that these young women though married and looking after children are *emotionally isolated*. They have not adjusted to being tied to home and are cut off from those in whom they previously confided their frustrations. It should be added that they are also unable in this situation to acquire the knowledge and skill about childbirth, child rearing and home management that have been transmitted down the generations and which are likely there-fore to embody the fruits of long-tested experience. Working class women without access to telephone, motor car and the social and professional group activities open to middle class women, when they move house, could be expected to suffer most acutely from the kind of separation Kessel describes. However, before such views are endowed with authority they should perhaps be supported by more than subjective impressions. The 'isolation' of indi-viduals who attempt suicide should perhaps be examined with the aid of objective indices to ascertain whether they are merely victims of circumstances or whether their isolation reflects in part, as it has proved in so many other settings, the difficulties of long-standing personality traits.

The peak for both sexes in Kessel's study is in the 24–34 age group and it is in that age group that the rates for the widowed and divorced most notably exceed expectation. When allowance is made for age, the married and single show similar rates but among the married there is a large number of separated persons. The *marriages* of 30 per cent. of males and 26 per cent. of females had been broken by *separation or divorce*, and in one-sixth of these the break had been within a month of the act of self-injury. In most other studies where an adequate number of cases was investigated a preponderance of single, widowed, separated and divorced were found (Whitlock and Shapira, 1967; Bridges and Koller, 1966; Taylor *et al.*, 1964; Sclare and Hamilton 1963; Middleton *et al.*, 1961).

Kessel (1965) was able to demonstrate the *type of area* in which the highest rates for self-poisoning were to be found. They were the old central areas of Edinburgh with overcrowded tenements and an apartment area developed in the late 1950s to rehouse those living in slum areas. The next highest rates were in the factory suburbs with low-standard property where employment was insecure and in an area where post-war housing estates were rapidly spreading. There were highly significant correlations with overcrowd-ing, the proportion of people living out of a family setting and criminality but not with the proportion of single-room households or numbers living in hostels. Thus the associated social factors were not identical with those Sainsbury (1955) found for suicide in London.

Social *disorganization* in the area where the subject lived was matched by disorganization in the background of their lives. 'A broken parental home, a disorganized marriage, a disorganized life-pattern, living in disorganized districts are often found together in the history of people who poison themselves. This is the background against which precipitating social factors are superimposed.' Greer and his associates (1966) have shown a relationship between attempted suicide and parental loss and, further, that those from broken homes significantly often blame disharmony in their own marital relationship for their suicide attempt.

There emerges a general agreement that some disruption of relationships with a key-figure in the subject's life is the most frequent precipitant of acts of self-injury: in the teenage group, quarrels with boy- or girl-friend and reaction to the authority of parents; in the married, a high degree of disharmony with the spouse. Kessel (1965) found such disruption present in 85 per cent. among men and 69 per cent. among women. He also found that 70 per cent. of single men and 59 per cent. of single women had poor relationships with whoever was the principal figure in their situation. A closely similar picture appears to be presented by attempted suicide in cultures far removed from those in which the studies discussed here have been conducted. In Yap's study (1958) in Hong Kong the impulsive self-injury following some event in which the subject experiences rejection, humiliation, threat to a personal relationship or is made to feel resentment and aggression that can find no direct outlet are unmistakably similar.

The *precipitant* for the act is often multiple. Worries about work or being in debt, the manifold irritations of poor housing mount up till some perhaps trivial quarrel produces a crisis.

When *motive* was investigated, physical illness (equally with material circumstances) though undoubtedly present and operative in a number of cases, is mentioned by patients less often than would be expected.

When the material studied is comprehensive and not confined to persons referred for psychiatric investigation and when the diagnosis of a psychiatric condition is made on positive features other than the suicide attempt as in Kessel's study (1965), between 20 and 25 per cent. of persons are found to have no psychiatric illness. For those who can be given a *psychiatric diagnosis*, the commonest condition among women is depression (43 per cent.), and among men abnormal personality (30–40 per cent.). The distinction between these two main categories which in each sex accounted for almost 70 per cent. of the diagnoses would be unlikely to prove very sharp when submitted to detailed scrutiny. The suddenness with which depression with suicidal impulses may be triggered by frustration or rejection in a psychopathic subject is well known. Moreover, in most series the depression seldom exhibits psychotic features and in the neurotic and reactive cases personality difficulties of long standing are often present in some degree.

Alcohol abuse is a persistent theme in these studies but covers much more than established dependence on alcohol. People drink before the act, either to give themselves Dutch courage, or to potentiate the action of the drug chosen. Drinking may precipitate an impulsive act; and it may be used as a defence against the depression which is the background of a deliberate one. Suicide may also be the reaction of one spouse to alcoholism in the partner. This does not exhaust the ways in which alcohol contributes. There are subjects who make determined attempts at suicide while intoxicated but in whom, after recovery, no relevant illness, adverse situation or clear suicidal intention can be established. Prevarication is the explanation in some cases but appears improbable in others. It is likely that in some subjects self-destructive tendencies would remain latent were it not for their release by consumption of alcohol. Kessel (1965) found that 39 per cent. of men and 8 per cent. of women in his Edinburgh study were alcoholics. The variation in association with alcohol from area to area is probably affected by cultural factors (Whitlock and Shapira, 1967).

Stengel and Cook (1958), Harrington and Cross (1959) and Kessel (1965) have provided a fascinating examination of *intention* too complex to be more than glanced at here. The act seems to have been unpremeditated in about two-thirds of the cases; and in about one-third previous warning of the intention has been given. Very often a setting is chosen where intervention is likely. Once they have been resuscitated, there are few who still wish to take their lives; and there are many who have never worked out the consequences of their act in terms of living or dying. Taking these things into account, one must conclude that possibly four out of five of these people did not have death in view, but rather a change in their immediate situation.

Stengel's view is borne out that there is a strong element of 'alarm signal' or 'appeal' to the human environment, conscious or unconscious. The dramatic circumstances and the near approach to death make these subjects the focus of attention so that their plight can be recognized. It also causes self-examination, remorse and a possible change of attitude in others, particularly the key-figure at whom the act seems to be directed. The motive of influencing or putting compulsion on others is often there beneath the surface.

This is one side of the picture. On the other, we have to take account of the chaotic, shifting and above all intense emotion in which many suicidal attempts are made. Sixty per cent. of the patients in one of the large series claimed that they intended to die and, if little credence can be placed on such statements, as Kessel points out, the insistence of 25 per cent. who denied that they sought death cannot be taken at its face value either. Many of these patients are labouring under emotions in which depression, humiliation, anger, despair and a desire to terminate or escape from an intolerable situation are blended. If there is no deliberate intention to die neither is there any clear intention to survive. Inherently dangerous methods of self-destruction are used and, if it were not for the incoordination inevitably associated with an impulsive act, the sheer inability of most women to use physically destructive methods and the ineffectiveness of barbiturates under modern conditions of resuscitation, many more would succumb.

The failure of many patients to complete the suicidal act later may owe something to a change in personal relationship that is initiated by their dramatic appeal. However, in many others interpersonal relationships are too feeble, shallow or damaged as a result of previous personality deficiencies to be transformed by one dramatic incident. Yet either no further attempt is made, or the next one is just as impulsive, undirected and futile as the last. *Ten per cent. of people who attempt suicide ultimately complete the act* and we have as yet no firm evidence to indicate that it is in their failure to secure an adequate response to their appeal that they differ from the remaining 90 per cent. Exaggerated emphasis should not be placed on those elements in suicidal acts that may lead the untrained and inexperienced to underestimate their danger. One is at times alarmed by the readiness with which doctors, inexperienced in psychiatry, are prepared to dismiss suicidal attempts as 'dramatic gestures', 'attention seeking acts' on grounds no better than that the dose of poisonous substance used was not lethal.

It is unwise to dismiss some cases as trivial 'hysterical' gestures, and to judge the seriousness of intent either by the amount of poison taken or by the degree of physical damage done. In these matters purely accidental factors may be decisive. Any tendency to give the 'benefit of the doubt' by setting down an overdose or coal gas poisoning (especially in the elderly) as accidental, does a disservice to the patient. Only a psychiatric investigation of all those who are brought into hospital for resuscitation will disentangle from the rest the estimated 10 per cent. who will eventually, if untreated, repeat the act with fatal consequences. Investigation should be automatic and early, as soon after admission as possible, before defences have been put up by all the parties concerned and while they are still open to influence. Maddison and Mackey (1966) approaching the phenomenon as a clinical problem make a case for developing individualized management programmes to provide treatment for 'the almost endless variety of behaviours and motives which is subsumed under the general term "suicidal".'

Stengel's other contention (1958) that 'the experience of the suicidal attempt signifies death, survival and a new beginning' seems to receive some confirmation from that group of subjects who find in the experience a catharsis and a turning point in their lives after which their own attitude to others is modified. In others a punitive motive is present. In others still the underlying emotions are too fleeting, the motivation too confused, intelligence, insight or candour too limited for adequate description of the act to be possible.

Tuckman and Youngman (1963 a,b), Farberow, Schneidman and Neuringer (1966) and Cohen, Motto and Seiden (1965) have made studies directed towards formulating a *profile predictive of suicide* based on hospital patients. Cohen *et al.* confirmed Kessel's opinion that classification by apparent 'seriousness of intent' had little prognostic value. The predictive factors uncovered tend to repeat the complex of environmental and personal characteristics described above as connected with suicide, many of which are outside the psychiatrist's control. The majority of those who make the dangerous gamble of self-injury are seen by a psychiatrist for the first time after the act.

Prophylaxis

COMMUNITY ACTION. Organized efforts to prevent suicide go back to the first decade of this century when, in 1906, voluntary organizations with a religious background were set up in London and New York. Since then other agencies have sprung up both in the United States and Europe and are extending their activities. They fall roughly into two groups. Those like the Salvation Army Antisuicide Bureau (1906) in London, the Samaritans, (1953, in London) and the National Save-a-Life League (1906, in New York) are lay volunteers who offer a 'first-aid' service which aims at being available by telephone day and night to listen, befriend and give preventive counselling. Referral to psychiatrist or hospital can follow if necessary but the guiding principle is Durkheim's opinion that what the potential suicide needs is to end his isolation and to feel that he is wanted by and contributory to some group. The other type of service, notably in Vienna and Los Angeles, is under professional direction. The Vienna service (1947) based on the university neuropsychiatric clinic uses lay workers for preventive counselling and also deals with all cases of attempted suicide. The Los Angeles Suicide Prevention Center (1958) employs only professional staff but seeks to coordinate the interest of other official and volunteer agencies. It also uses the material which comes to the Center in a programme of research.

It is impossible to evaluate the effectiveness of these and other preventive counselling services. Relatively to their small resources both in money and staff they deal with large numbers of cases. There are strong arguments for strengthening and extending them both to deal with more cases and to follow up the contacts made. Stengel (1964*b*) makes a plea for a wide reorientation of attitude in the community at large towards potential suicides and other groups in need of care. He sees in this an answer both to acute social problems such as suicide and old age and to the problem of how leisure is to be occupied when shorter working hours become the rule.

CLINICAL VIGILANCE. The suicidal state is in most instances a potentially avoidable phenomenon, although there is as yet no exact method for differentiating individuals with high suicidal risk from other psychiatric patients. The characteristics of such individuals can be assembled from retrospective studies of suicidal patients. In providing a list of features in such a predictive profile we have drawn upon enquiries that have already been quoted and we have used also a list of criteria published by Stengel, although only some of the items have been selected and others have been modified. The following then is a predictive profile that can be used in clinical practice.

Patients with two of the following features should be considered as presenting some suicidal risk and those with more than two as being a serious risk.

1. Depression with guilt feelings, self accusation, self-depreciation, nihilistic ideas, and great motor restlessness. Pokorny (1964) has concluded that the risk for those diagnosed as suffering from depressive illness was 25 times the expected rate for a normal population of similar composition.

2. Severe insomnia with persistent disproportionate concern about it. Regular early morning wakening with restlessness and intrusion of distressing thoughts carries a high risk.

3. Severe hypochondriacal preoccupations associated with delusional and near delusional convictions of physical disease such as venereal disease, cancer, cardiac illness.

4. A history of a previous suicidal attempt.

5. Male sex and age over 55 years.

6. A history of alcoholism or drug addiction.

7. The presence of a disabling, painful or serious physical illness particularly in a previously active, robust and energetic man.

8. Social isolation and an unsympathetic attitude of relatives which is either real or exaggerated by the patient.

9. Suicidal preoccupation and talk. Suicidal preoccupations that have been extracted with some difficulty from the patient, concealed from the family and not confided to anyone constitute a serious risk.

10. A history of suicide in the family. According to some workers (Hilgard *et al.*, 1960) there is an increased risk of psychiatric disorder, including suicidal behaviour, as the patient reaches the age at which some familial figure, significant in his youth, died, especially if this death was by suicide.

11. Unemployment and financial difficulty, particularly if these represent a steep decline in fortune.

12. Towards the end of a period of depressive illness when the depressive mood persists but initiative and power of decision are recovering.

The administration of hypotensive drugs perhaps deserves mention. The effect of reserpine in the production of severe depressive symptoms is widely known and the substance is now rarely used. However, it is less well appreciated that depression is a common side-effect of many hypotensive drugs including guanethidine and methyldopa. In a recent enquiry into consummated suicide (Barraclough and Sainsbury, 1967) 28 per cent. of the patients had been receiving these drugs.

OTHER SOCIAL AND MEDICAL MEASURES. When we look at the means employed in suicidal attempts we can see opportunities for prevention. Most studies agree in showing that an overdose of barbiturates is the method employed in approximately 50 per cent. of cases. Salicylates and other drugs vary in proportion from study to study but usually account for a further 30 per cent. Age and sex have an effect on the method used. The numbers using barbiturates and coal gas rise with age and the proportion using salicylate falls. Those who use violent methods are usually men. Kessel (1965) has shown that the use of barbiturates has shown a steep rise since the 1940s and of other psychotrophic preparations since 1955. The drugs used are almost always obtained legally by prescription sometimes for an earlier illness or for another person in the household.

There are a number of measures relating to the choice and administration of drugs which could make a variable contribution to prophylaxis. Mortality after self-poisoning by aspirin is relatively high and Kessel has recommended the control of its sale in large quantities and outside pharmacies. Care not to over-prescribe dangerous drugs and a clearance of any supplies that remain after an episode of illness would remove what constitutes a temptation at critical moments. Most of those who take drugs would be unlikely to resort to other methods. Provision for the treatment of alcoholism would probably exert some effect on suicide rates. Automatic admission of all cases of self-poisoning to hospital followed by prompt medical and psychiatric treatment is important. Attention should be directed towards emotional and inter-personal problems during the first few days after recovery as it will increase the effectiveness of medical care.

The definition of the social features associated with suicide and attempted suicide are perhaps the most impressive achievements of epidemiological and social psychiatry. Both from a clinical and social point of view the suicidal state appears to a large extent a potentially recognizable and treatable one. The translation of these observations into practical action and the assessment of the results of such action remain as tasks for the future.

PREVENTIVE PSYCHIATRY
General Background

The last two decades have seen a resurgence of interest in the possibility of preventing mental disorder. Clinical work with neurotic disorders has increased very much, and has interested the psychiatrist in the personality setting of these conditions and the biological and environmental background. These are phenomena within the limits of normal variation although at its extremes. There are no clues to the cerebral mechanisms involved. Psychiatrists who seek to formulate their ideas about the circumstances in which individuals thrive or break down have been led to search for abnormal patterns of rearing and early learning. We now generally believe that abnormal relationships, emotional deprivations and traumas during the early formative years of personality development are common and play a part in causation. To some extent systematic enquiries have supported these beliefs.

Sigmund Freud did much to direct interest towards the experiences and the psychological interactions of childhood. But it is doubtful whether inspirations derived from the consulting room could have exerted such a far-ranging influence had the cultural climate not been receptive to it. A universal and lasting effect on the work of the psychiatric clinic has been made by adding a new historical dimension to the psychiatric examination. This has been particularly pronounced in relation to the neuroses. Here looking before and after has come to stay and most psychiatrists would agree that history-taking in this sense is both relevant and illuminating even if hindsight is difficult to translate into useful practical action. The *historical, family-oriented approach* has permeated a wide range of practical disciplines concerned with the social and psychological problems of individuals and families. This is so, whether we are concerned with the effects of neglect, cruelty or institutionalization on children, or whether we are confronting behaviour disorder, delinquency, sexual deviation, addiction or crime. The outlook of the community at large, particularly in economically advanced societies, has been influenced by the same philosophy. Novelists, biographers, artists and thinkers have found inspiration in the observations of the psychiatric clinic; and even the average educated man is more inclined than he was three decades ago to speculate about the unsolved human problems he sees around him and to try to interpret them in terms of individual motivation and individual psychopathology. We have grown aware that socio-economic progress may foster prosperity, but it leaves many social problems unaffected and aggravates others. With increasing affluence there has been no diminution of crime, alcoholism and racial hatred. In the attempt to resolve such problems inspiration has been sought in abnormal psychology. A strong impetus has been lent to the *search for the potentially preventable causes* of morbid phenomena particularly where there was good reason for regarding these as extreme variants of the norm. However, early efforts have also served to reveal the great difficulty of obtaining precise information in relation to such questions; not only does retrospective information have to be interpreted with reserve but enquiries in this field tend to uncover an intricate maze of inter-related factors. Child psychiatry which stands most immediately to gain from discoveries in this area therefore still largely lacks firm theoretical and factual foundations.

The most promising time for the application of a preventive programme would be in childhood; and for it we lack at present any solid basis. It may be that careful and disciplined observation can lead to effective prophylaxis before aetiological factors are defined. Cook prevented scurvy and Snow cholera with no knowledge as to how these conditions were caused. However, our ambitions are higher and less practical. What is proposed in theories of prevention is not any one specific measure directed towards one form of psychiatric illness in which certain circumstances have been consistently observed in association with that illness, but a comprehensive programme aimed at averting mental disorders in general.

One of the reasons advanced for developing, in the immediate future, a preventive approach in psychiatry is that the problems of mental ill-health in society are so vast and pressing that action cannot be delayed until the decades of work needed to uncover aetiological factors in mental disorder are completed. In a recent lecture on suicide in Australia, Saint (1965) observed that one person in ten bears the mark of Thanatos. Ten per cent. of the population are alienated or detached from their neighbours. They live in a state of aggressive and resentful variance with others, or labour under feelings of unworthiness. As individuals they often show patterns of illness which may be frankly psychiatric in nature or wear a somatic disguise; or they may indulge in irresponsible behaviour including alcoholism, drug addiction and suicide. In the light of some studies 10 per cent. would appear to be an underestimate.

It is considered by exponents of preventive psychiatry that certain situations are already ripe for a preventive approach. Since the investigations of Lindemann (1944) into the aftermath of the fire at the Coconut Grove Nightclub great importance has been attached by many workers in this field to the value of anticipating and handling 'life-crises'. They define a crisis as a short period of disorganization of psychological equilibrium in which an individual strives to resolve some problem and re-establish emotional balance. They contend, that given help, the result may be beneficial as the individual may be enabled to make a more effective response in the future. If unaided he may decline to a lower efficiency, into emotional instability, preoccupation, feelings of guilt and persistent hostility. The outcome of crises such as puberty, physical illness and disabilities, old age, bereavement, the sudden challenges of a new job or promotion at work, is decided in part by the individual's resources of personality but also by the help and advice that he is able to secure. It is pointed out that such crises present a particularly favourable opportunity for intervention, in that all parties concerned are eager to receive advice and to make the necessary adaptations to avert damage. However, most agencies concerned with mental health work are too inflexible to make a prompt response to meet or to change the situation.

Another concept widely applied is that of the 'target' population (Caplan, 1964). These are persons particularly subject to stress, such as prospective parents, migrants and adolescents. Caplan considers that there is a case for preventive intervention in such groups to improve the quality of their interpersonal relationships and avert breakdown. Yet another group are the 'carriers'; subjects who are not themselves ill but adversely affect the mental health of their dependents through the distorted relationships that they establish. At 'Well-baby Clinics' Caplan (1961) has identified some 10 per cent. of mothers as 'carriers'.

'Crisis intervention' has been the subject of many publications; a recent volume edited by Parad (1965) was devoted to it. The basic assumption of workers in this field is that the family has to be considered as a unit. It is held that the one-generation family unit in a highly mobile society is in a particularly vulnerable situation. Failure to make roots in the community exposes such families to severe stress in periods of crisis, since the typical American community, while welcoming at a superficial level, does not evince deep feelings of responsibility for members experiencing prolonged difficulties. The underlying assumption made here, that urban communities are largely composed of one generation families with consequent isolation of younger and older generations alike, has been recently submitted to critical tests and found wanting (see p. 544). Intervention at an early stage of the life-span is regarded as important and many programmes are directed towards children and their families. According to Caplan, individuals (also the family group or the group as constituted by the inmates of an institution) function as systems in constant interchange with their environment. Crises create tensions within the system and disturbance of equilibrium can be regained through adjustments, through internal changes or by alterations in the relations of the system to the external world. This presupposes that the kind of action needed to restore equilibrium in a specific situation is known and that, in the presence of emotional disturbance or mental disorder, such external or internal adjustment would have the desired effect. It is thought that these forms of intervention should be evaluated frequently and changed if found to be unproductive.

Two main routes of casework with families emerge. One of these proceeds through traditional agencies such as, for example, counselling provided at a family agency (analogous to the Marriage Guidance Council of Great Britain) where disharmony in marriage can be eased and sound attitudes towards the marriage relationship fostered or an unhappy marriage averted as a result of appropriate advice. The second is case-finding undertaken experimentally in the first place at pre-natal and post-natal clinics, schools, community health centres, group service agencies and in other settings. The technique in each case is twofold (a) to cushion or reduce the impact of stress and (b) to encourage and support family members in mobilizing and using their capacities.

At the Community Mental Health Center in Boston anticipatory guidance is offered by

Caplan and his associates in a form of mental health consultation which he describes as more than education, yet more restricted in its aims than psychotherapy. Since the programme needed to provide even a limited service for intervening in crises within the community would be very great, the suggestion is made that psychiatrists, psychologists and psychiatric social workers would be best employed as instructors working through general practitioners, nurses, school-teachers, clergymen and others with a supervisory role, who would in fact act as counsellors or therapists. As there is a general shortage of personnel this would inevitably cause existing psychiatric resources to be 'spread thin' so as to make services more widely available to more people. However, in emphasizing the need for primary prevention along these lines Caplan (1961) disclaims any intention to belittle the importance of early treatment and arrest of illness or of attempts to reduce the disablement that established illnesses produce. In the case of adult psychiatry primary prevention is regarded as only one facet of a comprehensive community mental health scheme in which mental hospitals have their place.

Considerable importance is attached to the role of the family doctor in preventive work. His responsibility extends to the whole family unit. He is in an ideal position to assess to what extent disability is likely to have arisen from stresses and hardships within the family. He is also well-placed to assess the effects that any illness in one of its members is likely to exert economically, psychologically and socially on the whole group. He can make arrangements for treatment that produce the least possible dislocation and damage to the life of the family and arrange for domiciliary care for mother or child wherever possible as an alternative to separating them by hospital admission. This is a time-honoured role for the family doctor but one that under modern conditions has tended to fall into disuse. It should be remembered, however, that Caplan and many other writers on this subject are addressing themselves primarily to an American audience.

Not only in America but also in Europe and Great Britain, social psychiatry has to contend with the difficulties of having a wide variety of uncoordinated institutions and agencies undertaking family casework. The task of integration is formidable, and is made no easier by lack of the personnel who are to make contact with the family in the home. The prospects are very remote that we shall be able to train an adequate staff to undertake ambitious programmes of prophylaxis, as well as those of therapy. It is true that the available resources have to be realistically deployed; and some system of priorities seems to be called for. Caplan takes the view that selection of cases for treatment can no longer be left to the haphazard processes of patient-demand, nor are referrals to be based on therapeutic predictions. He says that the 'community implications of our treatment' should also be given weight. The phrase is an indefinite one. If it is meant to imply that the degree of suffering, hardship, danger or disability, incurred by the individual is to be replaced as the criterion for selection by an assessment of social consequences (bound at the present time to be vague and subjective, to say the least), then there will be few psychiatrists prepared to follow him. Until more objective evidence is available about the results of preventive work, the responsibility of the psychiatric team, on pragmatic as well as humane grounds, will be in the first place towards the sick and disabled.

Primary Prevention

Gruenberg (1957) has made the point that measures for control of mental disorder, as far as present knowledge will permit, should not be paralysed by a sense of ignorance

about the aetiology of schizophrenia. His contributions and those brought together in
'Prevention of Mental Disorders in Children' (Caplan, 1961) serve to bring home the
sharp limitations placed on primary prevention by present ignorance. However, they also
bring out the fact that there is more knowledge about the aetiology of certain forms of mental
disorder and subnormality, particularly those that arise through various forms of damage
in childhood, than is sometimes appreciated.

Gruenberg points out that the approach should be the same as the public health approach
to any other group of illnesses. 1. To give first priority to prevent what is preventable.
This is of course subject to severe limitations and does therefore not imply that this line
of action should claim the major share of available resources. 2. To give second priority
to terminating or arresting what can be terminated or arrested; that is secondary prevention. 3. To give third priority to reducing disability from disorders which have not been
prevented, terminated or arrested. Under the first heading of primary prevention maternal
and child welfare services should be examined to ascertain that present knowledge is being
applied to reduce the number of children born with lifelong handicaps of brain functioning:
rhesus incompatibility, congenital syphilis, rubella, malnutrition and other deprivations
during pregnancy still take some toll. Again toxaemias of pregnancy which have some association with mental deficiency, behaviour disorders and epilepsy are potentially avoidable.
The control of environmental hazards might serve to reduce iodine deficiency, brain injury,
poisoning and drug intoxication and threats to foetal brain development possibly emanating from other sources such as radiation and food additives. Efforts aimed at keeping the
family unit intact as far as possible by providing domiciliary care and support for key
members of the family when they require treatment can also contribute something of value.

A number of workers have advanced suggestions about practical action or further
research in this area. Tarjan (1961) believes that current knowledge of genetics should be
applied in more diagnostic and scientific counselling centres made available for the average
family. Diagnostic screening should make it possible to avert the worst consequences of
phenylketonuria and galactosaemia. The immunization of mothers against rubella, elimination of known defects in obstetric practice and the choice of child-bearing time when the
mother is in the best state of general health would all make a substantial contribution.

The views of Pasamanick and his associates (Pasamanick and Knobloch, 1961; Knobloch
et al., 1956) have become well known. He has advanced the concept of a continuum of
reproductive casualty leading at one extreme to the death of a foetus and at the other fading
off into the reversible physiological discomforts of 'normal birth' with, in between, minor
brain damage causing varying degrees of intellectual defect or personality damage. He
considers that in a subtle form the latter are far more common than generally appreciated;
and, in interaction with emotional deprivation, are the underlying aetiological factors of a
variety of neuropsychiatric disorders in children. The validity of the conclusions of this
group has been called in question but they have provided a strong stimulus to research in a
neglected area. The prospective enquiry being conducted by the National Institute into
neurological diseases and blindness in 50,000 pregnant women in which the children are
to be followed up over a six-year period should yield observations that resolve some controversial issues in this field. They may also have important implications for prevention.

As far as counselling parents is concerned, the problem of applying even real advances
in the knowledge of child development is greater than is sometimes supposed. It may be
that the attitudes of even well-intentioned parents to their children are at times harmful.
However, after a careful evaluation of attempts to educate parents, Brim (1961) could find

no evidence that this educational programme changed either the parents or their children. A number of workers have advanced suggestions about appropriate timely intervention aimed at averting adverse influences on personality development, to compensate for the ill-effects of rejection and over-solicitude, to reverse the development towards neuroses such as school phobia in its early stages and to help the family to cope with the bereaved or deprived child (Klein and Lindemann, 1961). There is however no evidence at the present time that such activities, which are immensely difficult and costly to provide on an adequate scale for preventive purposes, exert any effect. Biber (1961) asks what are the best relationships between children and teaching staff, within staffs, between school and parents, and between school and the wider community, for the mental health of the schoolchild. It is not possible to provide clear and reliable answers at the present time. Practical solutions have to be provided on the strength of good sense, imagination, insight and trial and error. In these ways child psychiatrists of modest critical and scientific outlook can make a useful contribution.

Secondary Prevention

Under this heading Gruenberg has some difficulty in suggesting a definitive list of disorders which are subject to ready diagnosis and effective treatment so that the progress of illness may be halted or its duration shortened. He suggests that depressive states of a certain type and intensity, general paralysis, pellagra, toxic deliria, conversion hysteria, cretinism and also phenylpyruvic oligophrenia may logically at the present stage, be included under the heading of secondary prevention. He advocates that treatment services for such a list of disorders should be instituted and case-finding procedures adopted.

To this list certain other disorders can be added. Although there is no clear evidence that early treatment of schizophrenia influences the ultimate prognosis, it would be wise and reasonable to act on the assumption that differences in response between cases that present acutely and those of insidious onset are in part due to earlier treatment of the former. Careful evaluation may of course prove this assumption to be ill-founded. Again in relation to severely incapacitating neuroses such as situational phobias and obsessive-compulsive neuroses later presentation at the psychiatric clinic appears to be correlated with poorer prognosis, and earlier referral for treatment would be desirable and perhaps effective.

One of the Expert Committees of the World Health Organization mental health section devoted a report (1957) to what is in effect secondary prevention. It emphasizes the importance of providing out-patient care and averting hospital admission wherever possible and appropriate. Early diagnosis, active treatment and after-care to lessen the risks of relapse and chronicity will inspire a measure of confidence in the public that will eventually open up possibilities for research into prophylaxis. The report goes on 'it will be advisable however, to guard against the successful psychiatrist coming to be looked upon as an all-round behaviour expert and being swamped with requests for advice in respect of general life problems which, though very important for the individual, may be more or less outside the competence of the mental health specialist. Generally speaking, it will, indeed, always be necessary to limit the range of activities according to the scope of the existing services . . . .'

Although the report is ten years old at the time of writing this chapter, its recommendations have not lost their relevance.

Tertiary Prevention

Under this heading Gruenberg includes such measures as *fostering more enlightened attitudes in the public* towards chronically disabled patients, the provision of various forms of social protection for them, the creation of sheltered workshops and supervised residential care outside hospital. He refers also to the need to organize mental hospitals along more liberal and open lines.

The subject of *institutionalization* and its effects on psychiatric patients has received a good deal of attention in recent years. It has become clear that long-term hospitalization exerts effects on patients which have to be differentiated from the features conferred by the illness from which they suffer. Among the pioneers who directed attention to the effect of the hospital environment was T. P. Rees (1955). He held that the capacity for taking social responsibility atrophies like muscle when disused. He therefore contrived ways in which patients could continue to exercise some responsibility so as to facilitate their earlier discharge towards independent life. In *Institutional Neurosis* (1966) Barton described the clinical features of this syndrome as apathy, lack of initiative, loss of interest in things and events not immediately personal or present, submissiveness, lack of interest in the future and an inability to make plans for it. There is deterioration in personal habits and standards generally. Individuality atrophies and the patient becomes resigned to the existing situation and resists discharge. Barton attributes the phenomenon to a number of overlapping factors among which the most important are loss of contact with the outside world, enforced idleness, the authoritarian attitude of medical and nursing staff, loss of personal possessions, interruption of activities that emphasize individuality, sedatives, the ward atmosphere and dwindling of future prospects.

In his description of the 'total institution' Goffman (1957) has widened the concept by describing the features that the mental hospital milieu has in common with other institutions. Both engender changes in their inmates that are in some respects similar. The American concept of the 'social breakdown syndrome' is similar to that of the English concept of 'institutionalization' but hospital treatment is considered only one of the factors. Gruenberg and Zusman (1964) describe the susceptibility and 'the overwhelming loss of confidence in his past patterns and feeling and thinking' that an attack of psychiatric illness can produce in a patient entering hospital. In this situation the pressures exerted by the institution are of importance, for the 'social identities and personal standards' it offers tend to be accepted and take the place of standards that have been disrupted.

The place of the patient's pre-morbid personality and social background have perhaps been uncritically ignored in the sweeping condemnations of ten to fifteen years ago. As Wing (1962) has pointed out, susceptibility to institutional pressures may include factors that led to hospital admission in the first place—lack of ties with the community, poverty, age and social position. Moreover those who tend to retreat from social relationships and social responsibilities may also be disposed to opt for a social environment where 'interaction can be minimal'. Wing considered that in schizophrenics, who constitute a majority of long-term hospital patients, the symptoms of illness could be distinguished from those of institutionalization. He suggested that blunting of affect, disordered speech, delusions and hallucinations are inherent in schizophrenia regardless of the setting. Dependency, apathy about leaving, lack of interest in outside events and resignation result from being in an institution.

Although the effects of institutionalization may at first have been somewhat exaggerated, the influence of a movement aimed at transforming the atmosphere of mental hospitals has notable achievements to its credit. To take only one group of factual observations, the suicide rate among mental hospital patients in the United Kingdom remained steady for many years around 50 per 100,000—some four times the national average. The introduction of E.C.T. produced no change but since 1956 it has declined slowly to about 36 per 100,000.

In the United States attempts have been made to reduce the prevalence of the 'social breakdown syndrome' in an experiment which made use of 'a comprehensive community-orientated unit' providing a continuous flexible programme of psychiatric care for the whole population (Brandon and Gruenberg, 1966). The findings suggested that the annual incidence of this condition in non-geriatric adult patients had been reduced to 50 per 100,000 after being perhaps twice as high two years previously.

From 1955 to 1960 a joint commission analysed and evaluated the needs and resources of the mentally ill in the United States of America. Late in 1961 President Kennedy appointed a cabinet level committee to review the report and on the basis of their work he sent his Message to Congress. 'We need a new type of health facility, one which will return mental health care to the mainstream of American medicine and at the same time upgrade mental health services.' The new *Community Mental Health Center* was to provide a complete range of care in the community with strong emphasis on prevention. Over a 3-year period 150 million dollars was made available for use by the state for constructing centres. To qualify for federal funds centres were to provide at least 5 essential elements of service: (a) in-patient services; (b) out-patient services; (c) partial hospitalization services including at least *day care*; (d) emergency services 24 hours per day with at least one of (a)–(c); (e) consultation and education services available to community agencies and professional personnel.

Emphasis was laid on the importance of continuity of care, easy transfer from one type of care to another and inter-availability of records and information. Moreover, research and evaluation were described as essential constituents of an adequate service. The results of evaluation of this large nationwide programme will be awaited with interest. It is to be hoped that the results will demonstrate that the quality of care received by seriously deranged and psychotic patients who have benefited more from modern advances than any other group suffering from psychiatric disorders will not have been prejudiced. It would be a Pyrrhic victory if the launching of what is in effect an experiment in preventive psychiatry were to cause a decline in the quality of care that can be provided in a more traditional hospital setting by attracting away resources and personnel that are in such short supply.

Conclusions

The most essential feature of any psychiatric service is that the benefit it confers should outweigh any harm or damage that it does. Since the effects of programmes of primary prevention are at present quite unknown the authors believe that in the list of priorities secondary and tertiary prevention should come before primary prevention. This means the provision of services of excellent quality to ensure early diagnosis and treatment and promote effective rehabilitation. For the present, no country in the world disposes of an adequate service for therapy. Neither the resources available for such services nor their organization in integrated entities comes up to satisfactory standards even in highly developed countries. In modern society a wide range of services seek to secure the skills of the psychiatrist: the courts, the approved schools and prisons, workers in the public health services, educationists and clergymen, not to speak of the family doctors who have come to appreciate that the techniques of psychiatric examination and case-taking and the insights they engender are invaluable for illuminating some of the problems in their own fields. Within limits, this kind of activity has its value. It can, amongst other things, help the psychiatrist to widen his perspectives and to see some of his problems from a new angle. It may even stimulate him to formulate fresh questions and hypotheses. In some limited fields sufficient factual knowledge may become available to justify experiments in prevention. Suicide and delinquency are notable examples and psychiatrists should join hands with those expert in other disciplines in the mounting of prophylactic experiments the results of which are carefully evaluated.

But in most areas the primary need is for more research. We need to have much more knowledge about those constituents in a child's familial and social environment that decide whether he matures into a healthy and effective or unstable and sick person. If a psychiatrist permits uncritical enthusiasm for action in the community to outweigh all other considerations he runs other risks. If he is to advance knowledge he must remain acutely conscious of the extent of his ignorance. Once he convinces himself that he knows, he will learn nothing new.

It may be admitted, on the other hand, that the humility he needs as a scientist may incapacitate him as a public spokesman. As Ruesch (1965) recently wrote 'rarely are data on mental health so self-evident that they need not be backed by unfaltering conviction'. However, the dangers he runs in espousing the cause of prevention with exaggerated optimism are probably the greater. In forming a judgement as to whether the community is ripe to receive the lessons of preventive psychiatry, it has to be noted that campaigns against alcoholism, smoking, dangerous driving and even obesity have met with singularly little success. These preventive campaigns sought to modify habits that kill and which within certain limits can be changed by voluntary action. Even such a simple measure as fluoridation of water, whose value has been fully authenticated, has encountered astonishing difficulties. Personal qualities such as self-esteem, independence, tolerance for others, capacity for kindliness and enduring affection in human relationships, insight, and the ability to handle conflicts are central to most concepts of mental health. In the course of treatment and rehabilitation the psychiatrist is often engaged in helping patients, and those suffering from neuroses in particular, to mature towards such attributes in the hope of creating lasting gains in stability and social adjustment. However, in seeking to carry his activity beyond the confines of the clinic, certain problems arise which have to be faced squarely. Mental health conceived in these terms entails judgements of value. Are communities prepared to permit psychiatrists to attempt to bring about changes in such fundamental attitudes and personal qualities in the population as a whole? Is there any evidence that with the techniques at our disposal we can achieve success? Above all, desirable as such qualities may be from the point of view of widely accepted humane values, there is as yet no satisfactory evidence that they are related to vulnerability to breakdown. In the light of this, what priority in the allocation of resources are we to give to preventive work with these or similar concepts as its starting point? Should we be justified in diverting resources from the treatment of patients in the early stages of illness?

Further it has to be remembered that the effect of advice aimed at securing more effective and harmonious social adjustment may be the opposite of what is intended. At the turn of the century the great physiologist Lawrence Henderson said that a man encountering a doctor for the first time had a fifty to fifty chance of not coming to harm. The creation of iatrogenic disability is not peculiar to physicians. The risk is run equally by psychiatrists. There is just not enough information to predict with any reliability the effects of preventive counselling; and the psychiatrist or social worker who is prepared confidently to offer advice to a patient to change his job or his wife, move his home or alter his habits may not only fail to alleviate stress but cause serious damage.

However, this chapter ought to end on a positive note, muted though this may be. A small body of knowledge has accumulated in relation to social and environmental factors and some of this is ripe for application. In the case of suicide, for example, attention needs to be focused on the lonely and the isolated, the aged and bereaved, those in poor health physically, those prone to alcoholic excess and those who have undergone a shift from relative affluence to poverty. To some extent the known facts about delinquency demand application in prophylaxis. We have acquired a good deal of knowledge of the conditions under which mentally subnormal individuals may reach their full potential in intelligence, the practical effectiveness of which they are capable and the conditions under which they become apathetic, wholly dependent, illiterate or even speechless. Again we have learnt to define some of the social variables that contribute to the unhappiness of the aged and perhaps to their chances of becoming sick. At the least, long-term institutionalization could be reduced if existing knowledge were applied more often and at earlier stages of illness.

If investigation of crude overall indices such as social class, income and social isolation have not shed a great deal of light on the causes of mental disorder, it is possible that it is in the social network of the family that the relevant social pressures are exerted and have to be studied. In the course of the past few decades a certain consensus of opinion has developed among psychiatrists of different schools about the character of the family setting from which subjects suffering from disorders such as anxiety neurosis, anorexia nervosa or homosexuality are drawn. Enquiries aimed at describing precisely and arriving at reliable measures of these settings are in progress in different parts of the world, and from them may come observations with implications for preventive programmes. Psychiatrists are in a uniquely privileged position for obtaining systematic observation on such matters. The value of their observations will be enhanced if they do not permit themselves to forget the possible contributions of biological factors. And their influence on the community at large will be all the greater if they bear in mind the mental hygiene movement in the early years of this century and the fate it ordained for itself by its exaggerated claims.

REFERENCES

The page of the text on which the item of literature is mentioned is given in italics after each reference.

ABEL, E. (1923) Famine and epidemics in Russia. *Münch. med. Wschr.*, *70*, 485.—*357*.

ABÉLY, X. (1944a) Diminution de l'aliénation mentale pendant la guerre. *Presse méd.*, *52*, 179.—*787*.

—— (1944b) Diminution des psychoses affectives pendant la guerre. *Presse méd.*, *52*, 227.—*787*.

ABRAHAM, K. (1927) Notes on the psycho-analytical investigation and treatment of manic-depressive insanity and allied conditions (1911). Selected Papers, p. 137. Institute of Psychoanalysis. London. L. and V. Woolf—*195*.

ABRAMSON, H. A. (1956) Lysergic acid diethylamide (LSD-25). XIX As an adjunct to brief psychotherapy, with special reference to ego enhancement. *J. Psychol.*, *41*, 199.—*437*.

—— (1957) Verbatim recording and transference studies with lysergic acid diethylamide. *J. nerv. ment. Dis.*, *125*, 444.—*437*.

——, JARVIK, M. E., KAUFMAN, M. R., KORNETZKY, C., LEVINE, A. and WAGNER, M. (1955) Lysergic acid diethylamide. I Physiological and perceptual responses. *J. Psychol.*, *39*, 3.—*438*.

ACHESON, R. M. and FOWLER, G. B. (1967) On the inheritance of stature and blood pressure. *J. chron. Dis.*, *20*, 731.—*588*.

ACKNER, B. (1954) Depersonalization, I and II. *J. ment. Sci.*, *100*, 838, 854.—*123*.

——, COOPER, J. E., GRAY, C. H. and KELLY, M. (1962) Acute porphyria: a neuropsychiatric and biochemical study. *J. Psychosom. Res.*, *6*, 1.—*360*.

——, and PAMPIGLIONE, G. (1959) An evaluation of the sedation threshold test. *J. Psychosom. Res.*, *3*, 271.—*204*.

ADAMS, G. F. (1965) Prospects of patients with strokes: with special reference to the hypertensive hemiplegic In: Proc. Conf. held London June 1965, ed. J. N. Agate. London: Pitman.—*596, 599*.

——, and HURWITZ, L. J. (1963) Mental barriers to recovery from strokes. *Lancet*, *2*, 533.—*600*.

——, McQUITTY, F. M. and FLUIT, M. Y. (1958) Rehabilitation of the elderly invalid at home: an experiment in restoration of activity after illness amongst old people in their homes in Belfast. Nuffield Provincial Hospitals Trust. London.—*562*.

ADAMS, R. (1942) Marihuana. *Bull. N.Y. Acad. Med.*, *18*, 705.—*427*.

ADIE, W. J. (1924) Pyknolepsy: a form of epilepsy occurring in children with a good prognosis. *Brain*, *47*, 96.—*673*.

AINSWORTH, M. D. *et al.* (1962) Deprivation of maternal care: a reassessment of its effects. Wld Hlth Org. Publ. Hlth Papers, No. 14. Geneva: W.H.O.—*29, 636, 637*.

de AJURIAGUERRA, J., HÉCAEN, H. and ANGELERGUES, R. (1960) Les apraxies: variétés cliniques et latéralisation lésionelle. *Rev. Neurol.*, *102*, 566.—*496*.

AKELAITIS, A. J. (1944) Atrophy of basal ganglia in Pick's disease. A clinico-pathological study. *Arch. Neurol. Psychiat. (Chic.)*, *51*, 27.—*619*.

ÅKESSON, H. A. (1961) Epidemiology and genetics of mental deficiency in a Southern Swedish population. Uppsala. Univ. of Uppsala.—*694*.

ALANEN, Y. O. (1958) The mothers of schizophrenic patients. *Acta psychiat. neurol. scand.*, *33*, Suppl. 124.—*263*.

——, REKOLA, J., STEWEN, A., TUOVINEN, M., TAKALA, K. and RUTANEN, E. (1963) Mental disorders in the siblings of schizophrenic patients. *Acta psychiat. scand.*, *39*, Suppl. 169.—*245*.

de ALARCÓN, R. (1964) Hypochondriasis and depression in the aged. *Geront. clin.*, *6*, 266.—*570*.

—— and RATHOD, N. H. (1968) Prevalence and early detection of heroin abuse. *Brit. med. J.*, *2*, 549.—*414*.

ALEXANDER, L. (1940) Wernicke's disease: identity of lesions produced by B₁—avitaminosis in pigeons with hemorrhagic polioencephalitis occurring in chronic alcoholism in man. *Amer. J. Path.*, *16*, 61.—*353*.

—— (1942) The vascular supply of the strio-pallidum. *Ass. Res. nerv. ment. Dis. Proc.* (1940), *21*, 77.—*439*.

—— (1948) The socio-psychological structure of the S.S. *Folia psychiat. neerl.*, *51*, 2.—*159*.

ALLENTUCK, S., and BOWMAN, K. M. (1942) The psychiatric aspects of marihuana intoxication. *Amer. J. Psychiat.*, *99*, 248.—*427*.

ALLERS, R. (1920) Psychogenic disturbance in the environment of a foreign language. Delusion of persecution in the linguistically isolated. *Z. ges. Neurol. Psychiat. 60*, 287.—*149*.

ALLISON, R. S. (1962) The Senile Brain: a Clinical Study. London: Arnold.—*499*.

ALSTRÖM, C. H. (1950) A study of epilepsy in its clinical, social and genetic aspects. *Acta psychiat. neurol. scand.*, Suppl. 63.—*452, 482*.

——, GENTZ, C. and LINDBLOM, K. (1943) Pulmonary tuberculosis of mental patients, especially schizophrenics. *Acta tuberc. scand.*, Suppl. 9.—*307*.

ALZHEIMER, A. (1907) On a peculiar disease of the cerebral cortex. *Allg. Z. Psychiat.*, *64*, 146.—*613*.

ÅMARK, C. (1951) A study in alcoholism. *Acta psychiat. neurol. scand.*, Suppl. 70.—*391, 393*.

ANCHERSEN, P. (1956) Chronic barbituric acid poisoning. *T. norske Laegeforen.*, *76*, 979.—*416*.

ANDERSON, E. W. (1936) Prognosis of depressions of later life. *J. ment. Sci.*, *82*, 559.—*213*.

—— (1942a) Psychiatric syndromes following blast. *J. ment. Sci.*, *88*, 328.—*502*.

ANDERSON, E. W. (1942b)Abnormal mental states in survivors, with special reference to collective hallucinations. *J. roy. Nav. med. Serv.*, *28*, 361.—*115*.

—— and MALLINSON, W. P. (1941) Psychogenic episodes in the course of major psychoses. *J. ment. Sci.*, *87*, 383.—*281*.

—— and RAWNSLEY, K. (1954) Clinical studies of lysergic acid diethylamide. *Mschr. Psychiat. Neurol.*, *128*, 38.—*436*.

ANDERSON, W. M. and DAWSON, J. (1962) The clinical manifestations of depressive illness with abnormal acetyl-methyl-carbinol metabolism. *J. ment. Sci.*, *108*, 80.—*204*.

—— and —— (1963) Verbally retarded depression and sodium metabolism. *Brit. J. Psychiat.*, *109*, 225.—*204*.

ANDREW, W. and WINSTON-SALEM, N. C. (1956) Structural alterations with ageing in the nervous system. *J. chron. Dis.*, *3*, 575.—*535*.

ANDREWS, G. and HARRIS, M. (1964)The Syndrome of Stuttering. London: Heinemann—*642, 654*.

ANGST, J. (1966) Zur Aetiologie und Nosologie Endogener Depressiver Psychosen. Berlin: Springer.—*197, 198*.

—— and PERRIS, C. (1967) Zur Nosologie endogener Depressionen. *Arch. Psychiat. Nervenkr.* (in press). —*188, 198*.

ANTHONY, E. J. (1957) An experimental approach to the psychopathology of childhood: encopresis. *Brit. J. med. Psychol.*, *30*, 146.—*648*.

ANTONI, N. (1946) Dreamy states, epileptic aura, depersonalization and psychaesthenic fits. *Acta psychiat. neurol. scand.*, *21*, 1.—*94, 460*.

ARIETI, S. (1946) Histopathologic changes in cerebral malaria and their relation to psychotic sequels. *Arch. Neurol. Psychiat. (Chic.)*, *56*, 79.—*383*.

ASHCROFT, P. B. (1941) Traumatic epilepsy after gunshot wounds of the head. *Brit. med. J.*, *1*, 739.—*505*.

ASHEM, B. (1963) The treatment of a disaster phobia by systematic desensitization. *Behav. Res. Ther.*, *1*, 81. —*186*.

ASHER, C. and ROBERTS, J. A. F. (1949) A study on birthweight and intelligence. *Brit. J. soc. Med.*, *3*, 56.—*706*.

ASHER, R. (1949) Myxoedematous madness. *Brit. med. J.*, *2*, 555.—*367*.

—— (1951) Munchausen's syndrome. *Lancet. 1*, 339.—*115*.

ASTRUP, C. and ØDEGAARD, Ø. (1960) Internal migration and mental disease in Norway. *Psychiat. Quart.*, *34*, Suppl. 116.—*784*.

ATKINSON, M. W., GARSIDE, R. F., KAY, D. W. K., ROMNEY, D. and ROTH, M. (1968) The contribution of environmental and hereditary factors in the aetiology of schizophrenia—a preliminary report. *Proc. 4th Wld Congr. Psychiat. Madrid, 1966. Excerpta med. int. Congr.* Series No. 150. p. 1777.—*251*.

BABCOCK, H. and LEVY, L. (1940) Manual of Directions for the Revised Examination of the Measurement of Efficiency of Mental Functioning. Chicago: Stoelting.—*492*.

BABINSKI, M. J. (1901) Definition of hysteria. *Rev. neurol. (Paris)*, *9*, 1074.—*112*.

von BAEYER, W. (1935) The Genealogy of Psychopathic Swindlers and Liars. Leipzig: Thieme.—*104, 111*.

von BAGH, K. (1941) Anatomical findings in thirty cases of systemic atrophy of the cerebral cortex (Pick's disease). *Arch. Psychiat. Nervenkr.*, *114*, 68.—*619*.

—— (1946) Clinical and Pathological Studies in Thirty Cases of Circumscribed Atrophy of the Cerebral Cortex. Helsinki.—*619*.

BAILLARGER, J. (1853–4) Note on the type of insanity with attacks characterized by two regular periods, one of depression and one of excitation. *Bull. Acad. Nat. Méd. (Paris)*, *19*, 340.—*188*.

BAKER, A. A. (1963) Letter: Abortion and the psychiatrist. *Brit. med. J.*, *2*, 867.—*377*.

——, MORISON, M., GAME, J. A. and THORPE, J. G. (1961) Admitting schizophrenic mothers with their babies. *Lancet, 2*, 237.—*373*.

BALL, J. R. B. (1965) Trans-sexualism: a descriptive and comparative study to attempt to establish possible aetiological factors. Thesis submitted to University of Newcastle upon Tyne.—*164, 165*.

—— (1966) The aetiological background of trans-sexualism: a comparative study of trans-sexuals with homosexual, exhibitionist and neurotic controls. To be published.—*169*.

—— and KILOH, L. G. (1959) A controlled trial of imipramine in the treatment of depressive states. *Brit. med. J.*, *1*, 1052.—*573*.

BARBOUR, R. F., BORLAND, E. M., BOYD, M. M., MILLER, A. and OPPÉ, T. E. (1963) Enuresis as a disorder of development. *Brit. med. J.*, *2*, 787.—*646*.

BARKER, J. C., THORPE, J. G., BLAKEMORE, C. B., LAVIN, N. I. and CONWAY, C. G. (1961) Letter: Behaviour therapy in a case of transvestism. *Lancet. 1*, 510.—*166*.

BARKER, P. A., ASHCROFT, G. W. and BINNS, J. K. (1960) Imipramine in chronic depression. *J. ment. Sci.*, *106*, 1447.—*199*.

BARON, D. N., DENT, C. E., HARRIS, H., HART, E. W. and JEPSON, J. B. (1956) Hereditary pellagra-like skin rash with temporary cerebellar ataxia, constant renal amino-aciduria, and other bizarre biochemical features. *Lancet, 2*, 421.—*725*.

BARR, M. L. and HOBBS, G. E. (1954) Chromosomal sex in transvestites. *Lancet, 1*, 1109.—*165*.

BARRACLOUGH, B. M., NELSON, B. and SAINSBURY, P. (1968) The diagnositic classification and psychiatric treatment of 25 suicides. Proc. 4th Int. Conf. for Suicide Prevention, Los Angeles, October 1967. —*791*.

—— and SAINSBURY, P. (1967) Personal communication.—*797*.

BARRY, H. and LINDEMANN, E. (1960) Critical ages for maternal bereavement in psychoneuroses. *Psychosom. Med.*, *22*, 166.—*5*.

BARSA, J. A. and KLINE, N. S. (1955) Combined reserpine-chlorpromazine therapy in disturbed psychotics. *Amer. J. Psychiat.*, *111*, 780.—*334*.

BARSLUND, I. and DANIELSEN, J. (1963) Temporal epilepsy in monozygotic twins. *Epilepsia (Amst)*. 4, 138.—*460*.
BARTHOLEMEW, A. A. (1961) Intoxication and habituation to glutethimide (Doriden). *Med. J. Aust.*, 2, 51.—*431*.
BARTON, R. (1966) Institutional Neurosis, 2nd ed. Bristol: Wright.—*338, 804*.
BATES, J. A. V. (1962) The Surgery of Epilepsy. In: Modern Trends in Neurology, ed. D. Williams, p. 125. London: Butterworth.—*481*.
BATT, J. C., KAY, W. W., REISS, M. and SANDS, D. E. (1957) The endocrine concomitants of schizophrenia. *J. ment. Sci.*, 103, 240.—*253*.
BÄTTIG, F. (1952) Beitrag zur Frage des Transvestitismus: Dissertation. Zurich: Buchdrukerai Fluntern.—*166*.
BAUER, J. (1921) The Constitutional Disposition of General Disease. Berlin: Springer.—*83*.
BEAMISH, P. and KILOH, L. G. (1960) Psychoses due to amphetamine consumption. *J. ment. Sci.*, 106, 337. —*422, 483*.
BEARD, G. M. (1880) American Nervousness. Richmond, Va: Treat.—*82*.
BECK, A. T., WARD, C. H., MENDELSON, M., MOCK, J. and ERBAUGH, J. (1961) An inventory for measuring depression. *Arch. gen. Psychiat.*, 4, 561.—*36*.
BECK, E. (1930) The problem of heredity in the symptomatic psychoses. *Mschr. Psychiat. Neurol.*, 77, 38.—*344*.
BECKETT, A. H. and ROWLAND, M. (1965) Determination and identification of amphetamine in urine. *J. Pharm. Pharmacol.*, 17, 59.—*421*.
BEIDLEMAN, B. (1954) Mongolism: a selective review. *Amer. J. ment. Defic.*, 50, 35.—*720*.
BELL, D. S. (1965) Comparison of amphetamine psychosis and schizophrenia. *Brit. J. Psychiat.*, 111, 701. —*299, 422*.
——— and TRETHOWAN, W. H. (1961) Amphetamine addiction and disturbed sexuality. *Arch. gen. Psychiat.*, 4, 74.—*422*.
BELL, J. (1934) Huntington's chorea. *Treas. hum. Inherit.*, 4, Part 1.—*624*.
BELL, K. M., (1965) The development of community care. *Publ. Admin.*, 4, 419.—*562*.
BENDA, C. E. (1947) Mongolism and Cretinism. London: Heinemann.—*721, 727*.
BENDER, L. (1940) The Goodenough Test (Drawing a Man) in chronic encephalitis in children. *J. nerv. ment. Dis.*, 91, 277.—*672*.
——— (1959) Autism in children with mental deficiency. *Amer. J. ment. Defic.*, 64, 81.—*681*.
——— (1961) Clinical research from in-patient services for children, 1920–1957. *Psychiat. Quart.*, 35, 88.—*684*.
——— (1962) Developmental neuropsychiatry: the future in child psychiatry. In: The Future of Psychiatry, ed. P. H. Hock and J. Zubin. New York: Grune & Stratton.—*640*.
——— (1963) Mental illness in childhood and heredity. *Eugen. Quart.*, 10, 1.—*685*.
——— and FARETRA, G. (1961) Pregnancy and birth problems of children with psychiatric problems. *Proc. 3rd Wld Congr. Psychiat.*, Montreal, p. 1329.—*684*.
——— and SCHILDER, P. (1933) Encephalopathia alcoholica. *Arch. Neurol. Psychiat. (Chic.)*, 29, 990.—*354*.
BENDER, M. B. (1945) Extinction and precipitation of cutaneous sensations. *Arch. Neurol. Psychiat. (Chic.)*, 54, 1.—*495*.
——— and FURLOW, L. T. (1945) Phenomenon of visual extinction in homonymous fields and psychologic principles involved. *Arch. Neurol. Psychiat. (Chic.)*, 53, 29.—*495*.
BENEDETTI, G. (1952) The Alcohol Hallucinoses. Stuttgart: Thieme.—*297, 300, 403*.
——— (1964) Klinische Psychotherapie. Bern.—*262*.
BENNETT, D. R., ZU RHEIN, G. M. and ROBERTS, T. S. (1962) Acute necrotizing encephalitis. *Arch. Neurol. (Chic.)*, 6, 96.—*513*.
BENTON, A. L. (1961) The fiction of the 'Gerstmann syndrome'. *J. Neurol. Neurosurg. Psychiat.*, 24, 176.—*497*.
BERESFORD-COOKE, K. (1964) Occupational therapy in the rehabilitation of the psychiatric geriatric patient at Crichton Royal. Parts 1 and 2. *Occup. Ther. J.* 27, 21.—*565*.
BERG, J. M. (1962) Meningitis as a cause of severe mental defect. *Proc. Lond. Conf. sci. Study ment. Defic.*, 1, 160.—*708*.
——— and KIRMAN, B. H. (1959) Syphilis as a cause of mental deficiency. *Brit. med. J.*, 2, 400.—*707*.
BERGMANN, K. (1966) Observations on the causation of neurotic disorder in old age with special reference to physical illness. *Proc. 7th Int. Congr. Geront.* Vienna, p. 623.—*577*.
BERINGER, K. (1927) Mescaline Intoxication. Berlin: Springer.—*435*.
——— (1932) Clinical symptoms of hashish intoxication: psychological disturbances. *Nervenarzt*, 5, 346.—*428*.
——— (1934) The Russo-German syphilis expedition into Burjato-Mongolia and its significance for the pathogenesis of parenchymatous syphilis. *Nervenarzt*, 7, 217,—*520*.
BERZE, J. (1910) Heredity or Dementia Praecox. Vienna: Deuticke.—*250*.
——— (1914) Primary Insufficiency of Psychic Activity. Vienna: Deuticke.—*265*.
BETHELL, M. F. (1965) Toxic psychosis caused by inhalation of petrol fumes. *Brit. med. J.*, 2, 276.—*432*.
BEVERFELT, E. (1962) Health and needs of non-attendants of old age health and welfare centres. In: Social Welfare of the Ageing, eds. J. Kaplan and G. J. Aldridge. New York: Columbia Univ. Press.—*560*.
BEWLEY, T. (1965) Heroin addiction in the United Kingdom (1954–64). *Brit. med. J.* 2, 1284.—*424*.
——— (1966) Recent changes in the pattern of drug abuse in the United Kingdom. *Bull. Narcot.*, 18, No. 4. 1. —*421*.
BIBER, B. (1961) Mental health principles in the school setting. In: Prevention of Mental Disorders in Children, ed. G. Caplan. New York: Basic Books.—*803*.
BICKFORD, J. A. R. and ELLISON, R. M. (1953) The high incidence of Huntington's chorea in the Duchy of Cornwall. *J. ment. Sci.*, 99, 291.—*623*.
BIESELE, J. J., SCHMID, W. and LAWLIS, M. G. (1962) Mentally retarded schizoid twin girls with 47 chromosomes. *Lancet*, 1, 403.—*722*.
BINSWANGER, L. (1933) On Flight of Ideas. Zurich: Füssli.—*195*.

BINSWANGER, L. (1945) Insanity as a problem of life history and as mental illness. *Mschr. Psychiat. Neurol.*, *110*, 129.—*227*.

BINSWANGER, O. (1898) Presenile dementia. *Münch. med. Wschr.*, *52*, 252.—*611*.

BIRNBAUM, K. (1908) Psychoses with Formation of Delusions and Paranoid Imaginations in the Degenerated. Halle.—*149*.

BJERNER, B. (1949) Alpha depression and lowered pulse rate during delayed actions in serial reaction test; study in sleep deprivation. *Acta physiol. scand.*, *19*, suppl. 65.—*381*.

BLACK, D. A. K., McCANCE, R. A. and YOUNG, W. F. (1944) A study of dehydration by means of balance experiments. *J. Physiol.* (Lond.), *102*, 406.—*358*.

BLACKER, C. P. (1937) A Social Problem Group. London: Oxford Univ. Press.—*704*.

——— (1948) Neurosis and the Mental Health Services. London: Oxford Univ. Press.—*632*.

BLACKWELL, B. (1963a) Letter: Tranylcypromine. *Lancet*, *1*, 167.—*202*.

——— (1963b) Hypertensive crises due to monoamine-oxidase inhibitors. *Lancet*, *2*, 849.—*202*.

——— and MARLEY, E. (1964) Interaction between cheese and monoamine-oxidase inhibitors in rats and cats. *Lancet*, *1*, 530.—*202*.

BLAKE, B. G. (1965) The application of behaviour therapy to the treatment of alcholism. *Behav. Res. Ther.*, *3*, 75.—*409, 410*.

BLAKEMORE, C. B., THORPE, J. G., BARKER, J. C., CONWAY, C. G. and LAVIN, N. I. (1963a) The application of faradic aversion conditioning in a case of transvestism. *Behav. Res. Ther.*, *1*, 29.—*166, 185*.

———, ———, ———, ——— and ——— (1963b) Follow-up note to the application of faradic aversion conditioning in a case of transvestism. *Behav. Res. Ther.*, *1*, 191.—*166*.

BLAU, A. (1936) Mental changes following head trauma in children. *Arch. Neurol. Psychiat.* (Chic.), *35*, 723.—*505*.

BLESSED, G., TOMLINSON, B. E., and ROTH, M. (1968) The association between quantitative measures of dementia and of degenerative changes in the cerebral grey matter of elderly subjects. *Brit. J. Psychiat.* *114*, 797.—*595, 602, 604, 605, 607*.

BLEULER, E. (1911) Dementia Praecox or the Group of Schizophrenias. Vienna. (Trans. J. Zinkin, 1950), New York: Int. Univ. Press.—*237*.

——— (1916) Textbook of Psychiatry. Berlin: Springer.—*548*.

——— (1921) The Autistic Thinking without Discipline in Medicine and its Conquest. Berlin: Springer.—*268*.

BLEULER, M. (1941a) Course of Illness, Personality and Family History in Schizophrenics. Leipzig: Thieme.—*245, 251, 311*.

——— (1941b) Remission of schizophrenia after shock therapy. *Z. ges. Neurol. Psychiat.*, *173*, 553.—*309*.

——— (1943) The Clinical Features of the Late Schizophrenias. *Fortschr. Neurol. Psychiat.*, *15*, 259.—*580*.

——— (1949) Textbook of Psychiatry (8th ed. of E. Bleuler's Textbook). Berlin: Springer.—*421*.

——— (1951) Psychiatry of cerebral diseases. *Brit. med. J.*, *2*, 1233.—*494, 526*.

——— *et al.* (1952) Unpublished material personally communicated.—*393*.

——— (1954) Endocrinological Psychiatry. Stuttgart: Thieme.—*253, 366, 368*.

——— (1963) Conception of schizophrenia within the last fifty years and today. *Proc. roy. Soc. Med.*, *56*, 945.—*246*.

BLISS, E. L., MIGEON, C. J., BRANCH, C. H. H. and SAMUELS, L. T. (1955) Adrenocortical function in schizophrenia. *Amer. J. Psychiat.*, *112*, 358.—*252*.

BOARD, F., WADESON, R. and PERSKY, H. (1957) Depressive affect and endocrine functions. *Arch. Neurol. Psychiat.* (Chic.), *78*, 612.—*203*.

BOATMAN, J. J. and SZUREK, S. A. (1960) A clinical study of childhood schizophrenia. In: The Aetiology of Schizophrenia, ed. D. D. Jackson. New York: Basic Books.—*686*.

BODIAN, M., WHITE, L. L. R., CARTER, C. O. and LOUW, J. H. (1952) Congenital duodenal obstruction and mongolism. *Brit. med. J.*, *1*, 77.—*722*.

van BOGAERT, L. (1945) A case of sub-acute sclerotic leuco-encephalitis. *J. Neurol. Psychiat.*, *8*, 101.—*513*.

———, van MAERE, M. and de SMEDT, E. (1940) Sur les formes familiales precoces de la maladie d'Alzheimer. *Mschr. Psychiat. Neurol.*, *102*, 249.—*613*.

BOGEN, E. (1932) The human toxicology of alcohol. In: Alcohol and Man, ed. Emerson. New York: Macmillan.—*392*.

BOLTON, N., BRITTON, P. G. and SAVAGE, R. D. (1966) Some normative data on the WAIS and its indices in an aged population. *J. clin. Psychol.*, *22*, 184.—*492*.

———, SAVAGE, R. D. and ROTH, M. (1967) The Modified Word Learning Test and the aged psychiatric patient. *Brit. J. Psychiat.*, *113*, 1139.—*492, 555*.

BONCOUR, G. P. (1910) Tics in schoolchildren and their interpretation. *Progr. méd.* (Paris), *26*, 495.—*654*.

BOND, D. D. (1958) Discussion following a paper on behavioural changes in nonpsychotic volunteers following the administration of taraxein, the substance obtained from serum of schizophrenic patients by R. G. Heath and his colleagues, read at the 113th annual meeting of the American Psychiatric Association, 1957. *Amer. J. Psychiat.*, *114*, 919.—*255*.

BONHOEFFER, K. (1903) On beggars and vagrants in big cities: prostitutes. *v. Lisztsche Z.*, *23*, 106.—*715*.

——— (1910) Symptomatic Psychoses. Berlin.—*342, 483*.

BÖÖK, J. A. (1953a) A genetic and neuropsychiatric investigation of a North-Swedish population. *Acta genet.* (Basel), *4*, 1.—*189, 239, 249*.

——— (1953b) Schizophrenia as a gene mutation. *Acta genet.* (Basel), *4*, 133.—*249*.

BOSS, M. (1952) Psychopathologie der Liebesstorungen. Bern: Huber.—*166*.

BOTWINICK, J. and BIRREN, J. E. (1951) The measurement of intellectual decline in the senile psychoses. *J. cons. Psychol.*, *15*, 145.—*603*.

BOURDILLON, R. E., CLARKE, C. A., RIDGES, A. P., SHEPPARD, P. M., HARPER, P. and LESLIE, S. A. (1965). 'Pink spot' in the urine of schizophrenics. *Nature* (Lond.), *208*, 453.—*256*.

BOWLBY, J. (1944) Forty-four juvenile thieves; their characters and home-life. *Int. J. Psychoanal.*, *25*, 19.—*636*.

——— (1946) Forty-four Juvenile Thieves. London: Baillière.—*636*.

——— (1951) Maternal Care and Mental Health. W. H. O. Monograph Series, No. 2, Geneva.—*636*.

——— (1953) Some pathological processes set in train by early mother-child separation. *J. ment. Sci.*, *99*, 265.—*29*.

——— (1958) A note on mother-child separation as a mental health hazard. *Brit. J. med. Psychol.*, *31*, 247.—*636*.

——— (1960) Separation anxiety. *Int. J. Psychoanal.*, *41*, 89.—*6*.

BOWLEY, A. H. (1943) The Natural Development of the Child, 2nd ed. Edinburgh: Livingstone.—*655*.

BOXALL, J. S. and CHAUVEL, P. J. (1966) Attempted suicide: a review of 100 consecutive cases at a district hospital. *Med. J. Aust.*, *1*, 264.—*378*.

BOYCOTT, A. E., DAMANT, G. C. C. and HALDANE, J. S. (1908) The prevention of compressed air illness. *J. Hyg.* (Camb.), *8*, 342.—*439*.

BOYD, D. A. Jnr, (1942) Mental disorders associated with childbearing. *Amer. J. Obstet. Gynec.*, *43*, 148 and 335.—*374*.

BRAATELIEN, N. T. and GALLAVAN, M. (1950) Brain tumours in mental patients. *Dis. nerv. Syst.*, *11*, 207.—*525*.

BRADLEY, C. (1937) The behaviour of children receiving benzedrine. *Amer. J. Psychiat.*, *94*, 577.—*674*.

BRADLEY, P. B., DENIKER, P. and RADOUCO-THOMAS, C. (eds.) (1959) Neuropsychopharmacology, Vol. I. Amsterdam: Elsevier.—*334*.

———, FLÜGEL, F. and HOCH, P. (eds.) (1964) Neuropsychopharmacology, Vol. 3. Amsterdam: Elsevier.—*334*.

BRAIN, W. R. (1941) Visual disorientation with special reference to lesions of the right cerebral hemisphere. *Brain.* *64*, 244.—*496*.

——— (1951) Diseases of the Nervous System, 4th ed. Oxford: Oxford Univ. Press.—*445*.

———, GREENFIELD, J. G. and RUSSELL, D. S. (1943) Discussion on recent experiences of acute encephalomyelitis and allied conditions. *Proc. roy. Soc. Med.*, *36*, 319.—*513*.

BRANDER, T. (1935) On the significance of exogenous factors in the origin of mental defect, shown by sixteen investigations in twins. *Mschr. Kinderheilk.*, *63*, 276.—*702*.

BRANDON, S. and GRUENBERG, E. M. (1966) Measurement of the incidence of the chronic severe social breakdown syndrome. In: Evaluating the Effectiveness of Mental Health Services. *Milbank. mem. Fd. Quart.*, *44*, 129.—*805*.

———, and SMITH, D. (1962) Amphetamines in general practice. *J. Coll. gen. Practit.*, *5*, 603.—*420*.

BRANDRUP, E. and KRISTJANSEN, P. (1961) A controlled clinical test of a new psycholeptic drug (Haloperidol). *J. ment. Sci.*, *107*, 778.—*334*.

von BRAUNMÜHL, A. (1930) Changes of basal ganglia in Pick's disease. *Z. ges. Neurol. Psychiat.*, *124*, 214.—*617*.

BREMER, J. (1951) A social psychiatric investigation of a small community in northern Norway. *Acta psychiat. neurol.* (Kbh.), suppl. 62.—*540*.

BREUTSCH, W. L. (1952) Specific structural neuropathology of the central nervous system (rheumatic, demyelinating, vasofunctional etc.) in schizophrenia. *Proc. 1st Int. Congr. Neuropath.*, *1*, 487.—*258*.

BREW, M. F. and SEIDENBERG, R. (1950) Psychotic reactions associated with pregnancy and childbirth. *J. nerv. ment. Dis.*, *111*, 408.—*374*.

BRIDGE. E. M. (1949) Epilepsy and Convulsive Disorders in Children. New York: McGraw-Hill.—*672*.

BRIDGES, P. K., and KOLLER, K. M. (1966) Attempted suicide: a comparative study. *Comprehens. Psychiat.* *7*, 240.—*793*.

BRIERLEY, H. (1968) The habituation of forearm muscle blood-flow in phobic subjects. To be published.—*96*.

BRIM, O. G. (1961) Methods of educating parents. In: Prevention of Mental Disorders in Children, ed. G. Caplan. New York: Basic Books.—*802*.

BRITISH MEDICAL JOURNAL (1961) Annotation: Drugs of addiction and habituation. *Brit. med. J.*, *1*, 1523.—*420*.

BRODIE, B. B. and COSTA, E. (1962) Some current views on brain monoamines. *Psychopharmac. Serv. Cent. Bull.*, *2*, 1.—*199*.

BROWN, F. (1961) Depression and childhood bereavement. *J. ment. Sci.*, *107*, 754.—*5*.

BROWN, F. W. (1942) Heredity in psychoneuroses. *Proc. roy. Soc. Med.*, *35*, 785.—*68*, *103*.

BROWN, G. W., CARSTAIRS, G. M. and TOPPING, G. (1958) Post-hospital adjustment of chronic mental patients. *Lancet*, *2*, 685.—*340*.

———, MONCK, E. M., CARSTAIRS, G. M. and WING, J. K. (1962) Influence of family life on the course of schizophrenic illness. *Brit. J. prev. soc. Med.*, *16*, 55.—*340*.

———, PARKES, C. M. and WING, J. K. (1961) Admissions and readmissions to three London mental hospitals. *J. ment. Sci.*, *107*, 1070.—*339*.

BROWN, J. L. (1960) Prognosis from presenting symptoms of preschool children with atypical development. *Amer. J. Orthopsychiat.*, *30*, 382.—*686*.

BROWNING, T. B., ATKINS, R. W. and WEINER, H. (1954) Cerebral metabolic disturbances in hypothyroidism; clinical and electroencephalographic studies of the psychoses of myxoedema and hypothyroidism. *A.M.A. Arch. intern. Med.*, *93*, 938.—*367*.

BRUCE, J. and RUSSELL, G. F. M. (1962) Pre-menstrual tension. A study of weight changes and balances of water, sodium and potassium. *Lancet*, *2*, 267.—*372*.

BRUGGER, C. (1928) The genetical position of Propfschizophrenie. *Z. ges. Neurol. Psychiat.*, *113*, 348.—*243*, *703*.

BRUNSWICK, M. R. (1929) Postscript to Freud's 'History of a Case of Infantile Neurosis'. Vienna: Deuticke.—*283*.

BUCCI, L. (1963) A familial organic psychosis of Alzheimer type in six kinships of three generations. *Amer. J. Psychiat.*, *119*, 863.—*613*.

BUCKE, M. (1962) Leisure-time activities of elderly people in the United Kingdom. In: Social Welfare of the Ageing, ed. J. Kaplan and G. J. Aldridge. New York: Columbia University Press.—*561*.

BÜHLER, C., HETZER, H. and TUDOR-HART, B. (1927) Sociological and psychological studies of the first year of life. *Quell, Forsch. Z. Jugendk.*, No. 5. Jena: Fischer.—*655, 708*.

BUMKE, O. (1924) Textbook of Mental Diseases. Berlin: Springer.—*467*.

BURCH, P. R. J. (1964a) Manic depressive psychosis: some new aetiological considerations. *Brit. J. Psychiat.*, *110*, 808.—*196*.

—— (1964b) Schizophrenia: some new aetiological considerations. *Brit. J. Psychiat.*, *110*, 818.—*196, 247*.

—— (1964c) Involutional psychosis: some new aetiological considerations. *Brit. J. Psychiat.*, *110*, 825.—*196*.

BURDACH, K. F. (1819–26) Vom Baue und Leben des Gehirns. Leipzig: Thieme.—*537*.

BÜRGER, M. (1957) Altern und Krankheit. Leipzig: Thieme.—*535*.

—— (1957) Die chemische Bimorphose des menschlichen Gehirns. Abhandlungen der Sachsischen Akademic der Wissenschaften zu Leipsig, Mathematisch-naturwissen-schaftliche Klasse, 45, 1.—*535*.

BURT, C. G., GORDON, W. F., HOLT, N. F. and HORDERN, A. (1962) Amitriptyline in depressive states: a controlled trial. *J. ment. Sci.*, *108*, 711.—*230*.

BURT, C. L. (1946) Intelligence and Fertility. Occasional papers on Eugenics, No. 4. London: Hamilton.—*701*.

—— (1948) The Young Delinquent, 4th ed. London: Univ. of London Press.—*716*.

BUSFIELD, B. L., WECHSLER, H. and BARNUM, W. J. (1961) Studies of salivation in depression. II Psychological differentiation of reactive and endogenous depression. *Arch gen. Psychiat.*, *5*, 472.—*204*.

BUSSE, E. W., DOVENMUEHLE, R. H. and BROWN, R. G. (1960) Psychoneurotic reactions of the aged. *Geriatrics*, *15*, 97.—*577*.

BYERS, R. K. and LORD, E. E. (1943) Late effects of lead poisoning on mental development. *Amer. J. Dis. Child.*, *66*, 471.—*443*.

BYKOV, K. (1959) The Cerebral Cortex and the Internal Organs (transl. R. Hodes). Moscow: Foreign Languages. Publ. House.—*24*.

CADE, J. F. J. (1949) Lithium salts in treatment of psychotic excitement. *Med. J. Aust.*, *2*, 349.—*232*.

CAIRNS, H. (1952) Disturbances of consciousness with lesions of the brain-stem and diencephalon. *Brain*, *75*. 109.—*498, 526*.

CAMBRIDGE-SOMERVILLE YOUTH STUDY, The (1951) See POWERS and WITMER.—*631*.

CAMERON, A. J. (1964) Heroin addicts in a casualty department. *Brit. med. J.*, *1*, 594.—*425, 430*.

CAMERON, D. E. (1963) The processes of remembering. *Brit. J. Psychiat.*, *109*, 325.—*610*.

CAMERON. N. (1938) Reasoning, regression and communication in schizophrenia. *Psychol. Monogr.*, *50*, No. 1.—*268*.

—— (1939) Schizophrenic thinking in a problem-solving situation. *J. ment. Sci.*, *85*, 1012.—*266*.

CAMP, W. A. and WOLFF, H. G. (1961) Studies on headache. Electroencephalographic abnormalities in patients with vascular headache of the migraine type. *Arch. Neurol. (Chic.)*, *4*, 475.—*454*.

CANNON, W. B. (1928) Feelings and Emotions. The Wittenberg Symposium. Worcester (Mass.), p. 257.—*138*.

CAPLAN, G. (ed.) (1961) Prevention of Mental Disorders in Children: Initial Explorations. New York: Basic Books.—*800, 801, 802*.

—— (1964) Principles of Preventive Psychiatry. London: Tavistock.—*800*.

CAPON, N. B. (1950) Development and behaviour of children. *Brit. med. J.*, *1*, 859.—*630*.

CAPSTICK, A. (1960) Recognition of emotional disturbance and the prevention of suicide. *Brit. med. J.*, *1*, 1179.—*542*.

CARDON, P. V., SOKOLOFF, L., VATES, T. S. and KETY, S. S. (1961) The physiological and psychological effects of intravenously administered epinephrine and its metabolism in normal and schizophrenic men. I Effects on heart rate, blood pressure, blood glucose concentration and the EEG. *J. psychiat. Res.*, *1*, 37.—*437*.

CARLSSON, A., FUXE, K., HAMBERGER, B. and LINDQVIST, M. (1966) Biochemical and histochemical studies on the effects of imipramine-like drugs and (+)—amphetamine on central and peripheral catecholamine neurones. *Acta physiol. scand.*, *67*, 481.—*201*.

CARMICHAEL, E. A. (1953) Hemiplegia of early onset and the results of hemispherectomy. Lumlian Lectures delivered to the Royal College of Physicians, April 1953.—*676, 733*.

CARNEY, M. W. P., ROTH, M. and GARSIDE, R. F. (1965) The diagnosis of depressive syndromes and the prediction of E.C.T. response. *Brit. J. Psychiat.*, *111*, 659.—*188, 210, 222, 225, 572*.

CARPELAN, H. (1957) Mental disorders in thyroidectomized patients: a psychosomatic study of 53 cases. *Acta psychiat. neurol. scand.*, *32*, Suppl., 116.—*366*.

CARR-SAUNDERS, A. M., MANNHEIM, H. and RHODES, H. C. (1942) Young Offenders: An Enquiry into Juvenile Delinquency. Cambridge: Cambridge Univ. Press.—*638*.

CARTER, A. B. (1949) The prognosis of certain hysterical symptoms. *Brit. med. J.*, *1*, 1076.—*105*.

CARTER, C. and MacCARTHY, D. (1951) Incidence of mongolism and its diagnosis in the newborn. *Brit. J. soc. Med.*, *5*, 83.—*720*.

CASLER, L. (1965a) The effects of extra tactile stimulation on a group of institutionalized infants. *Genet. Psychol. Monogr.* (Provincetown) *71*, 137.—*637*.

—— (1965b) The effects of supplementary verbal stimulation on a group of institutionalized infants. *J. Child Psychol.*, *6*, 19.—*637*.

—— (1968) Perceptual deprivation in an institutional setting. In: Early Experience and Behaviour: Psychological and Physiological Effects of Early Environmental Variation, ed. G. Newton and S. Levine. Springfield, Ill.: Thomas, Awaiting publication.—*637*.

CATTELL, R. B. (1943) The measurement of adult intelligence. *Psychol. Bull.*, 40, 153.—538.

—— (1948) A Guide to Mental Testing. 2nd ed. London: Univ. of London Press.—728.

CATTERSON, A. G., BENNETT, D. H. and FREUDENBERG, R. K. (1963) A survey of long-stay schizophrenic patients. *Brit. J. Psychiat.*, 109, 750.—338.

CAVANAGH, J. B., FALCONER, M. A. and MEYER, A. (1958) Some pathogenic problems of temporal lobe epilepsy. In: Temporal Lobe Epilepsy, ed. M. Baldwin and P. Bailey. Springfield, Ill.: Thomas.—468, 480.

—— and MEYER, A. (1956) Aetiological aspects of Ammon's horn sclerosis associated with temporal lobe epilepsy. *Brit. med. J.*, 2, 1403.—451, 468.

CAWTE, J. E. (1968) Diverse, cruel, poor and brutal nations. In preparation.—790.

CEDERMARK, J. (1942) On the symptoms, course and prognosis of cranial and cerebral injuries. *Acta. chir. scand.*, 86, Suppl. 75.—503.

CERLETTI, U. and BINI, L. (1938) Electroshock. *Boll. Accad. med. Roma*, 64, 36.—235.

CHAPMAN, J. (1966) The early symptoms of schizophrenia. *Brit. J. Psychiat.*, 112, 225.—274.

CHAUDHRY, M. R., and POND, D. A. (1961) Mental deterioration in epileptic children. *J. Neurol. Neurosurg. Psychiat.*, 24, 213.—673.

CHAZAN, M. (1962) School phobia. *Brit. J. educ. Psychol.*, 32, 209.—663.

CHENEY, C. O. and DREWRY, P. H. (1938) Results of non-specific treatment in dementia praecox. *Amer. J. Psychiat.*, 95, 203.—310

CHESTER, B., MCCLELLAND, H. A., ROTH, M. and KAY, D. W. K. (1969) A 1–3 year follow-up study of 196 cases of schizophrenia. To be published.—311.

CHODOFF, P. and LYONS, H. (1958) Hysteria, the hysterical personality and 'hysterical' conversion. *Amer. J. Psychiat.*, 114, 734.—104, 108.

CLARK, D. F. (1963a) Fetishism treated by negative conditioning. *Brit. J. Psychiat.*, 109, 404.—164.

—— (1963b) The treatment of monosymptomatic phobia by systematic desensitization. *Behav. Res. Ther.*, 1, 63.—186.

CLARK, D. H. (1964) The ward therapeutic community and its effects on the hospital. Symposium on Mental Hospital Psychiatry, Middlesex Hospital, January 1964.—327.

CLARK, J. A. (1962) The prognosis of drug addiction. *J. ment. Sci.*, 108, 411.—426.

CLARKE, A. D. B., CLARKE, A. M. and REIMAN, S. (1958) Cognitive and social changes in the feebleminded— three further studies. *Brit. J. Psychol.*, 49, 144.—705.

CLARKE, A. M., and CLARKE A. D. B. (1958) Mental Deficiency: the Changing Outlook. London: Methuen. —29, 705.

CLAUSEN, J. A. and KOHN, M. L. (1959) Relation of schizophrenia to the social structure of a small city. In: Epidemiology of Mental Disorder, ed. B. Pasamanick. Washington: Bailey.—238.

CLECKLEY, H. M. (1941) The Mask of Sanity. London: Kimpton.—111, 156.

CLEGHORN, R. A. (1951) Adrenal cortical insufficiency: psychological and neurological observations. *Canad. med. Ass. J.*, 65, 449.—368.

de CLÉRAMBAULT, G. (1942) Psychiatric Writings. Paris.—275.

CLOW, H. E. and ALLEN, E. B. (1951) Manifestations of psychoneuroses occurring in later life. *Geriatrics*, 6. 31.—577.

CLOWARD, R. A. and OHLIN, L. E. (1961) Delinquency and Opportunity. A Theory of Delinquent Gangs, London: Routledge.—659.

COBB, W. A. (1950) In: Electroencephalography, ed. D. Hill and G. Parr. London: Macdonald.—464.

COHEN Committee (1956) Report on the Medical Care of Epileptics. London: H.M.S.O.—481.

COHEN, A. K. (1956) Delinquent Boys. London: Routledge.—659.

COHEN, B. D., GRISELL, J. L. and AX, A. F. (1961) The effects of voluntary sleep loss on psychological and physiological functions. *Proc. 3rd. Wld Congr. Psychiat.*, 2, 986.—381.

COHEN, E., MOTTO, J. A. and SEIDEN, R. H. (1966) An instrument for evaluating suicidal potential: a preliminary study. *Amer. J. Psychiat.*, 122, 886.—796.

COHEN, M. E. et al. (1951) The high familial prevalence of neuro-circulatory asthenia (anxiety neurosis, effort syndrome). *Amer. J. hum. Genet.*, 3, 126.—68.

COHN, R. and NARDINI, J. E. (1958–9) The correlation of bilateral occipital slow activity in the human EEG with certain disorders of behaviour. *Amer. J. Psychiat.*, 115, 44.—71.

COLLEGE OF GENERAL PRACTITIONERS (1960) A survey of the epilepsies in general practice. A report by the Research Committee. *Brit. med. J.*, 2, 416.—450, 673.

—— (1962) Morbidity statistics from general practice. Vol. III (Disease in general practice). Studies on Medical and Population Subjects No. 14. (Research Committee of the Council) London: General Register Office, H.M.S.O.—589.

COLLIER, J. (1947) Anoxaemia. In: Price's Textbook of the Practice of Medicine. 7th ed. London: Oxford Univ. Press.—439.

COLLINS, R. T. (1943) Affect in schizophrenic reaction types. *J. ment. Sci.*, 89, 21.—313.

COLWELL, C. and POST, F. (1959) Community needs of elderly psychiatric patients. *Brit. med. J.*, 2, 214.—567.

COMFORT, A. (1965) The Process of Ageing. London: Weidenfeld.—536.

CONLON, M. F. (1963) Addiction to chlorodyne. *Brit. med. J.*, 2, 1177.—432.

CONNELL, P. H. (1958) Amphetamine Psychosis. (Maudsley Monograph No. 5) Institute of Psychiatry, London: Chapman.—299, 422, 483.

CONRAD, K. (1937a) Heredity and epilepsy. *Z. ges. Neurol. Psychiat.*, 159, 521.—450, 452, 454.

—— (1937b) Review of selection-free investigations into relatives of epileptics. *Z. psych. Hyg.*, 10, 167. —452, 703.

—— (1958) Die beginnende Schizophrenie Versuch einer Gestaltanalyse des Wahns. Stuttgart: Thieme. —315.

CONRAD, K. (1960) The symptomatic psychoses. In: Psychiatrie der Gegenwart, Vol. 2, 369. Berlin: Springer-Verlag.—*347*.

CONSTANTINIDIS, J., GARRONE, G., TISSOT, R. and de AJURIAGUERRA, J. (1965) L'incidence familiale des altérations neurofibrillaires corticales d'Alzheimer. *Psychiat. et Neurol. (Basel)*, *150*, 235.—*613*.

COOKE, W. R. (1945) The differential psychology of the American woman. *Amer. J. Obstet. Gynec.*, *49*, 457.—*372*.

COOPER, A. B. and EARLY, D. F. (1961) Evolution in the mental hospital. *Brit. med. J.*, *1*, 1600.—*338*.

COOPER, A. J., MAGNUS, R. V. and ROSE, M. J. (1964) A hypertensive syndrome with tranylcypromine medication. *Lancet*, *1*, 527.—*202*.

COOPER, B. (1961) Grouping and tranquillizers in the chronic ward. *Brit. J. med. Psychol.*, *34*, 157.—*334*.

COOPER, J. E. (1963) A study of behaviour therapy in thirty psychiatric patients. *Lancet*, *1*, 411.—*187*.

COPPEN, A. J. (1959) Body-build of male homosexuals. *Brit. med. J.*, *2*, 1443.—*170*.

——— (1965a) The prevalence of menstrual disorders in psychiatric patients. *Brit. J. Psychiat.*, *111*, 155.—*372*.

——— (1965b) Mineral metabolism in affective disorders. *Brit. J. Psychiat.*, *111*, 1133.—*203*.

———, MALLESON, A. and SHAW, D. M. (1965) Effects of lithium carbonate on electrolyte distribution in man. *Lancet*, *1*, 682.—*203*.

———, and SHAW, D. M. (1963) Mineral metabolism in melancholia. *Brit. med. J.*, *2*, 1439.—*203*.

———, ——— and FARRELL, J. P. (1963) Potentiation of the antidepressive effect of a monoamine-oxidase inhibitor by tryptophan. *Lancet*, *1*, 79.—*200*.

CORSELLIS, J. A. N. (1951) Sub-acute sclerosing leuco-encephalitis: a clinical and pathological report of two cases. *J. ment. Sci.*, *97*, 570.—*513, 514*.

——— (1962) Mental Illness and the Ageing Brain. Maudsley Monograph, No. 9. London: Oxford University Press.—*604, 605, 607*.

——— and BRIERLEY, J. B. (1954) An unusual type of presenile dementia. *Brain*, *77*, 571.—*614*.

COSIN, L. Z., MORT, M., POST, F., WESTROPP, C. and WILLIAMS, M. (1957) Persistent senile confusion: a study of 50 consecutive cases. *Int. J. soc. Psychiat.*, *3*, 195.—*554*.

———, ———, ———, ——— and ——— (1958) Experimental treatment of persistent senile confusion. *Int. J. soc. Psychiat.*, *4*, 24.—*560, 610*.

COSTA, E., GESSA, G. L., HIRSCH, C., KUNTZMAN, R. and BRODIE, B. B. (1962) On current status of serotonin as a brain neurohormone and in action of reserpine-like drugs. *Ann. N.Y. Acad. Sci.*, *96*, 118.—*200*.

COSTELLO, C. G. and SELBY, M. M. (1965) The relationship between sleep patterns and reactive and endogenous depression. *Brit. J. Psychiat.*, *111*, 497.—*210*.

COWIE, J., COWIE, V. and SLATER, E. (1968) Delinquency in Girls. London: Heinemann.—*639, 657, 716*.

COWIE, V., COPPEN, A. and NORMAN, P. (1960) Nuclear sex and body-build in schizophrenia. *Brit. med. J.*, *2*, 431.—*70*.

——— and GAMMACK, D. B. (1966) Serum proteins in Huntington's chorea. *Brit. J. Psychiat.*, *112*, 723.—*621*.

——— and SEAKINS, J. W. T. (1962) Urinary alanine excretor in a Huntington's chorea family. *J. ment. Sci.*, *108*, 427.—*621*.

COX, L. B. (1934) Observations on the nature, rate of growth and operability of the intracranial tumours derived from 135 patients. *Med. J. Aust.*, *1*, 182.—*525*.

CRAMER, F., PASTER, S. and STEPHENSON, C. (1949) Cerebral injuries due to explosion waves—'cerebral blast concussion'. A pathologic, clinical and electro-encephalographic study. *Arch. Neurol. Psychiat.*, *(Chic.)*, *61*, 1.—*502*.

CRAMMER, J. L. (1957) Rapid weight-changes in mental patients. *Lancet*, *2*, 259.—*254*.

——— (1959) Water and sodium in two psychotics. *Lancet*, *1*, 1122.—*202, 254*.

CRAVIOTO, H., KOREIN, J. and SILBERMAN, J. (1961) Wernicke's encephalopathy. A clinical and pathologica study of 28 autopsied cases. *Arch. Neurol. (Chic.)*, *4*, 510.—*355*.

CREAK, E. M. (1963a) Schizophrenia in early childhood. *Acta paedopsychiat. (Basel)*, *30*, 42.—*685*.

——— (1963b) Childhood psychosis: a review of 100 cases. *Brit. J. Psychiat.*, *109*, 84.—*685*.

——— and GUTTMANN, E. (1935) Chorea, tics and compulsive utterances. *J. ment. Sci.*, *81*, 834.—*382*.

——— and INI, S. (1960) Families of psychotic children. *J. Child Psychol. Psychiat.*, *1*, 156.—*685*.

CREUTZFELDT, H. G. (1920) On a peculiar focal disease of the central nervous system. *Z. ges. Neurol. Psychiat.*, *57*, 1.—*619*.

CRITCHLEY, M. (1943) Shipwreck-survivors. London: Churchill.—*356*.

——— (1949) Punch-drunk syndromes: the chronic traumatic encephalopathy of boxers. From: Hommage à Clovis Vincent. Paris: Maloine.—*505*.

——— (1953) The Parietal Lobes. London: Arnold.—*490, 499*.

——— (1957) Medical aspects of boxing, particularly from a neurological standpoint. *Brit. med. J. 1*, 357.—*505*.

——— (1964) Developmental Dyslexia. London: Heinemann.—*678*.

CROME, L., KIRMAN, B. H. and MARRS, M. (1955) Rhesus incompatibility and mental deficiency. *Brain*, *78*, 514.—*728*.

CRONHOLM, B. and OTTOSSON, J-O. (1963a) Reliability and validity of a memory test battery. *Acta psychiat. scand.*, *39*, 218.—*36*.

——— and ——— (1963b) The experience of memory function after electroconvulsive therapy. *Brit. J. Psychiat.*, *109*, 251.—*235*.

CRUZ-COKE, R., ETCHEVERRY, R., and NAGEL, R. (1964) Influence of migration on blood-pressure of Easter Islanders. *Lancet*, *1*, 697.—*589*.

CUMMING, E. and HENRY, W. E. (1961) Growing Old: the Process of Disengagement. New York: Basic Books.—*545*.

CUMMING, G. (1961) The Medical Management of Acute Poisoning. London: Cassell.—*417*.

CURRAN, D. (1930) Huntington's chorea without choreiform movements. *J. Neurol. Psychopath.*, *10*, 305.—*624*.

—— (1937) The differentiation of neuroses and manic-depressive psychoses. *J. ment. Sci.*, *83*, 156.—*220*.

—— and GUTTMANN, E. (1949) Psychological Medicine. A short introduction to psychiatry with an appendix on psychiatry associated with war conditions, 3rd ed. Edinburgh: Livingstone.—*6*.

—— and MALLINSON, W. P. (1944) Recent progress in psychiatry: psychopathic personality. *J. ment. Sci.*, *90*, 266.—*59*.

—— and PARR, D. (1957) Homosexuality: an analysis of 100 male cases seen in private practice. *Brit. med. J.* *1*, 797.—*171*.

CURTIUS, F. (1933) Disseminated Sclerosis and Heredity. Leipzig: Thieme.—*530*.

CUSHING, H. (1932) Intracranial Tumours: Notes upon a series of 2,000 verified cases with surgical-mortality percentages pertaining thereto. Springfield, Ill.: Thomas.—*525*.

DAHLBERG, G. (1941) Rare psychological defects from the point of view of the population. Proc. 7th Int. Genet. Congr., 1939. Cambridge.—*700*.

DAHLGREN, K. G. (1945) On Suicide and Attempted Suicide. Lund: Lindstedts.—*378*.

DALTON, K. (1959) Menstruation and acute psychiatric illnesses. *Brit. med. J.*, *1*, 148.—*205*.

—— (1960) Schoolgirls' behaviour and menstruation. *Brit. med. J.*, *2*, 1647.—*716*.

—— The Premenstrual Syndrome. London: Heinemann.—*372*.

DANZIGER, L. (1946) Prognosis in some mental disorders. *Dis. nerv. Syst.*, *7*, 229.—*309*.

DAVIES, D. L., SHEPHERD, M. and MYERS, E. (1956) The two-year prognosis of 50 alcoholic addicts after treatment in hospital. *Quart. J. Stud. Alcohol.*, *17*, 485.—*412*.

DAVIS, C. M. (1928) Self-selection of diet by newly weaned infants. *Amer. J. Dis. Child.*, *36*, 651.—*644*.

—— (1935) Choice of formulas made by three infants throughout the nursing period. *Amer. J. Dis. Child.*, *50*, 385.—*644*.

DAVIS, D. R. (1962) Birth order and maternal age of homosexuals: letter. *Lancet*, *1*, 540.—*169*.

DAVISON, K. (1964) Episodic depersonalization. *Brit. J. Psychiat.*, *110*, 505.—*124*.

—— (1966) Schizophrenia-like psychoses associated with organic brain diseases. Preliminary observations on 50 patients. *Newcastle med. J.*, *29*, 67.—*258, 301*.

DAWSON, J. R. (1933) Cellular inclusions in cerebral lesions of lethargic encephalitis. *Amer. J. Path.*, *9*, 7.—*513*.

—— (1934) Cellular inclusions in cerebral lesions of epidemic encephalitis. *Arch. Neurol. Psychiat. (Chic.)*, *31*, 685.—*513*.

DEAN, G. (1963) The Porphyrias. London: Pitman.—*359, 360*.

DELAY, J. and DENIKER, P. (1952) Le traitement des psychoses par une méthode neurolytique dérivée de l'hibernothérapie. (Le 4560 RP utilisé seul en cure prolongée et continuée). In: *C. R. Congr. Méd. Aliénist. Neurol., Luxembourg 1952*. Paris. p. 514.—*329*.

—— and DESCLAUX, P. (1945) Encephalography in degenerative dementing processes of the brain. *Rev. neurol.* 77, 212.—*626*.

——, NEVEU, P., LERIQUE, J. and DESCLAUX, P. (1944) On some results of pneumoencephalography and EEG in the diagnosis of cerebral atrophies. *Rev. neurol.* 76, 263.—*626*.

——, PICHOT, P., LEMPERIÈRE, T., NICHOLAS-CHARLES, P. J. and QUÉTIN, A-M. (1959) Étude psychophysiologique et clinique de la psilocybine. In: Les Champignons Hallucinogenes du Mexique, ed. R. Heim and G. Wasson. Paris: Le Muséum nat. d'Histoire naturelle. p. 287.—*436*.

DENBER, H. C. B., and BIRD, E. G. (1957) Chlorpromazine in the treatment of mental illness. IV Final results with analysis of data on 1,523 patients. *Amer. J. Psychiat.*, *113*, 972.—*333*.

—— and MERLIS, S. (1955) Studies on mescaline: action in schizophrenic patients. Clinical observations and brain wave patterns, showing effects before and after electric convulsive treatments. *Psychiat. Quart.*, *29*, 421.—*435*.

DENNY-BROWN, D. (1945) Disability arising from closed head injury. *J. Amer. med. Ass.*, *127*, 429.—*508*.

—— and RUSSELL, W. R. (1941) Experimental cerebral concussion. *J. Physiol*, 99, 153.—*499*.

DESPERT, J. L. (1952) Suicide and depression in children. *Nerv. Child.* 9, 378.—*669*.

DESROCHERS, J. L., PARENTEAU, A. and HARDY, J. (1961) La réduction de la masse cérébral dans le traitement de l'épilepsie incontrôlable non focalisée. *Canad. med. Ass. J.*, *85*, 827.—*481*.

DICKINSON, C. J. (1965) Neurogenic Hypertension. Oxford: Blackwell.—*590*.

—— and THOMPSON, A. D. (1961) A post mortem study of the main cerebral arteries with special reference to the cause of strokes. *Clin. Sci.*, *20*, 131.—*587, 595*.

DIETHELM, O. and ROCKWELL, F. V. (1943) Psychopathology of ageing. *Amer. J. Psychiat.*, *99*, 553.—*577*.

DIMSDALE, H., LOGUE, V. and PIERCY, M. (1963) A case of persisting impairment of recent memory following right temporal lobectomy. *Neuropsychologia*, *1*, 287.—*527*.

DIVRY, P. (1947) Cerebral ageing. *J. belge Neurol. Psychiat.*, *47*, 65.—*614*.

—— (1952) La pathochimie générale et cellulaire des processus séniles et préseniles. *Proc. 1st Int. Congr. Neuropath., 1952*, *2*, 313.—*614*.

DOHRENWEND, B. P. (1957) The Stirling County Study. A research program on relations between sociocultural factors and mental illness. *Amer. Psychol.* 12, 78.—*782*.

DOLLARD, J. and MILLER, N. E. (1950) Personality and Psychotherapy: an analysis in terms of learning, thinking and culture. New York: McGraw-Hill.—*409*.

DORRELL, W. (1963a) Letter: Tranylcypromine. *Lancet*, *1*, 388.—*202*.

—— (1963b) Letter: Tranylcypromine and intracranial bleeding. *Lancet*, *2*, 300.—*202*.

DOUGLAS, J. W. B. and BLOMFIELD, J. M. (1958) Children under Five. London: Allen, G.—*638, 645*.

DOWLING, R. H. and KNOX, S. J. (1963) Transvestism and fertility in a chromosomal mosaic. *Postgrad. med. J.*, *39*, 665.—*165*.

DOWNES, D. M. (1966) The Delinquent Solution: A Study in Subcultural Theory. London: Routledge.—*659.*

DREW, G. C., COLQUHOUN, W. P. and LONG, H. A. (1958) Effect of small doses of alcohol on a skill resembling driving. *Med.-leg. J. (Camb.), 26,* 94.—*392.*

DUBLIN, L. I. (1963) Suicide. New York: Ronald Press.—*788, 789.*

DUKOR, B. (1951) Probleme um den Transvestitismus. *Schweiz. med. Wschr., 81, 516.*—*166.*

DUNBAR, F. (1943) Psychosomatic Diagnosis. New York: Hoeber.—*589.*

DURKHEIM, E. (1897) Suicide (Trans. 1952) London: Routledge and Kegan Paul.—*777, 789.*

EARL, C. J. C. (1936) The affective-instinctive psychology of imbecile children. *Brit. J. med. Psychol., 15,* 266.—*717.*

EARLE, K. M., BALDWIN, M. and PENFIELD, W. (1953) Incisural sclerosis and temporal lobe seizures produced by hippocampal herniation at birth. *Arch. Neurol. Psychiat., (Chic.), 69,* 27.—*450.*

EARLY, D. F. (1960) The Industrial Therapy Organisation (Bristol). A development of work in hospital. *Lancet, 2,* 754.—*338.*

EAST, W. N. (1938) Responsibility in mental disorder, with special reference to algolagnia. *J. ment. Sci., 84,* 203.—*168, 717.*

EASTCOTT, H. H. G., PICKERING, G. W. and ROB, C. G. (1954) Reconstruction of internal carotid artery in a patient with intermittent attacks of hemiplegia. *Lancet, 2,* 994.—*595.*

EATON, J. W. and WEIL, R. J. (1955) Culture and Mental Disorders: a comparative study of the Hutterites and other populations. Glencoe, U.S.A.: The Free Press.—*189.*

EDGAR, G. W. F. (1963) Progressive myoclonus epilepsy as an inborn error of metabolism comparable to storage disease. *Epilepsia (Amst.), 4,* 102.—*451.*

EDGE, J. R. and NELSON, I. D. M. (1964) Survey of arrangements for the elderly in Barrow-in-Furness, 1 and 2. *Med. Care, 2,* 7.—*563.*

EDWARDS, J. H. (1960) The simulation of mendelism. *Acta genet. (Basel), 10,* 63.—*196, 247.*

—— (1963) The genetic basis of common disease. *Amer. J. med., 34,* 627.—*247.*

——, HARNDEN, D. G., CAMERON, A. H., CROSSE, V. M. and WOLFF, O. H. (1960) A new trisomic syndrome. *Lancet, 1,* 787.—*722.*

EHRINGER, H. and HORNYKIEWICZ, O. (1960) Distribution of noradrenaline and dopamine (3-hydroxytyramine) in the human brain and their behaviour in diseases of the extrapyramidal system. *Klin. Wschr., 38,* 1236.—*517.*

EINARSON, L., NEEL, A. V. and STRÖMGREN, E. (1944) On the Problem of Diffuse Brain Sclerosis with Special Reference to the Familial Forms. *Acta jutlandica, XVI, 1, (Copenhagen).*—*531.*

EISENBERG, L. (1956) The autistic child in adolescence. *Amer. J. Psychiat., 112,* 607—*679, 681.*

—— and KANNER, L. (1956) Childhood Schizophrenia Symposium, 1955/6. Early infantile autism, 1943–1955. *Amer. J. Orthopsychiat., 26,* 556.—*679, 680.*

EITINGER, L. (1959) Prognosis and therapeutic results in schizophrenia and the schizophreniform states. In: Congress Report, *2,* 150. Second Int. Congr. for Psychiat., Zurich, 1957. Zurich: Orell Füssli Arts.—*302.*

—— (1960) The symptomatology of mental disease among refugees in Norway. *J. ment. Sci., 106,* 947.—*149.*

EKBLAD, M. (1955) Induced abortion on psychiatric grounds. *Acta psychiat. neurol. scand.,* Suppl. 99.—*378, 760.*

—— (1961) Prognosis after sterilization on social-psychiatric grounds. A follow-up study of 225 women. *Acta psychiat. scand.,* Suppl. 161.—*760.*

EKMAN, G. (1951) On the number and definition of dimensions in Kretschmer's and Sheldon's constitutional systems. Essays in Psychology. Uppsala: Almquist.—*193.*

ELITHORN, A. (1959) Discussion on psychosurgery: prefrontal leucotomy and depression. *Proc. roy. Soc. Med., 52,* 203.—*222.*

ELLINGER, P. and BENESCH, R. (1945) Biosynthesis of 'nicotinamide' in the human gut. *Lancet, 1,* 432.—*353.*

ELLIS, H. (1928) In: Studies in the Psychology of Sex, Vol. 7. New York: Davis.—*164.*

ELSÄSSER, G. (1952) The Descendants of Mentally Ill Pairs of Parents. Stuttgart: Thieme.—*197, 245.*

—— and GRÜNEWALD, H. W. (1953) Schizophrene oder schizophrenieeänliche Psychosen bei Hirntraumatikern. *Arch. Psychiat. Nervenkr., 190,* 134.—*301.*

ENGEL, G. L. and ROMANO, J. (1944) Delirium: II Reversibility of the electroencephalogram with experimental procedures. *Arch. Neurol. Psychiat., (Chic.), 51,* 378.—*345, 485.*

—— and —— (1959) Delirium, a syndrome of cerebral insufficiency. *J. chron. Dis., 9,* 260.—*345.*

ENGELHARD, J. L. B. (1912) On puerperal psychoses and the influence of gestation period on psychiatric and neurological disease already in existence. *Z. Geburtsh. Gynäk., 70,* 727.—*374.*

EPSTEIN, A. W. (1961) Relationship of fetishism and transvestism to brain and particularly to temporal lobe dysfunction. *J. nerv. ment. Dis., 133,* 247.—*495.*

ERNST, K. (1956) 'Geordnete Familienverhältnisse' späterer Schizophrener im Lichteeiner Nachuntersuchang. *Arch. Psychiat. Nervenkr., 194,* 355.—*263, 303.*

ESQUIROL, J-E-D. (1838) Mental Maladies: a Treatise on Insanity, trans. E. K. Hunt (1845). Philadelphia: Lea and Blanchard.—*776.*

ESSEN-MÖLLER, E. (1946) A family with Alzheimer's disease. *Acta psychiat. neurol. scand., 21,* 233.—*613.*

—— (1956) Individual traits and morbidity in a Swedish rural population. *Acta psychiat., neurol. scand.,* suppl. *100.*—*239, 540.*

—— (1961) On classification of mental disorders. *Acta psychiat. scand., 37,* 119.—*484.*

—— (1963) Twin research in psychiatry. *Acta psychiat. scand., 39,* 65.—*240, 241, 246.*

EWALD, G. (1928) Psychoses in acute infections, etc. In: Handbook of Mental Diseases, ed. Bumke, vol. 7. Berlin: Springer.—*373.*

EY, H., BERNARD, P. and BRISSET, C. (1963) Manuel de Psychiatrie. Paris: Masson.—*13.*

EYSENCK, H. J. (1947) Dimensions of Personality. London: Kegan Paul.—*70, 704.*

—— (1952) The Scientific Study of Personality. New York.: Macmillan.—*9.*

—— (1959) Learning theory and behaviour therapy. *J. ment. Sci., 105,* 61.—*410.*

—— (1960a) Personality and behaviour therapy. *Proc. roy. Soc. Med., 53,* 504.—*184, 185.*

—— (ed.) (1960b) Behaviour Therapy and the Neuroses. London: Pergamon.—*24, 184, 185.*

—— (ed.) (1960c) Handbook of Abnormal Psychology. London: Pitman.—*9, 63.*

—— and RACHMAN, S. (1965a) The Causes and Cures of Neurosis. London: Routledge.—*184, 186.*

—— and —— (1965b) The application of learning theory to child psychiatry. In: Modern Perspectives in Child Psychiatry, ed. J. G. Howells, Ch. VI. London: Oliver & Boyd.—*649, 661, 663.*

FAERGEMAN, P. M. (1945) Psychogenic Psychoses. (trans. 1963) London: Butterworth.—*303.*

FAIRHALL, L. T. and NEAL, P. A. (1943) Industrial manganese poisoning. *Nat. Inst. Hlth. Bull.,* No. 182.—*444.*

FALCONER, M. A. (1958) Discussion on surgery of temporal lobe epilepsy. *Proc. roy. Soc. Med., 51,* 613.—*481.*

——, HILL, D., MEYER, A., MITCHELL, W. and POND, D. A. (1955) Treatment of temporal lobe epilepsy by temporal lobectomy: a suvey of findings and results. *Lancet, I,* 827.—*480.*

——, ——, —— and WILSON, J. L. (1958) Clinical, radiological and EEG correlations with pathological changes in temporal lobe epilepsy and their significance in surgical treatment. In: Temporal Lobe Epilepsy, ed. M. Baldwin and P. Bailey, p. 396. Springfield: Ill.: Thomas.—*480.*

FALRET, J. P. (1853–54) Clinical Lectures on Mental Medicine. General Symptomatology. Paris: Baillière.—*188.*

—— (1864) On Mental Diseases. Paris: Baillière.—*188.*

FARBEROW, N. L. and SHNEIDMAN, E. S. (eds.) (1961) The Cry for Help. New York: McGraw-Hill.—*792.*

——, —— and NEURINGER, C. (1966) Case history and hospitalization factors in suicides of neuro-psychiatric hospital patients. *J. nerv. ment. Dis., 142,* 32.—*796.*

FARIS, R. E. L. (1934) Cultural isolation and the schizophrenic personality. *Amer. J. Sociol., 40,* 155.—*786.*

—— and DUNHAM, H. W. (1939) Mental Disorders in Urban Areas. Chicago: Univ. of Chicago Press.—*238, 786.*

FELDMAN, R. G., CHANDLER, K. A., LEVY, L. L. and GLASER, G. H. (1963) Familial Alzheimer's disease. *Neurology (Minneap.), 13,* 811.—*613.*

von FELSINGER, J. M., LASAGNA, L. and BEECHER, H. K. (1956) The response of normal men to lysergic acid derivatives (di- and mono-ethylamides); correlation of personality and drug reactions. *J. clin. exp. Psychopath., 17,* 414.—*436.*

FEUCHTWANGER, E. and MAYER-GROSS, W. (1938) Brain injury and schizophrenia. *Schweiz. Arch. Neurol. Psychiat., 41,* 17.—*301, 509.*

FISH, F. J. (1962) Schizophrenia. Bristol: Wright.—*265.*

FISHER, G. W., MURRAY, F., WALLEY, M. R. and KILOH, L. G. (1960) A controlled trial of imipramine in the treatment of nocturnal enuresis in mentally subnormal patients. *Amer. J. ment. Defic., 67,* 536.—*647.*

FISHER, M. (1951) Occlusion of internal carotid artery. *Arch. Neurol. Psychiat. (Chic.), 65,* 346.—*596.*

FISHER, R. A. (1927) Elimination of mental defect. *J. Hered., 18,* 529.—*699.*

FLECK, S., CORNELISON, A. R., NORTON, N. and LIDZ, T. (1957) The intrafamilial environment of the schizophrenic patient. III Interaction between hospital staff and families. *Psychiatry (Washington), 20,* 343.—*246.*

——, LIDZ, T. and CORNELISON, A. (1963) Comparison of parent-child relationships of male and female schizophrenic patients. *Arch. gen. Psychiat., 8,* 1.—*262.*

FLEMINGER, J. J. and GRODEN, B. M., (1962) Clinical features of depression and the response to imipramine (Tofranil). *J. ment. Sci., 108,* 101.—*222.*

FLINK, E. B. *et al.* (1954) Magnesium deficiency after prolonged parenteral fluid administration and after chronic alcoholism complicated by delirium tremens. *J. Lab. clin. Med., 43,* 169.—*402.*

FØLLING, A. (1934) Excretion of phenylpyruvic acid in urine as metabolic anomaly in connection with imbecility. *Nord. med. T., 8,* 1054.—*724.*

de FONSECA, A. F. (1959) Analise Heredo-clinica das Perturbacoes Afectivas: estudo de 60 pares de gameos e seus consanguineos. Diss. med. Oporto, Faculdade da Universidade do Porto (Portugal).—*196.*

FORD, C. E., JONES, K. W., MILLER, O. J., MITTWOCH, U., PENROSE, L. S. RIDLER, M. and SHAPIRO, A. (1959) The chromosomes in a patient showing both mongolism and the Klinefelter syndrome. *Lancet, I,* 709.—*721.*

FORD, C. S. and BEACH, F. A. (1951) Patterns of Sexual Behaviour. New York: Harper.—*171.*

FORMANEK, R. (1939) The problem of the symptomatic origin of psychoses. *Z. ges. Neurol. Psychiat., 165,* 78.—*344.*

FORSSMANN, H, and THUWE, I. (1965) 120 children born after application for therapeutic abortion refused. *Acta psychiat. scand., 41,* 71.—*378.*

FOULDS, G. A. (1962) A quantification of diagnostic differentiae. *J. ment. Sci., 108,* 389.—*210.*

FOULKES, S. H. and ANTHONY, E. J. (1957) Group Therapy: the Psychoanalytic Approach. London: Penguin.—*182.*

FOWLIE, H. C., COHEN, C. and ANAND, M. P. (1963) Depression in elderly pat'ents with subnutrition. *Geront. clin., 5,* 215.—*568.*

FRANK, R. T. (1931) The hormonal causes of premenstrual tension. *Arch. Neurol. Psychiat., (Chic.), 26,* 1053.—*371.*

FRASER, T. R. (1947) The Incidence of Neurosis among Factory Workers. Med. Res. Cl. Industrial Hlth. Res. Board, Report No. 90. London: H.M.S.O.—*716*.

FREEDMAN, A. M. (1963) Treatment of drug addiction in a community general hospital. *Comprehens. Psychiat.*, *4*, 199.—*425*.

———, SAGER, C. J., RABINER, E. L. and BROTMAN, R. E. (1963) Response of adult heroin addicts to a total therapeutic programme. *Amer. J. Orthopsychiat.*, *33*, 890.—*426*.

FREEMAN, F. N., HOLZINGER, K. J. and MITCHELL, B. D., (1928) Adopted Children. Twenty-seventh Yearbook part 1, p. 103.—*705*.

FREEMAN, H. L. and KENDRICK, D. C. (1960) A case of cat phobia. *Brit. med. J.*, *2*, 497.—*186*.

FREEMAN, W. (1962) Lobotomy after 65. *Geriatrics*, *17*, 15.—*575*.

FREMMING, K. H. (1951) The expectation of mental infirmity in a sample of the Danish population. Occasional papers on Eugenics, No. 7. London: Eugenics Society.—*104, 189, 239*.

FREUD, A. (1928) Introduction to the Technique of Child Analysis. New York: Nervous and Mental Disease Publication.—*633*.

FREUD, S. (1884) Uebar Coca. *Centralbl. ges. Therap.* (*Wien*), *2*, 289.—*429*.

——— (1927) The Ego and the Id, trans. J. Rivière. London: Hogarth.—*195*.

FRIEDHOFF, A. J. and van WINKLE, E. (1962) Isolation and characterization of the compound from the urine of schizophrenics. *Nature*, *194*, 897.—*256*.

FRÖSHAUG, H. and YTREHUS, A. (1963) The problems of prognosis in schizophrenia. *Acta. psychiat. scand.*, *39*, Suppl. 169.—*310*.

FRY, A. (1962) Addiction to glutethimide: letter. *Brit. med. J.*, *2*, 673.—*431*.

FUCHS, H. (1961) Suicidal acts. *Öst. Ärzteztg* (*Vienna*), *19*.—*790*.

GADDUM, J. H. (1953) Antagonism between lysergic acid diethylamide and 5-hydroxytryptamine. *J. Physiol.*, (*Lond.*), *121*, 15 P.—*256*.

GALDSTON, I. (1947) On the aetiology of depersonalization. *J. nerv. ment. Dis.*, *105*, 25.—*123*.

GAMPER, E. (1927) The question of polioencephalitis haemorrhagica in chronic alcoholics. Anatomical findings in alcoholic Korsakov and their relation to the clinical picture. *Zbl. ges. Neurol. Psychiat.*, *47*, 830.—*355*.

——— (1928) The problem of polioencephalitis haemorrhagica in chronic alcoholics. *Dtsch. Z. Nervenheilk.*, *102*, 122.—*392*.

——— (1931) The position of the diencephalon in the psychocerebral apparatus. *Med. Klin.*, *27*, 41.—*527*.

GANROT, P. O., ROSENGREN, E. and GOTTFRIES, C. G. (1962) Effect of iproniazid on monoamines and mono-amine-oxidase in human brain. *Experientia*, *18*, 260.—*200*.

GANSER, S. J. M. (1898) On a peculiar type of twilight state. *Arch. Psychiat. Nervenkr.*, *30*, 633.—*114*.

GARDNER, E. A., BAHN, A. K. and MACK, M. (1964) Suicide and psychiatric care in the ageing. *Arch. gen. Psychiat.*, *10*, 547.—*544*.

GARRONE, G. (1962) Statistical and genetic study of schizophrenia in Geneva from 1901 to 1950. *J. Génét. hum.*, *11*, 91.—*239, 245*.

GARRY, J. W. and LEONARD, T. J. (1963) Trial of amitriptyline in chronic depression. *Brit. J. Psychiat.*, *109*, 54.—*230*.

GARSIDE, R. F., KAY, D. W. K. and ROTH, M. (1965) Old age mental disorders in Newcastle upon Tyne. Part III A factorial study of medical, psychiatric and social characteristics. *Brit. J. Psychiat.*, *111*, 939. —*541, 545, 577, 778, 787*.

GASTAUT, H. and FISCHER-WILLIAMS, M. (1959) In: Handbook of Physiology, ed. J. Field. Section 1 Neuro-physiology, Vol. 1, p. 329. Baltimore: Amer. Physiol. Soc.—*447*.

GATFIELD, P. D. and GUZE, S. B. (1962) Prognosis and differential diagnosis of conversion reactions: a follow-up study. *Dis. nerv. Syst.*, *23*, 623.—*105*.

von GEBSATTEL, V. E. (1928) Compulsive thinking on time in melancholia. *Nervenarzt*, *1*, 275.—*134, 195*.

GELDER, M. G. and MARKS, I. M. (1966) Severe agoraphobia: a controlled prospective trial of behaviour therapy. *Brit. J. Psychiat.*, *112*, 309.—*92, 95, 187*.

———, ———, SAKINOFSKY, I. and WOLFF, H. H. (1964) Behaviour therapy and psychotherapy in phobic disorders: alternative or complementary procedures? Paper given at Learning Theory Symposium of 6th Internat. Congr. Psychother., London.—*186*.

GELLERSTEDT, N. (1932-1933) Our knowledge of cerebral changes in normal involution of old age. *Upsala Läk. Förh.*, *38*, 193.—*535, 607*.

GELLHORN, E. (1943) Autonomic Regulations. New York: Interscience.—*85, 257*.

GERARD, D. L. and HOUSTON, L. G. (1953) Family setting and social ecology of schizophrenia. *Psychiat. Quart.*, *27*, 90.—*786*.

GERSTMANN, J. (1927) Fingeragnosie und Isolierte Agraphie. Ein neues Syndrom. *Z. ges. Neurol. Psychiat.*, *108*, 152.—*496*.

GESELL, A. L. and AMATRUDA, C. S. (1941) Developmental Diagnosis. New York: Harper.—*708*.

——— and ILG, F. L. (1937) Feeding Behaviour of Infants: a Paediatric Approach to the Mental Hygiene of Early Life. Philadelphia: Lippincott.—*655*.

GIBBENS, T. C. N. (1957) The sexual behaviour of young criminals. *J. ment. Sci.*, *103*, 527.—*70, 171*.

GIBBONS, J. L. (1960) Total body sodium and potassium in depressive illness. *Clin. Sci.*, *19*, 133.—*203*.

——— (1963) Electrolytes and depressive illness. *Postgrad. med. J.*, *39*, 19.—*203*.

——— and McHUGH, P. R. (1962) Plasma cortisol in depressive illness. *J. psychiat. Res.*, *1*, 162.—*203*.

GIBBS, E. L., GIBBS, F. A. and FUSTER, B. (1948) Psychomotor epilepsy. *Arch. Neurol. Psychiat.* (*Chic.*), *60*, 331.—*476*.

GILLES, H. (1949) The schizophrenic disorders. In: Modern Practice in Psychological Medicine, ed. J. R. Rees. London: Harper.—*272, 315.*

GILLESPIE, R. D. (1933) Mental and physical symptoms of presenile dementia. *Proc. roy. Soc. Med., 26,* 1080. —*625.*

GITTELMAN, R. K., KLEIN, D. F. and POLLACK, M. (1964) Effects of psychotropic drugs on long-term adjustment: a review. *Psychopharmacologia (Berl.), 5,* 317.—*335.*

GJESSING, R. (1947) Biological investigations in endogenous psychoses. *Acta. psychiat. neurol. scand.,* Suppl. *47,* 93.—*254.*

——— and GJESSING, L. (1961) Some main trends in the clinical aspects of periodic catatonia. *Acta. psychiat. scand., 37,* 1.—*254, 335.*

GLATT, M. M. (1959) Hazards of meprobamate: letter. *Brit. med. J., 1,* 587.—*431.*

——— (1961a) Drinking habits of English (middle class) alcoholics. *Acta. psychiat. scand., 37,* 88.—*391.*

——— (1961b) Treatment results in an English mental hospital alcoholic unit. *Acta. psychiat. scand., 37,* 143. —*407, 412.*

——— (1961c) Pavlov or Freud?: letter. *Lancet, 1,* 1112.—*408.*

——— (1962) Delirium tremens: letter. *Brit. med. J., 2,* 988.—*401.*

——— (1964a) Addiction to chlorodyne.: letter. *Brit. med. J., 1,* 309.—*432.*

——— (1964b) Drug dependence: letter. *Brit. med. J., 2,* 1073.—*414.*

GLAUS, A. (1931) On the combination of schizophrenia and epilepsy. *Z. ges. Neurol. Psychiat., 135,* 450.—*470.*

GLOWINSKI, J. and AXELROD, J. (1964) Inhibition of uptake of tritiated noradrenaline in the intact rat brain by imipramine and structurally related compounds. *Nature, 204,* 1318.—*201.*

GLUECK, S. S. and GLUECK, E. T. (1950) Unravelling Juvenile Delinquency. London: Oxford Univ. Press.—*5, 70, 656.*

GLYNN, J. D. and HARPER, P. (1961) Behaviour therapy in a case of transvestism: letter. *Lancet, 1,* 619.—*166.*

GODDARD, H. H. (1914) Feeble-mindedness. New York: Macmillan.—*715.*

GOFFMAN, E. (1957) Charactersitics of total institutions. In: Proc. Symposium on Preventive and Social Psychiatry, Walter Reed Army Institute of Research, April 1957. Washington D.C.—*804.*

GOLDBERG, E. M. and MORRISON, S. L. (1963) Schizophrenia and social class. *Brit. J. Psychiat., 109,* 785.—*238, 786.*

GOLDBERG, S. C., KLERMAN, G. L. and COLE, J. O. (1965) Changes in schizophrenic psychopathology and ward behaviour as a function of phenothiazine treatment. *Brit. J. Psychiat., 111,* 120.—*329, 332.*

GOLDFARB, A. I. (1962) The psychotherapy of elderly patients. In: Medical and Clinical Aspects of Ageing, ed. H. T. Blumenthal. New York: Columbia Univ. Press.—*576.*

GOLDFARB, H. (1943) The affects of early institutional care on adolescent personality. *Child Develop., 14,* 213. —*660.*

GOLDFARB, W. (1961) Childhood Schizophrenia. Cambridge, Mass.: Harvard Univ. Press.—*685.*

GOLDIN, S. and MacDONALD, J. E. (1955) The Ganser state. *J. ment. Sci., 101,* 267.—*114.*

GOLDSTEIN, H. H., WEINBERG, J. and SANKSTONE, M. I. (1941) Shock therapy in psychosis complicating pregnancy. *Amer. J. Psychiat., 98,* 201.—*373.*

GOLDSTEIN, K. (1930) The Organism. New York: Amer BK.—*485, 489.*

——— (1939) The significance of special mental tests for diagnosis and prognosis in schizophrenia. *Amer. J. Psychiat., 96,* 575.—*316.*

——— (1942) After Effects of Brain Injuries in War. Their Evaluation and Treatment. New York: Grune.—*127, 485, 489, 512.*

——— and KATZ, S. E. (1937) The psychopathology of Pick's disease. *Arch. Neurol. Psychiat. (Chic.), 38,* 473. —*485, 489.*

GOLDSTEIN, L., MURPHREE, H. B., SUGERMAN, A. A., PFEIFFER, C. C. and JENNEY, E. H. (1963) Quantitative electorencephalographic analysis of naturally occurring (schizophrenic) and drug-induced psychotic states in human males. *Clin. Pharmacol. Ther., 4.* 10.—*258.*

GOODMAN, L. S. and GILMAN, A. Z. (1965) The Pharmacological Basis of Therapeutics, 3rd ed. New York: Macmillan.—*416.*

GOODMAN, N. and TIZARD, J. (1962) Prevalence of imbecility and idiocy among children in a Metropolitan area. *Brit. med. J., 1,* 216.—*694.*

GOOLKER, P. and SCHEIN, J. (1953) Panel discussion: psychophysiological properties of adrenal cortex: recent unpublished advances; psychic effects of ACTH and cortisone. *Psychosom. Med., 15,* 589.—*369.*

GOSTLING, J. V. T. (1967) Herpetic encephalitis. *Proc. roy. Soc. Med., 60,* 693.—*513.*

GOTTESMAN, I. I. (1962) Differential inheritance of the psychoneuroses. *Eugen. Quart., 9,* 223.—*67.*

——— (1963) Heritability of personality: a demonstration. *Psychol. Monogr. 77,* No. 9, Serial No. 572.—*67.*

——— and SHIELDS, J. (1966) Schizophrenia in twins: 16 years' consecutive admissions to a psychiatric clinic. *Brit. J. Psychiat., 112,* 809.—*241.*

——— and ——— (1967) A polygenic theory of schizophrenia. *Proc. nat. Acad. Sci. (Wash.), 58,* 199.—*248.*

GOWERS, W. R. (1908) Heredity in diseases of the nervous system. *Brit. med. J., 2,* 1541.—*611.*

GRAD, J. and SAINSBURY, P. (1963) Evaluating a Community Care Service. In: Trends in the Mental Health Services, ed. H. Freeman and J. Farndale. London: Pergamon.—*563.*

——— and ——— (1966) Evaluating the effectiveness of mental health services. *Milbank mem. Fd Quart., 44* 246.—*563.*

——— and ——— (1968) The effects that patients have on their families in a community care and a control psychiatric service. A two year follow-up. *Brit. J. Psychiat., 114,* 265.—*564.*

GREEN, M. A., STEVENSON, L. D., da FONSECA, J. E. and WORTIS, S. B. (1952) Cerebral biopsy in patients with presenile dementia. *Dis. nerv. Syst., 13,* 303.—*616.*

GREENE, R. and DALTON, K. (1953) The premenstrual syndrome. *Brit. med. J.*, *1*, 1007.—*371*.

GREENFIELD, J. G. (1938) Contribution to discussion on the presenile dementias: symptomatology, pathology and differential diagnosis. *Proc. roy. Soc. Med.*, *31*, 1450.—*591*.

—— and BOSANQUET, F. D. (1953) The brain stem lesions in Parkinsonism. *J. Neurol. Neurosurg. Psychiat.*, *16*, 213.—*612*.

GREER, S. (1966) Parental loss and attempted suicide: a further report. *Brit. J. Psychiat.*, *112*, 465.—*794*.

—— and GUNN, J. C. (1966) Attempted suicides from intact and broken parental homes. *Brit. med. J.*, *2*, 1355.—*794*.

——, —— and KOLLER, K. M. (1966) Aetiological factors in attempted suicide. *Brit. med. J.*, *2*, 1352.—*794*.

GREGORY, I. (1958) Studies of parental deprivation in psychiatric patients. *Amer. J. Psychiat.*, *115*, 432.—*5*.

GREVING, H. (1941) Pathophysiological contributions on physical changes in endogenous psychoses, especially in schizophrenia. *Arch. Psychiat. Nervenkr.*, *112*, 613.—*254*.

GRIFFITHS, R. (1954) The Abilities of Babies, a Study in Mental Measurement. Univ. of London Press.—*728*.

GRINKER, R. R. and SPIEGEL, J. P. (1945) War neuroses in flying personnel overseas and after return to the U.S.A. *Amer. J. Psychiat.*, *101*, 619.—*181*.

GRIST, N. R. (1967) Acute viral infections of the nervous system. *Proc. roy. Soc. Med.*, *60*, 696.—*513*.

GRUENBERG, E. M. (1957) Application of control methods to mental illness. *Amer. J. publ. Hlth*, *47*, 944.—*801*.

—— (1961) A Mental Health Survey of Older People. New York: Utica.—*540*.

—— and ZUSMAN, J. (1964) The natural history of schizophrenia. *Int. Psychiat. Clin.*, *1*, 699.—*804*.

GRUHLE, H. W. (1915) Self-description and empathy. *Z. ges. Neurol. Psychiat.*, *28*, 148.—*272*.

—— (1936) On the psychoses of epilepsy. *Z. ges. Neurol. Psychiat.*, *154*, 395.—*470*.

GRÜNTHAL, E. (1927) Clinical and anatomical investigations on senile dementia. *Z. ges. Neurol. Psychiat.*, *111*, 763.—*605*.

—— (1936) The presenile and senile diseases of the brain and spinal cord. In: Bumke and Foerster's Handbook of Neurology, Vol. XI, p. 466. Berlin: Springer—*297*.

GUNTHER, M. and PENROSE, L. S. (1935) Genetics of epiloia. *J. Genet.*, *31*, 413.—*723*.

GUNZBURG, H. C. (1958a) Educational problems in mental deficiency. In: Mental Deficiency: the Changing Outlook. eds. A. M. Clarke and A. D. B. Clarke, ch. XII. London: Methuen.—*718*.

—— (1958b) Vocational and social rehabilitation of the feeble-minded. In: Mental Deficiency: the Changing Outlook. eds. A. M. Clarke and A. D. B. Clarke, ch. XIV, London, Methuen.—*735*.

—— (1960) Social Rehabilitation of the Subnormal. London: Baillière.—*714*.

GURNEY, C., HALL, R., HARPER, M., OWEN, S. G., ROTH, M. and SMART, G. A. (1967) A study of the physical and psychiatric characteristics of women attending an out-patient clinic for investigation for thyrotoxicosis. Communication to the Scottish Society for Experimental Medicine. Glasgow 1967.—*363*.

—— ROTH, M. and GARSIDE, R. F. (1970) Use of statistical techniques in classification of affective disorders. *Proc. roy. Soc. Med.*, *63*, 232.—*90, 94, 97*.

——, —— and HARPER, M. (1966) The differentiation of hyperthyroidism and psychiatric disorder: a computer analysis of physical signs, psychiatric features and laboratory findings. To be published.—*96*.

GUTTMANN, E. (1936a) On some constitutional aspects of chorea and on its sequelae. *J. Neurol. Psychopath.*, *17*, 16.—*382*.

—— (1936b) The effect of benzedrine on depressive states. *J. ment. Sci.*, *82*, 618.—*420*.

—— (1942) Aphasia in children. *Brain*, *65*, 205.—*676*.

—— (1943) Post-contusional headache. *Lancet*, *1*, 10.—*509*.

—— (1946) Late effects of closed head injuries: psychiatric observations. *J. ment. Sci.*, *92*, 1.—*502, 507*.

—— and CREAK, M. (1940) A follow-up study of hyperkinetic children. *J. ment. Sci.*, *86*, 624.—*655*.

—— and HORDER, H. (1943) Head injuries in children and their after-effects. *Arch. Dis. Childh.*, *18*, 139.—*505*.

—— and MACLAY, W. S. (1936) Mescaline and depersonalization: therapeutic experiments. *J. Neurol. Psychopath.*, *16*, 193.—*435*.

—— and MAYER-GROSS, W. (1940) Psychology of mutilation and disablement. *Lancet*, *2*, 185.—*671*.

——, —— and SLATER, E. T. O. (1939) Short-distance prognosis of schizophrenia. *J. Neurol. Psychiat.*, *2*, 25.—*310, 312*.

—— and SARGANT, W. (1937) Observations on benzedrine. *Brit. med. J.*, *1*, 1013.—*420*.

—— and WINTERSTEIN, C. E. (1938) Disturbances of consciousness after head injuries: observations on boxers. *J. ment. Sci.*, *84*, 347.—*505*.

GUZE, S. B. and PERLEY, M. J. (1963) Observations on the natural history of hysteria. *Amer. J. Psychiat.*, *119*, 960.—*105*.

HAGEN, F. W. (1870) Studies in the Field of Medical Psychology. Erlangen.—*289*.

HAGNELL, O. (1966) A Prospective Study on the Incidence of Mental Disorder. Stockholm: Norstedts.—*782*.

HAHN, R. D. and CLARK, E. G. (1946) Asymptomatic neurosyphilis: prognosis. *Amer. J. Syph.*, *30*, 513.—*518*.

HAKIM, S. and ADAMS, R. D. (1965) The special clinical problem of symptomatic hydrocephalus with normal cerebrospinal fluid pressure. *J. neurol. Sci.*, *2*, 307.—*629*.

HALDANE, J. B. S. (1941) The relative importance of principal and modifying genes in determining some human diseases. *J. Genet.*, *41*, 149.—*621*.

HALL, M. B. (1952) Our present knowledge about manic-depressive states in childhood. *Nerv. Child*, *9*, 319.—*668*.

HALL, R., OWEN, S. G. and SMART, G. A. (1964) Paternal transmission of thyroid autoimmunity. *Lancet*, *2*, 115.—*366*.

HALLGREN, B. (1950) Specific dyslexia ('congenital word blindness'); a clinical and genetic study. *Acta psychiat. neurol. scand.*, Suppl. 65.—*677*.

—— (1957) Enuresis: a clinical and genetic study. *Acta psychiat. neurol. scand.*, *32*. Suppl. 114.—*645*.

—— and Sjögren, T. (1959) A clinical and genetico-statistical study of schizophrenia and low-grade mental deficiency in a large Swedish rural population. *Acta psychiat. scand.*, *35*, Suppl. 140.—*243, 245*.

HAMBURGER, C. (1953) The desire for change of sex as shown by personal letters from 465 men and women. *Acta endocr.* (Munksgaard), *14*, 361.—*164, 166*.

——, Stürup, G. K. and Dahl-Iverson, E. (1953) Transvestism: hormonal psychiatric and surgical treatment. *J. Amer. med. Ass. 152*, 391.—*166*.

HAMILTON, G. V. T. (1929) A Research in Marriage. New York: Boni Liveright.—*170*.

HAMILTON, Max. (1960) A rating scale for depression. *J. Neurol. Neurosurg. Psychiat.*, *23*, 56.—*36*.

——, Hordern, A., Waldrop, F. N. and Lofft, J. (1963) A controlled trial on the value of prochlorperazine, trifluoperazine and intensive group treatment. *Brit. J. Psychiat.*, *109*, 510.—*334*.

——, Smith, A. G. L., Lapidus, H. E. and Cadogan, E. P. (1960) A controlled trial of thiopropazate di-hydrochloride (Dartalan), chlorpromazine and occupational therapy in chronic schizophrenics. *J. ment. Sci.*, *106*, 40.—*334*.

—— and White, J. M. (1959) Clinical syndromes in depressive states. *J. ment. Sci.*, *105*, 985.—*98, 222, 224*.

—— and —— (1960) Factors related to the outcome of depression treated with ECT. *J. ment. Sci.*, *106*, 1031.—*218*.

HAMILTON, M., Pickering, G. W., Roberts, J. A. F. and Sowry, G. S. C. (1954a) Aetiology of essential hypertension: I The arterial pressure in the general population. *Clin. Sci.*, *13*, 11.—*588*.

——, ——, —— and —— (1954b) Aetiology of essential hypertension: II. Scores for arterial blood pressures adjusted for differences in age and sex. *Clin. Sci.*, *13*, 37.—*588*.

——, ——, —— and —— (1954c) Aetiology of essential hypertension: IV. The role of inheritance. *Clin. Sci.*, *13*, 273.—*588*.

HANFMANN, E. and Kasanin, J. S. (1942) Conceptual Thinking in Schizophrenia. New York: Nervous and Mental Disease Publ.—*316*.

HANSEN, E. (1963) Reading and writing difficulties in children with cerebral palsy. In: Minimal Cerebral Dysfunction, ed. R. C. MacKeith and M. Bax. London: Nat. Spastics Soc.—*689*.

HARE, E. H. (1956) Mental illness and social conditions in Bristol. *J. ment. Sci.*, *102*, 349.—*786*.

—— and Shaw, G. (1965a) Mental Health in a New Housing Estate. Maudsley Monograph No. 12. London: Oxford University Press.—*783*.

—— and —— (1965b) A study of family health: I Health in relation to family size. *Brit. J. Psychiat.*, *111*, 461.—*783*.

—— and —— (1965c) A study of family health: II A comparison of the health of fathers, mothers and children. *Brit. J. Psychiat.*, *111*, 467.—*783*.

HARPER, M., Gurney, C., Savage, R. D. and Roth, M. (1965) Forearm blood flow in normal subjects and patients with phobic anxiety states. *Brit. J. Psychiat.*, *111*, 723.—*86*.

—— and Roth, M. (1962) Temporal lobe epilepsy and the phobic anxiety-depersonalization syndrome. Part 1. A comparative study. *Comprehens. Psychiat.*, *3*, 129.—*88, 460*.

HARRIS, J. S. and Cooper, H. A. (1937) Late results of encephalitis lethargica. *Med. Press*, *194*, 12.—*515*.

HARRINGTON, J. A. and Cross, K. W. (1959) Cases of attempted suicide admitted to a general hospital. *Brit. med. J.*, *2*, 463.—*378, 795*.

—— and Letemendia, F. J. J. (1958) Persistent psychiatric disorders after head injuries in children. *J. ment. Sci.*, *104*, 1205.—*505*.

HARVALD, B. (1954) Heredity in Epilepsy. Copenhagen: Munksgaard.—*452*.

HAŠKOVEC, L. and Ryšánek, K. (1967) The action of reserpine in imipramine-resistant depressive patients: clinical and biochemical study. *Psychopharmacologia* (Berl.), *11*, 18.—*202*.

HASLAM, J. (1809) Observations on Madness. 2nd ed., p. 120. London: F. & C. Rivington.—*281*.

HAWKINGS, J. R., Jones, K. S., Sim, M. and Tibbetts, R. W. (1956) Deliberate disability. *Brit. med. J.*, *1*, 361.—*115*.

HEAD, H. (1926) Aphasia and Kindred Disorders of Speech. New York: Macmillan.—*50*.

HEATH, R. G. (1962a) Brain centres and control of behaviour—man. In: The First Hahnemann Symposium on Psychosomatic Medicine, p. 228. Philadelphia: Lea & Febiger.—*258*.

—— (1962b) Common characteristics of epilepsy and schizophrenia: clinical observations and depth electrode studies. *Amer. J. Psychiat.*, *118*, 1013.—*258*.

——, Martens, S., Leach, B. E., Cohen, M. and Angel, C. (1957) Effect on behaviour in humans with the administration of taraxein. *Amer. J. Psychiat.*, *114*, 14.—*255*.

——, ——, ——, ——, and Feighley, C. A. (1958) Behavioural changes in non-psychotic volunteers following the administration of taraxein, the substance obtained from serum of schizophrenic patients. *Amer. J. Psychiat.*, *114*, 917.—*255*.

HEBB, D. O. (1961) Sensory deprivation: facts in search of a theory. *J. nerv. ment. Dis.*, *132*, 40.—*379*.

HEBBELINCK, M. (1965) Paper read at Institute on the Prevention and Treatment of Alcoholism reported in *Brit. med. J.*, *2*, 164.—*410*.

HÉCAEN, H. (1962) Clinical symptomatology in right and left hemisphere lesions. In: Interhemispheric Relations and Cerebral Dominance (ed. V. B. Mountcastle). Baltimore: Johns Hopkins Press.—*496*.

—— and Angelergues, R. (1963) La Cécité Psychique. Étude Critique de la Notion d'Agnosie. Paris: Masson.—*497*.

HEIDENHAIN, A. (1928) Klinische und anatomische Untersuchungen über eine eigenartige organische Erkrankung des Zentralnervensystems im Praesenium. *Z. ges. Neurol. Psychiat.*, *118*, 49.—*620*.

HEIM, R. and WASSON, R. G. (1959) Les champignons hallucinogènes du Mexique: études ethnologiques, taxonomiques, biologiques, physiologiques, et chimiques. Paris. Le Muséum National d'Histoire Naturelle de Paris.—*438*.

HEINRICH, A. (1939) The normal EEG and its relation to age. *Z. Alternsforsch.*, *I*, 345.—*626*.

HELGASON, T. (1964) Epidemiology of mental disorders in Iceland. A psychiatric and demographic investigation of 5395 Icelanders. *Acta. psychiat. scand.*, *40*, Suppl. 173.—*189, 239*.

HELLMANN, I. (1949) Discussion: Toilet training in early childhood. *Proc. roy. Soc. Med.*, *42*, 907.—*646*.

HELWEG-LARSEN, P. *et al.* (1952) Famine disease in German concentration camps; complications and sequels with special reference to tuberculosis, mental disorders and social consequences. *Acta psychiat. neurol. scand.*, Suppl. 83.—*357*.

HENDERSON, D. K. and GILLESPIE, R. D. (1950) Textbook of Psychiatry. 7th ed. London: O.U.P.—*755, 756*.

HENDERSON, Y. and HAGGARD, H. W. (1927) Noxious Gases and the Principles of Respiration Influencing their Action. New York: Amer. Chemical Soc.—*440*.

HENDIN, H. (1964) Suicide and Scandinavia: a Psychoanalytic Study of Culture and Character. New York: Grune & Stratton.—*788*.

HEPPENSTALL, M. E. and HILL, D. (1943) Electroencephalography in chronic post-traumatic syndromes. *Lancet*, *I*, 261.—*510*.

HERNER, T. (1961) Treatment of mental disorders with frontal stereotaxic thermo-lesions. A follow-up study of 116 cases. *Acta psychiat. scand.*, *36*, Suppl. 158.—*336, 337*.

HERON, A. and CHOWN, S. M. (1961) Ageing and the semi-skilled: a survey of manufacturing industry on Merseyside. Medical Research Council Memorandum, *40*. H.M.S.O.—*560*.

HERON, W. (1961) Cognitive and physiological effects of perceptual isolation. In: Sensory Deprivation, ed. P. Solomon *et al.* Cambridge, Mass.: Harvard University Press.—*379*.

HERSOV, L. (1960a) Persistent non-attendance at school. *J. Child. Psychol.* *I*, 130.—*663*.

—— (1960b) Refusal to go to school. *J. Child Psychol.*, *I*, 137.—*663*.

HERSOV, L. A. and RODNIGHT, R. (1960) Hartnup disease in psychiatric practice: clinical and biochemical features in three cases. *J. Neurol. Neurosurg. Psychiat.*, *23*, 40.—*725*.

HESS, W. R. (1954) Diencephalon: Autonomic and Extrapyramidal Functions. New York.: Grune & Stratton. —*201*.

HESTON, L. L. (1966) Psychiatric disorders in foster home reared children of schizophrenic mothers. *Brit. J. Psychiat.*, *112*, 819.—*252*.

——, LOWTHER, D. L. W. and LEVENTHAL, C. M. (1966) Alzheimer's disease: a family study. *Arch. Neurol.*, *15*, 225.—*613*.

HEUYER, G. and LAMACHE, A. (1929) Le mentisme. *Encéphale*, *24*, 325 and 444.—*128*.

HEWITT, L. E. and JENKINS, R. L. (1946) Fundamental Patterns of Maladjustment. Michigan Child Guidance Institute. Springfield, Ill.—*637*.

HILGARD, J. R., NEWMAN, M. F. and FISK, F. (1960) Strength of adult ego following childhood bereavement. *Amer. J. Orthopsychiat.*, *30*, 788.—*797*.

—— and —— (1963) Parental loss by death in childhood as an aetiological factor among schizophrenic and alcoholic patients compared with a non-patient community sample. *J. nerv. ment. Dis.*, *137*, 14.—*393*.

HILL, D. (1948) The relationship between epilepsy and schizophrenia: EEG studies. *Folia psychiat. (neerl.)* Congress Number *51*, 95.—*454, 473*.

—— (1952) EEG in episodic psychotic and psychopathic behaviour: a classification of data. *Electroenceph. clin. Neurophysiol.* *4*, 419.—*71*.

—— (1958) Discussion on surgery of temporal lobe epilepsy. Indications and contra-indications to temporal lobectomy. *Proc. roy. Soc. Med.*, *51*, 610.—*480*.

—— and WATTERSON, D. (1942) Electroencephalographic studies of psychopathic personalities. *J. Neurol. Psychiat.*, *5*, 47.—*72, 139*.

HILLARP, N-Å., FUXE, K. and DAHLSTRÖM. A. (1966) Demonstration and mapping of central neurons containing dopamine, noradrenaline and 5-hydroxytryptamine and their reactions to psychopharmaca. *Pharmacol. Rev.*, *18*, 727.—*200*.

HILLBOM, E. (1951) Schizophrenia-like psychoses after brain trauma. *Acta psychiat. neurol. scand.*, Suppl. 60. 36.—*509*.

—— (1960) After-effects of brain injuries. *Acta psychiat. neurol. scand.*, *35*, Suppl. 142.—*128, 301, 451, 483, 503, 505, 506, 509*.

HILLIARD, L. T. and KIRMAN, B. H. (1957) Mental Deficiency. London: Churchill.—*713, 714, 733*.

HIMWICH, W. A., COSTA, E. and HIMWICH, H. E. (1959) In: Biological Psychiatry, ed. J. H. Masserman. New York: Grune & Stratton.—*535*.

HINTON, J. M. (1963) Patterns of insomnia in depressive states. *J. Neurol. Neurosurg. Psychiat.*, *26*, 184.—*210*.

HIRSCHFELD, M. (1944) Sexual Anomalies and Perversions: Physical and Psychological Development and Treatment. New York: Emerson.—*170*.

HIRSCHMANN, J. (1962) Zur Kriminologie der Sexualdelikte des alterden Mannes. *Geront. clin. Addiment*, *115*. —*578*.

HOBSON, W. and PEMBERTON, J. (1955) The Health of the Elderly at Home. London: Butterworth.—*540*.

HOCH, P. H. (1961) Social psychiatry. In: Psychiatric der Gegenwart, Vol. III, p. 9. Berlin: Springer-Verlag. —*238*.

—— and CATTELL, J. P. (1959) The diagnosis of pseudoneurotic schizophrenia. *Psychiat. Quart.*, *33*, 17. —*325*.

—— and POLATIN, P. (1949) Pseudoneurotic forms of schizophrenia. *Psychiat. Quart.*, *23*, 248.—*296*.

HOFF, E. C. (1961) The aetiology of alcoholism. *Quart. J. Stud. Alcohol.* Suppl. 1, 57.—*393, 394.*

HOFFER, A. (1957) Adrenolutin as a psychotomimetic agent. In: Tranquillizing Drugs, ed. H. E. Himwich, p. 73. Washington: Amer. Ass. Advancement of Science.—*255.*

—— and OSMOND, H. (1962) The association between schizophrenia and two objective tests. *Canad. med. Ass. J.,* 87, 641.—*255.*

——, —— and SMYTHIES, J. (1954) Schizophrenia: a new approach. II Result of a year's research. *J. ment. Sci.,* 100, 29.—*255, 437.*

HOFMANN, A. (1955) Discovery of d-lysergic acid diethylamide—LSD. Sandoz Excerpta (Sandoz Pharmaceuticals, Hanover, N.J.). Vol. 1, No. 1.—*435.*

HOGBEN, L. T. (1933) The limits of applicability of correlation technique in human genetics. *J. Genet.,* 27, 376. —*701.*

—— (1941) Genetic variation and human intelligence. Proc. 7th Internat. Genet. Congr., 1939. Cambridge. —*701.*

HOLBOURNE, A. H. S. (1943) Mechanics of head injuries. *Lancet,* 2, 438.—*500.*

HOLLINGSHEAD, A. B. and REDLICH, F. C. (1954) Social stratification and schizophrenia. *Amer. sociol. Rev.,* 19, 302.—*785.*

—— and —— (1958) Social Class and Mental Illness: a Community Study. New York: Wiley.—*785.*

HOLLISTER, L. E. and FRIEDHOFF, A. J. (1966) Effects of 3,4-dimethoxyphenylethylamine in man. *Nature (Lond.),* 210, 1377.—*256.*

——, TRAUB, L. and PRUSMACK, J. J. (1960) Use of thioridazine for intensive treatment of schizophrenic refractory to other tranquillizing drugs. *J. Neuropsychiat.,* 1, 200.—*333.*

HOLMBOE, R. and ASTRUP, C. (1957) A follow-up study of 255 patients with acute schizophrenia and schizophreniform psychoses. *Acta psychiat. neurol. scand.,* 32, Suppl. 115.—*310.*

HOLT, L. E., SNYDERMAN, S. E., DANCIS, J. and NORTON, P. M. (1960) The treatment of a case of maple syrup urine disease. *Fed. Proc.,* 19, 10.—*725.*

HOMBURGER, A. (1926) Lectures on Psychopathology of Childhood. Berlin: Springer.—*649, 653.*

HOME OFFICE (1959–1965) Reports to the United Nations by Her Majesty's Government in the United Kingdom on the working of the International Treaties on Narcotic Drugs. London: H.M.S.O.—*424, 430.*

HOOD, H. and WADE, O. L. (1968) Use of amphetamines in general practice. *Lancet,* 2, 96.—*420.*

HOPKINS, B. and ROTH, M. (1953) Psychological test performance in patients over sixty. II Paraphrenia, arteriosclerotic psychoses and acute confusion. *J. ment. Sci.,* 99, 451—*549, 554.*

HOPKINSON, G. (1964) A genetic study of affective illness in patients over 50. *Brit. J. Psychiat.,* 110, 244.—*196.*

HORDERN, A., BURT, C. G., HOLT, N. F. and CADE, J. F. J. (1965) Depressive States: a Pharmacotherapeutic Study. Springfield, Ill.: Thomas.—*98.*

—— and HAMILTON, M, (1963) Drugs and moral treatment. *Brit. J. Psychiat.,* 109, 500.—*334.*

——, HOLT, N. F., BURT, C. G. and GORDON, W. F. (1963) Amitriptyline in depressive states: phenomenology and prognostic considerations. *Brit. J. Psychiat.,* 109, 815.—*230, 573.*

van der HORST, L. (1932) Psychological aspect of Korsakov syndrome. *Mschr. Psychiat. Neurol.,* 83, 65.—*405.*

HOSKIN, J. O. and FRIEDMAN, M. I. (1967) Psychiatry in New Britain: suicide by hanging. In preparation.—*790.*

HOSKINS, R. G. (1946) Biology of Schizophrenia. New York: Norton.—*254.*

HOWELLS, W. W. (1952) A factorial study of constitutional type. *Amer. J. Phys. Anthropol.,* 10, 91.—*193.*

HSIA, D. Y. Y., DRISCOLL, K. W., TROLL, W. and KNOX, W. E. (1956) Detection by phenylalanine tolerance tests of heterozygous carriers of phenylketonuria. *Nature (Lond.),* 178, 1239.—*725.*

HUDSON, H. S. and WALKER, H. I. (1961) Withdrawal symptoms following ethchlorvynol (placidyl) dependence. *Amer. J. Psychiat.,* 118, 361.—*418.*

HUGHES, E. M. (1925) Social significance of Huntington's chorea. *Amer. J. Psychiat.,* 81, 537.—*624.*

HUNT, H. F. (1943) The Hunt-Minnesota Test of Organic Brain Damage. Minneapolis: Univ. of Minnesota Press.—*492.*

HUNTER, D. (1959) Health in Industry. London: Pelican.—*443.*

HURST, E. W. (1944) A review of some recent observations on demyelination. *Brain,* 67, 103.—*439.*

HUTCHINSON, D. C. S., FLENLEY, D. C. and DONALD, K. W. (1964) Controlled oxygen therapy in respiratory failure. *Brit. med. J.* 2, 1159.—*441.*

HUXLEY, J., MAYR, E., OSMOND, H. and HOFFER, A. (1964) Schizophrenia as a genetic morphism. *Nature,* 204, 220.—*250.*

HUXLEY, J. S. (1942) Evolution: The Modern Synthesis. London: Allen.—*695.*

HYDE, R. W. and CHISHOLM, R. M. (1944) Studies in medical sociology. III. The relation of mental disorder to race and nationality. *New. Engl. J. Med.,* 231, 612.—*390.*

HYDÉN, H. (1955) Nucleic acids and proteins. In: Neurochemistry, ed. K. A. C. Elliott, *et al.* Springfield, Ill.: Thomas.—*610.*

ILLINGWORTH, R. S. (1960) The Development of the Infant and Young Child, Normal and Abnormal. Edinburgh: Livingstone.—*706, 709.*

—— (1963) The clumsy child. In: Minimal Cerebral Dysfunction, ed. R. C. MacKeith and M. Bax. London: Nat. Spastics Soc.—*689.*

INGHAM, J. G. and ROBINSON, J. O. (1964) Personality in the diagnosis of hysteria. *Brit. J Psychol.,* 55, 276. —*104.*

INGLIS, J. (1957) An experimental study of learning and 'memory function' in elderly psychiatric patients. *J. ment. Sci.,* 103, 796.—*554.*

—— (1959) A paired associate learning test for use with psychiatric patients. *J. ment. Sci.,* 105, 440.—*492.*

INGRAM, T. T. S. (1956) A characteristic form of over-active behaviour in brain-damaged children. *J. ment. Sci.*, *102*, 550.—*690.*

—— (1959) Specific developmental disorders of speech in childhood. *Brain, 82*, 450.—*683.*

—— (1963) Chronic brain syndromes in childhood other than cerebral palsy, epilepsy and mental defect. In: Minimal Cerebral Dysfunction, ed. R. C. MacKeith and M. Bax. London: Nat. Spastics Soc.—*691.*

INOUYE, E. (1960) Observations on forty twin index cases with epilepsy and their co-twins. *J. nerv. ment. Dis.*, *130*, 401.—*452.*

—— (1961) Similarity and dissimilarity of schizophrenia in twins. *Proc. 3rd Wld Congr. Psychiat.*, Montreal, *1*, 524.—*241.*

INTERDEPARTMENTAL COMMITTEE on Morphine and Heroin Addiction (1926) Report: Drug Addiction. London: H.M.S.O.—*414.*

INTERDEPARTMENTAL COMMITTEE on Drug Addiction (1961) Report: Drug Addiction. London: H.M.S.O. —*414.*

—— (1965) Second Report (The Brain Report): Drug Addiction. London: H.M.S.O.—*414, 432, 774.*

IRELAND, W. W. (1898) Mental Affections of Children. London: Churchill.—*632.*

ISBELL, H. (1963) In: Textbook of Medicine (Cecil-Loeb), ed. P. B. Beeson and W. McDermott, 11th ed. London: Saunders.—*426.*

——, ALTSCHUL, S., KORNETSKY, C. H., EISENMAN, A. J., FLANARY, H. G. and FRASER, H. F. (1950) Chronic barbiturate intoxication. *Arch. neurol. Psychiat.*, *(Chic.), 64*, 1.—*416, 418.*

——, BELLEVILLE, R. E. FRASER, H. F., WIKLER, A. and LOGAN, C. R. (1956) Studies on lysergic acid diethylamide (LSD-25). *Arch. Neurol. Psychiat.*, *(Chic.), 76*, 468.—*438.*

——, FRASER, H. F.. WIKLER, A., BELLEVILLE, R. E. and EISENMAN, A. J. (1955) Experimental study of aetiology of 'rum-fits' and delirium tremens. *Quart. J. Stud. Alcohol, 16*, 1.—*393.*

ISSERLIS, L. (1923) The relation between home conditions and the intelligence of school children. *Spec. Rep.*, *Ser. med. Res. Coun. (Lond.)*, No. 74.—*705.*

JACKSON, D. D. (1960) A critique of the literature on the genetics of schizophrenia, In: Etiology of Schizophrenia ed. D. D. Jackson. New York: Basic Books.—*240, 241.*

JACKSON, H. (1946) Contribution to discussion on cortical atrophy. *Proc. roy. Soc. Med., 39*, 423.—*626.*

JACOBS, P. A., BAIKIE, A. G., COURT BROWN, W. M. and STRONG, J. A. (1959) The somatic chromosomes in mongolism. *Lancet*, 1, 710.—*721.*

——, BRUNTON, M., MELVILLE, M. E., BRITTAIN, R. P. and McCLEMONT, W. F. (1965) Aggressive behaviour, mental subnormality and the XYY males. *Nature (Lond.), 208*, 1351.—*691.*

JACOBSON, E. (1938) Progressive Relaxation. Chicago: University of Chicago Press.—*185.*

JAHN, D. and GREVING, H. (1936) Investigations into the physical symptoms of catatonic stupor and fatal catatonia. *Arch. Psychiat. Nervenkr., 105*, 105.—*254.*

JAHRREIS, W. (1926) On a case of chronic systematized obsessional illness. *Arch. Psychiat. Nervenkr., 77*, 596. —*283.*

JAKOB, A. (1921) On peculiar diseases of the central nervous system with pathological findings. *Z. ges. Neurol. Psychiat., 64*, 147.—*619.*

—— (1923) Die Extrapyramidalen Erkrankungen. Berlin: Springer.—*619.*

JAMES, I. P. (1960) Temporal lobectomy for psychomotor epilepsy. *J. ment. Sci., 106*, 543.—*467.*

—— (1962) The recognition and management of addiction and chronic intoxication with sedative drugs *Med. J. Aust., 2*, 277.—*432.*

—— (1963) Drug-withdrawal psychoses. *Amer. J. Psychiat., 119*, 880.—*418.*

—— (1967) Suicide and mortality amongst heroin addicts in Britain. *Brit. J. Addict., 62.*—*427.*

JANET, P. (1893–4) The Mental State of the Hysterics. Paris: Rueff.—*107.*

—— (1907) The Major Symptoms of Hysteria. New York: Macmillan.—*107.*

—— (1908) Obsessions and Psychasthenia. Paris: Alcan.—*82, 120, 130, 132.*

—— (1910) The Psychological Automatism. Paris: Alcan.—*107.*

JANIGER, O. (1959) The use of hallucinogenic drugs in psychiatry. *Calif. Clinician*, July-August 1959.—*436.*

JANSEN, J and MONRAD-KROHN, G. H. (1938) On Creutzfeldt-Jakob's disease. *Z. ges. Neurol. Psychiat., 163*, 670.—*620.*

JANSSON B. (1964) Psychic insufficiencies associated with child-bearing. *Acta. psychiat. scand., 39*, Suppl. 172. —*374.*

JASPER, H. (1949) Diffuse projection systems: the integrative action of the thalamic reticular system. *Electroenceph. clin. Neurophysiol., 1*, 405.—*498.*

—— and DROOGLEVER-FORTUYN, J. (1947) Experimental studies on the functional anatomy of petit mal epilepsy. *Res. Publ. Ass. nerv. ment. Dis., 26*, 272.—*448, 498.*

—— and KERSHMAN, J. (1941) Electroencephalographic classification of epilepsies. *Arch. Neurol. Psychiat.*, *(Chic.), 45*, 903.—*464.*

—— and —— (1949) Classification of the EEG in epilepsy. *Electroenceph. clin. Neurophysiol.*, Suppl. 2, 123.—*446.*

——, PERTUISSET, B. and FLANIGIN, H. (1951) EEG and cortical electrograms in patients with temporal lobe seizures. *Arch. Neurol. Psychiat.*, *(Chic.), 65*, 272.—*463.*

JASPERS, K. (1909) Home-sickness and crime. *Arch. Krim Anthrop.* 35, 1.—*716.*

—— (1910) Eifersuchtswahn. Ein Beitrag zur Frage: 'Entwicklung einer Persönlichkeit oder 'Prozess'. *Z. ges. Neurol. Psychiat., 1*, 567.—*400.*

JASPERS, K. (1913a) General Psychopathology. Trans. from 7th ed. by J. Hoenig and M. W. Hamilton 1963: London: Manchester Univ. Press.—*58, 176, 274.*

———— (1913b) Causality and understanding of life and psychosis in dementia praecox (schizophrenia). *Z. ges. Neurol. Psychiat.*, *14*, 158.—*276.*

———— (1926) Strindberg and Van Gogh, 2nd edn. Berlin: Springer.—*287.*

———— (1945) General Psychopathology, 5th edn. Berlin: Springer. (1st edn. 1913).—*692.*

JEFFERSON, G. (1944) The nature of concussion. *Brit. med. J.*, *I*, 1.—*499.*

———— (1950) Localization of function in the cerebral cortex. *Brit. med. Bull.*, 6, 1535.—*526.*

JELLINEK, E. M. (1946) Phases in drinking history of alcoholics; analysis of survey conducted by official organ of Alcoholics Anonymous. *Quart. J. Stud. Alcohol*, 7, 1.—*391.*

———— (1947) Recent Trends in Alcoholism and Alcohol Consumption. New Haven: Hillhouse.—*390.*

———— (1952) The phases of alcohol addiction. In: Mental Health; Second Report of the Alcoholism Subcommittee. *Wld Hlth Org. techn. Rep. Ser.*, *48*, 26. Geneva: W.H.O.—*413.*

———— (1960) The Disease Concept of Alcoholism. New Haven: Hillhouse.—*395.*

JERSILD, A. T. (1957) Psychology of Adolescence. New York: Macmillan.—*662.*

JERVIS, G. A. (1939) The genetics of phenylpyruvic oligophrenia. *J. ment. Sci.*, *85*, 719.—*724.*

———— (1945) The pre-senile dementias. In: Mental Disorders in Later Life, ed. O. J. Kaplan. London: Oxford Univ. Press.—*611, 612, 620.*

———— (1954) The pre-senile dementias. In: Mental Disorders of Later Life, ed. O. J. Kaplan. 2nd ed. London: Oxford Univ. Press.—*620.*

———— (1963) Huntington's chorea in childhood. *Arch. Neurol. (Chic.)*, 9, 244.—*723.*

JOHANSON, E. (1958) A study of schizophrenia in the male. *Acta psychiat. neurol. scand.*, *33*, Suppl. 125.—*245, 311.*

———— (1964) Mild paranoia. *Acta psychiat. scand.*, *40*, Suppl. 177.—*152, 293, 295, 400.*

JOHNSON, J. (1965) Sexual impotence and the limbic system. *Brit. J. Psychiat.*, *III*, 300.—*495.*

JOKL, E. and GUTTMANN, E. (1932) Neuropsychiatric casuistry from the physiology of athletics. *Z. ges. Neurol. Psychiat.*, *141*, 343.—*671.*

JOLLIFFE, N., BOWMAN, K. M., ROSENBLUM, L. A. and FEIN, H. D. (1940) Nicotinic acid deficiency encephalopathy. *J. Amer. med. Ass. 114*, 307.—*353.*

———, GOODHART, R., GENNIS, J. and CLINE, J. K. (1939) The experimental production of vitamin B₁ deficiency in normal subjects. *Amer. J. med. Sci.*, *198*, 198.—*354.*

JONES, D. C. and CARR-SAUNDERS, A. M. (1927) The relation between intelligence and social status among orphan children. *Brit. J. Psychol.*, *17*, 343.—*705.*

JONES, D. P. and NEVIN, S. (1954) Rapidly progressive cerebral degeneration (subacute vascular encephalopathy) with mental disorder, focal disturbances and myoclonic epilepsy. *J. Neurol. Neurosurg. Psychiat.*, *17*, 148.—*620.*

JONES, E. (1954) Sigmund Freud: Life and Work. Vol. I, Ch. VI. New York: Basic Books—*429.*

JONES, G. and McCOWAN, P. K. (1949) Leucotomy in the periodic psychoses. *J. ment. Sci.*, *95*, 101.—*219.*

JONES, H. E. (1929) Homogamy in intellectual abilities. *Amer. J. Sociol.*, *35*, 369.—*701.*

JONES, H. G. (1960) The behavioural treatment of enuresis nocturna. In: Behaviour Therapy and the Neuroses, ed. J. H. Eysenck. Oxford: Pergamon.—*185.*

JONES, M. *et al.* (1952) Social Psychiatry: a study of therapeutic communities. London, Routledge.—*182, 183.*

———— and SCARISBRICK, R. (1946) Effect of exercise on soldiers with neurocirculatory asthenia. *Psychosom. Med. 8*, 188.—*83.*

JONES, M. C. (1924) A laboratory study of fear: the case of Peter. *Pedag. Semin.*, *31*, 308.—*184.*

de JONG, R. N. (1944) Methyl bromide poisoning. *J. Amer. med. Ass.*, *125*, 702.—*444.*

JUDA, A. (1934) The number and the psychiatric state of descendants of mentally defective and normal schoolchildren. *Z. ges. Neurol. Psychiat.*, *151*, 244.—*703.*

———— (1939a) The aetiology of mental deficiency. New investigations of twins from special schools. *Z. ges. Neurol. Psychiat.*, *165*, 90.—*702.*

———— (1939b) New psychiatric and genealogical investigations on twins from special schools and their families: twin propositi and partners. *Z. ges. Neurol. Psychiat.*, *166*, 365.—*702.*

JUNG, C. G. (1909) The Psychology of Dementia Praecox, trans. Brill. Nerv. & Ment. Dis. Monogr., No. 3. New York.—*265.*

JUNG, R. (1949) Studies of cerebral electrical changes after ECT. *Arch. Psychiat. Nervenkr.*, *183*, 206.—*468.*

KAADA, B. R. (1959) Contribution to discussion on methods and analysis of drug-induced behaviour in animals. In: Neuropsychopharmacology, Vol. I. ed P. B. Bradley, P. Deniker and C. Raduco-Thomas. Amsterdam: Elsevier.—*86.*

KAHN, E. (1928) Psychopathic personalities. In: Bumke's Handbook of Mental Diseases, 5, 227. Berlin: Springer.—*173.*

KAIJ, L. (1960) Alcoholism in Twins: Studies on the Etiology and Sequels of Abuse of Alcohol. Stockholm: Almquist & Wiksell.—*393.*

KALINOWSKY, L. B. and HOCH, P. H. (1961) Somatic Treatments in Psychiatry. New York, Grune & Stratton.—*234.*

———— and KENNEDY, F. (1943) Observations in electric shock therapy applied to problems of epilepsy. *J. nerv. ment. Dis.*, *98*, 56.—*479.*

KALLMANN, F. J. (1938) The Genetics of Schizophrenia. New York: Augustin.—*245, 288, 324.*

———— (1946) The genetic theory of schizophrenia. *Amer J. Psychiat.*, *103*, 309.—*245.*

KALLMANN F. J. (1950) The genetics of psychoses: An analysis of 1,232 twin index families. *Congr. int. Psychiat.*, 6, 1.—*196*.

—— (1951) Comparative adaptational, social and psychometric data on life histories of senescent twin pairs. *Amer. J. hum. Genet.*, 3, 65.—*536*.

—— (1952) Comparative twin study on the genetic aspects of male homosexuality. *J. nerv. ment. Dis.*, 115, 283.—*169*.

——, BARRERA, S. E., HOCH, P. and KELLY, D. M. (1941) Role of mental deficiency in incidence of schizophrenia. *Amer. J. ment. Defic.*, 45, 514.—*703*.

—— and ROTH, B. (1956) Genetic aspects of preadolescent schizophrenia. *Amer. J. Psychiat.*, 112, 599. —*670, 685*.

—— and SANDER, G. (1948) Twin studies on ageing and longevity. *J. Hered.*, 39, 349.—*536*.

KAMP, L. N. (1964) Autistic syndrome in one of a pair of monozygotic twins. *Psychiat. Neurol. Neurochir.* 67, 143.—*681*.

KANNER, L. (1943) Autistic disturbances of affective contact. *Nerv. Child*, 2, 217.—*678*.

—— (1951) Child Psychiatry. 2nd ed. Oxford: New York: Thomas.—*631, 679*.

KANT, O. (1940) Types and analysis of the clinical pictures of recovered schizophrenics. *Psychiat. Quart.*, 14, 676.—*313*.

—— (1941a) Study of a group of recovered schizophrenic patients. *Psychiat. Quart.*, 15, 262.—*310, 313*.

—— (1941b) The relation of a group of highly improved schizophrenic patients to one group of completely recovered and another group of deteriorated patients. *Psychiat. Quart.*, 15, 779.—*313*.

—— (1943) Clinical analysis of schizophrenic deterioration; investigation aided by sodium amytal interviews. *Psychiat. Quart.*, 17, 426.—*306*.

KARAGULLA, S. (1950) Evaluation of electric convulsion therapy as compared with conservative methods of treatment in depressive states. *J. ment. Sci.*, 96, 1060.—*218*.

KÅSS, E. N., RETTERSTÖL, N. and SIRNES, T. B. (1959) Barbiturate intoxication and addiction as a public health problem in Oslo. *Bull. Narcot.*, 11, 15.—*416*.

KAWI, A. A. and PASAMANICK, B. (1958) The association of factors of pregnancy with reading disorders in childhood. *J. Amer. med. Assoc.*, 166, 1420.—*688*.

KAY, D. W. K. (1959) Observations on the natural history and genetics of old age psychoses: a Stockholm material, 1931-1937 (Abridged). *Proc. roy. Soc. Med.*, 52, 791.—*568, 580, 585, 604*.

—— (1962) Outcome and cause of death in mental disorders of old age: a long-term follow-up of functional and organic psychoses. *Acta psychiat. scand.*, 38, 249.—*549, 581, 584, 604*.

—— (1663) Late paraphrenia and its bearing on the aetiology of schizophrenia. *Acta psychiat. scand.*, 39, 159. —*302*.

—— (1964) The genetics of stuttering. In: The Syndrome of Stuttering, Ch. 7. (see G. Andrews and M. Harris). London.—*652*.

——, BEAMISH, P. and ROTH, M. (1962) Some medical and social characteristics of elderly people under state care. *Sociol. Rev.*, Monograph No. 5. University of Keele.—*533, 541, 562*.

——, —— and —— (1964a) Old age mental disorders in Newcastle upon Tyne. Part I A study of prevalence. *Brit. J. Psychiat.*, 110, 146.—*540, 541, 577, 603*.

——, —— and —— (1964b) Old age mental disorders in Newcastle upon Tyne. Part II A study of possible social and medical causes. *Brit. J. Psychiat.*, 110, 668.—*540, 541, 545, 547, 561, 578, 778, 787*.

—— and BERGMANN, K. (1966) Physical disability and mental health in old age. *J. psychosom. Res.*, 10, 3. —*586, 781*.

——, ——, GARSIDE, R. F. and ROTH, M. (1966) A four-year follow-up study of a random sample of old people originally seen in their own homes. A physical, social and psychiatric enquiry. Comm. to the IVth Wld Congr. Psychiat., Madrid, Sept. 1966.—*603, 608, 778*.

—— and LEIGH, D. (1954) The natural history, treatment and prognosis of anorexia nervosa based on a study of 38 patients. *J. ment. Sci.*, 100, 411.—*124*.

—— and ROTH, M. (1955) Physical accompaniments of mental disorder in old age. *Lancet*, 2, 740.—*549, 586, 599*.

—— and —— (1961) Environmental and hereditary factors in the schizophrenias of old age ('late paraphrenia') and their bearing on the general problem of causation in schizophrenia. *J. ment. Sci.*, 107, 649. —*238, 293, 301, 302, 580, 581, 582*.

—— and SCHAPIRA, K. (1965) The prognosis in anorexia nervosa. Rep. of Symp. Göttingen, 1965, ed. J. E. Meyer and H. Feldmann. Stuttgart: Thieme.—*126*.

KEELER, W. R. (1958) Autistic patterns and defective communication in blind children with retrolental dysplasia. In: Psychopathology of Communication, ed. P. H. Hoch and J. Zubin. New York: Grune.—*682*.

KELLY, D. H. W. (1966) Measurement of anxiety by forearm blood flow. *Brit. J. Psychiat.*, 112, 789.—*86*.

—— and SARGANT, W. (1965) Present treatment of schizophrenia—a controlled follow-up study. *Brit. med. J.*, 1, 147.—*310*.

—— and WALTER, C. J. S. (1968) The relationship between clinical diagnosis and anxiety, assessed by forearm blood flow and other measurements. *Brit. J. Psychiat.*, 114, 611.—*96*.

KEMP, T. (1936) Prostitution. New York: Stechert.—*715*.

KENT, E. A. and WEINSAFT, P. (1963) Treatment of depression in the aged with opipramol. *J. Amer. Geriat. Soc.*, 11, 663.—*573*.

KESSEL, W. I. N. (1960) Psychiatric morbidity in a London general practice. *Brit. J. prev. soc. Med.*, 14, 16. —*542, 781*.

—— (1965) Self poisoning, I & II. *Brit. med. J.*, 2, 1265, 1336.—*790, 792, 793, 794, 795, 798*.

—— and COPPEN, A. (1963) The prevalence of common menstrual symptoms. *Lancet*, 2, 61.—*193, 371, 372*.

KESSEL W. I. N. and GROSSMAN, G. (1961) Suicide in alcoholics. *Brit. med. J.*, 2, 1671.—*412.*

—— and SHEPHERD, M. (1962) Neurosis in hospital and general practice. *J. ment. Sci.*, 108, 159.—*542.*

—— and WALTON, H. (1965) Alcoholism. London. Pelican.—*390, 393, 395, 396, 409.*

KETY, S. S. (1958) In: Chemical Pathology of the Nervous System, ed. Folch-Pi. 3rd Int. Neurochem. Symp. August 1958. London: Pergamon.—*255.*

—— (1959) Biochemical theories of schizophrenia, I and II. *Science, (Washington)*, 129, 1528, 1590.—*256, 257.*

KEUHL, F. A., ORMOND, R. E. and VANDENHEUVEL, W. J. A. (1966) Occurrence of 3,4-dimethoxyphenylacetic acid in urines of normal and schizophrenic individuals. *Nature (Lond.)* 211, 606.—*256.*

KEYS, A. (1952) The cholesterol problem. *Voeding*, 13, 539.—*590.*

——, MICKELSEN, O., MILLER, E. V. O. and CHAPMAN, C. B. (1950) The relation in man between cholesterol levels in the diet and in the blood. *Science, (Washington)*, 112, 79.—*590.*

KIDD, C. B. (1962a) Social attitudes to the elderly sick. *Geront. clin.*, 4, 33.—*566.*

—— (1962b) Criteria for admission of the elderly to geriatric and psychiatric units. *J. ment. Sci.*, 108, 68. —*563.*

—— and McKECHNIE, A. A. (1967) Prediction and outcome among old people in North-East Scottish mental hospitals. *Hlth Bull. (Edinb.)*, 25, 1.—*539.*

—— and SMITH, V. E. M. (1966) A regional survey of old people in North-East Scottish mental hospitals. *Scot. med. J.*, 11, 132.—*539, 564.*

KIDD, M. (1964) Alzheimer's disease: an electronmicroscopical study. *Brain*, 87, 307.—*607.*

KIELHOLZ, P. and BATTEGAY, R. (1963) The treatment of drug addicts in Switzerland. *Comprehens. Psychiat.*, 4, 225.—*426.*

KILOH, L. G. (1961) Pseudo-dementia. *Acta psychiat. scand.*, 37, 336.—*210, 484, 569.*

—— and BALL, J. R. B. (1961) Depression treated with imipramine: a follow-up study. *Brit. med. J.*, 1, 168. —*222.*

——, —— and GARSIDE, R. F. (1962) Prognostic factors in treatment of depressive states with imipramine. *Brit med. J.*, 1, 1225.—*222, 225, 230, 573.*

—— and BRANDON, S. (1962) Habituation and addiction to amphetamines. *Brit. med. J.*, 2, 40.—*420.*

—— and GARSIDE, R. F. (1963) The independence of neurotic depression and endogenous depression, *Brit. J. Psychiat.*, 109, 451.—*13, 188, 205, 210, 222.*

KIMURA, D. (1961) Some effects of temporal lobe damage on auditory perception. *Canad. J. Psychol.*, 15, 156. —*495.*

KIND, H. (1958) Psychiatry of hypophysical insufficiency with special reference to Simmond's disease. *Fortschr. Neurol. Psychiat.*, 26, 501.—*368.*

—— (1966) The psychogenesis of schizophrenia: a review of the literature. *Brit. J. Psychiat.*, 112, 333.—*262.*

KING, A. (1963) Primary and secondary anorexia nervosa syndromes. *Brit. J. Psychiat.*, 109, 470.—*125.*

—— and LITTLE, J. C. (1959) Thiopentone treatment of the phobic anxiety-depersonalization syndrome: a preliminary report. *Proc. roy. Soc. Med.*, 52, 595.—*102.*

KINSBOURNE, M. and WARRINGTON, E. K. (1963) The relevance of delayed acquisition of finger sense to backwardness in reading and writing. In: Minimal Cerebral Dysfunction, ed. R. C. MacKeith and M. Bax. London: Nat. Spastics Soc.—*678, 690.*

KINSEY, A. C., POMEROY, W. B. and MARTIN, C. E. (1948) Sexual Behaviour in the Human Male. Philadelphia: Saunders.—*159, 161, 168, 170, 538, 715.*

——, ——, —— and GEBHARD, P. H. (1953) Sexual Behaviour in the Human Female. Philadelphia: Saunders.—*170, 538.*

KIRBY, G. H. (1921) Guides for History-taking and Clinical Examination of Psychiatric Cases. Albany (N.Y.). *36, 46.*

KIRCHHOF, J. (1942) Depressive illness, especially endogenous mood changes as seen in clinical practice. *Z. ges. Neurol. Psychiat.*, 174, 89.—*217.*

KIRSHNER, N., GOODALL, M. C. and ROSEN, L. (1958) Metabolism of dl-adrenaline-2-C^{14} in the human. *Proc. soc. exp. Biol. (N.Y.)*, 98, 627.—*255.*

KLÄSI, J. (1922) On the Significance and Origin of Stereotypies. Berlin: Karger.—*271.*

KLEBANOFF, L. B. (1959) Parental attitudes of mothers of schizophrenic, brain-injured and normal children. *Amer. J. Orthopsychiat.*, 29, 445.—*686.*

KLEIN, D. C. and LINDEMANN, E. (1961) Preventive intervention in individual and family crisis situations. In: Prevention of Mental Disorders in Children, ed. G. Caplan. New York: Basic Books.—*803.*

KLEIN, M. (1937) Psychoanalysis of Children. 2nd edn. London: Hogarth.—*633.*

KLEIN, R. and MAYER-GROSS, W. (1957) The Clinical Examination of Patients with Organic Cerebral Disease. London: Cassell.—*48.*

KLEINSCHMIDT, H. J. WAXENBERG, S. E. and CUKER, R. (1956) Psychophysiology and psychiatric management of thyrotoxicosis: a two year follow-up study. *J. Mt Sinai Hosp.*, 23, 131.—*366.*

KLEIST, K. (1908) Studies of Psychomotor Symptoms in Mental Patients. Leipzig: Klinkhardt.—*623.*

—— (1913) Involutional paranoia. *Allg. Z. Psychiat.*, 70, 1.—*148, 297.*

—— (1921) Autochthonous psychoses of degeneration. *Z. ges. Neurol. Psychiat.*, 69, 1.—*215, 298.*

—— (1943) The catatonias. *Nervenarzt.* 16, 1.—*308.*

KLEITMAN, N. (1963) Sleep and Wakefulness, rev. ed. Univ. of Chicago.—*641.*

KLINEFELTER, H. F., REIFENSTEIN, E. C. and ALBRIGHT, F. (1942) Syndrome characterized by gynecomastia, aspermatogenesis without A-leydigism, and increased excretion of follicle-stimulating hormone. *J. clin. Endocr.*, 2, 615.—*722.*

KLINTWORTH, G. K. (1962) A pair of male monozygotic twins discordant for homosexuality. *J. nerv. ment. Dis.*, *135*, 113.—*170*.

KLOPFER, B. (1946) The Rorschach Technique. New York: World Book Co.—*317*.

KLÜVER, H. (1928) Mescal. London: Kegan Paul.—*433*.

——— and BUCY, P. C. (1938) An analysis of certain effects of bilateral temporal lobectomy in the rhesus monkey, with special reference to 'psychic blindness'. *J. Psychol.*, *5*, 33. —*494*.

——— and ——— (1939) Preliminary analysis of functions of the temporal lobes in monkeys. *Arch. Neurol. Psychiat.*, *(Chic.)*, *42*, 979.—*86*.

KNAPP, P. H. (1952) Amphetamine and addiction. *J. nerv. ment. Dis.*, *115*, 406.—*421*.

KNAUER, A. and MALONEY, W. J. M. A. (1913) Psychic action of mescaline. *J. nerv. ment. Dis.*, *40*, 425. —*433*.

KNIGHT, G. C. (1964)The orbital cortex as an objective in the surgical treatment of mental illness. The results of 450 cases of an open operation and the development of stereotactic approach. *Brit. J. Surg.*, *51*, 114. —*336, 575*.

KNOBLOCH, H. and PASAMANICK, B. (1959) Syndrome of minimal cerebral damage in infancy. *J. Amer. med. Ass.*, *170*, 1384.—*77, 688*.

———, RIDER, R., HARPER, P. and PASAMANICK, B. (1956) The neuropsychiatric sequelae of prematurity: a longitudinal study. *J. Amer. med. Ass.*, *161*, 581.—*802*.

KOCH, G. (1963) Die Erblichkeit der Epilepsien. *Psychiat. Neurol. Neurochir.*, *66*, 153.—*453*.

KOCH, J. L. A. (1891) The Psychopathic Inferiorities. Ravensburg: Dorn.—*56*.

KOHN, M. L. and CLAUSEN, J. A. (1955) Social isolation and schizophrenia. *Amer. sociol. Rev.*, *20*, 265.—*786*.

KOLLE, K. (1931) Primary Paranoia. Leipzig: Thieme.—*293, 580*.

KÖNG, E. (1963) Minimal cerebral palsy: the importance of its recognition. In: Minimal Cerebral Dysfunction, ed. R. C. MacKeith and M. Bax. London: Nat. Spastics Soc.—*689*.

KOPIN, I. J. (1959) Tryptophan loading and excretion of 5-hydroxyindoleacetic acid in normal and schizophrenic subjects. *Science (Washington)*, *129*, 835.—*257*.

KOSVINER, A., MITCHESON, M. C., MYERS, K., OGBORNE, A., STIMSON, G. V., ZACUNE, J. and EDWARDS, G. (1968) Heroin use in a provincial town. *Lancet*, *1*, 1189.—*415, 429*.

KRAEPELIN, E. (1904) Vergleichende Psychiatrie. *Zentbl. Nervenheilk.*, *15*, 433.—*790*.

——— (1909-13) Psychiatry, 8th ed. Leipzig: Thieme.—*297, 548*.

——— (1920) Symptoms of mental disease. *Z. ges. Neurol. Psychiat.*, *62*, 1.—*293*.

——— and LANGE, J. (1927) Psychiatry, Vols. 1 and 2. 9th ed. Leipzig: Thieme.—*444*.

KRAL, V. A. (1951) Psychiatric observations under severe chronic stress. *Amer. J. Psychiat.*, *108*, 185.—*122*.

——— (1962) Senescent forgetfulness: benign and malignant. *Canad. med. Ass. J.*, *86*, 257.—*603, 607*.

KRAMER, F. and POLLNOW, H. (1932) Uber eine hyperkinetische Erkrankung im Kindesalter. *Mschr. Psychiat. Neurol.*, *82*, 1.—*654, 690*.

KRANZ, H. (1936) Lives of Criminal Twins. Berlin: Springer.—*65, 658*.

KRAPF, E. (1928) Epilepsie und Schizophrenie. *Arch. Psychiat. Nervenkr.*, *83*, 547.—*470*.

KRAULIS, W. (1931) Heredity of hysterical reactions. *Z. ges. Neurol. Psychiat.*, *136*, 174.—*103, 155*.

KREISLER, O., LIEBERT, E. and HORWITT, M. K. (1948) Psychiatric observations on induced vitamin B complex deficiency in psychotic patients. *Amer. J. Psychiat.*, *105*, 107.—*351*.

KREITMAN, N., SAINSBURY, P., PEARCE, K. and COSTAIN, W. R. (1965) Hypochondriasis and depression in out-patients at a general hospital. *Brit. J. Psychiat.*, *111*, 607.—*142*.

KRETSCHMER, E. (1918) Der Sensitive Beziehungswahn. Berlin: Springer—*294*.

——— (1936) Physique and Character. 2nd ed. revised Miller. London: Routledge.—*69, 191, 251*.

——— (1948) Hysteria, Reflex and Instinct. Stuttgart: Thieme.—*112*.

KRINGLEN, E. (1965) Obsessional neurotics: a long term follow-up. *Brit. J. Psychiat.*, *111*, 709.—*132, 136, 137*.

——— (1966) Schizophrenia in twins: an epidemiological-clinical study. *Psychiatry (Washington)*, *29*, 172. —*241*.

——— (1967) Heredity and Environment in the Functional Psychoses. London: Heinemann.—*248*.

KURLAND, L. T. (1959) The incidence and prevalence of convulsive disorders in a small urban community. *Epilepsia (Amst).*, *1*, 143.—*450*.

KUSHLICK, A. (1961) Subnormality in Salford. In: A report on the mental health services of the City of Salford for the year 1960, ed. M. W. Susser and A. Kushlick. Salford Health Department.—*694*.

——— (1964) Prevalence of recognized mental subnormality of I.Q. under 50 among children in the South of England with reference to the demand for places for residential care. Paper to the Int. Copenhagen Conf. on the Sci. Study of Ment. Retardation, Copenhagen. August 1964.—*694*.

——— (1965) Community care for the subnormal—a plan for evaluation. *Proc. roy. Soc. Med.*, *58*, 374.—*694, 720*.

——— (1966) A community service for the mentally subnormal. *Soc. Psychiat.*, *1*, 73.—*694*.

KUROSAWA, R. (1962) Untersuchung der atypischen endogenen Psychosen. *Folia psychiat. neurol. Jap.*, *16*, 187. —*197*.

LABHARDT, F. (1963) Die Schizophrenieähnlichen Emotionspsychosen. Berlin: Springer.—*303*.

LA BROSSE, E-H., AXELROD, J. and KETY, S. S. (1958) O-methylation, the principal route of metabolism of epinephrine in man. *Science, 128*, 593.—*255*.

LANDIS, C. and BOLLES, M. M. (1950) Textbook of Abnormal Psychology. 2nd ed. New York: MacMillan.—*9*.

LANDOLT, H. (1960) Die Temporallappenepilepsie und ihre Psychopathologie. *Bibl. psychiat. neurol. (Basel)* 112.—*451, 454, 459, 462*.

Lane, M. R. (1961) Maple syrup urine disease. *J. Paediat. 58*, 80.—*725*.

Lang, T. (1940) Studies on the genetic determination of homosexuality. *J. nerv. ment. Dis.*, 92, 55.—*169*.

Lange, J. (1922) Catatonic Symptoms in Manic Illnesses. Berlin: Springer.—*221, 311*.

———— (1928) The endogenous and reactive affective disorders and the manic-depressive constitution. In: Handbook of Mental Diseases, ed. Bumke, Vol. 6. Berlin: Springer.—*191, 192, 194*.

———— (1929) Crime as Destiny: Studies of Criminal Twins. Leipzig: Thieme.—*65*.

Lange, W. (1909) Hoelderlin: A Pathography. Stuttgart.—*287*.

Langfeldt, G. (1937) The prognosis in schizophrenia and the factors influencing the course of the disease. *Acta psychiat. neurol. scand.*, suppl. *13*.—*302, 308, 309, 483*.

———— (1959) The prognosis in schizophrenia. In: Congress Report. *1*, 220. Second Int. Congr. Psychiat., Zurich 1957. Zurich: Orell Füssli Arts.—*302*.

———— (1960) Diagnosis and prognosis of schizophrenia. *Proc. roy. Soc. Med.*, 53, 1047.—*483*.

———— (1961) The erotic jealousy syndrome: a clinical study. *Acta psychiat. neurol. scand.*, 36, suppl. 151, 7.—*400*.

Lapouse, R. and Monk, M. A. (1958) An epidemiologic study of behaviour characteristics in children. *Amer. J. publ. Hlth*, 48, 1134.—*634*.

Larsson, T. and Sjögren, T. (1954) A methodological, psychiatric and statistical study of a large Swedish rural population. *Acta psychiat. neurol. scand.*, suppl. *89*.—*189, 239, 703*.

————, ———— and Jacobson, G. (1963) Senile dementia. *Acta psychiat. scand.*, *39*, suppl. 167.—*603, 604, 612*.

Laurence, D. R. (1963) Unwanted and dangerous interactions between drugs. *Prescribers' J.*, 3, 46.—*202*.

Lehmann, H. E. (1964) Pharmacotherapy of schizophrenia. Paper delivered to the American Pathological Association. Ann. conf. 1964. New York.—*335*.

Leighton, A. H. *et al.* (1959–1963) Stirling County Study of Psychiatric Disorder and Sociocultural Environment, Vols. I–III. New York: Basic Books.—*782*.

Leighton, D. C., Harding, J. S., Macklin, D. B., Hughes, C. C. and Leighton, A. H. (1963) Psychiatric findings of the Stirling County Study. *Amer. J. Psychiat.*, *119*, 1021.—*781*.

Leishman, A. W. D. (1959) Hypertension—treated and untreated: a study of 400 cases. *Brit. med. J.*, *1*, 1361.—*598*.

Lejeune, J., Gautier, M., Lafourcade, J., Berger, R. and Turpin, R. (1964) Délétion partielle du bras court du chromosome 5. Cinquième cas de syndrome du cri du chat. *Ann. Genet. (Paris)*, 7, 7.—*722*.

————, ———— and Turpin, R. (1959) Génétique. Les chromosomes humaines en culture des tissues. Presented by M. Léon Binet. *C.R. Acad. Sci., (Paris)*, 248, 602.—*720*.

Lemkau, P., Tietze, C. and Cooper, M. (1941, 1942, 1943) Mental hygiene problems in an urban district I–IV. *Ment. Hyg.*, 25, 624; 26, 100; 26, 275 and 27, 279.—*694, 781*.

Lennox, W. G. (1942) Mental defect in epilepsy and the influence of heredity. *Amer. J. Psychiat.*, 98, 733.—*454*.

———— (1945) The petit mal epilepsies, their treatment with Tridione. *J. Amer. med. Ass.*, 129, 1069.—*457*.

———— (1947) Sixty-six twin pairs affected by seizures. *Res. Publ. Ass. nerv. ment. Dis.*, 26, 11.—*452*.

———— (1951) Heredity of epilepsy as told by relatives and twins. *J. Amer. med. Ass.*, 146, 529.—*452*.

———— (1954) Social and emotional problems of epileptic child and his family. *J. Pediat.*, 44, 596.—*452*.

———— and Lennox, M. A. (1960) Epilepsy and Related Disorders. Vol. 1. London: Churchill.—*482*.

————, Gibbs, E. L. and Gibbs, F. A. (1945) The brain-wave pattern; an hereditary trait. *J. Hered.*, 36, 233.—*71*.

Leonhard, K. (1934) Atypical endogenous psychoses in the light of family research. *Z. ges. Neurol. Psychiat.*, *149*, 520.—*197*.

———— (1935) Exogenous schizophrenias and symptomatic components in the clinical picture of idiopathic schizophrenia. *Mschr. Psychiat. Neurol.*, 91, 249.—*298*.

————, Korff, I. and Schulz, H. (1962) Temperament in families with monopolar and bipolar phasic psychoses. *Psychiat. Neurol. (Basel)*, *143*, 416.—*196*.

Lesser, L. I., Ashenden, B. J. Debuskey, M. and Eisenberg, L. (1960) Anorexia nervosa in children. *Amer. J. Orthopsychiat.*, 30, 572.—*664*.

Letemendia, F. and Pampiglione, G. (1958) Clinical and electroencephalographic observations in Alzheimer's disease. *J. Neurol. Neurosurg. Psychiat.*, 21, 167.—*559*.

Levitt, J. and Taran, L. M. (1948) Some of the problems in the education of rheumatic children. *J. Pediat.*, 32, 553.—*381*.

Lévy-Valensi, J. (1925) Mental automatism and chronic delusional illness with hallucinations. *Paris méd.*, 2, 213.—*271*.

Lewin, B. (1950) The Psychoanalysis of Elation. New York: Norton.—*195*.

Lewin, L. (1931) Phantastica, Narcotic and Stimulating Drugs. London: Routledge.—*427*.

Lewis, A. J. (1934) Melancholia: a clinical survey of depressive states. *J. ment. Sci.*, 80, 277.—*195*.

———— (1935a) Problems of obsessional illness. *Proc. roy. Soc. Med.*, 29, 325.—*68*.

———— (1935b) Neurosis and unemployment. *Lancet*, 2, 293.—*140*.

———— (1942) Discussion on differential diagnosis and treatment of post-contusional states. *Proc. roy. Soc. Med.*, 35, 607.—*508*.

———— (1950) Section XX, Psychological Medicine. In: A Textbook of the Practice of Medicine, ed. F. W. Price, 8th ed., pp. 1924 and 1933. London: H.M.S.O.—*225*.

Lewis, E. O. (1929) An investigation into the incidence of mental deficiency. Report of the Mental Deficiency Committee (Wood Report), London.—*694, 703, 718*.

———— (1933) Types of mental deficiency and their social significance. *J. ment. Sci.*, 79, 298.—*693, 703*.

Lewis, H. H. (1954) Deprived Children (the Mershal experiment). A Social and Clinical Study. London: Oxford University Press.—*637*.

Lewis, N. D. C. (1949) Criteria for early differential diagnosis of psychoneurosis and schizophrenia. *Amer. J. Psychother.*, 3, 4.—*123*.

Leyton, G. B. (1946) Effects of slow starvation. *Lancet*, 2, 73.—*356*.

Liddell, D. W. (1953) Observations on epileptic automatism in a mental hospital population. *J. ment. Sci.*, 99, 732.—*468, 476*.

——— (1958) Investigations of EEG findings in presenile dementia. *J. Neurol. Neurosurg. Psychiat.*, 21, 173.—*559*.

Lidz, T., Cornelison, A. R., Fleck, S. and Terry, D. (1957a) The intrafamilial environment of the schizophrenic patient. I The father. *Psychiatry (Washington)*, 20, 329.—*246*.

———, ———, ——— and ——— (1957b) The intrafamilial environment of schizophrenic patients. II Marital schism and marital skew. *Amer. J. Psychiat.*, 114, 241.—*246*.

———, ———, Terry, D. and Fleck, S. (1958a) The intrafamilial environment of the schizophrenic patient. VI The transmission of irrationality. *Arch. neurol. psychiat. (Chic.)*, 79, 305.—*246, 266, 317*.

———, Fleck, S., Cornelison, A. R. and Terry, D. (1958b) The intrafamilial environment of the schizophrenic patient. IV Parental personalities and family interaction. *Amer. J. Orthopychiat.*, 28, 764.—*246, 266, 317*.

van Liere, E. J. (1942) Anoxia: Its Effect on the Body. Chicago: Univ. of Chicago Press.—*440*.

Lin, T-Y., (1953) A study of the incidence of mental disorder in Chinese and other cultures. *Psychiatry, (Washington)*, 16, 313.—*540*.

Lindemann, E. (1944) Symptomatology and management of acute grief. *Amer. J. Psychiat.*, 101, 141.—*799*.

Lindman, F. T. and McIntyre, D. M. (eds.) (1961) The Mentally Disabled and the Law. The Report of the American Bar Foundation on the Rights of the Mentally Ill. University of Chicago Press.—*740, 749, 758, 769*.

Lindsley, D. B., Bowden, J. W. and Magoun, H. W. (1949) Effect upon the EEG of acute injury to the brain stem activating system. *Electroenceph. clin. Neurophysiol.*, 1, 475.—*500*.

Lingjaerde, P., Skaug, O. E. and Lingjaerde, O. (1960) The determination of thyroid function with radio-iodine (1–131) in mental patients. *Acta psychiat. neurol. scand.*, 35, 498.—*253*.

Liss, L. (1960) Senile brain changes: histopathology of the ganglion cells. *J. Neuropath. exp. Neurol.*, 19, 559.—*607*.

Little, J. C. (1966) Physical prowess and neurosis: a study in specific vulnerability. Threatened physical prowess as an aetiological factor in the genesis of some neurotic states in the male. Thesis submitted for the degree of M.D. University of Bristol.—*143*.

Ljungberg. L. (1957) Hysteria. Copenhagen; Munksgaard.—*104, 117*.

Lloyd, E. A. and Clark, L. D. (1959) Convulsions and delirium incident to glutethimide (Doriden) withdrawal (a case report). *Dis. nerv. Syst.*, 20, 524.—*418*.

Locher, R. (1941) On the sudden death of mental patients and the acute catatoniform syndrome with fatal outcome. *Mschr. Psychiat. Neurol.*, 103, 278.—*307*.

Loewe, S. (1950) Active principles in Cannabis and pharmacology of Cannabinoles. *Arch. exper. Path. Pharmacol.*, 211, 175.—*427*.

Loewy, H. (1908) Die Aktionsgefuhle. *Prag. med. Wschr.*, 33, 443.—*121*.

Logan, R. F. L. (1965) The burden of the aged in society and on medical care. In: Medicine in Old Age. Proc. Conf. held at the Royal College of Physicians of London, 1965. Pitman.—*533*.

López Ibor, J. J. (1950) La Angustia vital. Patología general psychosomaticá, ed. Paz Montalvo. Madrid.—*90*.

——— (1962) The 'target' symptoms in the treatment of depressions. *Comprehens. Psychiat.*, 3, 15.—*222*.

——— (1966) Neuroses as Mood Disorders. Madrid: Editorial Gredos.—*90*.

Lorr, M. (1953) Multidimensional scale for rating psychiatric patients. *Vet. Adm. tech. Bull.*, 6, 1.—*36*.

Lovaas, O. L. (1967) A programme for the establishment of speech in non-speaking children. In: Early Childhood Autism, ed. J. K. Wing. London: Pergamon.—*684*.

Lovett-Doust, J. W. (1962) Consciousness in schizophrenia as a function of the peripheral microcirculation. In: Physiological Correlates of Psychological Disorders, Ch.: 4, 61, ed. R. Roessler and N. S. Greenfield. Madison, Wisconsin: University of Wisconsin Press.—*258*.

Lovibond, S. H. (1954) The object-sorting test and conceptual thinking in schizophrenia. *Aust. J. Psychol.*, 6, 52.—*266*.

——— (1963) The mechanism of conditioning treatment of enuresis. *Behav. Res. Ther.*, 1, 17.—*185*.

Lowenthal, M. F. (1964a) Lives in Distress. New York: Basic Books.—*545, 786*.

——— (1964b) Social isolation and mental illness in old age. *Amer. sociol. Rev.*, 29, 54.—*546*.

——— (1965) Antecedents of isolation and mental illness in old age. *Arch. gen. Psychiat.*, 12, 245.—*546, 561*.

Lubin, A. (1950) A note on Sheldon's table of correlations between temperamental traits. *Brit. J. Psychol. statist. Sect.*, 3, 186.—*193*.

Lubin, B. (1965) Adjective check lists for measurement of depression. *Arch. gen. Psychiat.*, 12, 57.—*36*.

Lucero, R. J. and Meyer, B. Y. (1951) A behaviour rating scale suitable for use in mental hospitals. *J. clin. Psychol.*, 7, 250.—*36*.

Lukianowicz, N. (1959) Survey of various aspects of transvestism in the light of our present knowledge. *J. nerv. ment. Dis.*, 128, 36.—*164*.

Lundborg, H. (1912) Heredity in progressive myoclonus epilepsy. *Z. ges. Neurol. Psychiat.*, 9, 353.—*451*.

Lundquist, G. (1961) A comparative study of pathogenesis, course and prognosis of delirium tremens. *Acta psychiat. Scand.*, 36, 443.—*401*.

Lundström, R. (1952) Rubella during pregnancy: its effects upon perinatal mortality, the incidence of congenital abnormalities and immaturity. A preliminary report. *Acta paediat. (Upsala)*, 41, 583.—*707*.

LUNDSTRÖM, R. (1962) Rubella during pregnancy: a follow-up study of children born after an epidemic of rubella in Sweden, 1951, with additional investigations on prophylaxis and treatment of maternal rubella. *Actapaediat. (Upsala)*, *51*, suppl. 133.—*707*.

LUTZ, J. (1945) Some remarks on the problems of schizophrenia in children. *Z. Kinderpsychiat.*, *11*, Heft. 6. —*670*.

LUXENBURGER, H. (1930) Heredität und Familientypus der Zwangsneurotiker. *Arch. Nervenkr. Psychiat.*, *91*, 590.—*68*.

——— (1933) Distribution of occupation and social class in the families of persons suffering from hereditary mental disorders. *Eugenik*, *3*, 34.—*703*.

LYNN, R. (1963) Russian theory and research on schizophrenia. *Psychol. Bull.*, *60*, 486.—*24*.

MCADAM, W. and MCCLATCHLEY, W. T. (1952) The electroencephalogram in aged patients of a mental hospital. *J. ment. Sci.*, *98*, 711.—*557*.

MCCARTHY, P. D. and WALSH, D. (1966) Suicide in Dublin. *Brit. med. J.*, *1*, 1393.—*788*.

MACLAY, W. S. and WILSON, I. G. H. (1950) Mental health services in England and Wales. In: Proc. Congr. Int. Psychiat. Paris: Hermann.—*754*.

MCCLELLAND, H. A., ROTH, M., NEUBAUER, H. and GARSIDE, R. F. (1968) Some observations on a case-material based on patients with certain common schizophrenic symptoms. Proc. IVth Wld Congr. Psychiat., Madrid, 1966. p. 2955. Excerpta Medica Foundation. Amsterdam.—*122, 260, 303*.

MCCLURE, J. L. (1962) Reactions associated with tranylcypromine. *Lancet*, *1*, 1351.—*202*.

MCCONAGHY, N. (1959) The use of an object-sorting test in elucidating the hereditary factor in schizophrenia. *J. Neurol. Neurosurg. Psychiat.*, *22*, 243.—*246, 266*.

———, JOFFE, A. D. and MURPHY, B. (1967) The independence of neurotic and endogenous depression. *Brit. J. Psychiat.*, *113*, 479.—*225*.

MCCORD, W. and MCCORD, J. (1960) Origins of Alcoholism. Stanford: Stanford University Press.—*393*.

MCDONALD, A. D. (1964) Intelligence in children of very low birth weight. *Brit. J. prev. soc. Med.*, *18*, 59.—*706*.

MACDONALD, E. M. (1960) Occupational Therapy in Rehabilitation. London: Baillière.—*565*.

MCFARLAND, R. A. (1932) The psychological effects of oxygen deprivation (anoxaemia) on human behaviour. *Arch. Psychol., Columbia University*, No. 145.—*440*.

MACFARLANE, J. W., ALLEN, L. and HONZIG, M. P. (1954) A Developmental Study of the Behaviour Problems of Normal Children between Twenty-one Months and Fourteen Years. Berkeley: Univ. of California Press.—*635*.

MCFIE, J. (1960) Psychological testing in clinical neurology. *J. nerv. ment. Dis.*, *131*, 383.—*48, 498*.

——— (1963) An introduction to the problem of 'minimal brain damage'. In: Minimal Brain Dysfunction. ed. R. C. MacKeith and M. Bax. London: Nat. Spastics Soc.—*687*.

MCGEER, E. G., BROWN, W. T. and MCGEER, P. L. (1957) Aromatic metabolism in schizophrenia. II Bidimensional urinary chromatograms. *J. nerv. ment. Dis.*, *125*, 176.—*255*.

MCGHIE, A. (1961) A comparative study of the mother-child relationship in schizophrenia. I The interview. II Psychological testing. *Brit. J. med. Psychol.*, *34*, 195, 209.—*266*.

MCINNES, R. G. (1937) Observations on heredity in neurosis. *Proc. roy. Soc. Med.*, *30*, 895.—*68, 103*.

MCINTOSH, J. and FILDES, P. (1914–15) A comparison of the lesions of syphilis and 'parasyphilis' together with evidence in favour of the identity of these two conditions. *Brain*, *37*, 141.—*520*.

MACIVER, I. N., FREW, I. J. C. and MATHESON, J. G. (1958) The role of respiratory insufficiency in the mortality of severe head injuries. *Lancet*, *1*, 390.—*501*.

MACKEITH, R. C. and BAX, M. (1963) Minimal Cerebral Dysfunction. National Spastics Soc. London.—*687*.

MACKENZIE, D. Y. and WOOLF, L. I. (1959) Maple syrup urine disease. *Brit. med. J.*, *1*, 90.—*725*.

MACKINNON, P. C. B. and MACKINNON, I. L. (1956) Hazards of the menstrual cycle. *Brit. med. J.*, *1*, 555. —*373*.

MCMENEMEY, W. H. (1940) Alzheimer's disease. A report of six cases. *J. Neurol. Psychiat.*, *3*, 211.—*614*.

——— (1941) Dementia in middle age. *J. Neurol. Psychiat.*, *4*, 48.—*628*.

——— (1961) Immunity mechanisms in neurological disease. *Proc. roy. Soc. Med.*, *54*, 127.—*621*.

MACMILLAN, D. (1960) Preventive geriatrics: opportunities of a community mental health service. *Lancet*, *2*, 1439.—*566*.

——— (1963) Recent developments in community mental health. *Lancet*, *1*, 567.—*566*.

MADDISON, D. and MACKEY, K. H. (1966) Suicide: the clinical problem. *Brit. J. Psychiat.*, *112*, 693.—*796*.

MAGOUN, H. W. (1958) The Waking Brain. Springfield, Ill. Thomas.—*463*.

MAHLER, M. S. (1961) On sadness and grief in infancy and childhood. In: Psychoanalytic Study of the Child, ed. R. S. Eissler, Vol. 16. London: Hogarth.—*686*.

MAIER, H. W. (1922) On insurance hebephrenia. *Z. ges. Neurol. Psychiat.*, *78*, 422.—*296*.

MALAMUD, N. (1959) Heller's disease and childhood schizophrenia. *Amer. J. Psychiat.*, *116*, 215.—*685*.

———, HAYMAKER, W. and PINKERTON, H. (1950) Inclusion encephalitis: with a clinico-pathologic report of three cases. *Amer. J. Path.*, *26*, 133.—*513*.

——— and RENDER, N. (1939) Course and prognosis of schizophrenia. *Amer. J. Psychiat.*, *95*, 1039.—*310*.

——— and WAGGONER, R. W. (1943) Genealogic and clinico-pathologic study of Pick's disease. *Arch. Neurol. Psychiat. (Chic.)*, *50*, 288.—*619*.

MALLISON, R. (1947) The diagnostic value of the encephalogram in cerebral atrophies of the involutional age. Rep. of Kongr. Neurol. Psychiat., Tübingen, p. 154.—*626*.

MALMROS, H. (1950) Relation of nutrition to health: statistical study of effect of war-time on arteriosclerosis, cardiosclerosis, tuberculosis and diabetes. *Acta med. scand.*, suppl. *246*, 137.—*590*.

MALZBERG, B. (1960) The Alcoholic Psychosis. Glencoe, Ill.: The Free Press.—*390.*

MANDELBROTE, B. M. and FOLKARD, S. (1961) Some problems and needs of schizophrenics in relation to a developing psychiatric community service. *Comprehens. Psychiat.*, *2*, 317.—*340.*

—— and WITTKOWER, E. D. (1955) Emotional factors in Grave's disease. *Psychosom. Med.*, *17*, 109.—*365.*

MANSON, M. M., LOGAN, W. P. D. and LOY, R. M. (1960) Ministry of Health Report, Public Health Medical Subjects, No. 101. London: H.M.S.O.—*707.*

MAPOTHER, E. and LEWIS, A. J. (1937) In: Price's Textbook of the Practice of Medicine. 5th ed., p. 1789. London: Oxford Univ. Press.—*207.*

MARAZZI, A. S. and HART, E. R. (1955) The possible role of inhibition at adrenergic synapses in the mechanism of hallucinogenic and related drug actions. *J. nerv. ment. Dis.*, *122*, 453.—*435.*

MARCHAND, L. and AJURIAGUERRA, J. (1948) Epilepsies. Paris: Desclée.—*456, 457, 465.*

MARIA, G. (1956) Ricerche elettroencefalografiche nel pavor nocturnus. *Cervello*, *32*, 101.—*643.*

MARIUZ, M. J. and WALTERS, C. J. (1963) Enuresis in non-psychotic boys treated with imipramine. *Amer. J. Psychiat.*, *120*, 597.—*647.*

MARJERKISON, G. and KEOGH, R. P. (1967) Electroencephalographic changes during brief periods of perceptual deprivation. *Percept. mot. Skills*, *24*, 611.—*380.*

MARKS, I. M. (1967) Classification of phobic states. Communication to R.M.P.A. Quarterly Meeting, Feb. 1967.—*95.*

—— and GELDER, M. G. (1965) A controlled retrospective study of behaviour therapy in phobic patients. *Brit. J. Psychiat.*, *111*, 561.—*95, 103, 186.*

—— and —— (1966a) Different ages of onset in varieties of phobia. *Amer. J. Psychiat.*, *123*, 218.—*92.*

—— and —— (1966b) Common ground between behaviour therapy and psychodynamic methods. *Brit. J. med. Psychol.*, *39*, 11.—*180.*

—— and —— (1967) Transvestism and fetishism: clinical and psychological changes during faradic aversion. *Brit. J. Psychiat.*, *113*, 711.—*166.*

MARRIOTT, H. L. (1947) Water and salt depletion, I–III. *Brit. med. J.*, *1*, 245, 285 and 328.—*358.*

MARSH, D. O., SCHNIEDEN, H. and MARSHALL, J. (1963) A controlled clinical trial of alpha methyldopa in Parkinsonian tremor. *J. Neurol. Neurosurg. Psychiat.*, *26*, 505.—*517.*

MARTIN, F. M. (1962) The selection of relevant social variables. In: The Burden on the Community. The Epidemiology of Mental Illness: a Symposium. Nuffield Provincial Hospitals Trust. London.—*786.*

——, BROTHERSTON, J. H. F. and CHAVE, S. P. W. (1967) Incidence of neurosis in a new housing estate. *Brit. J. prev. soc. Med.*, *11*, 196.—*783.*

MARTIN, M. E. (1958) Puerperal mental illness. A follow-up study of 75 cases. *Brit. med. J.*, *2*, 773.—*377.*

MASON, A. (1962) Fatal reaction associated with tranylcypromine and methylamphetamine. *Lancet*, *1*, 1073.—*202.*

MASON, C. F. (1956) Pre-illness intelligence of mental hospital patients. *J. consult. Psychol.*, *20*, 297.—*307.*

MASON, J. W. (1959) Psychological influences on the pituitary-adrenal cortical system. In: Recent Progress in Hormone Research. XV. New York: Academic Press.—*86.*

MASSERMAN, J. H. (1943) Behaviour and Neurosis. Chicago: Univ. of Chicago Press.—*4, 138.*

MATHES, P. (1924) Female constitutional types especially in the intersexual type. In: Biology and Pathology of the Female, ed. J. Halban and L. Seitz. Berlin: Urban and Schwarzenburg.—*83.*

MATHEWS, J. (1967) Personal communication.—*790.*

MATUSSEK, P. (1963) Wahn. In: Psychiatrie der Gegenwart, ed. H. W. Gruhle *et al.* Berlin: Springer-Verlag.—*294.*

MAY, A. R. (1964) Principles underlying community care. Symposium on Mental Hospital Psychiatry, Middlesex Hospital, 1964.—*339.*

MAYER, W. (1921) On paraphrenic psychoses. *Z. ges. Neurol. Psychiat.*, *71*, 187.—*288, 580.*

MAYER-GROSS, W. (1924) Self-descriptions from Confusional States. The Oneiroid Experience. Berlin.—*215, 299.*

—— (1931) Some symptoms of organic brain disease. *Arch. Psychiat. Nervenkr.*, *92*, 433.—*618.*

—— (1932) Schizophrenie. Bumke's Handbuch der Geisteskrankheiten. Vol. 9, p. 535. Berlin: Springer.—*310.*

—— (1935) On depersonalization. *Brit. J. med. Psychol.*, *15*, 103.—*120, 123.*

—— (1937) Irritability as a symptom in manic-depressives. *J. ment. Sci.*, *83*, 61.—*139.*

—— (1945) Electric convulsive treatment in patients over sixty. *J. ment. Sci.*, *91*, 101.—*549.*

—— (1948) Mental health survey in a rural area. A preliminary report. *Eugen. Rev.*, *40*, 140.—*694.*

—— and GUTTMANN, E. (1937) Schema for the examination of organic cases. *J. ment. Sci.*, *83*, 440.—*48.*

——, HARRIS, A. D. and LETEMENDIA, F. (1959) Comparison of abnormal behavioural states induced by psychotropic drugs in animals and man. In: Neuropsychopharmacology, ed. P. B. Bradley, P. Deniker and C. Radouco-Thomas, p. 108. London: Elsevier.—*351, 438.*

——, MOORE, J. N. P. and SLATER, P. (1949) Forecasting the incidence of neurosis in officers of the Army and Navy. *J. ment. Sci.*, *95*, 80.—*635.*

MAYS, J. B. (1952) A study of a delinquent community. *Brit. J. Delinq.*, *3*, 5.—*658.*

—— (1956) Delinquency areas II. *Brit. J. Delinq.*, *7*, 139.—*658.*

MEANS, J. H. (1937) The Thyroid and its Diseases. New York: Lippincott.—*727.*

MEDICAL DEFENCE UNION (1968) Memorandum: The Abortion Act, 1967. *Brit. med. J.*, *1*, 759.—*760.*

MEDICAL RESEARCH COUNCIL (1956) The Hazards to Man of Nuclear and Allied Radiation. London: H.M.S.O.—*700.*

—— (1963) Report to the Medical Research Council of the conference on phenylketonuria. *Brit. med. J.*, *1*, 1691.—*725.*

EE

MEDICAL RESEARCH COUNCIL (1965) Clinical trial of the treatment of depressive illness. *Brit. med. J.*, *1*, 881.—*573*.

MEDOW, W. (1922) A group of depressive psychoses in involutional age with unfavourable prognosis. *Arch. psychiat., Nervenkr.*, *64*, 480.—*297*.

MEDUNA, L. J. (1950) Clinical and biochemical indications of the convulsive and of the carbon dioxide treatment. *Proc. Congr. int. Psychiat.*, *4*, 135.—*357*.

—— and McCULLOCH, W. S. (1945) The modern concept of schizophrenia. *Med. Clin. N. Amer.*, *29*, 147.—*299*.

MEGGENDORFER, F. (1921) Clinical and genetic investigation of moral insanity. *Z. ges. Neurol. Psychiat.*, *66*, 208.—*322*.

—— (1926) Über die hereditäre Disposition zur Dementia senilis. *Z. ges. Neurol. Psychiat.*, *101*,—*604*.

—— (1930) Clinical and genetic observations in a case of pseudosclerosis spastica Jackob. *Z. ges. Neurol. Psychiat.*, *128*, 337.—*620*.

MENDELS, J. (1965a) Electroconvulsive therapy and depression. I The prognostic significance of clinical factors. *Brit. J. Psychiat.*, *111*, 675.—*222*, *225*.

—— (1965b) Electroconvulsive therapy and depression. II Significance of endogenous and reactive syndromes. *Brit. J. Psychiat.*, *111*, 682.—*225*.

—— (1965c) Electroconvulsive therapy and depression. III A method for prognosis. *Brit. J. Psychiat.*, *111*, 687.—*225*.

MENKES, J. H. (1959) Maple syrup disease. Isolation and identification of organic acids in the urine. *Pediatrics*, *23*, 348.—*725*.

——, HURST, P. L. and CRAIG, J. M. (1954) A new syndrome: progressive familial infantile cerebral dysfunction associated with an unusual urinary substance. *Pediatrics*, *14*, 462.—*725*.

MENTAL HEALTH ACT (1959) 7 and 8 Elizabeth, Ch. 72. London: H.M.S.O.—*736*.

MERRY, J. and ZACHARIADIS, H. (1962) Addiction to glue sniffing. *Brit. med. J.*, *2*, 1448.—*432*.

MESZAROS, A. F. and GALLAGHER, D. L. (1958) Measuring indirect effects of treatment on chronic wards. *Dis. nerv. Syst.*, *19*, 167.—*334*.

METRAKOS, J. D. (1963) The centrencephalic EEG in epilepsy. *Proc. 2nd int. Congr. hum. Genet.*, 1961, *iii*, 1792. Rome.—*453*.

METZNER, R. (1963) Re-evaluation of Wolpe and Dollard/Millar. *Behav. Res. Ther.*, *1*, 213.—*409*.

MEYER, A. (1944) The Wernicke syndrome. *J. Neurol. Psychiat.*, *7*, 66.—*527*.

—— (1956) Lésions observées sur les pièces operatoires prélevées chez les épileptiques temporaux. *Acta. neurol. psychiat. belg.*, *56*, 21.—*451*.

—— and BECK, E. (1954) Prefrontal Leucotomy and Related Operations. Edinburgh: Oliver.—*191*.

——, FALCONER, M. A. and BECK, E. (1954) Pathological findings in temporal lobe epilepsy. *J. Neurol. Neurosurg. Psychiat.*, *17*, 276.—*480*.

—— and McLARDY, T. (1950) Neuropathology in relation to mental disease. In: Recent Progress in Psychiatry, ed. Fleming. London: Churchill.—*439*.

MEYER, J-E. (1953) The localization of cerebral damage in early infancy in the border territories of the arteries. *Arch. Psychiat. Nervenkr.*, *190*, 328.—*706*.

—— (1959) Die Entfremdungserlebnisse (Depersonalization Experiences). Stuttgart: Thieme.—*121*.

—— (1961) Depersonalization in Adolescence. *Psychiatry*, *24*, 357.—*121*.

MEYER, V. and GELDER, M. (1963) Behaviour therapy and phobic disorders. *Brit. J. Psychiat.*, *109*, 19.—*186*, *187*.

—— and YATES, A. J. (1955) Intellectual changes following temporal lobectomy for psychomotor epilepsy. *J. Neurol. Neurosurg. Psychiat.*, *18*, 44.—*495*.

MEYER-MICKELEIT, R. W. (1953) Twilight attacks as a characteristic type of seizure in temporal epilepsy. *Nervenarzt*, *24*, 331.—*460*, *463*.

MIALL, W. E. and OLDHAM, P. D. (1963) The hereditary factor in arterial blood pressure. *Brit. med. J.*, *1*, 75.—*588*.

MICHAEL, R. P. and GIBBONS, J. L. (1963) Some inter-relationships between the endocrine system and neuropsychiatry. *Int. Rev. Neurobiol.*, *5*, 243.—*193*, *252*, *367*, *368*, *369*.

MIDDLETON, G. D., ASHBY, D. W. and CLARK, F. (1961) An analysis of attempted suicide in an urban industrial district. *Practitioner*, *187*, 776.—*793*.

MILLER, C. W. (1941) The paranoid syndrome. *Arch. Neurol. Psychiat.*, (*Chic.*), *45*, 953.—*289*.

MILLER, H. (1961) Accident neurosis I and II. *Brit. med. J.* *1*, 919, 992.—*508*.

MILLER, H. C. (1963) The Ageing Countryman. National Corporation for the Care of Old People. London.—*540*.

MILLER, J. D. and ROSS, C. (1968) Encephalitis: a four-year survey. *Lancet*, *1*, 1121.—*513*.

MILNE, M. D., CRAWFORD, M. A., GIRAO, C. B. and LOUGHBRIDGE, L. W. (1960) The metabolic disorder in Hartnup Disease. *Quart. J. Med.*, *29*, 407.—*725*.

MILNER, B. and PENFIELD, W. (1955) The effect of hippocampal lesions on recent memory. *Trans. Amer. neurol. Ass.*, *80*, 42.—*487*.

MINISTRY OF HEALTH and HOME OFFICE (1968) Memoranda on the Dangerous Drugs (Notification of Addicts: Supply to Addicts) Regulations, 1968. H M (68) 6 and 11.—*774*.

MINISTRY OF HOUSING AND LOCAL GOVERNMENT and MINISTRY OF HEALTH (1961) Services for Old People. Joint Circular No. 12/61, London: H.M.S.O.—*563*.

MINKOWSKA, F. (1937) Heredity of epilepsy and schizophrenia. *Arch. Klaus-Stift., Vererb.-Forsch.*, *12*, 33.—*469*.

MINKOWSKI, E. (1927) Schizophrenia, Paris: Payot.—*277*.

MINSKI, L. and GUTTMANN, E. (1938) Huntington's chorea: a study of thirty-four families. *J. ment. Sci.*, *84*, 21.—*622*.

MITCHELL, S. W. (1896) Remarks on the effects of Anhalonium Lewinii (The mescal button). *Brit. med. J.*, 2, 1625.—*433*.

MITCHELL, W., FALCONER, M. A. and HILL, D. (1954) Epilepsy with fetishism relieved by temporal lobectomy. *Lancet*, 2, 626.—*495*.

MITSUDA, H. (1957) Klinisch-erbbiologische Untersuchungen der endogen Psychosen. *Acta genet. (Basel)*, 7, 361.—*244*.

——— (1962) The concept of atypical psychoses from the aspect of clinical genetics. *Folia psychiat., neurol. Jap.* 16, 214.—*197, 244*.

MITTLER, P. (1967) The psychological assessment of autistic children. In: Early Childhood Autism, ed. J. K. Wing. London: Pergamon.—*681*.

MJÖNES, J. (1949) Paralysis agitans: a clinical and genetic study. *Acta psychiat. scand.*, Suppl. 54.—*516*.

MONCRIEFF, A. (1960) Biochemistry of mental defect. *Lancet*. 2, 273.—*724*.

MONEY, J. (1963) Cytogenetic and psychosexual incongruities with a note on space-form blindness. *Amer. J. Psychiat.*, 119, 820.—*165*.

MONIZ, E., LIMA, A. and DE LACERDA, R. (1937) Hémiplégies par thrombose de la carotide interne. *Presse med.*, 45, 977.—*596*.

MOONEY, H. B. (1965) Pathologic jealousy and psychochemotherapy. *Brit. J. Psychiat.*, 111, 1023.—*400*.

MOREAU DE TOURS, J. J. (1845) Du haschsch et de l'aberration mentale: Études Psychologiques. Paris: Fortin Masson.—*428*.

MOREL, F. and WILDI, E. (1952) Communication to the 1st International Congress of Neuropathology. Rome. —*614*.

MORGAN, W. P. (1896) A case of congenital word blindness. *Brit. med. J.*, 2, 1378.—*677*.

MORRIS, J. N. (1959) Health and social class. *Lancet*, 1, 303.—*786*.

———, HEADY, J. A., RAFFLE, P. A. B., ROBERTS, C. G. and PARKS, J. W. (1953) Coronary heart-disease and physical activity of work. I and II. *Lancet*, 2, 1053 & 1111.—*590*.

MORRISON, S. L. (1964) Alcoholism in Scotland. *Hlth Bull.* Dep. Hlth Scotl. (Edinburgh), 22, No. 7.—*389*.

——— and MORRIS, J. N. (1959) Epidemiological observations on high blood pressure without evident cause. *Lancet*, 2, 864.—*588*.

MORTON, J. H., ADDITON, H., ADDITON, R. G., HUNT, L. and SULLIVAN, J. J. (1952) Exhibit presented at New York Academy of Medicine, quoted by Greene and Dalton.—*372*.

MORTON, L. T. (1956) Daniel McNaughton's signature. *Brit. med. J.*, 1, 107.—*764*.

MORUZZI, G. and MAGOUN, H. W. (1949) Brain stem reticular formation and activation of the EEG. *Electroenceph. clin. Neurophysiol.*, 1, 455.—*500*.

MOWRER, O. H. (1950) Learning Theory and Personality Dynamics. New York: Ronald.—*647*.

MÜLLER, C. (1957) Further observations on the course of obsessional disorders. *Mschr. Psychiat. Neurol.*, 133, 80.—*134*.

MÜLLER, J. (1944) Schizophrenic and endocrine pathology. *Arch. Klaus-Stift. Verberb.-Forsch.*, 19, 53.—*252*.

MUNCIE, W. (1948) Psychobiology and Psychiatry. 2nd ed. London: Kimpton.—*33, 50*.

MURPHY, G. (1947) Personality: a Biosocial Approach to Origins and Structure. New York: Harper.—*9*.

MURPHY, T. L., CHALMERS, T. C., ECKHARDT, R. D. and DAVIDSON, C. S. (1948) Hepatic coma: clinical and laboratory observations on 40 patients. *New Engl., J. Med.*, 239, 605.—*360*.

MYERSON, A. and BOYLE, R. D. (1941) The incidence of manic-depressive psychosis in certain socially important families. *Amer. J. Psychiat.*, 98, 11.—*703*.

——— and NEUSTADT, R. (1942) Bisexuality and male homosexuality. *Clinics*, 1, 932.—*170*.

MYRIANTHOPOULOS, N. C. (1966) Huntington's chorea. *J. med. Genet.*, 3, 298.—*621*.

NEVIN, S. (1967) On some aspects of cerebral degeneration in later life. *Proc. roy. Soc. Med.*, 60, 517.—*620*.

NEW YORK STATE MENTAL HEALTH RESEARCH UNIT. (1955) A special census of suspected referred mental retardation. Onondaga County, New York. Technical Rep.—*694*.

NEWMAN, H. H., FREEMAN, F. N. and HOLZINGER, K. J. (1937) Twins: A study of Heredity and Environment. Chicago: Univ. of Chicago Press.—*64, 698, 702*.

NEWTON, R. D. (1948) The identity of Alzheimer's disease and senile dementia and their relationship to senility. *J. ment. Sci.*, 94, 225.—*611*.

NIELSEN, J. (1963) Geronto-psychiatric period-prevalence investigation in a geographically delimited population. *Acta psychiat., scand.*, 38, 307.—*540, 542*.

NISBET, N. H., MACKENZIE, M. S. and HAMILTON, M. C. (1966) Follow-ups of elderly discharged patients. *Lancet*, 1, 1314.—*565*.

NOACK, C. H. (1964) Enuresis nocturna. *Med. J. Aust.*, 1, 191.—*647*.

NORRIS, V. (1959) Mental Illness in London. Maudsley Monographs No. 6. London: Institute of Psychiatry and Chapman Hall.—*189, 239*.

NORTHFIELD, D. W. C. (1958) Discussion on surgery of temporal lobe epilepsy. *Proc. roy. Soc. Med.*, 51, 607. —*480*.

NØRVIG, J. (1948) State care for mental defectives. In: Danish Psychiatry. Copenhagen: Munksgaard.—*732*.

NYE, F. I. (1958) Family Relationships and Delinquent Behaviour. New York: Wiley.—*656*.

NYMGAARD, K. (1959) Studies on the sedation threshold. *Arch. gen. Psychiat.*, 1, 530.—*204*.

NYSTRÖM, S. (1964) On the relation between clinical factors and efficacy of ECT in depression. *Acta psychiat., scand.*, 40, Suppl. 181.—*225*.

OAKLEY, D. (1965) Senile dementia; some aetiological factors. *Brit. J. Psychiat.*, *111*, 414.—*604*.

OBERNDORF, C. P. (1950) Role of anxiety in depersonalization. *Int. J. Psychoanal.*, *31*, 1.—*123*.

OBRIST, W. D. (1954) The electroencephalogram of normal aged adults. *Electroenceph. clin. Neurophysiol.*, *6*, 235.—*557*.

O'CONNOR, N. and FRANKS, C. M. (1960) Childhood upbringing and other environmental factors. In: Handbook of Abnormal Psychology, ed. H. J. Eysenck. London: Pitman Medical.—*74, 636, 644, 646*.

—— and TIZARD, J. (1956) The Social Problem of Mental Deficiency. London: Pergamon.—*714*.

O'CONNOR, W. A. (1948) Some notes on suicide. *Brit. med. J. Psychol.*, *21*, 222.—*174*.

ØDEGAARD, Ø. (1932) Emigration and insanity. *Acta psychiat., scand.*, Suppl. 4.—*784*.

—— (1946) A statistical investigation of the incidence of mental disorder in Norway. *Psychiat. Quart.*, *20*, 381.—*189, 239*.

—— (1954) Incidence of mental diseases in Norway during World War II. *Acta psychiat. neurol. scand.*, *29*, 333.—*787*.

—— (1956) The incidence of psychoses in various occupations. *Int. J. soc. Psychiat.*, *2*, 85.—*785*.

—— (1957) Occupational incidence of mental disease in single women. *Living Condit. Hlth*, *1*, 169.—*785*.

—— (1962) Psychiatric epidemiology (abridged). *Proc. roy. Soc. Med.*, *55*, 831.—*777, 784*.

—— (1963) Mental disease in Norwegians with a high-school background. *Acta psychiat., scand.*, *39*, 31.—*785*.

OLIPHANT, J., EVANS, J. I. and FORREST, A. D. (1960) Huntington's chorea—some biochemical and therapeutic aspects, *J. ment. Sci.*, *106*, 718.—*625*.

OLTMAN, J. E., BRODY, B. S., FRIEDMAN, S. and GREEN, W. F. (1949) Frontal lobotomy; clinical experience with 107 cases in state hospital. *Amer. J. Psychiat.*, *105*, 742.—*337*.

ONARI, K. and SPATZ, H. (1926) Pathological contribution to Pick's circumscribed cerebral atrophy. *Z. ges. Neurol. Psychiat.*, *101*, 470.—*617*.

O'NEAL, P., BERGMAN, J., SCHAFER, J. and ROBINS, L. N. (1960) The relation of childhood behaviour problems to adult psychiatric status. A 30 year follow-up of 262 subjects. In: Child Development and Child Psychiatry, ed. C. Shagass and B. Pasamanick. New York: Amer. Psychiat. Ass.—*668*.

—— and ROBINS, L. N. (1958) The relation of childhood behaviour problems to adult psychiatric status. A 30 year follow-up study of 150 subjects. *Amer. J. Psychiat.*, *114*, 961.—*668*.

—— and —— (1959) Childhood patterns predictive of adult schizophrenia: a 30 year follow-up study. *Amer. J. Psychiat.*, *115*, 385.—*668*.

——, —— and SCHMIDT, E. H. (1956) A psychiatric study of attempted suicide in persons over 60 years of age. *Arch. neurol. Psychiat.*, (*Chic.*), *75*, 275.—*542*.

ORDONEZ SIERRA, J. (1962) Heredopsiquiatria Genetica de la Psicosis Maniaco-Depressiva. Madrid.—*196*.

ORME, J. E. (1957) Non-verbal and verbal performance in normal old age, senile dementia and elderly depression. *J. Geront.*, *12*, 408.—*538*.

——, LEE, D. and SMITH, M. R. (1964) Psychological assessment of brain damage and intellectual impairment in psychiatric patients. *Brit. J. soc. clin. Psychol.*, *3*, 161.—*492*.

ORTON, S. T. (1937) Reading, Writing and Speech Problems in Children. New York: Norton—*683*.

O'SHEA, H. E., ELSOM, K. O. and HIGBE, R. V. (1942) Studies of the B-vitamins in the human subject: IV Mental changes in experimental deficiency. *Amer. J. med. Sci.*, *203*, 388.—*351, 354*.

OSMOND, H., SMYTHIES, J. R. and HARLEY-MASON, J. (1952) Schizophrenia: a new approach. *J. ment. Sci.*, *98*, 309.—*256*.

OSNOS, R. B. J. (1963) The treatment of narcotic addiction. *New York J. Med.*, *63*, 1182.—*425*.

OSWALD, I. (1962) Sleeping and Waking: Physiology and Psychology. New York: Elsevier.—*641*.

—— and THACORE, V. R. (1963) Amphetamine and phenmetrazine addiction: physiological abnormalities in the abstinence syndrome. *Brit. med. J.*, *2*, 427.—*421*.

OTTOSSON, J. O. (1960a) Experimental studies in the mode of action of electroconvulsive therapy. *Acta psychiat. scand.*, *35*, suppl. 145, 5.—*235, 468*.

—— (1960b) Effect of lidocaine on the seizure discharge in electroconvulsive therapy. *Acta Psychiat., scand.*, *35*, suppl. 145, 7.—*235, 468*.

—— (1960c) Experimental studies of memory impairment after electroconvulsive therapy. The role of the electrical stimulation and of the seizure studied by variation of stimulus intensity and modification by lidocaine of seizure discharge. *Acta psychiat., scand.*, *35*, suppl. 145, 103.—*235, 468*.

OUNSTED, C. (1953) The factor of inheritance in convulsive disorders in childhood. *Proc. roy. Soc. Med.*, *45*, 865.—*452*.

—— (1955) The hyperkinetic syndrome in epileptic children. *Lancet*, *2*, 303.—*690*.

OVERHOLSER, W. (1954) Psychiatry and the law. *Ment. Hyg.* (New York), *38*, 243.—*755*.

OVERZIER, C. (1958) Transvestitismus und Klinefelter Syndrom. *Arch. Psychiat., Nervenkr.*, *198*, 198.—*165*.

PAEDIATRIC SOCIETY OF THE S. E. METROPOLITAN REGION (1962) The Needs of Mentally Handicapped Children. Report of a working party set up by the Paediatric Society of the S.E. Metropolitan Region. National Society for Mentally Handicapped Children, London.—*734*.

PAFFENBARGER, R. S. Jr., STEINMETZ, C. H., POOLER, B. G. and HYDE, R. T. (1961) The picture puzzle of the post-partum psychoses. *J. chron. Dis.*, *13*, 161.—*374*.

PAGE, J. D. (1947) Abnormal Psychology: A Clinical Approach to Psychological Deviants. New York: McGraw-Hill.—*9, 692*.

PAI, M. N. (1946) Personality defects and psychiatric symptoms after cerebrospinal fever in childhood: meningococcal encephalopathy. *J. ment. Sci.*, *92*, 389.—*114*.

PAILTHORPE, G. W. (1932) Studies in the Psychology of Delinquency. London: H.M.S.O.—*717*.

PAINE, R. S. (1960) Evaluation of familial biochemically determined mental retardation in children, with special reference to amino aciduria. *New. Engl., J. Med.,* 262, 658.—*724.*

———— (1962) Minimal chronic brain syndromes in children. *Develop. Med. Child Neurol.,* 4, 21.—*688.*

PANSE, F. (1942) Die Erbchorea. Leipzig.—*301, 624.*

PARAD, H. T. (ed.). (1965) Crisis Intervention: Selected Readings. New York: Family Service Ass. Amer. —*800.*

PARE, C. M. B. (1956) Homosexuality and chromosomal sex. *J. psychosom. Res.,* 1, 247.—*169.*

———— (1963) Potentiation of monoamine-oxidase inhibitors by tryptophan. *Lancet,* 2, 527.—*200.*

————, REES, L. and SAINSBURY, M. J. (1962) Differentiation of two genetically specific types of depression by the response to anti-depressants. *Lancet,* 2, 1340.—*197.*

PARKER, N. (1964a) Homosexuality in twins: a report on three discordant pairs. *Brit. J. Psychiat.,* 110, 489. —*170.*

———— (1964b) Close identification in twins discordant for obsessional neurosis. *Brit. J. Psychiat.,* 110, 496. —*66.*

———— (1964c) Twins: a psychiatric study of a neurotic group. *Med. J. Aust.,* 2, 735.—*66.*

PARKES, C. M. (1964) Recent bereavement as a cause of mental illness. *Brit. J. Psychiat.,* 110, 198.—*546.*

PARR, D. J. (1957) Homosexuality in clinical practice. *Proc. roy. Soc. Med.,* 50, 651.—*171, 173.*

———— (1957) Alcoholism in general practice. *Brit. J. Addict.,* 54, 25.—*389.*

PARSONS, P. L. (1965) Mental health of Swansea's old folk. *Brit. J. prev. soc. Med.,* 19, 43.—*540, 542, 560, 607.*

PARSONS-SMITH, B. G., SUMMERSKILL, W. H., DAWSON, A. M. and SHERLOCK, S. (1957) The electroencephalograph in liver disease. *Lancet,* 2, 867.—*361.*

PARTRIDGE, M. (1949) Some reflections on the nature of affective disorders arising from results of prefrontal leucotomy. *J. ment. Sci.,* 95, 795.—*222.*

PASAMANICK, B. and KNOBLOCH, H. (1961) Complications of pregnancy. In: Prevention of Mental Disorders in Children, ed. G. Caplan. New York: Basic Books.—*802.*

————, ROBERTS, D. W., LEMKAU, P. W. and KREUGER, D. B. (1959) A survey of mental disease in an urban population: prevalence by race and income. In: Epidemiology of Mental Disorder, ed. B. Pasamanick. Pub. No. 60 of the Amer. Ass. for the Advancement of Science, Washington.—*781.*

PATAU, K., SMITH, D. W., THERMAN, E., INHORN, S. L. and WAGNER, H. P. (1960) Multiple congenital anomaly caused by an extra autosome. *Lancet,* 1, 790.—*722.*

PATERSON, A. (1944) Disorders of personality after head injury. *Proc. roy. Soc. Med.,* 37, 556.—*505.*

———— and ZANGWILL, O. L. (1944) Disorders of visual space perception associated with lesions of the right cerebral hemisphere. *Brain,* 67, 331.—*501.*

PATTERSON, R. M., BAGCHI, B. K. and TEST, A. (1948) Prediction of Huntington's chorea; electroencephalographic and genetic study. *Amer. J. Psychiat.,* 104, 786.—*624.*

PAUL, N. L., FITZGERALD, E. and GREENBLATT, M. (1956) Five-year follow-up of patients subjected to three different lobotomy procedures. *J. Amer. med. Ass.,* 161, 815.—*335.*

PAVLOV, I. P. (1941) Conditioned Reflexes and Psychiatry. New York: Int. Pubs.—*20, 72.*

PAYNE, R. W. (1960) Cognitive Abnormalities In: Handbook of Abnormal Psychology, ed. N. J. Eysenck, Ch. VI. London: Pitman.—*492.*

———— (1962) An object classification test as a measure of over-inclusive thinking in schizophrenic patients. *Brit. J. soc. clin. Psychol.,* 1, 213.—*266.*

PEARL, R. and PEARL, R. D. (1934) The Ancestry of the Long-Lived. Baltimore: Johns Hopkins.—*536.*

PENFIELD, W. (1936) Epilepsy and surgical therapy. *Arch. Neurol. Psychiat.,* (Chic.), 36, 449.—*506.*

———— (1952) Epileptic automatism and the centreencephalic integrating system. In: Patterns of organization in the central nervous system. *Res. Publ. Ass. nerv. ment. Dis.,* 30, 513.—*463.*

———— (1954) In: Brain Mechanisms and Consciousness, ed. J. F. Delafresnaye. Oxford: Blackwell.—*487.*

———— and JASPER, H. (1947) Highest level seizures. *Res. Publ. Ass. nerv. ment. Dis.,* 26, 252.—*498.*

———— and ———— (1954) Epilepsy and the functional anatomy of the human brain. London. J. and A Churchill.—*468.*

———— and KRISTIENSEN, K. (1951) Epileptic seizure patterns. Springfield, Ill.: Thomas.—*458.*

———— and MILNER, B. (1958) Memory deficit produced by bilateral lesions in the hippocampal zone. *Arch. Neurol. Psychiat.,* (Chic.), 79, 475.—*355.*

———— and PAINE, K. (1955) Results of surgical therapy for focal epileptic seizures. *Canad. med. Ass. J.,* 73, 515.—*480.*

———— and SHAVER, M. (1945) Incidence of traumatic epilepsy and headache after head injury in civil practice. *Res. Publ. Ass. Res. nerv. ment. Dis.,* 24, 620.—*506.*

———— and STEELMAN, H. (1947) The treatment of focal epilepsy by cortical excision. *Ann. Surg.,* 126. 740. —*506.*

PENROSE, L. S. (1934) Method of separating relative aetiological effects of birth order and maternal age, with special reference to mongolian imbecility. *Ann. Eugen. (Camb.),* 6, 108.—*720.*

———— (1949a) The Biology of Mental Defect. London: Sidgwick.—*695, 700.*

———— (1949b) The incidence of mongolism in the general population. *J. ment. Sci.,* 95, 685.—*720.*

———— (1949c) Birth injury as cause of mental defect. *J. ment. Sci.,* 95, 373.—*706.*

———— (1963) The Biology of Mental Defect. 3rd ed. London: Sidgwick.—*707, 708, 722.*

PERLEY, M. J. and GUZE, S. B. (1962) Hysteria—the stability and usefulness of clinical criteria. *New Engl. J. Med.,* 266, 421.—*5, 105.*

PERRIS, C. (1966) A study of bipolar (manic-depressive) and unipolar recurrent depressive psychoses. *Acta., psychiat. scand.,* suppl. 194.—*197, 198.*

PERSKY, H. (1957) Adrenal cortical function in anxious human subjects. *Arch. neurol. psychiat. (Chic.)*, 78, 95.—86.

——, HAMBURG, D. A., BASOWITZ, H., GRINKER, R. R., SABSHIN, M., KORCHIN, S. J., HERZ, M., BOARD, F. A. and HEATH, H. A. (1958) Relation of emotional responses and changes in plasma hydrocortisone level after stressful interview. *Arch. neurol. psychiat., (Chic.)*, 79, 434.—86.

PETERMAN, M. G. (1946) Convulsions in childhood: a twenty year study of 2,500 cases. *Amer. J. Dis. Child.*, 72, 399.—672.

PIAGET, J. (1932) Judgement and Reasoning in the Child. (Trans. from French). New York: Harcourt.—656.

PICK, A. (1892) On the relation of senile cerebral atrophy and aphasia. *Prag. med. Wschr.*, 17, 165.—617.

PICKERING, G. W. (1955) High Blood Pressure. London: Churchill.—588.

—— (1965) Hyperpiesis: high blood pressure without evident cause: essential hypertension. *Brit. med. J.*, 2, 959, 1021.—590.

PIERCY, M. (1964) The effects of cerebral lesions on intellectual function: a review of current research trends. *Brit. J. Psychiat.*, 110, 310.—48, 493, 497, 499.

—— and SMYTH, V. (1962) Right hemisphere dominance for certain non-verbal intellectual skills. *Brain*, 85, 775.—497.

PINCUS, G. and HOAGLAND. H. (1950) Adrenal cortical responses to stress in normal men and in those with personality disorders. I Some stress responses in normal and psychotic subjects. II Analysis of pituitary-adrenal mechanism in man. *Amer. J. Psychiat.*, 106, 641, 651.—252.

PINKERTON, P. (1958) Psychogenic megacolon in children: the implications of bowel negativism. *Arch. Dis. Child.*, 33, 371.—648.

PIPPARD, J. (1955) Rostral leucotomy: a report on 240 cases personally followed up after 1½–5 years. *J. ment. Sci.*, 101, 756.—222.

—— (1962) Leucotomy in Britain today. *J. ment. Sci.*, 108, 249.—335.

PITTMAN, D. J. and SNYDER, C. R. (1962) Society, Culture and Drinking Patterns. New York: Wiley.—390.

PLATT, R. (1947) Heredity in hypertension. *Quart. J. Med.*, 16, 111.—589.

—— (1959) The nature of essential hypertension. *Lancet*. 2, 55.—588.

POHLISCH, K. (1941) Heredity in mental diseases. Proc. 7th Int. Genet. Congr. Edinburgh, 1939. p. 239. Cambridge. Cambridge Univ. Press.—621.

POKORNY, A. D. (1964) Suicide rates in various psychiatric disorders. *J. nerv. ment. Dis. 139*, 499.—797.

POLLACK, M. and GITTELMAN, R. K. (1964) The siblings of schizophrenic patients: a review. *Amer. J. Orthopsychiat.*, 34, 868.—685.

POLLIN, W., CARDON, P. V. Jr. and KETY, S. S. (1961) Effects of amino acid feedings in schizophrenic patients treated with iproniazid. *Science (Washington)*, 133, 104.—255.

—— and GOLDIN, S. (1961) The physiological and psychological effects of intravenously administered epinephrine and its metabolism in normal and schizophrenic men. II Psychiatric observations. *J. Psychiat. Res.*, 1, 50.—437.

POLLITT, J. (1957) Natural history of obsessional states. *Brit. med. J.*, 1, 194.—135.

POLONIO, P. (1957) A structural analysis of schizophrenia. *Psychiatria (Basel)*, 133, 351.—313.

—— and FIGUEIREDO, M. (1955) On structure of mental disorders associated with childbearing. *Mschr. Psychiat. Neurol.*, 130, 304.—374.

—— and SLATER, E. (1954) A prognostic study of insulin treatment in schizophrenia. *J. ment. Sci.*, 100, 442.—312.

POND, D. A. (1957) Psychiatric aspects of epilepsy. *J. Indian. med. Prof.*, 3, 1441.—455, 462, 470.

—— (1961) Psychiatric aspects of epileptic and brain-damaged children I and II. *Brit. med. J.*, 2, 1377, 1454.—76, 451.

—— (1962) The schizophrenic-like psychoses of epilepsy (Discussion). *Proc. roy. Soc. Med.*, 55, 316.—472.

—— (1965) The neuropsychiatry of childhood. In: Modern Perspectives in Child Psychiatry, ed. J. G. Howells, Ch. XIX. London: Oliver and Boyd.—673, 674.

—— and BIDWELL, B. H. (1960a) A survey of epilepsy in fourteen general practices. II Social and psychological aspects. *Epilepsia (Amst.)*, 1, 285.—450, 481.

——, —— and STEIN, L. (1960b) A survey of epilepsy in fourteen general practices. I Demographic and medical data. *Psychiat. Neurol. Neurochir.*, 63, 217.—450.

POPPER, K. R. (1963) Conjecture and Refutations: the Growth of Scientific Knowledge. London. Routledge.—5, 27.

POSKANZER, D. C., BROWN, A. E. and MILLER, H. (1962) Musicogenic epilepsy caused only by a discrete frequency band of church bells. *Brain*, 85, 77.—451.

POST, F. (1951) The outcome of mental breakdown in old age. *Brit. med. J.*, 1, 436.—549.

—— (1956) Body weight changes in psychiatric illness; a critical review of the literature. *J. psychosom. Res.*, 1, 219.—210.

—— (1962a) The Significance of Affective Symptoms in Old Age. Maudsley Monograph 10. London: Oxford Univ. Press.—572.

—— (1962b) The impact of modern drug treatment on old age schizophrenia. *Geront. clin. (Basel)*, 4, 137.—585.

—— (1965) The Clinical Psychiatry of Late Life. London: Pergamon.—585.

—— (1966) Persistent Persecutory States of the Elderly. London: Pergamon.—581.

POWERS, E. and WITMER, H. (1951) An experiment in the prevention of delinquency. The Cambridge-Somerville Youth Study. New York: Columbia Univ. Press.—631.

PRATT, R. T. C. (1951) An investigation of the psychiatric aspects of disseminated sclerosis. *J. Neurol. Neurosurg. Psychiat.*, 14, 326.—109, 530.

PRATT, R. T. C. (1953) Personal communication.—*607*.

PRECHTL, H. F. R. (1960) The Long Term Value of the Neurological Examination of the Newborn Infant. (Little Clubs Clinics in Developmental Medicine). London: Heinemann.—*76, 706*.

—— and STEMMER, C. J. (1962) The choreiform syndrome in children. *Develop. Med. Child Neurol.*, *4*, 119. —*690*.

PRENTISS, D. W. and MORGAN, F. P. (1896) Anhalonium Lewinii: a study of the drug with special reference to its action on man, with report of experiments. *Ther. Gaz.* (3rd series), *12*, 577.—*433*.

PRIBRAM, K. H. (1963) The new neurology: memory, novelty, thought and choice. In: EEG and Behaviour, ed. G. H. Glaser, Ch. VI. New York: Basic Books.—*488*.

PRICE, W. H. and WHATMORE, P. B. (1967a) Criminal behaviour and the XYY male. *Nature (Lond.)*, *213*, 815. —*691*.

—— and —— (1967b) Behaviour disorders and patterns of crime among XYY males identified at a maximum security hospital. *Brit. med. J.*, *1*, 533.—*691*.

PRIMROSE, E. J. R. (1962) Psychological Illness: a Community Study. London: Tavistock.—*540*.

PRINZHORN, H. (1923) Arts of the Mentally Ill. Berlin: Springer.—*328*.

PRINZMETAL, M. and BLOOMBERG, W. (1935) The use of benzedrine for the treatment of narcolepsy. *J. Amer. med. Ass.*, *105*, 2051.—*420*.

PRITCHARD, M. and GRAHAM, P. (1966) An investigation of a group of patients who have attended both the child and adult departments of the same psychiatric hospital. *Brit. J. Psychiat.*, *112*, 603.—*668*.

PRYCE, I .G. (1958) The relationship between glucose tolerance, body weight and clinical state in melancholia. *J. ment. Sci.*, *104*, 1079.—*211*.

——(1964) The relationship between 17-hydroxycorticosteroid excretion and glucose utilization in depressions. *Brit. J. Psychiat.*, *110*, 90.—*211*.

PUGH, T. F., JERATH, B. K., SCHMIDT, W. M. and REED, R. B. (1963) Rates of mental disease related to child-bearing. *New. Engl. J. Med.*, *268*, 1224.—*373*.

PURTELL, J. J., ROBINS, E. and COHEN, M. E. (1951) Observations on clinical aspects of hysteria. Quantitative study of 50 hysteria patients and 156 control subjects. *J. Amer. med. Ass.*, *146*, 902.—*105*.

QUASTEL, J. H. and WHEATLEY, A. H. M. (1933) The effects of amines on oxidations of the brain. *Biochem. J.* *27*, 1609.—*416, 435*.

RACHLIN, H. L. (1935) A follow-up study of Hoch's benign stupor cases. *Amer. J. Psychiat.*, *92*, 531.—*319*.

RACHMAN, S. and COSTELLO, C. G. (1961) The aetiology and treatment of children's phobias—a review. *Amer. J. Psychiat.*, *118*, 97.—*185*.

RAFTOS, J., JULIAN, D. G. and VALENTINE, P. A. (1964) The prolonged use of alpha methyldopa in the treatment of hypertension. *Med. J. Aust.*, *1*, 837.—*202*.

RAINER, J. D., MESNIKOFF, A., KOLB, L. C. and CARR, A. (1960) Homosexuality and heterosexuality in identical twins. *Psychosom. Med.*, *22*, 251.—*170*.

RAMER, T. (1946) The prognosis of mentally retarded children. *Acta psychiat. (Kbh.)*, Suppl. 41.—*715*.

RAWNSLEY, K. and LOUDON, J. B. (1962) Factors influencing the referral of patients to psychiatrists by general practitioners. *Brit. J. prev. soc. Med.*, *16*, 174.—*781*.

RAYMOND, M. J. (1956) Case of fetishism treated by aversion therapy. *Brit. med. J.*, *2*, 854.—*164, 186*.

RAYNOR, R. B., PAINE, R. S. and CARMICHAEL, E. A. (1959) Epilepsy of late onset. *Neurology (Minneap.)*, *9*, 111.—*451*.

RAZRAN, G. (1961) The observable unconscious and the inferable conscious in current Soviet psychophysiology: interoceptive conditioning, semantic conditioning and the orienting reflex.—*Psychol. Rev.* 68, 81.—*24*.

REES, J. R. (1947) The case of Rudolf Hess. London: Heinemann—*322*.

REES, T. P. (1957) Back to moral treatment and community care. *J. ment. Sci.*, *103*, 303.—*334*.

—— and GLATT, M. M. (1955) The organization of a mental hospital on the basis of group participation. *Int. J. Group Psychother.*, *5*, 157.—*804*.

REES, W. L. (1944) Physical constitution, neurosis and psychosis. *Proc. roy. Soc. Med.*, *37*, 635.—*217*.

—— (1950a) Body size, personality and neurosis. *J. ment. Sci.*, *96*, 168.—*70*.

—— (1950b) Body build, personality and neurosis in women. *J. ment. Sci.*, *96*, 426.—*70*.

—— (1950c) A factorial study of physical constitution in women. *J. ment. Sci.*, *96*, 619.—*70*.

—— (1953) The premenstrual tension syndrome and its treatment. *Brit. med. J.*, *1*, 1014.—*371, 372*.

—— (1960) Constitutional factors and abnormal behaviour. In: Handbook of Abnormal Psychology, ed. H. J. Eysenck. London: Pitman.—*68*.

—— and EYSENCK, H. J. (1945) A factorial study of some morphological and psychological aspects of human constitution. *J. ment. Sci.*, *91*, 8.—*70, 192*.

REGISTRAR-GENERAL (1953) Statistical Review of England and Wales for the year 1949. (Suppl. on General Morbidity, Cancer and Mental Health). London: H.M.S.O.—*787*.

—— (1964) Statistical Review of England and Wales for the year 1960. (Suppl. on Mental Health) London: H.M.S.O.—*183, 239, 540*.

—— (1966) Tables: Medical. London: H.M.S.O.—*589*.

REID, D. D. (1960) Epidemiological Methods in the Study of Mental Disorder. Wld Hlth Org. Publ. Hlth, Paper No. 2. Geneva.—*777*.

RENNIE, T. A. C. (1939) Follow-up study of 500 patients with schizophrenia admitted to the hospital from 1913–1923. *Arch. Neurol. Psychiat.*, *(Chic.)*, *42*, 877.—*310, 312*.

RENNIE, T. A. C. (1942) Prognosis in manic-depressive psychoses. *Amer. J. Psychiat.*, *98*, 801.—*217*.

RESNICK, O., KRUS, D., RASKIN, M. and FREEMAN, H. (1963) Reserpine action in subjects treated with mono-amine oxidase inhibitors. *Arch. gen. Psychiat.*, *8*, 481.—*200*.

RETTERSTÖL, N. and SUND, A. (1964) Drug addiction and habituation. *Acta psychiat., scand.*, *40*, suppl. 179. —*417, 418, 423, 426, 431*.

REY, J. H. and COPPEN, A. J. (1959) Distribution of androgyny in mental patients. *Brit. med. J.*, *2*, 1445.—*70*.

———, POND, D. A. and EVANS, C. C. (1949) Clinical and electroencephalographic studies of temporal lobe function.—*Proc. roy. Soc. Med.*, *42*, 891.—*71*.

RICHARDSON, I. M. (1964) Age and Need: a study of older people in north-east Scotland. London: Livingstone. —*547*.

RIMLAND, B. (1964) Infantile Autism: the Syndrome and its Implications for a Neural Theory of Behaviour. New York: Appleton.—*680*.

ROBBINS, L. R. and VINSON, D. B. (1960) Objective psychologic assessment of the thyrotoxic patient and the response to treatment: preliminary report. *J. clin. Endocr.*, *20*, 120.—*365*.

ROBERTS, J. A. F. (1939) Intelligence and family size. *Eugen. Rev.*, *30*, 237.—*698, 701*.

——— (1940) Studies on child population: V Resemblance in intelligence between sibs. *Ann. Eugen. (Camb.)*, *10*, 293.—*698*.

ROBERTS, J. M. (1959a) Prognostic factors in the electro-shock treatment of depressive states. I Clinical features from history and examination. *J. ment. Sci.*, *105*, 693.—*222*.

——— (1959b) Prognostic factors in the electro-shock treatment of depressive states. II The application of specific tests. *J. ment. Sci.*, *105*, 703.—*204*.

ROBERTS, W. W. (1960) Normal and abnormal depersonalization. *J. ment. Sci.*, *106*, 478.—*123*.

ROBERTSON, E. E. and BROWNE, N. L. M. (1953) Review of mental illness in the old age group. *Brit. med. J.*, *2*, 1076.—*549*.

———, LE ROUX, A. and BROWN, J. H. (1958) The clinical differentiation of Pick's disease. *J. ment. Sci.*, *104*, 1000.—*618, 619*.

ROBIN, A. A. (1958) A retrospective controlled study of leucotomy in schizophrenia and affective disorders. *J. ment. Sci.*, *104*, 1025.—*337*.

ROBINS, E. (1957) Discussion of R. G. Heath's 'Clinical studies with taraxein'. In: Transactions of the Fourth Conference on Neuropharmacology, ed, H. A. Abramson. Josiah Macy Jr. Foundation, New York.—*255*.

RODNIGHT, R. and AVES, E. K. (1958) Body fluid indoles of normal and mentally ill subjects. I Preliminary survey of the occurrence of some urinary indoles. *J. ment. Sci.*, *104*, 1149.—*256*.

ROGERS, M. E., LILIENFELD, A. M. and PASAMANICK, B. (1955) Prenatal and paranatal factors in the development of childhood behaviour disorders. *Acta psychiat. neurol. scand.*, suppl. 102.—*76*.

ROGERS, W. J. B. (1953) Personal communication.—*648*.

ROGINA, V. (1954) Psychoses due to nicotinic acid deficiency. *Neuropsihijatrija*, *2*, 50.—*352*.

ROHR, K. (1961) Contribution to information on the so-called "schizophrenic reaction". Family picture and catamneses. *Arch. Psychiat. Nervenkr.*, *201*, 626.—*303*.

ROMANO, J. and ENGEL, G. L. (1944) Delirium: I EEG data. *Arch. Neurol. Psychiat.*, *(Chic.)*. *51*, 356.—*485*.

ROME, H. P. and BRACELAND, F. J. (1952) Psychological response to ACTH, cortisone, hydrocortisone and related steroid substances. *Amer. J. Psychiat.*, *108*, 641.—*369*.

ROMNEY, D. M. (1967) Aspects of cognitive dysfunction in nuclear schizophrenics and their parents and siblings. Thesis submitted for the degree of Ph.D., University of Newcastle-upon-Tyne.—*252*.

ROSANOFF, A. J. (1931) Sex-linked inheritance in mental deficiency. *Amer. J. Psychiat.*, *88* (*11*), 289.—*702*.

———, HANDY, L. M. and ROSANOFF, I. A. (1934) Criminality and delinquency in twins. *J. crim. Law Criminol.*, *24*, 923.—*65, 452*.

——— and ——— (1935) Huntington's chorea in twins. *Arch. Neurol. Psychiat.*, *(Chic.)*, *33*, 839.—*621*.

———, ——— and PLESSET, I. R. (1935) The aetiology of manic-depressive syndromes with special reference to their occurrence in twins. *Amer. J. Psychiat.*, *91*, 725.—*197*.

———, ———, and ——— (1941) The aetiology of child behaviour difficulties, juvenile delinquency and adult criminality with special reference to their occurrence in twins. *Psychiat. Monogr.*, I. Sacramento.—*65, 658*.

ROSE, J. T. (1963) Reactive and endogenous depressions—response to ECT. *Brit. J. Psychiat.*, *109*, 213. —*222*.

ROSENTHAL, D. (1959) Some factors associated with concordance and discordance with respect to schizophrenia in monozygotic twins. *J. nerv. ment. Dis.*, *129*, 1.—*242*.

——— (1960) Confusion of identity and the frequency of schizophrenia in twins. *Arch. gen. Psychiat.*, *(Chic.)*, *3*, 297.—*241, 242*.

——— (1961) Sex distribution and severity of illness among samples of schizophrenic twins. *J. psychiat.*, *Res.*, *1*, 26.—*242*.

——— (1962a) Problems of sampling and diagnosis in the major twin studies of schizophrenia. *J. psychiat. Res.*, *1*, 116.—*242*.

——— (1962b) Familial concordance by sex with respect to schizophrenia. *Psychol. Bull.*, *59*, 401.—*242*.

——— (ed) (1963) The Genain Quadruplets. New York: Basic Books.—*241, 243*.

ROSENTHAL, S. H. and GUDEMAN, J. E. (1967a) The self-pitying constellation in depression. *Brit. J. Psychiat.*, *113*, 485.—*225*.

——— and ——— (1967b) The endogenous depressive pattern: an empirical investigation. *Arch. gen. Psychiat.*, *(Chic.)*, *16*, 241.—*225*.

ROSSI, J. J., STACH, A. and BRADLEY, N. J. (1963) Effects of treatment of male alcoholics in a mental hospital. *Quart. J. Stud. Alcohol.*, *24*, 91.—*411, 412*.

ROTH, M. (1949) Disorders of the body image caused by lesions of the right parietal lobe. *Brain, 72*, 89.—*496.*
——— (1951) Changes in the EEG under barbiturate anaesthesia by electro-convulsive treatment and their significance for the theory of ECT action. *Electroenceph. clin. Neurophysiol., 3*, 261.—*199, 473.*
——— (1955) The natural history of mental disorder in old age. *J. ment. Sci., 101*, 281.—*301, 549, 580, 585, 609.*
——— (1959a) The phobic anxiety-depersonalization syndrome. *Proc. roy. Soc. Med., 52*, 587.—*90, 92, 93, 94.*
——— (1959b) Mental health problems of ageing and the aged, *Bull. Wld Hlth Org., 21*, 527. Geneva.—*548, 562.*
——— (1960) The phobic anxiety-depersonalization syndrome and some general aetiological problems in psychiatry. *J. Neuropsychiat., 1*, 293.—*92.*
——— (1962) The desire to be ill. *Univ. Durham med. Gaz., 57*, 2.—*115.*
——— (1963) Neurosis, psychosis and the concept of disease in psychiatry. *Acta psychiat., scand., 39*, 128. —*294, 302, 304, 581.*
——— (1964) The contribution of specific and non-specific factors to the results of pharmacological treatment for psychiatric disorder. In: Neuropsychopharmacology, ed. P. B. Bradley, F. Flügel and P. Hoch, Vol. *3*, p. 113. Amsterdam: Elsevier.—*335.*
——— (1966) Problems of the aged in the light of epidemiological findings. Proc. IVth Wld Congr. Psychiat., 1966, Madrid. London. Excerpta Medica Foundation.—*547.*
——— (1967) The clinical interview and psychiatric diagnosis: have they a future in psychiatric practice? *Comprehens. Psychiat., 8*, 427.—*36.*
——— (1967) Psychiatric aspects of old age. In: Social and Genetic Influences on Life and Death, ed. R. Platt and A. S. Parkes, p. 163. Edinburgh: Oliver & Boyd.—*547.*
——— (1969) The classification of affective disorders. In: Symposium om Depressions—behandling, ed. B· Cronholm and F. Sjoqvist, pp. 9–47. Uppsala: Appelberg.—*94, 95, 97, 227, 375.*
——— and BALL, J. R. B. (1963) Psychiatric aspects of intersexuality In: Intersexuality, ed. A. J. Marshall and C. N. Armstrong, Ch. 9. London: Academic Press.—*165, 172.*
——— and GARSIDE, R. F. (1962) Some characteristics common to ECT and prefrontal leucotomy and their bearing on the mode of action of the two treatments. *J. Neuropsychiat., 3*, 221.—*199.*
———, ——— and GURNEY, C. (1965) Clinical-statistical enquiries into the classification of anxiety states and depressive disorders. In: Proc. Leeds Symp. on Behav. Disorders, 1965, ed. F. A. Jenner, p. 175.—*95, 131.*
———, GREEN, J. and OSSELTON, J. W. (1960) The EEG in mental disorders of old age. Unpublished observations.—*560.*
——— and GURNEY, C. (1971) The classification and clinical differentiation of anxiety states from depressive disorders I. In preparation.—*94.*
——— and HARPER, M. (1962) Temporal lobe epilepsy and the phobic anxiety-depersonalization syndrome. Part II Practical and theoretical considerations. *Comprehens. Psychiat., 3*, 215.—*86, 94.*
——— and HOPKINS, B. (1953) Psychological test performance in patients over 60. I Senile psychosis and the affective disorders of old age. *J. ment. Sci., 99*, 439.—*538, 549.*
——— and KAY, D. W. K. (1956) Affective disorders arising in the senium. II Physical disability as an aetiological factor. *J. ment. Sci., 102*, 141.—*586, 781.*
———, ———, SHAW, J. and GREEN J. (1957) Prognosis and pentothal induced electroencephalographic changes in electro-convulsive treatment. *Electroenceph. clin. Neurophysiol., 9*, 225.—*199, 233.*
——— and ——— (1969) Symptomological and aetiological diagnosis in psychiatry. To be published.—*484.*
——— and MORRISSEY, J. D. (1952) Problems in the diagnosis and classification of mental disorder in old age. *J. ment. Sci., 98*, 66.—*549, 609.*
——— and ROSIE, J. M. (1953) The use of ECT in mental disease with clouding of consciousness. *J. ment. Sci., 99*, 103.—*386.*
———, TOMLINSON, B. E. and BLESSED, G. (1967) The relationship between quantitative measures of dementia and of degenerative changes in the cerebral grey matter of elderly subjects. *Proc. roy. Soc. Med., 60.*, 254. —*605.*
ROTHLIN, E. (1957) Lysergic acid diethylamide and related substances. *Ann. N.Y. Acad. Sci., 66*, 668.—*437.*
——— (ed.) (1961) Neuropsychopharmacology Vol. 2. Amsterdam: Elsevier.—*334.*
ROTHSCHILD, D. (1947) The clinical differentiation of senile and arteriosclerotic psychoses. *Geriatrics, 2*, 155. —*590.*
——— (1956) Senile psychoses and psychoses with arteriosclerosis. In: Mental Disorders in Late Life, ed. O. J. Kaplan. Stanford, California: Stanford Univ. Press.—*605.*
ROTHSTEIN, H. J. (1941) A Study of Aments with Special Abilities. M.A. Thesis, Columbia University.—*730.*
ROYAL COLLEGE OF PHYSICIANS OF EDINBURGH (1963) The Care of the Elderly in Scotland. Publication No. 22. Edinburgh.—*560.*
ROYAL COMMISSION on the Law Relating to Mental Illness and Mental Deficiency (1957) Report. London: H.M.S.O.—*736.*
ROYAL MEDICO-PSYCHOLOGICAL ASSOCIATION (1960) The Recruitment and Training of the Child Psychiatrist. London.—*632.*
RÜDIN, E. (1909) On the Clinical Symptoms of Mental Illness in Prisoners Condemned to a Life Sentence. Munich: Lehmann.—*261.*
——— (1953) Ein Beitrag zur Frage der Zwangskrankheit insbesondere ihrer hereditären Beziehungen. *Arch. Psychiat. Nervenkr., 191*, 14.—*68.*
RUESCH, J. (1951) Chronic Disease and Psychological Invalidism: A Psychosomatic Study. Berkeley: Univ. of California Press.—*145.*

RUESCH J. (1965) Social psychiatry: an overview. *Arch. gen. Psychiat.*, (*Chic.*) *12*, 501.—*805*.
RUF, H. (1952) Experiments on the prolongation of induced epileptiform convulsions in the cat. *J. ment. Sci.*, *98*, 454.—*468*.
RÜMKE, H. C. (1963) Problems in the Field of Neurosis and Psychotherapy. Oxford: Blackwell.—*177*.
RUNGE, W. (1911) Psychoses during pregnancy and puerperium. *Arch. Psychiat. Nervenkr.*, *48*, 545.—*259*.
RUPP, C. and FLETCHER, E. K. (1940) A five to ten year follow-up of 641 schizophrenic cases. *Amer. J. Psychiat.*, *96*, 877.—*310*.
RUSSELL, B. (1956) Portraits from Memory and other Essays. London: Allen & Unwin.—*575*.
RUSSELL, G. F. M. (1960) Body weight and balance of water, sodium and potassium in depressed patients given electro-convulsive therapy. *Clin. Sci.*, *19*, 327.—*203, 211*.
——— and MEZEY, A. G. (1962) An analysis of weight gain in patients with anorexia nervosa treated with high calorie diets. *Clin. Sci.*, *23*, 449.—*126*.
RUSSELL, R. W. R. (1961) Observations on the retinal blood-vessels in monocular blindness. *Lancet*, *2*, 1422. —*596*.
RUSSELL, W. R. (1934) The after-effects of head injury. *Edin. med. J.*, *41*, 129.—*502*.
——— (1951) Disability caused by brain wounds; review of 1,166 cases. *J. Neurol. Neurosurg. Psychiat.*, *14*, 35.—*451*.
RUTTER, M., GREENFELD, D. and LOCKYER, L. (1967) A five to fifteen year follow-up of infantile psychosis. II Social and behavioural outcome. *Brit. J. Psychiat.*, *113*, 1183.—*685*.
——— and LOCKYER, L. (1967) A five to fifteen year follow-up of infantile psychosis. I Description of sample. *Brit. J. Psychiat.*, *113*, 1169.—*675*.
RYLANDER, G. (1961) Forensic psychiatry in relation to legislation in different countries. An international review. In: Psychiatrie der Gegenwart, Vol. 3, p. 397. Berlin: Springer.—*738, 755*.
RYLE, J. A. (1948) The Natural History of Disease. 2nd ed., p. 446. Oxford: Univ. Press.—*3*.

SACHS, E. Jr. (1950) Meningiomas with dementia as the first and presenting feature. *J. ment. Sci.*, *96*, 998.—*527, 528*.
SAINSBURY, P. (1955) Suicide in London. Maudsley Monograph No. 1. London: Inst. of Psychiatry: Chapman. —*777, 789, 791, 794*.
——— (1962) Suicide in later life. *Geront. clin.*, (*Basel*)., *4*, 161.—*544, 561, 790*.
——— (1968a) The diagnostic classification and psychiatric treatment of 25 suicides. Proc. 4th Int. Conf. for Suicide Prevention, Los Angeles, October 1967.—*791*.
——— (1968b) Suicide and depression. In Recent Developments in Affective Disorders, eds. A. Coppen and A. Walk. London: Royal Medico-Psychological Ass.—*791*.
SAINT, E. G. (1965) Suicide in Australia. *Med. J. Aust.*, *1*, 911.—*799*.
SANDISON, R. A., SPENCER, A. M. and WHITELAW, J. D. A. (1954) The therapeutic value of lysergic acid diethylamide in mental illness. *J. ment. Sci.*, *100*, 491.—*437*.
——— and WHITELAW, J. D. (1957) Further studies in the therapeutic value of lysergic acid diethylamide in mental illness. *J. ment. Sci.*, *103*, 332.—*437*.
SAPHIR, W. (1945) Chronic hypochloraemia simulating psychoneurosis. *J. Amer. med. Ass.*, *129*, 510.—*358*.
SARASON, S. B. (1953) Psychological Problems in Mental Deficiency. New York: Harper.—*705*.
SARGANT, W. and SHORVON, H. J. (1945) Acute war neurosis. *Arch. neurol. psychiat.* (*Chic.*), *54*, 231.—*181*.
——— and SLATER, E. (1940) Acute war neuroses. *Lancet*, *2*, 1.—*181*.
——— and ——— (1963) Introduction to Physical Treatment in Psychiatry, 4th ed. Edinburgh: Livingstone. —*182, 234*.
SARGENT, P. (1921) Some observations on epilepsy. *Brain*, *44*, 312.—*505*.
SAVAGE, R. D. (1964) Electro-cerebral activity, extraversion and neuroticism. *Brit. J. Psychiat.*, *110*, 98.—*71*.
SCHACHTER, M. (1952) The cyclothymic states in the pre-pubescent child. *Nerv. Child*, *9*, 357.—*668*.
SCHECKEL, C. L. and BOFF, E. (1964) Behavioural effects of interacting imipramine and other drugs with d-amphetamine, cocaine and tetrabenazine. *Psychopharmacologia*, (*Berl.*), *5*, 198.—*201*.
SCHEERER, M., ROTHMANN, E. and GOLDSTEIN, K. (1945) A case of 'idiot savant': an experimental study of personality organization. *Psychol. Monogr.*, *58*. No. 4.—*730*.
SCHEID, K. F. (1937) Febrile Episodes in Schizophrenic Psychoses. Leipzig: Thieme.—*285*.
SCHENK, V. W. D. (1959) Re-examination of a family with Pick's disease. *Ann. hum. Genet.*, *23*, 325.—*617*.
SCHIELE, B. C. and BROZEK, J. (1948) 'Experimental neurosis' resulting from semi-starvation in man. *Psychosom. Med.*, *10*, 31.—*357*.
SCHILDER, P. (1914) Selbstbewusstsein und Persönnlichkeits bewusstsein. Monographien aus d. Gesamtgebiet d. Neurologie u. Psychiatrie. Berlin: Springer.—*120*.
——— (1920) On the development of thoughts. *Z. ges. Neurol. Psychiat.*, *59*, 250.—*268, 274*.
——— (1928) 'Depersonalization'. In: Introduction to Psychoanalytic Psychiatry. *Nerv. ment. Dis. Monogr.*, Series 50.—*120*.
——— (1935) The image and appearance of the human body. *Psyche Monogr. No. 4*. London.—*120*.
SCHNABEL, I. (1921) Prognosis of psychiatric disturbances in childhood and adolescence from the material of the Zurich Psychiatric Clinic, 1870–1920. *Z. ges. Neurol. Psychiat.*, *68*, 241.—*670*.
SCHNEIDER, C. (1925) Contribution to the problem of schizophrenia, 4th communication. On a general theory of schizophrenic symptoms. *Z. ges. Neurol. Psychiat.*, *96*, 572.—*274*.
SCHNEIDER, K. (1920) The stratification of emotional life and the structure of the depressive states. *Z. ges. Neurol. Psychiat.*, *59*, 281.—*194*.

SCHNEIDER, K.(1923) Psychopathic Personalities. 9th ed. (1950) Vienna: F. Deuticke.—*59, 75*.
—— (1925) Nature and diagnosis of schizophrenia. *Z. ges. Neurol. Psychiat.*, *99*, 542.—*315*.
—— (1926) Studies of the Personality and Life History of Registered Prostitutes. Berlin: Springer.—*715*.
—— (1942) Mental Symptoms and Psychiatric Diagnosis. Leipzig: Thieme.—*320*.
—— (1952) Über den Wahn. Stuttgart. Thieme.—*274*.
SCHOLZ, W. (1951) Die Krampfschädigungen Des Gehirns. Berlin: Springer.—*468*.
SCHOU, M. (1963) Normothymotics, 'mood-normalizers': are lithium and imipramine drugs specific for affective disorders? *Brit. J. Psychiat.*, *109*, 803.—*232*.
SCHREBER, D. P. (1903) Memories of a Nervous Patient (trans. I. Macalpine and R. A. Hunter, 1955). London: Dawson.—*276*.
SCHROEDER, H. A. (1958) Degenerative cardiovascular disease in the Orient. I Atherosclerosis. II Hypertension. *J. chron. Dis.*, *8*, 287; 312.—*588*.
SCHROEDER, P. (1922) Degenerationspsychosen; Dementia Praecox. *Arch. Psychiat. Nervenkr*, *66*, 1.—*298*.
—— (1925) Hallucinating. *Z. ges. Neurol. Psychiat.*, *101*, 599.—*274*.
—— (1926) On degenerative psychoses. *Z. ges. Neurol. Psychiat.*, *105*, 539.—*215*.
SCHULER, E. A. and PARENTON, V. J. (1943) Recent epidemic of hysteria in a Louisiana high school. *J. soc. Psychol.*, *17*, 221.—*664*.
SCHULZ, B. and LEONHARD, K. (1940) Erbiologischklinische Untersuchungen an insgesamt 99 iw Sinne Leonhards typischen bzw. atypischen Schizophrenien. *Z. ges. Neurol. Psychiat.*, *168*, 587.—*243, 302*.
SCHÜRMANN, K. (1951) Psychological changes found with pathology of the chiasma opticum. *Dtsch. Z. Nervenheilk.*, *165*, 35.—*527*.
SCHWAB, G. (1925) Examination of the psychological and developmental condition of infants up to the age of three. *Jb. Kinderheilk.*, *107*, 86.—*708*.
SCHWARTZ, C. J. and MITCHELL, J. R. A. (1961) Atheroma of the carotid and vertebral arterial systems. *Brit. med. J.*, *2*, 1057.—*595*.
SCLARE, A. and HAMILTON, C. M. (1963) Attempted suicide in Glasgow. *Brit. J. Psychiat.*, *109*, 609.—*793*.
SCOTT, P. D. (1957) Homosexuality, with special reference to classification. *Proc. roy. Soc. Med.*, *50*, 655.—*173, 174*.
—— and WILLCOX, D. R. C. (1965) Delinquency and the amphetamines. *Brit. J. Psychiat.*, *111*, 865.—*420*.
SCOTTISH RESEARCH COUNCIL (1949) The Trend of Scottish Intelligence. London: Univ. London Press. —*694, 701*.
SCOVILLE, W. B. and MILNER, B. (1957) Loss of recent memory after bilateral hippocampal lesions. *J. Neurol. Neurosurg. Psychiat.*, *20*, 11.—*487, 495, 527*.
SEAGER, C. P. (1960) A controlled study of post-partum mental illness. *J. ment. Sci.*, *106*, 214.—*375*.
—— and FLOOD, R. A. (1965) Suicide in Bristol. *Brit. J. Psychiat.*, *111*, 919.—*791*.
SECHEHAYE, M. (1954) Introduction à une Psychothérapie des Schizophrènes. Paris: Presses Universitaires. —*262*.
SEDMAN, G. (1966) Depersonalization in a group of normal subjects. *Brit. J. Psychiat.*, *112*, 907.—*123*.
—— and KENNA, J. C. (1965) The use of LSD-25 as a diagnostic aid in doubtful cases of schizophrenia. *Brit. J. Psychiat.*, *111*, 96.—*437*.
SEELERT, H. (1929) Observations on the problem of the origin of schizophrenia symptoms. *Mschr. Psychiat. Neurol.*, *71*, 215.—*259*.
SELBY, G. and LANCE, J. W. (1960) Observations on 500 cases of migraine and allied vascular headache. *J. Neurol. Neurosurg. Psychiat.*, *23*, 23.—*454*.
SERAFETINIDES, E. A. and FALCONER, M. A. (1962) The effects of temporal lobectomy in epileptic patients with psychosis. *J. ment. Sci.*, *108*, 584.—*480*.
SHAGASS, C. and JONES, A. L. (1958) A neurophysiological test for psychiatric diagnosis: results in 750 Patients. *Amer. J. Psychiat.*, *114*, 1002.—*71, 204*.
—— and SCHWARTZ, M. (1963) Psychiatric correlates of evoked cerebral cortical potentials. *Amer. J. Psychiat.*, *119*, 1055.—*204*.
SHAKOW, D. (1946) The Nature of Deterioration in Schizophrenic Conditions. Nerv. ment. Dis. Monograph No. 70. Coolidge Foundation.—*307*.
SHAPIRO, M. B. and NELSON, E. H. (1955) An investigation of the nature of cognitive impairment in co-operative psychiatric patients. *Brit. J. med. Psychol.*, *28*, 239.—*492*.
——, POST, F., LOEFVING, B. and INGLIS, J. (1956) 'Memory function' in psychiatric patients over 60; some methodological and diagnostic implications. *J. ment. Sci.*, *102*, 233.—*554*.
SHAW, C. R. and McKAY, H. D. (1942) Juvenile Delinquency and Urban Areas. Univ. of Chicago Press.—*790*.
SHEEHAN, H. L. and SUMMERS, V. K. (1949) The syndrome of hypopituitarism. *Quart. J. Med.*, *18*, 319.—*368*.
SHELDON, J. H. (1948) The Social Medicine of Old Age. Published for the Trustees of the Nuffield Foundation. London.—*540*.
SHELDON, W. H., STEVENS, S. S. and TUCKER, W. B. (1940) The Varieties of Human Physique. London: Harper.—*63*.
—— and —— (1942) The Varieties of Temperament. London: Harper.—*63*.
SHENFIELD, B. E. (1962) American experience in ageing as viewed by a European. In: Social Welfare of the Ageing. ed. J. Kaplan and G. J. Aldridge. New York: Columbia University Press.—*562*.
SHENKEN, L. I. (1960) Psychotherapy in a case of bestiality. *Amer. J. Psychother.*, *14*, 728.—*168*.
—— (1964) Some clinical and psychopathological aspects of bestiality. *J. nerv. ment. Dis.*, *139*, 137.—*168*.
SHEPHERD, M. (1961) Morbid Jealousy: some clinical and social aspects of a psychiatric symptom. *J. ment. Sci.*, *107*, 687.—*400*.

844 REFERENCES

SHEPHERD, M. COOPER, B. BROWN, A. C. and KALTON, G. W. (1966) Psychiatric Illness in General Practice. London: Oxford Univ. Press.—*778, 781*.

SHERIDAN, M. D. (1964) Final report of a prospective study of children whose mothers had rubella in early pregnancy. *Brit. med. J.*, *2*, 536.—*707*.

SHERLOCK, S. (1955) Acute hepatic failure. *Brit. med. J.*, *1*, 1383.—*360, 361*.

——, SUMMERSKILL, W. H., WHITE, L. P. and PHEAR, E. A. (1954) Portal-systemic encephalopathy: neurological complications of liver disease. *Lancet*, *2*, 453.—*361*.

SHIELDS, J. (1954) Personality differences and neurotic traits in normal twin schoolchildren. *Eugen. Rev.*, *45*, 213.—*66*.

—— (1962) Monozygotic Twins Brought up Apart and Brought up Together. London: Oxford Univ. Press. —*64, 702*.

—— (1965) Review of 'Psychiatric Illnesses in Identical Twins' by Pekka Tienari. *Brit. J. Psychiat.*, *111*, 777.—*241*.

SHIPLEY, W. C. (1940) A self administering scale for measuring intellectual impairment and deterioration. *J. Psychol.*, *9*, 371.—*492*.

SHOCK, N. W. (1964) Intrinsic factors in ageing. In: Age with a Future. Proc. 6th Int. Congr. Geront., Copenhagen, 1963, ed. P. F. Hansen. Copenhagen: Munksgaard.—*534*.

SHORVON, H. J., HILL, J. D. N. BURKITT, E. and HALSTEAD, H. (1946) The depersonalization syndrome. *Proc. roy. Soc. Med.*, *39*, 779.—*121, 131*.

SIEGAL, M., NISWANDER, G. D., SACHS, E. and STRAVOS, D. (1959) Taraxein, fact or artifact? *Amer. J. Psychiat.*, *115*, 819.—*255*.

SILVERMAN, D. (1941) Prognosis in schizophrenia: a study of 271 cases. *Psychiat. Quart.*, *15*, 477.—*310*.

SIM, M. (1963) Abortion and the psychiatrist. *Brit. med. J.*, *2*, 145.—*377, 378*.

——, TURNER, E. and SMITH, W. T. (1966) Cerebral biopsy in the investigation of presenile dementia. I Clinical aspects. *Brit. J. Psychiat.*, *112*, 119.—*616*.

SIMCHOWICZ, T. (1910) Histologische Studien uber die senile Demenz. *Histol. u. histopath. Arb. u. d. Grosshirnrinde, Jena.*, *4*, 267.—*603*.

SIMON, H. (1927) Active treatment in mental hospital. *Allg. Z. Psychiat.*, *87*, 97.—*328*.

SINGER, M. T. and WYNNE, L. C. (1965a) Thought disorder and family relations of schizophrenics. III Methodology using projective techniques. *Arch. gen. Psychiat.*, *12*, 187.—*317*.

—— and —— (1965b) Thought disorder and family relations of schizophrenics. IV Results and implications. *Arch. gen. Psychiat.*, *12*, 201.—*317*.

SJÖBRING, J. (1963) La Personnalité: Structure et Développement. Paris: Doin et Deren.—*61*.

SJÖGREN, H. (1964) Paraphrenic, melancholic and psycho-neurotic states in the presenile-senile period of life. A study of 649 patients in the functional division. *Acta psychiat. scand.*, *40*, suppl. 176.—*577*.

SJÖGREN, T. (1932) Clinical and genetical investigation on oligophrenia in a peasant population of northern Sweden. *Acta psychiat. scand.*, suppl. 2.—*705*.

—— (1935) Genetical investigations of Huntington's chorea in a Swedish peasant population. *Z. menschl. Vererb.-u. Konstit.-Lehre*, *19*, 131.—*621*.

—— (1948) Genetic-statistical and psychiatric investigation of a west Swedish population. *Acta psychiat. neurol.*, (Kbh.), suppl. 52.—*239, 307*.

—— and LARSSON, T. (1959) Changing age-structure in Sweden and its impact on mental illness, especially senile psychosis. *Wld Hlth Bull.*, *21*, 569. Geneva. W.H.O.—*540*.

——, SJÖGREN, H. and LINDGREN, A. G. H. (1952) Morbus Alzheimer and morbus Pick: genetic, clinical and patho-anatomical study. *Acta psychiat. scand.*, suppl. 82.—*611, 612, 613, 614, 617*.

SJÖQVIST, F. (1965) Psychotropic drugs (2) Interaction between monoamine-oxidase (MAO) inhibitors and other substances. *Proc. roy. Soc. Med.*, *58*, 967.—*202*.

SJÖVALL, T. (1947) Preliminary studies on possible serum toxicity in schizophrenia. *Acta psychiat. neurol. (Kbh).*, suppl. 47, 105.—*255*.

SKALWEIT, W. (1934) Constitution and Progress in Schizophrenia. Leipzig: Thieme.—*317*.

SKOOG, G. (1965) Onset of anancastic conditions. *Acta psychiat. scand.*, *41*, suppl. 184.—*131, 133*.

SLATER, E. (1938) The periodicity of manic-depressive insanity. *Z. ges. Neurol. Psychiat.*, *162*, 794.—*194*.

—— (1943) The neurotic constitution. *J. Neurol. Psychiat.*, *6*, 1.—*62, 704*.

—— (1945) Neurosis and sexuality. *J. Neurol. Neurosurg. Psychiat.*, *8*, 12.—*83*.

—— (1947) Genetical causes of schizophrenic symptoms. *Mschr. Psychiat. Neurol.*, *113*, 50.—*314*.

—— (1951) Evaluation of electric convulsion therapy as compared with conservative methods of treatment in depressive states. *J. ment. Sci.*, *97*, 567.—*218*.

—— (1953) Psychotic and neurotic illnesses in twins. *Spec. Rep. Ser. med. Res. Coun. (Lond.)*, No. 278.—*66, 242, 245, 251*.

—— (1958) The monogenic theory of schizophrenia. *Acta genet. (Basel)*, *8*, 50.—*249*.

—— (1961) Hysteria 311. *J. ment. Sci.*, *107*, 359.—*66, 104, 117*.

—— (1962) Birth order and maternal age of homosexuals. *Lancet*, *1*. 69.—*169*.

—— (1965) The diagnosis of 'hysteria'. *Brit. med. J.*, *1*, 1395.—*106*.

——, BEARD, A. W., and GLITHERO, E. (1963) The schizophrenia-like psychoses of epilepsy. I–V *Brit. J. Psychiat.*, *109*, 95.—*258, 454, 470, 473, 483*.

—— and SLATER, P. (1944) A heuristic theory of neurosis. *J. Neurol. Psychiat.*, *7*, 49.—*62*.

—— and —— (1947) A study in the assessment of homosexual traits. *Brit. J. med. Psychol.*, *21*, 61. —*169*.

SLATER, P. (1945) Scores of different types of neurotics on tests of intelligence. *Brit. J. Psychol.*, *35*, 40. —*704*.

SLAVSON, S. R. (1950) Analytic Group Psychotherapy. New York: Columbia Univ. Press.—*183*.

SMITH, A. D. M. (1960) Megaloblastic madness. *Brit. med. J.*, 2, 1840.—*355*.

SMITH, C. M. (1958) A new adjunct to the treatment of alcoholism: the hallucinogenic drugs. *Quart. J. Stud. Alcohol.*, *19*, 406.—*437*.

SMITH, J. C. (1925) Atypical psychoses and heterologous hereditary taints. *J. nerv. ment. Dis.*, *62*, 1.—*299*.

———— (1930) The aetiological relationships of mental deficiency illuminated by investigations on twins. *Z. ges. Neurol. Psychiat.*, *125*, 678.—*702*.

SMITH, K. and SINES, J. O. (1960) Demonstration of a peculiar odour in the sweat of schizophrenic patients. *Arch. gen. Psychiat.*, 2, 184.—*256*.

SMITH, W. T., TURNER, E. and SIM, M. (1966) Cerebral biopsy in the investigation of presenile dementia. II Pathological aspects. *Brit. J. Psychiat.*, *112*, 127.—*616*.

SNYDER, C. R. (1958) Alcohol and the Jews. Yale Univ. Center of Alcohol Studies, Monograph No. 1, Chicago: Free Press.—*390*.

SØBYE, P. (1948) Heredity in essential hypertension and nephrosclerosis. A genetic clinical study of 200 propositi suffering from nephrosclerosis. *Op. dom. Biol. hered. hum.* (Kbh), *16*.—*588*.

SOLLMANN, T. (1948) Manual of Pharmacology. 7th ed. London: Saunders.—*429*.

SOLYOM, L. and BEACH, L. (1961) Further studies upon the effects of the administration of ribonucleic acid in aged patients suffering from memory (retention) failure. *Neuropsychopharmacol.*, 2, 351.—*610*.

SPATZ, H. (1938) Systemic atrophies. A well-defined group of hereditary diseases in the nervous system. *Arch. Psychiat. Nervenkr.*, *108*, 1.—*611*.

SPEER, E. (1927) Special psychotherapy in schizophrenia. *Z. ges. Neurol. Psychiat.*, *109*, 641.—*325*.

SPENCER, J. C. (1955) Delinquents and their neighbours. *Approved Schls Gaz.*, *49*, 46.—*658*.

SPILLANE, J. D. (1947) Nutritional Disorders of the Nervous System. Edinburgh: Livingstone.—*401*.

———— (1951) Nervous and mental disorders in Cushing's syndrome. *Brain*, 74, 72.—*367*.

SPITZ, R. A. (1945) Hospitalism. *Psychoanal. Stud. Child.* 1, 53.—*660*.

SPITZER, R. L., FLEISS, J. L., BURDOCK, E. I. and HARDESTY, A. S. (1964) The mental status schedule: rationale, reliability and validity. *Comprehens. Psychiat.*, 5, 384.—*55*.

SPROTT, W. J. H. (1956) Delinquency areas I. *Brit. J. Delinq.*, 7, 137.—*658*.

SROLE, L., LANGNER, T. S., MICHAEL, S. T., OPLER, M. K. and RENNIE, T. A. C. (1962) Mental Health in Metropolis: The Midtown Manhattan Study. In: Thomas A. C. Rennie Series in Social Psychiatry. New York: McGraw-Hill.—*781*.

STAEHELIN, J. E. (1944) Psychopathology of diseases of the diencephalon and mesencephalon. *Schweiz. Arch. Neurol. Psychiat.*, 53, 374.—*12*.

STAFFORD-CLARK, D. and TAYLOR, F. H. (1949) Clinical and electroencephalographic studies of prisoners charged with murder. *J. Neurol. Neurosurg. Psychiat.*, *12*, 325.—*72*.

STANLEY, R. J. and GUNZBURG, H. C. (1957) A survey of residential licences from a mental deficiency hospital. *Int. J. soc. Psychiat.*, 2, 207.—*714*.

STAUDENMEIER, L. (1912) Magic as an Experimental Science. Leipzig: Akadem, Verlagsgesellschaft.—*276*.

STAUDER, K. (1934) Lethal catatonia. *Arch. Psychiat. Nervenkr.*, *102*, 614.—*285, 307*.

STEIN, B. M., McCORMICK, W. F., RODRIGUEZ, J. N., and TAVERAS, J. M. (1962) Postmortem angiography of cerebral vascular system. *Arch. Neurol.* (*Chic.*), 7, 545.—*596*.

STENGEL, E. (1943) A study of the symptomatology and differential diagnosis of Alzheimer's and Pick's disease. *J. ment. Sci.*, *89*, 1.—*616*.

———— (1945) A study of some clinical aspects of the relationship between obsessional neurosis and psychotic reaction types. *J. ment. Sci.*, *91*, 166.—*129, 134, 283*.

———— (1963) Attempted suicide: its management in the general hospital. *Lancet*, *1*, 233.—*793*.

———— (1964a) In: Disorders of Language, ed. A. V. S. de Reuck and M. O'Connor, p. 285. London: Churchill.—*504*.

———— (1964b) Suicide and Attempted Suicide. London: Penguin.—*792, 797*.

————and COOK, N. G. (1961) Contrasting suicide rates in industrial communities. *J. ment. Sci.*, *107*, 1011.—*789*.

————, ———— and KREEGER, I. S. (1958) Attempted Suicide: its Social Significance and Effects. Maudsley Monograph, 4. Institute of Psychiatry: London.—*542, 792, 795, 796*.

STENSTEDT, A. (1952) A study in manic-depressive psychoses. Clinical, social and genetic investigations. *Acta psychiat. neurol.* (Kbh)., suppl. 79.—*196, 792*.

———— (1959) Involutional melancholia: an aetiological, clinical and social study of endogenous depression in later life with special reference to genetic factors. *Acta psychiat. neurol. scand.*, 34, suppl. 127.—*196, 214, 568*.

STEPHENS, J. H. and KAMP, M. (1962) On some aspects of hysteria: a clinical study. *J. nerv. ment. Dis.*, *134*, 305.—*104*.

STERTZ, G. (1926) On Pick's atrophy. *Z. ges. Neurol. Psychiat.*, *101*, 729.—*617*.

STEVENS, J. D. and DUNN, A. L. (1958) Thyroid function in mental diseases. *Dis. nerv. Syst.*, *19*, 338.—*253*.

STEVENSON, G. S. (1946) The prevention of personality disorders. In: Personality and the Behaviour Disorders, ed. J. M. Hunt. New York: Ronald.—*323*.

von STOCKERT, F. G. (1943) Psychic disturbances in typhus fever. *Dtsch. med. Wschr.*, *69*, 506.—*383*.

STOGDILL, C. G. (1965) School achievement, learning difficulties and mental health. *Can. ment. Hlth*, XIII, 5. (Suppl.).—*677*.

STOLL, W. A. (1947) Lysergic acid diethylamide, a 'phantasticum' derived from the ergot group of drugs. *Schweiz. Arch. Neurol. Psychiat.*, 60, 279.—*437*.

————and BRACK, K. E. (1957) Diagnostic and therapeutic experiences with institutional patients with thyroid disorders. *Psychiat. et Neurol.* (*Basel*), *133*, 167.—*253*.

STORCH, A. (1922) On archaic thinking in schizophrenia. *Z. ges. Neurol. Psychiat.*, *78*, 500.—*277*.

STOTT, D. H. (1957) Physical and mental handicaps following a disturbed pregnancy. *Lancet*. *1*, 1006.—*76, 656*.

—— (1959) Evidence for pre-natal impairment of temperament in mentally retarded children. *Vita hum.*, *2*, 125.—*656*.

STRANSKY, E. (1914) Schizophrenia and intra-psychiatric ataxia. *Jb. Psychiat. Neurol.*, *36*, 485.—*264*.

STRAUS, E. W. (1928) The experience of time in endogenous depression and psychopathic moods. *Mschr. Psychiat. Neurol.*, *68*, 640.—*195*.

—— (1948) On obsession. Nerv. & Ment. Dis. Monogr. No. 73. New York.—*134*.

STRAUSS, A. A. and LATHINEN, L. E. (1947) Psychopathology and Education of the Brain-injured Child. New York: Grune.—*706*.

STRELETZKI, F. (1961) Psychoses in the course of Huntington's chorea with special reference to the formation of delusions. *Arch. Psychiat. Nervenkr.*, *202*, 202.—*301*.

STRINGARIS, M. G. (1933) Clinical observations in psychoses due to hashish. *Arch. Psychiat. Nervenkr.*, *100*, 522.—*428*.

—— (1939) Addiction to Hashish. Berlin: Springer.—*428*.

STRÖMGREN, E. (1950) Statistical and genetic population studies within psychiatry-methods and principal results. *Actual. sci. ind.* No. 1101. Paris.—*239*.

STRONGIN, E. I. and HINSIE, L. E. (1939) A method for differentiating manic-depressive depressions from other depressions by means of parotid secretions. *Psychiat. Quart.*, *13*, 697.—*204*.

STUMPFL, F. (1936) The Origin of Crime Demonstrated in the Life History of Twins. Leipzig: Thieme. —*65, 658*.

STÜRUP, G. K. (1952) The treatment of criminal psychopaths at Herstedvester. *Brit. J. med. Psychol.*, *25*, 31. —*182, 184*.

SUGERMAN, A. A., GOLDSTEIN, L., MURPHEE, H. B., PFEIFFER, C. C. and JENNEY, E. H. (1964) EEG and behavioural changes in schizophrenia. *Arch. gen. Psychiat.*, *10*, 340.—*258*.

SULSER, F., BICKEL, M. H. and BRODIE, B. B. (1964) The action of desmethylimipramine in counteracting sedation and cholinergic effects of reserpine-like drugs. *J. Pharmacol. exp. Ther.*, *144*, 321.—*201*.

SVED, S. and WAINRIB, B. (1962) Effects of intravenous administration of ribonucleic acid upon failure of memory for recent events in presenile and aged individuals. In: Recent Advances in Biological Psychiatry, ed. J. Wortis. London: Heinemann.—*610*.

SVENDSEN, B. B. (1953) Fluctuation of Danish psychiatric admission rates in World War II: initial decrease and subsequent increase. *Psychiat. Quart.*, *27*, 19.—*787*.

SWINSCOW, D. (1951) Some suicide statistics. *Brit. med. J.*, *1*, 1417.—*792*.

SYDENSTRICKER, V. P. (1943) The neurological complications of malnutrition. Psychic manifestations of nicotinic acid deficiency. *Proc. roy. Soc. Med.*, *36*, 169.—*343*.

——, CLECKLEY, H. M. and GEESLIN, L. E. (1939) Nicotinic acid in the treatment of atypical psychotic states. *J. Amer. med. Ass.*, *112*, 2107.—*353*.

SYKES, M. K. and TREDGOLD, R. F. (1964) Restricted orbital undercutting: a study of its effects on 350 patients over 10 years, 1951–1960. *Brit. J. Psychiat.*, *110*, 609.—*136, 219, 222, 336, 575*.

SYMONDS, C. P. (1942) Differential diagnosis and treatment of post-contusional states. *Proc. roy. Soc. Med.*, *35*, 601.—*507*.

—— (1948) Epilepsy. *Brit. med. J.*, *1*, 533.—*456*.

—— (1949) Concussion and contusion of the brain and their sequelae. In: Injuries of the Brain and Spinal Cord and their Coverings, ed. S. Brock. New York: Williams & Wilkins.—*500*.

—— (1962) The schizophrenic-like psychoses of epilepsy (Discussion). *Proc. roy. Soc. Med.*, *55*, 311.—*473*.

—— and CAIRNS, H. (1950) Brain abscess. In: British Encyclopaedia of Medical Practice, 2nd ed., *3*, 67. London: Butterworth.—*525*.

—— and RUSSELL, W. R. (1943) Accidental head injuries. Prognosis in service patients. *Lancet*, *1*, 7.—*508*.

TAFT, L. T. and GOLDFARB, W. (1964) Prenatal and perinatal factors in childhood schizophrenia. *Develop. Med. Child Neurol.*, *6*, 32.—*685*.

TAIT, A. C., HARPER, J. and MCCLATCHLEY, W. T. (1957) Initial psychiatric illness in involutional women. I Clinical aspects. *J. ment. Sci.*, *103*, 132.—*214*.

TAKESADA, M., KAKIMOTO, Y., SANO, I. and KANEKO, Z. (1963) 3,4-Dimethoxyphenylethylamine and other amines in the urine of schizophrenic patients. *Nature (Lond.)*, *199*, 203.—*256*.

TALLAND, G. A. (1965) Deranged Memory. London: Academic Press.—*487*.

TANGERMANN, R. (1942) Spontaneous remissions in schizophrenia. *Allg. Z. Psychiat.*, *121*, 36.—*310*.

TANNER, J. M. (1951) Current advances in the study of physique. Photogrammetric anthropometry and an androgyny scale. *Lancet*, *1*, 574.—*70*.

TARJAN, G. (1961) Organic aetiological factors. In: Prevention of Mental Disorders in Children, ed. G. Caplan. New York: Basic Books.—*802*.

TAYLOR, D. T. E., HART, F. D. and BURLEY, D. (1964) Suicide in South London: an analysis of the admissions for attempted suicide in one medical unit of a general hospital. *Practitioner*, *192*, 251.—*793*.

TAYLOR, J. A. A. (1953) A personality scale of manifest anxiety. *J. abnorm. soc. Psychol.*, *48*, 285.—*36*.

TAYLOR, S. (1949) The psychopath in our midst. A Danish solution. *Lancet*, *1*, 32.—*183*.

TAYLOR, S. J. L. and CHAVE, S. (1964) Mental Health and Environment. London: Longmans.—*781, 783*.

TERMAN, L. M. and MERRILL, M. A. (1937) Measuring Intelligence. London: Harrap.—*728*.

—— and MILES, C. C. (1936) Sex and Personality. New York: McGraw-Hill.—*169, 171*.

TERRY, R. D., GONATAS, N. K. and WEISS, M. (1964) Ultrastructural studies in Alzheimer's presenile dementia. *Amer. J. Path.*, 44, 269.—*607*.

TETLOW, C. (1955) Psychoses of child-bearing. *J. ment. Sci.*, 101, 692.—*375*.

TEUBER, H. L., BATTERSBY, W. S. and BENDER, M. B. (1951) Performance of complex visual tasks after cerebral lesions. *J. nerv. ment. Dis.*, 114, 413.—*493*.

—— and BENDER, M. B. (1948) Critical flicker frequency in defective fields of vision. *Fed. Proc.*, 7, 1.—*493*.

—— and —— (1950) Perception of apparent movement across acquired scotomata in the visual field. *Amer. Psychol.*, 8, 271.—*493*.

THOMAS, J. C. S. (1963) Monoamine-oxidase inhibitors and cheese. *Brit. med. J.*, 2, 1406.—*202*.

THORPE, F. T. (1942) Shock treatment in psychosis complicating pregnancy. *Brit. med. J.*, 2, 281.—*373*.

—— (1960) Electrocoagulation of the cerebral orbital projection in the persistent depressive psychoses of the elderly. *J. ment. Sci.*, 106, 771.—*575*.

TIENARI, P. (1963) Psychiatric illnesses in identical twins. *Acta psychiat. scand.*, 39, suppl. 171.—*241*.

TIZARD, J. (1960a) Public health aspects of severe mental subnormality. *Roy. Soc. Hlth J.*, 80, 327.—*734*.

—— (1960b) Residential care of mentally handicapped children. *Brit. med. J.*, 1, 1041.—*717*.

—— and GRAD, J. C. (1961) The Mentally Handicapped and their Families. London: Oxford Univ. Press. —*717*.

TODD, J., COLLINS, A. D., MARTIN, F. R. R. and DEWHURST, K. E. (1962) Mental symptoms due to insulinomata. Report on two cases. *Brit. med. J.*, 2, 828.—*369, 370*.

TOMLINSON, B. E., BLESSED, G. and ROTH, M. (1968a) Observations on the brain in non-demented old people. *J. neurol. Sci.*, 7, 331.—*607*.

——, —— and —— (1968b) Unpublished observations.—*535*.

TOOLAN, J. M. (1962) Suicide and suicidal attempts in children and adolescents. *Amer. J. Psychiat.*, 118, 719. —*669*.

TOOTH, G. C. (1950) Studies in mental illness in the Gold Coast. Colonial Research Publications No. 6. London: H.M.S.O.—*383*.

—— and NEWTON, M. P. (1961) Leucotomy in England and Wales, 1942–1954. Ministry of Health Reports on Public Health and Medical Subjects, No. 104. London: H.M.S.O.—*335*.

TOWNSEND, P. (1957) The Family Life of Old People. London: Routledge.—*545, 561*.

—— (1962) The Last Refuge: a survey of residential institutions and Homes for the aged in England and Wales. London: Routledge.—*562*.

—— (1964) The place of older people in different societies. *Lancet*, 1, 159.—*544*.

—— and WEDDERBURN, D. (1965) The Aged in the Welfare State. London: G. Bell.—*546, 547*.

TRAPP, C. E. and JAMES, E. B. (1937) Comparative intelligence ratings in 4 types of dementia praecox. *J. nerv. ment. Dis.*, 86, 399.—*307*.

TREDGOLD, A. F. (1947) A Text-book of Mental Deficiency. 7th ed. London.—*702, 707, 719, 731*.

TREDGOLD, R. F. (1964) Psychiatric indications for termination of pregnancy. *Lancet*, 2, 1251.—*378*.

—— and SODDY, K. (1963) Text-book of Mental Deficiency (A. F. Tredgold), 10th ed. London: Baillière. —*733*.

TUCKMAN, J, and YOUNGMAN, W. F. (1963a) Suicide risk among persons attempting suicide. *Publ. Hlth Rep.* (*Wash.*), 78, 585.—*796*.

—— and —— (1963b) Identifying suicide risk groups among attempted suicides. *Publ. Hlth Rep.* (*Wash.*), 78, 763.—*796*.

TUCZEK, (1933) Combination of Manic-Depressive and Schizophrenic Heredity. Zurich: Orell Füssli.—*299*.

TUNE, G. S. (1964) Psychological effects of hypoxia: review of certain literature from the period 1950 to 1963. In: *Percept. mot. Skills*, 19, 551.—*440*.

TUNSTALL, J. (1966) Old and Alone: a Sociological Study of Old People. London: Routledge.—*562*.

TURNER, E. A. (1958) Bilateral temporal lobotomy for psycho-motor epilepsy. *Electroenceph. clin. Neurophysiol.* 10, 119.—*481*.

UNNA, K. (1943) Antagonistic effect of N-Allylnormorphine upon morphine. *J. Pharmacol.*, 79, 27.—*423*.

VAILLANT, G. E. (1963) Manic-depressive heredity and remission in schizophrenia. *Brit. J. Psychiat.*, 109, 746.—*313*.

——, SEMRAD, E. V. and EWALT, J. R. (1964) Current therapeutic results in schizophrenia. *New. Engl. J. Med.*, 271, 280.—*310*.

VALLANCE, M. (1965) Alcoholism: a two year follow-up study of patients admitted to the psychiatric department of a general hospital. *Brit. J. Psychiat.*, 111, 348.—*393, 394, 411*.

VAUGHAN, G. F. and CASHMORE, A. A. (1954) Encopresis in childhood. *Guy's Hosp. Rep.*, 103, 360.—*648*.

VENABLES, P. H. and WING, J. K. (1962) Level of arousal and the subclassification of schizophrenia. *Arch. gen. Psychiat.*, 7, 114.—*258*.

VESSIE, P. R. (1932) On transmission of Huntington's chorea for three hundred years. Bures family group. *J. nerv. ment. Dis.*, 76, 553.—*621*.

VICKERS, G. (1965) Medicine, psychiatry and general practice. *Lancet*, 1, 1021.—*780*.

VICTOR, M. and HOPE, J. M. (1958) The phenomenon of auditory hallucinations in chronic alcoholism. *J. nerv. ment. Dis.*, 126, 451.—*403*.

——, TALLAND, G. A. and ADAMS, R. D. (1959) Psychological studies of Korsakoff's psychosis: I General intellectual functions. *J. nerv. ment. Dis.*, 128, 528.—*405*.

VISLIE, H. (1956) Puerperal mental disorders. *Acta psychiat. neurol. scand.*, suppl. 111.—*374*.

VISPO, R. H. (1962) Pre-morbid personality in the functional psychoses of the senium. A comparison of ex-patients with healthy controls. *J. ment. Sci.*, *108*, 790.—*547, 577*.

VOGT, C. and VOGT, O. (1952) Altérations anatomiques de la schizophrenie et d'autres psychoses dites fonction-elles. *1st Int. Congr. Neuropath.*, *1*, 515.—*258*.

VOGT, M. (1954) The concentration of sympathin in different parts of the central nervous system under normal conditions and after the administration of drugs. *J. Physiol. (Lond.)*, *123*, 451.—*199*.

WADA, J. and GIBSON, W. C. (1959) Behavioural and EEG changes induced by injection of schizophrenic urine extract. *Arch. neurol. psychiat. (Chic.)*, *81*, 747.—*255*.

WAGSTAFFE, W. W. (1928) The incidence of traumatic epilepsy after gunshot wound of the head. *Lancet*, *2*, 861.—*505*.

WALDENSTRÖM, J. and HAEGER-ARONSEN, B. (1963) Different patterns of human porphyria. *Brit. med. J.*, *2*, 272.—*359, 360*.

WALKER, A. R. P., MORTIMER, K. L., DOWNING, J. W. and DUNN, J. A. (1960) Hypertension in African populations. *Brit. med. J.*, *2*, 805.—*588*.

WALSHE, F. M. R. (1931) Intracranial tumours; a critical review. *Quart. J. Med.*, *24* (old series), 587.—*525*.

WALSHE, J. M. (1951) Observations on symptomatology and pathogenesis of hepatic coma. *Quart. J. med.*, *20*, 421.—*361*.

WALTER, W. G. (1950) In: Electroencephalography, ed, J. D. N. Hill and G. Parr. London: Macmillan.—*673*.

WALTHARD, K. M. (1926) On the adaptation to severe organic defects. *Schweiz. med. Wschr.*, *56*, 1065.—*671*.

WALTHER-BÜEL, H. (1951) Psychiatry of Cerebral Tumours and the Problem of Focal Syndromes and of Psychological Localization. Vienna: Springer-Verlag.—*524*.

WALTON, D. (1958) The diagnostic and predictive accuracy of the modified word learning test in psychiatric patients over 65. *J. ment. Sci.*, *104*, 1119.—*555*.

—— and BLACK, D. A. (1957) The validity of a psychological test of brain-damage. *Brit. J. med. Psychol.*, *30*, 270.—*36, 492, 555*.

——, WHITE, J. G., BLACK, D. A. and YOUNG, A. J. (1959) The modified word learning test: a cross valida-tion study. *Brit. J. med. Psychol.*, *32*, 213.—*492*.

WALTON, H. J. (1961) Group methods in hospital organisation and patient treatment as applied in the psychi-atric treatment of alcoholism. *Amer. J. Psychiat.*, *118*, 410.—*182*.

WALTON, J. N., KILOH, L. G., OSSLETON, J. W. and FARRALL, J. (1954) The electroencephalogram in pernicious anaemia and subacute combined degeneration of the cord. *Electroenceph. clin. Neurophysiol.*, *6*, 45.—*355*.

WARD, A. A. Jr. (1961) Epilepsy. *Int. Rev. Neurobiol.*, *3*, 137.—*447*.

de WARDENER, H. E. and LENNOX, B. (1947) Cerebral beri-beri. (Wernicke's encephalopathy). *Lancet.*, *1*, 11. —*353, 354*.

von WARTBURG, J. P. (1965) Paper read at Institute on the Prevention and Treatment of Alcoholism, report in *Brit. med. J.*, *2*, 164.—*393*.

WATTS, A. F. and VERNON, P. E. (1950) Reading Ability. London: Churchill.—*677*.

WATTS, C. A. H. and WATTS, B. M. (1952) Psychiatry in General Practice. London: Churchill.—*540*.

WAYNE, E. J. (1960) Clinical and metabolic studies in thyroid disease. I and II. *Brit. med. J.*, *1*, 1,78.—*94, 363*.

WEATHERALL, M. (1954) Drugs and porphyrin metabolism. *Pharmacol. Rev.*, *6*, 133.—*360*.

WECHSLER, D. (1958) The Measurement of Adult Intelligence. 4th ed. Baltimore: Williams & Wilkins.—*492*.

WECKOWICZ, T. E. and BLEWETT, D. B. (1959) Size constancy and abstract thinking in schizophrenic patients. *J. ment. Sci.*, *105*, 909.—*274*.

WEINBERG, I and LOBSTEIN, J. (1936) The inheritance of manic-depressive insanity. *Psychiat. Neurol. (Basel)*, *1*, 339.—*189*.

WEINSTEIN, S., SEMMES, J., GHENT, L. and TEUBER, H. L. (1956) Spatial orientation in man after cerebral in-jury. II Analysis according to concomitant defects. *J. Psychol.*, *42*, 249.—*493*.

WEISENBURG, T. H. and McBRIDE, K. E. (1935) Aphasia. New York: Commonwealth Fund.—*50*.

WEITBRECHT, H. J. (1952) Typology of depressive psychoses. *Fortschr. Neurol. Psychiat.*, *20*, 247.—*195*.

—— (1933) Offene Probleme bei affektiven Psychosen. *Nervenarzt*, *24*, 187.—*225*.

WELFORD, A. T. (1962) On changes of performance with age. *Lancet*, *1*, 335.—*537, 538, 560*.

—— (1963) Social, psychological and physiological gerontology—an experimental psychologist's approach. In: Processes of Ageing, eds. R. H. Williams, C. Tibbitts and W. Donahue, Vol. I, p. 115. New York: Atherton.—*537, 538*.

WELLS, H. K. (1956) Pavlov and Freud, Vol. I. Ivan P. Pavlov: toward a specific psychology and psychiatry. London: Lawrence.—*21*.

WELNER, J. and STRÖMGREN, E. (1958) Clinical and genetic studies on benign schizophreniform psychoses based on a follow-up. *Acta psychiat. neurol. scand.*, *33*, 377.—*302*.

WENDT, G. G. (1959) Das Erkrankungsalter bei der Huntingtonschen chorea. *Acta genet. (Basel)*, *9*, 18.—*622*.

WERNICKE, K. (1881) Text-book of Cerebral Diseases, p. 229. Berlin: Karger.—*353*.

—— (1906) Fundamentals of Psychiatry. Leipzig Thieme.—*289*.

WEST, D. J. (1959) Parental figures in the genesis of male homosexuality. *Int. J. soc. Psychiat.*, *5*, 85.—*172*:

—— (1960) Homosexuality. London: Penguin.—*172*.

—— (1963) The Habitual Prisoner. London: Macmillan.—*261*.

WEST, J. B., LAHIRI, S., GILL, M. B., MILLEDGE, J. S., PUGH, L. G. and WARD, M. P. (1962) Arterial oxygen saturation during exercise at high altitude. *J. appl. Physiol.*, *17*, 617.—*440*.

WEST, R. (1943) The pathology of stuttering. *Nerv. Child*, *2*, 96.—*653*.

WESTLAKE, E. K., SIMPSON, T. and KAYE, M. (1955) Carbon dioxide narcosis in emphysema. *Quart. J. Med.*, 24, 155.—*357*.

WESTPHAL, C. (1871) Die Agoraphobie: eine Neuropathischerscheinung. *Arch. Psychiat. Nervenkr.*, 3, 138. —*86, 92*.

WHEELAN, L. (1959) Familial Alzheimer's disease. *Ann. hum. Genet.*, 23, 300.—*613*.

WHITE, L. E. and HAIN, R. F. (1959) Anorexia in association with a destructive lesion in the hypothalamus. *Arch. Path. (Chic.)*, 68, 275.—*124*.

WHITE, M. A. (1949) A study of schizophrenic language. *J. abnorm. soc. Psychol.*, 44, 61.—*286*.

WHITEHEAD, J. A. (1965) A comprehensive psycho-geriatric service. *Lancet*, 2, 583.—*566*.

WHITEHORN, J. C. and ZIPF, G. K. (1943) Schizophrenic language. *Arch. Neurol. Psychiat. (Chic.)*, 49, 831. —*286*.

WHITLOCK, F. A. and EDWARDS, J. E. (1968) Pregnancy and attempted suicide. *Comprehens. Psychiat.*, 9, (1), 1. —*378*.

——— and SCHAPIRA, K. (1967) Attempted suicide in Newcastle-upon-Tyne. *Brit. J. Psychiat.*, 113, 423.—*793, 795*.

WHYTE, L. L. (1962) The Unconscious before Freud. London: Tavistock.—*15*.

WIENER, N, (1961) Cybernetics. New York: Wiley—*142*.

WIKLER, A. (1957) The Relation of Psychiatry to Pharmacology. Baltimore: Williams & Wilkins.—*344, 438, 439*.

——— and RASOR, R. W. (1953) Symposium on drug addiction. Psychiatric aspects of drug addiction. *Amer. J. Med.*, 14, 566.—*418*.

WILD, C., SINGER, M. T., ROSMAN, B., RICCI, J. and LIDZ, T. (1965) Measuring disordered styles of thinking. *Arch. gen. Psychiat.*, 13, 471.—*317*.

WILDERMUTH, H. (1923) Schizophrenic signs in the healthy child. *Z. ges. Neurol. Psychiat.*, 86, 166.—*669*.

WILKINS, L. T. (1960) Delinquent Generations. Home Office Research Unit Report, No. 3. London: H.M.S.O. —*659*.

WILLIAMS, D. (1941a) The electroencephalogram in acute head injuries. *J. Neurol. Psychiat.*, 4, 107.—*503*.

——— (1941b) The electroencephalogram in chronic post-traumatic states. *J. Neurol. Psychiat.*, 4, 131.—*503*.

——— (1941c) The significance of an abnormal electroencephalogram. *J. Neurol. Psychiat.*, 4, 257.—*72*.

WILLIAMS, H. L., LUBIN, A, and GOODNOW, J. J. (1959) Impaired performance with acute sleep loss. *Psychol. Monogr.*, 73. No. 14. (Whole No. 484).—*381*.

———, QUESNEL, E., FISH, V. W. and GOODMAN, L. (1942) Studies in senile and arteriosclerotic psychoses. *Amer. J. Psychiat.*, 98, 712.—*591*.

WILLIAMS, M. and PENNYBACKER, J. (1954) Memory disturbance in third ventricular tumours. *J. Neurol. Neurosurg. Psychiat.*, 17, 115.—*487*.

WILLIAMS, R. D., MASON, H. L., POWER, M. H. and WILDER, R. M. (1943) Induced thiamine (Vitamin B$_1$) deficiency in man. *Arch. intern, Med.* 71, 38.—*354*.

WILLIAMSON, J., STOKOE, I. H., GRAY, S., FISHER, M., SMITH, A., McGHEE, A. and STEPHENSON, E. (1964) Old people at home: their unreported needs. *Lancet*, 1, 1117.—*540, 547, 560*.

WILMANNS, K. (1914) The psychopathies. In: Handbook of Neurology, ed. M. Lewandowsky. Berlin: Springer. —*56*.

——— (1922) Schizophrenia. *Z. ges. Neurol. Psychiat.*, 78, 325.—*270*.

——— (1940) On murder in the prodromal stage of schizophrenia. *Z. ges. Neurol. Psychiat.*, 170, 583.—*262*.

WILSON, P. (1908) In: Report of the Royal Commission on the Feeble-minded. 8, 123.—*717*.

WILSON, S. A. K. (1935) The epilepsies. In: Handbook of Neurology, ed. Bumke and Foerster. 9, 1.—*454, 459*.

WING, J. K. (1962) Institutionalism in mental hospitals. *Brit. J. soc. clin. Psychol.*, 1, 38.—*804*.

——— (1963) Rehabilitation of psychiatric patients. *Brit. J. Psychiat.*, 109, 635.—*337*.

——— (1964a) Longstay schizophrenic patients and the results of rehabilitation. Symp. on Mental Hospital Psychiatry, Middlesex Hospital, 1964.—*339*.

——— (1964b) The family management of schizophrenia and the principles of community care. Symp. on Mental Hospital Psychiatry, Middlesex Hospital, 1964.—*341*.

——— (ed.) (1967) Early Childhood Autism. London: Pergamon.—*680, 682*.

———, BENNETT, D. H., and DENHAM, J. (1964) The industrial rehabilitation of longstay schizophrenic patients. Medical Research Council Memorandum, No. 42. London: H.M.S.O.—*338, 339*.

———, BIRLEY, J. L. T., COOPER, J. E., GRAHAM, P. and ISAACS, A. D. (1967) Reliability of a procedure for measuring and classifying 'Present Psychiatric State'. *Brit. J. Psychiat.*, 113, 499.—*55, 778*.

——— and BROWN, G. W. (1961) Social treatment of chronic schizophrenia: a comparative survey of three mental hospitals. *J. ment. Sci.*, 107, 847.—*338, 340*.

———, MONCK, E., BROWN, G. W. and CARSTAIRS, G. M. (1964) Morbidity in the community of schizophrenic patients discharged from London Mental Hospitals in 1959. *Brit. J. Psychiat.*, 110, 10.—*310, 339*.

———, O'CONNOR, N. and LOTTER, V. (1967) Autistic conditions in early childhood: a survey in Middlesex. *Brit. med. J.*, 3, 389.—*680, 682*.

WINNICOTT, D. W. (1931) Clinical Notes on Disorders of Childhood. London: Heinemann.—*654*.

WINOKUR, G. (1967) Genetic principles in the clarification of clinical issues in affective disorder. Amer. Ass. for the Advancement of Science, 134th Meeting.—*197*.

——— and CLAYTON, P. (1967) Family history studies. I Two types of affective disorders separated according to genetic and clinical factors. Recent Advances in Biological Psychiatry, 9, 33.—*198*.

WITTENBORN, J. R. (1955) Wittenborn Psychiatric Rating Scales. New York: Psychological Corp.—*36*.

WITTKOWER, E. D. (1949) Psychosomatic medicine. In: Modern Practice in Psychological Medicine, ed. J. R. Rees. New York: Harper.—*589*.

WOLF, A., and COWEN, D. (1952) Histopathology of schizophrenia and other psychoses of unknown origin. In: The Biology of Mental Health and Disease. London: Cassell.—*257*.

WOLF, C. (1934) Castration in Male Sex Perverts and Sex Criminals. Basel: Schwabe.—*370.*

WOLFF, H. G. and CURRAN, D. (1935) Nature of delirium and allied states. *Arch. Neurol. Psychiat. (Chic.)*, 33, 1175.—*348.*

WOLPE, J. (1954) Reciprocal inhibition as the main basis of psychotherapeutic effects. *Arch. Neurol. Psychiat. (Chic.)*, 72, 205.—*184.*

——— (1958) Psychotherapy by Reciprocal Inhibition. Stanford: Stanford University Press.—*24, 184, 185.*

——— (1961) The systematic desensitization treatment of neuroses. *J. nerv. ment. Dis.*, 132, 189.—*184, 185.*

WOLTMAN, H. W. (1924) The mental changes associated with pernicious anaemia. *Amer. J. Psychiat.*, 80 (3), 435.—*355.*

WOOD, P. (1941) Da Costa's syndrome (or effort syndrome). *Brit. med. J.*, 1, 767, 805.—*361.*

WOODBURY, D. M., TIMIRAS, P. S. and VERADAKIS, A. (1957) Influence of adrenocortical steroids on brain function and metabolism. In: Hormones, Brain Function and Behaviour, ed. H. Hoagland. New York: Academic Press.—*203.*

WOODFORD-WILLIAMS, E., McKEON, J. A., TROTTER, I. S. and WATSON, D. (1962) The day-hospital in the community care of the elderly. *Geront. clin. (Basel)*, 4, 241.—*566.*

WOODSIDE, M. (1965) Hospital and community experience of 150 psychogeriatric patients. A follow-up one year after admission. *Geront. clin. (Basel)*, 7, 286.—*565.*

WOODWARD, M. (1955) Low intelligence and Delinquency. Institute for the Study and Treatment of Delinquency. London.—*716.*

WOOLF, L. I. (1961) Aminoaciduria. *Brit. med. Bull.* 17, 224.—*725.*

WOOLLEY, D. W. and SHAW, E. (1954a) Some neurophysiological aspects of serotonin. *Brit. med. J.*, 2, 122. —*256.*

——— and ——— (1954b) A biochemical and pharmacological suggestion about certain mental disorders. *Proc. nat. Acad. Sci. (U.S.A.)*, 40, 228.—*437.*

WOOTTON, B. (1959) Social Science and Social Pathology. London: G. Allen.—*6, 637, 780.*

WORLD HEALTH ORGANIZATION (1952) Drugs liable to produce addiction. Third Report of the Expert Committee on Drug Addiction. *Wld Hlth Org. techn. Rep. Ser.*, 57. Geneva.—*413.*

——— (1954) The mentally subnormal child. *Wld Hlth Org. techn. Rep. Ser.*, 75, Geneva.—*730.*

——— (1957) Addiction-producing drugs. Seventh report of the Expert Committee. *Wld Hlth Org. techn. Rep. Ser.*, 116. Geneva.—*413.*

——— (1957) The psychiatric hospital as a centre for preventive work in mental health. *Wld Hlth Org. techn. Rep. Ser.*, 134. Geneva.—*803.*

——— (1961) Epidemiological and Vital Statistics Report, Vol. 14, No. 5.—*788.*

——— (1964) Addiction-producing drugs. *Wld Hlth Org. techn. Rep. Ser.*, 273. Geneva.—*414.*

WORSTER-DROUGHT, C., GREENFIELD, J. G. and McMENEMEY, W. H. (1940) A form of familial presenile dementia with spastic paralysis (including the pathological examination of a case). *Brain*, 63, 237.—*612, 614.*

———, HILL, T. R. and McMENEMEY, W. H. (1933) Familial presenile dementia with spastic paralysis. *J. Neurol. Psychopath.*, 14, 27.—*620.*

WORTIS, H., BUEDING, E., STEIN, M. H. and JOLLIFFE, N. (1942) Pyruvic acid studies in the Wernicke Syndrome. *Arch. Neurol. Psychiat. (Chic)*, 47, 215.—*353.*

WRIGGLESWORTH, R. (1963) The importance of recognizing minimal cerebral dysfunction in paediatric practice. In: Minimal Cerebral Dysfunction, eds. R. C. MacKeith and M. Bax. London: Nat. Spastics Soc.—*691.*

WYCIS, H. T. and SPIEGEL, E. A. (1956) Treatment of certain types of chorea, athetosis and tremor by stereo-encephalotomy. *J. int. Coll. Surg.*, 25, 202.—*625.*

WYNNE, L. C. (1968) Schizophrenics and their families: recent research findings and implications. Mental Health Fund. 6th Annual Lecture. London.—*317.*

——— and SINGER, M. T. (1963) Thought disorder and family relations of schizophrenics. II A classification of forms of thinking. *Arch. gen. Psychiat.*, 9, 199.—*317.*

WYRSCH, J. (1941) Contribution to our knowledge of the course of schizophrenia. *Z. ges. Neurol. Psychiat.*, 172, 797.—*309.*

——— (1942) On theory and clinical observations of paranoid schizophrenia. *Mschr. Psychiat. Neurol.*, 106, 57.—*288.*

——— (1944) Selbstverstümmelung eines Transvestiten. *Schweiz. med. Wschr.*, 74, 657.—*164.*

YAP, P. M. (1958) Suicide in Hong Kong. London: Oxford Univ. Press.—*794.*

YARROW, J. L. (1964) Separation from parents during early childhood. In: Review of Child Development Research, ed. M. L. Hoffman and L. N. W. Hoffman. New York. (Russell Sage Foundation).—*638.*

YATES, A. J. (1958) The application of learning theory to the treatment of tics. *J. abnorm. soc. Psychol.*, 56, 175. —*186.*

YATES, P. O. and HUTCHINSON, E. C. (1961) Cerebral Infarction: The Role of Stenosis of the Extracranial Cerebral Arteries. M. R. C. Spec. Rep. Ser., No. 300. London: H.M.S.O.—*595.*

YOUNG, D. and SCOVILLE, W. B. (1938) Paranoid psychosis in narcolepsy and possible danger of benzedrine treatment. *Med. Clin. N. Amer.*, 22, 637.—*422.*

ZANGWILL, O. L. (1964) Neurological studies and human behaviour. *Brit. med. Bull.*, 20, 43.—*488, 490.*

ZAPPELLA, M. and COWIE, V. (1962) A note on the time of diagnosis in mongolism. *J. ment. Defic. Res.*, 6, 82. —*720.*

ZAWUSKI, G. (1960) On the heredity of Alzheimer's disease. *Arch. Psychiat. Nervenkr.*, 201, 123.—*613.*

ZIEGLER, G. K. and PAUL, N. (1954) On the natural history of hysteria in women. *Dis. nerv. Syst.*, *15*, 301.—*105*.

ZIEGLER, L. H. (1939) Depression as the chief symptom. *Psychiat. Quart.*, *13*, 689.—*219*.

ZIEGLER, F. J., IMBODEN, J. B. and MEYER, E. (1960) Contemporary conversion reactions: a clinical study. *Amer. J. Psychiat.*, *116*, 901.—*104*.

ZISKIND, E. (1957) Inculcation in Psychotherapy. Presentation volume for Charlotte Bühler, Verlag für Psychologie. ed. C. J. Hogrefe. Göttingen.—*178*.

——— (1964) A second look at sensory deprivation. *J. nerv. ment. Dis.*, *138*, 223.—*379*.

——— (1965) An explanation of mental symptoms found in acute sensory deprivation: researches 1958–1963. *Amer. J. Psychiat.*, *121*, 939.—*379*.

———, GRAHAM, R. W., KUNINOBU, L. and AINSWORTH, R. (1963) The hypnoid syndrome in sensory deprivation. In: Recent Advances in Biological Psychiatry. Vol. 5, Ch. 28. New York: Plenum Press.—*379*.

ZONDEK, H. and WOLFSOHN, G. (1944) Myxoedema and psychosis. *Lancet*, *2*, 438.—*367*.

ZUBEK, J. P. and WELCH, G. (1963) Electroencephalographic changes after prolonged sensory and perceptual deprivation. *Science*, *139*, 1209.—*380*.

ZUNG, W. W. K. (1965) A self-rating depressive scale. *Arch. gen. Psychiat. (Chic.)*, *12*, 63.—*36*.

ZURING, J. (1946) The Family Life of Schizophrenics. Amsterdam: Elsevier.—*324*.

INDEX